The 1997 World Book

YEAR BOOK

The Annual Supplement to The World Book Encyclopedia

▪▪▪ A REVIEW OF THE EVENTS OF 1996 ▪▪▪

World Book, Inc.

a Scott Fetzer company

Chicago ▪ London ▪ Sydney ▪
Toronto

World Book, Inc.
525 W. Monroe
Chicago, IL 60661

ISBN 0-7166-0497-3
ISSN 0084-1439
Library of Congress Catalog Card Number: 62-4818

Printed in the United States of America.

Staff

Contributors

Contributors not listed on these pages are members of *The World Book Year Book* editorial staff.

- **ALEXIOU, ARTHUR G.**, B.S.E.E., M.S.E.E.; Assistant secretary, Committee on Climatic Changes and Ocean. **[Ocean]**

- **ANDREWS, PETER J.**, B.A., M.S.; Free-lance writer; biochemist. **[Chemistry]**

- **APSELOFF, MARILYN FAIN**, B.A., M.A.; Professor of English, Kent State University, Ohio. **[Literature for children]**

- **ALLINSON, GARY D.**, Ph.D.; Professor of East Asian studies, University of Virginia. **[World Book supplement: Japan; Tokyo]**

- **BARBER, PEGGY**, B.A., M.L.S.; Associate executive director for public policy and programs, American Library Association. **[Library]**

- **BARNHART, BILL**, B.A., M.S.T., M.B.A.; Financial markets columnist, *Chicago Tribune*. **[Stocks and bonds]**

- **BAYNHAM, SIMON**, B.A., M.A., Ph.D.; Consultant, Research Institute for the Study of Conflict and Terrorism, London. **[Africa Special Report: Africa: Continent in Crisis]**

- **BOYD, JOHN D.**, B.S.; Economics/corporate reporter, *Knight-Ridder Financial News*. **[Economics; International trade; Manufacturing]**

- **BRADSHER, HENRY S.**, A.B., B.J.; Foreign affairs analyst. **[Asia and Asian country articles]**

- **BRETT, CARLTON E.**, B.A., M.S., Ph.D.; Professor of geological sciences, University of Rochester. **[Paleontology]**

- **BRODY, HERB**, B.S.; Senior editor, *Technology Review* magazine. **[Internet]**

- **BUERKLE, TOM**, B.A.; Correspondent, *International Herald Tribune*. **[Europe and Western European nation articles]**

- **CAMPBELL, GEOFFREY A.**, B.J.; Free-lance writer. **[Civil rights; Courts; Supreme Court of the United States]**

- **CAMPBELL, LINDA P.**, B.A., M.S.L.; Senior reporter, *Fort Worth Star-Telegram*. **[Civil rights; Courts; Supreme Court of the United States]**

- **CARDINALE, DIANE P.**, B.A.; Assistant communications director, Toy Manufacturers of America. **[Toys and games]**

- **CASEY, MICHAEL T.**, B.S., M.A.; Assistant editor, *Kansas City Star*. **[Automobile]**

- **CATES, WARD MITCHELL**, Ed.D.; Associate professor, Lehigh University **[World Book supplement: Computerized instruction]**

- **CLARK, KAREN LIN**, B.S.; Solutions editor, *San Diego Union-Tribune*. **[World Book supplement: San Diego]**

- **CORNELL, VINCENT J.**, B.A., M.A., Ph.D.; Andrew W. Mellon assistant professor of religion, Duke University. **[Islam]**

- **CROMIE, WILLIAM J.**, B.S., M.S.; Science writer, Harvard University. **[Space exploration]**

- **DeFRANK, THOMAS M.**, B.A., M.A.; Washington correspondent, *New York Daily News*. **[Armed forces]**

- **DeLANCEY, MARK W.**, B.A., M.A., Ph.D.; Professor of government and international studies, University of South Carolina. **[Africa and African country articles]**

- **DELPAR, HELEN**, Ph.D., Professor of history, University of Alabama. **[World Book supplement: Exploration]**

- **DILLON, DAVID**, B.A., M.A., Ph.D.; Architecture critic, *The Dallas Morning News*. **[Architecture]**

- **DIRDA, MICHAEL**, B.A., M.A., Ph.D.; Writer and editor, *The Washington Post Book World*. **[Poetry]**

- **DOLD, R. BRUCE**, B.S.J., M.S.J.; Deputy editorial page editor, *Chicago Tribune*. **[Elections Special Report: How Americans Elected Their President]**

- **DUCKETT, LUCINDA**, B.A.; Assistant chief of staff, (Sidney) *Daily Telegraph*. **[Australia]**

- **EATON, WILLIAM J.**, B.S., M.S.; Curator, Humphrey Fellows Program, University of Maryland. **[U.S. govt. articles]**

- **ELLIS, GAVIN**, Assistant editor, *New Zealand Herald*. **[New Zealand]**

- **FARR, DAVID M. L.**, D.Phil.; Professor emeritus of history, Carleton University. **[Canada; Canadian provinces]**

- **FEWSMITH, JOSEPH**, Ph.D.; Associate professor of international relations, Boston University. **[China Special Report: China After Deng]**

- **FISHER, ROBERT W.**, B.A., M.A.; Free-lance writer. **[Labor]**

- **FITZGERALD, MARK**, B.A.; Midwest editor, *Editor & Publisher*. **[Newspaper]**

- **FIXICO, DONALD L.**, B.A., M.A., Ph.D.; Professor of history, Western Michigan University. **[Indian, American]**

- **FOX, THOMAS C.**, B.A., M.A.; Editor/associate publisher, *National Catholic Reporter*. **[Roman Catholic Church]**

- **FRICKER, KAREN**, B.A., M.A.; Director of publications, The Public Theater. **[Theater]**

- **FRIEDMAN, EMILY**, B.A.; Health-care columnist, *Journal of the American Medical Association*. **[Health-care issues]**

- **GADOMSKI, FRED**, B.S., M.S.; Meteorologist, Pennsylvania State University. **[Weather]**

- **GALUSZKA, PETER** B.A.; Cleveland bureau chief, *Business Week* magazine. **[Russia Special Report: Life in the New Russia]**

- **GARVIE, MAUREEN**, B.A., B.Ed., M.A.; Teacher and writer, Queen's University. **[Canadian literature]**

- **GATTY, BOB**, Editor, Periodicals News Service. **[Food]**

- **GIBSON, ERIC**, former Executive editor, *ARTnews*. **[Art]**

- **GOLDEN, CARON**, B.A.; Free-lance writer and editor. **[San Diego]**

- **GOLDNER, NANCY**, B.A.; Dance critic, *The Philadelphia Inquirer*. **[Dancing]**

- **HARAKAS, STANLEY SAMUEL**, B.A., B.D., Th.D.; Professor emeritus, Holy Cross Greek Orthodox School of Theology. **[Eastern Orthodox Churches]**

- **HAVERSTOCK, NATHAN A.**, A.B.; Affiliate scholar, Oberlin College. **[Latin America and Latin American country articles]**

- **HELMS, CHRISTINE**, B.A., Ph.D.; Foreign affairs analyst; author. **[Middle East and Middle Eastern country articles; North African country articles]**

- **HENDERSON, HAROLD**, B.A.; Staff writer, Chicago *Reader* **[Chicago]**

- **HERMANN, RICHARD C.**, M.D.; Staff psychiatrist, McLean Hospital, and research fellow, Harvard Medical School. **[Psychology]**

- **HOFFMAN, ANDREW J.**, B.S., M.S., Ph.D.; Visiting assistant professor, Northwestern University. **[Environmental pollution]**

- **HOWELL, LEON**, A.B., M.Div.; Free-lance writer. **[Religion]**

- **HUSTON, ROBERT**, Free-lance writer. **[United Kingdom Special Report: Will the British Monarchy Survive?]**

- **JOHANSON, DONALD C.**, B.S., M.A., Ph.D.; President, Institute of Human Origins. **[Anthropology]**

- **JONES, TIM**, B.S.; Media writer, *Chicago Tribune*. **[Telecommunications]**

- **KILGORE, MARGARET**, B.A., M.B.A.; Editor, Phillips-Van Buren, Incorporated. **[Los Angeles]**

- **KING, MIKE**, Reporter, *The Montreal Gazette*. **[Montreal]**

- **KLINTBERG, PATRICIA PEAK** B.A.; Editor, *Farm Journal*. **[Farm and farming]**

- **KLOBUCHAR, LISA**, B.A.; Free-lance editor and writer. **[Biographies]**

- **KORMAN, RICHARD**, Associate editor, *Engineering News-Record*. **[Building and construction]**

- **LAWRENCE, AL**, B.A., M.A., M.Ed.; Executive director, United States Chess Federation. **[Chess]**

- **LEWIS, DAVID C.**, M.D.; Professor of medicine and community health, Brown University. **[Drug abuse]**

- **LIEBENSON, DONALD**, Free-lance writer, *Los Angeles Times* and *Chicago Tribune*. **[Deaths Special Report: George Burns: A Comedian's Comedian; Popular music Special Report: Ella Fitzgerald: First Lady of Song]**

- **LITSKY, FRANK**, B.S.; Sportswriter, *The New York Times*. **[Olympic Games Special Report: The 1996 Olympics; Sports articles]**

- **MANLY, LORNE**, former Editor-in-chief, *Folio*. **[Magazine]**

- **MARCH, ROBERT H.**, A.B., M.A., Ph.D.; Professor of physics, University of Wisconsin at Madison. **[Physics]**

- **MARSCHALL, LAURENCE A.**, Ph.D.; Professor of physics, Gettysburg College. **[Astronomy]**

- **MARTY, MARTIN E.**, Ph.D.; Fairfax M. Cone distinguished service professor, University of Chicago. **[Protestantism]**

- **MATHER, IAN J.**, B.A., M.A.; Diplomatic editor, *The European*, London. **[Ireland; Northern Ireland; United Kingdom]**

- **MATHESON, KATY**, M.A.; Free-lance writer **[World Book supplement: Ballet]**

- **MAUGH, THOMAS H., II**, Ph.D.; Science writer, *Los Angeles Times*. **[Biology]**

- **MAYES, BARBARA A.**, B.A.; Free-lance editor and writer. **[Nobel Prizes; Pulitzer Prizes]**

- **McLEESE, DON**, B.A., M.A.; Columnist/critic-at-large, *Austin American-Statesman*. **[Popular music]**

- **MESSENGER, ROBERT**, B.A.; Editor, Scott, Foresman and Co. **[Washington, D.C.]**

- **MINER, TODD**, B.S., M.S.; Meteorologist, Pennsylvania State University. **[Weather]**

- **MORITZ, OWEN**, B.A.; Free-lance writer. **[New York City]**

- **MORRIS, BERNADINE**, B.A., M.A.; Free-lance fashion writer. **[Fashion]**

- **MULLINS, HENRY T.**, B.S., M.S., Ph.D.; Professor of earth sciences, Syracuse University. **[Geology]**

- **NGUYEN, J. TUYET**, M.A.; Bureau chief, United Nations correspondent, United Press International. **[Population; United Nations]**

- **OGAN, EUGENE**, B.A., M.A., Ph.D.; Professor emeritus of anthropology, University of Minnesota. **[Pacific Islands]**

- **PAULSGROVE, ROBIN**, B.A.; Fire chief, Austin (Texas) Fire Department **[World Book supplement: Fire Department]**

- **PEARCE, FRED**, Free-lance author/journalist. **[Farm and farming Special Report: Mad Cow Disease]**

- **PRIESTAF, IRIS**, B.A., M.A., Ph.D.; Geographer and vice president, David Keith Todd Consulting Engineers, Incorporated. **[Water]**

- **RAPHAEL, MARC LEE**, B.A., M.A., Ph.D.; Professor of religion, College of William and Mary. **[Judaism]**

- **ROSE, MARK J.**, B.A., M.A., Ph.D.; Managing editor, *Archaeology* magazine. **[Archaeology]**

- **RUBENSTEIN, RICHARD E.**, B.A., M.A., J.D.; Professor of conflict resolution and public affairs, George Mason University. **[Terrorism]**

- **SAVAGE, IAN**, B.A., M.A., Ph.D.; Assistant professor of economics and transportation, Northwestern University. **[Aviation; Transportation]**

- **SEGAL, TROY**, B.A.; Free-lance writer. **[Television]**

- **SHAFORTH, FRANK**, B.A., law; Policy and federal relations director, National League of Cities. **[City]**

- **SHAPIRO, HOWARD S.**, B.S.; Cultural arts editor, *The Philadelphia Inquirer*. **[Philadelphia]**

- **SOLNICK, STEVEN L.**, B.A., M.A., Ph.D.; Professor of political science, Columbia University. **[Baltic states and other former Soviet republic articles]**

- **STEIN, DAVID LEWIS**, B.A., M.S.; Urban affairs columnist, *The Toronto Star*. **[Toronto]**

- **STUART, ELAINE**, B.A.; Managing editor, Council of State Governments. **[State government]**

- **TANNER, JAMES C.**, B.S.J.; News editor—energy, *The Wall Street Journal*. **[Petroleum and gas]**

- **TATUM, HENRY K.**, B.A.; Associate editorial page editor, *The Dallas Morning News*. **[Dallas]**

- **THIEME, JOHN A.**, B.A., M.Phil., Ph.D.; Professor of new literature in English, University of Hull. **[Literature]**

- **THOMAS, PAULETTE**, B.A.; Reporter, *The Wall Street Journal*. **[Bank]**

- **TOCH, THOMAS W.**, B.A., M.A.; Associate editor and education correspondent, *U.S. News & World Report*. **[Education]**

- **TONRY, MICHAEL**, A.B., LL.B.; Professor of law and public policy, University of Minnesota Law School. **[Prison]**

- **von RHEIN, JOHN**, B.A., M.A.; Music critic, *Chicago Tribune*. **[Classical music]**

- **WALTER, EUGENE J., Jr.**, B.A.; Free-lance writer. **[Conservation; Zoos]**

- **WATSON, BURKE**, B.A.; Assistant suburban editor, *Houston Chronicle*. **[Houston]**

- **WINEGRAD, DILYS PEGLER**, M.A., Ph.D.; Director and curator, Arthur Ross Gallery, University of Pennsylvania. **[Computer Special Report: ENIAC Celebrates a Birthday]**

- **WOLCHIK, SHARON L.**, M.A., Ph.D.; Director, Russian and East European studies, George Washington University. **[Eastern European country articles]**

- **WOODS, MICHAEL**, B.S.; Science editor, *The Toledo* (Ohio) *Blade*. **[AIDS; Computer; Drugs; Electronics; Energy supply; Medicine; Mental health; Public health; Safety]**

- **WUNTCH, PHILIP**, B.A.; Film critic, *The Dallas Morning News*. **[Motion pictures]**

- **ZOBELL, CHARLES**, B.A.; Managing editor, *Las Vegas Review-Journal*. **[World Book supplement: Las Vegas]**

Contents

Cross-Reference Tabs

A tear-out page of Cross-Reference Tabs for insertion in *The World Book Encyclopedia* appears before page 1.

The Year in Brief 10

A month-by-month review of the major news stories of 1996.

World Book Year Book Update

36 to 416

The major world events of 1996 are reported in more than 250 alphabetically arranged Update articles—from "Afghanistan" and "Africa" to "Zaire" and "Zoos." Included are Special Reports that provide an in-depth focus on especially noteworthy developments.

Page 436

The Year's

Major News Stories

From the reelection of the presidents of the United States and Russia to the tragic crashes of two U.S. airliners with the loss of all lives, 1996 was a year of memorable news events. On these two pages are stories that *Year Book* editors picked as some of the most important of the year, along with details on where to find information about them in *The World Book Year Book*.   The Editors

Ending welfare as we knew it

On August 1, the U.S. Congress gave final passage to a bill to overhaul the nation's welfare system. President Bill Clinton, who had promised in 1992 to "end welfare as we know it," signed the bill while expressing reservations about it. See **Clinton, Bill,** page 139; **Congress of the United States,** page 148.

▲
Yeltsin remains at the helm

After winning reelection as president of Russia in July, despite concerns about his health, Boris N. Yeltsin takes the oath of office on August 9. In the autumn, after suffering a third heart attack, Yeltsin underwent coronary bypass surgery. See **Russia,** page 337.

◀ **Rwandans go home**

Rwandans who had fled the ethnic warfare that raged in Rwanda in 1994 board United Nations trucks at a refugee camp in Burundi in August to return home. Rwandan refugees in Zaire also returned to Rwanda by the hundreds of thousands. See **Africa,** page 38; **Burundi,** page 98; **Zaire,** page 416.

◀ Airline crashes

A piece of a TWA airliner that exploded shortly after takeoff from New York City en route to Paris on July 17 floats in the Atlantic Ocean. The crash was still being investigated at year-end. In May, a ValuJet airliner caught fire and crashed into the Florida Everglades. The crashes raised fears about airline safety. See **Aviation,** page 80; **Disasters,** page 176.

New Israeli prime minister

Benjamin Netanyahu, candidate of the conservative Likud Party, wins a narrow election victory over Israeli Prime Minister Shimon Peres on May 29 to become the nation's new prime minister. Netanyahu promised to take a harder line in Israeli-Palestinian peace discussions. See **Israel,** page 247; **Middle East,** page 280; **Netanyahu, Benjamin,** page 287.

◀ A royal divorce

Britain's Prince Charles and Princess Diana, separated for three years, are granted a divorce in August. Opinion polls find that only 34 percent of Britons still see a need for a royal family. See **United Kingdom,** page 391; **United Kingdom** Special Report: **Will the British Monarchy Survive?** page 394.

▲
Clinton wins reelection

U.S. President Bill Clinton is the decisive victor in the November 5 election, becoming the first Democrat since Franklin Delano Roosevelt to win a second term in the White House. See **Clinton, Bill,** page 139; **Elections,** page 187; **Elections** Special Report: **How Americans Elected Their President,** page 188.

Mad Cow disease

British scientists announce in March that 10 cases of a rare degenerative brain disease may have been caused by eating beef from cattle infected with a disorder called bovine spongiform encephalopathy, or "mad cow disease." As a result, tens of thousands of British cattle are slaughtered. See **Farm and farming** Special Report: **Mad Cow Disease,** page 210; **United Kingdom,** page 391.

Unabomber suspect arrested ▶

Theodore J. Kaczynski, thought to be the so-called Unabomber who killed 3 people and injured 23 others with mail bombs over a 17-year period, is escorted by law enforcement officers in Helena, Montana, after his April 3 arrest. See **Crime,** page 158; **Terrorism,** page 380.

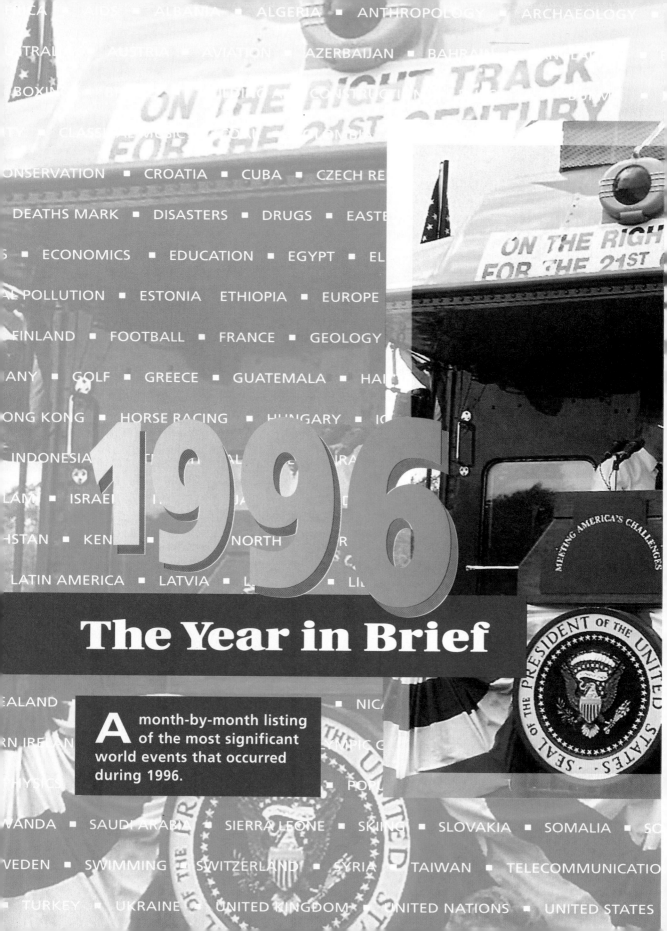

ON THE RIGHT TRACK
FOR THE 21ST CENTURY

ON THE RIGHT
FOR THE 21ST

MEETING AMERICA'S CHALLENGES

1996

The Year in Brief

A month-by-month listing of the most significant world events that occurred during 1996.

January
1996

S	M	T	W	TH	F	S
	1	2	3	4	5	6
7	8	9	10	11	12	13
14	15	16	17	18	19	20
21	22	23	24	25	26	27
28	29	30	31			

5 Japanese Prime Minister Tomichi Murayama announces his resignation.

6 A record-breaking blizzard sweeps up the East Coast of the United States, dumping 30.7 inches (78 centimeters) of snow on Philadelphia, 20.6 inches (52.3 centimeters) on New York City, and 18.2 inches (46 centimeters) on Boston.

8 François Mitterrand, the former French president who championed a unified Europe, dies in Paris.

Columnist William Safire calls First Lady Hillary Rodham Clinton a "congenital liar" in his column in *The New York Times*. The column relates Mrs. Clinton's role in Whitewater, a failed Arkansas real-estate deal that is being investigated by Congress. The attack draws a strong negative reaction from the president and is characterized by Democrats as election-year, partisan politics.

9 Chechen rebels raid the town of Kizlyar in neighboring Dagestan, seize a hospital and apartment building, and take 3,400 hostages, whom they announce they will shoot a few at a time until Russian troops withdraw from Chechnya.

15 Astronomers release photographs of the universe as it was 10 billion years ago. The pictures, which reveal hundreds of previously unknown galaxies, were taken by the Hubble Space Telescope. Looking farther out into space than any previous optical instrument, the telescope captured light that took at least 10 billion years to cross the universe.

17 American astronomers report that they have detected planets orbiting two stars in the galaxy. Because the stars are similar to the sun, the planets may be warm enough to contain liquid water and thus capable of supporting life.

Sheik Omar Abdel Rahman, a radical Islamic fundamentalist from Egypt, is sentenced by a federal district judge in New York City to life in prison after being convicted of plotting a series of bombings and assassinations aimed at pressuring the United States to end support of Israel and Egypt.

Ryutaro Hashimoto, Liberal Democratic Party head, is named prime minister of Japan.

18 Greece's Socialist Party elects Costas Simitis to replace Andreas Papandreou as prime minister.

23 The murder trial of Yigal Amir, the Israeli accused of assassinating Prime Minister Yitzhak Rabin in November 1995, begins in Tel Aviv.

A four-day blizzard, which began on January 6, cripples New York City as well as much of New England and the Middle Atlantic states.

23 In his State of the Union message, President Bill Clinton offers his vision of limited government and implies that the coming election campaigns should focus on values rather than budget. In response, Republicans call Clinton an elitist and the last defender of the status quo.

24 Prime Minister of Poland Jozef Oleksy resigns his office after being accused of passing state secrets to Soviet KGB agents before Communist rule in Poland was toppled in 1989.

26 Hillary Rodham Clinton testifies before a grand jury about the sudden reappearance of papers detailing her legal services for a failed Arkansas savings and loan company involved in the Whitewater affair. It is the first time a First Lady has been subpoenaed by a grand jury.

28 The Dallas Cowboys beat the Pittsburgh Steelers 27 to 17 to win football's Super Bowl XXX.

28 John E. du Pont, an heir to the du Pont chemical fortune, is arrested for allegedly shooting an Olympic wrestling champion, who lived and trained on du Pont's Pennsylvania estate.

February
1996

S	M	T	W	TH	F	S
				1	2	3
4	5	6	7	8	9	10
11	12	13	14	15	16	17
18	19	20	21	22	23	24
25	26	27	28	29		

1 Congress passes a sweeping communications bill allowing telephone and cable television companies to compete in each other's markets. President Bill Clinton signs the bill into law on February 8.

3 An earthquake of 7.0 magnitude strikes China's Yunnan Province, killing more than 250 people and injuring at least 15,000 others.

5 The Nepalese government announces that archaeologists working in Nepal believe they have uncov-

A bomb planted by the Irish Republican Army explodes on February 18 aboard a double-decker bus in central London, killing one person and injuring eight others.

10 In Japan, a highway tunnel collapses, trapping 20 motorists under a mountain. Rescuers are unable to reach the victims in time, and all 20 die.

12 Republican Party caucuses in Iowa provide the first major contest among Republican presidential contenders. Senator Bob Dole of Kansas wins, but by a narrow margin. On February 18, Senator Phil Gramm of Texas withdraws from the race and endorses Dole as the only candidate who can unite the factions within the Republican Party.

15 An oil tanker runs aground off the coast of Wales, spilling approximately 19 million gallons (72 million liters) of oil into the sea.

16 Eleven passengers die when an Amtrak train and a commuter train collide in suburban Maryland, outside of Washington, D.C.

18 An explosion on a double-decker bus in central London kills one person and injures eight. Police suspect the Irish Republican Army.

20 Russian troops launch an assault on Novogroznensky, the stronghold of Chechnya rebels.

Patrick Buchanan, campaigning on themes relating to the economic insecurity of the average American, wins the New Hampshire Republican presidential primary. Bob Dole comes in second.

23 Two of Saddam Hussein's sons-in-law who defected from Iraq in 1995 and later returned are executed by members of their own clan. The wives of the men were granted divorces on February 19.

24 Cuban military jets shoot down two civilian planes operated by a Miami-based Cuban refugee group. The United States charged Cuba with violating international law.

25 Two bombs explode in Israel, killing 27 people. The militant Muslim group, Hamas, claimed credit for the suicide bombings, the worst since the Israeli-Palestinian peace accords went into effect in September 1993.

29 Television and entertainment-industry executives meet with President Clinton at the White House and promise to set up, by January 1997, a voluntary system for rating violence on TV programs.

Discovery of a virus that may cause Kaposi's sarcoma, a cancer commonly found among men infected with the AIDS virus, is reported by scientists at the University of California at San Francisco.

The U.S. House of Representatives approves legislation that would end farm subsidies and regulation of crop production.

Princess Diana, wife of the heir to the throne of Great Britain, announces that she has agreed to divorce Prince Charles. The couple have two sons, William and Henry.

ered the birthplace of Buddha, the 6th-century B.C. religious figure born an Indian prince.

7 Haiti's new president, René Préval, is sworn in, replacing outgoing Jean-Bertrand Aristide.

9 A bomb explodes in London, destroying an office complex. The Irish Republican Army takes credit for the blast that kills two people and injures 100.

A single atom of a new metallic element is discovered by an international team of scientists working in Germany. It is added to the Periodic Table as element 112.

March
1996

S	M	T	W	TH	F	S
					1	2
3	4	5	6	7	8	9
10	11	12	13	14	15	16
17	18	19	20	21	22	23
24	25	26	27	28	29	30
31						

2 Australians, after 13 years of Labor government, sweep the conservatives into power.

3 A suicide bombing kills 20 people on a Jerusalem bus, the second bus bombing in a week.

4 Israel's fourth suicide bombing in a year carried out by the militant Muslim group Hamas kills 14 people and injures more than 100 at a busy Tel Aviv shopping mall.

5 Two brake factories in Dayton, Ohio, are struck by members of the United Auto Workers union. Within a week, three-quarters of General Motors North American auto and truck assembly plants shut down for lack of brake parts, idling 83,000 workers.

7 China fires test missiles into the Taiwan Strait, between Taiwan and the Chinese mainland. The missile tests are intended to intimidate the Taiwanese as they prepare for their first presidential election. On March 12, the Chinese navy and air force launch military exercises in the strait. In response, the United States sends warships into the area.

8 Stock and bond prices fall more than 3 percent in the worst drop in four years, nearly triggering a shutdown of the New York Stock Exchange. Market analysts interpret the drop as a response to a U.S. government announcement that job growth has been greater than expected.

Dr. Jack Kevorkian is acquitted in a Michigan court of two counts of assisting in suicides.

12 Senator Bob Dole wins seven Republican state primaries on so-called Super-Tuesday, giving him more than two-thirds of the 996 convention delegates needed to win the Republican nomination. On March 14, Steve Forbes withdraws from the race.

13 A gunman in Dunblane, Scotland, opens fire on a school gym class, killing 16 young children and a teacher. The man then turns the gun on himself.

14 The U.S. Food and Drug Administration (FDA) approves indinavir, the third and reportedly most effective of a new class of drugs designed to combat the virus that causes AIDS. Called protease inhibitors, the new drugs attack an enzyme that the virus needs in order to multiply.

16 Nigerian voters turn out in large numbers for municipal elections, the first stage in a plan to return the country from military to civilian rule.

19 A fire in a disco in Manila, the Philippines, packed with students celebrating the end of the school year, kills more than 150 people.

Sarajevo is united under Bosnian government control after Serbs relinquish Grbavica, the last Serbian-controlled suburb. On March 18, arsonists torched houses as Serbs abandoned the district.

Nelson Mandela, president of South Africa, is granted a divorce from his wife, Winnie Mandela.

An earthquake in northwestern China destroys some 50,000 buildings, leaving 24 people dead and 10,000 homeless.

20 A jury in Los Angeles returns a verdict of guilty in the trial of Eric and Lyle Menendez, accused of the 1989 murder of their parents.

A federal appeals court judge rules against the use of race as a criterion for admission to a college or university even for the "wholesome practice of correcting perceived racial imbalance." The case involved the University of Texas's affirmative action program.

21 The United Automobile Workers union and General Motors Corporation reach tentative agreement to end a strike at Dayton, Ohio, brake factories, which shut down GM automobile and truck assembly plants across North America.

France and Belgium ban the importation of British beef in the wake of a March 20 announcement by a British health minister that a new strain of Creutzfeld-Jakob disease had been found in 10 British citizens and that the neurological disease had "most likely" been transmitted through "exposure" to beef from cattle afflicted with bovine spongiform encephalopathy (BSE), the so-called "mad cow" disease. On March 25, the European Union bans the importation of British beef.

23 In Taiwan's first presidential election, incumbent Lee Teng-hui wins a resounding victory in a vote that is viewed as symbolic of Taiwan's move toward independent-nation status.

25 Law enforcement officers arrest two members of the Freemen, an antigovernment group, at a northeastern Montana ranch. Other members of the group retreat to a ranch building, which is then surrounded by officers.

26 Bob Dole wins California's Republican primary and declares himself the winner of the battle for the Republican presidential nomination.

The residents of Dunblane, Scotland, mourn the death of 16 primary school children and a teacher who were gunned down in the school gymnasium on March 13.

April
1996

S	M	T	W	TH	F	S
	1	2	3	4	5	6
7	8	9	10	11	12	13
14	15	16	17	18	19	20
21	22	23	24	25	26	27
28	29	30				

1 Russian forces halt their bombing and artillery assaults in the breakaway republic of Chechnya after Russian President Boris N. Yeltsin calls for a unilateral cease-fire.

3 U.S. Secretary of Commerce Ronald H. Brown and a delegation of American business leaders are killed when the military plane in which they are riding crashes into a mountain while attempting to land in Dubrovnik, Croatia.

Fifty-three-year-old Theodore J. Kaczynski, suspected of being the Unabomber, is arrested at a remote site in Montana. Over a 17-year period, the Unabomber produced package bombs that killed 3 people and maimed more than 20 others.

6 Fighting again breaks out in the six-year-old Liberian civil war when forces controlled by Charles Taylor attempt to arrest Roosevelt Johnson, rival faction leader, on murder charges. Thousands of citizens take refuge in the United States embassy in Monrovia, the capital.

11 Israel begins an air offensive against Lebanese centers of the Hezbollah (Party of God) terrorist organization with a helicopter bombing in Beirut.

Jessica Dubroff, a 7-year-old attempting to become the youngest pilot to fly across the United States, dies when the plane she is flying with her father and a flying instructor crashes after taking off from a Cheyenne, Wyoming, airport.

14 A "Fight the Right" march by an estimated 13,000 people representing 500 organizations is held in San Francisco to protest what the organizers termed the "radical right" and its influence on U.S. politics.

British golfer Nick Faldo wins the 60th Masters tournament at Augusta, Georgia, for the third time, with a 12-under-par 276.

15 The United States agrees to return to Japan 10 military installations on Okinawa, which is approximately 20 percent of the land the U.S. military occupies on the Japanese island.

18 An Israeli artillery barrage, fired into a United Nations peacekeeping camp, kills more than 100 Lebanese civilians. The attack, deadliest yet in Israel's Grapes of Wrath offensive against Hezbollah guerrillas in southern Lebanon, is described as a "grave error" by Israeli Prime Minister Peres.

Egyptian gunmen, believed to be Islamic Group members, open fire on Greek tourists outside a Cairo hotel. Eighteen are killed in the most violent attack since foreign tourists became targets of the fundamentalist Muslim group in 1992.

22 The chairmen of Nynex Corporation and Bell Atlantic announce that the two Baby Bell companies will merge in a deal valued at $22.1 billion, creating the nation's largest telecommunication firm. The announcement was preceded by the April 1 announcement of the merger of two other Baby Bells—Pacific Telesis and SBC Communications.

24 The main assembly of the Palestine Liberation Organization, bowing to the demands of Palestinian leader Yasir Arafat, votes to strike from the organization's 32-year-old charter those clauses that call for destroying the Jewish state of Israel.

Congressional and White House negotiators, after seven months of stop-gap spending measures and partial government shutdowns, agree on a permanent budget for fiscal year 1996, which began on October 1, 1995.

The trial of Shoko Asahara, of the Japanese Aum Shinrikyo sect, opens in Tokyo. Shoko Asahara, who claims to be Christ, is accused of masterminding the 1995 gas attack on the Tokyo subways, which resulted in the death of 12 and the injury of 5,500 people.

27 U.S. Secretary of State Warren Christopher brokers an end to Israel's Grapes of Wrath military operation against Hezbollah guerrillas.

28 An Australian gunman methodically kills more than 30 people, including several children and a baby, at a historic colonial prison, a popular tourist attraction in Port Arthur, Tasmania.

28 President Bill Clinton testifies, by videotape in a closed White House session, as a witness for the defense of two of his former partners in the failed Whitewater real estate venture.

29 Three Muslim refugees are killed and dozens wounded when Serbs, armed with rocks and sticks, attack Muslims attempting to visit houses and cemeteries they had not seen since the war.

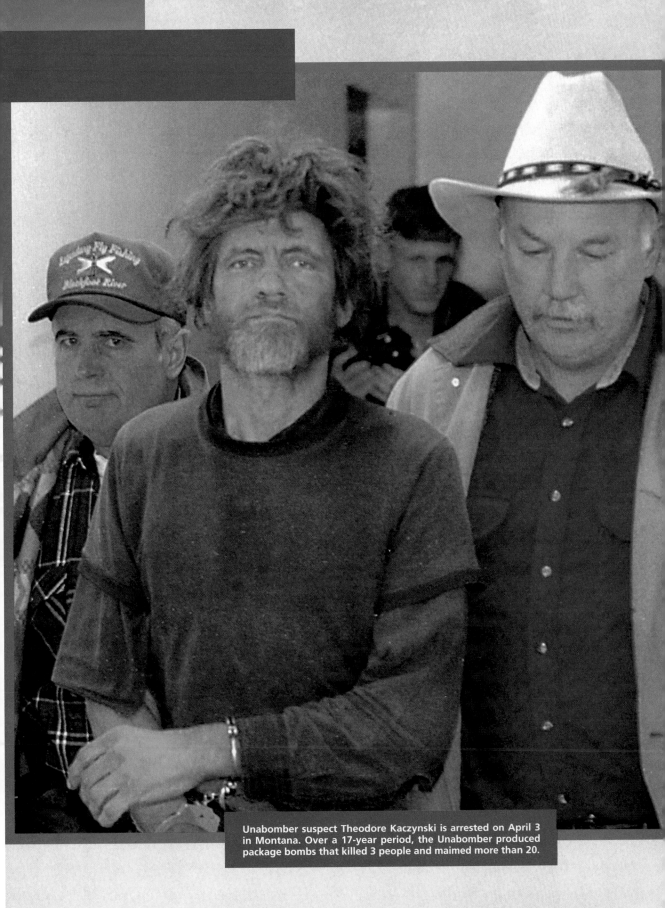

Unabomber suspect Theodore Kaczynski is arrested on April 3 in Montana. Over a 17-year period, the Unabomber produced package bombs that killed 3 people and maimed more than 20.

May
1996

S	M	T	W	TH	F	S
				1	2	3	4
5	6	7	8	9	10	11
12	13	14	15	16	17	18
19	20	21	22	23	24	25
26	27	28	29	30	31	

3 Fuel prices across the nation rise during the previous 10 weeks by an average of about 17 cents, or 15 percent. During the previous six days, prices go up by more than 5 cents.

4 Grindstone wins the Kentucky Derby and is the first horse in 37 years to win by a nose.

5 More than 2,500 refugees flee Monrovia, Liberia, on a Nigerian freighter, and tens of thousands flee

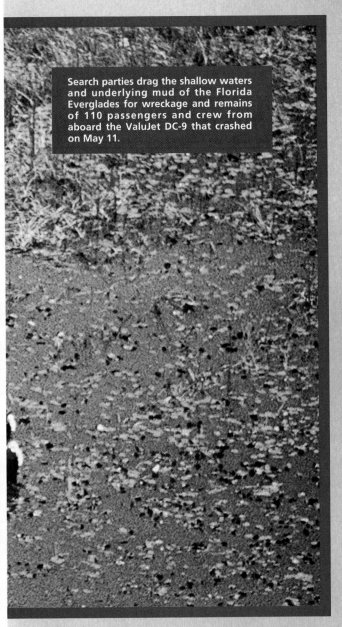

Search parties drag the shallow waters and underlying mud of the Florida Everglades for wreckage and remains of 110 passengers and crew from aboard the ValuJet DC-9 that crashed on May 11.

9 Ohio State University announces the discovery, in the university's Byrd Polar Research Center, of Rear Admiral Richard Byrd's diary of his May 9, 1926, flight to the North Pole. Examination of the diary has led one navigation specialist to conclude that Bryd not only fell short of his destination, but was aware that he had not succeeded.

Director of the National Institute of Allergy and Infectious Diseases Anthony S. Fauci announces that scientists at his institute have discovered the protein that allows the AIDS virus to gain admittance into cells of the human immune system.

10 The political base of India's Congress Party, in power for most of the nation's nearly 50 years of independence, is shattered in a general election.

11 A ValuJet DC-9, en route to Atlanta with 105 passengers and 5 crew members, crashes into the Florida Everglades, disappearing into the shallow water and mud of the wetlands.

15 Kansas Senator Robert Dole, majority leader of the Senate and Republican candidate for president, announces he will resign from the Senate to devote all of his time to his campaign.

16 Admiral Jeremy Boorda, Chief of Naval Operations and a member of the Joint Chiefs of Staff, kills himself.

20 The Supreme Court strikes down a referendum-based provision of the Colorado Constitution that both nullified existing civil rights protections for homosexuals and barred passage of any future antidiscrimination laws. In an opinion joined by five other justices, Anthony M. Kennedy wrote that the Colorado provision, which he characterized as "grounded in animus," violated the Constitution's equal protection guarantee.

22 Federal agents in San Francisco arrest seven representatives of China's two state-owned arms companies on charges of smuggling illegal arms into the United States. Bureau of Alcohol, Tobacco, and Firearms agents believe the guns were en-route to street gangs.

24 Japan's largest banks announce, with uncharacteristic candor, huge losses from bad debts, which have accumulated over a number of years.

28 A Little Rock, Arkansas, jury convicts James McDougal, Susan McDougal, and Governor Jim Guy Tucker, former business partners of President Bill Clinton, of fraud and other crimes associated with a series of bad loans issued in the 1980's by an Arkansas savings and loan association.

29 Benjamin Netanyahu, leader of the conservative Likud Party, defeats the incumbent Shimon Peres, leader of the Labor Party, by a margin of less than one percentage point in Israel's first direct election for prime minister.

by foot in the wake of renewed violence in the Liberian civil war, which has raged, intermittently, since 1989.

José María Aznar, Spain's first conservative leader since the country emerged from the Franco dictatorship in 1975, is sworn in as prime minister by King Juan Carlos.

6 The Federal Bureau of Investigation announces that the incidence of serious crime has dropped for the fourth consecutive year; homicides led the decrease, with an 8 percent drop in 1995.

21

June
1996

S	M	T	W	TH	F	S
						1
2	3	4	5	6	7	8
9	10	11	12	13	14	15
16	17	18	19	20	21	22
23	24	25	26	27	28	29
30						

1 H. D. Deve Gowda, leader of the multiparty United Front, is sworn in as prime minister of India.

2 Chad's citizens vote in a presidential election for the first time in the 36 years the country of 6 million people has been independent from France.

5 Trustees of the Hospital Insurance Trust Fund, which oversees Medicare funds, officially report that the fund that pays hospital bills for the elderly and disabled will be depleted by 2000 and will run a deficit by 2001 unless the current law is changed.

6 Chester DePratter and Stanley A. South, professors at the University of South Carolina, announce the discovery of the site of a 1562 French fort, Charlesfort, on Parris Island, near Beaufort, South Carolina. The fort predates the Roanoke (North Carolina) settlement by more than 20 years.

7 A Charlotte, North Carolina, church of predominately black membership is torched by arsonists—the 32nd such arson in the nation in 18 months.

10 The U.S. Supreme Court rules unanimously that police can stop drivers for supposed traffic violations when officers are, in fact, looking for evidence of other illegal activities.

Guerrillas of the Hezbollah, or the Party of God, terrorist organization ambush Israeli soldiers, killing five, in an Israeli security zone in southern Lebanon. Israel, claiming the attack violates the agreements that ended the heavy Israeli shelling of Lebanon in May, retaliates with artillery strikes.

11 Majority Leader Bob Dole resigns from the U.S. Senate to devote his time to running for the presidency on the Republican ticket.

A U.S. serviceman surveys the ruins of a military apartment building in Dhahran, Saudi Arabia, blown apart on June 25 by a group suspected to be anti-American Muslim terrorists. The explosion left 19 Americans dead and some 400 people wounded.

12 Trent Lott, senator from Mississippi, defeats Thad Cochran, senior senator from Mississippi, for Republican leadership of the U.S. Senate. Lott's election as Senate majority leader, in conjunction with Newt Gingrich's speakership of the House of Representatives, marks the first time that Republicans from the South have led both houses of Congress.

A panel of three federal judges declare major parts of a new law intended to regulate indecent material on the global computer network unconstitutional and block enforcement of the law.

13 The 14 Freemen remaining at the right-wing, antigovernment group's remote Montana ranch surrender to federal agents, ending an 81-day siege by federal authorities. At least five of the group face charges of threatening to kill a federal judge and circulating millions of dollars in bogus checks.

16 The Chicago Bulls score 87 to 75 against the Seattle SuperSonics to win the team's fourth National Basketball Association championship in six years.

19 The U.S. Census Bureau announces that the gap between the wealthiest 20 percent of American households and the remaining 80 percent is wider today than it has been since 1946 when World War II ended; 46.9 percent of the nation's aggregate income now goes to 20 percent of its households.

21 Officials of the U.S. Defense Department announce that Persian Gulf War troops may have been exposed to nerve gas when American soldiers, after the end of the war, in March 1991, destroyed an Iraqi ammunition depot that contained rockets armed with gas—possibly sarin or mustard. American troops who served in the Persian Gulf have reported a variety of illnesses.

Britain agrees to stop obstructing European Union (EU) business and accept a settlement of the three-month beef dispute with its (EU) partners.

23 Andreas Papandreou, the former Prime Minister of Greece who dominated Greek political life for most of the previous quarter century, dies at age 77.

25 A truck bomb, believed to have been the work of anti-American Muslim terrorists, blows up a military apartment complex in Dhahran, a city in eastern Saudi Arabia. The explosion kills 19 American servicemen and wounds more than 400 people, 250 of whom are American.

26 To mark the United Nations-sponsored World Anti-Drugs Day, China convicts 1,725 people of drug trafficking, and at least 260 of the convicted are taken directly from the courtroom to the execution ground and shot.

28 Islamic political leader Necmettin Erbakan is named Prime Minister of Turkey, an Islamic nation that has been committed to secular government since the establishment of a republic in October 1923.

23

July
1996

S	M	T	W	TH	F	S
		1	2	3	4	5	6
7	8	9	10	11	12	13
14	15	16	17	18	19	20
21	22	23	24	25	26	27
28	29	30	31			

2 Federal agents seize high-powered rifles and hundreds of pounds of a bomb-making compound from the house of 1 of the 12 Viper Militia members arrested July 1 for conspiring to blow up government buildings in Phoenix, Arizona.

3 Russian voters turn their backs on the nation's Communist past and reelect Boris Yeltsin president by an unexpectedly wide margin over Gennadiy Zyuganov, Communist Party leader.

4 Storms dump up to 22 inches (55.8 centimeters) of rain across nine central and southern Chinese provinces, flooding at least 1.75 million acres (700,000 hectares) of farmland. As many as 270 people are dead, and hundreds of thousands flee their homes for higher ground.

6 Steffi Graf, in a 6-3, 7-5 victory over Spanish tennis champion Arantxa Sánchez Vicario, takes her seventh Wimbledon and 20th Grand Slam title. On July 7, Dutch tennis champion Richard Krajicek takes the Wimbledon crown by beating MaliVai Washington 6-3, 6-4, 6-3 in the first final in 110 years to be played by two unseeded men.

10 Russia bombards two villages 20 miles south of Grozny, the destroyed Chechen capital. Launched less than one week after Boris Yeltsin was reelected president, the attack violates Russia's peace accord with Chechen rebel leaders.

11 Results of a study announced at the 11th international AIDS conference in Vancouver, Canada, reveal that combinations of drugs, new and old, suppress HIV, the virus that causes AIDS, below the level of detection for significant periods of time. The findings suggest that people with AIDS, like diabetics, may live relatively normal life spans through daily drug therapy.

13 Matching the winning streak set half a century ago by Citation, a six-year-old bay named Cigar captures his 16th straight race by taking the Arlington Citation Challenge by 3½ lengths.

15 Dow Jones Industrial stocks fall 161 points—continuing a trend that began when the government reported on July 5 that employment was booming and wages rising.

17 Trans World Airlines Flight 800, en route to Paris from New York City, explodes above the Atlantic just off the coast of Long Island, killing all 230 passengers and crew aboard the Boeing 747-100.

Columbia University seismologists announce that the inner core of Earth spins independently of the

The 1996 Olympic Games open in Atlanta, Georgia, on July 19 with a gala pageant featuring a silhouetted homage to the athletes of ancient Greece. More than 10,000 athletes from 197 nations participate in the opening of the centennial games.

rest of the planet and faster, making the core virtually a planet within a planet.

19 The centennial Summer Olympics open in Atlanta with a gala pageant featuring legendary heavyweight boxer Muhammad Ali—the final athlete to bear the torch to light the Olympic flame.

21 The Japanese government warns the public not to eat raw meat after announcing that some 8,000 people have been stricken with food poisoning.

25 The Tutsi-dominated Burundi military concludes a coup d'état, which began on July 24, in which President Sylvestre Ntibantunganya, a Hutu, is replaced by Pierre Buyoya, a Tutsi.

27 A pipe bomb packed with nails and screws explodes amid a tightly packed crowd at a late-night rock concert in Atlanta's Centennial Olympic Park, killing one woman and injuring 111 other people.

30 The Federal Election Commission (FEC) sues the Christian Coalition for illegally promoting conservative Republican candidates, such as Newt Gingrich, Jessie Helms, and Oliver North. Calling the coalition's nonpartisan posture a sham, FEC chairman Lee Ann Elliott announces that Democrats and members of her own Republican Party voted to bring the suit, which alleges that the coalition illegally contributed money to various conservative candidates.

1 Mohamed Farah Aideed, the clan leader who humiliated U.S. forces during the 1993 peacekeeping mission in Somalia, dies from wounds received during street fighting in Mogadishu, the capital.

2 Congress approves a 90-cent, two-stage minimum-wage increase to $5.15 an hour.

4 Followers of Somalia's slain warlord Mohamed Farah Aideed name his son, Hussein, who served with U.S. Marines in Somalia, as their new leader.

August
1996

S	M	T	W	TH	F	S
				1	2	3
4	5	6	7	8	9	10
11	12	13	14	15	16	17
18	19	20	21	22	23	24
25	26	27	28	29	30	31

6 A National Aeronautics and Space Administration official confirms that scientists have identified compounds and minerals related to bacterial action on a meteorite that fell from Mars approximately 16 million years ago. The presence of polycyclic aromatic hydrocarbons and magnetite and iron sulfide offers evidence that a primitive form of microscopic life may once have existed on Mars.

Chechen rebels audaciously assault and retake Grozny, the provincial capital, from Russian control. The attack leaves scores of Russian soldiers dead and the Russian army humiliated. On August 30, Russian national security adviser Alexander Lebed announces that he and Chechen leaders agree that the future status of the republic of Chechnya will be postponed.

9 Boris Yeltsin is sworn in as the first democratically elected president of an independent Russia at a pared-down Kremlin ceremony. Stiff and visibly shaky during the inauguration, Yeltsin speaks only during the oath of office.

10 Sections of six Western states experience intermittent power failures, which on a sweltering day shut down air conditioners from Texas west to California and north to Oregon.

Robert Dole accepts the Republican nomination for president of the United States at the Republican National Convention in San Diego on August 15. He is joined on the speaker's platform by his wife, Elizabeth Dole, and by the vice presidential nominee, Jack Kemp, and his wife, Joanne Kemp.

REPUBLICAN NATIONAL CONVENTION

On August 29, Bill Clinton accepts the nomination for president of the United States at the Democratic National Convention in Chicago. He is joined on the speaker's platform by his wife, Hillary Rodham Clinton, and their daughter, Chelsea.

13 Scientists, releasing photographs of the Jovian moon, Io, taken from the Galileo spacecraft, announce that the moon may once have had or may still have a global ocean, suggesting the existence of liquid water capable of supporting life.

14 Robert Dole, former majority leader of the U.S. Senate, is nominated as the Republican candidate for president of the United States at the party's convention in San Diego. Jack Kemp, former pro-football player, New York congressman, and member of the Cabinet of President George Bush, is nominated for vice president.

16 In the first test of the Clinton Administration's "don't ask, don't tell" policy regarding homosexuals in the U.S. military, a 41-year-old female Air Force major is acquitted of charges of sodomy and conduct unbecoming an officer by a seven-member jury at Lackland Air Force Base in San Antonio, Texas.

17 At a national convention in Valley Forge, Pennsylvania, Ross Perot is tapped as the presidential nominee of the Reform Party, the political organization that the 66-year-old Texas billionaire founded following his 1992 race for the presidency.

18 West African leaders meeting in Abuja, Nigeria, chose Ruth Perry, a former Liberian senator, as head of an interim government of Liberia. Liberia's leading warlords, in attendance at the meeting, agree to the appointment.

22 President Bill Clinton signs welfare-reform legislation that ends the federal guarantee of cash assistance for poor children, which has been part of the nation's social system since instituted during President Franklin Delano Roosevelt's New Deal.

28 President Bill Clinton and Vice President Al Gore are nominated at the Democratic Party convention in Chicago as the party's candidates for president and vice president of the United States.

A British court grants Charles, Prince of Wales, and Princess Diana a divorce. Diana, who will share with Charles equal access to their sons, William and Harry, receives a lump-sum settlement of $26 million. She retains her Kensington Palace apartment and the title of princess, but relinquishes the right to be Queen of England and the honorific title HRH—her royal highness.

30 President Saddam Hussein of Iraq sends tens of thousands of his troops toward the Kurdish enclaves in northern Iraq that were set up by the United States and its Western allies at the end of the 1991 Gulf War for the protection of Kurds.

September
1996

S	M	T	W	TH	F	S
1	2	3	4	5	6	7
8	9	10	11	12	13	14
15	16	17	18	19	20	21
22	23	24	25	26	27	28
29	30					

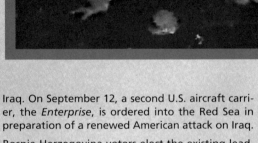

3 The United States launches missile strikes against Iraqi air defenses in southern Iraq in retaliation for Iraqi aggression against a Kurdish faction in the no-fly zone of northern Iraq.

4 Following the American missile strikes against Iraq, 400,000 Iraqi troops pull back from a contested Kurdish enclave in northern Iraq.

5 Fran, a Class 3 hurricane, slams into Cape Fear, North Carolina, with 115-mile- (185-kilometer-) per-hour winds. Ripping through Wilmington, Raleigh, and Durham, North Carolina, Fran leaves 17 people dead and damages exceeding $1 billion in its wake. On September 7, rivers in areas of Virginia and West Virginia flood their banks from the heavy rainfall unleashed during the hurricane's journey inland.

President Boris Yeltsin announces that he will undergo heart surgery.

6 The U.S. Department of Labor announces that the unemployment rate during August 1996 dropped to 5.1 percent, the lowest level in seven years.

8 Tennis star Steffi Graf captures the women's final of the U.S. Open with a 7-5, 6-3 victory over Monica Seles. Pete Sampras beats Michael Chang 6-1, 6-4, 7-6 to take the men's final.

9 Without firing a shot, the Kurdistan Democratic Party (KDP) forces backed by Saddam Hussein take the northern Iraqi city of Sulaimaniya, headquarters and stronghold of the Patriotic Union of Kurdistan. KDP leader Massoud Barzani now controls all of the cities of Iraq's Kurdish region.

11 The United States dispatches F-117 stealth fighters to Kuwait and B-52 bombers to other parts of the Middle East in preparation for another attack on Iraq. On September 12, a second U.S. aircraft carrier, the *Enterprise*, is ordered into the Red Sea in preparation of a renewed American attack on Iraq.

17 Bosnia-Herzegovina voters elect the existing leaders of the nation's three major ethnic groups to a three-member presidency. Muslim Bosnian President Alija Izetbegovic, Bosnian Serb separatist Momcilo Krajisnik, and the ethnic Croat Kresimir Zubak will govern under the chairmanship of Izetbegovic, who received the most votes.

25 Firefights between Israeli soldiers and Palestinians leave at least five dead and hundreds wounded in a series of clashes along Israel's West Bank. The vi-

A satellite image captures the swirling, 115-mile- (185-kilometer-) per-hour winds and eye of Hurricane Fran before it slams into North America at Cape Fear, North Carolina, on September 5.

olence is triggered by news that Israeli Prime Minister Benjamin Natanyahu authorized opening a new entrance to an archaeological tunnel along the western wall of Jerusalem's Temple Mount, which is sacred to both Jews and Muslims. Visitors use the tunnel to tour the archaeological layers of Jerusalem's history. On September 27, violence, raging in five West Bank cities and Gaza, spreads to Jerusalem. On September 29, President Bill Clinton invites Israeli Prime Minister Benjamin Netanyahu, Palestinian leader Yasir Arafat, King Hussein of Jordan, and Hosni Mubarak of Egypt to Washington to explore solutions to the violence.

27 The war-ravaged Afghani capital of Kabul, abandoned on September 26 by troops loyal to President Burhanuddin Rabbani, is captured by fundamentalist Islamic guerrillas. The rebel group, called the Taliban, proclaims the establishment of a strict Islamic state before executing former communist leaders. Men are told not to shave or trim beards. Women are forbidden to work outside the home, and girls are ordered out of schools. A traditional Islamic criminal code, prescribing stoning and the severing of hands, is instituted.

October
1996

S	M	T	W	TH	F	S
		1	2	3	4	5
6	7	8	9	10	11	12
13	14	15	16	17	18	19
20	21	22	23	24	25	26
27	28	29	30	31		

1 A federal district judge rules that third-party presidential candidate Ross Perot has no constitutional right to be included in presidential debates between Bill Clinton and Bob Dole, the Democratic and Republican candidates for president.

2 President Bill Clinton announces that the emergency summit meeting between Yasir Arafat and Benjamin Netanyahu has failed to resolve differences

The New York Yankees, after 18 years without a championship, are unable to contain their joy at winning baseball's World Series on October 26 by beating the Atlanta Braves 3-2 in game six.

The number of births by unmarried women also declined in 1995, by 4 percent.

5 Steam and ash from the erupting Loki volcano blasts 33,000 feet (10,058 meters) above Iceland, diverting all flights from the area. Since the eruption began on October 1, molten rock, flowing from a 5-mile (8-kilometer) fissure, has melted through 2,000 feet (609 meters) of ice in a glacier that covers nearly 10 percent of the island.

6 As agreed at the Washington, D.C., summit by Israeli Prime Minister Benjamin Netanyahu and Palestinian leader Yasir Arafat, negotiators meeting at Erez Crossing, in the Gaza Strip, concentrate on working out a timetable for a Palestinian takeover of the city of Hebron.

8 The 78-year-old Pope John Paul II is operated on for what doctors in Rome described as an inflamed appendix.

12 Thousands of U.S. citizens and immigrants of Hispanic ancestry march on Washington's National Mall to display ethnic pride and protest what is perceived as the country's growing anti-immigrant, anti-Hispanic attitude.

14 Stocks making up the Dow Jones industrial average climb 62 points in a single day to send the average past 6,000 for the first time in history.

17 Appearing on national television, President of Russia Boris Yeltsin dismisses Alexander Lebed as his national security chief.

19 Scientists in Melbourne, Australia, announce the discovery, on the island of Tasmania, of a shrub that they believe to be some 40,000 years old and, thus, the world's oldest living organism. Called King's Holly, the single plant stands 26 feet (7.8 meters) high and grows along a mountain gully for nearly 1 mile (1.6 kilometers).

20 Japan's Liberal Democrats, the country's major conservative party, take 239 of 500 seats in the key lower house of Parliament.

25 Toronto, Canada's largest city, is paralyzed when thousands of angry citizens fill downtown streets, protesting the provincial government's budget cuts, which are expected to profoundly affect welfare, public-hospital, and university funding.

26 After 18 years without a championship, the New York Yankees win baseball's World Series by beating the Atlanta Braves 3-2 in game six.

30 While thousands of Hutu refugees, who have lived in Zairian camps since the 1994 Rwandan civil war, flee into Burundi, the armies of Zaire and Rwanda lob artillery shells across their joint border. Hutu-dominated Zaire accuses Tutsi-dominated Rwanda of sending troops to reenforce Tutsi rebels in Zaire. Denying the charge, Rwanda claims Zaire is carrying out Tutsi genocide.

between the Palestinian and Israeli leaders. They do, however, agree that negotiators will continue to debate stalled provisions of the Oslo Accords.

3 Defense Secretary William Perry announces that up to 7,500 American troops will remain in Bosnia through mid-March 1997. Approximately 15,000 troops are currently stationed in Bosnia as part of a one-year peacekeeping mission.

4 The National Center for Health Statistics discloses that the number of births by teen-age mothers dropped in 1995, for the fourth consecutive year.

November
1996

S	M	T	W	TH	F	S
					1	2
3	4	5	6	7	8	9
10	11	12	13	14	15	16
17	18	19	20	21	22	23
24	25	26	27	28	29	30

3 Scuba divers complete a three-month deep sea-search for wreckage from Trans World Airlines flight 800. The Paris-bound airplane crashed into the ocean off the tip of New York's Long Island in July. In one of the largest salvage missions in the history of the U.S. Navy, divers recover almost 95 percent of the plane.

5 President Bill Clinton wins a landslide victory over former Senator Robert Dole. Clinton, the first Democratic president to win re-election since Franklin Roosevelt, dominates the balloting in all regions of the country except the South and Midwestern plains states. Despite GOP fears before the election that Democrats would also sweep House and Senate races, Republicans maintain control of both houses of Congress.

6 Pakistani citizens party in the streets in celebration of news that opposition forces have ousted Prime Minister Benazir Bhutto and dismantled her government. Police release Bhutto from a 24-hour house arrest, but her husband, a cabinet minister, remains in custody. President Farooq Leghari deposed Bhutto on November 5.

7 The United States launches an unmanned spaceship as a first step in a 10-year plan to explore Mars. Scheduled to begin orbiting Mars in September 1997, the ship was designed to study the atmosphere and map the planet's surface

9 India begins an emergency airlift of food and medicine to those left stranded by flood waters, which came in the wake of a November 7 cyclone that killed at least 1,000 people and ravaged the country's southeast coast. The storm leveled houses and devastated one of the country's most fertile growing regions.

12 Two airliners collide over India, killing all 351 people aboard. Shortly after takeoff, a Saudi Arabian jumbo jet slams into a Kazal Airlines plane that is approaching the New Delhi airport. It is the third deadliest crash and the worst midair collision in aviation history.

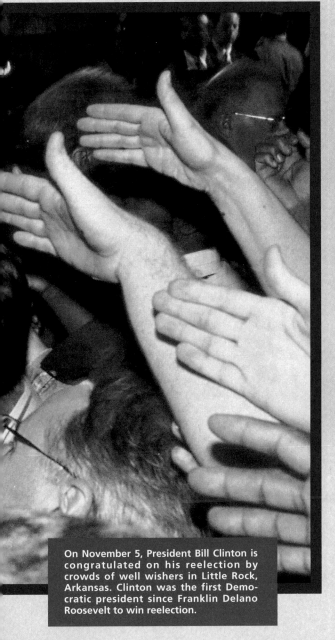

On November 5, President Bill Clinton is congratulated on his reelection by crowds of well wishers in Little Rock, Arkansas. Clinton was the first Democratic president since Franklin Delano Roosevelt to win reelection.

13 A U.S. Army drill sergeant pleads guilty to having had sexual relations with three female recruits. Three men who train recruits face charges of rape and sexual harassment against women recruits. The Army will expand its investigation into allegations of sexual harassment in its ranks.

15 President Bill Clinton announces that the United States will keep a military force in Bosnia for 18 more months. In 1995, Clinton said U.S. troops would occupy the war-torn Balkan nation for only one year.

18 Federal officials arrest a Central Intelligence Agency officer on charges he spied for Russia. Harold J. Nicholson, who allegedly has passed U.S. secrets to Moscow for two years, is the highest ranking officer at the agency ever charged with espionage.

19 Scientists announce that a 2.33-million-year-old jaw found in Ethiopia offers evidence that the human family line—genus *Homo*—is 400,000 years older than once believed. The jaw might provide an evolutionary link between humans' ancient ancestors and the more ape-like *australopithecine*.

20 The U.S. government agrees to pay $4.8 million to 12 people injected with radioactive plutonium or uranium in secret experiments performed from 1944 to 1974. The announcement follows an 18-month investigation, which concluded that the government endorsed the injection of radioactive material into several patients in Rochester, New York.

21 Russian scientists reveal that the country has been without photo reconnaissance satellites for nearly two months. It marks the first time since the early 1960's that Moscow has been without "spy photos" that keep tabs on military maneuvers in other countries.

23 A hijacked plane crashes into the Indian Ocean near the Comoro Islands off the east coast of Africa, killing at least 123 of the 175 people on board. After terrorists ignore warnings that the plane is running out of fuel, Ethiopian Airlines flight 961 crashes only 500 yards from shore, narrowly missing a class of scuba-diving students, More people die in this incident than in any other previous hijacking.

29 The International Tribunal on War Crimes in the former Yugoslavia hands down its first verdict, sentencing a former soldier of the Bosnian Serb army to 10 years in prison for his role in the massacre of Muslim civilians in 1995.

30 French truck drivers begin lifting highway barricades, ending a 12-day strike that constrained the economy of much of Western Europe.

December 1996

S	M	T	W	TH	F	S
1	2	3	4	5	6	7
8	9	10	11	12	13	14
15	16	17	18	19	20	21
22	23	24	25	26	27	28
29	30	31				

3 An explosion rips through a crowded commuter train during the height of rushhour in Paris, France. The blast kills two people and wounds seven. Although no terrorist group claims responsibility for the attack, police suspect it is the work of Algerian Muslim militants opposed to French support for Algeria's military-backed government.

4 The United States launches a spacecraft that will be the first Mars landing in 20 years and will deliver a remote-controlled roving vehicle to Mars. The vehicle will cruise the planet's landscape, taking pictures.

5 President Bill Clinton nominates Madeleine K. Albright to serve as secretary of state during the president's second term. Albright, U.S. chief delegate to the United Nations, will be the first woman to head the State Department. Clinton also chooses William S. Cohen, a Republican senator from Maine, to replace William Perry as secretary of defense and names the national security adviser, Anthony Lake, director of the Central Intelligence Agency.

6 Alan Greenspan, chairman of the board of the Federal Reserve System, rocks the world's financial community when he warns that a continued increase in stock prices could cause the market to crash. Stock prices dive following Greenspan's remarks, but quickly rebound after Greenspan makes no move to hike interest rates.

8 A U.S. congressman joins forces with the Sudanese ambassador to the United States to free three Red Cross workers held hostage for nearly 40 days in a Sudanese rebel camp. Rebels drop demands for $2.5 million in ransom after Representative Bill Richardson, from New Mexico, and Ambassador Mahdi I. Mohamed promise the rebels five tons of rice, four Jeeps, nine radios, and a health-survey for the disease-ridden camp.

9 The U.S. Energy Department announces it will dispose of 52.5 tons (53.34 metric tons) of plutonium—more than half of the national stockpile—from old nuclear weapons, by using it as fuel and by solidifying it and then putting it into storage.

10 Iraq, for the first time in six years, begins pumping oil abroad. Iraqi President Saddam Hussein reopens a 616-mile (991-kilometer) pipeline—which Turkey shut down in 1990 to protest Iraq's invasion of Kuwait—less than 24-hours after the United Nations approves a plan to allow Iraq to sell $1 billion of oil, twice every six months, in order to buy food and medical supplies.

12 Scientists reveal that a third human species, *Homo erectus*, lived at the same time as Neanderthals and *Homo sapiens* (human beings). Researchers conclude that *Homo erectus*, an ancient human ancestor that evolved 1.8 million years ago, did not die out until about 27,000 to 53,000 years ago.

13 President Bill Clinton nominates William M. Daley, brother of Chicago Mayor Richard Daley, as commerce secretary and Bill Richardson, a U.S. representative from New Mexico, as chief delegate to the United Nations. Clinton also ends weeks of speculation by announcing that Attorney General Janet Reno will serve a second term.

17 Gunmen kill six Western Red Cross workers in the separatist republic of Chechnya, while the workers are sleeping in a guarded compound. The murders place peace efforts and the future of international aid in jeopardy.

18 Marxist guerrillas storm the Japanese ambassador's house in Lima, Peru, and take 490 hostages. Members of the Túpac Amaru rebel group vow to kill the hostages unless the Peruvian government frees their jailed comrades.

20 President Bill Clinton fills out a Cabinet for his second term. He nominates Federico Peña as secretary of energy, Rodney Slater as secretary of transportation, Alexis Herman as secretary of labor, and Andrew Cuomo as secretary of housing and urban development.

24 Clashes erupt in Belgrade, Serbia, between government supporters and its opposition. Violence breaks out after hundreds of riot police and supporters of President Slobodan Milošević pour into the capital for a progovernment rally. The rally is held in the same area where about 20,000 government protesters have gathered daily since local elections were annulled in November.

29 The civil war in Guatemala ends after government officials and guerrillas sign a peace treaty. At least 100,000 people were killed during the 36-year conflict.

Madeline Albright, U.S. ambassador to the United Nations, addresses the White House press corp after being nominated for Secretary of State by President Bill Clinton on December 5. Albright is the first woman to be nominated to head the Department of State.

1996

World Book Year Book Update

The major events of 1996 are summarized in more than 250 alphabetically arranged articles, from "Afghanistan" to "Zoos." In most cases, the article titles are the same as those of the articles in *The World Book Encyclopedia* that they update. Included are Special Reports that offer in-depth looks at subjects, ranging from the career of comedian George Burns to the economic and social conditions of modern Russia. The Special Reports can be found on the following pages under their respective Update article titles.

Afghanistan

Afghanistan. A fundamentalist Muslim militia group, the Taliban, captured Afghanistan's capital, Kabul, on Sept. 27, 1996, and claimed power as the new national government. However, with the fall of Kabul, the country remained divided among four armed factions. The Taliban controlled the southern two-thirds. The forces of Burhanuddin Rabbani, the leader who had controlled Kabul, and his defense minister, Ahmad Shah Massoud, retreated to the northeast. A regional warlord, Abdul Rashid Dostam, ruled the Uzbek and Turkman ethnic minorities in the northwest, and a Hazara ethnic group held the north-central region.

It was widely believed that Pakistan had created and armed the Taliban because Pakistan wanted Afghanistan at peace but under Pakistani influence. Pakistan denied that it supported the Taliban. Meanwhile, Rabbani's forces received weapons and other aid flown in from India, Russia, and Iran.

The Taliban first appeared in 1994 as a reaction to the civil war that had been raging since the 1992 collapse of the nation's Communist regime. The Taliban was controlled by a shadowy council headed by a former guerrilla warrior and Muslim teacher, Muhammad Umar. Twice in 1995 and again in May 1996, Taliban troops failed to capture Kabul from the south, but their attacks wreaked further destruction on the city, whose population had fallen from 2 million to 1 million people since 1992. One faction leader who had repeatedly attacked Kabul, Gulbuddin Hikmatyar, was named Rabbani's prime minister on June 17, 1996.

Kabul taken, former president killed. On September 5, the Taliban launched an offensive east of the capital. Taliban troops defeated Massoud's forces at Sarobi, and Massoud's troops withdrew from Kabul on September 26. The following day, the Taliban took control of the city.

Taliban troops found Najibullah, the last Communist president, at the United Nations (UN) compound in Kabul, where he had taken refuge after his government fell. Najibullah was shot and his body hanged outside the presidential palace.

Taliban's Islamic system. The day Kabul fell, Umar named Mohammad Rabbani, a *mullah* (Muslim religious teacher) unrelated to the defeated president, to head a ruling interim council. Umar stated the Taliban would enforce a "complete Islamic system" in Afghanistan, which included a strict Islamic legal code and severe restrictions on women. The UN warned that Afghanistan would lose needed foreign aid if these policies continued, but Taliban officials defied the warnings.

Alliance. On October 10, Massoud, Dostam, and a Hazara leader announced an alliance to resist further Taliban attacks. There was little hope that fighting would soon end.   □ Henry S. Bradsher

See also **Asia** (Facts in brief table). In *World Book*, see **Afghanistan**.

Africa

Poverty and both civil and political instability were serious concerns in Africa in 1996. However, the climate for economic growth and democracy seemed more positive than in many past years. African immigrants in Europe, women's issues, and disease in Africa became worldwide concerns in 1996.

Africa's economies. Several reports indicated Africa experienced economic growth at rates ranging from 2.3 to 3.8 percent in 1996. A few countries in Africa experienced negative growth in 1996, and eight African countries experienced growth rates of 6 percent or higher. Most impressive was Uganda, which had a 10-percent growth rate. However, Africa's population growth continued to outpace its economic growth, resulting in an overall 0.6-percent drop in *per capita income* (national income divided by total population). Africa's population was expected to increase by 300 million people in the next 15 years, reaching 1.25 billion by 2025.

Economic statistics in Africa presented a mixed picture in 1996. Some countries, such as Uganda, made strong economic progress. However, the economies of Liberia, Somalia, and Zaire were greatly affected by war or civil disorder. Mining and industrial production were on the upswing, as were the prices of many African exports. However, the rate of increase of most export prices slowed in 1996, suggesting a future stagnation—or even decline—of economic growth.

The problems underlying Africa's economic woes remained unsolved. Among these were high transportation costs, heavy debt burdens, stagnant agricultural production, high unemployment, civil strife, recurrent drought, and high import burdens. Africa was receiving less foreign investment than other parts of the developing world, and its share of world trade dropped considerably during most of the 1990's.

Progress toward democracy. By some measures, Africa made substantial progress toward democracy during the 1990's. In some countries, military rulers disappeared, though they sometimes reappeared as civilian rulers. Elections were held in many countries, but the polling was often neither open, fair, nor competitive.

A military government in Sierra Leone, while engaged in a civil war, established and pursued an electoral process in 1996. A civilian, Ahmad Tejan Kabbah, was elected president and took the reins of power. The government achieved a cease-fire with rebels and began negotiations for a settlement.

In Uganda, President Yoweri Kaguta Museveni was reelected in May, and Museveni's supporters won a majority of seats when a new parliament was elected in June. Although partisan political activities were banned and Museveni used state resources to

Rwandan refugees, after fleeing camps in Burundi, await medical treatment in January at a temporary camp along Burundi's border with Tanzania.

woo electors, observers declared the elections free. The existence of a rebel group in the north, the Lord's Resistance Army, did not influence the election to any great extent.

Cape Verde President Antonio Mascarenhas Monteiro was reelected in February. Mathieu Kérékou, a former president of Benin, defeated incumbent President Nicéphore Sogolo in the March election in Benin. In São Tomé and Pri'ncipe, President Miguel Trovoada was returned to office in a runoff election in July. Also in July, President Idriss Deby won reelection in Chad in a process that foreign observers described as generally free and fair. However, seven of Deby's opponents boycotted the elections and characterized them as rigged.

Success stories—South Africa and Mali. South Africa continued to make democratic progress in 1996, approving a new constitution with strong human-rights protection. Local elections were successfully conducted in June in the conflict-torn KwaZulu region. Political parties began to seek alliances as they prepared for the next round of elections. The African National Congress, the Nationalist Party, and Inkatha remained the major political players.

Mali, in West Africa, remained a model of democratic success. In 1992, Mali's military government had sponsored multiparty elections, in which Alpha Oumar Konare was elected president. After taking office, he fostered popular participation and openness in government. These policies won support at home and abroad, attracting foreign aid and investment. United States Secretary of State Warren Christopher chose to begin his Africa visit in autumn 1996 in Mali to symbolize American support for democracy in Africa.

Other African countries did not embrace the democratic election process in 1996. March elections in Zimbabwe returned Robert Mugabe to office in what appeared to be a multiparty poll. In reality, government oppression prevented opposition parties from mounting campaigns.

A *coup d'état* (overthrow) in Niger in January ousted the elected president, Mahamane Ousmane. He was replaced by an army officer, Ibrahim Bare Mainassara. Bare Mainassara quickly had a new constitution ratified and won election to the presidency. To ensure his own election, he replaced the official vote-counting body with one of his choosing. Opposition leaders claimed the elections were a fraud. France, Niger's former colonial ruler, and the United States criticized the electoral process.

Gambia, Equatorial Guinea, and Nigeria. Gambia had a democratic form of government until 1994, when a coup overthrew the president and installed military rule under Captain Yahya Jammeh. In August 1996, Jammeh conducted a referendum on a new constitution, which was widely criticized for its human-rights shortcomings and the limits it set on presidential eligibility. The opposition took no part

in writing the document, and voters had only four days to study it before the September election. Jammeh won the presidency after several opponents had been disqualified.

What observers characterized as perhaps the most antidemocratic election in Africa in 1996 occurred in Equatorial Guinea. Citizens voted by selecting a picture of their candidate from a table while being observed by police agents.

Nigeria, the most populous country in Africa, with the continent's second largest economy, remained in the grip of a military dictatorship under General Sani Abacha. Abacha's regime continued to imprison Mashood Abiola, who had been elected president in a democratic election in 1993. Nigeria held local governmental elections in March 1996, which gave the appearance of returning the country to civilian rule.

Army mutinies flared in several African nations in 1996. A nine-day mutiny in the Central African Republic in May was especially violent. France sent in troops to quash the uprising, a move unpopular in France and in the Central African Republic. Destruction and looting occurred despite the intervention. Foreign nationals, including the members of the American Peace Corps, were evacuated. Another former French colony, Guinea, experienced a brief mutiny in early February. The rebels held President Lansana Conté prisoner for a brief time.

Liberia and Somalia. Anarchic conditions continued to prevail in Liberia and Somalia in 1996. In Liberia, the 1995 Abuja Agreement broke down. Major fighting erupted early in 1996 between the West-African peacekeeping force, ECOMOG, and one of several rebel groups. Large-scale fighting erupted in Monrovia, the capital, in April. A cease-fire was achieved in July, and a political agreement was signed in August. All sides agreed to choose a new head of state, and Ruth Perry, who had once been a senator, was named state council chairman.

Prospects for peace in Somalia brightened briefly in August after the death of one of the major factional leaders, Mohamed Farah Aideed. These hopes soon faded, however, when Aideed's son and successor stated his intention to "exterminate" his opponents. Hopes for peace rose again in October when the major faction leaders agreed to a cease-fire and promised to remove the blockades that divided Mogadishu, the capital, into factional enclaves.

Conditions in Rwanda and Burundi continued to be affected by ethnic rivalries in 1996. Mass slaughter in Rwanda in 1994 resulted in the deaths of at least 500,000 people and caused over 2 million people to become refugees. Hutu refugees, afraid of reprisals by the Tutsi-led government in Rwanda, refused to return home. The situation changed, however, in November 1996 when fighting in and around refugee camps in eastern Zaire prompted a massive refugee exodus back to their Rwandan homeland.

A similar Hutu-Tutsi conflict in Burundi led to the deaths of as many as 10,000 people per month in 1996. However, the genocide that many feared did not take place in 1996.

Zaire seemed to have the potential of becoming as chaotic and violent as Rwanda and Burundi in 1996. Its dictator, Mobutu Sese Seko, was out of the country for much of the year to receive treatment for cancer. In autumn 1996, conditions in the eastern provinces deteriorated as Tutsi Zairians fought Hutu refugee militias. Zaire's regular army became involved in the fray as well. Zaire and Rwanda exchanged artillery fire across the border several times in the late months of 1996. The number of refugees that remained in eastern Zaire following the mass exodus of Rwandan refugees in November remained unknown at the end of 1996.

Angola. Peace persisted in Angola through 1996. Some progress was made in demobilizing the National Union for the Total Liberation of Angola (UNITA) forces and integrating them into the national army. However, the country remained partitioned between government and UNITA sectors. In 1996, the United Nations (UN) peacekeeping force in Angola was the largest such force deployed anywhere in the world. Alioune Blondin Beye, the UN special representative in Angola, predicted that the operation would prove to be a success before withdrawal of the force, which was scheduled for 1997.

Crisis response force proposed. Africa's numerous crises placed heavy demands on the rich nations of the world for emergency relief and diplomacy. At times, the United States and other Western countries considered sending peacekeeping forces to troubled areas. In 1996, the idea of an African crisis response force gained popularity. African nations would provide the troops for such a force, while external donors would contribute financial and logistical support, equipment, and training.

The United States pressured South Africa to take a lead in developing such a force. The South African government, however, remained reluctant to champion the idea. High-ranking U.S. officials visited several African countries during 1996 and asked for promises of support troops for the proposed African crisis response force.

AIDS. There was some evidence in 1996 that the AIDS epidemic was slowing in Africa. Still, the continent remained the most severely affected in the world. Of the world's known cases of HIV infection, 63 percent (19.2 million) were in Africa. (HIV is the virus that causes AIDS.) Some 7.6 million Africans had died of AIDS by 1996. Botswana, Kenya, Malawi, Uganda, Zambia, and Zimbabwe were among the hardest-hit countries. Estimates put Malawi's adult HIV-infection rate at 1 in 8. In Kenya, more than 300,000 children had been orphaned by AIDS. The toll that AIDS had taken on the educated classes was reflected in declining economic growth in severely affected countries.

Many governments mounted AIDS education campaigns. While such programs were sometimes successful, they were often undermined by claims of "miracle" cures, which caused people to abandon safe sexual practices. In Malawi, since the outbreak of the AIDS epidemic, more than 1 million people had visited a traditional doctor who claimed to have an herbal AIDS cure.

Other diseases also took a great toll in Africa in 1996. A West African meningitis outbreak left 10,000 people dead. Nigeria, Burkina Faso, Niger, Mali, and Chad were most affected by the disease. The incidence of tuberculosis and malaria continued to increase during the year. Two outbreaks of Ebola hemorrhagic fever, the viral illness that had struck Zaire in 1995, occurred in Gabon in 1996, though the number of infections and deaths was low.

Female genital mutilation, also known as female circumcision, long practiced in northern and western Africa, had come under increasing criticism in Europe and America by 1996. In Africa, women's groups began to attack the practice as well, and it was outlawed in several countries. Prosecution under these laws was rare, however, and such measures had little impact.

The case of Fauziya Kasinga, a young woman from Togo who fled to the United States to avoid female genital mutilation and a forced marriage, focused attention on the issue during the year. American authorities had jailed Kasinga upon her arrival in 1994 as an illegal immigrant. She remained in detention until April 1996. In May, a U.S. court granted her *asylum* (the right to remain in one nation because of political conditions or persecution in another country).

African emigration in Europe. The large immigration of Africans to Europe, much of it illegal, remained a major European political issue in 1996. In France, which attracted many immigrants from former French colonies in Africa, the politics of immigration became especially heated.

Polygamy, the practice of marrying more than one wife, proved to be a particularly difficult issue in France. Thousands of polygamous families emigrated to France from former colonies and continued to practice polygamy in their new home. The practice was largely ignored by authorities until both French and immigrant African women displayed their opposition to the practice. In 1996, the French government outlawed the practice of polygamy among immigrants in France.

Meanwhile, France also tightened controls on immigration, restricted access to asylum, and, in some cases, forced the removal of immigrants to their home countries. These measures were largely designed to affect African immigrants in France or would-be immigrants to France.   □ Mark DeLancey

See also the various African country articles; **Africa** Special Report: **Continent in Crisis.** In *World Book,* see **Africa.**

Facts in brief on African political units

Country	Population	Government	Monetary unit*	Foreign trade (million U.S.$)	
				Exports†	Imports†
Algeria	29,170,000	President Liamine Zeroual; Prime Minister Ahmed Ouyahia	dinar (55.68 = $1)	11,137	8,648
Angola	11,819,000	President José Eduardo dos Santos	readj. kwanza (201,994.00 = $1)	2,989	1,140
Benin	5,732,000	President Mathieu Kerekou	CFA franc (514.47 = $1)	163	493
Botswana	1,574,000	President Sir Ketumile Masire	pula (3.53 = $1)	1,800	1,800
Burkina Faso	10,846,000	Popular Front Chairman, Head of State, & Head of Government Blaise Compaoré	CFA franc (514.47 = $1)	105	536
Burundi	6,751,000	Interim President Pierre Buyoya; Prime Minister Pascal-Firmin Ndimira	franc (221.15 = $1)	121	224
Cameroon	13,993,000	President Paul Biya	CFA franc (514.47 = $1)	1,369	732
Cape Verde	413,000	President Antonio Mascarenhas Monteiro; Prime Minister Carlos Alberto Wahnon de Carvalho Veiga	escudo (82.97 = $1)	5	210
Central African Republic	3,473,000	President Ange Patasse	CFA franc (514.47 = $1)	150	142
Chad	6,718,000	President Idriss Deby	CFA franc (514.47 = $1)	157	186
Comoros	700,000	President Mohamed Taki Abdoulkarim	franc (385.85 = $1)	22	69
Congo	2,734,000	President Pascal Lissouba; Prime Minister David Charles Ganao	CFA franc (514.47 = $1)	1,070	583
Djibouti	603,000	President Hassan Gouled Aptidon; Prime Minister Barkat Gourad Hamadou	franc (165.00 = $1)	16	219
Egypt	65,319,000	President Hosni Mubarak; Prime Minister Kamal Ahmed al-Ganzouri	pound (3.39 = $1)	3,475	10,218
Equatorial Guinea	420,000	President Teodoro Obiang Nguema Mbasogo; Prime Minister Serafin Seriche Dougan	CFA franc (514.47 = $1)	62	60
Eritrea	3,718,000	President Isaias Afworki	Ethiopian birr	no statistics available	
Ethiopia	58,338,000	President Negasso Gidada	birr (6.00 = $1)	372	1,033
Gabon	1,394,000	President El Hadj Omar Bongo; Prime Minister Paulin Obame	CFA franc (514.47 = $1)	2,314	740
Gambia	1,183,000	Chairman, Armed Forces Provisional Ruling Council, & Head of State Yahya Jammeh	dalasi (10.01 = $1)	35	208
Ghana	18,480,000	President Jerry John Rawlings	cedi (1,732.13 = $1)	1,252	2,175
Guinea	7,100,000	President Lansana Conté	franc (1015.00 = $1)	622	768
Guinea-Bissau	1,119,000	President João Bernardo Vieira	peso (18,036.00 = $1)	33	63
Ivory Coast	15,192,000	President Henri Konan Bédié	CFA franc (514.47 = $1)	2,878	2,354
Kenya	29,889,000	President Daniel T. arap Moi	shilling (55.75 = $1)	1,593	2,196
Lesotho	2,159,000	King Letsie III; Prime Minister Ntsu Mokhehle	maloti (4.59 = $1)	109	964
Liberia	3,236,000	State Council Chairman Ruth Perry	dollar (1 = $1)	396	272
Libya	5,773,000	Leader of the Revolution Muammar Muhammad al-Qadhafi; General People's Committee Secretary (Prime Minister) Abd al Majid al-Qaud	dinar (0.36 = $1)	11,213	5,356

Country	Population	Government	Monetary unit*	Foreign trade (million U.S.$)	
				Exports†	Imports†
Madagascar	13,673,000	Interim President and Prime Minister Norbert Lala Ratsirahonana	franc (3,950.00 = $1)	371	544
Malawi	11,522,000	President Bakili Muluzi	kwacha (15.36 = $1)	325	495
Mali	11,459,000	President Alpha Oumar Konare; Prime Minister Ibrahima Boubacar Keita	CFA franc (514.47 = $1)	343	608
Mauritania	2,390,000	President Maaouya Ould Sid Ahmed Taya	ouguiya (138.77 = $1)	437	222
Mauritius	1,141,000	President Sir Cassam Uteem; Prime Minister Navin Ramgoalam	rupee (20.49 = $1)	1,347	1,930
Morocco	28,032,000	King Hassan II; Prime Minister Abdellatif Filali	dirham (8.73 = $1)	4,665	8,539
Mozambique	17,117,000	President Joaquím Alberto Chissano; Prime Minister Pascoal Manuel Mocumbi	metical (11,140.50 = $1)	17	78
Namibia	1,621,000	President Sam Nujoma; Prime Minister Hage Geingob	rand (4.59 = $1)	1,300	1,100
Niger	9,769,000	President, Niger National Council, Ibrahim Bare Mainassara; Prime Minister Boukary Adji	CFA franc (514.47 = $1)	226	309
Nigeria	118,157,000	Head of State, Chairman, Federal Executive Council Sani Abacha	naira (22.00 = $1)	9,923	7,513
Rwanda	7,078,000	President Pasteur Bizimungu	franc (329.49 = $1)	82	335
São Tomé and Príncipe	138,000	President Miguel Trovoada	dobra (2,385.13 = $1)	6	32
Senegal	8,762,000	President Abdou Diouf; Prime Minister Habib Thiam	CFA franc (514.47 = $1)	456	967
Seychelles	75,000	President France Albert René	rupee (5.05 = $1)	52	207
Sierra Leone	4,727,000	President Ahmad Tejan Kabbah	leone (870.00 = $1)	25	135
Somalia	7,083,000	No functioning government	shilling (2,620 = $1)	81	81
South Africa	43,325,000	State President Nelson Mandela	rand (4.59= $1)	26,912	29,608
Sudan	29,631,000	President Umar Hasan Ahmad al-Bashir	pound (1,400.00 = $1)	509	1,059
Swaziland	904,000	King Mswati III; Prime Minister Bannabas Sibusiso Dlamini	lilangeni (4.59 = $1)	632	734
Tanzania	31,400,000	President Benjamin William Mkapa; Prime Minister Omar Ali Juma	shilling (596.00 = $1)	683	1,678
Togo	4,402,000	President Gnassingbé Eyadéma	CFA franc (514.47 = $1)	209	385
Tunisia	9,218,000	President Zine El Abidine Ben Ali; Prime Minister Hamed Karoui	dinar (0.99 = $1)	5,475	7,903
Uganda	19,806,000	President Yoweri Kaguta Museveni; Prime Minister Kintu Musoke	shilling (1,093.50 = $1)	461	1,056
Zaire	46,691,000	President Mobutu Sese Seko	new zaire (29,407.69 = $1)	419	382
Zambia	9,973,000	President Frederick Chiluba	kwacha (1,274.50 = $1)	1,088	988
Zimbabwe	11,764,000	President Robert Mugabe	dollar (10.60 = $1)	1,882	2,241

*Exchange rates as of Oct. 25, 1996, or latest available data.   †Latest available data.

In 1996, refugees from Rwanda who had fled to Zaire are forced to move again, some into neighboring Tanzania and others back into Rwanda. More than 1 million Rwandans have become refugees since 1994, when civil war and mass murder resulted in the death of more than 500,000 people.

AFRICA

CONTINENT IN CRISIS

Recent moves toward greater democratization across Africa raised the hopes of millions of people— but the future remained uncertain.

By Simon Baynham

To many observers, 1996 has produced a familiar pattern of African disaster stories. In Liberia, there has been no real end to the civil war that began with the 1990 assassination of President Samuel Doe. In Somalia, struggles among competing clans have suggested that the collapse of central authority will prevail well into the future. In 1996, tens of thousands of refugees crossed from Somalia into Kenya and Ethiopia; from Rwanda and Burundi into Tanzania; and from Zaire back into Rwanda. Civil war or extensive fighting has run unabated in Angola, Sudan, and in regions of the western Sahara.

Yet the picture is not entirely bleak. Several countries that were identified in the past with racial or tribal hatreds remained largely at peace under democratic rule throughout 1996—Ethiopia, Namibia, Mozambique, and South Africa. Elsewhere, substantial change has taken place with free, or relatively free, elections in Gambia, São Tomé and Príncipe, Niger, Zimbabwe, and Sierra Leone, where, despite civil war, military rulers returned the country to civilian rule following multiparty elections in February and March 1996.

For the past six years, a remarkable phenomenon has changed African political life. In what has been termed the "second liberation" (the first was the end of colonial rule), authoritarian regimes have been forced into liberalizing politics as well as economies. During these six years, 36 of Africa's 54 countries held multiparty elections. A peaceful change of government was the result of 14 of these elections. In other countries, reasonably free elections resulted in the governing party retaining its power. Only in a minority of African countries have governing elites held on to office by steadfastly refusing to permit multiparty elections or by engaging in blatant electoral fraud.

A turning of the tide

When Zambian President Kenneth Kaunda suffered spectacular electoral defeat at the hands of Federick Chiluba in October 1991, after nearly 30 years of single-party rule, the world saw the culmination of a people's exasperation over intolerable living conditions. The change of government, the result of the first free elections since independence, also illustrated an entire continent's anger and disillusionment with politicians who had promised freedom and prosperity in the early days of independence. In the majority of cases, these leaders had brought the people greater oppression and poverty than they had experienced under the yoke of colonial domination.

With the surge toward competitive party politics and democratization, Africa appeared to be headed in 1996 toward the freedom and prosperity for which so many had once hoped. The political wheel, however, has threatened to come full circle. Africa may well return to the point at which it stood soon after independence, when multiparty politics in most countries were soon abolished in favor of one-party or military government. As recent history has shown, the term democratization has involved more than the proliferation of political parties. It also has involved economic freedom, freedom of the mass media, and an extension of human rights. More widely, the democratic principle has emphasized the rule of law for all citizens and the concept of accountable, transparent government.

Most of the African countries that emerged as independent states during the 1960's failed to achieve even the basic requirements of democracy. During the three decades between independence and 1990, only Botswana, Gambia, and Mauritius maintained effective multiparty systems. Of these, there was only a single state, Mauritius, in which the existing government permitted the opposition to take

Glossary

Authoritarian:
favoring obedience
to authority instead
of individual free-
dom; totalitarian.

Coup d'état: a sud-
den and decisive act in
politics, usually bring-
ing about a change of
government unlawfully
and by force.

Hegemony: political
domination, especially
the leadership or domi-
nation of one state or
power over others in a
group.

The author

Simon Baynham,
Director of Research
from 1989 to 1996 at
London's Africa
Institute of South
Africa, is currently
Consultant at the
Research Institute for
the Study of Conflict
and Terrorism, also in
London.

office following free and fair elections. The conditions that brought about this failure of democracy were remarkably similar across Africa, as was illustrated by the immediate postindependence era.

The era of authoritarian rule

In the vast majority of African countries, the politicians who had won elections at independence set about eliminating their rivals. In most cases, by the time of the first or second postindependence election, the ruling government had begun to restrict or even to ban opposition parties. Many opposition leaders were persecuted, imprisoned, or in some instances killed. Others simply gave up and joined the governing party. In some cases, countries actually became independent with a single-party system already in place, notably the former Portuguese colonies—Angola, Guinea-Bissau, Mozambique—as well as such countries as Guinea, Mali, and Niger. In other countries, such as Ivory Coast and Tunisia, one-party states evolved because of the overwhelming domination of the ruling party. Thus, Africa's democratic elections often have been aptly described as "one man, one vote—once."

Single-party systems thus became the general pattern in Africa for some 30 years. During the decades of one-party rule, governments adopted a standard defense against accusations of dictatorship. It was asserted that newly independent states structured along tribal lines were "not suited" for multiparty democracy. Leaders claimed that Western-style liberal democracy would be inflammatory and dangerous in such volatile emergent societies. As one-party regimes consolidated their hold on power, they had no time for the notion of a "leader of the opposition." Instead, there was a clear concept of the political opposition as the enemy.

In the majority of cases, the abolition of legal means of organizing opposition meant that the only method of removing illiberal regimes was to resort to violence. Military *coups d'état* (takeovers), rather than elections, therefore became the main mechanism for changing governments. By the late 1980's, 31 African states had experienced successful army takeovers, and 16 of these states had experienced more than one coup. During the era from 1960 to 1990, the normal tendency among military rulers who had seized power by force was to bring civilians gradually into their governments—often by the formation of a single legal political party. In this way, military regimes were transformed into single-party dictatorships.

Economic decline

The failure of both single-party and military regimes to promote either national unity or decent standards of living gave prodemocracy forces a new lease on life. The democracy movement had its origins in the aftermath of independence, when the primary objective of Africa's new regimes was to retain power at any price, rather than to deal with pressing economic problems. As living standards declined, dissatisfaction with the ruling elite was channeled into a desire for democracy.

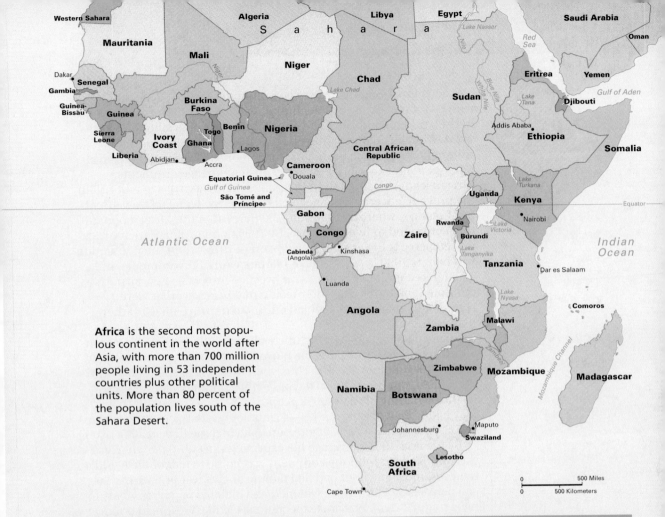

Western Sahara · Algeria · Libya · Egypt · Saudi Arabia · Oman
Mauritania · Mali · Niger · Chad · Eritrea · Yemen
Dakar · Senegal · Burkina Faso · Sudan · Djibouti · Ethiopia · Somalia
Gambia · Guinea-Bissau · Guinea · Benin · Nigeria · Central African Republic
Sierra Leone · Ivory Coast · Togo · Ghana · Cameroon · Uganda · Kenya
Liberia · Equatorial Guinea · Gabon · Congo · Zaire · Rwanda · Burundi · Tanzania
Angola · Zambia · Malawi · Comoros
Namibia · Botswana · Zimbabwe · Mozambique · Madagascar
South Africa · Swaziland · Lesotho

Africa is the second most populous continent in the world after Asia, with more than 700 million people living in 53 independent countries plus other political units. More than 80 percent of the population lives south of the Sahara Desert.

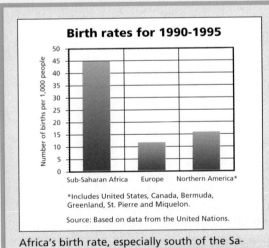

Birth rates for 1990-1995

Number of births per 1,000 people

Sub-Saharan Africa · Europe · Northern America*

*Includes United States, Canada, Bermuda, Greenland, St. Pierre and Miquelon.

Source: Based on data from the United Nations.

Africa's birth rate, especially south of the Sahara, is much higher than the world average. But its death rate is also higher than the world rate. Average life expectancy in sub-Saharan Africa is about 52 years compared with about 74 for Europe and 77 for North America.

Population projections

Population (thousands)

- Sub-Saharan Africa
- Europe
- Northern America*

*Includes United States, Canada, Bermuda, Greenland, St. Pierre and Miquelon.

Source: Based on data from the United Nations.

Population in sub-Saharan Africa continues to increase rapidly. Projections to 2020 show population steadily rising, whereas population is predicted to grow more slowly in North America, and even to level out and decrease in Europe.

The failure of many African governments to deal successfully with economic crisis has meant that while poor countries elsewhere in the world have sprung ahead, those in Africa have lurched backward. While droughts, famines, and other climatic factors contributed to economic problems, the major causes have been development policies adopted by many postcolonial governments. African leaders wanted to industrialize their countries in a hurry. In the process, governments neglected and often wrecked the agricultural sector—where in 1996 some 60 percent of the African population continued to live and work. By 1990, food production in Africa was 20 percent lower than it had been in 1970, when the population was half its 1990 level. To make matters worse, governments often squandered limited resources on prestige projects—new airports, multiple-lane highways, and presidential palaces—that were regarded by many as misguided efforts to improve image rather than economic strength.

Financial mismanagement, unchecked population growth, chronic corruption, and irresponsible borrowing from abroad contributed further to economic decline. Thus, there was less to spend on education and health care, crucial factors in the continent's development. By the beginning of the 1990's, people in Africa were poorer than they had been a decade earlier—a situation in sharp contrast to conditions in Southeast Asia, where percapita income had steadily risen.

By the mid-1990's, average life expectancy in sub-Saharan Africa was only 52 years, and the continent was home to half of the world's refugees, most of whom had fled famine or civil war or both. As the gap between rich and poor widened, the inability of governments to meet popular demands and expectations led to widespread political instability. This manifested itself in secessionist wars, tribal and religious clashes, violent demonstrations, and the widespread incidence of coups, countercoups, rebellions, and riots.

Africa's recent democratic revolution

Against this background of escalating economic crisis and political turmoil, Africa has been subject to both internal and external pressures for democratization. The process has been dubbed "Africa's democratic revolution."

Some of the external forces that have been exerted on Africa can be traced to radical developments in central and eastern Europe. There can be no doubt that political and economic reforms in the former Soviet Union, such as *glasnost* (political openness) and *perestroika* (economic restructuring), had a major impact on the socialist thinking of many single-party African states. Few observers could have predicted that the liberal changes introduced from the mid-1980's by former Soviet leader Mikhail Gorbachev would unleash forces that would have such profound repercussions. The rapid replacement of seemingly entrenched and highly repressive regimes in Eastern Europe blew winds of change across Africa. This had major consequences for the continent, stimulating demands for

In 1996, voters in Sierra Leone wait for hours to place their ballots in the country's first free democratic elections in more than 10 years, *above*.

South African President F. W. De Klerk turns over the power of his office in May 1994 to Nelson Mandela, elected president in the country's first multiracial elections, *left*. South Africa's relatively smooth transition from white-minority government to free democracy is widely regarded In Africa as an example to other nations of the continent.

democratic freedom and an end to single-party *hegemony* (political domination). As former President of Tanzania Julius Nyerere remarked in early 1990, "what is happening in Romania, Hungary, and East Germany can also happen here if we don't change."

From Algeria in the north to Swaziland in the south, and from Tanzania in the east to Togo in the west, Africa's military and one-party dictatorships came under verbal and physical attack as never before. In a host of countries, an increasingly impoverished and deeply disillusioned populace joined hands to demand political reform, government accountability, and free elections. These citizens included trade unionists, the unemployed, students, civil servants, and even army personnel. Echoing events in eastern Europe, popular political movements in Africa have often been characterized by public unrest and bloodshed. In many cases, "copycat" demon-

Somalians demonstrate for an end to war and instability at a peace rally in the capital, Mogadishu, in 1993. Life in the East African country has been dominated by civil war throughout the 1990's.

strations have spread from a country's capital to its outlying regions and even across frontiers to adjacent African states.

Pressure for a radical shakeup in Africa has also come from Western governments, as well as from lending organizations such as the World Bank and the International Monetary Fund (IMF). The United Kingdom, France, the United States, and other countries have made it clear that financial aid is conditional on political reform and evidence of free elections. International organizations and banks have made loans dependent on constitutional reform and abolition of human rights abuses. Largely as a consequence of external pressure, more than 30 African countries abandoned their experiments with socialism, in favor of the largely free-market policies preached by the World Bank and IMF.

The response of Africa's leaders

The responses of Africa's ruling elites to both internal and external demands for freedom, political democracy, and responsible government have been mixed. To date, the response of leaders might be divided into three categories. First, there are those leaders who recognized the approaching changes before popular revolts removed them from office. Thus, elections were held, averting potential civil unrest. In January 1991, for example, voters in the former Portuguese colonial islands of Cape Verde and São Tomé and Príncipe swept sitting politicians from power after 15 years of single-party domination. In March 1991, the West African republic of Benin became the third modern convert to multiparty democracy, when free elections ushered in a new president, Nicéphore Soglo, after 19 years of tyrannical rule under President Mathieu Kérékou. Zambia, which saw the departure of Kenneth Kaunda in 1991, has been placed in this category.

A second category of leaders also recognized the approach of change, but attempted to "manage" it in order to hold on to office. Zaire's President Mobutu Sese Seko has been a perfect example of this type of leader. He has held continuous office since his 1965 *coup d'état* and has successfully remained a step ahead of all opposition. He has accomplished this by encouraging the creation of scores of opposition parties in a time-honored strategy of "divide and rule."

The third group of leaders has been labeled "recalcitrants" or "die-hards." These have been primarily military leaders who have set themselves resolutely against reform. They have remained adamant that the power of the ruling regime will be maintained at all costs. Sudan's fundamentalist Islamic dictator General Umar Hasan Ahmad al-Bashir, who has shown no sign of moving with the political tide, has been labeled a "die-hard." Sudan has been engulfed by civil war for 30 of its 40 years of independence. Other leaders painted as "die-hards" include Libya's Colonel Muammar al-Qadhafi, in power since his 1969 coup, and Nigeria's General Sani Abacha, who took power in the 1993 overthrow of another military dictator.

In fact, Nigeria—Africa's most populous country and the continent's leading oil producer—has never been a single-party state but has spent nearly all of its independent existence under military rule. A heavily regulated transitional program for the restoration of democratic, civilian rule was instituted in 1986. However, in June 1993, the military government negated the results of the presidential election. The apparent winner, Chief Moshood Abiola, was not allowed to take office and was eventually imprisoned by General Sani Abacha. In October 1995, Abacha promised that Nigeria would be returned to democratic civilian rule by October 1998, but the announcement was greeted with skepticism both in and out of the country.

Events in the early 1990's cannot have escaped the attention of such hardline rulers. In March 1991, for example, Mali's military dictator, General Moussa Traoré, was ousted and arrested by his own army. This followed four days of antigovernment, prodemocracy riots in which hundreds of civilians died. The new military rulers restored civilian multiparty elections in March 1992, and the following month Alpha Oumar Konare was installed as president. In Ethiopia, in May 1991, following years of civil war, opposition forces toppled the embattled regime of Marxist hardliner Lieutenant

A funeral service is held for more than 300 Tutsi victims of a July 1996 massacre by Hutu rebels. Burundi's two major ethnic groups, the Hutu and the Tutsi, have long been in conflict.

In Liberia, a rebel soldier stands guard in Monrovia, the capital. Fighting in Liberia's six-year civil war erupted again in 1996.

Colonel Mengistu Haile-Mariam. A democratic constitution, providing for a federal system of government, was approved in December 1994. Free elections followed in May 1995.

Obstacles to political stability

For all of the euphoria that has been generated by changes in recent years, formidable hurdles have remained to the spread of democracy on the continent. Political freedom has often been mistaken as a cure for all the causes of popular discontent. Herein lies the danger. If democracy fails to deliver material prosperity, there could be a rapid return to the disenchantment that often leads to the reestablishment of dictatorship. This has been seen in Zambia, where President Chiluba has been grappling with the economic disaster inherited from Kenneth Kaunda. In short, multiparty systems have had to deal with the same financial problems faced by their predecessors. As such, the fragility of African economies has posed a considerable threat to democratic consolidation and will continue to do so.

Another major obstacle to democratic stability has been the problem of disputed electoral results. In Angola, the democratic transition from one-party rule by the Popular Movement for the Liberation of Angola (MPLA) was disrupted after the National Union for the Total Liberation of Angola (UNITA) rejected the September 1992 elections. In June 1993 in Nigeria, the military government annulled the presidential poll on the grounds that the election had been rigged.

Many African governments have publicly accepted the requirement for more democracy. Frequently, however, this has not been accompanied by an equal commitment to the liberties upon which democracy is based: tolerance, a free and vigorous press, and genuine freedom of assembly and speech. As could be seen in the 1992 run-off elections in Kenya and Cameroon, it was quite possible to have a multiparty system in which the opposition parties and mass media were intimidated and therefore rendered largely ineffective.

Moreover, many governments have continued to maintain strong military and police forces whose loyalties—often tribally reinforced — lie with the ruling political elite. These armed units frequently have been resistant to democracy. This was graphically illustrated in Burundi by the October 1993 coup attempt by a rebel faction of the Tutsi-dominated army, when the newly elected president was killed. In other countries, including Zaire, the armed forces have been used as a counterweight to the forces of liberalization. African governments have also been faced with the thorny question of how to demobilize both government and rebel troops to form a new unified army, as was being attempted in 1996 in Angola and Mozambique. Given the importance of military force in African political life, this has been a key stumbling block to the democratic transition.

The final barrier to institutionalizing democracy in Africa has been tribal conflict. Unfortunately, the drive for democracy has often led to the polarization of ethnic groupings, when new political parties crystallize mostly on the basis of tribal, regional, and religious affiliations. Such divisions often have placed the unity and stability of a multitribal country under severe strain. As has been seen in countries like Burundi, Rwanda, and Liberia, such wars have destroyed infrastructure and seriously disrupted the vital agricultural sector, which has remained the economic basis of most African families. In fact, mass starvation in Africa, contrary to widespread belief, has resulted more from warfare than drought. Famine has never occurred on the continent unless war has coincided with drought—as has been the case in Ethiopia, Eritrea, and southern Sudan.

Toward lasting freedom and democracy

Despite tribal rivalries and the horrors of famine and civil war, Africa's second liberation has indeed been set in motion, and the principle of legal political opposition has begun to take root across the continent. If the 1970's and 1980's were the "lost" decades, the 1990's have provided new signs of hope. Between June 1990 and June 1991, no fewer than nine African dictators lost power. In the same 12 months, more African states introduced multiparty politics than in the entire previous quarter century. The vast majority of the continent's countries have held free elections or have adopted significant democratic reforms. The remaining single-party and non-party states have grown increasingly vulnerable to similar pressures.

Assessing the future

The growth of freedom in Africa will not be a steady or uniform process. Two British scholars of Africa, Christopher Clapham and John Wiseman, have attempted to rank sub-Saharan nations into four broad categories. The first category consisted of nine states—including Botswana, South Africa, and the Seychelles—where prospects for continuing democracy were judged high. The second group consisted of 16 "marginal" countries possessing some criteria for optimism for future democracy. Among these states were Ghana, Malawi, and Tanzania. In the 16 states comprising the third category, which included Angola, Mozambique, and Togo, chances of sustainable democracy were assessed as being slight. The fourth category consisted of seven states where professors Clapham and Wiseman found no plausible prospects for democracy: Chad, Equatorial Guinea, Liberia, Rwanda, Somalia, Sudan, and Zaire.

The demise of authoritarian rule across much of Africa has been greeted with a mixture of joy and apprehension. It is one thing to topple a brutal dictatorship, but another thing altogether to construct a workable democracy. The lack of a democratic tradition in most African countries has made this goal especially difficult. The inability of opposition forces to achieve internal unity has raised doubts about the sustainability of democracy. What has never been in doubt, however, has been the commitment to change from ordinary Africans, millions of whom have waited for hours in the blazing sun in order to vote.

The point of view that Africa has not been "ready" for political democracy has been revised as both inaccurate and patronizing. In its place, a new outlook has evolved—that Africa must find its own route to representative and open government. Thus, for the remainder of the 1990's and into the early part of the next century, a crucial challenge confronts the continent: to maintain popular support for economic reforms that inevitably will make most people poorer in the short term, but better off in the long term; and to accomplish economic reform without destroying the ambition and will to succeed in the meantime. With Africa's vast agricultural and mineral potential, it is a challenge that remains well within the grasp of the continent's 700 million citizens. ■ ■ ■

AIDS. In March 1996, the U.S. Food and Drug Administration (FDA) approved ritonavir and indinavir, which are from a new class of HIV drugs called protease inhibitors. (HIV, or human immunodeficiency virus, is the virus that causes AIDS.) The new drugs disrupt the action of an enzyme, HIV protease, that is critical for reproduction of the virus. The combination of older drugs and the protease inhibitors decreases the amount of HIV in a patient's blood to undetectable levels. Scientists cautioned, however, that research was needed to determine if HIV would develop resistance to the drugs or reemerge from hiding places in the body if treatment were discontinued.

In June, the FDA also approved nevirapine, one of a new class of HIV drugs that stop the action of the reverse transcriptase enzyme, which is necessary for HIV's reproduction. Nevirapine blocks the *receptor,* or docking site, where the enzyme fits on a cell.

Cofactors identified. On May 10, researchers at the National Institute of Allergy and Infectious Diseases (NIAID) in Bethesda, Maryland, reported the identification of a long-sought cofactor necessary for HIV to infect cells. Scientists have known since 1984 that HIV infects immune system cells by attaching itself to CD4, a protein present on the surface of the cell. They were also aware that a *cofactor,* a joint factor that worked with the CD4, was necessary for actual infection. In the 1996 study, NIAID researchers identified the cofactor as another cell-surface protein, named fusin, that permits the cell and HIV to fuse. NIAID researchers suggested that the discovery could lead to new ways of blocking infection.

In June, five separate research groups announced another cofactor, a cell-surface protein called CKR5, the receptor for *chemokines* (immune-system chemicals that summon blood cells to inflammation sites). CKR5 acts as a docking site allowing HIV to enter a cell—a necessary step for the virus to reproduce. Researchers noted that chemokines can block the most common strain of HIV from entering cells. This discovery, scientists claimed, may lead to new treatments that replicate the action of chemokines.

Natural immunity. In September, scientists at the National Cancer Institute announced the discovery of a mutated gene for CKR5, which protects some people against infection with HIV and slows the progression of AIDS in others. Researchers identified CKR5 in a study of 1,850 people at high risk of infection and concluded that about 1 percent of white Americans inherit a mutated, or abnormal, gene for CKR5 from both parents. These people have complete immunity to HIV infection. About 20 percent of whites inherit a mutated gene from one parent and can become infected but the infection advances slowly, taking some three years longer than it does in people without the mutated gene. Almost no black people inherit the CKR5 mutation. Researchers believe that blacks inherit other forms of HIV immunity not yet identified.

New HIV test. On June 3, the FDA approved the first viral load blood test, the Amplicor HIV-1 Monitor, which measures the amount of HIV in a patient's blood. In the past, physicians monitored the progression of HIV infection indirectly, by checking the number of CD4 T-cells in a patient's blood. Because HIV kills these immune system cells, they decline in number as the infection progresses. Studies showed, however, that viral load was a more reliable indicator of HIV-infection progress.

AIDS cases. The U.S. Centers for Disease Control and Prevention (CDC) in Atlanta, Georgia, reported in August that as of Dec. 31, 1995, there had been 513,486 known AIDS cases and 319,849 AIDS-related deaths in the United States since 1981. The CDC estimated that between 650,000 and 900,000 people in the United States were infected with HIV in 1996.

The World Health Organization (WHO) in Geneva, Switzerland, reported in July that 1.3 million people worldwide died from AIDS-related illnesses in 1995, bringing the total since 1981 to 5.8 million. WHO also estimated that more than 90 percent of the estimated 21.8 million people infected with HIV in 1996 live in developing countries.

☐ Michael Woods

See also **Drugs.** In *World Book,* see **AIDS.**
Air pollution. See Environmental pollution.
Alabama. See State government.
Alaska. See State government.

Albania. Irregularities during the 1996 elections led European Union (EU) leaders to question Albania's commitment to political and economic reform. After the second round of elections, in June, President Sali Berisha's Democratic Party held 122 seats in the 140-seat Albanian parliament, an unexpectedly high number. Charges of election tampering by the government after the first round, in May, led to public protests, which ended in violent clashes with the police. Leaders of the Socialist Party, the chief party in opposition to the Democratic Party, denounced the results of the first balloting and boycotted the second round.

Election controversy. International observers found irregularities in 17 of 115 electoral districts. Several countries, including the United States and Italy, called for new elections. The European Union threatened in June to suspend cooperation with Albania. The Council of Europe, an organization of European countries dedicated to human rights and social progress, urged the government and the opposition to meet to resolve their differences.

The government ordered new elections in 17 districts but refused to completely annul the original election. Under diplomatic pressure from other countries, the socialists agreed to participate in local elections in October, which the Democrats also won by a wide margin. All parties in the election vowed to continue to support privatization and to work for

Albania

Albanian police and protesters clash in Tiranë on May 28, one of several violent protests against a government widely accused of election fraud.

closer integration with the rest of Europe. But the Socialists continued to demand talks with the government to discuss reforms, including the repeal of the "antigenocide law." This law prohibited former high Communist Party officials from holding public office until 2002. The Socialist Party was thus handicapped in the elections because the law prevented many of its leaders from running for office.

Economic recovery. President Berisha's party benefited from an economic recovery that included a 16-percent growth rate in 1995 and a drop in inflation to 6 percent. A national voucher privatization plan, which began in October 1995, was scheduled to privatize 350 large and medium-sized companies by the end of 1996. The government also announced plans to privatize the banking sector and open it to additional foreign investment. Foreign investors continued to receive very favorable terms.

Surveys found that most Albanians felt that their economic situation had improved since the overthrow of Communism. But many were dissatisfied with Berisha's style of governing and with the large-scale corruption in his administration. Critics also charged that corruption in the banking sector prevented Albania from fully benefiting from the large number of foreign loans it received in recent years.

☐ Sharon L. Wolchik

See also **Europe** (Facts in brief table). In *World Book,* see **Albania.**

Algeria. Algerian President Liamine Zeroual strove in 1996 to create a stable political climate for national elections. Terrorism continued unabated, however, claiming nearly 2,000 lives a month in 1996. Algeria's civil strife had begun when the military took control in 1992 to prevent a parliamentary election victory by the Islamic Salvation Front (FIS), an Islamic political party. Since the takeover, more than 50,000 Algerians have died.

Muslim extremists. Numerous assassinations and bombings undermined Zeroual's claim in 1996 that the violence was residual. The Armed Islamic Group (GIA), an extremist Islamic militant party, kidnapped and murdered seven French monks early in the year. On June 30, Ahmed Sahnoun, a respected *imam* (Islamic prayer leader) of Algiers, the capital, survived an assassination attempt. On August 1, a bomb killed Bishop Pierre Claverie of the port city of Oran. Car bombs in Algiers in February and September killed nearly 20 and wounded more than 100. Extremists continued to target journalists, killing more than 60 since mid-1993.

The Muslim groups suffered their own setbacks. GIA members apparently killed suspected collaborators in their own ranks. Meanwhile, a power struggle broke out between the GIA and the Islamic Salvation Army, the armed wing of FIS. In July 1996, GIA leader Djemal Zitoun was reported to have been killed in a clash with security forces.

Political reforms. In September, the government sponsored a National Conference of Understanding, intended as a prelude to a constitutional referendum. Algerians approved the constitutional referendum on November 28. Although a number of politicians pledged to reject violence and promote democracy, the conference failed to achieve consensus. Conspicuously absent were several secular parties—by their own choice—and the outlawed FIS.

President Zeroual's referendum for political reform included a ban on ethnic and religious parties, a proposal that met with stiff opposition.

Economy. In 1995, 140,000 new jobs had been created, but job applications had concurrently increased by 18 percent. Moreover, new jobs were mainly in civil service and agriculture instead of industry, which had suffered a loss of capacity due to civil strife. Joblessness had fueled extremism among the Muslim young. In 1996, 60 percent of Algerian youth aged 16 to 30 were unemployed.

Growth in agriculture and in the oil and gas industry had fueled a 4.3 percent increase in Algeria's gross domestic product in 1995. Rising oil prices and growing foreign investment suggested better economic prospects for 1996.　　　　□ Christine Helms

See also **Africa** (Facts in brief table). In *World Book*, see **Algeria**.

Angola. See Africa.

Animal. See **Conservation; Zoology; Zoos**.

Anthropology. Important fossil discoveries of distant human ancestors highlighted anthropology in 1996. New discoveries shed light on the relationship between Neanderthals and modern human beings. Scientists also announced that a third human species may have walked the earth at the same time as Neanderthals and *Homo sapiens*.

Oldest member of genus *Homo*. In December 1996, scientists at the Institute of Human Origins in Berkeley, California, announced that they had found the oldest known fossil of a *Homo* specimen along with some stone tools. *Homo* is the genus to which human beings belong.

They found an upper jaw in Hadar, Ethiopia—the site where a large sample of *Australopithecus afarensis* fossils, including the fossil skeleton "Lucy," had been unearthed. "Lucy" is the famous *Australopithecus afarensis* fossil skeleton discovered in Ethiopia in 1974. The new *Homo* jaw, deeply arched, was unmistakably distinct from the shallower *Australopithecus* palate. *Australopithecus* is a genus of humanlike creatures, which anthropologists regard as the earliest *hominids* (having to do with the family of primates that includes human beings).

Also scattered in the sediment containing the fossil jaw were crude stone artifacts that researchers believe were associated with the *Homo* specimen. Conditions at the site allowed for very precise dating. The jaw was found to be about 2.3 million years

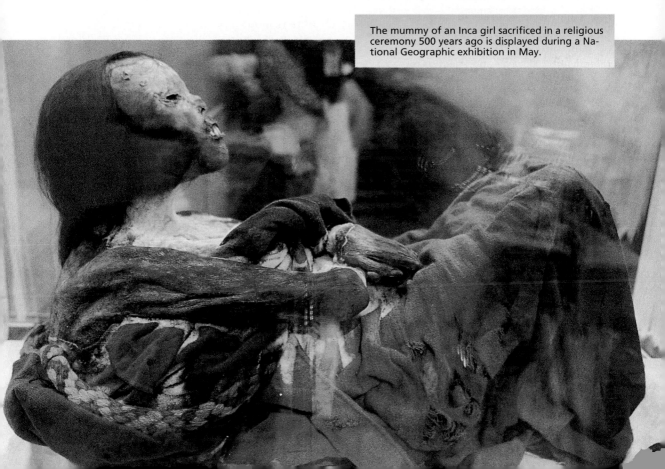

The mummy of an Inca girl sacrificed in a religious ceremony 500 years ago is displayed during a National Geographic exhibition in May.

Anthropology

old. Previous *Homo* specimens had been dated to no earlier than 1.9 million years old. The discovery of the jaw appeared to extend known human origins by some 400,000 years. Before they can classify the *Homo* fossil, anthropologists will have to wait for the discovery of more complete specimens.

Neanderthals. New evidence concerning the place of Neanderthals in human evolution came to light in 1996. The Neanderthals were a species of prehistoric, humanlike creatures that died out more than 30,000 years ago. Jean-Jacques Hublin of the Museum of Man in Paris and his colleagues identified fossil remains from the French site of Arcy-sur-Cure as Neanderthal. Although fragmentary, the fossil remains enabled the French team, using computer technology, to examine the inner ear arrangement of the semicircular canals in Neanderthals. Inner ear structures are important in helping human beings maintain balance.

The semicircular canals of the Neanderthal fossils were smaller than those found in modern human ears. Also, the configuration of these canals was quite different from the structures seen in modern humans. The distinctive anatomy of the inner ear bolstered the argument that Neanderthals were not the ancestors of *Homo sapiens*, but a unique species, *Homo neanderthalensis.* Through *radiocarbon* dating (a process of determining age by measuring radiocarbon content), the Hublin team determined the age of the Arcy-sur-Cure fossils to be about 34,000 years old, making them among the youngest Neanderthal fossils yet found.

A third human species may have coexisted on earth with Neanderthals and *Homo sapiens* as recently as 30,000 years ago, scientists revealed in December 1996. After reexamining fossil sites in Java, a team of scientists, led by paleontologist Carl C. Swisher of the Berkeley Geochronology Center in California, claimed that *Homo erectus,* a species of human being previously thought to have died out 300,000 years ago, lived as late as 27,000 to 53,000 years ago. Anthropologists believe that Neanderthals died out 30,000 years ago, and that *Homo sapiens* evolved between 200,000 and 100,000 years ago.

Australopithecus bahrelghazali. In 1996, Michael Brunet, a paleontologist, reported the discovery of a hominid fossil from Chad in central Africa. The fossil consisted of the front portion of a hominid *mandible* (lower jaw) with seven teeth. While many details of the teeth were similar to those of "Lucy," the chin area was more modern in appearance. The fossil was, therefore, assigned to a new species, *Australopithecus bahrelghazali* (Bahrel Ghazal is a riverbed). The fossil's age was estimated to be 3 million to 3½ million years old.

☐ Donald C. Johanson

See also **Archaeology.** In *World Book,* see **Anthropology.**

Archaeology. Significant archaeological finds in 1996 expanded knowledge of *prehistory* (the period of human history before writing) and yielded ancient treasures. Researchers also unearthed traces of the 1607 fort in Jamestown, Virginia, the first permanent English settlement in North America.

Neanderthals and modern humans. French archaeologists studying fossils unearthed in 1996 at Arcy-sur-Cure, an important archaeological site in France, discovered stone tools and ornaments that led them to reexamine how late Neanderthals and humans interacted. The Neanderthals were a species of prehistoric people that died out more than 30,000 years ago. Some of the Arcy-sur-Cure stone tools and artifacts reflected skills characteristic of Neanderthals. Other pieces found at the site were characteristic of human skills of the period. The archaeologists speculated that the discovery of artifacts that reveal contemporary Neanderthal and human skills in a single place suggest that Neanderthals and early humans may have interacted sufficiently to trade both objects and skills.

Early artifacts in Australia. Major archaeological finds in 1996 indicated that Australia may have been inhabited by humans much earlier than the previously accepted date of 60,000 years ago. Richard Fullagar of the Australian Museum in Sydney announced the discovery of thousands of engraved circles on rock faces at a site in the Northern Territory. Scientists gauged the age of the deposits surrounding the engraved rocks to be 75,000 years old. Other artifacts, including stone tools and starch grains, were excavated at deeper levels of the same deposit and were dated at 116,000 years old. An even deeper layer, dated at up to 176,000 years, yielded further stone tools and starch grains. The findings, if confirmed, would change scientists' views about the beginnings of human habitation in Australia.

Early winemaking. The earliest known evidence of wine was found in 1996 in a jar excavated at Hajji Firuz Tepe, an ancient village in Iran. Archaeologist Patrick McGovern of the University of Pennsylvania Museum analyzed residue in the jar and found it to contain substances related to winemaking. The jar itself had been dated to be about 7,400 years old. Before this find, the earliest evidence of wine was residue in a jar found at another Iranian site, Godin Tepe, dated at about 5,500 years old.

Serpent Mound redated. Scientific evidence completed in 1996 revealed that Serpent Mound, an American Indian earthwork in the shape of a meandering snake, was completed approximately 2,000 years later than previously believed. The mound, located in Ohio, was thought to have been constructed by Indians known as the Adena, who lived from approximately 1000 to 100 B.C.

Serpent Mound, which was first excavated in the 1800's, had never been dated scientifically. A recent excavation yielded two carbon samples, which were

58

journalist examines a solid gold vessel from the legendary "Trojan Gold" exhibited in Moscow in
April. The gold, unearthed in Turkey in the 1800's by archaeologist Heinrich Schliemann, disappeared from Berlin in 1945 and only reappeared in Moscow after the fall of the Soviet Union in 1991.

Archaeology

subsequently dated to between A.D. 1000 and 1140. The new evidence indicated that the mound must have been built by a much later group of American Indians, known as the Fort Ancient culture.

Scythian tomb. A Ukrainian-Polish archaeological team unearthed a spectacular Scythian tomb in Ukraine in August 1996. The Scythians were nomadic warriors who lived north of the Black Sea from about 700 to 200 B.C. The tomb, which included the remains of a prince, yielded perfectly preserved artifacts, including a dazzling Greek silver cup carved with images of fighting animals, and domestic objects, such as a cookstove, suggesting that the Scythians led a more settled way of life than archaeologists previously believed.

Jamestown. In September, William Kelso, director of archaeology at the Association for the Preservation of Virginia Antiquities, announced the discovery of the 1607 fort at Jamestown, Virginia. Traces of sections of the fort and more than 100,000 artifacts had been found during a 3-year excavation.

English colonists, who landed at the site in May 1607, immediately built the fort, which was attacked by Indians in less than two weeks. Over the last 3 1/2 centuries, the James River eroded much of the site, convincing many archaeologists that the fort was irretrievably lost. However, the discovery of traces of a curved *bastion*—a section of the fort's palisade of upright timbers, which bulged outward to provide a better line of fire—helped the archaeological team authenticate the remains of the fort. The bastion precisely matched detailed descriptions that were made in 1610.

African religion in colonial America. Archaeologists from the University of Maryland found evidence that many slaves in colonial America practiced religious beliefs and rituals that were brought from Africa, probably in secret, alongside the practice of Christian beliefs. In an Annapolis house built in the 1700's, archaeologist Mark Leone discovered three caches of objects that had been placed under a hearth and in the northeast corners of ground-floor workrooms. (Why such caches were typically placed in a northeast corner remained unknown.) Among the objects found were straight pins, beads, white buttons, a brass ring, and a bell. Such objects had been linked to West African religious concepts about the *cosmos* (the universe perceived as an orderly system) and the spirit world.

From the excavation and the discovery of more than 20 other caches—always in northeast corners—in Maryland and Virginia, Leone concluded that the pattern suggested the widespread continuation of African religious beliefs. The adoption of European-made objects, such as white buttons, into African-based rituals indicated the beginnings of a distinct African American culture. □ Mark Rose

See also **Anthropology; Geology.** In *World Book,* see **Archaeology.**

Architecture in the United States in 1996 continued to move in multiple directions. Architects touched every stylistic base from classic modernism to angry deconstructionism. (Deconstructionism is a design form that celebrates and highlights the fragments of a building, rather than the structure as a whole.) No innovative theories or compelling trends emerged—only a smørgasbørd of familiar ideas with a few exotic decorations.

Disney's Celebration. The most publicized project of 1996 was Celebration, the Disney Company's $2-billion town, which opened in November near Disney World in Orlando, Florida. Based on "America's best neighborhoods," Celebration was given a traditional main street with a city hall, post office, bank, and shops designed by Philip Johnson, Michael Graves, and other celebrity architects. The town was designed to house 20,000 residents and contains a school, hospital ("wellness center" in Disneyese), and houses that ranged in price from $110,000 to $750,000. The first 350 lots were snapped up, but it remained to be seen whether Celebration would become a real community or another Disney attraction.

Peter Eisenman's Aronoff Center of Design and Art, which opened in October at the University of Cincinnati, was among the most controversial designs of the year. Looking like an avalanche from certain perspectives, the structure is a collage of sharp angles and colliding planes. Inside, however, Eisenman provided a logical plan and lively studios for the university's College of Design, Architecture, Art, and Planning.

The Olympics. Unlike the 1992 Olympics in Barcelona, Spain, the 1996 games in Atlanta left a meager architectural legacy. The most valuable long-term contributions were new public parks, especially the 21-acre (8.4 hectare) Centennial Olympic Park with its dramatic fountain and towers designed by EDAW, Inc., of San Francisco.

The museum and library boom that began in 1995 continued into 1996 with Chicago's $46-million Museum of Contemporary Art, which opened in July. Designed by Josef Paul Kleihues of Berlin, the museum—located at Chicago Avenue and Mies van der Rohe Way—pays homage in its design to both the city's architectural heritage and to Mies, one of the most influential architects of the 1900's. The modular plan and decorative metalwork recall the architecture of Chicago's Louis Sullivan. Its precise geometry and surprising transparency owe much to the modernism of Mies. While some visitors might complain about the steep front stairs (32 steps) and the prickly aluminum panels on the exterior, the museum's interior is superb, particularly the galleries on the upper floor, which offer spectacular views of the city and Lake Michigan.

Several museums were also renovated in 1996. Tod Williams and Billie Tsien's $25-million expansion of the Phoenix Art Museum opened in September. The

60

Peter Eisenman's deconstructionist Aronoff Center at the University of Cincinnati is opened in October to critical acclaim and wide media attention.

architects doubled the museum's size by creating new galleries, a theater, and a sculpture pavilion dominated by a 93-foot- (28-meter-) high translucent fiberglass cone for concerts and other public events.

Additions to San Diego's Museum of Contemporary Art in La Jolla, California, were opened to the public in March. Venturi, Scott Brown Associates enlarged the existing Irving Gill building with a long arcing facade, new exhibition galleries, and a cafe. At the back of the museum, they created gardens and terraces linking the museum to the Pacific Ocean.

The new San Francisco Main Public Library, which opened in April, combines the orderliness of beaux-arts classicism with the exuberance of modernism. At the sides facing historic Marshall Square, Pei Cobb Freed and Partners designed uniform facades, with tall windows and gridded stone walls. But in back, the building dissolves into a jumble of cubes, squares, and vaults that suggest the diversity and complexity of a modern library. The most exhilarating space is a six-story rotunda that spirals upward, inviting visitors to join what the architects called "a spatial dance."

Controversial renovation. The controversial addition to architect Louis Kahn's Salk Institute for Biological Studies, also in La Jolla, finally opened in November. Designed by Anshen & Allen, the addition consists of two concrete lab buildings immediately east of the original complex, connected by a brick courtyard. The buildings replaced a dense eucalyptus grove that was part of Kahn's procession from nature to architecture to infinity. By slavishly repeating the proportions and materials of the original buildings, the architects created structures more dull than dangerous. Kahn's sublime composition of building, sea, and sky survived.

The 1996 Pritzker Prize, a $100,000 award given annually for lifetime contributions to architectural design, was awarded to José Rafael Moneo of Spain. A modernist by training and temperament, Moneo nevertheless has drawn extensively on historic forms and construction methods. The National Museum of Roman Art in Mérida, Spain, which launched his international career, combines ancient ruins with the latest museum technology. Moneo's other important contributions include the Pilar and Joan Miró Foundation headquarters in Palma de Mallorca, the restoration of Villa-Hermosa Palace in Madrid, and the San Pablo Airport in Seville, Spain.

Philip Johnson. The jolliest architectural event of 1996 was architect Philip Johnson's 90th birthday in July. The celebration lasted for weeks in the form of parties, interviews, symposia, and exhibitions, including several at New York City's Museum of Modern Art. The honoree predicted that he would live to be at least 100 and announced new projects, including a church in Dallas for the largest homosexual congregation in the nation. ☐ David Dillon

See also **Art.** In *World Book,* see **Architecture.**

Argentina. On July 26, 1996, President Carlos Saúl Menem announced the resignation of Domingo Cavallo, the minister of economy, who was widely credited for playing a major role in stabilizing Argentina's economy and bringing inflation under control. Cavallo was replaced by the former Central Bank president Benjamín Roque Fernández.

While improving Argentina's credit rating abroad, Cavallo's policies were criticized for straining the middle class, raising unemployment to a record 17 percent, and increasing poverty. On the day of Menem's announcement, 30,000 people in Buenos Aires, the capital, protested Cavallo's recent plans to cut the family allowances for workers earning more than $1,000 a month and to tax food vouchers, a part of the pay package for millions of Argentines.

In August, Fernández, as the new minister of economy, announced equally unpopular austerity measures that awaited congressional approval: raising the retirement age for women from 60 to 65; increasing the price of diesel fuel and oil, 40 and 10 percent respectively; and taxing purchases, such as private education and health and life insurance.

Crackdown on tax evaders. In June, the government toughened efforts to crack down on tax evaders. With only about half of the Argentines paying their taxes, the treasury was losing an estimated $24 billion annually—more than half the national budget of $40 billion. The new measure required Argentines traveling outside the country or making purchases of more than $10,000 to present certificates proving they had paid their taxes.

Labor confrontation. On September 27, an estimated 70,000 workers demonstrated outside the presidential palace to protest unemployment and a government plan to reform trade unions, including the union-run health programs. In support of the protesters, millions of Argentines did not go to work and brought the country to a standstill.

Military as entrepreneur. After a decade of cuts that had trimmed the annual defense budget by 75 percent, Argentina's armed forces turned to money-making ventures for relief. The military, the nation's largest landowner, unveiled plans in early 1996 to lease land on military bases for such commercial enterprises as shopping malls and to sell some of its businesses, including arms factories. The goal was to raise more than $1 billion over the next decade—revenue needed to build housing, provide adequate military training, and purchase modern equipment and weapons.

Argentina's army leased land to farmers and used army trucks to transport commercial cargo in rural areas. The navy employed ships to carry maritime cargo and to provide tourist excursions around Patagonia in the south of Argentina. Both the air force and navy rented airfields for auto races, and officers of all three branches rented out their often plush clubs for private functions.

Loony radio. A popular weekly radio program called Radio La Colifata (Loony Radio), broadcast from Borda Psychiatric Hospital in Buenos Aires, was honored in April by broadcasters in Argentina. Alfredo Olivera, the 29-year-old psychology graduate student who founded the program, accepted the award along with a Borda patient involved in the radio show. Olivera asserted that people learn not to fear mental illnesses when they hear the patients on the air "making fun of themselves or speaking intelligently about issues of the day."

Madonna as "Evita." In January, when filming began in Buenos Aires of the movie version of the musical *Evita,* Argentines were sharply polarized over the selection of Madonna, an American celebrity known for her sexually explicit music videos, to play the title role. President Menem called the musical "a libelous interpretation" of the life of Eva (Evita) Duarte de Perón, the wife of former President Juan Perón. Since her death from cancer in 1952, Evita has been revered in Argentina for her work on behalf of the poor. In spite of protests, throngs of fans attempted to catch a glimpse of the star or to obtain roles as extras in the movie, which opened in New York City on Nov. 12, 1996. ☐ Nathan A. Haverstock

See also **Latin America** (Facts in brief table). In *World Book,* see **Argentina.**

Arizona. See State government.
Arkansas. See State government.

Armed forces. The United States launched cruise missile strikes against Iraq in 1996, five years after U.S. and allied forces had defeated the Iraqi military in the Persian Gulf War. President Bill Clinton ordered the strikes in response to Iraqi leader Saddam Hussein's invasion of the Kurdish "safety zone" in northern Iraq, where Kurds had fled in 1991 to escape Hussein's forces after their Gulf War defeat. In 1996, Kurdish factions fought each other for supremacy in the mountains of the safety zone.

In September, U.S. Navy ships and an attack submarine in the Persian gulf launched 31 cruise missiles at Iraqi air defense installations, and Air Force B-52 heavy bombers fired 13 missiles from the air. Simultaneously, President Clinton ordered a substantial extension of the "no-fly zone" in southern Iraq, where Hussein's aircraft had been prohibited since the Gulf War in 1991. The president wanted to deter Hussein from attacking Saudi Arabia and Kuwait, Iraq's neighbors to the south.

On Sept. 11, 1996, after Iraqi forces fired missiles against U.S. aircraft patrolling the Kurdish safety zone, Clinton ordered eight F-117 stealth fighters to Kuwait, four B-52 bombers to a base in the Indian Ocean, and a second aircraft carrier into the Persian Gulf. Patriot surface-to-air missile batteries were also deployed from their base in Texas. On September 13, 5,000 combat troops from Fort Hood, Texas, were ordered to Kuwait to join 1,200 American troops al-

Army Sergeant Heather Johnsen, first woman member of the honor guard at the Tomb of the Unknown Soldier, patrols in Arlington National Cemetery in March.

ready there. However, in October, most observers claimed Hussein was more in control of northern Iraq than he had been before U.S. military actions.

Saudi bombing. On June 25, a bomb planted in a truck parked near a housing compound at Dhahran, Saudi Arabia, exploded, killing 19 American soldiers and wounding more than 400 other people. Besides Air Force personnel stationed in Saudi Arabia, victims included Saudis and Bangladeshis.

Several members of the U.S. Congress later alleged that the U.S. Army had underestimated the terrorist threat to American forces in Saudi Arabia and that security procedures had been lax. Military officials denied the charges, but in the aftermath of the bombing, the U.S. tightened security procedures. Several thousand troops were transferred to an isolated Saudi air force base in the desert to avoid further attacks. In August, the Army ordered 5,000 troops to join the 21,000 already serving in the Persian Gulf to promote peace and stability.

Bosnia peacekeeping. More than 18,000 American servicemen were stationed in the Balkans during 1996 as part of a North Atlantic Treaty Organization (NATO) peacekeeping operation to enforce the December 1995 agreement ending the ethnic fighting in Bosnia-Herzegovina. Despite fears that U.S. troops might suffer heavy casualties, only six soldiers died in Bosnia during 1996, all the result of accidents. U.S. officials continued to assert that American troops would be out of Bosnia by the end of 1996. But in October, NATO officials stated that at least 7,500 American peacekeepers would be required to remain in the Balkans well into 1997.

Okinawa cutbacks. The United States agreed in April to restore to Japan about 20 percent of the land that has been occupied by the U.S. military on Okinawa. The agreement involved 11 U.S. military installations, including a Marine Corps air station at Futenma that was to be turned over to Japan within seven years. Most American troops and equipment would be moved to bases on Japan's main islands, though U.S. troop strength on Okinawa would remain at 27,000.

The agreement to reduce the U.S. military presence resulted from public pressure generated by the sexual assault of a Japanese schoolgirl by three American servicemen in 1995. The marines were convicted by a Japanese court in March 1996. Two marines were given seven-year prison terms, and the third was sentenced to six years in prison.

Taiwan tensions. Heightened tensions between China and Taiwan in March 1996 prompted President Clinton to order the U.S. aircraft carrier *Independence* and three other warships into the Taiwan Strait in a show of support for Taiwan. China was conducting massive live-ammunition naval maneuvers in the strait in an attempt to intimidate Taiwanese voters casting ballots in their first direct election for president. The Taiwan Strait separates mainland China from Taiwan, which China claims as a province. In mid-March, the president ordered the carrier *Nimitz* and several other ships into the strait to underline U.S. concern. The election proceeded as scheduled.

Boorda suicide. Admiral Jeremy M. Boorda, the chief of naval operations, committed suicide on May 16 at his house at the Washington Navy Yard. Boorda had been chief of naval operations since March 1994 and was the only enlisted man in U.S. history to become the Navy's top officer.

Boorda's death came just hours before reporters from *Newsweek* magazine were scheduled to question him about two decorations for valor in combat in Vietnam. Boorda had stopped wearing the medals in 1995, after allegations were made that he was not entitled to wear them. However, military officials were divided on the issue. Secretary of Defense William J. Perry said after Boorda's death that the admiral had at worst committed a technical violation of military regulations.

Ron Brown killed. The U.S. Air Force announced on Aug. 6, 1996, that it was disciplining 16 officers as a result of the April 3 plane crash in Croatia that killed U.S. Secretary of Commerce Ron Brown and 34 others. Brown was leading a delegation of business leaders to inspect the war-torn Balkans when his Air Force T-43A plane veered off course in its approach to an airfield near the city of Dubrovnik in a rainstorm and crashed on a mountaintop.

In June, an Air Force investigation concluded that the plane, a military version of the Boeing 737 passenger jet, crashed as a result of pilot error and because senior officers had ignored directives to inspect the airfield at Dubrovnik to determine if U.S. planes could safely land there in bad weather. Brigadier General William E. Stevens, the commander of the wing to which the plane was assigned, and his deputy, Colonel John E. Mazurowski, were charged with "dereliction of duty," a punishment just short of a court-martial. They had been relieved of their commands in May.

Plane crashes. The military was plagued by an unusually high number of airplane crashes during 1996. Naval investigators concluded that a January F-14 crash in Nashville that killed the pilot and four others was the result of the pilot's "showing off" for his parents. The Navy temporarily grounded its entire fleet of F-14 Tomcat fighter planes in February after six crashes had occurred within 18 months. In March, the Marine Corps ordered a two-day grounding of all nonessential flight operations after six planes had crashed in a six-week period. On August 17, an Air Force C-130 cargo plane accompanying President Clinton on a vacation crashed shortly after takeoff from Jackson, Wyoming, killing nine people.

Scandals. The armed forces were rocked by a series of scandals in 1996. On August 6, the U.S. Naval Academy in Annapolis, Maryland, expelled 15 midshipmen for various drug-related offenses. Five other midshipmen previously had been court-martialed on drug charges and given prison sentences. The Academy had announced in May that admissions screening would be toughened to weed out applicants who might be prone to criminal conduct.

In September, a first-year female midshipman and a male U.S. Air Force cadet were indicted for the 1995 murder of a 16-year-old girl in Texas. Also in September 1996, a Naval Academy chaplain was accused of exposing himself to young girls at a department store.

In November, the U.S. Army charged a captain and two drill sergeants at the Ordnance Center of the Aberdeen Proving Ground in Maryland with rape or sexual harassment of more than 12 female recruits. The Army planned to interview every woman recruit who had been through training at the center over the previous two years.

Supreme Court rulings. In a landmark decision on June 26, the U.S. Supreme Court ruled that the Virginia Military Institute's (VMI) 157-year-old policy of excluding women was unconstitutional. The court decided 7-1 that an alternative women's program established by VMI at a nearby women's college was "distinctly inferior" to what VMI offered to male cadets. On September 21, VMI announced that it would admit women.

The ruling also applied to The Citadel, an all-male military academy at Charleston, South Carolina. Officials announced on June 28 that The Citadel would accept women for the first time in its 153-year history. In August, four female applicants passed physical fitness tests and were admitted.

On June 3, the Supreme Court unanimously ruled that the military death penalty was constitutional, which left intact death sentences imposed on eight imprisoned servicemen. The court ruled that President Ronald Reagan's guidelines issued in 1984, allowing the death penalty in military cases, were within the authority of the president as commander-in-chief of the armed forces.

Weapons systems. Despite recent cutbacks in weapons procurement, development continued on a few new weapons, including the Air Force's F-22 advanced tactical fighter, a new generation of nuclear attack submarines, a new air-to-surface missile for the Air Force and Navy, an advanced amphibious assault ship, and an arsenal ship. The first Seawolf nuclear attack submarine successfully completed sea trials in July. The Navy issued a $1.4-billion contract for the V-22 Osprey tilt-rotor aircraft.

Defense budget. The Clinton Administration's defense budget for the 1997 fiscal year, released March 4, 1996, requested spending authority of $242.6 billion, a reduction of about $10 billion from the fiscal 1996 budget approved by Congress. After adjusting for inflation, defense spending would decline by 6 percent, the 12th consecutive year of lower outlays. The $38.9 billion Clinton requested for weapons was the lowest level in seven years.

The largest weapons request was $3.5 billion for four Aegis missile ships. The Administration also requested $2.8 billion for ballistic missile defense programs, $2.6 billion for a dozen F/A- 8 Hornet attack jets, $2.3 billion for eight C-17 airlift jets, $2 billion for the F-22 tactical fighter, $1.2 billion for four V-22 Osprey tilt-wing planes, $920 million for a Seawolf nuclear attack submarine, and $684 million for the B-2 stealth bomber. On September 30, President Clinton signed a bill for $244 billion in defense spending, of which $44 billion was for weapons.

Command changes. On December 5, President Clinton nominated Republican Senator William S. Cohen of Maine as secretary of defense. William Perry resigned from the post shortly after Clinton was reelected to his second term. In March, Air Force General Joseph W. Ralston became vice chairman of the Joint Chiefs of Staff. In July, J. Paul Reason became the Navy's first African American four-star admiral, and Carol Mutter became the first woman lieutenant general in the Marine Corps. In August, Admiral Jay L. Johnson was named to succeed the late Admiral Boorda as chief of naval operations.

☐ Thomas M. DeFrank

In *World Book,* see the articles on the branches of the armed forces.

Armenia. On Sept. 22, 1996, President Levon Ter-Petrosian won a second five-year term, defeating former Prime Minister Vazgen Manukyan the first ballot. Ter-Petrosian won 52 percent of the vote to Manukian's 41 percent. Protesting accusations of election fraud, thousands demonstrated in Yerevan, and riots erupted on September 25. In the wake of the violence, Ter-Petrosian ordered the arrest of eight parliamentary deputies, including Manukyan.

During the campaign, Ter-Petrosian called for normalization of relations with Turkey, Armenia's longtime adversary. However, Armenia concluded military cooperation agreements with countries traditionally hostile to Turkey: It signed a treaty with Greece in June and with Bulgaria in September; and a similar pact reportedly was under negotiation with Syria. In September, Armenian and Russian troops conducted joint exercises near the Turkish border.

The 1994 cease-fire agreement in the Armenian-Azerbaijani war over the enclave of Nagorno-Karabakh continued to hold in 1996. Armenia had seized the chiefly Armenian enclave from Azerbaijan in 1993. In May 1996, Russian Foreign Minister Yevgeny Primakov attempted to broker a peaceful resolution to the conflict. Both sides exchanged limited numbers of war prisoners, but made little real progress toward a treaty. ☐ Steven L. Solnick

See also **Asia** (Facts in brief table); **Azerbaijan.** In *World Book,* see **Armenia.**

Art. A marble cupid in the foyer of the French Cultural Services in New York City became the focus of an intriguing puzzle in 1996. In January, art historian Kathleen Weil-Garris Brandt of New York University's Institute of Fine Arts, in New York City, identified the cupid as an unknown, early work by the Renaissance sculptor and painter Michelangelo.

The sculpture is an armless, youthful male figure twisting slightly on legs missing below the knees, with head tilting backward and slightly upward to the left. It had been purchased in Rome and transported to the United States in the early 1900's by architect Stanford White, who designed the building—once a private residence—where the sculpture now stands.

Brandt's attribution, if correct, would be a spectacular find. Only one Michelangelo sculpture—an early relief at London's Royal Academy of Arts—exists outside Italy. Philippe de Montebello, director of the Metropolitan Museum of Art in New York City, immediately endorsed Brandt's finding and announced his intention to exhibit the sculpture at the earliest possible opportunity.

Yet almost from the moment Brandt's assertion appeared in *The New York Times,* the sculpture was surrounded by controversy. Rumors that it might be a Michelangelo had been circulating in scholarly circles for decades, but until 1996 no one had publicly attributed the statue to him. Over the months, one Michelangelo authority after another, both in the United States and Europe, came out against the attribution. In October 1996, Brandt presented her case in *The Burlington Magazine,* a scholarly journal. The Metropolitan Museum remained committed to its promised exhibition, though at the end of 1996 it had not set a date for it.

Nazi legacy. On October 29 and 30, Christie's auction house sold approximately 8,000 works of art stolen primarily from Austrian Jews in the 1930's and 1940's by German Nazis. Nearly all the owners were eventually killed during the Holocaust, the systematic extermination by Nazi Germany of 11 million people, including 6 million Jews, during World War II (1939-1945). The auction netted $14.5 million.

The objects—paintings, drawings, books, and pieces of decorative art—had been among approximately 10,000 unclaimed works of art turned over to Austria by Allied forces after the war. The Allies stipulated that Austria continue the search for the owners or sell the works and donate the proceeds to Holocaust survivors. In the late 1960's, the Austrian government mounted a search for the missing owners or their heirs. By the early 1980's, however, only about 100 works of art had been returned, and Austria had granted itself title to the remaining pieces, which were stored in a monastery or displayed in state museums, government offices, and embassies.

Austria kept the existence of the art trove a secret until *ARTnews* magazine broke the story in 1984, forcing the government to make a more con-

Girl with the Pearl Earring is 1 of 20 paintings by Dutch artist Jan Vermeer shown at the National Gallery in Washington, D.C., in early 1996.

certed restitution effort. In 1995, Austria transferred ownership of what remained to the Federation of Austrian Jewish Communities, which allocated 88 percent of the sale's proceeds to Jewish survivors of the Holocaust and the rest to non-Jewish Austrian survivors. The sale was the latest event in the contentious, painful, and continuing problem of art treasures looted during World War II.

Another sensation event was the spring 1996 releasing in France of "Le Musee Disparu" ("The Missing Museum"), a chronicle of the Nazi confiscation of art from French Jewish collectors. "Le Musee Disparu" revealed that the French, like the Austrians, had made little effort to trace the art's owners or their heirs in the years following the war. Shamed

into action, the French government by late summer had established a site on the World Wide Web for publication of the list of unclaimed works.

Vermeer and modern politics. In February, "Vermeer in America," a retrospective of 20 of the 35 known works of Dutch artist Jan Vermeer at the National Gallery of Art in Washington, D.C., ended its 90-day run. The show fell victim to two U.S. government shutdowns and two snowstorms. The shutdowns, the result of a budget battle between the U.S. Congress and President Bill Clinton, similarly affected every other public museum in Washington. The Vermeer show was the first retrospective of the Dutch master staged since Vermeer's death in 1675. In addition, the National Gallery was one of only two venues for the exhibit—the other being the Maurit-shuis museum at The Hague, in the Netherlands. As a result, the closures of the show, widely considered a once-in-a-lifetime event, became one of the most prominent of the shutdown's dislocations. The National Gallery reissued tickets that had become unusable during the shutdowns and extended its hours to make up for lost time. On the exhibit's last day, Feb. 11, 1996, lines formed at dawn outside the museum.

Important exhibitions of 1996 included "Picasso and Portraiture: Representation and Transformation" at New York City's Museum of Modern Art (MOMA); "Olmec Art of Ancient Mexico" at the National Gallery; "Abstraction in the Twentieth Century: Total Risk, Freedom, Discipline" at the Guggenheim Museum in New York City; and "Splendors of Imperial China: Treasures from the National Palace Museum, Taipei" at the Metropolitan Museum. The Taipei exhibition, which began a six-city U.S. tour at the Met, was nearly derailed by protests in Taiwan against sending irreplaceable cultural treasures out of the country. Because of the uproar, 23 of the exhibit's choicest works were held back.

Notable retrospectives in 1996 included those of American Pop/Funk artist Edward Kienholz at the Whitney Museum of American Art in New York City and American modernist Jasper Johns at MOMA. "Cézanne" at the Philadelphia Museum of Art was the first exhibit of the works of French Postimpressionist in 60 years. The large numbers of people who attended the show provided 1996's best example of "cultural tourism"—the staging of "blockbuster" shows to attract huge crowds—a practice marking an important shift in the way museums present and justify themselves to the public. Until the early 1990's, museums emphasized the cultural, intellectual, and even spiritual values of their collections and exhibitions. With money tight and local governments looking at every grant and tax-exemption, museums adopted a more pragmatic approach, promoting shows as tourist magnets and engines of local economic activity.

Museums. In 1996, U.S. art museums continued to present a contradictory image. While they managed to mount ambitious exhibitions and undertake grandiose expansions, the strains of functioning in a period of rising costs and dwindling financial resources continued to extract a visible toll.

In February 1996, MOMA realized long-standing ambitions for more space in a convenient location by buying an adjacent hotel and two brownstones in a $50-million deal. The purchase added 250,000 square feet (23,000 square meters) to the museum's existing 350,000 square feet (32,200 square meters). Like most museums, MOMA had been hard pressed for room to show its permanent collection, particularly its holdings of contemporary art, which typically are larger than art made prior to World War II and thus take up more gallery space. The new quarters were not expected to be ready for at least 10 years.

In June 1996, the Museum of Contemporary Art in Chicago solved its space problem by moving into a new building five times larger than its previous quarters. Designed by German architect Josef Paul Kleihues, the new museum includes 45,000 square feet (4,100 square meters) of gallery space, a library, a theater, classrooms, and a cafe.

Financial strains, however, were also visible in 1996. In April, Vermont's Shelburne Museum, a small institution with a collection that includes important Impressionist works, announced plans to sell 22 works of art in hopes of raising $25 million to help pay operating expenses. The sell-off was the largest ever undertaken by a museum and violates professional guidelines, which stipulate that works of art can be sold only to purchase other works of art. The Shelburne, like many other small institutions, was eating into its endowment principal to cover a deficit.

In March, financial woes led two California museums—the Newport Harbor Art Museum in Newport Beach and the Laguna Art Museum in Laguna Beach—to announce a merger. While the combined institution, known as the Orange County Museum of Art, ran into opposition from some patrons fearing that the Laguna museum would be closed, local courts rejected two appeals to halt the merger.

In March, the Los Angeles County Museum of Art ended a 2 ½-year search for a new director by naming Graham W. J. Beal, director of the Joslyn Art Museum in Omaha, Nebraska, to the post. The unprecedented length of the vacancy at the helm of one of America's top museums symbolized how the stresses of fund-raising, board room battles, and art world politics had taken the luster off a once prestigious and alluring job.

Additional proof of this trend in May was the resignation of Robert T. Buck, director since 1983 of the Brooklyn Museum in New York City. Buck cited his desire to spend more time organizing exhibitions and writing—once a large part of a director's job—and less time coping with financial crises. In recent years, the Brooklyn Museum had been particularly hard hit by declining public and private support.

Acquisitions. In January, MOMA paid at least $1 million for "Untitled Film Stills," a series of 69 black-and-white self-portraits taken between 1977 and 1980 by Cindy Sherman. In the photos, Sherman mimics the costumes and conventions of 1950's *film noir*. The series was considered one of the earliest and most important examples of post-modern photography, in which artists make themselves the subject and blur the boundaries between truth and fiction. MOMA's purchase of the series, as well as the price it paid, represented the strongest endorsement yet of the artistic developments of the 1980's.

☐ Eric Gibson

See also **Architecture.** In *World Book,* see **Art and the arts; Painting; Sculpture.**

Territorial disputes flared in Asia during 1996, spurring a continuing race for more modern weapons. China fired missiles at Taiwan in an attempt to influence voting in Taiwan's first direct election for president. But none of the disputes came to blows, and except for Afghanistan, the area had little fighting.

The angriest dispute was over eight uninhabited rocky islets and reefs 125 miles (200 kilometers) northeast of Taiwan. They were claimed by China (which called them the Diaoyu Islands), Japan (which called them the Senkakus), and Taiwan. China's claim won loud support in Hong Kong, the British dependency that was to revert to China in 1997.

The dispute intertwined history, rising nationalism, fishing rights, and the possibility that undersea oil exists near the islands. Japan claimed to have won the islands as spoils of war from China in 1895, but then had lost control of them as a result of being defeated in World War II (1939-1945). Japan reclaimed the islands in 1972.

In February 1996, China confirmed that its oil exploration ship had been operating inside the area that Japan claimed as the islands' territorial waters. In July, the Japanese Youth Federation, a small right-wing group, reportedly with gangster connections, built a light tower on one of the islets, symbolizing Japanese ownership. By the time the group returned in September to repair typhoon damage to the tower, a diplomatic storm had arisen, fueled by China's long-held, anti-Japanese feelings over that nation's invasion of China before World War II.

Anti-Japanese demonstrations were held in Taiwan and Hong Kong. Japan sent coast guard and police vessels to the area to fend off attempts by Taiwan and Hong Kong to assert their ownership. In September, Taiwan's defense minister stated that war could not be ruled out. China postponed a ministerial visit to Japan, warning that relations would suffer further if Japan did not halt the Youth Federation's actions. At year-end, Japan showed little sign of trying to control the group.

Other island hostilities. Another feud unresolved at year-end swirled around ownership of three tiny islands between Japan and South Korea in the Sea of Japan. Japan called the islands Takeshima, and South Korea called them Tokdo. At stake were valuable fishing rights in the surrounding waters. Japan had ignored a South Korean coast guard unit stationed on the islands since 1956. But on Feb. 20, 1996, both nations declared 200-mile (320-kilometer) economic zones that encompassed the islands. Angry demonstrations erupted in South Korea, reviving memories of Japan's Korean occupation from 1910 to 1945. The South Korean government began to tear down the Japanese-built capital building in

Seoul, which blocked the public's view of Korea's historic royal palaces on a hillside.

Emotions boiled over into fierce competition to host the World Cup soccer tournament in 2002. The international soccer federation ruled that Japan and South Korea would cohost the tournament.

Tensions flared over islands in the South China Sea after China ratified the United Nations Law of the Sea convention on May 15, 1996. China used the convention as a basis for extending its economic zone to include the Paracel Islands. China had seized the atolls from South Vietnam in 1974, but after North Vietnam overran the South, the Communist government claimed ownership. Indonesia challenged the legality of China's action.

China stated it would make additional zone claims in the future, an apparent reference to the Spratly Islands—numerous atolls in the South China Sea. Brunei, China, Malaysia, the Philippines, Taiwan, and Vietnam claimed ownership of the Spratlys, though no clashes over them occurred during 1996.

Russia ignored Japan's desire to regain possession in 1996 of islands at the southwest end of the Kurile chain just northeast of Japan's northern island of Hokkaido. The former Soviet Union had captured the islands from Japan at the end of World War II.

Arms race. India and Pakistan's long-standing feud over the state of Kashmir triggered an arms race between the two nations that also involved China, a long-time friend of Pakistan. According to United States officials, China was supplying equipment for Pakistan's nuclear program in violation of international agreements to halt the spread of nuclear weapons. But on May 10, the United States declared that it would not impose sanctions on China. On May 11, China stated that it would provide assistance to nuclear facilities that are covered only by international inspections to ensure their peaceful use.

Missile issues. Another controversy arose in August with U.S. press reports that China had secretly supplied Pakistan with blueprints and equipment for building a factory to produce Chinese- designed M-11 medium-range missiles. Earlier, the United States had imposed—and then lifted—limited economic sanctions on China for selling M-11 parts and launchers to Pakistan, violating China's pledge to observe an international agreement on missiles.

India produced its own medium-range missiles. According to press reports, observers believed that both India and Pakistan had developed nuclear warheads for such missiles. Both countries refused to sign an international ban on nuclear weapons tests.

Authorities in Taiwan and Hong Kong seized illegal shipments from Chinese vessels destined for Pakistan. Hong Kong officials also seized artillery being

A Taiwanese student burns a Chinese flag during a March rally to protest China's firing of missiles at Taiwan to intimidate voters in the first direct presidential election.

Country	Population	Government	Monetary unit*	Foreign trade (million U.S.$)	
				Exports†	Imports†
Afghanistan	22,468,000	No functioning government	afghani (4,750.00 = $1)	188	616
Armenia	3,683,000	President Levon Ter-Petrosian	dram (not available)	248	661
Australia	18,532,000	Governor General William Deane; Prime Minister John Howard	dollar (1.26 = $1)	53,097	60,317
Azerbaijan	7,719,000	President Heydar A. Aliyev	manat (4,230.00 = $1)	550	681
Bangladesh	125,790,000	President Shahabuddin Ahmed; Prime Minister Sheikh Hasina Wajed	taka (42.61 = $1)	3,173	6,496
Bhutan	1,716,000	King Jigme Singye Wangchuck	ngultrum (35.60 = $1)	67	98
Brunei	295,000	Sultan Sir Hassanal Bolkiah	dollar (1.42 = $1)	2,296	1,695
Burma (Myanmar)	48,454,000	Prime Minister, State Law and Order Restoration Council Chairman Than Shwe	kyat (5.94 = $1)	847	1,272
Cambodia (Kampuchea)	10,778,000	King Norodom Sihanouk; Prime Minister Prince Norodom Ranariddh; Prime Minister Hun Sen	riel (2,300.00 = $1)	284	479
China	1,246,260,000	Communist Party General Secretary and President Jiang Zemin; Premier Li Peng	yuan (8.30 = $1)	119,830	114,577
Georgia	5,485,000	President Eduard Shevardnadze	lari (not available)	140	250
India	968,972,000	President Shankar Dayal Sharma; Prime Minister H. D. Deve Gowda	rupee (35.61 = $1)	30,542	34,402
Indonesia	203,480,000	President Suharto; Vice President Try Sutrisno	rupiah (2,325.50 = $1)	45,417	40,918
Iran	70,111,000	Leader of the Islamic Revolution Ali Hoseini-Khamenei; President Ali Akbar Hashemi-Rafsanjani	rial (3,000.00 = $1)	16,000	18,000
Japan	125,646,000	Emperor Akihito; Prime Minister Ryutaro Hashimoto	yen (113.25 = $1)	443,274	336,080
Kazakstan	17,341,000	President Nursultan Nazarbayev	tenge (not available)	5,064	3,882
Korea, North	24,713,000	Supreme Commander Kim Chong-il; Premier Kang Song-san	won (2.15 = $1)	1,020	1,640
Korea, South	45,836,000	President Kim Yong-sam; Prime Minister Yi Hong-Ku	won (827.90 = $1)	125,453	135,216
Kyrgyzstan	4,899,000	President Askar Akayev	som (not available)	380	439

shipped from North Korea to Syria. Hong Kong officials also discovered a missile launcher for an advanced American-made Sidewinder air-to-air missile. The discovery seemed to confirm suspicions in the United States that Israel was helping China acquire sensitive American technology.

Weapons sales. Many Asian countries bought arms legally. China purchased SU-27 jet fighter bombers, submarines, and warships from Russia. Vietnam bought Russian SU-27s, while Singapore, Malaysia, and Thailand ordered American-made warplanes. The United States hesitated over selling F-16's to Indonesia because of its controversial rule in East Timor, a former Portuguese possession.

Mongolian voters, after 75 years under Communism, ousted the mainly Communist Mongolian People's Revolutionary Party (MPRP) in elections on June 30, 1996. The MPRP won only 25 of 76 seats in parliament. A four-party, democratic coalition won 50 seats, and its general secretary, Mendsaykhany Enkhsaykhan, a 41-year-old economist, was elected prime minister. Despite the efforts of some old Communist officials to hang onto their jobs and block reforms, the prime minister reduced the size of the government. However, in a low voter turnout, the MPRP won many local elections on October 7.

Mongolia's economy continued a recovery that had begun in 1993. But in February, forest fires in

Country	Population	Government	Monetary unit*	Foreign trade (million U.S.$)	
				Exports†	Imports†
Laos	5,154,000	President Nouhak Phoumsavan; Prime Minister Khamtai Siphandon	kip (920.00 = $1)	348	587
Malaysia	20,970,000	Paramount Ruler Tuanku Ja'afar ibni Al-Marhum Tuanku Abdul Rahman; Prime Minister Mahathir bin Mohamad	ringgit (2.50 = $1)	73,715	77,615
Maldives	270,000	President Maumoon Abdul Gayoom	rufiyaa (11.77 = $1)	50	268
Mongolia	2,506,000	President Punsalmaagiyn Ochirbat; Prime Minister Mendsaykhany Enkhsaykhan	tugrik (466.67 = $1)	324	223
Nepal	23,028,000	King Birendra Bir Bikram Shah Dev; Prime Minister Sher Bahadur Deuba	rupee (56.78 = $1)	349	1,378
New Zealand	3,647,000	Governor General Dame Catherine Tizard; Prime Minister James B. Bolger	dollar (1.41 = $1)	13,746	13,957
Pakistan	148,562,000	President Farooq Leghari; Interim Prime Minister Meraj Khalid	rupee 40.22 = $1)	7,365	8,889
Papua New Guinea	4,496,000	Governor General Wiwa Korowi; Prime Minister Sir Julius Chan	kina (1.33 = $1)	2,642	1,450
Philippines	70,270,000	President Fidel Ramos	peso (26.29 = $1)	13,304	22,546
Russia	146,381,000	President Boris Yeltsin	ruble (5,442.00 = $1)	78,290	46,680
Singapore	2,899,000	President Ong Teng Cheong; Prime Minister Goh Chok Tong	dollar (1.42 = $1)	118,263	124,502
Sri Lanka	18,815,000	President Chandrika Kumaratunga; Prime Minister Sirimavo Bandaranaike	rupee (57.05 = $1)	3,798	5,192
Taiwan	21,918,000	President Li Teng-hui; Vice President Lien Chan	dollar (27.30 = $1)	93,000	85,100
Tajikistan	6,444,000	President Emomali Rahmonov; National Assembly Chairman Safarali Rajabov	ruble (5,442.00 = $1)	707	690
Thailand	60,046,000	King Phumiphon Adunyadet; Prime Minister Banharn Silapa-archa	baht (25.50 = $1)	45,236	54,438
Turkmenistan	4,279,000	President Saparmurat Niyazov	manat (not available)	1,939	777
Uzbekistan	23,846,000	President Islam Karimov	sum (not available)	3,100	2,900
Vietnam	77,780,000	Communist Party General Secretary Do Muoi; President Le Duc Anh; Prime Minister Vo Van Kiet	dong (11,020.00 = $1)	3,600	5,000

*Exchange rates as of Oct. 25, 1996, or latest available data.   †Latest available data.

the northeast burned an area the size of Maine, destroying up to a fifth of Mongolia's evergreen forest and killing 26 people. A cholera outbreak in August killed 10 people.

Laos. The ruling People's Revolutionary Party put less emphasis on its Communist origins than on authoritarian nationalism during 1996. At its sixth party congress in March, delegates ousted Khamphoui Keoboualapha from the party leadership. But when the National Assembly shuffled the cabinet on April 20, he remained a deputy prime minister, though with less control of foreign investment.

Macao held elections on September 22 for a legislative assembly that was to serve until 2001, which meant the legislators would remain in office after Portugal turned Macao over to China in 1999. China approved the five-year terms, unlike in Hong Kong, where China had announced it would abolish the advisory legislature upon taking control in 1997.

Free trade zone. At a September 1996 meeting sponsored by the United Nations, North Korea announced that foreign investors would spend $300 million in its section of a free-trade and investment zone along the Tumen River, where North Korea, China, and Russia meet. The three nations plus South Korea and Mongolia had agreed in 1995 to develop the area. North Korea's investment was mainly for a hotel and casino.

Boat people. The number of Vietnamese "boat people" in Asian camps dwindled during 1996 as host countries pressured them to go home, and the United Nations stopped funding the camps in June. Most of the 1 million people who had fled Vietnam in boats after the Communist takeover in 1975 had found refuge in other countries. But those considered jobseekers rather than political refugees had been refused resettlement and had ended up in detention camps.

Malaysia began closing its detention camps in April, and Indonesia closed its last camp in September. China wanted the camps in Hong Kong closed before it took over the region, but many of the 17,000 Vietnamese in the camps fought police efforts to send them home.

The last refugees from the Hmong tribe of Laos began moving from camps in Thailand to the United States in July. Before 1973, the Hmong had fought with American forces against Vietnamese-backed Lao Communists.

European ties. The first Asia-Europe meeting was held in Bangkok, Thailand, in March 1996. The conference brought together 10 Asian countries and the 15 nations of the European Union (EU). The Asian participants were China, Japan, South Korea, and the seven members of the Association of Southeast Asian Nations (Brunei, Indonesia, Malaysia, the Philippines, Singapore, Thailand, and Vietnam). EU officials sought closer ties with Asia, which once was under European colonial influence, but which in 1996 looked to the United States for most of its trade, technology, higher education, and defense. The attendees, heads of government except for some of the European representatives, agreed on a strong partnership in trade and investment, but the agenda avoided sensitive human rights issues.

Child labor was a sensitive issue in Asia during 1996. The International Labor Organization, an affiliate of the United Nations, stated that at least 15 percent of Asian children ages 10 to 14 were employed. Some were virtual slaves. In India, Pakistan, and Nepal, an estimated 1 million child workers had been sold into servitude by poor parents in 1996. The children worked long hours under primitive conditions with little hope of escape.

In some Asian countries, it was cheaper to have low-paid children produce goods than to buy machinery. Western pressure to end child labor often eliminated jobs and forced children into begging. Some governments tried to improve their educational systems, but budget problems limited the number of schools that could be established.

The Internet, the worldwide computer network, was censored in parts of Asia. Fearing its potentially disruptive influence, China, Singapore, and Vietnam tried to control access. ☐ Henry S. Bradsher

See also the articles on the individual Asian nations. In *World Book,* see **Asia.**

Astronomy. In 1996, astronomers studied a rock believed to be from Mars and examined data from a spacecraft orbiting Jupiter. They found new planets and were able to see the universe just as it was after the formation of the earliest galaxies. An amateur astronomer discovered a bright new comet.

Evidence of life on Mars. A team of scientists led by David S. McKay of the National Aeronautics and Space Administration's (NASA) Johnson Space Center in Houston announced in August that a meteorite found in Antarctica in 1984 offered strong evidence that primitive forms of life once existed on Mars. Astronomers believed that the rock was blasted off Mars about 16 million years ago when an asteroid collided with the planet. The rock then orbited the sun until, pulled by Earth's gravity, it fell to Antarctica 13,000 years ago.

The chemical composition of the rock, known as ALH 84001, was almost identical to that of rocks sampled by the Viking spacecraft on Mars in 1976. Microscopic studies revealed tiny globules of carbonate material, which may have been produced by living organisms. In addition, tiny egg-shaped and hair-shaped structures on the globule surfaces resembled the fossils of ancient microorganisms that geologists have found in rocks on Earth.

Galileo studies Jupiter. In December 1995, after traveling for six years and 2 billion miles (3.2 billion kilometers), the Galileo spacecraft reached Jupiter and began sending back data on the planet and its moons, including close-up views of Jupiter since the Voyager missions of the early 1980's.

One of Galileo's tasks was to gather data from a probe it had released in mid-1995. The probe arrived at Jupiter just hours before Galileo and plunged into the Jovian atmosphere. It radioed measurements to Galileo for 57 minutes before being destroyed by Jupiter's high temperature and pressure. Data radioed from the probe indicated that the planet had been formed from the same cloud of interstellar gas that formed the sun. Additional data revealed that there was less water vapor, lightning, and cloud cover in Jupiter's atmosphere than previously thought and that planetary winds reached speeds of more than 300 miles (480 kilometers) per hour.

Galileo's flights past Jupiter's moons revealed that Io and Ganymede may have their own magnetic fields, making them the first satellites in the solar system known to have such fields. Images of Europa, another moon that Galileo flew by, showed that it may have an ocean of liquid water under its ice-covered surface, making it the only known place in the solar system, other than Earth, that scientists believe may possess water in a liquid state.

New planets. The discovery of an object circling the star 51 Pegasi in 1995 marked the beginning of a boom in the discovery of new solar systems. In 1996, so many additional planets were detected around stars that these planets began to outnumber those

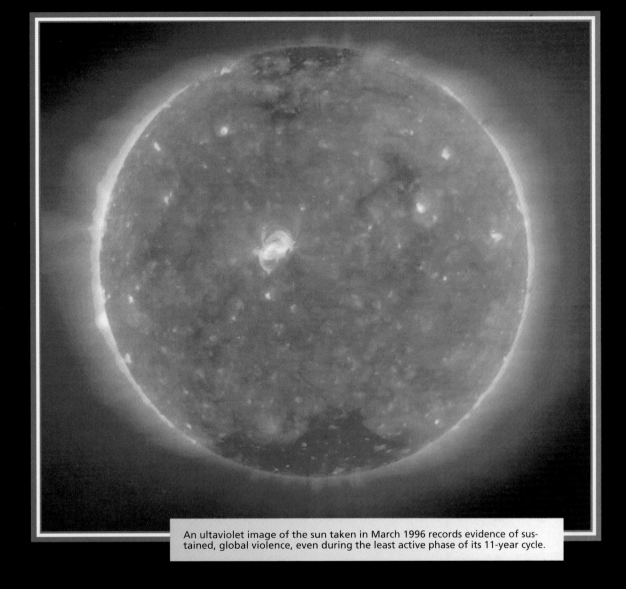

An ultaviolet image of the sun taken in March 1996 records evidence of sustained, global violence, even during the least active phase of its 11-year cycle.

of our own solar system. Astronomers Geoffrey Marcy and Paul Butler at San Francisco State University identified such planets—sometimes called "exoplanets" or "extrasolar planets"—around the stars 47 Ursae Majoris (in the Big Dipper), 70 Virginis, 55 Rho[1] Cancri, Tau Bootis, and Upsilon Andromedae.

George Gatewood of the Allegheny Observatory in Pittsburgh announced the discovery of a planet—and the possibility of a second—orbiting a star close to our sun, Lalande 21185. Scientists did not believe that the new planets were similar to Earth or likely to harbor life, and none was actually photographed directly. All were too faint and too close to bright stars to be distinguished. Instead, their presence was inferred by observing the stars and noting the small wobble a planet causes when its gravitational force pulls the star back and forth.

The earliest galaxies. In January 1996, astronomers released a picture of the way the universe looked not long after the big bang, the theoretical cosmic explosion in which the universe may have originated. The picture, called the Hubble Deep Field, was a composite of over 300 images taken of a small area in the Big Dipper by the Hubble Space Telescope during a 10-day period. Because the exposure was so long, astronomers could see fainter objects than seen before. Several of these objects were thought to be the most distant galaxies—so far away that their light took billions of years to reach Earth. When astronomers looked at these far-away galaxies, they were seeing them as they were at least 10 billion years ago, at a time shortly after the big bang.

In September, astronomers led by Sam Pascarelle of Arizona State University at Tempe announced that the Hubble Space Telescope had recorded images of some of the building blocks of galaxies—clusters of about 1 billion stars—in the Hercules constellation. Such "pregalactic" clusters may have merged to form the great oval- and spiral-shaped galaxies of the later stages of the universe—including the giant spiral of the Milky Way.

Comets Hyakutake and Hale-Bopp. In January, Japanese amateur astronomer Yuji Hyakutake discovered a comet that now bears his name. Northern observers were able to see Comet Hyakutake with the naked eye during late March, April, and May. In March, astronomers at the Max Planck Institute in Germany announced the ROSAT satellite had detected X rays from the comet, the first X rays ever detected from a comet. Comet Hale-Bopp, discovered in 1995 by Alan Hale and Thomas Bopp, became visible with binoculars in autumn 1996. Astronomers predicted that when Comet Hale-Bopp reached its maximum brightness in spring 1997, it would be brighter than Hyakutake.

□ Laurence A. Marschall

See also **Space exploration.** In **World Book,** see **Astronomy.**

Australia. John Howard succeeded Paul Keating as prime minister after early elections on March 2, 1996, gave Howard's Liberal Party 77 seats in the House of Representatives. Keating's Australian Labor Party, which had governed the nation for 13 years, captured only 49 seats. Howard's majority enabled his party to govern without a coalition. Keating retired after 26 years in politics, turning party leadership over to his deputy, Kim Beazley.

The economy continued to improve during 1996, though the 3.5 percent growth was less than the 4.9 percent achieved in 1995. Government figures released in July 1996 showed inflation at 3 percent, which remained steady for most of the year. However, unemployment began to rise, reaching 8.8 percent by August.

The new government faced its first test on August 20, when it handed down a budget that cut spending by $26.72 billion over four years. (All monetary figures in this article are in Australian dollars.) The budget called for reductions that included programs for *Aborigines* (native people), health, and education. The government announced it would raise the tax-free threshold for low- to middle-income families, allowing them to earn more before paying income tax.

Foreign relations with several of Australia's neighbors, notably China, Indonesia, the Philippines, and Vietnam, were damaged in May when Foreign

Australia's new prime minister, John Howard (left) and his family sing the national anthem to celebrate his Liberal Party's victory in the March elections.

Minister Alexander Downer abolished a program that had provided Asian countries with $124 million a year in loans and grants for noncommercial infrastructure projects, such as roads, bridges, and power stations. On June 18, Downer falsely told Parliament that none of the affected countries had complained about the program being discontinued. On June 26, Downer apologized, stating he had "inadvertently misled" Parliament. A Senate inquiry later found that Australia stood to lose large business deals with the Asian nations, including $1.5 billion in shipbuilding contracts.

Immigration. On July 3, the government announced a cut in overall immigration quotas and a shift toward immigrants who had business and English-language skills. A program allowing elderly parents to join their immigrant children in Australia was also cut. However, the quota of immigrants with certain work skills was increased.

On September 10, a new independent member of Parliament, Pauline Hanson, called for a complete halt to immigration, especially from Asia. Prime Minister Howard came under pressure to denounce Hanson's comments because they were damaging to relations with Asian neighbors, but he defended her right to free speech.

Environmental issues. On July 19, Australia refused to join 134 nations, including the United States, meeting in Geneva, Switzerland, in agreeing to reduce emissions of "greenhouse gases" to certain target levels. (Greenhouse gases are thought to contribute to global warming.) Australia sided with Russia and the 13 nations of the Organization of Petroleum Exporting Countries in opposing the targets, arguing that Australia was highly dependent on fossil fuels and had little opportunity to switch to alternative power sources. Australia's refusal sparked widespread condemnation from other governments and environmental groups.

On October 9 in southern New South Wales, the agriculture department released 16 rabbits that biologists had infected with a deadly virus as part of a program to eliminate huge populations of wild rabbits. The infected rabbits were to spread disease among the rabbit population. Rabbits had been overrunning Australia, decimating the vegetation needed by ranchers and farmers to feed sheep and cattle. Farmers welcomed the program, saying they hoped it would wipe out as much as 80 percent of the wild rabbit population in two years. By October, the virus had infected and killed an estimated 50 million rabbits in other mainland states. In November, workers released rabbits at 280 other sites nationwide.

Living standard. A July report by the United Nations (UN) stated that Australia's gap between rich and poor was the widest in the world. The richest 20 percent of households had an income 10 times higher than the income of the poorest 20 percent. Australia's standard of living, based on health, life expectancy, education, income, and opportunity, was the 11th highest in the world.

Euthanasia. On Sept. 22, 1996, a 66-year-old cancer patient became the first person to end his life voluntarily under a law enacted in the Northern Territory in 1995. At his command, a machine injected him with a lethal drug. The law, the first in the world to legalize *euthanasia* (mercy killings), applied only to the Northern Territory, though terminally ill Australians could travel there for assisted suicide.

Medical, religious, and right-to-life groups campaigned to repeal the law. On July 24, 1996, the Supreme Court of the Northern Territory dismissed an appeal to overturn it. In September, a federal legislator introduced a bill that would negate the territorial measure. The federal High Court decided on November 15 to consider an appeal to overturn the law.

Aborigines. On May 17, Bob Bellear became the nation's first Aboriginal judge. He was appointed to the New South Wales District Court.

In October, a group of Aborigines from the Dunghutti tribe was granted $738,000 in compensation for Aborigine-inhabited, government-owned land in northern New South Wales that had been sold to housing developers. It was the first successful claim under the Native Title Act. The act clarified a 1992 High Court ruling, known as the Mabo decision, that recognized the entitlement of native people to their traditional land only when the land was owned by the government. The New South Wales settlement was expected to influence the outcome of 400 other native title claims.

In September 1996, archaeologists found engravings and enormous sculpted boulders near Kununurra in Australia's far north. The artifacts suggested that Aborigines have occupied Australia for 176,000 years—nearly three times longer than scientists previously had thought. Some experts, however, debated the accuracy of the dating method used.

Helicopter crash. On June 12, Australia suffered its worst peacetime military accident in 30 years, when 18 soldiers were killed and 10 seriously injured in a midair collision between two Black Hawk helicopters. The incident happened during a night training exercise in north Queensland. Fifteen of the dead were commandos from the Special Air Service regiment. A military board of inquiry into the accident was convened in Perth on September 18.

Hobart massacre. On April 28, a gunman killed 35 people and injured 18 others at a historic site at the former penal colony of Port Arthur near Hobart, the capital of Tasmania. It was the world's worst peacetime massacre by a single gunman in recent history. The gunman, armed with two high-powered assault rifles, took 30 minutes to shoot 32 of his victims. He took three hostages to a nearby guesthouse and killed them during a 20-hour siege. The siege ended when he set fire to the house and tried to escape with his clothes on fire. Police arrested the man identified as Martin Bryant. In November, Bryant pleaded not guilty to 72 charges. In December, he was found guilty and sentenced to life imprisonment.

Gun laws. On May 10, in response to a public outcry over the Hobart massacre, the prime minister announced strict new gun controls, including a total ban on all automatic and semiautomatic rifles and pump-action shotguns. Other firearms remained legal but had to be licensed.

More than 100,000 gun owners staged demonstrations in state capitals on June 1 to protest new gun controls. On July 1, the government imposed a 0.2 percent rate increase for federal health insurance for a year to fund a program to compensate gun owners for turning in their weapons to the police.

Olympics. Australia won 41 medals, its highest number ever, at the 1996 Olympic Games in Atlanta, Georgia. Swimmer Kieren Perkins won the 1,500-meter freestyle after barely qualifying in earlier trials.

Media barons. In March, Australia's richest man, Kerry Packer, handed control of his $2.8-billion media empire to his son James. In September, Rupert Murdoch appointed his son, Lachlan, managing director of News Limited, Australia's biggest newspaper publishing company. □ Lucinda Duckett

See also **Asia** (Facts in brief table); **Howard, John.** In *World Book,* see **Australia.**

Austria struggled to define its place in the European Union (EU) in 1996 as the government imposed tough austerity measures in a bid to qualify for the planned single EU currency. The measures provoked a strong public backlash, reflected in the results of the October voting for Austria's seats in the European Parliament.

Difficulties forming a government were apparent from the start of the year as the center-left Social Democratic Party, which won the most votes in national elections in December 1995, and the conservative People's Party negotiated for nearly three months before coming to an agreement. The coalition, which had governed Austria since 1987, agreed on March 7, 1996, to retain the Social Democratic leader, Franz Vranitzky, as chancellor and the People's Party leader, Wolfgang Schuessel, as vice chancellor and foreign minister. The cornerstone of the coalition agreement was a strict, two-year budget package, the very issue that divided the coalition and forced early parliamentary elections in 1995.

The budget was designed to reduce the government deficit by $9.7 billion in 1996 and 1997, bringing the deficit to just below 3 percent of gross domestic product, the EU ceiling for a single currency. The package included significant cutbacks in welfare programs, including a reduction in paid maternity leave—from 2 years to 18 months—and cutbacks in unemployment benefits and student aid. It also in-

creased taxes on the wealthy and on interest income. The coalition agreed to trim the government by closing two ministries and eliminating 10,000 civil service jobs. The government cutbacks triggered a sharp slowdown in the economy and weakened public support for the government and for monetary union, which many Austrians blamed for the austerity measures.

Election setback. The discontent enabled the highly conservative Freedom Party of Jörg Haider to score its best result yet in the October 13 voting for Austria's seats in the European Parliament. Haider campaigned against the Maastricht Treaty on European Union, the blueprint for the single currency, as well as closer EU political integration, arguing instead for a "Europe of the fatherlands." The Freedom Party won 27.6 percent of the vote, up from 21.9 percent in the December 1995 national election, and took 7 of the 21 seats. The Social Democrats won 29.1 percent of the vote, their worst result in a national ballot, while the People's Party led with 29.6 percent. Both parties won 7 seats. In a simultaneous local election, the Social Democrats lost majority control of the city council in Vienna for the first time since 1920. Vranitzky resisted pressure to resign over the results, blaming his party's losses on apathy and low voter turnout. □ Tom Buerkle

See also **Europe** (Facts in brief table). In *World Book,* see **Austria; European Union.**

Automobile. Automakers had anticipated that 1996 would be a good year, and they were not disappointed. Through the first nine months of the year, sales of light vehicles in the United States reached 11.6 million units, or 3.2 percent more than sales for the same period in 1995. Rising sales of light trucks, such as the Ford S-series pickup, Chevrolet C/K pickup, and Dodge Caravan minivan, enabled the Big Three—General Motors Corp. (GM), Ford Motor Co., and Chrysler Corp.—to take 73 percent of the U.S. market share through the first nine months of 1996, the same share they had held in 1995. The share held by Japanese automakers fell slightly to 22.7 percent of the market, while European manufacturers experienced a gain to 4.3 percent.

Rising sales, however, increased the profits of only one of the Big Three. During the first nine months of 1996, Chrysler recorded net earnings of $2.7 billion, compared with $985 million for the same period in 1995. Chrysler benefited from a continuing buyer demand for light trucks.

Ford saw its profits fall 7 percent in the first nine months of the year. The number-two automaker earned $3.2 billion through September, compared with $3.5 billion for the same period a year earlier. Ford's profits were hurt by the high costs of launching new vehicles, such as the Ford Escort, Mercury Tracer, and F-series trucks. Analysts predicted that Ford would benefit from the new models in 1997.

GM's profits also dropped during the first nine months of 1996. The nubmer-one automaker reported a profit of $4.2 billion, compared with $5 billion for the same period a year earlier. GM's earnings fell nearly $1 billion because of a strike by workers in GM's Dayton, Ohio, facilities.

Light-truck sales increase. Buyer demand for light trucks remained strong in 1996, continuing a trend that had begun in the 1980's. Although Americans still bought more cars in 1995 (8.6 million) than light trucks (6.1 million), by September 1996, the gap was narrowing, with light-truck sales climbing to 4.9 million units, a 7.5 percent increase over the same period in 1995. Light trucks also accounted for 43 percent of industry sales, or 2 percent more than in the first nine months of 1995. Analysts predicted that light-truck sales would rise during the rest of the decade and eventually account for 45 to 50 percent of light-vehicle sales.

To lure light-truck buyers into their showrooms, automakers continued to produce more models of pickups, sport utility vehicles, and minivans in 1996. In addition, manufacturers such as GM, Toyota, Nissan, and Mercedes-Benz planned to boost truck production in the United States before the end of the decade to meet buyer demand.

New light-truck models. Light-truck introductions by Ford and Chrysler in 1996 underscored how the manufacturers planned to cater to motorists' tastes. Ford's full-sized, four-door sport utility vehicle, the Expedition, was designed to attract buyers who wanted a vehicle larger than the Ford Explorer. The Expedition was developed to compete with the Chevrolet Tahoe and GMC Yukon.

Chrysler introduced the Dodge Dakota, a medium-sized pickup truck. The Dakota's rugged styling was borrowed from the popular Dodge Ram pickup, and its engineering improvements from the Jeep Wrangler. Chrysler hoped that the Dakota's unique size—larger than the Chevrolet S-series pickups and the Ford Ranger, but smaller than the Ram and other full-sized pickup trucks—would increase sales.

GM added new minivans in 1996, to make that segment of its light-truck line more competitive. The Chevrolet Venture, Oldsmobile Silhouette, and Pontiac Trans Sport featured steel bodies, which replaced the plastic bodies of older versions, as well as such popular new features as dual power-sliding side doors.

New car models. Automakers premiered several new car models in 1996, including the Toyota Camry. The Camry had consistently ranked among the top 10 best-selling cars in the United States, with U.S. sales rising from 52,700 cars in 1983 to 328,600 cars in 1995. The new Camry featured conservative styling and a standard 4-cylinder engine that produced 133 horsepower, 8 more than the previous model.

Pontiac's Grand Prix adopted a more aggressive look, wider track, and longer wheel base than previous models. Designers hoped the changes would attract buyers who preferred cars with more flair and greater performance. The new Grand Prix sedan came with a standard 160-horsepower V6 engine, while the coupe featured a 195-horsepower engine.

First electric car. In 1996, GM launched the first electric car, the EV1, since those of the early 1900's. The EV1 was available for lease only to selected customers through 25 Saturn dealerships in California and Arizona. It contained 26 batteries, which allowed the car to travel 70 to 90 miles (113 to 145 kilometers) before needing to be recharged. Several states, including California, had mandated that auto manufacturers must make 10 percent of their vehicles emission free by the year 2003.

Chrysler takeover averted. Billionaire Kirk Kerkorian, who had been threatening to take over Chrysler since April 1995, reached an agreement with the Auburn Hills, Michigan, company in February. Kerkorian called off his hostile bid in exchange for a seat on the board of directors for an executive of Tracinda Corp., Kerkorian's holding company.

Labor disputes. A March 5 to 22 walkout by members of the United Auto Workers (UAW) union at two brake parts facilities in Dayton, Ohio, choked off supplies to GM's North American plants. The strike shut down 26 assembly plants and forced the layoffs of nearly 180,000 workers at GM plants and non-GM supplier facilities. Workers struck primarily over GM's attempts to move work from their plants to outside facilities, a practice called outsourcing. The same issue also played a role in a three-week strike in October by members of the Canadian Auto Workers union, which shut down some GM assembly plants and parts facilities in North America.

The issue of protecting jobs was at the heart of the UAW's bargaining with the Big Three in 1996. In the fall, the union won agreements from Ford, Chrysler, and GM to maintain minimum employment at 95 percent of the work force for the next three years. UAW members at Ford and Chrysler approved the contract without work stoppages. GM workers staged two local strikes which were settled after GM and the UAW reached a national contract.

Airbag danger. Federal regulators proposed rules in 1996 to protect children from airbags. According to the National Highway Traffic Safety Administration, an independent agency of the U.S. government, at least 26 children under the age of 12 had been killed by the force of deploying airbags since 1993. The agency proposed that manufacturers include warning labels in vehicles instructing motorists to never put rear-facing child seats in front seats and to make sure that children wear safety belts. The agency suggested that manufacturers of airbags develop products that would inflate at a rate based upon passenger size, which would be determined by sensor-equipped dashboards. ☐ Mike Casey

In *World Book,* see **Automobile.**

FOCUS ON

Automobiles 1996

The 1997 models reflect the continuing market for light trucks and sport utility vehicles. Sedan and sports-car design displays the influence of the rounded styling introduced in the 1986 Ford Taurus, which was redesigned in 1996.

The 1997 Pontiac Grand Prix GTP Sedan sports a wider track and longer wheel base than previous models.

The 1997 XK8 is the first Jaguar to feature a V8 engine under its traditionally sleek hood.

Automobile racing. The world of Indy-car racing was fragmented in 1996 by a power struggle in which the new Indy Racing League (IRL) began competing in opposition to Championship Auto Racing Teams (CART), the long-time establishment. Although almost all major teams and drivers stayed with CART, the IRL staged five races, including its cornerstone, the Indianapolis 500.

It was also a year of tragedy. Scott Brayton, who had won the pole position for the Indianapolis 500, was killed in a crash during practice nine days before the race. Jeff Krosnoff, an Indy-car rookie, was killed when he crashed in a CART race July 14 in Toronto. Drag racer Blaine Johnson, who led the National Hot Rod Association's (NHRA) top-fuel division, was fa-

tally injured when he crashed at 309 miles (497 kilometers) per hour August 31 in Clermont, Indiana. Emerson Fittipaldi (Indy cars) and Dale Earnhardt (stock cars) were also injured in collisions.

IRL. In 1995, IRL founder Tony George, the head of the Indianapolis Motor Speedway, had decreed that the first 25 spots in the Indianapolis 500 would be reserved for the IRL point leaders. That meant that such famous drivers as Fittipaldi, Al Unser, Jr., Michael Andretti, Bobby Rahal, and other CART drivers would have to compete for only eight spots. In 1996, many drivers and their teams largely ignored the IRL.

In April, the IRL announced that it wanted to reduce costs so less-affluent teams could be competi-

Ford's new 1997 Expedition is a luxurious, full-sized, four-door sport utility vehicle, which was designed to appeal to the buyer who wants a larger vehicle than the Ford Explorer.

For 1997, Toyota introduces a new version of its popular Camry LE, featuring more aerodynamic styling and a quieter, more powerful ride.

The 1997 Dodge Dakota 4x4 Club Cab Sport combines the rugged styling of the Dodge Ram pickup truck with the appeal of a midsize truck.

tive. Its rules outlawed all present Indy-type cars, beginning in 1997. Meanwhile, its drivers raced in older cars. IRL cars would cost significantly less— $260,000 for a chassis and $75,000 for an engine.

Because most of the veterans stayed with CART, the field of 33 cars at the 1996 Indianapolis 500, on May 26, included 17 rookies, 3 of whom had never raced an Indy car before. Buddy Lazier, in a Reynard-Ford, won the race by seven-tenths of a second, about eight car lengths. Only two months before, Lazier had broken his back in a crash.

CART. The day of the Indianapolis 500, CART ran a rival race, the U.S. 500, in Brooklyn, Michigan. There was a 12-car crash on the final turn of the last pace lap. Jimmy Vasser, starting from the pole posi-

tion, crashed his Reynard-Honda in that accident, but ran the race in his team's slower backup car and still won by almost 11 seconds.

In all, CART ran 16 races, including two in Canada, one in Brazil, and one in Australia. Michael Andretti won five races and Vasser four. Vasser won the series title.

NASCAR. Dale Jarrett starred in the National Association for Stock Car Racing's 31-race Winston Cup series for late-model sedans. Driving a Ford, he won three major races—the Daytona 500, February 18 in Daytona Beach, Florida; the Coca-Cola 600, May 26 in Concord, North Carolina; and the Brickyard 400, August 3 in Indianapolis. However, his inconsistency hurt him in the battle for the title and allowed Terry

Labonte to become the Winston Cup champion for the second time.

Formula One. There were 16 Grand-Prix races—11 in Europe and one each in Australia, Brazil, Argentina, Canada, and Japan—for the world drivers championship. To reduce speeds and make races safer, new rules trimmed the engine size from 3.5 liters to 3.0. Great Britain's Damon Hill took the title with 97 points to 78 for his Williams-Renault teammate, Gilles Villeneuve of Canada.

Endurance. An Oldsmobile Mark III won the first two triple-crown races—the 24 Hours of Daytona, February 3 and 4 in Daytona Beach, Florida, and the 12 Hours of Sebring, March 16 in Sebring, Florida. In the 24 Hours of LeMans, held June 15 and 16 in France, the Oldsmobile, while running in 15th place, dropped out halfway through the race with a faulty gearbox. The winner was a TWR Porsche codriven by Davy Jones of the United States (the runner-up at Indianapolis), Manuel Reuter of Germany, and Alexander Wurz of Austria. At age 22, Wurz was the youngest winner ever at LeMans.

Dragsters. The NHRA ran 20 major competitions in 1996. The season champions were Kenny Bernstein in the top-fuel division, John Force for the sixth time in seven years in funny cars, and Jim Yates in pro stock. In June, Bernstein drove the quarter-mile in the record time of 4.603 seconds. ☐ Frank Litsky

In *World Book,* see **Automobile racing.**

Aviation

Aviation. On June 11, 1996, executives of British Airways and American Airlines, a subsidiary of Dallas-based AMR Corp., announced an alliance. The airlines would coordinate schedules for nearly 500 weekly flights across the North Atlantic, jointly market their services, allow the interchange of frequent-flyer programs, and offer connections on each other's flights. However, no equity would be exchanged and the firms would remain separate entities.

The proposed deal led to an outcry from other airlines, including Britain's Virgin Atlantic Airways and a number of U.S. airlines that did not have access rights to London's Heathrow Airport. The alliance, which would control 60 percent of the air traffic between the United States and Great Britain, also attracted the attention of both Britain's Office of Fair Trading and the U.S. Department of Justice, which feared a possible reduction in competition.

Aircraft manufacturing. Fokker NV, the Dutch airplane manufacturer, declared bankruptcy in March. The company dated back to World War I (1914-1918), when it made the plane flown by Manfred von Richthofen, the "Red Baron." Fokker was saved from closure in July, when the Dutch industrial systems group Stork NV purchased the company for $180 million. Fokker's core businesses—maintenance, repair, and technical support—were organized into a new company, Fokker Aviation.

Airbus Industrie, the consortium of aircraft manu-

facturers in France, Great Britain, Germany, and Spain, announced in February that it will build a 550-seat aircraft to rival Seattle-based Boeing Aircraft Company's proposed 747-600. Plans called for Airbus's A3XX to be available in the early 2000's. Airbus, founded in 1970, announced in July that it would form a single, integrated company by 1999. In December 1996, Boeing announced plans to acquire rival McDonnell Douglas Corp., of St. Louis, Missouri, creating the largest aerospace manufacturer in the world.

National airlines. Kenya Airways continued the global trend toward privatization of state-owned airlines, with the sale of 51 percent of its stock to private shareholders in March and April 1996. The airline sold 26 percent of its stock to Dutch carrier KLM in 1995. Indonesian state airline Garuda stated that it would sell shares as well. Garuda's financial advisers hoped to find a foreign airline for a partner in 1997 and to sell shares to the public in 1998.

Spain's Iberia, Italy's Alitalia, and Air France remained in state ownership, but all three airlines continued to experience financial problems. The European Commission, an agency of the European Union, allowed Spain to give recovery aid to Iberia in 1992 and 1996. Similarly, it approved the French government's aid package to Air France in 1994 and 1996. British Airways, KLM, Scandinavian Airline Systems (SAS), and other airlines challenged the commission's decision before the European Court, arguing that state aid to Air France resulted in unfair competition. Alitalia, which had lost money for the past eight years, applied to the commission for permission to receive Italian government aid as well.

New airlines. In April, the London-based Virgin Group purchased EuroBelgian Airlines of Brussels, the second-largest airline in Belgium. The new airline, to be called Virgin European Airways, was to provide low-cost scheduled flights within Europe.

In September, Pan American World Airways returned to the skies, providing service from Miami to New York and Los Angeles. The new company was formed by a group of executives, some from the former Pan Am, who purchased rights to the name and logo from the carrier, which went bankrupt in 1991.

Airline accidents. A ValuJet Airlines DC-9 enroute from Miami to Atlanta, Georgia, crashed in the Florida Everglades on May 11, 1996, killing all 110 people aboard. The low-cost airline, formed in 1993, had grown to operate 51 aircraft. Concern was raised that rapid growth had affected its maintenance and operating procedures after Federal Aviation Administration (FAA) officials found that a fire aboard the plane caused the crash. The FAA grounded Atlanta-based ValuJet on June 17, 1996, after a study of the airline's procedures found "serious deficiencies." ValuJet resumed operations September 30, with fewer planes and tighter maintenance controls.

Claims by Department of Transportation Inspec-

Airbus Industrie, the French-based aircraft manufacturer, unveils plans in February 1996 for a 550-passenger "super-jumbo" jet, designed to compete with the Boeing 747-600.

tor General Mary Schiavo that the FAA knew of problems at ValuJet before May 11 but did not take action raised concern about the FAA's dual role. Since the creation of the FAA in 1958, the agency had both promoted aviation and ensured safety, objectives that have sometimes conflicted. FAA Administrator David Hinson and Transportation Secretary Frederico Peña proposed that the FAA be reconstituted with just a safety enforcement role.

A Trans World Airlines (TWA) Boeing 747 exploded on July 17, less than one-half hour after it left New York City bound for Paris. The aircraft burst into a fireball and crashed into the Atlantic off Long Island, killing all 230 people aboard. Despite similarities with the 1988 bombing of a Pan American World Airways 747 over Lockerbie, Scotland, investigators remained unable to determine the cause of the TWA explosion months after the accident.

Changes to 737. By the end of 1996, federal investigators had still not found the probable cause of the crashes of Boeing 737's near Pittsburgh in 1994 and Colorado Springs, Colorado, in 1991. However, suspicion centered on the rudder. In August, the FAA proposed nine improvements to the 200 through 500 series of 737's, most involving changes to the rudder- and wing-control surfaces. The National Transportation Safety Board, a U.S. government agency that makes safety recommendations to the FAA, proposed its own changes to the 737 in Oc-

tober. The recommendations of both agencies were to be further revised before being implemented.

The Global Positioning System (GPS), developed by the U.S. military, was adapted for civilian aviation use and tested on European aircraft in 1996. The 24 GPS satellites have enabled military and civilian users to locate precise positions or plot navigational routes. Because of security concerns, only Defense Department-approved users have been given access to the most precise measurements, those needed by airplanes as they approach runways or fly over areas without radar equipment. Differential GPS (DGPS), the system adapted for civilian aviation, includes ground stations that correct satellite data. British, Dutch, French, and German planes equipped with DGPS used it to relay their positions to ground controllers. The controllers allowed the test planes to fly closer together than the 60-mile (111-kilometer) distance demanded of planes using conventional, less accurate navigation. The system was expected to increase airspace capacity and to cut flight times.

Industry profits. World airlines earned more in 1996 than in any previous year in the 1990's. The director general of the International Air Transport Association predicted in April that airlines would post a net profit of $6 billion in 1996, compared with a profit of $5.2 billion in 1995. The airlines lost $15.6 billion from 1990 to 1993.   □ Ian Savage

In *World Book,* see **Aviation.**

Azerbaijan. In April 1996, Azeri President Heydar A. Aliyev met with Armenian President Levon Ter-Petrosian to discuss the eight-year-long war over the disputed Armenian enclave of Nagorno-Karabakh. In a joint declaration, the two presidents agreed to maintain the cease-fire that has held since May 1994 and to release prisoners of war. Armenian troops continued to occupy Nagorno-Karabakh, as well as approximately 20 percent of Azerbaijan.

In May 1996, Russian Foreign Minister Yevgeny Primakov, after three days of intense shuttle diplomacy between Armenia, Nagorno-Karabakh, and Azerbaijan, brokered a further agreement for the exchange of prisoners and hostages. The International Red Cross later reported that, despite their pledges, all parties continued to hold prisoners.

Russia accused Azerbaijan of providing supplies to the rebels in the breakaway Russian republic of Chechnya. In April, Moscow police arrested Ayaz Mutalibov, the former leader of Azerbaijan's Communist Party. Mutalibov had been sought by Azeri authorities since 1992 on charges of participating in a series of armed coup attempts in Azerbaijan. But after 30 days, Russian authorities refused to extradite Mutalibov to Azerbaijan and released him from custody.   □ Steven L. Solnick

See also **Armenia; Asia** (Facts in brief table). In *World Book,* see **Azerbaijan.**

Bahamas. See **West Indies.**

Bahrain. Violent antigovernment riots, bombings, and arson rocked Bahrain in 1996. The unrest alarmed the Arab states of the Persian Gulf, where Bahrain remained the key financial center.

Bombs exploded in three luxury hotels and two restaurants in early 1996, bringing the number of deaths from the violence between December 1994 and June 1996 to 25. The crisis deepened in June, when at least 44 Bahrainis were arrested and accused of a pro-Iranian plot to oust Bahrain's ruling Al Khalifa family.

The Al Khalifas are Sunni Muslims, one of the two primary sects of Islam. Sixty percent of Bahrainis (and most Iranians) are, however, Shiite Muslims, the other great division of Islam. Violence began in December 1994 with widespread demands for the restoration of parliament, which the ruling family had dissolved in 1975.

Bahraini authorities responded harshly to the continuing unrest. In March 1996, a man was executed for the 1995 killing of a policeman. It was the first execution in Bahrain since the mid-1970's. In July, three additional men received death sentences. By mid-year, more than 600 men and women had been detained, and more than 100 sentenced to prison.   □ Christine Helms

See also **Middle East** (Fact in brief table). In *World Book,* see **Bahrain.**

Ballet. See **Dancing.**

Bangladesh installed a new government in 1996, ending two years of political turmoil. Hasina Wajed ousted Khaleda Ziaur Rahman (known as Zia) and became prime minister on June 23. On October 9, former chief justice Shahabuddin Ahmed was sworn in as president, a largely ceremonial office.

Wajed, popularly known as Sheikh Hasina, headed the Awami League (AL). Her father and AL founder, Mujibur Rahman, had led Bangladesh to independence in 1971. He was killed in 1975 during a coup by military officers, who later received amnesty. On Aug. 13, 1996, Wajed's government began arresting the leaders of that coup.

Political turmoil. Wajed had refused to accept the result of 1991 parliamentary elections that brought Zia's Bangladesh Nationalist Party (BNP) to power, though international observers had called the elections free and fair. Wajed accused Zia's government of acting illegally. In 1994, Zia began organizing general strikes to pressure the government to turn over power to a neutral regime that would organize new elections. Finally, Zia called elections for Feb. 15, 1996, but the AL boycotted them, charging that the government would cheat. Only about 15 percent of the voters turned out, and they gave the BNP a sweeping victory. The AL continued violently disruptive strikes that hurt economic development.

Second election. Unable to maintain order, Zia resigned on March 30 so a neutral caretaker government could organize new elections. Muhammad Habibur Rahman was sworn in April 3 to head the interim government. The specter of a military coup arose briefly on May 20, when the BNP president, Abdur Rahman Biswas, fired the army chief of staff, but no coup attempt materialized.

In parliamentary elections on June 12, which observers called fair, the AL won 146 of the 300 seats, and the BNP won 116 seats. The Jatiya Party, led by a former president, Hussain Mohammad Ershad, won 32 seats. AL, in a coalition with Jatiya, formed a new government headed by Wajed.

As leader of the opposition, Zia promised cooperation to work for democracy. But on November 10, BNP members began a boycott of Parliament, accusing the AL of repressing its party workers and of holding some as political prisoners.

The economy. While Bangladesh remained an impoverished land, economic prospects improved somewhat after political turmoil ended. On August 20, the World Bank, an agency of the United Nations, called for economic reforms and tighter limits on government spending.

Nature's wrath. On May 13, a tornado swept through northern Bangladesh, killing more than 500 people and injuring 33,000 others. July storms on the Bay of Bengal left more than 100 Bangladeshi fishermen missing.   □ Henry S. Bradsher

See also **Asia** (Facts in brief table). In *World Book,* see **Bangladesh.**

Bank. Bolstered by a continuing expansion of the United States economy, banks posted strong earnings in 1996. For the first half of 1996, earnings for the nation's 10,100 banks totaled $25.8 billion. The nation's 2,050 savings and loans (S&L's) posted earnings of $5.1 billion. In the third quarter, major bank stocks collectively rose 27 percent, one of the strongest growth rates among all U.S. industries.

Steady interest rates kept the banking industry humming. The Federal Reserve System (commonly known as the Fed), the nation's central bank and top banking regulator, held interest rates low, apparently satisfied that inflation was in check. In the past, the Fed had increased interest rates when it feared that inflation was heating up. A higher interest rate makes it more expensive for businesses to borrow and expand and, thus, slows the economy.

On January 31, the Fed reduced the federal funds rate—the interest rate that member banks of the Fed charge each other for short-term loans—from 5.5 to 5.25 percent. The federal funds rate has often influenced the rate consumers pay for mortgages and loans. In the fall, low unemployment, which exerts upward pressure on wages and so can trigger inflation, prompted speculation that the Fed would raise interest rates. However, the consumer price index—a measure of prices that consumers pay for goods and services—increased just 2.9 percent for the 12-month period ending in July 1996. The Fed, at its closely watched meeting on September 24, kept the federal funds rate at 5.25 percent.

The only weak spot for bank profits was consumer debt. Banks, competing heavily in credit card services, allowed consumers to load up on both the number of credit cards and amount of credit. In the first half of 1996, banks wrote off bad credit card loans at an annual rate of 4.48 percent, the highest rate since 1992. In addition, two-thirds of the $3.8-billion in uncollectible bank loans written off in the second quarter of 1996—up 36 percent from the same period in 1995—represented bad debts from consumers who could not pay their credit card bills.

S&L woes continue. On Sept. 28, 1996, the U.S. Congress approved a plan to shore up the Savings Association Insurance Fund, which insures thrift deposits up to $100,000. The declining number of thrifts S&L's and the thrift industry's big losses in the 1980's had nearly depleted the fund. The losses resulted from the failure of more than 1,000 S&L's because of poor government regulation of the industry, mismanagement and fraud, and competition from other financial institutions. The government bailed out the thrift industry by taking control of the failed S&L's, selling some of their assets, and spending approximately $150 billion in taxpayer dollars to reimburse investors.

Under the new plan, the thrift industry was required to make a one-time payment of $4.7 billion into the insurance fund. Banks also agreed to aid the fund by paying 1.3 cents for each $100 of bank deposits. (Banks already were paying into their own Federal Deposit Insurance Corporation.) The cost to the banks was expected to reach about $12 billion over the next 20 years. Banks also agreed to pick up some of the annual $793-million cost of government bonds that financed part of the S&L bailout. In exchange for helping their competitors, banks were relieved of many regulations that they contended were unnecessarily burdensome. For example, Congress ruled that small banks in sound financial condition would be examined by U.S. regulators every 18 months instead of every 12 months.

The cost of reneging. In another development related to the S&L cleanup, the Supreme Court of the United States ruled 7-2 on July 1 that Congress had erred in enacting part of a 1989 law that bailed out the S&L industry. In the 1980's, government regulators had induced healthy S&L's to acquire failing thrifts by promising that the purchasers could use special accounting rules that would make the S&L's appear more profitable. However, the 1989 law—the Financial Institutions Reform, Recovery, and Enforcement Act—revoked these accounting advantages. As a result, many of the combined S&L's became insolvent and were seized by the government. The Supreme Court ruling, which required the government to compensate investors in the seized S&L's, may well have added another $10 billion to $20 billion to S&L bailout costs.

High court decisions. The Supreme Court in 1996 issued a number of rulings favorable to the banking industry. On June 3, the justices unanimously ruled that banks could set nationwide credit-card policies based on the laws of one state, even if those policies violate consumer protection laws in other states. Many banks relocated their credit card subsidiaries to states that permits banks to impose higher credit-card fees than those states with strict consumer laws. Consumer groups expressed unhappiness with the ruling.

Another unanimous Supreme Court ruling on March 26 allowed national banks to sell insurance at branch offices in communities with fewer than 5,000 residents. Although that practice has long been permitted under a 1916 federal law, some states had restricted the ability of banks to sell insurance.

Glass-Steagall Act. In spring 1996, Congress once again tried—and failed—to rewrite the Glass-Steagall Banking Act of 1933, the central law governing the businesses in which banks may engage. On July 31, 1996, however, the Fed proposed new rules reversing a provision of the banking act that barred banks from selling securities. Under the new rules, banks would be allowed to expand the amount of corporate debt and equity underwriting they can undertake to 25 percent of the revenue in their securities subsidiaries, up from the 10 percent permitted previously.

Easing mergers. On Aug. 23, the Fed proposed new rules making it easier for banks to win government approval for acquiring other banks. Among other changes, the rules limited the time for public comment on proposed acquisitions and streamlined the application process. Community activists opposed the changes. A 1977 law required banks to lend money in poorer areas of communities where they do business. Community groups often have used the approval process for acquisitions as an opportunity to gain commitments from banks for increased lending in such neighborhoods.

Auditing the Fed. The Fed came under rare scrutiny in an audit conducted by the General Accounting Office (GAO), the investigative arm of Congress, and published in March 1996. The GAO reported that between 1988 and 1994, the Fed's annual operating expenses rose by 50 percent to $2 billion—more than double the rate of inflation for that period. In addition, the GAO found that while the number of employees rose only 4 percent during that period, staff compensation jumped by 53 percent. The GAO also questioned the Fed's contracting and procurement procedures and criticized the system for constructing several expensive new banks. In addition, the Fed was criticized for amassing a $3.7 billion contingency fund, which the GAO said should be returned to the U.S. Treasury.   □ Paulette Thomas

In *World Book,* see **Bank.**

Baseball. A memorable 1996 season produced the greatest home-run barrage in major-league history and ended with the New York Yankees dethroning the Atlanta Braves as World Series champions. In December, the owners of the 30 National and American league clubs ended four years of labor unrest by agreeing to a collective-bargaining agreement with their players.

Labor agreement. In January 1996, the owners of American and National league clubs voted to introduce interleague play in the 1997 season, with each team playing 15 or 16 games against teams in the other league. In March 1996, the owners voted to create a revenue-sharing program in which certain profits would be pooled and shared among owners. Both measures needed approval by the players union. Negotiators for the owners and players union reached a tentative agreement that gave players collective bargaining rights and a contract that would run from 1996 to 2000, but the owners voted on November 6 to reject the deal. It received only 12 affirmative votes of the 23 needed for approval.

In November 1996, the owners went back to the players seeking changes in the deal. When the players refused, Acting Commissioner Arthur (Bud) Selig, who had at first repudiated the collective-bargaining agreement, reversed himself and pleaded with the owners to accept it. On November 26, the owners approved the contract by a vote of 26 to 4. On

December 5, the Players Association also approved the contract and agreed to extend interleague play through 1998.

Major-league players had gone on strike in 1994 in opposition to a team salary cap and other revenue-sharing measures. The strike lasted 232 days, wiping out the last 52 days of the 1994 regular season, the play-offs and World Series, and caused the 1995 season to begin three weeks late. Many fans were disillusioned by the strike. Attendance in the 1995 season fell significantly and the owners and players lost $1 billion.

Salaries. Jerry Reinsdorf, chairman of the Chicago White Sox, had led the fight against the collective-bargaining agreement, arguing that owners needed to restrain player salaries. However, in November, soon after the owners initially voted down the agreement, Reinsdorf signed Albert Belle, a gifted free-agent outfielder, to the richest contract in baseball history—$55 million over five years. Atlanta then re-signed John Smoltz, who had just won the Cy Young Award as the National League's best pitcher, for $31 million over four years.

Regular season. The Cleveland Indians (99-62) had the best record in the major leagues in 1996 and won the American League's Central Division title by 14½ games. The Yankees (92-70) won the Eastern Division by 4 games and the Texas Rangers (90-72) won the Western Division by 4½. The division winners were joined in the play-offs by the Baltimore Orioles, whose record of 88-74 was the best among teams that did not win a division title.

In the National League, the 1996 division winners were Atlanta (96-66) by 8 games in the Eastern Division, the St. Louis Cardinals (88-74) by 6 games in the Central, and the San Diego Padres (91-71) by 1 game over the Los Angeles Dodgers in the Western. The Dodgers (90-72) won the wild-card play-off berth.

Play-offs. In the first round of the American League play-offs, the Yankees eliminated Texas, 3 games to 1, and Baltimore defeated Cleveland, 3 games to 1. The Yankees won the league championship series with Baltimore, 4 games to 1, winning the first game when a 12-year-old fan leaned over the right-field wall and caught a ball that might have been caught by an outfielder. It was ruled a home run.

The National League play-offs started with a pair of sweeps—Atlanta by 3-0 over Los Angeles and St. Louis by 3-0 over San Diego. In the championship series, Atlanta fell behind St. Louis, 3 games to 1, but swept the last three games by 14-0, 3-1, and 15-0. The Braves then advanced to the World Series for the fourth time in five years.

World Series. The Yankees had a new general manager, Bob Watson; a new manager, Joe Torre; new power hitters in Cecil Fielder, Darryl Strawberry, and Charlie Hayes, acquired late in the season, and strong relief pitching. Atlanta had excellent starting pitchers in Smoltz, Greg Maddux, and Tom Glavine.

The World Series was held October 20 to 26. The Yankees started badly, losing at home by 12-1—the worst loss in their 187 World Series appearances—and then losing again by 4-0. But they won the next four games, 5-2, 8-6 in 10 innings, 1-0, and 3-2. With the final 3-2 victory, the Yankees won their 23rd World Series championship, their first since 1978. Relief pitcher John Wetteland, who earned a save in every Yankee victory, was voted the most valuable player of the series.

Stars. First baseman Mark McGwire of the Oakland A's hit 52 home runs, the highest in one season in the major leagues since George Foster's 72 home runs for the Cincinnati Reds in 1977. First baseman

Andres Galarraga of the Colorado Rockies drove in 150 runs, the most since Tommy Davis's 153 for Los Angeles in 1962. Albert Belle drove in 148 runs for Cleveland, the most in the American League since Ted Williams and Vern Stephens each drove in 149 runs for the Boston Red Sox in 1949.

The regular season ended with 4,962 homers, the most in the 128-year history of the major leagues. Many other home-run records were set in 1996: 257 by one team (Baltimore); 7 players on one team with 20 home runs or more (Baltimore); 17 major-league players with 40 homers or more; 43 players with 30 or more; and 83 players with 20 or more.

Outfielder Tony Gwynn of San Diego won his third consecutive National League batting title with

Final standings in major league baseball

American League

Eastern Division

	W.	L.	Pct.	G.B.
New York Yankees	92	70	.568	
Baltimore Orioles*	88	74	.543	4
Boston Red Sox	85	77	.525	7
Toronto Blue Jays	74	88	.457	18
Detroit Tigers	53	109	.327	39

Central Division

	W.	L.	Pct.	G.B.
Cleveland Indians	99	62	.615	
Chicago White Sox	85	77	.525	14½
Milwaukee Brewers	80	82	.494	19½
Minnesota Twins	78	84	.481	21½
Kansas City Royals	75	86	.466	24

Western Division

	W.	L.	Pct.	G.B.
Texas Rangers	90	72	.556	
Seattle Mariners	85	76	.528	4½
Oakland Athletics	78	84	.481	12
California Angels	70	91	.435	19½

American League champions—New York Yankees (defeated Baltimore, 4 games to 1)

World Series champions—New York Yankees ((defeated Atlanta 4 games to 2)

Offensive leaders

Batting average—Alex Rodriguez, Seattle	.358
Runs scored—Alex Rodriguez, Seattle	141
Home runs—Mark McGwire, Oakland	52
Runs batted in—Albert Belle, Cleveland	148
Hits—Paul Molitor, Minnesota	225
Stolen bases—Kenny Lofton, Cleveland	75
Slugging percentage—Mark McGwire, Oakland	.730

Leading pitchers

Games won—Andy Pettitte, New York	21
Earned run average (162 or more innings)—	
Juan Guzman, Toronto	2.93
Strikeouts—Roger Clemens, Boston	257
Saves—John Wetteland, New York	43
Shut-outs—Pat Hentgen, Toronto; Ken Hill, Texas;	
Rich Robertson, Minnesota (tie)	3
Complete games—Pat Hentgen, Toronto	10

Awards[†]

Most Valuable Player—Juan Gonzalez, Texas
Cy Young—Pat Hentgen, Toronto
Rookie of the Year—Derek Jeter, New York
Manager of the Year—Joe Torre, New York; Johnny Oates, Texas (tie)

National League

Eastern Division

	W.	L.	Pct.	G.B.
Atlanta Braves	96	66	.593	
Montreal Expos	88	74	.543	8
Florida Marlins	80	82	.494	16
New York Mets	71	91	.438	25
Philadelphia Phillies	67	95	.414	29

Central Division

	W.	L.	Pct.	G.B.
St. Louis Cardinals	88	74	.543	
Houston Astros	82	80	.506	6
Cincinnati Reds	81	81	.500	7
Chicago Cubs	76	86	.469	12
Pittsburgh Pirates	73	89	.451	15

Western Division

	W.	L.	Pct.	G.B.
San Diego Padres	91	71	.562	
Los Angeles Dodgers*	90	72	.556	1
Colorado Rockies	83	79	.512	8
San Francisco Giants	68	94	.420	23

National League champions—Atlanta Braves (defeated St. Louis, 4 games to 3)

Offensive leaders

Batting average—Tony Gwynn, San Diego	.353
Runs scored—Ellis Burks, Colorado	142
Home runs—Andres Galarraga, Colorado	47
Runs batted in—Andres Galarraga, Colorado	150
Hits—Lance Johnson, New York	227
Stolen bases—Eric Young, Colorado	53
Slugging percentage—Ellis Burks, Colorado	.639

Leading pitchers

Games won—John Smoltz, Atlanta	24
Earned run average (162 or more innings)—	
Kevin Brown, Florida	1.89
Strikeouts—John Smoltz, Atlanta	276
Saves—Jeff Brantley, Cincinnati;	
Todd Worrell, Los Angeles (tie)	44
Shut-outs—Kevin Brown, Florida	3
Complete games—Curt Schilling, Philadelphia	8

Awards[†]

Most Valuable Player—Ken Caminiti, San Diego
Cy Young—John Smoltz, Atlanta
Rookie of the Year—Todd Hollandsworth, Los Angeles
Manager of the Year—Bruce Bochy, San Diego

*Qualified for wild-card play-off spot.
[†]Selected by the Baseball Writers Association of America.

New York Yankees third baseman Charlie Hayes gathers in an easy fly ball to conclude the 1996 World Series. New York defeated the Atlanta Braves, 4 games to 2.

an average of .353. It was Gwynn's seventh title overall, tying Rogers Hornsby's record of the 1920's and Stan Musial's record of the 1950's and 1960's. Alex Rodriguez, the 21-year-old Seattle Mariners shortstop, hit .358 to claim the American League batting title. Paul Molitor of the Minnesota Twins was the 21st player in major-league history to reach 3,000 career hits. Pitcher Roger Clemens of Boston tied his 10-year-old major-league record by striking out 20 batters in one game.

Outstanding veterans who retired in 1996 included outfielder Dave Winfield of Cleveland at age 44, outfielder Andre Dawson of the Chicago Cubs at age 42, and shortstop Ozzie Smith of St. Louis at age 41. Kirby Puckett, Minnesota's star center fielder, retired

at age 35 due to vision problems. Tommy Lasorda, the 68-year-old manager of the Los Angeles Dodgers, retired after a mild heart attack. Lasorda had managed the Dodgers for 20 years.

Hall of Fame. In 1996, the Hall of Fame veterans committee elected American league pitcher Jim Bunning, Negro Leagues pitcher Bill Foster, and managers Earl Weaver and Ned Hanlon to the Baseball Hall of Fame. However, for the first time since 1971, veteran baseball writers failed to give any eligible player enough votes to be elected into the Hall of Fame. The players who came closest in the voting were pitcher Phil Niekro, first baseman Tony Perez, and pitcher Don Sutton. ☐ Frank Litsky

In *World Book,* see **Baseball.**

Basketball. Old reliables won the major basketball championships of the 1995-1996 season. The Chicago Bulls captured the National Basketball Association (NBA) title for the fourth time in six years under Coach Phil Jackson. The University of Tennessee won the National Collegiate Athletic Association (NCAA) women's title for the fourth time in 10 years under Coach Pat Summitt, and the University of Kentucky became the NCAA men's champion.

Professional. The Bulls finished the NBA's regular season with a 72-10 record, winning more games than any other team in the league's history. From March 1995 to April 1996, they won 44 consecutive games at home. Guard Michael Jordan and forward Scottie Pippen dominated games, as they did in a 110-102 victory over the Indiana Pacers, in which Jordan scored 44 points and Pippen 40.

The Bulls, in need of a power forward, traded before the season for 34-year-old Dennis Rodman of San Antonio. With his unpredictable behavior, Rodman made every game an adventure. In March, he head-butted a referee, which cost him a $20,000 fine and a six-game suspension by the league. However, he also led the league in rebounding for the fifth consecutive year.

The NBA expanded from 27 to 29 teams in 1995, with the addition of 2 teams in Canada—the Toronto Raptors and Vancouver Grizzlies. During the regular season, the teams played 82 games each. The Grizzlies set a league record in their first season by suffering the worst-ever losing streak in the NBA—23 games.

The division winners were the Bulls, the Orlando Magic (60-22), the Seattle SuperSonics (64-18), and the San Antonio Spurs (59-23). Another 12 teams also made the play-offs.

The Bulls raced through the play-offs, beating the Miami Heat (3 games to 0), the New York Knicks (4-1), and Orlando (4-0). Seattle reached the finals by defeating the Sacramento Kings (3-1), the Houston Rockets (4-0), and the Utah Jazz (4-3).

In the finals in June, the Bulls won the first three games before Seattle won the next two. The Bulls won the sixth game, with Rodman collecting 19 rebounds (11 offensive, which tied an NBA record) and took the title, 4 games to 2. Jordan averaged 27.3 points a game in the finals and was voted most valuable player in both the regular season and play-offs.

After the play-offs, the Bulls negotiated one-year contracts with Jordan ($30 million, the most ever in any sport), Rodman ($6 million), and Coach Jackson ($2.25 million). In July, the league and the players guaranteed that there would be a 1996-1997 season by signing a six-year collective-bargaining agreement, which had been reached in August 1995.

People. Jordan was voted the league's most valuable player in the regular season for the fourth time. With a 30.4-point-per-game average, he also won the scoring title for the eighth time. Jackson

The 1995-1996 college basketball season

College tournament champions

NCAA	(Men)	Division I:	Kentucky
		Division II:	Fort Hays State
		Division III:	Rowan
NCAA	(Women)	Division I:	Tennessee
		Division II:	North Dakota State
		Division III:	Wisconsin-Oshkosh
NAIA	(Men)	Division I:	Oklahoma City
		Division II:	Albertson College (Id.)
	(Women)	Division I:	Southern Nazarene (Okla.)
		Division II:	Western Oregon
NIT	(Men)	Nebraska	
Junior College	(Men)	Division I:	Sullivan College (Ky.)
		Division II:	Penn Valley (Mo.)
		Division III:	Sullivan County (N.Y.)
	(Women)	Division I:	Trinity Valley (Tex.)
		Division II:	Lansing (Mich.)
		Division III:	Central Lakes (Minn.)

Men's college champions

Conference	School
American West	Cal Poly SLO (reg. season)
	Southern Utah (tournament)
Atlantic Coast	Georgia Tech (reg. season)
	Wake Forest (tournament)
Atlantic Ten	
Eastern Division	Massachusetts*
Western Division	Virginia Tech—George Washington (tie)
Big East	
Big East 7	Georgetown
Big East 6	Connecticut*
Big Eight	Kansas (reg. season)
	Iowa State (tournament)
Big Sky	Montana State*
Big South	North Carolina-Greensboro*
Big Ten	Purdue (reg. season)
Big West	Long Beach State (reg. season)
	San Jose State (tournament)
Colonial	Virginia Commonwealth*
Conference USA	
Red Division	Tulane
White Division	Memphis
Blue Division	Cincinnati*
Ivy League	Princeton
Metro Atlantic	Iona—Fairfield (tie; reg. season)
	Canisius (tournament)
Mid-American	Eastern Michigan*
Mid-Continent	Valparaiso*
Mid-Eastern	South Carolina State*—Coppin State (tie; reg. season)
Midwestern	Wisconsin-Green Bay (reg. season)
	Northern Illinois (tournament)
Missouri Valley	Bradley (reg. season)
	Tulsa (tournament)
North Atlantic	Drexel*
Northeast	Mount Saint Mary's (Md.) (reg. season)
	Monmouth (N.J.) (tournament)
Ohio Valley	Murray State (reg. season)
	Austin Peay (tournament)
Pacific Ten	UCLA (reg. season)
Patriot League	Colgate*
Southeastern	Mississippi State (tournament)
Eastern Division	Kentucky
Western Division	Mississippi State
Southern	Western Carolina (tournament)
North Division	Davidson (reg. season)
South Division	Western Carolina (reg. season)
Southland	Northeast Louisiana*
Southwest	Texas Tech*
Southwestern	Mississippi Valley*—Jackson State (tie; reg. season)
Sun Belt	Arkansas-Little Rock—New Orleans* (tie; reg. season)
Trans America	Central Florida (tournament)
Eastern Division	Charleston (S.C.)
Western Division	Samford—Southeastern Louisiana (tie)
West Coast	Santa Clara—Gonzaga (tie; reg. season)
	Portland (tournament)
Western Athletic	Utah (reg. season)
	New Mexico (tournament)

*Regular season and conference tournament champion.

Basketball

was voted coach of the year. Jordan and Pippen made the all-star team with center David Robinson of San Antonio, power forward Karl Malone of Utah, and point guard Anfernee Hardaway of Orlando. Three Bulls—Jordan, Pippen, and Rodman—were voted to the all-defensive team.

A year after he broke Magic Johnson's career record for assists, Utah's John Stockton broke Maurice Cheeks's all-time record of 2,310 steals. Johnson, who retired four years before after testing positive for HIV, the virus that causes AIDS, returned to the Los Angeles Lakers at age 36, played the last half of the season, and then retired again.

College men. Kentucky was the preseason favorite, and during the season it shared the number-one position in the polls at various times with the University of Massachusetts and the University of Kansas. When the regular season ended, the NCAA chose 64 teams for its championship tournament and gave top seeds to Kentucky (28-2), Massachusetts (31-1), the University of Connecticut (30-2), and Purdue (25-5).

The University of California, Los Angeles (UCLA), the defending champion, was knocked out in the first round, 43-41, by Princeton's controlled game. The University of Georgia upset Purdue, 76-69, in the second round. Mississippi State upset Connecticut, 60-55, in a regional semifinal.

The Final Four in East Rutherford, New Jersey, had two favorites—Kentucky and Massachusetts—and two outsiders—Syracuse and Mississippi State. In the semifinals March 30, Kentucky eliminated Massachusetts, 81-74, and Syracuse, the fourth-place team in the Big East Conference, defeated Mississippi State, 77-69. In the final game on April 1, Kentucky, a 14-point favorite, held off Syracuse, 76-67. Kentucky's Tony Delk sank a record-tying seven three-point shots against Syracuse's zone defense and was voted the most valuable player of the Final Four.

Most selectors chose Marcus Camby, Massachusetts' 6-foot-11-inch (211-centimeter) center, as player of the year and Gene Keady of Purdue as coach of the year. The consensus All-America team comprised Camby, Ray Allen of Connecticut, Allen Iverson of Georgetown, Kerry Kittles of Villanova, and Tim Duncan of Wake Forest.

College women. The University of Connecticut, the defending NCAA champion, ranked first in the preseason polls. But the team lost this ranking after losing its opening game to Louisiana Tech. During the remainder of the season, Louisiana Tech and the University of Georgia battled for top ranking.

When the regular season ended, the five leaders in the Associated Press media poll were Louisiana Tech (28-1), Connecticut (30-3), Stanford University (25-2), the University of Tennessee (26-4), and Georgia (23-4). All but Georgia became regional top seeds in the NCAA tournament, which had expanded to 64 teams from 48.

National Basketball Association standings

Eastern Conference

Atlantic Division	W.	L.	Pct.	G.B.
Orlando Magic*	60	22	.732	—
New York Knicks*	47	35	.573	13
Miami Heat*	42	40	.512	18
Washington Bullets	39	43	.476	21
Boston Celtics	33	49	.402	27
New Jersey Nets	30	52	.366	30
Philadelphia 76ers	18	64	.220	42

Central Division	W.	L.	Pct.	G.B.
Chicago Bulls*	72	10	.878	—
Indiana Pacers*	52	30	.634	20
Cleveland Cavaliers*	47	35	.573	25
Atlanta Hawks*	46	36	.561	26
Detroit Pistons*	46	36	.561	26
Charlotte Hornets	41	41	.500	31
Milwaukee Bucks	25	57	.305	47
Toronto Raptors	21	61	.256	51

Western Conference

Midwest Division	W.	L.	Pct.	G.B.
San Antonio Spurs*	59	23	.720	—
Utah Jazz*	55	27	.671	4
Houston Rockets*	48	34	.585	11
Denver Nuggets	35	47	.427	24
Dallas Mavericks	26	56	.317	33
Minnesota Timberwolves	26	56	.317	33
Vancouver Grizzlies	15	67	.183	44

Pacific Division	W.	L.	Pct.	G.B.
Seattle SuperSonics*	64	18	.780	—
Los Angeles Lakers*	53	29	.646	11
Portland Trail Blazers*	44	38	.537	20
Phoenix Suns*	41	41	.500	23
Sacramento Kings*	39	43	.476	25
Golden State Warriors	36	46	.439	28
Los Angeles Clippers	29	53	.354	35

*Made play-offs

NBA champions—Chicago Bulls (defeated Seattle SuperSonics, 4 games to 2)

Individual leaders

Scoring	G.	F.G.	F.T.	Pts.	Avg.
Michael Jordan, Chicago	82	916	548	2,491	30.4
Hakeem Olajuwon, Houston	72	768	397	1,936	26.9
Shaquille O'Neal, Orlando	54	592	249	1,434	26.6
Karl Malone, Utah	82	789	512	2,106	25.7
David Robinson, San Antonio	82	711	626	2,051	25.0
Charles Barkley, Phoenix	71	580	440	1,649	23.2
Alonzo Mourning, Miami	70	563	488	1,623	23.2
Mitch Richmond, Sacramento	81	611	425	1,872	23.1
Patrick Ewing, New York	76	678	351	1,711	22.5
Juwan Howard, Washington	81	733	319	1,789	22.1

Rebounding	G.	Off.	Def.	Tot.	Avg.
Dennis Rodman, Chicago	64	356	596	952	14.9
David Robinson, San Antonio	82	319	681	1,000	12.2
Dikembe Mutombo, Denver	74	249	622	871	11.8
Charles Barkley, Phoenix	71	243	578	821	11.6
Shawn Kemp, Seattle	79	276	628	904	11.4
Hakeem Olajuwon, Houston	72	176	608	784	10.9
Patrick Ewing, New York	76	157	649	806	10.6

Those seeds held up with one exception. Georgia defeated Louisiana Tech, 90-76, in a regional final, so the same four teams from the previous year's Final Four returned to Charlotte, North Carolina. In the semifinals March 29, Tennessee held off Connecticut, 88-83 in overtime, and Georgia beat Stanford, 88-76. In the championship game two nights later, Tennessee easily defeated Georgia, 83-65.

Georgia's star player, Saudia Roundtree and Connecticut's Jennifer Rizzotti, both point guards, won player-of-the-year polls. Among the other All-Ameri-

Chicago Bulls stars Michael Jordan (23) and Dennis Rodman (91) battle for a rebound in Game 6 of the NBA finals in June against the Seattle SuperSonics.

ca choices were 6-foot-7-inch (201-centimeter) Kara Wolters of Connecticut, Vickie Johnson of Louisiana Tech, and Latasha Byears of DePaul.

International. The United States won the men's and women's gold medals in the Atlanta Olympics. Neither team came close to losing a game as both teams won by an average of about 30 points.

The men's team consisted of 12 NBA professionals: David Robinson, Shaquille O'Neal, Hakeem Olajuwon, Scottie Pippen, Karl Malone, Grant Hill, Charles Barkley, Gary Payton, Anfernee Hardaway, John Stockton, Reggie Miller, and Mitch Richmond. The coach was Len Wilkens of the Atlanta Hawks.

Ten of the 12 women's players had been playing in professional leagues overseas. They turned down contracts as high as $300,000 a year and accepted $50,000 each to spend one year as the United States national team and eventually the Olympic team. Among them were Lisa Leslie, Teresa Edwards, Katrina McClain, and Sheryl Swoopes. Tara VanDerveer took a leave from Stanford and coached them to a 60-0 record.

After the Olympics, many of the women chose to stay in the United States to play in one of the two new professional leagues. The American Basketball League started in the fall of 1996 with eight teams. The Women's NBA, owned by the National Basketball Association, planned to begin in June 1997 as a summer league. □ Frank Litsky

In *World Book,* see **Basketball.**

Belarus. On April 2, 1996, presidents Alexander Lukashenko of Belarus and Boris Yeltsin of Russia signed a treaty creating a "community of sovereign republics." While the treaty recognized Russia and Belarus as "sovereign and equal," it outlined mutual coordination of economies, foreign policies, and policing of common outside borders. The signing of the treaty triggered a series of protests in the capital, Minsk, by nationalists opposed to reunification.

President Lukashenko publicly called for a return to a state-controlled economy in 1996. Dissent over integration with Russia and economic reforms led to a constitutional crisis and a showdown between Lukashenko and parliament. In September, a constitutional court criticized Lukashenko's proposal for a new Belarusian constitution, which would vastly expand the powers of the presidency.

Lukashenko called a referendum for November 24 to ratify his new constitution. Prime Minister Mikhail Chigir resigned in protest. Lukashenko's opponents called the referendum part of a larger scheme by the president to set up a dictatorship. The referendum was approved by more than 70 percent of the voters. Lukashenko promptly utilized his new powers. On November 26, he set up a hand-picked parliament composed of his allies. The former parliament was dissolved. □ Steven L. Solnick

See **Europe** (Facts in brief table); **Russia.** In *World Book,* see **Belarus.**

Belgium. The year 1996 was dominated by two crime cases that shook the faith of many Belgians in their country's government and judicial system and prompted demands for fundamental reform.

Ring of child sexual abusers. Authorities investigating the disappearance of a 14-year-old girl on August 9 uncovered a group of men who authorities believe may have been responsible for the abduction, sexual abuse, and murder of several girls. On August 15, police found the missing girl, as well as a 12-year-old who disappeared in May, alive and locked in the basement of a house owned by the chief suspect, Marc Dutroux, near the southern city of Charleroi. Over the next three weeks, police searching houses owned by Dutroux found the bodies of two 8-year-old girls and two teen-age girls who were abducted in 1995. The two younger girls had been starved to death.

Revulsion at the crimes quickly turned into anger at authorities when it became known that Dutroux had been convicted previously of abduction and rape, that he had won early release from prison in 1992, and that he had been investigated for the 1995 kidnappings. The arrest of a Charleroi policeman for suspected involvement in an auto-theft ring related to Dutroux fanned suspicions of a cover-up. After mass demonstrations in October 1996 and a demand by King Albert II for judicial reform, Prime Minister Jean-Luc Dehaene promised constitutional changes to clean up the judicial system.

Progress in Cools case. After a five-year investigation, six men were arrested in September for the 1991 murder of a former vice prime minister, Andre Cools. The murder, considered Belgium's worst political crime, was believed to be related to corruption within Cools's Socialist Party. The six men arrested included Alain Van der Biest, a former Cools protégé and minister in the French-speaking southern region of Wallonia.

Earlier in 1996, a Belgian judge issued an international arrest warrant for Serge Dassault, chairman of the French aircraft maker Dassault Aviation SA, for questioning into alleged defense kickbacks, which were part of the web of corruption related to Cools. Guy Coëme, a former defense minister, was convicted of fraud in a separate kickback case and forced to resign from parliament.

Austerity continued. Using special decree powers, the government in October announced $3.2-billion in tax increases for 1997, increased spending cuts, and plans to sell gold reserves and other assets to reduce the national debt by $11.6 billion. The measures were intended to qualify Belgium to join a single European currency in 1999. □ Tom Buerkle

See also **Europe** (Facts in brief table). In *World Book,* see **Belgium; European Union.**

Belize. See Latin America.

Benin. See Africa.

Bhutan. See Asia.

Biology. Major new clues into the nature and origin of life were reported in 1996 by scientists in Europe and the United States. In April, Belgian and American researchers announced that they and colleagues in several other countries had identified each of the more than 12 million *bases* (chemical subunits), in their exact sequence, encoding the complete genetic blueprint of a yeast called *Saccharomyces cerevisiae.* Later in the year, a U.S. research group reported that it had accomplished the same feat with a primitive bacterialike microorganism called *Methanococcus jannaschii.* Both accomplishments were viewed as milestones on the road to sequencing the human *genome* (complete genetic makeup), which consists of more than 3 billion bases.

The yeast research was carried out in a collaborative effort by 92 laboratories around the world. The feat marked the first time that scientists had worked out the complete sequence of bases in an organism whose genes are packaged in a cell nucleus.

Researchers at the Institute for Genomic Research in Rockville, Maryland, reported in August that they had sequenced the 1,739,933 bases in the genes of *M. jannaschii,* a member of a primitive type of bacteria called Archaea that live in hot deep-sea vents. Researchers had previously sequenced the genes of another type of bacterium. With the 1996 sequencing feats, scientists had thus obtained the genetic blueprints for representatives of each of the three main branches of life: Archaea; Prokaria, a group that contains all other known kinds of bacteria; and Eukarya, organisms whose genes are contained in a cell nucleus, a group that includes all plants and animals.

Investigators hoped that by comparing the three sequences, they would learn more about the common ancestors of all three branches of life—the primitive organisms that lived shortly after life began more than 3.5 billion years ago. And because humans, bacteria, and yeast share many genes, the discoveries were expected to also provide new information about human biology.

Tool-using crows. Scientists once believed that human beings could be defined by their ability to make and use tools, but that belief was shattered more than 20 years ago by the discovery that chimpanzees and other primates are also proficient in tool use. In January, researchers at Massey University in New Zealand reported that crows, too, can make and use tools.

The scientists observed crows on New Caledonia, an island near New Zealand. They noted that the birds fashion leaves or twigs into long, narrow tools with hooks or barbs at the end that can be used to fish insects from wood or from under leaves. The birds even carry the tools between trees or foraging locations and store them securely on their perches when they are not using them.

Frozen sperm-producing cells. A new technique for freezing sperm-producing tissues, which could produce a form of biological immortality for males of many species, was reported in May by researchers at the University of Pennsylvania in Philadelphia. The technique could help men with abnormally low sperm production and aid in efforts to save endangered species.

It has long been possible to freeze sperm cells for future reproductive use, but the process is tricky, and the sperm survival rate is often low. The University of Pennsylvania scientists found that it is easier and more reliable to freeze sperm-producing *stem cells.* Moreover, with stem cells it is possible to produce virtually unlimited quantities of sperm. Thawed human stem cells could be implanted in a man's testes to restore his fertility or placed in the testes of a host animal; the resulting sperm cells could then be used to fertilize an egg cell in the laboratory.

The researchers demonstrated the feasibility of using host animals to generate sperm by implanting rat-sperm stem cells in the testes of mice, which then produced healthy rat sperm. In another possible application of this technique, stem cells from an endangered animal could be implanted in a host animal that would produce large quantities of sperm to impregnate females of the endangered species. As of late 1996, the scientists had not yet shown

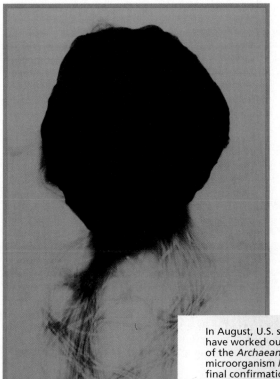

In August, U.S. scientists report that they have worked out the full genetic sequence of the *Archaeans* (a primitive form of life) microorganism *Methanococcus jannaschii*— final confirmation that the bacterialike Archaeans are a separate branch of life.

that sperm produced with the aid of a host animal can fertilize an egg cell, but they saw no reason why it should not work.

A hint of global warming. The growing season for plants in many countries in the Northern Hemisphere was a week longer in the mid-1990's than it was 20 years earlier, researchers at the Scripps Institution of Oceanography in La Jolla, California, reported in July. Their studies, based on atmospheric readings of carbon dioxide, a gas absorbed by plants as they grow, indicated that spring had been coming slightly earlier each year. The scientists stated that the lengthening growing season was most likely a result of global warming.

Chameleon fish. The tropical flounder can change its coloring within eight seconds to blend in almost perfectly with its natural background, researchers at the University of California at San Diego reported in February. Perhaps more surprisingly, the scientists noted, the fish also did a creditable job in laboratory tests at blending in with a checkerboard and a pattern of black spots. The investigators found that the key to the flounder's ability to camouflage itself lies in at least six types of surface skin markings, including H-shaped blotches, small dark rings, and small spots. The fish can adjust the darkness of these various markings to blend in with its background. □ Thomas H. Maugh II

In *World Book,* see **Biology; Botany; Zoology.**

Boating. In May 1996, Steve Fossett, a 52-year-old American, set another record for sailing across the Pacific Ocean. Fossett, a Chicago securities dealer, made his record-breaking voyage on the *Lakota,* a 60-foot (18-meter) *trimaran* (sailboat with three hulls set side by side). He sailed the Pacific Ocean east to west in 19 days 15 hours 18 minutes, breaking by almost 14 days the record set by the clipper ship *Sword Fish* in 1853. In August 1995, Fossett and his crew had set a 20 days-12 hours-53 minutes record for sailing the Pacific west to east.

In June 1996, 58 boats raced across the Atlantic, from Plymouth, England, to Newport, Rhode Island. Frenchman Loick Peyron, in the 60-foot (18-meter) trimaran *Fujicolor,* was the first to finish. The wind died in the last four hours, however, and his time of 10 days 10 hours missed the record by 50 minutes. Visibility was so poor in the last week of the race that four of the boats were involved in collisions with commercial ships.

The Newport-to-Bermuda race in June attracted 146 yachts, including the three-month-old sloop *Boomerang II,* the newest yacht in the maxi class, which finished first in 57 hours 31 minutes 50 seconds. After all other entries had finished and handicaps were computed, the 82-foot (25-meter) *Boomerang II* also was declared the winner on corrected time. *Boomerang II* was owned and skippered by George Coumantaros of New York City, who was

sailing in the biennial race for the 22nd time.

Eleven international clubs made $100,000 deposits to challenge New Zealand for the America's Cup races in 1999 and 2000. Challengers included clubs from the United States, the U.S. Virgin Islands, Australia, Great Britain, Japan, Spain, France, Russia, and Hong Kong. Leading skippers Dennis Conner of the United States and John Bertrand of Australia were expected to enter by the 1997 deadline.

Powerboats. *Pico/American Dream* and its driver, Dave Villwock of Kirkland, Washington, ended *Miss Budweiser'*s five-year championship reign during the May-to-November, 11-race series for the fastest racing powerboats—the turbine-powered hydroplanes. Villwock and *Pico* also won the showcase race of the series, the Gold Cup in Detroit on June 2, and Villwock was voted top driver of the season. Chip Hanauer of Tukwila, Washington, who had won 10 previous Gold Cups, suffered a concussion in practice for this year's Gold Cup. A week later, he withdrew as *Miss Budweiser'*s driver.

The National Marine Manufacturers Association, an industry trade group, said the boat market continued to be good. In 1995, it said, 650,000 boats were sold in the United States—a 22-percent increase. The total included 200,000 small jet boats that sold for $1.1 billion. □ Frank Litsky

In *World Book,* see **Boating; Sailing.**

Bolivia. See **Latin America.**

Bosnia-Herzegovina. In 1996, Bosnia-Herzegovina (often called Bosnia) began to see effects of the peace treaty brokered in November 1995 in Dayton, Ohio, and signed one month later in Paris by Bosnian, Croatian, and Serbian leaders. But obstacles to peace remained in 1996. Tensions among Muslims, Croats, and Serbs continued, threatening the agreements made to end the war. International peacekeeping forces and humanitarian organizations continued to play an important role in maintaining stability in the region. Under the Dayton plan, Bosnia was split into two substates—a Muslim-Croat federation and a Serb republic. While elections were held in September to form a new federal government, local elections were postponed, due to widespread irregularities in voter registration.

Fighting ends. On January 19, Muslim, Croat, and Serb forces completed their withdrawal from the zones of separation established by the Dayton agreement. The exchange of territory was marked by violence on both sides. Bosnian Serbs destroyed many houses and other buildings in Sarajevo, the Bosnian capital, before returning the city to Bosnian government control in February. At the urging of Bosnian Serb leaders, most Serbs left Sarajevo before control was relinquished. Numerous violent incidents occurred against Muslims in Serb-held areas such as Banja Luka and the western part of Mostar, against Serbs in Sarajevo, and against Croats who lived in

Bugojno, which was controlled by Muslims.

In January, May, and October, mass graves were discovered near the town of Sanski Most, which had been in Bosnian Serb hands during much of the war. The numbers of bodies found in these graves were fewer than in the huge mass grave found in Srebrenica in 1995, which contained the remains of approximately 2,000 people, but Bosnian sources claimed there were many more mass graves in the area around Sanski Most.

On Oct. 3, 1996, the United States announced that 7,500 of its soldiers would remain in Bosnia until March 1997 to cover the withdrawal of NATO forces. The withdrawal had been due to be completed by Dec. 20, 1996.

Diplomacy. The United Nations (UN) lifted sanctions against the Bosnian Serbs in February. Bosnian Muslim, Croat, and Serb leaders and the leaders of Croatia and Yugoslavia signed an arms reduction agreement on June 14. On June 18, the UN lifted its arms embargo on all former Yugoslav republics.

Bosnian Serb leaders, including Radovan Karadzić and Ratko Mladić, commander of the Bosnian Serb armed forces, defied international calls that they surrender to the UN International Criminal Tribunal for the former Yugoslavia. The tribunal issued international arrest warrants for Karadzić and Mladić in July. Under international pressure, including a June 26 ultimatum from Yugoslav leaders, Karadzić dele-

gated his powers as Bosnian Serb president to Vice President Biljana Plavšić on June 30. But Karadzić retained much power behind the scenes and continued as chairman of the Serbian Democratic Party. In mid-July, he agreed to remove himself from politics and resigned from the presidency on July 19.

Economy. International efforts began in 1996 to rebuild Bosnia's shattered economy. Officials of the International Monetary Fund prepared a $90-million loan to support peace in Bosnia. Bosnian officials planned to use the loan for pensions, social security, and disability benefits, as well as jobs for demobilized soldiers. By September, Bosnia had received $880 million of a $1.89-billion assistance package from the international community.

Elections. Federal elections were held September 14. The Muslim Party of Democratic Action emerged as the strongest force from the Muslim-Croat Federation, winning 16 of 28 seats set aside for the federation in the 42-seat national House of Representatives. The Serbian Democratic Party won 9 of 14 legislative seats reserved for Serbian representatives. Former Bosnian president Alija Izetbegović, a Muslim, was elected chairman of Bosnia's new three-person presidency.   □ Sharon L. Wolchik

See also **Croatia; Europe** (Facts in brief table); **United Nations; Yugoslavia.** In *World Book,* see **Bosnia-Herzegovina.**

Botswana. See Africa.

Residents of the Bosnian city of Mostar enjoy a peaceful day on the Neretva River in June. The stone bridge, a landmark, was destroyed during the war.

Bowling. The most exciting bowler of 1996 turned out to be not one of the many stars of the Professional Bowlers Association (PBA) tour for men or the Ladies Pro Bowlers Tour for women. Instead, he was Earl Anthony, a 58-year-old member of the PBA Seniors tour.

In the 1970's and 1980's, Anthony won a record 41 tournaments on the PBA Tour and was voted bowler of the year six times. When he turned 50 years old, Anthony joined the seniors tour, but retired in 1991 because of arthritis. He returned in July 1996, finishing second and third in his first two tournaments. On September 26, he won the Naples Senior Classic in Naples, Florida. Anthony had the highest per-game average on the tour (226.95 pins) and was second in earnings with $35,810.

Dave Davis led the seniors tour in earnings with $63,815 and won the American Bowling Congress (ABC) Senior Masters. Dale Eagle won the PBA senior championship and John Denton the Showboat Senior Invitational. In all, the PBA Seniors tour comprised 13 tournaments paying $1.5 million in prize money.

PBA Tour. The 29 tournaments carried $4.5 million in purses. They were dominated by 37-year-old Walter Ray Williams, Jr. Williams won five tournaments (no other player won more than two). He led the PBA in scoring—with 225.37 pins per game—and in earnings—$241,330. Bob Learn, Jr., was second in earnings with $236,232. Learn's total included a $100,000 bonus for bowling a perfect 300 game April 6 in winning the Flagship Open in his hometown of Erie, Pennsylvania.

In the major tournaments, Dave D'Entremont won the Brunswick World Tournament of Champions, Ernie Schlegel the ABC Masters, Butch Soper the PBA national championship (Williams placed second), and Dave Husted the Bowling Proprietors Association of America (BPAA) United States Open.

LPBT. On the $1.5-million, 22-tournament women's tour, Wendy Macpherson enjoyed the greatest success. She led in tournament victories (three) and earnings ($117,155). Tammy Turner won twice before a stress fracture of the lower back forced her to miss the autumn tournaments.

Lisa Wagner won the Women's International Bowling Congress Queens tournament for her 30th tour victory, a record. Kim Adler won the Hammer Players Championship, Carol Gianotti-Block the Sam's Town Invitational, and rookie Liz Johnson the BPAA United States Open.

The women's tour, like the others, was struggling to retain sponsors in 1996. The LPBT, ABC, BPAA, and other bowling organizations formed Bowling Inc., a marketing conglomerate aimed at finding new sponsors and television exposure and generally rekindling interest in the sport. The PBA chose not to join the group.   □ Frank Litsky

In *World Book,* see **Bowling.**

Boxing. The confusing picture in boxing's heavyweight division became even more confused in 1996 when the unthinkable happened. After giving up his World Boxing Council (WBC) heavyweight title, Mike Tyson, the world's top heavyweight, lost his World Boxing Association (WBA) title to Evander Holyfield.

Heavyweight. In 1990, when the undefeated Tyson was the universally recognized heavyweight champion, he lost the title to James (Buster) Douglas. Tyson later regained the title, spent three years in an Indiana prison on a rape conviction, and returned to boxing in 1995.

In 1996, the ferocious and intimidating Tyson appeared unbeatable. He stopped Frank Bruno of the United Kingdom (U.K.) in three rounds March 16 in Las Vegas, Nevada, to win the WBC title. Tyson then met Bruce Seldon September 7 in Las Vegas. Tyson stopped Seldon after 109 seconds of the first round, taking Seldon's WBA title.

The 30-year-old Tyson then held both the WBC and WBA titles. The WBC ordered Tyson to defend its title in a match against its top-ranked challenger, Lennox Lewis, of the U.K. Tyson, however, gave up the WBC crown in September, choosing instead to defend the WBA title against Holyfield.

On November 9 in Las Vegas, Tyson lost the WBA title, too, when the 34-year-old Holyfield, a heavy underdog, became the aggressor. He floored Tyson once and beat him in 11 rounds. The loss was only

World champion boxers

World Boxing Association

Division	Champion	Country	Date won
Heavyweight	Evander Holyfield	U.S.A.	11/96
	Mike Tyson	U.S.A.	9/96
	Bruce Seldon	U.S.A.	4/95
Light heavyweight	Virgil Hill	U.S.A.	9/92
Middleweight	William Joppy	U.S.A.	6/96
	Shinji Takahara	Japan	12/95
Welterweight	Ike Quartey	Ghana	6/94
Lightweight	Orzubek Nazarov	Russia	10/93
Featherweight	Wilfredo Vasquez	Puerto Rico	5/96
	Eloy Rojas	Venezuela	12/93
Bantamweight	Daorung Chuwatana	Thailand	10/96
	Nana Konado	Ghana	1/96
	Veerapol Sahaprom	Thailand	9/95
Flyweight	Jose Bonilla	Venezuela	11/96
	Saen Sor Ploenchit	Thailand	2/94

World Boxing Council

Division	Champion	Country	Date won
Heavyweight	Vacant	------	------
	Mike Tyson	U.S.A.	3/96
	Frank Bruno	Great Britain	9/95
Light heavyweight	Roy Jones	U.S.A.	11/96
	Fabrice Tiozzo	France	6/95
Middleweight	Keith Holmes	U.S.A.	3/96
	Quincy Taylor	U.S.A.	8/95
Welterweight	Pernell Whitaker	U.S.A.	3/93
Lightweight	Jean-Baptiste Mendy	France	4/96
	Vacant	------	------
	Miguel Gonzalez	Mexico	8/92
Featherweight	Luisíto Espinoza	Philippines	12/95
Bantamweight	S. Singhamanassuk	Thailand	8/10/96
	Vacant	------	------
	Wayne McCullough	Ireland	7/95
Flyweight	Yuri Arbachakov	Russia	6/92

Tyson's second as a professional. The victory gave Holyfield his third heavyweight championship, making him only the second heavyweight besides Muhammad Ali to win the title three separate times. Tyson earned $30 million for the match, and Holyfield earned $11 million.

Michael Moorer won the International Boxing Federation (IBF) heavyweight title in a split decision over Axel Schulz of Germany June 22 in Dortmund, Germany. Moorer then retained the title by defeating Frans Botha of South Africa in the 12th round on November 9 in Las Vegas.

Other divisions. The most competitive division in 1996 was welterweight, where the champions were Pernell Whitaker of the United States (WBC), Ike Quartay of Ghana (WBA), and Felix Trinidad of Puerto Rico (IBF). Light heavyweight Virgil Hill, the WBA champion most of the last 11 years, successfully defended his title for the 22nd time.

Amateur. Cuba dominated the 1996 Atlanta Olympics, taking 4 gold and 4 silver medals out of 12 weight divisions. Felix Savon, Cuba's 28-year-old heavyweight, repeated his 1992 gold-medal Olympic performance and extended his 10-year unbeaten streak internationally. Two weeks before the Olympics began, two of Cuba's best fighters fled from their Mexican training camp and defected to the United States.   □ Frank Litsky

In *World Book*, see **Boxing.**

Brazil. On Oct. 10, 1996, the Brazilian government indefinitely postponed action on a decree, which was signed January 9 by President Fernando Henrique Cardoso, that allowed citizens to appeal the government's land allocations to indigenous peoples (native Indians). Indian rights groups, conservationists, the Roman Catholic Church, and left-wing politicians attacked the new decree. By the April deadline for filing appeals, more than 1,000 private companies, ranchers, miners, and state governments had challenged claims to more than 300 land reserves.

Violence against the poor. On April 17, police in the Amazon state of Pará opened fire on protesters blocking a highway, killing 19 and wounding at least 50. The protesters were members of a landless peasant movement, which had aggressively campaigned in recent years for land reform. Police blamed protesters for the violence, but a videotape by a local television crew revealed that police fired the first shots.

On April 30, former state police officer Marcus Vinicius Borges Emanuel was sentenced to 309 years in prison for his self-confessed role in the brutal 1993 killing of eight homeless youths in Rio de Janeiro. (The sentencing, however, was symbolic because under Brazilian law the maximum time that can be served is 20 years.) Six of the victims of the Candelária Massacre, as the case was called, were killed while sleeping in the doorway of the Can-

delária Cathedral.

Troubled banks. On March 20, Banco do Brasil, Latin America's largest bank, reported that it had lost $4.3 billion in 1995, a figure that exceeded the bank's net worth. In response, the Brazilian government announced a rescue plan to increase the capital of the state-run financial institution by $8 billion.

While bank officials blamed losses on unpaid loans and a drop in earnings due to the weakness of the Brazilian currency, several senators demanded an investigation. President Cardoso, however, averted the investigation of Banco do Brasil, the fifth major Brazilian financial institution to require a federal bailout since he took office in 1995.

Farias killed. On June 23, 1996, Paulo César Cavalcante Farias, the suspected mastermind of an influence-peddling scheme that prompted the resignation of former President Fernando Collor de Mello in 1992, was found shot to death in Maceio, the capital of the northeast state of Alagoas. Local police hastily ruled that Farias's 28-year-old girl friend, Suzana Marcolino, shot him and then committed suicide. But Brazilians were skeptical, as Farias had been scheduled to testify within a week in a corruption case connected to the previous Brazilian administration.

New heart surgery. Heart surgeons from the United States and elsewhere converged on a small hospital near Curitiba in southern Brazil during 1996 to observe the Brazilian surgeon Randas J. V. Batista perform a promising new procedure. Batista had developed a method for surgically removing a section of muscle in the main pumping chamber of hearts, thus increasing mechanical efficiency. Several U.S. physicians began using the technique under vastly better operating conditions than Batista's at the rural Brazilian hospital. Although many specialists called for more research on the technique, the operation could allow many patients to avoid the risks and complications of heart transplants, resume normal daily lives, and reduce the use of medications.

Brasília's population exceeds target. With a population exceeding 2 million in 1996, Brasília was more than four times larger than city planners expected it to be by the year 2000. The carefully planned capital city of Brazil, inaugurated in 1960, has become a growing metropolitan area, which includes 16 unplanned suburbs of mostly poor residents.

Michael Jackson in Rio. In a February 1996 court battle, Michael Jackson, the American pop musician, won the right to use the hillside slum of Santa Marta in Rio de Janeiro as a backdrop for a music video entitled "They Don't Care About Us." Local officials feared the video might further tarnish Rio's reputation abroad and hurt its chances of attracting the Olympics in 2004.   □ Nathan A. Haverstock

See also **Latin America** (Facts in brief table). In *World Book,* see Brazil.

British Columbia. See Canadian provinces.
Brunei. See Asia.

Building and construction.

Two new towers were officially designated the tallest buildings in the world in 1996. In April, the Council on Tall Buildings and Urban Habitat, a professional and research organization located at Lehigh University in Bethlehem, Pennsylvania, voted to end the reign of Chicago's Sears Tower, completed in 1974, as the world's tallest building.

Reaching new heights. The council's executive committee decided that Sears, standing at 1,454 feet (443 meters) tall, had been surpassed not once but twice by the Petronas Twin Towers located in Kuala Lumpur, Malaysia. The two structures both topped out at 1,483 feet (452 meters).

A controversy raged over whether the spires of the Petronas Twin Towers and the television antennas on the Sears Tower should be counted in calculating the height of the buildings. Chicago school children wrote letters to the council to plead the case for the Sears Tower.

In the end, the Petronas's spires were designated as structural, while the television antennas atop Sears Tower were not. Sears dropped to third tallest building in the world, and the sentimental favorite—New York City's 1931 Empire State Building—fell to seventh place.

Enron's Dabhol plant. In India, construction of an electric power plant in Dabhol, a small city south of Bombay, got back on track in 1996. Indian Prime Minister H. D. Deve Gowda on July 9 approved a guarantee to purchase power from the plant, which was being built by the Houston-based Enron Development Corporation. The Indian state of Maharashtra, where the plant is located, had sued in an Indian court to break Enron's original contract. In August 1995, the state forced Enron to suspend work on the project, following allegations of kickbacks and padded costs.

After Enron negotiated new terms with the state, international lenders hesitated to fund the project until the federal government of India guaranteed to underwrite costs.

While Enron and seven other foreign firms operating in India were able to obtain federal guarantees covering various projects, the suspension of Enron's original Dabhol agreement chilled the atmosphere for foreign investment in power plants in India and other developing nations.

U.S. construction. In 1996, the United States construction industry experienced its fifth straight year of modest expansion due to slow, steady growth in the national economy and unchanged interest rates resulting from the strict policies of the Federal Reserve system, the nation's central bank. The total value of construction contracts awarded in 1996 hit $322 billion, up from $305 billion in 1995.

Media reports of layoffs by large corporate employers did not cause consumer confidence to dip. Single-family-home construction rose 3 percent, with 1.1 million new units constructed in 1996, according to F. W. Dodge, a forecasting company based in New York City. Other types of construction also fared well.

Hotel construction increased 30 percent, a respectable showing after 1995's 56-percent increase. Average hotel-room occupancy rates of about 70 percent promised to keep hotel construction at high levels for several years.

Los Angeles subway trouble. Problems continued to plague the $5.8-billion Los Angeles subway project during 1996. Over Fourth of July weekend, a contractor-owned tunnel-boring machine became stuck in the Red Line's North Hollywood-Universal City tunnel. The machine—more than 300 feet (90 meters) long—had to be dug out entirely by hand before work on the project could be resumed.

While the 3.2-mile (5.1-kilometer) downtown section of the subway was in operation in 1996, outlying sections still under construction had fallen behind schedule by several years and over budget by more than $1 billion.

In 1996, the Los Angeles subway project became mired in litigation. Contractors, project consultants, and the Los Angeles County Metropolitan Transportation Authority (MTA) all filed lawsuits, accusing project managers of corruption and safety violations. Hollywood Boulevard property owners—claiming property damage from tunnel construction beneath their streets—also filed lawsuits. Throughout Los Angeles, house and business owners filed lawsuits. Controversy surrounded the project's every move.

Morrison Knudsen saved by merger. One of America's oldest engineering and construction companies, Morrison Knudsen Corporation of Boise, Idaho, avoided financial disaster by merging with the Washington Construction Group, Incorporated. Under the court-approved agreement, Morrison Knudsen, which had lost hundreds of millions of dollars under former chairman and chief executive William Agee, went into planned bankruptcy. While shareholders sustained major losses, the corporation was able to continue as part of a larger, financially sounder organization.

Olympic Stadium engineer suspended. Disciplinary action against an engineer made headlines in 1996. An engineer who helped design the Olympic Stadium in Atlanta, Georgia, was suspended from practice for three years under an agreement signed in June.

The engineer had discovered a weakness in a stadium light tower on March 10, 1995, but failed to notify construction personnel to stop work. Days later, an ironworker died when the light tower collapsed.   □ Richard Korman

See also **Malaysia.** In *World Book,* see **Building construction; Skyscraper.**

The World's 25 Tallest Buildings

Building	Height feet	meters
1. Petronas Tower 1 (Kuala Lumpur, Malaysia)	1483	452
2. Petronas Tower 2 (Kuala Lumpur, Malaysia)	1483	452
3. Sears Tower (Chicago, U.S.)	1450	442
4. Jin Mao Building (Shanghai, China)	1379	421
5. One World Trade Center (New York City, U.S.)	1368	417
6. Two World Trade Center (New York City, U.S.)	1362	415
7. Empire State Building (New York City, U.S.)	1250	381
8. Central Plaza (Hong Kong)	1227	374
9. Bank of China Tower (Hong Kong)	1209	369
10. T & T Tower (Kaohsiung, Taiwan)	1140	348
11. Amoco Building (Chicago, U.S.)	1136	346
12. John Hancock Center (Chicago, U.S.)	1127	344
13. Shun Hing Square (Shenyang, China)	1066	325
14. Sky Central Plaza (Guangzhou, China)	1056	322
15. Baiyoke Tower II (Bangkok, Thailand)	1050	320
16. Chrysler Building (New York City, U.S.)	1046	319
17. NationsBank Plaza (Atlanta, U.S.)	1023	312
18. First Interstate World Center (Los Angeles, U.S.)	1018	310
19. Texas Commerce Tower (Houston, U.S.)	1000	305
20. Ryugyong Hotel (Pyongyang, North Korea)	984	300
21. Two Prudential Plaza (Chicago, U.S.)	978	298
22. First Interstate Bank Plaza (Houston, U.S.)	972	296
23. Landmark Tower (Yokohama, Japan)	971	296
24. 311 South Wacker Drive (Chicago, U.S.)	959	292
25. Jubilee St./Queen's Rd. Central (Hong Kong)	958	292

Source: "The 100 Tallest Buildings in the World" published by the Council on Tall buildings and Urban Habitat

In May, the Petronas Towers in Kuala Lumpur, Malaysia, top out at a record-breaking 1,483 feet (452 meters) to become the world's two tallest buildings.

Bulgaria. The Socialist government of Prime Minister Zhan Videnov came under increasing pressure in 1996 from international and domestic groups. Videnov survived a vote of no-confidence in the legislature June 13, but popular protests against the government's economic policies continued.

Under international pressure, the government announced in May that it would speed up the privatization process it had begun in 1994. The private sector accounted for approximately 50 percent of the nation's gross domestic product by 1996, but industry remained largely in state hands.

Bulgaria's economy remained one of the worst among the former Soviet satellite states. In 1996, the nation faced its worst economic situation since the overthrow of Communist rule in 1989. In July, the government increased the price of fuel, cigarettes, and alcohol and raised some tax rates. The price of electricity skyrocketed, and telephone and postal rates rose significantly.

On November 4, Petar Stoyanov, running as an anti-Communist, won a runoff election to become the new president of Bulgaria. Although the presidency was a largely ceremonial office, Stoyanov's clear victory was seen as a blow to the stability of Videnov's Socialist government.   □ Sharon L. Wolchik

See also **Europe** (Facts in brief table). In *World Book,* see Bulgaria.

Burkina Faso. See Africa.

Burma. The struggle continued in 1996 between the *junta* (military group holding power after a revolution) ruling Burma, which is officially named Myanmar, and the opposition National League for Democracy. The League had won parliamentary elections in 1990, but the junta, known as the State Law and Order Restoration Council, imprisoned many League members and refused to allow parliament to convene.

League leader Daw Aung San Suu Kyi held a three-day party conference in May 1996 on the compound of her home, where she had been under house arrest from 1989 until 1995. A few days prior to the meeting, the junta had arrested 238 League members in an unsuccessful attempt to prevent the conference from taking place. The junta did allow 10,000 people to gather outside the house to hear an address by Suu Kyi, who assured the crowd that the League would not bend to junta pressure.

Tightening the law. The junta announced on June 7, 1996, that anyone undermining the stability of the state would be imprisoned from 5 to 20 years. The new law was interpreted as being aimed at Suu Kyi. Nevertheless, 5,000 supporters gathered at Suu Kyi's compound on June 8 to hear her reaffirm that the League would carry out its responsibility as the duly elected representatives of the Burmese people.

By September, the junta had arrested at least 60 more League members. Nevertheless, Suu Kyi

prepared to hold another League conference. This time, police successfully prevented the meeting from taking place, and for the first time, they kept a crowd from gathering to hear Suu Kyi's weekly address, a practice she had begun in 1995.

In December 1996, Suu Kyi was again restricted to the confines of her house when university students began another round of demonstrations against the junta. Authorities closed secondary schools and stationed troops at two universities in an effort to quell protests.

Foreign attitudes. Western governments criticized the junta for its continued repression of democratically elected representatives. In contrast, the Association of Southeast Asian Nations (ASEAN) in July 1996 granted Burma observer status, a step toward full ASEAN membership, possibly in 1997. However, after the September crackdown on the League, ASEAN members expressed doubts whether Burma was eligible for membership.

Drug lord. On Jan. 5, 1996, the rebel Khun Sa surrendered his 10,000-man army to Burma's military, after years of fighting for independence for the Shan ethnic minority. Khun Sa was also an opium and heroin producer. There was little evidence indicating his arrest curtailed the drug business.

□ Henry S. Bradsher

See also **Asia** (Facts in brief table). In *World Book,* see **Burma.**

Burundi. Burundi teetered on the brink of ethnic war between the minority Tutsi and the majority Hutu in 1996. The Tutsi continued to dominate the army and government, while the Hutu organized in the countryside. The legacy of the 1995 Hutu slaughter of Tutsi in Rwanda continued to haunt Burundi.

Moving toward war. During 1996, Burundi moved closer to full-fledged civil war. The most consistent pattern was that of Hutu attacks on Tutsi in rural areas, followed by severe reprisals by the Tutsi-dominated army. It was estimated that about 10,000 people were killed each month in 1996 and that some 150,000 had been killed in the previous 2 ½ years.

Refugee numbers swelled as Hutu fled to Tanzania, Uganda, Zaire, and Rwanda, and as Tutsi flocked to the Burundi capital, Bujumbura. Hutu refugees abroad posed economic and social problems in host countries and were recruited by Hutu rebel groups, such as the Zaire-based National Council for the Defense of Democracy, led by Leonard Nyangoma.

Western reluctance. The United Nations Secretary General Boutros Boutros-Ghali repeatedly advocated initiatives to prevent collapse in Burundi. In 1996, however, the major world powers refused to intervene. Burundi's leaders viewed international intervention as a potential threat to their hold on the country. Some Hutu leaders opposed intervention as well, suspecting that an international presence in

Burundi might thwart their own goals. Any intervention force, thus, could expect to encounter opposition from both sides.

The United States offered logistical and financial support—but no troops—for an intervention force. African states under the leadership of Tanzania's former president, Julius Nyerere, proposed an intervention force relying largely on African resources. The plan was not well received in Bujumbura.

July coup. In late July, President Sylvestre Ntibantunganya, a Hutu, was deposed in a *coup d'état* (overthrow) led by former President Pierre Buyoya, an officer in the Tutsi-dominated army. Buyoya stated that his aims were to impose control on the army, end attacks on Hutu, and negotiate a settlement of the conflict. Violence continued to mount, however, culminating in the murder of Archbishop Joachim Ruhuna in September.

Neighboring states, led by Nyerere with the support of the Organization of African Unity (OAU), undertook an embargo of Burundi, closing all transport routes into the landlocked country. The immediate result was increased suffering for the people.

□ Mark DeLancey

See also **Africa** (Facts in brief table); **Rwanda; Zaire.** In *World Book,* see **Burundi.**
Bus. See Transit.
Business. See Bank; Economics, Labor; Manufacturing.

Cabinet, U.S. President Bill Clinton's Cabinet lost one of its prominent members on April 3, 1996. Secretary of Commerce Ron Brown, 54, was killed in a plane crash while on a trade mission to Bosnia-Herzegovina and Croatia. Thirty-two other Americans, including executives of United States business firms, also died in the crash.

Brown was the first Cabinet secretary in over 150 years to die in the line of duty. He was aboard a U.S. Air Force jet that slammed into a mountainside near Dubrovnik, Croatia, during a severe storm. An investigation disclosed that the pilot was off course at the time of the crash. The Air Force subsequently disciplined top officers of the squadron for inadequate attention to safety concerns.

President Clinton led the mourners at funeral services for Brown, a leading black political figure who was involved in strategy and fund-raising in the president's 1992 election campaign. Brown managed civil rights activist Jesse Jackson's presidential bid in 1988 and later became chairman of the Democratic National Committee. The president named a former political adviser U.S. Trade Representative Mickey Kantor to replace Brown as head of the Commerce Department.

Appointments. In February, Alice M. Rivlin, director of the Office of Management and Budget (OMB), was appointed vice chairman of the Federal Reserve Board. Her appointment filled a vacancy caused by the departure of Alan S. Blinder, who

Bodyguards escort Burundian President Sylvestre Ntibantunganya to safety during the July coup.

President Bill Clinton stands with the family of Secretary of Commerce Ron Brown at Brown's funeral in April. Brown was killed in a plane crash in Croatia while on a trade mission.

stepped down when his term expired at the end of January. In April, President Clinton selected Franklin D. Raines, vice chairman of the Federal National Mortgage Association (better known as Fannie Mae) to succeed Rivlin as head of the OMB.

Cabinet changes. President Clinton made several Cabinet changes after his reelection in November 1996. He nominated Madeline K. Albright, U.S. ambassador to the United Nations, to replace Warren Christopher as secretary of state and Maine Republican Senator William Cohen to succeed William Perry as secretary of defense. Clinton tapped National Security Adviser Anthony Lake to replace John Deutch as director of the Central Intelligence Agency. Within the White House, North Carolina business execu-

tive Erskine Bowles was named chief of staff, succeeding Leon Panetta. Samuel (Sandy) Berger was selected to head the National Security Council.

In December, President Clinton nominated candidates to fill the rest of the seats in his Cabinet that were vacated by members who resigned following his reelection. Clinton nominated William M. Daley as secretary of commerce, Rodney Slater as secretary of transportation, Federico F. Peña as secretary of energy, Andrew M. Cuomo as secretary of housing, and Alexis Herman as secretary of labor. Congress must confirm the appointments before the nominees can be installed in office.

☐ William J. Eaton

In *World Book*, see **Cabinet.**

Cage, Nicolas (1964–), an American motion-picture actor, won the Academy Award in March 1996 for best actor of 1995 for his portrayal of a Hollywood agent on a suicidal drinking binge in *Leaving Las Vegas.* Known for impassioned, unconventional performances, Cage often has received mixed reviews from critics and audiences.

Nicolas Cage was born Nicolas Coppola on Jan. 7, 1964, in Long Beach, California. He began acting as a teen-ager and dropped out of high school after passing the General Educational Development (GED) test during his junior year. His first screen role was a small part in the 1982 film *Fast Times at Ridgemont High.* However, as the nephew of celebrated film director Francis Ford Coppola, he found it difficult to win movie roles and changed his name to Cage.

Nicolas Cage's most commercially successful film was *Moonstruck* (1987), in which he played a one-handed baker who romances a widow played by Cher. His other films include *Birdy* (1984), *Peggy Sue Got Married* (1986), *Raising Arizona* (1987), *Vampire's Kiss* (1989), *Wild at Heart* (1990), *Honeymoon in Vegas* (1992), *It Could Happen to You* (1994), *Kiss of Death* (1995), and *The Rock* (1996). Cage is married to actress Patricia Arquette.

□ Lisa Klobuchar

California. See **Los Angeles; San Diego; State government.**

Cambodia. Clashes in 1996 between the parties of Cambodia's governing coalition triggered international concern about the government's stability. The fighting occurred between the National United Front for an Independent, Neutral, Peaceful, and Cooperative Cambodia (known as FUNCINPEC) and the Cambodian People's Party (CPP).

FUNCINPEC, led by Prince Norodom Ranariddh, a son of King Norodom Sihanouk, took the largest number of votes in the 1993 elections supervised by the United Nations. It was, however, forced to form a coalition government with the second-place CPP, which before the election had run a Vietnamese-backed Communist slate headed by Hun Sen.

In March 1996, Prince Ranariddh, the first prime minister, accused Hun Sen, the second prime minister, of refusing to share power and threatened to withdraw from the government. Hun Sen replied that any attempt to dissolve the government would be met with military force. In June, Hun Sen taunted Ranariddh for not carrying out his threat and stated that the government would continue without Ranariddh or his followers.

Khmer Rouge defections. The Khmer Rouge, the Communist movement that ruled Cambodia from 1975 to 1979, split into two factions in 1996—one led by a hardline Communist and the other led by a defector eager to make peace with the government. Ieng Sary, a foreign minister during the

Khmer Rouge regime and leader of its guerrilla forces, asked the government in 1996 to recognize his newly formed political party made up of Khmer Rouge defectors. Pol Pot, leader of the fractured Khmer Rouge, denounced Sary and vowed that the Khmer Rouge would continue its fight against the government.

New evidence indicated that during the Khmer Rouge rule at least 1.5 million people—a quarter of Cambodia's population—had been killed. Ieng Sary had been sentenced to death in 1979 for genocide. In 1996, he denied responsibility for the 1975-1979 deaths, despite extensive testimony about his personal role in atrocities.

In August 1996, Pol Pot accused Ieng Sary of stealing money earned from gem mining and logging in Khmer Rouge-controlled areas. These earnings were the Khmer Rouge's main resource of revenue after China cut off aid to the group in 1990.

After a dispute between Prince Ranariddh, who condemned Ieng Sary, and Hun Sen, who as a former Khmer Rouge leader defended him, the two prime ministers recommended amnesty for Ieng Sary as a step toward national reconciliation. Sihanouk granted amnesty September 14. But the government insisted that Ieng Sary could not enter politics while remaining a regional warlord. □ Henry S. Bradsher

See also **Asia** (Facts in brief table). In *World Book,* see **Cambodia.**

Cameroon reaped benefits from major foreign investment, officially announced a new constitution, and conducted municipal elections in 1996.

Financing was approved for the petroleum pipeline from Chad to Cameroon's Atlantic port of Kribi. Financed by international corporations, the pipeline was developed to generate future revenues for Cameroon from transported crude oil.

In January, the ruling regime announced a new constitution that guaranteed legislative and presidential elections in 1997. However, many viewed the constitutional process as illegitimate, and provisions for greater legislative independence and restrictions on presidential powers failed to satisfy this opposition.

Cameroon's municipalities conducted multiparty elections in March. Afterward, the central government appointed representatives to supervise cities where opposition candidates had won, marring the election process. Strikes and riots followed.

A border conflict with Nigeria remained tense in 1996. Discussions in Togo in February failed to prevent a major armed clash in May. A United Nations observer team was sent to the disputed area to end the conflict and keep the peace.

In July, African leaders gathered in Cameroon's capital, Yaoundé, for the annual summit of the Organization of African Unity. □ Mark DeLancey

See also **Africa** (Facts in brief table); **Nigeria.** In *World Book,* see **Cameroon.**

In 1996, the government of Prime Minister Jean Chrétien, stunned by the razor-thin defeat of a 1995 *referendum* (a bill or political question submitted to the people for a direct vote) proposing Quebec's separation from the Canadian federation, moved carefully to counter a revival of the separatist threat. The government's response took two forms. The first involved changing Canada's federal system to make Quebec a more comfortable participant in the union. The second response was a serious attempt to spell out the negative consequences of separation should Quebec vote in a future referendum to create a sovereign state.

The softer approach. Chrétien moved swiftly in early 1996 to carry out the second of two promises he had made to Quebeckers while campaigning against the referendum. The first, fulfilled in December 1995, was the passage by Parliament of a resolution recognizing Quebec's distinct language, culture, and civil law. The largely symbolic measure had long been sought by Quebec nationalists. Then, on Feb. 2, 1996, Parliament granted final approval to legislation giving Quebec a veto over changes to Canada's constitution. British Columbia and Ontario were allowed a veto, as was a prairie bloc consisting of Alberta, Manitoba, and Saskatchewan, and an Atlantic bloc consisting of New Brunswick, Newfoundland, Nova Scotia, and Prince Edward Island.

Delegating power. The government also moved to delegate more powers to the provinces, a process it called "rebalancing" the federation. Rebalancing limited the federal government's spending power and facilitated government withdrawal from certain jurisdictions in which it had been the dominant player. These included job training, forestry, mining, tourism and recreation, and public housing.

Plans for the transfer of these jurisdictions dominated a meeting of the premiers of Canada's 10 provinces, including Quebec, held on June 20 and June 21 in Ottawa, the capital. At the conference, the federal government confirmed its intention to withdraw from job training over the next three years and to turn over to the provinces $2 billion in annual funding.

The federal government made it plain, however, that it was not prepared to transfer control over health care and antipoverty programs to the provinces. At a meeting in Jasper, Alberta, from August 21 to August 23, several premiers argued that the federal government had lost the right to dictate eligibility requirements, payment levels, and other standards for social programs managed by the provinces because it had cut financial support for these programs so substantially. All the premiers, except Lucien Bouchard of Quebec, agreed to establish a council to work with the federal government on a power-sharing plan. Bouchard contended that the federal government should have no authority over social programs. Chrétien's government, however, rejected the idea of provincial standards for national programs, contending that such a system was unenforceable. The government also cited surveys showing that Canadians considered the country's current system of government-financed, single-payer medical care vital to the quality of their lives and essential to their sense of national identity.

Quebeckers to the Cabinet. In an effort to reach out to the citizens of Quebec, Chrétien strengthened Quebec's representation in his Cabinet. On January 25, Stéphane Dion, a political scientist from Montreal with strong federalist views, was named minister of intergovernmental affairs with a mandate to explore constitutional change with the provinces. Pierre Pettigrew, a management consultant, received the minor post of minister for international cooperation. On October 4, Pettigrew was promoted to minister for human resources.

The tougher line. The Chrétien government's tougher line against *secession* (formal separation from the federal union) was formally launched by Minister of Justice Allan Rock on September 27. While Quebec citizens on Oct. 30, 1995, narrowly voted down independence, Separatists, led by the premier of Quebec, continued to push for succession. According to Rock, Quebeckers must be offered a stark choice: separation or not. The consequences of secession must be plain. Rock also asserted that Quebeckers do not have the right to act unilaterally in setting the conditions for secession.

Rock also announced that the federal government would ask the Supreme Court of Canada to rule on the legality of secession. Three questions would be posed. First, as Canada's constitution has no provision for secession, is it legal for Quebec to declare independence unilaterally? Second, does the right to self-determination, claimed by Quebec, imply the right to independence? Third, in any conflict between domestic and international law over Quebec's secession, which law should take precedence?

Rock's strategy was politically hazardous because it risked alienating moderate opinion in Quebec. Indeed, both Daniel Johnson, the leader of Quebec's Liberal Party, and Quebecker Jean Charest, the federalist leader of the Progressive Conservative Party (PCP), criticized the plan as dangerous. They argued that the federal government should emphasize changes in the existing federation as a safer road in the conflict. Rock, however, hoped that a Supreme Court ruling favorable to the government's position would deter the moderate majority of Quebeckers from voting for what would then be the illegal step

Thousands of demonstrators pack Queen's Park in Toronto on October 26 to protest cutbacks in social services by the government of Ontario.

The Ministry of Canada*

Jean Chrétien—prime minister
Herbert Eser Gray—solicitor general of Canada; leader of the government in the House of Commons
Lloyd Axworthy—minister of foreign affairs
Pierre Pettigrew—minister of human resources development
Douglas Young—minister of national defence; minister of veterans affairs
Arthur C. Eggleton—minister for international trade
Jane Stewart—minister of national revenue
Ralph E. Goodale—minister of agriculture and agri-food
Diane Marleau—minister of public works and government services
Ron Irwin—minister of Indian affairs and Northern development
Fred J. Mifflin—minister of fisheries and oceans
Joyce Fairbairn—leader of the government in the Senate; minister with special responsibility for literacy
Sheila Copps—deputy prime minister; minister of Canadian heritage
Lucienne Robillard—minister of citizenship and immigration
John Manley—minister of industry; minister for the Atlantic Canada Opportunities Agency; minister of Western economic diversification; minister responsible for the Federal Office of Regional Development—Quebec
David Charles Dingwall—minister of health
Paul Martin—minister of finance
David Anderson—minister of transport
Marcel Massé—president of the Treasury Board; minister responsible for infrastructure
Stéphane Dion—president of the Queen's Privy Council for Canada; minister of intergovernmental affairs
Anne McLellan—minister of natural resources
Allan Rock—minister of justice; attorney general of Canada
Hedy Fry—secretary of state (multiculturalism/ status of women)
Fernand Robichaud—secretary of state (agriculture and agri-food, fisheries and oceans)
Ethel Blondin-Andrew—secretary of state (training and youth)
Lawrence MacAulay—secretary of state (veterans; Atlantic Canada Opportunities Agency)
Christine Stewart—secretary of state (Latin America and Africa)
Raymond Chan—secretary of state (Asia-Pacific)
Jon Gerrard—secretary of state (science, research, and development; Western economic diversification)
Douglas Peters—secretary of state (international financial institutions)
Alfonso Gagliano—minister of labor; deputy leader of the government in the House of Commons
Martin Cauchon—secretary of state (Federal Office of Regional Development—Quebec)
Sergio Marchi—minister of the environment
Don Boudria—minister for international cooperation; minister responsible for la Francophonie
*As of Dec. 31, 1996.

Premiers of Canadian provinces

Province	Premier
Alberta	Ralph Klein
British Columbia	Glen Clark
Manitoba	Gary Filmon
New Brunswick	Frank McKenna
Newfoundland	Brian Tobin
Nova Scotia	John Savage
Ontario	Mike Harris
Prince Edward Island	Keith Milligan
Quebec	Lucien Bouchard
Saskatchewan	Roy Romanow

Government leaders of territories

Northwest Territories	Don Morin
Yukon Territory	Piers MacDonald

of independence. Such a ruling threatened to also hurt Quebec's chances of winning international diplomatic recognition as a new nation.

Rock's announcement of a Supreme Court review, which would take at least a year, drew an angry response from the separatist government of Quebec. Claiming that secession was a strictly political act, the Parti Québécois (PQ) government declared that it would not participate in the case and would ignore any Supreme Court ruling.

In six by-elections held on March 25, Chrétien's Liberal Party easily retained a seat in the Toronto area and two others in Labrador and Newfoundland. In Quebec, Liberals Stéphane Dion and Pierre Pettigrew also won election. But a third Liberal, running

in a strongly nationalist section of Quebec, went down to a resounding defeat. The by-elections maintained party standings in the 295-seat House of Commons: Liberals, 176; Bloc Québécois, 53; Reform Party, 51; New Democratic Party, 9; Progressive Conservative Party, 2; Independent, 4.

Budget. Finance Minister Paul Martin delivered a budget to the House of Commons on March 6. The budget, looking forward to 1997 as an election year, contained few tax increases and few major cuts in government services. Martin continued his plan of steadily cutting both spending and the federal deficit. Program expenditures (not including interest on the public debt) were set at $109.4 billion, down from $113.8 billion in 1995-1996. (All monetary figures are in Canadian dollars.) Interest on the national debt was estimated at $47.8 billion, 36 percent of government revenues. Martin predicted that in 1996-1997, the budget deficit would fall to $24.3 billion, 3 percent of Canada's *gross domestic product* (GDP)—the total value of all goods and services produced within the country. He had set this goal when the Liberals took office in 1993. For 1997-1998, he predicted a shortfall of $17 billion, 2 percent of the GDP.

In an attempt to slow the rising cost of old-age benefits, the budget introduced a new Seniors Benefit program of tax-free payments that would replace the current Old Age Security program in 2001. Since 1954, benefits had been paid to every citizen regardless of income. Government pensions were to be reduced or eliminated for wealthier senior citizens. Benefits would be eliminated for single pensioners with an annual income of $52,000, down from the current $85,000, and eliminated for couples with a combined income of $78,000, down from $170,000. However, the new plan would not affect Canadians who had turned 60 by the end of 1995, or their spouses, regardless of their ages.

Disharmony over harmonizing. The finance minister announced on April 22, 1996, that three Atlantic provinces—Nova Scotia, New Brunswick, and Newfoundland—had agreed to "harmonize" their provincial sales taxes with the 7-percent federal goods and service tax (GST). The blended 15-percent sales tax, to take effect in April 1997, would apply to sale goods as well as to services previously covered by the GST. The government agreed to pay the provinces $961 million to make up for any lost tax income.

All other provinces except Quebec, which had already partly harmonized its sales tax with the GST, rejected the blended sales tax. They feared a loss of revenue and an extra tax burden on consumers. Opponents of the tax also criticized Chrétien and the Liberals for failing to keep their 1993 campaign promise to abolish the tax.

Public pressure over that promise forced Sheila Copps, Chrétien's deputy prime minister and minister of Canadian heritage, to resign from the Cabinet and give up her seat in Parliament on May 1, 1996. During the campaign, Copps had vowed to abolish the GST or resign from politics. But Copps easily won a hastily arranged by-election in her Hamilton, Ontario, voting district on June 17 and returned to her positions in the Cabinet.

Legislation. The 1996 parliamentary session saw little notable legislation. Social policy was the main field of action. A long-discussed reform of the unemployment insurance system was approved by the House of Commons on May 14. The changes required employees to work longer before becoming eligible for benefits. It also cut benefit levels and the amount of time benefits could be collected. The changes were opposed by noisy demonstrations in Quebec and in the Atlantic provinces.

Political opponents Lucien Bouchard (left), premier of Quebec, and Jean Chrétien (right), prime minister of Canada, attend the opening of a United Nations meeting in Montreal in May.

The House of Commons of the second session of the 35th Parliament convened on Feb. 27, 1996. As of Nov. 1, 1996, the House of Commons consisted of the following members: 178 Liberal Party, 53 Bloc Québécois, 50 Reform Party, 9 New Democratic Party, 2 Progressive Conservative Party, 2 Independents, and 2 Independent Liberals. This table shows each legislator and party affiliation. An asterisk (*) denotes those who served in the 34th Parliament.

Alberta
Diane Ablonczy, Ref.
Leon E. Benoit, Ref.
Judy Bethel, Lib.
Cliff Breitkreuz, Ref.
Jan Brown, Ind.
David Chatters, Ref.
Ken Epp, Ref.
Deborah Grey, Ref.*
Art Hanger, Ref.
Hugh Hanrahan, Ref.
Stephen Harper, Ref.
Grant Hill, Ref.
Dale Johnston, Ref.
David Kilgour, Lib.*
John Loney, Lib.
Preston Manning, Ref.
Ian McClelland, Ref.
A. Anne McLellan, Lib.
Bob Mills, Lib.
Charlie Penson, Ref.
Jack Ramsay, Ref.
Jim Silye, Ref.
Monte Solberg, Ref.
Ray Speaker, Ref.
Myron Thompson, Ref.
John Williams, Ref.

British Columbia
Jim Abbott, Ref.
David Anderson, Lib.
Margaret Bridgman, Ref.
Raymond Chan, Lib.
John Cummins, Ref.
Harbance Singh Dhaliwal, Lib.
John Duncan, Ref.
Paul E. Forseth, Ref.
Jack Frazer, Ref.
Hedy Fry, Lib.
Bill Gilmour, Ref.
Jim Gouk, Ref.
Herb Grubel, Ref.
Richard M. Harris, Ref.
Jim Hart, Ref.
Sharon Hayes, Ref.
Jay Hill, Ref.
Daphne Jennings, Ref.
Keith Martin, Ref.
Philip Mayfield, Ref.
Ted McWhinney, Lib.
Val Meredith, Ref.
Nelson Riis, N.D.P.*
Bob Ringma, Ref.
Svend J. Robinson, N.D.P.*
Werner Schmidt, Ref.
Mike Scott, Ref.
Darrel Stinson, Ref.
Chuck Strahl, Ref.
Anna Terrana, Lib.
Randy White, Ref.
Ted White, Ref.

Manitoba
Reg Alcock, Lib.
Lloyd Axworthy, Lib.*

Bill Blaikie, N.D.P.*
Marlene Cowling, Lib.
Ronald J. Duhamel, Lib.*
Ron Fewchuk, Lib.
Jon Gerrard, Lib.
Elijah Harper, Lib.
John Harvard, Lib.*
Jake E. Hoeppner, Ref.
David Iftody, Lib.
Glen McKinnon, Lib.
Rey D. Pagtakhan, Lib.*
David Walker, Lib.*

New Brunswick
Guy H. Arseneault, Lib.*
Harold Culbert, Lib.
Charles Hubbard, Lib.
George S. Rideout, Lib.*
Pierrette Ringuette-Maltais, Lib.
Fernand Robichaud, Lib.
Andy Scott, Lib.
Elsie Wayne, P.C.
Douglas Young, Lib.*
Paul Zed, Lib.

Newfoundland
George S. Baker, Lib.*
Gerry Byrne, Lib.
Bonnie Hickey, Lib.
Fred J. Mifflin, Lib.*
Lawrence D. O'Brien, Lib.
Jean Payne, Lib.
Roger Simmons, Lib.*
Brian Tobin, Lib.*

Northwest Territories
Jack Iyerak Anawak, Lib.*
Ethel Blondin-Andrew, Lib.*

Nova Scotia
Dianne Brushett, Lib.
Mary Clancy, Lib.*
David C. Dingwall, Lib.*
Francis G. LeBlanc, Lib.*
Ron MacDonald, Lib.*
Russell MacLellan, Lib.*
John Murphy, Lib.
Geoff Regan, Lib.
Roseanne Skoke, Lib.
Harry Verran, Lib.
Derek Wells, Lib.

Ontario
Peter Adams, Lib.
Sarkis Assadourian, Lib.
Jean Augustine, Lib.
Sue Barnes, Lib.
Colleen Beaumier, Lib.
Reginald Belair, Lib.
Mauril Bélanger, Lib.
Eugène Bellemare, Lib.*
Maurizio Bevilacqua, Lib.*
Jag Bhaduria, Ind. Lib.

Raymond Bonin, Lib.
Don Boudria, Lib.*
Bonnie Brown, Lib.
John Bryden, Lib.
Charles Caccia, Lib.*
Murray Calder, Lib.*
Barry Campbell, Lib.
John Cannis, Lib.
Marlene Catterall, Lib.*
Brenda Chamberlain, Lib.
Shaughnessy Cohen, Lib.
David M. Collenette, Lib.
Joe Comuzzi, Lib.*
Sheila Copps, Lib.*
Rex Crawford, Lib.*
Roy Cullen, Lib.
Paul DeVillers, Lib.
Stan Dromisky, Lib.
Arthur C. Eggleton, Lib.
John English, Lib.
John Finlay, Lib.
Jesse Flis, Lib.*
Joe Fontana, Lib.*
Beryl Gaffney, Lib.*
Roger Gallaway, Lib.
John Godfrey, Lib.
Bill Graham, Lib.
Herb Gray, Lib.*
Ivan Grose, Lib.
Albina Guarnieri, Lib.*
Mac Harb, Lib.*
Ed Harper, Ref.
Leonard Hopkins, Lib.*
Tony Ianno, Lib.
Ron Irwin, Lib.
Ovid L. Jackson, Lib.
Jim Jordan, Lib.*
Jim Karygiannis, Lib.*
Stan Keyes, Lib.*
Bob Kilger, Lib.*
Gar Knutson, Lib.
Karen Kraft Sloan, Lib.
Walt Lastewka, Lib.
Derek Lee, Lib.*
Gurbax Singh Malhi, Lib.
John Maloney, Lib.
John Manley, Lib.*
Sergio Marchi, Lib.*
Diane Marleau, Lib.*
Larry McCormick, Lib.
Dan McTeague, Lib.
Peter Milliken, Lib.*
Dennis J. Mills, Ind. Lib.*
Maria Minna, Lib.
Andy Mitchell, Lib.
Ian Murray, Lib.
Robert D. Nault, Lib.*
John Nunziata, Lib.*
Pat O'Brien, Lib.
John O'Reilly, Lib.
Gilbert Parent, Lib.*
Carolyn Parrish, Lib.
Janko Peric, Lib.
Douglas Peters, Lib.

Jim Peterson, Lib.*
Beth Phinney, Lib.*
Jerry Pickard, Lib.*
Gary Pillitteri, Lib.
Julian Reed, Lib.
John Richardson, Lib.
Allan Rock, Lib.
Brent St. Denis, Lib.
Benoît Serré, Lib.
Alex Shepherd, Lib.
Bob Speller, Lib.*
Paul Steckle, Lib.
Christine Stewart, Lib.*
Jane Stewart, Lib.
Paul Szabo, Lib.
Andrew Telegdi, Lib.
Peter Thalheimer, Lib.
Paddy Torsney, Lib.
Rose-Marie Ur, Lib.
Tony Valeri, Lib.
Lyle Vanclief, Lib.*
Joseph Volpe, Lib.
Tom Wappel, Lib.*
Susan Whelan, Lib.
Bob Wood, Lib.*

Prince Edward Island
Wayne Easter, Lib.
Lawrence MacAulay, Lib.*
Joe McGuire, Lib.*
George Proud, Lib.*

Quebec
Warren Allmand, Lib.*
Mark Assad, Lib.*
Gérard Asselin, B.Q.
Claude Bachand, B.Q.
Eleni Bakopanos, Lib.
Richard Bélisle, B.Q.
Michel Bellehumeur, B.Q.
Stéphane Bergeron, B.Q.
Maurice Bernier, B.Q.
Yvan Bernier, B.Q.
Gilles Bernier, Ind.*
Robert Bertrand, Lib.
Pierre Brien, B.Q.
René Canuel, B.Q.
André Caron, B.Q.
Martin Cauchon, Lib.
Jean J. Charest, P.C.*
Jean Chrétien, Lib.*
Jean-Guy Chrétien, B.Q.
Paul Crête, B.Q.
Madeleine Dalphond-Guiral, B.Q.
Michel Daviault, B.Q.
Pierre de Savoye, B.Q.
Maud Debien, B.Q.
Bernard Deshaies, B.Q.
Stéphane Dion, Lib.
Nunzio Discepola, Lib.
Antoine Dubé, B.Q.
Gilles Duceppe, B.Q.*
Maurice Dumas, B.Q.

Members of the Canadian Senate

The Senate of the second session of the 35th Parliament convened on Feb. 27, 1996. As of Nov. 1, 1996, the Senate consisted of 51 Liberals, 50 Progressive Conservatives, and 3 Independents. The first date in each listing shows when the senator was appointed. The second date in each listing shows when the senator's term expires. A senator's term expires when the senator reaches the age of 75. Senators appointed before 1965 need not retire at the age of 75. An * denotes the two senators who were appointed before 1965. Though Orville H. Phillips was appointed in 1963, he has elected to retire at the age of 75. Thus, his end-of-term date of 1999 is indicated.

Michel Dupuy, Lib.
Gilbert Fillion, B.Q.
Sheila Finestone, Lib.*
Alfonso Gagliano, Lib.*
Christiane Gagnon, B.Q.
Patrick Gagnon, Lib.
Michel Gauthier, B.Q.
Maurice Godin, B.Q.
Monique Guay, B.Q.
Michel Guimond, B.Q.
Jean-Marc Jacob, B.Q.
Francine Lalonde, B.Q.
Jean Landry, B.Q.
François Langlois, B.Q.
René Laurin, B.Q.
Laurent Lavigne, B.Q.
Raymond Lavigne, Lib.
Ghislain Lebel, B.Q.
Nic Leblanc, B.Q.*
Réjean Lefebvre, B.Q.
Gaston Leroux, B.Q.
Jean H. Leroux, B.Q.
Clifford Lincoln, Lib.
Yvan Loubier, B.Q.
Jean-Paul Marchand, B.Q.
Paul Martin, Lib.*
Marcel Massé, Lib.
Réal Ménard, B.Q.
Paul Mercier, B.Q.
Osvaldo Nunez, B.Q.
Denis Paradis, Lib.
Philippe Paré, B.Q.
Bernard Patry, Lib.
Pierre S. Pettigrew, Lib.
Pauline Picard, B.Q.
Louis Plamondon, B.Q.*
Roger Pomerleau, B.Q.
Lucienne Robillard, Lib.
Yves Rocheleau, B.Q.
Benoît Sauvageau, B.Q.
Bernard St-Laurent, B.Q.
Benoît Tremblay, B.Q.
Stéphan Tremblay, B.Q.
Suzanne Tremblay, B.Q.
Pierrette Venne, B.Q.*

Saskatchewan
Vic Althouse, N.D.P.*
Chris Axworthy, N.D.P.*
Morris Bodnar, Lib.
Garry Breitkreuz, Ref.
Bernie Collins, Lib.
Simon de Jong, N.D.P.*
Ralph E. Goodale, Lib.
Elwin Hermanson, Ref.
Allan Kerpan, Ref.
Gordon Kirkby, Lib.
Lee Morrison, Ref.
Georgette Sheridan, Lib.
John Solomon, N.D.P.
Len Taylor, N.D.P.*

Yukon Territory
Audrey McLaughlin, N.D.P.*

Province	Term
Alberta	
Joyce Fairbairn, Lib.	1984-2014
Jean B. Forest, Lib.	1996-2001
Ronald D. Ghitter, P.C.	1993-2010
Daniel Hays, Lib.	1984-2014
Nicholas W. Taylor, Lib.	1996-2002
Walter Patrick Twinn, P.C.	1990-2009
British Columbia	
Jack Austin, Lib.	1975-2007
Pat Carney, P.C.	1990-2010
Edward M. Lawson, Ind.	1970-2004
Len Marchand, Lib.	1984-2008
Raymond J. Perrault, Lib.	1973-2001
Gerry St. Germain, P.C.	1993-2012
Manitoba	
Sharon Carstairs, Lib.	1994-2017
Duncan J. Jessiman, P.C.	1993-1998
Janis G. Johnson, P.C.	1990-2021
Gildas L. Molgat, Lib.	1970-2002
Mira Spivak, P.C.	1986-2009
Terrance R. Stratton, P.C.	1993-2013
New Brunswick	
John G. Bryden, Lib.	1994-2012
Erminie J. Cohen, P.C.	1993-2001
Eymard G. Corbin, Lib.	1984-2009
Mabel M. DeWare, P.C.	1990-2001
Noel A. Kinsella, P.C.	1990-2014
Joseph P. Landry, P.C.	1996-1997
Rose-Marie Losier-Cool, Lib.	1995-2012
Brenda Robertson, P.C.	1984-2004
Louis J. Robichaud, Lib.	1973-2000
Jean-Maurice Simard, P.C.	1985-2006
Newfoundland	
Ethel M. Cochrane, P.C.	1986-2012
C. William Doody, P.C.	1979-2006
P. Derek Lewis, Lib.	1978-1999
Gerald R. Ottenheimer, P.C.	1987-2009
William J. Petten, Lib.	1968-1998
William Rompkey, Lib.	1995-2011
Northwest Territories	
Willie Adams, Lib.	1977-2009
Nova Scotia	
John M. Buchanan, P.C.	1990-2006
Gérald J. Comeau, P.C.	1990-2021
J. Michael Forrestall, P.C.	1990-2007
Alasdair B. Graham, Lib.	1972-2004
Michael Kirby, Lib.	1984-2016
Finlay MacDonald, P.C.	1984-1998
John M. Macdonald, P.C.*	1960-
Wilfred P. Moore, Lib.	1996-2017
Donald H. Oliver, P.C.	1990-2013
John B. Stewart, Lib.	1984-1999
Ontario	
Norman K. Atkins, P.C.	1986-2009
Peter Bosa, Lib.	1977-2002
Anne C. Cools, Lib.	1984-2018
Consiglio Di Nino, P.C.	1990-2013
Richard J. Doyle, P.C.	1985-1998

Province	Term
Ontario cont'd	
John T. Eyton, P.C.	1990-2009
Jean-Robert Gauthier, Lib.	1994-2004
Jerahmiel S. Grafstein, Lib.	1984-2010
Stanley Haidasz, Lib.	1978-1998
James F. Kelleher, P.C.	1990-2005
William M. Kelly, P.C.	1982-2000
Colin Kenny, Lib.	1984-2018
Wilbert Joseph Keon, P.C.	1990-2010
Marjory LeBreton, P.C.	1993-2015
Michael Arthur Meighen, P.C.	1990-2014
Lorna Milne, Lib.	1995-2009
Lowell Murray, P.C.	1979-2011
Landon Pearson, Lib.	1994-2005
P. Michael Pitfield, Ind.	1982-2012
Marie-P. Poulin, Lib.	1995-2020
Richard J. Stanbury, Lib.	1968-1998
Peter Stollery, Lib.	1981-2010
Andrew Thompson, Lib.	1967-1999
Eugene Whelan, Lib.	1996-1999
Prince Edward Island	
Doris M. Anderson, Lib.	1995-1997
M. Lorne Bonnell, Lib.	1971-1998
Orville H. Phillips, P.C.*	1963-1999
Eileen Rossiter, P.C.	1986-2004
Quebec	
W. David Angus, P.C.	1993-2012
Lise Bacon, Lib.	1994-2009
Gérald A. Beaudoin, P.C.	1988-2004
Roch Bolduc, P.C.	1988-2003
Guy Charbonneau, P.C.	1979-1997
Michel Cogger, P.C.	1986-2014
Pierre De Bané, Lib.	1984-2013
Philippe D. Gigantès, Lib.	1984-1998
Jacques Hébert, Lib.	1983-1998
Céline Hervieux-Payette, Lib.	1995-2016
Leo Kolber, Lib.	1983-2004
John Lynch-Staunton, P.C.	1990-2005
Shirley Maheu, Lib.	1996-2006
Léonce Mercier, Lib.	1996-2001
Pierre Claude Nolin, P.C.	1993-2025
Marcel Prud'homme, Ind.	1993-2009
Maurice Riel, Lib.	1973-1997
Jean-Claude Rivest, P.C.	1993-2018
Pietro Rizzuto, Lib.	1976-2009
Fernand Roberge, P.C.	1993-2015
Charlie Watt, Lib.	1984-2019
Dalia Wood, Lib.	1979-1999
Quebec divisional	
Normand Grimard, P.C.	1990-2000
Thérèse Lavoie-Roux, P.C.	1990-2003
Saskatchewan	
Raynell Andreychuk, P.C.	1993-2019
James Balfour, P.C.	1979-2003
Eric A. Berntson, P.C.	1990-2016
Leonard J. Gustafson, P.C.	1993-2008
Herbert O. Sparrow, Lib.	1968-2005
David Tkachuk, P.C.	1993-2020
Yukon Territory	
Paul Lucier, Lib.	1975-2005

Canada, provinces, and territories population estimates

	1996 estimates
Alberta	2,789,528
British Columbia	3,855,140
Manitoba	1,143,083
New Brunswick	762,501
Newfoundland	570,711
Northwest Territories	66,568
Nova Scotia	942,796
Ontario	11,252,425
Prince Edward Island	137,312
Quebec	7,389,137
Saskatchewan	1,022,537
Yukon Territory	31,452
Canada	**29,963,631**

City and metropolitan populations

	Metropolitan area 1996 estimates	City 1991 census
Toronto, Ont.	4,410,269	635,395
Montreal, Que.	3,365,160	1,017,666
Vancouver, B.C.	1,883,679	471,844
Ottawa-Hull	1,039,307	
Ottawa, Ont.		313,987
Hull, Que.		60,707
Edmonton, Alta.	890,771	616,741
Calgary, Alta.	853,711	710,677
Quebec, Que.	699,035	167,517
Winnipeg, Man.	680,285	616,790
Hamilton, Ont.	657,230	318,499
London, Ont.	420,614	303,165
Kitchener, Ont.	404,216	168,282
St. Catharines-Niagara	391,086	
St. Catharines, Ont.		129,300
Niagara Falls, Ont.		75,399
Halifax, N.S.	344,135	114,455
Victoria, B.C.	315,168	71,228
Windsor, Ont.	294,063	191,435
Oshawa, Ont.	281,922	129,344
Saskatoon, Sask.	223,524	186,058
Regina, Sask.	199,243	179,178
St. John's, Nfld.	175,249	95,770
Chicoutimi-Jonquière	167,854	
Chicoutimi, Que.		62,670
Jonquière, Que.		57,933
Sudbury, Ont.	166,661	92,884
Sherbrooke, Que.	148,925	76,429
Trois-Rivières, Que.	142,028	49,426
Thunder Bay, Ont.	130,006	113,946
Saint John, N.B.	129,380	74,969

Estimates are for July 1, 1996. Source: Statistics Canada.

On May 9, the House of Commons by a vote of 153 to 76 passed legislation that amended the federal Human Rights Act to prohibit discrimination on the basis of sexual orientation. The measure applied only to employees of the federal government and of federally regulated businesses, about 10 percent of Canada's work force. Seven provinces had already passed similar legislation. Opponents of the amendment argued that adopting such protections for homosexuals would lead to the legalization of same-sex marriages and to adoption of children by gay couples.

The economy gave mixed signals in 1996. The domestic market was weak, with low consumer spending and an unemployment rate stuck at about 9.5 percent for the sixth consecutive year. But export trade boomed, led by a wave of trucks and minivans crossing the border to the United States. Canada continued to be the strongest exporter among the seven leading industrialized countries and the most dependent upon foreign trade.

Some promising signs of job growth emerged, especially in manufacturing and in full-time positions. Inflation remained low, reflecting consumer caution and fears of unemployment, which held down wage increases. The consumer price index was 2 percent in November. The GDP grew at a somewhat faster rate than in 1995, with the mid-1996 estimate set at $789.5 billion.

Military controversies. In 1996, Canada's military forces continued to be embroiled in controversies over misconduct while serving with United Nations (UN) peacekeeping missions. (Advance troops under UN jurisdiction arrived in Somalia in December 1992; the remaining troops left in March 1995.) In 1995, charges of violence against Somali civilians committed by Canadian soldiers in 1993 and evidence of racial prejudice had led to the disbandment of the Canadian Airborne Regiment and the establishment of an official inquiry into the actions of Canadian officers in the Somalia mission.

One focus of the investigation was a charge of document tampering leveled at General Jean Boyle, who was involved in releasing information about the Somalia mission to the public. Boyle was appointed chief of Canada's defense staff in January 1996. Boyle claimed ignorance of the tampering, which he blamed on subordinates lacking "moral fiber." An investigation in March cleared Boyle of wrongdoing. Although Boyle's leadership was widely questioned, he was defended by Minister of National Defense David Collenette, who had appointed him.

On October 4, however, Collenette resigned his post over a breach of ethical guidelines governing Cabinet ministers. Collenette admitted having written to the Immigration and Refugee Board on behalf of a constituent. His resignation was seen as a convenient way for the Chrétien government to dispose of a minister who had become a political embarrassment. Doug Young became the new defense minister. On October 8, Boyle also resigned as chief of Canada's defense staff, saying that the armed forces deserved a leader unburdened by controversy.

Peacekeeping operations. Despite the controversies, Canadian forces maintained a leading role in peacekeeping operations. In early 1996, 1,000 Canadian troops joined the UN peacekeeping force in Bosnia. In February, Canada's offer to shoulder the cost of 700 Canadian troops in the North Atlantic Treaty Organization (NATO) mission in Haiti averted a threatened veto of the operation by China. China had insisted that the force should consist of only 1,200 troops, while other members of the Security Council argued for 1,900. A Canadian general was chosen overall commander of the mission.

In November, Chrétien spearheaded a UN effort to organize a multinational relief force to assist refugees in the African country of Rwanda. The prime minister offered 1,500 troops. Lieutenant General Maurice Baril, commander of Canada's land forces, was chosen to lead the mission. However, the plan was called off when refugees returned to their homeland, Rwanda.

Canada-United States relations. An agreement signed on April 2 put aside, for at least 5 years, a 15-year controversy over Canadian subsidies of soft-wood lumber, one of the most contentious disputes between Canada and the United States. Softwood lumber was Canada's third-largest export to the United States and accounted for 36 percent of the U.S. soft-lumber market. U.S. lumber producers had claimed that Canada was subsidizing its lumber exports through the low harvesting fees levied on the lumber companies by the provinces.

Under the terms of the agreement, lumber producers in British Columbia, Quebec, Alberta, and Ontario would pay an export tax on all shipments exceeding 14.7 billion board feet per year (the average export level for the three previous years). In 1995, the four provinces shipped a record 16.2 billion board feet of soft lumber to the U.S. The provinces were to keep any taxes they collected. Industry analysts expected that even if export levels reached those of 1995, 91 percent of Canadian soft-lumber exports would still enter the United States market tax free. For its part, the United States agreed not to file any complaints about Canadian lumber exports with the Canadian government for five years.

On July 15, 1996, a panel of the World Trade Organization (WTO) unanimously ruled that Canada was not violating the terms of the North American Free Trade Agreement (NAFTA) by imposing *tariffs* (taxes placed on goods that one nation imports from another) as high as 350 percent on imported dairy products and poultry. In an attempt to protect domestic dairy and poultry producers, Canada in 1995 had levied high tariffs on imported eggs, dairy products, and poultry. The United States, which wanted to enter the $12-billion Canadian dairy and poultry market, argued that the tariffs were illegal under the terms of NAFTA, which was designed to eliminate all tariffs between the United States and Canada by 1998.

The panel based its decision on the failure by the United States to complain about Canada's high tariffs on yogurt and ice cream in 1993, when the WTO's rules on tariffs were renegotiated. The panel's decision was of limited comfort to Canada's 32,000 dairy and poultry farmers. The WTO rules stipulated that by 2001 Canada must begin to phase out its tariffs.

Federal spending in Canada
Estimated budget for fiscal 1996-1997*

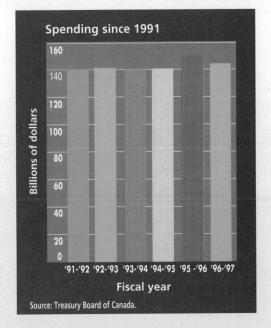

Department or agency	Millions of dollars†
Agriculture and agri-food	1,992
Canadian heritage	2,559
Citizenship and immigration	692
Environment	554
Finance	71,147
Fisheries and oceans	1,323
Foreign affairs and international trade	3,445
Governor general	10
Health	1,823
Human resources development	24,339
Indian affairs and northern development	4,190
Industry	3,684
Justice	745
National defence	10,555
National revenue	2,204
Natural resources	771
Parliament	274
Privy Council	160
Public works and government services	4,056
Solicitor general	2,562
Transport	1,774
Treasury board	1,432
Veterans affairs	1,939
Total	**142,230**

Spending since 1991

Source: Treasury Board of Canada.

* April 1, 1996, to March 31, 1997.
† Canadian dollars; $1 = U.S. $0.74 as of Oct. 25, 1996.

NORAD renewed. On March 25, 1996, Canada and the United States renewed for five years the agreement governing the operation of the North American Aerospace Defense Command (NORAD). NORAD was established in 1957 to alert Canada and the United States of any military strike through North American air space. In 1991, NORAD's mission was expanded to include interception of drug traffickers. Canada contributed $300 million annually, or 10 percent of the system's cost.

Chrétien intruder tried. On June 28, 1996, a provincial judge in Ontario found André Dallaire, 34, guilty of the attempted murder of Prime Minister Chrétien. Dallaire had broken into the prime minister's residence in November 1995 and waved a knife at Chrétien's wife. Dallaire, who was diagnosed as suffering from schizophrenia, was declared not criminally responsible for his act and sentenced to a group home near Montreal.

The Royal Canadian Mounted Police came under severe criticism for failing to detect the intruder and for their lax response to the Chrétiens' call for help. In spring 1996, four junior officers suspended in the incident were reinstated. A supervisor involved in the scandal resigned in August rather than face disciplinary action. ☐ David M. L. Farr

See also **Canadian provinces; Canadian territories; Chrétien, Jean; Montreal; Toronto.** In *World Book*, see **Canada; Quebec.**

Canadian literature.

The Canadian literary scene in 1996 showed particular strength and vitality in the field of adult fiction. Rohinton Mistry's *A Fine Balance* (1995), about urban life in India, and Margaret Atwood's *Alias Grace*, based on the notorious case of convicted 19th-century murderess Grace Marks, were 1996 semi-finalists for Great Britain's prestigious Booker Prize. The year was also distinguished by the publication of retrospective collections by Alice Munro *(Selected Stories)* and Mavis Gallant *(Selected Stories of Mavis Gallant)*.

Strong work from writers at midcareer included *Oyster,* Australian-born Janette Turner Hospital's novel about two women in the Australian outback, and Guy Vanderhaeghe's *The Englishman's Boy,* which shifts between Hollywood in the 1920's and the Cypress Hills Indian massacre in Saskatchewan in the late 1800's. W. P. Kinsella's *If Wishes Were Horses* is an exquisitely sentimental journey, while Matt Cohen's *Last Seen* is the surreal tale of a man whose brother may have returned from the dead.

First novels. An exceptional crop of first novels included *Fall on Your Knees,* a family saga set on Cape Breton Island in Nova Scotia, by award-winning playwright Ann-Marie MacDonald, and *The Cure for Death by Lightning* by Gail Anderson-Dargatz, a coming-of-age story set in British Columbia during World War II (1939-1945). Claudia Casper's *The Reconstruction* tells the story of a sculptor reshaping her own identity as she constructs a life-sized model of a 3-million-year-old human ancestor. Yann Martel's novel of identity, *Self,* relates the story of a young man who suddenly and unexpectedly turns into a woman. Poet Dionne Brand's *In Another Place, Not Here* captures the experiences of West Indians in the multicultural milieu of modern Toronto.

Witnesses to war. Several works reflected the urgency of revisiting the events of World War II as the number of eyewitnesses dwindles. *Fugitive Pieces,* a widely admired first novel by poet Anne Michaels, is about a child survivor of the Holocaust. Janice Kulyk Keefer's *The Green Library* moves between contemporary Toronto and Ukraine during World War II, and Katherine Govier's *Angel Walk* looks back on the wartime activities of a woman photographer. *You Went Away,* an intimate novel by Timothy Findley, captures the war years of the family of an alcoholic air force officer.

Nonfiction writers also looked back on World War II. *Carved in Stone* by Manny Drukier, who survived his boyhood in a Polish ghetto, vividly portrays a lost community and his last moments with family members. *The Guns of Victory: A Soldier's-Eye View*, the second volume of World War II memoirs by George Blackburn, offers stunning vignettes of Canadian soldiers in Europe.

Millennium musings. The juxtaposition of the approaching turn of the millennium and the apparent end of an era of Canadian prosperity was examined by a number of writers. In *Dreams of Millennium: Report from a Culture on the Brink*, Mark Kingwell examines how anxieties over the coming of the year 2001 affect North American culture. In *Boom, Bust and Echo: How to Profit from the Coming Demographic Shift,* demographer David Foot and journalist Daniel Stoffman use population studies to predict future trends in health care, education, politics, and the workplace. *In Search of a New Left: Canadian Politics After the Neoconservative Assault* by James Laxer offers a blueprint for a new kind of social democracy with greater citizen control. Canada's increasingly self-interested economic policy is the theme of *Shakedown: How the New Economy Is Changing Our Lives* by pollster Angus Reid.

Life stories. In *Red China Blues: My Long March from Mao to Now,* journalist Jan Wong recounts her growing disillusion with the political philosophy of Chinese leader Mao Zedong. In *Back on the Rez,* Mohawk journalist Brian Maracle describes his withdrawal from urban life to a Six Nations Reserve. Bob Rae, former premier of Ontario, offers a funny and eloquent account of his public life in *From Protest to Power: Personal Reflections of a Life in Politics.*

Widely respected feminist journalist Doris Anderson tells the story of her radicalization in *Rebel Daughter.* James Raffan's *Fire in the Bones: Bill Mason and the Canadian Canoeing Tradition* affectionately recalls a leading Canadian filmmaker and wilderness lover, who died in 1988. The moving story of the secret relationship between an imprisoned con man and a girl living near his penitentiary is retold in *The Convict Lover* by Merilyn Simonds.

Other notable publications. The Canadian media are the focus of *A Dream Betrayed on the CBC* by Anthony Manera, a former president of the Canadian Broadcasting Corporation, and *From Politics to Profits*, Minkoi Sotiron's exploration of the erosion of quality in Canada's newspapers. *A History of Reading* by anthologist Alberto Manguel explores how people are moved and changed by what they read.

Poetry. *Nightwatch: New and Selected Poems* spans three decades of Dennis Lee's career. *Dancing in the Dark: Poems and Short Stories* presents varied compositions by David Donnell. *A Really Good Brown Girl* by Marilyn Dumont, a *Metis* (Canadian of mixed Indian and European ancestry), evokes her childhood in Alberta, while Gregory Scofield employs city imagery in his autobiographic *Native Canadiana: Songs from the Urban Rez.*

Children's books. *How Smudge Came* by Nan Gregory tells the gentle story of a developmentally handicapped woman and a puppy. *Sarah and the People of Sand*, written by W. D. Valgardson and illustrated by Ian Wallace, is the story of an Icelandic girl and her Cree neighbors in Manitoba in the 1870's. In Carol Matas's *After the War*, a 15-year-old survivor of a Nazi concentration camp returns to her family home in Poland. Kit Pearson set an exciting psychological ghost story, *Awake and Dreaming,* on Vancouver Island in British Columbia. *Stephanie's Ponytail* is Robert Munsch's latest publication.

Awards. Winners of the 1996 Governor-General's Award for books in English were Guy Vanderhaeghe for *The Englishman's Boy* (fiction); E. D. Blodgett for *Apsotrophes: Woman at a Piano* (poetry); Colleen Wagner for *The Monument* (drama); John Ralston Saul for *The Unconscious Civilization* (nonfiction); Paul Yee for *Ghost Train* (children's literature-text); Eric Beddows for *The Rooster's Gift* (children's literature-illustration); and Linda Gaboriau for *Stone and Ashes* (translation).

Winners for French-language books were Marie-Claire Blais for *Soifs* (fiction); Serge Patrice Thibodeau for *Le Quatuor de l'Errance Suivi de La Traversée du Desert* (poetry); Norman Chaurette for *Le Passage de l'Indiana* (drama); Michel Freitag for *Le Naufrage de l'Universite* (nonfiction); Gilles Tibo for *Le Secret de Madame Lumbago* (children's literature-text); and Christiane Teasdale for *Systems de Survie—Dialogue Sure les Fondements Moraux du Commerce et de la Politique* (translation).

Alias Grace by Margaret Atwood won the Giller Prize, and Keath Fraser took the Chapters/Books in Canada First Novel Award for *Practical Anatomy*

☐ Maureen McCallum Garvie

See also **Literature.** In *World Book,* see **Canadian literature.**

Books by two of Canada's most admired writers were acclaimed in 1996. *Alias Grace* by Margaret Atwood, *left,* took the Governor-General's Award for fiction. *Selected Stories* by Alice Munro, *right,* offered a retrospective of her life work.

Canadian provinces.

In 1996, Canadian provinces continued to stress balanced budgets as crucial government priorities. Alberta and Saskatchewan competed to be the first province to eliminate its debt. The laggards in the race to reduce expenditures—the large provinces of Ontario and Quebec—faced strikes and demonstrations by public-sector unions and students as they slashed their budgets.

Alberta, rich in oil, gas, and other natural resources, achieved another year of spectacular success in budget cutting in 1996. On June 24, the Progressive Conservative Party (PCP) government of Premier Ralph Klein announced that the $506-million deficit forecast for fiscal year 1995-1996 had been turned into a $1.1-billion surplus, thanks to unexpectedly high oil and income tax revenues.

Since taking office in 1992, the PCP had slashed public services in order to reduce Alberta's $6.2-billion public debt. Although happy with the debt reduction, provincial taxpayers wanted increased spending on social and health services. Klein announced on June 24, 1996, that the entire budget surplus would go toward paying off the debt, which he predicted would be eliminated by 2010, 12 years earlier than had been forecast. But Klein also allocated $375 million in savings from interest payments on the debt to health, education, and programs for seniors (all amounts in Canadian dollars).

British Columbia. Strengthened by a change in leadership, the New Democratic Party (NDP) narrowly won a second mandate to govern British Columbia in an election held on May 28, 1996. Glen Clark, an aggressive 38-year-old former labor organizer, was elected leader of the NDP on February 18, succeeding Premier Michael Harcourt. Harcourt, in office since 1991, had announced his resignation on Nov. 15, 1995, after the NDP was accused of accepting illegal political contributions. Clark was sworn in as premier on February 22.

Immediately after his appointment as premier, Clark began a vigorous campaign to boost the NDP's public standing, which had trailed that of the opposition Liberal Party in opinion polls for three years. In April 1996, Clark's administration froze electric power rates, automobile insurance premiums, and university tuition. In a budget released on April 30—just hours before setting the date for provincial elections—the NDP cut the tax rate for small businesses by $29 million and the provincial income tax for low- and moderate-income taxpayers by 1 percentage point, effective on July 1.

Although the NDP captured a majority in the legislature—winning 39 of 75 seats—the party lost 11 of the seats it had held before the election and gathered only 39 percent of the popular vote. The Liberals, who won 42 percent of the vote, took only 33 seats, though this represented a significant increase from the 14 seats held before the election. Smaller parties won the remaining three seats.

On July 2, Finance Minister Andrew Petter admitted that instead of showing a promised $14-million surplus for the 1995-1996 fiscal year, the budget would actually generate a $235-million deficit. Petter blamed the turnaround on an over-optimistic projection of increased forestry revenues made when the April 30 budget was reintroduced. The revelation embarrassed the Clark government, which was accused of deliberately suppressing the bad news until after the election.

After ignoring the land claims of the Nisga'a Indians for more than 100 years, the government of British Columbia and the federal government reached a settlement with the band on March 22. The Nisga'a were granted absolute ownership of 1,210 square miles (3,134 square kilometers) of land south of the Alaska Panhandle as well as timber rights to a wider area. The band also received 27 percent of the total catch in the rich Nass River salmon run and a one-time $200-million grant. Although the deal aroused bitter opposition from the commercial fishing and timber industries as well as from some non-Indian residents of British Columbia, the settlement was expected to be a model for negotiations with 47 other native tribes in the province.

Manitoba suffered several outbreaks of labor unrest by public employees in 1996. A three-day walkout by about 800 prison guards beginning on May 4 followed a riot at Headingley Correctional Institution near Winnipeg on April 25 and 26. Seven guards and 30 inmates were injured.

At least 1,000 nursing home workers stayed off the job in July and August. The workers, mostly food service and housekeeping staff, claimed that other workers whose jobs required similar training and skills were paid more. The dispute ended on August 20, when the workers accepted a new contract equalizing pay and providing more job security.

About 3,000 home-care workers struck from mid-April to mid-May over government plans to contract out 25 percent of home-care services to private companies. The workers returned to their jobs after the government agreed to contract only 20 percent of home-care services and imposed a two-year freeze on privatizing such services in rural areas.

After a stormy passage through the legislature, a bill to privatize the Manitoba Telephone System passed on November 28. Heavily in debt and engaged in operations in direct competition with private telephone companies, the Manitoba system had been barely profitable in recent years.

New Brunswick—led by Premier Frank McKenna, who commanded an overwhelming Liberal Party majority in the legislature—continued in 1996 on its course of attracting new investment and putting its financial house in order. The budget, presented on February 15, forecast a surplus of $92.9 million on spending of $4.4 billion. The surplus would be used to reduce the province's debt, which was expected to total $5.3 billion at the end of the fiscal year 1996-1997. More than 3,000 public jobs were eliminated in the province during the previous three years, many through retirement and attrition.

In September 1996, New Brunswick opened Canada's first privatized elementary school. Built and maintained by a real-estate company, the Evergreen School in Moncton was leased to the government, which operated the educational program.

Also in September, New Brunswick, in an effort to increase parental authority over schools, became the first Canadian province to replace elected school boards with parent councils. The councils were to advise school superintendents and supply the members of two provincial school boards—one for English-language schools, the other for French-language schools. The provincial boards were given a veto over curriculums and budgets and some power over staffing arrangements, though the province's Ministry of Education would have final approval over hiring teachers and principals. Critics claimed that the new system would actually diminish parental authority by transferring more power to the education ministry.

Newfoundland gained a new premier on January 26 when Brian Tobin, the former federal fisheries minister who had directed Canada's efforts in a fishery dispute with Spain in 1995, succeeded retiring Premier Clyde Wells as head of the Liberal Party. The Liberals easily won reelection on Feb. 22, 1996, taking 37 seats in the 48-member legislature. The PCP captured nine seats, while the NDP took one. An independent candidate won the remaining seat.

On August 5, Newfoundland signed an agreement with a consortium of oil companies to develop Canada's second offshore oil field, Terra Nova. Expected to begin production in 2001, Terra Nova, about 220 miles (350 kilometers) southeast of St. John's, was expected to yield an estimated 400 million barrels of oil.

On July 9, 1996, Newfoundland, the federal government, and the Innu Indian nation agreed to move about 500 Innu from a desolate island on the Labrador coast to a more favorable site at Sango Bay on the mainland. The Innu, who had been relocated on Davis Inlet in 1967, encountered extreme living conditions. The community's appalling situation, which included high rates of suicide, alcoholism, and drug abuse, became widely known in 1993, when six young natives tried to kill themselves. The move to the new site, which has a good water supply, a protected harbor, and plentiful fishing, was expected to cost $85 million, to be provided by the federal government.

Nova Scotia, with fewer than 1 million inhabitants, boasts 13 universities, one of the largest concentrations of such institutions in Canada. In April 1996, after several years of talks, eight universities and colleges in Halifax announced an agreement to streamline their operations in order to reduce operating expenses. Under the plan, Nova Scotia Teachers College, in Truro, closed. Dalhousie University, the province's largest university, absorbed the 1,400 students in engineering, architecture, or planning who were attending the Technical University of Nova Scotia. Dalhousie and five other universities in Halifax formed a group called the Metro Halifax University Consortium to reduce administrative operations and to share services.

Nova Scotia's budget, released in April, was the province's first overall balanced budget in 25 years. It guaranteed a $2.1-million surplus for fiscal year 1996-1997 and offered taxpayers a 3.4-percent reduction in the provincial income tax rate. The change, to take effect in 1997, would give Nova Scotia the third lowest income tax rate in Canada. The budget followed three years of austerity in program spending, the elimination of hundreds of public service jobs, and a reduction in or freeze on civil service salaries.

Ontario. The PCP government of Premier Michael Harris worked in 1996 to implement its 1995 campaign pledge to cut provincial spending, lower Ontario's income tax, and produce a balanced budget within five years. On Jan. 29, 1996, Ontario's legislature passed a sweeping Savings and Restructuring Act that modified at least 40 statutes so that the government could more easily reduce or eliminate social services. The law allowed the government to close hospitals, charge user fees for the provincial drug plan, control physicians' services, and soften environmental laws. If fully implemented, the law would result in about $6 billion in spending cuts.

On February 26, a government plan to cut the number of Ontario's public employees by 13 percent over a two-year period triggered the largest strike by Canadian civil servants since 1991. About 55,000 of the 67,400 members of the Ontario Public Service Employees' Union stayed off the job until April 1, 1996. In the contract that ended the strike, the union failed to win the full severance package it had sought. But the pact strengthened the rights of employees whose jobs were to be turned over to private companies and provided greater job security for workers with seniority. On April 11, the Harris government announced a plan to eliminate 10,600 public sector jobs—about 13 percent of the provincial work force—as well as welfare benefits for people attending college or vocational schools by 1998.

The provincial budget, presented on May 7, 1996, by Finance Minister Ernie Eves, announced a 30-percent reduction in the provincial tax rate, to be fully implemented by fiscal year 1998-1999. The provincial rate, which was 58 percent of federal tax payable, was dropped to 54 percent effective July 1, 1996, and was scheduled to drop to 49 percent on Jan. 1, 1997. Savings to Ontario taxpayers were projected at $1.2 billion in fiscal year 1996-1997.

Anger over the Harris government's cutbacks in

Flood waters surge through the streets of Chicoutimi, Quebec, in mid-July, after unusually heavy rainfall caused rivers to overflow their banks and dams to collapse.

social services triggered a massive protest in Toronto on October 25 and 26, 1996. Tens of thousands of demonstrators marched through the city during the "Metro Days of Action," Ontario's fifth such protest organized by labor and social activists since the PCP took office in 1995.

Prince Edward Island. Catherine Callbeck, the first woman to be elected premier of a Canadian province, stunned her supporters on Aug. 6, 1996, by announcing her resignation. Appointed premier in 1993, Callbeck led the Liberal Party to an electoral win the same year. But with 1996 opinion polls showing the PCP leading for the first time in a decade, Callbeck decided not to proceed with another election.

Callbeck claimed she had achieved the goals she

had set for herself in 1993—to balance the budget and reform the health and educational systems. Callbeck was succeeded as Liberal Party leader and premier by one of her ministers, Keith Milligan. The Milligan government was soundly defeated in the November 18 election by the PCP under Pat Binns. The PCP, which benefited from voter anger with Callbeck's austerity measures, captured 18 seats. The NDP took only one seat.

The largest marine salvage operation in Canada's history was completed on July 30 with the recovery of the *Irving Whale*, a barge that sank in the Gulf of St. Lawrence in September 1970. An attempt to raise the barge in August 1995 had been halted by a federal court because of environmental concerns. The

Quebec, which in 1996 had one of the highest provincial unemployment rates—11.5 percent—in Canada; to contain a $3.9-billion deficit; to reform the educational system; and to improve social and economic conditions in the Montreal region. He reiterated, however, that his long-term goal was still independence for Quebec.

Bernard Landry, head of the new department of economy and finance, announced a plan on March 11, 1996, to slash spending by $1.1 billion in fiscal year 1996-1997. Spending estimates for the year, released on March 27, 1996, revealed the first real reduction in Quebec's outlays in 25 years.

The centerpiece of the budget, released on May 9, was a promise to cut the deficit from $3.2 billion in fiscal year 1996-1997 to zero by 1999-2000. The budget did not call for a tax hike but restricted tax breaks for businesses and middle-income wage earners. In contrast to previous PQ budgets, the budget made no reference to the prospect of sovereignty, the assumption being that Quebec would remain part of Canada for the immediate future.

Bouchard stressed that Quebec must moderate its insistence on the primacy of the French language and allow the use of bilingual commercial signs. He made it clear that an independent Quebec must be prepared to enter into a partnership with the rest of Canada. These views were rejected by hard-line separatists in the PQ at a policy convention on November 22 through 24, 1996, in Quebec. By threatening resignation and calling for tighter party discipline, Bouchard forced the PQ to accept his views.

One of the worst natural disasters ever to strike Canada occurred on July 19 and 20 when floods devastated the Saguenay River Valley between Lac-Saint-Jean and the St. Lawrence River in southern Quebec. Ten people died and at least 15,000 residents were forced from their houses. The floods, which caused an estimated $600 million in damages, resulted from heavy rainfall that caused rivers to overflow their banks and several dams to collapse.

Saskatchewan projected its third consecutive budget surplus in fiscal year 1996-1997. On a provincial budget of almost $5 billion issued on March 28, 1996, the NDP government of Premier Roy Romanov predicted a $358-million surplus, most of it from the sale of the government's partial stake in the Cameco Corporation, a uranium company. Taxes remained stable, and a deficit-reduction surtax, introduced in 1992, was eliminated for low-income families and scaled back for higher-income taxpayers.

Saskatchewan's 30 regional health boards, the centerpiece of a new medical care system that emphasized maintaining health, received additional funding on Aug. 20, 1996. Rural residents had complained about being forced to travel to larger towns for surgery and other special procedures.

☐ David M. L. Farr

In *World Book,* see the various province articles.

barge contained 3,400 tons (3,100 metric tons) of heavy fuel oil and 2,900 gallons (10,976 liters) of toxic polychlorinated biphenyls (PCB's) in its heating system. The salvage operation in July was completed without a significant oil or PCB's spill or structural damage to the barge.

Quebec. Lucien Bouchard, leader of the separatist Parti Québécois (PQ), resigned his seat in Canada's Parliament to become premier of Quebec on Jan. 29, 1996. He replaced Premier Jacques Parizeau, who resigned after the narrow defeat of an October 1995 referendum on independence for Quebec.

Bouchard made it clear that he was in no hurry to hold another referendum on sovereignty. His priorities, he stated, were to improve the economy in

Canadian territories. The New Democratic Party (NDP) swept to victory in territorial elections in the Yukon Territory on Sept. 30, 1996, ousting Premier John Ostashek and his Yukon Party government. The NDP, which has won three of the last four elections, took 11 seats in the territory's 17-seat legislature, a gain of 5. The Yukon Party, which won office in 1992, captured only 3 seats, down from the 7 held before the vote. The Liberal Party won 2 seats.

The NDP's success was attributed to voter dissatisfaction with Yukon Party policies. Ostashek's government, facing budgetary problems, had suspended collective bargaining with the territory's 3,000 civil servants and teachers and rolled back salaries. Increased taxes and levies on fuel and tobacco and a controversial wolf kill had also aroused voter anger.

Piers McDonald, leader of the NDP, became the Yukon Territory's new premier on Oct. 19, 1996. He promised to enact labor reforms and to make the settlement of native (Indian) land claims a priority for his government. Such claims had proceeded slowly under Ostashek's administration.

Diamond mine. Employment in the Northwest Territories, which had a jobless rate of about 17 percent, was expected to receive a much-needed boost with the establishment of what would be the first diamond mine in North America. The $750-million open-pit mine was to be located at Lac de Gras, about 190 miles (300 kilometers) north of Yellowknife, the territorial capital. About 1,000 workers would be required to build the mine, and 830 employees would be needed to operate the facility.

The mine's principal owner was BHP Minerals Canada Limited, a subsidiary of an Australian mining corporation. Annual revenues were projected at $500 million (Canadian dollars), with mining expected to begin in late 1998 and continue for 25 years.

A federal environmental review panel granted provisional approval to the project on June 21, 1996, but listed 29 concerns about the environment and economic benefits for four local native bands, who have land claims to the mine site. The federal Cabinet approved the project in August, but withheld water licenses and land-use permits pending the satisfactory establishment of environmental safeguards and the completion of benefit agreements. On November 1, the federal government, the leaders of the four bands, and BHP Minerals signed an agreement formally approving the mining project.

New parks. Canada gained a new national park in June with the establishment of Tuktut Nogait east of Inuvik in the western Arctic. The park, which encompasses 6,310 square miles (16,340 square kilometers) of tundra, is a calving ground for 100,000 caribou. It is the fourth national park to be established in the western Arctic. ☐ David M. L. Farr

In *World Book,* see **Northwest Territories; Yukon Territory.**

Cape Verde. See Africa.

Census. The U. S. Supreme Court ruled unanimously in March 1996 that the federal government need not revise 1990 census figures to adjust for an undercount of some 4 million people, primarily urban African Americans and Hispanics. The ruling was a setback for civil rights groups and cities, such as Chicago, Los Angeles, and New York, that sued to require the Census Bureau to use statistical sampling techniques to achieve a more reliable count. The Supreme Court's decision upheld the Administration of President George Bush in its refusal to change the final figures despite widespread agreement that the 1990 estimate was off by about 2 percent because of the Bureau's failure to count 4.8 percent of the African American population and 5.2 percent of the Hispanic population living in major metropolitan areas. The issue was important to leaders of large cities because census figures are used to set funding levels in federal programs, and it was important to minority groups, since census figures are used to allocate seats in the House of Representatives. Ironically, the Census Bureau announced before the court ruling that, as a cost-cutting measure, it would use statistical sampling techniques to count 10 percent of all households in the next census. Combining sampling techniques with traditional door-to-door and mail census measurements will cut nearly $1 billion from the estimated $4.8-billion cost of the constitutionally mandated decennial count.

Changes in composition of U.S. population. The Census Bureau projected a much-changed profile for the United States in the year 2050. A far greater percentage of the population will be Hispanic and Asian American. In a March 13 report, bureau experts stated that they expect the percentage of non-Hispanic whites to drop from 73.6 percent of the population in 1995 to 52.8 percent in 2050. In contrast, the proportion of Hispanic Americans was projected to rise from 10.2 percent in 1995 to 24.5 percent in 2050. Asian Americans were projected to increase from 3.3 percent of the populace to 8.2 percent in the next 55 years. The percentage of African Americans was projected to rise only slightly—from 12 percent to 13.6 percent by 2050. Overall, the U.S. population was projected to increase by 50 percent in the next half century—from 262 million in 1995 to 394 million by the middle of the 21st century.

Older brides and grooms. On March 12, the Census Bureau reported that the average age of Americans at the time of first marriage had changed significantly since the early 1960's. According to the results of a survey conducted by the bureau in 1994, the average age of brides was 24.5 years, compared to 20 years in the 1960's, and 26.7 years for grooms, compared to 22 in the 1960's. ☐ William J. Eaton

See also **Population.** In *World Book,* see **Census; Population.**

Central African Republic. See Africa.

Chad. See Africa.

Chemistry. New insights into the chemical structure of spider silk were reported in January 1996 by scientists at Cornell University in Ithaca, New York. The researchers described how silk components come together to produce a fiber stronger and more elastic than any synthetic fiber.

The best spider silk is the thread called a dragline that a spider uses to build the frames of its webs and to drop down onto prey. Scientists would like to learn how to make this fiber synthetically.

Researchers had long known that spider dragline silk is a protein, and they had identified the *amino acids* (protein building blocks) it is composed of. They had also isolated the spider genes containing the coded instructions for making the silk, and they had placed those genes into bacteria to produce bioengineered dragline silk. To make the best silk, however, investigators needed to learn how the different components of the silk protein are put together.

The new findings, reported by three Cornell researchers—biophysicist Lynn W. Jelinski, chemist Alexandra H. Simmons, and physicist Carl A. Michal—provided a partial answer to that question. Their chief tool was a technique called magnetic resonance imaging (MRI), which uses powerful magnetic fields to produce images of tissues. With an MRI scanner, they found that dragline silk contains three kinds of amino acid chains, each with its own role.

The toughness of silk fibers, the scientists discovered, comes from highly ordered crystalline segments called beta sheets. The elasticity results from semicrystalline segments that are chemically similar to the beta sheets but with a more irregular arrangement. Pieces of these segments can shift and support weaker sections in response to stress. These segments form long chains with the beta sheets and are also linked to the third component, a gelatinlike, disordered chain of amino acids. This final component forms an outside sheath.

Knowing how dragline silk is constructed has provided clues to how synthetic fibers that are as good as or better than spider silk could be made. Stronger ropes, better bulletproof vests, more comfortable seat belts, and superfine sutures for microsurgery are just a few of the possible uses for such silk.

A close look at friction. Mechanical systems need lubrication and periodic replacement, which costs industry billions of dollars each year. With a better understanding of friction at the molecular scale, it should be possible to build systems that last longer and use less energy. In May, two researchers at Harvard University in Cambridge, Massachusetts, reported a major step toward that goal.

Chemists Charles M. Lieber and Paul E. Sheehan used an atomic force microscope, an instrument that can move atoms and other small amounts of matter, to measure the friction of crystals sliding against other crystals. Pushing a tiny crystal of molybdenum oxide along the surface of molybdenum disulfide, a common lubricant, they found that there was much less friction in one direction than in other directions.

With a computer model, the chemists demonstrated that the low-friction slide was made possible by the crystals lining up so that the surface atoms of the molybdenum oxide could slip between the sulfur atoms of the lubricant. In other directions, however, the atoms banged against each other. This finding provided a fundamental reference for future work in developing low-friction materials.

Destroying CFC's. A simple process can turn chlorofluorocarbons (CFC's), chlorine-containing chemicals that have been found to destroy ozone in the upper atmosphere, into smaller compounds that pose no environmental hazard. That finding was announced in January 1996 by chemists Robert H. Crabtree and Juan Burdeniuc of Yale University in New Haven, Connecticut. Their process could not rid the atmosphere of CFC's, but it could be used to destroy CFC's that were being held in storage.

CFC's had been used since the 1930's in air conditioners, refrigerators, manufacturing processes, and aerosol cans. But in 1987, most of the world's CFC-producing nations signed a treaty to end production of the chemicals by the year 2000 (the date was later changed to the end of 1995). By 1996, the manufacture of CFC's was banned in 139 countries.

The treaty came about in response to the finding that CFC's drift to the upper atmosphere. There, high-energy sunlight breaks the compounds apart, releasing chlorine atoms. These atoms react with molecules of ozone—a form of oxygen consisting of three linked atoms—converting them to ordinary oxygen. Because ozone protects the planet from ultraviolet radiation, the build-up of CFC's in the upper atmosphere was hazardous to life on Earth.

Although CFC's were no longer being manufactured in 1996, tons remained in storage, posing a continuing potential threat to the ozone layer. CFC's are very durable compounds, and test methods for destroying them were expensive and inconvenient.

The solution to this problem came from an unexpected source—sodium oxalate, a chemical commonly found in rhubarb leaves. Crabtree and Burdeniuc found that simply running CFC's over a powdered bed of sodium oxalate at 554 °F (290 °C) causes them to break down into carbon, carbon dioxide, sodium chloride (table salt), and sodium fluoride.

New element created. The artificial creation of element 112, the heaviest element ever made, was reported in February 1996 by scientists at the Society for Heavy Ion Research Laboratory in Darmstadt, Germany. The researchers made the new element by bombarding a small piece of lead with zinc *ions* (electrically charged atoms), which caused some of the zinc and lead nuclei to fuse. The new atoms were very unstable and lasted only a fraction of a second before breaking apart.　　☐ Peter J. Andrews

In *World Book,* see **Chemistry.**

Chess. In 1996, 22-year-old Gata Kamsky became the first United States player to challenge a reigning world chess champion since Bobby Fischer defeated Boris Spassky of the former Soviet Union in 1972. In July 1996, however, Kamsky lost 7.5 to 10.5 to Russia's Anatoly Karpov, the International Chess Federation (FIDE) champion, in Elista, Russia.

In February, the other official world chess champion—Professional Chess Association (PCA) title holder Garry Kasparov of Russia—defeated the world's most powerful chess computer, Deep Blue. The computer, owned by International Business Machines Corporation (IBM) of Armonk, New York, can analyze 200 million chess moves per second.

Hungarian-born Zsuzsa Polgar, 26, of New York City, won the Women's World Chess Championship by defeating reigning champion Xie Jun, 25, of China, in Spain on February 20. Zsuzsa, the oldest of the three famous chess-playing Polgar sisters, won by a score of 8.5 to 4.5. Twenty-year-old Judith Polgar, the youngest of the sisters, rose to become the 10th-ranked overall player in the world in 1996.

The 32nd World Chess Olympiad, a biennial competition involving teams from more than 100 nations, was held from September 15 to October 2 in Yerevan, Armenia. Russia won the gold medal; Ukraine took the silver; and the United States captured the bronze.

Tournaments. Dmitry Gurevich of Chicago posted a perfect 7-to-0 score to win the U.S. Masters on March 10 in Oak Brook, Illinois. In July, Alex Yermolinsky of Euclid, Ohio, won the U.S. Interplay Invitational Championship in Parsippany, New Jersey. Anjelina Belakovskaya of New York City won the Interplay Women's Invitational Championship. On August 16 in Alexandria, Virginia, Gabriel Schwartzman, 19, of Gainesville, Florida, won the U.S. Open Chess Championship.

School Championships. A record 1,712 young chess players converged on Tucson, Arizona, from May 3 to 5 for the National Elementary School Chess Championship. Samson Benen of New York City and Rubin Miller of Dayton, Ohio, became individual co-champions. Hunter College Elementary School of New York City won the team championship.

At the National Junior High School Chess Championship in Orlando, Florida, in April, Vinay Bhat of San Jose, California, a young master only 11 years old, took individual honors over 872 competitors. Woodlands School of Hartsdale, New York, won the team championship. In Somerset, New Jersey, at the National High School Chess Championship, local master Dean Ippolito, 17, won the individual title in a field of 1,100 competitors. Masterman High School of Philadelphia became team champion.

On June 1, more than 1,500 young players took on the world's best adult players on the aircraft carrier *Intrepid* in New York City.   □ Al Lawrence

See also **Computer.** In *World Book,* see **Chess.**

Chicago in 1996 mourned the loss of Joseph Cardinal Bernardin, head of the city's Roman Catholic Archdiocese, who died of cancer on November 14. Bernardin was widely known as a mediator who sought to resolve conflict within the Roman Catholic community and to promote dialogue and cooperation among all religions. In September 1996, he had been awarded the Presidential Medal of Freedom.

In August, the cardinal had revealed that his pancreatic cancer, diagnosed in 1995, had spread. His condition was untreatable, he said, and he had less than a year to live. He told a packed news conference that he was "at peace."

Democratic Convention. Chicago basked in the national spotlight August 26 to 29, as it hosted the Democratic National Convention, its first political convention in 28 years. The Democratic Party nominated President Bill Clinton and Vice President Al Gore for a second term. Meanwhile, the city largely avoided memories of the 1968 Democratic National Convention, also held in Chicago. At that time, violent clashes between protesters and the police dominated the news. But Mayor Richard M. Daley was able to manage dissent and present the city's good side to the more than 20,000 convention delegates and media representatives.

School reform. In a drastic move to improve Chicago's public schools, the city's School Reform Board of Trustees, on September 30, placed 109 of the city's 557 public schools on academic probation. Fewer than 15 percent of students at the schools on probation were reading at or above national norms. The schools were given one year to reach this level. Principals and teachers at schools on academic probation were subject to removal by the board.

On March 27, the school board reversed previous "social promotion" policies. Under these policies, elementary school students were promoted to a higher grade even though they had failed to master the skills of their current grade level.

Airport battle. In October, the Chicago Park District took possession of Meigs Field, a small airport near downtown Chicago, after the airport's 50-year lease expired on September 30. Mayor Daley had announced in September that he intended to demolish Meigs Field to make way for a new lakefront park. But Daley's plans were put on hold while state officials opposed to closing the airport, including Illinois Governor Jim Edgar, challenged the action.

Redevelopment projects. Efforts to renovate parts of the city progressed in 1996. A stretch of Chicago's famous Lake Shore Drive was diverted away from the lakefront as part of a project to reclaim about 10 acres (4 hectares) of park land. By 1997, the strip of land was to be converted into a campuslike park connecting several attractions in the area, including, the Shedd Aquarium, Adler Planetarium and Field Museum of Natural History.

State Street, downtown Chicago's most venerable

shopping district, was reopened to vehicular traffic in October, in time for the Christmas shopping season. The street had been closed to vehicles and the area redesigned as a pedestrian mall in 1979. The $24.5-million project included restoration of street lamps and subway entrances in the Beaux-arts style of the early 1900's.

Chicago's Museum of Contemporary Art (MCA) formally reopened at a new location on the Near North Side in July 1996. First opened in "temporary" quarters in 1967, the MCA's original building was too small to display the museum's entire permanent collection. In addition to galleries displaying works of visual art, the new museum, which was built at a cost of $46 million, was designed by German archi-

tect Josef Paul Kleihues to accommodate fully staged dance, theater, and musical performances.

Conservation project. In April 1996, 34 public and private groups created the Chicago Region Biodiversity Council to coordinate the preservation and restoration of about 200,000 acres (80,900 hectares) of scattered prairies, wetlands, and forests that lie between Milwaukee, Wisconsin, Chicago, and Gary, Indiana. The initiative was intended to serve as a model for managing natural resources in an urban area. It was coordinated by the Nature Conservancy and initially funded with $700,000 from the United States Forest Service.   □ Harold Henderson

In *World Book,* see Chicago.

Children's books. See Literature for children.

Roman Catholic cardinals and bishops file into Chicago's Holy Name Cathedral on Nov. 20, 1996, for the funeral mass for Joseph Cardinal Bernardin.

Chile. On June 25, 1996, Chile became the fifth member of South America's Southern Cone Common Market (known as Mercosur). The agreement, signed in San Luís, Argentina, opened Chile's markets to unrestricted trade with Argentina, Brazil, Paraguay, and Uruguay, while allowing Chile to continue independent trade agreements with non-Mercosur countries.

In March, the Agricultural Ministry announced the successful eradication of the Mediterranean fruit fly in all regions except one in the north. The controversial 30-year campaign, during which toxic pesticides were widely spread in rural and populated urban areas, allowed Chile to substantially increase its exports of apples, grapes, avocados, and other fruit to Asia. According to the Agricultural Ministry, Chile hoped to increase the $1 billion annual value of its agricultural exports by one-half by the end of the century.

In March 1996, arms merchants from more than 400 companies and 43 nations displayed their wares at Chile's International Air and Space Show in the capital, Santiago. According to the U.S. Defense Department, merchants hoped arms sales to Latin American nations would total $3.6 billion to $5.2 billion by the year 2000. Chile's own armed forces, which receive 10 percent of the profits (approximately $400 million annually) from national copper sales, were a prime target for merchants.   □ Nathan A. Haverstock

See also **Latin America** (Facts in brief table). In *World Book,* see **Chile.**

China. As the Chinese Communist Party celebrated its 75th anniversary on July 9, 1996, it grappled with problems of leadership, economics, and China's political role in the world. Jiang Zemin, general secretary of the party, as well as the nation's president and chairman of the powerful Central Military Commission, tried to arrange a new form of collective leadership to prevent a power struggle once Deng Xiaoping, the ailing party patriarch, was dead.

The key issue for the party was the growing degree of capitalism in the economy. In 1978, Deng had removed many Communist restrictions on free enterprise and had introduced some elements of capitalism into China's basically socialistic system. Since 1978, China had developed the world's fastest growing economy. However, the gap between rich and poor had widened, and the party's control over society weakened. In 1996, some party leaders wanted to impose tighter, more Communistic economic and social rules.

At the annual late-summer leadership conference at Beidaihe, a beach resort, party leaders discussed reviving the title of chairman used by Mao Zedong, who had led the party to power in 1949 and died in 1976. The party abolished the post of chairman in 1982. Giving the title to Jiang was seen as a step toward ensuring stability. Party leaders also discussed designating hardline Premier Li Peng and the more liberal Qiao Shi vice chairmen of China. In 1996, Qiao

Shi was number three in the party hierarchy after Jiang and Li. The 15th party congress, scheduled for late 1997, must ratify the title changes before they could be implemented.

Political sniping continued despite official efforts to suppress it. Qiao, the top official of China's parliament, the National People's Congress, called for faster-moving reforms. In September 1996, he warned of threats to reform by conservative elements in the party. Deng's son, Deng Pufang, spoke on July 9 in defense of his father's reforms, which implied he was criticizing Jiang and more conservative leaders.

The party tried to crack down on the public's questioning of its methods. While claiming to build a "spiritual civilization," officials in September attempted to tighten control over the dissemination of information. They blocked Chinese language sites on the *Internet* (the worldwide computer network) and replaced the head of a liberal newspaper.

The crackdown included new moves against dissidents. On October 9, a prodemocracy activist, Liu Xiaobo, was sentenced without trial to three years in a labor camp for writing in support of Tibetan self-determination. Former student leader Wang Dan was given an 11-year sentence for subversion.

Strike Hard, a national campaign against crime, was launched in April 1996. The government increased the number of *capital offenses* (crimes punishable by death), from 21 in 1980 to 68 in 1996. In the first three months of 1996, 162,000 people were arrested, and more than 1,000 were executed.

By August, authorities were pressing regional officials to arrest local crime bosses. An estimated 10,000 criminal gangs, with a membership of 500,000 to 1 million, were active in China in 1996. Gang members were mostly unemployed youths and former prisoners. Gangs were involved in more than one-third of China's serious crimes, including crimes involving firearms, which rose 20 percent in 1996.

Orphans. Human Rights Watch, an American civil rights organization, announced in January that thousands of children in China were allowed to die every year from medical neglect and starvation in China's state-run orphanages. A Chinese doctor, who worked in a Shanghai orphanage before fleeing China in 1995, supplied evidence that children with disabilities were denied treatment and allowed to die because they were unlikely candidates for adoption. Officials denied the allegation, but later publicly stated that China lacked the money to care for all of the nation's orphaned and disabled children.

Trouble in Tibet. On June 1, 1996, Chinese authorities presided at Tibetan Buddhist ceremonies initiating a 7-year-old boy as the incarnation of the Panchen Lama, the second most important religious leader of Tibet after the Dalai Lama. Chinese officials used the initiation to argue that Tibet was historically a part of China.

In May 1995, the Dalai Lama, living in exile in India, had proclaimed another boy the incarnated Panchen Lama. The previous Panchen Lama died in 1989. The Chinese had denounced the Dalai Lama's selection as another effort to separate Tibet from China. On May 29, 1996, Chinese officials admitted that the boy chosen by the Dalai Lama, together with his family, had been taken into custody.

Also in May, Tibetan monks at Ganden Monastery attacked police for banning photographs of the Dalai Lama, and rioting broke out in other monasteries. In May and July, two monks died while serving prison sentences for opposing Chinese rule. In August, Chinese officials stated that an education campaign was underway in Tibet to instill love of the Communist Party and respect for its laws.

Xinjiang separatism. A Communist directive in May 1996 stated that stability in Xinjiang, China's western province, was endangered by a separatist movement and religious unrest. Muslims of the Uighur ethnic majority in Xinjiang had long opposed Chinese rule and the influx of Chinese settlers. At least four antigovernment organizations were reported operating in Xinjiang during 1996, and some government officials were known to have been assassinated. But the government denied reports that 450 soldiers and 20 other people had been killed in street clashes during 1996. The government reportedly arrested more than 5,000 Uighurs during 1996.

Summer floods along the Yangtze River and in other parts of China killed at least 2,700 people in 1996 and left more than 4.4 million homeless. The 1996 disaster brought the number of deaths caused by summer floods in China to 20,000 since 1990. The Yellow River, the source of China's worst recorded floods, crested at a record level in 1996, but did not overflow its dikes.

China fired missiles into the sea within 30 miles (48 kilometers) of Taiwan's two main ports shortly before Taiwan's first direct presidential elections on March 23. China feared that Taiwan might be moving closer to declaring itself an independent nation. In 1949, after mainland China was taken over by Communists, Chiang Kai-shek's Nationalist government established itself on the island of Taiwan. Since then, officials of both Taiwan and China claimed to represent all of China.

Some 150,000 Chinese troops participated in military exercises across the Taiwan Strait, the channel that separates China from Taiwan. The United States moved two naval battle groups closer to Taiwan as a warning to China. In April, China refused to resume talks on cooperation with Taiwan, but called for political talks in August. Taiwanese businessmen had more than $20 billion invested in China, and China apparently wanted to keep ties open in order to attract capital needed for modernization.

Satellite launch failures. On Feb. 15, 1996, a rocket set to lift a communications satellite into or-

bit exploded, killing six people and seriously injuring 57 others. On August 18, a similar rocket failed to lift a U.S.-made satellite into proper orbit, the fifth failure in three years. China had hoped to become a global player in the satellite-launching industry.

Nuclear tests. China detonated nuclear devices underground on June 8 and July 29, 1996, but announced that the July blast—the 44th Chinese nuclear explosion detected abroad—would be the last.

U.S. trade relations. During May and June 1996, a long-standing dispute over Chinese piracy of compact discs (making and selling discs without paying royalties to copyright holders) nearly caused a trade war. The United States threatened to impose *tariffs* (taxes on imported goods) on $2 billion worth of Chinese imports. After China promised to crack down on the piracy, the two nations agreed on the protection of intellectual property rights.

U.S. customs inspectors found widespread fraud in the shipment of Chinese-made clothing to the United States. To evade U.S. quotas, the clothing bore false labels from other countries. High technology equipment sold to China for civilian uses turned up in arms factories, further straining China's relations with the United States.

On March 6, 1996, the U.S. State Department reported that China continued "to commit widespread and well-documented human rights abuses." Nonetheless, on May 20, U.S. President Bill Clinton announced he was renewing China's "most favored nation" status, which gave China broad trade privileges with America.

Economic problems. China's population increased by 13.5 million people in 1996. Chinese leaders, worried about meeting future food demands, urged farmers to grow more grain. Worldwatch Institute, a U.S. organization, warned in April that by the year 2030 China might need to import nearly twice the 1995 total of all world grain exports. Other experts doubted that the situation would become that desperate.

In 1996, industrial output in China continued to rise, but at a slower rate. Cars and other new luxury goods piled up because poorly paid workers could not afford them. State-owned industries employed 100 million workers, but many operated at a loss and were given government subsidies, which drained the national budget. The government, however, did not dare close industries or fire unneeded workers for fear of political repercussions.

Premier Li in a March 5 report to the National People's Congress claimed that China was achieving tremendous economic advances. But he also noted problems of high inflation, corruption, "poor public order in some places," stagnant farm production, and a wide gap in incomes.　　　□ Henry S. Bradsher

See also **Asia** (Facts in brief table); **China** Special Report: **China After Deng; Taiwan.** In *World Book,* see **China.**

CHINA AFTER DENG

Deng Xiaoping transformed China into a global
economic power. As he fades from the scene,
new leaders vying for control face an array of
problems unleashed by Deng's reforms.

By Joseph Fewsmith

In 1996, China's paramount leader, 93-year-old Deng Xiaoping, was physically incapacitated and could no longer be considered politically active. As he faded from the scene, there were increasingly frequent signs that new leaders were jockeying for power, including transparent efforts to curtail the influence of the Deng family. Chinese leaders also moved to distance themselves from Deng. This was ironic, but understandable. While Deng realized China's century-old dream of regaining a position of "wealth and power," an achievement for which he deserves an honored place in Chinese history, a new regime must establish its own agenda. Furthermore, Deng's reforms left many difficult problems for any new leadership to resolve.

China's internal difficulties were compounded by a variety of international problems, stemming from the nation's emergence not only as a major economic player, but also as a significant political power. In 1996, the world was wary of China, uncertain whether the Asian giant wanted to join the international system or change it. Problems were particularly acute in China's own backyard, where it had territorial disputes with many of its neighbors. In 1995 and 1996, conflict with Taiwan—which China regarded as a renegade province—boiled over in extensive military exercises that were intended as a show of power but had the potential for shaking the peace and stability of the western Pacific.

China, in turn, had its own concerns about other nations, particularly about the United States. By the mid-1990's, Chinese leaders had developed a growing tendency to view the United States as attempting to "contain" China. This tendency fed a strain of nationalist feeling, which began to influence the development of Chinese domestic politics.

Deng Xiaoping's fading from the political scene marked an important turning point in Chinese history and in China's relations with the world. Deng's 18-year reign as China's leader unleashed changes in China's life as radical in their way as the transformation of Chinese society set into motion by Mao Zedong, who led the Chinese Communist Party (CCP) to power in 1949 and died in 1976. Deng's passing may be of greater significance than Mao's. It would inevitably bring fundamental changes to China's political system, and, unlike Mao's death, bring into question the viability of Communist rule in China. Even if the CCP remained in power, which seemed likely, the nature of its rule would nevertheless change.

Deng's life

Deng Xiaoping became a Communist during his stay in France as a work-study student in the early 1920's. He joined the Chinese Communist Party in 1924. When fighting between the Chinese Communists and the ruling Nationalists broke out in China in 1927, Deng threw himself into revolutionary work. As one of the military leaders who led the CCP to victory in 1949, he developed a reputation as an outstanding military strategist as well as a skilled administrator. After the revolution succeeded, Deng worked briefly in his native province in southwestern China before moving to Beijing, the capital, where in 1956 he was appointed general secretary of the CCP, then one of China's highest posts.

Although Deng was closely associated with Mao Zedong during the revolutionary years, he was always more practical than the visionary, indeed utopic, Mao. As Mao's policies became more radical during the late 1950's and early 1960's, Deng increasingly found himself at odds with the top leader. When Mao launched the Cultural Revolution in 1966, which was an attempt to return Chinese society to Communist principles, Deng, after president Liu Shaoqi, became the second most prominent victim of Mao's purges of party officials. While exiled from power, Deng worked part-time in a tractor factory in rural Jiangxi province in south-central China.

Deng's exposure to the outside world during his stay in France, his experience as a pragmatic and capable administrator, and his victimization during the Cultural Revolution all contributed to his zeal for reform once he returned to power. Convinced that China had wasted 20 years on meaningless disputes over ideology, Deng determined to set ideology aside and concentrate on economic development. The slogans "practice is the sole criterion of truth" and "seek truth from facts" captured the pragmatic ethos of Deng's goals.

Deng's reforms

Deng's economic reforms began in the countryside. For 20 years, China under Mao had squeezed wealth from the countryside by forcing peasants to join communes. Communes were both economic and political units that, in theory, were to promote growth by eliminating small-sized, individual farms and to encourage all workers to labor for the whole community. In reality, communes destroyed economic opportunities, undermined incentives, and bound peasants under tight political control. The result was rural stagnation. For two decades, rural incomes barely rose and actually declined in many areas. In 1978, more than one-quarter of China's rural population earned an annual per capita income of less than 50 yuan ($25 at the then prevailing exchange rate) and lived in dire poverty.

The author

Joseph Fewsmith is an Associate Professor in the department of international relations at Boston University.

In 1978, local reform-minded officials associated with Deng began allowing peasants to grow their own grain on individual plots of land. Peasants could not own the plots, but after paying a fixed amount of grain to the state as a tax, they were allowed to sell surpluses at markets. This system, which became known as the household responsibility system, gave peasants an incentive to tend their crops carefully. Peasants soon grew more grain—and made more money—under this system than under the old commune system. In 1983, communes were dissolved throughout the country.

Reform of China's industrial sector was more complex. Deng had two problems: The first problem involved prices. The prices of manufactured goods in China had been frozen for two decades despite great changes in the range of products and the types of technology used to make them. The economy could not function efficiently with prices that did not reflect changes in supply and demand. Deng's second problem involved the products themselves. For years, state-owned factories had produced whatever the state's plan dictated, and all profits were turned back to the state. Deng realized that China's factories needed to be given incentives to make products people wanted to buy.

China under Deng followed a step-by-step approach to reform the industrial sector. Plans were drawn for new pricing policies and an increased emphasis on market forces both for what kind of products state-owned factories would produce and the quantity.

However, local factories—referred to as township and village enterprises—developed differently. Most of these facilities did not exist when Deng came to power. His plan allowed townships and villages to develop, operate, and own industries that from their inception were to make market-driven products. Large numbers of peasants, freed from agriculture by Deng's rural reforms, sought and found employment in these factories. The factories became such a large part of the industrial sector that by 1996 they were manufacturing more than one-half of China's total industrial production. Goods produced in the township and village enterprises made up 20 percent of China's exports in 1996.

After agricultural and industrial reform, Deng's third goal was to open China's economy to the world—a decision that had an enormous impact on the nation's economic development. In 1978, China's *foreign trade* (the combined total of exports and imports) amounted to only $21 billion. By 1995, the figure had risen 13-fold to over $280 billion, and China could claim 11th place among the world's trading nations. China's global focus has also permitted foreign investment, particularly from Hong Kong. Businesses based in Hong Kong invested heavily in the rural enterprises, which used inexpensive labor to produce goods for the international market.

Prosperity's problems

Rural and industrial reforms coupled with opening China to the outside world produced one of the remarkable economic growth stories of recent times. In 1978, when Deng came to power, the average income of Chinese peasants amounted to the equivalent of only $72 a year. Urban residents fared somewhat better at the equivalent of

Revolutionary leaders
China's top Communist leader, Mao Zedong, *above left,* worked closely with Deng Xiaoping, *above right,* during the nation's early revolutionary years. But Deng became a prominent victim of Mao's purges during the Cultural Revolution, which began in 1966.

Producing for profit
Peasant farmers bring their produce to sell on market day in Guilin, an inland city in southeastern China. Under Deng, peasants began to cultivate individual plots without state interference, giving them incentives to increase production for their own profit. Mao Zedong's commune system tied the peasants to the land economically and politically.

Workers check computer monitors in a factory in Shenzhen, an experimental free-market zone in southeast China, where economic growth has soared. Deng's industrial reforms created factories that produced the type of goods dictated by the marketplace, a radical departure from Mao's state-owned factories, which made goods dictated by a central plan.

$158 a year. By 1996, income had risen significantly. The World Bank estimated that China's per capita income was approximately the equivalent of earning $1,500 per year. This was more like the rate of middle-income, rather than developing, countries. Many experts predicted that China would be one of the world's largest economies by early to mid-21st century.

The rapid economic progress and change that took place in China under Deng's reforms also brought great social problems. Because rural reforms brought about more efficient use of labor, many people became either underemployed or unemployed. Despite the growth of rural industries, which in 1996 provided jobs for more than 100 million workers, as many as 150 million remained underemployed. In the search for a better life, many peasants migrated to urban areas. This was not allowed before Deng came to power. Although most of the migrants to the cities found work, many turned to crime.

Many peasants who stayed in the countryside, particularly those in poorer inland areas, found themselves squeezed by the low prices paid for their grain, the high prices of fertilizer, and the taxes imposed on them. The resulting peasant discontent touched off large and small disturbances throughout rural China. Outbreaks of violence in the provinces alarmed the leadership, and one leader was quoted as saying, "If there are problems in the villages, no one in the present regime can hold onto power."

The economy's mixture of market and nonmarket forces, the traditional importance of personal connections in Chinese society, and the breakdown of social norms contributed to a massive rise in corruption. The newly emerging middle class discovered that money could buy power, and bribery of officials at all levels became rampant. A decade of official campaigns against corruption failed to stem the tide.

China's social problems occurred against a backdrop of other complicating factors. The people retained little faith in Marxism as an ideology. Their increased well-being did not come from the state's control of the means of production, as Marx taught, but rather from

Shoppers find an extensive array of domestic and imported goods in a department store in Zhengzhou, testifying to Deng's success at refocusing China's economy on the consumer.

A surging global economy

Deng Xiaoping's agricultural and industrial reforms paved the way for explosive growth in China's world trade. When Deng came to power in 1978, China's foreign trade totaled only $21 billion. In the 1990's, China's exports and imports were calculated in hundreds of billions of dollars.

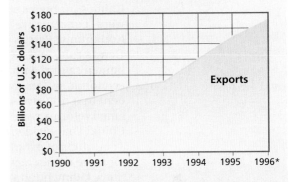

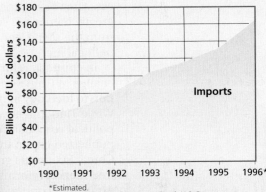

*Estimated.
Sources: International Monetary Fund; U.S. Department of Commerce, International Trade Administration.

the interplay of market forces, the hallmark of capitalism. Another factor was the growing independence of China's provinces, which increasingly pursued their own interests with less regard for Beijing's directives.

A range of political forces

As in other societies undergoing rapid and unsettling transitions, China's problems stirred political responses. Broadly speaking, there were "conservative" and "reformer" forces at work within the Communist Party's political elite. Both groups were active for most of Deng's rule. In the Chinese context, conservatives sought to combine limited reform with a continuation of Communist ideology and an economic system guided by state plans. Long before a crucial incident that occurred in June 1989, conservatives felt that market-oriented reforms were undermining the basis of Communist rule in China. That incident occurred in Tiananmen Square in Beijing. Thousands of people, most of them students, staged a demonstration for more democracy in China. The military crushed the demonstrations, killing hundreds, perhaps thousands, of protesters in the process. After Tiananmen, the influence of conservative leaders was greatly increased. While a number of conservative leaders passed from the scene, conservatism remained a potent force in Chinese political life.

In contrast, reformers, like Deng, envisioned a much greater change to China's economic system. In general, they paid less attention to ideology and were willing to allow market forces to dominate. While Tiananmen was a major setback for reformers, they staged a political comeback after January 1992, when Deng went on a highly publicized trip to the Shenzhen Special Economic Zone in southeast China. Economic growth in the zone had soared under experimental free-market reforms. Nevertheless, social problems as a result of explosive economic growth raised doubts about the immediate future for reforms as Deng's influence waned.

A tier of younger leaders were waiting to take control once Deng was out of the picture. Most of these men fell into two camps: neoauthoritarians or neoconservatives. Neoauthoritarians believed in the use of state power to bring about a rapid shift to a complete market economy. They believed that rapid change would not only promote economic development but would also lessen many social problems by removing some of the underlying economic causes. In their quest to modernize China, neoauthoritarians looked to the examples of the authoritarian market economies of East Asia, especially Taiwan, South Korea, and Singapore.

Neoconservatives sought a slower transition to a market economy. They envisioned a greater role for the state in direct management of the economy. Although both neoauthoritarians and neoconservatives desired a strong central government, neoconservatives, generally, were more inclined to look for an ideological system that could again focus the loyalty of the people. Neoauthoritarians instead looked to

Shanties in the shadow of newly constructed skyscrapers in Shenzhen provide makeshift shelter for peasant laborers seeking work in the city, *above*.

the construction of efficient bureaucratic systems and reliance on laws and regulations to attain their goals.

China's leaders of both conservative and reform persuasion were challenged by Chinese society itself, which underwent very rapid changes. The period in which Chinese society was described as a passive "sea of blue ants"— a reference to the blue Mao jackets that everyone wore—has long passed. New generations with new desires have come to the fore. The opening up of China and the growth of the economy generated new tastes—often influenced by Hong Kong and Taiwan pop culture—and a growing affluence with which to satisfy those tastes. Diversification of the economy and greater job mobility made the people less dependent on the state. Chinese society displayed an energy and vitality not evident 20 or even 10 years before. China watchers came to believe that as the Chinese population became wealthier and better educated, new voices would demand to be heard. Whether the government would attempt to accommodate or repress rising social demands remained to be seen.

In the late 1980's and particularly following the Tiananmen crackdown, many Chinese youth looked to the West rather than to Communist ideology as a source of political and social idealism. By the mid-1990's, however, the government of China had recaptured a degree of legitimacy that seemed impossible only a few years before.

Police apprehend drug traffickers along China's border with Burma. Crime of all kinds has risen in China in great part because of the immense social change that accompanied Deng's economic reforms.

CHINA'S LEADERSHIP IN 1996

Li Peng, premier of the State Council of the People's Republic of China, *top row, left.*

Jiang Zemin, president of the People's Republic of China and general secretary of the Chinese Communist Party, *top row, right.*

Zhu Rongji, vice premier of the State Council of the People's Republic of China, *bottom row, left.*

Li Ruihuan, chairman of the National Committee of the Chinese People's Political Consultative Conference, *bottom row, right.*

China's new younger leaders, *above,* have risen through bureaucracies and tend to be more cautious than Deng Xiaoping.

The government's success resulted in part from its ability to reduce inflation and trigger the unprecedented economic boom, which began in the early 1990's. The government also used nationalist feelings to bolster this legitimacy. This was possible because of a widespread feeling that the United States and other nations were trying to hold China down.

China, however, found that promoting nationalism could backfire. In March 1996, China attempted to disrupt Taiwan's pending presidential elections by aiming unarmed missiles at Taiwan ports. China then prepared to test live ammunition near Taiwan, triggering the United States to move two aircraft carrier battle groups into the area as a show of support for the elections. Stirred by nationalism, Chinese students planned protest demonstrations at the U.S. embassy in Beijing. The Chinese government, fearing violence, stopped the protests. The government also canceled commemorations of the start of the Sino-Japanese War of 1937 for fear the ceremonies would spiral out of control.

A new generation of leaders

For 18 years, the forces unleashed by Deng's reforms were more or less contained by the old political system. The same political formula was unlikely to work indefinitely. With the death of Deng and the passing of the generation that fought and won the revolution, it was inevitable that political power would pass to a younger generation.

The new, younger leaders were less ideological and more bureaucratic than their elders. They included General Secretary Jiang Zemin, Premier Li Peng, Vice Premier Zhu Rongji, Qiao Shi, the head of China's legislative body, the National People's Congress (NPC), and

Li Ruihuan, chairman of the National Committee of the Chinese People's Political Consultative Conference. They were described often as technocrats and had spent their careers in bureaucracies. Whereas the elder revolutionaries seemed confident in their ability to unleash and then rein in social forces, the younger generation appeared to be more cautious, which suggested that China's political system would evolve slowly under new leadership. This might be good for China, which has had more than its share of upheaval during the past 100 years.

The new leaders' tendency toward caution could be upset for two reasons: First, there were clear differences among these leaders that were likely to worsen as the succession struggle unfolded. Li Peng has been closely identified with the conservative wing of the Communist Party, and Jiang Zemin had expressed approval of some neoconservative ideas. In contrast, Zhu Rongji fell into the neoauthoritarian school of thought, and Qiao Shi appeared to be most responsive to public opinion and the need for law.

Second, it was inevitable that new issues would arise to exacerbate the tensions among the leadership. Whether the issues were economic policy, rural riots, or a new round of social protests similar to Tiananmen Square in 1989, China's leaders were bound to respond in different ways. Some would seek to contain and repress protest, while others would seek ways to incorporate new demands into China's social fabric. Just how the divided leadership responded to emerging social and economic issues would determine to a great extent the shape of China's political future.

China's global influence

The domestic political changes underway in China in 1996 would have a major influence on the world. As one of the five permanent members of the United Nations Security Council, China exerted considerable influence on international affairs. With 1.2 billion people, China's other major influence was economic. China represented both a huge export market and a labor market, which many foreign investors had already recognized by 1996.

If China's political transition was peaceful, if its political system was opened gradually, and if its economy was internationalized, then China could take its place as a responsible member of the world community. If, however, China was to repress the emerging forces or try to co-opt them through nationalism, then it could be a disruptive force. The political transition underway was likely to determine whether China was to become an influential citizen of the world, a disruptive force—or something in between. ■ ■ ■

Chrétien, Jean, Canada's prime minister since 1993, saw his Liberal Party government remain generally popular throughout the country in 1996, except in his native province of Quebec. However, polls released in May showed that Chrétien's own approval rating had fallen to 47 percent, down 21 points from the previous year. In Quebec, his performance ratings languished at 24 percent.

Chrétien contended that a certain slippage in popularity was to be expected after three years in office. But critics accused the prime minister of lacking qualities of leadership. They also pointed to voter dissatisfaction with cutbacks in government services and the Liberals' handling of the Quebec problem. Political opponents also criticized Chrétien's reversals on promises made during the 1993 electoral campaign, such as his pledges to eliminate the unpopular goods and services tax.

Conservative course. During 1996, Chrétien continued to pursue a political agenda a little to the right of center that recalled many of the policies of Prime Minister Brian Mulroney, his Progressive Conservative Party predecessor. Chrétien implemented the North American Free Trade Agreement, though he had railed against the pact when he served as the leader of the opposition in the House of Commons.

In its 1996-1997 budget, Chrétien's government continued to reduce the federal deficit to a level lower than that attempted by the Progressive Conservatives. He introduced sweeping changes in Canada's social programs and gave the provinces more flexibility to carry them out.

Quebec problem. Chrétien's greatest challenge continued to be the threat posed by Quebec's independence movement. The prime minister seemed ill at ease in coping with the political dynamics in his home province. His dismal ratings in Quebec were especially worrisome for a leader whose party controlled only 19 of Quebec's 75 seats in the House of Commons. Most of these seats were in the Montreal area, which has a large English-speaking population. In French-speaking areas of Quebec, the Liberals commanded little or no support.

Although many Canadians believed Chrétien should take a firm line with the separatists, the prime minister resisted this approach, reluctant to embark on policies that might antagonize moderate opinion in Quebec. Instead, he worked to transfer more federal powers to the provinces, warned Quebeckers of the economic losses they would face if they embraced separatism, and made job creation for all Canadians a priority. As Canada moved toward a general election in 1997, Chrétien wrestled with the daunting problem of convincing his fellow Quebeckers that their best interests lay with an undivided Canada. □ David M. L. Farr

See also **Canada.** In *World Book,* see **Chrétien, Jean.**

City. In mid-1996, attention became focused on the state of the world's cities. The global human population was approximately 5.6 billion and growing at the rate of about 250,000 a day. Nearly half the total—2.5 billion—lived in cities, compared with only one-third of the population in the mid-1900's. Estimates showed that the trend toward expansion of urban areas would continue into the next century. By 2025, the world population was expected to double to 10.6 billion. Experts projected that two-thirds—about 7 billion people—would live in cities.

United Nations population report. In May, the United Nations Fund for Population Activities (UNPF) issued a report entitled "The State of World Population 1996." United Nations (UN) statistics showed that there were 14 *megacities* (metropolitan areas with more than 10 million residents) in the world in 1996. By the year 2015, the report predicted, this number would grow to 27. Furthermore, the list of the world's 10 largest cities would be almost completely changed. With the exception of the world's largest city—Tokyo, with an estimated 1996 population of 28.7 million—all of the 10 largest cities by 2015 were expected to be in developing nations: Bombay, India; Lagos, Nigeria; Shanghai; Jakarta, Indonesia; São Paulo, Brazil; Karachi, Pakistan; Beijing; Dhaka, Bangladesh; and Mexico City.

In the face of such rapid growth, the report noted, developing countries would be hard pressed to provide adequate public and social services to ever-increasing numbers of people. A spokesman for the United Nations Fund for Population Activities, during a press conference announcing the publication of the report, remarked that proper planning and social investment would determine whether the emerging cities of the 2000's become "engines of economic activity and centers of culture and creativity or slums that breed poverty, crime, disease, and environmental degradation."

City Summit. Delegates representing 171 countries met in Istanbul, Turkey, in June 1996 for the United Nations Conference on Human Settlements—also known as Habitat II. Unlike previous international conferences, this self-described "city summit" gave municipal leaders an important role.

During a speech to the delegates, Wally N'Dow, head of the UN Center for Human Settlements and secretary-general of the conference, remarked that if nations would redirect just 5 percent of their military budgets toward improving their cities during the next 10 years, the world would be able to begin dealing effectively with the problems posed by increasing urban growth. "The resources exist to bring safe water and sanitation and a roof over the head of people everywhere—women, men, and children on this planet earth, our global village," N'Dow said.

The 12-day Istanbul conference was the second UN-sponsored international conference held to discuss the future of the world's cities. The first conference, known as Habitat I, was held in Vancouver, Canada, in 1976. The Vancouver conference was dominated by participants from central governments, and while many ambitious promises about the future were made, virtually none were achieved. Instead, the conference bogged down in ideological bickering among the industrialized and developing nations and the countries of the former Soviet bloc.

The rapid urbanization of developing nations, characterized by high birth rates and rural migration, created social and environmental pressures—such as inadequate water supplies, traffic jams, pollution, overcrowded dwellings, and sanitation problems—that dominated the agenda in Istanbul. In many developing cities, sewage was being released into streams and oceans. India, the world's second most populous country after China in 1996, had 3,000 cities and towns, but only eight complete waste-water-treatment plants. About 500 million people in cities around the world were homeless or poorly housed. In Addis Ababa, the capital of Ethiopia, 79 percent of the population was either homeless or lived in inadequate housing. More than 50 percent of the populations of Bogotá, Colombia, and Jakarta, Indonesia, lived in substandard housing or were homeless. Such problems were familiar to industrialized cities, but not as serious, because growth has been far slower and resources far greater.

Even as central governments turned their attention and resources away from cities in 1996, rapid growth meant cities took on more responsibility for their own futures. The convergence of different races and cultures within growing cities fostered more democratic, open political pressures. Nowhere has this change to local government been more in evidence than Latin America. There, a reaction against dictatorships and debt crises has encouraged a massive transfer of decision-making authority and spending power from federal to city governments. Since 1986, more than 12,000 cities and towns in Latin America have elected mayors and councilors—a new generation of city politicians with new ideas for improving their cities.

The 1996 City Summit concluded that the emerging trend was moving toward cities that are self-dependent, rather than dependent on a central government. The increased participation of local leaders as in Istanbul and in countries around the world in 1996 was seen as a potential source of strength and hope for future change. Looking ahead, the increasing importance of cities seemed certain to force other changes in the world.

Suburbanization. A study of U.S. census data published in June by Harvard University's Joint Center for Housing Studies revealed that population growth in suburbs surrounding major U.S. cities was 10 times greater than in cities proper. From 1990 to 1994, city population (within city boundaries) of

50 largest cities in the world

Rank	Urban center*	Population
1.	Tokyo-Yokohama, Japan	28,743,000
2.	Mexico City, Mexico	24,645,000
3.	São Paulo, Brazil	22,241,000
4.	Seoul, South Korea	19,606,000
5.	New York City, U.S.	14,639,000
6.	Osaka-Kobe-Kyoto, Japan	14,105,000
7.	Bombay, India	13,874,000
8.	Calcutta, India	13,116,000
9.	Rio de Janeiro, Brazil	13,048,000
10.	Buenos Aires, Argentina	12,364,000
11.	Teheran, Iran	12,146,000
12.	Manila, Philippines	11,624,000
13.	Jakarta, Indonesia	11,459,000
14.	Cairo, Egypt	11,412,000
15.	Moscow, Russia	10,838,000
16.	Los Angeles, U.S.	10,473,000
17.	Delhi, India	10,426,000
18.	Lagos, Nigeria	10,280,000
19.	Karachi, Pakistan	9,704,000
20.	London, U.K.	8,831,000
21.	Paris, France	8,772,000
22.	Lima, Peru	8,109,000
23.	Istanbul, Turkey	7,856,000
24.	Taipei, Taiwan	7,671,000
25.	Essen, Germany	7,339,000
26.	Shanghai, China	7,262,000
27.	Bogotá, Colombia	7,010,000
28.	Bangkok, Thailand	6,831,000
29.	Madras, India	6,707,000
30.	Chicago, U.S.	6,546,000
31.	Pusan, South Korea	5,924,000
32.	Santiago, Chile	5,904,000
33.	Beijing, China	5,890,000
34.	Hong Kong	5,864,000
35.	Bangalore, India	5,848,000
36.	Dhaka, Bangladesh	5,512,000
37.	Lahore, Pakistan	5,148,000
38.	Tianjin, China	5,091,000
39.	Nagoya, Japan	5,073,000
40.	Madrid, Spain	4,836,000
41.	Milan, Italy	4,804,000
42.	Kinshasa, Zaire	4,721,000
43.	St. Petersburg, Russia	4,703,000
44.	Baghdad, Iraq	4,692,000
45.	Barcelona, Spain	4,558,000
46.	Belo Horizonte, Brazil	4,512,000
47.	Shenyang, China	4,501,000
48.	Ahmadabad, India	4,318,000
49.	Hyderabad, India	4,264,000
50.	Ho Chi Minh City, Vietnam	4,143,000

*An urban center is a continuous built-up area, similar to a metropolitan area, having a population density of at least 5,000 persons per square mile (1,900 per square kilometer).
Source: 1996 estimates based on data from the U.S. Bureau of the Census.

50 largest cities in the United States

Rank	City	Population*	Percent change in population since 1990	Unemployment rate†	Mayor‡
1.	New York City	7,333,253	+0.1	7.8%	Rudolph W. Giuliani (R, 12/97)
2.	Los Angeles	3,448,613	-1.1	8.3	Richard J. Riordan (R, 6/97)
3.	Chicago	2,731,743	-1.9	5.2	Richard M. Daley (D, 4/99)
4.	Houston	1,702,086	+4.4	6.6	Bob Lanier (NP, 12/99)
5.	Philadelphia	1,524,249	-3.9	6.2	Edward G. Rendell (D, 1/00)
6.	San Diego	1,151,977	+3.7	5.5	Susan Golding (NP, 12/00)
7.	Phoenix	1,048,949	+6.6	3.8	Skip Rimsza (NP, 12/99)
8.	Dallas	1,022,830	+1.5	4.8	Ronald Kirk (NP, 5/99)
9.	San Antonio	998,905	+6.8	5.4	William E. Thornton (NP, 6/97)
10.	Detroit	992,038	-3.5	4.5	Dennis Archer (D, 1/98)
11.	San Jose	816,884	+4.4	3.7	Susan Hammer (NP, 12/98)
12.	Indianapolis	752,279	+2.9	3.5	Stephen Goldsmith (R, 12/99)
13.	San Francisco	734,676	+1.5	4.3	Willie L. Brown, Jr. (D, 1/00)
14.	Baltimore	702,979	-4.5	5.9	Kurt L. Schmoke (D, 12/99)
15.	Jacksonville, Fla.	665,070	+4.7	3.9	John A. Delaney (R, 7/99)
16.	Columbus, Ohio	635,913	+0.5	3.2	Gregory S. Lashutka (R, 12/99)
17.	Milwaukee	617,044	-1.8	4.0	John O. Norquist (D, 4/00)
18.	Memphis	614,289	-0.7	4.8	W. W. Herenton (D, 12/99)
19.	El Paso	579,307	+12.4	13.5	Larry Francis (NP, 7/97)
20.	Washington, D.C.	567,094	-6.6	4.3	Marion S. Barry, Jr. (D, 1/99)
21.	Boston	547,725	-4.6	4.3	Thomas M. Menino (D, 1/98)
22.	Seattle	520,947	+0.9	4.5	Norman B. Rice (NP, 12/97)
23.	Austin	514,013	+10.4	3.5	Bruce Todd (NP, 6/97)
24.	Nashville	504,505	+3.3	3.4	Philip Bredesen (D, 9/99)
25.	Denver	493,559	+5.5	4.2	Wellington E. Webb (D, 6/97)
26.	Cleveland	492,901	-2.5	5.2	Michael R. White (D, 12/97)
27.	New Orleans, La.	484,149	-2.6	7.4	Marc Morial (D, 5/98)
28.	Oklahoma City, Okla.	463,201	+4.2	3.4	Ronald J. Norick (NP, 4/98)
29.	Fort Worth, Tex.	451,814	+0.9	4.7	Kenneth Barr (NP, 5/97)
30.	Portland, Ore.	450,777	+2.7	4.2	Vera Katz (NP, 12/00)
31.	Kansas City, Mo.	443,878	+2.1	4.0	Emanuel Cleaver II (D, 4/99)
32.	Charlotte, N.C.	437,797	+10.6	3.3	Pat McCrory (R, 11/99)
33.	Tucson, Ariz.	434,726	+6.4	3.7	George Miller (D, 12/99)
34.	Long Beach, Calif.	433,852	+1.1	8.3	Beverly O'Neill (D, 6/98)
35.	Virginia Beach, Va.	430,295	+9.5	5.5	Meyera E. Oberndorf (NP, 6/00)
36.	Albuquerque, N. Mex.	411,994	+7.1	5.4	Martin J. Chavez (D, 11/97)
37.	Atlanta, Ga.	396,052	+0.5	4.0	Bill Campbell (D, 12/97)
38.	Fresno, Calif.	386,551	+9.2	12.6	Jim Patterson (NP, 1/01)
39.	Honolulu, Hawaii	385,881	+2.3	5.6	Jeremy Harris (D, 1/01)
40.	Tulsa, Okla.	374,851	+2.1	3.7	M. Susan Savage (D, 5/98)
41.	Sacramento, Calif.	373,964	+1.2	6.2	Joe Serna, Jr. (D, 11/00)
42.	Miami, Fla.	373,024	+4.0	7.6	Joe Carollo (R, 11/97)
43.	St. Louis, Mo.	368,215	-7.2	4.7	Freeman R. Bosley, Jr. (D, 4/97)
44.	Oakland, Calif.	366,926	-1.4	5.1	Elihu Mason Harris (NP, 12/98)
45.	Pittsburgh, Pa.	358,883	-3.0	5.0	Thomas Murphy (D, 12/97)
46.	Cincinnati, Ohio	358,170	-1.6	4.6	Roxanne Qualls (D, 11/97)
47.	Minneapolis, Minn.	354,590	-3.7	3.2	Sharon Sayles Belton (D, 12/97)
48.	Omaha, Nebr.	345,033	+2.8	3.1	Hal Daub (R, 6/97)
49.	Las Vegas, Nev.	327,878	+27.0	5.5	Jan Laverty Jones (D, 6/99)
50.	Toledo, Ohio	322,550	-3.1	4.9	Carlton Finkbeiner (D, 12/97)

*1994 estimates (source: U.S. Bureau of the Census).
†June 1996 unemployment figures are for metropolitan areas (source: U.S. Bureau of Labor Statistics).
‡The letters in parentheses represent the mayor's party, with *D* meaning Democrat, *R* Republican, *I* Independent, and *NP* nonpartisan. The date is when the term of office ends (source: mayors' offices).

America's 39 largest cities increased by 1.7 million. Suburban populations during the same period grew by 17 million. In major cities, the study found, the average annual growth rate per 1,000 residents was 0.6. In suburbs, the rate was 15.1 per 1,000 residents.

This trend toward "suburbanization" presented challenges across the United States. In the mid-1990's, the governments of Los Angeles, Detroit, Washington, D.C., Boston, St. Louis, Atlanta, and Pittsburgh represented less than a quarter of their metropolitan areas. San Francisco represented less than one-tenth. Representatives from suburban legislative districts have come to dominate the majority of state legislatures.

While the percentage of people living in urban areas around major world cities has continued to grow, the percentage of people living within the cities has actually declined. The population within the city limits of Paris accounted for only one-fifth of the metropolitan population in the mid-1990's, and in Barcelona it accounted for about one-half. This trend pressured national governments to devote fewer resources to the cities and to place increased emphasis on metropolitan or regional governments.

New concept of "city." In the past, the largest cities in the world dominated world affairs. Size was synonymous with global economic power. But, in coming years, this may cease to be the case. In the 1990's, São Paulo, Mexico City, Shanghai, and Bombay joined the elite list of the world's largest cities. But despite their size, these cities were not as economically prosperous as large cities have been in the past. In the early 2000's, 17 megacities are expected to emerge in developing countries in Asia, Africa, and Latin America.

Just as "focusing" became a popular business strategy in the 1990's, cities that took advantage of the global marketplace became more dominant by focus than size. San Diego, the same size as Detroit, the former world automobile capital, appeared poised to capitalize on its diverse language and culture and its port facilities on the Pacific Rim to far surpass Detroit in global power and importance.

One of the most striking changes in urban population trends has come through the emergence of unofficial "city-states" that span regions and countries. These may one day replace the traditional model of cities as communities of fixed political boundaries. Italy's Po Valley, for example, contains a string of cities where the world's top fashion industry has flourished. Similarly, in America, "Silicon Valley," the suburban area between San Jose and San Francisco, is a cluster of cities that has become home to some of the world's most prolific developers of computers and other electronic products. These areas may best represent the trend of cities in the 21st century—interdependent centers of human creativity and commerce. □ Frank Shafroth

In *World Book*, see **City.**

Civil rights. California voters on Nov. 5, 1996, approved a measure to end all forms of affirmative action by public agencies in that state. Affirmative action refers to policies aimed at increasing the numbers of people from certain social groups and minorities—for example, women, African Americans, Hispanic Americans, and disabled people—in employment, education, business, government, and other areas. In general, affirmative action is intended to benefit groups that are thought to have suffered from discrimination.

In voting for the measure, California became the first state to go so far in dismantling government-imposed affirmative action. The measure—the California Civil Rights Initiative or Proposition 209—declared that the state "shall not discriminate against or grant preferential treatment to any individual or group on the basis of race, sex, color, ethnicity, or national origin in the operation of public employment, public education, or public contracting." A lawsuit to block the new law and another to compel immediate enforcement were filed after the vote.

Texaco controversy. Texaco Incorporated of White Plains, New York, the object of a lawsuit charging widespread racist employment practices, became embroiled in a controversy over allegedly racist remarks by company officials. On November 4, *The New York Times* reported on a meeting of Texaco officials during which they had allegedly made racial remarks. The remarks were secretly taped by Richard A. Lundwall, at the time a Texaco human resources coordinator, who allegedly offered to shred a document involved in a two-year racial discrimination suit against the company. The suit had been filed on behalf of 1,500 current and former black employees of Texaco.

The president of Texaco condemned the remarks, suspended several officials with pay, and announced a racial sensitivity program for company employees. Black leaders, however, called for a boycott of the company. On November 15, Texaco agreed to pay $176.1 million to settle the discrimination suit. The settlement included $115 million in cash, $26.1 million in pay raises over five years for black employees, and $35 million for sensitivity and diversity training programs. The settlement was subject to court approval. On November 19, federal prosecutors charged Lundwall with obstruction of justice for his alleged role in destroying documents.

College admissions. On March 19, the U.S. Court of Appeals for the Fifth Circuit in New Orleans, Louisiana, ruled that state-funded colleges and universities could not consider race in admissions decisions as a means of creating a diverse student body. The court decided that in 1992 the University of Texas School of Law in Austin had violated the constitutional rights of four white applicants by using admissions procedures that evaluated some black and Hispanic candidates separately. Although

An estimated 6,000 people march through Los Angeles on April 7 to protest the beating of two illegal immigrants by Riverside County deputies.

the ruling applied only to schools in Texas, Louisiana, and Mississippi, it cast doubt on all public university admissions policies based on the Supreme Court's 1978 *Bakke v. Board of Regents* decision, which forbade quotas in admissions to achieve racial balance but permitted the consideration of race as one factor in evaluating applicants. On July 1, 1996, the Supreme Court declined to review the decision.

Sex discrimination. The Virginia Military Institute (V.M.I.) in Lexington, Virginia, and The Citadel in Charleston, South Carolina—the only two state-funded, all-male military colleges in the United States—agreed to admit women students after the Supreme Court ruled on June 26 that V.M.I.'s gender-based admissions policy violated the equal protection guarantees of the 14th Amendment to the Constitution. In a 7 to 1 ruling, the justices declared that V.M.I.'s alternative program for female students at a nearby women's college was inadequate. The decision left the school with the options of admitting women or becoming a private institution.

Despite the Supreme Court decision, V.M.I. continued to deny admission forms to women. On September 10, the Justice Department filed an emergency motion with the circuit court demanding that the school admit women immediately. On September 20, V.M.I.'s governing board voted 9 to 8 to allow women into the program. The school planned to admit women students in the fall of 1997.

The 154-year-old Citadel, which had also waged a lengthy legal battle against admitting women and had established a separate women's program, announced on June 28, 1996, that it would accept both men and women into the same program. Four women enrolled in the fall of 1996.

Church fires. Arsons at small, African American churches in Southern states became a civil rights issue as African American leaders and some members of Congress questioned whether the federal government was doing enough to find the perpetrators and to determine if the attacks were racially motivated. Suspicious fires damaged or destroyed dozens of black churches in 11 Southern states, but a review of arson reports by a major news service revealed that criminals were targeting white churches as well.

Some civil rights leaders blamed the attacks on a nationwide climate of racial intolerance. On June 8, President Bill Clinton stated that although the federal government had failed to find evidence of a national racist conspiracy, racial hostility was a driving force in a number of the fires. He ordered increased federal efforts toward halting the fires and arresting the arsonists.

The exact number of fires and arrests differed according to what organization was reporting statistics. The Associated Press (AP) news service reported on July 4 that its review of federal, state, and local records revealed 73 fires at black churches and 75 fires at white churches between January 1995 and

July 1996. The AP said racism was clearly a motive in fewer than 20 of the cases. In September 1996, the Justice Department reported that approximately 100 people had been charged with setting fire to black churches since January 1995, and 34 percent of those charged were black. In October 1996, the National Fire Protection Association, a trade group in Quincy, Massachusetts, reported that arsonists had torched an estimated 520 churches in 1994, the last year for which data were available. According to the association, the church arsons had steadily fallen since 1980 when a record 1,420 churches were burned.

On June 7, 1996, members of the burned Macedonia Baptist Church near Sumter, South Carolina, filed a civil suit against the Christian Knights of the Ku Klux Klan, a white supremacist group in Mt. Holly, North Carolina. The church sued after two men connected to the supremacist group were charged with deliberately setting the June 1995 fire.

Homosexual rights. On May 20, 1996, the Supreme Court struck down an amendment to the state constitution of Colorado that banned state and local laws protecting homosexuals from discrimination. Voting 6 to 3, the justices ruled that the government cannot single out a group of people and deny them protections extended to others.

☐ Linda P. Campbell and Geoffrey A. Campbell

See also **Supreme Court of the United States.** In *World Book,* see **Civil rights.**

Classical music. In 1996, symphony orchestras in the United States commissioned more new works and programmed a higher percentage of works by U.S. composers than ever before. However, orchestras also faced declining public funding, constrained private contributions, and smaller audiences.

Both the number and variety of educational concerts rose as orchestras sought to attract new audiences, cultivate a new generation of listeners, and fill a growing void in public-school music programs. Orchestras also increased programs aimed at minorities. Although the total number of concerts remained relatively stable, a growing number of orchestras sought to escape the concert routine by offering pop music and theme-based concerts. A surge in the number of teen-age performers in concert halls proved to be a novel way of boosting a struggling classical music industry.

Tighter budgets caused friction between orchestra boards and musicians. In September 1996, strikes over wages silenced the Atlanta (Georgia) Symphony Orchestra, the Oregon Symphony in Portland, and the Philadelphia Orchestra.

In Philadelphia, one issue reflected an emerging problem for U.S. orchestras—the loss of income from recordings. With sales in the classical recording business falling, particularly in the standard symphonic repertory, record companies were cutting back their U.S. contracts. After EMI Classics ended its recording

The opera house, La Fenice, in Venice, Italy, is destroyed by a fire set by an arsonist on January 29. Reconstruction was expected to take three years.

contract with the Philadelphia Orchestra in August 1996, the orchestra's board announced it was cutting from the musicians' contracts a guaranteed payment from recordings and other media work. On September 16, the musicians went on strike. It ended on November 18 after the musicians' union and the board agreed to set up a jointly run company to oversee the orchestra's media work.

Record companies defended their cutbacks by noting that musicians' fees have made U.S. orchestras about 50 percent more expensive to record than their European counterparts. But the record companies themselves had contributed to the problem by flooding the market with less expensive compact disc reissues of classic performances. Most consumers preferred the cheaper classics over the more expensive modern recordings of the same music.

New operas. One of the most critically praised new operas in 1996 was *Emmeline,* the first opera by American composer Tobias Picker, with a libretto by J. D. McClatchy. The opera, based on Judith Rossner's 1980 novel of the same name, tells the true story of a factory worker who inadvertently marries her own son. The opera was premiered by the Santa Fe (New Mexico) Opera on July 27, 1996.

Brain Opera, an audience-participation piece that weaves together live and recorded music and speech as well as music transmitted over the Internet, was Tod Machover's contribution to the new Lincoln Center Festival '96 in New York City in July and August. Machover directs the Experimental Media Facility at the Massachusetts Institute of Technology in Cambridge. Critical opinion was divided between those who considered *Brain Opera* a prototype for opera in the 21st century and those who found it pretentious and empty.

Les Enfants Terribles—A Dance Opera Spectacle, the third work in composer Philip Glass's trilogy inspired by works by the French artist-director Jean Cocteau, premiered on June 4 at the Spoleto Festival USA in Charleston, South Carolina. Glass's collaborator was choreographer Susan Marshall.

The Picture of Dorian Gray, by American composer Lowell Liebermann, based on the 1890 novel by British author Oscar Wilde, was given its world premiere by the Opera de Monte-Carlo in Monaco in May 1996. The Houston Grand Opera staged the premiere of *Florencia en el Amazonas (Florence on the Amazon),* an opera by Mexican composer Daniel Catan, based on the stories of Colombian author Gabriel García Márquez, on October 25.

Two operas by Luciano Berio, Italy's most eminent living composer, highlighted international celebrations of Berio's 70th birthday. *Outis (Nobody),* based on the ancient Greek legend of Ulysses, premiered on October 5 at the La Scala Opera in Milan, Italy. Greek scholar Dario Del Corno wrote the libretto. The Lyric Opera of Chicago staged the U.S. premiere of Berio's acclaimed and complex 1984 work *Un Re in Ascolto (A King Listens)* on Nov. 9, 1996.

Symphonic, instrumental, and chamber music. American composer William Bolcom saw four premieres of his works played by the Baltimore Symphony Orchestra in 1996. On April 11, the orchestra presented *Gaea,* a three-part work for piano and orchestra written for two soloists, each of whom was playing with the left hand only. Leon Fleisher's performance of Piano Concerto No. 1 for Left Hand was followed by Gary Graffman's presentation of Concerto No. 2 for Left Hand. The two then played the pieces together as Concerto for Two Pianos Left Hand and Orchestra. On June 13, flutist James Galway and the Baltimore Symphony premiered Bolcom's Lyric Concerto for Flute and Orchestra.

The Los Angeles Philharmonic on May 23 presented the U.S. premiere of *Antiphonies* by Harrison Birtwistle, Great Britain's leading modernist composer. Three of Birtwistle's chamber and ensemble pieces—*Slow Frieze, Pulse Shadows: Meditations on Paul Celan,* and *Bach Measures*—had their premieres in April and May as part of "Secret Theatres," a major retrospective of Birtwistle's music at London's South Bank Centre.

Steven Stucky's *Pinturas de Tamayo (Paintings of Tamayo),* inspired by canvases by Mexican artist Rubino Tamayo, had its first presentation on March 28 by the Chicago Symphony Orchestra. The Ensemble Modern of Frankfurt, Germany, gave the first performance of American composer John Adams's *Scratchband* in Washington, D.C., on April 15. Ellen Taaffe Zwilich's Triple Concerto was premiered on February 7 by the Kalichstein-Laredo-Robinson Trio, for whom it was written, with the Minnesota Orchestra. American composer Joan Tower had her *Rapids* for piano and orchestra introduced by the University of Wisconsin Festival Orchestra in Madison on March 2.

Notable deaths in 1996 included those of Japanese composer Toru Takemitsu, 65, American Morton Gould, 82, and conductor Rafael Kubelik, 82. Takemitsu was the most important composer to bridge the musical worlds of East and West with materials drawn from traditional Japanese music and modernism of the 1900's. Gould, also a conductor and pianist, wrote music that successfully absorbed jazz and popular music into the language of the concert hall. Kubelik served as musical director of the Chicago Symphony Orchestra, the Royal Opera at Covent Garden, London, and the Metropolitan Opera, New York City. Miriam Gideon and Louise Talma, two of America's leading women composers, died, both at age 89. Also mourned was Dorothy Maynor, 85, an American soprano whose highly successful concert and recital career helped pave the way for later black artists. ☐ John von Rhein

See also **Popular music.** In *World Book,* see **Classical music; Opera.**

Clinton, Bill. President Bill Clinton was reelected on Nov. 5, 1996, the first Democratic president to win a second term in office since Franklin D. Roosevelt in 1936. Clinton swept to a decisive victory, taking 31 states and the District of Columbia to win 379 electoral votes. However, Clinton received only 49 percent of the popular vote, compared with 41 percent for Robert Dole and 8 percent for Ross Perot, the Reform Party candidate.

As 1996 began, the government shut-down that had begun in December 1995 continued, with Clinton and the Republican-led Congress locked in a budget stand-off. The government resumed services on Jan. 6, 1996, after Clinton and the Congress compromised on a budget. Clinton accepted the Republican concept of balancing the federal budget over a seven-year period. But he resisted Republican Party (GOP for Grand Old Party) attempts to enact deep reductions in projected Medicare outlays to help pay for a massive cut in income taxes, which Clinton said would benefit only wealthy Americans.

Legislation. From this stormy start, President Clinton and Congress compromised to pass major bills dealing with welfare, immigration, health care, telecommunications, and the minimum wage.

On April 10, the president vetoed a bill that would have banned a late-term abortion procedure. The Senate could not override his veto. But Clinton went along with Congress and signed on September 21 the controversial "Defense of Marriage Act," which denied federal recognition of same-sex marriages.

In August, Clinton moved away from traditional Democratic Party positions when he signed a welfare reform bill that ended federal cash assistance for poor families as an entitlement. The bill split Democrats in Congress, with liberals strongly criticizing it, some moderate Democrats voting for it, and Republicans supporting the measure. For Clinton, who promised to "end welfare as we know it" during his 1992 campaign, signing the welfare bill appeared to be an election-year necessity.

Clinton pleased Democrats by signing a bill on August 20 that raised the United States minimum wage from $4.25 to $5.15 an hour.

Personal and ethical issues kept the president on the defensive in 1996. His wife, Hillary Rodham Clinton, was called to testify before a federal grand jury by Kenneth Starr, the independent counsel conducting an investigation of Whitewater, a failed Arkansas real estate venture in which the Clintons had invested. In early 1996, missing records concerning Hillary Clinton's legal work for Madison Guaranty Savings & Loan of Little Rock, Arkansas, were discovered in the Clinton's private quarters in the White House. The first lady said she did not know how the records got there.

The owners of Madison Guaranty Savings & Loan in the 1980's, James McDougal and Susan McDougal, were partners with the Clintons in the Whitewater

President Bill Clinton campaigns in Michigan in August during a four-day, whistle-stop tour aboard his "21st Century Express" train.

Development Corporation. The McDougals were tried and convicted of filing fraudulent loan applications in an unrelated case. The president testified for the defense, on videotape, from the White House.

On August 29, the same night that the president accepted the Democratic Party nomination in Chicago, one of his close advisers, Dick Morris, was forced to resign after it was reported that he had carried on an affair with a prostitute.

The GOP-led Congress was expected to probe further into charges that the Clinton Administration improperly obtained Federal Bureau of Investigation files of more than 600 people, including prominent Republicans. Contributions to the Democratic Party from Indonesian business executives were expected to be the focus of congressional investigations as well.

Foreign policy. In mid-April, the president withdrew U.S. troops from Haiti after they helped keep the peace following the return to power of elected Haitian President Jean-Bertrand Aristide.

Clinton suffered a setback on May 29 when Benjamin Netanyahu beat Shimon Peres, whom Clinton endorsed, to become prime minister of Israel. In October, Clinton hosted a meeting in Washington between Netanyahu, Palestinian leader Yasir Arafat, and King Hussein of Jordan, which failed to produce significant progress toward peace between Israelis and Palestinians.

In September, the president ordered missile at-tacks on Iraq's military forces in retaliation for Iraqi leader Saddam Hussein's backing of a Kurdish faction in northern Iraq. Republican opponents said the U.S. attacks did nothing to weaken Saddam Hussein and were not backed by U.S. allies in the region.

In November, the president announced that he would keep some U.S. forces in Bosnia for an additional 18 months. Clinton had deployed troops there in November 1995 to help maintain peace among Serbs, Croats, and Bosnian Muslims.

Resignations. After the election, President Clinton was faced with rebuilding his Cabinet for his second term. Secretary of State Warren Christopher resigned the day after the election, and Secretary of Defense William Perry announced he would leave his post at the end of 1996. The president also accepted the resignations of Secretary of Energy Hazel O'Leary, Secretary of Labor Robert Reich, and Secretary of Housing and Urban Development Henry G. Cisneros. Leon Panetta, White House chief of staff, served notice he would return to his home state of California. Clinton named Erskine B. Bowles, a North Carolina businessman, to replace Panetta.

☐ William J. Eaton

See also **Congress of the United States; Democratic Party; Elections** Special Report: **How Americans Elected Their President; United States, Government of the.** In *World Book,* see **Clinton, Bill.**
Clothing. See Fashion.

Colombia. On Jan. 22, 1996, Fernando Botero Zea, former defense minister and President Ernesto Samper Pizano's 1994 campaign manager, publicly accused Samper of soliciting and knowingly accepting $6 million from Colombia's Cali drug cartel during the 1994 presidential campaign. The charge contributed to the political turmoil in a nation already ravaged by rampant drug corruption and rebel armies.

Botero's accusations were followed by a flurry of cabinet resignations. Leading politicians from the Liberal and Conservative parties, business leaders, and students demanded Samper's resignation. On June 12, 1996, however, Colombian House of Representative members, many of whom were themselves under investigation for campaign corruption, voted 111 to 43 to drop the charges against the president, which freed him from the threat of impeachment.

The United States reacted to the vote by publicly revoking Samper's U.S. visa on July 11. U.S. State Department spokesman Nicholas Burns commented, "People who knowingly assist narco-traffickers are not welcome in the U.S."

On September 5, Vice President Humberto de la Calle urged President Samper to resign, saying the country appeared "to be falling to pieces." On September 10, de la Calle himself resigned, citing the administration's irreparable "loss of credibility."

Rebel attacks. In August, rebels believed to belong to the Revolutionary Armed Forces of Colombia and the National Liberation Army carried out at least 10 attacks on police and military posts. In the worst attack, 500 rebels overran an army base in the southern Putumayo territory, leaving 54 soldiers dead, 17 wounded, and 26 missing—the highest casualty toll from a single guerrilla action in 40 years, according to Colombian military spokesmen.

Foreign-owned oil companies developed a novel and expensive strategy to defend themselves against the continuing violence in Colombia. In August, British Petroleum (BP) signed a three-year agreement with the Defense Ministry. For $54 million to $60 million, Colombia's armed forces were to provide an elite and highly mobile battalion to protect the 550-mile (885-kilometer) BP pipeline, which was under construction. In addition to the new outlay for protection, foreign-owned oil companies since 1992 had paid Colombia $250 million annually in "war taxes." According to military intelligence experts, the industry also had been paying rebel forces for "protection" to the tune of another $140 million annually. □ Nathan A. Haverstock

See also **Latin America** (Facts in brief table). In *World Book,* see **Colombia.**

Colorado. See **State government.**

Common Market. See **Europe.**

Commonwealth of Independent States. See **Armenia; Azerbaijan; Belarus; Georgia; Kazakstan; Kyrgyzstan; Russia; Ukraine; Uzbekistan.**

Comoros. See **Africa.**

Computer. The number of people who owned a personal computer (PC) continued to rise in 1996. The trend was fueled by falling prices, improved power and performance of the machines, and the wealth of information available on the World Wide Web. As PC's became more commonplace, manufacturers began to rethink and refine their concept of a computer's role in the typical household.

"Convergence" was a term used in the computer industry to describe a new trend in 1996—the blending of home computers with consumer electronics (such as TV's, VCR's, and home audio systems). In 1996, two major consumer electronics firms introduced PC's designed around this principle.

In June, Sony Corporation of Park Ridge, New Jersey, announced its first entry into the home PC market—VAIO (for Video-Audio Integration and Operations). VAIO was designed to offer multimedia performance with high-quality audio and video playback capabilities. A Sony-designed, multichannel speaker system and a monitor based on the company's popular Trinitron TV technology were options.

Toshiba America Inc. of New York City unveiled its new Infinia line of PC's in September. Infinias were offered with an optional TV/FM radio tuner with remote control and featured car-radiolike controls for volume, tuning, and switching from TV to PC. Toshiba expected the Infinia to sell for between $2,150 and $3,550, depending on options selected.

The PC of the future? Efforts intensified in 1996 to develop a new generation of inexpensive personal computers designed specifically for accessing the Internet. The devices, sometimes called *information appliances* or *network computers,* were envisioned as simplified versions of traditional PC's that would sell for about $500.

In February, Oracle Corporation of Redwood City, California, demonstrated a prototype of its new Network Computer (NC). The NC had no disk drive to permanently store programs. Instead, it was designed to download operational programs each time the user connected to the Internet. In April, Microsoft Corporation of Redmond, Washington, announced plans to develop a similar device, which it called the Simply Interactive Personal Computer (SIPC). Microsoft, however, did not plan to manufacture the SIPC. Rather, it would specify standards for SIPC hardware and software.

Man versus machine. In February, Russian chess master Garry Kasparov defeated a computer named Deep Blue, designed by International Business Machines (IBM) of Armonk, New York, in the first series of regulation chess matches between a computer and a master-class chess player. Deep Blue took the first game—the first time in history that a machine defeated a grand master under tournament rules. However, Kasparov won the match, 3 games to 1, with 2 draws. □ Michael Woods

See also **Internet.** In *World Book,* see **Computer.**

The University of Pennsylvania throws a party for the 50-year-old computer that introduced the world to the age of information.

By Dilys Pegler Winegrad

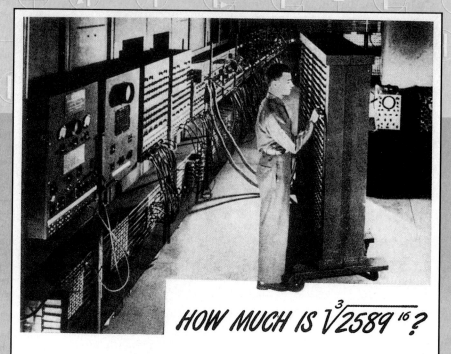

HOW MUCH IS $\sqrt[3]{2589}^{16}$?

The Army's ENIAC can give you the answer in a fraction of a second!

that's a stumper? You should see *some* ENIAC's problems! Brain twisters that to paper would run off this page and ond . . . addition, subtraction, multi-, division — square root, cube root, . Solved by an incredibly complex circuits operating 18,000 electronic tipping the scales at 30 tons!

IAC is symbolic of many amazing ces with a brilliant future for you! egular Army needs men with apti-entific work, and as one of the first he post-war era, you stand to get ground floor of important jobs

AR ARMY SERVES THE NATION NKIND IN WAR AND PEACE

which have never before existed. You'll find that an Army career pays off.

The most attractive fields are filling quickly. Get into the swim while the getting's good! 1½, 2 and 3 year enlistments are open in the Regular Army to ambitious young men 18 to 34 (17 with parents' consent) who are otherwise qualified. If you enlist for 3 years, you may choose your own branch of the service, of those still open. Get full details at your nearest Army Recruiting Station.

A GOOD JOB FOR YOU
U. S. Army
CHOOSE THIS FINE PROFESSION NOW!

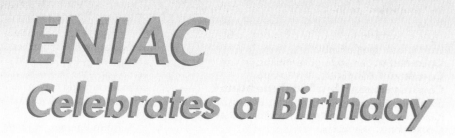

ENIAC
Celebrates a Birthday

There was a birthday party on February 14, 1996, for one of the nation's most influential baby boomers. The party was thrown by faculty and students at the Moore School of Electrical Engineering, at the University of Pennsylvania in Philadelphia, and the guest of honor was ENIAC—the Electronic Numerical Integrator and Computer. Conceived during World War II, but born during the postwar years, ENIAC was the world's first large-scale, all-electronic, general-purpose, digital computer, making it something like the founding father of today's computer. As part of the birthday celebration, another baby boomer, Vice President Al Gore, switched on a portion of ENIAC, and the machine was tested through the simple addition of two numbers. Although ancient as computers go, ENIAC passed the test with flying colors, giving both the right answer and an impressive demonstration of how and where the computer age began.

Number crunching

Like other advances in technology, ENIAC was designed to do the work of many people, but at a faster rate. For about 200 American women—mathematicians who were called "computers" by the U.S. Army's Ordnance Department—the home front during World War II was that department's Ballistic Research Laboratory (BRL). The mission was calculating firing tables for artillery. The enemy was time. Hour after hour, day after day, each woman, working in assembly-line fashion, calculated one portion of the complicated formulas.

The women, working at a BRL substation at the University of Pennsylvania's Moore School, calculated the trajectories, or possible flight paths, of artillery shells. Ultimately, their calculations would be compiled into tables used by gunners to aim their weapons accurately. To create such tables, the women had to calculate between 2,000 and 4,000 trajectories for every pairing of artillery shell and weapon. Using a desktop electromechanical calculator, each mathematician needed up to 40 hours to calculate a trajectory. The BRL team also employed the Moore School's differential analyzer, an analog computer that derived calculations from the movement of gears and rods. Although the differential analyzer could compute a trajectory in about 20 minutes, resetting the machine's rods and gears for each new trajectory required up to two hours. Under these time restraints, it took up to two months to complete a single firing table. At first, this pace met the demands of the military, but as the war escalated, the women could not keep up with the production of new weapons. The enemy—time—would win unless the army discovered a new, faster method of calculation. In the end, a solution was proposed, not by the army, but by two young civilians, physicist John W. Mauchly and graduate student J. Presper Eckert.

John W. Mauchly spent August 1942 at the Moore School of Electrical Engineering attending a government-sponsored class on the electronic devices and techniques used in weapons systems and was recruited to join the draft-depleted faculty. Discussions with Eckert on the feasibility of a high-speed calculating machine led Mauchly to

Preceding page:

The U.S. Army, which funded the development of ENIAC, uses the computer in its post-World War II recruiting advertisements.

The author

Dilys Pegler Winegrad is the director and curator of the Arthur Ross Gallery at the University of Pennsylvania in Philadelphia. She has written extensively about the history of the university.

How far have we come since 1946?

- One person using a desktop calculator took up to 40 hours to calculate one trajectory, or the flight path of an artillery shell fired from a gun.

- ENIAC calculated a trajectory in 30 seconds—4,800 times faster than the human calculator. J. Presper Eckert, front left, and John W. Mauchly, center, designed ENIAC.

- ENIAC-on-a-Chip, a computer chip designed to replicate ENIAC's capabilities, is no bigger than a thumbnail. The prototype, enlarged at left, measures less than one-tenth of an inch (2 by 2 millimeters) square.

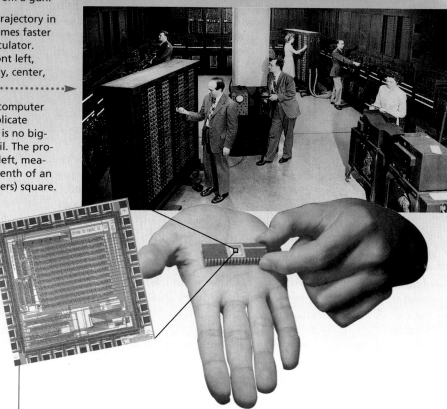

compose a memo on the subject entitled "The Use of High Speed Vacuum Tube Devices for Calculation," a theoretical outline for a new type of electronic computation. Mauchly's initial interest in using vacuum tubes for high-speed electronic calculation had nothing to do with the war effort. He simply wanted a faster way to solve "the problem of the weather"—his research specialty.

J. Presper Eckert, a talented University of Pennsylvania graduate student in electrical engineering, was intrigued by Mauchly's ideas on electronic computation and set about finding solutions to problems that would have to be addressed before high-speed vacuum tubes could be employed in calculating complex equations, particularly the problem of how to keep vacuum tubes from continuously failing. Although only in his early 20's, Eckert had already developed an electronic device for recording the measurements of magnetic fields on film. He had also helped design Moore School's differential analyzer.

By March 1943, the BRL was desperately behind schedule. Lieutenant Herman H. Goldstine, who headed the BRL substation at the Moore School, learned of Mauchly's ideas for electronic digital calculation and recognized the possible significance of the ideas to the army. In April 1943, Mauchly and Eckert—with the assistance of John G. Brainerd, the Moore School's director of war research—submitted a proposal to the army. Within weeks, University of Pennsylvania trustees and the army reached an agreement to produce a computer, which was classified as Project PX. Mauchly and Eckert successfully completed the project. They built a computer capable of calculating a trajectory in about 30 seconds, but Project PX was not completed until after the Japanese had surrendered on September 2, 1945.

ENIAC's place in computing history

Mechanical devices for counting go back further than ENIAC's 50 years. The first mechanical counter—the abacus—was created some 2,500 years ago and remains in use today. Another device, the slide rule, was invented in 1621 and was widely used until the 1970's, when it was superseded by the hand-held electronic calculator.

In 1822, Englishman Charles Babbage produced a working prototype of what may be considered the first mechanical computer. He designed the "Difference Engine," as he called it, to solve problems using a mathematical technique called the method of difference. Babbage never actually built his machine.

Herman Hollerith, an American inventor, created an electric tabulating machine that read data from punched cards. It was first used to tabulate the 1890 U.S. census and was the first calculator powered by electricity.

In 1942, physics professor John V. Atanasoff and graduate student Clifford Berry at Iowa State College at Ames, Iowa, completed a computer capable of solving a complex system of algebraic equations. Although the Atanasoff-Berry Computer could only be programmed to calculate a single kind of equation and was very slow, its circuitry included vacu-

Vacuum tubes

Most vacuum tubes consisted of a glass bulb from which almost all air had been removed. Inside the bulb were metal electrodes. An electric current was applied through wires at the base of the tube. This caused subatomic particles called electrons to flow from the cathode, the negative electrode, to the anode, the positive electrode. The vacuum tube also contained a wire grid between the cathode and the anode to control the amount of electrons flowing through the tube.

Vacuum tubes controlled electric current in all electronic devices—radios, televisions, and computers—until the 1950's, when the smaller, cheaper, and more reliable transistor was invented.

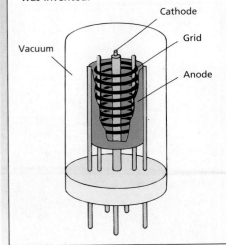

145

Major developments in computer technology

Difference Engine

- Invented by Englishman Charles Babbage in the 1820's
- First design of an automatic calculating machine
- Designed to calculate mathematical tables
- First full-scale working model not built until 1991

Electric Tabulating Machine

- Invented by American Herman Hollerith in 1888
- Electric machine that read punched cards
- Tabulated the results of the 1890 census in the United States

um tubes—a system that Atanasoff demonstrated to John Mauchly in 1941.

Because World War II ended before the completion of ENIAC, responsibility for the machine's 1945 test run was handed to scientists at Los Alamos National Laboratory in New Mexico, a research center that developed and tested nuclear weapons. ENIAC was programmed to compute calculations connected with thermonuclear reactions. As a result of the laboratory's successful simulation of a nuclear blast based on ENIAC's calculations, the federal government continued to support computer technology, and for more than a decade, ENIAC churned out numbers for military-sponsored scientific research.

The "electronic brain"

After ENIAC's first public demonstration on February 14, 1946, journalists described it as an "electronic brain." They predicted that it would introduce "a new epoch in the scope of human thought." While the reporters may have accurately predicted the influence of the new technology, they did exaggerate its capability. What ENIAC did best was to perform time-consuming, routine calculations, thus freeing humans for more creative thinking. ENIAC worked well, and it worked fast. In one second, it could add or subtract 5,000 sums or multiply two 10-digit decimals 300 times. The speed was achieved through electronic digital circuitry and the nearly 18,000 vacuum tubes. Most computers that existed before ENIAC employed electrical relay switches in their circuitry to perform calculations. Although the Atanasoff-Berry Computer had vacuum tubes, it still used mechanical devices for storing numbers. ENIAC's vacuum tubes made the machine all-electronic. It needed no movable parts to calculate problems or store numbers.

ENIAC was also the first computer that could be programmed. Earlier computers had been wired to do only one kind of calculation. ENIAC's functions could be altered. However, this was no small task. Because the machine was not capable of storing instructions, reprogramming required resetting thousands of switches and unplugging and replugging innumerable electrical cords, all by hand. However tedious the process, the fact that it could be programmed made ENIAC the first general-purpose digital computer.

The machine was also described as "large-scale."

While the description actually referred to the magnitude of the problems ENIAC could handle, its physical bulk was impressive. The computer, weighing 30 short tons (27 metric tons), occupied a room 30 by 50 feet (9 by 15 meters). Its 40 panels, 3 feet (0.9 meter) in depth, were arranged to form an 80-foot- (24-meter-) long U-shape. According to popular myth, when ENIAC was switched on, the lights of Philadelphia dimmed. In fact, ENIAC, which pulled 174 kilowatts of electricity at start-up, had its own special power lines.

The 50th anniversary celebration

To celebrate ENIAC's 50th birthday, Jan Van der Spiegel and Fred Ketterer—professors at the Moore School of Electrical Engineering—asked students to create a new product that would dramatically demonstrate how far computer technology had advanced since 1946. Three students—Titi Alailima, James Tau, and Lin Ping Ang—designed a computer chip that replicated ENIAC's operations. Measuring only 0.3 by 0.3 inch (8 by 8 millimeters), ENIAC-on-a-Chip required less than 0.5 watt of electrical power to operate its 250,000 tiny transistors.

The original ENIAC has become a treasured antique, a piece of Americana preserved by the Smithsonian Institution in Washington, D.C. Sections of the computer have been loaned, however, to the University of Pennsylvania. For the 50th anniversary party, the Smithsonian granted permission to the university to attempt to resurrect these sections. After replacing several hundred vacuum tubes and filling in gaps with a modern personal computer, engineers managed to get one of ENIAC's 40 original panels back into operation.

When Vice President Gore switched on the machine, ENIAC was instructed to add two numbers: 46—for the year 1946—and 50—for its age. ENIAC successfully added the two numbers, marking both the anniversary and John W. Mauchly's and J. Presper Eckert's enormous achievement. By convincing military scientists and technical experts of the value and practicability of electronic digital computers, Mauchly and Eckert provided a crucial base for the staggering technological advances that have followed. A top-secret, wartime project laid the foundation for a new industry based not on humanity's capacity for destruction, but rather its inexhaustible creativity. ■ ■ ■

Differential Analyzer
- Invented by American Vannevar Bush in 1930
- Analog computer that calculated equations from the movement of gears and shafts
- Designed to solve mathematical problems for research about electric circuitry

Z2
- Invented by the German Konrad Zuse in 1941
- Electromechanical digital calculator, which used second-hand telephone relay switches in its circuitry
- Computed mathematical calculations for airplane designs

Atanasoff-Berry Computer
- Invented by Americans John V. Atanasoff and Clifford Berry in 1942
- First digital computer using vacuum tubes in the electronic circuitry
- Designed to solve certain complex mathematical equations for research in math and physics

Mark I
- Invented by American Howard H. Aiken in 1943
- Electromechanical digital calculator, with switching devices in the circuitry
- First used for mathematical computations needed by the U.S. Navy during World War II

Colossus
- Invented by Englishman T. H. Flowers in 1943
- Electronic digital computer with about 1,500 vacuum tubes
- Decoded secret messages from the German secret-code machine, Enigma

ENIAC
- Invented by Americans John W. Mauchly and J. Presper Eckert in 1945
- First electronic digital computer that could be programmed to perform more than one kind of mathematical computation
- Originally designed to calculate the trajectory of artillery shells

Congress of the United States.

Partisan clashes between the Republican-controlled United States Congress and Democratic President Bill Clinton subsided in 1996 as Americans voiced their opposition to radical changes in government policy. President Clinton moved toward the political center and his Republican (GOP for Grand Old Party) opponents moderated their positions. As a result, the second session of the 104th Congress approved—and Clinton signed into law—a number of ground-breaking bills, including legislation dealing with welfare, farm subsidies, telecommunications, health care, immigration, and terrorism.

Budget compromise. The flow of legislation marked a sharp turnaround from 1995, when confrontation between GOP forces in Congress and the president led to two shutdowns of the federal government and a prolonged deadlock over budget priorities. The Senate and the House of Representatives voted early in January 1996 to end the stalemate and reopen the government, backing off from the revolutionary conservative policies outlined in the Republican Party's 1994 Contract with America (an outline of planned legislation upon which conservatives ran in the 1994 Congressional election).

While Congress approved a series of stopgap measures in the first quarter of 1996 in order to keep the government going, agreement on a spending plan for the 1996 fiscal year was not reached until April 26, seven months after the fiscal year began on Oct. 1, 1995. The budget signed by Clinton reduced nondefense appropriations to $223.8 billion, compared to $246.1 billion in the previous year. A total of $264.3 billion was allocated for defense programs. While Congress forced Clinton to accept deeper spending cuts than he preferred, Clinton, citing a program to balance the budget by 2002, blocked a Republican plan to give major tax cuts to families.

Another budget battle was averted when Congress reached an agreement with President Clinton on a spending bill shortly before the Oct. 1, 1996, start of the 1997 fiscal year. The final bill was approved 370 to 37 in the House and 84 to 15 in the Senate. While the $600-billion budget cut $30 billion in spending, it did reflect major Republican concessions, including an additional $6.5 billion for education and other domestic programs. Some programs targeted for elimination by the GOP, such as Goals 2000, a plan for improving the quality of U.S. schools, were retained.

State of the Union. The president, facing a reelection bid in November 1996, distanced himself from traditional Democratic themes in his January 23 State of the Union Address. Observers noted that Clinton sounded like his Republican opponents when he declared, "The era of big government is over." He seized on many GOP issues, such as fighting crime and balancing the budget. But the president also took advantage of a popular feeling that Republicans were largely to blame for the two shutdowns of federal services. Democrats in Congress gave the president a prolonged standing ovation when he declared: "Never, ever shut the federal government down again."

The telecommunications bill. To keep pace with new technology, Congress on February 1 approved a sweeping overhaul of federal communications laws. The legislation, which sailed through the House on a 414-to-16 vote and won Senate approval in a 91-to-5 roll call, was signed into law by Clinton on February 8.

The law opened the door for increased competition in radio, television, and telephone service and reduced restrictions on media ownership. It allowed broadcast companies to own television stations reaching 35 percent of U.S. households, up from 25 percent under the previous law. The law also lifted limits on the number of TV or radio stations a company could own and gave telephone companies the right to compete in the cable television business. Control of cable TV rates, enacted in 1992, were to be lifted by 1999, except for basic cable service. The measure also allowed regional telephone companies, known as the "Baby Bells," to operate long-distance telephone service and long-distance carriers to offer regional phone service.

In addition, the law imposed criminal penalties for the distribution of pornographic materials to children on the Internet, the global computer network. It also required makers of TV sets to install a device called the V chip that would enable parents to block violent programs.

Farm subsidies cut. Congress also enacted a bill to cut back many federal farm subsidies. The "Freedom to Farm Act," passed by Congress in February and signed into law on April 4, marked the most sweeping changes in agriculture law since the 1930's. The law was designed to phase out payments to farmers for not planting such crops as corn, wheat, rice, and cotton. Price guarantees for peanuts and sugar, however, were to continue as were price supports for dairy products.

Tough measures on terrorism. Congress, responding to the president's request, overwhelmingly approved an antiterrorism bill, which authorized the spending of $1 billion over four years to combat terrorism. It banned entry into the United States of foreigners who are members of groups deemed by the U.S. government to be terrorist organizations. Penalties were imposed for raising funds or contributing to known terrorist groups. The bill also contained provisions that placed a time limit on the filing of appeals for death sentences.

Congress passed line-item veto legislation, expanding the chief executive's powers to pick and choose pieces of legislation by vetoing one or more items in a bill without turning down the entire measure. The provision was designed to prevent lawmakers from inserting special-interest benefits into bills.

Under the bill, which Clinton signed on April 9, 1996, the president was given the right to reject tax breaks affecting fewer than 100 people or 10 businesses. While the law barred any specific veto of spending on federal entitlement programs, such as social security, it allowed a president to block expansion of such benefits. The added power was given to the president for an eight-year trial period and went into effect on Jan. 1, 1997.

The law proved to be controversial because it transferred some of Congress's constitutional power over federal spending to the executive branch of the government, altering the separation of powers outlined in the Constitution. The same day Clinton signed the bill into law, the National Treasury Employees Union filed a lawsuit challenging the law's constitutionality. Other groups announced that they also would consider filing lawsuits.

Increasing the minimum wage. In a victory for Democrats, on Aug. 2, 1996, Congress increased the federal minimum hourly wage from $4.25 to $5.15. While Republican leaders opposed the legislation, they yielded to pressure from GOP moderates to bring the bill to a vote. It passed the House 281 to 144. All 47 Senate Democrats were joined by 27 Republicans to pass the bill raising the minimum wage by 50 cents on Oct. 1, 1996, and an additional 40 cents on Oct. 1, 1997. The bill also included $21.4 billion in tax breaks to business.

Welfare reform. Perhaps the most far-reaching legislation passed by the 104th Congress ended the federal guarantee of assistance to poor families with children and gave control over the welfare program to state governments. The bill passed the House 328 to 101, with Democrats evenly split for

and against it. The Senate approved it 78 to 21, with 25 Democrats in favor and 21 opposed.

The bill, signed into law by the president on August 22, denied welfare benefits to heads of households who were not employed after two years of receiving benefits and placed a five-year lifetime limit on welfare aid for most recipients. The measure also denied most welfare benefits to legal immigrants and cut the federal food stamp program by $24 billion over a six-year period. The welfare bill was expected to reduce spending by $55 billion by 2002.

Opponents charged that the bill would plunge 1 million children into poverty and leave a gaping hole in the nation's safety net for the poor. The president said he would propose changes in the law early in 1997 to restore benefits for legal immigrants and provide more funds for the food stamp program.

Health insurance made portable. Congress overwhelmingly approved a bill that would enable workers to retain health insurance coverage when they change jobs and would limit denial of coverage to individuals with preexisting medical conditions. The measure also authorized a trial program in which

Trent Lott, the junior senator from Mississippi, defeats Thad Cochran, senior senator from Mississippi, on June 12 to become majority leader of the U.S. Senate.

Members of the United States House of Representatives

The House of Representatives of the first session of the 105th Congress consisted of 207 Democrats, 227 Republicans, and 1 independent (not including representatives from American Samoa, the District of Columbia, Guam, Puerto Rico, and the Virgin Islands), when it convened on Jan. 7, 1997. There were 197 Democrats, 236 Republicans, 1 independent, and 1 vacancy when the second session of the 104th Congress convened. This table shows congressional district, legislator, and party affiliation. Asterisk (*) denotes those who served in the 104th Congress; dagger (†) denotes "at large."

Alabama
1. Sonny Callahan, R.*
2. Terry Everett, R.*
3. Bob Riley, R.
4. Robert Aderholt, R.
5. Bud Cramer, R.*
6. Spencer Bachus, R.*
7. Earl Hilliard, D.*

Alaska
†Donald E. Young, R.*

Arizona
1. Matt Salmon, R.*
2. Ed Pastor, D.*
3. Bob Stump, R.*
4. John Shadegg, R.*
5. Jim Kolbe, R.*
6. J. D. Hayworth, R.*

Arkansas
1. Marion Berry, D.
2. Vic Snyder, D.
3. Asa Hutchinson, R.
4. Jay Dickey, R.*

California
1. Frank Riggs, R.*
2. Wally Herger, R.*
3. Vic Fazio, D.*
4. John Doolittle, R.*
5. Robert T. Matsui, D.*
6. Lynn Woolsey, D.*
7. George E. Miller, D.*
8. Nancy Pelosi, D.*
9. Ronald V. Dellums, D.*
10. Ellen Tauscher, D
11. Richard Pombo, R.*
12. Tom Lantos, D.*
13. Fortney H. (Peter) Stark, D.*
14. Anna Eshoo, D.*
15. Tom Campbell, R.*
16. Zoe Lofgren, D.*
17. Sam Farr, D.*
18. Gary Condit, D.*
19. George Radanovich, R.*
20. Calvin Dooley, D.*
21. William M. Thomas, R.*
22. Walter H. Capps, D.
23. Elton Gallegly, R.*
24. Brad Sherman, D.
25. Howard McKeon, R.*
26. Howard L. Berman, D.*
27. James E. Rogan, R.
28. David Dreier, R.*
29. Henry A. Waxman, D.*
30. Xavier Becerra, D.*
31. Matthew Martinez, D.*
32. Julian C. Dixon, D.*
33. Lucille Roybal-Allard, D.*
34. Esteban E. Torres, D.*
35. Maxine Waters, D.*
36. Jane Harman, D.*
37. Juanita Millender-McDonald, D.*
38. Steve Horn, R.*
39. Edward Royce, R.*
40. Jerry Lewis, R.*
41. Jay Kim, R.*
42. George E. Brown, Jr., D.*
43. Kenneth Calvert, R.*
44. Sonny Bono, R.*
45. Dana Rohrabacher, R.*
46. Loretta Sanchez, D.
47. C. Christopher Cox, R.*
48. Ronald C. Packard, R.*
49. Brian Bilbray, R.*
50. Bob Filner, D.*
51. Randy (Duke) Cunningham, R.*
52. Duncan L. Hunter, R.*

Colorado
1. Diana DeGette, D.
2. David E. Skaggs, D.*
3. Scott McInnis, R.*
4. Bob Schaffer, R.
5. Joel Hefley, R.*
6. Daniel Schaefer, R.*

Connecticut
1. Barbara B. Kennelly, D.*
2. Sam Gejdenson, D.*
3. Rosa DeLauro, D.*
4. Christopher Shays, R.*
5. James H. Maloney, D.
6. Nancy L. Johnson, R.*

Delaware
†Michael Castle, R.*

Florida
1. Joe Scarborough, R.*
2. Allen Boyd, D.
3. Corrine Brown, D.*
4. Tillie Fowler, R.*
5. Karen Thurman, D.*
6. Clifford B. Stearns, R.*
7. John Mica, R.*
8. Bill McCollum, R.*
9. Michael Bilirakis, R.*
10. C. W. Bill Young, R.*
11. Jim Davis, D.
12. Charles Canady, R.*
13. Dan Miller, R.*
14. Porter J. Goss, R.*
15. Dave Weldon, R.*
16. Mark Foley, R.*
17. Carrie Meek, D.*
18. Ileana Ros-Lehtinen, R.*
19. Robert Wexler, D.
20. Peter Deutsch, D.*
21. Lincoln Diaz-Balart, R.*
22. E. Clay Shaw, Jr., R.*
23. Alcee Hastings, D.*

Georgia
1. Jack Kingston, R.*
2. Sanford Bishop, D.*
3. Mac Collins, R.*
4. Cynthia A. McKinney, D.*
5. John Lewis, D.*
6. Newt Gingrich, R.*
7. Bob Barr, R.*
8. Saxby Chambliss, R.*
9. Nathan Deal, R.*
10. Charlie Norwood, R.*
11. John Linder, R.*

Hawaii
1. Neil Abercrombie, D.*
2. Patsy T. Mink, D.*

Idaho
1. Helen Chenoweth, R.*
2. Michael Crapo, R.*

Illinois
1. Bobby Rush, D.*
2. Jesse L. Jackson, Jr., D.*
3. William O. Lipinski, D.*
4. Luis Gutierrez, D.*
5. Rod R. Blagojevich, D.
6. Henry J. Hyde, R.*
7. Danny Davis, D.
8. Philip M. Crane, R.*
9. Sidney R. Yates, D.*
10. John Edward Porter, R.*
11. Gerald Weller, R.*
12. Jerry F. Costello, D.*
13. Harris W. Fawell, R.*
14. J. Dennis Hastert, R.*
15. Thomas W. Ewing, R.*
16. Donald Manzullo, R.*
17. Lane A. Evans, D.*
18. Ray LaHood, R.*
19. Glenn Poshard, D.*
20. John Simkus, R.

Indiana
1. Peter J. Visclosky, D.*
2. David McIntosh, R.*
3. Tim Roemer, D.*
4. Mark Souder, R.*
5. Steve Buyer, R.*
6. Danny L. Burton, R.*
7. Edward A. Pease, R.
8. John Hostettler, R.*
9. Lee H. Hamilton, D.*
10. Julia M. Carson, D.

Iowa
1. Jim Leach, R.*
2. Jim Nussle, R.*
3. Leonard Boswell, D.
4. Greg Ganske, R.*
5. Tom Latham, R.*

Kansas
1. Jerry Moran, R.
2. Jim Ryun, R.
3. Vince Snowbarger, R.
4. Todd Tiahrt, R.*

Kentucky
1. Edward Whitfield, R.*
2. Ron Lewis, R.*
3. Anne Northup, R.
4. Jim Bunning, R.*
5. Harold (Hal) Rogers, R.*
6. Scotty Baesler, D.*

Louisiana
1. Robert L. Livingston, Jr., R.*
2. William J. Jefferson, D.*
3. W. J. (Billy) Tauzin, R.*
4. Jim McCrery, R.*
5. John Cooksey, R.
6. Richard Hugh Baker, R.*
7. Chris John, D.

Maine
1. Thomas Allen, D.
2. John Baldacci, D.*

Maryland
1. Wayne T. Gilchrest, R.*
2. Robert Ehrlich, Jr., R.*
3. Benjamin L. Cardin, D.*
4. Albert Wynn, D.*
5. Steny H. Hoyer, D.*
6. Roscoe Bartlett, R.*
7. Elijah Cummings. D.*
8. Constance A. Morella, R.*

Massachusetts
1. John W. Olver, D.*
2. Richard E. Neal, D.*
3. James McGovern, D.
4. Barney Frank, D.*
5. Martin Meehan, D.*
6. John Tierney, D.
7. Edward J. Markey, D.*
8. Joseph P. Kennedy II, D.*
9. John Joseph Moakley, D.*
10. William Delahunt, D.

Michigan
1. Bart Stupak, D.*
2. Peter Hoekstra, R.*
3. Vernon Ehlers, R.*
4. Dave Camp, R.*
5. James Barcia, D.*
6. Frederick S. Upton, R.*
7. Nick Smith, R.*
8. Debbie Stabenow, D.
9. Dale E. Kildee, D.*
10. David E. Bonior, D.*
11. Joseph Knollenberg, R.*
12. Sander M. Levin, D.*
13. Lynn Rivers, D.*
14. John Conyers, Jr., D.*
15. Carolyn Kilpatrick, D.
16. John D. Dingell, D.*

Minnesota
1. Gil Gutknecht, R.*
2. David Minge, D.*
3. Jim Ramstad, R.*
4. Bruce F. Vento, D.*
5. Martin O. Sabo, D.*
6. William P. Luther, D.*
7. Collin C. Peterson, D.*
8. James L. Oberstar, D.*

Mississippi
1. Roger Wicker, R.*
2. Bennie Thompson, D.*
3. Charles Pickering, R.
4. Mike Parker, R.*
5. Gene Taylor, D.*

Missouri
1. William L. (Bill) Clay, D.*
2. James Talent, R.*
3. Richard A. Gephardt, D.*
4. Ike Skelton, D.*
5. Karen McCarthy, D.*
6. Pat Danner, D.*
7. Roy Blunt, R.
8. Jo Ann Emerson, R.*
9. Kenny Hulshof, R.

Montana
†Rick Hill, R.

Nebraska
1. Doug Bereuter, R.*
2. Jon Christensen, R.*
3. Bill Barrett, R.*

Nevada
1. John Ensign, R.*
2. Jim Gibbons, R.

New Hampshire
1. John E. Sununu, R.
2. Charles Bass, R.*

New Jersey
1. Robert E. Andrews, D.*
2. Frank LoBiondo, R.*
3. H. James Saxton, R.*
4. Christopher H. Smith, R.*
5. Marge Roukema, R.*
6. Frank Pallone, Jr., D.*
7. Bob Franks, R.*
8. William Pascrell, D.
9. Steven Rothman, D.
10. Donald M. Payne, D.*
11. Rodney Frelinghuysen, R.*
12. Mike Pappas, R.
13. Robert Menendez, D.*

New Mexico
1. Steven H. Schiff, R.*
2. Joe Skeen, R.*
3. William B. Richardson, D.*

New York
1. Michael Forbes, R.*
2. Rick Lazio, R.*
3. Peter King, R.*
4. Carolyn McCarthy, D.
5. Gary L. Ackerman, D.*
6. Floyd H. Flake, D.*
7. Thomas J. Manton, D.*
8. Jerrold Nadler, D.*
9. Charles E. Schumer, D.*
10. Edolphus Towns, D.*
11. Major R. Owens, D.*
12. Nydia Velázquez, D.*
13. Susan Molinari, R.*
14. Carolyn Maloney, D.*
15. Charles B. Rangel, D.*
16. José E. Serrano, D.*
17. Eliot L. Engel, D.*
18. Nita M. Lowey, D.*
19. Sue Kelly, R.*
20. Benjamin A. Gilman, R.*
21. Michael R. McNulty, D.*
22. Gerald B. Solomon, R.*
23. Sherwood L. Boehlert, R.*
24. John McHugh, R.*
25. James Walsh, R.*
26. Maurice Hinchey, D.*
27. William Paxon, R.*
28. Louise M. Slaughter, D.*
29. John J. LaFalce, D.*
30. Jack Quinn, R.*
31. Amo Houghton, R.*

North Carolina
1. Eva Clayton, D.*
2. Bob Etheridge, D.
3. Walter Jones, Jr., R.*
4. David Price, D.
5. Richard Burr, R.*
6. Howard Coble, R.*
7. Mike McIntyre, D.
8. W. G. (Bill) Hefner, D.*
9. Sue Myrick, R.*
10. Cass Ballenger, R.*
11. Charles H. Taylor, R.*
12. Melvin Watt, D.*

North Dakota
†Earl Pomeroy, D.*

Ohio
1. Steve Chabot, R.*
2. Rob Portman, R.*
3. Tony P. Hall, D.*
4. Michael G. Oxley, R.*
5. Paul E. Gillmor, R.*
6. Ted Strickland, D.
7. David L. Hobson, R.*
8. John A. Boehner, R.*
9. Marcy Kaptur, D.*
10. Dennis Kucinich, D.
11. Louis Stokes, D.*
12. John R. Kasich, R.*
13. Sherrod Brown, D.*
14. Thomas C. Sawyer, D.*
15. Deborah Pryce, R.*
16. Ralph Regula, R.*
17. James A. Traficant, Jr., D.*
18. Bob Ney, R.*
19. Steven LaTourette, R.*

Oklahoma
1. Steve Largent, R.*
2. Tom Coburn, R.*
3. Wes Watkins, R.
4. J. C. Watts, R.*
5. Ernest Jim Istook, R.*
6. Frank Lucas, R.*

Oregon
1. Elizabeth Furse, D.*
2. Robert Smith, R.
3. Earl Blumenauer, D.*
4. Peter A. DeFazio, D.*
5. Darlene Hooley, D.

Pennsylvania
1. Thomas M. Foglietta, D.*
2. Chaka Fattah, D.*
3. Robert A. Borski, Jr., D.*
4. Ron Klink, D.*
5. John Peterson, R.
6. Tim Holden, D.*
7. W. Curtis Weldon, R.*
8. Jim Greenwood, R.*
9. E. G. (Bud) Shuster, R.*
10. Joseph M. McDade, R.*
11. Paul E. Kanjorski, D.*
12. John P. Murtha, D.*
13. Jon Fox, R.
14. William J. Coyne, D.*
15. Paul McHale, D.*
16. Joseph Pitts, R.
17. George W. Gekas, R.*
18. Michael Doyle, D.*
19. William F. Goodling, R.*
20. Frank Mascara, D.*
21. Philip English, R.*

Rhode Island
1. Patrick Kennedy, D.*
2. Robert Weygand, D.

South Carolina
1. Mark Sanford, R.*
2. Floyd Spence, R.*
3. Lindsey Graham, R.*
4. Bob Inglis, R.*
5. John M. Spratt, Jr., D.*
6. James Clyburn, D.*

South Dakota
†John Thune, R.

Tennessee
1. William Jenkins, R.
2. John J. Duncan, Jr., R.*
3. Zach Wamp, R.*
4. Van Hilleary, R.*
5. Bob Clement, D.*
6. Bart Gordon, D.*
7. Ed Bryant, R.*
8. John S. Tanner, D.*
9. Harold E. Ford, D.*

Texas
1. Max Sandlin, D.
2. Jim Turner, D.
3. Sam Johnson, R.*
4. Ralph M. Hall, D.*
5. Pete Sessions, R.
6. Joe Barton, R.*
7. Bill Archer, R.*
8. Kevin Brady, R.
9. Nick Lampson, D.
10. Lloyd Doggett, D.*
11. Chet Edwards, D.*
12. Kay Granger, R.
13. William Thornberry, R.*
14. Ron Paul, R.
15. Rubén Hinojosa, D.
16. Silvestre Reyes, D.
17. Charles W. Stenholm, D.*
18. Sheila Jackson Lee, D.*
19. Larry Combest, R.*
20. Henry B. Gonzalez, D.*
21. Lamar S. Smith, R.*
22. Tom DeLay, R.*
23. Henry Bonilla, R.*
24. Martin Frost, D.*
25. Ken Bentsen, D.
26. Richard K. Armey, R.*
27. Solomon P. Ortiz, D.*
28. Frank Tejeda, D.*
29. Gene Green, D.*
30. Eddie Bernice Johnson, D.*

Utah
1. James V. Hansen, R.*
2. Merrill Cook, R.
3. Christopher Cannon, R.

Vermont
†Bernard Sanders, Ind.*

Virginia
1. Herbert H. Bateman, R.*
2. Owen B. Pickett, D.*
3. Robert Scott, D.*
4. Norman Sisisky, D.*
5. Virgil Goode, D.
6. Robert Goodlatte, R.*
7. Thomas J. (Tom) Bliley, Jr., R.*
8. James P. Moran, Jr., D.*
9. Frederick C. Boucher, D.*
10. Frank R. Wolf, R.*
11. Thomas Davis III, R.*

Washington
1. Rick White, R.*
2. Jack Metcalf, R.
3. Linda Smith, R.
4. Doc Hastings, R.*
5. George Nethercutt, R.*
6. Norman D. Dicks, D.*
7. Jim McDermott, D.*
8. Jennifer Dunn, R.*
9. Adam Smith, D.

West Virginia
1. Alan B. Mollohan, D.*
2. Robert E. Wise, Jr., D.*
3. Nick J. Rahall II, D.*

Wisconsin
1. Mark Neumann, R.*
2. Scott Klug, R.*
3. Ron Kind, D.
4. Gerald D. Kleczka, D.*
5. Thomas Barrett, D.*
6. Thomas E. Petri, R.*
7. David R. Obey, D.*
8. Jay Johnson, D.
9. F. James Sensenbrenner, Jr., R.*

Wyoming
†Barbara Cubin, R.*

Nonvoting representatives
American Samoa
Eni F. H. Faleomavaega, D.*

District of Columbia
Eleanor Holmes Norton, D.*

Guam
Robert Underwood, D.*

Puerto Rico
Carlos Romero-Barceló, D.*

Virgin Islands
Victor O. Frazer, Ind.

certain workers in certain states set aside part of their paycheck, tax-free, to pay for medical services. Clinton signed the bill in August.

Defeated measures. Some GOP-backed measures were defeated in the Republican-controlled Congress in 1996. A constitutional amendment to require a two-thirds majority in both houses of Congress to raise federal taxes failed in the House. The measure was 37 votes short of the required two-thirds majority for constitutional amendments.

Clinton vetoed several measures passed by Congress in 1996. In April, he vetoed Republican-backed bills that would have required him to abolish the Agency for International Development, the United States Information Agency, or the Arms Control and Disarmament Agency. He voted another bill that would have banned late-term abortions. Clinton also used his veto power on May 2 to kill a measure that would have limited awards in product liability lawsuits.

Foreign policy. On foreign policy issues, Congress supported by a 286-to-141 vote President Clinton's decision to continue most-favored-nation trading status for China. Congress also approved a measure that allowed U.S. citizens whose businesses were confiscated by the government of President Fidel Castro of Cuba to sue foreign firms currently operating those businesses in Cuba. Clinton signed the bill, strongly opposed by many foreign governments, but he invoked a provision to delay the filing of such lawsuits.

Ethics problems continued to plague both the House and the Senate in 1996. Former chairman of the House Ways and Means Committee, Dan Rostenkowski, a Democrat from Illinois, pleaded guilty to two counts of mail fraud on April 9 and was sentenced to 17 months in prison and fined $100,000. Rostenkowski lost his seat in the House in the 1994 elections, which followed his indictment on corruption charges.

On September 18, the Senate Ethics Committee cleared Republican Senator Alfonse D'Amato of New York of charges that he broke Senate rules when he made a one-day profit of $37,125 from a stock trade in 1993. The panel said that D'Amato may have gotten preferential treatment from a brokerage firm, but no evidence indicated that he was aware of it. House Minority Leader Richard A. Gephardt was cleared of the charge that he failed to properly report his ownership of a vacation property.

Gingrich's woes. The popularity of Speaker of the House Newt Gingrich fell sharply in 1996. Many House initiatives were either blocked or watered down by the Senate, and Republican moderates rebelling against Gingrich's leadership.

The House Ethics Committee pressed ahead with its investigation of Gingrich's chairmanship of GOPAC, a fund-raising organization, from 1986 to 1995. At issue was whether Gingrich unlawfully received as much as $250,000 from GOPAC to help

A sculpture of Lucretia Mott, Susan B. Anthony, and Elizabeth Cady Stanton, crusaders for women's rights, is moved in 1996 from the Capitol's basement into the Rotunda, where sculptures had previously honored only men.

Members of the United States Senate

The Senate of the first session of the 105th Congress consisted of 45 Democrats and 55 Republicans when it convened on January 7, 1997. The first date in each listing shows when the senator's term began. The second date in each listing shows when the senator's term expires.

State	Term	State	Term	State	Term
Alabama		**Louisiana**		**Ohio**	
Richard C. Shelby, R.	1987-1999	John B. Breaux, D.	1987-1999	John H. Glenn, Jr., D.	1974-1999
Jeff Sessions, R.	1997-2003	Mary L. Landrieu, D.	1997-2003	Mike DeWine, R.	1995-2001
Alaska		**Maine**		**Oklahoma**	
Theodore F. Stevens, R.	1968-2003	Olympia Snowe, R.	1995-2001	Don Nickles, R.	1981-1999
Frank H. Murkowski, R.	1981-1999	Susan E. Collins, R.	1997-2003	James M. Inhofe, R.	1994-2003
Arizona		**Maryland**		**Oregon**	
John McCain III, R.	1987-1999	Paul S. Sarbanes, D.	1977-2001	Ron Wyden, D.	1996-1999
Jon Kyl, R.	1995-2001	Barbara A. Mikulski, D.	1987-1999	Gordon Smith, R.	1997-2003
Arkansas		**Massachusetts**		**Pennsylvania**	
Dale Bumpers, D.	1975-1999	Edward M. Kennedy, D.	1962-2001	Arlen Specter, R.	1981-1999
Tim Hutchinson, R.	1997-2003	John F. Kerry, D.	1985-2003	Rick Santorum, R.	1995-2001
California		**Michigan**		**Rhode Island**	
Barbara Boxer, D.	1993-1999	Carl Levin, D.	1979-2003	John H. Chafee, R.	1976-2001
Dianne Feinstein, D.	1993-2001	Spencer Abraham, R.	1995-2001	Jack Reed, D.	1997-2003
Colorado		**Minnesota**		**South Carolina**	
Ben N. Campbell, R.	1993-1999	Paul D. Wellstone, D.	1991-2003	Strom Thurmond, R.	1955-2003
Wayne Allard, R.	1997-2003	Rod Grams, R.	1995-2001	Ernest F. Hollings, D.	1966-1999
Connecticut		**Mississippi**		**South Dakota**	
Christopher J. Dodd, D.	1981-1999	Thad Cochran, R.	1978-2003	Thomas A. Daschle, D.	1987-1999
Joseph I. Lieberman, D.	1989-2001	Trent Lott, R.	1989-2001	Tim Johnson, D.	1997-2003
Delaware		**Missouri**		**Tennessee**	
William V. Roth, Jr., R.	1971-2001	Christopher S. (Kit) Bond, R.	1987-1999	Fred Thompson, R.	1994-2003
Joseph R. Biden, Jr., D.	1973-2003	John Ashcroft, R.	1995-2001	Bill Frist, R.	1995-2001
Florida		**Montana**		**Texas**	
Bob Graham, D.	1987-1999	Max Baucus, D.	1978-2003	Phil Gramm, R.	1985-2003
Connie Mack III, R.	1989-2001	Conrad Burns, R.	1989-2001	Kay Bailey Hutchison, R.	1993-2001
Georgia		**Nebraska**		**Utah**	
Paul Coverdell, R.	1993-1999	J. Robert Kerrey, D.	1989-2001	Orrin G. Hatch, R.	1977-2001
Max Cleland, D.	1997-2003	Chuck Hagel, R.	1997-2003	Robert F. Bennett, R.	1993-1999
Hawaii		**Nevada**		**Vermont**	
Daniel K. Inouye, D.	1963-1999	Harry M. Reid, D.	1987-1999	Patrick J. Leahy, D.	1975-1999
Daniel K. Akaka, D.	1990-2001	Richard H. Bryan, D.	1989-2001	James M. Jeffords, R.	1989-2001
Idaho		**New Hampshire**		**Virginia**	
Larry E. Craig, R.	1991-2003	Robert C. Smith, R.	1990-2003	John W. Warner, R.	1979-2003
Dirk Kempthorne, R.	1993-1999	Judd Gregg, R.	1993-1999	Charles S. Robb, D.	1989-2001
Illinois		**New Jersey**		**Washington**	
Carol Moseley-Braun, D.	1993-1999	Frank R. Lautenberg, D.	1982-2001	Slade Gorton, R.	1989-2001
Richard J. Durbin, D.	1997-2003	Robert G. Torricelli, D.	1997-2003	Patty Murray, D.	1993-1999
Indiana		**New Mexico**		**West Virginia**	
Richard G. Lugar, R.	1977-2001	Pete V. Domenici, R.	1973-2003	Robert C. Byrd, D.	1959-2001
Dan R. Coats, R.	1989-1999	Jeff Bingaman, D.	1983-2001	John D. Rockefeller IV, D.	1985-2003
Iowa		**New York**		**Wisconsin**	
Charles E. Grassley, R.	1981-1999	Daniel P. Moynihan, D.	1977-2001	Herbert Kohl, D.	1989-2001
Tom Harkin, D.	1985-2003	Alfonse M. D'Amato, R.	1981-1999	Russell D. Feingold, D.	1993-1999
Kansas		**North Carolina**		**Wyoming**	
Sam Brownback, R.	1997-2003	Jesse A. Helms, R.	1973-2003	Craig Thomas, R.	1995-2001
Pat Roberts, R.	1997-2003	Lauch Faircloth, R.	1993-1999	Mike Enzi, R.	1997-2003
Kentucky		**North Dakota**			
Wendell H. Ford, D.	1974-1999	Kent Conrad, D.	1987-2001		
Mitch McConnell, R.	1985-2003	Byron L. Dorgan, D.	1992-1999		

fund his 1990 reelection campaign. The panel also widened its inquiry into Gingrich's use of tax-exempt contributions to finance a televised college course that he taught and whether he used the course to promote his conservative agenda. On December 21, a House subcommittee found that Gingrich had used tax-exempt money for political purposes and that he provided the committee with inaccurate information about the role of a political action committee. Gingrich admitted to the charges and apologized.

Elections. Majority Leader Robert Dole resigned his Senate seat on June 11 to devote full time to his ampaign for the U.S. presidency. Trent Lott, a Republican senator from Mississippi, became majority leader on June 12. Lott, a staunch conservative, was first elected to Congress in 1972. He became Republican whip of the House of Representatives in 1980. In 1988, Lott was elected to the Senate. He became Senate majority whip in 1994.

In national elections on November 5, the GOP lost nine seats in the House but retained control, with a 227 to 207 majority over the Democrats. The Republicans picked up two seats in the Senate to increase their majority to 55 to 45. □ William J. Eaton

See also **Democratic Party; Elections; Lott, Trent; Republican Party; United States, Government of the.** In *World Book,* see **Congress of the United States.**

Connecticut. See State government.

Conservation. In 1996, the United States National Park Service tottered on the edge of insolvency. According to service officials, the U.S. Congress between 1983 and 1996 allowed the service's annual budget (adjusted for inflation) to decline by $202 million. During the same period, the visitor count at the nation's national parks rose from 207 million to 270 million. The increase in visitors and decreased funding meant that maintenance projects, such as those for bridges, roads, and campgrounds, were postponed for lack of funds. These projects were estimated in 1996 to cost more than $4 billion.

Cost-cutting measures by the park service in 1996 included closing campgrounds in the Great Smoky Mountains National Park on the North Carolina-Tennessee border, Glacier National Park in Montana, and Yellowstone National Park in Wyoming. Yosemite National Park in California employed only 3 of the 19 rangers considered to be the minimum necessary to police the park's 800 square miles (2,070 square kilometers) of back country. Nearly 900 seasonal positions for rangers throughout the park system went unfilled in 1996.

In July, Congress considered two major national park financial relief bills, which were backed by many Republicans and Democrats, as well as by President Bill Clinton. The first bill would allow the parks to charge more realistic entrance fees. For example, a carload of people entering Yellowstone in 1996

paid $10 per vehicle for a week's stay—the same price charged in 1916, when Congress established the National Park Service. The second bill would allow the National Park Service to annually choose 10 corporate sponsors that would contribute money—up to approximately $100 million—in exchange for the right to advertise in the parks. The second bill did not pass. However, in November 1996, Secretary of the Interior Bruce Babbitt announced that a three-year pilot program of new or increased fees was to be phased in at 100 parks during 1997. Under the pilot program, 80 percent of the fees was to help fund the specific parks that collected them and the remainder of the money was to help fund the National Park Service..In the past, all park fees went to the general revenue fund of the U.S. Treasury.

Everglades restoration. On Feb. 19, 1996, Vice President Al Gore announced a Clinton Administration plan to restore the Everglades, the vast wetlands that cover most of south Florida and include Everglades National Park, Big Cypress National Preserve, and several smaller refuges. The core of the plan was an engineering project that would recreate the system's natural *hydrologic patterns* (pertaining to hydrology, the science of water). Beginning in 1906, Florida had drained parts of the Everglades for agriculture. Later, canals and levees were built to divert water from Lake Okeechobee north of the Everglades to supply Miami and the towns around it. Over time, the reduced water flow, as well as pollution from runoff of agricultural chemicals, mostly from sugar plantations, had greatly altered the ecology of the Everglades.

The Clinton plan called for the purchase of at least 100,000 acres (40,500 hectares) of farmland south of Lake Okeechobee. The land would be restored to marshlands, which would function as natural water filters. The project would cost $1.5 billion over seven years and would be financed in part by a penny-per-pound tax on sugar, a proposal that infuriated sugar growers. Under a Florida law passed in 1994, the growers were already being forced to pay more than $320 million over a 20-year period in environmental cleanup costs. Moreover, both houses of Congress had passed bills with less ambitious plans for Everglades restoration. By year-end, it was unclear as to how the restoration would proceed.

Grand Canyon flooding. On March 6, 1996, officials opened tubes at the Glen Canyon Dam allowing the Colorado River to surge through the Grand Canyon for the first time since the dam was completed in 1964. The torrent of water flowed for seven days, duplicating the once annual spring floods that for thousands of years nourished the floor of the canyon. It was hoped that the flooding would restore canyon-floor beaches, stir up sediment to nourish plants, and cut new channels to provide habitats for endangered fish.

The Glen Canyon Dam was built to provide elec-

Water is released from Glen Canyon Dam into the Colorado River in March, simulating spring floods that had once nourished the floor of the Grand Canyon until the construction of the dam in 1964.

trical power and drinking water for seven Western states. The Colorado River, severely restricted by the dam, changed from warm and muddy into a clear, cold flow, which eroded the canyon's beaches and damaged fish spawning grounds. After the dam was closed again, Interior Secretary Babbitt declared that the artificial flood was a success and provided researchers with data for planning future floods.

Smog at Big Bend. A whitish-gray haze blanketing Big Bend National Park in Texas in 1996 was caused by two coal-fired electrical plants operating over the Rio Grande border in northern Mexico, according to reports by the National Park Service and the U.S. Environmental Protection Agency. The agencies stated that the plants annually generated

250,000 tons (226,800 metric tons) of sulfur dioxide—a colorless gas that interacts with sunlight and other airborne chemicals to create smog. Visibility that once ranged for 50 to 100 miles (80 to 160 kilometers) in all directions was often reduced in 1996 to as little as 9 miles (14 kilometers).

Under the environmental provisions of the North American Free Trade Agreement (NAFTA), ratified by Mexico, the United States, and Canada in 1993, industries were subject to their home country's environmental laws. The electrical plants complied with Mexico's emission standards, which were less rigorous than U.S. standards.

The Mexican government insisted that the U.S. statistics were incorrect and that pollution was not a problem. Mexican officials also countered that industrial and automobile pollution generated in the United States was responsible for the smog. Faced with a weak economy, Mexicans resented the idea that they should spend billions of pesos to improve scenic views for American hikers. U.S. scientists stressed that the acidic haze would likely pollute human water supplies in the area, as well as harm plants and animals. But Mexico planned to build two more electrical plants in the north.

Yellowstone wolves. Gray wolves introduced into Yellowstone National Park in 1995 proved to be thriving in 1996. The animals had been absent from the West for 70 years because of an eradication program mounted in the 1920's. In late January 1996, 17 additional wolves were brought from Canada and released in the park. The wolves reproduced ahead of expectations, and the population stood at 50 to 65 by mid-May. Wildlife biologists decided it would no longer be necessary to airlift wolves from Canada to reach a target population of 100.

Wolves did stray outside the park to sites in Montana and Wyoming, which angered ranchers. Fearing for their livestock, ranchers opposed reintroduction and attempted to halt the program through legal action. Other local citizens, however, were more enthusiastic about wolf reintroduction, partly because it generated a tourist boom. In surveys, visitors said wolves were the animals they most wanted to see while visiting Yellowstone. The wolves also accomplished another major objective of the program—restoring a natural balance by preying on the park's overly large elk population.

Mysterious manatee deaths. By mid-1996, 304 dead manatees had washed up on the Florida coast, topping the previous record of 206 for all of 1990. Caribbean manatees numbered only about 2,000 to 2,600 animals in 1996. Some have been killed every year by powerboat propellers or crushed by floodgates, but the 1996 deaths puzzled biologists because most of the animals were not injured. The scientists speculated that red tides may have caused some deaths. A red tide is a natural phenomenon caused by algal microorganisms that collect in "blooms." The algae carry brevetoxin, which has killed large numbers of fish and seabirds in past years. More than half the tissue samples from the dead manatees revealed brevetoxin levels 50 to 100 times higher than normal.

A glut of gulls. The U.S. Fish and Wildlife Service in late May poisoned 6,000 herring and great black-backed gulls at the Monomoy National Wildlife Refuge, islands south of Cape Cod, Massachusetts. The gulls commandeer nesting territory and eat the chicks of roseate terns, an endangered species, and piping plovers, a species designated as threatened.   □ Eugene J. Walter, Jr.

In *World Book,* see **Conservation.**

Costa Rica. See **Latin America.**

Courts. On Dec. 3, 1996, in Honolulu, Hawaii, Circuit Court Judge Kevin S. C. Chang ruled that the state's ban on same-sex marriages violated the state Constitution because the state had demonstrated "no compelling state interest" in denying marriage licenses to homosexual couples. Although Chang initially ordered the state to begin issuing licenses, he put the order on hold on December 4 to allow state attorneys to appeal to the Hawaii Supreme Court. (Federal courts have no jurisdiction in the case.)

The case drew national attention and prompted both state and federal legislators throughout the United States to introduce legislation that would allow other states not to honor the union of homosexual couples married in Hawaii. The Defense of Marriage Act, signed by President Bill Clinton on September 21, denied federal recognition of same-sex marriages and exempted states from recognizing same-sex marriages performed in other states.

Free speech. On June 12, a panel of three federal judges in Philadelphia ruled that a law banning indecency on the Internet, the worldwide computer network, violated the First Amendment's guarantee of free speech. The Communications Decency Act, signed by President Clinton on February 8, made it illegal to post "indecent" or "patently offensive" words or pictures on the Internet where children could find them. Penalties included up to two years in prison and a $250,000 fine. Judge Stewart R. Dalzell noted, "As the most participatory form of mass speech yet developed, the Internet deserves the highest protection from governmental intrusion."

Assisted suicide. On March 8, a jury found Jack Kevorkian, a physician, not guilty of violating Michigan law by assisting in the suicides of Merian Frederick, 72, who had amyotrophic lateral sclerosis (commonly called Lou Gehrig's disease), and Ali Khalili, 61, who had bone cancer. On May 14, Kevorkian was also acquitted of charges that he illegally aided in the suicides of Sherry Miller, 43, who had multiple sclerosis, and Marjorie Wantz, 58, who suffered chronic pain after several botched operations.

The debate over medically assisted suicides was further fueled by two rulings in federal appeals courts. On March 6, the Ninth U.S. Circuit Court of Appeals struck down a Washington state law that prohibited doctors from helping terminally ill patients commit suicide. In an 8-to-3 decision, the court ruled that patients have a constitutional right to a "dignified and humane death." On April 2, the Second U.S. Circuit Court of Appeals struck down a similar New York State law. The court ruled that the law violated the constitution because its restrictions were not tied to a "legitimate state interest."

Smoking liability. In 1996, the number of states suing the tobacco industry for the cost of treating smoking-related illnesses rose to 14. The states sought billions of dollars to reimburse their Medicaid programs and to gain bans on cigarette advertisements aimed at young people. On March 28, Texas became the first state to sue the tobacco companies in federal court, alleging violations of federal racketeering and antitrust laws in an attempt to recoup more than $4 billion in Medicaid outlays since 1980 to treat tobacco-related illnesses.

On May 24, 1996, a three-judge panel of the Fifth U.S. Circuit Court of Appeals dismissed a class-action lawsuit on behalf of millions of smokers against cigarette manufacturers. The panel ruled unanimously that the case would be too unwieldy because of its size. However, plaintiffs' lawyers said they would continue to press their cases in separate actions in all 50 states.

Presidential immunity. On January 9, a three-judge panel of the Eighth U.S. Circuit Court of Appeals rejected President Clinton's contention that presidents are immune from being sued while in office. Ruling 2 to 1, the panel decided that former Arkansas state employee Paula Corbin Jones could proceed with a 1994 sexual-harassment lawsuit against Clinton. The case was delayed again on June 24, 1996, when the U.S. Supreme Court agreed to hear an appeal from Clinton on whether all proceedings should be delayed until he leaves office. The court had previously ruled that presidents are immune from suits over official activities when in office, but had not ruled on whether presidents may be sued while they are in office for incidents that oc-

curred before taking office. The Supreme Court was to hear the case in 1997.

O. J. Simpson. On Sept. 17, 1996, the civil trial of former football star and sports commentator O. J. Simpson opened in Santa Monica, California. The families of Nicole Brown Simpson, Simpson's ex-wife, and Ronald Goldman, Nicole Simpson's friend, sued O. J. Simpson for monetary compensation for the wrongful deaths of Nicole Simpson and Goldman. O. J. Simpson had been acquitted in October 1995 in a criminal trial for the murders of his ex-wife and Goldman. To win the wrongful-death suit, lawyers for the plaintiffs needed to convince only 9 of the 12 jurors that a "preponderance of evidence" demonstrated Simpson was responsible for the murders.

Abortion clinic violence. On March 18, 1996, John C. Salvi III was convicted of the 1994 murder of two receptionists at abortion clinics in Brookline, Massachusetts. He was sentenced to two life-in-prison terms without possibility of parole, plus an additional 18 to 20 years for the attempted murders of five other people. Relying on an insanity defense, Salvi's lawyers claimed that, although Salvi committed the killings, he suffered from serious mental problems. On Nov. 29, 1996, Salvi committed suicide in his prison cell in Walpole, Massachusetts.

◻ Linda P. Campbell and Geoffrey A. Campbell

See also **Crime; Supreme Court of the United States.** In *World Book,* see **Court.**

Jack Kevorkian (center) confers in court in February with a witness whose mother committed suicide, allegedly with Kevorkian's assistance.

Crime. A series of mail-bomb attacks that had baffled law-enforcement officials for 17 years may have been solved in April 1996 with the arrest in rural Montana of Theodore J. Kaczynski, 53. Kaczynski was accused of being the so-called Unabomber, an antitechnology zealot who had killed 3 people and injured 23 others with mail bombs.

Mass killings in Scotland, Tasmania. A Dunblane, Scotland, man carrying several handguns walked into a Dunblane elementary school on March 13 and opened fire, killing 16 children and a teacher. The gunman, Thomas Hamilton, also wounded 12 other children and two teachers. At the end of the shooting spree, Hamilton killed himself.

On April 28, a gunman armed with two high-powered assault rifles killed 35 people and wounded 18 others near Hobart, Tasmania. The suspect in the murders, 28-year-old Martin Bryant, pleaded guilty in November and was sentenced to life in prison.

FBI, CIA agents accused of spying. A Federal Bureau of Investigation (FBI) agent, Earl Edwin Pitts, was arrested in December on charges that for five years, in the late 1980's and early 1990's, he sold classified information to the former Soviet Union. Pitts was only the second FBI agent in the bureau's history to be accused of spying.

In November, an officer of the Central Intelligence Agency (CIA), Harold J. Nicholson, was charged with spying for Russia. Nicholson was accused of providing the Russians with the identities of newly trained CIA agents who were scheduled for foreign assignments.

"Freemen" siege ends peacefully. A stand-off in Montana between FBI agents and an antigovernment group calling itself the Freemen ended without bloodshed on June 13 when the last 16 members of the group surrendered. The 81-day confrontation was one of the longest armed sieges in U.S. history. The stand-off, at a remote farm complex outside the town of Jordan, began on March 25 when FBI agents arrested two Freemen on charges of fraud and making death threats.

Killing for love. A young man and woman from Texas faced murder charges in late 1996, accused of killing a rival for the man's affections. The suspects, David Graham and Diane Zamora, were freshmen at, respectively, the U.S. Air Force Academy and the U.S. Naval Academy at the time of their arrest in September. They were charged with slaying an acquaintance, Adrianne Jones, in November 1995 while all three were attending high school in north Texas. Police investigators said that Zamora, Graham's girlfriend, became enraged when she learned that Graham and Jones had had a sexual encounter together. The investigators said Zamora talked Graham into a joint murder plot. The two were awaiting trial at year-end.

Urban crime. Violent crime in the nation's large cities dropped by 8 percent in 1995, according to an annual survey by the FBI. But U.S. Attorney General Janet Reno commented, "This is no time to rest on our laurels. Crime is still too high."

No major American city could match New York City for a sustained decline in violent crime. In October, the police department reported that violent crime, continuing a downward trend that began in 1991, had fallen 15 percent from 1995. The number of murders in the city, which reached a record 2,245 in 1990, was down to fewer than 1,000 toward the end of 1996. That was the lowest number of murders in New York City since 1968.

The drop in crime in New York City was attributed to more criminals being in prison, to a possible decline in crack-cocaine usage, and—perhaps most of all—to the efforts of New York City Mayor Rudolph W. Giuliani to fight crime in the streets.

Violent crime, especially murder, remained especially high in New Orleans, Louisiana, which had the nation's highest homicide rate in 1996. In the last week of November, 13 people were murdered in the city of fewer than 500,000 people, including three employees of a French Quarter pizza restaurant who were herded into a freezer and shot. New Orleans Mayor Marc Morial pledged in 1996 to cut the city's murder rate in half. □ David Dreier

See also **Australia; Terrorism; United Kingdom; United States, Government of the.** In *World Book,* see **Crime.**

Croatia. In 1996 Croatian leaders, with the leaders of Bosnia and Serbia, came under continued pressure from international organizations and governments to live up to the commitments made in the 1995 Dayton accords. The international community complained about Croatia's lack of cooperation in the arrest of Bosnian war criminals. Six Croats had been indicted by the International War Crimes Tribunal in 1996.

The Croatian Democratic Union (HDZ), the ruling party, faced greater challenges from domestic opponents once the war in Bosnia was ended. President Franjo Tudjman was criticized for his actions against the city council of Zagreb, the capital, and for interfering with freedom of the press. Tudjman repeatedly refused to allow an opposition party candidate elected to the mayorship of Zagreb to take office. On April 30, he dismissed the entire city council, but Croatia's constitutional court reversed this action. Tudjman also took steps to hinder the activities of journalists critical of the government.

Despite these problems, Croatia formally joined the Council of Europe in November 1996. The council is an advisory body that promotes economic and social cooperation among European countries. Council membership was seen as a major step toward membership in the European Union. But Tudjman maintained that Croatia would resist international pressure to create close economic ties between itself

Mourners drop wreaths into the Straits of Florida in March to honor four Cuban Americans shot down by Cuban jet fighters in February.

and the other republics of the former Yugoslavia.

On April 3, United States Commerce Secretary Ronald Brown and 30 members of a U.S. delegation died in a plane crash near Dubrovnik. The delegation was visiting the region to discuss U.S. aid in reconstruction and investment.

In September, rebel Serbs completed the demobilization of their troops in Eastern Slavonia, the last part of Croatia still held by Serbs. President Tudjman declared that Croatian Serbs who were innocent of war crimes and accepted Croatia as their country would be permitted to remain in Croatia.

The Croatian economy continued to show signs of recovery in 1996. Inflation stood at 3.5 percent in 1996. Despite positive signs, the economy continued to reflect the impact of the war. Unemployment was expected to drop to 15.5 percent in 1996. Tourism recovered somewhat in 1996 but was 40 percent of its prewar level.

Croatian and Yugoslav leaders met in January and March to discuss steps toward normalizing their relations. Agreements were reached on opening a major oil pipeline and reestablishing highway, rail, and air traffic between the two capitals. On August 23, the nations signed an agreement in Belgrade to normalize relations. Formal diplomatic relations followed in early September. □ Sharon L. Wolchik

See also **Europe** (Facts in brief table); **Yugoslavia.** In *World Book,* see **Croatia.**

Cuba. On Feb. 24, 1996, Cuban MiG jet fighters shot down two small airplanes belonging to Brothers to the Rescue, a Miami-based Cuban exile organization. The incident occurred in international air space, but south of the 24th parallel, Cuba's legally defined air defense identification zone. A third plane belonging to the organization allegedly was traveling in Cuban air space, but was not fired upon. Brothers to the Rescue was patrolling the waters between Cuba and Florida searching for Cuban refugees. The group also claimed to have made unauthorized flights in the past, dropping antigovernment leaflets over Cuba.

Transcripts of radio communications between the Cuban pilots and the military's ground control revealed that the pilots were aware that they were firing upon unarmed aircraft. Also, the Cuban pilots did not contact the targeted planes, warn them of a possible attack, or attempt to escort them out of the area—actions that are required by international law.

U.S. punitive measures. President Bill Clinton characterized the incident as "an appalling reminder of the nature of the Cuban regime" and imposed punitive measures on Cuba, including the suspension of all charter flights between the two countries. He asked the U.S. Congress to enact legislation allowing some of the $100 million in frozen Cuban assets in the United States to be used to compensate the families of the four downed aviators.

On March 12, President Clinton signed into law

the Helms-Burton Bill, named for its two Republican sponsors, Senator Jesse Helms of North Carolina and Representative Dan Burton of Indiana. The legislation allowed U.S. citizens to sue foreign companies that profit from the use of Cuban properties taken from Americans after the 1959 Cuban revolution. Among other highly controversial measures, the new law also denied U.S. visas to executives of these foreign companies and to their families.

The Central Committee of Cuba's Communist Party met on March 23 and 24, 1996, to discuss the impact of the actions of the United States on the struggling Cuban economy and the future of foreign investment in Cuba. Party leaders agreed to address the economic crisis by cracking down on anti-Communist Cubans and reversing the modest free-market reforms begun in 1993.

At the March 1996 meeting, General Raúl Castro Ruz, defense minister and President Fidel Castro's brother, criticized self-employed workers and academics, calling them "Trojan horses" planted by the United States to undermine Communism.

Pope John Paul II and President Castro met for the first time on November 19 in Rome. Following the meeting, the Vatican confirmed plans for a papal visit to Cuba in 1997.   □ Nathan A. Haverstock

See also **Latin America** (Facts in brief table). In *World Book,* see Cuba.

Cyprus. See Middle East.

Czech Republic.
Despite a growing free-market economy, the coalition government of Prime Minister Václav Klaus failed in 1996 to win a majority in the parliamentary elections held May 31 and June 1. Klaus's moderate Civic Democratic Party captured only 29.6 percent of the vote. His coalition partners, the Christian Democratic Union and the Civic Democratic Alliance, won 8.1 percent and 6.3 percent respectively. The totals gave the coalition only 99 seats—2 seats short of a majority.

Parliamentary shift. The moderately liberal Social Democrats took 26.4 percent of the vote. This increased the party's presence in the Chamber of Deputies from 16 to 61 seats and gave it the power to influence the formation of a government.

After the coalition failed to establish a majority necessary to form a government, Czech President Václav Havel brokered a deal between the coalition parties and the Social Democrats. Havel persuaded the Social Democrats to allow Prime Minister Klaus to form a minority government. In return, Miloš Zeman, leader of the Social Democrats, became speaker of the parliament. Klaus's government survived a no-confidence vote on July 25, after the Social Democrats walked out in a dispute over the return of confiscated property to the Roman Catholic Church.

The economy of the Czech Republic grew by about 5 percent in 1996. Unemployment remained under 3 percent, and inflation fell to approximately

8.5 percent by midyear. Foreign investment continued to grow. The country's trade deficit, however, also increased, reaching $3.1 billion by late July. The Czech Republic continued to trade primarily with developed Western countries.

International affairs. In 1996, the Czech Republic was again criticized by human rights groups and by U.S. government officials for its policies toward a minority group called the Rom (also known as Gypsies). Czech leaders insisted that their country's citizenship law, which left many Rom without citizenship, was fair. Despite this issue, the Czech Republic continued to make progress toward membership in NATO and the European Union.

After World War II, millions of ethnic Germans were expelled from the Sudetenland, then a primarily ethnic-German area of Czechoslovakia. Many fled to Germany. In 1995, Czech and German officials began working to draft a reconciliation agreement on the Sudeten German issue. In 1996, they were still struggling to find mutually agreeable language in which Germany would apologize for the excesses of Nazi rule and the Czechs would apologize for the expulsion of ethnic Germans. In addition, many Czechs wanted the Sudeten Germans to drop their demands to reclaim or receive compensation for their lost property.   □ Sharon L. Wolchik

See also **Europe** (Facts in brief table). In *World Book,* see **Czech Republic; Sudetenland.**

Dallas.
On June 14, 1996, the first 11 miles (18 ' kilometers) of a light-rail, mass transportation system opened in Dallas. The line provided commuter service from downtown to the Oak Cliff section of south Dallas. Plans called for the Dallas Area Rapid Transit (DART) line to be extended to north Dallas by early 1997 and for the construction of 53 miles (85 kilometers) of additional line by 2010. Completion of the first phase convinced four of DART's member cities to vote on August 10 to remain in the system.

Drought. During 1996, Dallas suffered its worst drought since 1978. By July, the city had received only half its normal annual rainfall of 33.7 inches (85.6 centimeters). Fortunately, a long-range lake development plan, established after the great drought of the early 1950's, kept city officials from requiring water rationing.

Texas Instruments (TI) announced plans on Feb. 20, 1996, for a $2-billion expansion at its Dallas headquarters. The new plant construction was part of a company bid to gain a larger share of the worldwide semiconductor market. On May 29, TI chairman, President, and Chief Executive Officer Jerry R. Junkins, 58, died after suffering a heart attack. Junkins was one of Dallas's top civic leaders.

Schools superintendent Chad Woolery resigned August 5 to accept an executive post with the Voyager Foundation, a nonprofit organization that provides educational after-school programs. During

Woolery's three-year tenure, student test scores and attendance improved, and the drop-out rate declined. There were, however, public clashes at school board meetings. A June 11 board meeting was canceled after the New Black Panther Party threatened to attend bearing firearms. The New Black Panthers were angry that Bill Keever, a white man, was appointed school board president while no African American held a leadership position. Woolery subsequently created the position of chief of staff and appointed an African American to the post. Almost 90 percent of the students in the Dallas public schools are Hispanic or African American.

City council member Paul Fielding was indicted on June 21 on federal charges of extortion and bankruptcy fraud. Fielding was accused of using his position to gain a lucrative cleaning contract for a client, of lying during a bankruptcy proceeding, and of conspiring to defraud investors.

Downtown development. The Dallas City Council created a special downtown taxing district on June 26 to encourage more residential and retail development. New taxes collected in the district have been earmarked to build parking garages and make other improvements. The plan is expected to raise $140 million over the next 15 years.

Trinity plan. A long-range, multibillion-dollar plan to turn the flood-prone Trinity River into an economic asset won support during an August 23 meeting of federal, state, and local officials. The U.S. Army Corps of Engineers agreed to proceed with design studies of the project, and the Texas Department of Transportation has drawn plans to build a freeway along one of the levees. Plans also include building lakes, parks, and high-rise residential units.

The Dallas Cowboys football team won its third Super Bowl victory—27-17 over the Pittsburgh Steelers—in four years on Jan. 28, 1996. However, Cowboys star wide receiver Michael Irvin was indicted in April on charges of felony cocaine and marijuana possession. On July 15, Irvin pleaded "no contest" and was sentenced to four years' probation and 800 hours of community service and fined $10,000. Prior to the trial, Dallas police officer Johnnie Hernandez was arrested on charges of attempting to hire a federal agent posing as a hit man to kill Irvin. Officer Hernandez alleged that Irvin had threatened Irvin's girlfriend, who was to be a witness at the drug possession trial. Hernandez pleaded guilty on August 2 and received a six-year prison term.

The Dallas Mavericks basketball team was sold on May 1 by Donald Carter to a group of Dallas investors headed by land developer Ross Perot, Jr., and automobile dealer David McDavid. Perot, with city and possibly state financing, planned to build a multibillion-dollar sports arena complex with shops and apartments to serve as the new home of the Mavericks. □ Henry K. Tatum

See also **City.** In *World Book,* see **Dallas.**

Dancing. Lincoln Kirstein, the most influential advocate of ballet in the United States, died on Jan. 5, 1996, at the age of 88. By bringing choreographer George Balanchine from Europe to the United States in 1933, Kirstein in effect sowed the seeds of a classical dance tradition in this country. In the 1930's, ballet was synonymous in the public's mind with the former Soviet Union. Through the example of Balanchine's ballets and teaching methods, Kirstein advanced the idea of a native style—contemporary in spirit and danced by Americans, yet as technically rigorous and pure as the Russian school of which Balanchine himself was a product.

In 1934, the two men founded the School of American Ballet in New York City, from which developed a series of companies that in 1948 became the New York City Ballet. Kirstein poured his private fortune into ensuring the stability of the school and Balanchine's artistic freedom as director. But it was his moral and intellectual commitment as much as his patronage that made him such a unique figure.

Uncertain future. Kirstein's death triggered further speculation about City Ballet's future. Patrons who had worried that the company has largely abandoned the classical tradition could take no comfort in the new works presented in 1996 at the New York State Theater in New York City. Three of the five works were by choreographers from modern dance. The other two ballets—*Reliquary*, a tribute to Balanchine and Russian-born composer Igor Stravinsky—and *Tchaikovsky Pas de Quatre*, choreographed by Peter Martins, the company's artistic director, suggested to many observers that Martins was running out of steam. Martins was also criticized for not developing his principal dancers into mature artists.

American Ballet Theater. Generating more excitement were the dancers of the American Ballet Theater (ABT) of New York City under the guidance of Kevin McKenzie. Among those attracting particular attention were Paloma Herrera, Jose Manuel Carreno, Vladimir Malakhov, and Angel Corella. ABT's most ambitious repertory undertaking in 1996 was the May 3 premiere of Twyla Tharp's *The Elements*, during the troupe's season at the Metropolitan Opera House in New York City. But it was Tharp's reworking of *Americans We* to highlight the virtuosity of Herrera and Corella that caused a sensation.

Tharp also formed a new company for which she created three new pieces: *Heroes,* a large-scale work to a new score by American composer Philip Glass; *66,* a parody of American life—named for the famed highway—set to 1950's and 1960's music; and *Sweet Fields,* accompanied by American sacred choral music. Under the title *Tharp!,* this program began a 20-city tour on Sept. 20, 1996, in Berkeley, California.

Premieres. On April 19, Merce Cunningham's *Ocean* had its first American performance at the University of California. *Ocean* is the last work that Cunningham and composer John Cage, his collaborator

Opulent sets and costumes frame the dancers of the Paris Opera Ballet during its June staging of Marius Petipa's *La Bayadère* in New York City.

for nearly 50 years, conceived before Cage's death in 1992. According to Cage's specifications, the 90-minute dance is performed in the round, with 112 musicians sitting in a circle behind the audience. The score, by Andrew Culver, is based on Cage's notations. Although Cunningham's choreography was not a radical departure from past work, *Ocean* was hailed as a luminous summation of Cunningham's esthetic and a beautiful monument to the Cunningham-Cage enterprise. Cunningham used an old Cage score for another new work, *Rondo,* that received its U.S. premiere on June 19, 1996, at the American Dance Festival in Durham, North Carolina.

Debuting on October 3 at Berkeley's Zellerbach Hall was Pina Bausch's *Nur Du (Only You).* Although Bausch's German-based Tanztheater Wuppertal has been a frequent visitor to the United States, *Nur Du* is her first work inspired by American culture. (The title is taken from a hit song by the Platters, a group popular in the 1950's.) To prepare the piece, Bausch and her group prowled streets, churches, and homeless shelters in California and Texas for material.

The Trisha Brown Dance Company. Trisha Brown celebrated the 25th anniversary of her company with an eventful week at New York City's Brooklyn Academy of Music, where she opened the theater's annual Next Wave Festival on October 1. Continuing her exploration of music from the classical canon, she turned to chamber pieces by Austrian composer Anton Webern. *Twelve-Ton Rose* (a pun on Webern's system of composition called twelve-tone rows) was the one completely new dance. Brown also expanded a 1994 solo work, *If you could see me*—danced by Brown with her back to the audience—into a duet *You can see us,* performed with guest artist Mikhail Baryshnikov. Brown's retrospective programming revived choreography from the 1960's and reintroduced former colleague Steve Paxton, who joined Brown in improvisational duets.

The Joffrey Ballet of Chicago was still struggling in 1996, eight years after the death of founder Robert Joffrey, to find its artistic identity and financial footing. Having moved to Chicago from New York City in 1995, the group's debut season, May 22 to June 2, 1996, was presented as part of Chicago's Spring Festival of Dance. While some of the company's premieres were created by artistic director Gerald Arpino, most were by relatively unknown choreographers.

Lincoln Center Festival '96. New York City spawned a new summer arts festival, Lincoln Center Festival '96, which ran from July 22 to August 11. In the dance arena, the Lyon National Opera Ballet of France presented the American premiere of Maguy Marin's satirical update of the 1870 classic *Coppelia.* Instead of taking place in a charming village square, Marin's version is set in a drab housing project. The hero is bedazzled not by a pretty mechanical doll

but by a chorus line of men and women all wearing short, tight dresses and high heels. Also presented at the festival was *Sweet Release,* choreographed by Judith Jamison, artistic director of the Alvin Ailey American Dance Theater, to a commissioned score by jazz composer Wynton Marsalis.

Changes in Canada. James Kudelka, artist-in-residence at the National Ballet of Canada in Toronto since 1992, became the troupe's artistic director on June 1, 1996. Kudelka replaced Reid Anderson, director from 1989 to 1995, who had resigned in protest when the Ontario Arts Council cut the company's subsidy by $425,000 (Canadian dollars), about 25 percent of its government allotment. Budget cuts had also forced the company to reduce its roster from 71 to 59 dancers. Anderson took over the Stuttgart Ballet in Germany.

Kudelka trained at the National Ballet School and from 1972 to 1981 and was a member and soloist with the National Ballet, where he created his first choreography in 1980. In 1981, he joined Montreal's Les Grandes Ballets Canadiens, where he served as resident choreographer from 1984 to 1990. Among the tasks facing Kudelka as head of the National Ballet was raising funds for the company's new Ballet Center. Only half the cost of the $12-million facility was contributed by the government.

☐ Nancy Goldner

In *World Book,* see **Ballet; Dance.**

Agnew, Spiro (1918-September 17), U.S. vice president (1969–1973) under Richard Nixon, known for his colorful, alliterative attacks—"nattering nabobs of negativism," "pusillanimous pussyfooters"—on anti-Viet Nam War protesters and the media. Agnew was forced to resign on Oct. 10, 1973, after plea bargaining to avoid prison on tax evasion charges.

Amsterdam, Morey (1914?-October 28), wisecracking comedian best remembered for his role on television's "The Dick Van Dyke Show" of the early 1960's.

Annabella (1909-September 18), French film actress who achieved only modest success in Hollywood but was acclaimed by French audiences for her work in such films as René Clair's *Le Million* and *Quatorze Juillet* and Marcel Carné's *Hôtel du Nord.*

Ahern, Kathy (1949-July 6), golf prodigy who joined the Ladies Professional Golf Association Tour at the age of 17 and won three major L.P.G.A. tournaments before injuries ended her career in the late 1970's.

Allen, Mel (1913-June 16), sports announcer who was the Southern-tinted, ebullient voice of the New York Yankees from 1939 to 1964.

Ayres, Lew (1908-December 30), actor who was best known for his performance in *All Quiet on the Western Front* and his portrayal of Dr. Kildare in 9 films.

Azikiwe, Nnamdi (1904-May 11), first president of Nigeria who attempted to forge alliances between the nation's dominant ethnic groups.

Bainbridge, Kenneth (1904-July 14), physicist who built Harvard's first cyclotron and headed Project Trinity, the first atomic-bomb test.

Balsam, Martin (1919-February 13), Academy-award-winning actor best remembered for his role as a detective who is murdered in Alfred Hitchcock's *Psycho.*

Belli, Melvin (1907-July 9), histrionic lawyer of the famous and infamous, dubbed the King of Torts, who achieved fame through his 1964 defense of Jack Ruby, the man who killed Lee Harvey Oswald.

Beradino, John (1917-May 19), professional baseball player and actor who appeared in "Our Gang" comedies and for 33 years played physician Steve Hardy on the soap opera "General Hospital."

Berman, Pandro S. (1905-July 13), Hollywood producer of more than 100 films, including *Gunga Din, The Blackboard Jungle,* and the Astaire and Rogers musicals *Top Hat* and *The Gay Divorcee.*

Bernardin, Joseph Cardinal (1928-November 14), Roman Catholic archbishop of Chicago, the nation's second largest archdiocese, who was credited with helping resolve troubling issues within the church.

Bessel, Ted (1939-October 8), television director and actor who appeared in more than 30 productions, including "That Girl," in which he played the boyfriend, Donald Hollinger.

Bokassa, Jean-Bedel (1919-November 3), self-proclaimed emperor of the Central African Republic.

Bombeck, Erma (1927-April 22), humorist, columnist, and best-selling author who gently poked fun at housekeeping, parenting, and postwar, suburban life.

McGeorge Bundy, foreign policy adviser to presidents Kennedy and Johnson

Audrey Meadows, television actress

Greer Garson, motion-picture actress

Boorda, Admiral Jeremy (1938-May 16), chief of Naval Operations and member of the Joint Chiefs of Staff who was the first sailor in U.S. naval history to climb from enlisted man to four-star admiral.

Bowser, Arda C. (1889-September 7), last surviving member of the first National Football League championship team—the Canton, Ohio, Bulldogs—and the inventor of the kicking tee.

Brodsky, Joseph (1940-January 28), exiled Russian poet who won the Nobel prize in 1987 and was named U.S. poet laureate in 1991.

Brother Adam (1898-September 1), English Benedictine monk and bee breeder, whose experiments produced the Buckfast Superbee, widely regarded as the healthiest and most prolific honey producer ever bred.

Brown, Ron (1941-April 3), U.S. secretary of commerce and former Democratic National Committee chairman.

Brownell, Herbert (1904-May 1), Eisenhower Administration attorney general who played a key role in implementing Supreme Court desegregation decisions.

Bundy, McGeorge (1919-September 16), influential foreign policy adviser who advocated enlarging American involvement in the Vietnam War.

Burke, Admiral Arleigh A. (1901-January 1), former U.S. chief of naval operations who was the Navy's most celebrated destroyer squadron commander of World War II.

Burns, George (1896-March 9), vaudeville, radio, and television comedian who with partner and wife Gracie Allen helped redirect American comedy.

Carné, Marcel (1906-November 1), French film director whose *Les Enfants du Paradis* is considered one of the great motion-picture classics.

Caesar, Irving, (1895-December 17), lyricist of more than 1,000 songs, including *Tea for Two, Swanee,* and *Just a Gigolo.* Caesar was one of the last links to New York City's legendary Tin Pan Alley.

Chancellor, John (1927-July 12), newsman who for 41 years at NBC television reported political conventions, space shots, wars, and the news of the day and broadcast thoughtful analyses and unqiue commentaries.

Chaplin, Lita Grey (1908-January 6), actress who at 12 years old won a lead role in *The Kid,* which also starred Charlie Chaplin. She married Chaplin at age 16 and divorced him at age 18.

Cherrill, Virginia (1908-November 14), actress who starred as a blind flower girl in the Charlie Chaplin silent film *City Lights.*

Christine, Virginia (1920-July 24), film and television actress who was best known for the persona she created—Mrs. Olson—for Folger's coffee commercials.

Clark, Ossie (1942-August 6), British fashion designer whose romantic clothes and frenetic lifestyle helped define "mod" in 1960's London.

Clarke, Henry (1919-April 26), high-fashion photographer, from 1950 to the 1970's, for *Vogue* magazine.

Colbert, Claudette (1903-July 30), stage and screen star who was best known for her unflappable characters in classic screwball comedies, including Frank Capra's *It Happened One Night,* for which she won the 1934 Academy Award for best actress, and Preston Sturges's *The Palm Beach Story* (1942).

Colby, William (1920-April 27), Central Intelligence Agency (CIA) director who was responsible for moving control and accountability for the CIA into the executive branch of the U.S. government.

Collins, Tommy (1929-June 3), featherweight boxer who in 1953 was beaten so savagely by the lightweight champion, Jimmy Carter, that the fight sparked an outcry for boxing reform, which led to the "three-times down rule."

Condon, Richard (1915-April 9), novelist and political satirist who wrote *The Manchurian Candidate, Winter Kills,* and *Prizzi's Honor.*

Conover, Willis (1920-May 17), "Voice of America Jazz Hour" host who was tagged "most famous American virtually no American has ever heard of."

Cray, Seymour (1925-October 5), computer pioneer who headed the design team of the first transistor-based computer and was honored as the father of the supercomputer industry.

Davies, Ronald (1904-April 18), federal judge who in 1957 ordered the forced integration of Little Rock, Arkansas, schools.

Dominguín (1926-May 8), leading Spanish bullfighter, whose style in the bull ring was chronicled by Hemingway in *The Dangerous Summer* (1959) and whose charm out of the ring attracted the likes of Picasso and film actress Ava Gardner.

Gene Kelly, dancer and
motion-picture actor

Erma Bombeck, newspaper
columnist and humorist

Kenneth Bainbridge,
physicist

Dove, Ulysses (1947-June 11), choreographer whose
works were performed by the Alvin Ailey American
Dance Theater and the New York City Ballet.

Dru, Joanne (1922-September 10), movie actress who
starred in such classic Westerns as Howard Hawks's
Red River and John Ford's *She Wore a Yellow
Ribbon*.

Duras, Marguerite (1914-March 3), French novelist
whose works included the 1984 novel *L'Amant* and
the 1960 screenplay *Hiroshima, Mon Amour*.

Edwards, Vince (1928-March 11), actor famed for playing "Ben Casey" in the popular TV show of the 1960's.

Elder, Lonne (1931-June 11), playwright who wrote the
modern classic *Ceremonies in Dark Old Men* and
screenplay for the
film *Sounder*.

Erdos, Paul (1913-
September 20),
mathematician who
was credited with
founding the field of
discrete mathemat-
ics, which laid the
foundation for com-
puter science.

Finley, Charlie (1919-
February 18), major-
league baseball-team
owner who is credit-
ed with instituting
the designated hit-
ter, colored uni-
forms, and nighttime
World Series games.

Carl Sagan,
astronomer and author

Fitzgerald, Ella (1917-June 15), preeminent jazz vocalist of her generation, dubbed "first lady of song."

Garson, Greer (1903-April 6), film actress noted for her
portrayals of noble women, including Eleanor Roosevelt in *Sunrise at Campobello, Madame Curie*, and
Mrs. Miniver, for which she received the 1942 Academy Award for best actress.

Gordon, Irving (1915-December 1), songwriter who
penned hundreds of tunes, including "Unforgettable"
for Nat King Cole.

Guillikson, Tim (1951-May 4), former tennis pro who
coached Mary Joe Fernandez, Martina Navratilova,
and Pete Sampras.

Helm, Brigitte (1905-June 11), German film actress of
the silent era who played the good Maria and her evil,
robotic twin in the Fritz Lang classic *Metropolis*.

Hemingway, Margaux (1955-June 29), fashion model,
actress, and granddaughter of Ernest Hemingway who
was described as having "the face of a generation."

Hill, Julian (1904-January 28), research chemist who discovered nylon in the 1930's.

Hiss, Alger (1904-November 15), diplomat who was accused of spying for the former Soviet Union and convicted of perjury in 1950 for alleged lying during his
1948 appearance before the House Committee on Un-
American Activities, which was investigating Communists in the State Department.

Hooker, Evelyn (1907-November 18), psychologist who
researched homosexual men in the 1950's. Hooker
shocked the world by suggesting that homosexuality
is not a psychological disorder.

Hummert, Anne (1905-July 5), inventor of radio soap
opera who spun many of the classic radio serials, including *Helen Trent, Ma Perkins*, and *Stella Dallas*.

Hurd, Cuthbert (1911-May 22), mathematician and
computer scientist who was instrumental in the development of the first IBM general computer and headed
the first independent computer software company.

Israel, Frank (1945-June 10), architect of Los Angeles
vernacular structures and designer of sets for such
films as *Star Trek: The Motion Picture*.

Jellicoe, Sir Geoffrey (1900-July 17), a leading British
landscape architect whose designs included the British
memorial to John F. Kennedy at Runnymede on the
Thames River.

165

Deaths

P. L. Travers, author of Mary Poppins books

Spiro Agnew, U.S. vice president 1969–1973

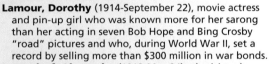

Minnie Pearl, country comedian and storyteller

Jenco, Lawrence M. (1934-July 19), Roman Catholic priest who was held hostage for 18 months in the 1980's by Islamic radicals in Lebanon.

Jordan, Barbara (1936-January 27), the first African-American woman from the South to serve in the U.S. House of Representatives since Reconstruction.

Junkins, Jerry R. (1937-May 29), Texas Instruments chairman who rose from the factory floor to top executive and was credited with reviving the American computer-chip industry.

Juyewardene, Junius Richard (1906-November 1), former president of Sri Lanka who led efforts to modernize and reshape the country politically.

Keane, Molly (1905-April 22), Anglo-Irish novelist of manners whose works included *Conversation Piece* and *Good Behavior.*

Kelly, Gene (1912-February 2), dancer, actor, director, and choreographer who redefined the Hollywood musical with athleticism and ingenuity. He starred in such classic musicals as *Singin' in the Rain, On the Town,* and *An American in Paris.*

Kerr, Walter (1913-October 9), theater critic from 1951 until 1983, first for the *New York Herald Tribune* and then *The New York Times,* celebrated for the wit and intelligence of his criticism.

Kieslowski, Krzysztof (1942-March 14), Polish film director who achieved acclaim for his trilogy *Three Colors (Blue, White, Red).*

Kirstein, Lincoln (1907-January 5), writer, critic, and cultural figure who, with George Balanchine, founded and directed both New York City's School of American Ballet and the influential New York City Ballet.

Kosterlitz, Hans W. (1903-October 28), researcher who discovered enkephalins, opiate-like substances in the brain, which led to the discovery endorphins.

Kraus, Hans (1905-March 6), specialist in physical medicine and rehabilitation who had been called the father of sports medicine.

Kubelik, Rafael (1914-August 11), conductor for the Chicago Symphony Orchestra, the Royal Opera at Covent Garden, London, and the Bavarian Radio Symphony Orchestra of Munich, Germany.

Lacoste, René (1904-October 12), legendary French tennis star who invented the metal racket and lent his name and nickname—the Crocodile—to a line of sports clothes and its reptilian logo.

Lamour, Dorothy (1914-September 22), movie actress and pin-up girl who was known more for her sarong than her acting in seven Bob Hope and Bing Crosby "road" pictures and who, during World War II, set a record by selling more than $300 million in war bonds.

Langsdorf, Alexander (1912-May 24), physicist who produced the plutonium used as a source of energy in the first atomic test bomb and the atomic bomb dropped on Nagasaki, Japan, in 1945.

LaRue, Lash (1917-May 21), 1940's star of two dozen "B" movie Westerns who, in his prime as the Cheyenne Kid, could pluck a flower with a single flick of his trademark bullwhip.

Lasser, David (1902-May 5), founder of the American Institute of Aeronautics and Astronautics and author of the highly influential *The Conquest of Space,* source of the idea that rocket propulsion made space travel possible.

Roger Tory Peterson, naturalist and illustrator

Leakey, Mary (1913-December 9), anthropology-clan matriarch who discovered 3.7-million-year-old footprints made by human ancestors.

Leary, Timothy (1920-May 31), Harvard psychologist and 1960's guru who introduced a generation to psychedelic drugs and coined the phrase "turn on, tune in, and drop out."

Lenard, Mark (1928-November 22), actor who gained fame in his role as Sarek of Vulcan, father of Mr. Spock, in the TV and film series "Star Trek."

Lews, Henry (1932-January 26), the first African American conductor and musical director of a major American orchestra. He broke racial barriers when he conducted the New Jersey Symphony Orchestra.

Lorengar, Pilar (1928-June 2), lyric soprano best known for her roles in the operas of Mozart.

Marmur, Julius (1926-May 20), geneticist and biochemist whose early research on DNA contributed to unlocking the mysteries of heredity.

Mastroianni, Marcello (1924–December 18), Italian actor who is best remembered for his depiction of suave, Latin lovers and his starring roles in Federico Fellini's *La Dolce Vita* and *8½*.

McCampbell, David (1910-June 30), naval aviation "ace of aces" who during World War II shot down 32 Japanese planes. McCampbell received the Medal of Honor for leading his air group into a formation of 60 planes and personally dispatching 9 enemy aircraft in 95 minutes.

McNeill, Don (1907-May 7), good-natured host of the daily radio program "Don McNeill's Breakfast Club" from 1933 to 1968.

Meadows, Audrey (1924-February 3), actress who starred as Alice, wife of Ralph Kramden, on the early television show "The Honeymooners."

Milne, Christopher Robin, (1920-April 20), son of A. A. Milne, the author of *Winnie the Pooh,* who modeled the character Christopher Robin after his son.

Mitchell, Joseph (1908-May 24), writer whose nonfiction stories of ordinary, if eccentric, lives were featured in *The New Yorker* from the 1930's to the 1960's.

Mitford, Jessica (1917-July 23), leading muckraking journalist who wrote *The American Way of Death*. Mitford was one of the eccentric Mitford sisters immortalized in sister Nancy's *The Pursuit of Love* and *Love in a Cold Climate.*

Mitterrand, François (1916-January 8), longest serving president of France who forged the French Socialist Party. When Mitterrand took office in 1981, socialists gained power for the first time since 1936.

Claudette Colbert, stage and film actress

John Chancellor, television newscaster and commentator

Monroe, Bill (1911-September 9), musician who fused gospel harmonies and Celtic fiddling, blues, and folk songs into a sound that came to be called bluegrass for Monroe's band, the Blue Grass Boys.

Montana, Patsy (1914-May 3), pioneer country-music star whose 1935 hit, "I Want to Be a Cowboy's Sweetheart" was the first million-seller hit for a female country singer.

Morris, Greg (1934-September 5), actor who portrayed the electronics wizard Barney Collier on the 1970's television series "Mission: Impossible."

Muskie, Edmond (1915-March 26), Democrat from Maine who served his state as governor and U.S. senator. Muskie was nominated for vice president in 1969. He ran for his party's nomination in the 1972 presidential primaries.

Nath, Pandit Pran (1918-June 13), Indian classical singer whose mastery of the 600-year-old kirana style and whose encyclopaedic knowledge of raga transformed him from naked singing saint to concert artist.

Niarchos, Stavros (1910-April 15), Greek shipping magnate famed for his rivalry with fellow shipping magnate Aristotle Onassis.

Overmyer, R. F. (Robert Franklyn) (1936-March 22), a commander of the space shuttle Challenger and a member of Apollo 17 support crew.

Packard, David (1913-March 27), computer pioneer who started Hewlett-Packard in a garage in 1939.

Packard, Vance (1914-December 9), prolific author who railed against materialism, manipulation in advertising, and commercialization in such books as *The Status Seekers* and *The Hidden Persuaders.*

Papandreou, Andreas (1919-June 23), former prime minister of Greece who dominated Greek political life for much of the last 25 years.

Pearl, Minnie (1912-March 4), country comedian and storyteller whose regular appearances on "The Grand Ole Opry" spanned more than half a century.

Peterson, Roger Tory (1908-July 28), ornithologist whose classic 1934 *Field Guide to the Birds* instructed and inspired generations of bird watchers.

Deaths

Prowse, Juliet (1937-September 14), dancer whose career was launched when her dancing on the 1959 *Can-Can* movie set was pronounced "immoral" by visiting Soviet leader Nikita·Khrushchev.

Reichstein, Tadeus (1897-August 1), Noble Prize-winning chemist who isolated corticosterone (or cortisone), the steroid used to reduce inflammation, from adrenal gland hormones.

Rozelle, Pete (1926-December 6) former National Football League commissioner who instituted the Super Bowl games in 1967.

Rudolph, Arthur (1906-January. 3), scientist who developed the Saturn V booster that in 1969 transported U.S. astronauts to the moon.

Sagan, Carl (1934-December 20), astronomer and Pulitzer Prize-winning author, best known for his 13-part TV series "Cosmos." Sagan supported the possibility that life exists elsewhere in the universe.

Schwab, Leon (1911-January 6), cofounder of the Hollywood pharmacy Schwab's Drugstore, a hang-out for movie actors in the 1930's and 1940's. Actress Lana Turner was said to have been discovered while sipping a soda in Schwab's.

Shakur, Tupac (1971-September 13), controversial, best-selling rapsinger and Billboard chart-topper who was murdered in a drive-by shooting following a Las Vegas prizefight.

Siegel, Jerry (1914-January 28), cocreator of Superman, the character who first donned his cape in 1938.

Rafael Kubelik, conductor

Snell, George (1903-June 6), Nobel Prize-winning biologist whose work on genetics laid the basis for organ transplantation.

Snyder, Jimmy "The Greek" (1922-April 20), odds maker and regular on the television show "The NFL Today."

Stevenson, McLean (1929-February 15), actor who played Henry Blake on the TV series "M*A*S*H*."

Stokes, Carl (1927-April 4), Cleveland major, 1967 to 1971, who was the first African American mayor of a major U.S. city.

Suenens, Leo Jazef (1904-May 6), Belgian cardinal dubbed "the architect of 20th century Catholicism."

Taylor, Charles F. (1894-June 22), mechanical engineer who worked for Orville and Wilbur Wright and helped design the Whirlwind engine for Charles Lindbergh's plane *The Spirit of St. Louis.*

Terra, Daniel J. (1911-June 28), business executive and collector of American paintings who founded the Terra museums in Chicago and Giverny, France.

Tiny Tim (1932-November 30), ukulele-playing singer who crooned "Tiptoe Through the Tulips With Me" in his trademark falsetto, making the song a novelty hit in the 1960's.

Toumanova, Tamara (1919May 29), child-prodigy ballerina who became famliar to American audiences in the 1930's and 1940's.

Travers, P. L. (Pamela Lyndon) (1899–April 23), English writer who penned *Mary Poppins.*

Trilling, Diana (1905-October 23), cultural critic whose essays and critiques appeared in *The New Yorker, The Atlantic, The Saturday Review,* and *The Nation.* Trilling was the wife of writer Lionel Trilling.

Tudor, David (1926-August 13), composer and pianist whose association with composer John Cage resulted in Tudor's appointment as director of the Merce Cunningham Dance Company in 1992.

Tuttle, Elbert P. (1897-June 23), former chief justice of the old U.S. Court of Appeals for the Fifth Circuit who was awarded the Presidential Medal of Freedom in 1980 for his role in the 1950's and 1960's in extending civil rights to black Southerners. President Jimmy Carter said that Tuttle had "helped make the constitutional principle of equal protection a reality of American life."

van der Post, Laurens (1906-December 15), author of 25 works of fiction and nonfiction who became a spiritual mentor to Great Britain's Prince Charles and godfather to Prince William.

Van Fleet, Jo (1915-June 10), Tony and Academy award-winning actress known for her portrayals of strong, proud women in such films as *East of Eden* and *Cool Hand Luke* and on stage in Tennessee Williams's *Camino Real.*

Versalle, Richard (1933-January 15), operatic tenor who died of a heart attack after singing the line "You can only live so long" during the opening scene of *The Makropulos Case.*

Walenda, Angel (1968-May 3), circus performer who continued to walk the high wire on an artificial limb after losing a leg to cancer.

Wanderone, Rudolf Walter (1906?-January 18), charming pool hustler who in the 1960's adopted the name Minnesota Fats.

Watson, Johnny "Guitar" (1924-May 17), flamboyant rhythm and blues guitarist and singer whose unique sound was described by rock musician Frank Zappa as "an icepick to the forehead."

Weston, Jack (1925-May 3), balding, rotund character actor who appeared in the cult film classics *Wait Until Dark* and *The Ritz.*

Whittle, Sir Frank (1907-August 8), British inventor who at age 21 conceived of jet propulsion in a college thesis and at age 30 built the first jet engine.

Yaoting, Sun (1902-December 19), the last eunuch to serve China's last emperor, Pu Yi.

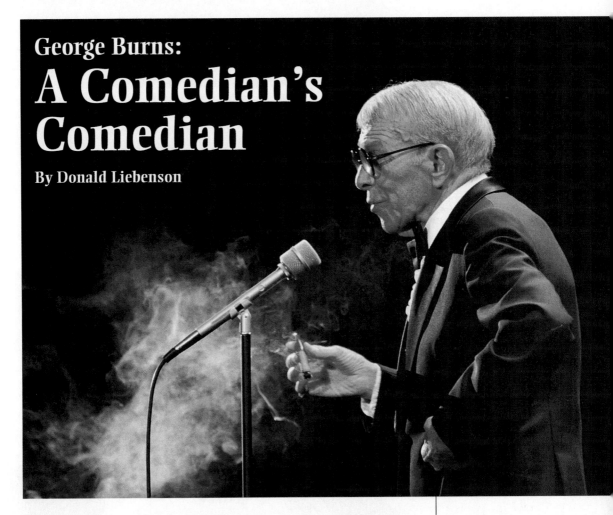

George Burns:
A Comedian's Comedian

By Donald Liebenson

O n his 90th birthday, comedian George Burns quipped, "I can't afford to die. I'd lose a fortune. I'm booked." And more than once he remarked that he would retire from show business on the day he died. On March 9, 1996, at age 100, Burns died at his home in Beverly Hills. His passing closed the final chapter of a remarkable show business story that spanned more than 90 years.

George Burns was among the last of a generation of entertainers who began their careers on the vaudeville stage. In the 1920's, he formed with Gracie Allen, whom he later married, one of the most beloved comedy teams of the 20th century. After Allen's death in 1964, Burns became a star in his own right as an actor and fixture on nightclub and concert stages around the world. He was also a popular author, who published several books chronicling his long career. His last book, *100 Years, 100 Stories,* was on the bestseller lists at the time of his death.

The author

Donald Liebenson writes about entertainment for the *Los Angeles Time*s and the *Chicago Tribune.*

His comic trademarks were his gravelly voice, rapid-patter singing style, and ever-present cigar, which he frequently puffed for emphasis between jokes. Much of his gentle humor was directed at himself: "If I get a laugh," he once said, "I'm a comedian. If I get a small laugh, I'm a humorist. If I get no laughs, I'm a singer. If my singing gets big laughs, then I'm a comedian again." In the latter part of his career, his age became the source for some of his most memorable one-liners: "It's nice to be here," he would announce to audiences. "At my age, it's nice to be anywhere." Indeed, to mark his 100th birthday, Burns had scheduled appearances at the London Palladium and Caesars Palace in Las Vegas. But his health had deteriorated since an accident in July 1994, when he slipped and fell in the shower, and he was forced to cancel.

Early life and career

George Burns, whose real name was Nathan Birnbaum, was born on Jan. 20, 1896. He was the 9th of 12 children in a family that lived in a small apartment on New York City's Lower East Side. "Nattie," as he was called by his family, was five years old when he performed for his first audiences by dancing on sidewalks accompanied by an organ grinder who worked the neighborhood.

When Burns was seven years old, his father died. He earned money shining shoes, selling newspapers, and running errands. His show business career began in earnest when he formed the Pee Wee Quartet with three other neighborhood boys. He quit school when he was in the fourth grade.

Burns stars with his wife and partner, Gracie Allen, in "The George Burns and Gracie Allen Show," which ran on CBS Television from 1950-1958. The show is recognized as one of the most innovative programs of its day.

Burns would do any kind of act to break into vaudeville. He sang, danced, and was a trick roller skater. He appeared with dogs and even with trained seals. He also performed under many guises: He was the "Company" of Fry and Company, "Williams" of Brown and Williams, and "Links" of Burns and Links. He might appear in the same city billed as Jimmy Delight one week and Billy Pierce the next. "I never knew what my name was," he joked, recalling those early years. "After playing a theater, I would have to change my name. The booker who booked me would never give me another job if he knew who I was."

Burns and Allen

This all changed in 1923, when Burns teamed up with a 17-year-old Irish-American actress, Grace Ethel Cicile Rosalie Allen. Burns intended for "Gracie" to play the straight man while he cracked the jokes, but their roles were quickly reversed when Burns noticed that audiences laughed more at her setups than at his punch lines.

"Dizzy," the title of their first routine, summed up Gracie's appeal. Her character was a woman whose fractured logic made perfect sense to her, but confounded everyone else. As Burns described it, her character would put salt in the pepper shaker and pepper in the salt shaker so if she ever mixed them up, she would be right. After three years as a comedy team, the couple were married on Jan. 7, 1926, in Cleveland.

Burns and Allen went on to become vaudeville headliners. They also made guest appearances on radio shows and made a series of one- and two-reel short subject films, most of which Burns wrote.

In 1932, the team debuted their own radio show on the Columbia Broadcasting System (CBS) and appeared in their first feature film, *The Big Broadcast,* opposite Bing Crosby. They appeared in a total of 14 films, most memorably in *International House* (1933), with W. C. Fields, and *A Damsel in Distress* (1937), in which they danced with Fred Astaire.

The duo's radio show remained on the air until 1950, when they switched to television. "The George Burns and Gracie Allen Show"

Burns co-stars with Walter Matthau in *The Sunshine Boys* (1975), his first film role in 35 years. The performance earned him an Academy Award for Best Supporting Actor.

ran for eight years. Defying convention, Burns narrated each week's episode and spoke directly to the camera. At the end of each program, they performed a stand-up routine that ended with Burns's signature remark, "Say good night, Gracie." Allen retired from show business in 1958 and died of heart disease six years later.

Solo career

Burns continued as a solo performer. He starred in two subsequent television series, "The George Burns Show" (1959-1960) and "Wendy and Me" (1964-1965), but neither was successful. He kept busy working the nightclub circuit and appearing on television talk and variety shows.

It was not until Burns was 79 years old that he became a star in his own right. In 1975, Jack Benny, Burns's closest friend, was slated to star in the film version of Neil Simon's *The Sunshine Boys.* When Benny became ill, Burns, who had not appeared in a film in 35 years, stepped in to play vaudevillian Al Lewis opposite Walter Matthau, who portrayed his embittered, estranged partner, Willie Clark. For this performance, Burns received an Academy Award for Best Supporting Actor.

His next film, two years later, was his most popular. He played the title role, opposite John Denver, in *Oh God!* (1977). Its success inspired two sequels, *Oh God! Book II* (1980) and *Oh God! You Devil* (1984). More critically acclaimed was *Going in Style* (1979), in which Burns and co-stars Art Carney and Lee Strassberg played three bored retirees who decide to rob a bank.

Burns was also a late bloomer in the recording studio. In 1980, he released the album, *I Wish I Were 18 Again.* Other recordings followed, including *George Burns in Nashville* and *Young at Heart.* In 1990, he earned a Grammy Award in the Best Spoken or Nonmusical Recording category for his narration of his book *Gracie: A Love Story.* That same year, he received an Emmy Award for Outstanding Individual Achievement in Informational Programming for *A Conversation With George Burns.* In 1995, he was honored by the Screen Actors Guild with that organization's first Life Achievement Award.

In his later concert appearances, Burns told show business anecdotes, sang obscure, rapid-patter songs, and joked about his age, his beloved cigars, and dating younger women: "I would go out with women my age. But there *are* no women my age."

Part of what endeared Burns to audiences was his indefatigable spirit. "If you can fall in love with what you're going to do for a living," he told a reporter, "you've got it made. I fell in love with show business 90 years ago, and I love it just as much today." ■ ■ ■

For further reading:

Burns, George. *Gracie: A Love Story.* Putnam, 1988.

Gottfried, Martin. *George Burns and the Hundred-Year Dash.* Simon & Schuster, 1996

Democratic Party. The Democratic Party retained control of the presidency in 1996. President Bill Clinton became the first Democrat to win a second term since Franklin D. Roosevelt in 1936. Democrats, however, lost their battle to regain a majority of seats in both houses of Congress in the Nov. 5, 1996, election.

A family picnic. In August 1996, for the first time since the violent 1968 Democratic Convention, the Democratic Party returned to Chicago to nominate a candidate for president. In 1968, the convention was characterized by bloody street battles outside the convention walls and a Democratic civil war inside the hall. In 1996, the convention was likened to a family picnic. In stark contrast to the 1996 Republican Convention, which struggled to unite warring conservative and moderate factions, the Democrats joined hands and danced the *macarena* (a Latin dance hit that swept the country in 1996) during a convention at which partying may have overshadowed politics.

Speakers concentrated on pulling the American public's collective heartstrings. Wheelchair-bound actor Christopher Reeve, who became *quadriplegic* (unable to move his arms, legs, and body below the neck) after falling from a horse and breaking his neck, made a stirring plea for government funding to help people with disabilities. Gun-control advocate Sarah Brady, whose husband, Jim, was wounded during an assassination attempt on former President Ronald Reagan in 1981, barely mentioned politics in her speech that focused on children who have been killed by gunfire.

First Lady Hillary Rodham Clinton and Vice President Al Gore each used the convention pulpit to advocate for children and endorse family issues. Hillary Clinton, in a direct counterattack on Republican jibes at her book *It Takes a Village*, defended her efforts to protect and improve the lives of children. Gore illustrated the dangers of teen-age smoking by telling the story of his sister's death from lung cancer.

The president's wish list. After campaigning on a whistle-stop train tour, President Bill Clinton arrived in Chicago to accept his party's nomination on August 29. In his acceptance speech, Clinton announced a series of programs he hoped to initiate in his second term. His plans included a children's reading program that would help improve skills in grade school-aged children; a large tax break for people who profit from the sale of a house; a welfare-to-work program that would help place 1 million welfare recipients in jobs by the year 2000 and give tax credits to businesses that employ former welfare recipients; and a $1.9-billion plan to clean up the environment. Clinton said the cost of these programs—a total of about $9.5 billion—could be met by slashing corporate subsidies. He vowed to put an end to big government and create a balanced budget.

Victory and defeat. Throughout 1996, President Clinton maintained a large lead in the polls over Republican challenger Robert Dole. Following the convention, Clinton's polling numbers bounced even higher. Democrats vying for other offices, though, struggled to outpace Republican candidates. Democrats clung to the hope that Clinton's popularity meant that voters would back the party in the November election.

Clinton easily defeated Dole, taking 379 electoral votes to Dole's 159 and winning 31 states and the District of Columbia. However, Republicans kept their majority control of both the House of Representatives and the Senate. In the Senate, the Democrats lost two seats, giving the Republicans a 55-to-45 majority. In the House, the Democrats picked up 9 seats, cutting the Republican majority to 20 seats. The Democrats had lost control of Congress when Republicans were swept into power in the 1994 elections.

Races were closer than expected in many instances. Some Republicans either lost or nearly lost their seats to Democratic challengers. Loretta Sanchez, a Democrat from California, beat long-time Congressman Robert Dornan by a handful of votes. In the battle to replace retiring Illinois Democratic Senator Paul Simon, Richard Durbin, a Democratic congressman, won a surprising landslide victory over challenger Al Salvi, who pumped millions of dollars from his personal fortune into his campaign.

Actor Christopher Reeve speaks about the plight of disabled people at the Democratic National Convention held in August in Chicago.

Sarah Brady, whose husband, Jim (on the screen above her), was wounded during a 1981 assassination attempt on President Ronald Reagan, addresses the Democratic National Convention in August on the need for gun control.

Campaign financing reform. The Democratic Party came under fire in 1996 for receiving funds from foreign sources. Officials at the Democratic National Committee (DNC) acknowledged mistakes and returned several contributions that were challenged as illegal or improper. President Clinton called for a ban on all political contributions from noncitizens as part of sweeping campaign finance reform.

The Los Angeles Times reported on Sept. 21, 1996, that the DNC received an illegal $250,000 contribution from Cheong Am, a South Korean electronics company. The DNC returned the money after press inquiries were made. The funds were solicited by John Huang, vice chairman of the DNC. Republicans demanded an investigation into the matter.

Common Cause, a citizen's watchdog group, charged on October 9 that both the Democratic and Republican parties had committed "massive" violations of campaign finance laws by spending millions on television ads supporting Clinton and Dole, respectively. Earlier in 1996, the U.S. Supreme Court had ruled that spending limits in the campaign finance laws did not apply to political parties if they acted independently of their candidates in buying ads. Critics claimed the decision opened a gigantic loophole in the laws designed to limit outlays in presidential elections.   □ William Eaton

See also **Clinton, Bill; Congress; Elections; Republican Party.** In *World Book,* see **Democratic Party.**

Denmark enjoyed a strong economy in 1996. Although the European Union (EU) forecast Danish economic growth would slow to 1.3 percent, below the EU average, unemployment in Denmark was expected to fall to 6.1 percent in 1996, well below the EU average of nearly 11 percent. Part of the decline in unemployment reflected a government requirement that people drawing unemployment benefits must enroll in training courses or other programs designed to speed their return to the work force.

Budgetary rigor. The government pursued restrictive spending policies that lowered the deficit to a projected 0.9 percent of gross domestic product in 1996. That figure was well below the 3 percent deficit ceiling for countries wishing to join a single European currency, scheduled to begin in 1999. As a result, EU finance ministers agreed on June 3, 1996, that Denmark met the deficit requirement for monetary union, the only country besides Ireland and Luxembourg to do so. The Danish government, however, indicated it would heed public skepticism and exercise its option not to adopt a single EU currency. In September, Denmark asked its EU partners to grant Denmark privileged status and closely tie the Danish crown's value to the planned single currency.

Troubled relations with Denmark's EU partners were caused by a constitutional challenge to the country's signing of the 1992 Treaty on European Union, also called the Maastricht Treaty after the Dutch town where it was signed. The Danish Supreme Court ruled in August 1996 that the challenge, brought by 11 Danish citizens, could proceed. The plaintiffs argued that the powers granted to the EU under the Maastricht Treaty violated Danish constitutional limits on the transfer of sovereignty. The case aroused fears in other EU members that Denmark would be a reluctant partner in new talks, begun in March, aimed at reinforcing the treaty.

Denmark angered its EU partners in October by blocking European retaliation against U.S. trade sanctions on foreign firms that trade with Cuba. The Danish government contended that the measures exceeded EU authority and infringed on national powers. Denmark withdrew its veto after the wording of the proposed law was redrafted.

Rival motorcycle gangs continued violent confrontations in 1996. An antitank missile fired at the Hell's Angels gang's headquarters in central Copenhagen, the capital, on October 6 killed 2 people and injured 19 others. The Danish Parliament responded by passing a law barring gang clubhouses from residential areas. Clashes between the Hell's Angels and Bandidos resulted in the death of at least 9 people and injured nearly 50 from 1994 to 1996 in Denmark, Sweden, Finland, and Norway.   □ Tom Buerkle

See also **Europe** (Facts in brief table). In *World Book,* see **Denmark; European Union.**

Dinosaur. See **Paleontology.**

Disabled. The United States Department of Justice on Feb. 8, 1996, filed civil suits against Days Inn of America, Inc., and its parent company, HFS Inc., both of Parsippany, New Jersey, charging that five new Days Inn hotels failed to meet federal standards for public buildings and businesses as required by the 1990 Americans with Disabilities Act (ADA). The suits, which were the first to challenge compliance with the ADA's new-construction provisions, resulted from a Justice Department investigation of 28 franchised hotels built in 17 states since 1992, when the Americans with Disabilities Act went into effect. Investigators for the Justice Department found that all 28 hotels failed to accommodate the needs of disabled people, as prescribed by the 1990 law. Later, 23 of the 28 hotels negotiated settlements with the Justice Department prior to the filing of the suits.

As part of an omnibus spending bill signed by President Bill Clinton on Sept. 30, 1996, federal spending for the education of disabled children rose to $4 billion for fiscal 1997, an increase of nearly $800 million over fiscal 1996. The money was to fund the Individuals with Disabilities Education Act, the primary federal program for disabled children. The government estimated that 5.4 million U.S. children were classified as disabled in 1996, of whom more than half were considered learning disabled rather than physically disabled.   □ Carol L. Hanson

In *World Book,* see **Disabled.**

Disasters. A flood in southern China, which killed more than 2,700 people and left 4.4 million people homeless, was the greatest single disaster of 1996. At least 6,800 people died in storms or floods, and some 1,750 people were killed in aircraft crashes. Disasters that resulted in 25 or more deaths in 1996 include the following:

Aircraft crashes

February 6—Puerto Plata, Dominican Republic. A Birgen Air Boeing 757 flying from the Dominican Republic to Germany crashes into the Atlantic Ocean about 13 miles (21 kilometers) offshore. All 189 people on board die in the crash.

February 29—Arequipa, Peru. A Boeing 737 crashes 5 miles (8 kilometers) from Arequipa, killing all 123 people on board. The flight was en route from Lima to Rodriguez Ballon Airport.

April 3—Dubrovnik, Croatia. U.S. Commerce Secretary Ron Brown and 34 others die when a military jet crashes into St. John Mountain as the jet approaches Dubrovnik Airport during a storm.

May 4—Sudan. Forty-eight passengers and five crew members die when a Sudanese Federal Airlines jet en route to Khartoum crashes during a sandstorm.

May 11—Near Miami, Florida. A ValuJet DC-9, en route to Atlanta with 105 passengers and 5 crew members, crashes into into the shallow waters, mud, and deep underlying peat of the Everglades. Divers hunt the snake- and alligator-infested waters for bodies and wreckage.

July 15—Eindhoven, Netherlands. The crash of a Belgian Hercules C-130 military cargo plane at Eindhoven Airport leaves at least 26 crew members and military passengers dead.

July 17—Long Island, New York. Trans World Airlines (TWA) Flight 800, en route to Paris from New York's Kennedy International Airport, explodes 13,700 feet (4,175 meters) above the Atlantic just off the coast of Long Island, killing all 230 passengers and crew members aboard the Boeing 747-100.

August 29—Svalbard Islands, Arctic Circle. A Russian jetliner crashes into a mountain on the Norwegian island of Spitsbergen, killing all 141 crew members and passengers, most of whom are Russian and Ukrainian miners and their families.

September 25—Den Helder, Netherlands. A World War II-vintage DC-3 Dakota, flown primarily for pleasure trips, goes down in the Wadden Sea, killing 32 passengers and crew members.

October 2—Ancón, Peru. Seventy passengers and crew members die when Aeroperu Flight 603, en route to Santiago, Chile, from the Peruvian capital of Lima, crashes into the Pacific Ocean when the cockpit instruments of the Boeing 757 fail shortly after take-off.

October 24—Manta, Ecuador. An American-owned cargo jet explodes and slams into a church tower just after take-off. The raining debris crushes or ignites surrounding houses, killing 30 people.

October 31—São Paulo, Brazil. Brazil's TAM airline Flight 402, a Fokker-100, bound for Rio de Janeiro, crashes into a densely populated São Paulo neighborhood, killing all 95 passengers and crew members as well as 8 people on the ground.

November 7—Imota, Nigeria. A Nigerian passenger plane crashes into a swamp while en route to Lagos. The plane, which departed from Port Harcourt, carried 141 people. There are no survivors.

November 12—India. Shortly after take-off from the New Delhi airport, a Saudi Arabian jumbo jet slams into a Kazal Airlines plane approaching the airport. All 349 passengers and crew members aboard the two planes are killed. It is the fourth deadliest crash in aviation history.

November 23—Comoros Islands, Africa. A hijacked plane crashes into the Indian Ocean near the Comoros Islands off the east coast of Africa, narrowly missing a scuba diving class. At least 123 of the 175 people on board die in the crash.

Earthquakes

February 3—Lijiang region, China. An earthquake kills at least 250 people and injures more than 14,000 others.

February 17—Irian Jaya, Indonesia. An earthquake and tsunamis kill at least 62 people in eastern Indonesia.

Explosions and fires

January 31—Shaoyang City, China. Ten tons of military dynamite explode in an illegal explosives warehouse in the basement of an apartment building. The explosion kills 77 people and injures more than 400 people.

January 31—Columbo, Sri Lanka. A suicide bomber rams a truck filled with explosives into the gates of the Central Bank of Sri Lanka killing 86 people and injuring more than 1,400 others.

March 19—Quezon City, Philippines. A fire causes the death of more than 150 people in a disco in a suburb of Manila.

June 11—São Paulo, Brazil. A lunchtime explosion in a suburban shopping mall kills 44 people and leaves 100 injured.

June 29—Sichuan Province, China. An explosion in a firecracker factory kills at least 36 workers and passers-by and injures another 52 people. The factory, which was operated privately without authorization, had been closed in April for reasons of safety.

July 17—Shenzhen, China. Smoke from a fire in a ground-floor restaurant spreads upstairs into a hotel, killing 29 guests and injuring another 18 in this boom town near Hong Kong, where Chinese economic reforms began.

A rescue crew searches for bodies in the debris of a 12-story apartment building that collapsed near Cairo, Egypt, on October 27, killing more than 60 people.

A section of wing from Trans World Airlines Flight 800 floats in the Atlantic Ocean off the coast of Long Island, New York, in July. The crash killed 230 people.

August 14—Arequipa, Peru. An errant rocket ignited during a fireworks display knocks a high-tension cable down onto a crowd of onlookers, electrocuting 35 people, some of whom burst into flames.

November 16—Dagestan, Russia. At least 32 people are killed by an explosion that levels a building housing Russian military officers. The cause of the blast is unknown, though some officials suspect it was a terrorist act by Chechen separatist forces.

November 22—Hong Kong. A fire in a high-rise apartment building, which burned for 21 hours before being extinguished, kills 39 people and injures 81 others. It is the deadliest blaze in the British dependency in 39 years.

Shipwrecks

January 19—Near Sumatra. More than 100 people die when an Indonesian ferry sinks off the northern tip of Sumatra.

February 18—Philippines. At least 54 people drown when a ferry capsizes off the Philippine coast. A low tide forced the ferry to wait before entering the port of Cadiz. While the ferry was waiting, waves overturned the boat.

February 29—Near Kampala, Uganda. At least 81 people drown after a boat capsizes on Lake Victoria, near Bumba Island, 75 miles (121 kilometers) east of Kampala.

May 21—Mwanza, Tanzania. More than 600 people, many of whom were students, drown when a 441-capacity ferry carrying at least 729 passengers lists and capsizes.

July 31—Guwahati, India. At least 42 people drown when a ferry carrying approximately 70 people capsizes in the Noa Dihing River in the state of Assam near the Chinese border.

Storms and floods

January 6-9—East Coast, United States. A blizzard socks the Eastern Seaboard, killing at least 150 people, and dumping up to 35 inches (89 centimeters) of snow on 12 states.

June 2—Yunnan Province, China. Two mountain landslides, triggered by heavy rains, kill at least 79 people and injure 77 in the 23 pits of the Daping gold mine.

June 3—Islamabad, Pakistan. Temperatures of 120 °F (49 °C) in the provinces of Punjab and Sindh cause at least 186 people to die.

June 16—Hyderabad, India. A cyclone lashes the coastal areas in southeastern India with heavy rain, killing at least 120 people.

June 23—Rajasthan, India. Flooding caused by unusually heavy rains leaves 43 dead in the northern state of Rajasthan and 326 dead nationwide.

July 4—China. Storms, which began in late June, dump up to 22 inches (55.8 centimeters) of rain across nine central and southern provinces, flooding as much as 1.75 million acres (700,000 hectares) of farmland and killing 31,000 head of livestock. As many as 500 people are killed, and thousands are forced to flee their homes for higher ground.

July 15—Bangladesh and eastern India. Four days of torrential monsoon rains produce flooding and landslides that leave as many as 135 people dead and 1.9 million homeless.

July 27—Bangladesh. Seasonal monsoons and the resulting floods kill at least 290 Bangladeshis.

July 27—Central America. Hurricane Cesar

sweeps over the Central American isthmus, leaving 35 people dead in its wake.

July 28—South Korea. Torrential rains trigger landslides that kill 68 soldiers and civilians in military camps near the North Korean border.

July 31—Taiwan. The worst typhoon to hit Taiwan in 30 years floods large areas of the island and kills 44 people.

August 7—Spain. At least 70 people camping in the Pyrenees Mountains die and 180 are injured when a sudden torrential rain causes flash flooding that covers the campground in mud and debris.

August 18—Southern China. More than 2,700 people have died as the result of flooding, which since the seasonal rains began in late June, has ruined 8 million acres (3.2 million hectares) in crops, destroyed nearly 1 million buildings, and left 4.4 million people homeless.

August 22-24—Kashmir. Trekking in the Himalayan Mountains toward a shrine to the Hindu god Shiva, 240 of a group of more than 50,000 pilgrims die from exposure during a blizzard that blasts the area for three days.

August 25—Lahore, Pakistan. Floods in the Punjab Province inundate more than 1,100 villages, killing 40 people and leaving tens of thousands of people homeless.

September 10—China. A typhoon hits the southern Chinese province of Guangdong, killing at least 114 people and leaving more than 200,000 people homeless.

October 21—Andhra Pradesh and Tamil Nadu, India. Six days of torrential rains flood vast areas of two coastal states in southern India, killing at least 92 and leaving tens of thousands homeless.

November 6—Hyderabad, India. A cyclone pounds India's southeast coast, killing more than 1,000 people. Storm waters flood acres of rice fields and villages, leaving tens of thousands homeless.

December 26—Malaysia. A tropical storm rages in Sabah, Malaysia, on the island of Borneo for more than three hours, leaving 106 people dead and more than 3,000 people homeless. Hardest hit is Keningau south of Kota Kinabalu, the state capital, where 102 drown or are buried under debris.

Other disasters

February 25—Israel. A bomb planted in a bus kills 24 people near Jerusalem, and 3 more people are killed by a bomb planted at a hitchhiking post for soldiers near the coastal city of Ashkelon.

May 13—Sind Province, Pakistan. Approximately 50 people drown when a bus carrying 64 people falls from a bridge into an irrigation canal.

June 25—Haiti. At least 30 children die of acute kidney failure after taking Haitian-produced liquid acetaminophen contaminated with diethylene glycol, an ingredient of automobile antifreeze.

July 8—Nepal. A packed Nepalese bus plunges over a cliff and into a river, killing 25 passengers and injuring an additional 35 people.

July 15—India. More than 55 pilgrims are killed when thousands of worshipers stampede during religious festivals at overcrowded Hindu shrines in the cities of Ujjain and Hardwar.

September 16—Yemen. Health officials announce that Yemen's two-month-old cholera outbreak has killed 77 people.

October 15—New Delhi, India. The federal government announces that an outbreak of dengue fever, which has claimed 158 lives and led to the hospitalization of more than 3,000 people since August 29, is classified an epidemic.

October 17—Guatemala City, Guatemala. A melee before a World Cup qualifying soccer match ends in a stampede, during which 78 fans are crushed to death and 127 others are injured.

October 27—Cairo, Egypt. A 12-story residential building in the Cairo suburb of Heliopolis collapses, killing more than 60 people. Armed with a permit to add only a single floor, the owner of the building added an additional five stories to the building's original seven.

December 30—Sesapani, India. A bomb explodes under a train, killing at least 60 passengers.

See also **Aviation; Transportation; Weather.** In *World Book,* see **Disaster.**

Dole, Elizabeth (1936–   ), in 1996, took a year's leave of absence from her position as president of the American Red Cross to campaign for her husband, former Senator Bob Dole, Republican candidate for president of the United States.

Elizabeth Hanford Dole was born on July 20, 1936, in Salisbury, North Carolina. She earned a political science degree from Duke University in Durham, North Carolina, in 1958, and a law degree from Harvard University in Cambridge, Massachusetts, in 1965.

In 1966, Dole was appointed an assistant in the Department of Health, Education, and Welfare. She held a series of consumer advocacy posts in the administrations of presidents Lyndon B. Johnson and Richard M. Nixon. In 1973, Nixon appointed her to the Federal Trade Commission (FTC). She married Bob Dole in 1975 and resigned her FTC post when he announced he would seek the 1980 Republican presidential nomination.

Under President Ronald Reagan, Elizabeth Dole served as assistant to the president for public liaison from 1981 to 1983 and secretary of transportation from 1983 until 1987. She served in the Administration of President George Bush from 1988 to 1991 as secretary of labor. □ Lisa Klobuchar

See also **Elections** Special Report: **How Americans Elected Their President; Republican Party.**

Dominican Republic. See **Latin America.**

Drought. See **Water; Weather.**

Drug abuse. Illicit drug use, especially among 12- to 17-year-olds, increased in recent years, according to the National Household Survey on Drug Abuse (NHSDA) released in August 1996. The report asked United States residents about their drug use. The survey revealed that illicit drug use by teenagers increased from 5.3 percent in 1992 to 10.9 percent in 1995 (the latest year for which figures were available). Since 1992, marijuana use increased more than 200 percent, and cocaine use increased more than 260 percent. The NHSDA survey also reported that 12.8 million U.S. residents age 12 and older had used an illegal substance during the month preceding the survey.

Herbal Ecstasy. In 1996, the Federal Drug Administration (FDA) launched an investigation into a "natural" drug called ephedra. FDA officials linked the drug to the deaths of 15 people. The drug, often sold in health food stores under brand names such as Herbal Ecstasy or Cloud Nine, is an ancient Chinese medicine called *ma huang*. It contains the chemical ephedrine, a substance commonly found in over-the-counter decongestants, energy-enhancers, and weight loss aids. Excessive use of ephedra can cause anxiety, dizziness, seizures, and stroke.

Heroin's increasing popularity. Heroin use among young people, middle-class professionals, and entertainers was on the rise in 1996. An increasing supply of purer forms of heroin allowed users to inhale rather than inject the substance, contributing to its popularity. However, treatment clinics reported that most users were still over the age of 30, male, and preferred injection to inhalation.

Smoking. President Bill Clinton called for the FDA to regulate cigarettes in 1996. The FDA restricted tobacco advertising in magazines with high-teen readerships, outdoors near schools and playgrounds, on clothing or bags, and at sporting events. In addition, the FDA mandated that cigarette vending machines be put in places that were inaccessible to people under the age of 18.

Courts also took a stand against the tobacco industry in 1996. On August 9, a Florida jury awarded $750,000 to a man who developed lung cancer after smoking for many years. The cigarette maker of the brand the man smoked had failed to sufficiently inform the public about the danger of its product, and was thus found liable for the man's illness. Only once before had a jury ordered a tobacco company to pay damages in a lawsuit related to the health effects of smoking.

Alcohol. According to a University of Michigan study released in 1996, alcohol use among 14-year-olds increased by 50 percent from 1992 to 1994. Binge drinking—having four or more drinks in one session—also increased. One-fifth of 10th-grade respondents reported having been intoxicated in the 30 days preceding the survey.　　　□ David Lewis

In *World Book,* see **Drug Abuse.**

Drugs. On April 19, 1996, the first drugs designed to cure peptic ulcers were approved by the U.S. Food and Drug Administration (FDA). *Peptic ulcers,* ulcers in the stomach or the *duodenum* (the top of the small intestine), affected about 5 million Americans in 1996.

Once believed to be caused by stomach acids, ulcers were treated with a special diet and antacids. Although this treatment relieved symptoms, it did not provide a cure. The 1984 discovery of the bacterium *Helicobacter pylori* as the actual cause of most ulcers offered the possibility of a cure. The new treatment consists of a combination of two drugs: clarithromycin, sold as Biaxin, an antibiotic that kills the bacteria; and omeprazole, sold as Prilosec, which halts acid production in the stomach.

Cancer drugs. On March 29, 1996, President Bill Clinton announced the FDA would use new guidelines to speed up the approval of cancer drugs. With the new program, the FDA can approve a drug if the manufacturer can prove it effectively shrinks cancerous tumors, a strong indicator that a drug will prolong the life of a patient. After FDA approval, the manufacturer must complete studies of the long-term effectiveness of the drug.

The FDA also announced it would approve cancer drugs that have already been tested and approved in any of 26 foreign countries, which have approval standards similar to the FDA's. U.S. physicians who use these drugs must provide information to the FDA about treatment outcomes.

On May 16, the FDA approved Gemzar, the first new treatment for pancreatic cancer in 30 years. Pancreatic cancer is difficult to treat because patients tend to be without recognizable symptoms until the disease becomes advanced. Less than 10 percent of pancreatic cancer patients live more than a year after diagnosis. Clinical trials showed that Gemzar, compared to conventional treatment, increased patients' survival by about 1.5 months.

On May 29, the FDA approved a new ovarian cancer drug, topotecan, sold under the brand name Hycamtin. The first of a new class of antitumor drugs called camptothecins, Hycamtin interferes with an enzyme needed for tumor growth. The new drug offers a second line of therapy for patients who are not responding to other treatments. In the United States, ovarian cancer annually strikes some 26,700 women and kills about 14,800.

Multiple sclerosis drug. On May 17, the FDA approved the first drug to slow the progression of multiple sclerosis (MS), a chronic nerve disorder that affects about 250,000 Americans. As the disease progresses, it causes increasing disabilities, including weakness, loss of coordination, speech and vision problems, and in some cases paralysis.

The new genetically engineered drug, Avonex, is based on interferon, a virus-fighting protein of the immune system. In tests, Avonex slowed the rate of progress of the disease by as much as 40 percent.

Stroke treatment. On June 18, the FDA approved tissue plasminogen activator (TPA), the first drug that can minimize damage from *acute ischemic stroke,* a sudden loss of brain function caused by a blood clot. TPA dissolves blood clots and restores normal blood flow. Strokes annually afflict about 500,000 Americans, kill about 150,000, and are the leading cause of long-term adult disability.

Experts warned that TPA minimizes stroke damage only if patients recognize symptoms and seek emergency care within three hours. If more time elapses, the drug can cause bleeding in the brain. Also, a physician must determine that a blood clot, not a *cerebral hemorrhage* (bleeding in the brain), is the cause of the stroke. Symptoms of stroke, which usually occur suddenly, include weakness, numbness on one side of the body, blurred vision, slurred speech, dizziness or loss of coordination, mental confusion, and personality changes.

Whooping cough vaccine. On July 31, the FDA approved a new whooping cough vaccine that is less likely than the older vaccine to cause the severe but rare side effects: fever, excessive drowsiness, irritability, vomiting, and painful swelling at the site of the injection. The old vaccine may also be linked to extremely rare neurologic illnesses. Although whooping cough, or pertussis, is a contagious and potentially fatal respiratory disease, some parents have refused to have their children vaccinated because of the adverse side effects.

The new vaccine, called Tripedia, is used for the first four shots in the vaccination series, usually given at 2, 4, 6, and 18 months. The older form of the vaccination is used for the last shot in the series, given when a child is between the ages of 4 and 6 years. Unlike the old vaccine, Tripedia is an *acellular vaccine,* a vaccine that does not contain the whole whooping cough microbe. Researchers believed the acellular form accounts for the diminished side effects.

Antiobesity drug. On April 30, the FDA approved a diet drug for the first time since 1974. The antiobesity prescription drug, dexfenfluramine, is sold under the brand name Redux.

Dexfenfluramine increases levels of the brain chemical serotonin, tricking the body into feeling full. In one study, 60 percent of the people taking the drug—while also following a strict diet and exercise routine—lost 10 percent of body weight in the course of a year. Only 30 percent of those on just the diet and exercise routine lost 10 percent or more.

The FDA cautioned that dexfenfluramine should be used only under a physician's supervision. It may cause a rare and sometimes fatal form of high blood pressure. Critics of the drug asked the FDA to withhold approval because of reports that large doses—30 times greater than a normal dose—caused brain damage in laboratory animals, but the FDA concluded that the risk was not clear. □ Michael Woods

See also **AIDS; Medicine.** In *World Book,* see **Drugs.**

Eastern Orthodox Churches. In February 1996, Ecumenical Patriarch Bartholomew, the head of the Orthodox Church in Constantinople (Istanbul, Turkey), reestablished the Orthodox Church of Estonia as an autonomous church under his authority. Estonian Orthodox Christians and the Estonian government requested this measure to sever connections to the authority of the Russian Orthodox Church. Prior to the annexation of Estonia by the former Soviet Union in 1940, the Estonian Church had been independent. After the fall of the Soviet Union in 1991, the church remained under the Patriarchate of Moscow. In response to Bartholomew's decision, Patriarch Alexé II of Moscow, who supported the Russian-speaking Orthodox Christians in Estonia, broke ties with Bartholomew. In May 1996, the two sides agreed to form two separate churches in Estonia.

The Bulgarian Church split officially in July when members of the church governing body under Metropolitan Pimen declared themselves as the proper authority in the Bulgarian Orthodox Church. The *schism* (division) began in 1992, when the government invalidated the former Communist government's 1971 approval of the election of Patriarch Maxim. At that time, Pimen became the head of a new synod, but Maxim and the Holy Synod refused to recognize his authority. In November 1995, the government established Maxim as the official patriarch—an act not recognized by other Orthodox Churches.

Call for tolerance. In February 1996, Serbian Orthodox Patriarch Pavle called for the people of the former nation of Yugoslavia to see beyond "narrow political and factional criteria" as the new republics tried to attain peaceful coexistence. After an attack on a Belgrade mosque in May, Pavle promised support of religious tolerance to Mufti Hamdija Jusufspahic, the leader of Belgrade's Muslim community.

Parthenios III, Greek Orthodox Patriarch of Alexandria and All Africa, died of a heart attack at age 76 on July 23. Parthenios, influential in Eastern Orthodox and worldwide Christian affairs, was elected in 1991 as one of eight copresidents of the World Council of Churches, an organization of Orthodox, Protestant, Old Catholic, and Anglican churches.

New American archbishop. Archbishop Iakovos of the Greek Orthodox Archdiocese of North and South America retired on July 29, 1996, after serving 37 years as archbishop. On July 30, the Holy Synod of the Ecumenical Patriarchate elected Metropolitan Spyridon of Italy, an American-born clergyman, to succeed Archbishop Iakovos. The Holy Synod named Spyridon Archbishop of the Greek Orthodox Archdiocese of America and created three new metropolitanates in Canada, Central America, and South America. Spyridon, 52, was also given the title of *Exarch* (representative) of the Ecumenical Patriarchate for all four regions. □ Stanley S. Harakas

See also **Religion.** In *World Book,* see **Eastern Orthodox Churches.**

Economics

Economics. The world economy strengthened slightly in 1996, as leading industrial nations recovered somewhat from a sharp 1995 slowdown, and developing nations with market economies turned in impressive gains. Most nations making a transition from state-run economies to market-based systems also made headway.

Worldwide economic output, a measure of goods and services produced above inflation (the pace of price increases), was expected to grow 3.8 percent in 1996 after a 3.5 percent gain in 1995, according to the International Monetary Fund (IMF). The IMF is a United Nations agency that provides economic guidance and loans to member nations.

However, those figures mask sharp differences between 1995 and 1996. For example, 1995 was marked by significant weakness in the economic growth of Japan and Western Europe, as well as a sharp slowdown in the United States that left its economy barely growing at year-end. By contrast, in late 1996 the IMF predicted global expansion would continue, with both output and trade growing faster than they had done historically.

U.S. output grew 2 percent in 1995, with only a 0.3-percent gain in the final three months. Yet in 1996, output in the first three quarters grew at rates of 2 to 4.7 percent.

Recovery in many other industrial nations was slower. In much of Europe, economic growth in early 1996 was restrained by weakness lingering from late 1995. Some nations, led by Germany, cut interest rates to fuel growth. These and other measures were likely to boost Europe's output in late 1996. But Germany and France were expected to grow 1.4 percent and 1.1 percent respectively in 1996, below 1995's pace of 1.9 percent for Germany and 2.2 percent for France. Both countries were projected to grow faster in 1997. Italy's 1995 growth rate of 3 percent led major industrial nations, but the Italian economy lost speed in 1996 when its key exports slowed. It was projected to edge up to 2.2 percent in 1997.

Western European nations shifted policies in 1996 as they prepared to adopt a single currency and monetary system by 1999. To form a European monetary union, they were required to meet economic targets in such areas as budget deficits and inflation. Some nations had trouble meeting the timetable, casting doubt over the union.

Industrial picture. The United Kingdom's 1995-1996 economic slowdown was much less severe than other world industrial countries. The nation's output grew 2.5 percent in 1995 and was expected to slow to 2.2 percent in 1996 before rising again in 1997. Signs of developing inflation prompted the Bank of England to hike interest rates. Inflation occurs when consumer prices rise rapidly.

Japan had suffered a deep slowdown that kept its economic growth below 1 percent in 1994 and

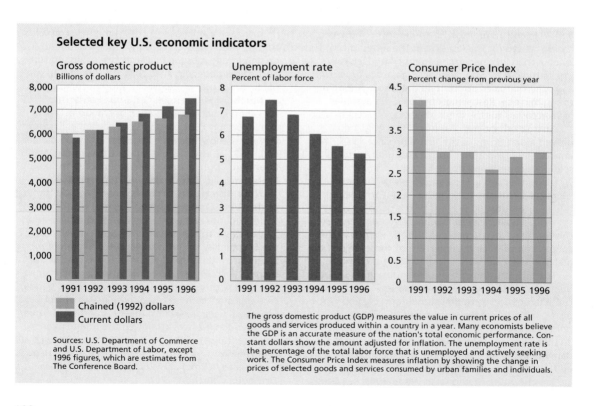

Selected key U.S. economic indicators

Gross domestic product
Billions of dollars

Unemployment rate
Percent of labor force

Consumer Price Index
Percent change from previous year

■ Chained (1992) dollars
■ Current dollars

Sources: U.S. Department of Commerce and U.S. Department of Labor, except 1996 figures, which are estimates from The Conference Board.

The gross domestic product (GDP) measures the value in current prices of all goods and services produced within a country in a year. Many economists believe the GDP is an accurate measure of the nation's total economic performance. Constant dollars show the amount adjusted for inflation. The unemployment rate is the percentage of the total labor force that is unemployed and actively seeking work. The Consumer Price Index measures inflation by showing the change in prices of selected goods and services consumed by urban families and individuals.

1995. It established a healthier recovery in 1996, when it was projected to grow 3.5 percent. Canada slowed toward an estimated 1.4-percent growth rate in 1996 after growing by 2.3 percent in 1995. Amid subdued inflation, Canada's central bank lowered interest rates, and the nation's output was projected to grow 3.2 percent in 1997.

Smaller industrial nations showed variety in their economies. Norway and Ireland continued to experience robust growth with low inflation, but Spain, Sweden, and Finland saw their export-led expansions slow. Austria and Belgium were expected to gradually perk up as their most important export markets, Germany and France, regained strength. Australia and New Zealand saw solid growth.

In the developing world, economies were smaller but growth rates more dynamic. In 1996, output rose to 6.3 percent from 5.9 percent in 1995. In 1996, Mexico was recovering from 1995's sharp financial and economic crisis. Growth resumed in Argentina, and Venezuela laid plans to get its economy growing in 1997 after several years of decline. African nations strengthened economically. Middle Eastern nations turned in mixed performances, from overheating economies to threatened slowdowns. The rapidly growing Asian nations of Indonesia, Malaysia, and Thailand began restraining their economies to prevent overheating. China's growth cooled from the fast-paced early 1990's, and its inflation rate declined. In India, rising inflation pressure and high interest rates risked economic disruption.

Former Soviet-bloc nations in Europe and Asia, which were shifting toward market economies, were finally projected in 1996 to achieve slight growth in output after years of contraction. The improvement, however, was mainly due to growth in Eastern European countries, which were more industrialized and had made a faster shift. In Russia, Ukraine, and Bulgaria, real growth was not expected until 1997.

The United States economy slowed to a 0.3-percent growth rate in the final three months of 1995. But in the first quarter of 1996, it recovered despite a series of business-closing winter storms and a lengthy strike against its largest automaker, General Motors, to post a 2-percent gain in the gross domestic product (GDP). The GDP is the value of all goods and services produced within the country and is the main gauge of output after inflation. The GDP picked up speed, rising to a robust 4.7-percent rate for the April-June quarter of 1996. It then tapered off again to a more sustainable 2-percent pace in the July-September quarter. Economists generally expected 1996 to close with moderate growth.

During the 1995 slowdown, the central bank of the United States, called the Federal Reserve System or the Fed, lowered short-term interest rates a scant 0.25 percent in July and again in December. With recovery still uncertain in January 1996, the Fed then cut interest rates another 0.25 percent and then held rates steady.

The fast second-quarter growth rate brought new fears of inflation to financial markets. The stock market, meanwhile, soared to new heights. By early June, veteran market watchers were warning that stock prices had increasingly become speculative rather than based on fundamental values. The market moved lower in June and plunged in July. Inflation indicators each month continued to show wages and prices holding at around 3 percent. Inflation fears waned, and the stock market hit record highs. In October, the benchmark Dow Jones Industrial Average pierced the 6,000 mark for the first time. Labor markets remained tight with low unemployment rates of 4.9 to 5.6 percent.

The economy and politics. The year began with Democratic President Bill Clinton and a Republican-led Congress battling over economic policies. Compromise legislation produced a 90-cent minimum wage hike and major welfare reforms. Republican presidential candidate former Senator Robert Dole made weak growth and a tax cut the center of his campaign, but his message failed to resonate with voters as the economy hummed along. While Clinton was reelected president, Republicans maintained control of Congress, which calmed nerves on Wall Street. Stock prices soared. □ John D. Boyd

In *World Book,* see **Economics.**

Ecuador. On Aug. 10, 1996, Abdala Bucarám Ortíz, 44, of the center-left Roldosista Party, was sworn in for a four-year term as Ecuador's president. A descendant of Lebanese immigrants, Bucarám had formerly served as police commissioner in the Guayas province and mayor of Guayaquil. Bucarám had run unsuccessfully in 1988 and 1992 as the presidential candidate for the Roldosista Party, which he founded in 1982 in honor of his brother-in-law, former President Jaime Roldós Aguilera, who was killed in an airplane crash in 1981.

The populist rhetoric and flamboyance of Bucarám's 1996 campaign, which earned him the nickname *El Loco* (the madman), worried Ecuador's business leaders. But once in office, Bucarám pledged that his administration would continue the free-market reforms of his predecessor, Sixto Durán Ballén, while strengthening social programs for the poor.

On Jan. 14, 1996, when tensions along the border with Peru increased, Israel confirmed the sale of four Kfir fighter planes to Ecuador. The U.S. government, one of four nations responsible for overseeing the July 1995 peace agreement between Ecuador and Peru, approved the deal. The United States was required to sanction the deal, because the engines of the aircraft were manufactured by the U.S. company General Electric. □ Nathan A. Haverstock

See also **Latin America** (Facts in brief table). In *World Book,* see **Ecuador.**

Education. A record 51.7 million students entered U.S. elementary and secondary schools in the fall of 1996, and another 14.4 million students enrolled in colleges and universities. Schools struggled to find room for the students. In New York City there was a shortage of 91,000 seats, and classes were held in hallways, storage rooms, and cafeterias.

The nation also spent a record amount of money educating its students in 1996. Elementary and secondary school spending reached $318 billion, while colleges and universities spent nearly $211 billion.

The quality of the nation's educational system was a major concern to Americans in 1996. Many of the nation's governors and corporate leaders gathered in Palisades, New York, in March for the National Education Summit. Led by Louis V. Gerstner, Jr., chairman of International Business Machines, Inc. (IBM), of Armonk, New York, and Tommy Thompson, governor of Wisconsin and chairman of the National Governors Association, the summit members promised to work toward setting higher academic standards in every state within two years.

The public echoed this concern as well. Polls, including a June sampling by the newspaper *USA Today,* revealed that people polled believed that improving elementary and secondary schools was the most important task facing the nation. They rated the need to make college less expensive as the third greatest challenge, after the reduction of crime.

Report cards issued on the nation's schools gave the public reason for concern. In November, the National Education Goals Panel, a bipartisan organization set up by the Charlottesville Education Summit of 1989 to monitor the progress of U.S. schools, released its annual report. The panel determined that, while some states had made progress toward some goals, the nation as a whole had not. The panel reported in 1996 that parents were reading to their children more and math achievement was up in grades 4 and 8, but it also noted that reading scores remained flat in grades 4 and 8 and dropped in grade 12. It also reported that drug use in schools was on the rise. The panel concluded that many schools were not educating students very well.

National standards. The movement to raise standards in core subjects got a boost in April, when an organization of educators and scholars published history standards for elementary and secondary schools. The organization, the National Center for History in the Schools, published standards in 1995 that were attacked by conservatives who said that they painted an overly negative portrait of the nation's past and ignored many important historical figures. The new standards were more balanced, many historians and educators agreed.

Setting high standards in English, however, was more difficult. The National Council of Teachers of English and the International Reading Association—organizations representing the nation's English and reading teachers—in March 1996 released a set of 12 vague language arts standards. Representatives of the two organizations, polarized by debates over how to teach reading and what students should read, could not agree on more detailed standards.

School reform. Several states and cities introduced programs in 1996 to spur local educators to raise standards. In January, officials of the Maryland State Board of Education announced that the state's students would have to pass 10 rigorous end-of-course exams to graduate from high school: three exams in English, three in social studies, two in math, and two in science. In April, the New York State Board of Regents voted to require that, beginning in the year 2000, students pass the state's Regents exams to earn a high school diploma. In previous years, students could choose between taking the Regents exams and the less difficult State Competency Tests. The Chicago Board of Education launched a program in January 1996 to reward schools that raised test scores and lowered dropout rates with monetary grants. The money was earmarked for educational programs at the winning schools.

In September, two noted school reformers, E. D. Hirsch, Jr., and Theodore Sizer, published new books detailing their blueprints for improving the nation's schools. In *The Schools We Need: And Why We Don't Have Them,* Hirsch argued that all students should study a common curriculum to ensure that they acquire a broad range of knowledge. Sizer, however, wrote that schools should teach students mental skills, such as creative and independent thinking. In *Horace's Hope: What Works for the American High School,* he called for schools to teach a smaller number of subjects in more detail, and for in-depth projects or "exhibitions" to replace standardized tests.

Ebonics. In December, the Oakland, California, school board declared that many of its African American students speak a language that reflects West African and Niger-Congo roots. The language, called "Ebonics" (from the words "ebony" and "phonics") by some linguists, is not merely a dialect of standard English, according to the school board, but a distinct language. The board hoped that recognizing Ebonics as a separate language would help students as they learn standard English. Critics of the move called it a ploy to allow the school district to get federal funds available for bilingual programs.

Education and the presidential race. In January, President Bill Clinton stressed the importance of using technology to improve education. In March, the President participated in NetDay96, a program in which major communications corporations and 20,000 volunteers helped connect 3,000 California schools to the Internet, a global web of computer networks that operate over telephone lines. President Clinton proposed in June to offer $1,500-a-year tax credits for the first two years of college. He pledged billions of dollars for physical repairs to public schools and proposed creating a voluntary national corps of one million tutors to help all students learn to read by the third grade. In July, Republican presidential candidate Robert Dole attacked the nation's teachers' unions, branding them opponents of reform in public education.

Tuition vouchers. A long-running national debate over *school vouchers,* tax dollars given to parents to pay their children's tuition at private schools, flared in 1996, after Robert Dole in July pledged to spend $5 billion a year on vouchers for private and parochial school tuitions if elected president. Dole argued that the plan would spur improvements in public schools by making them compete with private schools for students. President Clinton attacked the plan as destructive to public schools.

In August, more than 1,800 Cleveland students entered private religious schools on vouchers. Under a program created by the Republican-controlled Ohio legislature, as many as 2,000 of Cleveland's low-income students received up to $2,250 for tuition at any participating private or suburban public school. Program opponents filed a court challenge, claiming that the program violated the constitutional separation of church and state. An Ohio court upheld the program in July. The ruling was appealed.

In Wisconsin, the state's legislature passed a law expanding a five-year-old voucher program for low-income students in Milwaukee to include parochial schools. The move was challenged, however, and in August, a state court prevented the law from going into effect. Milwaukee and Cleveland had the only school systems with voucher programs in 1996.

The Milwaukee program was also controversial because three of the 17 private schools admitting voucher students during the 1995-1996 school year closed, and the leaders of two of the schools were charged with fraud involving the voucher program. Still, a national survey—the Phi Delta Kappa/Gallup Poll, released in August—found that 36 percent of the people polled favored allowing parents to send their children to private schools at public expense, up from about 25 percent in 1993.

The quality of the nation's teachers was also a major issue in 1996. The National Commission on Teaching and America's Future, a bipartisan panel funded by the Rockefeller Foundation and the Carnegie Corporation, issued a sharply worded report in September warning that low admission standards and weak program requirements in teacher training programs were threatening the quality of the nation's instructors. Written by a 26-member panel headed by Governor James B. Hunt of North Carolina, the report, "What Matters Most," noted that only about half of U.S. teacher-training institutions were accredited. It called for tougher standards for teacher education and licensing, paying teachers on the basis of performance, and greater spending on teaching rather than on administration.

School privatization. A bold experiment in school reform—the hiring of a private, for-profit company to run the Hartford, Connecticut, school system—collapsed in January 1996. The Hartford school board canceled its contract with Educational Alternatives, Inc. (EAI), a Minneapolis-based company, in a dispute over finances and the company's performance. EAI launched the "privatization" movement in education in the early 1990's. Its misfortunes in Hartford left it without a public school contract. Another company in the for-profit school business, the Edison Project, LP, expanded from 4 to 12 schools in the autumn of 1996.

Higher education. The U.S. Supreme Court handed down two landmark decisions involving the nation's colleges and universities in 1996. In June, by a vote of 7 to 1, the court ruled that the Virginia Military Institute, an all-male academy partially funded by Virginia taxpayers, violated the constitution by barring female students. In September, the university's board of trustees voted to admit women in 1997 rather than become a fully private college. The Citadel, a South Carolina school that was the nation's only other state-supported, all-male military college, admitted four female students in August 1996, just one year after admitted its first woman student, Shannon Faulkner.

In July, the Supreme Court dealt a blow to affirmative action in higher education (the taking into account of a person's race, gender, or ethnic background in school admissions and in employment hiring decisions, to encourage diversity among students and faculty). The court let stand a lower federal ruling in the case of *Hopwood v. Texas,* which barred the University of Texas law school from considering race in admissions. The lower court ruled that the school's affirmative action policy violated the rights of white students who were denied admission to the school, despite higher admissions test scores.

The rising cost of college was a troubling reality for many families in 1996. Tuition at four-year public colleges and universities rose 6 percent, twice the rate of inflation. Four-year private colleges hiked their tuition bill an average of 5 percent. In 1996, it took about 95 days of income for the average family to pay a student's tuition, compared with 52 days in 1976. The cost of a year at Yale, Harvard, and other elite private colleges surpassed $30,000 in 1996.

Some schools bucked the trend and cut tuitions in 1996—only to find that increases in enrollment made the schools stronger financially. For example, when Muskingum College, a liberal-arts school in Ohio, cut its 1996-1997 tuition by 29 percent, its enrollment climbed more than 36 percent, generating an extra $250,000 in revenue. The benefits of such price-cutting experiments to both students and colleges caused higher education experts to predict that the price-cutting would spread.   □ Thomas Toch

In *World Book,* see **Education.**

Egypt. Egyptian President Hosni Mubarak became increasingly concerned in 1996 about the fate of the Arab-Israeli peace process. Early in the year, a series of deadly bombings in Israel by Palestinian militants heightened antipeace sentiment among many Israelis. Mubarak and United States President Bill Clinton convened The Summit of the Peace Makers at Sharm ash Shaykh, Egypt, on March 13. Attended by 27 world leaders, the summit was aimed at finding ways to combat terrorism. It was also intended to show support for Israeli Prime Minister Shimon Peres, a key architect of the Arab-Israeli peace agreements. Peres, however, lost reelection in May.

Arab League summit. Alarmed by the new Israeli government's rejection of the principle of exchanging land for peace, which was the basis of the peace talks, Mubarak sponsored an Arab League summit on June 22 and 23 in Cairo. The meeting, attended by all 21 Arab League members except Iraq, was the first such summit since Iraq's 1990 invasion of Kuwait. The Arab states issued a strong warning that regional tensions would revive if Israel failed to abide by the terms of the peace process.

Tension with Israel. Mubarak's first meeting with new Israeli Prime Minister Benjamin Netanyahu on July 18, 1996, failed to allay his fears. Netanyahu said Israel would withdraw troops from the West Bank town of Hebron, but added that the formula of land for peace was open to "differing interpreta-

tions." Mubarak was annoyed by Israeli criticism of reports that Egypt had imported Scud-missile material from North Korea.

Massacre. Islamic militants shot and killed 17 Greek tourists and an Egyptian outside a Cairo hotel on April 18. The Islamic Group, Egypt's largest militant organization, announced it carried out the killings to avenge an Israeli attack on Lebanon earlier that month and claimed that the Greeks had been mistaken for Israelis. The attack was the most lethal since the extremists began their attacks against tourists in 1992 as a way of unseating Mubarak and establishing an Islamic government. Previous to the April 19 massacre, the Islamic group had killed 8 tourists in more than 20 attacks.

The Egyptian government, which relies heavily on more than $3 billion a year in tourism revenues, reacted swiftly to the attack. Some 1,500 suspected extremists were detained at police roadblocks or arrested during massive sweeps through Cairo shantytowns. Since militants began their violent campaign against the government in 1992, more than 920 Egyptians have been killed and as many as 26,000 have been detained by the police.

☐ Christine Helms

See also **Israel; Middle East** (Facts in brief table). In *World Book,* see **Egypt**.

El Salvador. See **Latin America** (Facts in brief table).

Egyptian workers begin a preservation program in 1996 to save the Great Sphinx from wind, pollution, and time. The 4,500-year-old statue is located in the desert near Giza.

Elections. President Bill Clinton easily won a second term in the 1996 presidential election, defeating Republican challenger former Senator Robert Dole of Kansas. The president captured electoral votes in 31 states and Washington, D.C. He took 379 electoral votes to Dole's 159. Clinton received 49 percent of the popular vote, compared with 41 percent for Dole and 8 percent for Ross Perot, the Reform Party candidate. Only 49 percent of registered voters went to the polls, the lowest voter turnout since 1924.

Republicans retain control. Republicans, who had won control of both the United States Senate and House of Representatives from the Democrats in 1994, held onto their Congressional majorities. In the Senate, the Republicans (GOP for Grand Old Party) picked up 2 seats to increase their majority to 55 seats. In the House, Democrats gained 9 seats, but the GOP retained a 20-seat majority.

Thirteen conservative Republican House freshmen were defeated after serving a single term. But 58 others won reelection, and the GOP took most of the open seats in the southern states.

Newly elected GOP senators were reported to be more conservative than their predecessors. In the House, the election appeared to be a victory for moderates. In both parties, moderates appeared to hold the balance of power on closely contested issues.

Senate incumbents reelected. Incumbent GOP senators Theodore Stevens of Alaska, Larry E. Craig of Idaho, Mitch McConnell of Kentucky, Thad Cochran of Mississippi, Robert C. Smith of New Hampshire, Pete V. Domenici of New Mexico, James M. Inhofe of Oklahoma, Fred Dalton Thompson of Tennessee, Phil Gramm of Texas, and John W. Warner of Virginia were all reelected. Incumbent Democratic senators to win reelection were Joseph R. Biden, Jr., of Delaware, Tom Harkin of Iowa, Carl Levin of Michigan, Paul Wellstone of Minnesota, Max Baucus of Montana, and John D. Rockefeller IV of West Virginia.

The only incumbent not reelected was Larry Pressler, a Republican from South Dakota, who lost his seat to Democratic representative Tim Johnson.

Other Senate races. A record number of senators—14—retired in 1996, creating sharp competition in many states. Republican candidates Jeff B. Sessions of Alabama, Tim Hutchinson of Arkansas, and Chuck Hagel of Nebraska all won seats formerly held by Democrats who did not run for reelection. In other contests not involving incumbents, Democrats and Republicans retained seats vacated by members of their own party.

In a widely watched race, Democrat John Kerry defeated Massachusetts GOP Governor William F. Weld. In Maine, Republican Susan E. Collins beat Democrat Joseph Brennan. In Georgia, Max Cleland, a Democrat, edged out Republican Guy Millner to retain the seat vacated by Democratic Senator Sam Nunn. In Louisiana, Democrat Mary L. Landrieu narrowly beat conservative Republican Woody Jenkins.

Republican Senator Strom Thurmond, who was born in 1902 and served in the Senate longer than any other member, coasted to victory over Democrat Elliott Close in South Carolina. GOP Senator Jesse Helms won a rematch with Democrat Harvey Gantt in North Carolina. In Illinois, Representative Richard Durbin, a Democrat, defeated Republican Al Salvi to retain the seat vacated by retiring Democratic Senator Paul Simon. In Colorado, GOP Representative Wayne Allard beat Democrat Thomas Strickland.

In Kansas, freshman representative Sam Brownback, a Republican, easily defeated Democrat Jill Docking to fill out the unexpired term of presidential nominee Robert Dole. In another Senate race in Kansas, Republican Representative Pat Roberts crushed Democrat Sally Thompson.

In a bitter New Jersey contest, Representative Robert G. Torricelli, a Democrat, defeated Republican Richard A. Zimmer. In Wyoming, Republican Mike Enzi won against Democrat Kathy Karpan. Democrat Jack Reed defeated GOP candidate Nancy J. Mayer in Rhode Island to win the seat vacated by veteran Democrat Claiborne Pell.

State races. In gubernatorial races, the national totals remained unchanged—17 Democratic governors, 32 Republican governors, and one independent. Democrat Jeanne Shaheen became the first woman governor of New Hampshire. In West Virginia, former Republican Governor Cecil H. Underwood recaptured the governor's office from the Democrats. Voters in the state of Washington elected Democrat Gary Locke, who became the first Chinese-American governor of a mainland state. In Indiana, Lieutenant Governor Frank L. O'Bannon, a Democrat, defeated Indianapolis Mayor Stephen Goldsmith to replace Evan Bayh as governor.

Republican governors Marc Racicot of Montana, Edward Schafer of North Dakota, and Michael Leavitt of Utah were reelected. Democratic governors Thomas Carper of Delaware, Mel Carnahan of Missouri, James B. Hunt, Jr., of North Carolina, and Howard Dean of Vermont also were returned to office.

The number of houses of representatives under Democratic control increased from 46 to 49, with the party winning majorities in the California, Michigan, and Illinois houses. Senate chambers under Republican control decreased from 50 to 44.

On ballot issues, California voters decided to halt affirmative action programs for women and minorities in public employment, education, and contracting. The outcome appeared likely to shape the national debate over affirmative action programs.

☐ William J. Eaton

See also **Clinton, Bill; Congress of the United States; Democratic Party; Elections** Special Report: **How Americans Elected Their President; Republican Party; State government.** In *World Book,* see **Election; Election campaign.**

How Americans Elected Their PRESIDENT

In a process many people take for granted after more than 200 years, Americans elected a new president on Nov. 5, 1996.

By R. Bruce Dold

The author:

R. Bruce Dold is the deputy editorial page editor of the *Chicago Tribune*. He won a Pulitzer Prize in 1994 for editorial writing.

A s the 1996 United States presidential primary season began in earnest in January, President Bill Clinton enjoyed a comfortable—but not insurmountable—lead over his Republican challengers for a second term. Clinton's lead came despite the Republican Party's near dominance of national politics after its historic takeover of the U.S. House of Representatives and Senate in the November 1994 elections. Republicans had also used congressional committee hearings to draw attention to controversies in the White House and allegations of financial misdealings during Clinton's terms as governor of Arkansas.

Clinton's troubles were not serious enough to allow another Democrat a chance at the presidential nomination. Nine Republican candidates, on the other hand, announced that they would seek their party's nomination for president.

Along with the election itself and the conventions of the major political parties, the presidential primaries are a key part of the process of electing the president. The candidate is selected in a series of state primary elections and *caucuses* (party meetings). These contests begin early in the election year and determine the number of delegates each candidate will have at the party's convention.

The candidate with the most delegates is formally nominated at the convention.

Almost from the beginning of the Clinton presidency in 1993, Senator Bob Dole of Kansas was widely expected to be the Republican nominee in 1996. First elected to the Senate in 1968, Dole was the Senate majority leader from 1985 to 1987 and reclaimed that position in 1995. In the intervening years, he was the Senate minority leader. Dole ran unsuccessfully for vice president in 1976 as President Gerald R. Ford's running mate, and he failed in bids for the Republican presidential nomination in 1980 and 1988.

The Republican challengers

Dole faced eight challengers. Several came from the conservative wing of the party, including journalist/television commentator Patrick Buchanan, Senator Phil Gramm of Texas, Representative Robert Dornan of California, and former State Department official and radio talk show host Alan Keyes. Moderates such as millionaire publisher Malcolm (Steve) Forbes, Jr., former Tennessee Governor Lamar Alexander, Indiana Senator Richard Lugar, and businessman Maurice Taylor also entered the campaign.

Buchanan showed some early strength when he won the Louisiana caucuses on February 6. He stunned the Republican Party leadership when he finished second to Dole in the closely watched Iowa caucuses on February 12 and won the New Hampshire primary on February 20.

Buchanan, who ran unsuccessfully for the Republican nomination in 1992, campaigned as an outspoken opponent of abortion, and he drew considerable support from Christian conservatives, who had achieved greater prominence in the party. Buchanan supported economic nationalism, and he opposed immigration and the North American Free Trade Agreement (NAFTA). His populist, antiestablishment campaign broke with many traditional Republican beliefs.

Forbes and Alexander appealed to moderate Republican voters in the early primaries. Forbes, who spent $25 million of his own fortune on his campaign, crusaded for a flat tax, a proposal to replace the graduated income tax with a single rate of 17 percent and eliminate most deductions. Forbes argued that a flat tax would reduce or eliminate the need for the Internal Revenue Service, make it easier for all taxpayers to calculate their own taxes without paying for professional assistance, and stimulate economic growth. Forbes's only primary wins were in Delaware and Arizona.

Alexander campaigned as an outsider who would reform politics in Washington, D.C. He touted Tennessee's economic growth during his two terms as governor from 1979 to 1987, his accomplishments in public education, and his tenure as secretary of education under President George Bush. Alexander failed to draw significant support after his third-place finishes in Iowa and New Hampshire, however. Dornan and Keyes drew some conservative support away from Buchanan but ultimately had little impact on the campaign.

THE PRIMARIES

Major Republican candidates

Patrick J. Buchanan

Experience: Newspaper columnist, television commentator, former director of communications for President Ronald Reagan.

Date entered race: March 20, 1995.

Primaries or caucuses won: 2 (New Hampshire and Missouri)

Exited race: Aug. 12, 1996.

Robert J. Dole

Experience: United States Senator from Kansas.

Date entered race: April 10, 1995.

Primaries or caucuses won: 46

Clinched nomination: March 26, 1996.

Malcolm (Steve) Forbes

Experience: Magazine publisher.

Date entered race: Sept. 22, 1995.

Primaries or caucuses won: 2 (Arizona and Delaware)

Exited race: March 14, 1996.

Republican presidential candidates in 1996 who failed to win any primaries or caucuses:

Lamar Alexander, former governor of Tennessee and secretary of education under President George Bush.

Bob Dornan, U.S. congressman from California.

Phil Gramm, U.S. senator from Texas.

Alan Keyes, former State Department official and ambassador to the United Nations Economic and Social Council.

Richard Lugar, U.S. senator from Indiana.

Maurice Taylor, businessman from Detroit.

Clinton, meanwhile, enjoyed the luxury of having no serious primary opposition. As Republican rivals aired criticisms of Dole, Clinton's lead in public opinion polls grew.

But Dole regained his footing as the primary campaign turned to the South, which had become an important stronghold for the Republicans during the 1980's. Dole swept the Southern primaries, continuing the trend that began in 1984 of Southern States voting as a bloc in the primaries for the eventual Republican nominee. Dole's victories in Georgia, Maryland, and several other states on March 5 forced Alexander and Lugar out of the race. A week later, Dole clinched the nomination by winning Oregon and the six Southern states that voted a week later on so-called Super Tuesday.

Forbes's withdrawal after Super Tuesday left Buchanan as the only challenger to Dole. Although Buchanan claimed only one more victory, in the Missouri caucuses, he continued his campaign to the Republican convention in August.

Even though Dole had secured the nomination, the criticism from Republican primary opponents had hurt his candidacy. He had fallen far behind Clinton in most opinion polls. Dole sought to spark his campaign with a stunning development: He resigned from the Senate in June to devote himself to the campaign. Dole ended his run as the longest-serving Republican leader of the Senate in its history. His surprise resignation, however, failed to lift his standing in the polls as the Republicans prepared for their August national convention in San Diego.

The conventions

Republicans and Democrats gathered for their national nominating conventions in August 1996. The Democrats convened in Chicago, making this the 25th time Chicago had hosted a political convention—a greater number than any other city in the nation. San Diego, on the other hand, where the Republicans gathered, had never been the site of a national political convention.

Most political observers agreed that there was little left to decide when the two parties convened in 1996 and that the conventions were tame compared with past gatherings. Since the 1970's, the selection of the nominees had been settled before the conventions opened. The conventions had largely become an opportunity for the parties to formally adopt their

Issues frequently debated during the Republican primaries:

Tax cuts: All Republican candidates favored cutting taxes and simplifying the federal tax code. Forbes favored a flat tax of 17 percent, and Buchanan and Gramm wanted a flat tax of 16 percent. All candidates favored cutting taxes on investment income.

Welfare reform: The Republican candidates agreed that the welfare system needed overhauling and supported the welfare reform bill that President Bill Clinton signed in August. Most candidates favored giving the states block grants in order to run welfare progams and wanted to place lifetime limits on the amount of time welfare recipients could receive benefits.

Immigration: Pat Buchanan made immigration an issue in the primaries with his call to build a wall along a portion of the border of the United States and Mexico to prohibit illegal immigration into the United States. He also called for a five-year moratorium on legal immigration. Most candidates opposed welfare to illegal immigrants.

Abortion: Nearly all Republican candidates opposed abortion, but some, such as Buchanan, Dornan, and Keyes, were more vocal about their opposition. Forbes was the only Republican candidate who supported a woman's right to an abortion.

Balanced budget: All candidates wanted to balance the federal budget. Dole wanted to cut government programs and expenses slowly to achieve a balanced budget by 2002. Others, such as Gramm, wanted to balance the budget in five years or less. Most of the candidates favored cutting one or several large federal agencies, such as the Department of Education or the Internal Revenue Service.

Morality: Most of the Republican candidates decried what they saw as moral decay in the United States. Dole blamed Hollywood and the entertainment industry for producing morally debased movies, and the other candidates strongly supported "family values."

Dole chooses Kemp

Bob Dole chose Jack Kemp, *right*, as his vice presidential running mate in August 1996. Kemp was a former member of the United States House of Representatives and also served as secretary of housing and urban development under President George Bush.

THE CONVENTIONS

The Reform Party Ticket

In August, Ross Perot chose economist Pat Choate as his Reform Party running mate, *above*, offering voters another choice besides the traditional Republican and Democratic candidates.

The Democrats

In 1996, President Bill Clinton retained Vice President Al Gore on the Democratic presidential ticket. Clinton was attempting to become the first Democratic president to be reelected to a second term since Franklin D. Roosevelt in 1936.

platforms (statements of belief) and to proclaim the virtues of their nominee through national television exposure.

Bob Dole was nominated as the Republican Party presidential candidate on August 14 and accepted the nomination the next day. Dole chose Jack Kemp, a former U.S. congressman and secretary of Housing and Urban Development, as his running mate. The Republican platform called for constitutional amendments to require a balanced federal budget, put limits on congressional terms in office, protect the rights of crime victims, and deny citizenship to children born in the United States to illegal immigrants. The Republican platform was also firmly opposed to abortion.

Clinton accepted the Democratic Party presidential nomination on August 29. The Democratic platform reflected Clinton's move to the political center. The platform supported the death penalty, mandatory life sentences for criminals who commit three violent offenses, and Clinton's commitment to welfare reform. The platform supported abortion rights but added a clause that stated the party respected those who disagreed. With the memory of their 1994 loss of the House and Senate still fresh in their memories, the Democrats also embraced a theme traditionally associated with Republicans—the need for a smaller federal government.

Ross Perot won the Reform Party presidential nomination on August 17. Perot chose Pat Choate, an economist, as his running mate.

The fall campaign

After the Republican convention, Bob Dole pulled nearly even with Clinton in some opinion polls. But by early September, Dole had lost all of those gains and was even further behind Clinton than before the conventions.

Dole centered his campaign around the issue of taxes, promising a 15 percent income-tax cut. Dole also stepped up his criticism of Clinton for several ethics controversies surrounding the president, including contributions totaling hundreds of thousands of dollars that the Democrats took from foreign business interests. After the U.S. Department of Health and Human Services released a report in August showing marijuana use among teen-agers had nearly doubled in three years, Dole accused Clinton of ignoring drug abuse. A Dole campaign ad used footage of Clinton on MTV, a television network geared to teen-agers, laughing about his own experimentation with marijuana when he was a college student.

The Republican nominee also attempted to convince voters that the president was too liberal for the American public. But most voters were not swayed.

In addition, missteps bedeviled the Dole campaign. He drew unwanted attention to his age by referring to the Los Angeles Dodgers baseball team as the "Brooklyn Dodgers," even though the team had moved from Brooklyn to Los Angeles after the 1957 season. At an

A breakdown of delegates to the 1996 Republican and Democratic conventions

Participants	Democratic delegates	Republican delegates
Total delegates	4,320	1,990
Male	50%	66%
Female	50%	34%
White	67%	90%
Black	20%	3%
Asian	3%	1%
Hispanic	9%	2.5%
Union member	28%	3%

Sources: The Democratic National Committee, the Republican National Committee, and the Associated Press.

THE CAMPAIGN

Robert J. Dole

Party: Republican
Age: 73
Experience: U.S. congressman, 1961-1969; Republican nominee for vice president, 1976; U.S. senator, 1969-1996.

Dole ran as a moderate conservative in favor of gradually reducing the size of the federal government and shifting more power to the states. He also stressed the importance of maintaining strong moral values and reasserting U.S. interests around the world.

Stances on issues:

Abortion: Dole opposed abortion except when the mother's life was in danger or in cases of rape or incest. He favored giving states the right to impose waiting periods and require parental notification.

Federal budget: Dole favored a constitutional amendment to require a balanced budget. He called for balancing the budget by the year 2002.

Crime: Dole favored the death penalty, stricter penalties for convicted violent felons, the building of more prisons, the death penalty for international drug traffickers, and prosecuting as adults youths who commit three violent crimes.

Economy: Dole wanted to help U.S. business by reducing taxes, balancing the budget, opening new markets for U.S. products, and reducing governmental regulations. Dole believed that tax cuts would spur development, create jobs, and raise incomes, allowing the government to collect more tax income.

Gun control: Dole supported instant background checks and mandatory sentencing of criminals who use a gun while committing a crime.

Health care: Dole supported health-care reform, advocating tax incentives for small businesses to help them provide health care to their employees, making health costs tax deductible, and limiting the amount of damages that juries can award in medical malpractice suits.

Taxes: Dole proposed a 15 percent personal income tax cut and wanted to cut the top tax rate on investment gains from 28 to 14 percent. He also wanted to require a three-fifths majority of Congress to raise taxes.

Welfare: Dole supported the recent welfare bill that ended the open-ended welfare system. He favored giving the states control over welfare and requiring welfare recipients to find work within two years.

William J. Clinton

Party: Democrat
Age: 50
Experience: Arkansas attorney general, 1977-1979; governor of Arkansas, 1979-1981 and 1983-1992; U.S. President, 1993-

Clinton ran as a moderate liberal and supported traditional liberal causes, such as raising taxes on the wealthy and abortion rights. But he also embraced some conservative ideas, such as reducing the size of the federal government and welfare reform.

Stances on issues:

Abortion: Clinton supported a woman's right to have an abortion. He opposed late-term abortions except when the life or health of the mother was threatened.

Federal budget: Clinton opposed a constitutional amendment to require a balanced budget, but he called for balancing the budget by 2002.

Crime: Clinton supported the death penalty and expanded its use with the passage of the 1994 Crime Bill to cover terrorism, large-scale drug trafficking, and the murder of law enforcement officials. The bill also banned many assault weapons.

Economy: Clinton signed a bill increasing the minimum wage in August 1996. He claimed that the economy of the United States had the highest growth rate of any major country in the world since 1993. Clinton claimed that the economy had produced more than 10.5 million jobs since 1993.

Gun control: Clinton supported gun control. He signed the Brady Bill, which required a five-day waiting period to purchase firearms. He also signed the 1994 Crime Bill, which banned many assault weapons.

Health care: Clinton supported a bill to guarantee health care for people with preexisting conditions and to allow people to continue coverage when they shift jobs. He favored allowing people who have lost their jobs to retain health-care coverage for up to a year.

Taxes: Clinton favored simplifying the tax code but opposed a flat tax. He proposed a middle class tax cut and a $1,500-per-year tax credit to help pay for college.

Welfare: Clinton signed the Welfare Reform Bill, which required recipients to find work within two years of accepting welfare and limited lifetime benefits to five years. The bill also shifted the responsibility for administering welfare to the states.

appearance in Chico, California, Dole fell off a reviewing stand when a railing collapsed. He was unhurt, but the image reminded voters that Dole was 73 years old.

Clinton focused his campaign on the theme that he would "build a bridge to the 21st Century," an attempt to convince voters that he had a more centrist, forward-thinking vision than Dole and to remind them that he was much younger than his opponent. Clinton recognized that the Democrats had lost control of the U.S. House of Representatives in 1994 because voters perceived them as too liberal and out of touch with concerns of the public. But he also was aware that the new Republican leadership had lost public support because voters regarded its agenda as extremely conservative.

As the campaign wore on, Clinton stepped up his criticism of Dole. A campaign ad criticized "The real Bob Dole" for voting against Medicare (government-funded health insurance for the elderly), gun control, and education funding.

As the incumbent president, Clinton gained a great advantage from the relatively healthy state of the U.S. economy. Clinton repeatedly reminded audiences that 10.5 million new jobs had been created during his Administration. The nation's unemployment rate stood at a relatively low 5.2 percent in September 1996. When Dole accused Clinton of being a "tax-and-spend liberal," the president countered that the federal budget deficit had declined in each year of his Administration and had reached its lowest level since 1981.

The two top candidates debate

Dole and Clinton agreed to participate in two presidential debates. Their campaign staffs also agreed to one vice presidential debate. Ross Perot and his vice presidential running mate, economist Pat Choate, asked to participate in the debates. But the independent Commission On Presidential Debates, which organized the debates, ruled that they would not be allowed to participate, because Perot had failed to demonstrate that he had a reasonable chance of winning the presidency. The decision largely eliminated any chance of Perot becoming a significant factor in the campaign.

Dole and Clinton both performed well in the two debates, held in Hartford, Connecticut, and San Diego. Dole emphasized his tax-cut plan and conservative philosophy in the first debate. "I trust the people. The president trusts the government," Dole said, attempting to explain the basic difference between himself and Clinton.

But some Republicans criticized Dole for not challenging the president more aggressively in the debate. Dole was more sharply critical of Clinton's ethics in the second debate. The president ignored the attacks and focused on the achievements of his Administration.

In the campaign's final weeks, Dole attempted several last-minute gambits. He sharply criticized the news media for what he said was a liberal bias in favor of Clinton, and he railed at the seemingly complacent voters with the plaintive call, "Wake up, America." He sent his campaign manager, Scott Reed, on a mission to Texas to ask Ross

POLLS AND POLLING

The art of polling

Pollsters consider several things in their efforts to assemble accurate polls. They try to write balanced questions that will draw out each respondent's views. Pollsters also try to interview large numbers of people so that their poll results reflect the views of the population as a whole.

Phrasing the questions

How a question is phrased can affect the results of a poll. The first question, *right*, calls for a simple yes or no response. The second question offers alternative positions. Most pollsters would say that the second question would reflect the views of the population more accurately than the first question.

Do you agree or disagree with this statement: Any able-bodied person can find a job and make ends meet.

Some people feel that any able-bodied person can find a job and make ends meet. Others feel there are times when it is hard to get along and some able-bodied people are not able to find work. Whom do you agree with most?

Sampling

A sample is the number of people that pollsters question. Sampling error is a term pollsters use to assess the chance that the sample is not representative of the general population. Sampling error is expressed as a number of percentage points above and below the reported percent. Larger samples have smaller sampling errors.

Results of a preelection poll with a sampling error of 3 percentage points

	Level of support reported in poll	Actual level of support with sampling error
Candidate A	49 percent	46 percent to 52 percent
Candidate B	46 percent	43 percent to 49 percent
Undecided	5 percent	

Sampling and sampling error

The table, *right*, shows that sampling error falls with larger polling samples.

Sample Size	Sampling error
200	±9 percentage points
400	±6 percentage points
600	±5 percentage points
1,000	±4 percentage points
1,500	±3 percentage points

Perot to drop out of the race and endorse Dole. But the trip became an embarrassment to Dole when Perot refused to quit and ridiculed the request as "weird."

Election results

Negative campaigning and the perception that Clinton would be an easy winner appeared to have an impact on Election Day. Only 49 percent of the voting age population went to the polls.

Voters gave Clinton the victory, though by a smaller margin than many experts had expected. After the campaign, President Clinton emerged as the youngest president ever to win reelection, and the first Democrat to win two terms since Franklin D. Roosevelt in 1936.

Clinton received 49 percent of the popular vote; Dole, 41 percent; and Perot, 8 percent. (Minor third-party and independent candidates won the rest of the vote.) Clinton's performance was a better showing than the 43 percent he received in 1992, but it fell short of the majority vote the president wanted.

Clinton's victory in the Electoral College vote was more commanding. He won 379 electoral votes to Dole's 159. The Electoral College is a group of representatives chosen by the voters of each state to elect the president and vice president. Every state has as many votes in the Electoral College as the total of its senators and representatives in Congress. In the election, the candidate who wins a *plurality* (the highest number) of a state's popular votes usually receives all the state's electoral votes.

A dramatic gap in the support of women and minorities was the key to Clinton's victory, according to exit polling figures compiled by the Cable News Network and *Time* magazine. Men split their vote evenly between Dole and Clinton, but the president held a 54 percent to 38 percent advantage among women. Analysts attributed this gender gap to the president's support of abortion rights, gun control, and women's health issues.

Clinton shows strength with minorities

Election results showed that the Democratic Party retained its traditional support among minority groups. Clinton held an 84 percent to 12 percent advantage among African American voters and won the Hispanic vote by 72 percent to 21 percent. Dole had a narrow edge among white voters, 46 percent to 43 percent, but Clinton enjoyed greater support among voters who earned less than $50,000 a year.

The most significant factor in Clinton's reelection, however, appeared to be voters' confidence in the U.S. economy. Several surveys found that about 55 percent of voters believed the economy was in excellent or good shape, and a large majority of those voters supported Clinton. Historically, presidents have rarely failed to be reelected during a time of economic expansion.

The president's victory, however, was tempered by the Democrats' failure to regain control of the House or Senate. Republicans gained two seats in the Senate to hold a 55 to 45 advantage. Although the GOP lost seats in the House, it still held the majority. For at least two more years, the Democratic president would have to negotiate with Republican leadership of Congress. ...

POPULAR VOTE

Alabama:	Dole, 51%	Clinton, 43%
Alaska:	Dole, 51%	Clinton, 33%
Arizona:	Clinton, 47%	Dole, 44%
Arkansas:	Clinton, 54%	Dole, 37%
California:	Clinton, 51%	Dole, 38%
Colorado:	Dole, 46%	Clinton, 44%
Connecticut:	Clinton, 52%	Dole, 35%
Delaware:	Clinton, 52%	Dole, 37%
Dist. of Columbia:	Clinton, 85%	Dole, 9%
Florida:	Clinton, 48%	Dole, 42%
Georgia:	Dole, 47%	Clinton, 46%
Hawaii:	Clinton, 57%	Dole, 32%
Idaho:	Dole, 52%	Clinton, 34%
Illinois:	Clinton, 54%	Dole, 37%
Indiana:	Dole, 47%	Clinton, 42%
Iowa:	Clinton, 50%	Dole, 40%
Kansas:	Dole, 54%	Clinton, 36%
Kentucky:	Clinton, 46%	Dole, 45%
Louisiana:	Clinton, 52%	Dole, 40%
Maine:	Clinton, 52%	Dole, 31%
Maryland:	Clinton, 54%	Dole, 38%
Massachusetts:	Clinton, 62%	Dole, 28%
Michigan:	Clinton, 52%	Dole, 38%
Minnesota:	Clinton, 51%	Dole, 35%
Mississippi:	Dole, 49%	Clinton, 44%
Missouri:	Clinton, 48%	Dole, 41%
Montana:	Dole, 44%	Clinton, 41%
Nebraska:	Dole, 53%	Clinton, 35%
Nevada:	Clinton, 44%	Dole, 43%
New Hampshire:	Clinton, 50%	Dole, 40%
New Jersey:	Clinton, 53%	Dole, 36%
New Mexico:	Clinton, 49%	Dole, 41%
New York:	Clinton, 59%	Dole, 31%
North Carolina:	Dole, 49%	Clinton, 44%
North Dakota:	Dole, 47%	Clinton, 40%
Ohio:	Clinton, 47%	Dole, 41%
Oklahoma:	Dole, 48%	Clinton, 40%
Oregon:	Clinton, 47%	Dole, 37%
Pennsylvania:	Clinton, 49%	Dole, 40%
Rhode Island:	Clinton, 60%	Dole, 27%
South Carolina:	Dole, 50%	Clinton, 44%
South Dakota:	Dole, 46%	Clinton, 43%
Tennessee:	Clinton, 48%	Dole, 46%
Texas:	Dole, 49%	Clinton, 44%
Utah:	Dole, 54%	Clinton, 33%
Vermont:	Clinton, 54%	Dole, 31%
Virginia:	Dole, 47%	Clinton, 45%
Washington:	Clinton, 51%	Dole, 36%
West Virginia:	Clinton, 51%	Dole, 37%
Wisconsin:	Clinton, 49%	Dole, 39%
Wyoming:	Dole, 50%	Clinton, 37%

Source: The Associated Press.

Electronics

Electronics. A number of consumer manufacturers announced that they would begin to market digital video disc (DVD) players by the end of 1996. However, concerns in the industry, mainly about preventing the unauthorized copying of DVD movies, delayed the introduction of DVD until after December. Manufacturers expected DVD technology—which has applications in computer software and information storage systems, as well as in home entertainment—to generate wide public interest. Several computer makers said they would begin selling personal computers with DVD drives in 1997.

DVD's look like the ordinary CD's used for music and computer CD-ROM data, but they can store much more information. A single DVD can hold a typical, full-length movie—with digital sound and a picture three times sharper than a video cassette—and still have space left over. DVD players offer many special features. For example, the extra space on a DVD can be used to store alternative soundtracks in different languages. A DVD player may also have a built-in system that blocks out films that exceed the ratings limit preselected by a parent.

Toshiba America Information Systems, Inc. of Irvine, California, announced that its first DVD players would go on sale for $599 and $699. Unlike VCR's, these machines were not able to record programs. DVD movies were expected to become available in large numbers in 1997.

V-chips. A new federal law, signed by President Bill Clinton in February 1996, required manufacturers to install a special chip in most new television sets sold in the United States by 1998. The *V-chip* (short for "violence chip") is a microprocessor that can block programs that contain violence, sex, or profane language. The law also gave broadcast and cable television companies one year to voluntarily develop a violence rating system similar to the one already used for movies. This would help parents identify which programs the V-chip should block.

Speed record. In March, three separate groups of researchers at an optical fiber conference in San Jose, California, announced that they had successfully transmitted digital information through an optical fiber at the rate of one *terabit* (one trillion bits) per second. One terabit of information is equal to about 300 years of a daily newspaper. However, practical use of this capability was still years in the future.

Sales of electronics equipment, components, and related products in the first half of 1996 rose by 11 percent compared to 1995, the Electronic Industries Association (EIA) reported in August. A 17-percent increase occurred in computer and computer-related equipment sales. □ Michael Woods

See also **Television.** In *World Book,* see **Electronics.**

Employment. See Economics; Labor.
Endangered species. See Conservation.

Energy supply. On March 12, 1996, the U.S. Department of Energy (DOE) began operating the Defense Waste Processing Facility (DWPF), the largest nuclear waste processing plant in the United States, at the DOE's Savannah River site in South Carolina.

The $2.4-billion facility was designed to *vitrify* (convert into a glasslike material) highly radioactive liquid waste resulting from the production of nuclear weapons. Vitrification involves mixing the waste with sandlike particles of tough glass. The mixture then is melted and poured into stainless-steel canisters to cool and harden. Each canister holds about 4,000 pounds (1,800 kilograms) of the mixture.

The DOE estimated that by the year 2021, the DWPF will have converted 34 million gallons of liquid nuclear waste, which is stored in 51 underground tanks, into 6,000 canisters of vitrified waste that can be stored safely for long periods without contaminating the environment. Plans were made to store the canisters temporarily at Savannah River until a permanent waste storage facility could be completed.

Solar Two, a new solar electric power plant, went into operation in June 1996 in the Mojave Desert near Daggett, California. The $39-million experimental plant, funded by both private utilities and the DOE, was designed to test whether solar energy could be stored economically to later produce electricity.

The plant consisted of 1,926 movable mirrors that focus sunlight on the top of a 300-foot (90-meter)

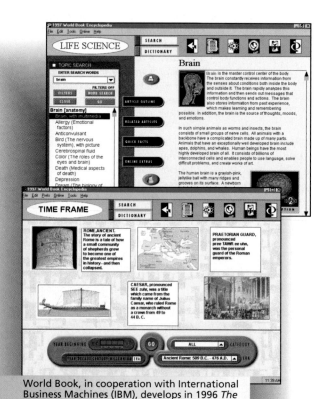

World Book, in cooperation with International Business Machines (IBM), develops in 1996 *The World Book Multimedia Encyclopedia,* a state-of-the-art version of *The World Book* on CD-ROM, available in retail stores early in 1997.

tower. Sunlight heats molten sodium and potassium nitrates that flow through pipes. After being heated, the chemicals are stored in insulated tanks until needed to heat water into steam to turn a turbine generator.

Solar Two replaced Solar One, an earlier plant that used sunlight to produce steam directly but could not operate at night or on cloud-covered days. Solar Two was scheduled to continue in operation until 1998, when scientists would evaluate its performance.

Nuclear power. In January 1996, the world's first advanced boiling water reactor (ABWR) nuclear power plant went into operation in Japan. Named Kashiwazaki-Kariwa 6, the 1,356-megawatt plant was designed and built by the General Electric Company and a group of Japanese partners.

In a boiling water reactor, the water inside the reactor is allowed to boil, and the steam from the core directly moves the turbines. In pressurized water reactors, used in most U.S. nuclear power plants, water in the reactor is pressurized so that it is heated beyond its boiling point but does not boil. The pressurized water heats another water supply outside the reactor that creates the generating steam.

The new ABWR was developed for the next generation of American nuclear power plants. Its reactors have features intended to improve safety, reduce construction and operating costs, and reduce time needed for construction.

Energy production. In September, the DOE reported that the United States produced 34.196 quadrillion British thermal units (Btu's), or "quads," of energy in the first half of 1996, an increase from the 33.964 quads produced in the first half of 1995. A Btu is the amount of energy needed to raise the temperature of 1 pound (0.45 kg) of water by 1 °F (0.56 °C).

Energy consumption increased from 43.455 quads in the first half of 1995 to 45.670 quads in the first half of 1996. Coal was the largest source of energy, followed by natural gas, crude oil, nuclear electric power, hydroelectric power, and geothermal power. Imports, mainly of crude oil, made up the difference between production and consumption of energy.

Wind was the world's fastest-growing energy source during 1995, according to an August 1996 report by the Worldwatch Institute, a research organization based in Washington, D.C. Wind power generating capacity rose to 4,900 megawatts in 1995, up from 3,700 megawatts in 1994. Since 1990, wind power capacity annually rose by 20 percent, a greater increase than with any other form of energy. The rapid growth indicated that wind power, which accounted for less than 1 percent of the world's electricity in 1996, could become an important energy source in the 21st century. □ Michael Woods

See also **Petroleum and gas.** In *World Book,* see Energy supply; Nuclear energy.

Engineering. See Building and construction.
England. See United Kingdom.

Environmental pollution. The British Coast Guard declared a full environmental alert on Feb. 15, 1996, when the tanker *Sea Empress,* fully laden with about 36 million gallons (136 million liters) of crude oil, ran aground off the coast of Wales and began leaking oil from its torn hull. Before being refloated a week later, the ship had spilled more than 16 million gallons (61 million liters) of oil, fouling some 100 miles (160 kilometers) of coastline.

Oil from the spreading slick killed as many as 25,000 sea birds and threatened the fish populations that local communities depend on for their livelihood. Estimates for the cost of cleaning up the spill ranged as high as $15.4 million.

Global warming. The Earth's average surface temperature climbed to a record high in 1995, scientists at the British Meteorological Office and the National Aeronautics and Space Administration (NASA) reported in January 1996. This finding lent support to the concern of many scientists that the burning of fossil fuels was warming the Earth's climate.

The British measured an average temperature of 58.72 °F (14.84 °C), while researchers at NASA's Goddard Institute for Space Studies in New York City recorded an average of 59.7 °F (15.39 °C). Both measurements confirmed that 1995 was the warmest year in the nearly 150 years (since 1856) that climatic records have been kept. Previously, the warmest year on record had been 1990.

The global temperature average for 1995 made the five-year period from 1991 through 1995 the warmest of any five-year period since 1856. This was despite the cooling effect of the 1991 Mount Pinatubo volcanic eruption in the Philippines, which cast aloft a sun-reflecting haze of dust and ash. Many scientists expect the Earth's surface temperature to rise another 1.8 to 6.3 °F (1.0 to 3.5 °C) by the year 2100, with a best-estimate average rise of 3.6 °F (2.0 °C). A United Nations (UN) scientific panel concluded that this observed warming was "unlikely to be entirely natural in origin." Previously, few scientists had been willing to make such a statement.

Many researchers attribute global warming, at least in part, to the accumulation in the atmosphere of gases that trap the heat of sunlight. These so-called greenhouse gases, notably carbon dioxide, are released when coal, natural gas, petroleum products, and wood are burned. Some climatologists think that continued warming could reduce crop yields, raise global sea levels, and create erratic weather patterns. The latter might already be occurring, some scientists speculated. They pointed to record amounts of snowfall in the Northeastern United States in 1996, a record heat wave that hit Chicago in 1995, and the worst flooding in recorded history in the Mississippi basin in 1993.

Antarctic ice melting? One result of global warming long feared by scientists appeared to be underway in the 1990's—the melting of the vast West Antarctic Ice Sheet. *Glaciologists* (scientists who study glaciers) of the British Antarctic Survey reported in January that atmospheric warming had caused five floating ice shelves in the northwest part of the continent to shrink drastically over the previous 50 years. The most recent loss of ice occurred in 1995, when a 500-square-mile (1,300-square-kilometer) area of the Larsen Ice Shelf broke apart in less than two months.

Many scientists, however, questioned whether global warming was to blame for the diminishing ice. They noted that a warmer atmosphere would increase evaporation from the oceans and bring heavier precipitation to many parts of the world, including Antarctica. Global warming should thus actually increase the size of the ice sheets. Moreover, researchers said, Antarctica was not warming uniformly.

Good news for the ozone layer. A finding that may bode well for the ozone layer in the upper atmosphere was reported in May 1996 by researchers at the National Oceanic and Atmospheric Administration (NOAA) in Washington, D.C. For the first time, the NOAA investigators said, ground-level air measurements had detected a reduction in chlorine concentrations. Chlorine, a component of many industrial chemicals, is the substance most responsible for the thinning of the ozone layer.

Ozone is a molecular form of oxygen consisting of three linked oxygen atoms. Ozone in the upper atmosphere acts as a barrier against the sun's ultraviolet light and is thus essential to life on Earth. Chlorine from chemicals that drift into the upper atmosphere reacts with ozone, transforming it to ordinary oxygen. Because it takes two to three years for ground-level chlorine to migrate to the upper atmosphere, the NOAA scientists predicted that ozone destruction would start to decline in 1998 or 1999. The ozone blanket would then begin to slowly recover. The turnaround could be credited to the 1987 Montreal Protocol, a United Nations treaty that led to an international ban on the use of ozone-destroying chemicals by the end of 1995.

Endocrine disrupters. A possible new environmental threat to human health was revealed in the 1996 book *Our Stolen Future* by Theo Colborn, a senior scientist at the World Wildlife Fund, an international conservation organization. Colborn and his coauthors, Dianne Dumanoski and John Peterson Myers, proposed that synthetic chemicals mimicking natural hormones such as estrogen can disrupt fertility, fetal development, and other vital processes. These pollutants, called endocrine-disrupting chemicals, include compounds used in plastics, detergents, and pesticides. The book argued that endocrine-disrupting chemicals may be causing a decline in human sperm counts, an epidemic of breast and prostate cancer, and damage to fetuses that leads to such consequences as reduced intelligence, hyperactivity, and violent behavior.

These conclusions were controversial, however. For one thing, the scientific community was divided on whether sperm counts were really declining. Furthermore, many scientists argued that the amounts of most synthetic chemicals in the environment are minuscule compared with naturally occurring plant hormones that can produce the same effects. Most experts agreed that the data on endocrine disrupters were simply not conclusive enough to state with certainty what effects these chemicals can have on the human body.

Three Gorges Dam. The largest hydroelectric project in history, the Three Gorges Dam in China, came under intense criticism from environmentalists in 1996. As a result, the United States government refused to provide loans for the project.

Construction on the $25-billion dam on the Yangtze River was well underway in 1996 and was scheduled for completion in 2009. The dam would be the largest in the world, spanning 6,864 feet (2,092 meters), rising 610 feet (186 meters), and creating a reservoir 400 miles (644 kilometers) long. Plans called for the dam to house 26 sets of turbines and generators with a total electrical generating capacity of 18,200 megawatts. The dam would boost China's supply of electric power by 10 percent.

Environmentalists charged, however, that the dam was a disaster in the making, and their opposition prompted the board of the U.S. Export-Import Bank to vote in May 1996 not to supply funding for the project. The bank is an independent government agency that provides loans and loan guarantees to U.S. companies to assist them in competing with foreign companies for business overseas. Several large American companies, including Caterpillar Inc., a maker of earth-moving equipment, had hoped to obtain financing from the bank to help them sell equipment to China for the construction of the dam.

According to the bank's president, Martin Kamarck, the Chinese government had made no plans for building treatment plants for the expected 265 billion gallons (1 trillion liters) of sewage and industrial waste that would be discharged into the reservoir each year. Nor had the government made any provision for cleaning up the thousand-year-old landfills of solid wastes, garbage, and toxic materials that lie in the areas to be flooded.

Milestone year for electric cars. Despite a decision by the California Resources Board to delay a requirement that 2 percent of the vehicles sold in that state be "nonpolluting" by 1998, 1996 was a big year for electric automobiles. Four major automakers—Saturn, Honda, Toyota, and Chrysler—announced plans to produce electric vehicles anyway. Researchers at the University of California at Davis had estimated the annual demand for electric cars in California at 100,000 vehicles.   □ Andrew J. Hoffman

In *World Book,* see **Environmental pollution.**

Equatorial Guinea. See Africa.

A workman clears oil-soaked seaweed from a beach in Wales in February after the tanker *Sea Empress* ran aground, spilling more than 16 million gallons (60.5 million liters) of oil.

Erbakan, Necmettin (1926–) became prime minister of Turkey on June 28, 1996, by forming a ruling coalition made up of his party, the conservative Islamic Welfare Party (IWP), and two pro-Western, non-Islamic parties. Erbakan was Turkey's first Islamist prime minister since the country became a republic in 1923.

Erbakan's government was charged with improving the nation's 80-percent inflation rate. He announced his intention of banning *usury* (the practice of lending money at interest) and forming closer ties to other Islamic countries through economic union. He also supported withdrawal from the North Atlantic Treaty Organization (NATO).

Erbakan, born in Sinop, Turkey, graduated from Istanbul Technical University. After earning a doctoral degree from Aachen Technical University in Germany, he taught at Istanbul Technical University until taking over leadership of the Union of Chambers of Commerce and Industry in 1965.

First elected to parliament in 1969, Erbakan formed his first Muslim political party in 1970. In 1971, the Turkish military banned the party, but Erbakan reestablished it in 1972 under a new name. In turn, this party was banned in 1980. Erbakan assumed leadership of the IWP in 1987.

☐ Lisa Klobuchar

See also **Turkey.**

Eritrea. See Africa.

Estonia. Relations between Estonia and neighboring Russia deteriorated significantly during 1996. Russia continued to claim that Estonian laws discriminated against Russian-speaking citizens, most of whom moved to Estonia between 1939 and 1991, when the country was part of the Soviet Union. Estonia, for its part, complained that Russia was meddling in the internal affairs of Estonia. In May 1996, the Estonian parliament bowed to international pressure and dropped a requirement that candidates for local office pass an Estonian language test.

Ethnic tensions were not the only source of conflict between the two countries. Throughout 1996, Russian and Estonian negotiators continued to disagree over the exact location of the Russian-Estonian border. Also, in April, Russian officials claimed that Estonia owed Russia $170 million for currency that Estonia failed to return when it introduced its own currency. Estonia countered that Russia owed Estonia about $80 million that had been frozen in accounts when Estonia left the Soviet Union.

On Sept. 20, 1996, President Lennart Meri was elected to a second five-year term by a specially convened electoral college. The special vote was required after the Estonian parliament deadlocked on three presidential ballots. ☐ Steven L. Solnick

See also **Europe** (Facts in brief table). In *World Book,* see Estonia.

Ethiopia. See Africa.

Europe

The countries of Europe struggled in 1996 to define the economic, political, and security arrangements that would guarantee the region's stability into the next century. The nations of the European Union (EU), an organization of 15 Western European countries, forged ahead with plans to issue a single currency despite worries that the effort was slowing growth and keeping unemployment high. The EU also began negotiations on constitutional reforms intended to enable the union to accept new members from Eastern Europe. The North Atlantic Treaty

Bosnian Serbs, fearing reprisals from Muslim-Croat police deployed to transfer territory, flee the suburbs of Sarajevo along a snow-covered mountain road in February.

Organization (NATO), a defense alliance between 14 Western European countries, Canada, and the United States, also pursued reforms designed to enhance Europe's role in its own defense and to enable the alliance to accept new members from Eastern Europe. NATO's task of restoring peace in the former Yugoslavia, however, proved more difficult, forcing the alliance to extend its troop presence there.

European economic growth stalled in early 1996 because of the economic turbulence related to the adoption of a single currency and the interest-rate increases of 1995. While growth resumed in the second half of 1996, it was too weak to significantly reduce unemployment. The EU predicted that growth would average 1.6 percent for the full year, down from 2.4 percent in 1995. Almost 18 million people, 10.9 percent of the work force of Western Europe, were without jobs in 1996.

Single currency doubts. The weakness of the economy cast doubt on the ability of EU governments to reduce their budget deficits to qualify for Economic and Monetary Union, a 1992 pact estab-

Facts in brief on European countries

Country	Population	Government	Monetary unit*	Foreign trade (million U.S.$) Exports†	Imports†
Albania	3,512,000	President Sali Berisha; Prime Minister Aleksander Gabriel Meksi	lek (108.10 = $1)	112	621
Andorra	73,000	Co-sovereigns bishop of Urgel, Spain, and the president of France; Prime Minister Marc Forne	French franc & Spanish peseta	30	not available
Austria	8,040,000	President Thomas Klestil; Chancellor Franz Vranitzky	schilling (10.72 = $1)	45,031	55,340
Belarus	10,113,000	President Alekandr Lukashenko	ruble (not available)	4,156	4,644
Belgium	10,166,000	King Albert II; Prime Minister Jean-Luc Dehaene	franc (31.38 = $1)	137,272 (includes Luxembourg)	125,617
Bosnia-Herzegovina	3,777,000	Chairman of the collective presidency Alija Izetbegović	dinar (not available)	no statistics available	
Bulgaria	8,692,000	President Zhelyu Zhelev; Prime Minister Zhan Videnov	lev (227.90 = $1)	4,157	4,316
Croatia	4,470,000	President Franjo Tudjman	kuna (5.41 = $1)	4,633	7,583
Czech Republic	10,317,000	President Václav Havel; Prime Minister Václav Klaus	koruna (26.90 = $1)	21,640	25,308
Denmark	5,191,000	Queen Margrethe II; Prime Minister Poul Nyrup Rasmussen	krone (5.84 = $1)	48,981	43,168
Estonia	1,516,000	President Lennart Meri	kroon (12.16 = $1)	1,302	1,663
Finland	5,144,000	President Martti Ahtisaari; Prime Minister Paavo Lipponen	markka (4.57 = $1)	29,658	23,214
France	58,399,000	President Jacques Chirac; Prime Minister Alain Juppé	franc (5.14 = $1)	286,536	274,335
Germany	81,640,000	President Roman Herzog; Chancellor Helmut Kohl	mark (1.52 = $1)	509,528	445,753
Greece	10,499,000	President Konstandinos Stephanopoulos; Prime Minister Costas Simitis	drachma (239.05 = $1)	9,392	21,489
Hungary	10,044,000	President Arpad Goncz; Prime Minister Gyula Horn	forint (158.93 = $1)	12,435	15,046
Iceland	274,000	President Olafur Grimsson; Prime Minister David Oddsson	krona (66.79 = $1)	1,803	1,755
Ireland	3,578,000	President Mary Robinson; Prime Minister John Bruton	pound (punt) (0.62 = $1)	43,702	32,269
Italy	57,210,000	President Oscar Scalfaro; Prime Minister Romano Prodi	lira (1,529.55 = $1)	(includes San Marino) 190,019	167,694
Latvia	2,522,000	President Guntis Ulmanis; Prime Minister Andris Skele	lat (0.56 = $1)	1,283	1,916
Liechtenstein	31,000	Prince Hans Adam II; Prime Minister Mario Frick	Swiss franc	no statistics available	

lishing a common currency and central bank among EU members, scheduled to begin in 1999. In January 1996, Foreign Minister Carlos Westendorp of Spain said the currency's introduction might have to be delayed if the credibility of the project were to be salvaged. Valery Giscard d'Estaing, the former French president, suggested that the deficit criteria be softened to take the weak economy into account. To qualify for joining in the single currency at its introduction, countries needed to reduce their *deficits* (annual debts) to 3 percent of *gross domestic product* (the value of all goods and services produced in a country during a given period).

Europe's political leaders, led by Chancellor Hel-

mut Kohl of Germany and President Jacques Chirac of France, remained determined to launch the single currency, to be called the euro, on schedule. They considered monetary union essential to developing closer political integration. Countries on the EU's northern and southern fringes doubled their efforts in 1996 to qualify for monetary union, instituting drastic spending cuts and tax increases to reduce their budget deficits in 1997. These countries' leaders believed they needed to participate in monetary union to retain an influence over European economic policy and full access to the EU single market.

At a meeting in Dublin, Ireland, on Dec. 13, 1996, EU leaders agreed to measures designed to pave the

Country	Population	Government	Monetary unit*	Foreign trade (million U.S.$) Exports†	Imports†
Lithuania	3,697,000	President Algirdas Brazauskas	litas (4.00 = $1)	2,698	3,010
Luxembourg	414,000	Grand Duke Jean; Prime Minister Jean-Claude Juncker	franc (31.38 = $1)	137,272 (includes Belgium)	125,617
Macedonia	2,196,000	President Kiro Gligorov	denar (40.51 = $1)	1,055	1,199
Malta	370,000	President Ugo Mifsud Bonnici; Prime Minister Eddie Fenech Adami	lira (0.36 = $1)	1,519	2,448
Moldova	4,463,000	President Mircea Snegur; Prime Minister Andrei Sangheli	leu (4.63 = $1	720	822
Monaco	33,000	Prince Rainier III	French franc	no statistics available	
Netherlands	15,674,000	Queen Beatrix; Prime Minister Wim Kok	guilder (1.71 = $1)	165,572	146,150
Norway	4,373,000	King Harald V; Prime Minister Thorbjoern Jagland	krone (6.46 = $1)	41,744	32,707
Poland	38,549,000	President Aleksander Kwasniewski; Prime Minister Wlodzimierz Cimoszewicz	zloty (2.82 = $1)	17,042	21,383
Portugal	9,817,000	President Jorge Sampaio; Prime Minister Antonio Guterres	escudo (153.60 = $1)	22,632	32,435
Romania	22,720,000	President Ion Iliescu; Prime Minister Nicolae Vacaroíu	leu (3,329.50= $1)	7,548	9,424
Russia	146,381,000	President Boris Yeltsin	ruble (5,442.00 = $1)	78,290	46,680
San Marino	26,000	2 captains regent appointed by Grand Council every 6 months	Italian lira	190,019 (includes Italy)	167,694
Slovakia	5,397,000	President Michal Kovac; Prime Minister Vladimir Meciar	koruna (31.08 = $1)	8,549	8,488
Slovenia	1,948,000	President Milan Kucan; Prime Minister Janez Drnovsek	tolar (139.33= $1)	8,286	9,452
Spain	39,729,000	King Juan Carlos I; Prime Minister José María Aznar	peseta (128.25 = $1)	73,293	92,503
Sweden	8,862,000	King Carl XVI Gustaf; Prime Minister Goran Persson	krona (6.59 = $1)	79,918	64,446
Switzerland	7,332,000	President Jean-Pascal Delamuraz	franc (1.26 = $1)	77,670	77,006
Turkey	64,293,000	President Süleyman Demirel; Prime Minister Necmetlin Erbakan	lira (95,122.00 = $1)	21,600	35,710
Ukraine	51,219,000	President Leonid Kuchma	hryvna (1.78 = $1)	11,289	10,716
United Kingdom	58,987,000	Queen Elizabeth II; Prime Minister John Major	pound (0.63 = $1)	242,038	265,320
Yugoslavia	10,842,000	President Zoran Lilić; Prime Minister Radoje Kontić	new dinar (5.04 = $1)	no statistics available	

*Exchange rates as of Oct. 25, 1996, or latest available data.   †Latest available data.

way for the euro: a stability pact to enforce low budget deficits after monetary union; an exchange-rate mechanism to link the euro to currencies not participating initially; and legislation guaranteeing contracts after the euro replaces national currencies.

EU reform. The EU began negotiations on revising the bloc's governing treaties at an intergovernmental conference in Turin, Italy, on March 29. The reforms were intended to enable the EU to accept as many as a dozen new members from Eastern and Southern Europe in the early 2000's. Expectations of the outcome were limited, however, by a rising tide of anti-EU sentiment in many countries, particularly in the United Kingdom. The main reforms discussed

were allowing groups of EU countries to develop joint policies without hindrance from other EU members, a key aim of France and Germany; limiting the right of individual countries to veto EU policies; and developing closer cooperation in fighting international crime and drug trafficking. The negotiations were expected to continue until mid-1997.

EU expansion into Eastern Europe was expected to be delayed beyond the target date of 2000 set by most former Soviet bloc countries. The European Commission, the EU executive agency in charge of preparing for the acceptance of new members, attributed the delay, in part, to the slow pace of economic and political reform in those countries.

205

Fragile peace in former Yugoslavia. The former Yugoslav republic of Bosnia-Herzegovina (often called Bosnia) enjoyed its first peace in five years in 1996 as Serbs, Muslims, and Croats began implementing an American-brokered settlement. Prospects for a lasting peace remained uncertain because the war's legacy of mistrust left the ethnic communities deeply divided. Fear of reprisals prevented most of the country's 2 million refugees from returning to their homes.

A NATO-led force of 60,000 soldiers, most of whom entered Bosnia in January and February 1996, maintained peace throughout the year. The force supervised the removal of troops and heavy weapons from battle lines between the three communities and enabled civilian reconstruction efforts to begin. Foreign donors led by the EU, the United States, and the World Bank, an international agency that lends money to countries, pledged $1.89 billion in assistance to rebuild highways, utility lines, and housing destroyed during the war.

Presidential and parliamentary elections went ahead as scheduled on Sept. 14, 1996, though the strong showing by nationalist Muslim, Serb, and Croat candidates in their respective regions helped to reinforce Bosnia's ethnic divisions. Alija Izetbegović, the Muslim leader, automatically became head of the three-person Bosnian presidency after polling more votes than the leading Serb and Croat candidates. Izetbegović later met in Paris with President Slobodan Milošević of Serbia and agreed to resume diplomatic and commercial relations between Bosnia and Yugoslavia, which consists of the federation of Serbia and Montenegro. International monitors postponed municipal elections scheduled for Bosnia for September 1996 until 1997 because of alleged widespread electoral fraud.

Frustration over the failure of authorities to arrest suspected war criminals also hindered peace-building efforts. However, the UN International Criminal Tribunal for the Former Yugoslavia did convict Dražen Erdemović, a Croat who fought with the Bosnian Serbs, and sentenced him to 10 years in prison in November 1996. Erdemović confessed to taking part in the slaughter of more than 1,000 Muslim civilians near the town of Srebrenica in July 1995.

U.S. President Bill Clinton announced on Nov. 15, 1996, that he would extend a U.S. troop presence in Bosnia, which had been set to expire in December, by up to 18 months. NATO endorsed the plan, which created a stabilization force of 30,000 soldiers.

Protests in Serbia erupted after President Milošević's ruling Socialist Party overturned the results of municipal elections. A coalition of five opposition parties claimed to have won the November 17 elections in 15 of the country's 18 biggest cities, including the capital, Belgrade. Daily street protests involving as many as 100,000 people posed the biggest challenge to Milošević's nine-year tenure in office.

NATO reform. NATO took steps in 1996 to adapt to the post-Cold War world. Foreign ministers of the 16 NATO allies agreed to give European members the right to organize military operations without the participation of the United States. The agreement, reached at a meeting in Berlin on June 3, satisfied a European desire for greater autonomy from the United States in defense matters and established a procedure for NATO to lend forces and equipment, including U.S.-controlled items such as troop transports and reconnaissance satellites, to the Western European Union, the EU's defense arm. The agreement also created a European deputy to the American general who commands NATO forces. The European deputy was to control European operations.

The reforms were welcomed by France, which had promised to rejoin NATO's integrated military command if Europeans were given greater control. France, while remaining a NATO member, expelled NATO troops from its soil and withdrew French forces from NATO command in 1966. France's ties with the alliance and with the United States were strained in 1996, however, when President Clinton refused a request from French President Chirac to replace the American commander of NATO's southern forces with a European. President Clinton said such a change was unacceptable because the bulk of the forces in the region were American, including the Sixth Fleet in the Mediterranean Sea.

NATO enlargement and Russia. The alliance also attempted to develop plans to accept new members from Eastern Europe while forging closer ties with Russia, which continued in 1996 to view the expansion of NATO as a threat to Russian security. In September, U.S. Secretary of State Warren Christopher proposed that NATO sign a charter with Russia providing for closer political consultations and security cooperation. Defense Secretary William Perry offered to bring more Russian officers into NATO's command structure, building on Russia's participation in the NATO-led force in Bosnia. However, Russian Prime Minister Viktor Chernomyrdin declared firm opposition to enlargement at a security conference in Lisbon in December, saying it would create a dangerous new dividing line in Europe. Nevertheless, the conference of the Organization for Security and Cooperation in Europe agreed to seek further cuts in conventional weapons, a step NATO hoped would soften Russian opposition to expansion.

President Clinton set the first firm timetable for NATO expansion, stating on October 22 that NATO should accept its first Eastern European members in 1999. Poland, Hungary, and the Czech Republic were considered to be the leading candidates for entry.

Beef crisis. Europe's beef market collapsed, and relations between Great Britain and its EU partners were seriously strained after the British government announced on March 20, 1996, that people who ate beef from cattle with the neurological disease bovine spongiform encephalopathy (BSE), also known as "mad cow disease," may risk developing Creutzfeldt-Jakob disease, a fatal, degenerative disease of the human brain. The EU imposed a worldwide ban on British beef exports, worth about $750 million a year. Prime Minister John Major criticized the ban as a violation of the EU single market and retaliated by blocking more than 100 EU proposals or pieces of legislation. Both sides called a truce at a summit meeting in Florence, Italy, on June 20. EU leaders agreed to lift the export ban in stages if Britain adopted new safety measures, including the slaughter of up to 4 million animals believed to be at risk of the disease. Britain did not present plans for a slaughter until December, however, and there was little sign of a lifting of the ban at year-end.

Opening to Asia. EU leaders held a summit meeting with leaders of 10 Asian nations in Bangkok in March and agreed to attempt to increase trade and investment between the two regions. European leaders had been concerned by the increased attention the United States paid to Asia. They hoped the meeting with the heads of government of Japan, South Korea, China, and the members of the Association of South East Asian Nations would bolster Europe's diplomatic and commercial presence in the world's fastest-growing markets.

Clash over Cuba. Transatlantic trade tensions flared after U.S. President Clinton in March signed the Helms-Burton Bill, named for its Republican sponsors, Senator Jesse Helms and Representative Dan Burton. The law allowed U.S. citizens to sue foreign companies that profit from the use of Cuban properties expropriated from Americans after the 1959 Cuban revolution. The EU challenged the legality of the law at the World Trade Organization in Geneva, Switzerland, and adopted its own legislation to shield European companies. The EU also adopted a tougher stance toward Cuba, suspended talks on economic cooperation, and increased its support for democracy and human rights.

The Channel Tunnel was the scene of a major accident in 1996. A fire in a truck being carried by train from France to England brought the train to a halt inside the tunnel on November 18. The blaze caused minor injuries to the 34 passengers and severe damage to one of the project's two tunnels. Authorities suspended passenger service in the other tunnel until December 4, to review safety procedures. Eurotunnel, the company that operates the project, estimated the fire cost at least $380 million in damages and lost revenue. The accident came just six weeks after Eurotunnel won an agreement from its bankers to ease interest payments on its $15 billion debt. □ Tom Buerkle

See also the various European country articles. In *World Book,* see **Europe; European Union;** and the various country articles.

Explosion. See **Disasters.**

Farm and farming. For the first time in 60 years, United States farmers planted spring crops in 1996 with few restrictions from the federal government. The Agriculture Improvement and Reform Act, dubbed the "freedom to farm law," was signed by President Bill Clinton on April 4, 1996, ending government control over the production of corn, cotton, rice, and wheat.

Under the new law, farmers were to receive $36.7 billion in payments that were to gradually decline over seven years. Payments to farmers in 1996 totaled $5.7 billion. The amount a farmer received was calculated on past production of a subsidized crop. Thus a farmer who was required to plant corn in 1995 could plant soybeans in 1996 and receive a payment based on past corn plantings.

American farmers took advantage of the new flexibility to plant more corn and soybeans and less rice and cotton. Corn acreage was up 11 percent, and soybean planting increased 3 percent. The U.S. Department of Agriculture (USDA) reported in November that the increase in acreage yielded 9.2 billion bushels of corn—22 percent more than the 1995 crop. Wheat at 2.3 billion bushels was 5-percent higher. Increased planting of soybeans resulted in the second largest crop ever. The 1996 crop—2.4 billion bushels—was 8 percent above 1995's crop.

Farmers devoted 6 percent less acreage to rice in 1996 than they had in 1995, but harvested 2-percent more rice. Cotton acreage dropped a steep 16 percent. However, remarkably good weather in California pushed the cotton harvest 2 percent above the 1995 level of 18.2 million bales.

Environmental programs renewed. The "freedom to farm law" retained the Conservation Reserve Program, a plan created in 1985 that had idled 36.4 million acres (14.7 million hectares) of land highly susceptible to erosion. The USDA drew up new criteria aimed at forcing all but the most environmentally sensitive land back into crop production. "Freedom to farm" created the Environmental Quality Incentive Program to help livestock and crop producers reduce pollution in order to improve water quality around their operations. The new farm law also renewed the Wetlands Reserve Program begun in 1985. The program called for retiring 130,000 acres (52,600 hectares) of wetlands from agricultural use. Half the acreage would be idled for 30 years, the remainder permanently.

Crop insurance. In a pilot program, private companies offered farmers in Iowa and Nebraska federally backed Crop Revenue Coverage on 1996 corn and soybean crops. The policies insured farmers against low yields and allowed them to take advantage of crop price increases. Premiums were at least 40 percent higher than traditional coverage, but nevertheless proved to be popular. The USDA allowed winter wheat growers in most states to buy the new coverage for their 1997 crops.

An Oklahoma rancher in May gazes across land in the grip of the worst drought to hit the Great Plains since the Dust Bowl days of the 1930's.

World grain supplies. Global grain production was up in 1996, but so was consumption. World wheat production jumped 8 percent over 1995, yet supplies were the second lowest since the USDA began keeping records in 1960. India grew more wheat than the United States for the second year in a row. Argentina, Australia, Canada, and the European Union (EU) all reported larger wheat crops than in 1995. Earlier in the 1990's, the EU had spent billions of dollars to subsidize exports of wheat, but in 1996, it levied a tax on the crop to discourage exporting to nonmember countries.

Global production of small grains rose 11 percent mainly because of larger barley crops in Western Europe and Canada. Global oilseed production was up

due to larger soybean crops in Brazil and the United States. Increased rice production in China and Vietnam and near-record U.S. yields kept total production stable.

Global production of cotton, the lone crop not suffering from short supplies, was at 87 million bales, off by 5 percent from 1995. Increases in Australia, Egypt, and India were not large enough to offset smaller crops in Brazil and China.

U.S. prices rise. Despite the overall bounty of U.S. agriculture, reserves of barley, corn, oats, rice, and wheat declined. With surpluses heading downward, U.S. commodity prices reacted upward. Short stocks also translated to a 3.5 percent retail food price increase in the United States. It was the first time in the 1990's that food prices rose more than the rate of inflation.

U.S. agricultural exports hit a record $60 billion in 1996, the second year in a row that agriculture was the nation's top exporting industry. In addition to increased worldwide demand, a favorable exchange rate made U.S. products affordable overseas. Export sales of red meat, poultry, fruits, vegetables, and snack foods eclipsed sales of bulk grains.

Beef exports increased 8 percent because of large supplies and lower prices. Still, health concerns over beef prevented exports from rising even higher. For example, Japan cooled its desire for U.S. beef in the wake of an outbreak of food poisoning, but beef exports to Mexico nearly doubled. In contrast, pork exports were up 40 percent. Farmers sold hogs rather than buy expensive feed. Fewer hogs drove up the price of pork, as did strong demand from Canada and Japan, increasing returns to hog farmers. China, Hong Kong, Mexico, and Russia bought the most U.S. poultry, and 1996 poultry exports jumped 23 percent.

In 1996, two-thirds of U.S. farm exports went to 18 Asian and North American countries. Yet, the USDA estimated that questionable trade barriers used by the same countries cost U.S. farmers $2.7 billion in lost export sales. For example, fungus infestations in U.S. wheat caused China to cancel agreements to purchase 1.1 million short tons (1 million metric tons) of the grain. China had not refused such wheat in the past, but instead took a discount on the price. Still, U.S. sales of cotton, grains, red meat, poultry, and vegetables to China totaled $2 billion in 1996.

NAFTA versus WTO. In 1996, the North American Free Trade Agreement (NAFTA), a pact to eliminate trade barriers among Canada, Mexico, and the United States that took effect in 1994, came into conflict with a rewritten global trade agreement signed in 1994. The treaty, called the General Agreement on Tariffs and Trade (GATT), created the World Trade Organization (WTO) to enforce GATT rules.

On Jan. 1, 1996, Canada replaced its *import quotas* (certain quantities of items to be imported each year) with tariffs on U.S. dairy, poultry, eggs, and other products—some as high as 350 percent of the price. (A tariff is a tax placed on goods that one nation imports from another.) Under GATT rules, Canada could convert its quotas to tariffs. It had until the year 2001 to reduce its tariffs by 15 percent. The high 1996 rates meant that, even after the 15 percent reduction, Canadian dairy and poultry producers would still be protected from U.S. competition after 2001. The U.S. dairy industry charged that the Canadian action circumvented NAFTA, which required tariffs between the two countries to gradually disappear over 10 years. However, in July, a WTO arbitration panel upheld Canada's position that GATT superseded NAFTA.

Beef scare. In July, an epidemic caused by *Escherichia coli* bacteria sickened more than 9,000 people in Japan. In 1993, *E. coli* had been responsible for a major U.S. outbreak of food poisoning in the Pacific Northwest. The cause proved to be contaminated ground beef. At first, Japan blamed U.S. beef for its epidemic and cut imports of red meat by 40 percent. However, the government later admitted it could not determine the source of the *E. coli*. By year-end, U.S. beef sales to Japan were at the same level as in 1995, but Japan planned to tighten meat inspection.

Meat safety. The 1993 *E. coli* outbreak in the United States had led to more strict federal regulation of meat and poultry slaughter and processing plants. In 1996, processing plants were given up to 42 months to develop plans that incorporated the Hazard Analysis and Critical Control Point (HACCP) system into their inspection procedures. HACCP was originally devised by the Pillsbury Corp. of Minneapolis, Minnesota, to produce food safe for consumption by U.S. astronauts. Since 1904, inspectors have depended upon sight, smell, and touch to detect contaminated meat. Visual inspections continued in 1996, but new regulations required inspectors and plants to focus on prevention.

Delaney ditched. In July, Congress passed the Food Quality Protection Act, which repealed the 1958 Delaney clause that banned all cancer-causing substances from processed food regardless of how small the quantity. In practice, the Delaney clause prevented the Environmental Protection Agency from using scientific advances that made it possible to measure substances in parts-per-billion. Thus, the goal of banning all cancer-causing substances was impossible to attain. The new standard, which applied to both processed and raw foods, allowed residues that pose no reasonable risk of harm, particles so small that they have a 1-in-1 million chance of causing cancer.

Genetically improved crops. Soybean and cotton plants genetically altered for new desirable traits were harvested on a commercial scale for the first time in 1996. The soybean plants were altered for genetic resistance to a widely used, potent herbicide called Roundup, enabling plants to withstand spraying to kill weed infestations in the field. The altered cotton plants had a gene for producing a protein lethal to tobacco budworms and cotton bollworms, pests that feed on cotton buds and bolls. The new cotton plants grown in parts of Texas and Mississippi's Delta region required pesticide spraying because corn planting in the area attracted infestations of corn earworm, which is the same pest as the cotton budworm. In the Far West, where less crop switching occurred, the new cotton thrived without spraying. ☐ Patricia Peak Klintberg

See **Farm and farming** Special Report: **Mad Cow Disease**. See also **Weather**. In *World Book*, see **Agriculture; Farm and farming**.

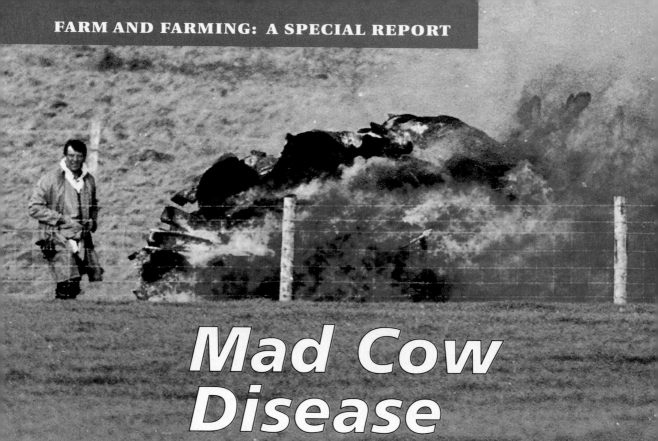

Mad Cow Disease

Panic hit the beef industry and the British public as "mad cow disease" killed animals and contaminated the beef supply.

By Fred Pearce

Above:

Cattle infected with BSE, or "mad cow disease," are burned to prevent further spread of the disease into the food chain.

It was Europe's public health bombshell of the 1990's. On March 20, 1996, the United Kingdom's (UK) health minister Stephen Dorrell announced the discovery of 10 cases among young people of an unusual form of the rare and deadly Creutzfeldt-Jakob disease (CJD) and said that the victims had "most likely" contracted the disease from exposure to contaminated beef.

CJD, a degenerative disease of the human brain affects one person in a million each year around the world. After infection, it normally takes many years before the symptoms show themselves. And in the handful of known cases, CJD was generally associated with people aged 60 or older. But here was a strain that seemed to be attacking the young, and there had been 10 cases in the UK among people under age 42 during the previous two years. The suspect beef was said to have come from cattle infected with a similar brain-wasting condition, contracted from commercial feed. The popular press and media dubbed it "mad cow disease," but it was known scientifically as *bovine spongiform encephalopathy*, or BSE .

A matter for concern

The government statements brought both panic and recrimination. After years of official denials, the admission of a possible link between BSE and CJD set alarm bells ringing throughout Europe. Overnight the European Union (EU) banned British beef exports. Some British supermarkets and hamburger outlets switched to foreign beef. Beef sales across much of Europe, particularly in Germany, collapsed, regardless of where the meat had come from. Slaughter houses and cattle markets emptied.

The European Commission demanded that the British government set up measures to eradicate BSE. Its tone antagonized many British Conservative politicians, who were already opposed to European interference in UK affairs. The UK government tried to have the export ban lifted and temporarily withdrew cooperation on other EU business. In June, after protracted and bitter negotiations between London and Brussels (where the EU has its headquarters), the UK agreed to the selective slaughter and destruction of cattle likely to be infected so as to remove them from the human food chain. But which cows and how many were to be killed? As the year went on, those issues became fraught with complexity.

Perhaps most alarming was the idea that if the CJD victims had indeed contracted the disease from BSE-infected beef, they had probably done so before 1989, when rigorous controls on cattle feed were introduced. Because of the length of time that CJD takes to develop, these victims could be just the first of many. It did not matter that ministers claimed the route of infection had been largely eliminated by 1990.

The use of the unspecific phrase "most likely" in Dorrell's March 20 statement highlighted the fact that there was no direct scientific proof that BSE could be transmitted to human beings. But government assurances, given on the basis of scientific advice that the risk in eating beef was extremely small, only added to the sense of concern. A small risk was not the same as no risk, and the media quickly caught on to that fact. "Beef warning sparks panic," headlined *The Guardian* newspaper on March 21, "Many millions in potential danger." A number of eminent scientists, notably Richard Lacey, professor of microbiology at the University of Leeds, warned that in the next decade there might be thousands of deaths among people who, in the late 1980's, had eaten beef infected with BSE.

The background to the crisis

BSE and CJD, along with a sheep disease called scrapie, belong to a range of diseases that infect the brains of animals, giving the brain a spongy appearance. This gave rise to the technical name *spongiform encephalopathy*. The infective agent is a little-known protein called a

Glossary

Encephalopathy: any disease of the brain.

Epidemiology: the branch of medicine dealing with the causes, distribution, and spread of diseases in a community, especially of infectious diseases.

Microbiology: the science dealing with microorganisms—that is, organisms too small to be seen without a microscope.

Neuropathology: the study of diseases of the nervous system.

The author:

Fred Pearce is a freelance journalist on environmental affairs. He has covered the beef crisis for *New Scientist* magazine since March 1996.

A slow, fatal group of diseases

So-called mad cow disease belongs to a group of untreatable, fatal illnesses called *transmissible spongiform encephalopathies* (TSE's). The agent that causes TSE's is neither a bacteria nor a virus, but a little-understood type of protein called a prion. Scientists believe that prions invade normal protein molecules in the membrane of the brain, causing them to refold into abnormal forms, which themselves bring on more abnormal refolding in a cascading effect. Unfortunately, there is no immune response or inflammation, as brain tissue becomes spongy and death finally ensues.

A TSE of cattle

Bovine spongiform encephalopathy (BSE)— "mad cow disease"—was first diagnosed in 1986 in the United Kingdom. In 1988, the UK banned the use of feed supplements thought to be the culprit in spreading BSE, and the number of cases dropped. Nevertheless, more than 155,000 cases have been identified among British cattle, the most of any nation.

Other animal TSE's

An animal TSE called scrapie has been common to sheep for at least 200 years. Other TSE's of animals appear to be of more recent origin. For example, a TSE of mink was first reported in 1947, and since the mid-1980's, scientists have diagnosed TSE's in cats, mule deer, and certain zoo animals.

Human TSE's

There are four human TSE's, all very rare. Creutzfeldt-Jakob disease; kuru, found among a tribe in New Guinea; Gerstmann-Straussier syndrome; and fatal familial insomnia. There may be a genetic factor to some human TSE's.

Mysterious, slow-acting diseases

Infection	Host population	Mode of transmission	Symptoms
Scrapie 	Certain breeds of sheep that usually are more than four years old; found in all parts of the world except Australia and New Zealand.	Unknown.	Irritability and restlessness; later scratching, biting, and rubbing of the skin, from which the name derives; patchy loss of wool, tremors, weight loss, weakness in the hindquarters.
Bovine spongiform encephalopathy	Mature cattle, mainly in the United Kingdom.	Most likely commercial feed supplements containing parts of sheep infected with scrapie. Can possibly be transmitted from an infected cow to her calf.	A progressive degeneration of the nervous system that lasts from less than 2 weeks to 14 months. Symptoms include a stumbling or high-stepping gait, changes in temperament, scratching, and weight loss.
Kuru 	Mainly the women and children of an isolated tribe in Papua New Guinea called the Fore.	Eating infected tissue of the brain in a ritual ceremony for a dead tribal member. The women and children ate brain tissue. The men ate muscle tissue, which may not transmit the disease or which may require a longer incubation period.	Neurological weakness, palsy, and uncoordinated movements, but no deterioration of mental function; on average, patients die about one year after the onset of symptoms.
Creutzfeldt-Jakob disease	Human populations worldwide, though there is an increased incidence among Libyan Jews and in areas of Chile, England, Hungary, Slovakia, and the United States. Average age of patients is 63.	Unknown.	In about 20 percent of cases, muscular spasms, reduced mental function, loss of higher brain function, and abnormal behavior. About 90 percent of patients die within one year of developing symptoms, 5 percent die within the second year of symptoms, and 5 percent experience slow neurological deterioration that delays death for up to 10 years.

Source: *Encyclopaedia of Microbiology*, Volume 4, Academic Press, 1992.

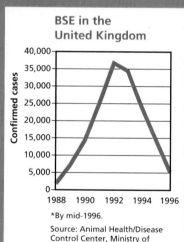

BSE in the United Kingdom

*By mid-1996.

Source: Animal Health/Disease Control Center, Ministry of Agriculture, United Kingdom.

Gathering the evidence

A researcher examines the brain tissue of an infected cow, *top*. A graph of confirmed cases of BSE in the UK, *above*, shows a peak in 1992. Because of BSE's long incubation period—usually four years—most infections occurred in the late 1980's.

prion, whose existence was for many years disputed by scientists. Since 1986, biologists have known that spongiform encephalopathy can be transmitted from sheep to cattle. Meat and bone meal from sheep carcasses, some infected with scrapie, have been incorporated into commercial cattle feed since the 1920's. But the technique that was used to extract the bone meal was able, in most cases, to remove the danger of such transmission.

Rendering plants, or centers that process the inedible parts of slaughtered animals, once used a solvent to extract the tallow (a fatty substance used in making soap and cosmetics), thus leaving a protein-rich bone meal that could be added to animal feed. During this process, the infective agent responsible for scrapie was largely neutralized. But in about 1980, UK rendering plants replaced solvent extraction by heat treatment to separate the tallow. Using heat was cheaper, but the temperature attained was not high enough to kill off the infectious material. This change, as a Scottish scientist named Derek Mould in 1965 warned, increased the infectivity of scrapie.

In 1985, a cow on a dairy farm in Kent, England, became the first to go "mad." At first, it was edgy and uncoordinated, then aggressive, then lame—and then it died. Under the microscope, its brain was found to be riddled with holes, like a sponge. Scientists had seen their first case of BSE, and quickly identified its source as cattle feed that included the remains of sheep infected with scrapie.

Delayed reaction

Although the diagnosis was swift, the UK government delayed until mid-1988 before setting up an inquiry to make recommendations on what to do. The delay allowed the disease to spread far and fast. By the time of the inquiry, there were thousands of cases of BSE, and tens of thousands of other animals infected but not yet showing symptoms. Within weeks of his appointment, the inquiry's chairman, Oxford University biologist Richard Southwood, had persuaded ministers to ban sheep and cattle remains from cattle feed and to order the sick cattle to be destroyed.

The intention was to stop the spread of the disease among cattle rather than to protect humans. Scientists in the late 1980's, as Southwood later recalled in a 1996 magazine interview, remained fairly confident that BSE could not be passed on to humans.

The scientists reasoned that humans had been exposed to scrapie for hundreds of years with no ill effects, and they saw no reason to believe that BSE would be different. But as they would eventually realize, the fact that scrapie could not be transmitted from sheep to humans was no guarantee that BSE might not make that jump.

It was not until November 1989, four years after the first case, that the government accepted Southwood's second recommendation, which was to ban certain cattle organs known to harbor BSE, such as the brain and spinal cord, from human food. At the same time, ministers set up a permanent body to monitor the situation, the Spongiform Encephalopathy Advisory Committee (SEAC), and launched a scientific program to evaluate changes in patterns in the occurrence of CJD in humans which might be attributed to BSE. This CJD surveillance unit was set up at the Western General Hospital in Edinburgh, Scotland.

"Doomsday scenario"

One day in September 1995, James Ironside, a neuropathologist at the CJD surveillance unit, examined the spongy brain of a teen-age victim of CJD and discovered something that was, until then, unique. He already knew that young CJD victims were extraordinarily rare: In the UK, there had been just one case in a person under 30 years old in the previous 25 years. But the pattern of degenerating brain tissue revealed under the microscope was new to him. In all spongiform diseases, *fibrils,* or threads, of protein form in the brain. In this young victim, the protein fibrils had turned into large clumps, and there were a lot of them.

As several similar cases followed in the ensuing weeks, it dawned on Ironside, and on Robert Will, head of the CJD surveillance unit, that these might represent the "doomsday scenario" that the unit had been set up to watch for—that is, changes in patterns in human CJD. With no common factors among its victims other than eating beef, the most likely explanation of this new form of CJD was that it was a human form of mad cow disease. And if BSE could pass to humans, most of the population of the UK was potentially at risk. In March 1996, Will blew the whistle after he and Ironside had uncovered 10

British beef banned

- Austria
- Australia
- Belgium
- Canada
- Cyprus
- Finland
- France
- Germany
- Greece
- Holland
- Italy
- Japan
- Jordan
- New Zealand
- Portugal
- Singapore
- South Africa
- Spain
- Sweden
- United States

Farmers suffer

British farmers, *top,* fight desperately to save the collapsing beef market by protesting against the European Union (EU) ban on British beef in March 1996. However, some countries, such as the United States in 1988, had already imposed a ban after reports of BSE in the late 1980's.

Allaying public fears

Hamburger and fast-food chains in the UK responded to public fears about BSE by switching temporarily to non-British beef.

unusual cases of CJD in young people, two of them teen-agers. By October, four more cases of the new variant CJD had emerged.

There was something subtly different about these cases. Whereas traditional elderly sufferers from CJD became forgetful and developed odd behavior, these younger victims became chronically depressed and anxious. But what convinced Will that he was looking at a new form of CJD was the state of the dissected brains of its victims: none showed fibrils, just great blotches of telltale protein. Press reports about the issue compelled the UK government to react. In consultation with SEAC, the fateful government statement was issued in the House of Commons on March 20, and the crisis finally broke.

Loss of confidence

The revelations profoundly damaged the UK beef industry, and public confidence was shaken. Many charged that since 1988 the government had acted to protect the farming and food-processing industries rather than the consumer. Some public health scientists had been warning for years that humans could catch BSE. Among them were Harash Narang, a microbiologist in the government's own Public Health Laboratory Service, and Stephen Dealler, a consultant microbiologist at Burnley Hospital. These scientists alleged that the regulations put in place in 1989 and 1990 to prevent infection had been poorly implemented by farmers, slaughterhouses, and feed manufacturers, and poorly policed by government inspectors. In the aftermath of the March revelations, the SEAC made recommendations to tighten up these rules.

Part of the crisis in public confidence arose from the difficulties scientists and politicians have with the word "safe." Throughout the early 1990's, ministers and their advisers had repeatedly said "British beef is safe," even though scientists were by then acknowledging the possibility that BSE might be transmissible to humans. Even the government's chief medical officer, Kenneth Calman, agreed that "the theoretical risk has always been acknowledged." The 1996 crisis, therefore, inevitably brought a widespread mistrust of public pronouncements.

But scientists proved as hard to rely on as politicians. They consistently underestimated how many cattle would contract BSE. In early 1989, Richard Southwood predicted there would eventually be 17,000 to 20,000 cases before the disease was wiped out. As confirmed cases soared to a peak of 700 animals a week in mid-1992, predictions were revised to 100,000 cases. After that the incidence fell consistently, but by mid-1996, it was still at around 120 a week, and the total of confirmed cases was more than 160,000, with no end in sight. BSE cases had by then also shown up in Switzerland and Denmark, and in France. France, whose imports of British beef had gone up by nearly 20 percent since 1990, planned to double its funding for BSE research.

Furthermore, a disturbing number of new cases of BSE occurred in animals born after the feed ban. In theory, they should not have been exposed to scrapie. But in practice farmers had often continued to use old feed or feed intended for pigs and other farm animals—feed that still contained scrapie-infected material. A second possibility was that cows could pass on the disease to their calves, in the womb or from their milk. In 1990, the government had approved a research program intended to test this possibility. The interim results of this study, conducted by John Wilesmith of the Central Veterinary Laboratory in Weybridge, Surrey, were announced in early August 1996. They showed that there was a distinct chance that transmission from mother to calf could take place. The finding was based on studies of 600 calves for seven years, but researchers had not yet worked out how the disease was passed on.

The culling of the cattle

Following the March announcement, the British government officials and the SEAC argued that there was no public health purpose in a slaughter of British cattle. But they were assuming that the route of BSE into the human food chain was finally closed off, something that European veterinary experts and public health officials were less inclined to believe than most of their UK counterparts. These EU officials argued that, until the disease had been substantially eliminated from UK-bred cattle, the risk of transfers to humans was too great, whatever the safeguards. So they sided with Southwood, who said in March that "a slaughter of all animals born before early 1991" was probably necessary to slow the number of new cases and restore public confidence.

Finally, the British government agreed in June to the slaughter and destruction of all cattle aged 30 months or more. It was a mammoth task for slaughterhouses and rendering plants, which clearly could not cope with the more than half a million animals involved. Power stations and waste incinerators joined in the disposal of carcasses. But the whole agreement came under review again once scientists had discovered that the disease could be passed on from mother to calf.

When will it end?

For British farmers the central question at the end of 1996 was: how soon can cattle herds be purged of BSE? And epidemiologists were still grappling with this issue, which was made more complex by the discovery of possible mother-to-calf transmission of BSE among cattle. Few scientists expected maternal transmission to be able to sustain the epidemic forever, but they feared it would slow the pace of the disease's disappearance. British government officials suggested that BSE could linger on until the year 2008, though a study published in August by a team from Oxford University suggested that it might die out by 2001. On the strength of this study, the UK government sought a revision of the culling agreement with the EU.

For the British public, a more fundamental issue remained as 1996 ended: would there be a major human epidemic or not? Only time would tell. Scientists regarded the potential for a massive epidemic among humans as slight, but real. It would depend on whether any more cases of the new strain of CJD turned up relatively soon. Scientists hoped that by the end of 1997, they might know whether the 14 cases remained an unexplained, if tragic, oddity; if they represented the start of a small outbreak; or if they signaled the beginning of a major epidemic.

Direct scientific proof that BSE causes CJD in humans cannot be obtained without the ultimate—and obviously impossible—experiment: the injection of BSE into human subjects to test for the development of CJD. Meanwhile, in France, rhesus monkeys were deliberately injected with tissue from the brains of BSE-infected cows and developed symptoms strikingly similar to those of the young CJD victims. On the other hand, researchers at Queen Mary's College, London, injected BSE into mice genetically engineered to be more like humans in their response to CJD. But no fatalities occurred among the mice after more than a year. Such conflicting results do little to allay fears, but many researchers think that if there is an epidemic, it will be a small one.

James Ironside of the CJD surveillance unit agrees. He believes that, at worst, the disease might develop as it did when human growth hormone accidentally contaminated with CJD was given to some 2,000 people with dwarfism in the 1980's. Then, he said, doctors initially feared that most of the 2,000 Britons who had been given the treatment would develop fatal illness. Instead, by mid-1996, only 18 cases had been confirmed.

Until more conclusive evidence is in, the government, scientists, and the people of the United Kingdom can only wait and hope that the threat of a major outbreak will never be fulfilled.　■ ■ ■

Fashion took on a neater look in 1996, a trend that appeared midsummer when the 1997 men's styles were introduced at the New York City fashion shows. The male models had cut their shoulder-length hair, including their pony tails. The fresh, neater look was soon apparent at late-night clubs, where patrons were no longer showing up in see-through or cut-away clothes. Instead, the fashionable look was either long and slinky or short and slinky, usually black, but not glitzy.

In runway shows, the basic shapes for women's clothes were long and fitted. The basic pieces for any season were long jackets, slightly fitted tunics, and slender skirts. Even men's clothes cast off the over-sized look for one shaped closer to the body.

Minimalism. Simplicity remained the dominant look in high-fashion circles as it had been for several seasons. However, popular pared-down, spare shapes demanded accents to avoid the look of a uniform. Thus, a few decorative elements appeared in 1996. Jewelry returned, primarily big, rough-cut stones circling the neck, and bold metal belt buckles accenting the waistline.

Some new designs incorporated an old fabric—Spandex. For years, this stretch yarn was employed only in swimsuits and pantyhose. The new designs for 1997 used the stretch factor in blouses and tunics. Spandex was also used in pants and

Black remained *the* color for men's clothing in 1996. The all-black look even triggered the return of the black suit, largely unseen since the "corporate look" of the 1950's and early 1960's.

Exotic animal-print fabrics were a favorite with designers in 1996. Zebra, cheetah, jaguar, and ocelot prints turned up on slacks and blouses, cap, gloves, and scarf sets, and even on purses and shoes.

FOCUS ON

Fashion | 1996

Square toes and chunky heels, which appeared in 1996 on a wide variety of footwear—from conservative pump to high-fashion boot—caught on with both the young and the mature buyer.

skirts, helping to make the new fitted clothes truly fit. Leggings, traditionally made with stretch yarns, became even more important as part of the new lean look. They were upgraded from utilitarian to styles in bold colors and fanciful patterns.

Cracking the casual look. In the past decade, many companies that required more formal attire introduced dress-down Fridays. The concept was so enthusiastically received that some firms extended the casual look to the entire week. Just when beach clothes and athletic garb seemed to have taken over the world, a reaction set in. Some progressive companies in such fields as advertising and computers began introducing dress-up Fridays. They found it set them apart from their corporate competitors. The firms also found that many of their employees did not mind the change. Many employees enjoyed getting back into jackets.

French couture. Traditionally the most provocative trendsetter, French high fashion continued to lose its grip on popular taste. Yves Saint Laurent, who had ushered in the pants-suit era in the 1970's, produced no new vital concepts. Hubert de Givenchy's role at the House of Givenchy was taken over briefly by John Galliano, who focused on exotic evening dresses. In October 1996, Galliano replaced Gianfranco Ferré as head designer at Christian Dior.

Only Karl Lagerfeld in his made-to-order collection for Chanel influenced fashion in 1996. His very long suit jacket—as long as a coat—paired with skirts, pants, and leggings fit neatly with the new long, lean look, and was reproduced by ready-to-wear houses at less exalted prices.

Fur is back. For years, animal-rights advocates in Great Britain and the United States successfully protested the use of furs in clothing. But in 1996, ranch mink and fur from other commercially grown animals, not endangered species, moved back into the fashion spotlight. A number of couture designers used fur trimmings, such as Valentino's chinchilla collars. Young U.S. designers, such as YeoLee, Byron Lars, and Marc Jacobs, showed low-keyed styles in mole and sheared sable, which fit into the look of slender, understated fashion. South Korea and Japan were among the growing new markets for fur coats.

Exporting American fashion. Leading American fashion houses—including Calvin Klein, Donna Karan, and Ralph Lauren—developed plans in 1996 to begin wide exportation of products to Asia, as well as to Europe. Designers believed that American fashion, with its emphasis on separates, versatility, comfort, and informality, could be as successfully exported as American blue jeans have been during the last 30 years. In 1996, television and the Internet seemed to "soften" international boundaries of fashion, and Asia began to open its doors to American fashion and its designers.   □ Bernadine Morris

In *World Book,* see **Clothing; Fashion.**

Finland boasted one of Europe's strongest economies in 1996. The government forecast growth of 2.8 percent, down from 4.2 percent in 1995, but nearly double the average growth rate for the 15-nation European Union (EU). Inflation fell below 1 percent in 1996, an EU low, but unemployment, at about 16 percent, remained high.

On September 3, the government of Prime Minister Paavo Lipponen introduced a budget for 1997 that would reduce spending by 5 percent and cut the deficit to 1.4 percent of gross domestic product. The government claimed that such measures would lower interest rates, spur investment, foster the creation of jobs, and qualify Finland for charter membership in the EU monetary union, scheduled for 1999. On Oct. 12, 1996, the government tied the value of its currency, the markka, to other EU currencies by joining the bloc's exchange-rate mechanism. As a result, Finland was expected to meet all requirements for joining the single currency in 1997.

The government softened Finland's neutrality in April 1996 by joining Sweden in proposing that all EU members work together in international peacekeeping operations.   □ Tom Buerkle

See also **Europe** (Facts in brief table). In *World Book,* see **European Union; Finland.**

Fire. See Disasters.

Flood. See Disasters.

Florida. See State government.

Food. In July 1996, United States President Bill Clinton signed legislation that set a new standard for the allowable amount of residue from pesticides and other chemicals in agricultural products and processed foods. The new law prohibited any chemical that, if consumed at average levels over a lifetime, would result in more than one case of cancer per 1 million people in the United States. The law also required the U.S. Environmental Protection Agency to establish human tolerance levels for agricultural chemicals, taking into account the increased vulnerability of infants and children to the chemicals. The new law replaced the 1958 Delaney Clause, which had prohibited any trace of cancer-causing chemicals in food. The Grocery Manufacturers of America, the National Food Processors Association, and other food-industry groups praised the new standard, stating that it would lead to the use of safer, more effective chemicals in food production.

Fat substitute. In January 1996, the U.S. Food and Drug Administration (FDA) approved the use of a fat substitute called olestra in snack foods. Frito-Lay, the largest U.S. snack manufacturer, began test-marketing potato chips made with olestra in April under an agreement with Procter & Gamble (P&G), the developer of olestra. P&G also began test-marketing its own brand of potato chips made with the fat substitute.

Both Frito-Lay and P&G asked the FDA to allow

less explicit language on package labels for products containing olestra. In approving the fat substitute, the FDA required labels to include language in a black box stating, "Olestra may cause abdominal cramping and loose stools. Olestra inhibits the absorption of some vitamins and other nutrients. Vitamins A, D, E, and K have been added." Frito-Lay reported that after reading the label, 75 percent of consumers in its survey were uncertain of the product's safety, or they believed it to be unsafe. P&G found similar results in its consumer surveys. The FDA gave P&G time to conduct consumer surveys and propose labeling alternatives.

The Center for Science in the Public Interest (CSPI), a Washington, D.C.-based health advocacy group, appealed the FDA's approval of olestra. The CSPI stated that the snacks had undergone limited testing with children and may cause adverse health effects. The group asked the FDA to require more explicit labeling language. The group also pledged to launch campaigns in the test markets to inform consumers of the health effects of olestra, and it established a telephone hot line for consumers to report adverse reactions.

Fat labeling. In August 1996, the CSPI released a major study on a type of fat called "trans fat" in brand name and restaurant foods. According to the study, many foods made with partially hydrogenated oil, vegetable shortening, or margarine also contained damaging amounts of trans fat. CSPI senior scientist Margo Wootan stated that trans fat raises cholesterol levels as much as saturated fat.

The CSPI called on restaurants and food manufacturers to switch to liquid vegetable oil and to disclose the amount of trans fat in their products. Under 1996 labeling requirements, trans fat was not identified on labels, though it was included in total fat content. However, the Grocery Manufacturers of America stated that calls for trans fat labeling were premature because research data was inconclusive.

Fresh versus frozen. In February 1996, the FDA proposed to allow frozen fruits and vegetables packages to bear labels marked "healthy." The American Frozen Food Institute (AFFI), a trade association, had submitted test results to the FDA showing that frozen produce and fresh produce contained roughly the same amount of nutrients.

The AFFI also urged the U.S. Department of Agriculture (USDA) and the Department of Health and Human Services to revise the *1995 Dietary Guidelines for Americans* to include frozen foods. The AFFI claimed that the guidelines not only omitted the nutritional benefits of frozen vegetables but implied that only raw vegetables contained the necessary nutrients for good health.

USDA Undersecretary for Food, Nutrition, and Consumer Services Ellen Haas responded that the USDA was not attempting to misrepresent the quality and acceptability of frozen food. She said

the USDA would work to include frozen foods in nutrition information based on the guidelines.

The U.S. Congress settled the issue of fresh versus frozen labeling of poultry products by establishing that poultry products held at 26 °F (–3.3 °C) or higher temperatures may be labeled "fresh," while poultry products chilled to below 0 °F (–17.8 °C) would be labeled "frozen." Poultry at temperatures between 0 °F and 26 °F would carry neither label.

Eating out. Department of Commerce data for 1995, the most recent available, showed that 44 percent of U.S. food dollars were spent away from the home. The National Restaurant Association predicted 1996 food service sales at $312.9 billion, up 5 percent over 1995. According to the Commerce Department, fast-food establishments accounted for nearly half (47.8 percent) of restaurant sales. About one-third of all table-service restaurants served ethnic foods.

Yogurt in school-lunch programs. The USDA proposed to allow yogurt as an alternative for meat in school-lunch programs and other national feeding programs, stating that by including yogurt the number of food choices containing high levels of fat and cholesterol would be reduced. In comments to the USDA, the American Meat Institute sharply disagreed, noting that the USDA had withdrawn similar proposals in 1981, 1985, and 1989. ☐ Bob Gatty

In *World Book,* see **Food; Food supply.**

Football. A variety of problems struck both college and professional football in 1996. Among colleges, the bowl alliance created to crown an undisputed—if unofficial—national champion triggered confusion instead. Among the professionals, the Dallas Cowboys, 1995-1996 champions of the National Football League (NFL), had three of its players suspended for alcohol- or drug-related offenses, and the Canadian Football League (CFL) lost four franchises and appeared to be on the brink of failure.

College. While many coaches and athletic directors continued to advocate national champion playoffs for the major colleges, opposition continued from college presidents. The unofficial championship thus was left again to the polls and to an alliance of three major post-season bowl games: the Sugar, Orange, and Fiesta. The Big Ten and the Pacific 10 conferences continued to spurn the alliance and send their champions to the Rose Bowl.

The alliance hoped to match in one bowl—this time, the Sugar Bowl—the teams ranked first and second in the regular season by the Associated Press media poll and the USA Today/CNN coaches poll. These two polls ranked Florida State No. 1 and Arizona State No. 2. Each finished the season with an 11-0 record, the only undefeated and untied teams in Division I-A, where the major colleges played.

However, because Arizona State belonged to the Pacific 10, it was obliged to play in the Rose Bowl

Football

against Ohio State (10-1). It looked as if the Sugar Bowl would be a match-up between Florida State and the University of Nebraska, until the University of Texas upset Nebraska, 37 to 17, in the Big 12 championship game. Nebraska fell from second to sixth in the polls, and Florida moved up to third. This cost Nebraska a chance to win a third consecutive national championship and left Florida State matched with the University of Florida (11-1) in the Sugar Bowl. This was an attractive match-up, except for the fact that the teams had met November 30, when Florida was ranked first and Florida State second. Florida State won, 24 to 21, and there seemed to be little interest in a rematch.

On Jan. 1, 1997, Ohio State defeated Arizona State, 20 to 17, in the Rose Bowl in Pasadena, California. The following night, Florida dominated Florida State, 52 to 20, in the Sugar Bowl in New Orleans. The major polls then crowned Florida as the national champion.

Season. Great improvement was shown in 1996 by Arizona State, which had a 6-5 record in 1995, and the University of Houston, which finished with a 7-4 record—after winning just one game in 1995—and went to the Liberty Bowl. Notre Dame (8-3) was ranked 18th in the final polls. When it was not chosen for a major bowl, it turned down bids from two lesser bowls. After the season, Lou Holtz, who had a shaky relationship with his athletic director, quit after 11 years as Notre Dame's coach.

Danny Wuerffel, the University of Florida's senior quarterback, won every major player-of-the-year-award, including the Heisman Trophy. For the season, he completed 207 of 370 passes for 3,625 yards and 39 touchdowns. In the Heisman voting, the closest race since 1989, Wuerffel received 1,363 points to 1,174 for Troy Davis, Iowa State's junior running back. Davis rushed for 2,158 yards for a team with only a 2-9 record. Quarterback Jake Plummer of Arizona State, who passed for 2,575 yards and 23 touchdowns, finished third. Offensive tackle Orlando Pace of Ohio State won the Outland and Lombardi awards as the nation's outstanding lineman.

In November, Boston College threw 13 players off the team for betting on college and professional sports, including two players who allegedly bet against Boston College. Coach Dan Henning, already under fire for three losing seasons, later resigned.

Largely because the Southwest Conference had dissolved, two other conferences expanded. The Big 8 became the Big 12 by adding Texas, Texas A&M, Texas Tech, and Baylor. The 10-member Western Athletic Conference added Southern Methodist, Texas Christian, Rice, San Jose State, Tulsa, and Nevada-Las Vegas.

Tie games were eliminated by a new rule that creat-

Heisman Trophy winner Danny Wuerffel, of the University of Florida, fades back to pass. In 1996, he completed 207 of 370 passes for 3,625 yards.

ed overtime with equal alternate possessions until one team outscored the other. The rule led to some games that lasted until the fifth overtime.

Professional. In January 1996, in the NFL's National Conference play-offs, Dallas whipped the Philadelphia Eagles, 30 to 11, holding Ricky Watters to 39 yards rushing. Dallas then defeated the Green Bay Packers, 38 to 27, as Emmitt Smith, the Cowboys' star running back, rushed for 150 yards.

In the American Conference, the Pittsburgh Steelers eliminated first the Buffalo Bills, 40 to 21, and then the Indianapolis Colts, 20 to 16. The contest against the Colts ended when the Steelers batted away a Colts' last-second pass in the end zone.

Dallas met Pittsburgh January 28 in Tempe, Arizona, in the Super Bowl, a championship that an American Conference team had not won since 1984. This streak continued. While Pittsburgh held Dallas to 56 yards rushing, three interceptions, two by Larry Smith, helped the Cowboys win, 27 to 17.

Before the 1996 season, which began in September, the Cowboys were struck by the suspensions of defensive end Shante Carver (6 games) and wide receiver Michael Irvin (5 games). Emmitt Smith suffered knee and neck injuries, and the offensive line was hobbled. The Cowboys lost three of their first four games, but they rallied to a 10-6 record and a fifth consecutive division title.

When the Cleveland Browns moved to Baltimore in 1996, they became the Ravens because the NFL kept the

The 1996 college football season

College conference champions

Conference	School
Atlantic Coast	Florida State
Big East	Miami (Fla.)—Syracuse—Virginia Tech (tie)
Big Sky	Montana
Big Ten	Ohio State—Northwestern (tie)
Big Twelve	Texas
Big West	Nevada—Utah State (tie)
Conference USA	Southern Mississippi—Houston (tie)
Gateway	Northern Iowa
Ivy League	Dartmouth
Metro Atlantic	Duquesne
Mid-American	Ball State
Mid-Eastern	Florida A&M
Northeast	Robert Morris
Ohio Valley	Murray State
Pacific 10	Arizona State
Patriot	Bucknell
Pioneer	Dayton
Southeastern	Florida
Southern	Marshall
Southland	Troy State
Southwestern	Jackson State
Western Athletic	Brigham Young
Yankee	William & Mary

Major bowl games

Bowl	Winner	Loser
Alamo	Iowa 27	Texas Tech 0
Aloha	Navy 42	California 38
Amos Alonzo Stagg (Div. III)	Mount Union (Ohio) 56	Rowan (N.J.) 24
Blue-Gray	Blue 44	Gray 34
Carquest	Miami 31	Virginia 21
Citrus	Tennessee 48	Northwestern 28
Copper	Wisconsin 38	Utah 10
Cotton	Brigham Young 19	Kansas State 15
Fiesta	Penn State 38	Texas 15
Gator	North Carolina 20	West Virginia 13
Heritage	Howard 27	Southern 24
Holiday	Colorado 33	Washington 21
Independence	Auburn 32	Army 29
Las Vegas	Nevada 18	Ball State 15
Liberty	Syracuse 30	Houston 17
Orange	Nebraska 41	Virginia Tech 21
Outback	Alabama 17	Michigan 14
Peach	Louisiana State 10	Clemson 7
Rose	Ohio State 20	Arizona State 17
Sugar	Florida 52	Florida State 20
Sun	Stanford 38	Michigan State 0
NCAA Div. I-AA	Marshall 49	Montana 29
NCAA Div. II	Northern Colorado 23	Carson-Newman (Tenn.) 14
NAIA Div. I	Southwestern Oklahoma State 33	Montana Tech 31
NAIA Div. II	Sioux Falls (S.D.) 47	Western Washington 25

All-America team (as picked by AP)

Offense
Quarterback—Danny Wuerffel, Florida
Running backs—Troy Davis, Iowa State; Byron Hanspard, Texas Tech
Wide receivers—Reidel Anthony, Florida; Marcus Harris, Wyoming
Tight end—Pat Fitzgerald, Texas
Center—K. C. Jones, Miami
Other linemen—Chris Naeole, Colorado; Benji Olson, Washington; Orlando Pace, Ohio State; Juan Roque, Arizona State
All-purpose—Kevin Faulk, Louisiana State
Place-kicker—Marc Primanti, North Carolina State

Defense
Linemen—Peter Boulware, Florida State; Derrick Rodgers, Arizona State; Reinard Wilson, Florida State; Grant Winstrom, Nebraska
Linebackers—Canute Curtis, West Virginia; Pat Fitzgerald, North-western; Jarrett Irons, Michigan; Matt Russell, Colorado
Backs—Dré Bly, North Carolina; Chris Canty, Kansas State; Kevin Jackson, Alabama; Charles Woodson, Michigan
Punter—Noel Prefontaine, San Diego State

Player awards
Heisman Trophy (best player)—Danny Wuerffel, Florida
Lombardi Award (best lineman)—Orlando Pace, Ohio State
Outland Trophy (best interior lineman)—Orlando Pace, Ohio State

Browns' name, colors, and legacy for a future team in Cleveland. The Houston Oilers played to mostly empty seats at home while preparing to move to Nashville in 1998. The Seahawks stayed in Seattle after flirting with a move to Los Angeles.

Season. Green Bay (13-3), the second-year Carolina Panthers (12-4), and Dallas won the National Conference's division titles. They qualified for the play-offs with the three remaining conference teams with the best records—San Francisco (12-4), Philadelphia (10-6), and Minnesota (9-7).

The division winners in the American Conference were the Denver Broncos (13-3), New England Patriots (11-5), and Pittsburgh (10-6). The wild-card play-off teams were Buffalo (10-6), Indianapolis (9-7), and the second-year Jacksonville Jaguars (9-7).

People. Dan Marino of the Miami Dolphins became the first quarterback in NFL history to pass for 50,000 yards, and John Elway of Denver became the third to reach 45,000 yards. But overall, 1996 was a difficult year for quarterbacks, perhaps because half of the starters were at least 30 years old. Warren Moon of Minnesota was 40, and Jeff Hostetler of the Oakland Raiders, Jim Kelly of Buffalo, and Marino all were 35 or 36. All missed starts because of injuries.

Joe Gibbs, who coached the Washington Redskins to three Super Bowl victories, was elected to the Pro Football Hall of Fame with offensive tackle Dan Dierdorf, defensive tackle Lou Creekmur, defensive back Mel Renfro, and wide receiver Charlie Joiner. Another Hall of Fame member, Pete Rozelle, the NFL commissioner (1960 to 1989) who made pro football a television staple, died Dec. 6, 1996, at age 70 of brain cancer.

Other leagues. The Canadian Football League (CFL) struggled to survive in 1996. Four teams from the United States—San Antonio; Shreveport, Louisiana; Birmingham, Alabama; and Memphis, Tennessee—folded and the Baltimore franchise moved to Montreal, leaving nine CFL teams for the 1996 season, all from Canada. All finished the season, but only because the league gave three teams—Montreal, Ottawa, and British Columbia—financial assistance. After the 1996 season, the Ottawa Rough Riders, who had been in existence for 120 years, also folded. In December, CFL commissioner Larry Smith announced the he would resign after his contract expired in early 1997.

The Toronto Argonauts won the CFL's Grey Cup championship game November 24 in Hamilton, Ontario, defeating the Edmonton Eskimos, 43 to 37. Doug Flutie, the Toronto quarterback, was named the league's most valuable player for the regular season and the Grey Cup game.

The World League of American Football, an NFL-sponsored enterprise, played from April to June in six European cities. The league lost about $12 million in 1996, after losing $23 million in 1995. The Scottish Claymores, based in Edinburgh, beat Frankfurt, 20 to 17, to win the World Bowl June 23. □ Frank Litsky

In *World Book,* see **Football.**

National Football League final standings

American Conference

Eastern Division

	W.	L.	T.	Pct.
New England Patriots*	11	5	0	.687
Buffalo Bills*	10	6	0	.625
Indianapolis Colts*	9	7	0	.562
Miami Dolphins	8	8	0	.500
New York Jets	1	15	0	.062

Central Division

	W.	L.	T.	Pct.
Pittsburgh Steelers*	10	6	0	.625
Jacksonville Jaguars*	9	7	0	.562
Cincinnati Bengals	8	8	0	.500
Houston Oilers	8	8	0	.500
Baltimore Ravens	4	12	0	.250

Western Division

	W.	L.	T.	Pct.
Denver Broncos*	13	3	0	.813
Kansas City Chiefs	9	7	0	.562
San Diego Chargers	8	8	0	.500
Oakland Raiders	7	9	0	.438
Seattle Seahawks	7	9	0	.438

*Made play-offs

National Conference

Eastern Division

	W.	L.	T.	Pct.
Dallas Cowboys*	10	6	0	.625
Philadelphia Eagles*	10	6	0	.625
Washington Redskins	9	7	0	.562
Arizona Cardinals	7	9	0	.438
New York Giants	6	10	0	.375

Central Division

	W.	L.	T.	Pct.
Green Bay Packers*	13	3	0	.813
Minnesota Vikings*	9	7	0	.562
Chicago Bears	7	9	0	..438
Tampa Bay Buccaneers	6	10	0	.375
Detroit Lions	5	11	0	.313

Western Division

	W.	L.	T.	Pct.
Carolina Panthers*	12	4	0	.750
San Francisco 49ers*	12	4	0	.750
St. Louis Rams	6	10	0	.375
Atlanta Falcons	3	13	0	.188
New Orleans Saints	3	13	0	.188

Individual statistics (American Conference)

Leading scorers, touchdowns

	TD's	Rush	Rec.	Ret.	Pts.
Curtis Martin, New England	17	14	3	0	104
Terrell Davis, Denver	15	13	2	0	90
Michael Jackson, Baltimore	14	0	14	0	88
Tony Martin, San Diego	14	0	14	0	84
Carl Pickens, Cincinnati	12	0	12	0	74
Karim Abdul-Jabbar, Miami	11	11	0	0	66
Jerome Bettis, Pittsburgh	11	11	0	0	66
Shannon Sharpe, Denver	10	0	10	0	60
James Stewart, Jacksonville	10	8	2	0	60

Leading scorers, kicking

	PAT	FG	Longest	Pts.
Cary Blanchard, Indianapolis	27	36	52	135
Al Del Greco, Houston	35	32	56	131
Adam Vinatieri, New England	39	27	50	120
John Carney, San Diego	31	29	53	118
Mike Hollis, Jacksonville	27	30	53	117

Leading quarterbacks

	Att.	Comp.	Yds.	TD's	Int.
John Elway, Denver	466	287	3,328	26	14
Vinny Testaverde, Baltimore	549	325	4,177	33	19
Dan Marino, Miami	373	221	2,795	17	9
Mark Brunell, Jacksonville	557	353	4,367	19	20
Drew Bledsoe, New England	623	373	4,086	27	15
Jeff Hostetler, Oakland	402	242	2,548	23	14
Jeff Blake, Cincinnati	549	308	3,624	24	14
Chris Chandler, Houston	320	184	2,099	16	11
Stan Humphries, San Diego	416	232	2,670	18	13
Jim Harbaugh, Indianapolis	405	232	2,630	13	11

Leading receivers

	Passes caught	Total yards	Avg. gain	TD's
Carl Pickens, Cincinnati	100	1,180	11.8	12
Terry Glenn, New England	90	1,132	12.6	6
Tim Brown, Oakland	90	1,104	12.3	9
Tony Martin, San Diego	85	1,171	13.8	14
Keenan McCardell, Jacksonville	85	1,129	13.3	3
Wayne Chrebet, N.Y. Jets	84	909	10.8	3
Jimmy Smith, Jacksonville	83	1,244	15.0	7
Shannon Sharpe, Denver	80	1,062	13.3	10
Michael Jackson, Baltimore	76	1,201	15.8	14
O. J. McDuffie, Miami	74	918	12.4	8

Leading rushers

	Rushes	Yards	Avg.	TD's
Terrell Davis, Denver	345	1,538	4.5	13
Jerome Bettis, Pittsburgh	320	1,431	4.5	11
Eddie George, Houston	335	1,368	4.1	8
Adrian Murrell, N.Y. Jets	301	1,249	4.1	6
Curtis Martin, New England	316	1,152	3.6	14
Karim Abdul-Jabbar, Miami	307	1,116	3.6	11
Thurman Thomas, Buffalo	281	1,033	3.7	8
Napoleon Kaufman, Oakland	150	874	5.8	1
Chris Warren, Seattle	203	855	4.2	5
Garrison Hearst, Cincinnati	225	847	3.8	0

Leading punters

	Punts	Yards	Avg.	Longest
John Kidd, Miami	78	3,611	46.3	63
Chris Gardocki, Indianapolis	68	3,105	45.7	61
Darren Bennett, San Diego	87	3,967	45.6	66
Lee Johnson, Cincinnati,	80	3,630	45.4	67
Brian Hansen, N.Y. Jets	74	3,311	44.7	69

Individual statistics (National Conference)

Leading scorers, touchdowns

	TD's	Rush	Rec.	Ret.	Pts.
Terry Allen, Washington	21	21	0	0	126
Emmitt Smith, Dallas	15	12	3	0	90
Ricky Watters, Philadelphia	13	13	0	0	78
Irving Fryar, Philadelphia	11	0	11	0	66
Eddie Kennison, St. Louis	11	0	9	2	66
Cris Carter, Minnesota	10	0	10	0	60
Keith Jackson, Green Bay	10	0	10	0	60
Dorsey Levens, Green Bay	10	5	5	0	60
Wesley Walls, Carolina	10	0	10	0	60

Leading scorers, kicking

	PAT	FG	Longest	Pts.
John Kasay, Carolina	34	37	53	145
Jeff Wilkins, San Francisco	40	30	49	130
Chris Boniol, Dallas	24	32	52	120
Scott Blanton, Washington	40	26	53	118
Gary Anderson, Philadelphia	40	25	46	115

Leading quarterbacks

	Att.	Comp.	Yds.	TD's	Int.
Steve Young, San Francisco	316	214	2,410	14	6
Brett Favre, Green Bay	543	325	3,899	39	13
Brad Johnson, Minnesota	311	195	2,258	17	10
Ty Detmer, Philadelphia	401	238	2,911	15	13
Troy Aikman, Dallas	465	296	3,126	12	13
Kerry Collins, Carolina	364	204	2,454	14	9
Gus Frerotte, Washington	470	270	3,453	12	11
Dave Krieg, Chicago	377	226	2,278	14	12
Kent Graham, Arizona	274	146	1,624	12	7
Scott Mitchell, Detroit	437	253	2,917	17	17

Leading receivers

	Passes caught	Total yards	Avg. gain	TD's
Jerry Rice, San Francisco	108	1,254	11.6	8
Herman Moore, Detroit	106	1,296	12.2	9
Larry Centers, Arizona	99	766	7.7	7
Cris Carter, Minnesota	96	1,163	12.1	10
Brett Perriman, Detroit	94	1,021	10.9	5
Irving Fryar, Philadelphia	88	1,195	13.6	11
Isaac Bruce, St. Louis	84	1,338	15.9	7
Curtis Conway, Chicago	81	1,049	13.0	7
Bert Emanuel, Atlanta	76	931	12.3	6
Jake Reed, Minnesota	72	1,320	18.3	7

Leading rushers

	Rushes	Yards	Avg.	TD's
Barry Sanders, Detroit	307	1,553	5.1	11
Ricky Watters, Philadelphia	353	1,411	4.0	13
Terry Allen, Washington	347	1,353	3.9	21
Emmitt Smith, Dallas	327	1,204	3.7	12
Anthony Johnson, Carolina	300	1,120	3.7	6
Jamal Anderson, Atlanta	232	1,055	4.5	5
Edgar Bennett, Green Bay	222	899	4.0	2
Rodney Hampton, N.Y. Giants	254	827	3.3	1
Raymont Harris, Chicago	194	748	3.9	4
Robert Smith, Minnesota	162	692	4.3	3

Leading punters

	Punts	Yards	Avg.	Longest
Matt Turk, Washington	75	3,386	45.1	63
Sean Landeta, St. Louis	78	3,491	44.8	70
Todd Sauerbrun, Chicago	78	3,491	44.8	72
Tommy Thompson, San Francisco	73	3,217	44.1	65
Jeff Feagles, Arizona	76	3,328	43.8	68

France. President Jacques Chirac attempted in 1996 to regain the influence France had once wielded in Middle Eastern and African affairs. In April, Foreign Minister Hervé de Charette tried to negotiate a cease-fire in southern Lebanon between the Israeli army and the Islamic fundamentalist group Hezbollah. The United States criticized de Charette's attempt, claiming it conflicted with the diplomatic efforts of Secretary of State Warren Christopher.

In October, President Chirac, claiming he was being too closely guarded, got into a pushing match with Israeli security guards in Jerusalem. He also publicly blamed the Israeli government's intransigence for stalling the Middle East peace process. Israel dismissed the criticism as evidence of French bias in favor of the Palestinians.

In November, French Defense Minister Charles Millon urged the international community to intervene in Zaire, where refugees from Rwanda and Burundi were endangered by the armed conflicts around them.

Defense shakeup. President Chirac announced defense reforms in February aimed at transforming the military's pre-1991 role from one of national defense against potential Soviet aggression to a mobile force capable of intervening in distant crises. The reforms would end conscription in 1997 and phase in an all-volunteer army by 2002, reducing the number of military personnel by 150,000, to 350,000. The changes also included the scrapping of France's land-based nuclear missiles and the closure of its nuclear test site in the South Pacific, which Chirac briefly reactivated to the fury of Asian countries in 1995. The plan was expected to save $20 billion in arms spending over five years.

The government in October 1996 arranged to sell Thomson-CSF, the state-owned electronics company, to the Lagardère Group, owner of missile manufacturer Matra. The government abandoned the sale in November, however, after Lagardère's plan to sell the Thomson television business to Daewoo of South Korea triggered protests in France.

Economic growth virtually ground to a halt in early 1996, part of a broader European slowdown caused by turbulence on currency and bond markets in 1995. Even with a modest recovery in the second half, growth was forecast to be just 1.1 percent for the full year, half the rate of 1995.

Unemployment rose to a record high of 12.6 percent at the end of 1996, and criticism of the government's austerity policies grew even within the ruling conservative coalition parties. The government responded with tax breaks for companies that created jobs and with modest income-tax cuts over five years beginning with a $5-billion reduction in 1997.

Budget controversy. The government continued in 1996 to place top priority on reducing its budget deficit to qualify for a European single cur-

Danielle Mitterrand stands before the coffin of her husband, former French president François Mitterrand, at his state funeral on Jan. 11, 1996.

Gabon

rency, scheduled to be introduced in 1999. Prime Minister Alain Juppé's government relied on a one-time payment to the treasury of $7 billion from the state-owned telephone company, France Telécom, to decrease the deficit in the 1997 budget and qualify for first-round participation in the single currency. The tactic drew strong criticism from Germany, where officials feared the move would spur account-ing tricks across Europe that would weaken the sin-gle currency, but the European Commission en-dorsed the manuever in October 1996.

François Mitterrand, the Socialist president of France from 1981 to 1995, died of cancer on Jan. 8, 1996, at the age of 79. Eulogized as a national hero by both left- and right-wing (liberal and conserva-tive) politicians, Mitterrand generated as much con-troversy in death as in life. His longtime mistress, Anne Pingeot, and their daughter, Mazarine, ap-peared at his funeral alongside his wife, Danielle. In October, another woman, a Swedish journalist, dis-closed that Mitterrand had fathered her son as well.

Bank bailout. One year after obtaining a record $9.2-billion government rescue package, state-owned Crédit Lyonnais won approval from the Euro-pean Commission on September 25 for a fresh infu-sion of $765 million in French government aid. The bank, which claimed it needed the funds to keep from posting new losses, also negotiated with the French government and the commission for a final aid injection to prepare it for privatization. The gov-ernment meanwhile began investigating former di-rectors on suspicions of failing to control the lending surge that caused the bank's difficulties.

Corsican violence. Militant nationalists on the Mediterranean island of Corsica broke off secret ne-gotiations with the government and escalated what had been a low-level campaign of violence for great-er autonomy. The nationalists staged their first ma-jor attack on mainland France on October 5 by bombing the city hall of Bordeaux, where Prime Minister Juppé also serves as mayor. Juppé vowed that the government would not give in to terrorism.

Housing scandals. In 1996, Paris officials planned to sell some of the 1,389 apartments owned by the city because of scandals about their use by public officials. Sales were suspended in October, however, when a writer claimed that nearly one-third of the properties had been seized from Jews deported to Nazi death camps by the Vichy regime, which collaborated with Nazi Germany during World War II (1939-1945). □ Tom Buerkle

See also **Europe** (Facts in brief table). In *World Book,* see **European Union; France.**

Gabon. See Africa.

Gambia. See Africa.

Gas and gasoline. See Energy supply; Petroleum and gas.

Genetic engineering. See Biology; Medicine.

Geology. In July, seismologists Xiaodong Song and Paul G. Richards of Columbia University's Lam-ont-Doherty Earth Observatory in Palisades, New York, reported the first observations of evidence that Earth's solid inner core actually rotates 1.1 per-cent faster than the overlying mantle and crust. Sci-entists had long known from studying the path and speed of *seismic waves* (vibrations created by earth-quakes and explosions) that Earth's interior consists of a solid inner core surrounded by a *molten* (liquid) outer core with an overlying solid mantle and crust. The Columbia researchers studied seismic waves that had traveled through the center of the Earth to data-collection sites on the opposite side. By com-paring varied travel times of seismic waves from dif-ferent years, the researchers calculated the faster ro-tational speed of Earth's core.

Eighteen-hour day. In a study reported in July, planetary scientist Charles P. Sonett of the University of Arizona in Tucson and researchers at other univer-sities calculated that a day 900 million years ago was just over 18 hours, rather than 24 hours, long. Scien-tists had known that the gravitational pull of the sun and moon, which causes tidal changes, increases the distance of the moon from Earth and slows the rota-tion of Earth, resulting in longer days.

Sonett's team evaluated *tidal rhythmites* (very thin layers of sediment deposited by ancient tidal currents) in rocks of different ages from Australia and different areas of the United States. The tidal rhythmites left from the highest tides—during the full moon, new moon, and the first and third quar-ters—act as indicators of time intervals between tides. The researchers used the records of time intervals to calculate the length of a day 900 million years ago.

Earthquakes in the Pacific Northwest. Two studies reported in 1996 suggested that, in the past, large, devastating earthquakes occurred along the Cascadia subduction zone, an area of fault lines off the coast of the Pacific Northwest (northern Califor-nia, Oregon, Washington, and southern British Columbia in Canada).

In January, scientists at the Geological Survey of Japan and the University of Tokyo reported on the likely cause of a major *tsunami* (a large sea wave generated by an earthquake) that hit Japan on Jan. 26, 1700. By studying geological evidence and histor-ical records of earthquakes, the researchers inferred that the Cascadia subduction zone was the most likely source of the earthquake triggering the tsuna-mi. They estimated that the earthquake had a mag-nitude of 9—strong enough to have resulted from the fracture of more than 800 miles (1,300 kilome-ters) of the Cascadia subduction zone.

In a study reported in February 1996, Richard A. Meyers, a graduate student of geography at the Uni-versity of Calgary in Alberta, Canada, and fellow re-searchers used ground-penetrating radar to identify eight buried land forms probably created by earth-

In October, steam and ash from the Loki volcano, which lies under Iceland's Vatna-jokull glacier, is blasted 33,000 feet (10,058 meters) into the air. Molten rock from the eruption melted through 2,000 feet (609 meters) of glacial ice.

quakes along the coast of Washington state. Using radiocarbon dating methods on samples from those formations, the researchers estimated that earthquakes had occurred over the past 5,800 years with the latest event occurring about 300 years ago.

Mass extinction. During the past 600 million years, there have been five major mass extinction events. The largest of these extinctions occurred near the end of the Permian Period, about 2410 to 250 million years ago, when as many as 95 percent of all marine species became extinct. In 1996, two papers were published that identified oceanic *anoxia* (lack of oxygen) as a likely cause of the Permian extinction.

Geologists Paul B. Wignall and Richard J. Twichett of the University of Leeds in the United Kingdom found evidence of anoxia in ocean sediments from the Permian Period (from 290 million to 240 million years ago). They found deposits of uranium, which will not dissolve in water that lacks oxygen. Paleontologist Andrew H. Knoll of Harvard University in Cambridge, Massachusetts, and his colleagues further proposed that an upwelling of deep anoxic ocean water released toxic concentrations of carbon dioxide and hydrogen sulfide that killed vast numbers of marine organisms. The carbon dioxide released from the deep ocean water also would have led to extreme global warming, causing further environmental change and extinction. □ Henry T. Mullins

In *World Book,* see **Earth; Earthquakes; Geology.**

Georgia. In 1996, President Eduard Shevardnadze renewed efforts to settle two secessionist conflicts in Georgia. Russian troops under the auspices of the Commonwealth of Independent States (CIS), an alliance of former Soviet republics, continued to enforce cease-fires in Abkhazia and South Ossetia.

Shevardnadze pressured Russia and the CIS to act more aggressively to end the Abkhaz rebellion, which had created more than 200,000 refugees. In January, CIS leaders responded by imposing a short-lived economic and military blockade against Abkhazia. In July, a United Nations (UN) resolution supported Georgia's claim that its borders were not negotiable. In September, Georgian foreign minister Irakly Menagarishvili appealed to the UN to impose sanctions on Abkhazia.

In May, Georgian and South Ossetian leaders signed a memorandum that acknowledged both the territorial integrity of Georgia and the right of the Ossetian people to self-determination. This was seen as a first step toward a political settlement.

Both breakaway republics held elections in November 1996, Abkhazia to elect a parliament and South Ossetia to choose a president. UN and Georgian officials denounced the elections, calling them invalid and "unlawful." □ Steven L. Solnick

See also **Asia** (Facts in brief table). In *World Book,* see **Georgia.**

Georgia (state of). See **State government.**

Germany struggled economically in 1996 as a brief recession drove unemployment to its highest level since the end of World War II (1939-1945). Despite the difficulties and the unpopularity of some of the government's policies, Chancellor Helmut Kohl remained in power. In October 1996, he became the country's longest-serving leader of the 1900's, surpassing the 14-year rule of Konrad Adenauer, the chancellor who guided former West Germany's postwar recovery.

Election results. Politically, the tone for 1996 was set in elections in three states on March 24. Kohl's Christian Democratic Union held or increased its share of the vote in the states of Baden-Württemberg, Rhineland-Palatinate, and Schleswig-Holstein. Its junior coalition partner, the Free Democratic Party, which had failed in 12 consecutive state elections to win the minimum 5 percent of the vote required for seats, increased its share of the vote and won seats in all three states, campaigning for cuts in income taxes. The results were a setback for the opposition Social Democratic Party. The Social Democrats had campaigned for restrictions on immigration by ethnic Germans from Eastern Europe and for a postponement of European Monetary and Economic Union. According to the 1992 pact, a common currency and central bank among European Union members was scheduled to begin in 1999.

Economy. Strengthened by the election results, Kohl urged cutbacks in government spending and welfare benefits, saying Germany had been living beyond its means. In April 1996, the government announced plans to cut federal and state government spending in 1997. It also proposed to slash welfare spending by cutting sick pay from 100 percent to 80 percent of normal wages, raising the retirement age for women from 60 to 63, and allowing companies more flexibility in firing workers. The welfare measures were passed by parliament in September, and the federal budget was approved in late November.

The cuts were designed to restore the country's competitiveness and ensure that Germany would meet the low-deficit requirement for participation in a single European currency. However, a weak economy raised both the deficit and unemployment rates. The economy entered a brief recession in the first three months of the year. Although a recovery ensued, growth for all of 1996 was forecast by the European Commission to slow to 1.4 percent from 1.9 percent in 1995. The number of unemployed rose above 4 million—10 percent of the labor force—for the first time in October 1996. In November, the government cut $2 billion of spending and delayed a tax cut intended for 1997. Still, the government's own economic advisers predicted Germany would fail to meet the single-currency deficit requirement.

Labor strife. In January, the government had won support from unions and employers for a set of measures, including reductions in regulations and in-

In January, an African woman protests before the burned shell of an asylum for immigrants in Lübeck, Germany. At least 10 people died in the fire, which some believed had been set by an anti-immigrant group.

centives for investment, which were intended to cut unemployment in half by the year 2000. But in April 1996, unions and business failed to agree on a proposal to trade wage restraint for new jobs. In October, more than 100,000 workers went on strike to protest plans by major companies to implement the sick-pay cuts immediately rather than waiting for new contract negotiations. The companies backed down after a week of strikes.

Corporate troubles. Bremer Vulkan Verbund AG, Germany's largest shipbuilder, declared bankruptcy on February 21, citing 1995 losses of about $650 million. Chairman Friedrich Hennemann was arrested and charged with breach of trust in June 1996 for allegedly diverting $550 million of government funds designated for shipyards in eastern Germany to cover the company's losses in western Germany.

The chief executive of Thyssen AG, a major steel company, and nine other executives were arrested in August on charges of defrauding the government of $50 million in the takeover of a former East German metal-trading company in 1992. Thyssen sued Berlin's public prosecutor, calling the unprecedented arrest of a chief executive at his office "monstrous."

Volkswagen AG's three-year dispute with General Motors Corp. (GM) escalated when GM filed a civil lawsuit for alleged industrial espionage in March 1996. GM claimed that former executives, led by Jose Ignacio Lopez de Arriortua, took secret company

documents with them when they moved to Volkswagen in 1993. Lopez resigned in November 1996 and was charged with stealing secrets in December. Volkswagen denied the allegations but sought to settle with GM out of court.

Holocaust debate. Controversy erupted following the publication of a book by American scholar Daniel Goldhagen, who claimed that millions of ordinary Germans supported, participated in, or knew about the *Holocaust* (the extermination of European Jews and others by the Nazis during World War II). German critics called the book, *Hitler's Willing Executioners,* a flawed work that could harm German-American relations. The German public flocked to hear Goldhagen's defense of the work during his 1996 speaking tour of Germany.

Balkan refugees. At the end of 1996, Germany began returning some of the estimated 350,000 refugees who had sought asylum in the country during the war in Bosnia, from 1991 to 1995. An August 1996 agreement between the 16 German states and the federal government called for returning refugees by force after October 1, if they refused to leave voluntarily. Criminals were to be deported first, followed by single people and childless couples. Agreements with the Yugoslavian government to begin returning Serbian refugees in December and with the Bosnian government to return the first group of Bosnian refugees by June 30, 1997, followed. The southern German state of Bavaria initiated the first deportations on Oct. 9, 1996.

Deutsche Telekom AG, the state-owned telephone company, sold a 26-percent stake in November in Europe's largest stock offering. Demand was so great that the stock price jumped 20 percent on the first day of trading. The government hoped the offering would boost the stock market.

Graf charged. Peter Graf, the father of tennis star Steffi Graf, was charged in April with failing to declare $28 million of his daughter's income to German tax authorities. The case highlighted the rise in Germany of tax evasion, and it raised controversy about the government's treatment of Graf, who was charged eight months after being jailed and waited until November 1996 to be released on bail.

Terrorism. German authorities arrested a German woman and her Palestinian ex-husband on October 10 for a 1986 Berlin nightclub bombing that killed three people, including two U.S. soldiers. Prosecutors also issued arrest warrants for four Libyans and said evidence indicated that the Libyan government ordered the attack. In 1986, former U.S. President Ronald Reagan had blamed Libya for the attack and bombed Tripoli in retaliation.   □ Tom Buerkle

See also **Europe** (Facts in brief table). In *World Book,* see **Bosnia-Herzegovina; European Union; Germany; Yugoslavia.**

Ghana. See Africa.

Golf. By almost every standard, Tom Lehman was the golfer of the year in 1996. However, the year will probably be better remembered as the "Year of the Tiger," after Eldrick (Tiger) Woods, a charismatic, gentlemanly, 20-year-old college sophomore who turned professional in late 1996 and enjoyed huge success.

Woods. On Aug. 25, 1996, in Cornelius, Oregon, Woods rallied from 5 strokes down with 16 holes to play to win his third consecutive United States amateur championship. Three days later, he quit college, declared himself a professional, and signed long-term clothing and golf-club endorsement contracts worth more than $40 million.

Tournament officials of the Professional Golfers' Association (PGA) tour granted Woods sponsor exemptions so he could compete, but he was not assured a place on the 1997 PGA tour unless he won at least $150,000 in 1996. He did that and more. Playing only eight tournaments—one-third the number that most others played—Woods finished 25th in annual earnings with more than $790,000.

Grand Slam. At the Masters Tournament, held April 11 to 14 in Augusta, Georgia, Greg Norman began with a course-record 63 strokes and started the final round six strokes ahead. But his game fell apart on the last 10 holes, where he shot 5 bogeys and 2 double bogeys. Nick Faldo of Great Britain shot a final-round 67 and beat Norman by five strokes.

Tiger Woods blasts out of a sand trap and onto the green at the Quad City Classic in September 1996. He made his debut as a professional golfer in August.

In the U.S. Open June 13 to 16 in Bloomfield Hills, Michigan, on the same course where Ben Hogan won the U.S. Open title in 1941, Steve Jones finished with 278, beating Lehman and Davis Love III by one stroke. Jones had read Hogan's book prior to the Open and said that it taught him to focus on the next shot and not worry about what might happen.

There was excitement at the British Open July 18 to 21 in Lytham St. Annes, England, when 56-year-old Jack Nicklaus shot a 69 and a 66 in the first two rounds and was a stroke off the lead. But Nicklaus later faded, and Lehman, with a final score of 271, beat Ernie Els and Mark McCumber by two strokes.

In the PGA championship August 8 to 11 in Louisville, Kentucky, Kenny Perry led by a stroke until he bogeyed the last hole. Mark Brooks, who had been two strokes back, birdied that hole, and he and Perry finished at 277, one stroke ahead of Steve Elkington and Tommy Tolles. Brooks then birdied the first hole of a playoff round against Perry and won.

PGA Tour. Five years before, Lehman struggled on lesser tours in the United States, Asia, and Australia. In 1996, he won three tournaments, including the season-ending, $3-million Tour Championship. He took the earnings title with just over $1.78 million. Lehman also received the Vardon Trophy for low scoring average (69.32), and he won the PGA Player of the Year Award on a point system based on victories, scoring average, and earnings.

Seniors. Hale Irwin enjoyed a big year, winning the PGA Senior championship and finishing second in the Tradition, U.S. Senior Open, and the Senior Players Championship. Jim Colbert led in earnings with $1,627,890—a senior record—to $1,615,769, for Irwin. Colbert won five tournaments on the seniors tour, and John Bland won three.

Women. Laura Davies of Great Britain won the McDonald's Ladies Professional Golf Association (LPGA) Championship and the du Maurier Classic, two of the four major tournaments. She was voted LPGA Player of the Year. In the other majors, Patty Sheehan captured the Nabisco Dinah Shore, and Annika Sorenstam of Sweden won the U.S. Women's Open. Davies, Dottie Pepper, and Karrie Webb of Australia won four tournaments each on the tour. Webb was the earnings leader with a record-breaking $1,002,000, which was the most ever earned by a rookie on the LPGA or PGA tours.

Team. In the biennial President's Cup competition for men, played September 14 to 16 in Lake Manassas, Virginia, the United States won, 16½ to 15½, over a team of golfers from all continents except Europe. For reasons never made clear, the international players forced out their captain, David Graham of Australia, before the competition began. In the Solheim Cup matches for women, held September 20 to 22 in Chepstow, Wales, the United States rallied to defeat Europe, 17 to 11. □ Frank Litsky

In *World Book,* see **Golf.**

Gore, Albert, Jr. Vice President Albert Gore, Jr., was reelected on November 5 as President Bill Clinton's running mate in the 1996 presidential election. Although opinion polls suggested voters distrusted Clinton, Gore's reputation for integrity remained intact. Gore was also regarded as a potential presidential candidate in 2000. In one indication of Gore's increasing political influence, his top aide, Peter S. Knight, was named manager of the Clinton-Gore campaign.

With Clinton's backing, Gore played a larger role in government than most vice presidents. In January, he hosted Russian Prime Minister Viktor S. Chernomyrdin during trade talks in Washington, D.C. Following the talks, they signed an agreement allowing Russia a larger role in launching commercial satellites. After the crash of TWA Flight 800, on July 17, Clinton named Gore to head an aviation safety commission. Also in July, Gore was sent by the president to Moscow to meet with Russian President Boris N. Yeltsin in a top-level exchange.

Gore played an influential behind-the-scenes role in the passage of a major telecommunications bill signed into law on February 8. He also helped shape a proposal to invest $75 million of federal funds to restore the Florida Everglades.

□ William Eaton

See also **Telecommunications.** In *World Book,* see **Gore, Al.**

Gowda, H. D. Deve (1933–   ), was appointed prime minister of India on May 28, 1996. Gowda, leader of the Janata Dal (People's Party), headed the United Front coalition of 13 centrist, leftist, and regional parties. Earlier in May, the Bharatiya Janata Party (BJP) won the largest number of seats in India's general elections, but the BJP prime minister, Atal Behari Vajpayee, was unable to claim a majority in parliament and was forced to resign after two weeks. With the support of the Congress Party, Gowda's United Front won a confidence vote in parliament on June 12.

Haradanahalli Doddegowda Deve Gowda, the son of a farmer, was born on May 18, 1933, in Haradanahalli in the state of Karnataka. He graduated in civil engineering from Lakshamma Venkata-swamy Occupational Institute in 1952.

In 1962, Gowda was elected to the Karnataka Legislative Assembly, where he held several important posts, including chairman of the public accounts committee.

In 1991, he was elected to the Lok Sabha, India's lower house of parliament. Gowda became leader of the Janata Party in 1993 and chief minister of Karnataka in 1994. As chief minister, he supported the interests of farmers and members of the lower castes. □ Francesca Mitchell

See also **India.** In *World Book,* see **India.**

Great Britain. See **United Kingdom.**

Greece. The country's political leadership underwent dramatic change in 1996 with the death of Andreas Papandreou, the Socialist leader who dominated Greek politics for two decades. Costas Simitis, a moderate, was elected as his successor.

Papandreou dies. Andreas Papandreou founded the Panhellenic Socialist Movement, or PASOK, in 1974 after the fall of a military *junta* (dictatorship). With a combination of generous spending plans and anti-American and anti-European rhetoric, he guided PASOK to parliamentary victory in 1981 and served as prime minister for eight years, a post he lost in 1989 elections and regained in 1993. He was hospitalized in November 1995 with severe lung and kidney ailments and was forced to resign office in January 1996 as his health deteriorated. He died of heart failure on June 23 at the age of 77.

Costas Simitis, a law professor and former industry minister, was chosen on January 18 to succeed Papandreou as prime minister by the PASOK majority in parliament. He promised to reduce state control of the economy and cut public spending in an effort to bring down Greece's high inflation and interest rates, a legacy of the heavy borrowing carried out under Papandreou in the 1980's. Simitis said his pro-business policies would strengthen the economy and improve relations with Greece's European Union (EU) partners, which had criticized the previous government for failing to implement economic reform.

Simitis was elected chairman of PASOK after Papandreou's death and, seeking to strengthen his mandate, called an early election. He led PASOK to victory on Sept. 22, 1996. The Socialists won 41.5 percent of the vote and 162 seats in the 300-seat parliament. The conservative New Democracy Party won 38.1 percent of the vote and 108 seats. Party leader Miltiades Evert resigned after the defeat.

Economy. The EU predicted growth would remain steady at a rate of 2 percent in 1996, while inflation was expected to fall by 1.0 percent to 8.3 percent. On November 19, the government approved plans to raise taxes by $1.2 billion in 1997 to slash the deficit and give Greece a chance to join a single European currency soon after the year 2000. The plans provoked protest strikes throughout Greece.

Aegean conflict. Greece went to the brink of armed confrontation with Turkey in January over an uninhabited Aegean islet. The islet, known as Imia to Greeks and Kardak to Turks, was claimed by both countries. Mediation by the United States averted a conflict between the NATO allies. In July, Greece lifted its veto of a $4.3-billion EU aid program for Turkey and 11 other Mediterranean countries after the government in Ankara, the Turkish capital, agreed to submit the Aegean dispute to international arbitration. □ Tom Buerkle

See also **Europe** (Facts in brief table); **Turkey.** In *World Book,* see **European Union; Greece.**

Guatemala. On Jan. 14, 1996, Alvaro Arzú Irigoyen, 49, began a four-year term as Guatemala's president. He pledged to find a peaceful resolution to the 36-year-old civil war, in which more than 100,000 people—combatants and civilians—died.

During his first week in office, Arzú dismissed military leaders who had been linked to human rights abuses and criminal enterprises, including drug trafficking. Among those discharged were eight generals and several colonels, including Colonel Julio Roberto Alpirez, a former paid informant of the United States Central Intelligence Agency. Alpirez had been linked to the murders of a U.S. citizen in 1990 and the Guatemalan husband of another U.S. citizen in 1992.

Impressed by Arzú's action, rebels suspended hostilities during much of 1996, while awaiting the final negotiations of peace accords. On February 25, Arzú met with the leaders of the rebel Guatemalan National Revolutionary Union in Mexico City—the first meeting of a Guatemalan president with rebel leaders since the war began. On Dec. 29, 1996, the two sides signed the final peace agreement, which included a broad amnesty plan for members of the armed forces and rebel groups accused of human rights violations. □ Nathan A. Haverstock

See also **Latin America** (Facts in brief table). In *World Book,* see **Guatemala.**

Guinea. See Africa.

Guyana. See Latin America.

Haiti. On Feb. 7, 1996, René Préval, 53, took office as president for a four-year term. His inauguration was the first peaceful transfer of power from one democratically elected president to another since Haiti achieved independence from France in 1804.

On March 15, 1996, Préval announced plans to sell minority stakes in four state-owned industries. The move was designed to appease the U.S. Congress, which had withheld economic aid because of Haiti's poor performance setting up a free-market economy.

Violence escalated as the United Nations (UN) peacekeeping forces, which arrived in Haiti in March 1995, prepared to depart the country in February 1996. The agitators included dissidents among the more than 6,000 Haitian soldiers who had been demobilized when U.S. troops landed in September 1994 to restore democracy. After granting two extensions, the UN agreed to extend the peacekeeping mission to May 31, 1997.

On July 16, 1996, Lieutenant General Claude Raymond, a former army chief of staff, and three others were charged with committing terrorist acts intended "to destabilize public authority." On July 19, the leader of the Association of Unjustly Discharged Soldiers, André-Pierre Armand, who had warned of a plot to assassinate Préval, was himself assassinated, allegedly by former soldiers. □ Nathan A. Haverstock

See also **Latin America** (Facts in brief table). In *World Book,* see **Haiti.**

Hashimoto, Ryutaro (1937–   ), became prime minister of Japan on Jan. 11, 1996, heading a three-party coalition led by his own Liberal Democratic Party (LDP). He replaced Tomiichi Murayama of the Social Democratic Party, who resigned under pressure from his own party. Hashimoto was charged with improving Japan's economy, which had been gripped by a four-year recession.

Hashimoto's policies called for increased participation by Japan in world affairs, including gaining a seat on the United Nations (UN) Security Council and participation in UN peacekeeping missions. He also supported the continued presence of United States troops on Okinawa.

Hashimoto was born on July 29, 1937, in the capital, Tokyo. He earned a law degree from Keio University in 1960. In 1963, he was elected to the Japanese parliament, the Diet. Besides holding the posts of secretary general and president of the LDP, he had been minister of health and welfare, minister of transport, minister of finance, and minister of international trade and industry. In 1995, as party president, he was appointed deputy prime minister.

Hashimoto wrote *Vision of Japan,* published in an English translation in 1994. He is an expert in kendo, the sport of Japanese fencing. He has participated in two mountain-climbing expeditions to Mount Everest.

□ Lisa Klobuchar

Hawaii. See State government.

Health-care issues. The Health Insurance Portability and Accountability Act was signed by President Bill Clinton on Aug. 21, 1996, after a long political battle. The law was designed to protect members of employee groups from being denied insurance, or charged more, because of poor health histories. However, the law did not apply to most individuals buying insurance singly. The law also did not control the price of policies that insurers were required to offer.

The bill, originally introduced in Congress in 1995, had been held up for months by partisan fighting, especially over whether it would include medical savings accounts (MSA's), which Republicans favored, and coverage for mental health, which Democrats favored. MSA's are special tax-free savings accounts for small businesses, the self-employed, and the uninsured that would cover routine medical costs. The final version of the bill included a provision for a four-year trial of 750,000 MSA's. The Democrats withdrew the mental health provision, but it later was attached to another measure and passed.

Although President Clinton claimed that 25 million people would be aided by the law, most analysts believed its impact would be minimal. A study of U.S. Census Bureau data by the Employee Benefit Research Institute , released in April 1996, estimated that on any given day in 1996 more than 60 million Americans under age 65 were without any form of health insurance. The Institute is a private firm that studies workplace benefit issues.

Medicare and Medicaid. Political fighting over Medicare (which covers medical care for most people over 65 and some other groups) and Medicaid (which covers medical care of poor people, the disabled, and certain other groups) raged throughout 1996. No major changes in Medicare were passed, though Medicare trustees reported on June 5 that, at the current rate of spending, the fund that pays for hospital care would run a deficit of $53 billion by the year 2001.

In contrast, Medicaid faced potentially sweeping changes as a result of a historic welfare bill signed by President Clinton on August 22. Since the 1960's, people who were eligible for welfare were automatically eligible for Medicaid. Under the new law, people could be eligible for one or the other or both, but the two programs were no longer tied. The law also greatly limited welfare and medical benefits for legal immigrants. Illegal immigrants were ineligible for most federal programs.

Managed care backlash. The number of Americans belonging to health insurance arrangements known collectively as managed care—a form of health care that directs and sometimes limits patient services and referrals—continued to climb in 1996. However, the backlash against managed care also grew. Critics claimed that managed care plans prevented physicians from speaking freely with patients about alternative treatments, calling these practices "gag rules," and that plans made it difficult for patients to see specialists. On December 6, Medicare announced that gag rules could not be imposed on physicians treating patients whom Medicare sponsored. According to critics, some for-profit managed care plans were making enormous profits while constraining patients' access to care. Many states passed laws in 1996 to address such complaints.

Abortion. In April, President Clinton vetoed a bill outlawing partial-birth abortion, a rare late-term procedure used in extreme situations. A congressional attempt to override the veto failed in the Senate.

In September, the Food and Drug Administration (FDA) announced preliminary approval of mifepristone, also known as RU-486, a drug that induces abortion. FDA approval of RU-486 was strongly opposed by the antiabortion movement.

FDA head David Kessler announced his resignation in November. He had sought to have tobacco classified as a drug, creating a controversy that raged in state legislatures, Congress, and the media in 1996. Although tobacco firms claimed they were not responsible, 18 states filed suit against them to recover funds spent treating Medicaid patients with tobacco-related illnesses.

□ Emily Friedman

See also **Medicine.** In *World Book,* see Health.

Hobbies. See Toys and games.

Hockey

Hockey. In their first season at their new home in Denver, the Colorado Avalanche (formerly the Quebec Nordiques) won the Stanley Cup, becoming the 1995-1996 champions of the National Hockey League (NHL). This outcome surprised many fans because the Detroit Red Wings had so dominated the regular season.

Season. At the end of the previous season, Detroit reached the Stanley Cup finals, only to be swept by the New Jersey Devils in four games. In the 1995-1996 season, the Red Wings played like a team with a mission. In an 82-game season, they won 62 games, lost only 13, and tied 7. The 62 victories broke the previous NHL record of 60, which was set by the 1976-1977 Montreal Canadiens. Detroit's coach, Scotty Bowman, also coached that formidable Montreal team. The Red Wings boasted an exciting offense, tough defense, and five talented Russian players who often played as a unit. These factors helped the Red Wings win their division title, with 131 points. The league's next highest point total was Colorado's 104 points.

Play-offs. New Jersey, plagued by poor coach-player relationships, was not among the 16 NHL teams that qualified for the play-offs. Colorado performed better with each series, eliminating the Vancouver Canucks (4 games to 2), Chicago Blackhawks (4 to 2), and, finally, Detroit (4 to 1) to reach the finals. The Florida Panthers, in only their third season,

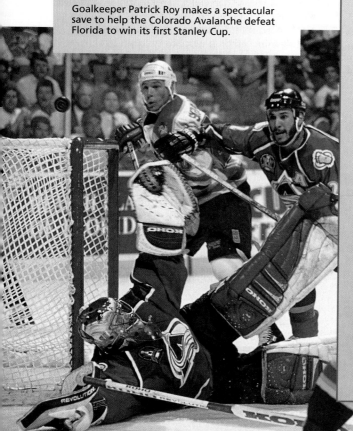

Goalkeeper Patrick Roy makes a spectacular save to help the Colorado Avalanche defeat Florida to win its first Stanley Cup.

National Hockey League standings

Western Conference

Central Division	W.	L.	T.	Pts.
Detroit Red Wings*	62	13	7	131
Chicago Blackhawks*	40	28	14	94
Toronto Maple Leafs*	34	36	12	80
St. Louis Blues*	32	34	16	80
Winnipeg Jets*	36	40	6	78
Dallas Stars	26	42	14	66
Pacific Division				
Colorado Avalanche*	47	25	10	104
Calgary Flames*	34	37	11	79
Vancouver Canucks*	32	35	15	79
Anaheim Mighty Ducks	35	36	8	78
Edmonton Oilers	30	44	8	68
Los Angeles Kings	24	40	18	66
San Jose Sharks	20	55	7	47

Eastern Conference

Northeast Division	W.	L.	T.	Pts.
Pittsburgh Penguins*	49	29	4	102
Boston Bruins*	40	31	11	91
Montreal Canadiens*	40	32	10	90
Hartford Whalers	34	39	9	77
Buffalo Sabres	33	42	7	73
Ottawa Senators	18	59	5	41
Atlantic Division				
Philadelphia Flyers*	45	24	13	103
New York Rangers*	41	27	14	96
Florida Panthers*	41	31	10	92
Washington Capitals*	39	32	11	89
Tampa Bay Lightning*	38	32	12	88
New Jersey Devils	37	33	12	86
New York Islanders	22	50	10	54

*Made play-offs

Stanley Cup champion—
Colorado Avalanche (defeated Florida Panthers, 4 games to 0)

Scoring leaders	Games	Goals	Assists	Pts.
Mario Lemieux, Pittsburgh	70	69	92	161
Jaromir Jagr, Pittsburgh	82	62	87	149
Joe Sakic, Colorado	82	51	69	120
Ron Francis, Pittsburgh	77	27	92	119
Peter Forsberg, Colorado	82	30	86	116
Eric Lindros, Philadelphia	73	47	68	115
Paul Kariya, Anaheim	82	50	58	108

Leading goalies (25 or more games)	Games	Goals against	Avg.
Ron Hextall, Philadelphia	53	112	2.17
Chris Osgood, Detroit	50	106	2.17
Jim Carey, Washington	71	153	2.26
Mike Vernon, Detroit	32	70	2.26
Martin Brodeur, New Jersey	77	173	2.34
Jeff Hackett, Chicago	35	80	2.40
Daren Puppa, Tampa Bay	57	131	2.46

Awards
Calder Trophy (best rookie)—Daniel Alfredsson, Ottawa
Hart Trophy (most valuable player)—Mario Lemieux, Pittsburgh
Jennings Trophy (team with fewest goals against)—
    Chris Osgood and Mike Vernon, Detroit
Lady Byng Trophy (sportsmanship)—Paul Kariya, Anaheim
Masterton Trophy (perseverance, dedication to hockey)—
    Gary Roberts, Calgary
Norris Trophy (best defenseman)—Chris Chelios, Chicago
Ross Trophy (leading scorer)—Mario Lemieux, Pittsburgh
Selke Trophy (best defensive forward)—Sergei Fedorov, Detroit
Smythe Trophy (most valuable player in Stanley Cup)—
    Joe Sakic, Colorado
Vezina Trophy (most valuable goalie)—Jim Carey, Washington

reached the finals by defeating such established teams as the Boston Bruins (4 games to 1), Philadelphia Flyers (4 to 2), and Pittsburgh Penguins (4 to 3).

In the final series, Colorado beat Florida in four straight games. The performance of star goalkeeper Patrick Roy, who joined the Avalanche late in the season after being traded from Montreal, was a key factor in Colorado's success. The final game was a five-hour, scoreless marathon lasting until 1:05 a.m., when the Avalanche's Uwe Krupp scored the game's only goal 4 minutes and 31 seconds into the third overtime period. Krupp had torn two knee ligaments early in the season and had not been expected to play until the next season.

International. The United States won the World Cup of Hockey, beating Canada 5-2 in Montreal in the last game of a three-game final series. The competition, which replaced the Canada Cup, involved eight teams, from Canada, Europe, and the United States, stocked with NHL players. Games were played from August 26 to September 14 in nine European, Canadian, and U.S. cities.

The World Cup overshadowed the world championships, held April 21 to May 5 in Vienna, Austria. The Czech Republic defeated Canada by a score of 4-2 to win the title. The United States beat Russia 4-3 in overtime to take third place.　　　　□ Frank Litsky

In *World Book*, see **Hockey**.

Honduras. See Latin America.

Hong Kong made preparations in 1996 for midnight, June 30, 1997, when it would cease to be a British dependency and become a special administrative region of China. British and Chinese officials, however, clashed over future conditions for the 6.3 million people of the area on China's south coast. The clashes stemmed, in part, from a history of troubled relations between China and Great Britain.

Chinese-British relations. Having lost a war to Britain, China in 1842 ceded Hong Kong island to Great Britain. Later, Britain took ownership of areas nearby and, in 1898, negotiated a 99-year lease for the adjacent New Territories. This increased the area under British control to 415 square miles (1,075 square kilometers).

China, which had long resented its 19th-century losses of territory to European colonial powers, was unwilling in the early 1980's to renew the lease on the New Territories, scheduled to expire in 1997. Britain decided that the area of Hong Kong it owned could not survive alone. Thus, in 1984, China and Great Britain negotiated a Joint Declaration, stating that Britain would turn over all of Hong Kong to China in 1997. The declaration further stated that Hong Kong, under Chinese ownership, would have a "high degree of autonomy." It would retain for 50 years its capitalist system, British common law, and international guarantees of human rights. China was willing to make these concessions because Hong Kong was economically important. In 1996, more than 60 percent of all foreign investment in China flowed through Hong Kong, and Hong Kong-based companies employed 6 million people in China.

However, when demonstrators for democracy were killed in 1989 in Tiananmen Square in Beijing, China's capital, British officials began to worry that China's human-rights and economic commitments to Hong Kong would not be honored.

Changes to come. In March 1996, a 150-seat Preparatory Committee, created by China in 1995 with 94 members from Hong Kong, announced that the popularly elected Legislative Council would be replaced in 1997 with a provisional legislature with appointed members. Critics claimed the change reflected China's anger that a Hong Kong political party critical of China's plans won the largest number of votes in the September 1995 legislative elections. Hong Kong's governor, Chris Patten, labeled China's change of plan "provocative." Critics also claimed that China was planning to change laws, suppress free press, and fire independent judges.

In March 1996, the Preparatory Committee also named a group, consisting mainly of Hong Kong's business and pro-China elite, to choose a chief executive to run Hong Kong after 1997. In December 1996, the group selected a wealthy, 59-year-old shipping magnate, Tung Chee-hwa.　　□ Henry S. Bradsher

In *World Book*, see **Hong Kong**.

Horse racing. Although Cigar lost three of his last four races, the 6-year-old bay was again the thoroughbred of the year in 1996. In November 1996, Cigar was retired as racing's all-time leading earner, with $9.9 million. Serena's Song, the 4-year-old filly who raced against colts in the 1995 Kentucky Derby and other races, was also retired after the 1996 season. She earned $3.28 million, the most ever won by a female.

Cigar raced throughout the world in 1996, even flying to the United Arab Emirates for the $4-million Dubai World Cup, which was held on March 27. He won the race and collected $2.4 million, the richest winner's purse in history. His winning streak reached 16 races, tying a North American record set nearly a half-century before by the legendary Citation. Cigar's streak ended August 10 in Del Mar, California, when he finished second to Dare and Go, a 35 to 1 shot. In the $4-million Breeders' Cup Classic, held October 26 at Woodbine near Toronto, Ontario, Cigar ran his last race. He finished third to Alphabet Soup and Louis Quatorze.

Three-year-olds. Despite finishing 12th in the Kentucky Derby, second in the Preakness, and second in the Belmont Stakes, Skip Away finished the 1996 season as the division leader among 3-year-olds. After the Triple Crown races, he won the Blue Grass, Ohio Derby, Haskell, and Woodbine Million, and he beat Cigar by an eyelash in the Jockey Club

Cigar claims his 16th consecutive victory July 13 at the Arlington Citation Challenge. His winning streak tied the record set nearly a half century ago by the legendary Citation.

Major horse races of 1996

Thoroughbred racing

Race	Winner	Value to winner
Arlington Million	Mecke	$600,000
Belmont Stakes	Editor's Note	$437,880
Breeders' Cup Classic	Alphabet Soup	$2,080,000
Breeders' Cup Distaff	Jewel Princess	$520,000
Breeders' Cup Juvenile	Boston Harbor	$520,000
Breeders' Cup Juvenile Fillies	Storm Song	$520,000
Breeders' Cup Mile	Da Hoss	$520,000
Breeders' Cup Sprint	Lit de Justice	$520,000
Breeders' Cup Turf	Pilsudski	$1,040,000
Derby Stakes (England)	Shaamit	$813,264
Hollywood Gold Cup Handicap	Siphon	$600,000
Irish Derby (Ireland)	Zagreb	$548,498
Japan Cup (Japan)	Singspiel	$1,685,293
Jim Beam Stakes	Roar	$360,000
Jockey Club Gold Cup	Skip Away	$600,000
Kentucky Derby	Grindstone	$869,800
King George VI and Queen Elizabeth Diamond Stakes (England)	Pentire	$458,015
Matrlarch Stakes	Wandesta	$420,000
Oaklawn Handicap	Gerl	$450,000
Pacific Classic Stakes	Dare and Go	$600,000
Pimlico Special Handicap	Star Standard	$360,000
Preakness Stakes	Louis Quatorze	$458,120
Prix de l'Arc de Triomphe (France)	Helissio	$815,600
Santa Anita Derby	Mr. Purple	$600,000
Super Derby	Editor's Note	$450,000
Travers Stakes	Will's Way	$450,000
Woodbine Million (Canada)	Skip Away	$600,000

Harness racing

Race	Winner	Value to winner
Cane Pace	Scoot to Power	$163,214
Hambletonian	Continentalvictory	$500,000
Little Brown Jug	Armbro Operative	$185,981
Meadowlands Pace	Hot Lead	$500,000
Messenger Stakes	Go for Grins	$166,540
Woodrow Wilson	Jeremys Gambit	$400,000

Sources: *The Blood Horse Magazine* and U.S. Trotting Association

Gold Cup on October 5 in Elmont, New York.

The Triple Crown winners were Grindstone in the Kentucky Derby May 4 in Louisville, Kentucky; Louis Quatorze in the Preakness May 18 in Baltimore, and Editor's Note in the Belmont Stakes June 8 in Belmont, New York. Five days after the Derby, Grindstone was retired because of a bone chip in a knee.

Harness. Jenna's Beach Boy, a 4-year-old pacing colt, set all-time records for races over a one-mile track (1 minute 47⅗ seconds) and a half-mile track (1 minute 49⅗ seconds). Four days after Jenna's Beach Boy's 1:49⅗, Stand Forever lowered the record to 1:49⅖. Jenna's Beach Boy won nine races, including the Cadillac Breeders Crown for older pacers.

Continentalvictory, a 3-year-old trotting filly, won the Yonkers Trot and the Hambletonian, the first two legs of trotting's triple crown, but was scratched from the final leg, the Kentucky Futurity, with a sprained ankle. Hennessey won the race.

Europe. Helissio, a 3-year-old colt, won the Prix de St. Cloud and Europe's prestigious Prix de l'Arc de Triomphe. The best harness horse was Coktail Jet, a 6-year-old trotter whose victories included the Elitlopp and the Prix d'Amerique.   □ Frank Litsky

In *World Book,* see **Horse racing.**

Hospital. See **Health-care issues.**

Housing. See **Building and construction.**

Houston residents saw nearly a year of tough bargaining end in September 1996 with an agreement to build a $265-million, retractable-roof baseball park downtown—a deal that would keep the Astros baseball team in Houston for at least 30 years. Team owner Drayton McLane, Jr., claiming he had lost $61 million since buying the team four years earlier, had warned city leaders that he would have to sell the Astros if a new facility were not built.

Stadium deal. The Astros had played in the Astrodome since it opened to worldwide acclaim in 1965. The Astrodome became less of a tourist attraction over the years, however, as other cities built new stadiums and the Astros failed to reach a World Series. McLane, a businessman from Temple, Texas, said he needed a ball park that would produce more revenue, like the new stadiums that drew big crowds in Denver, Cleveland, and Baltimore.

Astros fans had feared that McLane might sell the team to another businessman who wanted to move it to the Washington, D.C., area. Houston already had seen its National Football League team, the Oilers, agree to move to Nashville, Tennessee, in 1998, after team owner Bud Adams's demand for a downtown stadium was refused in 1995.

The plan for a new, 42,000-seat ballpark narrowly won approval from Harris County voters in a Nov. 5, 1996, referendum. Certain parts of the financing plan required approval from the Texas state legislature. The Astros were scheduled to begin playing in their new park in the year 2000.

Cancer doctor charged. Dr. Stanislaw Burzynski continued his struggle in 1996 to keep his Houston clinic open and to provide his experimental drug Antineoplaston to patients with terminal cancer. In late 1995, the doctor and his Burzynski Research Institute were named in a 75-count indictment charging mail fraud, violations of U.S. Food and Drug Administration (FDA) rules and Texas law, and contempt of a federal judge's 1983 order forbidding Burzynski to ship the drug across state lines.

The government had been trying for more than a decade to stop Burzynski, because his drug lacked FDA approval. Patients from all over the country came to Houston for Burzynski's treatment, and they pleaded with officials to allow Burzynski to continue offering them hope. U.S. District Judge Sim Lake ruled in February that Burzynski was breaking the law by dispensing the drug without FDA approval, but immediately stayed his ruling pending a decision from an appeals court. In April, a U.S. Circuit Court of Appeals agreed with Lake, but the FDA allowed about 400 patients to continue treatment. Burzynski's trial was set to begin in early 1997.

FBI sting. Several members of the Houston City Council came under investigation in the spring of 1996 after a sting operation conducted by the Federal Bureau of Investigation (FBI). Posing as Hispanic investors, FBI agents allegedly induced Houston Port Commissioner Betti Maldonado to offer illegal contributions to members of the Houston city council in exchange for a share in a downtown convention center hotel development project.

The investigation focused on councilmen John Castillo, Felix Fraga, and John Peavy, and on former councilman Ben Reyes. Maldonado and the councilmen denied wrongdoing, and none were immediately charged with a crime. However, Maldonado and Peavy later resigned their positions, and a federal grand jury continued to examine the case.

Bank robberies in the Houston area increased dramatically in 1996, for reasons that police could not explain. By late September, as the city's fiscal year was drawing to a close, police had recorded at least 57 bank heists, compared with only 42 in the previous year. The FBI's Houston office, which includes Harris County and some outlying areas, had investigated 135 bank robberies in fiscal 1996, compared with only 67 in 1995.

The most notorious robber was a man whom police called the "Polo Shirt Bandit," because of the type of shirt he wore. The bandit was believed to be responsible for 35 bank robberies in the Houston area and 3 others in Texas since 1989. On Nov. 27, 1996, police cornered the bandit after a high-speed car chase. The bandit shot himself in the head to avoid capture, but survived. □ Burke Watson

See also **City.** In *World Book*, see **Houston.**

Howard, John W. (1939–   ), became prime minister of Australia in March 1996, when his Liberal-National Party coalition defeated Paul Keating's Labor government, winning 94 out of 148 seats. The Labor Party had been in power for 13 years.

John Winston Howard was born on July 26, 1939, in Earlwood, New South Wales. He graduated from Sydney University in 1961 with a bachelor of laws degree and became a *solicitor* (lawyer). Howard entered politics in 1974 as a Liberal and was elected a Member of Parliament for the Sydney seat of Ben-nelong. He held various ministerial posts in the Liberal-National Party coalition government from 1975 to 1983, including treasurer and minister for finance. Following his party's defeat in 1983, Howard served as leader of the opposition from 1985 to 1989. After holding various ministerial posts in the shadow cabinet, Howard was again in 1995 appointed leader of the opposition. He was sworn in as prime minister on March 11, 1996.

The Liberal-Nationals, traditionally a conservative party promoting free-market economics, had shifted to the center of Australian politics in the 1990's. Howard pledged to retain the Medicare national health insurance program and set aside $1 billion (Australian dollars) to tackle environmental problems. Another major priority was reform of Australia's union laws. □ Francesca Mitchell

See also **Australia.**

American Michelle Kwan won the gold medal at the U.S. National Figure Skating Championships in January and the world championships in March.

Hungary in 1996 remained one of the most successful of former Communist nations in shifting to a free-market economy. Seeking to qualify for membership in NATO and the European Union, the Socialist-led government sought to improve Hungary's relations with neighboring countries.

Finance Minister Lajos Bokros, a key figure in Hungary's economic reforms, resigned in February, after the government failed to approve changes he proposed in funding social security. In May, Defense Minister Gyorgy Keleti resigned after it was revealed that the Hungarian armed forces sent eight fighter planes to Poland to join military exercises without Keleti's knowledge or the permission of parliament.

The government pledged to continue the austerity measures adopted in 1995. Inflation declined to 24 percent in 1996 from a high of 31 percent in 1995. However, social security continued to account for more than half of government spending.

The issue of ethnic minorities strained relations with Slovakia and Romania and threatened to undermine a treaty between Hungary and Slovakia. The treaty, which was ratified by the Slovak parliament in March 1996, included pledges of fair treatment for ethnic minorities living in each country. Despite the controversy, Hungary and Romania signed a similar treaty in September.   □ Sharon L. Wolchik

See also **Europe** (Facts in brief table). In *World Book,* see **Hungary.**

Ice skating. Fifteen-year-old Michelle Kwan of Torrance, California, and 24-year-old Todd Eldredge of South Chatham, Massachusetts, won individual gold medals at the 1996 World Figure Skating Championships in Edmonton, Canada. The championships, which were held March 17 to 24, attracted 196 skaters from 41 nations. As usual, Russians did well in ice dancing and pairs competition. Oksana Gritshuk and Yevgeny Platov won the ice dancing title for the third straight year, and Marina Eltsova and Andrei Bushkov won gold in the pairs competition.

This was the first time that Americans had swept the singles titles since Brian Boitano and Debi Thomas won in 1986. Kwan became the third youngest women's champion behind 14-year-old Sonja Henie of Norway in 1927 and 15-year-old Oksana Baiul of Ukraine in 1993. She clinched first place near the end of her free-skating routine, when she daringly substituted a triple toe loop for a less-difficult double axel. After a stunning free-skating routine, Lu Chen of China, the silver medalist, seemed astounded that she had not won.

Eldredge won the free-skating competition and the overall title over Ilia Kulik of Russia. Elvis Stojko of Canada, trying for his third consecutive world title, fell on a triple-triple combination in the short program and finished fourth overall.

As in 1995, most of the sport's outstanding skaters competed as professionals in 1996, outside the jurisdiction of the International Skating Union (ISU), skating's world governing body. They earned considerable money on tours, exhibitions, and made-for-television events. For the first time, the ISU offered prize money to so-called amateurs—$700,000 on a grand-prix circuit and $500,000 for the world championships.

Speed skating. Rintje Ritsma of the Netherlands won his third straight men's all-around championship at the European Speed Skating Championships, held January 20 and 21 in Heerenveen, the Netherlands. Gunda Niemann of Germany won her seventh women's European overall title in eight years. In February, Ritsma and Niemann also won the world championships in Inzell, Germany—Niemann for the fifth time in six years. Over the season, she also won World Cup titles for 1,500 meters and the combined 3,000/5,000 meters.

The world all-around sprint championships, held February 17 and 18 in Heerenveen, were won by Sergei Klevchenya of Russia and Christine Witty of West Allis, Wisconsin. In a breakthrough year, the 20-year-old Witty made a strong bid to succeed Bonnie Blair, the American who retired in March 1995, as the sport's top woman sprinter. □ Frank Litsky

In *World Book,* see **Ice skating.**

Iceland. See Europe.

Idaho. See State government.

Illinois. See State government.

Immigration. In 1996, an election year, the United States Congress passed two new laws that appeared to reflect an anti-immigrant mood in the country. The first bill, which cracked down on illegal immigration, was included in a major spending bill that overwhelmingly passed the House of Representatives in a 370-37 vote and the Senate in an 84-15 roll call vote. It was signed by President Bill Clinton on September 30. The second bill, which was part of a major revision of the American welfare system, denied certain benefits to legal immigrants. The welfare bill was signed into law by the president on August 22.

New border controls. A major segment of the immigration law signed into law on September 30 focused on controlling the U.S.-Mexican border. Backers of the legislation stated that the bill reflected popular response to the estimated 4 million illegal immigrants believed to be in the United States in 1996, a number that immigration officials estimated could grow by as many as 300,000 people a year.

The new law earmarked $12 million for the construction of a 14-mile (22.5-kilometer) fence south of San Diego to stop people from illegally crossing into the United States. A thousand new immigration agents were to be hired each year for five years to patrol the U.S.-Mexican border, and the support staff was to be increased by 1,500 positions.

Under the new law, the Immigration and Natu-ralization Service was to hire 1,200 additional investigators to deal with alien criminals, visitors who overstay visa limits, and U.S. employers who hire illegal immigrants. The punishment for smuggling illegal aliens was toughened to a mandatory three-year prison sentence. The maximum penalty for fraud related to immigration documents was raised from 5 to 15 years in prison.

The new law stipulated that citizens who sponsor immigrants must earn an annual income that is at least 25 percent higher than the poverty line, which the U.S. government defines as the amount of income that households need to eat adequately without spending more than a third of income on food. The law also stipulated that sponsors must sign affidavits guaranteeing that they would support the immigrants they sponsor for up to 10 years or until the immigrant becomes a citizen.

Welfare changes. President Bill Clinton angered liberal members of his own Democratic Party when he signed the welfare bill, which, among other provisions, denied food stamps to most legal immigrants. The measure also allowed the states to shut off cash aid and Medicaid benefits to most legal immigrants. However, states that provided emergency medical services to illegal aliens would be eligible for federal reimbursement. □ William J. Eaton

In *World Book,* see **Immigration.**

Income tax. See Taxation.

India. More than 340 million voters cast ballots between April 27 and May 7, 1996, in parliamentary elections that ousted the Congress Party, the party that held power for the nearly half century since India gained independence from Great Britain in 1947. The Congress Party and its allies won only 141 of 545 seats in the lower house of parliament. A Hindu nationalist party, the Bharatiya Janata Party (BJP), and allies won 194 seats. United Front, a group of 13 broadly leftist and regional parties supported by India's poor and those low in the Hindu caste system, won 111 seats.

BJP leader Atal Behari Vajpayee became prime minister on May 15, succeeding P. V. Narasimha Rao, who had been prime minister since 1991. But the BJP and allied Shiv Sena party were unable to win sufficient support from other parties to gain a parliamentary majority. The other parties opposed the coalition's antagonism toward Muslims and other Indian minorities, as well as its economic nationalism and other highly conservative policies. Rather than lose a confidence vote in parliament and be ousted, Vajpayee resigned on May 28, 1996.

President Shankar Dayal Sharma then named H. D. Deve Gowda as prime minister. Gowda was leader of the United Front, whose support in parliament had risen to 190 seats. Gowda took office on June 1. He won a confidence vote on June 12 with the backing of the Congress Party. On June 28, Gowda chose two Communists to serve as Cabinet ministers, the first Communists to serve as ministers in India.

Gowda was India's first regional leader to become prime minister. He had been head of the Janata Dal party in the state of Karnataka in southern India and as such was head of the state government. State leaders of other regional parties, most supported by voters low in the Hindu caste system, selected him to head the United Front in the national elections.

Gowda had earned credit for forward-looking economic policies in Karnataka, home to some of India's most advanced industries. He named as finance minister Palaniappan Chidambaram, a widely respected, Harvard-educated attorney who had been Rao's commerce minister. Chidambaram sought to sell government-owned industries, lower trade barriers, and encourage foreign investment.

Gowda's government was soon torn by factional disputes, but it stayed in power because no party wanted another election.

Bribery scandals. Police had discovered evidence in 1991 that politicians had accepted $18 million in kickbacks from an Indian business family, but little was done to prosecute them until January 1996. Under pressure from India's Supreme Court, the Central Bureau of Investigation began charging senior politicians. On March 1, the court took control of the bureau from Rao's government to ensure impartiality in the investigations. Eventually, seven members of Rao's Cabinet were forced to resign. BJP president L. K. Advani was also implicated, though the party had claimed that its members were honest while accusing Rao's party of being corrupt. The charges reinforced popular perceptions that India's entire political establishment was corrupt and that Rao's government was among the worst.

Rao as prime minister tried to stay out of the spreading scandal, but opposition politicians said that he, too, had been bribed. After being named in a criminal conspiracy case, Rao resigned as leader of the Congress Party. Sitaram Kesri, 80 years old, was elected as provisional party president.

Kashmir troubles. Muslim separatists continued guerrilla warfare in the Himalayan state of Jammu and Kashmir during 1996. Some 14,500 people had died in seven years of fighting for an independent state. Despite terrorist threats against voters by the separatists, Kashmir held legislative elections in September 1996, the first since 1987.

In May 1996, reports surfaced that four tourists, from Germany, Great Britain, and the United States, abducted by a shadowy Muslim military group were killed in Kashmir in July 1995. The reports, however, could not be confirmed.

In late August 1996, 50,000 Hindus on pilgrimage to a sacred cave site 12,725 feet (3,880 meters) high in the Himalayan Mountains in Kashmir were caught in a blizzard, which lasted for three days. More than 240 lightly dressed and ill-prepared pilgrims died of exposure.

Vetoing a nuclear ban. On August 20, India vetoed a United Nations (UN) treaty banning nuclear testing. Five nuclear powers signed the treaty on September 24, but without India, the pact could not come into force. Since the 1950's, India had been a leading advocate of banning nuclear tests, but it raised technical objections to the UN treaty. Western observers claimed the veto was India's attempt to protect its own nuclear weapons program from international restrictions.

India had felt threatened by China since China tested a nuclear device in 1974. India had also worried about the reported capability of Pakistan, with which India had fought several wars, to make nuclear weapons.

Economic slowdown. After rapid growth in 1995, Indian economic growth slowed in 1996. Interest rates as high as 21 percent crippled private investment. State governments lacked money for education and health programs.

Hundreds killed by cyclone. A *cyclone* (a violent windstorm) destroyed 250,000 village houses and killed more than 1,000 people on India's southeast coast on Nov. 6, 1996. □ Henry S. Bradsher

See also **Asia** (Facts in brief table); **Gowda, H. D. Deve.** In *World Book,* see **India.**

Indian, American.

On Jan. 23, 1996, U.S. Attorney General Janet Reno announced the return of four acres of land, considered sacred, to the Karuk Indians of northwestern California. The federal government had seized the site of the ancient Karuk village of Katimin after the owner's 1993 conviction for cultivating marijuana on the land. In July 1996, the Karuks used the site for the annual summer Brush Dance, a ceremony to renew the world and ensure the return of the salmon and acorns.

On May 24, President Bill Clinton signed an executive order giving protection to certain lands sacred to American Indians and making these lands accessible to religious practitioners.

Return of historical treasures. On July 6, the Iroquois Confederacy, an alliance of six Indian nations, held a ceremony at the Onondaga Nation in New York state to celebrate the return of 74 historic wampum strings and belts—beaded articles made from clam shells—from the Museum of the American Indian in New York City. The wampum strings had been used in trade, and the belts were records of treaties. In May, the Science Museum of Minnesota in St. Paul returned nine False Face masks to the Iroquois Confederacy. The objects, which are considered sacred, represent the faces of spirits and were used in healing ceremonies.

Controversial statue. In October, the National Capital Commission in Ottawa, Canada, agreed to remove a statue of a Canadian Indian from public display at the request of the Assembly of First Nations, an organization representing the native peoples of Canada. The statue was part of a monument to Samuel de Champlain, a French explorer from the 1600's. First Nations called the statue demeaning. It portrayed the Indian, wearing a loin cloth and sash, kneeling before Champlain.

Delaware Tribe. On Sept. 23, 1996, Ada Deer, assistant secretary for Indian Affairs at the U.S. Department of the Interior, formally released the Delaware Tribe of Eastern Oklahoma from the trusteeship of the Cherokee Nation. An 1866 treaty had recognized the Delaware as an independent tribe. In 1979, however, the acting deputy commissioner of the U.S. Department of the Interior—apparently unaware of the terms of the 1866 agreement—decided to engage in relations with the Delaware only through the Cherokee Nation. Reinstatement of the Delaware Tribe in 1996 followed legal reviews of the 1866 treaty and an 1867 treaty between the Cherokee and the Delaware.

Sacred Run. In March 1996, 35 runners began the 105-day, 2,600-mile (4,200-kilometer) "Sacred Run" from Los Angeles to Atlanta, Georgia, the site of the 1996 Olympic Games. The cofounder of the American Indian Movement, Dennis Banks, organized the run to send the message that "all life is sacred."

Casinos. On March 27, the U.S. Supreme Court ruled in a case between the Seminole Tribe and the state of Florida that tribes could not use federal courts to compel states "to negotiate in good faith" for approval of casinos—a stipulation of the Indian Gaming Regulatory Act of 1988.

On Sept. 23, 1996, a federal judge closed the Mescalero Apache casino in southern New Mexico, one of 11 Indian-operated casinos in the state. During 1996, both the Supreme Court of New Mexico and federal judges ruled that all the casinos were operating illegally because the tribes needed the approval of the state legislature, not just the approval of the governor. However, nine casinos owned by the Pueblo Indians and another Apache casino were allowed to stay open pending appeals. The Mescalero casino was allowed to reopen in November.

Education crisis. On September 4, approximately 200 Mohawk Indians seized a public grade school in Hogansburg, New York, to assert authority over their children's education. The St. Regis Mohawk Tribal Council, Akwasasne Mohawk Council, and Mohawk Nation Council of Chiefs formed their own unified school district. On September 12, however, Mohawk leaders dissolved the new school district when the Salmon River School District agreed to establish an eight-member council, made up of school board members and representatives from the Mohawk community, to address grievances of the Native Americans in the district. □ Donald L. Fixico

In *World Book,* see **Indian, American.**

Indiana. See **State government.**

Indonesia experienced its worst riots in more than two decades in 1996, after the government of President Suharto tried to weaken the political power of Megawati Sukarnoputri. Megawati, a daughter of Indonesia's former President Sukarno, was seen as a potential challenger to Suharto. Since 1993, she had headed the Democratic Party of Indonesia (PDI), consisting of nationalist and Christian forces in a nation predominately Islamic. The PDI had been one of only three political parties allowed by the government. In September, the United States stated it was postponing the sale of F-16 fighters to Indonesia because of the turmoil, but later announced the sale was on again.

Power play. In June 1996, the government arranged for a rebel PDI faction to remove Megawati as party leader. On July 27, police backed by the military tried to oust her supporters from the party's headquarters in Jakarta, the national capital, where they had been organizing daily antigovernment rallies. In the rioting that followed, at least 3 people were killed and 20 buildings burned.

The government feared that growing public unrest and the appeal of Megawati would challenge Suharto's control of parliament in elections due in 1997. Suharto and his army backers also feared that she might even run for president in 1998. But after Megawati's ouster as party leader, officials barred her from running for parliament by saying she was not on the official party ticket.

The army blamed the unrest on the new People's Democratic Party. The party was agitated over the low pay of industrial workers and the widening gap between rich and poor. Military officials compared the tiny party to the old Indonesian Communist Party, which the army had smashed in 1965.

Family affairs. Suharto's wife and closest political confidant, Siti Hartinah, died on April 28, 1996. Although stricken by the loss, the 75-year-old president showed no sign of ending his 30-year rule. He was said to be in good health for his age.

Suharto gave his son Hutomo Mandala Putra exclusive authorization to build a "national car." Hutomo got tax breaks to import the first cars from South Korea. This was widely seen as another example of corruption in the presidential family.

Squelching independence. In August, Suharto promoted his son-in-law, Prabowo Subianto, to the rank of major general after he led a May attack that led to the freeing of nine hostages in West Irian, the Indonesian half of the island of New Guinea. A group seeking independence for West Irian had taken the hostages. Earlier in his career, Prabowo had been accused of human rights violations in putting down dissidents seeking independence in East Timor, a former Portuguese colony before Indonesia seized it in 1975. □ Henry S. Bradsher

See also **Asia** (Facts in brief table). In *World Book,* see **Indonesia.**

International trade

International trade. Trade issues became controversial in the early months of 1996, a presidential election year in the United States, but concern over international trade cooled as the economy gathered strength during the year and leaders defused trade disputes.

World trade volume was estimated to grow by 6.7 percent in 1996, a slower increase than in the previous two years. This was because major trading nations in Europe suffered a substantial economic slowdown, and Asian nations' economies—while still aggressively growing—slowed to more sustainable growth rates. Japan, a leading trade nation, experienced healthier economic growth after years of near stagnation. Industrial nations were projected to increase trade in goods and services by more than 5 percent, a slowdown from the 7.8-percent increase in 1995. Developing countries were expected to increase trade volume by 11.3 percent for 1996, according to the International Monetary Fund, an agency of the United Nations.

NAFTA. As 1996 began, a new dispute simmered between the United States and Mexico over a provision in the North American Free Trade Agreement (NAFTA), which was supposed to allow freight trucks to move freely across the U.S. and Mexican border. (NAFTA is a 1994 treaty that united Mexico, Canada, and the United States into one of the world's largest free-trade zones.)

Before NAFTA, the movement of trucks was limited to a small zone near the international border. The new rules allowed Mexican trucks to haul cargoes through Texas and California, for example, and it allowed American trucks to drive into Mexico as far as the big market of Monterrey. The new regulations drew objections from U.S. unions, which feared job losses, and American officials in border states, who feared a rise in highway deaths and injuries if Mexican trucks failed to meet U.S. safety requirements. The United States suspended the trucking provision in late 1995 until it could negotiate extra safety procedures. The negotiations continued through 1996, and industry officials expected the administration of U.S. President Bill Clinton to settle the issue after his reelection.

A "tomato war" also broke out between Mexico and the United States in 1996. Before NAFTA went into effect, hefty U.S. *tariffs* (taxes on imports or exports) raised the price of Mexican tomatoes to equal the price of U.S. tomatoes. When NAFTA removed tariffs, Mexican tomatoes, which were cheaper to produce because of lower labor costs and the value of the peso in relation to the dollar, flooded the American market, raising the ire of American producers. The dispute triggered a U.S. investigation into whether Mexico was dumping tomatoes (selling at a price below cost of production). In late October, Mexico agreed to sell tomatoes in the United States at a price above an agreed upon floor.

Election pressure. In early 1996, Republicans were believed to have a good chance of ousting President Bill Clinton in the November 5 election. When populist Republican Patrick Buchanan made headway in early Republican caucuses and primaries, his nationalistic views thus had the potential to affect U.S. trade policy. Buchanan opposed NAFTA and the larger world trade pact, the General Agreement on Tariffs and Trade (GATT). Buchanan charged that GATT threatened U.S. sovereignty by subjecting some U.S. trade policies to the decisions of the World Trade Organization (WTO), which resolves tough disputes under GATT. In the first case WTO decided, on April 29, it ruled against applying U.S. pollution standards to gasoline imported from countries with lower pollution standards.

The eventual Republican presidential nominee, Senator Robert Dole of Kansas, also vowed the WTO would not be allowed to interfere with U.S. sovereignty. Dole, however, largely rejected protectionist arguments in favor of trade policies that were generally in line with those of the Clinton Administration. He did argue that the Clinton Administration was being outfoxed in trade negotiations with other countries. As the year progressed, the domestic economy strengthened, and foreign trade cooled as an election issue.

U.S. trade leadership. The Clinton Administration lost a powerful voice for American business interests overseas when Secretary of Commerce Ronald H. Brown died in an airplane crash on April 3 near Dubrovnik, Croatia. A U.S. Air Force jet carrying a group on a trade mission crashed into a mountain in stormy weather, killing all aboard.

Brown's death removed an energetic salesman for the Clinton Administration's policies and a strong defender of the Department of Commerce, which Congressional Republicans had tried to eliminate in 1995 and 1996. President Clinton named U.S. Trade Representative Mickey Kantor to head the Commerce Department, a move many interpreted as helping the department survive future budget fights. Deputy U.S. Trade Representative Charlene Barshefsky became acting trade representative and was pivotal in securing an agreement in December among most high-technology trading countries to end tariffs on computers by the year 2000. In December, President Clinton nominated Barshefsky to be permanent U.S. trade representative. William Daley was nominated to become commerce secretary.

China's rise. China's recent emphasis on boosting its exports to fuel economic growth showed up dramatically in U.S. statistics during 1996. In June, for the first time, and again in August, the United States posted a larger monthly trade deficit with China than with Japan. (A trade deficit is the shortfall between one country's exports to another country and its imports from that country.) The United States, for many years, had posted its largest trade deficit with Japan.

Police destroy pirated compact discs (CD's) in the streets of Beijing in February. China averted a trade war with the United States by cracking down on the illegal manufacture of CD's.

China's application to join the WTO remained on hold in 1996. For WTO entry, members must agree to follow certain trade rules. China's entry into WTO was blocked in part because the country has set no date for scaling back tariffs on imports.

During May and June 1996, the United States pushed a long-simmering disagreement over Chinese piracy of compact discs (reproduction of discs without permission or the payment of royalties to the copyright holder and the sail of such disks on the international market) to the brink of a trade war by threatening to impose punitive tariffs on $2 billion worth of Chinese imports. In July, China cracked down on manufacturers accused of piracy, and the two nations reached an agreement on intellectual property rights.

European Union (EU). The long-standing goal of uniting Europe's industrial nations in a single market economy slowly moved forward during 1996. Countries in the EU—an organization of 15 Western European countries that promotes cooperation among its members—attempted to set economic goals in such areas as inflation in order to permit the formation of a single European currency, called the euro, scheduled to go into circulation in 1999. The euro would replace all other forms of currency circulated in individual countries in the EU.

☐ John D. Boyd

In *World Book,* see **International trade.**

Internet. In 1996 the Internet (often called *the Net*) grew far beyond its origins as a computer network connecting a few dozen government and university scientists. *E-mail* (electronic mail), once considered a novelty, became a common way for businesses and individuals to exchange messages, documents, and computer files. Businesses rushed to take advantage of the new medium, pouring millions of dollars into colorful "home pages" on the World Wide Web, the graphics-based portion of the Net, to showcase products and services.

Presidential candidates in the 1996 United States election campaigned for the first time through the Internet. In the closing statement of his first debate with President Bill Clinton, Republican challenger Robert Dole invited Internet users to "tap into my home page"—a remark that would have been incomprehensible just four years before. (When Dole made a small error in reciting his web address during a televised debate, thousands of confused viewers wound up not at Dole's web site but at a parody of the Dole site that had a similar address.)

Traffic jams looming? Some computer industry analysts began to warn in 1996 that unless efforts were made to increase the capacity of communications networks that comprise the Internet, an on-line population explosion threatened to overload it. These experts claimed that users would one day experience long delays because the systems that route data traffic on the Net would become unable to keep up with the growing volume of data. Optimists noted that some upgrading was already underway.

Web software. New versions of the two most popular *web browsers* (applications that access the World Wide Web) came on the market in 1996. In August, Netscape Communications Corporation of Mountain View, California, began promoting its Navigator 3.0, an updated version of the browser used by about 85 percent of Internet users. Seeking to challenge Netscape's huge market share, Microsoft Corporation of Redmond, Washington, released its own web browser, Internet Explorer, in the spring and an updated version, Internet Explorer 3.0, in August. Experts predicted a major battle between the two firms for supremacy in the browser market.

Internet telephone service also emerged in 1996. Several companies marketed software that enabled users to make long-distance telephone calls over the Net, using their computers. Internet telephoning bypassed long-distance phone companies, and users paid only their regular connection fee. The sound quality, however, was erratic, and conversations needed to be arranged in advance. Still, American long-distance telephone companies, fearing competition from the Net, petitioned the U.S. government to regulate Internet phone service.

Censorship question. As more families and schools began to connect to the Internet, parents worried that their children would gain access to the Net's substantial volume of adult-oriented material. To address this concern, the U.S. Congress in February passed a law that imposed stiff penalties on anyone who sent obscene or "indecent" material through the Internet or an on-line service. The law was soon challenged in court by people who claimed it violated the First Amendment to the U.S. Constitution, which guarantees the right to free speech. In June, a panel of federal judges ruled unanimously that the law was unconstitutional. The U.S. Justice Department appealed the ruling to the U.S. Supreme Court, which said it would hear the case in 1997.

Providing equal access. The most important social issue regarding the Internet was how to ensure that its resources became accessible to everyone, especially to those who could not afford expensive computers and access fees. This desire to create equal access sparked a variety of plans aimed at connecting schools to the Internet. Some communities organized "Net Days," at which volunteers strung cables, set up computers, and installed the software needed for schools to access the Net. These festive events were compared to prairie barn raisings. Many communities also set up computers at libraries and other public buildings, so that people without a computer could explore the Net.   □ Herb Brody

See also **Computer; Telecommunications.** In *World Book,* see **Internet.**

Iowa. See **State government.**

Iran. Iran's attempts to evade the U.S. campaign to isolate its Islamic regime met with setbacks in 1996. In August, the United States approved economic sanctions against any foreign company or bank investing more than $40 million in the oil and gas industries of either Iran or Libya. The United States accused both countries of being "rogue states" that supported terrorism. The sanctions gained momentum after four suicide bombings in Israel by radical Islamic groups with alleged ties to Iran resulted in the deaths of 61 people between Jan. 1 and March 4, 1996.

Western nations condemned what was viewed as Iran's public support for the bombings. While Iran's official news agency called the attacks "divine retribution," the government insisted this did not reflect an official view and denied involvement. Nevertheless, Iran was excluded from an international conference on combating terrorism, which met in Egypt in mid-March.

German embarrassment. On March 14, Belgian customs officials discovered ammunition, including a 275-pound explosive mortar round armed with a timing device, in cargo being shipped from Iran to Germany. Western officials feared the arms may have been intended for Israeli or Jewish targets in Europe. The arms shipment was one of several incidents in 1996 that embarrassed Germany, which supports "critical dialogue" with its trading partner Iran.

More tension surrounded the trial in Germany of five men, an Iranian and four pro-Iranian Lebanese, for the 1992 murders of Iranian Kurdish dissident Sadiq Sharafkindi and three of his associates in a Berlin restaurant. In March 1996, Germany issued a warrant for the arrest of Iranian intelligence minister Ali Fallahian for his alleged role in ordering the killings. And in August, exiled former Iranian president Abol Hassan Bani Sadr testified at the trial that Iran's president, Ali Akbar Hashemi Rafsanjani, and spiritual leader, Ali Khamenei, ordered the killings.

Iranian Kurds. In late August, Iranian-backed Kurdish leader Jalal Talabani of the Patriotic Union of Kurdistan (PUK) attacked his Iraqi-backed rival Massoud Barzani, head of the Kurdish Democratic Party. (The Kurds, an ethnic group living in parts of Iran, Iraq, Syria, Armenia, and Turkey, seek an independent state.) Barzani received military support from Iraqi President Saddam Hussein, and by mid-September, PUK rebels were routed. However, Iran rearmed the PUK, which retook their positions in October. Iran claimed that 200,000 Kurds fled eastward, seeking Iran's assistance, and it called for international aid. Many of the refugees later returned to their homes. In July, more than 3,000 Iranian Revolutionary Guards entered Iraq and destroyed two Kurdish rebel bases during a three-day strike.

□ Christine Helms

See also **Iraq; Middle East** (Facts in brief table); **Turkey.** In *World Book,* see **Iran.**

Iraq again in 1996 became the focus of regional and international attention when the United States on September 3 and 4 fired 44 sea- and air-launched missiles at targets in southern Iraq. The United States also announced it was expanding the "no-fly" zone in southern Iraq, a move intended to keep Iraqi aircraft grounded.

The United States acted in retaliation for Iraq's military intervention among Kurdish factions in northern Iraq. (The Kurds are an ethnic group living in parts of Iran, Iraq, Syria, Armenia, and Turkey.) Iraqi troops supported the militia of Massoud Barzani's Kurdish Democratic Party (KDP) in a successful assault in late August against Sulaimaniya, a city held by rival militia leader Jalal Talabani of the Patriotic Union of Kurdistan (PUK). The PUK was quickly routed, and it fled to Iran. Barzani's move was motivated in part by the growing alliance between Talabani and Iran, which reportedly had supplied the PUK with arms and intelligence since 1995.

International reaction. Only the United Kingdom, Kuwait, and Israel supported the actions of the United States. Many nations, including key American allies in the West and Middle East, either urged restraint or condemned the U.S. actions. These nations feared Iraq could disintegrate if it were prevented from defending itself against domestic groups (such as the PUK) aided by outside powers (such as Iran). They warned that further U.S. force could foster anti-Americanism, destabilize the Arab-Israeli peace process, and embroil Turkey, Syria, and Iran in conflict. Under these pressures, the United States and Iraq both avoided further military action.

The Kurdish power struggle again erupted when the PUK, rearmed by Iran, recaptured nearly all of Sulaimaniya province, except the city of Irbil, the Kurdish capital, after a two-day blitz, which ended on October 14. The United States, which warned Iran and Iraq not to intervene, brokered a cease-fire between the PUK and KDP on October 23. The situation remained highly unstable, however. Since 1994, numerous cease-fires had been broken. More than 4,000 Kurds had died in interfactional fighting.

The renewal of Kurdish factionalism was a blow to the United States, which had hoped to topple Iraqi President Saddam Hussein. Under the protection of Operation Provide Comfort (OPC), a U.S.-led military alliance was set up at the end of the Persian Gulf War in 1991 to protect Iraqi Kurds from Iraqi troops, and U.S. intelligence agencies reportedly helped fund opposition to Hussein. Hostilities in 1996 prompted the United States to evacuate up to 6,000 people associated with these programs. In September, Iraq reportedly arrested and killed 100 members of the opposition Iraqi National Congress in Irbil.

United Nations (UN) sanctions. The Kurdish infighting delayed the implementation of a deal

The crew of the U.S.S. *Shiloh* fires 1 of 44 missiles launched against Iraq on September 3 and 4 in retaliation for Iraqi intervention in Kurdish factions.

signed May 20 by the UN and Iraq, allowing Iraq to sell $1 billion of oil twice in a six-month period in order to buy food and medical supplies.

The World Health Organization (WHO), a UN agency, announced in March that the health of Iraqis had deteriorated since sanctions were imposed after Iraq invaded Kuwait in August 1990. WHO reported that malaria, cholera, and typhoid had reached epidemic levels; infant mortality had doubled; the death rate for children under age 5 was six times higher than before 1990; and malnutrition was widespread. The oil-for-food program was designed to address these problems. Insecurity in northern Iraq raised concerns about the safety of UN inspectors who were to oversee the distribution of UN goods. However, Iraq began oil exports in mid-December. The lifting of sanctions had been contingent on Iraq proving it had destroyed its weapons of mass destruction, a condition that Iraq had finally accepted in late November.

Defectors slain. Two of Hussein's sons-in-law were slain by relatives on February 23, three days after returning to Baghdad from Jordan, where they had received political asylum in August 1995. The men had returned to Iraq with Hussein's blessing. Hours before the killings, it was announced that Hussein's daughters had divorced their husbands.

☐ Christine Helms

See also **Middle East** (Facts in brief table); **Turkey.** In *World Book,* see **Iraq.**

Ireland

Ireland held the rotating presidency of the European Union (EU) for six months in 1996, beginning July 1, and so led the negotiations aimed at creating a single currency for EU countries. The EU hoped to begin the circulation of a single currency in 1999.

The Irish economy continued to grow strongly in 1996. Some economists projected growth of 5 to 7 percent, making the economy one of the most dynamic among EU countries. Irish exports and company profits broke records in 1996. A healthy surplus made it possible for the coalition government, made up of the Fine Gael, Labour, and Democratic Left parties, to prepare for a tax-cutting budget in early 1997, as a prelude to the general election scheduled for the spring. In 1996, Fine Gael's share in the polls rose to 26 percent, which was sufficient for the party to continue to lead the coalition.

Social problems. Despite strong economic growth, unemployment remained high at 12.7 percent in 1996, compared with 14 percent in 1995. Social ills among the unemployed, including drug trafficking and other crimes, remained a major problem facing the Irish government. On June 26, 1996, Monica Guerin, an investigative journalist, was murdered by a gunman on a motorcycle when she stopped her car at a stoplight. Guerin had been reporting on drug-related crime. On July 25, in a session of the *Dail* (the lower house of Parliament), the government introduced six bills aimed at curbing organized

crime, including the freezing of assets of suspected drug dealers on the word of a senior police officer or revenue commissioner.

Peace talks stalled. Peace talks between the British and Irish governments and various political parties of Northern Ireland stalled in June. The Irish Republican Army (IRA), an unofficial military force fighting for uniting Northern Ireland with Ireland, had refused to surrender its weapons and in February had resumed terrorist bombings against Great Britain after a 17-month cease-fire. Agreeing that the IRA had broken pretalk conditions, Ireland joined Great Britain and refused to allow Sinn Fein, the political wing of the IRA, delegates seats at the June 10 opening of the forum, or peace talks, in Belfast. When the Democratic Unionist Party, an extreme Protestant group in favor of Northern Ireland remaining part of the United Kingdom, walked out, further discussions became pointless.

Divorce vote upheld. On June 12, the Supreme Court refused to overturn the November 1995 referendum in which a narrow majority of Irish voters supported the legalization of divorce. The court rejected a challenge by former senator Des Hanafin, chairman of the Anti-Divorce Campaign, who had objected to the use of government funds in the referendum campaign.

☐ Ian Mather

See also **Northern Ireland.** In *World Book,* see **Ireland.**

Islam

Islam. In 1996, developments in the Middle East and Southeast Asia were, at turns, hopeful, disturbing, and even ironic for followers of the Islamic faith.

Voice of moderation. In March, President Hosni Mubarak of Egypt appointed Sayed Muhammad Tantawi as the new Sheikh, or Grand Imam, of the Al-Azhar mosque in Cairo. Although Islam has no hierarchy, the Sheikh of Al-Azhar is regarded as the spokesman of the Sunnis, an Islamic sect that claims more than 80 percent of the world's 1 billion Muslims.

Prior to his appointment, Tantawi had been Egypt's Grand Mufti, or chief Islamic legal scholar, favoring Western practices, such as contraception and interest-earning bank accounts. He had also declared the practice of female genital mutilation to have no basis in Islamic law. Tantawi replaced Sheikh Gad al-Haq Ali Gad al-Haq, who died on March 15, a conservative whose 14-year tenure was marked by frequent criticism by Western governments. Tantawi's appointment drew criticism from conservative sheikhs at Cairo's Al-Azhar University.

Islamic scholar. In August, the Court of Cassation, Egypt's highest appeals court, upheld the conviction of author Nasr Abu Zeid on charges of *apostasy* (disbelief in the faith). Abu Zeid, a professor of Arabic literature at Cairo University, had asserted that some parts of the Koran, the holy book of Islam, should be read metaphorically rather than literally. In response to the alleged apostasy, a group of academics and lawyers had evoked an Islamic law, which forbids a Muslim woman to marry a non-Muslim man, to demand that Abu Zeid and his wife divorce. Earlier in 1996, the couple had moved to the Netherlands.

Israel's Muslims. The May elections in Israel, in which Jewish religious parties made broad gains, also resulted in the first two Muslim members of the *Knesset* (the Israeli parliament): Abdel Malek Dehemshe and Tawfiq Khatib. Dehemshe, a lawyer from Nazareth, and Khatib, the former mayor of Jarjuli, represented the Islamic Movement, which campaigned on a joint ticket with the secular Arab Democratic Party. The joint platform of the two parties called for a continuation of the Israeli-Palestinian peace process and equality between Israel's Arab citizens and the Jewish majority.

Peace in the Philippines. On September 2, Manuel Yan, chief negotiator for the Philippine government, and Nur Misuari, head of the Moro National Liberation Front (MNLF), signed a treaty that ended the 26-year civil war, which had claimed between 50,000 and 150,000 lives. The treaty provided for the MNLF, representing most of the more than 3 million Muslims in the Philippines, to oversee 14 provinces for 3 years. At the end of 3 years, a referendum was to be held to decide which provinces would join an autonomous Muslim region. □ Vincent J. Cornell

See also **Philippines.** In *World Book,* see **Islam; Muslims.**

Israel. Four suicide bombings in Israel killed 61 people and injured more than 200 between Feb. 25 and March 4, 1996, reopening a divide among Israelis over the Arab-Israeli peace process. The militant wing of the pro-Iranian group Hamas claimed responsibility for the bombs, saying they were to avenge Israel's assassination of Hamas bomb maker Yahya Ayyash in Gaza on January 5. Many observers believed the bombs were intended to disrupt the peace process prior to Israel's prime ministerial elections.

Election. Prime Minister Shimon Peres, leader of the Labor Party, narrowly lost the May 29 election to Likud leader Benjamin Netanyahu by 49.5 percent of the vote to 50.4 percent. After the assassination of Prime Minister Yitzhak Rabin in 1995 and prior to the bombings, Peres had held a commanding lead in opinion polls. Netanyahu contended during his campaign that Labor's policy of trading Israeli-occupied Arab land for peace risked Israel's security. He opposed Palestinian statehood, negotiations over the status of Jerusalem (claimed by both Israelis and Palestinians as their capital), and Israel's withdrawal from the Golan Heights, which it captured from Syria in the 1967 Arab-Israeli Six-Day War.

Peace stalled. Netanyahu sought to allay U.S. and Arab doubts about his commitment to peace, but the peace process was frozen after he took office on June 18. Netanyahu met Egyptian President Hosni Mubarak in July and Jordan's King Hussein in August, but initially refused to meet Palestinian leader Yasir Arafat.

The Israeli leader also refused to negotiate with Syria on the principle of trading land for peace, which had been accepted by representatives of Israel in the 1993 peace talks with the Palestinian Liberation Organization (PLO) in Oslo, Norway. Instead, Netanyahu reportedly sought a narrower agreement in which Syria would curtail the actions of guerrillas belonging to Hezbollah, an Islamic-fundamentalist group, in southern Lebanon. In exchange, Israel would reduce its presence in the Israeli-proclaimed "security zone" in Lebanon. Some 1,000 Israeli troops and 3,000 Israeli-sponsored South Lebanese Army (SLA) troops were stationed in southern Lebanon in 1996. Syria, which Netanyahu had blasted on June 27 as a supporter of terrorism, on August 2 flatly rejected negotiations not based on exchanging land for peace.

Occupied territories. Netanyahu sought to renegotiate the former Israeli government's pledge to withdraw Israeli troops from the West Bank city of Hebron. (The West Bank is an area Israel captured from Jordan in the 1967 Six-Day War.) Hard-line Israelis pressed Netanyahu to oppose concessions on Hebron, where 400 militant Jewish settlers lived amid 100,000 Palestinians. Netanyahu rejected an Israeli withdrawal from Hebron and the West Bank when he met with U.S. officials in Washington, D.C., on September 8 and 9.

On July 29, the Israeli government announced it planned to build two bridges across the Jordan River to the Golan Heights and two roads through the West Bank. On August 2, it lifted a four-year freeze on Jewish settlements in the West Bank and Gaza Strip. Israeli forces also destroyed a Bedouin Arab encampment on the West Bank to make room for an expanded Jewish settlement and, on August 27, bulldozed a building under construction by Palestinians in the Old City of Jerusalem.

Relations with Palestinians. Israeli President Ezer Weizman, fearing the stalemate could lead to a renewal of conflict, invited Arafat on August 25 to meet with him. The meeting took place on October 8, when Arafat made his first public visit to Israel.

Tensions had heightened on August 28, when Arafat called a four-hour general strike by Palestinians to protest Israeli actions. Under growing pressure, Netanyahu met Arafat on September 4 at the Gaza border crossing of Erez. The leaders vowed to continue negotiations.

Crisis. On September 24, violent clashes developed when Israel opened a new door to an existing tunnel below Jerusalem's Temple Mount, a site sacred to both Jews and Muslims. At least 15 Israelis and 58 Palestinians died in the violence, which brought Israeli troops and Palestinian police into pitched battles for the first time. Israel claimed the tunnel would improve tourists' access to holy sites,

Israeli soldiers patrol an archaeological tunnel under Jerusalem's Temple Mount during Israeli-Palestinian clashes in September, which were triggered when Israel ordered that a new tunnel entrance be opened in the Palestinian sector.

but Arabs saw it as an intrusion into their sector of Jerusalem and a sign that Netanyahu was not committed to peace.

U.S. President Bill Clinton tried to resuscitate the peace process by hosting a peace summit in Washington, D.C., beginning on October 1. It was attended by Netanyahu, Arafat, and King Hussein. Forty hours of intense negotiations ended on October 2 with no agreement, except that Israelis and Palestinians would continue a dialogue. The dialogue, which began on October 6 and was intended to resolve the issue of Israel's troop withdrawal from Hebron, remained stalemated.

Lebanon. On April 11, Israel launched a massive aerial and artillery campaign against Hezbollah guerrillas in southern Lebanon. Hezbollah had increased rocket attacks into northern Israel. The Israeli campaign was tacitly supported by the United States. But it raised an international furor on April 18, when 100 Lebanese were killed and another 100 wounded by Israeli artillery that hit a United Nations (UN) compound at Qana in southern Lebanon. The United States brokered a cease-fire.

Yigal Amir received a life sentence on March 27 for assassinating Prime Minister Rabin in 1995. Amir, who showed no remorse for the killing, opposed the Arab-Israeli peace process. □ Christine Helms

See also **Middle East** (Facts in brief table). In *World Book,* see **Israel.**

Italy made strides toward greater political stability in 1996 as voters elected a center-left (moderate to liberal) government that promised to modernize the economy and the constitution. The election—Italy's second in two years—was called after support collapsed in January for the government of Prime Minister Lamberto Dini.

The Olive Tree coalition won the April 21 election, capturing 292 seats in the 630-seat Chamber of Deputies, the lower house of parliament, and 157 seats in the 315-seat Senate. The coalition was composed of the Democratic Party of the Left (former Communists that emerged as Italy's largest party) and centrist groups led by Romano Prodi, an economist and former chairman of the state-owned holding company IRI. With the tacit support of the left-wing Refounded Communists, the coalition formed a government headed by Prodi as prime minister. The election dealt a harsh setback to the center-right Freedom Alliance led by media magnate Silvio Berlusconi, which had won the March 1994 election but saw its government collapse over corruption scandals. In 1996, the Freedom Alliance took 245 seats in the lower chamber and 116 in the Senate.

Budget. Prodi promised strict discipline to reverse the country's high inflation and interest rates. He sought to qualify Italy for the Economic and Monetary Union, a 1992 pact establishing a common currency and central bank scheduled to begin in

1999 among European Union (EU) members.

On Sept. 27, 1996, the government announced plans for $40 billion in spending cuts and tax increases in 1997, which were intended to lower the deficit to 3 percent of gross domestic product, the limit under monetary union. On November 24, the government also agreed to tie the value of the lira to other EU currencies, satisfying another requirement for monetary union.

The Northern League, a political party that won 59 chamber seats and 27 Senate seats in the election—about 10 percent of the vote—stepped up its demand for independence for a vaguely defined northern region dubbed Padania by the group's leader, Umberto Bossi. The league staged a symbolic declaration of independence in Venice on Sept. 15, 1996, but that event was overshadowed by larger unity rallies in Milan and other cities. Italy's major political parties had already agreed in July to set up a commission to propose constitutional reforms to allow regional and local authorities more power.

Corruption cases. A lengthy trial began in January on charges that former prime minister Silvio Berlusconi and 10 associates paid $240,000 in bribes to tax police to win favorable treatment for Fininvest, the holding company that controls Berlusconi's media empire. Berlusconi and another former prime minister, Bettino Craxi, along with Aldo Livolsi, chief executive of Berlusconi's television and advertising business, were ordered to stand trial in July on charges of making $6.5 million in illegal payments to Craxi's defunct Socialist Party. Craxi, living in exile in Tunisia, was convicted in absentia for a fourth time in April and sentenced to eight years' imprisonment for soliciting bribes on contracts for building the Milan metro.

Another former prime minister, Giulio Andreotti, went on trial in April on charges of involvement in the 1979 murder of a journalist. A separate trial, which began in 1995, charging Andreotti with Mafia involvement, was suspended after illness removed one judge from the proceedings. It was restarted in May 1996.

Nazi trial. A military court on August 1 found Erich Priebke guilty of involvement in the country's worst World War II atrocity, the March 1944 killing of 335 Italian men and boys. Citing a 30-year statute of limitations, the court freed the 83-year-old German and former Nazi SS captain. The decision provoked protest demonstrations until the government arrested Priebke again, but in response to a warrant issued by German authorities who wanted him extradited to Germany to stand trial for war crimes there. In October, Italy's highest appeals court ordered a retrial.   □ Tom Buerkle

See also **Europe** (Facts in brief table). In *World Book,* see **European Union; Italy.**

Ivory Coast. See **Africa.**
Jamaica. See **West Indies.**

Japan. Ryutaro Hashimoto was reelected prime minister on Nov. 7, 1996. In early elections on October 20, his conservative Liberal-Democratic Party (LDP) won 239 of the 500 seats of the lower house that dominates the Diet, the Japanese parliament. Elections were not mandatory until July 1997. Weak support for Hashimoto's previous ruling coalition had caused major newspapers and other influential forces to press for early balloting. Although Hashimoto fell 12 seats short of a parliamentary majority, his previous two coalition partners chose to stay out of the new government due to their dismal showing in the October election. Hashimoto's new cabinet was made up entirely of LDP members.

Before the elections took place, politicians were nervous over a new electoral system established in 1994. The new system set up 300 single-member voting districts, plus 200 seats to be filled by *proportional representation* (a system of electing legislature members so that each political party is represented in proportion to its share of the total vote cast). Under the old rules, multiseat voting districts pitted party members against each other, which often led candidates to spend huge sums of money to curry voter favor. The change was intended to make members more responsive to voters by encouraging discussion of policy choices rather than buying votes. Historians noted, however, that Japan had used single-member constituencies in the 1890's and again in the 1920's but abandoned them partly because they had led to corruption.

Hashimoto was initially elected prime minister shortly after Tomiichi Murayama resigned on Jan. 5, 1996. Murayama headed the small Social Democratic Party, one of the LDP's coalition partners. Hashimoto, a 58-year-old son of a bureaucrat, had gained prominence by rebuffing American complaints about unequal trade. He was considered to be a defender of political bosses and industrialists controlling the government.

Hashimoto's main opposition, the New Frontier Party, was led by Ichiro Ozawa, a former LDP backroom deal maker who had become an advocate of political and economic reform. Ozawa sparked opposition to the government's $6.3-billion plan to bail out seven mortgage lenders, whose real estate speculations had benefited politicians and organized crime just before property values dropped in the early 1990's. In March 1996, New Frontier members staged a sit-down in parliament to block action on the bailout. But the LDP won the standoff, and the New Frontier Party ended its obstructionist tactics. In June, the parliament approved the bailout. Thereafter, New Frontier and Ozawa lost public support.

Fatal food poisonings. Food infected with *Escherichia coli* bacteria killed 11 people, sickened more than 9,400, and caused a national scare that peaked in July 1996. More than 6,000 elementary school children were stricken in Sakai, a city near Osaka. The epidemic raised questions about national health standards, which in the past had been considered high. Officials, who tried to avoid worrying the public, were accused of moving too slowly after the first people died in May. Some experts suspected that the meat inspection system was inadequate. The source of the infection was never found.

Blood supply scandal. On August 29, police arrested Takeshi Abe, Japan's leading expert on hemophilia, a blood disorder in which clotting does not occur normally. Abe was accused of professional negligence by knowingly allowing in the 1980's the use of blood-clotting agents contaminated with HIV, the virus that causes AIDS, resulting in the infection of some 1,800 Japanese hemophiliacs. On March 29, 1996, a court had awarded $424,000 to each of more than 400 infected hemophiliacs who had brought suits against five drug companies and the government. The lawsuits charged that government health officials had been slow to regulate blood-clotting products despite knowing that untreated products carried a risk of AIDS.

Tension over the U.S. military on the island of Okinawa, the American military's main base of operation in east Asia, grew heated during 1996. In March, three U.S. servicemen were convicted and given prison sentences for raping a 12-year-old Okinawan girl. Public anger over the case turned into protests over U.S. occupation of more than 20 percent of the land on the island. Governor Masahide Ota refused to sign documents forcing private landowners to extend leases for U.S. bases.

On April 12, the United States announced plans to return a Marine air station to Japan. Later, the United States announced a plan to restore a fifth of the land it occupied to Japan. In return, Japan agreed to pay American moving expenses, which could reach $10 billion. The number of U.S. troops stationed in Japan (47,000) was to remain unchanged. Tokyo also promised more economic aid and benefits for Okinawa, the poorest part of the nation with the highest unemployment.

On August 28, Japan's Supreme Court ruled that the central government had the power to seize land on Okinawa for American use, thus overruling Governor Ota. However, on September 8, 60 percent of Okinawan voters supported a nonbinding referendum calling for a reduction of U.S. bases on Okinawa.

Clinton visit. U.S. President Bill Clinton visited Japan in mid-April. He and Hashimoto agreed to renegotiate the Japanese-American security treaty. The result was the biggest shift in Japanese military policy since World War II (1939-1945).

In 1981, the Japanese government had interpreted the country's postwar constitution as prohibiting any fighting alongside allies abroad. But, with Japan dependent upon the United States for security in Japan's increasingly well-armed and argumentative region of the world, Hashimoto opened the possibil-

ity of aiding U.S. forces in military conflicts outside Japanese territory. He also agreed on Japanese and American forces' providing logistical support—but not ammunition—to each other during military exercises, United Nations peacekeeping operations, and humanitarian missions abroad.

Economic problems persisted during 1996, six years after Japan's stock market collapsed. On average, property values had fallen 47 percent from 1992 to 1996. By mid-1996, financial institutions had written off almost $200 billion in bad loans, and more than $200 billion in unrepaid loans remained on the books.

An economic stimulus package worth $177.5 billion that the government had introduced in 1995 spurred economic growth in early 1996. But growth weakened later in the year, and many economists worried that the improvement was just an extravagant, temporary fix. Japan remained one of the world's richest, most economically successful countries, but public debt and the budget deficit soared. Japan's stubborn 3.5 percent unemployment rate stood at a 50-year high in 1996. Job shortages hit the young especially hard, with unemployment among people under the age of 25 nearly double the national rate. Big corporations, the traditional leaders in hiring, cut back on their employment of university graduates. School dropouts found fewer manufacturing jobs because many firms had moved production to countries with cheaper labor, such as China, where wages averaged only 4 percent of Japanese wages.

Declines in domestic production and, therefore, exports in combination with increased imports reduced the country's positive trade surplus. More imports were the result, in part, from the government's loosening of the retail distribution system, which had long favored Japanese goods.

Nuclear disputes. Japan planned to increase the amount of electricity generated by nuclear power from 31 percent in 1996 to 42 percent by 2010. But engineering blunders caused a fast-breeder reactor at Monju to leak coolant and overheat on Dec. 8, 1995. Officials tried to keep news of the accident from an already wary public. On Aug. 4, 1996, 60 percent of voters in Makai, on Japan's west coast, rejected the jobs and subsidies offered by the government to build a reactor there. Five other towns passed bylaws requiring referendums before reactors could be built, despite the central government's insistence that decisions on sites were in its domain.

Subway gassing trial. The trial of religious sect leader Shoko Asahara began on April 24. He faced charges that included ordering 26 killings, including the nerve gas attack in the Tokyo subway system March 20, 1995, that killed 12 people. The trial was expected to last several years.   □ Henry S. Bradsher

See also **Asia** (Facts in brief table); **Hashimoto, Ryutaro.** In *World Book,* see **Japan.**

Johnson, Michael (1967–), in 1996 at the Olympic Games in Atlanta, Georgia, became the first man in history to win gold medals in both the 200-meter and 400-meter events. He also set a world record of 19.32 seconds in the 200-meters.

Johnson's mastery of both the 200- and 400-meter events made him unique in the history of track sports. He was the only runner ranked number one in the world in both events, a feat he accomplished four times. He won world championships in the 200-meter in 1991 and in the 400-meter in 1993, the first athlete in history to have done so. At the 1995 world championships in Göteborg, Sweden, he won both events in the same meet. Johnson won 51 consecutive 400-meter races between 1988 and the summer of 1996.

Michael Johnson was born on Sept. 13, 1967, in Dallas. He attended Baylor University, in Waco, Texas.

Johnson competed in the 200-meter race at the 1992 Barcelona Olympic Games, but weakened by food poisoning, he failed to qualify for the finals. He did, however, win a gold medal in the 4-x-400-meter relay, helping set a world record of 2 minutes, 55.74 seconds.

Johnson received numerous awards, including Athlete of the Year in 1993. □ Lisa Klobuchar

See **Olympic Games** special report: **The 1996 Olympics.** See also **Track and field.**

Jordan. Jordan experienced serious social unrest in mid-August 1996 when the government lifted subsidies on bread, causing the price to double. Riots began in the southern city of Kerak and spread to nearby towns and to the capital, Amman. To quell the violence, King Hussein I deployed the army, suspended the country's parliament, and imposed a curfew. More than 570 people were arrested, of whom 145 faced trial.

The Jordanian government blamed Iraq for inciting the unrest. Other Jordanians blamed the crisis on worsening economic conditions. Unemployment, pegged officially at 15 percent, was actually closer to 25 percent. Some 18 percent of Jordan's 4.2 million people lived below the poverty line in 1996, which meant that their income was less than $146 a month.

Nonetheless, Jordan's economic policies were praised by the International Monetary Fund (IMF), an agency of the United Nations, which helped Jordan implement an economic reform program. The IMF noted that Jordan's *budget deficit* (the difference between government revenues and expenditures) in 1996 was only 3 percent of the gross domestic product (GDP—the total amount of goods and services produced within a nation). This was a sharp reduction from the 1991 deficit, which was 10 percent of the GDP.

Arab-Israeli peace process. Many Jordanians complained that the Arab-Israeli peace process had failed to produce economic benefits. Doubt was cast on the future of the peace process after the election of Benjamin Netanyahu as Israeli prime minister in May. Netanyahu, who favored opening new Jewish settlements in Israeli-occupied Arab territories, rejected the previous Israeli government's formula of trading occupied land for peace.

Foreign relations. King Hussein's efforts to assist the United States in isolating the Iraqi regime of Saddam Hussein also raised the ire of Jordanians, many of whom supported Iraq. In January, the king announced that Jordan would halve its trade with Iraq, worth $400 million a year.

However, King Hussein refused to support U.S. attacks against Iraq in September 1996. (The attacks followed Iraq's intervention in a dispute among Kurdish factions in northern Iraq.) The king announced Jordan would never permit its territory to be used to strike at a fellow Arab state. In February, the king permitted an Iraqi opposition group known as the Iraqi National Accord to open an office in Amman. Jordan granted asylum to prominent Iraqi General Nazar Khazraji, who defected in April.

Jordan and Saudi Arabia restored diplomatic relations in early 1996. Ties had been broken by the Saudis when King Hussein expressed sympathy for Iraq during the 1991 Persian Gulf War.

□ Christine Helms

See also **Middle East** (Facts in brief table). In *World Book,* see Jordan.

Judaism. In June 1996, three Orthodox Jewish political parties, holding 23 seats in the Israeli parliament, joined the coalition government of Prime Minister Benjamin Netanyahu, who was elected on May 29. As part of the coalition agreement, Netanyahu's conservative Likud party adopted Orthodox-supported policies: banning the importation into Israel of *nonkosher* meats (not acceptable in Jewish dietary laws); halting, temporarily, archaeological excavations at Jewish grave sites; and denying government recognition of non-Orthodox conversions to Judaism. (This nonrecognition was important because marriages, divorces, and burial services for Jews are the responsibility of the Orthodox Jewish rabbinate.)

Conservative, Reform, and Reconstructionist congregations, as well as secular organizations, opposed the new government policies and anticipated that recent Israeli Supreme Court decisions that had granted more recognition to non-Orthodox Judaism would be reversed. For example, a 1994 Supreme Court ruling allowed non-Orthodox Jews to serve on a city's religious council.

Funding for education programs. In 1996, Jewish federations, charitable organizations that in the past had focused on fund-raising for Israel and community services, donated much more money to synagogues for education and outreach programs to U.S. Jews. Organizations, such as the United Jewish Appeal (UJA)-Federation of Jewish Philanthropies of

New York, believed that the funding for education might counter the increased number of Jews who are no longer affiliated with the religion because of inter-marriage or assimilation. Although federations and synagogues traditionally had interacted very little, federation leaders, such as John Ruskay of the UJA-Federation, acknowledged the "importance of the synagogue in the development of Jewish identity."

Messianic Jews. In March, in San Antonio, Texas, two members of Hadassah, The Women's Zionist Organization of America, professed to be messianic Jews—Jews claiming a belief in Jesus. Because Hadassah is a secular community service organization, the leaders allowed the two to retain memberships. Nonetheless, the disclosure of the members' beliefs raised concerns about the growing number of messianic Jews in both secular Jewish organizations and synagogues and about the increased efforts to convert Jews to Christianity.

Rabbinical leaders and most Jews of the four branches of Judaism—Orthodox, Conservative, Reform, and Reconstructionist—consider messianic Jews converts to Christianity and, therefore, no longer Jewish. Messianic Jews, who practice Jewish religious traditions but believe that Jesus is the prophesied Jewish messiah, defend the movement as another branch of Judaism.

The Southern Baptist Convention (SBC), the largest Protestant denomination in the United States, passed a resolution in June calling on its members to direct their "resources toward the proclamation of the Gospel to the Jews." Larry L. Lewis, the president of the SBC's Home Mission Board, said that resolution was necessary because recent efforts between Jewish and Christian groups to discuss their faiths had become a substitute for seeking converts to Christianity.

The resolution threatened the long-running efforts of Jewish conservatives to forge alliances with their evangelical Christian counterparts in supporting Israel and opposing abortion and same-sex marriages. Many Jewish organizations, religious and secular, expressed concern over the resolution.

Jewish studies. On July 15, Thomas Bird, a Roman Catholic professor of Yiddish, resigned as director of Jewish Studies at Queens College in New York City, two weeks after he was appointed. Members of the Jewish Studies faculty objected to the appointment because Thomas did not speak Hebrew and was not Jewish. His critics reasoned that the head of the department should be a Jewish "role model" to Jewish students and the community. Numerous Jewish organizations supported the appointment, however, stressing that eligibility to serve in an academic position should not be based on religion, race, gender, or ethnicity.   □ Marc Lee Raphael

See also **Protestantism; Religion.** In *World Book,* see Jews; Judaism.

Kampuchea. See Cambodia.

Kansas. See State government.

Kazakstan. In 1996, President Nursultan Nazarbayev consolidated his powers and began to focus on economic reform. In January, a new parliament dominated by Nazarbayev's supporters was sworn in, ending nine months of presidential rule. Nazarbayev had dissolved the previous parliament in March 1995.

Even before the parliament met, however, Nazarbayev signed a new decree diminishing its powers and giving the president the right to name and dismiss government officials without parliamentary approval. Nazarbayev claimed that his victory in a 1995 national referendum and the need to accelerate economic reforms justified the decree.

In June 1996, a consortium of Kazak and Western firms reported finding massive oil and gas deposits along the Caspian Sea. Drilling was expected to begin in 1997. In July, the International Monetary Fund approved a $446-million line of credit to support economic reforms through 1998.

In 1996, Kazaks began to drop Russian endings (such as "yev") from their surnames. Place names changed during the rule of the former Soviet Union began to be restored. The government planned to stop using Russia's Cyrillic alphabet and urged that the Russian spelling of "Kazakhstan" be replaced by the traditional "Kazakstan."   □ Steven L. Solnick

See also **Europe** (Facts in brief table). In *World Book,* see Kazakstan.

Korea, North. Summer flooding in North Korea's main farming regions hurt food production in 1996 just as it had in 1995. In September 1996, two United Nations agencies reported that food rations for a large part of the population were "well below minimum quantities required." Widespread malnutrition was reported, as were signs of famine.

North Korea's secretive Communist government appealed for food aid from abroad. The nation needed an estimated 2.2 million short tons (2 million metric tons) of additional grain in 1996. By July, it had received about a third of that amount. Foreign experts said poor land utilization, lack of incentives to improve farming methods, and keeping 5 percent of the population tied up in the armed forces had created the nation's food problems. North Korea showed no signs of changing its policies.

Analysts believed economic output had declined 30 percent since 1991. Many factories were idle in 1996. North Korean diplomats abroad were caught smuggling and were involved in passing counterfeit U.S. money. The government sought foreign investment within tight limits. But it also discouraged investors by establishing high wages.

Hostile acts. On April 4, North Korea announced that it would no longer respect the Demilitarized Zone, a region that had separated North and South Korea since the end of the Korean War (1950-1953). To prove its point, North Korean troops briefly en-

South Korean troops board a submarine abandoned when North Korean spies infiltrated South Korea in September.

tered the zone. The violation seemed to be intended to force the United States into signing a new treaty to replace the 1953 armistice. On April 16, 1996, South Korea and the United States proposed that North Korea and China meet with them on the armistice issue. In May, the press reported that North Korea held secret talks with South Korea in China. On September 2, the North announced it wanted four-power talks to discuss a withdrawal of the 37,000 U.S. troops stationed in South Korea.

Power plants. America, Japan, and other donor nations were slow to fund a $4-billion program to build two nuclear power stations in North Korea. Under a 1994 plan, the plants were to replace facilities capable of producing nuclear weapons materials.

Missing soldiers. Unconfirmed reports in 1996 described inmates in North Korean labor camps as being American soldiers, missing in action (MIA) since the Korean War. In May, the United States paid North Korea $20 million for recovering the remains of more than 200 MIA's. In July, U.S. experts were allowed to help search for 8,100 MIA's. In September, a U.S. congressional subcommittee heard testimony that more than 900 U.S. soldiers might have been left behind when the war ended in 1953. □ Henry S. Bradsher

See also **Asia** (Facts in brief table). In *World Book,* see **Korea.**

Korea, South.

Former South Korean presidents Chun Doo Hwan and Roh Tae Woo were convicted in 1996 of mutiny, treason, and corruption. On August 26, Chun was sentenced to death, and Roh was given 22½ years in prison. In December, an appeals court reduced Chun's sentence to life imprisonment and cut Roh's prison term to 17 years.

The charges against Chun and Roh, both former army generals, stemmed from the 1979 overthrow that had led to Chun's presidency and declaration of martial law in 1980. Chun had eliminated other generals and civilian political leaders in his drive to return the nation to a dictatorship based on control by the army. He was held responsible for the military's crushing of prodemocracy demonstrators, mainly students rebelling against Chun's increasing power in the city of Kwangju. Over time, the government compensated the families of 288 civilians killed at Kwangju. However, the death toll was believed to be higher, and the massacre still echoed in the national politics of 1996.

Chun and Roh were also fined for taking bribes while in office. Chun admitted to having a $900 million slush fund, and Roh confessed to amassing $650 million. But both insisted they accepted gifts to use for political activities. Chun claimed that his fund had helped Roh win the presidential election of 1987, the first direct election for president, and Roh was believed to have helped Kim win in 1992.

Students demonstrated in 1996 for the unification of North Korea and South Korea. The government stated that their action "benefits the enemy" in the north. The police confronted some 7,000 students on the campus of Yonsei University in Seoul, the capital. On August 20, after a nine-day standoff, the police arrested the protest leaders.

In the 1980's, the South Korean public had supported student and worker protests against Chun and Roh's military rule. The demonstrations had forced Chun to replace the electoral college with direct election of the president. But in 1996, few people showed sympathy for demonstrators.

Spy submarine stranded. A submarine from North Korea went aground on South Korea's east coast on September 18, apparently while landing a commando team. Eleven North Koreans were found shot dead—possibly, the sub's crew—killed by fellow North Koreans. South Koreans captured one of the infiltrators and 13 of the 14 remaining men believed to have been on the submarine.

The trade deficit grew in 1996, as big companies moved more production to lower-wage nations. In September, after the stock market had dropped 22 percent in four months, the government announced foreign investors would be allowed to put more money into Korean stocks. □ Henry S. Bradsher

See also **Asia** (Facts in brief table). In *World Book,* see **Korea.**

Kuwait.

Eight Kuwaiti parliament members angered officials in the Persian Gulf region when the Kuwaitis called upon Bahrain in February 1996 to restore its parliament. In an attempt to contain prodemocracy riots, Bahrain had dissolved its parliament in 1975. The Kuwaiti government had been regarded by many Arabs as a model for political reform because it is the only Arab Gulf state with a *parliamentary assembly* (a congress that serves as the highest lawmaking body in a country). On Oct. 7, 1996, Kuwait held its second parliamentary election since the assembly was created after the 1991 Gulf War.

An Islamic court in Kuwait announced in May 1996 that Robert Hussein, a Kuwaiti Shiite Muslim who had declared himself a Christian convert, was an *apostate* (one who forsakes his religion). Under Islamic law, an unrepentant apostate can be put to death. However, the court ruled that the sentence would be decided by a civil, not an Islamic, court.

Some 140,000 Bedouins, descendants of Arab nomads, who fled during the 1990-1991 Iraqi occupation were not allowed to reenter Kuwait, which asserted that Bedouins are stateless and, therefore, not qualified for education or health benefits. Others claimed that Bedouins have lived in Kuwait for decades and should have equal rights.

□ Christine Helms

See also **Middle East** (Fact in brief table). In *World Book,* see **Kuwait.**

Kyrgyzstan. In 1996, President Askar Akayev continued to champion Western-style reforms in Kyrgyzstan. Akayev, a 51-year-old physicist, had been reelected in December 1995 with an overwhelming 75 percent of the popular vote.

Akayev wasted little time in capitalizing on his electoral triumph. In February 1996, more than 90 percent of the electorate supported his proposal to expand presidential powers. The government promptly resigned, clearing the way for Akayev to use his new authority to hand-pick new Cabinet ministers without the need for parliamentary approval.

In March, Kyrgyzstan joined Belarus, Kazakstan, and Russia in a new customs union intended to expand trade among the four countries. By pursuing greater integration with the former Soviet republics, Akayev hoped to create new jobs in Kyrgyzstan. He predicted that inflation would fall to between 15 and 20 percent in 1996 from the 1995 rate of 32 percent, which was already the lowest in the region.

The Kyrgyz economy also stood to benefit from the country's deposits of precious metals. In separate deals, American and Canadian firms in 1996 were awarded rights to mine Kyrgyz gold and silver deposits in conjunction with Kyrgyz companies. Several other joint mining ventures were scheduled to begin prospecting within one year. □ Steven L. Solnick

See also **Asia** (Facts in brief table). In *World Book,* see **Kyrgyzstan.**

Labor and employment. In 1996, the United States economy gained 2.4 million jobs, up from the 2 million created in 1995. The unemployment rate dropped to 4.9 percent in October, a level historically difficult to reduce without triggering inflation. The jobless rate averaged 5.45 percent through the first 11 months of 1996. Inflation remained at a low 3 percent in 1996. Despite the favorable job picture, U.S. workers continued to struggle with technological and competitive threats to job security. White-collar jobs were as vulnerable to "downsizing" and restructuring as blue-collar jobs had been in the 1970's and 1980's when the United States moved from a manufacturing to a service economy.

About 4.2 million "long-term" American workers lost their jobs between January 1993 and December 1995 because of mass layoffs or plant closings, according to a February 1996 survey by the U.S. Bureau of Labor Statistics (BLS). The survey also found that 70 percent of the displaced workers had found another job by early 1996.

Wages for workers in private industry and local and state government employees rose an average of 2.8 percent for the year ending on Sept. 30, 1996, according to the BLS. The wages of white-collar workers rose an average of 3.1 percent; blue-collar workers, 2.4 percent; and service workers, 2.2 percent.

Most major labor negotiations were resolved without a strike. The strikes that occurred often focused on *outsourcing*—the use of less-expensive nonunion contractors for work formerly done by company employees. Wages and benefits of union workers rose 2.6 percent in the year ending in September 1996. Wages and salaries alone increased 2.7 percent over the same period.

AT&T job cut. AT&T Corp., the long-distance telephone giant, announced on Jan. 2, 1996, that it planned to cut 40,000 jobs during the year, the largest single job cut ever in the telephone industry. AT&T, after coming under widespread criticism for the planned purge, claimed that only 18,000 employees would actually be laid off.

The oil industry avoided work stoppages in early February when the 44,500-member Oil, Chemical, and Atomic Workers International Union (OCAW) ratified a three-year contract with the American Oil Company (AMOCO), after rejecting three previous offers. Under the pact, hourly wages of about $19 were raised by 40 cents per hour. Wages were to go up about another 50 cents per hour on Feb. 1, 1997, and about 60 cents per hour on Feb. 1, 1998. Job security and medical benefits were also improved. Other major oil companies made similar offers to the OCAW after the union accepted the AMOCO proposal.

In the aerospace industry, outsourcing was the focus of a dispute between the International Association of Machinists and Aerospace Workers (IAM)

Changes in the United States labor force

	1995	1996
Civilian labor force	132,058,000	133,750,000
Total employment	124,900,000	126,494,000
Unemployment	7,404,000	7,236,000
Unemployment rate	5.6%	5.4%
Changes in real weekly earnings of production and nonsupervisory workers (private nonfarm sector)*	-0.4%	1.4%
Change in output per employee hour (private nonfarm sector)†	0.3%	0.3%

*Constant (1982) dollars. 1995 change from December 1994 to December 1995; 1996 change from October 1995 to October 1996 (preliminary data).

†Annual rate for 1995; for 1996, change is from third quarter 1995 to third quarter 1996 (preliminary data).

Source: U.S. Bureau of Labor Statistics.

The downside, of course, is it's your turn to clean the men's room.

and Lockheed Martin Aeronautical Systems of Marietta, Georgia. On March 13, 1996, IAM members at Lockheed plants in five states rejected a three-year pact that included a company plan to turn over union janitorial and groundskeeping jobs at a plant in Marietta to an outside contractor. In late March and early April, union workers at two Lockheed plants in California ratified the contract, which included a $2,000 lump-sum payment and 3-percent increases in the second and third years. On April 19, the remaining local unions again overwhelmingly rejected the proposal and authorized a strike. The stalemate ended when Lockheed agreed to retain the disputed jobs. IAM workers in Georgia, Mississippi, South Carolina, and West Virginia ratified the pact on April 21.

Detroit newspaper strike. A bitter strike by editorial employees of the *Detroit News* and the *Detroit Free Press* dragged on in 1996. The employees had walked off the job on July 13, 1995, in a dispute over a number of wage and benefit issues, including merit pay raises. In anticipation of the strike, the papers had "borrowed" workers from their parent companies, hired replacement workers and adult newspaper carriers, and accepted that there would be losses in circulation and advertising revenues.

The Teamsters Union, the largest of six unions representing the newspaper strikers, agreed to several concessions involving pension benefits. On April 24,

1996, the management of the *Free Press* declared an impasse in the strike, an action that allowed the paper to put its latest contract offer into effect. The *News* had declared an impasse when the strike began. The *Free Press* also eliminated a requirement that all employees join a union and refused to promise striking workers their old jobs when the strike was settled. During the strike, the newspapers and the six striking unions sporadically bargained for new contracts and filed charges and countercharges of unfair labor practices before the National Labor Relations Board. By December 1996, about half of the striking journalists from the papers had returned to work.

Automotive industry. The Ford Motor Company and Chrysler Corporation negotiated new three-year contracts with the United Automobile Workers (UAW) in September without a strike. The Ford pact, approved by the union on September 17, included both raises and cost-of-living adjustments that would boost the 1996 wage base of $17.98 per hour to $21.60 per hour by 1999. In addition, Ford improved pension benefits and offered a first-year $2,000 bonus. Ford also agreed to limit its use of outside contractors and to retain at least 95 percent of its UAW-represented work force during the life of the contract. The Chrysler pact, approved on September 29, contained similar provisions.

In contrast, relations between the UAW and General Motors Corporation (GM) remained stormy. In

1995, the local UAW struck the company at least seven times in disputes over what the union charged was "excessive" overtime and outsourcing. On March 5, 1996, a dispute over these issues at two GM brake manufacturing plants in Dayton, Ohio, flared into what became the largest U.S. auto strike since 1970. Before it ended 17 days later, 26 of GM's 29 North American plants had been shut down, nearly 180,000 workers idled, and numerous suppliers forced to curtail or halt operations. The agreement ending the strike included the resolution of more than 600 union health and safety complaints and a company guarantee to hire 417 new workers to ease overtime requirements. In return, GM, which is believed to have the highest production costs in the U.S. auto industry, won the right to continue using outside contractors to bolster the company's competitiveness. On Nov. 19, 1996, the UAW ratified a new three-year contract with GM, similar to the agreements signed with Ford and Chrysler.

Canadian strike. The settlement between GM and the UAW was delayed by a strike against General Motors of Canada by all 26,000 members of the Canadian Auto Workers (CAW) union. CAW members walked off the job beginning October 2 over a company plan to increase purchases from outside contractors and to sell off two unprofitable Canadian parts plants. The 20-day strike also idled 25,000 GM workers in the United States and Mexico. On October 23, the CAW ratified a new contract with GM of Canada that resembled the pact it had signed with Chrysler Canada Limited on September 17. On November 8 and 9, the CAW agreed to a similar contract with Ford Motor Company of Canada Limited, hours before a strike deadline. In all three contracts, workers gained some protection against outsourcing, but GM of Canada won the right to sell off the unprofitable plants.

In the airlines industry, the Air Line Pilots Association overwhelmingly ratified a new four-year pact with Delta Air Lines, one of the largest U.S. carriers, on April 24. Under the agreement, the company won the right to cut the pay of its 8,600 pilots by 2 percent and to require the pilots to pay their own health benefits as part of the company's $2-billion cost-cutting plan. The union accepted the cuts in exchange for a company promise to reinstate 472 furloughed pilots. The agreement called for wages to "snap back" to precontract levels if company profits improved. Delta pilots were also granted stock options and a profit-sharing plan.

The railroad industry was beset by contract negotiation impasses but avoided a government-imposed settlement. Contracts were up for negotiation between 35 major railroads and 8 unions, including the 32,000-member Transportation Communications International Union (TCU) and the United Transportation Union (UTU), the largest railroad union.

By spring, three unions had ratified new agreements. But in April, contract talks with the other five unions broke down, and four of them, including the TCU, voted to strike on May 17. The UTU agreed to binding arbitration. On May 8, President Bill Clinton named an emergency board to mediate the railroads' dispute with the TCU and another panel to handle binding arbitration between the UTU and the railroads. Ultimately, the arbitration panel imposed an agreement, rejected by the UTU in April, that boosted wages by 14.3 percent over five years. The railroads also agreed to pay workers lump-sum bonuses of 3 percent in 1996 and 3.5 percent in 1997. Three other unions settled by late July 1996.

Stalled negotiations between the TCU and the railroads, however, led President Clinton to appoint, on June 23, another emergency board to recommend terms for a settlement. On July 23, hours before a second strike deadline, the TCU and the railroads reached an agreement.

On July 30, the Brotherhood of Maintenance of Way Employees and Conrail agreed on a new contract after two years of talks. It was the first labor settlement with a railroad since the late 1970's that did not involve government intervention, a strike, or a company lockout.

Union membership slipped by 300,000 during 1995 (the most recent year for which data were available). The percentage of workers in unions also declined from 15.5 percent to 14.9 percent. The decline in membership was for the most part the result of the economy's huge shift from blue-collar to white-collar employment. Unions traditionally have had difficulty organizing white-collar employees.

Government policy. With the 1996 presidential and congressional elections in mind, nearly 260 Republican members of Congress joined with Democratic legislators on August 2 to pass an increase in the minimum wage. President Clinton signed the bill later in August. The legislation raised the minimum wage from $4.25 to $5.15 an hour, with a 50-cent rise taking effect on October 1 and another 40-cent hike scheduled for 1997.

In 1996, President Clinton signed bipartisan legislation that allows workers who change or lose their job to retain health-care benefits. Employers were required to provide immediate coverage for new employees who had worked for previous employers continuously for at least one year, even if new workers had preexisting medical problems.

In 1996, the Clinton Administration abandoned its efforts to provide federal job protection for striking workers. On February 2, a federal appeals court overturned a 1995 executive order banning companies from holding federal contracts worth more than $100,000 if they hire permanent replacements for strikers. □ Robert W. Fisher

See also **Economics; Manufacturing.** In *World Book,* see **Labor force; Labor movement.**
Laos. See Asia.

Terrorist guerrillas stormed the Japanese ambassador's residence in Lima, Peru, on Dec. 17, 1996, and took 490 hostages. Members of the Túpac Amaru, a Marxist, pro-Castro (Fidel Castro, leader of Communist Cuba), vowed to kill hostages one at a time unless the Peruvian government freed the rebel's jailed comrades. The guerrillas seized the residence during a reception honoring Japanese Emperor Akihito's birthday. Authorities believed the residence was targeted because Japan had supported Peruvian President Alberto Fujimori, who declared a war on terrorism when he was first elected to office in 1991. President Fujimori's brother and Peru's foreign and agricultural ministers, the president of the Supreme Court, and six members of the Peruvian congress were among the people taken hostage. Six officials of the U.S. embassy as well as the ambassadors from Japan, Brazil, Bolivia, Cuba, South Korea, Austria, and Venezuela were held captive.

Terrorist groups have waged a civil war in Peru for more than 15 years. Túpac Amaru rebel forces blasted onto the scene in 1984 with a machine-gun fire attack on the U.S. embassy. The middle-class Túpac Amaru favored intimidation through kidnapping and extortion, while a rival guerrilla faction, the Shining Path, engaged in more violent forms of terrorism. Since the late 1980's, when the Shining Path nearly toppled the government, Peru has used the military to cripple rebel ranks. Hundreds of rebels were arrested and jailed, including Lori Helene Berenson, a New York native and an alleged member of Túpac Amaru, who was convicted in 1995 of treason and sentenced to life in prison.

Japan and Peruvian officials were at odds regarding how to deal with the rebels. President Fujimori refused to meet or negotiate with the rebels. In order to combat rebel violence that has killed 30,000 people in 16 years, Fujimori has taken a hard line against terrorism. He has made it a policy to use fire power, rather than negotiations, to combat terrorism. Japan, which has put a priority on the safety of hostages and has a history of meeting terrorist demands to win the release of hostages, favored bargaining with the rebels.

Outbreaks of violence. Rebel armies in Colombia, Mexico, and Peru continued to mount attacks in 1996. In August, the violence resulted in at least 96 deaths when the Revolutionary Armed Forces of Colombia retaliated against government attempts to eliminate coca crops used to make cocaine. The situation was so chaotic that foreign oil companies contracted with Colombia's military to protect their oil wells and pipelines in Colombia.

In Mexico, where the Zapatista Revolutionary Army had staged violent attacks since 1994, a second rebel group, the Popular Revolutionary Army, attacked military and police posts in four different states in August 1996. Also in August, the Peruvian government declared a state of emergency in 11 provinces after the resurgence of the rebel army, the Shining Path, whose leader has been in jail since 1992.

Extraditions and indictments. The alert action of law enforcement institutions resulted in numerous extraditions and indictments. On January 15, Mexican authorities sent Juan García Abrego, the alleged kingpin of a cocaine smuggling cartel, to the United States, where he was on the Federal Bureau of Investigation's list of the 10 most wanted criminals.

On April 2, a federal judge in Argentina charged five current and former executives of the local subsidiary of the U.S. company, International Business Machines (IBM), with fraud. The IBM executives and 25 others were implicated in a bribery scheme involving a federal Argentine bank. Also in April, Dominican Republic authorities expelled two Haitians who had plotted the 1991 coup against Haiti's democratically elected government. Lieutenant Colonel Joseph Michel François and former Port-au-Prince mayor Franck Romain, who figured prominently in past Haitian oppression, were granted political asylum in Honduras on April 22, 1996.

United States courts, in 1996, played a role for some Latin Americans seeking justice. In January, the state-owned Chile Copper Corporation—known by its Spanish acronym, CODELCO—filed a lawsuit in Miami, Florida, against metal trading firms in Belgium and the United Kingdom. CODELCO claimed that a 1994 loss of $200 million was the result of an international business conspiracy.

On April 4, authorities in New York City indicted Venezuelan Orlando Castro Llanes on charges of conspiring to defraud more than $55 million from depositors at a Puerto Rican bank. Castro, a fugitive, was also wanted for his alleged role in the 1994 collapse of Venezuela's second-largest bank.

In September, the Argentine government agreed to an out-of-court settlement with José Siderman, 85, who sought justice in the Los Angeles County Superior Court for being kidnapped, tortured, and forced out of Argentina by the military dictatorship in 1976. Siderman was the first Latin American to use the U.S. judicial system to seek compensation for human rights abuses in a Latin American country.

The U.S. government also found itself in the defendant's box in 1996. On August 28, Latin Americans of Japanese descent filed a suit in the Federal District Court in Los Angeles, seeking reparation payments, like those already granted to Japanese Americans. More than 2,200 Latin Americans of Japanese de-

Guatemalans by the thousands crowd the main plaza of Guatemala City on December 29 to celebrate the end of Guatemala's 36-year civil war.

scent had been deported to the United States during World War II and forcibly interned. Of these, only 150 had been granted reparations.

New leaders. In 1996, two new presidents took office in the nations that share the island of Hispaniola. In February, René Préval replaced Jean-Bertrand Aristide as the president of Haiti. In August, in the Dominican Republic, Leonel Fernández Reyna succeeded Joaquín Balaguer Ricardo. Both presidents pledged to improve relations between their countries.

In January in Guatemala, former mayor of Guatemala City Alvaro Arzú Irigoyen squeaked to a narrow victory in the presidential runoff elections. In Ecuador, Abdala Bucarám Ortíz also won an upset victory over his conservative opponent in the July runoff elections. In September, Jules Wijdenbosch of the National Democratic Party won the presidential election in Suriname. In October elections in Nicaragua, conservative candidate José Arnoldo Alemán Lacayo defeated Daniel Ortega Saavedra of the left-wing Sandinista National Liberation Front.

Andean Community. At a March 10 meeting in Trujillo, Peru, the presidents of Bolivia, Colombia, Ecuador, Peru, and Venezuela established the Andean Community to replace the troubled, 27-year-old Andean Pact. The organization of the Andean Community, modeled on the European Union, broadened the scope of the countries' collaboration beyond merely economic matters. According to the new agreement, the foreign ministers of the five countries were to elect a secretary general with some executive powers to a rotating position.

Apparel industry. "This is obscene if this is happening," said talk show celebrity Kathie Lee Gifford in tearful remarks on her May 1, 1996, television show. Gifford was responding to allegations of appalling working conditions at the Global Fashions factory in San Pedro Sula, Honduras, which manufactured apparel for Wal-Mart's Kathie Lee Gifford clothing line.

In April, Wendy Diaz, a 15-year-old worker in the Global Fashions factory, had described for reporters in Washington, D.C., and New York City working conditions: verbal abuse, sexual harassment, 60- to 74-hour workweeks, and wages of 34 cents an hour.

Miami entertainment center. By 1996, Miami, Florida, was clearly established as the center of Latin America's entertainment industry and had been dubbed, by the *New York Times,* the Hollywood of Latin America. By 1996, Miami served as the headquarters for several major entertainment giants: Sony Discos and WEA Latina, the Latin music divisions of the world's two largest record companies; Univisión and Telemundo, the two major U.S. Spanish-language networks; and the cable channels MTV Latino and Gems.

Waterway poses environmental threat. Despite warnings from ecologists, work began in June on portions of the Hidrovia, a 2,000-mile- (3,200-kilometer-) long waterway that was to utilize existing rivers to provide an inland maritime highway for five South American countries: Bolivia, Paraguay, Argentina, Uruguay, and Brazil. The Hidrovia—stretching from Cáceres in west-central Brazil to Punta del Este, Uruguay, on the South Atlantic—was designed to open the resource-rich area to world commerce.

Ecologists warned that the new waterway—which would widen, deepen, and straighten the Paraguay River and its tributaries—would drain water from the Brazilian Pantanal, altering the ecosystem of the world's largest wetlands. The Pantanal is home to 90,000 plant varieties, 685 species of birds, 260 fish, 1,132 butterflies, 80 mammals, and 50 reptiles.

Archaeological controversy. The April 18 publication of conclusions from 20 years of research at the *Caverna de Pedra Pintada* (Cave of the Painted Rock), an archaeological site on the north shore of the Amazon River, triggered a controversy among specialists in early tropical civilization. The report's author, archaeologist Anna C. Roosevelt, argued that Amazonian people sustained a stable and relatively sophisticated civilization over 11,000 years ago.

The cave, according to Roosevelt of Chicago's Field Museum of Natural History, was a gathering place for people who hunted small game, caught fish and turtles, and foraged for plants, nuts, and fruits. Moreover, they left behind painted artwork: a blazing comet, simple stick figures, and prints of their hands.

Roosevelt's arguments challenged the long-held theory about the migration of people down the American continents. According to that theory, big-game hunters lived on the North American plains about 11,000 years ago and eventually migrated to South America, continuing their hunting lifestyle in the temperate highlands, not in the tropics of the Amazon. Archeologist Betty J. Meggers of the Smithsonian Institution defended this theory. She argued that although the Amazon may have had a more moderate climate, allowing for small foraging cultures, the climate was too harsh and the resources too scarce to sustain the sizeable, sedentary population that Roosevelt claimed could have existed.

U.S. relations. During the 1996 election year, office-seekers of both major U.S. parties were anxious to demonstrate to American voters their toughness on three Latin American issues: drug-trafficking, illegal immigration, and oppression in Cuba. In January, President Bill Clinton appointed General Barry R. McCaffrey to direct the Office of National Drug Control Policy. McCaffrey, 53, was the former commander of the Southern Command in the Panama Canal Zone, a primary operation center for the confiscation of narcotics destined for U.S. markets.

On August 22, President Clinton signed legislation reforming federal welfare, which allowed states to

Facts in brief on Latin America

Country	Population	Government	Monetary unit*	Foreign trade (million U.S.$) Exports†	Imports†
Antigua and Barbuda	67,000	Governor General James B. Carlisle; Prime Minister Lester Bird	dollar (2.70 = $1)	40	246
Argentina	35,394,000	President Carlos Saúl Menem	peso (1.00 = $1)	20,967	20,123
Bahamas	284,000	Governor General Orville Turnquest; Prime Minister Hubert Ingraham	dollar (1.00 = $1)	1,517	1,801
Barbados	264,000	Governor General Sir Clifford Husbands; Prime Minister Owen Arthur	dollar (2.01 = $1)	235	760
Belize	226,000	Governor General Sir Colville Young; Prime Minister Manuel Esquivel	dollar (2.00 = $1)	158	258
Bolivia	7,764,000	President Gonzalo Sánchez de Lozada Bustamente	boliviano (5.19 = $1)	1,101	1,424
Brazil	166,844,000	President Fernando Henrique Cardoso	real (1.03 = $1)	46,506	53,783
Chile	14,670,000	President Eduardo Frei Ruíz-Tagle	peso (459.03 = $1)	16,039	15,914
Colombia	36,155,000	President Ernesto Samper Pizano	peso (1,013.90 = $1)	9,764	13,853
Costa Rica	3,567,000	President José Maria Figueres Olsen	colón (215.46 = $1)	2,577	3,252
Cuba	11,176,000	President Fidel Castro	peso (1.00 = $1)	2,050	2,185
Dominica	71,000	President Crispin Anselm Sorhaindo; Prime Minister Edison James	dollar (2.70 = $1)	56	111
Dominican Republic	8,083,000	President Leonel Fernández Reyna	peso (13.78 = $1)	765	2,976
Ecuador	11,460,000	President Abdala Bucarám Ortíz	sucre (3,321.00 = $1)	4,307	4,193
El Salvador	6,020,000	President Armando Calderon Sol	colón (8.76 = $1)	998	2,853
Grenada	93,000	Governor General Reginald Palmer; Prime Minister Keith Mitchell	dollar (2.70 = $1)	20	107
Guatemala	11,226,000	President Alvaro Arzú Irigoyen	quetzal (6.05 = $1)	1,522	2,604
Guyana	854,000	President Cheddi Jagan	dollar (138.90 = $1)	414	485
Haiti	7,479,000	President René Préval; Prime Minister Rosny Smarth	gourde (15.12 = $1)	154	696
Honduras	5,969,000	President Carlos Roberto Reina Idiáquez	lempira (12.70 = $1)	1,061	1,219
Jamaica	2,485,000	Governor General Sir Howard Cooke; Prime Minister P. J. Patterson	dollar (34.15 = $1)	1,191	2,161
Mexico	97,038,000	President Ernesto Zedillo Ponce de León	new peso (7.87 = $1)	48,430	46,756
Nicaragua	4,709,000	President José Arnoldo Alemán Lacayo	gold córdoba (8.74 = $1)	525	949
Panama	2,718,000	President Ernesto Pérez Balladares	balboa (1.00 = $1)	583	2,404
Paraguay	5,208,000	President Juan Carlos Wasmosy	guaraní (2,090.00 = $1)	817	2,370
Peru	24,668,000	President Alberto Fujimori	new sol (2.56 = $1)	5,575	9,224
Puerto Rico	3,733,000	Governor Pedro Rosselló	U.S. dollar	21,800	16,700
St. Kitts and Nevis	41,000	Governor General Clement Athelston Arrindell; Prime Minister Denzil Douglas	dollar (2.70 = $1)	27	110
St. Lucia	146,000	Governor General George Mallet; Prime Minister Vaughan Lewis	dollar (2.70 = $1)	123	313
St. Vincent and the Grenadines	114,000	Governor General David Jack; Prime Minister James F. Mitchell	dollar (2.70 = $1)	43	135
Suriname	432,000	President Jules Wijdenbosch	guilder (410.00 = $1)	472	472
Trinidad and Tobago	1,335,000	President Noor Hassanali; Prime Minister Basdeo Panday	dollar (6.15 = $1)	1,866	1,130
Uruguay	3,221,000	President Julio Maria Sanguinetti	peso (8.49 = $1)	2,117	2,867
Venezuela	22,777,000	President Rafael Caldera Rodríguez	bolívar (470.13 = $1)	16,744	9,291

*Exchange rates as of Oct. 25, 1996, or latest available data.
†Latest available data.

cut assistance to illegal immigrants. On August 27, California Governor Pete Wilson signed an executive order that ended illegal immigrants' access to certain state benefits, including public housing, prenatal care, and child-abuse programs.

Helms-Burton bill. In February, the Cuban military shot down two unarmed U.S. civilian airplanes. In response, the U.S. Congress adopted a get-tough position with Cuba. Congress by an overwhelming majority passed the Helms-Burton Bill, which President Clinton signed on March 12.

Sponsored by Senator Jesse Helms of North Carolina and Representative Dan Burton of Indiana, the legislation restrained any future president from loosening the embargo on Cuba, which had been decreed by executive order in 1962. The law also penalized foreign companies that invested in property expropriated from American citizens after the 1959 Communist takeover in Cuba.

Several European and Western Hemisphere countries protested the new law. Both Canada and Mexico argued that it conflicted with the North American Free Trade Agreement. In Panama at the June 4 General Assembly of the Organization of American States, 23 of the 34 member nations approved a resolution condemning the law.   □ Nathan A. Haverstock

See also articles on the individual nations. In *World Book,* see **Latin America** and articles on the individual nations.

Latvia. In 1996, a new coalition government, headed by Prime Minister Andris Skele, was in power in Latvia. Skele, a businessman with no party affiliation, was the third person in three months to be invited to form a government by President Guntis Ulmanis. Skele's Cabinet included members from all of the parliament's major parties. In June, President Ulmanis was elected to another three-year term.

In June, Skele and the leaders of Estonia and Lithuania criticized the United States for renegotiating the 1992 Agreement on Conventional Forces in Europe with Russia. The United States agreed to allow up to 600 Russian armored vehicles to remain in the Pskov district, a Russian region on the Latvian border, until 1999. The Baltic leaders argued that the vehicles threatened their security.

In August 1996, the parliament passed a resolution stating that Soviet rule from 1940 to 1991 "amounted to an occupation of Latvia." The resolution also stated that the district of Abrene, the focus of ongoing negotiations with Russia, was unlawfully incorporated into Russia in 1944, when both countries were part of the Soviet Union. In response, Russian officials canceled Prime Minister Skele's scheduled visit to Moscow.   □ Steven L. Solnick

See also **Estonia; Europe** (Facts in brief table). In *World Book,* see **Latvia.**
Law. See **Civil Rights; Courts; Supreme Court of the United States.**

Lebanon. Lebanon, still recovering from the devastating 1975-1991 civil war, suffered a new setback in 1996 when Israel launched an intense aerial and artillery attack on southern Lebanon on April 11. Israel said it acted in retaliation for rocket attacks on northern Israel by the pro-Iranian Hezbollah, an Islamic fundamentalist guerrilla group. While the United States quietly supported the Israeli military campaign, international criticism intensified after April 18, when Israeli artillery killed more than 100 Lebanese people and injured another 100 at a United Nations compound in Qana, Lebanon. The victims, including women and children, were among some 500,000 refugees who had fled their homes during earlier Israeli attacks.

Fearful that the bombing would derail the Arab-Israeli peace process, the United States brokered a cease-fire on April 27. By then, some 200 Lebanese had been killed and more than 400 wounded. The raids caused an estimated $500 million in damage to Lebanese infrastructure, as Israel targeted bridges, roads, water storage facilities, public buildings, and two electrical substations in addition to guerrilla bases. This was a heavy blow to the government of Lebanese Prime Minister Rafik Hariri, whose multibillion-dollar development program to repair damage from the civil war doubled public debt to $8.3 billion between 1993 and mid-1996.

Elections. Pro-Syrian candidates swept the September elections for the 128-member parliament. The results were expected to bolster the government of Hariri, who won a seat along with 20 supporters. The elections were marred by charges of fraud and undue influence by Syria, which in 1996 kept 35,000 troops in Lebanon.

Social unrest. On February 29, the government blocked a general strike of 120,000 public workers when Lebanon's 50,000-strong army enforced a curfew for the first time since 1984. The workers had demanded a 76-percent pay increase, the repeal of a 1993 ban on demonstrations, and the end of a plan to close dozens of radio and television stations. The government had ordered some 200 radio and television stations to cease broadcasting by Nov. 30, 1996, and announced that only 4 private television stations and 12 radio stations would be licensed after that date. All stations granted licenses belonged to prominent businessmen and politicians, including Hariri.

Samir Geagea, once head of the powerful Christian militia Lebanese Forces, was charged in August with the 1987 murder of Prime Minister Rashid Karami. Geagea, who was already serving two life sentences for murder, had been the most prominent critic of Lebanon's pro-Syria government.

□ Christine Helms

See also **Middle East** (Facts in brief table); **Syria.** In *World Book,* see **Lebanon.**
Lesotho. See **Africa.**

Liberia. Prospects for a peaceful resolution to Liberia's civil war fared dismally during the first eight months of 1996. By the end of the year, however, hopes again ran high that the end of fighting and chaos was at hand.

Liberia's civil war began in 1989 when forces led by Charles Taylor attempted to overthrow Samuel Doe's military government. The war degenerated into a struggle between remnants of the Liberian army, Taylor's militia, and forces of several other ethnically-based groups. While Doe was overthrown and killed in 1990, the war continued. By 1996, the country was ravaged: The economy was destroyed; 80 percent of the population were refugees; and more than 150,000 people were dead.

Early in 1996, fighting broke out between the Nigerian-led peacekeeping army, ECOMOG, and a Liberian rebel group, Ulimo-J, led by Roosevelt Johnson. This clash undermined the Abuja Agreement, a peace plan that Liberia's warring factions had signed in August 1995. Many observers suspected that these groups were fighting over control of diamond smuggling north of Monrovia.

Fighting in the capital. By March 1996, rival Liberian groups were again at war in the countryside. On April 6, factional forces attempted to arrest Roosevelt Johnson in Monrovia, triggering large-scale fighting within the city, and chaos ensued. International agencies began evacuating foreign-aid workers on April 9. The United States

Child soldiers, used increasingly by Liberia's factional militias, patrol the streets of Monrovia, the capital, during the intense fighting in April.

flew many foreign nationals and even some Liberians out of the country. Crowds fled to the American embassy compound, where 20,000 people eventually took refuge.

A truce agreed to on April 19 lasted only a few days. By April 30, fighting was again widespread in Monrovia. U.S. Marines were forced to shoot into the crowds in the streets to protect the embassy compound. Thousands of Monrovians, attempting to escape the chaos and prospects of starvation and disease, boarded ships in the harbor. A few refugee-crowded ships managed to reach ports in nearby West African countries, where they posed serious dilemmas for local officials. Other ships were forced to return to Monrovia.

A new peace plan. Liberia's factional leaders agreed to a cease-fire in July and met with West African leaders in Abuja, Nigeria, in August to draft a new peace plan. The plan maintained the existing ruling structure. Ruth Perry, a woman who had once been a Liberian senator, was appointed head of state. The plan also called for demobilization of the militias by January 1997 and the scheduling of elections for May 1997. Prospects for the new agreement depended upon acceptance by the Liberian factions and strong international support for demobilization.   □ Mark DeLancey

See also **Africa** (Facts in brief table); **Nigeria.** In *World Book,* see **Liberia.**

Library.
A major concern for librarians in 1996 was that new technology continued to widen the gap between the "information rich" and the "information poor." Since people in many U.S. households did not own a computer—especially those living in rural areas and central cities—librarians worked to ensure that the nation's schools and libraries provide free and open access to information in all formats.

How connected are libraries? A 1996 survey by the National Commission on Libraries and Information Science, an independent agency of the U.S. government located in Washington, D.C., found that 44.6 percent of public libraries in 1996 were connected to some degree to the Internet, a global web of computer networks that operate over telephone lines, compared with 20.9 percent in 1994. However, only about 28 percent of public libraries were able to offer patrons access to the Internet and less than 25 percent were able to offer graphical access to the World Wide Web (the Web). The Web is a graphically oriented portion of the Internet. Of those libraries not yet connected to the Web, 60 percent expected to be by 1997.

Corporate aid in 1996 helped many libraries to reinvent themselves for the information age. The Microsoft Corporation of Redmond, Washington, launched a pilot project called Libraries Online! with the American Library Association (ALA) of Chicago. The project was designed to encourage research and develop new approaches for extending information technologies to underserved populations. The program funded demonstration projects in nine library systems and covered the cost of computer hardware, software, telecommunication, administrative and technical support, and staff training. In October 1996, Microsoft Chairman Bill Gates announced his intention to build on the successful pilot with a $10.5-million Libraries Online! initiative that would connect 41 more public library systems.

The MCI Foundation, a charitable organization established by MCI Communications Corp., invested $750,000 in Library-LINK, a three-year project with the ALA to help advance the technological capabilities of the nation's public libraries. Approximately 25 public library systems were to receive MCI Library-LINK grants and training between 1995 and 1997.

The Ameritech Foundation of Chicago, funded by telecommunications company Ameritech Corp., made a $2-million grant to the Library of Congress's National Digital Library (NDL) in April 1996. The NDL planned to make 5 million documents available over the Internet by 2000. The Ameritech funds were to be used to digitize primary sources that document American history from libraries across the country.

NetDay96. In March 1996, NetDay96, a public-private partnership to connect California's schools to the Internet, organized thousands of volunteers to wire 3,000 California schools and their libraries. President Bill Clinton and Vice President Al Gore were NetDay volunteers, working to connect Ygnacio Valley High School in Concord, California, to the Internet. Local companies donated wiring kits, and hundreds of engineers pitched in from local universities. NetDay96 continued throughout the year as a national grass-roots effort to wire schools so that they could network their computers and connect them to the Internet. The goal was to wire at least five classrooms and a library in every school in the United States by the fall of 1996.

The Telecommunications Reform Bill of 1996, which deregulated segments of the telecommunications industry, mandated affordable telecommunications rates for libraries, schools, and rural health care providers. In October, the Clinton Administration asked the Federal Communications Commission to mandate free Internet access and basic telecommunications services for schools and libraries.

The San Francisco Public Library's new main building opened in April with 300 public-access computer terminals. However, controversy over whether the library should concentrate on providing electronic access or more books raged when novelist Nicholson Baker in the Oct. 14, 1996, issue of *The New Yorker* accused the library of dumping thousands of books in its move to the high-tech library building.   □ Peggy Barber

See also **Internet; Telecommunications.** In *World Book,* see **Library.**

Libyan dictator Muammar al-Qadhafi greets Palestinian leader Yasir Arafat at a summit meeting of Muslim, Middle Eastern leaders held in Cairo in June.

Libya. Antigovernment violence in Libya in 1996 led observers to speculate about the stability of Muammar Muhammad al-Qadhafi's regime. In March, armed Libyan rebels clashed with security forces trying to recapture escaped prisoners near Benghazi, Libya's second-largest city. On July 9, a soccer riot in the Libyan capital of Tripoli left 50 people dead and scores of people injured. The riot began when the bodyguards of Qadhafi's son fired on spectators denouncing Qadhafi. In August, Libyan fighter jets reportedly bombed rebel hideouts near the Mediterranean port of Darnah.

The United Nations had placed economic sanctions on Libya in 1992 for its refusal to turn over agents indicted for the 1988 terrorist bombing of Pan Am Flight 103 over Lockerbie, Scotland. Libya has since come under increasing international pressure. In May 1996, the U.S. Congress passed an antiterrorism law that enabled relatives of Flight 103 victims to file a $1-billion class-action suit against Libya. Another U.S. law passed in 1996 mandated sanctions against foreign firms that invest heavily in Libya's oil industry.

In April, the United States threatened Libya with military action for allegedly building a chemical weapons factory in a mountain 40 miles (64 kilometers) outside Tripoli. □ Christine Helms

See also **Africa** (Facts in brief table). In *World Book,* see **Libya.**

Literature. The 1996 Nobel Prize for Literature was awarded to the 73-year-old Polish poet Wislawa Szymborska, formerly a prominent figure in the Solidarity campaign, but hitherto little known outside her own country. Much of her work belongs to an Eastern European tradition of parable-writing and demonstrates similarities with the writings of Poland's 1980 Nobel laureate, Czeslaw Milosz.

The United Kingdom. Historical themes continued to be particularly popular with novelists in 1996. Beryl Bainbridge's *Every Man for Himself* offered a fictional treatment of the maiden voyage of the *Titanic.* Lynne Truss's *Tennyson's Gift* poked fun at a number of famous Victorians who in the novel come together on the Isle of Wight during the summer of 1864. Shena Mackay's *The Orchard on Fire* offered a vivid picture of rural England in 1953, in which a school-girl heroine discovers the dark underside of a seemingly tranquil country town.

The recent vogue for spinoffs from literary classics continued in 1996 with sequels to Jane Austen's *Emma:* Emma Tennant's *Emma in Love* and Rachel Billington's *Perfect Happiness.* Tennant's *Elinor and Marianne* was a continuation of Austen's *Sense and Sensibility.* Glyn Hughes's *Brontë* and Peter Ackroyd's *Milton in America* took their departure points from writers in British literary history.

The year was notable for novels by distinguished women writers: Margaret Drabble's *The Witch of Ex-*

moor; Muriel Spark's *Reality and Dreams;* Penelope Lively's *Credo;* Doris Lessing's *Love, Again;* Fay Weldon's *Worst Fears;* and A. S. Byatt's *Babel Tower.*

Graham Swift won the Booker Prize for his novel *Last Orders,* generally regarded as his finest book since *Waterland* (1983). *Last Orders* tells the story of four Londoners who delve into their pasts as they travel to the coastal city of Margate to scatter the ashes of a friend, as his will has requested. Moving between the somber and the comic, Swift reveals the extraordinariness of ordinary lives. The Booker Prize recognizes writers from the British Commonwealth countries and former British colonies.

Ulster poet Seamus Deane's semiautobiographical novel *Reading in the Dark,* gives a graphic account of growing up in Londonderry in the 1940's and 1950's. Its boy narrator lives as much in a fantasy world as in the real world, but he gradually discovers how much political events have affected his own family's life. Other notable Irish novels of 1996 included Edna O'Brien's *Down by the River* and William Trevor's *After Rain.*

Notable collections of poetry included Craig Raine's *Clay: Whereabouts Unknown,* Christopher Logue's *Selected Poems,* John Fuller's *Stones and Fire,* Charles Boyle's *Paleface,* and U. A. Fanthorpe's *Safe as Houses.* The 1995 Nobel Prize winner, Seamus Heaney, won the 1996 Forward Prize for his poetry collection, *The Spirit Level,* which draws parallels between Greece and Ireland as a device for exploring the possibility of balance between competing forces in Northern Ireland.

Other European countries. Czech writer Milan Kundera, best known for his black comedy *The Unbearable Lightness of Being* (translated in 1984), published a collection of essays, *Testaments Betrayed,* as well as *Slowness,* a novel with two contrasting narratives that take place in a château in France. One, set in the 1700's, tells the story of the sexual education of a young nobleman; the other tells a contemporary story of a group of intellectuals gathered for a conference.

Interest in one of Italy's most highly regarded writers, Italo Calvino, continued unabated in 1996. A two-volume, 3,000-page collection of Calvino's nonfiction prose, which covered much of his output of literary criticism, was published during the year.

West Indies and Latin America. Three significant novels by British-based Guyanese writers appeared in 1996. Wilson Harris based *Jonestown* on the 1978 mass suicide and murder of the followers of the American "People's Temple" cult in Guyana's interior. Fred D'Aguiar's *Dear Future* moves between a thinly veiled version of Guyana and London, exposing political corruption in the former through the story of a boy's "visionary capacity." David Dabydeen's novel *The Counting House,* set in the 1800's, follows the fortunes of a young Italian couple who travel halfway around the world

to become indentured laborers on a plantation.

Earl Lovelace's first novel in 12 years, *Salt,* gives an account of ordinary people in Trinidad trying to attain "personhood" in the wake of a history dominated by slavery and abuses. Like some of Lovelace's other work, the story draws heavily on *Carnival* (pre-Lenten festival) images and gives a vivid picture of Trinidadian folk life.

James Woodall's *The Man in the Mirror of the Book* depicts the life of Argentine writer Jorge Luis Borges, one of the masters of modern short fiction. The Peruvian writer Mario Vargas Llosa published *Making Waves,* a collection of essays on literary and political topics, and *Death in the Andes,* a novel set in a remote part of his homeland.

In the United States, the 1996 National Book Award for fiction went to Andrea Barrett's *Ship Fever and Other Stories.* This collection of short stories weaves fictional and historical characters from the 1800's in their searches for truths about science and the human heart. The nonfiction winner was James Carroll's *An American Requiem: God, My Father, and the War that Came Between Us,* an autobiographical account of Carroll's priesthood in the Roman Catholic Church and his father's illustrious military career during the Vietnam War. Hayden Carruth's *Scrambled Eggs and Whiskey: Poems 1991–1995* won the poetry award. In the new National Book Award category of literature for young people, the winner was Victor Martinez's *Parrott in the Oven: Mi Vida,* the story of a young boy who learns to rise above the conflicts of his troubled family. Toni Morrison, the winner of the 1993 Nobel Prize for literature, received the 1996 National Book Foundation Medal for her contributions to American literature.

The Pulitzer Prize-winning novel of 1996 was Richard Ford's *Independence Day.* In this sequel to the 1986 *The Sportswriter,* Frank Bascombe, in the midst of a midlife crisis, spends a memorable Fourth of July with his troubled son. Jorie Graham's *The Dream of the Unified Field: Selected Poems* won the Pultizer Prize for poetry. American poet John Ashbery, praising Graham's collection, claimed the work was an "utterance that swings with the conviction of [William] Blake's." The award for biography went to Jack Miles's *God: A Biography,* which is not a biography in the traditional sense. Using techniques of literary analysis, Miles describes the multifaceted and developing character of God in the Hebrew Bible.

Another notable novel in 1996 was Amy Tan's *The Hundred Secret Senses,* which, like her previous novels, contrasts the lives of Chinese Americans born in the United States with those born in their ancestral homeland. This newest novel, which builds on a 100-year-old ghost story, contrasts the lives of two half-sisters who grew up in different countries.

David Foster Wallace's novel *Infinite Jest* was hailed as a powerful study of addiction, but the story also satirizes numerous aspects of American life, including politics and sports. Uncommon to the style of a novel, this mammoth text included over 400 footnotes.

One of the most highly regarded U.S. novelists, John Updike, produced what may come to be lauded as his most impressive achievement, *In the Beauty of the Lilies.* This saga, which begins in 1910, follows four generations of the Wilmot family and chronicles the secularization of American society and religion.

Frank McCourt's *Angela's Ashes: A Memoir* tells the story of the McCourt family's journey in the 1930's from the United States back to their native Ireland. In this promising debut, McCourt recalls childhood memories with dignity and humor despite the desperate poverty his family endures.

Laura E. Skandera-Trombley's *Mark Twain and the Company of Women,* a biographical account of Twain's life with his wife and three daughters, investigates the influence the four women had on his fiction. Other notable contributions to American literary biography included Jeffery Myers's *Robert Frost* and Robin G. Schultze's *The Web of Friendship: Marianne Moore and Wallace Stevens.*

Canada. In 1996, Canada's most famous living novelist, Margaret Atwood, published *Alias Grace,* a fictional account of the life of Grace Marks, a servant who was condemned to death for murder in the 1800's and subsequently reprieved. Atwood's attempt to solve the riddle surrounding the servant's identity draws on two popular feminine art forms of the 1800's: the keepsake album and the patchwork quilt.

The year was also distinguished by the publication of Alice Munro's retrospective collection *Selected Stories.* The works of Munro, one of Canada's best fiction writers, reveal the truths and often the darkness in the ordinary events of life.

Jack Hodgins's *The Macken Charm* uses a Vancouver Island wake and funeral as the starting point for a rich account of a larger-than-life family.

Chinese Canadian writer Evelyn Lau published her first novel, *Other Women,* a story of a failed love affair and the woman's all-consuming fantasies that will not let her forget her lover.

Australia and New Zealand. The year 1996 was notable for two particularly impressive Australian novels. In David Foster's *The Glade Within the Grove,* a Utopian commune founded by a group in 1968 is seen by one of the characters as a kind of "White Dreamtime," similar to the mythic time of Aboriginal folklore. David Malouf followed the success of his 1993 novel *Remembering Babylon* with *The Conversations at Curlow Creek,* which explores the Celtic legacy in Australia through a dialogue between an Irish convict about to be hanged and the Irish leader of the soldiers responsible for his execution.

Helen Garner, a writer best known for *Monkey Grip,* a classic novel about addiction, published a fine collection of essays, *True Stories.* Mudrooroo (formerly known as Colin Johnson), Australia's best-known Aboriginal writer, published *Us Mob—Struggle: An Introduction to Indigenous Australia.* Janette Turner Hospital's novel *Oyster* laid bare the violent and secretive past of a small Queensland town. Michael Wilding, a leading exponent of the new Australian short fiction that emerged in the late 1960's, compiled 30 years of this writing in *Somewhere New: New and Selected Stories.* Thomas Keneally, the author of *Schindler's List,* published a memoir of his youth, *Homebush Boy.* A collected edition of the poems of one of Australia's finest living writers, Dorothy Hewett, also appeared in 1996.

In Barbara Anderson's *The House Guest,* three very different New Zealanders try to unravel the mystery surrounding an American novelist who briefly stayed in the childhood home of one of the characters. Judy Corballis's *Tapu* gives a fictional account of an English missionary family sent to New Zealand to convert Maoris in the early 1800's.

Asia. Since the publication of Salman Rushdie's *Midnight's Children* in 1981, Indian fiction in English had undergone a remarkable upsurge. Two major Indian novels in English were published in 1996. The Canadian-based writer Rohinton Mistry won the Commonwealth Writers Prize for *A Fine Balance.* In this novel set in the 1970's, four very different characters come together in a Bombay flat during a "State of Internal Emergency" announced by Indira Gandhi. As they tell their stories, a picture of their past lives emerges, and their subsequent destinies prove to be linked in complex and unexpected ways. Amitav Ghosh published *The Calcutta Chromosome,* a novel about a computer clerk fascinated by a particular chapter in the history of malaria research.

An Echo of Heaven, by the Japanese writer Kenzaburo Oe, the 1994 Nobel Prize winner, was published in translation in 1996.

Africa. The Noma Award for Publishing in Africa was won by Kitia Touré from Ivory Coast. Touré's novel, *Destins Paralleles,* offers a panoramic critique of the corruption and inequalities of Ivorian society. Ben Okri's novel *Dangerous Love,* also reflecting the contemporary social disillusion felt by many African writers, deals with a young painter coming of age in a Nigeria of slums and the destitute.

The work of Salih al-Tayyib, one of Sudan's finest writers, became available to English-language readers with the translation of his novel *Bandarshah* in 1996. Using the same village setting as his earlier novel, *Season of Migration to the North,* the new novel comprises two linked stories in which the characters struggle to lead moral lives. Abdulrazak Gurnah treated a rather different subject in *Admiring Silence,* in which the alienated narrator who has lived in the United Kingdom for many years returns to his native Zanzibar in a largely futile attempt to find a sense of purpose and a homeland.　　□ John Thieme

See also **Canadian literature; Poetry; Pulitzer Prizes.** In *World Book,* see **Literature.**

Literature for children. The trend toward publishing multicultural books for children continued in 1996, and more historical fiction for children was published as well. Outstanding books of 1996 included the following:

Picture books. *The Paperboy* by Dav Pilkey (Orchard Bks.). The love of a paperboy for his dog shines in this tale of a typical morning. Ages 4 to 10.

The Aunt in Our House by Angela Johnson, illustrated by David Soman (Orchard Bks.). An aunt comes to stay and, despite her own sadness, brightens and warms the house. Ages 5 to 8.

The Butterfly Alphabet by Kjell B. Sandved (Scholastic). The alphabet is revealed on the wings of moths and butterflies in this stunning book of photographs. Ages 4 and up.

Cousin Ruth's Tooth by Amy MacDonald, illustrated by Marjorie Priceman (Houghton Mifflin). When Cousin Ruth loses a tooth, all of her zany relatives pitch in to help, just as they did in MacDonald's previous book, *Rachel Fister's Blister*. Ages 5 to 8.

When Willard Met Babe Ruth by Donald Hall, illustrated by Barry Moser (Harcourt Brace). Hall offers a nostalgic look at America through the eyes of Willard, a boy who meets Babe Ruth. When he grows up, Willard names his daughter Ruth after the legendary baseball player. Ages 7 and up.

Seeing Stars by Sharleen Collicott (Dial). Luminous paintings highlight the adventures of two animal friends who think they are going to the stars but end up in the sea. Ages 3 to 7.

The Toy Brother by William Steig (HarperCollins). A boy who tinkers in his father's lab and makes a potion that shrinks him must depend on his younger brother for help. Ages 5 to 8.

Wiley and the Hairy Man retold by Judy Sierra, illustrated by Brian Pinkney (Lodestar). In this Alabama folktale, Wiley must trick the Hairy Man three times in order to be rid of him. Ages 5 to 9.

When Birds Could Talk and Bats Could Sing by Virginia Hamilton, illustrated by Barry Moser (Scholastic). Tales from the author's African American heritage offer humor and wit and are illustrated in bright water colors. All ages.

The Six Servants by Jacob and Wilhelm Grimm, translated by Anthea Bell, illustrated by Sergei Goloshapov (North-South Bks.). Dark, dramatic illustrations set the mood for this tale of a prince and his helpers who try to win the princess. Ages 5 to 8.

Near Myths: Dug Up & Dusted Off by Robert Kraus (Viking). These spoofs of mythical characters are especially amusing if the reader knows the originals. Ages 8 to 10.

Crawlies Creep by David Pelham (Dutton). Delightful animals are brought to life through pop-ups, fold-out pages, and rhyming text. Ages 2 to 5.

The Old Man Who Loved Cheese by Garrison Keillor, illustrated by Anne Wilsdorf (Little, Brown). A man who loved the worst-smelling cheese loses his family in this hilarious story told in rhyme. All ages.

The Bunyans by Audrey Wood, illustrated by David Shannon (Scholastic). Paul Bunyon marries and has two children, both giants, and their antics result in many natural wonders. Ages 5 to 8.

Now I will Never Leave the Dinner Table by Jane Read Martin and Patricia Marx, illustrated by Roz Chast (HarperCollins). Patty Jane invents revenge when her baby-sitter sister makes her taste the spinach before she can leave the table. Ages 4 to 8.

White Wave: A Chinese Tale retold by Diane Wolkstein, illustrated by Ed Young (Harcourt Brace). A lonely farmer finds a magic snail that changes his life, but greed destroys his happiness. Ages 3 to 7.

The Bobbin Girl by Emily Arnold McCully (Dial). Rebecca, 10, works all day in a mill in 19th-century Lowell, Massachusetts, where conditions are terrible. The women walk out, and Rebecca does, too, although her family needs the money. Ages 6 to 9.

The Thanksgiving Visitor by Truman Capote, illustrated by Beth Peck (Knopf). Detailed paintings bring to life this autobiographical tale of a family gathering in 1932 rural Alabama. Ages 10 to 12.

Sam and the Tigers: A Retelling of Little Black Sambo by Julius Lester, illustrated by Jerry Pinkney (Dial). In this rich version of the 100-year-old tale, all of the characters are named Sam, and in the end, the

Officer Buckle and Gloria, the story of a policeman who gives boring safety tips and a dog who helps him, wins the 1996 Caldecott Medal for author and illustrator Peggy Rathman.

boy, Sam, is gloriously victorious. Ages 4 to 8.

Fiction. *Bruises* by Anke De Vries, translated by Stacey Knecht (Front Street/Lemniscaat). In this Dutch award-winner, Judith, abused by her mother, finds a friend and the courage to speak out. Ages 12 and up.

Sees Behind Trees by Michael Dorris (Hyperion). Walnut, a young Native American boy of the 1500's yearns for a grown-up name, but the partially sighted boy cannot prove himself worthy in the traditional ways. The elderly Gray Fire helps him to find his own way to adulthood. Ages 8 to 11.

Send Me Down a Miracle by Han Nolan (Harcourt Brace). When an artistic newcomer sees a vision, the preacher's daughter, Charity, is torn between independence and obeying her father. Ages 12 and up.

Black Horses for the King by Anne McCaffrey (Harcourt Brace). The book follows Galwyn's adventures working with the special horses brought by the future King Arthur to England to help rid the country of the hated Saxons. Ages 12 and up.

Mothers & Other Strangers by Budge Wilson (Harcourt Brace). This collection of stories provides a powerful study of nine characters, ages 18 to 77, and the turning points in their lives. Ages 12 and up.

Beyond the Western Sea: Book I, The Escape from Home; Book II, Lord Kirkle's Money by Avi (Orchard Bks.). In Book I, Maura and Patrick flee the potato famine in Ireland, and Laurence runs away from his grand home because of an unjust beating. The children board a ship in Liverpool for America, where their adventures continue in Book II. Ages 11 to 14.

Bad Girls by Cynthia Voigt (Scholastic). Mikey and Margalo are two newly enrolled fifth-grade girls who cause all sorts of problems in their school. Ages 8 to 12.

Officer Buckle knew more safety tips than anyone else in Napville.

Every time he thought of a new one, he thumbtacked it to his bulletin board.

Safety Tip #77

NEVER stand on a SWIVEL CHAIR.

Step by Wicked Step by Anne Fine (Little, Brown). An old diary in a spooky house prompts five children to reveal the problems in their own lives, and they discover what they have in common. Ages 9 to 12.

The Ornament Tree by Jean Thesman (Houghton Mifflin). Orphaned 14-year-old Bonnie moves in with cousins in 1918 Seattle and encounters boarders, money problems, and a special tree. Ages 12 and up.

Granny the Pag by Nina Bawden (Clarion). Catriona was raised by her leather-wearing, Harley-riding Gran. When her parents want her to live with them, a bitter custody battle ensues. Ages 9 to 12.

The Ballad of Lucy Whipple by Karen Cushman (Clarion). When Lucy's mother moves the family to a California mining camp in 1849, Lucy saves her money to get back to Massachusetts. Ages 10 to 14.

Jip, His Story by Katherine Paterson (Lodestar). The tale of Jip, an orphan on a "poor farm" in Vermont in 1855, conveys that period's attitudes toward poverty, mental illness, and education and provides a shocking conclusion. Ages 10 to 14.

Fantasy. *Zoe Rising* by Pam Conrad (HarperCollins). In this sequel to *Stonewords*, Zoe, at summer camp with friend Jedidiah, finds herself once more drawn back in time to disturbing episodes. Ages 9 and up.

Cold Shoulder Road by Joan Aiken (Delacorte). The spellbinding adventures of Is Twite and her cousin Arun involve smugglers and kidnappers and a mysterious sect. Ages 10 and up.

The Beduin's Gazelle by Frances Temple (Orchard Bks.). The sequel to *The Ramsay Scallop* focuses on two betrothed desert cousins, Halima and Aitayah, an uncle who tries to keep them apart, and a sheikh who wants Halima for his bride. Ages 12 and up.

The Wanderings of Odysseus: The Story of the Odyssey by Rosemary Sutcliff, illustrated by Alan Lee (Delacorte). This retelling of *The Odyssey* is illustrated with fine water colors. All ages.

The Son of Summer Stars by Meredith Ann Pierce (Little, Brown). In this last book of the Firebringer trilogy, Prince Jan of the unicorns sets out after his father and learns a crushing secret from him. Ages 12 and up.

Waterbound by Jane Stemp (Dial). Gem discovers a secret passage to an underground place, where the disabled and disfigured who were banished by the city have established the community of Waterbound. Ages 12 and up.

Nutcracker by E. T. A. Hoffmann, illustrated by Roberto Innocenti (Harcourt Brace). Dramatic paintings highlight the original Hoffmann tales. All ages.

Found by June Oldham (Orchard Bks.). In the frightening 21st century, Ren is sent from home, finds an abandoned baby, and learns to survive with the help of other outcasts. Ages 12 and up.

Poetry. *The Goof Who Invented Homework: And Other School Poems* by Kalli Dakos, illustrated by Denise Brunkus (Dial). This collection of 36 mostly funny poems recounts what can happen at school. Ages 7 to 11.

Food Fight: Poets Join the Fight Against Hunger with Poems To Favorite Foods edited by Michael J. Rosen (Harcourt Brace). Children's poets present 33 new works in this wide-ranging collection. All ages.

On the Wing by Douglas Florian (Harcourt Brace). Delightful, imaginative bird poems are combined with accurate paintings. Ages 4 to 8.

Sawgrass Poems: A View of the Everglades by Frank Asch, illustrated by Ted Levin (Harcourt Brace). Superb color photos and poems capture life and scenes in the threatened Everglades. Ages 5 to 9.

Make a Joyful Sound: Poems for Children by African-American Poets edited by Deborah Slier, illustrated by Cornelius Van Wright & Ying-Hwa Hu (Scholastic). A fine range of poets and subjects makes this a welcome collection. All ages.

Echoes for the Eye: Poems to Celebrate Patterns in Nature by Barbara Juster Esbensen, illustrated by Helen K. Davie (HarperCollins). Verse and water colors explore spirals in ferns and hurricanes, branches in veins and lightning, polygons in honeycombs, and more. Ages 8 to 12.

Falling Up by Shel Silverstein (HarperCollins). More comical drawings and poems continue the tradition of *Where the Sidewalk Ends* and *A Light in the Attic*. All ages.

Nonfiction books. *Ever Heard of an Aardwolf?* by Madeline Moser, illustrated by Barry Moser (Harcourt Brace). Striking engravings accompany brief descriptions of 20 unusual creatures. All ages.

The Bone Detectives by Donna M. Jackson, illustrated by Charlie Fellenbaum (Little, Brown). An actual murder is solved as forensic specialists reconstruct the victim's identity from skeletal remains. Ages 10 to 14.

Roman Numerals I to MM by Arthur Geisert (Houghton Mifflin). Pigs and other things are counted to show what the different letters of Roman numerals mean. Ages 7 to 9.

Squishy, Misty, Damp & Muddy: The In-Between World of Wetlands by Molly Cone (Sierra Club). Superb color photos and simple text reveal the importance of wetlands. Ages 6 to 9.

The Magic School Bus: Inside a Beehive by Joanna Cole, illustrated by Bruce Degen (Scholastic). Ms. Frizzle's students explore a beehive in a unique way, just as they did in *Inside a Hurricane* and *In the Time of the Dinosaurs*. Ages 8 and up.

Accidents May Happen: Fifty Inventions Discovered by Mistake by Charlotte Foltz Jones, illustrated by John O'Brien (Delacorte). This companion volume to *Mistakes that Worked* reveals how various things, including foods, toys, and paper were invented. Ages 8 and up.

Bill Pickett, Rodeo-Ridin' Cowboy by Andrea Pinkney, illustrated by Brian Pinkney (Harcourt Brace). Young Bill meets the challenge of wrestling steers and becomes famous as a rodeo cowboy. Ages 5 and up.

Stephen Biesty's Incredible Explosions by Richard Platt (DK Publishing). Twelve subjects, including a space station, windmill, Venice, and the human body, are opened and explained, revealing their inner workings. All ages.

Puppies, Dogs, and Blue Northers by Gary Paulsen, illustrated by Ruth Paulsen (Harcourt Brace). The story of how Paulsen's sled-dog puppies were raised (or raised him) leaves the reader wanting more. All ages.

Anastasia's Album compiled by Hugh Brewster (Hyperion). This collection of photographs of the youngest daughter of the last czar of Russia, from birth through her days as a prisoner of the revolutionaries, includes her own and her family's writings and provides insight into their lives. Ages 10 to 13.

Awards. Karen Cushman won the 1996 Newbery Medal for her novel *The Midwife's Apprentice*. The award is given by the American Library Association (ALA) for "the most distinguished contribution to children's literature" published the previous year. The ALA's Caldecott Medal for "the most distinguished American picture book for children" was awarded to Peggy Rathmann for *Officer Buckle and Gloria*.   □ Marilyn Fain Apseloff

In *World Book*, see **Caldecott Medal**; **Newbery Medal**; **Literature for children**.

Lithuania. In January 1996, Prime Minister Adolfas Slezevicius admitted to having shifted his personal savings only days before Lithuania's two largest commercial banks were declared insolvent in December 1995. President Algirdas Brazauskas demanded Slezevicius's resignation on Jan. 29, 1996, but the prime minister refused. On February 8, the parliament—including many members of Slezevicius's own Democratic Labor Party (DLP)—voted to remove Slezevicius from office. In his place, Brazauskas named economist Mindaugas Stankevicius, a minister in Slezevicius's Cabinet and a DLP member.

In June, Lithuania joined its neighbors Latvia and Estonia in protesting a decision by the United States to permit Russia to station up to 600 armored vehicles in a region bordering the Baltic States. Vytautas Landsbergis, leader of the Conservative Party, the DLP's chief opposition, suggested that Europe should provide the Baltic States with 600 antitank missiles to balance the Russian forces.

In parliamentary elections held on October 20, Lithuania's voters ousted the liberal DLP in favor of Landsbergis's nationalist Conservative Party. Landsbergis, who had been president of Lithuania during the 1991 breakup of the former Soviet Union, became the country's new prime minister.

□ Steven L. Solnick

See also **Latvia**; **Estonia**; **Europe** (Facts in brief table). In *World Book*, see **Lithuania**.

Los Angeles. On June 4, 1996, the Los Angeles City Council approved Mayor Richard J. Riordan's $4 billion budget. The budget allocated 49 percent of city funds for police and security, 18 percent for fire protection, 5 percent for sanitation, and the balance for administrative costs.

The mayor pledged to reinvigorate Hollywood, the once-fabled movie capital. While Hollywood has continued to attract 6 million tourists a year, its run-down condition prompted a plan calling for better street lighting, sidewalk benches, and increased street maintenance.

More public clinics. Los Angeles County announced on September 8 an ambitious program that would more than double—from 39 to 83—the number of outpatient medical clinics in the county. The plan fulfilled promises made in 1995 to the federal government in return for a bailout of the county's troubled public health system. The plan called for a shrinking of the expensive hospital system and a new focus on primary and preventive care at neighborhood clinics. Private medical groups would join the county facilities to care for the poor and those lacking health insurance.

Crime and punishment. The city council passed a ban in 1996 on the manufacture and sale of cheap handguns, known as Saturday night specials, within Los Angeles city limits. In 1995, the L.A. Police Department confiscated more than 1,400 of the "specials" that were all made in southern California. The measure, inspired by a similar law in West Hollywood, came seven years after Los Angeles banned the sale of assault rifles.

Meanwhile, the Twin Towers, an ultramodern $373-million jail facility built in 1994 to relieve overcrowding in county jails, stood empty for lack of maintenance funds. Since 1993, the sheriff of Los Angeles County had closed four jails for lack of operating funds, which resulted in overcrowding at the remaining jails and early release of prisoners. A 1996 investigation by *The Los Angeles Times* found that the average prisoner served less than a quarter of his or her sentence.

Welfare wins. In September 1996, the Los Angeles County Board of Supervisors was scheduled to consider a plan to shift $19 million from the general relief fund to pay for opening and operating the Twin Towers jail facility. The shift in funds would have reduced a recipient's monthly benefit check by $40. The proposal was withdrawn amid protests outside the building where the board met. Protesters warned that crime would rise if aid were cut.

Orange County financial plan. On May 15, United States bankruptcy Judge John E. Ryan approved a complex recovery plan to allow affluent Orange County, which is part of the greater Los Angeles metropolitan area, to emerge from the largest municipal bankruptcy filing in the nation's history. The county filed for bankruptcy protection

on Dec. 6, 1994, after the collapse of a $1.7-billion investment pool built on high-risk securities. Wall Street financiers fashioned a $920-million bond recovery plan, similar to a large equity loan, which allowed the county to mortgage many of its remaining real estate assets—including landfills and county buildings—to repay noteholders, vendors, and other creditors. Several lawsuits were still pending in 1996.

Economic upswing. The city's economy continued to recover in 1996 from the 1991-1992 recession and federal cutbacks in the aerospace industry. Mayor Riordan sought to improve the city's business climate through an overhaul of taxes and permit procedures. Los Angeles International Airport underwent an expansion of cargo-handling capacity to take advantage of current thriving business conditions with Pacific Rim countries.

The economic turnaround was fueled by improved business in the motion-picture and television industry, apparel design and manufacturing, and international trade. The Los Angeles Customs District maintained its position as number one in the nation. During 1995 and 1996, goods valued at $164.2 billion passed through the Los Angeles Customs District. Rankings were based on the total value of imports and exports passing through ports and airports that are part of the district.   □ Margaret A. Kilgore

See also **City.** In *World Book,* see **Los Angeles.**

Lott, Trent (1941-), a Republican senator from Mississippi, became majority leader of the United States Senate on June 12, 1996. Lott replaced Robert Dole, the Republican presidential candidate, when Dole resigned from the Senate to devote his energies to his campaign.

A staunch conservative, Lott has supported revising the tax system, including cutting the capital gains tax and eliminating the estate tax. He also has advocated reducing the size of government, including closing the energy and commerce departments.

Lott was born on Oct. 9, 1941, in Grenada County, Mississippi. He attended the University of Mississippi at Oxford, where he earned a bachelor's degree in public administration in 1963 and a law degree in 1967. His first political post was administrative assistant to William Colmer, a congressman from Mississippi. When Colmer retired in 1972, Lott was elected to succeed him. Lott became chairman of the House Republican Research Committee in 1979 and Republican whip in 1980.

In 1988, Lott was elected to the Senate. He became Senate majority whip after his reelection in 1994. He has served on the finance, commerce, science, transportation, and rules committees.

Lott and his wife, the former Patricia Thompson, have two grown children.   □ Lisa Klobuchar

See also **Congress of the United States**

Louisiana. See **State government.**

Los Angeles International Airport's new 28-story control tower, which became operational in March, provides air-traffic controllers with their first full view of the runways and gives the city a highly visible new landmark.

Lucid, Shannon (1943–), an American astronaut, in 1996 spent 188 days in space aboard the Russian space station, Mir, setting records for the longest space flight by a woman and by an American. Lucid began the mission on March 22 and returned to earth on September 26. On board, she served as a mission specialist, a person who conducts various experiments in space.

Lucid was born Jan. 13, 1943, in Shanghai, China, and grew up in Bethany, Oklahoma. She attended the University of Oklahoma, at Norman, where she earned a bachelor's degree in chemistry in 1963 and a doctorate in biochemistry in 1973. She worked as a research associate with the Oklahoma Medical Research Foundation from 1974 until 1978, when she was accepted into the astronaut candidate training program at the National Aeronautic and Space Administration (NASA) in Houston, Texas. Lucid became an astronaut in 1979.

From 1979 to 1985, Lucid served on a number of ground-based technical assignments at NASA. She functioned as a mission specialist on a total of five space flights—in 1985, 1989, 1991, 1993, and 1996. Lucid also served as chief of mission support and chief of astronaut appearances at NASA.

Shannon Lucid and her husband, Michael, have three children.   □ Lisa Klobuchar

See also **Space Exploration.**

Luxembourg. See Europe.

Magazine. Online magazines, or *webzines,* were the talk of the magazine industry in 1996. Publishers flocked to the World Wide Web on the Internet, building online versions of their print magazines or creating new titles altogether. Conde Nast Publications launched a site called *Swoon* for people in their 20's. Computer-magazine publisher CMP Publications attempted to build the *TV Guide* of the Internet with the debut of *NetGuide Live.* Time Inc. designed a health and cooking site called *Thrive@,* located on both the America Online service and its own Web site.

Microsoft magazine. Computer-software giant Microsoft Corporation of Redmond, Washington, introduced its online magazine, *Slate,* in June 1996. Microsoft hired Michael Kinsley, a former editor of the political magazine *The New Republic,* to create the online magazine, which covered politics and culture. But *Slate* was a disappointment to many Internet browsers. Some people in the media business also found *Slate* disappointing. A site called *Stale* even popped up, solely devoted to spoofing the content of Microsoft's webzine.

Still, Microsoft's entry into the publishing business had the managements of many magazine and newspaper companies worried. In addition to launching an adventure-travel webzine called *Mungo Park,* Microsoft planned to spend millions of dollars building a network of city and regional Web sites. These sites were planned as entertainment guides to each location, providing arts and entertainment listings and reviews. Traditional magazines and newspapers were concerned that such online services would lure away readers and advertisers.

Classic magazines return. The British humor magazine *Punch,* which folded in 1992, was revived in September 1996. Founded in 1841, the once world-famous magazine featured satire, reviews, and cartoons. United Newspapers Group, owner of the magazine, discontinued the magazine due to diminishing readership and revenues. A $5-million contribution from Egyptian-born businessman Mohamed al-Fayed enabled *Punch* to resume publication under a new editor, former newspaper columnist Peter McKay.

House & Garden magazine was also reborn in September. Conde Nast had stopped publication in 1993 after purchasing another upscale home-design magazine, *Architectural Digest,* from Knapp Communications. Perceiving that people had begun to devote more time and money to their homes and gardens, Conde Nast spent $40 million in 1996 to relaunch the magazine. The first issue of the new *House & Garden* eclipsed the advertising record set by *George,* the feature magazine about politics introduced by John F. Kennedy, Jr., in 1995; *House & Garden*'s comeback issue contained more advertising pages than any other first issue of a consumer magazine—207 pages compared to *George*'s 175.

Premiere **controversy.** The biggest magazine controversies of the year revolved around charges that magazine owners were meddling in the editorial product. In May, top editors at movie magazine *Premiere* resigned after David Pecker, chief executive officer (CEO) of the magazine's owner, Hachette Filipacchi Magazines, vetoed publication of an investigative piece on Planet Hollywood, a restaurant chain owned by movie actors, including Sylvester Stallone. Ronald Perelman, the CEO of New World Communications Group and half-owner of *Premiere,* was involved at the time in a joint venture with Planet Hollywood. Pecker said that *Premiere*'s readers did not want investigative stories.

Helen Gurley Brown retires. In January 1996, Helen Gurley Brown, editor-in-chief of *Cosmopolitan,* announced that she was stepping down after over 30 years at the women's magazine. When Brown took over the Hearst Magazines publication in 1965, *Cosmopolitan* was losing money and struggling to stay in print. Brown transformed it into a magazine about finding happiness both in relationships and at work and made the "Cosmo Girl" an international phenomenon. The American Society of Magazine Editors inducted Brown into its new Hall of Fame.
□ Lorne Manly

In *World Book,* see **Magazine.**

Maine. See **State government.**

Malawi. See **Africa.**

Malaysia. Prime Minister Mahathir bin Mohamad maneuvered during 1996 to keep tight control of his United Malays National Organization (UMNO), the nation's dominant political party. Mahathir has been president of the UMNO, as well as prime minister, since 1981 and at age 70 showed no signs of planning to retire.

On May 4, 1996, the UMNO's Supreme Council decided only Mahathir could be nominated for party president when elections, due every three years, were held on October 9. The council also decided that only Deputy Prime Minister Anwar Ibrahim could be nominated as deputy president of the UMNO. Any other nominees were disqualified. In the elections, two of Mahathir's supporters failed to win leadership jobs, shifting power toward Ibrahim.

After 39 years in power, the UMNO was widely seen as a source of patronage, and its leaders had obtained great personal wealth through the patronage system. The party regretted this image, so on July 6, the UMNO's Supreme Council announced an unprecedented ban on campaigning for party jobs. Observers saw the ban as a reaction to an increase in spending to win lucrative leadership positions.

Returning to the fold. Anwar, age 48, was reported to be unhappy in October when Razaleigh Hamzah, a 58-year-old prince of Kelantan state, rejoined the UMNO. Razaleigh had been one of the UMNO's most powerful leaders and Malaysia's finance minister, but he left the party in 1988 after losing a leadership contest with Mahathir. Razaleigh had formed an opposition party, but when it fared poorly against the UMNO, members voted to dissolve it. Razaleigh's return cast doubt on Anwar's role as Mahathir's ultimate heir.

Religious issues. Ethnic Malays, who are Muslim, constituted the UMNO's largest segment. However, Mahathir publicly opposed groups that advocated strict interpretations of Islamic law. In April, he criticized religious courts that made judgments according to Islamic tenets. Mahathir announced that he planned to restructure the nation's Islamic courts, which function parallel to the secular court system.

Economic goals. On May 6, Mahathir introduced in Parliament a five-year plan calling for annual economic growth of 8 percent. But a growing shortage of Malaysian laborers and skilled professionals raised doubts about the plan's feasibility.

Still, Malaysia's economic progress was symbolized in the capital, Kuala Lumpur, by the Petronas Towers. At 1,483 feet (542 meters) in height, the twin towers earned in 1996 the title of the world's tallest buildings. ☐ Henry S. Bradsher

See also **Asia** (Facts in brief); **Building and construction.** In *World Book,* see **Malaysia.**

Maldives. See Asia.

Mali. See Africa.

Malta. See Europe.

Manitoba. See Canadian provinces.

Manufacturing. In 1996, the manufacturing sector in the United States rebounded from a year of sluggish production activity and grew at a mild but steady rate. Although the 1995 downturn still haunted production lines in January 1996, factory output began to perk in February.

The year got off to a rocky start. January 1996 brought massive winter storms that shut down factories, distributors, and government offices for days across much of the eastern and central United States.

The 1995 and January 1996 factory slowdown was expected after the Federal Reserve System (the Fed), the nation's central bank, raised interest rates seven times during 1994 and early 1995. Rates were raised to prevent the economy's growth from triggering inflation, in which consumer prices rise rapidly.

Increased interest rates put a brake on economic growth—seen clearly in orders for factory goods and factory output—that so cooled the economy that the Fed began cutting interest rates again in mid-1995. Interest-rate cuts provide a manufacturing boost only after a lengthy lag period. So the factory sector continued to weaken for months. The overall U.S. economy grew by just 0.3 percent in the final quarter of 1995. This was slower than in the third quarter of 1995, when it grew by 3.8 percent. By early 1996, some economists warned that a manufacturing recession or downturn had set in.

Threats to manufacturing. Those fears were aggravated by special factors whose impact on factories was hard to predict. Political battles in late 1995 between U.S. President Bill Clinton, a Democrat, and a Republican-led Congress led to two shutdowns of much of the federal government, which spurred concerns that government purchases of manufactured goods in 1996 would be reduced.

The 1995 Christmas period—the biggest season of the year for U.S. retailers—was so weak that stores had trouble clearing their shelves of merchandise. This in turn dampened potential demand for new factory goods early in 1996.

A weak new year. January was the low point for U.S. industrial production in 1996. Production had declined 0.5 percent in October 1995 before it rose slightly during the rest of that year. Output fell by 0.2 percent in January 1996. Also in January, U.S. factories, mines, and utilities ran at only 82.4 percent of total available capacity.

The weakness in industrial production showed up in labor markets, as the nation's civilian unemployment rate edged up from 5.5 percent of the labor force in October 1995 to 5.8 percent in January 1996. The Fed, which had cut interest rates by a bare 0.25 percent in July 1995, responded to the growing signs of weakness in the economy by cutting rates an additional 0.25 percent in December 1995 and January 1996.

Rebound. Output at factories, mines, and utilities rebounded in February 1996. Production lines attempted to catch up after weather shutdowns, and the economy pulled out of its weakest period. The economy added 509,000 nonfarm civilian jobs, and the unemployment rate declined. But signs of weakness continued—new orders placed that month for factory goods fell by 1.5 percent.

Temporary setback. March brought a setback to manufacturing as it tried to regain its balance. A strike at brake factories supplying car assembly plants of General Motors—the nation's largest automaker—shut down car plants and related parts production in numerous states, which caused industrial output to drop to 0.5 percent. The strike briefly threw thousands out of work, and joblessness edged up.

Inflation fears. Despite weak industrial output, the gross domestic product (GDP)—the total value of goods and services produced in the United States—grew by a respectable 2 percent in the January-March quarter. It then strengthened to produce a 4.7-percent growth rate in the second quarter. This triggered fears in financial markets that the economy was growing too fast to keep inflation contained at an annual rate of 3 percent or less. Some worried that the Fed might raise interest rates to head off inflation.

However, inflation indicators from labor costs to consumer prices remained subdued. In a mid-July report to Congress, Fed Chairman Alan Greenspan said labor markets were tight and factories were running at a capacity rate, which traditionally meant wages and prices might rise. Yet, Greenspan said, prices of industrial materials were virtually flat.

The Fed held back from raising interest rates during the summer and early autumn, and the economy slowed. GDP rose by 2 percent in the third quarter.

Manufacturers' survey. In 1996, the monthly survey by the National Association of Purchasing Management (NAPM), a closely watched indicator of health in the manufacturing sector, asked purchasing managers at more than 300 industrial companies about output, new orders, employment, inventory levels, and other factors. The survey reflected lingering weakness in the factory sector despite gains in the overall economy.

An NAPM index reading below 50 percent indicates the factory sector is contracting. The reading remained below 50 percent through March, nudged up to 50.1 percent in April, then slipped to 49.3 percent in May. In June it rose to 54.3 percent, but in July it dropped to 50.2 percent. The index reported better numbers in August and September, dipped in October, but hit 52.7 percent in November.

One major part of the recovery of the manufacturing sector was the result of export orders, which remained under the 50-percent reading only in January and February. By late summer, export orders were growing faster than total orders for factory goods, as growth in demand from foreign buyers for U.S. products outpaced gains in demand from domestic buyers.

Mixed trends. Manufacturing trends remained mixed as the year moved toward a close. The government announced that total factory orders fell in June and August. Industrial output was virtually flat in July and up just slightly through September. Shipments in advance of Christmas appeared to herald higher holiday production than in 1995, but weak raw material prices suggested that demand for most factory goods was still not robust.

Weakness was evident in the amount businesses spent on capital equipment (equipment used to make goods or provide services), which increased by just 1.5 percent in 1996—to $603 billion—compared with a boost of 8.1 percent in 1995.

Productivity and costs. The government's measure of productivity—output per hours worked—fell by 1.2 percent in the rapidly weakening fourth quarter of 1995, gained 1.9 percent in the first quarter of 1996, and gained just 0.6 percent in the second quarter. Labor costs remained steady. By the end of September, total U.S. salary and benefit compensation had risen just 2.8 percent in the previous 12 months. The gain was slightly higher—3.1 percent—for manufacturing. □ John D. Boyd

In *World Book,* see **Manufacturing.**

Maryland. See **State government.**

Massachusetts. See **State government.**

Mauritania. See **Africa.**

Mauritius. See **Africa.**

Medicine. The first scientific evidence showing a direct link between smoking and lung cancer was reported in October 1996 by researchers at the University of Texas M. D. Anderson Cancer Center in Houston. The researchers reported finding that a chemical produced in the body from cigarette smoke damages a gene that protects against cancer.

The investigators exposed lung-tissue cells growing in a laboratory dish to a compound called BPDE, which the body manufactures from benzo(a)pyrene, a common constituent of tobacco smoke. They later examined a particular gene, known as p53, in those cells. The p53 gene is a so-called tumor-suppressor gene, which blocks the development of cancer by preventing uncontrolled cell division.

The researchers found that BPDE molecules formed strong chemical bonds with the p53 gene at three locations that would have prevented the gene from functioning and would presumably have become permanent *mutations* (changes) at those sites when the cells reproduced. Mutations at the very same places in the p53 gene are commonly seen in lung cancer.

Arthritis treated with new genes. The world's first gene therapy for rheumatoid arthritis was performed on a 68-year-old woman in July at the University of Pittsburgh in Pennsylvania. The disease, which causes pain, inflammation, and destruction of tissue in the joints, affects 2.1 million Americans.

Researchers removed cells from the woman's joint tissue and inserted into them a gene that blocks the action of *interleukin-1* (IL-1), a protein produced by the immune system. In rheumatoid arthritis, which many investigators think is an *autoimmune disease*—a disorder in which the immune system attacks the body's own tissues—large quantities of IL-1 are produced in the joints. IL-1 is the major cause of the symptoms of rheumatoid arthritis.

The researchers injected the modified cells into two knuckle joints in one of the woman's hands. The knuckles of the other hand were not treated. The disease-damaged knuckles of both hands were later surgically removed and replaced with artificial knuckles. At year-end, the scientists were examining both the treated and untreated knuckles to see what effect the gene therapy had produced.

Arthritis drugs. Three new genetically engineered drugs for the treatment of rheumatoid arthritis were being tested in the United States in 1996. Nearly 800 arthritis patients were involved in three separate clinical trials of the drugs. Most of the patients reported improvements in their symptoms and only minor side effects. In October, arthritis researchers said the drugs showed promise for treating the disease and even halting its progress.

New finding on hemoglobin. Hemoglobin, the major component of red blood cells, helps regulate blood pressure, researchers at Duke University in Durham, North Carolina, reported in March. The scientists discovered that as hemoglobin passes through the lungs, it picks up not only oxygen but also an unusual form of nitric oxide that it uses to make blood vessels widen.

The body controls the flow of blood by contracting and relaxing muscle cells surrounding the blood vessels. Scientists discovered in the 1980's that the cells lining blood vessels release nitric oxide, which has a relaxing effect on the muscle cells. That effect increases blood flow and reduces blood pressure.

This finding created a puzzle, however, because the iron atoms in hemoglobin readily bind with nitric oxide. Researchers wondered how the muscle cells obtain enough nitric oxide to function.

The Duke University investigators found that as hemoglobin passes through the lungs, it picks up a form of nitric oxide that differs from the form released by the cells lining blood vessels. The newly discovered type of nitric oxide, which they called super nitric oxide, is released to the blood vessels by hemoglobin molecules. In this way, hemoglobin seems able to expand or contract blood vessels to vary blood pressure and blood flow. The researchers said their discovery could lead to new ways of controlling blood pressure and treating heart attacks.

Skin-cancer gene found. In June, two groups of scientists in the United States, Australia, and Sweden identified the gene that causes basal cell carcinoma, a skin cancer that is the most common form of cancer in humans. About 750,000 Americans develop basal cell carcinoma each year. The disease is easily curable through surgical removal of the cancer, but the researchers predicted that their discovery would lead to a more convenient cure—a skin cream that will reverse the genetic fault.

Brain scans detect Alzheimer's. A highly sensitive brain-imaging technique can detect signs of Alzheimer's disease in high-risk individuals long before symptoms begin, scientists in Phoenix reported in March. They said the procedure may eventually permit routine diagnosis of the devastating brain disorder 10 to 20 years before an individual's mental functioning begins to obviously deteriorate.

The researchers, at Phoenix's Good Samaritan Regional Medical Center, used a technology called positron emission tomography (PET) to scan the brains of 33 people in their 50's and 60's. The subjects all had a family history of Alzheimer's but showed no symptoms of mental impairment. Eleven of the individuals had two copies of a gene called ApoE4, which is linked to a high risk of Alzheimer's. The other 22 people had no copies of ApoE4.

The PET images showed that the patients with two copies of ApoE4 had reduced activity in the same brain regions as patients who already have the symptoms of Alzheimer's disease. The researchers saw no reduction in brain function in the individuals with no copies of the gene.

No benefit seen from beta-carotene. Beta-carotene, a dietary supplement taken by millions of people, does not prevent heart disease or cancer, according to two large U.S. studies sponsored by the National Institutes of Health (NIH) in Bethesda, Maryland, and reported in January. Scientists had theorized that supplements of beta-carotene, found naturally in many fruits and vegetables, might protect against heart disease and cancer by counteracting destructive chemicals known as free radicals.

One of the NIH studies found hints that beta-carotene may actually be harmful. In that study, of 18,314 men and women at high risk for lung cancer, those who took beta-carotene and vitamin A for at least four years had a 28 percent higher incidence of lung cancer and a 17 percent higher death rate than those taking a *placebo* (inactive substance). The researchers qualified the finding, however, by stating that the people's preexisting cancer risk may have been a bigger factor than the supplements.

The second study lasted 12 years and included 22,071 male physicians who also took either beta-carotene supplements or a placebo. That study found that beta-carotene had no effect in preventing either cancer or heart disease, but neither did it find any risk involved with taking the supplement.

The researchers said the results of the two studies apply only to beta-carotene supplements. They recommended that people continue to eat a diet rich in natural beta-carotene and other nutrients.

Stabilizing the heart. In May, the FDA approved the expanded use of an implanted defibrillator, an electronic device that could prevent thousands of deaths annually from abnormal heart rhythms. The erratic rhythms, termed *ventricular fibrillation,* disrupt the normal pumping of blood and can lead to death within a few minutes. The defibrillator is surgically implanted in the abdomen and connected by a wire to the heart. The device senses the onset of ventricular fibrillation and sends an electric jolt to the heart to restore normal rhythm.

Help for sickle cell patients. Bone marrow transplants can cure many young children with sickle cell anemia, a study funded by the NIH concluded in August. In a five-year study, researchers at medical centers in the United States, Canada, Europe, and Brazil transplanted bone marrow from a brother or sister into 22 children with severe sickle cell anemia, a hereditary disorder that causes red blood cells to take on twisted sicklelike shapes. In the United States the disease strikes mainly African Americans.

Two years after being treated, 16 of the children in the study appeared cured. Four children were not helped, and two died. The researchers said the procedure carries a 10 percent chance of death. As a result, they said, it would probably be limited to the most severely ill patients.   □ Michael Woods

See also **AIDS; Drugs; Public Health.** In *World Book,* see **Medicine.**

Mental health. Physical differences in specific
areas of the brains of men and women may explain why women tend to have better verbal abilities than men, researchers at Johns Hopkins University in Baltimore, Maryland, reported in February 1996.

The researchers, led by psychiatrist Thomas Schlaepfer, used computerized imaging to calculate the amount of gray matter in 60 healthy men and women of similar ages. Gray matter, or the cerebral cortex, is the thin outer layer of nerve cells responsible for complex mental processes, such as thought, memory, and speech. The researchers found that in two areas of the brain involved with speech the women had 23.2 and 12.8 percent more gray matter than the men. Schlaepfer concluded that women's generally superior verbal abilities may have a physical basis, rather than, as previously thought, an educational basis or an environmental basis of some other origin.

Good grades. Believing in one's ability to do well in school and wanting to learn are more important for achieving good grades than natural ability or a desire to please parents, a report from Beaver College in Glenside, Pennsylvania, concluded in June. Psychologist Marianne Miserandino studied 77 third- and fourth-grade children with comparable above-average scores on standardized tests. She found that pupils who were confident of their abilities were more likely to enjoy and persist at school work. Those uncertain of their competence or wanting to

get good grades to make their parents happy tended to lose interest in school and get poorer grades. Miserandino concluded, "Talent and potential will be wasted unless children believe that they possess ability and have the freedom to use it."

Effects of mental stress. In June, researchers at Duke University Medical Center in Durham, North Carolina, reported that mental stress, which can increase the heart's need for oxygen while reducing blood supply to the heart, can be more important in triggering a cardiac event than physical exercise.

At the beginning of the study, 126 patients with cardiac artery disease received a series of mental stress tests, such as speaking before an audience, and traditional physical stress tests, monitoring heart action during exercise. During the next five years, patients who tested positive on the mental stress tests were found to be three times more likely to experience severe symptoms or to die from coronary artery disease. The Duke researchers recommended that physicians test heart patients for mental stress and suggest stress-management techniques.

Conflicts between a husband and wife are more likely to affect the hormone levels and immune system of the woman, even hours after an argument ends, according to a study at Ohio State University in Columbus, which was reported in July. During the 15-hour study, the researchers took blood tests of 90 married couples who engaged in conflict-management exercises. The researchers attempted to test the physiological responses of a woman when she reacted with acute frustration to her husband's "tuning out" during an argument.

Blood tests showed that women who reacted negatively to their husbands' emotional withdrawal experienced changes in the immune system and increases in stress-related hormone levels. Janice Kiecolt-Glasser, a professor of psychiatry and psychology at Ohio State, said the hormone levels remained elevated as wives apparently relived the conflict throughout the day. Researchers said that elevated hormone levels could render a person more vulnerable to illness.

Most manic-depressive patients stop taking lithium, the most frequently prescribed medication, too soon and risk a serious recurrence of their illness, according to a study by the Oregon Health Sciences University in Portland, which was reported in August.

Manic-depressive illness, or bipolar disorder, is a serious mental disorder that involves sharp mood swings, ranging from elation to deep depression. Psychiatrist Bentson H. McFarland and pharmacist Richard Johnson conducted a six-year study of 1,594 bipolar disorder patients treated with lithium. Most took lithium for only a few months and discontinued treatment without consulting their physicians, increasing the patients' risk of emergency psychiatric hospitalization.   □ Michael Woods

See also **Psychology.** In *World Book,* see **Brain; Mental illness.**

On May 1, 1996, workers in Mexico City peacefully protest the continuing effects of the economic crisis triggered by the 1994 devaluation of the peso.

Mexico. On Aug. 28, 1996, armed rebels of the Popular Revolutionary Army (known by the Spanish acronym EPR) attacked police and military posts in four Mexican states: Guerrero, Oaxaca, Chiapas, and México. The raids, which left 13 dead and 23 wounded, marked the second guerrilla uprising since the Zapatista attacks of January 1994.

Unlike the Zapatistas, who sought to negotiate a settlement with the government in 1996, the EPR vowed to use force to remove Mexico's long-dominant Institutional Revolutionary Party (PRI). The EPR's objective was a socialist "transition government," according to one EPR commander. Following the attacks, Zapatista rebels, while at pains to disassociate themselves from the EPR, broke off talks with the government on September 2, demanding the release of 20 prisoners.

Political corruption. In July, a commission investigating political corruption implicated President Ernesto Zedillo Ponce de León in a 1989 payment of $7 million to a company controlled by a supporter of the PRI. Zedillo, who had been a senior budget official in 1989, denied the accusations. On July 18, 1996, the PRI-dominated commission canceled the investigation.

Raúl Salinas investigation. In 1996, investigators tried to determine how Raúl Salinas de Gortari, brother of former President Carlos Salinas de Gortari, amassed more than $200 million while working as a civil servant with an annual salary of $190,000. During investigations, three Mexican billionaires admitted making payoffs to Raúl Salinas for lucrative acquisitions when the government of Carlos Salinas began privatizing the economy. On June 5, the U.S. Justice Department reported that the New York-based Citibank may have conducted transactions that allegedly concealed the sources of Salinas's money.

In February, Raúl Salinas was also charged with planning the 1994 assassination of PRI Secretary-General José Francisco Ruíz Massieu, the former brother-in-law of Carlos Salinas.

Purge of police force. On Aug. 16, 1996, Attorney General Antonio Lozano Gracia dismissed more than 700 commanders and agents of the Federal Judicial Police because of allegations of corruption. The dismissal of one-sixth of the agency's force led to a crime wave, which was attributed in part to the disgruntlement of dismissed officers. On December 2, President Zedillo dismissed Lozano for mishandling other high-profile corruption investigations.

Economic rebound. On July 25, Mexican authorities announced that Mexico would repay $7 billion of the $12.5 billion borrowed from the United States in 1995. By privately refinancing the loan on better terms, Mexico was able to repay much of the money it borrowed to recover from the financial crisis of 1994.

On Aug. 18, 1996, Mexico reported that its economy grew by 7.2 percent in the second quarter of 1996—the first sign of growth since the devaluation of the peso in December 1994. In July 1996, Mexico's census bureau reported that unemployment dropped to 5.8 percent from 7.3 percent in 1995. However, the figures did not account for the millions of people, working odd jobs, who do not show up on regular payrolls.

Guerrero massacre. In January 1996, 17 police officers and 4 government officials were arrested in the western state of Guerrero in connection with the June 1995 massacre of 17 peasants en route to an antigovernment rally. In March 1996, Guerrero's governor, Rubén Figueroa Alcocér, stepped down amid accusations of a cover-up of the killings. Although Mexico's Supreme Court in April implicated Figueroa and seven others in the cover-up, judicial authorities in Guerroro cleared him of charges in June.

Tabasco oil. On February 16, 1,000 protesters, led by the leftist Democratic Revolutionary Party, ended a three-week blockade of about 60 state-owned oil wells in the state of Tabasco. The protest was sparked by charges that Petroleos Mexicanos, the oil company owned by Mexico, had polluted local land and water, thereby destroying the livelihood of peasants.

Major league play. On August 17, more than 23,000 fans watched the New York Mets and the San Diego Padres in the first major-league, regular-season game played outside the United States or Canada. The game, one of a weekend series in Monterrey, sparked talk of possible major-league teams in Mexico. □ Nathan A. Haverstock

See also **Latin America** (Facts in brief table). In *World Book,* see **Mexico.**

Mfume, Kweisi (1948–), was named president and chief executive officer of the National Association for the Advancement of Colored People (NAACP) on Feb. 15, 1996. Mfume was given the task of revitalizing the organization, which was plagued by debt and scandals involving its former executive director, Benjamin F. Chavis, Jr.

Born in Baltimore, Maryland, on Oct. 24, 1948, Mfume was named Frizzell Gray. When Gray was 16, his mother died of cancer, and he left school to support his three sisters. Embittered over his difficult life, he joined a street gang.

While in his early 20's, Mfume abruptly decided to give up his gang life. He passed his General Educational Development (GED) exam in 1968 and became a popular radio-show host in Baltimore. He graduated magna cum laude from Morgan State University in 1976 and earned a master's degree from Johns Hopkins University in 1984. While in school, he changed his name to Kweisi Mfume *(kwah EE see oom FOO may),* which means "son of conquering kings" in Swahili.

Mfume served on the Baltimore City Council from 1978 to 1987. In 1986, he was elected to the United States House of Representatives, where he served as chairman of the Congressional Black Caucus from 1992 to 1994. □ Lisa Klobuchar

See also **Civil Rights.**

Michigan. See **Detroit; State government.**

279

Hopes of stability in the Middle East were dashed in 1996. The election of a hard-line Israeli government froze the Arab-Israeli peace process. Interfactional Kurdish fighting in northern Iraq threatened to embroil other states. And Islamic militants staged brazen terrorist acts. The American military confrontation with Iraq and its tacit support of an Israeli military campaign in southern Lebanon brought criticism from many Western and Arab allies of the United States.

Peace process. The Arab-Israeli peace process stalled after the leader of the conservative Likud party, Benjamin Netanyahu, won Israel's May 29 elections for prime minister. Although Netanyahu said he was committed to peace, he initially refused to meet with Palestinian leader Yasir Arafat after taking office on June 18. Netanyahu also indicated that peace agreements made by the previous Israeli government needed renegotiation.

Netanyahu narrowly beat Prime Minister Shimon Peres, the leader of Israel's Labor Party. Peres had held a commanding lead in polls until four suicide bombs by Islamic militants killed 61 people in Israel between February 25 and March 4. After the bombings, many Israelis concluded that trading "land for peace," as the Peres government had pledged to do, risked Israel's security.

Arab League. Alarmed by the Israeli election result, Arab League leaders convened their first summit since 1990 in Cairo, Egypt. When the summit ended on June 23, 1996, participants called on Netanyahu to reaffirm Israel's commitment to the exchange of land for peace and withdrawal of troops from the West Bank and Golan Heights. Israel captured the West Bank from Jordan and the Golan Heights from Syria in the 1967 Arab-Israeli Six-Day War. Arab League leaders demanded that Jewish settlers be removed from Israeli-occupied Arab territories. They also called for negotiations over Jerusalem, the "right of return" for Palestinian refugees, and the final status of the Palestinian self-rule area. The summit was attended by 21 of the 22 members of the Arab League. Iraq was not invited.

Crisis in Israel. On July 29, 1996, Israel announced it would build two bridges to the Golan Heights and two roads through the West Bank. It also lifted a four-year freeze on Jewish settlements in the West Bank. In August, Syria responded by rejecting peace talks that were not based on Israel's return of the Golan Heights, and it began moving troops toward the Golan Heights.

Arafat's call for a four-hour general strike on August 28 finally led to a meeting between him and Netanyahu at the Gaza border crossing of Erez on September 4. But a new crisis erupted on September 24 when Israel secretly opened a tunnel running below Jerusalem's Temple Mount, a site sacred to Muslims and Jews. Over the next four days, 15 Israelis and at least 58 Palestinians died in clashes.

The crisis prompted U.S. President Bill Clinton to host a peace summit in Washington, D.C., on October 1. The summit ended with participants agreeing on little except to begin a dialogue on October 6 on the long-delayed withdrawal of Israeli troops from the West Bank town of Hebron. (Under a peace accord signed in September 1995, Israel was supposed to withdraw most of its troops from Hebron by March 1996. Little had been achieved by mid-December.)

Kurdish infighting. U.S. policy suffered many setbacks when Iraq and Iran became involved in a power struggle between two Kurdish militias supported by the United States. (The Kurds are an ethnic group fighting to establish an independent state in parts of Iraq and Turkey.) In mid-September, Iraq intervened militarily to help the Kurdish Democratic Party take control of northeastern Iraq, which had been controlled by a rival group backed by Iran, the Patriotic Union of Kurdistan (PUK). On October 14, PUK, rearmed by Iran, recaptured most of its territory. Despite a cease-fire brokered by the United States on October 24, the situation remained volatile.

The crisis ended a U.S. covert operation in northern Iraq to topple Iraqi President Saddam Hussein and forced the United States to evacuate more than 2,000 Kurds who had worked with the U.S. or Iraqi opposition groups. Relief organizations also withdrew.

Attack on Iraq. The United States fired 44 missiles at air-defense targets in southern Iraq on September 3 and 4 to punish Baghdad for its military action in northern Iraq. The attack was harshly criticized by almost all of America's Western and Arab allies. Jordan and Saudi Arabia, strong U.S. allies, refused to allow the United States to launch air strikes from their soil. Many allies also condemned the American expansion of a "no-fly" zone over southern Iraq.

U.S. critics feared that Kurdish infighting and Iran's involvement could lead to Iraq's fragmentation, growing Islamic extremism, and increasing anti-Americanism. The prospect of a wider regional confrontation arose when Turkey, during the crisis, declared that it wanted to establish a security zone along its border with Iraq. Turkey added that it reserved the right to attack its own rebel Kurds, some of whom had established bases in northern Iraq.

Iraqi suffering. In late November, the United Nations (UN) approved an agreement allowing Iraq to sell a limited amount of oil to buy food and sup-

Boys carry a model of a rocket through the streets of Beirut in a march in May commemorating the martyrdom in the 680's of al-Husayn, a figure who is revered by Shi'ite Muslims and around whom militant Muslim groups have rallied.

Facts in brief on Middle Eastern countries

Country	Population	Government	Monetary unit*	Foreign trade (million U.S.$)	
				Exports†	Imports†
Bahrain	590,000	Amir Isa bin Salman Al Khalifa; Prime Minister Khalifa bin Salman Al Khalifa	dinar (0.38 = $1)	3,930	3,581
Cyprus	756,000	President Glafcos Clerides (Turkish Republic of Northern Cyprus: President Rauf R. Denktash)	pound (0.46 = $1)	1,229	3,690
Egypt	65,319,000	President Hosni Mubarak; Prime Minister Kamal Ahmed al-Ganzouri	pound (3.39 = $1)	3,475	10,218
Iran	70,111,000	Leader of the Islamic Revolution Ali Hoseini-Khamenei; President Ali Akbar Hashemi-Rafsanjani	rial (3,000.00 = $1)	16,000	18,000
Iraq	21,694,000	President Saddam Hussein	dinar (1,800.00 = $1)	10,400	6,600
Israel	5,797,000	President Ezer Weizman; Prime Minister Binyamin Netanyahu	new shekel (3.28 = $1)	19,028	29,632
Jordan	5,802,000	King Hussein I; Prime Minister Abd al-Karim al-Kabariti	dinar (0.71 = $1)	1,769	3,697
Kuwait	1,649,000	Amir Jabir al-Ahmad al-Jabir Al Sabah; Prime Minister & Crown Prince Saad al-Abdallah al-Salim Al Sabah	dinar (0.30 = $1)	12,945	7,144
Lebanon	3,117,000	President Ilyas Harawi; Prime Minister Rafiq al-Hariri	pound (1,551.00 = $1)	925	4,100
Oman	2,334,000	Sultan Qaboos bin Said Al Said	rial (0.39 = $1)	5,545	3,915
Qatar	572,000	Amir and Prime Minister Hamad bin Khalifa Al Thani	riyal (3.64 = $1)	3,181	1,891
Saudi Arabia	19,072,000	King & Prime Minister Fahd bin Abd al-Aziz Al Saud	riyal (3.75 = $1)	42,395	28,198
Sudan	29,631,000	President Umar Hasan Ahmad al-Bashir	pound (1,400.00 = $1)	509	1,059
Syria	15,686,000	President Hafiz al-Asad; Prime Minister Mahmud Zubi	pound (41.95 = $1)	3,970	4,616
Turkey	64,293,000	President Süleyman Demirel; Prime Minister Necmetlin Erbakan	lira (95,122.00 = $1)	21,600	35,710
United Arab Emirates	1,987,000	President Zayid bin Sultan Al Nuhayyan; Prime Minister Maktum bin Rashid al-Maktum	dirham (3.67 = $1)	24,000	20,000
Yemen	15,581,000	President Ali Abdallah Salih; Prime Minister Abd al-Aziz Abd al-Ghani	rial (130.00 = $1)	101	1,378

*Exchange rates as of Oct. 25,1996, or latest available data.
†Latest available data.

plies. UN sanctions imposed since the 1990 Iraqi invasion of Kuwait caused a dire health crisis in Iraq. In October, a UN official announced that 4,500 Iraqi children under 5 years of age died monthly due to famine and disease. In 1996, UN pleas for $40 million in relief for Iraq netted only $1.6 million. The United States said on October 30 that it would donate $7.3 million, but only if the money went to Iraqi Kurds. Iraqi oil began to be exported in December.

Stability in Saudi Arabia was in doubt after a massive truck bomb killed 19 U.S. troops and injured some 400 Americans, Saudis, and Bangladeshis in Dhahran on June 25. The Saudis arrested 40 suspects in connection with the blast. The suspects belonged to the Shiah sect of Islam, which is prevalent in Iran but followed by only 15 percent of the Saudi kingdom's 12 million people. The suspects were said to be members of the Saudi Hezbollah, which allegedly was linked to Lebanon's Hezbollah, Islamic fundamentalist guerrillas, and aided by Syria and Iran. The United States, angered by the Saudis' refusal to share intelligence about the suspects, said it had uncovered no evidence that implicated Iran.

The Dhahran bomb was the second in seven months to kill Americans in Saudi Arabia. In May 1996, four Saudis were beheaded for setting a bomb that exploded in Riyadh in November 1995, killing five Americans and two Indians.

Saudi extremists have accused the ruling Al Saud family of corruption, limiting political participation, and maintaining close ties with the United States. Extremists were angered in 1996 by what they viewed as a U.S. bias in favor of Israel in the Arab-Israeli peace process and America's tacit support for Israel's military campaign in southern Lebanon in April, which killed 200 Lebanese.

Palestinians went to the polls for the first time on January 20, electing Palestinian leader Arafat chairman of the Palestine National Authority (PNA). In addition, voters selected members of an 88-seat Palestine Legislative Council. Arafat took his oath of office on February 12. On April 24, the Palestine Liberation Organization's (PLO) National Council voted 504 to 54 to revoke a clause in its 32-year-old charter calling for Israel's destruction. Arafat, who was once condemned as a terrorist, visited the White House, where President Clinton on May 1 hailed Arafat's commitment to peace.

Arafat's triumph was uncertain, however. In March, he had been forced to clamp down on Muslim radicals after four suicide bombings in Israel. Nearly 400 suspected extremists were arrested, and on March 6, a Palestinian court sentenced a man, Mohammad Abu Wardeh, to life in prison for recruiting suicide bombers.

The death of a prisoner in police custody, the seventh since 1994, sparked demonstrations in the West Bank city of Nablus on Aug. 1, 1996. On August 2, 100 people were arrested following violent protests in Tulkarm by families of prisoners who were on hunger strikes. Some Palestinian officials acknowledged that the police, who until recently were guerrillas, needed better training.

Israel's regular partial or complete closings since 1994 of its border to Palestinian workers prompted fears that worsening economic conditions among Palestinians could fuel extremism. The closings were blamed for a decline in Palestinian health and the deaths in March of three Arab infants being transported to health facilities. By May 1996, only $27 million out of $1.5 billion pledged to the PNA by foreign donors had materialized. The Palestinian Central Bureau of Statistics said in February that Gaza's population would double to more than 1.8 million in 15 years, further straining its overstretched resources. Nearly 47 percent of the 2.2 million Arabs in Gaza and the West Bank were under 15 years old.

A U.S.-European rift opened on August 5 when President Clinton signed a law imposing sanctions on foreign companies and banks that invested more than $40 million in the further development of Iranian or Libyan oil industries. The United States considered those two states "pariahs" that sponsored terrorism. The European Union (EU) replied on October 1 that it would challenge the law before the World Trade Organization.

Rivalry between the United States and France emerged in foreign policy. The United States was riled by French President Jacques Chirac's trip to the Middle East in late October. Chirac was criticized by the Israelis for urging them to honor prior commitments to peace, but he was lauded by the new Palestinian parliament on October 23 when he said the creation of a Palestinian state would promote peace.

France, however, had been 1 of 27 countries to send its leader to an antiterrorism conference at the invitation of President Clinton after the suicide bombings in Israel. Known as the Summit of the Peacemakers, the conference was convened on March 13 at the Egyptian Red Sea resort of Sharm ash Shaykh. On April 27, France and the United States agreed to form a five-member monitoring group with Lebanon, Syria, and Israel to oversee the U.S.-brokered cease-fire between Israel and Lebanon.

Qatar. In October, the ruling Al Thani family announced that an agreement had been reached allowing the return of the former emir, Khalifa bin Hamad Al Thani, who had been deposed in 1995 by his son, Hamad bin Khalifa Al Thani. The deal ended lawsuits by Qatar, which had frozen the assets of the former emir, in exchange for his return of a reported $3 billion missing from the treasury after his ouster.

Chemical weapons. On Oct. 22, 1996, the United States announced it would contact 20,000 soldiers who served in the 1991 Gulf War to determine whether they may have been exposed to chemical weapons when two Iraqi munitions dumps were blown up by U.S. troops in March 1991. Thousands of veterans had complained of unexplained health problems, called Gulf War Syndrome.

Environment. Experts who attended a UN-sponsored international conference in Istanbul, Turkey, said on June 5, 1996, that competition over scarce water resources would soon replace oil as an excuse for war. On May 1, the UN's Food and Agriculture Organization warned that all five North African states bordering the Mediterranean Sea—Egypt, Tunisia, Algeria, Libya, and Morocco—would by 2000 be in crisis over maintenance of agricultural productivity due to a water shortage and the spread of deserts.

Aid to Bosnia. Arab countries agreed in 1996 to donate $100 million to Bosnia's Muslim-Croat federation to help defend themselves against Bosnian Serbs. (A 1995 peace plan ended Bosnia-Herzegovina's civil war by dividing it into two entities, one dominated by a Muslim-Croat federation and the other by Bosnian Serbs.) ☐ Christine Helms

See also articles on the various Middle Eastern countries. (Fact in brief table). In *World Book,* see **Middle East** and individual Middle Eastern country articles.

Mining. See Energy supply.

Minnesota. See State government.

Mississippi. See State government.

Moldova. See Europe.

Mongolia. See Asia.

Montana. See State government.

Montreal. In March 1996, residents of Montreal both mourned the loss of a revered sports and entertainment center and welcomed its multimillion-dollar replacement. The 72-year-old Forum, home of the Montreal Canadiens hockey team for 3,229 regular-season and 307 play-off games, hosted its last match on March 11. A capacity crowd cheered the Canadiens as they beat the Dallas Stars 4-1. In an emotional postgame ceremony, players and fans bade farewell to the place where the Canadiens—the National Hockey League's most victorious franchise—clinched half of its 24 championships.

On March 12, some 2,500 Forum fans attended a charity auction of memorabilia from the historic building, which had also hosted political and religious rallies, concerts, circuses, and even bullfights. On March 15, an elaborate parade beginning at the Forum kicked off the official move to the new $230-million Molson Centre. In the March 16 inaugural game at the Centre, the Canadiens defeated the New York Rangers 4-2. An open house at the Centre on March 17 attracted more than 151,000 visitors.

On August 13, the Montreal City Council approved a zoning change to allow redevelopment of the Forum into an entertainment complex, which would include motion-picture theaters, restaurants, and several large retail stores. Some local merchants, who feared that the complex would destroy their business, opposed the plan.

Stadium roof. Plans for another of Montreal's landmark buildings, Olympic Stadium, also attracted mixed reviews. On September 5, Serge Ménard, Quebec's minister of state for Montreal, publicly endorsed a decision by the Olympic Installations Board, which operates the Stadium, to replace the current retractable roof with a fixed one. The project, which would cost an estimated $30 million to $35 million, was to be completed by 1999.

Built for the 1976 Summer Olympic Games, the Olympic Stadium, which is currently home to the Montreal Expos baseball team, was equipped in 1987 with the world's first retractable stadium roof. The roof, however, never functioned properly, tore itself a number of times, and had not been opened since 1993. Claude Brochu, president of the Expos, expressed disappointment at the board's decision, insisting that baseball fans wanted to be able to watch games outside in pleasant weather.

The Montreal Casino, the biggest gambling house in Canada, became one of the world's biggest casinos with the July 12, 1996, opening of a new $73.8-million wing. Located on Ile Notre-Dame in the middle of the St. Lawrence River, the casino, which is housed in the French pavilion from the 1967 world's fair Expo 67, originally consisted of a European-style gaming house. The new wing, called Le Pavillon, increased the casino's total number of slot machines to 2,700 and the number of gaming tables to 105.

Airport shuttle. Aéroports de Montréal (ADM), the private company that operates Montreal International Airport (Mirabel) and Montreal International Airport (Dorval), announced plans on Feb. 20, 1996, to transfer all regularly scheduled commercial flights from Mirabel to Dorval by April 1997. The plan calls for Mirabel to continue handling charter flights and cargo shipments.

The $185-million estimated cost of the project was to be financed by a passenger surcharge. ADM predicted the move would boost traffic at both airports by 650,000 passengers within three years. Dorval handles about 5.9 million passengers annually. Mirabel serves an average of 2.4 million per year. Groups representing municipalities around Mirabel and Dorval sought a court injunction to block the shift until economic and environmental impact studies could be carried out.

Barnabé case continued. Richard Barnabé, a taxi driver who was beaten unconscious in a cell at the Montreal Urban Community (MUC) police station on Dec. 14, 1993, died on May 2, 1996, after spending 29 months in a coma. Before his death, four MUC police officers were found guilty and sentenced for the beating. After his death, 10 additional MUC officers, including a former police chief, were cited by an ethics committee for professional misconduct. □ Mike King

See also **Canada.** In *World Book,* see **Montreal.**

Motion pictures. Big-budget action-adventure movies shared box-office dollars in 1996 with dialogue-driven movies produced on a shoestring by independent film companies. The year also saw a growing interest in plotlines taken from the pages of classic literature and the reemergence of movies featuring strong women characters.

Looking Backward. The American movie industry seemed to be taking a look backward. Three of the year's biggest hits—*Independence Day, Twister,* and *Mission: Impossible*—traversed familiar terrain. Filmgoers with long memories recognized in *Independence Day* a spoof of the conventions of 1950's science-fiction films, while *Twister* used high technology to re-create some improbably busy days in the lives of tornado chasers. Both films rekindled the mood of 1970's disaster epics, such as *The Towering Inferno* and *The Poseidon Adventure. Mission: Impossible,* the project of producer-star Tom Cruise, represented a rethinking of one of television's most durable series.

The classics. On a less explosive note, classic literature continued to inspire filmmakers, some of whom took a radical approach. Director-star Kenneth Branagh transferred William Shakespeare's *Hamlet* to the 1800's and included such non-Shakespearean actors as Robin Williams, Billy Crystal, and Jack Lemmon among his cast. Baz Luhrmann, the Australian director of *Strictly Ballroom,* transplanted

Mel Gibson is a Scottish rebel in *Braveheart,* a film that earned the actor Academy Awards for best director and best picture.

Romeo and Juliet from Verona, Italy, to a contemporary, gang-infested setting called *Verona Beach.*

Franco Zeffirelli's adaptation of *Jane Eyre* proved disappointing, as did Trevor Nunn's recreation of *Twelfth Night.* But moviemakers' fresh discovery of Jane Austen continued with a popular version of *Emma,* which contained a charming performance by Gwyneth Paltrow as the matchmaking heroine. Henry James also enjoyed a cinematic comeback, with Nicole Kidman and Barbara Hershey giving superb performances in *The Portrait of a Lady.* Audiences awaited a new version of *Washington Square,* with Jennifer Jason Leigh cast in the role that won an Oscar for Olivia de Havilland in *The Heiress* in 1949.

Arthur Miller's *The Crucible,* filmed with Daniel Day-Lewis and Winona Ryder, seemed certain to figure in the year's Oscar race, while an adaptation of Thomas Hardy's *Jude the Obscure,* titled *Jude,* was a critical favorite.

Versions of *Anna Karenina, Great Expectations, Cousin Bette, Don Quixote, A Midsummer Night's Dream, The House of Mirth,* and *Mrs. Dalloway* were either planned or in production in 1996. The classics offered performers richer roles than did Hollywood action films.

Summer offerings. A steady flow of movies was available for the *megaplex* theaters (multiroom theaters with more than 18 screens) that dominated the filmgoers' landscape. The summer months and the year-end holidays continued to see the most intense rate of new releases. However, after the Fourth of July opening of *Independence Day,* box-office business in the summer of 1996 dwindled. Only *A Time to Kill,* a splashy version of an early John Grisham novel, proved a strong magnet for moviegoers during the late summer. Its star, newcomer Matthew McConaughey, became an instant celebrity.

Noticeable among the summer disappointments was *The Cable Guy,* an unconventional comedy starring the popular Jim Carrey as an emotionally needy cable installer. Carrey received a record-breaking $20 million for the film. Its failure to perform as expected made studio executives ponder the wisdom of paying the salaries asked by big-name actors.

The Disney Studio's animated entry *The Hunchback of Notre Dame* failed to win moviegoers in the manner of *The Lion King* or *Pocahontas.* Although some of Hunchback's fiery images seemed too mature for very young audiences, its startling, vivid imagery marked a decided advancement for animation.

Summer in the international market. The disappointing late summer box-office business in the United States could be traced to the omnipresence of the Olympic Games, televised from Atlanta, Georgia, in July. Ironically, international movie attendance during the late summer reached a new high. *Mission: Impossible* broke records in Spain, and *The Rock,* an adventure film teaming Sean Connery with Nicolas Cage, scaled new heights in Germany. In many instances, U.S. films proved stronger at the box office internationally than domestically. The Demi Moore-Alec Baldwin drama *The Juror* flopped stateside but was a success in Europe and Asia.

One reason for the surging international attendance was the upgrading of theaters in European and Asian cities. The *multiplex* (multiroomed theater with 18 or less screens) boom continued, with audiences in South Korea and Taiwan flocking to their first viewings in these multiscreen theaters.

Big roles for women. Perhaps the most significant box-office success of 1996 was *The First Wives Club.* Released in September—traditionally not a prime moviegoing month—the glossy comedy became a smash hit despite mixed reviews. More significantly, it headlined Goldie Hawn, Diane Keaton, and Bette Midler—three actresses who are in their 50's. *The First Wives Club* proved that hit films need not be limited to winter and summer releases and that mature women can attract audiences. The year turned out to be a strong one for veteran actresses. Lauren Bacall gained fresh accolades for *The Mirror Has Two Faces,* while Debbie Reynolds garnered strong reviews for *Mother.* Shirley MacLaine re-created the matriarch of the 1983 *Terms of Endearment* for the film's sequel, *The Evening Star.*

The most anticipated end-of-year film in 1996 was *Evita,* starring Madonna as the powerful Argentine political figure Eva Peron. Madonna's screen impact had never duplicated the sensation of her personal appearances, but many expected that *Evita* would become her signature role. Still, the film's virtually all-musical format was considered a risk.

Late releases. Music also played an intregal part in Woody Allen's *Everyone Says I Love You,* with a cast that included Julia Roberts and Goldie Hawn.

Disney's *101 Dalmatians* reversed convention by adapting a classic animated film into a live-action comedy. Glenn Close snarled her way through the role of villainous Cruella De Vil.

Mars Attacks!, with an all-star ensemble including Jack Nicholson as a fuzzy-minded U.S. president and Glenn Close as a snippy first lady, was at the center of speculation among year-end releases. Its director, Tim Burton, responsible for the first two *Batman* movies as well as *Ed Wood* and *Beetlejuice,* has always taken an unconventional path.

Other strongly hyped releases included *Ransom,* with Ron Howard directing Mel Gibson as a tycoon who attempts to turn the tables on his son's abductors; *Ghosts of Mississippi,* about the retrial of Medgar Evers' slayer Byron De La Beckwith; *The Preacher's Wife,* a remake of 1947's *The Bishop's Wife,* with Denzel Washington and Whitney Houston assuming roles originated by Cary Grant and Loretta Young; *In Love and War,* with clean-cut Chris O'Donnell portraying Ernest Hemingway and Sandra Bullock as the nurse who inspired *A Farewell to Arms; The People vs. Larry Flynt,* with Woody Harrelson as the notorious *Hustler* publisher who experiences a religious awakening; and *Michael,* in which John Travolta—like Denzel Washington in *The Preacher's Wife*—plays an angel.

Out of the mainstream. Small-scale, nonmainstream films continued to reap strong critical endorsements. John Sayles, America's leading independent director, had one of the biggest triumphs of his career with *Lone Star,* which delved into a multilayered mystery surrounding a Texas border town. Moviemaking brothers Joel and Ethan Coen had a similar success with *Fargo,* which took a comedic look at a Minnesota murder and contained a finely tuned performance by Frances McDormand as a rural sheriff.

Actors Campbell Scott and Stanley Tucci won praise as codirectors of *Big Night,* a look at rival Italian restaurants in the late 1950's. Following Mel Gibson's directing victory in *Braveheart,* more actors turned to the other side of the lens. Tom Hanks, Al Pacino, Barbra Streisand, Anthony Hopkins, Kevin Spacey, and Matthew Broderick all directed films in 1996, with various degrees of success.

Academy Award winners in 1996

The following winners of the 1995 Academy Awards were announced in March 1996:

Best Picture, *Braveheart*
Best Actor, Nicolas Cage, *Leaving Las Vegas*
Best Actress, Susan Sarandon, *Dead Man Walking*
Best Supporting Actor, Kevin Spacey, *The Usual Suspects*
Best Supporting Actress, Mira Sorvino, *Mighty Aphrodite*
Best Director, Mel Gibson, *Braveheart*
Best Original Screenplay, Christopher McQuarrie, *The Usual Suspects*
Best Screenplay Adaptation, Emma Thompson, *Sense and Sensibility*
Best Cinematography, John Toll, *Braveheart*
Best Film Editing, Mike Hill, Dan Hanley, *Apollo 13*
Best Original Dramatic Score: Luis Bacalov, *The Postman (Il Postino)*
Best Original Music or Comedy Score: Alan Menken and Stephen Schwartz, *Pocahontas*
Best Original Song, Alan Menken and Stephen Schwartz, "Colors of the Wind" from *Pocahontas*
Best Foreign-Language Film, *Antonia's Line* (Netherlands)
Best Art Direction, Eugenio Zanetti, *Restoration*
Best Costume Design, James Acheson, *Restoration*
Best Sound, Rick Dior, Steve Pederson, Scott Millan, David MacMillan, *Apollo 13*
Best Sound Effects Editing, Lon Bender, Per Hallberg, *Braveheart*
Best Makeup, Peter Frampton, Paul Pattison, Lois Burwell, *Braveheart*
Best Visual Effects, *Babe*
Best Animated Short Film, *A Close Shave*
Best Live-Action Short Film, *Lieberman in Love*
Best Feature Documentary, *Anne Frank Remembered*
Best Short Subject Documentary, *One Survivor Remembers*
Honorary Award, Kirk Douglas and Chuck Jones

Directorial highs and lows. For other directors, 1996 was an unpredictable year. Robert Altman had a major disappointment with *Kansas City,* while Italy's Lina Wertmuller faltered with *Ninfa Plebea.* Michael Cimino's *The Sunchaser* went almost unnoticed, attracting neither the acclaim of *The Deer Hunter* nor the infamy of *Heaven's Gate.*

However, John Schlesinger rebounded from a career slump with a sterling adaptation of the 1930's satirical novel *Cold Comfort Farm,* and Bernardo Bertolucci erased memories of the unfortunate *Little Buddha* with the sensual *Stealing Beauty.* Spike Lee had a flop with *Girl 6,* a comedy drama dealing with phone sex. Spike Lee's *Get On the Bus,* cinema's first look at 1995's Million Man March was a critical success, but a failure at the box office.

European movies and moviegoers. British filmmaker Mike Leigh, whose films, *Naked, High Hopes,* and *Life Is Sweet,* were art-house successes, continued to revitalize his country's film output with the intensely moving *Secrets and Lies.* In this movie, a black, professional woman discovers that her birth mother is a white factory worker. Danny Boyle's *Trainspotting,* which presented a group of young Scots drowning in drugs, aimlessness, and cynicism, was a smash hit in Great Britain.

Germany enjoyed a reemerging entertainment scene, and its movie industry prospered accordingly. As recently as 1991, no German-made film drew more than 400,000 viewers in its native land. But the comedy *Der Bewegte Mann* sold 6.5 million tickets, earning $48 million on an investment of $2.7 million. By contrast, films produced by German subsidiaries of Disney and Warner Bros. flopped at the box office. Brazil also saw a renaissance in moviegoing, with box-office figures rising 50 percent during the first part of 1996.

The sentimental Italian-made drama *Il Postino (The Postman)* was the highest-grossing foreign-language film in 1996 in the United States. Otherwise, the exportation of Italian films reached an all-time low. The market share of Italian films in other European countries was less than 2 percent. In the United States, the Italian market share slipped even lower.

Rare early film discovered. In September, a 1912 feature film, previously believed lost, came to light. *Richard III,* the second feature film ever made in the United States, was donated to the American Film Institute by William Buffum of Portland, Oregon. The film's original nitrate print had been painstakingly maintained by Buffum in his basement for 30 years. ☐ Philip Wuntch

See also **Cage, Nicolas; Sarandon, Susan.** In *World Book,* see Motion pictures.

Mozambique. See Africa.

Music. See Classical music; Popular music.

Myanmar. See Burma.

Nebraska. See State government.

Nepal. See Asia.

Netanyahu, Benjamin (1949–), on May 29, 1996, became the first prime minister of Israel to be elected directly by the people. Netanyahu, the chairman of the conservative Likud Party, was known for his hard-line position toward Israel's Palestinian population. Before being elected, he spoke out against the previous government's land-for-peace agreement with the Palestinian Liberation Organization (PLO). The agreement called for Israel to cede sovereignty over certain areas of the West Bank, land west of the Jordan River, to the local Palestinian population.

Netanyahu was born on Oct. 21, 1949, in Tel Aviv, Israel. He moved to the United States at the age of 14. In 1967, he returned to Israel to serve in an antiterrorist unit in the Israel Defense Forces. In 1972, he enrolled at the Massachusetts Institute of Technology (MIT), in Cambridge, Massachusetts, where he earned a bachelor's degree in architecture and a master's degree in business administration.

In 1982, Netanyahu became Israel's deputy chief of mission to the United States. He served in several diplomatic posts before being elected to the Knesset, Israel's parliament, in 1988. Netanyahu gained international attention as the chief Israeli spokesperson during the Persian Gulf War (1991). In 1991, he was named deputy minister in the office of the prime minister. ☐ Lisa Klobuchar

See also **Israel; Middle East.**

Netherlands. The economy of the Netherlands continued to outperform most of its European Union (EU) partners in 1996 as demand for Dutch products from consumers at home and abroad grew. The government forecast growth of 2.5 percent, compared with an EU average of 1.6 percent. Government policy continued to focus on restraining public spending to reduce the deficit and debt and qualify the Netherlands to participate in a single European currency, scheduled to begin in 1999. On Sept. 17, 1996, the government introduced a budget for 1997 containing spending cuts as well as reductions in income and social security taxes. The government claimed the package would reduce the deficit to 2.2 percent of gross domestic product, well below the 3 percent limit for entering monetary union.

Central banker. Wim Duisenberg, the director of the Dutch central bank, was expected to become the first president of the European Central Bank, which is to manage the single EU currency. Duisenberg was designated in May to succeed in 1997 Alexandre Lamfalussy as president of the European Monetary Institute, the forerunner of the central bank.

Corporate troubles. Fokker NV, the airplane maker that had been a symbol of Dutch manufacturing prowess since World War I, collapsed in early 1996. Daimler-Benz AG, the German parent company of Fokker, abandoned the company on January 22, after the Dutch government failed to provide aid to cover Fokker's large losses and debts. Fokker declared bankruptcy on March 15 and laid off some 5,600 workers, the country's largest mass layoff. Fokker's core businesses were reorganized in July into a new company, Fokker Aviation, while court-appointed administrators searched for a buyer.

Philips NV, the largest company in the Netherlands, announced plans in August to slash 6,000 jobs as part of a restructuring of its troubled consumer electronics business. The cuts, which hit hardest at its German subsidiary, Grundig, were designed to shift production of television sets, videocassette recorders, and stereo equipment from Europe to countries with lower labor costs, particularly in Southeast Asia.

Drugs dispute. The government of Prime Minister Willem Kok remained locked in a diplomatic struggle with France over Dutch drug laws and policies on their enforcement. French President Jacques Chirac canceled a five-nation summit meeting on drugs that was to have been held in Amsterdam in March. He claimed that Dutch laws, which included permitting the sale of marijuana at coffee shops, had made the Netherlands a conduit for the trafficking of drugs into France. The Dutch legislature tightened the laws on April 2 by voting to reduce the amount of marijuana that could legally be sold.

□ Tom Buerkle

See also **Europe** (Facts in brief table). In *World Book,* see **European Union; Netherlands.**

New York City.

Schools in New York City opened Sept. 4, 1996, to the worst overcrowding in 20 years. School officials said a surge in Caribbean and Asian immigrants, combined with a slow-paced construction program and a decline in the dropout rate, resulted in an enrollment of more than 1 million students—91,000 more than the system's 1,100 schools could handle. Overcrowding was reported in most of the city's 31 community school districts.

In response, Schools Chancellor Rudolph F. Crew announced on September 18 that the Board of Education would test a year-round school calendar, beginning next summer, modeled on programs in Los Angeles and Trenton, New Jersey. Students would be divided into four groups, with each group attending school for 45 days, followed by 15 days off. Schools would thus be only three-quarters filled at any one time, but would not lose any state aid.

In 1996, the Young Women's Leadership School, an all-girls junior high school, opened in a school district in the East Harlem section of Manhattan. The school was based on the premise that girls perform better in math and science if boys are not in the classroom. The experiment faced challenges from civil rights activists, who argued that girls-only schools violated the civil rights of boys.

Police Commissioner William Bratton, one of the nation's most visible and innovative police officials, resigned April 15 to head a private security firm. In his 27 months as commissioner, Bratton's ideas and hard-nosed enforcement were credited with a 27 percent drop in serious crime and a 40 percent decline in homicides. He was succeeded by former Fire Commissioner Howard Safir.

In an effort to increase participation and interest, sponsors of New York's Labor Day parade broke with tradition by moving the annual event from its traditional date on the first Monday to the first Saturday in September. The effort paid off, as the September 7 parade attracted the highest attendance in years. More than 200,000 participants, representing 100 unions, marched 25 blocks to the theme "America Needs a Raise."

Times Square facelift. The redevelopment of the 42nd Street/Times Square area of Manhattan continued at a rapid pace in 1996. Private investors poured millions of dollars into the renovation of old, run-down theaters and commercial buildings, promising to transform the area into a tourist-friendly district of shopping, entertainment, and restaurants. The much-publicized, $34-million renovation of the New Amsterdam Theater by the Walt Disney Company as a venue for Disney-produced live theater performances was to be completed by the spring of 1997.

A new visitors' center opened in June 1996, in the restored Selwyn Theater on 42nd Street, and new zoning restrictions took effect in November that forced out all but a few remaining X-rated businesses, which had dominated the area since the 1960's. City officials reported that efforts to "clean up" Times Square had led to a 42-percent drop in the area's crime rate since 1992.

Workfare agreement. Leaders of New York City's Transit Authority and the Transport Workers Union reached agreement Sept. 18, 1996, on a "workfare" contract that would permit welfare recipients to fill up to 500 cleaning jobs that become available through attrition. The agreement between the transit

A spectacular fire engulfs a Manhattan office building on March 1. The blaze drew more than 300 firefighters and brought morning rush-hour traffic to a standstill.

agency and one of the city's most militant unions was part of a new labor contract that guaranteed no layoffs through 1999. The agreement, however, alarmed leaders of other municipal unions who held agreements with the administration of Mayor Rudolph Giuliani stipulating that workfare participants would never fill jobs held by union workers.

Giuliani often cited workfare as one of his biggest accomplishments. Since he became mayor in January 1994, more than 34,000 people had been put to work cleaning New York's streets and parks, doing clerical work, and assisting janitors in city buildings in exchange for their welfare benefits. It was the city's largest public jobs program since the Great Depression of the 1930's.　　□ Owen Moritz

See also **City; Education.** In *World Book,* see **New York City.**

New Zealand on Oct. 12, 1996, held its first general election under a new system that provided for a combination of direct election of representatives and *proportional representation* (a system of electing legislators in which each political party is represented in proportion to its share of the total vote cast). The ruling National Party won 44 seats. The main opposition Labour Party took 37 seats, and the New Zealand First Party captured 17 seats. Prime Minister James Bolger and his National Party continued to govern until a coalition was formed in December.

The New Zealand First Party, under the new election system, held the balance of power, and its leader and founder, Winston Peters, a *Maori* (native New Zealander of Polynesian descent), negotiated in secret with the National Party and the Labour Party for nearly eight weeks following the election before a government could be organized. On December 11, New Zealand First finally formed a coalition with the National Party. James Bolger was again named prime minister, and Peters was made Bolger's deputy as well as treasury minister, an office of immense economic power.

The economy. New Zealand, between 1985 and 1995, transformed its highly regulated economy into a market-driven system through restructuring and deregulatory reforms. The international financial community reacted positively to the reforms, and the New Zealand dollar reached an eight-year high in 1996. The Reserve Bank reduced interest rates to lower the market price of the dollar, and thus encourage exports.

Treasury forecasts predicted that the economy would expand by 3.2 percent between March 1996 and March 1997, which was higher than the Reserve Bank's prediction of 2 percent. Budget surpluses allowed for a preelection round of income tax cuts, the first in nearly eight years. Inflation, which had been fueled by rising housing costs, was held at 2.3 percent for the fiscal year ending June 1996. Unemployment stood at 6.1 percent, one of the lowest rates among industrialized nations.

The Waitangi Tribunal, a judicial group set up in the 1970's to redress Maori grievances, recommended in June 1996 that the Maoris of the Taranaki region be compensated for the "horrific injustices" inflicted on them during the colonial period of the 1800's. The government, however, insisted that Maoris would have to accept compensatory settlements below the level of their demands.

Wild horses. Public protests forced the government to cancel plans to thin herds of wild horses on North Island in August. In October, the government announced a plan to offer surplus wild horses for sale.　　□ Gavin Ellis

See also **Asia** (Facts in brief table). In *World Book,* see **New Zealand.**

Newfoundland. See Canadian provinces.

Newsmakers

Remembering the Donner Party. In July 1996, more than 200 direct descendants of the ill-fated Donner Party, a group of 82 pioneers heading westward to California, gathered near Donner Pass in eastern California. They commemorated the 150th anniversary of a tragic incident. During the severe winter of 1846-1847, the pioneers became snowbound. Thirty-five of them died.

In late October 1846, the group, led by George and Jacob Donner, reached a pass later to be named Donner Pass in the Sierra Nevada Mountains, but a snowstorm had already blocked the pass. Unable to proceed or turn back, the settlers built crude shelters of logs, rocks, and hides. When their food supplies ran out, they ate their animals, mice, twigs, and their shoes. Finally, they were forced to consume their own dead. In December, a few members managed to struggle through the snow-blocked pass and sent back rescue workers, who brought the other survivors through.

At the reunion, the descendants downplayed the tragic nature of the event, maintaining that the survivors did what they had to do to survive. The gathering focused instead on the courageousness of the pioneers.

JFK Jr. ties the knot. Once described as "America's most eligible bachelor," John F. Kennedy, Jr., the 35-year-old son of President John F. Kennedy and Jacqueline Kennedy Onassis, married Carolyn Bessette, age 30, on Sept. 21, 1996. Kennedy was the cofounder and editor of *George* magazine, and Bessette worked in public relations for Calvin Klein, Ltd., in New York City.

The wedding took place in great secrecy at a private resort on secluded Cumberland Island, off the coast of Georgia. Guests were invited to the wedding just days before it took place. Among those in attendance were Massachussets Senator Edward M. Kennedy, the groom's uncle, and other Kennedy family members.

Tragedy on Everest. In Nepal, eight climbers attempting to climb Mount Everest were killed in May 1996, when a storm mustering strong winds and subzero temperatures suddenly struck. Mount Everest is the world's highest mountain, with a summit 29,028 feet (8,848 meters) above sea level.

Rob Hall, 36, of Christchurch, New Zealand, had succeeded in reaching the summit for the fifth time. But he was trapped on the way down when he stayed with his partner, Doug Hansen, 44, of Renton, Washington, who was overcome by altitude sickness and unable to continue. Hansen died during the night, but Hall, without oxygen, fluids, a tent, or a sleeping bag, survived long enough to speak to his wife in New Zealand over the radio, which was connected to the telephone at his base camp. He died before rescuers could reach him.

Others missing in the storm and presumed dead included Yasuko Namba, 47, of Tokyo, the second Japanese woman to climb Mount Everest, and three members of an expedition from India, who had reached the top from Tibet, up the north face of the mountain.

The highest helicopter rescue in history saved the lives of two climbers. Ming Ho Gau, 47, the first Taiwanese to climb Mount Everest, and Seaborne B. Weathers of Dallas were picked up by a Nepalese air force helicopter. The pilot, Colonel Madan K. Chetri, managed the rescue at 20,900 feet (6,370 meters) above sea level.

The death toll resulting from the storm surpassed what previously had been the worst accident on the mountain—an avalanche in 1989 that killed six Polish climbers.

Rare giant flower blooms. In July 1996, visitors flocked to the Royal Botanic Gardens in the Kew district of London to view a rare event—the blooming of a tropical plant known as a titan arum (*Amorphophallus titanium*). The plant, which is native to the Indonesian island of Sumatra, blooms, on average, only three times during its lifetime. The blossom usually gives off a strong and unpleasant odor. The specimen at Kew Garden, which measured 64 inches (162 centimeters) tall, had last bloomed in 1963.

Reporters and television crews from around the world came to London to cover the event. Many people, however, were somewhat disappointed that the blossom didn't deliver the horrible smell for which it is famous. "A bit disappointing," commented one Englishwoman who came to see the

A titan arum blooms at London's Royal Botanic Gardens in July. Crowds were disappointed by the blossom's lack of a characteristically foul odor.

plant. "It smells worse outside than it does here."

Byrd's flight reexamined. On May 9, 1926, Richard E. Byrd and pilot-mechanic Floyd Bennett became the first people to fly an airplane to the North Pole. Or so they said.

Rumors had persisted in the years since Byrd's flight that the two explorers actually turned back before reaching the pole. In 1996, archivists at Ohio State University in Columbus discovered Byrd's flight diary. They enlisted the aid of Dennis Rawlins, a specialist in navigation and science history from Baltimore. After carefully examining the diary, Rawlins found that notes and calculations in the diary indicated that Byrd and Bennett may have turned their plane around at least 2.25 degrees of latitude shy of the North Pole. Rawlins also found discrepancies in some navigational figures made by Byrd in the diary, which did not match those he used in other reports of the journey.

Campus crusader wins Templeton Prize. In 1996, the Templeton Prize for Progress in Religion went to William Bright, the 74-year-old founder of the Campus Crusade for Christ. The prize—700,000 British pounds ($1.07 million)—is awarded each year to the person recognized as most advancing the understanding of religion.

Bright was a successful businessman before devoting himself to student ministry. In 1951, he founded the Campus Crusade for Christ at the University of California, Los Angeles (UCLA). In 1996, the organization was active on more than 650 campuses in the United States and 470 campuses in other parts of the world.

Past winners of the Templeton Prize, which was established in 1972, include Mother Teresa, the Roman Catholic missionary, and Russian novelist Alexander Solzhenitsyn. Bright said he intended to use the prize to promote the benefits of fasting.

Girl pilot crashes. Seven-year-old Jessica Dubroff's attempt to become the youngest person to fly a plane across the continental United States made her a media celebrity in 1996. Her story, however, took a tragic turn on the morning of April 11, when her airplane appeared to stall just after take-off from an airfield near Cheyenne, Wyoming, and crashed nose-first into the ground. Jessica, her father, Lloyd Dubroff, and flight instructor Joe Reid were killed instantly. Flight regulations in the United States that permit children to handle the controls of an airplane in flight were widely criticized as contributing to the fatal crash.

Parents found guilty. A jury in May 1996 found a Michigan couple guilty of failing to "exercise reasonable parental control" over their teen-age son, violating a 1994 St. Clair Shores city ordinance that makes parents responsible for the conduct of their children. The couple's son, age 16, was first arrested in May 1995 for committing several burglaries. When the boy was arrested for a second time in September 1995, police searched his bedroom and found a handgun, a knife, stolen goods, a four-foot (1.2 meters) marijuana plant, and alcohol.

A six-person jury took less than 30 minutes to find the parents guilty. They were fined $100 each and ordered to pay court costs, but Michigan state law prevented them from being liable for $27,000 in damages that were the result of their son's burglaries. The youth served a one-year sentence in a juvenile detention facility.

International swim falls short. In June 1996, Australian swimmer Susie Maroney fell about 12 miles (19 kilometers) short of her goal of becoming the first person to swim the Straits of Florida—the stretch of ocean between Cuba and the United States—without assistance. At least 50 other swimmers have tried unsuccessfully to swim the straits, which are known for their strong currents.

Maroney, 21, was in the water for nearly 38 hours and swam a total of 88½ miles (142.4 kilometers), setting a world record. She swam most of the way inside a custom-built shark cage towed by a boat, but left the cage for a time after large waves began to toss the cage about. Maroney was not allowed to leave the water or hold onto the cage during the swim. She was treated for dehydration at a hospital in Key West, Florida, and released. In 1993, Maroney had set a world record for swimming around New York City's Manhattan Island in 7 hours, 7 seconds.

Spelling champ. At the 69th National Spelling Bee, which ended May 30 in Washington, D.C., 12-year-old Wendy Guey of West Palm Beach, Florida, took the $5,000 first prize when she correctly spelled *vivisepulture,* meaning "the act or practice of burying alive." Thirteen-year-old Nikki Dowdy of Houston came in second. Dowdy lost her bid for first place in the 13th round when she misspelled *cervicorn,* an adjective meaning branching like antlers.

Heeere's *Oleg!* Oleg Gordievsky, the former head of KGB operations in London, made a drastic career change in October 1996, when he debuted as the host of "Wanted," a new game show on British TV. A double agent who spied on the KGB, the intelligence agency of the former Soviet Union, for the British, Gordievsky defected to the West in 1985. Until the collapse of the Soviet Union in 1991, he was in hiding from Soviet authorities.

Described as "part 'Running Man', part 'Treasure Hunt'," *Wanted* pitted teams of contestants (called *runners*) against a team of *trackers*. The object of the game was for runners to flee across the British Isles without being detected by the trackers or appearing on camera. The longer the runners remained free, the more prizes they accumulated. The show was scheduled for an eight-week run.

Jackie O. auction. Personal effects from the estate of Jacqueline Bouvier Kennedy Onassis, who died of cancer in 1994, were snatched up by bidders at Sotheby's auction house in New York City in April 1996. Although celebrity items typically command high prices at auction, experts were shocked at the incredibly high prices fetched by some of Onassis's possessions.

Among the highest bids were $42,000 for a textbook of French verb conjugations, $211,000 for a *faux* (fake) pearl necklace featured in a famous 1962 photograph, and $2.6 million for Onassis's 40-carat

diamond engagement ring from her second husband, Greek millionaire Aristotle Onassis. In all, the auction grossed $34.5 million for a collection valued at just $4.6 million by Sotheby's.

Rauf suspended. Calling the U.S. flag "a symbol of oppression, of tyranny," Denver Nuggets star Mahmoud Abdul-Rauf was suspended by the National Basketball Association in March 1996, for refusing to stand while the national anthem was played before games. Rauf, who became a Muslim in 1991, later argued that standing for the anthem violated his religious beliefs, because the *Koran* (Islamic scriptures) forbids "nationalistic ritual." The suspension would have cost Rauf $31,707 per game. He compromised after missing only one game. Rauf and league officials agreed that he would stand and pray silently during the anthem.

Primary Colors was the subject of much speculation both inside and outside the nation's capital during the first half of 1996. The novel, the story of a fictional Southern governor's run for president of the United States, featured characters that bore a striking resemblance to President Clinton, his wife, Hillary Rodham Clinton, and members of his 1992 campaign staff. The identity of the book's author—listed only as "Anonymous"—was debated by Washington, D.C., insiders for several months. Nearly ev-

Dancers in Chicago attempt to master the "Macarena," the line-dance craze that swept the United States in 1996.

eryone agreed that the author must have been someone intimately familiar with the circumstances of Bill Clinton's 1992 presidential campaign.

In July, Joe Klein, a columnist for *Newsweek* magazine and a commentator for CBS News, admitted that he was the author of *Primary Colors.* Klein was immediately criticized by fellow journalists, who questioned his ethics. When asked by reporters if he had written the book, Klein had repeatedly and flatly denied doing so. He said that he had been "anguished" about this deception, but stated that he had an agreement with the book's publisher to keep his identity secret.

Klein resigned from CBS News on June 25. Richard Smith, president and editor in chief of *Newsweek,* said that he expected Klein to continue working for the magazine. At the time, more than 1 million copies of *Primary Colors* were in print, and the motion-picture rights to the story had been sold for $1.5 million.

Flag may bear Lincoln's blood. A small museum run by the Pike County Historical Society in Milford, Philadelphia, revealed that it may hold a unique piece of Americana. An American flag in the museum's collection bears a stain that may be a remnant of President Abraham Lincoln's blood.

Joseph Garrera, an amateur historian from Newton, New Jersey, said he was able to trace the flag's history to Ford's Theatre, where Lincoln was shot on April 14, 1865. The flag was donated to the historical society in 1954 by a man whose mother was in the cast of *Our American Cousin,* the play Lincoln was attending the night he was shot. Garrera found that, after the shooting, two flags were reported missing from the theater. One of them, he said, could have been used to cushion Lincoln's head as he lay dying from the head wound. Forensic testing showed that the stain was in fact human blood, but proof that the blood came from Abraham Lincoln was unlikely to be established.

Garrera reported his finding to several top Lincoln scholars, and many agreed with his conclusion. Although authenticity of historical artifacts is often not certain, Garrera stated that he was "95 percent" sure the flag was authentic.

Madonna gives birth. After a pregnancy that attracted international media attention throughout 1996, pop singer and actress Madonna delivered her first child on October 14. The baby girl was named Lourdes Maria Ciccone Leon. The father was Carlos Leon, 30, the star's former personal trainer.

Michael Jackson, "the King of Pop" and Lisa-Marie Presley, daughter of Elvis Presley, "the King of Rock and Roll," ended their 19-month marriage in 1996. Citing "irreconcilable differences," Presley filed for divorce on January 18. A spokesman for Jackson said the couple would "remain good friends."

In November 1996, Jackson's management an-

President John F. Kennedy's golf clubs and rocking chair are put on public display in April before bringing record prices at auction.

nounced that the star had remarried and was soon to become a father. Jackson reportedly met his new bride, 37-year-old Debbie Rowe, 15 years ago at the office of his plastic surgeon. The two were married in Sydney, Australia, where Jackson was on tour. The baby was due to be born in February 1997.

Protesters decry pageant. The Miss World beauty pageant became the center of a storm of controversy in November 1996. Critics of the pageant, which was held in Bangalore, India, staged protests—which frequently became violent—for weeks prior to the event. They said that the pageant violated Indian culture, dehumanized women, and promoted the use of cosmetics and plastic surgery. One man burned himself to death in protest, and a feminist group threatened to stage a mass suicide during the event, which was televised around the world on November 23. Extra security measures were put in place—smoking was banned, audience members were searched, and cigarette lighters were confiscated. The new Miss World, Irene Skliva of Greece, was crowned without incident.

Gorilla saves boy. On August 16, visitors to the Tropic World exhibit at the Brookfield Zoo outside Chicago were horrified when a 3-year-old boy tumbled more than 15 feet (4.6 meters) into an enclosure that contained seven gorillas. In the pit, Binti-Jua, a 160-pound, female western lowland gorilla, approached the dazed toddler and picked him up, gently cradling him in her arms. Shielding the boy from the other gorillas, Binti-Jua carried the child to an access door, where zookeepers took him to safety. The boy, suffering from head injuries, a broken hand, and several cuts and bruises, was taken to a nearby hospital.

Zoo officials said that Binti-Jua had been neglected by her mother as a baby and that trainers had taught her the basic parenting skills she needed to raise her own young. This training by human beings may explain why Binti-Jua apparently acted out of compassion for the injured child.

As soon as Tropic World reopened after the incident, visitors came in large numbers to see Binti-Jua. Many brought gifts and treats for the gorilla, calling her a heroine. Cards, letters, and more gifts poured into the zoo from around the world, prompting zoo administrators to assign Binti-Jua her own mailbox.

The pharaoh of beers. Using a recipe reconstructed during research about the culture of ancient Egypt, scientists at Great Britain's Cambridge University in 1996 brewed a type of beer that was popular among Egyptians more than 4,000 years ago. The researchers analyzed beer residues and desiccated loaves of bread recovered from ancient tombs to infer much about how the beer was crafted. It was customary for the ancient Egyptians to be entombed with food and beer to sustain them in the afterlife.

Ancient Egyptian art and writings indicate that beer enjoyed great popularity among both the nobility and common people of ancient Egypt. The beers created by ancient Egyptians bore names like Beautiful, Heavenly, and Joy Bringer. The scientists found that the brewing process was more elaborate than they had thought.

The finished product was an ale that appeared slightly cloudy and had a golden color. "It does not taste like any beer I've ever tried before," said Dr. Delwen Samuel, one of the Cambridge researchers. "It's very rich, very malty and has a flavor that reminds you a little of chardonnay."

Oldest American dies. Mary Thompson, whom the U.S. Social Security Administration had recorded as the oldest person in America, died of a heart attack August 3 in Florida. Thompson never had a birth certificate, but records kept by the Social Security Administration traced her life back to March 27, 1876, making her at least 120 years old. The Guinness Book of Records had listed Carrie White, who was 116 years old when she died in 1991, as the oldest American. According to Guinness, Jeanne Calment, a Frenchwoman who turned 121 in February 1996, was the world's oldest living person whose birth date could be authenticated.

Gigante fit to stand trial. On August 28, Vincent "the Chin" Gigante, the reputed head of New York's notorious Genovese crime family, was found by a federal judge to be physically and mentally competent to stand trial in March 1997. Gigante, 68, was charged with six counts of murder and three counts of conspiracy to commit murder. Authorities on the New York City crime scene believed Gigante became the country's most powerful crime figure af-

A gorilla comes to a child's rescue in August. The 3-year-old boy had fallen into the gorilla enclosure, and Binti-Jua gently carried him to safety.

ter the imprisonment of John Gotti in 1993.

Gigante was known for wandering the streets of Manhattan's Little Italy neighborhood dressed in pajamas and a bathrobe, mumbling to himself. His lawyers tried to portray Gigante as a harmless old man who was suffering from mental illness. But prosecutors argued that Gigante's behavior was simply a ploy to avoid prosecution. Although Gigante had been indicted in May 1990, prosecutors previously had been unable to establish that he was competent to stand trial.
☐ Peter Uremovic

Newspaper. The economics of publishing newspapers in the United States improved in 1996. The price of newsprint, the paper on which newspapers are printed, declined in 1996 for the first time since 1994. From a low of $420 per metric ton (2,200 pounds), in 1994, the cost of newsprint soared as high as $760 in early 1996, but declined to $600 by April.

One reason for the price decline was a campaign of aggressive cost-cutting by the newspaper companies themselves. *The Denver Post,* for example, trimmed the width of its print page to 12-½ inches (31.8 centimeters)—1 inch (2.5 centimeters) narrower than the standard broadsheet newspaper page. *The Post's* local competitor, the *Rocky Mountain News,* cited newsprint costs in a 1996 decision to end home delivery outside the Denver metropolitan area. Other major dailies, including *The Los Angeles Times* and *The Des Moines Register,* also stopped selling papers far from their local markets.

Sales of major newspaper companies in 1996 demonstrated the industry's improving health. In many cases, however, newspapers were held by large communications companies that also held television stations, which attracted potential buyers.

In the biggest deal of the year, the A. H. Belo Corporation, publisher of *The Dallas Morning News,* announced an agreement on September 26 to buy the Providence Journal Company, owner of *The Providence* (R.I.) *Journal-Bulletin* and nine TV stations. The purchase price was $1.5 billion.

Pulitzer Publishing Co., owner of the *St. Louis Post-Dispatch,* announced a $240-million deal in May to buy the stock of Scripps League Newspapers, Inc., a publisher of 16 small newspapers in the Midwest and West. In July, Media General, Inc., publisher of the *Tampa* (Florida) *Tribune,* agreed to pay $710 million for Park Acquisitions, the owner of 28 daily newspapers and 10 network-affiliated TV stations.

Industry downsides. A bitter newspaper strike in Detroit, stretching into its second year, continued to work hardship on both strikers and publishers. Union workers for *The Detroit News* and *Detroit Free Press* struck on July 13, 1995. The newspapers, using replacement employees, continued to publish without interruption. Independent audits, however, showed that the combined circulation of the newspapers was down 35 percent during the week and 31 percent on Sundays.

An industry report released in May 1996 showed that journalism school graduates were the most poorly paid college-educated workers joining the labor force. Graduates of journalism schools in 1996 could expect to earn an average annual income of only about $20,000 in their first year on the job. Moreover, at least one in five journalists under the age of 25 was paid a salary under the official poverty line of $15,141. □ Mark Fitzgerald

In *World Book,* see **Newspaper.**

Nicaragua. On Oct. 20, 1996, Nicaraguans elected José Arnoldo Alemán Lacayo of the conservative Liberal Alliance Party to a six-year term as president. Alemán's inauguration, scheduled for Jan. 10, 1997, would mark the first transfer of power from one democratically elected civilian to another in the country's history.

Alemán, a former mayor of the capital, Managua, defeated former President Daniel Ortega Saavedra of the Sandinista National Liberation Front. Alemán, who survived an assassination attempt in January 1996, promised free-market economic reforms and improved relations with the United States.

In March, the Nicaraguan government sold the logging rights to 153,000 acres to a Korean company. Nicaragua's Sumo Indians challenged the concession, claiming that some of the land belonged to them. As they prepared to take their case to court, the Sumos, with the help of the World Wildlife Fund in Washington, D.C., and Harvard University in Cambridge, Massachusetts, produced a survey of their ancestral land holdings. Conservationists hoped the Sumo project would draw attention to the alarming rate at which Central American forests were being cut—approximately 1,160 square miles (3,000 square kilometers) annually. □ Nathan A. Haverstock

See also **Latin America** (Facts in brief table). In *World Book,* see **Nicaragua.**

Niger. See **Africa.**

Nigeria, Africa's most populous country, continued to fall short of regional and world expectations in 1996. The country remained in the grip of a repressive dictatorship that showed little interest in genuine democratic reforms.

Military regime keeps a tight grip. The military government of General Sani Abacha came to power in a *coup d'état* (internal overthrow) in 1993. The military had invalidated the results of a presidential election that year when a candidate not to its liking, Moshood Abiola, won. Abiola was arrested on charges of treason in late 1993. At the end of 1996, he was still in prison.

In late 1995, General Abacha's government executed nine political dissidents. A sharp and immediate world outcry ensued. Led by the United States, Western nations imposed economic sanctions against Nigeria in an effort to force its government to return to democratic rule. The Commonwealth of Nations, an association of countries that were once part of the British Empire, suspended Nigeria's membership. At the same time, many Western countries refused travel visas to Nigerian government officials. These initiatives seemed to have had little effect on Nigeria's ruling regime.

Some world leaders—notably South Africa's President Nelson Mandela—advocated a boycott of Nigerian oil. Such a boycott could be expected to exert far greater economic pressure on Nigeria than sanctions. However, neither the United States nor European Union members, dependent on Nigerian oil exports, proved willing to undertake such a costly action. Mandela also spearheaded a campaign against Shell Oil, the major investor in Nigeria and the regime's economic mainstay. Like the boycott idea, this effort failed to produce any tangible results.

Promises of democracy. The regime vowed in 1996 that democracy would return to Nigeria by 1998, but only after a series of incremental steps to prepare the population. In March, local government elections were conducted on a nonpartisan basis. In June, the regime lifted its three-year ban on political parties. Also in 1996, the government announced the creation of six new states, resulting in a total of 36 governmental regions. However, a promised new constitution lagged behind schedule.

Given Nigeria's recent history, most Nigerians viewed the transition to democracy with cynicism. Further contributing to this cynicism was the murder of Moshood Abiola's wife, Kudirat, by three unknown gunmen on a Lagos street on June 4, 1996. Many Nigerians suspected government involvement in the crime. Nigerians also saw evidence of violent opposition to military rule in several bomb blasts—one in the Kano Airport and another in a major hotel—and in the January 17 crash of an airplane carrying Abiola's son.

An improving economic scene. In 1996, Shell Oil proceeded with the construction of a multibillion-dollar natural gas project. In March, Shell announced the discovery of a major new offshore oil field. In the first half of the 1990's, petroleum provided more than 90 percent of Nigeria's export income, though the country's oil wealth had done little to improve overall standards of living. Inflation in 1996 was reported to be at a rate of 40 percent or less, an improvement over previous years. Economic growth for 1995 was reported at 2.17 percent; for 1996, the government forecast a jump to 4.94 percent.

Regional diplomacy and conflicts. Nigeria continued to exercise leadership in West African affairs. Nigerian soldiers comprised the majority of an 8,000-member peacekeeping force in Liberia. The force, known as ECOMOG, remained in Liberia throughout 1996. At the same time, conflicts close to home distracted Nigeria. Its continuing dispute with Cameroon over the oil-rich Bakassi Peninsula flared hotly in 1996. The United Nations sent an observer team to the region, and Cameroon took the conflict to the International Court of Justice.

In May, many Nigerians were saddened by the death of Nnamdi Azikiwe, one of the country's founders. Born in 1904 and educated in the United States, Azikiwe had helped lead Nigeria to independence in 1960. ☐ Mark DeLancey

See also **Africa** (Facts in brief table); **Cameroon; Liberia; South Africa.** In *World Book,* see **Nigeria.**

Nobel Prizes in literature, peace, the sciences, and economics were awarded in October 1996 by the Norwegian Storting (parliament) in Oslo and by the Royal Swedish Academy of Sciences, the Karolinksa Institute, and the Swedish Academy of Literature in Stockholm. Each prize was worth $1.12 million.

The literature prize went to Polish poet Wislawa Szymborska, 73, whose spare, witty verse emphasizes interpersonal relationships and the oddities and unexpected turns of everyday life. Szymborska has long been revered in her native country, where her poetry has been set to rock music. The Nobel committee noted that Szymborska had been described as "the Mozart of poetry, not without justice in view of her wealth of inspiration and the veritable ease with which her words seem to fall into place."

Although Szymborska has described her poetry as personal rather than political, her first volume, *That's What We Live For* (1952), was heavily influenced by Communism. But in *Calling Out to Yeti* (1957), she compared Joseph Stalin, dictator of the former Soviet Union from 1929 to 1953, to The Abominable Snowman. Her volumes include *View with a Grain of Sand* (1967), *People on a Bridge* (1986), and *Sounds, Feelings, Thoughts* (1981).

The peace prize went to Roman Catholic Bishop Carlos Filipe Ximenes Belo, 48, and political activist Jose Ramos-Horta, 46, both of the former Portuguese colony of East Timor in Southeast Asia. The two men were honored for their attempts to end a conflict that began when Indonesia invaded East Timor in 1975. Since then, tens of thousands of people have died in the conflict. The Nobel committee noted that it had awarded the prize to Belo and Ramos-Horta because it did not want the conflict to be forgotten.

Belo, the spiritual leader of most East Timorese, who are overwhelmingly Roman Catholic, attempted to mediate a peaceful end to the conflict. He also spoke out at great personal risk against Indonesia's occupation forces. Ramos-Horta worked for East Timor's independence from Portugal, just before the Indonesian invasion. Since the invasion, he has lived in exile in Australia, where he has continued to serve as the chief spokesman for an independent East Timor.

The prize for physiology or medicine was shared by Australian-born Peter C. Doherty, 55, of St. Jude's Children's Research Hospital in Memphis, Tennessee, and Swiss Rolf M. Zinkernagel, 52, of the Institute of Experimental Immunology in Zurich, Switzerland. The two scientists were honored for proposing a theory that answered a basic and persistent question in immunology: How does the immune system recognize cells infected with a virus?

Doherty and Zinkernagel's theory developed from collaborative experiments with a mouse virus conducted in the early 1970's. The two scientists proposed that white blood cells, which detect and destroy infected cells, locate their targets by means of two proteins. The first, found on the surface of every body cell, is unique to each individual and helps the immune system distinguish the self from the non-self. The second is a fragment of an invading virus displayed on the surface of each infected cell.

The economics prize went to Briton James A. Mirrlees, 60, of Cambridge University in England and Canadian-born William Vickrey, 82, of Columbia University in New York City. Vickrey died on October 11, three days after winning the prize.

The two economists were honored for their groundbreaking and practical contributions to the theory of incentives, an area of economics dealing with cases in which information varies among decision makers. The Nobel committee credited the men with advancing the understanding of a wide range of economic situations, including tax systems, insurance, credit markets, and auctions. Before winning the economics prize, Vickrey was best known for his contributions to an economic system called time-of-day pricing, in which the price of a service, such as electric power or public transit, rises with demand.

The chemistry prize was shared by Americans Richard E. Smalley, 53, and Robert F. Curl, Jr., 63, of Rice University in Houston, and Briton Harold W. Kroto, 57, of the University of Sussex in Great Britain. The scientists were cited for their 1985 discovery of buckeyballs, a class of hollow, spherical carbon molecules made up of 60 or 70 interlocking carbon molecules. Buckeyballs are also known as fullerenes, after the American designer Buckminster Fuller, the developer of the geodesic dome, which the molecule resembles.

Since 1985, buckeyballs have gone from being a scientific oddity to the foundation of a well-established branch of chemistry. Their study may lead to the development of superstrong fibers or materials with unusual electrical or optical qualities.

The physics prize went to Americans David M. Lee, 65, and Robert C. Richardson, 59, of Cornell University in Ithaca, New York, and Douglas D. Osheroff, 52, of Stanford University in Palo Alto, California. The scientists won the prize for proving in 1972 that at extremely low temperatures, liquid helium-3, a rare form of helium, becomes superfluid—that is, able to flow without losing energy to friction the way ordinary fluids do. The scientists found that the phenomenon occurs when helium-3 is chilled to −459.67 °F. (−273.15 °C), almost absolute zero. Superfluidity in ordinary liquid helium was discovered in the 1930's, but converting helium-3 to that state had proved more difficult. Because superfluid helium has magnetic properties different from those of ordinary fluids, it can be used to observe directly the interactions of atoms and molecules. □ Barbara A. Mayes

In *World Book,* see **Nobel Prizes.**
North Carolina. See State government.
North Dakota. See State government.

Northern Ireland. On Jan. 23, 1996, a team led by former U.S. Senator George Mitchell proposed a solution for breaking the deadlock in peace talks between the British and Irish governments and various political parties of Northern Ireland. The British had demanded that the Irish Republican Army (IRA), an unofficial military force fighting for a united Ireland, surrender its weapons before its political wing, Sinn Féin, would be admitted to the talks. Mitchell's team recommended a gradual decommissioning of weapons as talks progressed. British Prime Minister John Major, however, side-stepped the recommendations and announced special elections for delegates to the forum, or peace talks.

Cease-fire ends. In response to the prime minister's announcement, the IRA ended its 17-month cease-fire by exploding a bomb in London's Docklands area on February 9. The bomb killed 2 people and injured 100. Additional bombs were set off in central London on February 18 and in a shopping center in Manchester, England, on June 15. An IRA mortar attack on a British army base at Osnabrück, Germany, followed on June 28. On October 7, two bombs exploded at the British Army's Northern Ireland headquarters in Lisburn. The resumption of violence by the IRA jeopardized a parallel cease-fire by Protestant groups that favor Northern Ireland remaining part of the United Kingdom (U.K.).

Forum elections. Elections for the forum took place on May 30. The Ulster Unionist Party (UUP), a Protestant group in favor of Northern Ireland's remaining part of the U.K., won the greatest number of seats. Sinn Féin secured 15 percent of the vote, giving it 15 seats. Government officials in London and Dublin, however, insisted that Sinn Féin could not take part in the forum and turned the party's delegation away from opening talks in Belfast on June 10. The Democratic Unionist Party, a Protestant group that is more extreme than the UUP, refused to accept Mitchell as chairman, accusing him of favoring Sinn Féin, and left the talks as well.

Confrontation. On July 7, members of the Orange Order, a 200-year-old Protestant organization, were blocked by the police from marching along a road next to a Catholic housing project at Drumcree, southeast of Belfast. A five-day confrontation ensued, and Protestants across Northern Ireland, angry at the police ban, erected barricades. More than 100,000 Orangemen planned to converge on Drumcree around July 12. At the last moment, police chief constable Sir Hugh Annesley allowed the Drumcree march. When police used batons to remove Roman Catholic protesters who tried to block the path of the Orangemen, violence broke out. Throughout Northern Ireland, Catholics expressed outrage at the police decision. □ Ian Mather

In *World Book,* see **Northern Ireland.**
Northwest Territories. See Canadian territories.

Norway. Prime Minister Gro Harlem Brundtland announced on October 23, 1996, that she would resign from office. Brundtland, 57, stated that she was relinquishing her job to Labor Party Chairman Thorbjoern Jagland to settle questions about her succession well ahead of parliamentary elections scheduled for September 1997. Jagland promised that the minority Labor government under his leadership would continue Brundtland's conservative budget policies.

The government in October forecast an unprecedented budget surplus of more than $6 billion for 1997, equivalent to about 5.1 percent of gross domestic product. The surplus was earmarked for a savings fund to pay the nation's retirement bills when the North Sea oil and gas wells have run dry.

Norway's economy enjoyed one of the strongest performances in Europe in 1996 because of rising oil prices. A dispute over how to share the prosperity triggered a 10-day strike in May by 37,000 engineering workers. The strike shut down the country's auto-parts industry and disrupted automobile production at Saab and Volvo in Sweden. Workers ended the walkout when employers agreed to lower the retirement age to 62 from 64. □ Tom Buerkle

See also **Europe** (Facts in brief table). In *World Book,* see **European Union; Norway.**

Nova Scotia. See **Canadian provinces.**

Nuclear energy. See **Energy supply.**

Nutrition. See **Food.**

O'Brien, Dan (1966–), an American decathlete, won the gold medal in the decathlon at the 1996 Olympics in Atlanta, Georgia. The decathlon is a 10-event competition in which competitors are awarded points for each event. Previously, O'Brien had won three world decathlon championships.

O'Brien was born on July 18, 1966, and given up for adoption. At the age of 2, he was adopted by Jim and Virginia O'Brien. O'Brien became the national high school decathlon champion in 1984 and was awarded an athletic scholarship to the University of Idaho in Moscow, Idaho.

At O'Brien's first international decathlon meet, the 1990 Goodwill Games in Seattle, Washington, the athlete won a silver medal. He won his first world and U.S. championships for decathlon in 1991. He was favored to win the gold medal at the 1992 Barcelona Olympics, but missed three pole vaults in the qualifying meet and did not make the team. Later that year, he set a new world record of 8,891 points. In 1993, he also set a world's record of 6,476 points in the heptathlon, a seven-event competition, and won the U.S. national and world decathlon championships. In 1994, he successfully defended his U.S. title and in 1995 won the U.S. and world championships. □ Lisa Klobuchar

See also **Olympic Games** Special Report: **The 1996 Olympics.**

Ocean. The National Aeronautics and Space Administration (NASA) announced in July 1996 that the TOPEX-Poseidon satellite, a joint project of the United States and France, was capable of mapping the topography of the ocean's surface to the unprecedented accuracy of 1.8 inches (4.6 centimeters). According to NASA, the accuracy was considerably greater than the project goal.

The TOPEX-Poseidon satellite bounced radar signals off the ocean's surface in order to measure the distance between the spacecraft and the sea surface. Data from these measurements allowed scientists to map the hills and valleys of water on the surface of the ocean created by the varying strength of gravitational attraction between undersea mountains and other kinds of terrain and the water above them. Because the satellite performed better than expected from its 1992 launch, ocean scientists were surprised at the unanticipated details revealed about ocean currents, sea level changes, and subsurface features.

Preliminary findings based on the first years of data collected from the satellite indicated that the sea level was rising at an astonishing rate of 0.2 inch (5 millimeters) per year—a rate that conflicted with results from coastal tide gauges. After discovering a mathematical error in the data-processing software, scientists estimated that the sea level was rising at a rate of 0.04 to 0.12 inch (1 to 3 millimeters) per year.

New life form. In August, scientists announced genetic proof of a third major branch of life on earth —tiny one-celled organisms, called *Archaea,* which live in the walls of hydrothermal vents on the sea floor. (The second branch of life includes plants and animals and a third, bacteria.) The genetic study was completed by researchers at The Institute for Genomic Research (TIGR) in Rockville, Maryland, the University of Illinois at Urbana-Champaign, and the Johns Hopkins University School of Medicine in Baltimore.

Archaea thrive in seawater temperatures and pressures that no other known life forms are able to withstand. Samples for the genetic study were collected from a Pacific Ocean vent at a depth of 8,060 feet (2,460 meters) where the water temperature is 185 °F (85 °C) and the water pressure is over 3,700 pounds per square inch (260 kilograms per square centimeter). The organisms exist without sunlight or oxygen and produce methane, a highly flammable gas.

The scientists completed the genetic blueprint of the *Archaea,* finding two-thirds of the genes totally new to biologists. Because *Archaea* are so genetically different from other life forms, scientists claimed this discovery would revolutionize human perception of the manner in which life can exist. J. Craig Venter, president of TIGR, noted that the ability of *archaea* to survive in such harsh conditions increases the likelihood that life could exist on other planets.

The Brent Spar saga. In July, a panel of scientists concluded that sinking the Brent Spar, a 300,000-

barrel oil storage buoy, would have little impact on the marine environment. The United Kingdom's Department of Trade and Industry commissioned the scientific impact analysis after Greenpeace, an international environmental organization, challenged the decision of Shell U.K., Ltd., a subsidiary of the Royal Dutch/Shell Group of Oil Companies, to scuttle the buoy. The Greenpeace activists, claiming the buoy would pose a serious toxic threat, temporarily thwarted plans by Shell to sink the buoy in the deep Atlantic off the west coast of Scotland.

The panel, chaired by John Shepherd of the Southampton Oceanography Centre in the United Kingdom, concluded that damage from the wreckage would be confined to a small area and that the wildlife on the sea floor would recover within 2 to 10 years. Shepherd noted that the amount of polychlorinated biphenyls (PCB's)—the toxic compounds posing the only real environmental danger—was extremely small since Shell had removed the main electrical components that contained PCB's. Although the panel members said that scuttling the Brent Spar would have little impact, they did not advocate disposing of other buoys in the same way. Shell announced plans to consider other disposal options but did not rule out dumping Brent Star at sea. □ Arthur G. Alexiou

In *World Book,* see **Ocean.**

Ohio. See **State government.**

Oklahoma. See **State government.**

Old age. See **Social Security.**

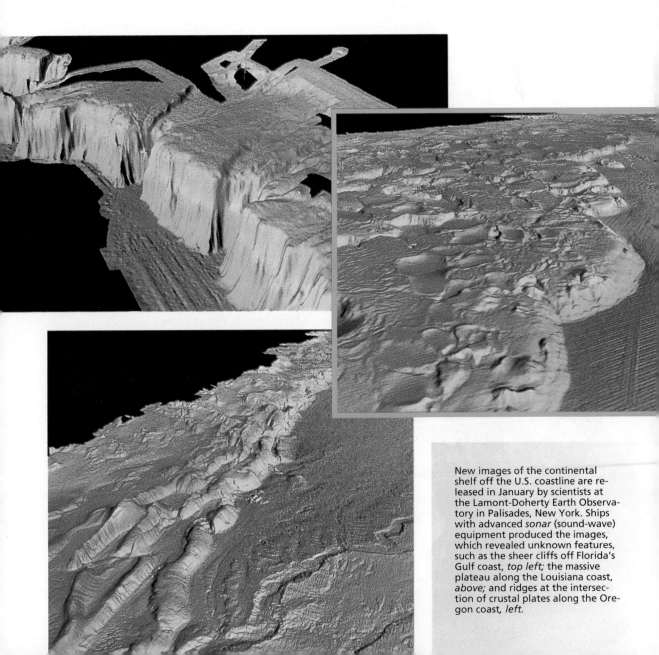

New images of the continental shelf off the U.S. coastline are released in January by scientists at the Lamont-Doherty Earth Observatory in Palisades, New York. Ships with advanced *sonar* (sound-wave) equipment produced the images, which revealed unknown features, such as the sheer cliffs off Florida's Gulf coast, *top left;* the massive plateau along the Louisiana coast, *above;* and ridges at the intersection of crustal plates along the Oregon coast, *left.*

The 1996 Olympics

The world's best athletes gathered in Atlanta, Georgia, to compete in the 1996 Summer Olympic Games and mark the 100th anniversary of the modern Olympics.

By Frank Litsky

In many ways, the 1996 centennial Olympic Games in Atlanta, Georgia, from July 19 to August 4, were the biggest ever. More athletes (10,778) competed than in any previous Olympics, including 40 percent more female athletes than in 1992. A record number of nations (197) took part; 79 nations won medals and 53 won gold medals—more than ever before. More professional athletes also took part in the games than ever before, including, for the first time, cyclists.

The competition in the 31 sports was often superlative. The time schedule was altered so Michael Johnson of the United States could try to become the first male runner to win the 200 and 400 meters in one Olympics, and the 28-year-old Texan succeeded. His crowning glory was an astounding world record of 19.32 seconds in the 200 meters. Marie-Jose Perec of France achieved the same double victory for women.

One of the most touching moments of the games involved the former boxing champion and Olympic gold medalist Muhammad Ali. In the opening ceremonies, his hands shaking from Parkinson's syndrome, Ali lighted the cauldron that housed the Olympic flame during the competition.

Tragedy tarnished the games, however, when a bomb exploded on July 27 in Atlanta's Centennial Olympic Park. The blast killed 1 person and injured 111 others.

Despite the bomb, the games continued as scheduled, and for the first time since 1968, the United States won the most medals in a nonboycotted Olympics. The United States won 101 medals, followed by Germany's 65, Russia's 63, China's 50, Australia's 41, and France's 37.

Decathlon gold medalist Dan O'Brien of the United States

1996 OLYMPIC MEDALISTS

ARCHERY

Men's individual
GOLD	Justin Huish, United States
SILVER	Magnus Petersson, Sweden
BRONZE	Oh Kyo-moon, South Korea

Men's team
GOLD	United States
SILVER	South Korea
BRONZE	Italy

Women's individual
GOLD	Kim Kyung-wook, South Korea
SILVER	He Ying, China
BRONZE	Olena Sadovnycha, Ukraine

Women's team
GOLD	South Korea
SILVER	Germany
BRONZE	Poland

BADMINTON

Men's singles
GOLD	Poul-Erik Hoyer-Larsen, Denmark
SILVER	Dong Jiong, China
BRONZE	Rashid Sidek, Malaysia

Men's doubles
GOLD	Rexy Mainaky and Ricky Subagja, Indonesia
SILVER	Cheah Soon Kit and Yap Kim Hock, Malaysia
BRONZE	S. Antonius and Denny Kantono, Indonesia

Women's singles
GOLD	Bang Soo-hyun, South Korea
SILVER	Mia Audina, Indonesia
BRONZE	Susi Susanti, Indonesia

Women's doubles
GOLD	Ge Fei and Gu Jun, China
SILVER	Gil Young-ah and Jang Hye-ock, South Korea
BRONZE	Qin Yiyuan and Tang Yongshu, China

Mixed doubles
GOLD	Gil Young-ah and Kim Dong-moon, South Korea
SILVER	Park Joo-bong and Ra Kyung-min, South Korea
BRONZE	Liu Jianjun and Sun Man, China

BASEBALL
GOLD	Cuba
SILVER	Japan
BRONZE	United States

BASKETBALL

Men
GOLD	United States
SILVER	Yugoslavia
BRONZE	Lithuania

Women
GOLD	United States
SILVER	Brazil
BRONZE	Australia

BEACH VOLLEYBALL

Men
GOLD	Karch Kiraly and Kent Steffes, United States
SILVER	Mike Dodd and Mike Whitmarsh, United States
BRONZE	John Child and Mark Heese, Canada

Women
GOLD	Jackie Silva and Sandra Pires, Brazil
SILVER	Monica Rodrigues and Adriana Samuel, Brazil
BRONZE	Natalie Cook and Kerri Ann Pottharst, Australia

BOXING

106 lbs. (48 kg)
GOLD	Daniel Petrov, Bulgaria
SILVER	Mansueto Velasco, Philippines
BRONZE	Oleg Kiryukhin, Ukraine, and Rafael Lozano, Spain

112 lbs. (51 kg)
GOLD	Maikro Romero, Cuba
SILVER	Bolat Djumadilov, Kazakhstan
BRONZE	Albert Pakeyev, Russia, and Zoltan Lunka, Germany

119 lbs. (54 kg)
GOLD	Istvan Kovacs, Hungary
SILVER	Arnaldo Mesa, Cuba
BRONZE	Raimkul Malakhbekov, Russia, and Vichairachanon Khadpo, Thailand

126 lbs. (57 kg)
GOLD	Somluck Kamsing, Thailand
SILVER	Serafim Todorov, Bulgaria
BRONZE	Floyd Mayweather, United States, and Pablo Chacon, Argentina

132 lbs. (60 kg)
GOLD	Hocine Soltani, Algeria
SILVER	Tontcho Tontchev, Bulgaria
BRONZE	Terrance Cauthen, United States, and Leonard Doroftei, Romina

139 lbs. (63.5 kg)
GOLD	Hector Vinent, Cuba
SILVER	Oktay Urkal, Germany
BRONZE	Bolat Niyazymbetov, Kazakhstan, and Fethi Missaoui, Tunisia

148 lbs. (67 kg)
GOLD	Oleg Saitov, Russia
SILVER	Juan Hernandez, Cuba
BRONZE	Marian Simion, Romania, and Daniel Santos, Puerto Rico

156 lbs. (71 kg)
GOLD	David Reid, United States
SILVER	Alfredo Duvergel, Cuba
BRONZE	Karem Tulaganov, Uzbekistan, and Ermakhan Ibraimov, Kazakhstan

165 lbs. (75 kg)
GOLD	Ariel Hernandez, Cuba
SILVER	Malik Beyleroglu, Turkey
BRONZE	Rhosii Wells, United States, and Mohamed Bahari, Algeria

178 lbs. (81 kg)
GOLD	Vassili Jirov, Kazakhstan
SILVER	Lee Sueng-bao, South Korea
BRONZE	Antonio Tarver, United States, and Thomas Ulrich, Germany

201 lbs. (91 kg)
GOLD	Felix Savon, Cuba
SILVER	David Defiagbon, Canada
BRONZE	Nate Jones, United States, and Luan Krasniqi, Germany

Over 201 lbs. (Over 91 kg)
GOLD	Vladamir Klitchko, Ukraine
SILVER	Paea Wolfgramm, Tonga
BRONZE	Alexei Lezin, Russia, and Duncan Dokiwari, Nigeria

CANOEING

Sprint

Men's 500-meter canoe singles

GOLD	Martin Doktor, Czech Republic
SILVER	Slavomir Knazovicky, Slovakia
BRONZE	Imre Pulai, Hungary

Men's 1,000-meter canoe singles

GOLD	Martin Doktor, Czech Republic
SILVER	Ivan Klementyev, Latvia
BRONZE	Gyorgy Zala, Hungary

Men's 500-meter canoe doubles

GOLD	Gyorgy Kolonics and Csaba Horvath, Hungary
SILVER	Nikolai Juravschi and Victor Reneischi, Moldova
BRONZE	Gheorghe Andriev and Grigore Obreja, Romania

Men's 1,000-meter canoe doubles

GOLD	Andreas Dittmer and Gunar Kirchbach, Germany
SILVER	Marcel Glavan and Antonel Borsan, Romania
BRONZE	Gyorgy Kolonics and Csaba Horvath, Hungary

Men's 500-meter kayak singles

GOLD	Antonio Rossi, Italy
SILVER	Knut Holmann, Norway
BRONZE	Piotr Markiewicz, Poland

Men's 1,000-meter kayak singles

GOLD	Knut Holmann, Norway
SILVER	Beniamino Bonomi, Italy
BRONZE	Clint Robinson, Australia

Men's 500-meter kayak doubles

GOLD	Kay Bluhm and Torsten Gutsche, Germany
SILVER	Beniamino Bonomi and Daniele Scarpa, Italy
BRONZE	Andrew Trim and Danny Cousins, Australia

Men's 1,000-meter kayak doubles

GOLD	Antonio Rossi and Daniele Scarpa, Italy
SILVER	Kay Bluhm and Torsten Gutsche, Germany
BRONZE	Andrian Dushev and Milk Kazanov, Bulgaria

Men's 1,000-meter kayak fours

GOLD	Germany
SILVER	Hungary
BRONZE	Russia

Women's 500-meter kayak singles

GOLD	Rita Koban, Hungary
SILVER	Caroline Brunet, Canada
BRONZE	Josefa Idem, Italy

Women's 500-meter kayak doubles

GOLD	Agneta Andersson and Susanne Gunnarsson, Sweden
SILVER	Birgit Fischer and Ramona Portwich, Germany
BRONZE	Anna Wood and Katrin Borchert, Australia

Women's 500-meter kayak fours

GOLD	Germany
SILVER	Switzerland
BRONZE	Sweden

Slalom

Men's canoe singles

GOLD	Michal Martikan, Slovakia
SILVER	Lucas Pollert, Czech Republic
BRONZE	Patrice Estanguet, France

Men's canoe doubles

GOLD	Frank Adisson and Wilfred Forgues, France
SILVER	Miroslav Simek and Jiri Rohan, Czech Republic
BRONZE	Andre Ehrenberg and Michael Senft, Germany

Men's kayak singles

GOLD	Oliver Fix, Germany
SILVER	Andraz Vehovar, Slovenia
BRONZE	Thomas Becker, Germany

Women's kayak singles

GOLD	Stepanka Hilgertova, Czech Republic
SILVER	Dana Chladek, United States
BRONZE	Myriam Fox-Jerusalmi, France

CYCLING

Road

Men's road race

GOLD	Pascal Richard, Switzerland
SILVER	Rolf Sorensen, Denmark
BRONZE	Max Sciandri, Great Britain

Men's time trial

GOLD	Miguel Indurain, Spain
SILVER	Abraham Olano, Spain
BRONZE	Chris Boardman, Great Britain

Women's road race

GOLD	Jeannie Longo-Ciprelli, France
SILVER	Imelda Chiappa, Italy
BRONZE	Clara Hughes, Canada

Women's time trial

GOLD	Zulfiya Zabirova, Russia
SILVER	Jeannie Longo-Ciprelli, France
BRONZE	Clara Hughes, Canada

Track

Men's sprint

GOLD	Jens Fiedler, Germany
SILVER	Marty Nothstein, United States
BRONZE	Curt Harnett, Canada

Men's individual pursuit

GOLD	Andrea Collinelli, Italy
SILVER	Philippe Ermenault, France
BRONZE	Bradley McGee, Australia

Men's team pursuit

GOLD	France
SILVER	Russia
BRONZE	Australia

Men's kilometer time trial

GOLD	Florian Rousseau, France
SILVER	Erin Hartwell, United States
BRONZE	Takanobu Jumonji, Japan

Men's points race

GOLD	Silvio Martinello, Italy
SILVER	Brian Walton, Canada
BRONZE	Stuart O'Grady, Australia

Women's sprint

GOLD	Felicia Ballanger, France
SILVER	Michelle Ferris, Australia
BRONZE	Ingrid Haringa, Netherlands

Women's individual pursuit

GOLD	Antonella Bellutti, Italy
SILVER	Marion Clignet, France
BRONZE	Judith Arndt, Germany

Women's point race
GOLD   Nathalie Lancien, France
SILVER   Ingrid Haringa, Netherlands
BRONZE   Lucy Tyler Sharman, Australia

Mountain Bike
Men's cross-country
GOLD   Bart Jan Brentjens, Netherlands
SILVER   Thomas Frischknecht, Switzerland
BRONZE   Miguel Martinez, France

Women's cross-country
GOLD   Paola Pezzo, Italy
SILVER   Alison Sydor, Canada
BRONZE   Susan DeMattei, United States

DIVING

Men's springboard
GOLD   Xiong Ni, China
SILVER   Yu Zhuocheng, China
BRONZE   Mark Lenzi, United States

Men's platform
GOLD   Dmitri Sautin, Russia
SILVER   Jan Hempel, Germany
BRONZE   Xiao Hailiang, China

Women's springboard
GOLD   Fu Mingxia, China
SILVER   Irina Lashko, Russia
BRONZE   Annie Pelletier, Canada

Women's platform
GOLD   Fu Mingxia, China
SILVER   Annika Walter, Germany
BRONZE   Mary Ellen Clark, United States

EQUESTRIAN

Individual events
Jumping
GOLD   Ulrich Kirchhoff, Germany
SILVER   Willi Melliger, Switzerland
BRONZE   Alexandra Ledermann, France

Dressage
GOLD   Isabell Werth, Germany
SILVER   Anky Van Grunsven, Netherlands
BRONZE   Sven Rothenberger, Netherlands

Three-day event
GOLD   Blyth Tait, New Zealand
SILVER   Sally Clark, New Zealand
BRONZE   Kerry Millikin, United States

Team events
Jumping
GOLD   Germany
SILVER   United States
BRONZE   Brazil

Dressage
GOLD   Germany
SILVER   Netherlands
BRONZE   United States

Three-day event
GOLD   Australia
SILVER   United States
BRONZE   New Zealand

FENCING

Individual Events
Men's foil
GOLD   Alessandro Puccini, Italy
SILVER   Lionel Plumenail, France
BRONZE   Franck Boidin, France

Men's epee
GOLD   Aleksandr Beketov, Russia
SILVER   Ivan Trevejo Perez, Cuba
BRONZE   Geza Imre, Hungary

Men's sabre
GOLD   Stanislav Pozdnyakov, Russia
SILVER   Sergei Sharikov, Russia
BRONZE   Damien Touya, France

Women's foil
GOLD   Laura Badea, Romania
SILVER   Valentina Vezzali, Italy
BRONZE   Giovanna Trillini, Italy

Women's epee
GOLD   Laura Flessel, France
SILVER   Valerie Barlois, France
BRONZE   Gyoengyi Szalay Harvathne, Hungary

Team events
Men's foil
GOLD   Russia
SILVER   Poland
BRONZE   Cuba

Men's epee
GOLD   Italy
SILVER   Russia
BRONZE   France

Men's sabre
GOLD   Russia
SILVER   Hungary
BRONZE   Italy

Women's foil
GOLD   Italy
SILVER   Romania
BRONZE   Germany

Women's epee
GOLD   France
SILVER   Italy
BRONZE   Russia

Gold-medal gymnast Shannon Miller of the United States

FIELD HOCKEY

Men
GOLD   Netherlands
SILVER   Spain
BRONZE   Australia

Women
GOLD   Australia
SILVER   South Korea
BRONZE   Netherlands

GYMNASTICS

Men
Team
GOLD   Russia
SILVER   China
BRONZE   Ukraine

All-around
GOLD   Li Xiaoshuang, China
SILVER   Aleksei Nemov, Russia
BRONZE   Vitaly Scherbo, Belarus

Floor exercise
GOLD   Ioannis Melissanidis, Greece
SILVER   Li Xiaoshuang, China
BRONZE   Aleksei Nemov, Russia

Pommel horse
GOLD — Li Donghua, Switzerland
SILVER — Marius Urzica, Romania
BRONZE — Aleksei Nemov, Russia

Rings
GOLD — Yuri Chechi, Italy
SILVER — Dan Burinca, Romania, and
Szilveszter Csollany, Hungary (tie)
BRONZE — None awarded

Vault
GOLD — Aleksei Nemov, Russia
SILVER — Yeo Hong-chul, South Korea
BRONZE — Vitaly Scherbo, Belarus

Parallel bars
GOLD — Rustam Sharipov, Ukraine
SILVER — Jair Lynch, United States
BRONZE — Vitaly Scherbo, Belarus

Horizontal bar
GOLD — Andreas Wecker, Germany
SILVER — Krasimir Dounev, Bulgaria
BRONZE — Vitaly Scherbo, Belarus; Aleksei Nemov,
Russia, and Fan Bin, China (tie)

Women
Team
GOLD — United States
SILVER — Russia
BRONZE — Romania

All-around
GOLD — Lilia Podkopayeva, Ukraine
SILVER — Gina Gogean, Romania
BRONZE — Simona Amanar, Romania, and
Lavinia Milosovici, Romania (tie)

Vault
GOLD — Simona Amanar, Romania
SILVER — Mo Huilan, China
BRONZE — Gina Gogean, Romania

Uneven parallel bars
GOLD — Svetlana Chorkina, Russia
SILVER — Amy Chow, United States, and
Bi Wenjiing, China (tie)
BRONZE — None awarded

Balance beam
GOLD — Shannon Miller, United States
SILVER — Lilia Podkopayeva, Ukraine
BRONZE — Gina Gogean, Romania

Floor exercise
GOLD — Lilia Podkopayeva, Ukraine
SILVER — Simona Amanar, Romania
BRONZE — Dominique Dawes, United States

JUDO

Men
Extra lightweight
GOLD — Tadahiro Nomura, Japan
SILVER — Girlamo Giovinazzo, Italy
BRONZE — Richard Trautmann, Germany, and
Dorjpalam Narmandakh, Mongolia

Half-lightweight
GOLD — Udo Quellmalz, Germany
SILVER — Yukimasa Nakamura, Japan
BRONZE — Israel Hernandez, Cuba, and
Henrique Guimares, Brazil

Lightweight
GOLD — Kenzo Nakamura, Japan
SILVER — Kwak Dae-sung, South Korea
BRONZE — Jimmy Pedro, United States, and
Christophe Gagliano, France

Half-middleweight
GOLD — Djamel Bouras, France
SILVER — Toshihiko Koga, Japan
BRONZE — Soso Liparteliani, Georgia,
and Cho In-chul, South Korea

Middleweight
GOLD — Jeon Ki-young, South Korea
SILVER — Armen Bagdasarov, Uzbekistan
BRONZE — Marko Spittka, Germany, and
Mark Huizinga, Netherlands

Half-heavyweight
GOLD — Pawel Nastula, Poland
SILVER — Kim Min-soo, South Korea
BRONZE — Stephane Traineau, France, and
Miguel Fernandes, Brazil

Heavyweight
GOLD — David Douillet, France
SILVER — Ernesto Perez, Spain
BRONZE — Harry van Barneveld, Belgium,
and Frank Moeller, Germany

Women
Extra lightweight
GOLD — Kye Sun, North Korea
SILVER — Ryoko Tamura, Japan
BRONZE — Yolanda Soler, Spain,
and Amarilis Savon, Cuba

Half-lightweight
GOLD — Marie-Claire Restoux, France
SILVER — Hyun Sook-hee, South Korea
BRONZE — Noriko Sagawara, Japan, and
Legna Verdecia, Cuba

Lightweight
GOLD — Driulis Gonzalez, Cuba
SILVER — Jung Sun-yong, South Korea
BRONZE — Isabel Fernandez, Spain,
and Marisbel Lomba, Belgium

Half-middleweight
GOLD — Yuko Emoto, Japan
SILVER — Gella Van de Caveye, Belgium
BRONZE — Jung Sung-sook, South Korea,
and Jenny Gal, Netherlands

Middleweight
GOLD — Cho Min-sun, South Korea
SILVER — Aneta Szczepanska, Poland
BRONZE — Wang Xianbo, China, and Claudia
Zwiers, Netherlands

Half-heavyweight
GOLD — Ulla Werbrouck, Belgium
SILVER — Yoko Tanabe, Japan
BRONZE — Ylenia Scapin, Italy,
and Diadenis Luna, Cuba

Heavyweight
GOLD — Sun Fuming, China
SILVER — Estela Rodriguez, Cuba
BRONZE — Johanna Hagn, Germany,
and Christine Cicot, France

MODERN PENTATHLON

GOLD — Aleksandr Parygin, Kazakhstan
SILVER — Eduard Zenovka, Russia
BRONZE — Janos Martinek, Hungary

RHYTHMIC GYMNASTICS

Individual
GOLD — Yekaterina Serebryanskaya, Ukraine
SILVER — Yanina Batyrchina, Russia
BRONZE — Yelena Vitrichenko, Ukraine

Team
GOLD — Spain
SILVER — Bulgaria
BRONZE — Russia

ROWING

Men
Single sculls
GOLD	Xeno Mueller, Switzerland
SILVER	Derek Porter, Canada
BRONZE	Thomas Lange, Germany

Double sculls
GOLD	Davide Tizzano and Agostino Abbagnale, Italy
SILVER	Kjetil Undset and Steffen Stoerseth, Norway
BRONZE	Frederick Kowal and Samuel Barathay, France

Lightweight double sculls
GOLD	Markus and Michael Gier, Switzerland
SILVER	Maarten van der Linden and Pepijn Aardwijn, Netherlands
BRONZE	Anthony Edwards and Bruce Hick, Australia

Quadruple sculls
GOLD	Germany
SILVER	United States
BRONZE	Australia

Coxless pair
GOLD	Steven Redgrave and Matthew Pinsent, Great Britain
SILVER	David Weightman and Robert Scott, Australia
BRONZE	Michel Andrieux and Jean-Christophe Rolland, France

Coxless four
GOLD	Australia
SILVER	France
BRONZE	Great Britain

Lightweight coxless four
GOLD	Denmark
SILVER	Canada
BRONZE	United States

Eights
GOLD	Netherlands
SILVER	Germany
BRONZE	Russia

Women
Single sculls
GOLD	Yekaterina Khodotovich, Belarus
SILVER	Silken Laumann, Canada
BRONZE	Trine Hansen, Denmark

Double sculls
GOLD	Marnie McBean and Kathleen Heddle, Canada
SILVER	Cao Mianying and Zhang Xiuyun, China
BRONZE	Irene Eljs and Eeke van Nes, Netherlands

Lightweight double sculls
GOLD	Constanta Burcica and Camelia Macoviciuc, Romania
SILVER	Teresa Bell and Lindsay Burns, United States
BRONZE	Rebecca Joyce and Virginia Lee, Australia

Quadruple sculls
GOLD	Germany
SILVER	Ukraine
BRONZE	Canada

Coxless pair
GOLD	Megan Still and Kate Slatter, Australia
SILVER	Missy Schwen and Karen Kraft, United States
BRONZE	Christine Gosse and Helene Cortin, France

Eights
GOLD	Romania
SILVER	Canada
BRONZE	Belarus

SHOOTING

Rifle
Men's air
GOLD	Artem Khadzhibekov, Russia
SILVER	Wolfram Waibel, Jr., Austria
BRONZE	Jean-Pierre Amat, France

Men's small bore, prone
GOLD	Christian Klees, Germany
SILVER	Sergei Beliaev, Kazakhstan
BRONZE	Jozef Gonci, Slovakia

Men's small bore, three position
GOLD	Jean-Pierre Amat, France
SILVER	Sergei Beliaev, Kazakhstan
BRONZE	Wolfram Waibel, Jr., Austria

Men's running target
GOLD	Yang Ling, China
SILVER	Xiao Jun, China
BRONZE	Miroslav Janus, Czech Republic

Women's air
GOLD	Renata Mauer, Poland
SILVER	Petra Horneber, Germany
BRONZE	Aleksandra Ivosev, Yugoslavia

Women's small bore, three-position
GOLD	Aleksandra Ivosev, Yugoslavia
SILVER	Irina Gerasimenok, Russia
BRONZE	Renata Mauer, Poland

Pistol
Men's air
GOLD	Roberto Di Donna, Italy
SILVER	Wang Yifu, China
BRONZE	Tanu Kiriakov, Bulgaria

Men's free
GOLD	Boris Kokorev, Russia
SILVER	Igor Basinski, Belarus
BRONZE	Roberto Di Donna, Italy

Men's rapid fire
GOLD	Ralf Schumann, Germany
SILVER	Emil Milev, Bulgaria
BRONZE	Vladimir Vokmyanin, Kazakhstan

Women's air
GOLD	Olga Klochneva, Russia
SILVER	Marina Logvinenko, Russia
BRONZE	Mariya Grozdeva, Bulgaria

Women's sport
GOLD	Li Duihong, China
SILVER	Diana Yorgova, Bulgaria
BRONZE	Marina Logvinenko, Russia

Shotgun
Men's trap
GOLD	Michael Diamond, Australia
SILVER	Josh Lakatos, United States
BRONZE	Lance Bade, United States

Men's double trap
GOLD	Russell Mark, Australia
SILVER	Albano Pera, Italy
BRONZE	Zhang Bing, China

Men's skeet
GOLD	Ennio Falco, Italy
SILVER	Miroslav Rzepkowski, Poland
BRONZE	Andrea Benelli, Italy

Women's double trap
GOLD	Kim Rhode, United States
SILVER	Susanne Kiermayer, Germany
BRONZE	Deserie Huddleston, Australia

SOCCER

Men
GOLD	Nigeria
SILVER	Argentina
BRONZE	Brazil

Women
GOLD	United States
SILVER	China
BRONZE	Norway

SOFTBALL

GOLD	United States
SILVER	China
BRONZE	Australia

SWIMMING

Men

50-meter freestyle
GOLD	Aleksandr Popov, Russia	:22.13
SILVER	Gary Hall, Jr., United States	
BRONZE	Fernando Scherer, Brazil	

100-meter freestyle
GOLD	Aleksandr Popov, Russia	:48.74
SILVER	Gary Hall, Jr., United States	
BRONZE	Gustavo Borges, Brazil	

200-meter freestyle
GOLD	Danyon Loader, New Zealand	1:47.63
SILVER	Gustavo Borges, Brazil	
BRONZE	Daniel Kowalski, Australia	

400-meter freestyle
GOLD	Danyon Loader, New Zealand	3:47.97
SILVER	Paul Palmer, Great Britain	
BRONZE	Daniel Kowalski, Australia	

1,500-meter freestyle
GOLD	Kieren Perkins, Australia	14:56.40
SILVER	Daniel Kowalski, Australia	
BRONZE	Graeme Smith, Great Britain	

100-meter backstroke
GOLD	Jeff Rouse, United States	:54.10
SILVER	Rodolfo Falcon, Cuba	
BRONZE	Neisser Bent, Cuba	

200-meter backstroke
GOLD	Brad Bridgewater, United States	1:58.54
SILVER	Tripp Schwenk, United States	
BRONZE	Emanuele Merisi, Italy	

100-meter breaststroke
GOLD	Fred Deburghgraeve, Belgium	1:00.65
SILVER	Jeremy Linn, United States	
BRONZE	Mark Warnecke, Germany	

200-meter breaststroke
GOLD	Norbert Rozsa, Hungary	2:12.57
SILVER	Karoly Guttler, Hungary	
BRONZE	Andrei Korneyev, Russia	

100-meter butterfly
GOLD	Denis Pankratov, Russia	:52.27*
SILVER	Scott Miller, Australia	
BRONZE	Vladislav Kulikov, Russia	

200-meter butterfly
GOLD	Denis Pankratov, Russia	1:56.51
SILVER	Tom Malchow, United States	
BRONZE	Scott Goodman, Australia	

200-meter individual medley
GOLD	Attila Czene, Hungary	1:59.91[†]
SILVER	Jani Sievinen, Finland	
BRONZE	Curtis Myden, Canada	

400-meter individual medley
GOLD	Tom Dolan, United States	4:14.90
SILVER	Eric Namesnik, United States	
BRONZE	Curtis Myden, Canada	

Triple gold medalist
Michelle Smith of Ireland

*World record. [†]Olympic record. ♦Heyns set a world record of 1:07.02 in the preliminaries.

4x100-meter freestyle relay
GOLD   United States   3:15.41[†]
SILVER   Russia
BRONZE   Germany

4x200-meter freestyle relay
GOLD   United States   7:14.84
SILVER   Sweden
BRONZE   Germany

4x100-meter medley relay
GOLD   United States   3:34.84*
SILVER   Russia
BRONZE   Australia

Women

50-meter freestyle
GOLD   Amy Van Dyken, United States   :24.87
SILVER   Le Jingyi, China
BRONZE   Sandra Volker, Germany

100-meter freestyle
GOLD   Le Jingyi, China   :54.50[†]
SILVER   Sandra Volker, Germany
BRONZE   Angel Martino, United States

200-meter freestyle
GOLD   Claudia Poll, Costa Rica   1:58.16
SILVER   Franziska van Almsick, Germany
BRONZE   Dagmar Hase, Germany

400-meter freestyle
GOLD   Michelle Smith, Ireland   4:07.25
SILVER   Dagmar Hase, Germany
BRONZE   Kirsten Vlieghuis, Netherlands

800-meter freestyle
GOLD   Brooke Bennett, United States   8:27.89
SILVER   Dagmar Hase, Germany
BRONZE   Kirsten Vlieghuis, Netherlands

100-meter backstroke
GOLD   Beth Botsford, United States   1:01.19
SILVER   Whitney Hedgepeth, United States
BRONZE   Marianne Kriel, South Africa

200-meter backstroke
GOLD   Krisztina Egerszegi, Hungary   2:07.83
SILVER   Whitney Hedgepeth, United States
BRONZE   Cathleen Rund, Germany

100-meter breaststroke
GOLD   Penelope Heyns, South Africa   1:07.73♦
SILVER   Amanda Beard, United States
BRONZE   Samantha Riley, Australia

200-meter breaststroke
GOLD   Penelope Heyns, South Africa   2:25.41[†]
SILVER   Amanda Beard, United States
BRONZE   Agnes Kovacs, Hungary

100-meter butterfly
GOLD   Amy Van Dyken, United States   :59.13
SILVER   Liu Limin, China
BRONZE   Angel Martino, United States

200-meter butterfly
GOLD   Susan O'Neill, Australia   2:07.76
SILVER   Petria Thomas, Australia
BRONZE   Michelle Smith, Ireland

200-meter individual medley
GOLD   Michelle Smith, Ireland   2:13.93
SILVER   Marianne Limpert, Canada
BRONZE   Lin Li, China

400-meter individual medley
GOLD   Michelle Smith, Ireland   4:39.18
SILVER   Allison Wagner, United States
BRONZE   Krisztina Egerszegi, Hungary

4x100-meter freestyle relay
GOLD   United States   3:39.29[†]
SILVER   China
BRONZE   Germany

4x200-meter freestyle relay
GOLD   United States   7:59.87[†]
SILVER   Germany
BRONZE   Australia

4x100-meter medley relay
GOLD   United States   4:02.88
SILVER   Australia
BRONZE   China

Gold medalist Kieren Perkins of Australia

SYNCHRONIZED SWIMMING

GOLD	United States
SILVER	Canada
BRONZE	Japan

TABLE TENNIS

Men's singles

GOLD	Liu Guoliang, China
SILVER	Wang Tao, China
BRONZE	Joerg Rosskopf, Germany

Men's doubles

GOLD	Kong Linghui and Liu Guoliang, China
SILVER	Lu Lin and Wang Tao, China
BRONZE	Lee Chul-seung and Yoo Nam-kyu, South Korea

Women's singles

GOLD	Deng Yaping, China
SILVER	Chen Jing, Taiwan
BRONZE	Qiao Hong, China

Women's doubles

GOLD	Deng Yaping and Qiao Hong, China
SILVER	Liu Wei and Qiao Yunping, China
BRONZE	Park Hae-jung and Ryu Ji-hae, South Korea

TEAM HANDBALL

Men

GOLD	Croatia
SILVER	Sweden
BRONZE	Spain

Women

GOLD	Denmark
SILVER	South Korea
BRONZE	Hungary

TENNIS

Men's singles

GOLD	Andre Agassi, United States
SILVER	Sergi Bruguera, Spain
BRONZE	Leander Paes, India

Men's doubles

GOLD	Todd Woodbridge and Mark Woodforde, Australia
SILVER	Neil Broad and Tim Henman, Great Britain
BRONZE	Marc-Kevin Goellner and David Prinosil, Germany

Women's singles

GOLD	Lindsay Davenport, United States
SILVER	Arantxa Sanchez Vicario, Spain
BRONZE	Jana Novotna, Czech Republic

Women's doubles

GOLD	Gigi Fernandez, and Mary Joe Fernandez, United States
SILVER	Jana Novotna and Helena Sukova, Czech Republic
BRONZE	Arantxa Sanchez Vicario and Conchita Martinez, Spain

TRACK AND FIELD

Men

100 Meters

GOLD	Donovan Bailey, Canada	:9.84*
SILVER	Frank Fredericks, Namibia	
BRONZE	Ato Boldon, Trinidad-Tobago	

200 Meters

GOLD	Michael Johnson, United States	:19.32*
SILVER	Frank Fredericks, Namibia	
BRONZE	Ato Boldon, Trinidad-Tobago	

400 Meters

GOLD	Michael Johnson, United States	:43.49[†]
SILVER	Roger Black, Great Britain	
BRONZE	Davis Kamoga, Uganda	

800 meters

GOLD	Vebjoern Rodal, Norway	1:42.58[†]
SILVER	Hezekiel Sepeng, South Africa	
BRONZE	Fred Onyancha, Kenya	

1,500 meters

GOLD	Noureddine Morceli, Algeria	3:35.78
SILVER	Fermin Cacho, Spain	
BRONZE	Stephen Kipkorir, Kenya	

5,000 meters

GOLD	Venuste Niyongabo, Burundi	13:07.96
SILVER	Paul Bitok, Kenya	
BRONZE	Khalid Boulami, Morocco	

10,000 meters

GOLD	Haile Gebrselassie, Ethiopia	27:07.34[†]
SILVER	Paul Tergat, Kenya	
BRONZE	Salah Hissou, Morocco	

Marathon

GOLD	Josia Thugwane, South Africa	2:12:36
SILVER	Lee Bong-ju, South Korea	
BRONZE	Eric Wainaina, Kenya	

110-meter hurdles

GOLD	Allen Johnson, United States	:12.95[†]
SILVER	Mark Crear, United States	
BRONZE	Florian Schwarthoff, Germany	

400-meter hurdles

GOLD	Derrick Adkins, United States	:47.54
SILVER	Samuel Matete, Zambia	
BRONZE	Calvin Davis, United States	

3,000-meter steeplechase

GOLD	Joseph Keter, Kenya	8:07.12
SILVER	Moses Kiptanui, Kenya	
BRONZE	Alessandro Lamruschini, Italy	

20-kilometer walk

GOLD	Jefferson Perez, Ecuador	1:20:07
SILVER	Ilya Markov, Russia	
BRONZE	Bernardo Segura, Mexico	

50-kilometer walk

GOLD	Robert Korzeniowski, Poland	3:43:30
SILVER	Mikhail Schennikov, Russia	
BRONZE	Valenti Massana, Spain	

4x100-meter relay

GOLD	Canada	:37.69
SILVER	United States	
BRONZE	Brazil	

4x400-meter relay

GOLD	United States	2:55.99
SILVER	Great Britain	
BRONZE	Jamaica	

High jump

GOLD	Charles Austin, United States	7 ft. 10 in.[†] (2.39 m)
SILVER	Artur Partyka, Poland	
BRONZE	Steve Smith, Great Britain	

Pole vault

GOLD	Jean Galfione, France	19 ft. 5 in.[††] (5.92 m)
SILVER	Igor Trandenkov, Russia	
BRONZE	Andrei Tivontchik, Germany	

Long jump

GOLD	Carl Lewis, United States	27 ft. 10¾ in. (8.50 m)
SILVER	James Beckford, Jamaica	
BRONZE	Joe Greene, United States	

Triple jump

GOLD	Kenny Harrison, United States	59 ft. 4¼ in.[†] (18.09 m)
SILVER	Jonathan Edwards, Great Britain	
BRONZE	Yoelbi Quesada, Cuba	

Shot-put
GOLD	Randy Barnes, United States	70 ft. 11¼ in. (21.62 m)
SILVER	John Godina, United States	
BRONZE	Aleksandr Bagach, Ukraine	

Discus
GOLD	Lars Riedel, Germany	227 ft. 8 in.[†] (69.40 m)
SILVER	Vladimir Dubrovshik, Belarus	
BRONZE	Vasily Kaptyukh, Belarus	

Hammer
GOLD	Balazs Kiss, Hungary	266 ft. 6 in. (81.24 m)
SILVER	Lance Deal, United States	
BRONZE	Oleksiv Krykun, Ukraine	

Javelin
GOLD	Jan Zelezny, Czech Republic	289 ft. 3 in. (88.16 m)
SILVER	Steve Backley, Great Britain	
BRONZE	Seppo Raty, Finland	

Decathlon
GOLD	Dan O'Brien, United States	8,824 pts.
SILVER	Frank Busemann, Germany	
BRONZE	Thomas Dvorak, Czech Republic	

Women

100 meters
GOLD	Gail Devers, United States	:10.94
SILVER	Merlene Ottey, Jamaica	
BRONZE	Gwen Torrence, United States	

200 meters
GOLD	Marie-Jose Perec, France	:22.12
SILVER	Merlene Ottey, Jamaica	
BRONZE	Mary Onyali, Nigeria	

400 meters
GOLD	Marie-Jose Perec, France	:48.25[†]
SILVER	Cathy Freeman, Australia	
BRONZE	Falilat Ogunkoya, Nigeria	

800 meters
GOLD	Svetlana Masterkova, Russia	1:57.73
SILVER	Ana Quirot, Cuba	
BRONZE	Maria Mutola, Mozambique	

1,500 meters
GOLD	Svetlana Masterkova, Russia	4:00.83
SILVER	Gabriela Szabo, Romania	
BRONZE	Theresia Kiesl, Austria	

5,000 meters
GOLD	Wang Junxia, China	14:59.88[†]
SILVER	Pauline Konga, Kenya	
BRONZE	Roberta Brunet, Italy	

10,000 meters
GOLD	Fernanda Ribeiro, Portugal	31:01.63[†]
SILVER	Wang Junxia, China	
BRONZE	Gete Wami, Ethiopia	

Marathon
GOLD	Fatuma Roba, Ethiopia	2:26:05
SILVER	Valentina Yegorova, Russia	
BRONZE	Yuko Arimori, Japan	

100-meter hurdles
GOLD	Ludmila Enquist, Sweden	:12.58
SILVER	Brigita Bukovec, Slovenia	
BRONZE	Patrica Girard-Leno, France	

400-meter hurdles
GOLD	Deon Hemmings, Jamaica	:52.82[†]
SILVER	Kim Batten, United States	
BRONZE	Tonja Buford-Bailey, United States	

10-kilometer walk
GOLD	Yelena Nikolayeva, Russia	41:49[†]
SILVER	Elisabetta Perrone, Italy	
BRONZE	Wang Yan, China	

4x100-meter relay
GOLD	United States	:41.95
SILVER	Bahamas	
BRONZE	Jamaica	

4x400-meter relay
GOLD	United States	3:20.91
SILVER	Nigeria	
BRONZE	Germany	

High jump
GOLD	Stefka Kostadinova, Bulgaria	6 ft. 8¾ in.[†] (2.05 m)
SILVER	Niki Bakogianni, Greece	
BRONZE	Inga Babakova, Ukraine	

Long jump
GOLD	Chioma Ajunwa, Nigeria	23 ft. 4½ in. (7.12 m)
SILVER	Fiona May, Italy	
BRONZE	Jackie Joyner-Kersee, United States	

Triple jump
GOLD	Inessa Kravets, Ukraine	50 ft. 3½ in.[†] (15.33 m)
SILVER	Inna Lasovskaya, Russia	
BRONZE	Sarka Kasparkova, Czech Republic	

Shot-put
GOLD	Astrid Kumbernuss, Germany	67 ft. 5½ in. (20.56 m)
SILVER	Sui Xinmei, China	
BRONZE	Irina Khudorozhkina, Russia	

Discus
GOLD	Ilke Wyludda, Germany	228 ft. 6 in. (69.66 m)
SILVER	Natalya Sadova, Russia	
BRONZE	Elina Zvereva, Belarus	

Javelin
GOLD	Heli Rantanen, Finland,	222 ft. 11 in. (67.94 m)
SILVER	Louise McPaul, Australia	
BRONZE	Trine Hattestad, Norway	

Heptathlon
GOLD	Ghada Shouaa, Syria	6,780 pts.
SILVER	Natalya Sazanovich, Belarus	
BRONZE	Denise Lewis, Great Britain	

VOLLEYBALL

Men
GOLD	Netherlands
SILVER	Italy
BRONZE	Yugoslavia

Women
GOLD	Cuba
SILVER	China
BRONZE	Brazil

WATER POLO

GOLD	Spain
SILVER	Croatia
BRONZE	Italy

Double gold medalist Michael Johnson of the United States

*World record. [†]Olympic record. [††]Equals Olympic record.

WEIGHTLIFTING§

119 lbs. (54 kg)
GOLD — Halil Mutlu, Turkey — 634 lbs. (287.5 kg)†
SILVER — Zhang Xiangsen, China
BRONZE — Sevdalin Minchev, Bulgaria

130 lbs. (59 kg)
GOLD — Tang Ningsheng, China — 678 lbs. (307.5 kg)*
SILVER — Leonidas Sabanis, Greece
BRONZE — Nikolay Pechalov, Bulgaria

141 lbs. (64 kg)
GOLD — Naim Suleymanoglu, Turkey — 739 lbs. (335 kg)*
SILVER — Valerios Leonidis, Greece
BRONZE — Xiao Jiangang, China

154 lbs. (70 kg)
GOLD — Zhan Xugang, China — 788 lbs. (357.5 kg)*
SILVER — Kim Myong, North Korea
BRONZE — Attila Feri, Hungary

168 lbs. (76 kg)
GOLD — Pablo Lara, Cuba — 810 lbs. (367.5 kg)
SILVER — Yoto Yotov, Bulgaria
BRONZE — Jon Chol, North Korea

183 lbs. (83 kg)
GOLD — Pyrros Dimas, Greece — 866 lbs. (392.5 kg)*
SILVER — Marc Huster, Germany
BRONZE — Andrzej Cofalik, Poland

201 lbs. (91 kg)
GOLD — Aleksei Petrov, Russia — 887 lbs. (402.5 kg)
SILVER — Leonidas Kokas, Greece
BRONZE — Oliver Caruso, Germany

218 lbs. (99 kg)
GOLD — Akakide Kakhiashvilis, Greece — 926 lbs. (420 kg)*
SILVER — Anatoli Khrapaty, Kazakhstan
BRONZE — Denis Gotfrid, Ukraine

238 lbs. (108 kg)
GOLD — Timur Taimazov, Ukraine — 948 lbs. (430 kg)
SILVER — Sergei Syrtsov, Russia
BRONZE — Nicu Vlad, Romania

238 lbs. (Over 108 kg)
GOLD — Andrey Chemerkin, Russia — 1,009 lbs. (457.5 kg)**
SILVER — Ronny Weller, Germany
BRONZE — Stefan Botev, Australia

Gold medalist Naim Suleymanoglu of Turkey

WRESTLING

Freestyle

106 lbs. (48 kg)
GOLD — Kim Il, North Korea
SILVER — Armen Mkrchyan, Armenia
BRONZE — Alexis Vila, Cuba

115 lbs. (52 kg)
GOLD — Valentin Dimitrov Jordanov, Bulgaria
SILVER — Namik Abdullayev, Azerbaijan
BRONZE — Maulen Mamyrov, Kazakhstan

126 lbs. (57 kg)
GOLD — Kendall Cross, United States
SILVER — Giuvi Sissaouri, Canada
BRONZE — Ri Yong Sam, North Korea

137 lbs. (62 kg)
GOLD — Tom Brands, United States
SILVER — Jang Jae-sung, South Korea
BRONZE — Elbrus Tedeyev, Ukraine

150 lbs. (68 kg)
GOLD — Vadim Bogiyev, Russia
SILVER — Townsend Saunders, United States
BRONZE — Zaza Zazirov, Ukraine

163 lbs. (74kg)
GOLD — Bouvaysa Saytiev, Russia
SILVER — Park Jang-soon, South Korea
BRONZE — Takuya Ota, Japan

181 lbs. (82 kg)
GOLD — Khadzhimurad Magomedov, Russia
SILVER — Yang Hyun-Mo, South Korea
BRONZE — Amir Reza Khadem, Iran

198 lbs. (90 kg)
GOLD — Rasull Khadem, Iran
SILVER — Makharbek Khadartsev, Russia
BRONZE — Eldari Kurtanidze, Georgia

220 lbs. (100 kg)
GOLD — Kurt Angle, United States
SILVER — Abbas Jadidi, Iran
BRONZE — Arawat Sabejew, Germany

287 lbs. (130 kg)
GOLD — Mahmut Demir, Turkey
SILVER — Aleksei Medvedev, Belarus
BRONZE — Bruce Baumgartner, United States

Greco-Roman

106 lbs. (48 kg)
GOLD — Sim Kwon-Ho, South Korea
SILVER — Aleksander Pavlov, Belarus
BRONZE — Zafar Gulyov, Russia

115 lbs. (52 kg)
GOLD — Armen Nazaryan, Armenia
SILVER — Brandon Paulson, United States
BRONZE — Andri Kalashnikov, Ukraine

* World record. **Equals world record. †Olympic record. §Winning weight is total of two lifts—snatch and clean and jerk.

126 lbs. (57 kg)
GOLD — Yuri Melnichenko, Kazakhstan
SILVER — Dennis Hall, United States
BRONZE — Sheng Zetian, China

137 lbs. (62 kg)
GOLD — Wlodzimierz Zawadzki, Poland
SILVER — Juan Luis Maren, Cuba
BRONZE — Mehmet Pirim, Turkey

150 lbs. (68 kg)
GOLD — Oyszard Wolny, Poland
SILVER — Ghani Yolouz, France
BRONZE — Aleksander Tretyakov, Russia

163 lbs. (74 kg)
GOLD — Feliberto Ascuy, Cuba
SILVER — Marko Asell, Finland
BRONZE — Jozef Tracz, Poland

181 lbs. (82 kg)
GOLD — Hamza Yerlikaya, Turkey
SILVER — Thomas Zander, Germany
BRONZE — Valeri Tsilent, Belarus

198 lbs. (90 kg)
GOLD — Vyacheslav Oleynyk, Ukraine
SILVER — Jacek Fafinski, Poland
BRONZE — Maik Bullmann, Germany

220 lbs. (100 kg)
GOLD — Andrzej Wronski, Poland
SILVER — Sergei Lishtvan, Belarus
BRONZE — Mikael Ljungberg, Sweden

287 lbs. (130 kg)
GOLD — Aleksandr Karelin, Russia
SILVER — Matt Ghaffari, United States
BRONZE — Sergei Moureiko, Moldova

★ **Medals Standings** ★

Country	Total	Gold	Silver	Bronze
United States	101	44	32	25
Germany	65	20	18	27
Russia	63	26	21	16
China	50	16	22	12
Australia	41	9	9	23
France	37	15	7	15
Italy	35	13	10	12
Korea	27	7	15	5
Cuba	25	9	8	8
Ukraine	23	9	2	12

YACHTING

Open
Laser
GOLD — Robert Scheidt, Brazil
SILVER — Ben Ainslie, Great Britain
BRONZE — Peer Moberg, Norway

Soling
GOLD — Germany
SILVER — Russia
BRONZE — United States

Star
GOLD — Marcello Ferreira and Torben Grael, Brazil
SILVER — Bobbie Lohse and Hans Wallen, Sweden
BRONZE — Colin Beashel and David Giles, Australia

Tornado
GOLD — Jose Luis Ballester and Fernando Leon, Spain
SILVER — Mitch Booth and Andrew Landenberger, Australia
BRONZE — Lars Grael and Kiko Pellicano, Brazil

Men
Finn
GOLD — Mateusz Kusznierewicz, Poland
SILVER — Sebastien Godefroid, Belgium
BRONZE — Roy Heiner, Netherlands

Mistral (boards)
GOLD — Nikolaos Kaklamanakis, Greece
SILVER — Carlos Espinola, Argentina
BRONZE — Gal Fridman, Israel

470
GOLD — Yevhen Braslavets and Ihor Maviyenko, Ukraine
SILVER — John Merricks and Ian Walker, Great Britain
BRONZE — Nuo Barreto and Vitor Rocha, Portugal

Women
Europe
GOLD — Kristine Roug, Denmark
SILVER — Margriet Matthijsse, Netherlands
BRONZE — Courtenay Becker-Dey, United States

Mistral (boards)
GOLD — Lee Lai-shan, Hong Kong
SILVER — Barbara Kendall, New Zealand
BRONZE — Alessandra Sensini, Italy

470
GOLD — Begona Via Dufresne and Theresa Zabell, Spain
SILVER — Alicia Kinoshita and Yumiko Shige, Japan
BRONZE — Olena Pakholchik and Rusiana Taran, Ukraine

Country	Population	Government	Monetary unit*	Foreign trade (million U.S.$) Exports†	Imports†
Australia	18,532,000	Governor General William Deane; Prime Minister John Howard	dollar (1.26 = $1)	53,097	60,317
Fiji	808,000	President Ratu Sir Kamisese Mara; Prime Minister Sitiveni Rabuka	dollar (1.39 = $1)	614	860
Kiribati	82,000	President Teburoro Tito	Australian dollar	5	37
Marshall Islands	57,000	President Kunio Lemari ††	U.S. dollar	4	63
Micronesia, Federated States of	131,000	President Bailey Olter	U.S. dollar	3	91
Nauru	12,000	President Lagumot Harris	Australian dollar	93	73
New Zealand	3,647,000	Governor General Dame Catherine Tizard; Prime Minister James B. Bolger	dollar (1.41 = $1)	13,746	13,957
Palau	18,000	President Kuniwo Nakamura	U.S. dollar	1	25
Papua New Guinea	4,496,000	Governor General Wiwa Korowi; Prime Minister Sir Julius Chan	kina (1.33 = $1)	2,642	1,450
Solomon Islands	404,000	Governor General Sir Moses Pitakaka; Prime Minister Solomon Mamaloni	dollar (3.60 = $1)	96	101
Tonga	99,000	King Taufa'ahau Tupou IV; Prime Minister Baron Vaea	pa'anga (1.21 = $1)	15	77
Tuvalu	10,000	Governor General Manuella Tulaga; Prime Minister Kamuta Latasi	Australian dollar	1	4
Vanuatu	178,000	President Jean Marie Leye; Prime Minister Maxime Carlot-Korman	vatu (111.03 = $1)	25	87
Western Samoa	177,000	Head of State Malietoa Tanumafili II; Prime Minister Tofilau Eti Alesana	tala (2.44 = $1)	9	95

*Exchange rates as of Oct. 25, 1996, or latest available data. †Latest available data. ††acting president

Pacific Islands. Financial troubles topped the list of problems for most Pacific Island nations during 1996. According to a United Nations report released in April, only Tonga and Fiji had gross domestic products higher than those of the 1980's. Living standards in some Pacific Island countries had declined because of population growth. But in Western Samoa and other nations primarily engaged in agriculture, natural disasters caused economic hardship. Except for Fiji and Papua New Guinea, most Pacific Island governments suffered from continuing deficits. France's nuclear tests in French Polynesia in September 1995 caused tourism to drop in 1996.

Pacific Island nations were among the world's nations that received the highest per capita foreign aid. But Australia cut aid to the Solomon Islands because of its failure to adopt a code controlling logging operations, which had been drafted in a regional forum. The World Bank and Australia threatened reductions in aid and loans to Papua New Guinea because of that country's failure to live up to terms agreed upon earlier. Government watchdogs and media raised accusations of various forms of financial mismanagement in Fiji, the Republic of the Marshall Islands, the Cook Islands, and Vanuatu.

Environmental issues. Scientists from the United States National Aeronautics and Space Administration detected high levels of pollution over the Pacific Islands in 1996. Most of the pollution came from Australia and East Africa. The Republic of the Marshall Islands began exploring the possibility of storing toxic waste from industrialized nations as a source of revenue. However, many islanders and outside observers were more concerned about the effects of logging, especially in Papua New Guinea and the Solomon Islands.

Western Samoa. In May 1996, Tofilau Eti Alesana began an unprecedented fifth term as prime minister. His Human Rights Protection Party formed a ruling coalition in parliament, voting him its leader. At age 72, he was the nation's longest-serving politician and one of the region's elder statesmen.

Vanuatu. In February 1996, in a confused session of Parliament, Maxime Carlot was chosen to succeed Serge Vohor as prime minister. Vanuatu had held national elections in December 1995, and Vohor had been chosen prime minister in a coalition government but resigned less than two months later to avoid facing a motion of no-confidence.

Marshall Islands. Amata Kabua, president since 1979, soon after the Marshall Islands gained independence from the United States, died on Dec. 19, 1996. Kunio Lemari, minister of transport and communications, was named acting president.

Papua New Guinea. Despite repeated efforts at mediation by Australia and other countries, Papua

New Guinea in 1996 could not end an armed revolt, which began in 1988, on Bougainville Island. Bougainville's giant copper mine had been Papua New Guinea's most important source of export income until 1989. The rebellion led to demands for the island's complete independence. The conflict also threatened relations with the Solomon Islands. The Solomons' government accused troops from Papua New Guinea of raiding villages and murdering citizens on islands near Bougainville. The Papuan government claimed that villagers on the islands provided the Bougainville rebels with arms and other supplies. In September, the rebels killed 12 Papuan troops, the government's worst defeat.

Fiji moved closer in 1996 to revising its constitution, which was instituted in 1987 after two military coups. A three-member review committee recommended moving away from the constitutional provisions that based government power entirely on ethnicity. Instead, the panel proposed that 12 seats in the lower house of Parliament be reserved for Fijians, 10 for East Indians, and 3 for members of other ethnic groups. The remaining 45 seats would be filled by open voting. The presidency would be reserved for an ethnic Fijian, subject to approval by the lower house. The upper house would have veto power over Fijian matters. ☐ Eugene Ogan

In *World Book,* see **Pacific Islands.**

Painting. See Art.

Pakistan. President Farooq Leghari dismissed the government of Prime Minister Benazir Bhutto on Nov. 5, 1996. President Leghari named Miraj Khalid as interim prime minister and called for new elections to take place on Feb. 3, 1997. Although the constitution required elections within three months of a government's dismissal, some members of Khalid's cabinet reportedly to be attempted to delay the voting until candidates suspected of corruption could be forced to withdraw.

Officials disclosed that Pakistan's economic problems were more serious than Bhutto had admitted. President Leghari requested that Shahid Javed Burki, a Pakistani vice president of the World Bank, a United Nations agency, serve as Khalid's chief economic adviser. Foreign aid, which had been withheld from Bhutto's government because of its record of corruption, was reinstated.

Corruption among government leaders and friends of Bhutto's ruling Pakistan People's Party (PPP) had been alleged for months by Pakistani newspapers. In June 1996, Transparency International, a European group that monitors corruption, listed Pakistan as Asia's most corrupt country. Some of the charges concerned Bhutto and her husband, Asif Ali Zardari. On June 9, the London newspaper *Sunday Express* reported that the couple had purchased through a third party a lavish country estate in southern England for $3.8 million. The paper reported that crates of antiques, among other items, were arriving at the mansion. Bhutto denied making any such purchases. In August, Bhutto created a vague new cabinet post for Zardari, naming him minister for investments with no clear duties. Zardari was widely reported to have become one of Pakistan's wealthiest men since his wife became prime minister. When Bhutto's government was dismissed, Zardari was jailed without being charged.

On September 20, Bhutto's younger brother Murtaza and six bodyguards were killed in a fight with police. The brother had founded a PPP breakaway group that opposed Bhutto. On December 18, Bhutto's husband was charged with murdering Murtaza.

Courting trouble. Bhutto and Leghari had clashed since March over judicial appointments. On June 13, the Supreme Court ordered the firing of 24 judges named by the government without judicial consultation. Bhutto refused to comply. She charged opposition groups with trying to use the judiciary system to overthrow her government.

Frequent fighting broke out throughout 1996 between Pakistan's diverse political, religious, and ethnic groups. In Karachi, the nation's economic and industrial center, law and order was in effect only sporadically as Muslim groups fought for political and economic gain. ☐ Henry S. Bradsher

See also **Asia** (Facts in brief table). In *World Book,* see **Pakistan.**

Paleontology in 1996 was dominated by the unearthing of a gigantic, carnivorous dinosaur, electrifying fossil finds, discoveries concerning the origins of sharks and fishes, and an intriguing new theory regarding the world's greatest known mass extinction.

A gigantic dinosaur. In May, paleontologist Paul Sereno of the University of Chicago announced the discovery of a huge predatory dinosaur, *Carcharodontosaurus* (shark-toothed reptile), in Saharan Morocco in Africa. Sereno and his team unearthed fossils of a five-foot (1.52-meter) skull and serrated, saberlike teeth from mid-Cretaceous 90-million-year-old riverbed deposits. Although fossil fragments of the species had been discovered in Egypt in the 1920's—and subsequently destroyed during World War II—Sereno's find made clear the size and nature of *Carcharodontosaurus*. Both *Carcharodontosaurus* and its close relative, *Giganotosaurus*—discovered in 1995 in South America—rivaled or surpassed the size of *Tyrannosaurus*. This new discovery led some paleontologists to conclude that South America and Africa remained connected at least as late as 100 million years ago. Prevailing scientific thought had held that the two continents were already separate in the Early Cretaceous Period, perhaps 50 million years earlier.

World's oldest fish. Important findings about the origins of vertebrates, animals with backbones, made news in early 1996. Ivan Sansom and Paul Smith

Paleontology

of the United Kingdom's University of Birmingham concluded that primitive fishes existed over 500 million years ago. The researchers carefully reexamined microscopic, scalelike fossils of a creature called *Anatolepis.* Previously, researchers had argued that this material represented fragments of shells of a primitive, horseshoe-shaped, crablike animal. Smith and his colleagues, however, demonstrated the presence of dentine, a tooth- and scale-forming substance found only in vertebrates. Their findings led some scientists to conclude that the origins of vertebrates go back 500 million years to the Cambrian Period—the geological period during which much of Earth's animal life originated.

Origins of sharks. In related research, Sansom and Smith, and Moya Smith, an anatomist at a London hospital, found evidence that may date the origin of sharks at least 25 million years earlier than previously believed. Scientists have long regarded sharks as among the most ancient of vertebrates. Previously, the oldest known shark fossils were 430 million years old. The Sansom and Smith team reported on the discovery of abundant fish scales in Colorado sandstone about 455 million years old. Some of the scales closely resemble those of sharks, possessing a toothlike structure with a pulp cavity from which many branched canals radiate.

Theory of a mass extinction. In 1996, researchers continued to seek causes of the world's most spectacular known mass extinction. Marine life narrowly escaped total extinction 240 million to 250 million years ago in a crisis that occurred toward the end of the Permian Period (from 290 million to 240 million years ago), when perhaps 95 percent of all marine animal species died out.

In July 1996, a team of scientists led by Andrew Knoll of Harvard University proposed a new geochemical theory for the mass extinction. Central to their theory was a suspected buildup of carbon-dioxide (CO_2) gas in the deep oceans over a long period of stagnation of the ocean. Ocean stagnation may have resulted from the warm climate and conglomeration of Earth's continents in a single land mass. Today's scattered continents and cold poles, by contrast, keep ocean waters circulating in alternately rising and sinking currents.

According to the theory, cooling of the planet caused a dramatic overturn of ocean waters approximately 250 million years ago. Many marine animals would have been poisoned by the influx of water-enriched CO_2. The animals most sensitive to CO_2 were in fact those that the fossil record reveals to have been most affected. The Knoll team's theory provided an important new look at the P-T mass extinction and suggested new avenues for research into other similar extinction events ☐ Carlton E. Brett

In *World Book,* see **Paleontology.**

Framed by a model of the dinosaur skull his team discovered in Morocco, paleontologist Paul Sereno speaks at a May news conference in Washington, D.C.

Panama. On June 21, 1996, President Ernesto Pérez Balladares admitted he had received $51,000 for his 1994 campaign from José Castrillón Henao, a reputed member of Colombia's Cali drug cartel. The president claimed he had not personally been aware of the contribution. The allegations surfaced in an investigation of campaign fundraiser Alfredo Alemán Chiari. Alemán had been the vice president of a bank allegedly used for money laundering and co-owner of an airline allegedly involved in transporting cocaine.

Earlier in 1996, Vice President Tomás Altamirano Duque announced, while President Pérez Balladares was out of the country, the pardon of more than 130 people who had been charged with human rights abuses during the past 21 years. Human rights groups criticized the pardons as well as pending legislation that would pardon nearly 1,000 other Panamanians.

On March 27, Federal District Judge William Hoeveler in Miami, Florida, denied a new trial to former Panamanian dictator General Manuel Antonio Noriega, who began serving a 40-year sentence in the United States for drug trafficking and other charges in 1992. Noriega's lawyers argued that the U.S. Justice Department had been aware during the trial that a witness had been bribed by the Cali cartel to testify against Noriega.   □ Nathan A. Haverstock

See also **Latin America** (Facts in brief table). In *World Book,* see **Panama.**

Papua New Guinea. See Asia; Pacific Islands.

Paraguay. On April 22, 1996, General Lino César Oviedo refused a presidential order to resign as army chief of staff, bringing Paraguay dangerously close to a military *coup* (takeover). Oviedo fled to the safety of an army barracks where he, in turn, demanded that President Juan Carlos Wasmosy step down. In an unusual show of support for democracy, leaders of neighboring countries, including Argentina and Brazil, offered military assistance to Wasmosy and dispatched diplomats to Paraguay during the crisis.

Wasmosy averted a coup by offering Oviedo the cabinet position of defense minister. When thousands of citizens protested, Wasmosy, on April 25, withdrew the appointment. Oviedo resigned from his army position without further incident. Calling himself a "soldier for democracy," he then announced he would run for president in 1998.

In June 1996, Paraguay began blasting rocks in the Paraguay River—the first stage of a plan to develop a 2,000-mile (3,200-kilometer) waterway linking the inland commerce of five South American countries to the south Atlantic. Ecologists protested the action as premature in light of studies indicating that the waterway could severely damage large Brazilian wetlands.   □ Nathan A. Haverstock

See also **Latin America** (Facts in brief table). In *World Book,* see **Paraguay.**

Pennsylvania. See Philadelphia; State government.

Peru. On Dec. 17, 1996, in Lima, the capital, the Túpac Amaru Revolutionary Movement—a Marxist, pro-Cuban rebel group—seized the residence of the Japanese ambassador to Peru during a party for the Japanese emperor's birthday. The 490 hostages included diplomats and business executives from around the world and chief Peruvian government officials.

On December 18, the Túpac Amaru released a French cultural attaché and the ambassadors from Canada, Germany, and Greece to negotiate on behalf of the rebels. The negotiations were complicated by the fact that Japan had often met the demands of terrorists in order to spare the lives of hostages. Peruvian President Fujimori, who is of Japanese descent and has enjoyed the support of the Japanese government and investors, has built a reputation on his firm stance against terrorists.

By December 31, the Túpac Amaru had released all but 81 of the hostages. Peruvian officials predicted a peaceful resolution to the crisis.

In August, the Peruvian government declared a state of emergency in 11 provinces after the resurgence of another rebel army, the Shining Path. The estimated 3,000 members of the two Peruvian rebel groups controlled areas in the Upper Huallaga Valley, where enough coca is grown to supply half of the world cocaine production.   □ Nathan A. Haverstock

See also **Latin America** (Facts in brief table). In *World Book,* see **Peru.**

Petroleum and gas. Prices of petroleum rose in 1996 as worldwide consumption increased for the third straight year and as the demand for oil unexpectedly exceeded the supply. Petroleum products were consumed at a rate of some 71.8 million barrels a day—a 2.5 percent increase over 1995. There are 42 gallons (159 liters) of oil in a barrel.

Expecting lower prices at the beginning of 1996, petroleum refiners in the United States and Europe delayed purchases of crude oil. To cut storage costs, refiners had adopted "just-in-time" inventory practices, shrinking their fuel stockpiles to low levels.

Furthermore, refiners expected the oil market to weaken with Iraq in 1996 selling 600,000 to 700,000 barrels a day, adding to the already high output of 26 million barrels a day from members of the Organization of Petroleum Exporting Countries (OPEC), an association of 11 countries that work together to maximize oil revenues. The United Nations (UN) had banned Iraq from exporting petroleum after its 1990 invasion of Kuwait. Due to economic hardships in Iraq, the UN again in 1996 offered the Iraqis an opportunity to hold a one-time, six-month oil sale to finance the purchase of food and medicine. In September, however, Iraqi conflicts with Kurds in northern Iraq forced the UN to postpone the sale until December.

Unexpected demand for oil. In 1996, start-up delays in new fields in non-OPEC areas, such as the North Sea, and the already lean stockpiles created a

Petroleum and gas

tight supply of oil. For the first time in several years, production failed to match, much less exceed, the rising demand for petroleum. The demand grew faster than predicted, partly because of the very cold 1995-1996 winter in the United States and Europe. Economic recovery in Europe and Asia also contributed to higher fuel use. In the United States, still the world's leading oil consumer, imports of petroleum surged.

Depleted supplies and increased demand resulted in much higher costs to consumers. In January 1996, American motorists were paying historically low gasoline prices, after adjustments for taxes and inflation. In late May, however, prices at the pump rose more than 20 cents a gallon to almost $1.40. By mid-October, after the summer travel season, the average retail price declined to $1.28 a gallon.

Trucking firms, airlines, and homeowners who heated with oil also felt the price increases. By 1996, the supplies of distillates—diesel fuel, kerosene jet fuel, and heating oil—had fallen to the lowest levels in years, but the demand sharply increased. The American Petroleum Institute in Washington, D.C., reported the deliveries of distillates by October had surged to over 3.5 million barrels a day in the United States, a 13 percent increase from October 1995.

Crude oil prices. Although analysts predicted the demand for petroleum would continue to escalate, there was much uncertainty whether crude oil prices would increase. West Texas Intermediate (WTI), the grade of crude oil that serves as the U.S. benchmark, had averaged between $17 and $18 a barrel in 1995. In early 1996, WTI began at approximately $19 a barrel and rose to nearly $26 before the price dropped in October.

John Lichtblau, chairman of the Petroleum Industry Research Foundation in New York City, estimated WTI prices averaged between $22 and $23 in 1996. For various reasons, including new expectations that Iraq would be allowed to export oil in limited quantities, Lichtblau estimated that WTI would average $20 to $22 in 1997. Although other estimates were as low as $18, upward revisions of price predictions were likely if cold winter weather drained fuel inventories.

The use of natural gas, considered to be a clean-burning fuel, increased throughout the world in 1996 with new natural gas fields in Asia providing fuel to generate electricity to meet growing power needs. According to the U.S. Energy Information Administration (EIA) in Washington, D.C., natural gas consumption in the United States exceeded 16 trillion cubic feet (453 billion cubic meters) in the first nine months of 1996—an increase of 100 billion cubic feet (2.8 billion cubic meters) from the September 1995 figures. According to the EIA, gas delivered to consumers averaged $3.20 per 1,000 cubic feet (28 cubic meters) in the first half of 1996—up from $2.71 in the first half of 1995. □ James C. Tanner

See also **Iraq; United Nations.** In *World Book,* see **Gas; Petroleum.**

Philadelphia. A major Philadelphia police scandal continued to unfold in 1996. The indictment of six police officers of North Philadelphia's 39th Police District in 1995 had led to a review of the arrests made by those officers. As a result, more than 160 criminal cases were thrown out in 1996. In one notorious case, a judge overturned the 1988 murder conviction of an admitted heroin dealer when evidence came to light that a former police officer had paid off the prosecution's star witness.

In late 1996, the city of Philadelphia settled a federal lawsuit filed by the National Association for the Advancement of Colored People (NAACP) and the American Civil Liberties Union (ACLU) in the wake of the police scandal. Mayor Edward Rendell and ACLU executive director Larry Frankel worked out an ambitious reform program for the police department. It included the creation of a watchdog post to monitor the department's internal affairs, increased supervision of the narcotics squad, and appointment of a 15-member police corruption task force, among other provisions.

School funding controversy. A plan to improve the education of Philadelphia's minority students embroiled city and state governments in legal wrangling that eventually reached the Pennsylvania Supreme Court. Commonwealth Court Judge Doris Smith ruled on August 20 that the state of Pennsylvania must allocate an additional $45.1 million in 1996 to fund a court-ordered school reform plan. The ruling climaxed weeks of hearings, during which Judge Smith threatened Philadelphia School Superintendent David Hornbeck with a charge of contempt of court.

On September 10, the Pennsylvania Supreme Court struck down Judge Smith's ruling. At the core of the controversy were financial realities similar to those troubling all big-city school systems in the United States. The Philadelphia School District's annual budget was $1.45 billion, of which 60 percent of funding came from the state. At the same time, per-pupil spending in the Philadelphia suburbs amounted to $2,000 more than that of the city.

Jury rules against city. In June, a federal jury found the city of Philadelphia liable for the 1985 confrontation between police and the radical group Move, which left 11 people dead. The city was ordered to pay $1.5 million to relatives of group members and to Ramona Africa, the only adult survivor of the event, which climaxed when police dropped a bomb that ignited an entire city block.

Interstate tire fire. On March 13, a tire fire broke out under a portion of Interstate 95, which runs through eastern Philadelphia. Fueled by thousands of illegally dumped tires, the extremely destructive fire so badly charred the eight-lane, elevated highway that a section 180 feet long (55 meters) had to be replaced. The highway, one of Philadelphia's busiest, could be reopened only after four

Smoke billows from a tire fire burning under a stretch of Interstate 95 in Philadelphia in March. The fire damaged one of the city's busiest highways.

months of costly repairs. In October, three Philadelphia teen-agers, suspected members of an arson ring, were charged with setting the fire.

Orchestra on strike. Musicians of the Philadelphia Orchestra voted 100 to 0 to strike, after failing to reach an agreement with management on a new contract. The strike, the orchestra's first since 1966, began on September 16, when a three-year contract expired. The orchestra, under the direction of Wolfgang Sawallisch, was to have opened its 1996-1997 concert season on September 17. The strike was settled on November 18.

New sports arena. On August 31, Philadelphia inaugurated a new $210-million sports arena, the CoreStates Center, on the occasion of the World Cup Hockey competition. The arena, which seats 21,000 people, provided a home for three sports franchises—the National Hockey League's Philadelphia Flyers, the National Basketball Association's Philadelphia 76ers, and the Major Indoor Lacrosse League's Philadelphia Wings.

Cézanne exhibit. Attendance at the Philadelphia Museum of Art broke records in 1996, when more than 1 million visitors attended the museum in the calendar year. Approximately 700,000 people came to see the only U.S. showing of a retrospective of the works of Paul Cézanne (1839-1906) which ran from May 30 to September 1.   □ Howard S. Shapiro

See also **City.** In *World Book,* see **Philadelphia.**

Philippines. On Sept. 2, 1996, the government signed a treaty ending about 25 years of civil war with the Moro National Liberation Front (MNLF), the main Muslim guerrilla group that had sought an independent state in the southern Philippines. In August, President Fidel V. Ramos had reached a peace agreement with Nur Misuari, head of the MNLF. Misuari had led the fight against Christian Filipino settlers on Mindanao and other southern islands that were the traditional homeland of Muslims. Estimates of the number killed during the conflict ranged from 50,000 to 150,000.

Peace terms. The agreement gave the nation's more than 3 million Muslims some autonomy and economic self-control in an area designated the Autonomous Region in Muslim Mindanao (ARMM), which covered over a quarter of the southern islands. Running unopposed, Misuari was elected governor of the ARMM, taking office on September 30.

The agreement called for the ARMM's 14 provinces to hold referendums in 1998 to decide whether the provinces should be controlled by an autonomous Muslim government. The agreement also provided for the integration of some of the 16,000 MNLF troops into the Philippine army and police.

Some leaders of the Christians, who outnumbered Muslims in many of the 14 provinces, were critical of the agreement. An MNLF splinter group, the hardline Moro Islamic Liberation Front, openly

317

On February 25, Filipinos celebrate the 10th anniversary of the bloodless ouster of former President Ferdinand Marcos, which led to the restoration of democracy.

opposed the signing. Pressing for total independence, Moro Islamic Liberation Front guerrillas ambushed army troops and raided towns.

Terrorism and kidnapping. Termination of MNLF hostilities and a recent decline of the New People's Army, a Communist insurgency, marked the end of the two major threats to Philippine stability that had arisen in the 1970's. Nevertheless, some New People's Army guerrillas turned to urban terrorism in 1996, though they claimed to target only corrupt and abusive employers.

Ordinary criminals also kidnapped businessmen for ransom. In May 1996, a Hong Kong consulting firm reported that foreign businessmen surveyed by the firm rated the Philippines as the most dangerous country in Asia. More than 600 kidnappings from 1992 through mid-1996 focused on wealthy Filipino businessmen of Chinese ancestry. In response to the rash of kidnappings, President Ramos established 56 courts to focus exclusively on kidnapping cases as part of a cleanup effort.

Political maneuvering throughout 1996 anticipated the 1998 presidential election. Ramos was constitutionally ineligible for another term and repeatedly stated that he intended to retire. However, a group of lawyers and businessmen collected signatures for a 1997 referendum that would amend the constitution to allow Ramos and other politicians a second term.

On Jan. 31, 1996, the largest party in Congress, Laban ng Demokratikong Pilipino (Struggle of Filipino Democrats—LDP), broke from its coalition with Ramos's Lakas-National Union of Christian Democrats to form an opposition. LDP leader, Edgardo Angara, was introduced as the country's next president at the party's May convention.

The Philippine vice president, Joseph Estrada, also maneuvered to run for the presidency in 1998, as did Miriam Defensor-Santiago, whom Ramos defeated in the election of 1992. Ramos's own party considered running the speaker of the Philippine House of Representatives, Jose de Venecia, for president, but his popularity was said to be low.

Economic growth in the first half of 1996 stood at more than 7 percent, significantly higher than in 1995. After years of budget deficits, the nation achieved in 1996 its third straight year of budget surpluses as a result of privatizing many state-owned businesses. In 1996, more than 75 percent of exports were manufactured goods, surpassing such traditional exports as sugar and coconut oil.

Tragedies. A fire in a discotheque near Manila, the national capital, killed more than 150 people, mainly teen-agers, on March 19. On February 18, an overloaded ferry that had failed safety inspections capsized, drowning at least 54.　　□ Henry S. Bradsher

See also **Asia** (Facts in brief). In *World Book,* see **Philippines.**

318

Physics. In January 1996, researchers at the Lawrence Livermore National Laboratory in Livermore, California, demonstrated that hydrogen, the lightest element, could become a metal under the right conditions. A tiny sample of liquid hydrogen, squeezed by the impact of a bullet, momentarily had the properties of a metal.

Hydrogen becomes a metal. In liquid or solid metals, the atoms' outermost electrons are loosely attached. Since the atoms are close together, as occurs in a liquid or a solid, the regions in which these electrons wander overlap, allowing free movement between atoms. The movement of these electrons in metals allows them to conduct electricity.

Hydrogen must be cooled below –423 °F (–253 °C) to be liquefied. It freezes to a solid below –435 °F (–259 °C). Even in a liquid or solid state, however, hydrogen clings to its single electron more tightly than other chemically similar elements. Thus, hydrogen must be compressed to bring its atoms close enough to permit electrons to jump from atom to atom. Unsuccessful attempts to produce metallic hydrogen have involved squeezing liquid or solid hydrogen in powerful presses.

The Livermore team—Samuel Weir, Arthur Mitchell, and William Nellis—took a different approach. Much higher pressures were reached, but only for an instant of time. They used a gas gun—sort of a big brother of an air rifle—to fire a one-inch (25-millimeter) pellet at a speed of 16,400 miles (26,400 kilometers) per hour. Bullets from an ordinary high-powered rifle reach speeds of about 1,000 miles (1,600 kilometers) per hour. At the end of the gun barrel was a sample of liquid hydrogen 0.02 inch (0.5 millimeter) thick, sandwiched between two sapphire disks. The shock of the impact quickly drove the pressure in the liquid to more than a million atmospheres, or 14 million pounds per square inch (1 million kilograms per square centimeter).

Although the high pressure lasted only a fraction of a *microsecond* (millionth of a second), this was sufficient time to measure the electrical resistance of the hydrogen with high-speed electronic equipment. As the hydrogen compressed, resistance fell rapidly. Above 1.4 million atmospheres, the hydrogen was able to conduct electricity as other metals do.

Metallic hydrogen is more than a laboratory curiosity. Planetary scientists have long attempted to understand the powerful magnetic fields of Jupiter and Saturn, the cores of which are made largely of hydrogen. Metallic hydrogen could sustain the strong electric currents required to generate their magnetic fields. The new information about the pressure and temperature at which hydrogen becomes metallic will help scientists better understand the core and surfaces of these planets.

Two places at the same time. In the world of quantum physics, it is possible for an atom to be in two places at once—at least hypothetically. (Quantum physics is based on the theory that radiant energy is transferred in pulsations and that each pulsation is a definite amount.) In May 1996, a team of physicists at the National Institute of Standards and Technology (NIST) in Boulder, Colorado, reported the first laboratory experiment in which one atom was separated by a space more than 100 times the diameter of that atom—that is, one atom was in two places at once.

The atom was a positive ion of *beryllium,* a metallic element, with one electron removed so that it would respond to electrical forces. The atom was caught in an electromagnetic trap and slowed to a near halt by laser beams. Using lasers to affect the spin of the atom's outer electron, the NIST scientists "teased" the single atom into two states—spin-up and spin-down—that forced the atom to move to one side or the other of the electromagnetic trap. Using other laser beams, the researchers pushed the two states of the single atom apart by about 80 nanometers (8 billionths of a meter).

Although the experiment had little practical significance, it provided a vivid demonstration of how the quantum world appears to contradict natural intuition about reality. It was also a notable example of techniques that enable scientists to manipulate and observe individual atoms.   □ Robert H. March

In *World Book,* see **Physics.**

Poetry. In 1996, two collections of poems were published that became sentimental favorites while receiving well-deserved praise. Jane Kenyon, the author of *Otherwise: New and Selected Poems,* died in 1995 from cancer at the age of 47. She left behind a body of work at once witty and wistful, by turns taking up the natural world of her small New England farm and her own self-aware reflections on mortality. Her description of a man eating yogurt offers the reader a glimpse of eternity. She evokes in a phrase the sensual feel of her husband's shirt. And she repeatedly captures her own deep, pervasive melancholy.

Virginia Hamilton Adair, 83, had written poetry for years, but *Ants on the Melon: A Collection of Poems* was her first published book of poetry. By no means are these "old-lady poems" about robins or daffodils, but rather tight, short lyrics, many in traditional forms. Several are extremely sensual, and others, like "Key Ring," read like strange omens. The narrator's grandfather has just given the little girl his keys to hold: "I asked, 'Do they unlock every door there is? / And what would I find inside?' / He answered, 'Mysteries and more mysteries. You can't tell till you've tried.' / Then as I swung the heavy ring around / the keys made a chuckling sound."

Hall and Hecht. Mortality dominated the work of two of the best-established poets in the United States, Donald Hall and Anthony Hecht. Among the four poems in *The Old Life,* Hall offers a lament for his wife, Jane Kenyon. The long title piece is an autobiography in loose, chatty, and exceptionally readable verse: "I wanted a Mickey Mouse / watch as much as, later in life, / I wanted a job, / a prize, or a woman. It disappeared / a month after my fifth birthday, and sixty years afterward / I grieve for it whenever / I regret something lost."

Anthony Hecht—whom 1987 Nobel laureate Joseph Brodsky called "the best poet writing in English today"—is a master of an exquisitely musical diction, with a subtle wit, and a mournful view of life. His 1996 collection, *Flight Among the Tombs,* is divided into two parts: a collection of poems called "Presumptions of Death"; and a collection including imitations of Horace, an elegy for American poet James Merrill, who died in 1995, and a long poem entitled "Proust on Skates," which ends: "It will not last, that happiness; nothing lasts; / But will reduce in time to the clear brew / Of simmering memory / Nourished by shadowy gardens, music, guests, / Childhood affections, and, of Delft, a view / Steeped in a sip of tea."

Robert Hass, the 1995–1996 American poet laureate, published *Sun Under Wood: Poems.* Hass's book mixes prosy long lines, Zen Buddhist reflections, and homages to Mexican artist Frida Kahlo and Hass's mother: "In grammar school, whenever she'd start to drink, / she panicked and made amends by baking chocolate cake. / And, of course, when we got home, we'd smell the strong, sweet smell / of the absolute darkness of the chocolate, / and be too sick to eat it."

Award winners. Hayden Carruth's *Scrambled Eggs & Whisky: Poems 1991–1995* celebrates love in old age, laments his daughter's illness, and looks back on his checkered past. His collection won the 1996 National Book Award for poetry. Jorie Graham's *The Dream of the Unified Field: Selected Poems* won the 1996 Pulitzer Prize for poetry.

Other notable collections. Gary Snyder's *Mountains and Rivers Without End* is a multifaceted epic poem, touching on American history, ecology, Chinese painting, Japanese No drama, Buddhist thought, and much else. Not precisely a continuous work, Snyder's book is a gathering of poems, many with the profound but simple lessons associated with haiku: "Over stone lip / the creek leaps out as one / divides in spray and streamers, / lets it all go."

In *Meadowlands,* Louise Gluck describes the breakup of a marriage while also retelling Homer's *The Odyssey.* This may sound improbable, but Gluck manages to make her poems convincing, touching, funny, and true to life. A. R. Ammons's *Brink Road* offers a huge variety of work, characterized by wit, beautiful word-music, and subjects ranging from the nature of the universe to "Tenure's Pleasures."

☐ Michael Dirda

See also **Literature; Pulitzer Prizes.** In *World Book,* see **Poetry.**

Poland. In a close election, Aleksander Kwasniewski, a former Communist, was elected president of Poland in November 1995. Winning with only 51 percent of the vote, Kwasniewski pledged to respect democracy and the market economy and reaffirmed Poland's desire to join the European Union (EU) and NATO. In 1996, however, a large segment of the public had switched allegiance to a coalition of opposition groups led by the trade organization Solidarity. By midyear, support for the Solidarity coalition equaled that of the governing coalition, and on September 1, the 16th anniversary of the founding of Solidarity, some 35,000 citizens demonstrated in support of the organization in Warsaw.

Prime Minister Jozef Oleksy resigned in January after being charged with serving as a spy for the Soviet Union, but was soon after elected leader of the Social Democratic Party, the senior partner in the coalition government. Oleksy was succeeded as prime minister by Wlodzimierz Cimoszewicz on February 7.

Government. Politics in Poland continued to be marked by conflict within the governing coalition. Leaders of the Polish Peasant Party (PSL), the junior party of the coalition, were less in favor of further privatization than their partners, the Social Democrats. After the dismissal of foreign trade minister Jacek Buchacz, a PSL member, in early September, party leaders threatened to leave the coalition. The leaders relented after PSL member Miroslaw Pietrewicz was appointed head of Poland's newly created treasury ministry.

Economy. After achieving a growth rate of 6.5 percent in 1995, Poland's economy remained strong in 1996. Polish leaders forecast a 17 percent inflation rate for the year. Foreign investment continued to grow rapidly, surpassing $10 billion. However, the trade deficit, which reached $3.1 billion in July, was much larger than in 1995.

Foreign affairs. The Polish public continued to support joining the European Union. Although the government maintained its desire to join NATO, leaders of the Party of Real Politics—a small, right-wing political party—warned that Russia's opposition to NATO expansion could make joining the alliance detrimental to Poland.

Poland joined the Organization for Economic Cooperation and Development (OECD) in July. But EU officials were dissatisfied with the slow pace Polish leaders were following in removing trade barriers, a precondition for achieving EU membership.

Polish military cooperation with Germany and NATO continued. German and Polish armed forces conducted several joint military exercises in 1996, and Polish troops participated in peacekeeping efforts in Bosnia.

☐ Sharon Wolchik

See also **Europe** (Facts in brief table). In *World Book,* see **Poland.**

Pollution. See Environmental pollution.

Popular music. In 1996, reunion tours by veteran 1970's bands, such as the flamboyantly theatrical Kiss and the punk band the Sex Pistols, received widespread attention.

For the first time in 17 years, Kiss toured with its original members—drummer Peter Criss, guitarist Ace Frehley, bassist Gene Simmons, and guitarist Paul Stanley. Kiss performed with the outlandish makeup and special effects that had electrified audiences in the 1970's. Tickets for the tour quickly sold out at arenas and stadiums across the country, with the concerts attracting many older fans who came costumed in the dress and makeup of their favorite Kiss members. The tour also proved popular with fans who had been too young to see Kiss perform during its prime.

A more notorious reunion was that of the Sex Pistols, the punk firebrands who had disbanded following a disastrous U.S. tour in 1978. The band, which released only one album in its brief existence, initially represented an assault on the values of the music industry, which the punks considered to be fat, greedy, and resistant to change. In 1996, however, the Sex Pistols dubbed their reunion the "Filthy Lucre Tour" and said it was an attempt to make the money they had foregone during the 1970's.

New wave returns. Sensing that the public had become more receptive to their music, other bands from the 1970's joined the Sex Pistols in returning to the scene. Among the leading "new wave" acts of the late 1970's, the Talking Heads regrouped as The Heads, without singer David Byrne, while Patti Smith's *Gone Again,* her first album in eight years, was critically hailed as one of the year's best releases.

Heroin. The increase in heroin use among rock musicians drew media attention throughout the summer, with magazines—including *Newsweek, Entertainment Weekly,* and *Rolling Stone*—devoting major stories to the topic. In May, singer Dave Gahan of Depeche Mode nearly died from a heroin overdose. Stone Temple Pilots canceled part of its 1996 tour while singer Scott Weiland underwent treatment for heroin addiction.

A number of rock bands experienced tragedy through drug overdoses during 1996. On May 25, Bradley Nowell of the band Sublime died of a heroin overdose. Jonathan Melvoin, the touring keyboardist for Smashing Pumpkins, met the same fate on July 12, forcing the band to interrupt its U.S. tour. The band's drummer, Jimmy Chamberlin, was arrested for possession and was fired from the band.

Amid the continuing controversy concerning drug abuse in rock, the music industry was accused of being so concerned with keeping acts profitable that it was willing to ignore or even assist addiction, rather than urge time off for recovery. While some managers and record company executives maintained that they had no right to meddle in the private lives of their artists, the National Academy of Recording

Grammy Award winners in 1996

Record of the Year, "Kiss from a Rose," Seal
Album of the Year, "Jagged Little Pill," Alanis Morissette
Song of the Year, "Kiss from a Rose," Seal
New Artist, Hootie and the Blowfish
Pop Vocal Performance, Female, "No More 'I love You's,'" Annie Lennox
Pop Vocal Performance, Male, "Kiss from a Rose," Seal
Pop Performance by a Duo or Group with Vocal, "Let Her Cry," Hootie and the Blowfish
Traditional Pop Vocal Performance, "Duets II," Frank Sinatra
Pop Instrumental Performance, "Mariachi Suite," Los Lobos
Rock Vocal Performance, Female, "You Oughta Know," Alanis Morissette
Rock Vocal Performance, Male, "You Don't Know How It Feels," Tom Petty
Rock Performance by a Duo or Group with Vocal, "Run Around," Blues Traveler
Hard Rock Performance, "Spin the Black Circle," Pearl Jam
Metal Performance, "Happiness in Slavery," Nine Inch Nails
Rock Instrumental Performance, "Jessica," Allman Brothers Band
Rock Song, "You Oughta Know," Glen Ballard and Alanis Morissette
Alternative Music Performance, "MTV Unplugged in New York," Nirvana
Rhythm-and-Blues Vocal Performance, Female, "I Apologize," Anita Baker
Rhythm-and-Blues Vocal Performance, Male, "For Your Love," Stevie Wonder
Rhythm-and-Blues Performance by a Duo or Group with Vocal, "Creep," TLC
Rhythm-and-Blues Song, "For Your Love," Stevie Wonder
Rap Solo Performance, "Gangsta's Paradise," Coolio
Rap Performance by a Duo or Group, "I'll Be There For You/You're All I Need to Get By," Method Man featuring Mary J. Blige
New-Age Album, "Forest," George Winston
Contemporary Jazz Performance, "We Live Here," The Pat Metheny Group
Jazz Vocal Performance, "An Evening with Lena Horne," Lena Horne
Jazz Instrumental Solo, "Impressions," Michael Brecker
Jazz Instrumental Performance, Individual or Group, "Infinity," McCoy Tyner
Large Jazz Ensemble Performance, "All Blues," Tom Scott
Latin Jazz Performance, "Antonio Brasiliero," Jobim
Country Album, "The Woman in Me," Shania Twain
Country Vocal Performance, Female, Alison Krauss
Country Vocal Performance, Male, "Go Rest High on That Mountain," Vince Gill
Country Performance by a Duo or Group with Vocal, "Here Comes the Rain," The Mavericks
Country Vocal Collaboration, "Somewhere in the Vicinity of the Heart," Shenandoah with Alison Krauss
Country Instrumental Performance, "High Tower," featuring Bela Fleck and Johnny Gimble
Bluegrass Album, "Unleashed," The Nashville Bluegrass Band
Country Song, "Go Rest High on That Mountain," Vince Gill
Rock Gospel Album, "Lesson of Love," Ashley Cleveland
Classical Album, "Debussy: La Mer," Pierre Boulez
Music Video, Long Form, "Secret World Live," Peter Gabriel
Music Video, Short Form, "Scream," Michael Jackson

Popular music

Arts and Sciences attempted to combat the rise of drug addiction among musicians through its Musi-Cares substance abuse program.

Death of Tupac Shakur. On September 13, one of the most popular and talented artists in the field of "gangsta" rap, Tupac Shakur, died of gunshot wounds he suffered on September 7 as he rode in a car driven by record-company executive Marion "Suge" Knight in Las Vegas, Nevada. His murderers escaped, and Las Vegas police said that Shakur's companions provided no leads. There was speculation that the 25-year-old Shakur had been the victim of a gang-style assassination.

Shakur's recordings were released under the name "2Pac." Early in 1996, his *All Eyez on Me* double CD went to the top of the charts immediately upon release and sold more than 5 million copies during its first three months. Although Shakur was mourned as a hero and a martyr by many rap fans, his death was widely seen as a sign that the days of gangsta rap's most violent expression were over.

Rap releases. A more positive sign for socially conscious rap came with the chart-topping success of the Fugees (short for "refugees"). The New Jersey trio sold more than 10 million copies of its breakthrough album, *The Score,* with "Fu-Gee-La," the album's first single, appealing to fans of melodic pop as well as hard-core rap.

The year's other major chart-topping rap breakthrough was *It Was Written,* the second album by Nas, which turned the acclaim he has long enjoyed among hip-hop fans into more widespread popularity.

Concert slump. With the Kiss tour a notable exception, 1996 was considered a disappointing year for the concert business. Some of the acts that had filled stadiums in the first half of the 1990's either disbanded, such as the Grateful Dead, or didn't tour, such as the Eagles, the Rolling Stones, R.E.M., and U2, leaving the field to acts who were unable to match the ticket sales of these supergroups.

Many of the major tours featured acts that had achieved their peak popularity in the 1970's. Styx, Steely Dan, Steve Miller, Pat Benatar, Peter Frampton, the Allman Brothers, REO Speedwagon, and other acts all toured during 1996, more than a decade since the release of their last hit records.

Lollapalooza, a festival-style touring package originally featuring alternative bands, continued its decline. The more metal-oriented 1996 line-up, featuring Metallica and Soundgarden, failed to attract the huge crowds the festival drew in the early 1990's.

Alanis Morissette. After dominating the Grammy awards, Canadian singer Alanis Morissette's *Jagged Little Pill* became the top-selling album ever by a female artist, with United States sales exceeding 12 million. Morissette continued touring throughout the year, returning to cities as often as three times to play ever larger arenas.

LeAnn Rimes and country's decline. After enjoying a boom through the mid-1990's, the popularity of country music began to decline, as album sales, touring business, and the number of radio stations playing it diminished. Many fans and members of the industry felt that the music had become too slick and had strayed too far from its roots, with many of its younger performers marketed on the basis of looks and image rather than depth of talent.

An exception to that criticism came with the breakthrough of teen-age country singer LeAnn Rimes, whose album *Blue* sold more than 123,000 copies in its first week of release. The hit title track had been written more than 30 years before for the late Patsy Cline, and Rimes's vocal style evoked memories of that country singer. Rimes, who turned 14 on August 28, impressed critics and audiences with her vocal range, emotional power, and performing poise. Her music attracted fans of all ages.

Jazz continued to renew itself through younger performers who were heavily influenced by the jazz masters of the past. Saxophonists Joshua Redman and James Carter, guitarist Mark Whitfield, and pianist Cyrus Chestnut joined the ranks of the most respected members of the younger jazz generation. All of these musicians were featured in *Kansas City,* a Robert Altman film that paid homage to the jazz of the 1930's.

The year's most noteworthy reissue, *Miles Davis and Gil Evans: The Complete Columbia Studio Recordings,* consisted of six compact discs featuring the collaboration between the famed trumpeter, Davis, and his favorite orchestral arranger, Evans. The recording includes such classic jazz albums as *Miles Ahead, Porgy and Bess,* and *Sketches of Spain.*

On June 15, singer Ella Fitzgerald died at her house in Beverly Hills, California, at the age of 78. Fitzgerald was mourned throughout the world as the most influential jazz vocalist since Billie Holiday.

The Beatles and Stones. *The Beatles Anthology,* an 8-volume set of videos featuring 10 hours of footage—including more than 5 hours of unseen footage—was released in late September. It became the top-selling music video in America.

The Rolling Stones Rock and Roll Circus joined the *Beatles Anthology* on video racks later in 1996. Shot as a television special in 1968, the show featured the Rolling Stones acting as circus ringmasters, introducing other superstar rockers, such as John Lennon, the Who, and Eric Clapton. The show, which had not been seen since its production in 1968, was given a premiere at the 1996 New York Film Festival in October.

On December 31, Buckingham Palace announced that Paul McCartney was to be knighted, the first rock star to be so honored.   □ Don McLeese

See also **Popular music** Special Report: **Ella Fitzgerald—First Lady of Song.** In *World Book,* see **Country music; Jazz; Popular music; Rock music.**

Ella Fitzgerald
First Lady of Song

A singer legendary for her taste, purity of sound, and stylistic innovations dies at age 79.

By Donald Liebenson

The author

Donald Liebenson writes about entertainment for the *Los Angeles Time*s and the *Chicago Tribune*.

Ella Fitzgerald, one of the most celebrated and influential jazz singers of her generation, died at the age of 79 on June 15, 1996. Often called the "First Lady of Song," Fitzgerald enjoyed the love of audiences, the respect of musicians, and the praise of critics. Like legendary trumpeter and singer Louis Armstrong, with whom she often performed and recorded, Fitzgerald introduced jazz to a mainstream audience. But her vast repertoire embraced a wide range of American music, including blues, pop, opera, and Broadway and Hollywood show tunes. Generations of singers were inspired by Ella Fitzgerald, and composers called her renditions of their songs definitive. "I never realized," lyricist Ira Gershwin once remarked, "just how good our songs really were until I heard them sung by Ella Fitzgerald." Fitzgerald was an intuitive singer, blessed with a warm, clear, and vibrant voice that a critic once said could make a military march sound like a love song. She also popularized the art of scat (improvised singing of wordless syllables). Singer Mel Tormé told biographer Stuart Nicholson, "Her notes float out in perfect pitch, effortless and, most important of all, swinging." Fitzgerald was honored with 13 Grammy Awards, the National Medal of Arts, and many honorary doctorate degrees from such universities as Dartmouth and Yale. In 1979, she was enshrined in the Hall of Fame of the jazz magazine *Down Beat*.

Ella Fitzgerald was born on April 25, 1917, in Newport News, Virginia. Most biographies and reference books list the year of her birth as 1918, but her 1993 biography confirmed that she was born one year earlier. Her parents were William Fitzgerald and Temperance Williams Fitzgerald. Her father left the family when she was young, and she moved with her mother and stepfather to Yonkers, New York.

As a child, Fitzgerald wanted to be a dancer and developed a dance routine, which she performed in local clubs. But she also listened to the radio and records and could imitate favorite singers, including Louis Armstrong, Bing Crosby, and the Boswell Sisters led by Connee Boswell.

Performing a solo act in the clubs of the 1940's, Fitzgerald comes under the influence of such musicians as Charlie Parker and Dizzy Gillespie, who were developing a new jazz style called bebop.

In 1932, Fitzgerald's mother died suddenly of a heart attack, and Fitzgerald went to live with her aunt in Harlem, a section of Manhattan that at the time was the national center of African American culture. She made her stage debut on November 21, 1934, at an amateur contest at Harlem's famed Apollo Theater. Although she intended to dance, she was intimidated by the enthusiastic response received by two dancers who appeared before her. She decided at the last minute to sing two of her mother's favorite songs, "The Object of My Affection" and "Judy," which Connee Boswell and the Boswell Sisters had popularized. She won first prize.

Watching in the wings was saxophonist Benny Carter, who took Fitzgerald to audition for bandleader Fletcher Henderson. Henderson did not hire her, but Chick Webb, another bandleader, took a chance on the teen-ager. Webb's trumpet player, Mario Bauza, called Fitzgerald "a diamond in the rough." During the band's residency at Harlem's Savoy Ballroom, Fitzgerald was a hit with audiences and rapidly established herself as a valuable addition to Webb's band.

In 1935, Ella Fitzgerald made her first recording with Webb, "Love and Kisses," for the Decca Records label. Three years later, at the age of 21, she became America's most popular female vocalist with her recording of "A-Tisket, A-Tasket," which she adapted from a nursery rhyme and childhood game. The song hit the top of the charts two weeks after it was released and stayed on the hit parade for 19 weeks. Fitzgerald sang it in the 1942 Abbott and Costello comedy, *Ride' Em Cowboy,* and later in the 1944 musical, *Two Girls and a Sailor.*

When Chick Webb died in 1939, Fitzgerald led the band, which was renamed "Ella Fitzgerald and Her Famous Orchestra." In 1942, however, she left to pursue a solo career.

In 1952, Fitzgerald takes her "Jazz at the Philharmonic" tour to Europe, where she performs to great acclaim with drummer Max Roach (at rear), trumpeter Roy Eldridge, and legendary pianist Oscar Peterson.

She began to be influenced by a new style of jazz known as bebop, pioneered by major jazz artists such as saxophonist Charlie Parker and trumpeter Dizzy Gillespie. Fitzgerald incorporated bebop's intricate rhythms into her singing. In 1945, she recorded "Flying Home," considered one of the most influential vocal jazz records of its time because of her dazzling scat singing. Two years later, Fitzgerald released a bebop version of George and Ira Gershwin's "Lady Be Good." These were creative high points in Fitzgerald's two-decade recording career with Decca, but most of the records she made for the label were lightweight novelty songs.

Fitzgerald's concert performances, however, secured her reputation as the premier jazz vocalist of the day. She toured with jazz entrepreneur Norman Granz's Jazz at the Philharmonic series, which included such jazz giants as Gillespie and Parker, trumpeter Roy Eldridge, and saxophonists Coleman Hawkins and Lester Young. Fitzgerald's show-stopping rendition of "How High the Moon" was considered the signature tune of the series.

In 1953, Fitzgerald chose Norman Granz as her personal manager and became the first artist to sign to his new record label, Verve. She developed a strong bond with Granz, and many people credited him with bringing Fitzgerald's talent to the widest possible audience. Their first collaboration—*The Cole Porter Songbook,* recorded in 1956—was a turning point in her career. It was followed by "song-books" devoted to the compositions of Irving Berlin, Harold Arlen, Duke Ellington, George and Ira Gershwin, Jerome Kern, Johnny Mercer, and Richard Rodgers and Lorenz Hart. These records are, in the words of one critic, "a massive recorded encyclopedia of American popular song" and established Fitzgerald as an internationally beloved jazz artist.

Fitzgerald continued to record for Verve after Granz sold the label in 1960. She also made several albums for Capitol Records. She became an audience favorite at festivals, clubs, and concert halls. During the 1970's and 1980's, she recorded many albums for Pablo Records, which Granz launched in 1973. Fitzgerald appeared in two major musical films: *Pete Kelly's Blues* (1955), a portrait of the 1920's jazz age, and *St. Louis Blues* (1958), a film biography of blues legend W. C. Handy. She made television appearances on variety and talk shows and appeared in a series of popular commercials for Memorex recording tape that featured the slogan, "Is it live or is it Memorex?"

Ella Fitzgerald was married in 1941 to Benny Kornegay. The marriage was annulled in mid-1942. In 1947, she married jazz bassist Ray Brown. They adopted a boy, Ray, Jr. The couple divorced in 1953 but continued to perform together.

In the last years of her life, Fitzgerald was in poor health. In 1993, both of her legs were amputated below the knee due to circulatory system complications from diabetes. She ceased to appear in public after the operation and died at her Beverly Hills, California, house.

Before Ella Fitzgerald's death, two tribute concerts had been planned for New York City's Carnegie Hall in July 1996. Fitzgerald performed there 26 times between 1947 and 1991. These concerts were staged as planned, but as memorials to Ella Fitzgerald's enduring legacy. Songs were performed and anecdotes told by more than 30 entertainers, including former colleagues as well as members of a new generation of jazz singers, all of whom had been inspired by the "First Lady of Song." ■ ■ ■

Notable recordings

In addition to the "song-book" series—

Ella and Louis (1956)
Ella Fitzgerald at the Opera House (1957)
Mack the Knife: Ella in Berlin (1960)
Let No Man Write My Epitaph—soundtrack (1960; rereleased in 1991 as *The Intimate Ella*)
Ella and Oscar (1975)
A Perfect Match: Ella and Basie (1980)

Compilations—

The Early Years
For the Love of Ella
First Lady of Song
The Best of the Songbooks

Population. The steady growth of the world's urban population was the focus of the State of the World Population report, published by the United Nations Population Fund (UNPF) in May 1996. In addition, urban growth was discussed at the United Nations Conference on Human Settlements, also known as Habitat II, in Istanbul, Turkey, from June 3 to June 14.

Megacities. The UNPF predicted that by the year 2005 about half of the estimated world population of 6.59 billion will live in cities. In mid-1996, the world population totaled 5.8 billion, of which about 2.6 billion—45 percent—lived in large cities. In its report, the UNPF explained that more and more people in developing countries were abandoning rural areas in search of the better economic opportunities and living conditions available in large cities. That migration trend will increase the population in many already-crowded cities and turn them into megacities, metropolitan areas with more than 10 million inhabitants. In 1995, 14 cities in the world qualified as megacities. By the year 2015, the number is expected to almost double, to 27 megacities.

According to UNPF, the world's annual urban growth rate in developing countries was estimated to be four times greater than that of the richest industrialized countries. Thus, Asia was predicted to have the most megacities in the 21st century, and in Latin America and North America, the development of megacities was predicted to be less pronounced.

The UNPF report stressed that urban growth "is inevitable and it should not be feared," because cities are centers for economic growth and social development. Cities provide capital and markets for enterprise, employment opportunities, better health care, and better living conditions, with electricity, sewers, heating, and garbage collection. For women in developing countries, cities present more chances for education and independence. Nevertheless, the report noted, urban growth also carries such risks as the collapse of basic services, intolerable environmental degradation, and increased social conflicts if city planners are not prepared for the massive influx of people.

Habitat II. Delegates to Habitat II, including about 20,000 city mayors, academics, business people, and national government representatives, also discussed concerns about urban life. According to the World Bank, in the mid-1990's, at least 600 million people lived in poverty in slums and shantytowns with no infrastructure for water or sewage. Such living conditions created innumerable public health problems and social instability. The delegates, in the congress's final declaration, endorsed "ensuring adequate shelter for all and making human settlements safer, healthier, more livable, equitable, sustainable, and more productive." ☐ J. Tuyet Nguyen

See also **Census; City.** In *World Book,* see **Food supply; Population.**

Portugal. The Socialist Party strengthened its political dominance in Portugal in January 1996 when Jorge Sampaio, a former Lisbon mayor and Socialist Party leader, was elected president. Sampaio received 52 percent of the vote, defeating Aníbal Cavaço Silva, the former prime minister, whose center-right Social Democratic Party lost control of parliament to the Socialists in October 1995.

Economic growth and a decline in the deficit in 1996 boosted the government's hopes of joining the European Union (EU) monetary union from the planned start in 1999. In October 1996, the government proposed tighter controls on public spending in order to lower the deficit in 1997 to 2.9 percent of gross domestic product, which is sufficiently low to join the single European currency.

The government continued to have problems, however, with domestic institutions, including soccer clubs, that evaded paying taxes. About $7 billion in taxes went unreported in 1996. On June 27, the parliament rejected a proposal that all revenues from the state-run gambling pool be given to soccer clubs to enable them to pay overdue taxes. In 1996, the soccer clubs received 50 percent of the gambling pool revenues. Those opposed to the proposal claimed that such a plan was unfair to salaried people, who bear the biggest tax burden. ☐ Tom Buerkle

See also **Europe** (Facts in brief table). In *World Book,* see **European Union; Portugal.**

Powell, Colin (1937–), a retired general of the United States Army and former chairman of the Joint Chiefs of Staff, became a prominent, if reluctant, political figure in 1996. Powell's name was put forth as a possible candidate for both president and vice president on the Republican ticket, and he was a featured speaker at the 1996 Republican National Convention.

Colin Luther Powell was born on April 5, 1937, in New York City. He joined the Reserve Officers' Training Corps (ROTC) while at the City College of New York, from which he graduated in 1958. After joining the Army, he served two tours of duty in Vietnam during the 1960's. In 1987, he became national security adviser in the Reagan Administration. In that post, he played a key role in the signing of the Intermediate-Range Nuclear Forces Treaty, an arms control agreement between the United States and the former Soviet Union.

Powell was appointed chairman of the Joint Chiefs of Staff in 1989 and became a national figure during the 1991 Persian Gulf War. After retiring from the Army in 1993, he completed an autobiography, *My American Journey* (1995). ☐ Lisa Klobuchar

See also **Republican Party.**

President of the United States. See **Clinton, Bill; United States, Government of the.**

Prince Edward Island. See **Canadian provinces.**

Prison. In January 1996, federal and state prisons and jails in the United States held an estimated 1,585,400 inmates, according to an August 1996 report by the U.S. Department of Justice's Bureau of Justice Statistics (BJS). The number was a historic high.

According to the BJS, the January 1996 U.S. prison and jail population rate was 600 inmates per every 100,000 people in the general population. The rate was nearly double what it had been in 1985, when there were 313 inmates per 100,000 population. Furthermore, the 1996 U.S. prison population rate was far higher than in European countries. In 1996, there were less than 60 inmates per 100,000 population in Sweden and the Netherlands, according to the BJS. Austria, England, France, Germany, and Italy had somewhat higher rates—ranging from 70 to 90 inmates per 100,000 population.

Female inmates. The BJS reported that the number of females sentenced to state and federal prison grew more slowly than the number of males. There were 6.5 percent more females and 6.8 percent more males in state and federal institutions in 1995 than there had been in 1994. However, between 1980 and January 1996, the number of male inmates grew by 226 percent, and the number of female inmates increased by 413 percent.

The BJS reported the same trend for jails in the United States. In 1985, 8 percent of inmates held in jails were women. By 1996, more than 10 percent were women. Between 1985 and January 1996, the number of male inmates increased by 98 percent, while the number of female inmates grew by 173 percent.

Across the nation, patterns varied widely as to the proportion of women serving prison sentences. In Oklahoma, for example, 10 percent of prisoners were women. In Maine, only 3 percent were women.

Prison conditions. Record numbers of inmates in prisons and jails in 1996 placed a burden on facilities. Many state prisons were extremely overcrowded, holding as many as 25 percent more inmates than the institutions had been designed to house. Federal prisons were even more overcrowded, housing 28 percent more inmates than they were designed to hold. Large prison populations reduced inmate privacy and strained vocational, educational, and recreational facilities, raising tension levels throughout the institutions.

In 1996, politicians who wanted to be perceived as "tough-on-crime" pressured prison managers in many states to reduce or deny long-standing, inmate privileges, such as television, smoking, use of athletic equipment, and college-level educational programs. The reinstatement of chain gangs for men as well as women was seriously debated in 1996 in several states. □ Michael Tonry

See also **Crime.** In *World Book,* see **Prison.**

Prizes. See **Nobel Prizes; Pulitzer Prizes.**

Protestantism. In August 1996, German courts cleared Dietrich Bonhoeffer, a well-known Protestant witness against Adolf Hitler, of charges of treason—more than 50 years after Bonhoeffer's death. Bonhoeffer, who was actively involved in the anti-Nazi resistance movement, was hanged on April 9, 1945, for participating in a 1944 plot to assassinate Adolf Hitler. Although Bonhoeffer had been in violation of the law of Nazi Germany, many Protestants have argued that he was a martyr to a morally corrupt legal system.

Archbishop Tutu retires. In June 1996, Desmond Tutu, the Anglican archbishop of Capetown, South Africa, retired after 10 years as the leader of the church in South Africa, Lesotho, Mozambique, Namibia, Swaziland, and the island of St. Helena.

Tutu, ordained an Anglican priest in 1961, received the Nobel Peace Prize in 1984 for his nonviolent campaign against the apartheid government of South Africa. On June 23, 1996, at a farewell service for Tutu, South African President Nelson Mandela presented the archbishop with South Africa's Order for Meritorious Service. Archbishop Njongonkulu Ndungane, Tutu's successor in the church, was invested on September 14.

Homosexuality. In May, the General Conference of the United Methodist Church (UMC) voted down a proposed announcement that the UMC was "unable to arrive at a common mind" on the subject of homosexuality. The UMC upheld the statement in the church's *Book of Discipline* that claims homosexuals are people of "sacred worth" but that homosexual practice is "incompatible with Christian teaching."

The Presbyterian Church (U.S.A.) in its July general assembly in Albuquerque, New Mexico, voted 313 to 236 to approve a report labeling homosexual practice a sin and declaring that active homosexuals should not be appointed as elders, deacons, or ministers.

In May, a court of the Episcopal Church dismissed heresy charges against Walter Righter, retired bishop of the Diocese of Iowa, for ordaining Barry Stopfel, a practicing homosexual, to the diaconate in 1990. Ten of the church's 300 bishops had sought a case against Righter to protest what they regarded as lax policies against the ordination of gay and lesbian clergy.

The Promise Keepers (PK), a movement of largely evangelical Christian men, attracted more than 1 million participants to 22 stadium events in 1996. PK promoted their cause of helping men "keep their promises" to spouses, families, God, their churches, and themselves. Founded in 1990 by former University of Colorado football coach Bill McCartney, the organization burgeoned in 1996 to support a $115-million budget and a staff of over 400.

Movement critics, who also increased in number, accused PK of being sexist, authoritarian, and antihomosexual. In response, the PK leadership took pains to be nonpolitical, pledged support to local churches, and emphasized racial reconciliation among men.

Southern Baptists. In June, the Cooperative Baptist Fellowship (CBF), a large dissenting group within the Southern Baptist Convention (SBC), voted not to break with the Convention, despite apparently unbridgeable gaps between the two factions. Resisting the denominational leadership's move to the theological and political right, the CBF grew from 400 churches in 1991 to 1,400 in 1996. Although remaining within the larger denomination, the CBF reaffirmed its support of independent Baptist seminaries and mission programs.

In June, the SBC, the largest Protestant body in the United States, called for a boycott of the Walt Disney Company for promoting "anti-Christian" and "anti-family" values. The church criticized Disney for extending benefits to the same-sex partners of employees and for supporting activities conducted by gay and lesbian organizations at Disney's parks.

Also in June, the SBC appointed a U.S. missionary to Jewish communities and approved a resolution calling for Baptists to convert Jews to Christianity. The resolution claimed other Christian denominations have engaged in dialogue with Jewish groups but have acted as though they "have neither right nor obligation to proclaim the Gospel to the Jewish people." The SBC's action drew criticism from leaders in the Jewish community.   ☐ Martin E. Marty

See also **Judaism; Religion.** In *World Book,* see **Protestantism.**

Psychology. Australian researchers implemented an extensive program in 1996 for early intervention and treatment of schizophrenia. Researchers found that early treatment and relapse detection might improve the outcome of this illness. Scientists also revealed in 1996 that women who were treated with estrogen during and after menopause reduced their risk of Alzheimer's disease.

Schizophrenia is a debilitating mental illness characterized by hallucinations and delusions, disorganization of thought and behavior, and deterioration in social and vocational functioning. The disease most commonly strikes people in late adolescence or early adulthood. Researchers have found that delaying treatment can worsen the condition and decrease chances for recovery. Unfortunately, many people fail to recognize their own disease or seek treatment in its early stages.

Researchers from the Early Psychosis Prevention and Intervention Centre (EPPIC) targeted a community in Melbourne, Australia. Through community education, the EPPIC team promoted early recognition of schizophrenia and its treatment in health-care facilities. Community outreach efforts were extensive. In later stages of the program, more than 60 percent of the patients were first evaluated by the EPPIC team in a nonpsychiatric setting, such as a patient's home, school, or in a general practitioner's office.

Most patients received outpatient treatment, although some required hospital care. Some patients received low dosages of neuroleptics, drugs commonly used to treat schizophrenia or severe mental disturbance. EPPIC researchers recommended a combination of medication and individual and family therapy to treat patients. Since schizophrenia most often begins in early adulthood, when issues of identity and role formation are underway, therapists placed great importance on treating a patient's social and vocational problems resulting from schizophrenia.

Preliminary evaluation suggested that the program was a success. Patients appeared to have fewer symptoms and to function better than before treatment. One goal of the program was to encourage secondary prevention—early detection and effective treatment—in mental health care.

Estrogen may decrease risk of Alzheimer's. A study by Columbia University researchers in New York City in 1996 provided the strongest evidence to date that replacement estrogen may decrease the risk of developing Alzheimer's disease (AD).

AD leads to progressive deterioration of memory, language, and judgment, typically in older people. AD is caused by a gradual destruction of neural cells in the brain, and affects more than 4 million people in the United States. About 100,000 people die from the disease every year. The personal, societal, and financial costs are immense, and available treatments have had little impact on the overall course of the illness.

Until recently, doctors knew of no causes for Alzheimer's disease, other than a possible *hereditary link* (the passing of physical or mental characteristics from one generation to the next). They knew of no way to prevent the disease. Since the late 1980's, researchers found that specific genes can either protect people from or make them more susceptible to the disease. Scientists had tested dozens of drugs to prevent or delay progression of Alzheimer's.

Previous studies suggested that women who receive estrogen replacement therapy may be less likely to develop AD. Women produce less and less of the hormone estrogen as they age. Estrogen replacement therapy is often prescribed for older women to prevent bone loss and other effects caused by decreased estrogen production. Scientists targeted estrogen in Alzheimer's research because the hormone appears to have a beneficial effect on brain cells.

The Columbia study followed 1,124 women for one to five years after the onset of menopause. The 156 women who received estrogen replacement therapy had a significantly lower risk of developing AD than the women who did not receive estrogen. Women taking estrogen for the longest periods had the lowest risk of developing the disease.

☐ Richard C. Hermann and Robert A. Lasser
In *World Book,* see **Psychology.**

Public health

Public health. Regulations to control the marketing of tobacco to teen-agers were issued in August 1996 by the United States Food and Drug Administration (FDA). The FDA predicted that the rules would reduce teens' use of cigarettes, smokeless tobacco, and other tobacco products by 50 percent.

The regulations outlawed slick tobacco advertisements in magazines read primarily by teen-agers; free cigarette samples; tobacco brand sponsorship of sporting, music, and cultural events; and cigarette vending machines except in adult facilities where children are not allowed. In addition, younger tobacco buyers were required to prove they are 18—the legal age for purchasing tobacco products in the United States—with a photo identification card.

The regulations were to be phased in over a two-year period beginning in early 1997. Advertising and tobacco companies were already moving in late 1996 to challenge the new rules in the courts.

World smoking surges. About 1.1 billion people around the world use tobacco regularly, according to a study reported in May by the World Health Organization (WHO), an agency of the United Nations. WHO found that while tobacco use in industrialized nations had decreased since the early 1980's, it was growing rapidly in less-developed countries. If the trend continues, WHO predicted, tobacco would cause about 10 million deaths a year worldwide by about the year 2020—7 million in developing countries. In the mid-1990's, an estimated 3 million people a year were dying of smoking-related illnesses.

Report urges exercise. The first U.S. surgeon general's report on exercise and health concluded in July 1996 that greater physical activity would improve the health of millions of Americans. The report stated that regular exercise can reduce the risk of heart disease, diabetes, high blood pressure, colon cancer, and other diseases. It emphasized that an average of 30 minutes daily of moderate exercise such as brisk walking and yard work is sufficient.

America's infant mortality rate declined to 8.4 deaths per 1,000 live births in 1993, the lowest rate ever recorded, the U.S. Centers for Disease Control and Prevention (CDC) in Atlanta, Georgia, reported in March 1996. The final 1993 rate represented a 1.8 percent decrease from the 8.5-per-1,000 rate in 1992. Preliminary CDC data indicated that the rate continued to decline in 1994 and may have dropped to 7.9 per 1,000, the CDC said.

Modern TB epidemic. About 3 million people around the world died from tuberculosis (TB) in 1995, more than in any other year in history, the WHO reported in March. At the peak of the TB epidemic that raged in the early 1900's, an estimated 2.1 million people died worldwide each year. The WHO warned that up to 500 million people around the globe could contract the disease by the year 2045 unless governments increase their funding of TB control programs.

Mad cow disease. British scientists in March reported a possible link between *bovine spongiform encephalopathy* (BSE), or "mad cow disease," and a rare but fatal human brain disorder called Creutzfeldt-Jakob disease (CJD). BSE is a fatal brain disease of cattle, first detected in British herds in the late 1980's. It was traced to feed supplements made from the remains of sheep afflicted with a related disease called scrapie. Researchers identified CJD cases that appeared to have been linked to bovine spongiform encephalopathy.

The CJD cases led many countries to ban imports of British beef. Representatives of the 15 countries in the European Union (EU) agreed in June 1996 to phase out the ban after the British government adopted a plan to control BSE in cattle.

Folic acid. The FDA in February ordered processed food manufacturers to begin fortifying grain products with folic acid by Jan. 1, 1998. Folic acid is a B-vitamin found in green, leafy vegetables and many fruits. The order, which was the first addition to the federally mandated list of nutrients used to enrich foods since 1943, came in response to evidence that babies born to women who have had an inadequate intake of folic acid are more prone to birth defects known as neural tube defects.   □ Michael Woods

See also **AIDS; Farm and farming** Special Report: **Mad Cow Disease; Medicine.** In *World Book,* see **Public health.**

Puerto Rico. On Sept. 10, 1996, Hurricane Hortense slammed into Puerto Rico with 80-mile- (130-kilometer-) per-hour winds and up to 20 inches (51 centimeters) of rain. In its wake, Hortense left 24 people dead and more than $200 million in damage. The United States government declared 26 cities and towns eligible for federal emergency aid.

In August, President Bill Clinton signed the Small Business Job Protection Act of 1996, which began phasing out tax breaks to U.S. companies in Puerto Rico. Anticipating a decline in U.S. investors, Puerto Rican authorities moved ahead with plans to create more jobs by increasing tourist revenues. Plans included improving the airport infrastructure, building new hotels, and restoring historic buildings.

On April 4, Orlando Castro Llanes, a Venezuelan fugitive, was indicted in New York City on charges of defrauding depositors in the Banco Progreso Internacional de Puerto Rico of more than $55 million.

On September 25, a judge of the Federal District Court of Puerto Rico levied a fine against three corporations owned by the Frank family of New York City: New England Marine Services, Bunker Group, and Bunker Group of Puerto Rico. In April, the corporations were found negligent in the 1994 oil spill that damaged tourist beaches in San Juan.

□ Nathan A. Haverstock

See also **Latin America** (Facts in brief table). In *World Book,* see **Puerto Rico.**

Pulitzer Prizes in journalism, letters, drama, and music were awarded on April 9, 1996, by Columbia University in New York City on the recommendation of the Pulitzer Prize Board.

Journalism. The public service award went to *The News & Observer* of Raleigh, North Carolina, for articles exposing major health and environmental problems caused by the largely unregulated waste disposal systems used by that state's corporate hog farms. *The Orange County* (California) *Register* won the investigative reporting prize for disclosing massive fraud at a southern California fertility clinic.

The New York Times took three prizes: spot news reporting, for Robert D. McFadden's articles written under deadline pressure; editorial writing, for Robert B. Semple, Jr.'s, commentaries on environmental issues; and feature writing, for Rick Bragg's articles on the Southern United States. *Newsday* on Long Island, New York, collected two prizes: explanatory journalism, for Laurie Garrett's coverage of a 1995 outbreak of Ebola hemorrhagic fever in Zaire; and beat reporting, for Bob Keeler's series on a progressive Roman Catholic parish on Long Island.

Alix M. Freedman of *The Wall Street Journal* won the national reporting prize for articles examining the tobacco industry. *The Christian Science Monitor* was awarded the international reporting prize for David Rohde's articles on atrocities in Bosnia-Herzegovina. The prize for commentary went to E. R. Shipp of the *New York Daily News* for columns on social issues. Robert Campbell, architecture critic of *The Boston Globe*, won the criticism award, and Herb Caen of the *San Francisco Chronicle* received a special award for columns on local affairs.

The spot news photography award went to freelance photographer Charles Porter IV for his picture of a fire fighter carrying a 1-year-old girl fatally injured in the 1995 bombing of a federal building in Oklahoma City, Oklahoma. The feature news photography award went to free-lance photographer Stephanie Welsh for images related to female genital mutilation in Kenya. Jim Morin of the *Miami* (Florida) *Herald* won the editorial cartooning prize.

Letters, drama, and music. The fiction award went to Richard Ford for his novel *Independence Day.* Jonathan Larson, who died on Jan. 25, 1996, posthumously won the drama prize for *Rent.* George Walker, honored for "Lilacs," became the first African American composer to win the music prize. Alan Taylor won the history prize for *William Cooper's Town: Power and Persuasion on the Frontier of the Early American Republic.* Jorie Graham took the poetry prize for *The Dream of the Unified Field.* The general nonfiction award went to Tina Rosenberg for *The Haunted Land: Facing Europe's Ghosts After Communism.* Jack Miles won the biography prize for *God: A Biography.* □ Barbara A. Mayes

In *World Book,* see **Pulitzer Prizes.**

Quebec. See **Canadian provinces.**

Reed, Ralph (1961–), executive director of the conservative Christian Coalition, continued to be an influential figure in American politics in 1996. He was also credited with playing a major role in the 1994 federal elections, in which the Republican Party gained a majority in Congress for the first time in 40 years.

Reed was born on June 24, 1961, in Portsmouth, Virginia. He became executive director of the National College Republicans during his senior year at the University of Georgia, in Athens, from which he graduated in 1983. The same year, he became a born-again Christian.

In 1984, Reed founded Students for America, a conservative, Christian-oriented group that participated in the reelection campaign of President Ronald Reagan. Later in 1984, he enrolled at Emory University, in Atlanta, where he earned a doctorate in American history.

Television evangelist Pat Robertson named Reed head of the newly formed Christian Coalition in 1989. The organization has actively supported candidates who have shared the social and political values supported by the Christian Coalition: cutting taxes, reducing the size of government, outlawing abortion, and restricting rights for gays and lesbians. Reed is the author of *Active Faith* (1996).

□ Lisa Klobuchar

See also **Religion; Republican Party.**

Reeve, Christopher (1952–), a motion-picture actor best known for his title roles in *Superman* films, became in 1996 a highly visible crusader for spinal cord research after he was paralyzed from the neck down as the result of a horseback riding accident. Reeve appealed for support for his cause at the Academy Awards ceremony in March and the Democratic National Convention in August.

Reeve was born Sept. 25, 1952, in New York City. He studied acting at the prestigious Juilliard School for Drama in New York City and earned a bachelor's degree from Cornell University in 1974. Reeve was in the cast of "Love of Life," a TV soap opera, from 1974 to 1976. In 1977, still an unknown, he landed the title role in *Superman* (1978). The film was a tremendous success and made Reeve an international star.

Reeve also has had extensive stage experience. In his first Broadway performance, in 1976, he played with Katharine Hepburn in *A Matter of Gravity.* In 1980, he portrayed a disabled Vietnam veteran in a Broadway production of *Fifth of July.*

Reeve's other movies include *Somewhere in Time* (1980), *Monsignor* (1982), *Deathtrap* (1982), and *Village of the Damned* (1995). He returned to acting for the first time following his accident in a made-for-television film that was screened in November.

□ Lisa Klobuchar

See also **Democratic Party.**

A British police officer, on June 21, turns away pagan worshipers wanting to celebrate the summer solstice at Stonehenge, a prehistoric stone monument.

Religion. In February 1996, the discovery of what was believed to be the birthplace of Buddha was announced by archaeologists from Nepal, India, Pakistan, Sri Lanka, and Japan. Prince Siddhartha Gautama, later known as Buddha, was born sometime before 500 B.C. According to Buddhist literature, Emperor Ashoka, who ruled over much of the Indian subcontinent, visited the birthplace in 249 B.C. and built a brick platform to hold a commemorative stone. In 1995, the archaeologists discovered the stone and platform in a chamber beneath an ancient temple in Lumbini, Nepal, about 200 miles (320 kilometers) southwest of the capital, Kathmandu.

The Church of Jesus Christ of Latter-day Saints, or the Mormon Church, celebrated in 1996 the 150th anniversary of the Mormons' trek from Nauvoo, Illinois, to the Salt Lake Valley in Utah. In 1846, anti-Mormon persecutions forced 11,000 Mormons to move. Although the anniversary commemorated early anti-Mormon sentiments, 1996 marked a significant milestone as well. The church announced that, for the first time, the majority of the 9 million members of this traditionally American religion lived outside of the United States.

The growth of the church paralleled efforts to change its image among mainstream Christian religions. Leaders emphasized the name *Church of Jesus Christ* rather than the *Mormon Church,* and the label *Latter-day Christians* rather than *Mormons.*

Church burnings. On July 3, President Bill Clinton signed into law the Church Arson Prevention Act of 1996, which made the destruction of religious property "on the basis of race, color, or ethnicity" a federal offense. The legislation, which appropriated money for federal investigations and provided compensations for victims, followed the burnings of 73 African American churches, mostly in the Southeast from Jan. 1, 1995, to June 30, 1996, according to figures tabulated by the Associated Press.

In May, the National Council of Churches brought together Protestant, Orthodox, Roman Catholic, Islamic, and Jewish organizations to establish the Burned Churches Fund to finance new church buildings. The religious coalition also placed newspaper advertisements condemning the racism believed to have motivated the attacks.

The national attention to the arsons led to charges that religious groups, politicians, and the media had exaggerated the role of racism. Although federal investigators found no evidence of a racist conspiracy, Deval Patrick, the U.S. assistant attorney general for civil rights, noted that many of the arsons were examples of a "climate of racial division."

The religious right. The Christian Coalition, an evangelical Christian organization, and conservative Roman Catholics dominated the writing of the party platform prior to the Republican National Convention in August. The platform included calls for a con-

Religious groups with 150,000 or more members in the United States*

African Methodist Episcopal Church	3,500,000
African Methodist Episcopal Zion Church	1,230,842
American Baptist Association	250,000
American Baptist Churches in the U.S.A.	1,507,934
Antiochian Orthodox Christian Archdiocese of North America	300,000
Armenian Apostolic Church of America	350,000
Armenian Church of America, Diocese of the	650,000
Assemblies of God	2,324,615
Bahá'í Faith	300,000
Baptist Bible Fellowship International	1,500,000
Baptist Missionary Association of America	230,171
Buddhists	780,000
Christian and Missionary Alliance	307,366
Christian Church (Disciples of Christ)	937,644
Christian Churches and Churches of Christ	1,104,931
Christian Methodist Episcopal Church	1,000,000
Christian Reformed Church in North America	211,154
Church of God (Anderson, Ind.)	209,945
Church of God (Cleveland, Tenn.)	722,541
Church of God in Christ	5,499,875
Church of God in Christ, International	250,000
Church of Jesus Christ of Latter-day Saints	4,613,000
Church of the Nazarene	597,841
Churches of Christ	1,651,103
Conservative Baptist Association of America	250,000
Coptic Orthodox Church	180,000
Episcopal Church	2,517,520
Evangelical Free Church of America	227,290
Evangelical Lutheran Church in America	5,199,048
Greek Orthodox Archdiocese of North and South America	1,500,000
Hindus	910,000
International Church of the Foursquare Gospel	222,658
International Council of Community Churches	500,000
International Pentecostal Holiness Church	150,133
Jehovah's Witnesses	945,990
Jews	5,900,000
Liberty Baptist Fellowship	150,000
Lutheran Church—Missouri Synod	2,596,927
Muslims	5,100,000
National Association of Free Will Baptists	210,305
National Baptist Convention of America, Inc.	3,500,000
National Baptist Convention, U.S.A., Inc.	8,500,000
National Missionary Baptist Convention of America	2,500,000
National Primitive Baptist Convention, Inc.	500,000
Orthodox Church in America	2,000,000
Pentecostal Assemblies of the World	1,000,000
Presbyterian Church in America	257,556
Presbyterian Church (U.S.A.)	3,698,136
Progressive National Baptist Convention, Inc.	2,500,000
Reformed Church in America	309,459
Roman Catholic Church	60,190,605
Salvation Army	443,246
Seventh-Day Adventist Church	775,349
Sikhs	190,000
Southern Baptist Convention	15,614,060
United Church of Christ	1,501,310
United Methodist Church	8,584,125
United Pentecostal Church International	550,000
Wisconsin Evangelical Lutheran Synod	414,874

*A majority of the figures are for the years 1994 and 1995. Includes only groups with at least 150,000 members within the United States.

Sources: Representatives of individual organizations; David B. Barrett, Editor, *The World Christian Encyclopedia; Yearbook of American and Canadian Churches 1996.*

stitutional amendment banning abortions, conservative immigration policies, and denial of civil rights protection for homosexuals. Although Republican presidential candidate Robert Dole lost the election, the Coalition helped elect a Republican majority to the U.S. Congress. However, at least nine House incumbents who had 100 percent voting records on the Coalition's agenda were defeated.

Supreme Court. Associate Justice Clarence Thomas announced in June that he had left the Episcopal Church and returned to the Roman Catholic Church into which he had been baptized. His decision marked the first time in the Supreme Court's history that the majority of the justices were not Protestants. While observers of the court have found little correlation between religious affiliation and court rulings, the event was a milestone marking the increased religious diversity of the United States.

U.S. seminarians. The number of students enrolled in programs at Protestant, Orthodox, and Roman Catholic theological seminaries accredited by the Association of Theological Schools reached 65,070 in the 1995-1996 academic year. One-third—21,736 —of the seminarians were women. The total number of students was almost double the 1972 figure of 32,922, with 3,358 women.　□ Leon Howell

See also **Civil Rights; Eastern Orthodox Churches; Islam; Judaism; Protestantism; Roman Catholic Church.** In *World Book,* see **Buddhism; Mormons; Religion.**

Republican Party.
The Republican Party in 1996 failed to win the presidency but retained control of both houses of the United States Congress. Republicans picked up two seats in the Senate to widen their majority but lost several seats in the House of Representatives, reducing their majority and increasing the influence of moderates in both parties.

The presidential race. After a series of divisive primary contests, the Republican Party (GOP for Grand Old Party) convened in August in San Diego for its national convention and united behind its presidential candidate, former Senate Republican majority leader Robert Dole of Kansas.

Dole got a slow start in his presidential quest, losing the New Hampshire Republican primary to conservative television commentator Patrick J. Buchanan. Another rival, multimillionaire Malcolm S. (Steve) Forbes, Jr., won primaries in Delaware and Arizona. When Dole began to win races in the more populous states, Forbes dropped out of contention on March 14, after financing his campaign with an estimated $23 million to $30 million of his own money. Buchanan halted his campaign on August 12, long after Dole clinched the GOP nomination.

In an unexpected move, Dole resigned his Senate seat on June 11 to devote himself to his campaign. The Senate GOP whip, Trent Lott of Mississippi, was elected to replace Dole as majority leader. Dole chose Jack Kemp, former professional football play-

Republican Party

er, New York congressman, and secretary of Housing and Urban Development, as his vice presidential running mate.

Dole put aside his long-term emphasis on balancing the federal budget and made a 15 percent federal income tax cut the main emphasis of his campaign. With President Bill Clinton claiming credit for a healthy economy and the American voters skeptical of Dole's ability to balance the budget and cut taxes, Dole was unable to defeat the president. Dole won 19 states, mainly in the South, the Great Plains, and the West, while Clinton took 31 states and the District of Columbia.

In Senate races, Republicans gained two seats, increasing their majority. With victories by GOP Senate candidates Tim Hutchinson in Arkansas, Jeff B. Sessions in Alabama, and Chuck Hagel in Nebraska, the GOP picked up three seats formerly held by Democrats. They lost only one of their own seats, when incumbent Republican senator Larry Pressler lost to Democrat Tim Johnson in South Dakota.

In other Senate races, conservative GOP candidates Patrick Roberts and Samuel Brownback in Kansas, Michael Enzi in Wyoming, Gordon Smith in Oregon, and Wayne Allard in Colorado replaced retiring Republicans. In Maine, Susan E. Collins, a moderate GOP candidate, took the seat vacated by Senator William S. Cohen.

In the House, Republicans lost some ground but retained a majority for the first time since 1928. Although Democrats gained at least nine seats, they still fell about 10 votes short of dethroning Speaker of the House Newt Gingrich in the 105th Congress. Twelve of the 70 GOP freshmen elected in 1994 who sought reelection were defeated, and nearly two dozen others struggled to win close contests against Democratic challengers. But a majority of the GOP representatives first elected in 1994 easily won second terms.

Barbour quits. After serving four years as chairman of the Republican National Committee, Haley Barbour announced that he would step down when his term ended in January 1997, to resume his career as a partner in a law and lobbying firm.

Party improprieties. In 1996, Simon C. Fireman, former vice chairman of Dole's campaign finance committee, pleaded guilty to making illegal contributions by funneling $69,000 to the GOP candidate through employees of his firm, Aqua-Leisure Industries. Fireman was sentenced to six months in prison and fined $1 million. Aqua-Leisure was fined $5 million. Democrats also charged that Jose Fanjul, a Cuban-born Spanish citizen who owned U.S.-based Flo-Sun Sugar Company, gave $234,000 of the firm's money to the Republican National Committee.

In July, the U.S. Department of Justice announced that it would not prosecute former Republican Senator Bob Packwood of Oregon on charges that he altered diaries that may have contained details of his misconduct. Packwood had resigned from the Sen-

Colin Powell, retired chairman of the Joint Chiefs of Staff, delivers an address in August at the Republican National Convention in San Diego.

ate in 1995 after the Senate ethics committee accused him of sexual harassment and influence peddling. Representative Ron Wyden, a Democrat, was elected to replace him.

Representative Enid Greene, a Republican from Utah, did not seek reelection in 1996 after her husband, Joseph Waldholtz, said he made illegal contributions to her 1994 campaign. Waldholtz pleaded guilty to felony charges, including bank fraud, and in November 1996 was sentenced to 37 months in prison. Greene was not charged with any crimes.

The bipartisan House ethics committee expanded its investigation into whether Speaker of the House Gingrich improperly used tax-exempt contributions for political purposes in a televised college course he

taught. In September, the committee and the nonpartisan outside counsel, James M. Cole, announced that the committee would investigate whether Gingrich lied to the committee or failed to provide it with complete information.

In December, the committee found that Gingrich had used tax-exempt money for political purposes. Gingrich admitted the truth of the charges and apologized to the committee.

◻ William J. Eaton

See also **Democratic Party; Elections** Special Report: **How Americans Elected Their President; Reed, Ralph; Robertson, Pat.**

In *World Book,* see Republican Party.

Rhode Island. See State government.

Elizabeth Dole, wife of the Republican presidential candidate, Robert Dole, greets delegates at the August convention in San Diego.

Robertson, Pat (1930–), a *televangelist* (television evangelist), continued in 1996 to be regarded as an influential figure in American politics, particularly the Republican Party, through the organizations he has founded—the Christian Broadcasting Network (CBN), the world's largest television ministry, and the Christian Coalition, a conservative organization.

Marion Gordon Robertson was born on March 22, 1930, in Lexington, Virginia. He graduated from Washington and Lee University in 1950 and earned a law degree from Yale in 1955. In 1956, he experienced a religious conversion and enrolled in New York Theological Seminary. He was ordained a Southern Baptist minister in 1961.

Robertson founded CBN in 1960, and his "700 Club," a Christian talk and call-in show, went on the air in 1967. In 1977, he founded CBN University (now Regent University), and CBN formed CBN Cable, a cable TV network, which aired religious and family-oriented programs. In 1980, CBN Cable was renamed the CBN Family Channel.

Robertson resigned his Baptist ordination in 1987 and launched an unsuccessful campaign for the 1988 Republican presidential nomination. Shortly after his defeat, he founded the Christian Coalition.

Robertson and his wife, Dede, have 4 children and 11 grandchildren. ☐ Lisa Klobuchar

Rodman, Dennis (1961–), a professional basketball player with the Chicago Bulls, won his fifth straight National Basketball Association (NBA) rebounding title in 1996. Rodman's rebounding skills helped carry the Bulls to a fourth NBA championship. His tireless, aggressive play and flamboyant style—including his tattoos, outlandishly dyed hair, and occasional cross-dressing—have made him a favorite among fans.

Dennis Keith Rodman, born May 13, 1961, in Trenton, New Jersey, grew up in Dallas, Texas. Under 6 feet (182 centimeters) tall as a teen-ager, he did not play high school ball. Rodman, after growing 8 inches (20 centimeters) after graduation, began his basketball career in 1982 at Cooke County Junior College in Gainesville, Texas. He transferred the following school year to Southeastern Oklahoma State University, in Durant, where he was recognized as a top college player, averaging 24 points and 18 rebounds per game.

Rodman was drafted by the Detroit Pistons in 1986 and contributed to the team's 1989 and 1990 NBA championships. In 1990 and 1991, he was named NBA defensive player of the year. In 1993, the Pistons traded him to the San Antonio Spurs, which traded him to the Bulls in 1995.

Rodman's autobiography, *Bad As I Wanna Be*, was a best seller in 1996. ☐ Lisa Klobuchar

See also **Basketball.**

Roman Catholic Church. On Nov. 14, 1996, Joseph Cardinal Bernardin, the archbishop of the Roman Catholic Archdiocese of Chicago, died of cancer at the age of 68. Since his ordination in 1966, Bernardin had played roles in major developments in Roman Catholicism in the United States.

On Aug. 12, 1996, Bernardin, known for his efforts to reconcile feuding church factions, announced the Catholic Common Ground Project, a series of meetings and papers through which Roman Catholics could discuss divisive issues. Bernardin drew both support and criticism from other bishops. James Cardinal Hickey, archbishop of Washington, D.C., protested that the true common ground for Catholics was the Bible and the teachings handed down from church leaders.

Pope John Paul II visited France in September 1996 to celebrate the 1,500th anniversary of the baptism of the Frankish King Clovis I. The visit renewed old debates about the role of the Roman Catholic Church in France. Emphasizing the separation of church and state, French President Jacques Chirac welcomed the pope in the name of the "republican and secular France." Instead of focusing on such issues as birth control and the role of women, which have drawn criticism in the past, the pope spoke about the obligation of wealthy countries to care for people "afflicted by life."

On November 19, Cuban President Fidel Castro and Pope John Paul II met for the first time in Rome. During the visit, the Pope confirmed his intention to visit Cuba in 1997 at Castro's invitation.

Criticism of the Vatican. Archbishop John R. Quinn, retired archbishop of San Francisco and leading figure in the U.S. hierarchy, called for broad reforms in the administrative authority of the church. In a June 29, 1996, address at Oxford University in Great Britain, Quinn charged that the Vatican bureaucracy had replaced the former "ecclesial model" of government that had allowed for more cooperation and open discussions about church matters. He noted that members of the Vatican staff and papal *nuncios* (ambassadors) had assumed authority traditionally conferred on local bishops and diocese.

Guatemala protest. On March 31, Sister Dianna Ortiz, an American nun, began a silent vigil near the White House to demand the release of U.S. government files about human rights abuses in Guatemala. In November 1989, Guatemalan military police kidnapped, tortured, and raped Ortiz. She claimed a U.S. Central Intelligence Agency (CIA) operative witnessed the event. On May 3, 1996, the U.S. State Department announced that there was no evidence that a CIA operative was involved in the case. On May 7, Ortiz ended her vigil when the Department released most of the files to the public and classified files to the U.S. Congress.

Call for excommunications. In March, Bishop Fabian Bruskewitz of Lincoln, Nebraska, called for the excommunication of Roman Catholics belonging to any of a dozen organizations that he declared "perilous to the Catholic faith." The list included five Masonic groups, two abortion-rights groups, a euthanasia organization, and four Roman Catholic church-reform organizations. One of the targeted groups, Call to Action—a 15,000-member national organization that promoted the ordination of women and marrriage for priests—claimed several U.S. bishops as members in 1996. Many Catholics in the diocese ignored the order, and many bishops criticized Bruskewitz for taking such a drastic measure without conferring with other church leaders.

Response to welfare reform. Many Roman Catholic leaders criticized the welfare-reform legislation passed by the U.S. Congress and signed into law by President Clinton on Aug. 22, 1996. The debate between Milwaukee Archbishop Rembert Weakland and Wisconsin Governor Tommy Thompson, a Roman Catholic, became the focus of the church's opposition. Criticizing Wisconsin Works (W-2), the state's proposal for ending welfare money to the poor and providing public funding for new jobs, Weakland declared that Catholic teaching holds that "the poor, especially children, have a moral claim on the resources of the community." Parts of the W-2 policy went into effect in October 1996. □ Thomas C. Fox

See also **Religion.** In *World Book,* see **Roman Catholic Church.**

Romania. In November 1996, Romania elected its first non-Communist government since the fall of dictator Nicolae Ceausescu in 1989. Emil Constantinescu became the country's new president, and his reformist coalition won a majority in the legislature.

In March 1996, the government had ousted the ultranationalist Party of Romanian National Unity from the coalition after its leader repeatedly criticized Romania's basic treaty with Hungary. The treaty was a precondition for membership in the European Union. A statement in support of autonomy for Hungarian minorities abroad released by delegates at a conference of ethnic Hungarians had caused concern in Romania, but the treaty was signed in September.

Romania reaffirmed its interest in joining the North Atlantic Treaty Organization (NATO) and adopted military reforms to move to a professional army. Romanian forces participated in NATO-sponsored military exercises in the Black Sea in August.

The economy continued to improve in 1996, as both industrial and agricultural output grew. Under pressure from the World Bank and the International Monetary Fund, Romania stepped up its privatization efforts. Energy shortages caused shutdowns and labor unrest early in the year. □ Sharon L. Wolchik

See also **Europe** (Facts in brief table). In *World Book,* see **Romania.**

Rowing. See **Sports.**

Russia. Uncertainty over the political and physical health of Russian President Boris Yeltsin dominated Russian affairs throughout 1996. After staging a stunning political comeback to win reelection as president in July, Yeltsin immediately entered a sanitarium, incapacitated by heart disease. Political turmoil surrounding Yeltsin overshadowed all other developments on the political landscape, including a stable but precarious economy, an uncertain cease-fire in the rebellion in Chechnya, and moves toward reintegration with several former Soviet republics.

Presidential campaign. As 1996 began, many Russian politicians and analysts were speculating that Boris Yeltsin would retire from politics and not seek reelection to a second term as president. Polls in January showed that Yeltsin had as little as 8 percent support among the Russian electorate. Yeltsin's persistent heart problems during 1995 had raised doubts about his health.

Russia's Communist Party had dominated the December 1995 parliamentary elections, winning 35 percent of the seats in the *Duma* (lower house of parliament). By contrast, the party of Prime Minister Viktor Chernomyrdin garnered just 12 percent of the seats. Although Yeltsin had not affiliated himself with any particular party, the outcome of the parliamentary vote revealed an unhappy public that seemed unlikely to grant Yeltsin another term.

Yeltsin's chief opponent, Communist Party leader Gennadiy Zyuganov, attacked Yeltsin for championing economic reforms that impoverished many Russians and weakened Russia as a world power. The Communists were split, however, between moderate socialists, who sought to erect a European-style welfare state, and hard-line Communists, who hoped to resurrect the institutions of Communist rule under the former Soviet Union.

On March 15, 1996, hard-line Communists in the Duma condemned the 1991 dissolution of the Soviet Union as "illegal." The move alarmed Russia's neighboring republics, who feared the Communists would attempt to restore the Soviet Union if they came to power. It also handed President Yeltsin an important weapon to convince voters that Zyuganov's Communist Party was the same authoritarian party that had run the former Soviet Union until 1991. This impression was deepened when the Communists released their economic program just a few weeks before the first round of voting. That document called for a wholesale reversal of privatization and a return to state control over the economy.

As the June 16 vote approached, Yeltsin appeared rejuvenated. He energetically portrayed the presidential contest as a choice between failed Communist programs of the past and his own commitment to democratic and market reforms. He secured a cease-fire in Russia's brutal war in Chechnya and vowed to abolish the unpopular military draft by the year 2000. Yeltsin received universally flattering cov-

Boris Yeltsin (center) takes the oath of office for his second term as president on August 9. Yeltsin appeared ill, and the ceremony lasted only 16 minutes.

erage from almost all national media outlets, which also ignored or criticized Yeltsin's chief opponents. Although media coverage of the election was biased, many journalists justified their actions by arguing that a victory by the Communists would mean a permanent end to freedom of the press.

The election. In the first round of voting on June 16, Yeltsin won 35 percent of the vote to Zyuganov's 32 percent. Retired army general Alexander Lebed, a fierce critic of corruption and the war in Chechnya, held third place. Lebed's surprisingly strong showing of 14 percent made his support critical in the subsequent runoff between Yeltsin and Zyuganov. To secure his support, Yeltsin promptly invited Lebed to join the government as national security advisor. Yeltsin also placed Lebed in charge of peace negotiations in Chechnya and fired Lebed's long-time enemy, Defense Minister Pavel Grachev. Yeltsin even hinted that he viewed the gruff, plainspoken Lebed as a likely successor.

On July 3, Yeltsin swept to victory with 54 percent of the popular vote. His margin of victory over Zyuganov was a remarkable 14 percentage points, amounting to 10 million votes. Yeltsin's triumph appeared to banish the threat of a Soviet Communist revival once and for all and promised to usher in a new era of political and economic consolidation.

Euphoria within the Russian political and economic elite over Yeltsin's victory, however, was short-lived. Even before the July 3 vote, Yeltsin dropped out of sight. In September, he acknowledged that he would require heart bypass surgery. Throughout the fall, he remained incapacitated, barely in control of events in the Kremlin. The situation triggered a new political crisis in Moscow, as potential successors jockeyed for power.

Contenders for power. In the immediate aftermath of the July voting, Alexander Lebed emerged as the clear favorite to succeed Boris Yeltsin. Lebed's populist image was increasingly attractive to Russian voters, especially as he vowed to use his new powers as national security advisor to root out corruption in the government and economy. Lebed also traveled to Chechnya and on August 31 secured a preliminary agreement on a peace treaty that would defer the question of Chechen independence for five years.

Lebed's growing popularity posed a threat to several powerful interests. Prime Minister Viktor Chernomyrdin, who had close ties to Russia's powerful oil and natural gas industry, feared that Lebed would threaten the connections between business and government that had emerged in post-Soviet Russia. Chernomyrdin's industrial allies had succeeded in maintaining tight control over Russia's valuable oil and gas reserves, and they viewed Lebed's attack on entrenched interests with alarm.

Lebed also ran afoul of Anatoliy Chubais, who had masterminded Yeltsin's reelection strategy.

Chubais had been rewarded after the election with an appointment as Yeltsin's chief of staff. Chubais was committed to consolidating the market and legal reforms begun in 1992, and Lebed's brand of populism threatened to undermine these achievements. Critics hinted that Chubais was also protecting his allies in key economic sectors and feared that Lebed's status as a political outsider could bring him to power with few ties to the status quo.

Finally, Lebed alienated much of the Russian military elite, even while championing the cause of military reform. His appointment as national security advisor was accompanied by the dismissal of several top generals in addition to Defense Minister Grachev, and Lebed's criticism of the conduct of the Chechen war was scathing. While Lebed's actions were popular among common soldiers, they were seen as directly threatening to Russia's senior military establishment.

In October 1996, these forces of opposition coalesced to force Lebed out. Interior Minister Anatoliy Kulikov, himself a target of criticism by Lebed, accused Lebed of plotting to overthrow the government. Yeltsin promptly fired Lebed, even though Kulikov offered no evidence to support his charge. Lebed did not challenge his dismissal. Instead, he called Yeltsin a "sick old man" and said that he would work to build an organization that could win the next presidential election, whenever it was held.

Yeltsin has surgery. On November 5, Yeltsin underwent heart surgery to bypass five blocked coronary arteries. Doctors called the seven-hour operation a success and said they expected Yeltsin to eventually resume a full workload. Days later, Yeltsin returned to the sanitarium but officially resumed presidential powers, which had been turned over to Prime Minister Chernomyrdin. In late December, Yeltsin resumed his day-to-day duties as president.

Economy. The Russian economy continued to contract in 1996, but at a slower rate than in previous years. Natural resource sectors showed some signs of recovery, while industrial output continued to stagnate. Inflation slowed to under 3 percent per month, and the ruble remained mostly stable. In February, the International Monetary Fund (IMF) signaled its approval of Russia's economic progress by granting a three-year, $10-billion loan.

In the second half of 1996, however, it became clear that the economy was closer to crisis than was apparent during the presidential campaign. Russia's budget deficit continued to grow, and the State Bank kept the government running by refinancing government bonds at high rates of interest. Alarmed by the bleak fiscal outlook, the IMF in October suspended loan payments until Russia could show signs of meeting revenue targets.

The weakness of the economy also prompted waves of strikes by workers protesting nonpayment of wages. Miners, teachers, and workers in transport and industry all engaged in strikes during 1996. Soldiers and scientists also protested poor economic conditions. In November, the director of Russia's top nuclear research laboratory committed suicide, calling attention to the critical lack of funding and resources affecting Russia's scientific community.

The "near abroad." On April 2, Boris Yeltsin signed a treaty with Belarus's President Alexander Lukashenko creating a new "community" with a common currency and shared political institutions. Five days earlier, Yeltsin had created a new customs union linking Russia, Belarus, Kazakstan, and Kyrgyzstan. Russian troops continued to police borders in Tadzhikistan and Georgia. The developments revealed the success of Moscow's policy of reestablishing its influence throughout the so-called "near abroad" of former Soviet republics. Only the three Baltic republics continued to resist expansion of Russia's sphere of influence.

Chechnya. On April 22, a Russian missile killed Dzhokhar Dudayev, leader of rebel forces in the breakaway republic of Chechnya. Dudayev had led Chechnya's independence drive since 1991, leading to Russia's invasion in December 1994. But Russia's hopes that Dudayev's death would weaken the spirit of the Chechen forces were dashed. In August 1996, Chechen fighters launched a surprise offensive against Russian troops in Grozny, the Chechen capital, and regained control of the nearly ruined city.

After intense bombardment failed to dislodge Chechen forces, newly appointed Russian security chief Alexander Lebed convinced Russian military leaders to stop the attack. Lebed then negotiated a draft peace accord with the Chechen leadership. The agreement was criticized by Russian nationalists for giving too much autonomy to Chechnya. Its fate was uncertain in the wake of Lebed's dismissal.

Bomb blast. At least 13 people were killed and dozens injured on November 10, when a powerful bomb exploded during a memorial service at a Moscow cemetery. A crowd of 150 people had gathered there to pay tribute to Mikhail Likhodei, the leader of a group of Russian veterans of the war in Afghanistan (1979-1989), who had been assassinated in November 1994.

The blast left a crater nearly five feet (1.5 meters) deep. Among the dead were Likhodei's widow, his mother, and Sergei Trakhirov, his successor as the head of the Afghan Veterans Invalids Fund. In 1993, the group had split into factions, which led to gang warfare. Investigators believed that the rival group, aiming to kill Trakhirov, was behind the bombing. Russian veterans of the Afghan war have frequently been associated with organized crime in Russia.

☐ Steven L. Solnick

See also **Belarus; Europe** (Facts in brief table); **Russia** Special Report: **Life in the New Russia.** In *World Book*, see **Russia.**

Life in the New Russia

Russians have gained new freedoms since the 1991 fall of Communism, but at what price?

By Peter Galuszka

Russians made a major commitment to political and economic reform in mid-1996. In the nation's first multichoice presidential election, the people chose Boris N. Yeltsin, thus voting to continue on the road to democracy and a free-market economy.

The critical turn came on July 3, the day of the second round of voting in the presidential elections. With 54 percent of the vote, Yeltsin, a Soviet-era-official-turned-democrat, was reelected president of Russia. Communist Party leader Gennadiy Zyuganov, who wanted to turn back the clock and bring back the "good life" of the bygone days of Communism, received only 40 percent of the vote.

The election outcome surprised many Western observers who had assumed that Zyuganov would be chosen in a backlash over the pain that Yeltsin's reforms had caused. While many Russians were glad to see the Soviet system collapse, they suffered greatly in the aftermath.

Most of the suffering was brought about by the sudden change from a centrally controlled economy to a free market. Yeltsin's economists freed prices in January 1992 and put an end to state financial support for many factories and services. Under Communism, subsidized housing, education, medical care, and vacations had been free or extremely inexpensive. By the mid-1990's, they were very costly. High-quality foreign goods, previously sold only in stores inaccessible to the average Russian, flooded the shelves. Few Russians, however, could afford them. Hyperinflation ate up the life savings of many Russians, living standards dropped sharply, and resentment grew. While the mass of citizens suffered, a small minority—mostly young businessmen or well-connected former Communists—raked in millions of dollars in sometimes illegal schemes. With old controls gone, crime became rampant.

Young entrepreneurs hawk their wares in Moscow's Red Square. Many Russians are able to earn more selling merchandise in the streets than professionals can earn practicing law or medicine.

New freedoms

Why, then, did Russians vote to continue economic reform? Many observers believe that it was because the Russian people came to enjoy the freedoms they experienced in the early post-Soviet years and feared losing them if the Communist Party returned to power. For the first time in decades, the media were no longer monitored by government censors. Newspapers, magazines, and radio and television programs were filled with information on subjects that had long been forbidden. The media began to criticize government policies, expose sources of environmental pollution, and discuss social problems such as poverty or drug and alcohol abuse. Under the Communist regime, few negative references to the government had been allowed; the health consequences of pollution had been hidden; and the existence of social problems had been vigorously denied. Western rock music, which the Soviet government once denounced as a corrupting influence on youth, was now aired on radio and television. By the early 1990's, most large Russian cities had FM rock music stations very much like those in the United States. The people could listen to foreign radio broadcasts—once electronically jammed by Communist censors.

Russians also came to treasure their new freedom to travel. Under Communist rule, travel was tightly controlled because the government suspected that many Russians would *defect* (leave their own country for another) if allowed beyond Russian borders. Most citizens were not allowed to travel out of Russia at all, and those who were, such as ballet stars or Olympic athletes, were followed and closely watched. By the 1990's, anyone could travel, as long as he or she had enough money and applied for the proper visas.

Russians after the fall of Communism also came to value the freedom to buy high-quality consumer goods. Under Communism, products that were commonplace in the West—foreign-made stereos, videocassette players, televisions, not to mention fashionable clothing, such as jeans—were only available to the privileged. Communist Party bureaucrats and foreign visitors bought such goods at special stores that the general public was not allowed to use. State stores, in which most people shopped, sold only poor-quality, Soviet-made goods, which were usually in short supply. People, usually women, stood in long lines to purchase whatever was available, a chore that, according to some estimates, took up as many as 15 hours per week.

Those who wanted decent goods often turned to the thriving black market. But if caught by the police, black-market shoppers could be imprisoned. Students who were caught dealing in the black market could expect that their chances to attend universities and pursue careers would be ruined. By the mid-1990's, most stores were fully stocked with expensive foreign goods. Voters in the 1996 elections did not want to take the chance that the Communists would tax foreign goods so heavily that store shelves would become empty again.

Finally, Russians, especially young people in their 20's and 30's, did not want to give up the freedom of finding good jobs and starting

The author

Peter Galuszka, Cleveland Bureau Chief for *Business Week,* served as the magazine's bureau chief in Moscow for six years.

Housing in Russia

A young mother and her child explore a new housing development in the Moscow suburb of Krasnogorsk. Many of Russia's new elite now live in such spacious, sub-urban-style housing, built on speculation by emerging entrepreneurs.

A young couple and their child squeeze their belongings into the limited space available to them in a typical, Soviet-era communal apartment in Moscow. Many young couples cannot afford to buy an apartment. In addition, a shortage of available apartments for all who can afford to buy them has pushed real estate prices to extremely high levels.

An elderly woman sleeps with her dog in a homeless camp near Red Square. Many older people are unable to make ends meet on limited pensions and have lost their apartments in Moscow's booming real estate market.

their own businesses. Under Communist rule, private businesses were illegal. Many people did offer small-scale services, such as tailoring or repairwork, but had to hide their activities for fear of arrest and imprisonment. After 1992, the government gradually transferred most state-run businesses to private control. By 1996, after one of the largest sell-offs of government property in history, almost 80 percent of the formerly state-run economy was in private hands.

It became possible to start new businesses and to seek out customers. Ambitious entrepreneurs formed banks, construction companies, advertising agencies, and insurance firms. Many enterprises that were started from scratch proved to be so successful that, according to estimates by the Russian State Committee of Statistics, more than 10,000 Russians earned 1 billion rubles ($200,000) per month in early 1996.

New challenges

Younger people proved more successful at forming businesses than older people. Graduates of the Moscow Aviation Institute—most of whom were under 30 years of age—were so ashamed of the poor reputation of Aeroflot, the Russian national airline, that they formed Transaero in the early 1990's. The new private airline flew late-model jetliners domestically and to such places as the Middle East and Europe. By 1994, Transaero was operating 75 flights per week.

Many older people, according to private business owners, were not willing to learn new business methods. They were less likely to experiment with innovative ideas. And they were less accommodating than younger people to retail and service customers—a trait that tourists and foreign companies establishing businesses in Russia were not willing to tolerate. Most older Russians neither started businesses nor were hired to work in businesses begun by others and were thus left out of the best opportunities in the new economy.

This difference in attitude between young and old was one of the greatest conflicts in Russia in the mid-1990's. Many older Russians did not believe that the new freedoms were worth the price they had to pay. Older people longed for the "good old days" of Communism, when most people lived in the small apartments assigned to them in badly constructed high-rise buildings or in old, converted single-family houses. While they may have had to share the bathroom and kitchen with other families, rent was inexpensive—usually the equivalent of $20 a month or less.

By the mid-1990's, many Russians had bought apartments of their own. But they had to deplete their savings to do so and were still required to pay maintenance fees that usually cost much more than $20 a month. Such living accommodations were hard for older Russians to achieve and maintain. In addition, the cost of Russian real estate began to soar in the early 1990's, especially in the beautiful, old buildings of the "hot" sections of Moscow and St. Petersburg. Many older people were forced or tricked out of their apartments in these areas so that the apartments could be turned into luxury units. By the

Working conditions

Elite young Russians, for whom cellular phones have become a status symbol, conduct business in a Moscow nightclub. By the mid-1990's, some of the new, young entrepreneurs were earning as much as 1 billion rubles ($200,000) per month from businesses they themselves had started.

mid-1990's, Moscow and St. Petersburg had some of the highest real estate prices in the world. Rent for plush apartments could cost more than $5,000 a month. Older people—living on pensions that were still only about $50 a month in early 1996—resented losing apartments they had lived in for decades, even if they could purchase another apartment that would truly be their own.

Another negative consequence of the new freedom in Russia was the fact that services upon which older Russians had long depended rose steeply in price. In the Soviet era, medical and dental care were either free or very inexpensive. The quality of care was not always good, and there was often a shortage of medications and supplies. Sometimes patients had to pay bribes even for minimal service. But medical care was accessible to all. By late 1992, medical care had become so expensive that even Russian families who pooled their savings could barely afford surgery for one of their members. This decline in the availability of health care, along with high rates of smoking and alcoholism and the prevalence of polluted air and water, led to a drop in the estimated life expectancy, especially for Russian men. According to the *Russian Statistical Yearbook*, life expectancy in 1991 was about 63 years for men and 74 years for women. By 1996, some sources estimated that men's life expectancy had fallen to 57 years. Women's had fallen to

Miners protest outside the Russian White House in Moscow, demanding payment of salaries owed to them by the state. By the time miners went on strike in February 1996, some had not been paid for six months.

71 years in the mid-1990's. In the United States, the average life expectancy for men in the mid-1990's was 76 years, and for women, 79 years.

Changing needs in education

The Russian education system, another source of pride for older Russians, suffered tremendous upheavals in the mid-1990's. Before the Bolshevik Revolution of 1917, only 40 percent of Russians could read and write. In 1990, the rate was 98 percent, making Russia one of the most literate nations on earth. Higher education may not have been on the level of the best colleges in the West, but Russia's universities turned out thousands of engineers, scientists, and doctors.

In the changing economy of the mid-1990's, education became more costly than many families could afford. A five-year law school program, which would have been free or inexpensive in Soviet days, cost about $2,000 per year by the mid-1990's. In addition, a law degree no longer carried with it the assurance of a substantial salary. Many older Russians with professional degrees found that their salaries barely allowed them to make ends meet in the new economy. They could no longer enjoy the trips and other luxuries that they and their children had long taken for granted.

Students, who saw the great amounts of money entrepreneurs were making, were tempted to abandon professional training for the business world. In 1996, in one of Moscow's top cardiological centers, the average physician earned about $75 a month, and senior physicians earned $150 a month. By comparison, a woman selling cosmetics part-time in Moscow's suburbs, for such firms as Avon and Mary Kay, earned an average of $300 to $400 a month. Many respected teachers, schooled in Marxism and Leninism, no longer knew how to prepare students for an economy they no longer understood.

Loss of services

For older Russians, the freedom to listen to Western rock music was far outweighed by the fact that they could no longer afford to attend classical cultural events. In the Soviet era, the state funded such insti-

tutions as orchestras and ballet and opera companies. When funding became unavailable in the mid-1990's, tickets to such institutions as the world-renowned Bolshoi Theatre were still relatively inexpensive by world standards, but became out of the reach of ordinary Russians. The Bolshoi and other troupes began to tap the new Russian banks for funding. They turned to touring and performing in other countries not out of national pride, but to earn income. For the average Russian, the less-expensive children's theater became the only affordable cultural program left.

Perhaps the most difficult concept for older Russians to grasp—and a major reason for the dramatic reduction in social services—was the change in status of the Russian workplace. Under the Soviet system, factories and other businesses served as far more than just centers of production. They were critically important providers of virtu-

The body of a prominent Russian banker, Ivan Kivelidi, is borne in a funeral procession by business and political associates. At the time of his death in 1995, many Russians believed that his murder by poisoning was ordered by the Russian *mafija* (organized criminal gangs).

347

ally all social services. Employees could leave their children at the company day-care center, shop at the company's special food stores, and vacation inexpensively in company-subsidized resorts and hotels in such attractive spots as the woods of the far north or the warm beaches of the Black Sea. The businesses were able to offer these services so cheaply because the state poured billions of rubles into subsidizing them.

After 1992, much of the state money was cut off, and businesses could not afford to pay for services for their workers. When factories and businesses were privatized, shareholders cut the services to scale down expenses and compete more effectively in the free market.

Workers suffer

Not only did workers at many factories and other businesses have to start paying for services that were once free, they also had to work at times for months without pay. Many companies became unable to meet payrolls. Industrial production in Russia dropped 40 percent from 1989 to 1996. In the new, free-market economy, many factories could find no market for the shoddy and outdated wares they once sold to other republics in the Soviet Union. Some factories were unable to get the raw materials they needed for their manufacturing processes. The coal-mining industry suffered from severe cash shortages because its government subsidies had been cut; mining had done little to implement free-market reforms, and the industries to which it supplied coal were unable to pay for it. More than 500,000 Russian coal miners went on strike on February 1, 1996, to protest their lack of wages—some of them had been unpaid for as long as six

An elderly man gazes into a Mercedes-Benz showroom in Moscow. Although more consumer goods have become available, fewer Russians—especially the elderly—can afford them.

months. The miners went back to work on February 3, after the Russian government promised to increase its funding for the coal industry and to pay part of the back wages immediately. More than 400,000 miners struck again in November, when the government fell behind in wage payments once more.

Workers in other areas suffered as well. Teachers, soldiers, doctors, and others who were employed by state-run industries were all affected by the government's monetary shortfall. President Yeltsin, in his reelection campaign, promised back payments of more than $1-billion for state workers. He fulfilled his promise on June 6, when he used government funds to pay civil servants' salaries. Although the International Monetary Fund, which agreed to lend Russia $10 billion for its economic transition, was not pleased by this move, some analysts suggest that it helped Yeltsin to win reelection.

Besides industrywide problems, workers also had to contend with reasons closer to home for not being paid. Corrupt company managers scrambled to steal as much money as possible as quickly as possible—often at the expense of their workers—because, unlike in Communist days, the managers could not be sure how long they would hold their positions. Some managers siphoned goods from their factory's assembly lines, selling them privately for their own profit and decreasing the profit for the factory. Others secretly sold off incoming raw materials, forcing their factory's assembly lines to stand idle until new materials arrived. Still other managers invested workers' salaries in high-interest government bonds and pocketed the interest instead of paying workers on time. A lack of foreign investment also handicapped Russian business. Chaotic conditions,

Young people in Moscow enjoy a heavy-metal rock concert. Banned under the Communists, such music can now be listened to freely.

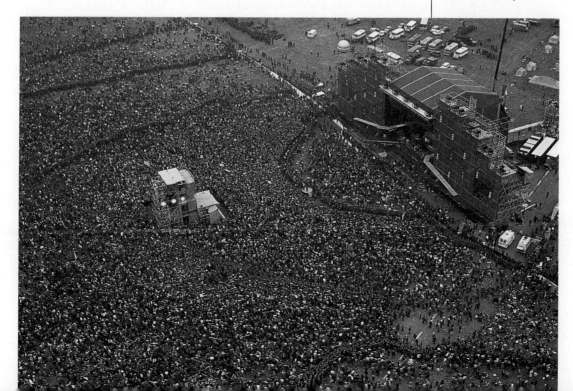

especially the lack of property laws and a workable tax system, kept out much potential investment.

Farmworkers suffered as much—if not more—than city workers after economic reforms were instituted. Agricultural production in the Soviet Union began to decline in 1929, when dictator Joseph Stalin forced independent farmers to work together on collective or state farms that were to be operated on socialist principles. A central governing body decided which crops should be grown and how the farmers should grow them, regardless of local conditions. The system discouraged new farming methods and employed more workers than necessary, so that all people would have jobs. Productivity fell, and a country that had been a grain exporter in prerevolutionary days was forced to import as much as 40 million short tons (36 million metric tons) of grain per year under the Soviets.

After the Soviet Union broke up, problems in agriculture remained. As with factory workers, state and collective farmworkers were accustomed to having the state subsidize services that they and their families enjoyed. When the state could no longer afford the subsidies, workers were expected to pay for the services themselves.

In addition, efforts to replace the old state and collective farm systems with private farms met with resistance. As late as the mid-1990's, a powerful lobby of conservative farm managers continued to back Russia's Communist-Party-dominated parliament in preventing the passage of laws that would allow the free sale of private farmland. Young people, who might have become farmers if they could own land, continued to leave farms for cities, where they could earn more money. This left mostly older workers to deal with the production problems on deteriorating state and collective farms.

Past experience had proved that both the land and the people were capable of growing enough food to meet the country's needs. Even after private farms were collectivized by the Communists, ordinary Russians were allowed to tend small private plots on the farms, and city dwellers could have gardens at their *dachas* (private country houses). These plots were so productive that, in the 1980's, they supplied more than 25 percent of the Soviet Union's agricultural output. By 1993, the private plots were producing 83 percent of all the potatoes grown in Russia and 40 percent of the meat. Nevertheless, mass production of food remained low. By some estimates, Russia imported 72 percent of the food its people consumed in the mid-1990's.

Widespread corruption

While younger Russians found it much easier than the older generation to seize new economic opportunities in post-Soviet days, their lives were by no means easy. Young men still faced a draft for army service at the age of 18, even though as many as 84 percent of them managed to avoid it. By law, they were obligated to serve in the army reserve until the age of 50.

Many young people who tried to become entrepreneurs were victimized by the Russian *mafija* (organized criminal gangs), which either drove them out of business to prevent competition or demanded protection money. Some of the more successful new business owners hired private security forces to protect them from the mafiosi. Those who could not afford protection were often gunned down in the street, in plain view of passers-by. The police were of little help. In the early 1990's, when mafija crime grew most rapidly, the police budget was so small that departments could not afford to equip officers with the fast cars and sophisticated weaponry needed to match those owned by rich gangsters. In addition, police salaries, which sources estimated were only about 30,000 rubles a month (less than $30) in mid-1993, encouraged corruption. In 1994, the budget for law enforcement was increased. Policemen's wages doubled, spending on cars and equipment rose, and the growth in the crime rate slowed.

Besides the mafija, many corrupt state officials, including the tax authorities, added to the burdens of would-be entrepreneurs. Bureaucrats had to be paid off so that a business would be allowed to continue. Competitors with connections to former Soviet officials could unleash inspectors, tax collectors, and various license-issuing bodies to destroy a fledgling business. Russia's billionaires usually made their money by using their links to state officials to export state-owned resources for huge profits.

Despite all of the hardships, as Russian voters went to the polls in mid-1996, they believed that they could once again make their country a strong world power. Russia remained rich in great reserves of oil, natural gas, precious metals, and timber. Its people remained among the best-educated in the world, eager to create opportunities for themselves in the new economic order. The tough reforms instituted since 1991 caused much distress. But they also cut annual inflation from 2,300 percent in 1992 to 130 percent a year in 1995, instilling hope for the future. In 1996, Russian voters decided not to turn back the clock. Instead, they opted to continue to use democracy and the free-market economy to remake their country. ■ ■ ■

For further reading:

Layard, Richard, and Parker, John. *The Coming Russian Boom: A Guide to New Markets and Politics.* Free Press, 1996.

Randolph, Eleanor. *Waking the Tempests: Ordinary Life in the New Russia.* Simon & Schuster, 1996.

Remnick, David. *Lenin's Tomb: The Last Days of the Soviet Empire.* Random House, 1993.

Rwanda. The legacy of genocide continued to dominate life in Rwanda in 1996. In 1994, the Hutu-controlled government had undertaken the mass killing of the minority Tutsi people. At least 500,000 Rwandans—many Tutsis and some moderate Hutus—were killed. The terror lasted until a Tutsi rebel group seized power. Two million people, mainly Hutu, then fled to neighboring countries such as Zaire and Burundi. After taking power, the Tutsi-dominated government tried to maintain order and convince refugees to return home—largely without success. The legacy of the war included a massive refugee problem, a lifeless economy, packed jails, and thousands of unwanted babies.

The refugee problem. Bringing refugees home proved to be a difficult task. Allowing them to remain in neighboring countries created political and social problems for the host countries and left the mostly Hutu refugees free to train and prepare for another round of killing. In this, they were aided by international arms dealers as well as the government of Zaire, within whose borders most of the refugees resided. Zaire profited from the refugee presence through the humanitarian attentions of international aid organizations.

The president of Zaire, Mobutu Sese Seko, once despised by his former allies—the United States, France, and Belgium—won their grudging support by allowing them to funnel aid to the refugees in Zaire. Occasionally, Mobutu showed signs of pressuring the refugees to leave. In February 1996, for example, he threatened to expel the 190,000 Rwandans from Kibumba Camp, 1 of about 30 refugee camps in Zaire. At the end of the year, a revolt in Zaire led to the closing of the camps and tens of thousands of the refugees were forced to return to Rwanda.

Bringing killers to justice. The government of Rwanda proceeded with arrests of citizens implicated in the mass murders of 1994. By mid-1996, the ruling regime had arrested about 80,000 people at a rate of up to 4,000 per month. Prisons were badly overcrowded, and conditions were vile for prisoners. The government had delayed trials, it claimed, because many of the nation's lawyers, prosecutors, and judges had been killed in 1994. Meanwhile, the government set out to train new legal professionals.

In 1996, the United Nations established a tribunal to try Rwandans accused of war crimes in the slaughter. By late 1996, however, only 21 Rwandans had been indicted, almost half of whom were still at liberty.

An especially bitter legacy of 1994 was the children who were progeny of brutal Hutu rape. These children, numbering in the thousands, and their mothers became objects of scorn and hatred.

◻ Mark DeLancey

See also **Africa** (Facts in brief table); **Zaire.**
In *World Book,* see **Rwanda.**

Safety. In March 1996, the National Research Council (NRC) recommended that new motor vehicles should carry labels to help consumers compare safety features. The NRC, an agency of the National Academy of Sciences in Washington, D.C., advised the U.S. Department of Transportation (DOT) to request that auto manufacturers voluntarily display safety stickers by the year 2000.

The stickers would include a safety score of "crash worthiness" and a list of crash-avoidance features, such as antilock brakes. Although the DOT has published crash test results comparing vehicles of a similar size and weight, the stickers would standardize comparisons for all vehicles. The NRC also recommended safety-feature brochures for glove boxes, safety handbooks, and information about vehicle safety on the Internet, the global computer network.

Baseball equipment. The U.S. Consumer Product Safety Commission (CPSC), an independent agency that is charged with protecting consumers, concluded in a June report that new safety equipment could prevent or reduce the severity of more than 58,000 baseball-related injuries to children each year. Of the 6 million children participating in organized baseball leagues and the 13 million in nonleague play in 1995, about 162,100 were treated for baseball-related injuries in hospital emergency rooms.

The CPSC recommended three kinds of equipment already available commercially: softer-than-standard balls to prevent severe head and neck injuries; batting helmets with face guards; and safety-release bases that have no parts sticking up that could cause injuries when a player slides into a base.

Lead dust on vinyl window blinds. In June, the CPSC advised parents with children under age 7 to remove imported vinyl miniblinds that may cause lead poisoning. The blinds—imported from China, Taiwan, Mexico, and Indonesia—contained lead that was added to stabilize the plastic. In the CPSC study, the plastic in the blinds deteriorated from prolonged exposure to sunlight and heat, leaving lead dust on the surface. Children could ingest the lead dust by touching the blinds and then putting their hands in their mouths. The CPSC said that blinds made without lead are labeled as such on the packaging.

Shopping carts. In February, researchers at Ohio State University (OSU) in Columbus urged parents to stop putting children in conventional shopping carts, which were found to be unstable. The researchers also concluded that infant seats and safety belts do not prevent the often serious head injuries resulting from falls. According to CPSC estimates, each year some 21,000 children under age 4 have required hospital treatment for injuries from overturned carts. The OSU researchers recommended that shopping carts be redesigned with a wider wheel base and lower center of gravity to increase stability.

Workplace violence. The Occupational Safety and Health Administration (OSHA), a Labor Department agency that promotes safe working conditions, issued guidelines in March to protect health-care and social-service employees, who make up more than two-thirds of the victims of workplace violence. Assaults on these employees have included attacks from patients, street gangs in emergency rooms, and violence in neighborhoods where social-service workers visit clients.

In the first federal guidelines on prevention of workplace violence, OSHA recommended that employers take the following precautions: install metal detectors, monitoring cameras, and panic buttons; design rooms to protect employees against entrapment; and provide proper maintenance of automobiles used in the field.

Automobile recall. In April, the Ford Motor Company of Dearborn, Michigan, recalled 8.7 million cars and trucks—the largest single recall by an auto manufacturer—from the model years 1988 to 1993 to replace ignition switches that could cause fires.

Ford acted after reports that short circuits in the ignition switches of 13 different models caused at least 1,100 fires and resulted in 21 injuries in the United States and 9 in Canada. Because the switches could ignite after the vehicles were turned off, some fires occurred in parked vehicles, destroying garages and houses. ☐ Michael Woods

In *World Book*, see **Safety**.

Sailing. See Boating.

San Diego. The major event of 1996 in San Diego was the Republican National Convention, held at the bayside San Diego Convention Center from August 12 to 15. About 1,990 delegates, 1,990 alternates, and their families, as well as 15,000 media representatives, arrived in the city beginning August 10. The San Diego Convention and Visitor's Bureau reported that the convention generated a total of $162 million for the local economy.

Bob Dole and Jack Kemp, ushered into the city across the San Diego Bay by boat, were officially nominated as the Republican Party's presidential and vice presidential candidates. Parties were held throughout the city in honor of Republican celebrities and the delegates. One exception was the party held at the San Diego Zoo by Democratic scion John F. Kennedy, Jr., to publicize his magazine, *George*.

Symphony bankrupt. The San Diego Symphony disbanded on January 14, when it could no longer pay its creditors and musicians because of deficit spending and failed fund-raising efforts. The symphony's board of directors tried to raise the necessary funds over the next few months but finally filed for Chapter 7 liquidation bankruptcy on May 31.

Top Gun school leaves San Diego. The last jets of the Navy Fighter Weapons School left the San Diego area for a new home at Fallon Naval Air Station in Nevada on May 29. The Top Gun school, where U.S. Navy pilots—"the best of the best"—

train in advanced dogfighting and other combat skills, had been at San Diego's Miramar Naval Air Station for almost 30 years. The school's move was a result of the Navy's plan to turn Miramar over to the Marine Corps as part of the base closing and realignment process.

Hotel del Coronado. San Diego's internationally famous Hotel del Coronado was acquired in September by the Travellers Group, a New York financial services company that already held a major interest in the property on Coronado Island. M. Larry Lawrence, the long-time owner of the hotel that has been used many times as a movie set, died on January 9 in Bern, Switzerland, where he had served for nearly two years as U.S. Ambassador.

Research institute receives gift. In May, the Scripps Research Institute announced that it had received a $100-million gift from L. Samuel Scaggs, head of one of the nation's largest drug and grocery retailers. The gift established a chemical biology program to encourage research into new approaches to drug design. It was one of the largest medical research donations in the history of American philanthropy and the largest to a San Diego institution. The funds will be distributed over the next 10 years.

Teachers' strike. The San Diego Teachers Association led a strike against the San Diego Unified School District from February 1 through February 8. The two groups came to a $4-million financial agreement that settled the dispute on February 9. The teachers accepted a proposal that will raise salaries by an average of 14.7 percent over three years. The funds for the increase were to come from anticipated state tax revenue or direct state grants. The agreement raised the average teacher's salary from $40,400 for the 1995-1996 school year under the old contract to $42,759 for 1995-1996 under the new contract. The average teacher's salary was projected to be $46,339 for the 1997-1998 school year, the third year of the new contract.

Giant pandas arrive. On Sept. 10, 1996, after four years of negotiations, the San Diego Zoo received two giant pandas from China. Shi Shi, a 16-year-old male, and Bai Yun, a 5-year-old female, were to be housed by the zoo for the next 12 years. The zoo spent more than $1 million designing and building a habitat for the pandas. It was to pay China $1 million annually for the loan of the animals. China agreed to use the money to preserve the critically endangered species in its natural habitat in China.

The zoo's arrangement with China was to allow scientists at the zoo's Center for the Reproduction of Endangered Species the chance to study how pandas use scent markings to communicate with each other. The zoo also hoped that the pair would mate and produce a panda cub, which would, by contractual agreement, belong to China. ☐ Caron Golden

See also **City**. In *World Book*, see **San Diego**.

Sarandon, Susan (1946–   ), an American motion-picture actress and five-time Academy Award nominee, won the 1995 Academy Award for best actress for her portrayal of Sister Helen Prejean, a nun who counsels a death-row inmate, in the film *Dead Man Walking.* Sarandon was born Susan Abigail Tomalin on Oct. 4, 1946, in New York City. She married Chris Sarandon, a graduate student and actor, in 1967. The couple were divorced in 1979.

Susan Sarandon graduated from Catholic University, in Washington, D.C., in 1968 with a degree in drama. During the 1970's, she appeared in a number of movie, theater, and television roles. She first gained attention for her role in the horror-movie spoof *The Rocky Horror Picture Show* (1975). Sarandon was first nominated for an Academy Award for her performance as a waitress training for a casino job in *Atlantic City* (1980), in which she co-starred with veteran actor Burt Lancaster. She gained critical and popular acclaim for her work in *Bull Durham* (1988), in which she portrayed a literature professor who mentored young minor-league baseball players. Her roles in *Thelma and Louise* (1991), *Lorenzo's Oil* (1992), and *The Client* (1994) also earned her best-actress nominations. In 1996, she provided the voice for the character Miss Spider in the animated film *James and the Giant Peach.*   □ Lisa Klobuchar

See also **Motion pictures.**

Saskatchewan. See **Canadian provinces.**

Saudi Arabia. Questions about the health of King Fahd and growing signs of Islamic extremism created unease in Saudi Arabia in 1996. After suffering a stroke in November 1995, King Fahd appointed a half-brother, Crown Prince Abdullah, regent in January 1996. Abdullah, heir to the throne, headed the National Guard, which is responsible for the kingdom's internal security.

King Fahd resumed his duties as king on February 21. The reversal was an apparent attempt to end rivalries among other members of the ruling Al Saud family, who resented Abdullah's power. Even so, Fahd's frail health allowed Abdullah to continue wielding enormous authority.

Terrorism. A 3,000-pound (1,300-kilogram) truck bomb detonated outside a foreign military housing complex in Dhahran on June 25. The bomb killed 19 United States service members and injured about 400 Americans, Saudis, and Bangladeshis. The complex housed a U.S.-led coalition known as Operation Southern Watch, which enforced a no-fly zone in southern Iraq. Since the 1991 Persian Gulf War, the United States had stationed more than 5,000 troops in Saudi Arabia.

Experts denied that the kingdom's stability was immediately threatened, but many saw the attack—which came only seven months after the bombing of a U.S. training center in Riyadh—as a sign of growing unhappiness with the Saudi ruling family and its

alliance with the United States. Critics accused the ruling family of corruption and failure to widen political participation. Discontent was most evident among Saudis under 30, who comprised some 70 percent of the population but were finding employment opportunities increasingly scarce.

Executions. Four young Saudis were beheaded on May 31 for the Riyadh bombing, which killed five Americans and two Indians in November 1995. In April 1996 the men claimed during televised confessions that they had links with foreign Islamic extremists. Saudis, who had assumed the bombing was entirely the work of foreign groups, were stunned by the confessions of their fellow countrymen.

U.S.-Saudi relations became strained after the bombings. U.S. security officials claimed the Saudis refused to allow them to interview the four men convicted in the Riyadh bombing and later executed.

In August, the two countries agreed to pay roughly $100 million each to move some 4,000 U.S. troops to a remote air base at Al Kharj, 60 miles (96.5 kilometers) south of Riyadh. The United States hoped the base would be more secure. The Saudis hoped the move would reduce the visibility of U.S. troops and stem criticism of their presence by Islamic conservatives. In September, the Saudis refused to support the U.S. bombing of Iraq. The refusal was attributed to Saudi fears of growing extremism and anti-Americanism.

Dissidents. Great Britain reversed itself on April 18 and decreed that Saudi dissident Muhammad Masari could remain for another four years in England. The British government had sought Masari's deportation, but in March, an immigration judge ruled that Masari's safety might be at risk if he were expelled. Britain was concerned that Masari's presence could jeopardize its $3 billion in annual sales of weapons to the Saudi kingdom. Masari headed the Committee for the Defense of Legitimate Rights in London, which accused the Saudi ruling family of corruption and mismanagement.

Anglo-Saudi relations were further strained in April 1996 when the British Broadcasting Corporation and a Saudi satellite network ended joint television broadcasts because of Saudi censorship of news reports. In addition, the Saudi company accused the British Broadcasting Corporation of biased reporting in a television documentary on human rights abuses in Saudi Arabia.

Economy. An increase in world oil prices was good news for the Saudi treasury, which remained dependent on oil sales for 70 percent of revenues. The kingdom has suffered huge budget deficits since the early 1980's but expected to earn some $37 billion from oil sales in 1996.   □ Christine Helms

See also **Middle East** (Facts in brief table). In *World Book,* see **Saudi Arabia.**

School. See **Education.**

Senegal. See **Africa.**

Sierra Leone. Political events in Sierra Leone led to positive results in 1996. Previously ruled by the military and torn by civil war, this small West African nation conducted democratic elections, returned to civilian rule, and negotiated a cease-fire with rebels.

In 1995, the military government, led by Valentine Strasser, had announced elections for 1996, a promise that was regarded widely with cynicism. On Jan. 16, 1996, the ruling body, the National Provisional Ruling Council (NPRC), arrested Strasser, sent him into exile, and replaced him with Brigadier General Julius Maada Bio. Bio affirmed his commitment to elections and declared his intention to meet with Foday Sankoh, who was the leader of the rebel group, the Revolutionary United Front.

Although the NPRC, behind the scenes, attempted to stall the elections, the head of the electoral commission, James Jonah, kept the election schedule on track. Polling took place, as scheduled, February 26-27 and March 15. Ahmed Tejan Kabbah of the Sierra Leone People's Party won the presidency. Upon taking office, Kabbah followed Bio's initiatives and met with Sankoh, who had already pledged a ceasefire. As a result, the cease-fire was extended, and peace talks were opened. ☐ Mark DeLancey

See also **Africa** (Facts in brief table). In *World Book,* see **Sierra Leone**.

Singapore. See Asia.

Skating. See Hockey; Ice skating; Sports.

Skiing. In the 1995-1996 World Cup professional season, the major winners among the men included Lasse Kjus and Atle Skaardal of Norway and Alberto Tomba of Italy. Among the most successful women were Katja Seizinger of Germany, Picabo Street of the United States, and Pernilla Wiberg of Sweden.

The overall champions of the previous year's World Cup tour had been Tomba in the men's division and Vreni Schneider of Switzerland among the women. After that season ended, Schneider retired at age 30. Tomba had a spectacular season, with seven victories in slaloms and four in giant slaloms. He could not repeat such a performance in 1995-1996, but he did win both events at the world championships, in February 1996 in Sierra Nevada, Spain.

At the end of the 1995-1996 World Cup tour, Lasse Kjus of Norway placed first, with 1,216 points, and Guenther Mader of Austria was second, with 1,000 points. Among the women, Katja Seizinger of Germany finished first, with 1,472 points, and Martina Ertl of Germany was second, with 1,059 points. Picabo Street was sixth, with 837 points. The 23-year-old Seizinger won the World Cup in the women's super giant slalom. Ertl took the giant slalom title.

No American woman had won a downhill event on the World Cup circuit until the 1994-1995 season, when Picabo Street won six downhill events. In the 1995-1996 season, she won three events and was again the season's downhill champion. The 1996-

Alberto Tomba of Italy captures the gold medal in the men's slalom event at the World Championships in Spain in February.

1997 season was only weeks old when Street badly injured her left knee in a spill while training in Vail, Colorado, and was out for the season.

Street (women's downhill) and Atle Skaardal (men's super giant slalom) were the only skiers to sweep the World Cup and world-championship titles in their disciplines. In the men's slalom, Tomba finished second to Sebastien Amiez of France.

In the world championships, 10 nations shared the 30 medals. Italy and Switzerland won five medals each, Austria and Norway four each, and the United States and Sweden three each. Italy won four gold medals, and Sweden won two.

Other winners. In cross-country skiing, the World Cup overall winners were Bjorn Dahlie of Norway among the men and Italy's Manuela Di Centa among the women. In ski jumping, Andreas Goldberger of Austria won the World Cup championship and the world ski-flying title. In Nordic combined (jumping and cross-country skiing), Norway's Knut Tore Apeland won top honors, and 19-year-old Todd Ludwick of Steamboat Springs, Colorado, became the first American world junior champion. Freestyle champions included Jonny Moseley of Tiburon, California (men's overall), Katarina Kubenk of Canada (women's overall), and Donna Weinbrecht of West Milford, New Jersey, who won the women's moguls for a record fifth year. ☐ Frank Litsky

In *World Book,* see **Skiing.**

Slovakia. Politics in Slovakia remained turbulent in 1996. Tensions continued between Prime Minister Vladimir Mečiar and President Michal Kovač.

In January, President Kovač's son, Michal Kovač, Jr., was charged in Slovakia with fraud in connection with his dealings with an import-export firm. In May, President Kovač sued Prime Minister Mečiar for slander and defamation after Mečiar accused him of being involved in the case. Also in May, Slovak authorities dropped their investigation of the 1995 kidnapping of Michal Kovač, Jr. The chief investigator on the case stated that the police could not decide whether it was a real kidnapping or a deception engineered by young Kovač himself.

In June, the two junior members of Mečiar's three-party coalition government—the Slovak National Party and the Slovak Workers Party—stopped supporting the coalition, although they did not formally withdraw from it. The parties sided with the opposition over issues that included the composition of the board overseeing the National Property Fund—which is in charge of Slovakia's privatization effort—and opposition membership in the parliamentary group that supervises the Slovak secret service. Coalition talks in late June and early July resulted in agreement to support the Mečiar government.

Legislation. Mečiar's government introduced several measures that were criticized by representa-

tives of the North Atlantic Treaty Organization (NATO), the European Union (EU), and various governments. Chief among these measures was a controversial "law on the protection of the republic," which would have made critics of the government subject to criminal prosecution and imprisonment. Opposition leaders and leaders of Slovakia's significant Hungarian minority feared the vaguely worded law could be used against Mečiar's critics for political reasons. President Kovač refused to sign the measure, and parliament declined to take it up again.

In August, a new law that reorganized Slovakia into eight administrative regions, instead of the previous three, went into effect. The reorganization downgraded the status of Bratislava, the capital of Slovakia and a stronghold of the political opposition, from that of an independent region to simply being a part of a larger administrative region. Opposition leaders charged that the new administrative divisions benefited Mečiar's party, Movement for a Democratic Slovakia.

Economic developments continued to be favorable in Slovakia in 1996. The private sector accounted for 62 percent of total gross domestic product. Inflation, which had been 7 percent at the end of 1995, dropped to 6.1 percent in May 1996. Unemployment, which had been 15 percent at the beginning of 1995, fell to 11.9 percent in May of 1996. However, political controversy and uncertainty continued to discourage foreign investors.

Foreign affairs. Criticism in 1996 from the international community threatened Slovakia's acceptance into European institutions. EU officials who visited Slovakia in early July criticized the government's policies regarding minority rights, the treatment of the opposition, and the proposed law on the protection of the republic. They said that these issues, in addition to inconsistent efforts toward economic reform, could exclude Slovakia from the first group of central European nations to join the EU.

Slovak leaders delivered Slovakia's completed EU questionnaire for membership in July. In September, a parliamentary commission on European integration was established. In keeping with the agreement among the coalition parties, the commission included members of opposition parties.

Although the Slovak parliament ratified a basic treaty with Hungary on March 26, the issue of Hungarian minorities in Slovakia continued to cause friction between the two countries. Delegates to a conference of ethnic Hungarians in Budapest released a statement supporting autonomy for Hungarian minorities abroad. In response, both Prime Minister Mečiar and President Kovač criticized the Hungarian declaration, and the Slovak public called for alterations to the March treaty. ☐ Sharon Wolchik

See also **Czech Republic, Europe** (Facts in brief table). In *World Book,* see **Slovakia.**

Slovenia. See **Europe.**

Goalkeeper Giovanni Cervona of AS Roma dives to block a pass to AC Milan's Roberto Baggio (right) in an Italian first division match played in February.

Soccer. Major League Soccer (MLS), a new, top-tier professional league, began its first season in the United States in 1996 and received greater public enthusiasm than anticipated. In October, D.C. United became the league's first champion. In international play, Germany won the European championship.

The MLS represented professional soccer's latest attempt to establish itself in the United States. When the sport's governing body—Fédération Internationale de Football Association (FIFA)—awarded the 1994 World Cup tournament to the United States, a condition was that the United States must establish a first-division league, as every other soccer-playing nation had done.

United States. Since the 1985 demise of the North American Soccer League, which emphasized big-name international players, there had been no major American league. That changed with the birth of the 10-team MLS. Seven teams—New York/New Jersey, Los Angeles, Washington, D.C., New England, Colorado, Kansas City, Missouri, and Columbus, Ohio—were privately financed. The remaining three teams—Dallas, Tampa Bay, and San Jose—were collectively owned and financed by the league.

The MLS emphasized American players. Each team was allowed to employ four foreign players. The teams played a 32-game regular season from April to September 1996, followed by a play-off series. In the championship game, played October 20

in Foxboro, Massachusetts, D.C. United defeated the Los Angeles Galaxy by a score of 3-2.

The league had hoped to attract crowds of 10,000 or even 20,000 per match. Instead, a game between Los Angeles and New York/New Jersey drew 69,255 fans to the Rose Bowl (thousands were turned away). Attendance averaged 17,416, and cable-television ratings were higher than expected.

The European championships were held in June in the United Kingdom. The semifinals were decided on penalty kicks, with Germany defeating England and the Czech Republic upsetting France. Germany won the final game, 2-1, at Wembley Stadium in London, in sudden-death overtime. A linesman ruled that a German player had been offside, but the call was overturned by the referee.

Other games. The United States defeated China in the U.S. Women's Cup in May and the Olympic Games in August. Nigeria won the Olympic men's gold medal by defeating Brazil in the semifinals, 4-3, and Argentina in the final, 3-2. Mexico's national team captured the CONCACAF Gold Cup and the U.S. Cup. In professional soccer, Juventus of Turin won the European Champions Cup. Bayern Munich won the UEFA Cup, Manchester United won the English Football Association Cup, and South Africa, in its first major tournament, the African Cup.

□ Frank Litsky

In *World Book,* see **Soccer.**

Social security. Trustees of the Social Security Trust Fund noted in their 1996 report that the fund would remain solvent through the year 2029. However, they warned that the Medicare Hospital Insurance Trust Fund would be bankrupt by the year 2001 unless changes were made to the program.

Medicare, which provides health insurance for 30 million elderly and disabled persons, was hit in the mid-1990's by high costs for advanced surgical procedures, home health care, nursing, and hospice care. During that same time, revenues from payroll taxes were lower than expected. The trustees noted that the Hospital Insurance Trust Fund had a surplus of $121 billion in mid-1996, but it would barely break even by the year 2000 and would run a deficit of $53 billion by 2001. Medicare Part B, which pays for doctor visits and other costs, is not in danger of insolvency; it is funded by the government and by premiums paid by beneficiaries. Secretary of the Treasury Robert Rubin, a trustee of the funds, suggested cutting Medicare costs by $116 billion over a 6-year period to keep the hospital fund solvent through 2006.

In March, President Bill Clinton signed into law an increase in the wages that retirees between the ages of 65 and 69 can earn without losing social security benefits. The ceiling was raised from $11,520 to $12,500 in 1996. It is scheduled to rise incrementally to $30,000 a year by 2002.   □ William J. Eaton

In *World Book,* See **Social security.**

Somalia. The most significant event in Somalia in 1996 was the death on August 1 of General Mohamed Farah Aideed, leader of the Somali National Alliance (SNA). The SNA has been one of the three major factions in the country's civil war, which began in 1991. Aideed died of wounds received during street fighting in the capital, Mogadishu. His death appeared to provide an opportunity for ending the war. However, nothing came of the short-lived cease-fire nor of a fragile, second peace agreement that resulted from Aideed's death.

Ongoing chaos. In 1996, Somalia remained in the grip of civil war. After the 1991 expulsion of dictator Mohamed Siad Barre, the northern part of Somalia declared independence and renamed itself Somaliland. Although unrecognized by most countries of the world, Somaliland has remained relatively stable under the rule of President Mohammed Ibrahim Egal.

Much of the remainder of Somalia, lacking any central government, had been ruled since 1991 by clan elders or by militia leaders. An area along the Ethiopian border had remained in the control of the Islamic fundamentalist Al Itahad (Islamic Unity)—a group that had followed a policy using terrorism to "liberate" the Somali minority in the Ogaden region of Ethiopia. In reprisal, the Ethiopian army staged an attack on Somalia in August 1996.

Three powerful militias—Aideed's SNA, Ali Mahdi Mohammed's Somali Salvation Alliance, and the forces of Osman Hassan Ali Atto—dominated Mogadishu, where the most severe fighting occurred in 1996. Aideed's opponents, upon hearing of his death, announced a cease-fire. Hopes ran high that faction leaders would reach a peace agreement.

Aideed the younger. On August 4, the SNA announced that Aideed's son, Hussein Aideed, had been chosen to succeed his father. An American citizen in his mid-30's, Hussein had been a soldier with the U.S. force sent to Somalia in 1992. This force was to provide security for international relief organizations, which were in Somalia to relieve mass starvation triggered by a combination of war and drought. Any hopes that Hussein might promote peace were short-lived. Upon taking charge of the SNA, he declared his intention of "exterminating" his enemies. On August 10, fighting again erupted between Aideed's and Mahdi's forces.

On October 15, the three major factions of the civil war announced another cease-fire. Fighting, however, again erupted in late October, this time between Aideed's and Atto's forces.

Relative calm prevailed through much of rural Somalia in 1996, though sporadic fighting occurred among clans. Because rainfall was generally sufficient in 1996, the grain harvest was expected to be 35 percent greater than in 1995.   □ Mark DeLancey

See also **Africa** (Facts in brief table); **Ethiopia**. In *World Book,* see **Somalia.**

South Africa. South Africa continued in 1996 to struggle with the problems of transition from *apartheid* (racial separation) to an open, democratic system of government. While the nation achieved progress in the political sphere, daunting social and economic problems remained.

Reconciliation and justice. One of South Africa's major challenges in 1996 was to reconcile racial and political differences after decades of apartheid. To root out excesses of the apartheid era, the government in 1996 indicted individuals implicated in political crimes under the old system of government.

Magnus Malan, former minister of defense, was the highest official put on trial. He was accused of ordering a raid on an African National Congress (ANC) headquarters that led to several deaths and, with several codefendants, went on trial for murder. Highly conservative political groups rallied to his defense. Individuals and groups long opposed to apartheid hoped for convictions but viewed the legal system—peopled by apartheid-era appointees—skeptically. In mid-October, the court found all the defendants innocent.

In a separate trial, Eugene de Kock, the alleged leader of an apartheid-era assassination squad, provided sensational testimony. De Kock testified that an operation called Long Reach, with ties to the then white-only South African government, had in

1986 assassinated Swedish Prime Minister Olof Palme. Palme's offense had been to criticize apartheid. De Kock was convicted in October of 89 crimes, including several murders.

The Truth and Reconciliation Commission, headed by former Archbishop Desmond Tutu, provided another means of cleansing the past. This government-appointed body was established to receive testimony about abuses under apartheid and to provide a forum for voluntary confession.

Some high-ranking individuals spoke before the commission during hearings that began in April 1996. Former State President Frederik Willem de Klerk, leader of the National Party, apologized for apartheid and its abuses of human rights but claimed the government had never knowingly participated in violent crimes to enforce apartheid.

A new constitution—and politics. After difficult negotiations, the Constitutional Assembly approved a new constitution on May 8. The new constitution included a bill of rights and created a federal system with a strong president and a two-house legislature. The constitution was slated to go into effect gradually over three years. In early December, the Supreme Court gave final approval to the new constitution and it was signed by President Mandela.

Political violence continued in the KwaZulu area, where ANC and Inkatha Freedom Party, a Zulu-based organization, loyalists have been fighting intensely for several years. The number of incidents declined in 1996, however, and after several delays, local KwaZulu elections were concluded without serious incident on June 26. In May, de Klerk announced that the National Party would leave the government to become a party of opposition. The party also undertook a campaign to broaden its base and to attract black voters.

Nelson Mandela, leader of the ANC and national hero of liberation, maintained his decision to retire at the end of his term in 1999. On July 7, 1996, he stated that his deputy, Thabo Mbeki, was Mandela's chosen successor. Younger and more reserved than Mandela, Mbeki has been recognized as a skilled behind-the-scenes politician who had developed powerful support in the party.

Difficult economic and social conditions continued to confront South Africa in 1996. The unemployment rate—about 33 percent overall and perhaps more than 40 percent among black workers—was among the highest in the world. The government's ambitious new housing plan proved very difficult to implement: As many as 8 million of South Africa's nearly 45 million people remained homeless.

□ Mark W. DeLancey

See also **Africa** (Facts in brief table). In *World Book,* see **South Africa.**

South America. See Latin America.

South Carolina. See State government.

South Dakota. See State government.

Space exploration. During 1996, U.S. astronaut Shannon W. Lucid spent 188 days in space, setting both a U.S. space endurance record and a world space endurance record for women. U.S. space shuttle crews flew seven missions. Two unmanned spacecraft were launched to Mars. And the U.S. government revised its space policy, transferring some activities to the private sector and reordering its priorities.

Japanese satellite retrieved. The space shuttle Endeavour, launched January 11, retrieved a Japanese scientific satellite in orbit since March 1995. Japanese astronaut Koichi Wakata used a 50-foot (15-meter) robot arm to snag the satellite and pull it into the shuttle's cargo bay. The crew also used the robot arm to place a small Flyer satellite into orbit. Flyer instruments checked the shuttle for atmospheric contamination and showed that the Global Positioning System, a group of satellites that precisely locate objects on Earth, could locate satellites in space. Endeavour's crew, during spacewalks, tested tools for assembling the planned International Space Station and a spacesuit designed to keep astronauts warm in temperatures below −75 °F (−59 °C). Endeavour landed at Kennedy Space Center (KSC) on the east coast of Florida on Jan. 20, 1996.

International missions. A Chinese Long March rocket exploded upon launch on February 14 and fell back to Earth, hitting a nearby village. Estimates of the number of people who died varied from 6 to more than 56. Another Long March rocket successfully lifted the Apstar 1A, a U.S.-built communications satellite, into orbit on July 3.

The European Space Agency launched an Ariane 5 rocket on June 4, but the rocket had to be destroyed when it veered off course less than a minute after launch. An investigation concluded that software errors in Ariane's guidance system caused the disaster.

A Russian spacecraft was launched to Mars on November 16 but fell back to Earth when its booster rocket malfunctioned. It landed in the Pacific Ocean near Chile. The unmanned space probe carried a small quantity of plutonium, which experts agreed would not pose any danger because of the ocean depth to which the probe remnants fell.

Unmanned flights. On February 17, the National Aeronautics and Space Administration (NASA) launched the first spacecraft that would orbit an asteroid, the Near Earth Asteroid Rendezvous (NEAR). Plans called for NEAR to reach its target, Eros, an asteroid some 25 miles (40 kilometers) long, in 1999 and orbit it for one year. Scientists hoped to gather information about Mathilde, another asteroid, which NEAR will fly by in 1997 on its way to Eros.

Life on Mir. The Russian space station Mir completed 10 years in orbit on Feb. 20, 1996. The next day, cosmonauts Yuri Onufrienko and Yuri Usachev arrived and worked with the two crew members already aboard Mir. The latter left on February 29 to return to Earth, leaving Onufrienko and Usachev to

American astronaut Shannon W. Lucid inventories supplies in March with Russian cosmonauts aboard the Russian space station Mir. Lucid spent 188 days in space, breaking American and international space endurance records.

welcome the American ship Atlantis and its crew.

Atlantis went into orbit on March 22 and docked with Mir the next day. Biochemist Shannon Lucid became the first American woman to fly aboard a foreign spacecraft. Two of the five other crew members aboard Atlantis took a spacewalk on March 27, the first walk between two manned spacecraft. The astronauts clamped debris collectors to Mir to determine how much space dust and grit strikes the station. Leaving Lucid aboard Mir, Atlantis returned to Earth, landing at Edwards Air Force Base (EAFB) in California on March 31.

On August 17, a Soyuz craft brought three more people to Mir, including Claudie Andre-Deshays, the first French woman in space. After 16 days aboard Mir, Andre-Deshays, Usachev, and Onufrienko left the station and returned to Earth on September 2.

Return to Mir. Atlantis flew back to Mir on September 16, following almost seven weeks of delays caused by booster problems, accidents, and hurricanes. The shuttle docked with Mir on September 18, and the crew delivered almost 5,000 pounds (2,268 kilograms) of food, water, and other supplies—the largest space resupply ever flown—and picked up Shannon Lucid. She broke the U.S. record of 115 days in space previously set in 1995 by Norman E. Thagard, also aboard Mir. Lucid also, on Sept. 7, 1996, broke the 169-day space flight record for women established by Russian cosmonaut Elena Kondakova, who worked aboard the station in 1995. Atlantis undocked on Sept. 23, 1996, and landed at KSC on September 26.

Electrifying flight. The shuttle Columbia roared into space on February 22 with four Americans, two Italians, and one Swiss. The team repeated an experiment that failed on a 1992 flight, releasing a satellite 5-feet (1.5-meters) in diameter attached to a long, insulated wire tether 12.8-miles (20-kilometers) long. The wire successfully produced 3,500 volts of electricity as it moved through Earth's magnetic field. However, the tether broke, ending the experiment. The problem was later traced to a small puncture in the insulation, which caused a short circuit.

The crew also performed microgravity and combustion experiments, which entailed setting small fires to test smoke detectors and fire extinguishers in weightless conditions. Although a computer circuit controlling the shuttle's rudder and brakes failed, the Columbia landed safely at KSC on March 9.

Inflatable construction. Endeavour flew again on May 19, carrying a Spartan satellite. Inside the satellite was an inflatable antenna. After it was deployed, the antenna expanded to 50 feet (15 meters) in diameter and sprouted three 92-foot (28-meter) supports. NASA planned to employ such inflatable structures both as inexpensive satellites and as space-station components. The Endeavour crew retrieved the Spartan and also released a satellite equipped with magnetic rods, which enabled Earth's magnetic field—rather than the usual system of costly steering jets—to stabilize the satellite in orbit.

Video games in space. Columbia returned to orbit on June 20 on a science mission. The seven-member crew of American, French, and Canadian astronauts grew small trees, played video games to test hand-eye coordination, and studied bone and muscle loss, growth of protein crystals, and development of fish embryos in the near absence of gravity. Columbia landed at KSC on July 7.

New space shuttle. On July 2, NASA selected Lockheed Martin Corporation to build the next generation of space shuttles. Lockheed Martin's plan, a wedge-shaped, fully reusable vehicle, was designed to take off vertically like a rocket and land horizontally like an airplane. NASA announced that it expected the wingless craft to cut the cost of putting 1 pound (0.45 kilogram) of payload into orbit from nearly $10,000 to $1,000 and to slash other repair and maintenance costs. The space agency budgeted $1 billion toward a half-sized prototype, known as X-33, to be in the air by 1999. Further plans called for launching the full-size, 127-foot (39-meter) Venture Star in about 2006.

New U.S. space policy. On Sept. 19, 1996, the U.S. government announced a major revision in its space policy, transferring some space activities traditionally handled by NASA, such as the launching and operation of spacecraft, to private companies. NASA would concentrate on exploration, science, and technology. The revised policy also emphasized unmanned missions and international cooperation.

Missions to Mars. NASA launched two missions to Mars in late 1996. The Mars Global Surveyor, sent into orbit on November 7, was expected to reach the planet in September 1997. Its purpose was to make detailed maps while orbiting Mars for 687 Earth days—the Martian year. Mars Pathfinder, launched on Dec. 4, 1996, was to land on Mars on July 4, 1997, putting a small roving robot on the Martian surface. The rover was designed to send back pictures and data on Martian weather, rocks, and soil.

Record shuttle flight. Columbia flew the last shuttle flight of 1996, blasting off from KSC on November 19. The Columbia flight was the first shuttle flight partially conducted by the private space-flight operations company United Space Alliance, a joint venture of Lockheed Martin Corp. and Rockwell International Inc. Columbia's five-member crew, including 61-year-old Story Musgrave—the oldest astronaut to fly in space—deployed and retrieved two scientific satellites and conducted two space walks. Columbia landed at the Kennedy Space Center on December 7, breaking the 1995 16-day Endeavour record for the longest U.S. shuttle mission.

☐ William J. Cromie

See also **Astronomy.** In *World Book,* see **Space exploration.**

Spain experienced a dramatic change of leadership in 1996 as voters ended 14 years of Socialist rule and elected a government led by the conservative Popular Party. The party, which ran a strong nationalist campaign, won 156 seats in the March 3 election, falling short of a majority in the 350-seat Chamber of Deputies but ahead of the 141 seats taken by the Socialist Workers' Party. To win the support of the Catalan Convergence and Union Party and form a government, the Popular Party was forced to hand major new powers to the country's 17 autonomous regions, including a greater share of income tax revenues.

Economic change. The victory enabled José María Aznar, a 43-year-old former tax inspector and Popular Party leader, to be sworn in as prime minister on May 6, replacing Felipe González Márquez, who had led Spain since 1982. Aznar promised to reduce government spending and deregulate the economy to stimulate growth and employment and qualify Spain to participate in European monetary union in 1999.

The government announced immediate spending cuts of $1.6 billion for 1996, mainly affecting public works programs. In June, the government adopted measures to deregulate the economy, aid small businesses, and reduce taxes on capital gains. It also announced plans to sell some state-owned assets, including shares in the communications monopoly Telef´ønica and the electricity generator Endesa. In September, the government announced new austerity measures designed to slash the budget deficit by a third in 1997—to 3 percent of gross domestic product, the maximum allowed under monetary union. The budget would cut spending by $6 billion, freezing the pay of government workers, and increase taxes.

Growth slows. The budget cuts slowed the economy, but the government claimed that the lower interest rates fostered by its policies would generate a strong recovery. The European Union forecast that Spanish growth would slow to 2 percent in 1996 from 3 percent in 1995. Unemployment remained at a high of 22 percent.

Death squads. A Supreme Court judge on April 30 dismissed allegations that Felipe González Márquez had approved death squads that were reported to have killed 27 people in a 1980's "dirty war" against the Basque separatist group ETA (the initials stand for Basque Homeland and Freedom in the Basque language). Such allegations were a major factor in the Socialists' defeat in the March election. Speculation about a cover-up revived in August when the Aznar government refused to declassify secret service documents requested by judges investigating the killings. The government cited reasons of national security. ☐ Tom Buerkle

See also **Europe** (Facts in brief table). In *World Book,* see **European Union; Spain.**

Sports

Sports. Among the sports stars of 1996 were a rash of home-run hitters in baseball, 20-year-old Tiger Woods in golf, a troubled Steffi Graf in tennis, Michael Jordan in professional basketball, and Michael Johnson in track and field. It was a year of soaring salaries and franchise values and soaring health problems.

Salaries for the best players in the National Basketball Association (NBA) escalated wildly. Jordan remained with the champion Chicago Bulls through the 1996-1997 season by signing for an annual $30 million, the highest salary ever paid in any sport. Center Shaquille O'Neal moved from the Orlando Magic to the Los Angeles Lakers for $120 million over seven years. Center Alonzo Mourning moved from the Charlotte Hornets to the Miami Heat for $112 million over seven years. Forward Juwan Howard stayed with the Washington Bullets for $100 million over seven years.

Athletes in other sports were paid record salaries as well. In baseball, outfielder Albert Belle signed a five-year, $55-million contract with the Chicago White Sox. In hockey, center Wayne Gretzky was earning $8.5 million with the Los Angeles Kings, but he was traded to the New York Rangers in February. In football, Dallas Cowboys quarterback Troy Aikman earned $6.25 million for the year.

Teams could afford the salaries because franchises were worth more. In Philadelphia, a 66-percent interest in the Flyers hockey team and the 76ers basketball team and in the old and new arenas where the teams played, sold for $250 million. A controlling share of the Dallas Mavericks basketball team was sold for $125 million. A 90-percent interest in the New York Islanders hockey team was purchased for $165 million.

Financial World magazine's annual survey of professional sports franchise values named the Dallas Cowboys football team the most valuable franchise, at an estimated value of $272 million. Next on the list were the Miami Dolphins (football) at $214 million, the New York Yankees (baseball) at $209 million, the New York Knicks (basketball) at $205 million, and the Baltimore Ravens (football) at $201-million. All 30 teams of the National Football League plus 11 baseball and 10 basketball teams were valued higher than the $126-million evaluation of the top-ranked hockey team—the Detroit Red Wings.

Health. John McSherry, a 51-year-old National League baseball umpire, collapsed in the first inning of an opening-day, April 1 game in Cincinnati, Ohio, and died of sudden cardiac arrest. McSherry stood 6 feet 2 inches (1.88 meters) and weighed more than 320 pounds (145 kilograms). Soon after, Eric Gregg and Rocky Roe, fellow major league umpires, took leaves of absence to enter weight-loss programs.

In February, Tommy Morrison, the 27-year-old former heavyweight champion of the World Boxing Order, tested positive for HIV, the virus that causes AIDS. Brett Butler, the 38-year-old center fielder of the Los Angeles Dodgers, underwent surgery in May for throat cancer. When he returned to the line-up in September, he broke his left hand. Lance Armstrong, a 25-year-old Texan and former world road-race cycling champion, underwent surgery in October to remove two lesions on his brain. Earlier that month, Armstrong had announced he had testicular cancer.

Drugs. The United States and Australia led the battle to pressure the international swimming federation, known as FINA, to eliminate illegal drug use by Chinese swimmers. The Americans and Australians were thus embarrassed when Jessica Foschi, a 15-year-old American, tested positive for steroids and Samantha Riley, a world record-holder from Australia, tested positive for a banned painkiller.

Foschi denied she had ever used bodybuilding anabolic steroids. But in February, FINA suspended her until August 1997. Riley said she had taken an analgesic drug in a prescription headache tablet, which her coach had given her by mistake. When FINA decided not to suspend Riley, U.S. swimming officials reinstated Foschi. However, FINA's ruling barred Foschi from international competition, including the 1996 Olympics, but the situation became academic when she failed to qualify for the U.S. team. Riley won a silver and a bronze medal at the Olympic Games.

NCAA. The National Collegiate Athletic Association (NCAA), the major governing body of college sports, shifted the balance of power to less than 100 colleges with the broadest and strongest athletic programs. It gave the highest decision-making positions to college presidents and chancellors, and it rejected proposals to weaken academic requirements for incoming freshmen.

The NCAA penalized Mississippi State, Florida State, and Michigan

With Egypt's ancient pyramids of Giza illuminated in the background, squash players compete under glass in an international competition held in May.

State, among others, for violating rules in conducting football programs. Auburn and New Mexico State were penalized for basketball violations.

Awards. In January, Olympic runner Michael Johnson was awarded two major multisport honors: the 1996 Jesse Owens International Trophy Award and the U.S. Olympic Committee (USOC) 1995 Sports-Man of the Year. In the Jesse Owens Award voting, Johnson's closest rivals were Haile Gebrselassie of Ethiopia and Jonathan Edwards of Great Britain, also from track and field. In the USOC voting, wrestler Bruce Baumgartner was second and Pete Sampras (tennis) third. Picabo Street (skiing) was voted USOC SportsWoman of the year, with runner Gwen Torrence second and Bonnie Blair (speed skating) third.

In March, Bruce Baumgartner, the 35-year-old world champion in super-heavyweight freestyle wrestling, was voted the Sullivan Award as America's outstanding amateur athlete of 1995. The award is voted upon each year by U.S. media and sports figures. The other finalists were Michael Johnson and Gwen Torrence in track and field, Tiger Woods in golf, Tommy Frazier in college football, Rebecca

Lobo and Lorenzen Wright in basketball, Shannon Miller and Dominique Moceanu in gymnastics, and Rebecca Twigg in cycling.

Among the winners in 1996 were—

Cycling. After Bjarne Riis of Denmark ended Miguel Indurain's five-year winning streak in the Tour de France, Indurain won the Olympic gold medal for Spain in the men's road time trial. Jeannie Longo-Ciprelli of France won the Olympic women's road race and the world-championship road time trial and broke the world one-hour record. Lance Armstrong, the United States's best road racer, won the Tour DuPont.

Diving. China won 5 of the 12 diving medals at the 1996 Olympic Games, the year's only major international competition. The U.S. outdoor championships produced two potential stars: 16-year-old Troy Dumais, who won two gold medals and one bronze medal in men's competition; and 14-year-old Erica Sorgi, who became the youngest American platform champion since Jenny Chandler in 1974.

Gymnastics. Yuri Checci of Italy won a third consecutive world title in rings, Vitaly Scherbo of Belarus a third consecutive title in floor exercise, and Pae Gil Su

of North Korea won a third in pommel horse at the world championships, held April 15-20 in San Juan, Puerto Rico. Romania's Gina Gogean won gold medals in the women's vault and floor exercise. There were no compulsory exercises and no team or all-around competitions.

Marathon. Uta Pippig of Germany won the Boston Marathon women's title for the third straight year. But Cosmas Ndeti, trying for his fourth win in a row, finished third, with Moses Tanui, a fellow Kenyan, taking the men's title. The New York Marathon produced surprise winners in Giacomo Leone of Italy among the men and Anuta Catuna of Romania among the women.

Rowing. Imperial College won the Grand Challenge Cup and Goldie Boat Club the Ladies' Challenge Plate, giving British eights the two major titles in the Henley Royal Regatta in July in Henley, England. In American collegiate competition, the men of Princeton University and the women of Brown University swept the national, Intercollegiate Rowing Association and Eastern sprint championships.

Other champions

Archery, world Olympic bow field champions: men, Andrea Parenti, Italy; women, Carole Ferriou, France

Biathlon, world champions: men's 20-kilometer, Sergei Tarasov, Russia; women's 15-kilometer, Emmanuelle Claret, France

Canoeing, World Cup whitewater champions: men's canoe, Adam Clawson, United States; men's kayak, Paul Ratcliffe, Great Britain; women's kayak, Lynn Simpson, Great Britain

Cricket, World Cup champion: Sri Lanka

Equestrian, World Cup champions: jumping, Hugo Simon, Austria; dressage, Anky van Grunsven, Netherlands

Fencing, U.S. foil champions: men, Nick Bravin, New York City; women, Felicia Zimmerman, Rochester, New York

Field hockey, Atlanta Six-Nation men's champion: Pakistan

Lacrosse, U.S. college champions: men, Princeton University; women, University of Maryland

Modern pentathlon, world women's champion: Yanna Dulgacheva-Shubenok, Belarus

Motorcycle racing, world 500-cc champion: Michael Doohan, Australia

Rugby, Tri Nations champion, New Zealand

Sled dog racing, Iditarod (Anchorage to Nome) champion: Jeff King, Denali Park, Alaska

Soap Box Derby, masters champion: Tom Scrofano, Conneaut, Ohio

Triathlon, world champions: men, Simon Lessing, Great Britain; women, Jackie Gallagher, Australia

Volleyball, World League men's champion: Netherlands

Weightlifting, European super heavyweight champion: Andrei Chemerkin, Russia   □ Frank Litsky

See also articles on the various sports. In *World Book,* see articles on the sports.

Sri Lanka. In 1996, the Sri Lankan army suffered its worst defeat in 13 years of civil war with the Liberation Tigers of Tamil Eelam (LTTE). The LTTE used terrorist tactics and guerrilla warfare in its fight to win an independent state in north and northeast Sri Lanka for the Tamils, a Hindu minority in a nation predominately Buddhist and Sinhalese.

On Dec. 5, 1995, the army had captured the LTTE's stronghold at Jaffna at the northern tip of Sri Lanka. On May 16, 1996, the army claimed control over the entire Jaffna peninsula, though soldiers continued to clear LTTE forces from jungles along the northeast coast. On July 18, the LTTE retaliated by attacking a large army base at Mullaitivu. Only about 35 of approximately 1,500 soldiers at the base survived the attack. The LTTE forces captured an estimated $50 million in weapons and ammunition before withdrawing.

The army then launched an offensive to capture Kilinochchi, a village that had become the LTTE political headquarters after the loss of Jaffna. Both sides sustained heavy losses before Kilinochchi fell on September 29. Sporadic LTTE attacks on police stations in eastern Sri Lanka continued in 1996.

Terrorism. On January 31, an LTTE suicide team rammed a bomb-laden truck into barriers at the 11-story Central Bank in downtown Colombo, Sri Lanka's capital. The explosion killed 88 people, wounded hundreds of others, and wrecked the country's financial district. On April 12, the military prevented two trawlers carrying bombs from blowing up naval gunboats and supply ships in Colombo Harbor. On July 24, however, two bombs exploded on a train in a suburb of Colombo, killing 64 people and wounding some 400. These attacks brought the number of civilians killed in Colombo by LTTE bombings to more than 2,500 since 1983. On July 4 in Jaffna, an LTTE suicide bomber tried to kill the government minister responsible for rebuilding the city. The minister survived the blast that killed 21 people.

President Chandrika Kumaratunga persisted in trying to find a political solution to the war. On January 16, she published a draft of proposals first made to the LTTE in August 1995 that gave more political and economic power to the Tamil minority. The government also allowed food convoys to enter rebel-held areas, where some 600,000 Tamils faced starvation. But the LTTE rejected negotiations.

Economy. By midyear, the government had exhausted defense funds for all of 1996—more than $700 million. Industrial production slowed due to lack of power, brought on by a drought that had reduced water levels in the reservoirs of hydroelectric plants, the nation's major power source.

One bright spot. Sri Lanka won the cricket World Cup on March 17. The victory over Australia raised war-battered morale.   □ Henry S. Bradsher

See also **Asia** (Facts in brief). In *World Book,* see **Sri Lanka.**

State government. In 1996, states were in their best financial position since fiscal 1980, and many cut taxes. Nationwide, state tax cuts totaled $3.6 billion, mostly in personal income taxes. New York's $2-billion tax cut was the largest. Legislatures in Connecticut, Indiana, and Georgia also passed major tax reductions.

Welfare reforms. In 1995, a number of states received waivers from the federal government, allowing them to make changes in federally funded welfare programs. Some states responded by requiring recipients to find jobs and get training. Many states limited benefits to two years. Others adopted "family caps" that denied benefits to children born to mothers already on welfare. Some states cut aid programs they had once offered to poor adults. Connecticut eliminated general assistance cash grants for employable people on Sept. 1, 1996. Pennsylvania's welfare reform also eliminated Medicaid, the federal and state medical assistance program for the poor, for 220,000 childless adults.

Legislation signed in August by President Bill Clinton ended guaranteed federal cash assistance for poor families. The law replaced this assistance with lump-sum payments to states, which were to decide how to distribute the funds. The federal law also placed a lifetime limit of five years on aid and required recipients to begin working within two years. The bill also eliminated benefits for legal immigrants who were not U.S. citizens.

State health activity. Massachusetts lawmakers expanded health insurance to 150,000 poor children and prescription drug assistance to low-income adults. The health services were to be financed by a 25-cents-a-pack cigarette tax hike.

By mid-1996, all states except Alaska and Wyoming had adopted some type of managed-care system for Medicaid. Managed care provides comprehensive health coverage for a fixed fee and is less expensive than conventional insurance.

At least 19 states had approved medical savings accounts, which were to allow people to put aside pretax income to use for medical expenses. Such plans were adopted in Louisiana, Ohio, and Wisconsin in 1996.

In efforts to protect patient rights, 33 states enacted laws in 1996 to regulate managed care plans. Many states ruled that insurers and health maintenance organizations (HMO's) could not prohibit doctors from discussing expensive treatments with patients. At least 23 states passed laws requiring health insurers to pay for a minimum hospital stay of 48 hours for mothers and newborns.

Indiana, Maine, Minnesota, Pennsylvania, Tennessee, New Jersey, and other states enacted laws in 1996 prohibiting health insurers from denying policies to, or raising the insurance premiums of, victims of domestic violence.

After Florida in 1995 sued tobacco companies in an effort to recover the costs of treating smoking-related diseases, attorneys general in at least 16 other states followed suit in 1996. Maryland sold off tobacco stock in its pension funds, expecting stock prices to drop if one of the lawsuits should succeed. Massachusetts became the first state to require tobacco makers to list ingredients on cigarette packages. Tobacco companies challenged this law in court.

Crime and punishment. As a result of recent state laws that lengthened prison terms for violent crimes, more offenders were behind bars in 1996. State spending on corrections rose by 15 percent during the fiscal year ending June 30, 1995. The number of state and local prisoners increased by almost 67,000, to more than 1 million in 1995, according to the most recent data available from the U.S. Department of Justice.

Virginia in 1996 passed tougher sentencing guidelines for offenders under the age of 18 and ruled that youngsters charged with violent crimes could be tried as adults. Texas committed $10.5 million to support community projects for middle-schoolers in areas with high juvenile crime rates.

Alaska passed a law in 1996 requiring parents of juvenile offenders to participate in their child's treatment and pay restitution for harm caused by the child. Under a law approved by voters in November, Arizona will try violent criminals age 15 or older as adults.

To relieve overcrowding in prisons, states resorted to alternative accommodations for prisoners. At least 12 states sent prisoners to out-of-state facilities operated by private companies or local governments. Private prisons and local jails in Texas housed thousands of inmates from other states. Georgia passed a law allowing private firms to build and operate new prisons there.

In April, Alabama's chain gangs, in which inmates are chained together for work details, attracted national attention when the state corrections commissioner announced he would expand them to include female inmates. Shortly after the announcement, Alabama's governor dismissed the commissioner, saying he did not want female chain gangs. In September, the state reached an agreement with a federal court to eliminate the use of chain gangs.

Speed limits. In 1995, Congress lifted the national maximum speed limit of 65 miles (105 kilometers) per hour on rural interstates. At least 22 states raised their speed limits in 1996 as a result of this action.

Education. In 1996, Illinois, Connecticut, Florida, and South Carolina approved public charter schools, which are not subject to the rules of the local public school district.

In the fall, nationwide school enrollment for kindergarten through 12th grade reached 52 million students, the highest level in 25 years. California schools set up about 20,000 new classrooms to meet a state goal of a maximum of 20 students per class, kindergarten through third grade. The state ap-

Selected statistics on state governments

State	Resident population*	Governor†	House (D)	House (R)	Senate (D)	Senate (R)	State tax revenue‡	Tax revenue per capita‡	Public school expenditures per pupil§
Alabama	4,252,982	Fob James, Jr. (R)	72	33	22	12#	$ 5,078,000,000	$1,190	$4,480
Alaska	603,617	Tony Knowles (D)	15	25	7	13	1,922,000,000	3,180	10,160
Arizona	4,217,940	Fife Symington (R)	22	38	12	18	6,223,000,000	1,480	4,330
Arkansas	2,483,769	Mike Huckabee (R)	86	13#	28	6#	3,392,000,000	1,370	4,370
California	31,589,153	Pete Wilson (R)	43	37	23	16**	53,269,000,000	1,690	4,930
Colorado	3,746,585	Roy Romer (D)	24	41	15	20	4,530,000,000	1,210	5,460
Connecticut	3,274,662	John G. Rowland (R)	97	54	19	17	7,474,000,000	2,280	8,710
Delaware	717,197	Tom Carper (D)	14	27	13	8	1,589,000,000	2,220	7,510
Florida	14,165,570	Lawton Chiles (D)	59	61	17	23	18,583,000,000	1,310	5,980
Georgia	7,200,882	Zell Miller (D)	106	74	34	22	9,487,000,000	1,320	5,550
Hawaii	1,186,815	Ben Cayetano (D)	39	12	23	2	2,874,000,000	2,420	6,280
Idaho	1,163,261	Phil Batt (R)	11	59	5	30	1,733,000,000	1,490	4,450
Illinois	11,829,940	Jim Edgar (R)	60	58	28	31	16,590,000,000	1,400	5,530
Indiana	5,803,471	Frank L. O'Bannon (D)	50	50	19	31	8,046,000,000	1,390	6,230
Iowa	2,841,764	Terry E. Branstad (R)	46	54	21	29	4,403,000,000	1,550	5,740
Kansas	2,565,328	Bill Graves (R)	48	77	13	27	3,765,000,000	1,470	5,900
Kentucky	3,860,219	Paul E. Patton (D)	64	36	20	18	6,285,000,000	1,630	5,970
Louisiana	4,342,334	Murphy J. (Mike) Foster (R)	77	27#	25	14	4,677,000,000	1,080	4,840
Maine	1,241,382	Angus King (I)	81	69**	19	15**	1,813,000,000	1,460	6,480
Maryland	5,042,438	Parris N. Glendening (D)	100	41	32	15	8,061,000,000	1,600	6,930
Massachusetts	6,073,550	William F. Weld (R)	129	29††	32	8	11,601,000,000	1,910	7,470
Michigan	9,549,353	John Engler (R)	58	52	16	22	17,723,000,000	1,860	7,130
Minnesota	4,609,548	Arne H. Carlson (R)	70	64	42	24**	9,328,000,000	2,020	6,150
Mississippi	2,697,243	Kirk Fordice (R)	84	34‡‡	34	18	3,599,000,000	1,330	4,190
Missouri	5,323,523	Mel Carnahan (D)	87	75#	19	15	6,752,000,000	1,270	5,080
Montana	870,281	Marc Racicot (R)	35	65	16	34	1,214,000,000	1,400	5,880
Nebraska	1,637,112	E. Benjamin Nelson (D)	unicameral (49 nonpartisan)				2,220,000,000	1,360	5,540
Nevada	1,530,108	Bob Miller (D)	25	17	9	12	2,698,000,000	1,760	5,260
New Hampshire	1,148,253	Jeanne Shaheen (D)	145	253§§	9	15	917,000,000	800	6,410
New Jersey	7,945,298	Christine Todd Whitman (R)	30	50	16	24	13,607,000,000	1,710	9,970
New Mexico	1,685,401	Gary E. Johnson (R)	42	28	25	17	2,844,000,000	1,690	5,650
New York	18,136,081	George E. Pataki (R)	95	54#	26	35	34,294,000,000	1,890	9,880
North Carolina	7,195,138	James B. Hunt, Jr. (D)	59	61	30	20	11,426,000,000	1,590	5,150
North Dakota	641,367	Edward T. Shafer (R)	26	72	19	30	959,000,000	1,490	4,710
Ohio	11,150,506	George V. Voinovich (R)	39	60	12	21	15,186,000,000	1,360	5,750
Oklahoma	3,277,687	Frank Keating (R)	65	36	33	15	4,416,000,000	1,350	4,460
Oregon	3,140,585	John Kitzhaber (D)	29	31	10	20	4,286,000,000	1,360	6,390
Pennsylvania	12,071,842	Tom J. Ridge (R)	99	104	20	30	18,262,000,000	1,510	7,400
Rhode Island	989,794	Lincoln C. Almond (R)	84	16	41	9	1,490,000,000	1,510	7,730
South Carolina	3,673,287	David Beasley (R)	53	70**	26	20	4,763,000,000	1,300	5,020
South Dakota	729,034	William J. Janklow (R)	23	47	13	22	694,000,000	950	5,070
Tennessee	5,256,051	Don Sundquist (R)	61	38	18	15	5,908,000,000	1,120	4,720
Texas	18,723,991	George W. Bush (R)	82	68	15	15#	20,289,000,000	1,080	5,590
Utah	1,951,408	Michael O. Leavitt (R)	20	55	10	19	2,676,000,000	1,370	3,910
Vermont	584,771	Howard Dean (D)	88	58##	17	13	801,000,000	1,370	7,470
Virginia	6,618,358	George Allen (R)	52	47**	20	20	8,784,000,000	1,330	5,890
Washington	5,430,940	Gary Locke (D)	42	56	23	26	10,196,000,000	1,880	6,110
West Virginia	1,828,140	Cecil H. Underwood (R)	74	26	25	9	2,732,000,000	1,490	6,900
Wisconsin	5,122,871	Tommy G. Thompson (R)	47	52	17	16	9,029,000,000	1,760	7,210
Wyoming	480,184	Jim Geringer (R)	18	42	9	21	667,000,000	1,390	6,110

*July 1, 1995 estimates (source: U.S. Bureau of the Census).
†As of December 1996 (source: state government officials).
‡1995 figures (source: U.S. Bureau of the Census).
§1995-1996 figures for elementary and secondary students in average daily attendance (source: National Education Association).
#One vacancy.

**One independent.
††One independent; one vacancy.
‡‡Three independents; one vacancy.
§§Two independents.
##Three progressive; one independent.

366

propriated $771 million to help schools hire more teachers and $200 million for new facilities. North Carolina granted schools $15 million to reduce the second-grade class size to 23 students per teacher.

State spending on education accounted for more than one-third of state budgets overall. Spending on education grew by 5 percent in a majority of states. Several states in 1996 revised formulas for distributing school funds to increase the funding of poorer school districts and decrease funding of richer ones. Alabama changed its school funding formula to comply with a 1993 court order. Arkansas distributed state funds to equalize the amount spent per pupil among poorer and richer districts and to help poor districts manage their debts. Illinois approved $52.5 million in grants to school districts, distributing the funds according to student enrollment in each district. South Dakota approved a new school funding formula, increasing the state share of funding, which was scheduled to go into effect in 1997. Arizona approved spending $70 million to help poor districts repair or build schools. The action came two years after the state supreme court ruled that the state's school finance system violated the U.S. Constitution.

Other states considered ways to meet court orders to finance school districts more fairly. New Jersey's supreme court set a Dec. 31, 1996, deadline for lawmakers to complete a new school finance plan. The state increased overall spending on schools by $47 million and used funds saved by cuts to wealthier districts to increase aid to needy districts by $60 million. A Wyoming task force examined how to comply with a state supreme court order to overhaul education by July 1997. Court suits challenged school finance systems in Ohio, Pennsylvania, New Hampshire, and Illinois.

Governors. Mike Foster was sworn in as governor of Louisiana on January 8. He was only the second Republican governor in the state's history. In June, Arkansas Lieutenant Governor Mike Huckabee, a Republican, replaced Democratic Governor Jim Guy Tucker. Tucker resigned after he was convicted on two felony counts involving illegal land deals. On June 13, a federal grand jury indicted Arizona Governor Fife Symington on 23 counts of fraud and extortion. He refused to step down before his trial, which was scheduled for 1997.

In gubernatorial elections on November 5, no incumbents lost. Voters reelected Republican incumbents in three states, and Democrats in four. New Hampshire elected its first woman governor, Democrat Jeanne Shaheen. The state of Washington elected its first governor of Chinese descent, Democrat Gary Locke. West Virginia elected former Governor Cecil Underwood, a Republican, and Indiana elected Democratic Lieutenant Governor Frank O'Bannon.

☐ Elaine Stuart

See also **Elections.** In *World Book,* see **State government** and the articles on the individual states.

Stocks and bonds. A powerful and unexpected rally after the November presidential election lifted U.S. stocks and bonds from what might have been an ordinary year to a dramatic ride for investors in 1996. Buying was spurred by a widespread belief that deficit spending and regulatory initiatives by the federal government would be curbed during at least two more years of stand-off between a Democratic president and a Republican-controlled Congress. Reports of mild price inflation at the consumer and producer levels, plus indications that the economy was slowing at year-end, delighted investors who feared the inflationary consequences of too-rapid economic growth.

After a brief decline in early January, the daily Dow Jones Industrial Average—a composite of the stock prices of 30 major companies—rose sharply through mid-February but leveled off through June at about 5,600. A potentially scary drop in technology stocks in mid-July took the entire market lower and raised fears that the six-year-old stock market advance, known as a bull market, had ended. But the July swoon merely set the stage for a new leg of the rally that pushed the Dow industrials up more than 800 points. In early December, the Dow stood at about 6,500, up 27 percent for the year, well above the historical annual return for stocks—about 11 percent. Broader stock market indexes also staged post-election rallies to all-time highs. The Standard & Poor's 500 index of 500 company stocks and the Nasdaq Composite Index of all stocks traded on the electronic Nasdaq Stock Market operated by the National Association of Securities Dealers were up 23 percent by early December.

A steady decline in interest rates on short- and long-term debt securities fueled the postelection stock market rally. Interest rates, which are expressed as "yields" in the bond market, fell, luring money away from fixed-income debt securities and into the stock market. Lower yields also boosted corporate profits, making investments in stocks more rewarding. After reaching 7.2 percent in June, the yield on the U.S. Treasury's 30-year bond fell to less than 6.4 percent in early December. Lower long-term interest rates make home mortgages cheaper for consumers. The yield on three-month Treasury bills peaked at 5.36 percent in early September, fell to about 5 percent in early October, and stood at about 5.13 percent in early December.

Winners and losers. The undisputed champion of the stock market in 1996 was International Business Machines Corporation (IBM), of Armonk, New York, the giant computer company whose fortunes helped lead the overall market sharply higher from late July. IBM, one of the 30 stocks in the Dow Jones industrial average, peaked at about $175 shortly before the stock market crash of October 1987, and sank fairly steadily to a low of about $40 in mid-1993. After a weak performance in the first half of 1996, IBM took

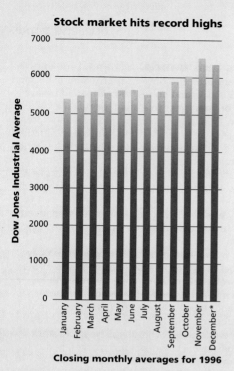

Stock market hits record highs

Closing monthly averages for 1996

*December figure is as of the 13th.

The Dow Jones Industrial Average climbed, from a dip in July 1996, more than 800 points to break 6,000 in October, then 6,500 in November.

Money pouring in to stock *mutual funds* (publicly sold pools of stocks and bonds) kept the demand for stocks high for most of the year. Through October 1996, investors pumped $192.6 billion into equity mutual funds, nearly double the $97.5 billion invested in the first 10 months of 1995. In the same period in 1996, more than $51 billion in initial public offerings of stock, up 89 percent from the first 10 months of 1995, soaked up some of the fresh money flowing to Wall Street.

International stock markets. The strength of the U.S. stock and bond markets diverted many investors from non-U.S. markets. But stock markets on either side of the border did well. The Toronto Stock Exchange index of 300 Canadian stocks broke the 6,000 mark for the first time in late November 1996, up 27 percent through the first 11 months of the year. The Financial Times-Stock Exchange index of 100 stocks traded on the London Stock Exchange gained just 9.5 percent to 4048.5 in early December. But the German Stock Index, known as the DAX Index, was up 27 percent for the year through early December.

The Nikkei 225 index of major Japanese companies traded on the Tokyo Stock Exchange rose 4.1 percent through early December to 20674.69, reflecting Japan's slow climb out of recession. Japan had been a major source of investment dollars into U.S. stocks and bonds. ☐ Bill Barnhart

In *World Book,* see **Bond; Investment; Stock.**

off from $90 in late July and jumped to more than $160 in early December. The advance reflected IBM's success in the markets for personal computers and mid-sized computers, as opposed to mainframe computers—large, multifunction machines—that had been the company's mainstay in the 1980's. In September 1996, IBM announced a new line of low-cost computers for people wanting easy access to the Internet.

Several computer technology stocks soared to extraordinary prices in May and, despite slumps in the second half, closed the year with impressive one-year gains. Iomega Corporation, a popular maker of computer disk storage systems, ended 1995 at $8.11 and rocketed to more than $55 a share in late May 1996. In early December, the stock was quoted at $23.50, nearly triple its 1995 closing price.

AT&T Corporation declined in 1996, reflecting stiff competition in the telecommunications industry and the company's decision to divest itself of its equipment business, named Lucent Technologies, Inc., and its computer systems business, named NCR Corporation. AT&T ended 1995 at $64.75 and traded at about $38 in early December 1996.

Stocks of gold mining companies fared poorly, as they did in 1995, as inflation stabilized, and the price of gold declined. Homestake Mining Company, for example, stood at about $15 in early December 1996, down from $15.50 at the end of 1995.

Sudan. Sudanese leader Umar Hasan Ahmad al-Bashir won election as president in March of 1996. Bashir's support of terrorism and failure to end a costly 13-year civil war devastated Sudan's economy and deepened the country's international isolation. Many Sudanese viewed the elections, the first since 1986, as a sham despite Bashir's claim that they gave his Islamic government a broad democratic mandate. Bashir had banned political parties since taking power in 1989.

Hassan al-Turabi, widely considered more powerful than Bashir, was elected speaker of parliament in April. Turabi's powerful National Islamic Front controlled the parliament, and his nomination as its speaker was unopposed.

Sanctions. The international community, which had hoped that the worsening state of the Sudanese economy would moderate its foreign affairs policies, was disappointed. The United Nations (UN) Security Council passed a resolution on April 26 imposing diplomatic sanctions if Sudan failed to turn over to international authorities three men suspected of a 1995 assassination attempt on Egyptian President Hosni Mubarak during a visit to Ethiopia.

The sanctions, which went into effect on May 10, 1996, required nations to reduce their diplomatic missions in Sudan and curb the entry of Sudanese officials and military officers. International and regional organizations were forbidden to hold conferences in

Women in eastern Khartoum, Sudan, receive military training as part of a government plan to battle rebels challenging Islamic law.

Sudan. Sudan claimed it was unable to find the suspects, but the United States announced in April that one of the men had left Sudan with official help.

A U.S.-backed effort to ban arms sales to Sudan and flights by Sudanese airliners was approved by the UN Security Council in August. Some states, such as Egypt, feared an arms embargo could fragment Sudan if the Arab, Islamic-dominated government in the north fell to the predominately Christian and animist rebels in the south.

Foreign relations. The United States removed all its government officials from Sudan in February. In April, it expelled a Sudanese diplomat at the UN. The United States accused the diplomat of aiding terrorists convicted in 1995 of planning to bomb the UN and other New York landmarks, as well as planning an assassination attempt on Egyptian President Mubarak during a 1993 trip he made to the United States.

Aviation. Three Sudanese plane crashes killed 144 people by mid-1996. A Sudanese airliner was diverted from Jordan to the United Kingdom on August 26 by 7 Iraqi hijackers who requested asylum. On March 24, two men opposed to Sudan's government hijacked a Sudan Airways plane and forced it to fly to the Eritrean capital of Asmara, where they surrendered. □ Christine Helms

See also **Middle East** (Facts in brief table). In *World Book*, see **Sudan**.

Supreme Court of the United States.

During its 1995-1996 term, the Supreme Court of the United States issued important rulings on sexual equality, civil rights, the death penalty, and states' rights.

Equal protection. One of the court's most controversial decisions came on June 26, when the justices ruled that the all-male Virginia Military Institute (V.M.I.) in Lexington, Virginia, violated constitutional equal protection guarantees by excluding women. Voting 7 to 1, the court ruled that the 157-year-old, state-supported school must admit women, because an alternate program set up for female students was inadequate. V.M.I. had started the separate women's training program after being sued by the U.S. Justice Department in 1990 to end the school's all-male status. V.M.I. had resisted a coeducational student body on the grounds that women were not suited to the school's strict, stressful, and physically rigorous environment. Justice Clarence Thomas did not take part in the case because his son was a V.M.I. student.

The Citadel in Charleston, South Carolina, the nation's only other all-male military institution receiving state funding, also established a separate women's program after the Fourth U.S. Circuit Court of Appeals ruled in 1995 that the school must admit female students. However, after the Supreme Court's decision in the V.M.I. case, The Citadel announced on June 28, 1996, that it would accept both men and

women into the same program. Four women enrolled as freshmen in fall 1996.

Voting districts. Extending a line of rulings that have changed the way state lawmakers draw voting boundaries, the court on June 13 struck down three congressional districts in Texas and one in North Carolina. In two 5-to-4 decisions, the justices pronounced districts unconstitutional when race was the main consideration in the way they were shaped. Defenders of the districts said they were designed to boost the chances of African Americans and Hispanics of winning seats in the U.S. Congress. In the Texas case, state officials also argued that the odd shapes of the districts resulted from efforts to protect the adjoining districts of veteran members of Congress.

The cases grew out of legislators' efforts to redraw voting districts to reflect population shifts revealed by the 1990 census. Largely because of those revisions, the number of African Americans in the U.S. House of Representatives increased from 24 to 39 after the 1992 elections. However, beginning in 1993, the court threw many of the new minority districts into doubt with rulings that outlawed using race as the key factor in designing voting districts.

Gay rights. In its first ruling involving gay rights in a decade, the court voted 6 to 3 to strike down a Colorado constitutional amendment that banned state and local laws protecting homosexuals from discrimination. The May 20 ruling concluded the government cannot single out a group of people and deny them protections that all other citizens enjoy. The Colorado amendment, supported by the majority of voters in a 1992 referendum, never went into effect. It was challenged by homosexual men and women and by the cities of Aspen, Boulder, and Denver, which had adopted gay-rights laws.

States' rights. On March 27, the court used a case involving Indian gambling casinos to restrict the power of Congress to allow states to be sued in federal court. The justices ruled 5 to 4 that a provision of the 1988 Indian Gaming Regulatory Act was unconstitutional because it violated state sovereignty. The law allowed Indian tribes to sue states in federal court if the states would not negotiate legalizing gambling casinos on reservations. The decision came in a dispute between the Seminole tribe and the state of Florida. At the time of the ruling, 200 Indian tribes were running 126 casinos in 24 states.

Death penalty appeals. The court voted 9 to 0 on June 28 to uphold a key portion of a new law strictly limiting the number of federal appeals that can be filed by state death-row inmates. The justices ruled that Congress can require inmates who want to file more than one federal appeal to meet stringent standards and obtain permission from an appellate court. Those restrictions were contained in the Antiterrorism and Effective Death Penalty Act of 1996, which President Bill Clinton signed on April 24. Even with those limitations, the Supreme Court justices reserved the

Activists celebrate the Supreme Court's decision in May that a Colorado amendment banning antidiscrimination laws for homosexuals was unconstitutional.

court's power to review death penalty appeals directly.

Punitive damages. In a May 20 decision, the court reversed a $2-million punitive-damages award. An Alabama jury had awarded the judgment to a man who had bought a new BMW automobile and then discovered that it had received a minor paint repair. The 5-to-4 ruling provided new guidelines on determining when punitive damages are excessive.

Punitive damages are awarded in some civil cases, such as personal-injury lawsuits and contract disputes, to punish wrongdoers. Some states had limited large punitive-damage awards, but the high court had declined to bar such awards in all cases. In the Alabama suit, the car owner claimed he was deceived because he had not been told that his $40,000 car had received a paint touch-up before he bought it. The jury concluded that the touch-up decreased the car's value by $4,000. The jurors then penalized BMW $4 million, because approximately 1,000 people across the United States had bought cars similarly touched-up. While the Alabama Supreme Court reduced the award to $2 million, the U.S. Supreme Court ruled that the amount was still excessive, based on the small amount of money the car owner actually lost.

Cable TV and the First Amendment. On June 28, the court upheld a key part of a 1992 law designed to shield children from sexually explicit programs on cable television and struck down two other provisions of the law. In a 7-to-2 vote, the court ruled that Congress can require cable systems to remove indecent programs from channels that independent programmers pay to lease. However, the justices voted 5 to 4 against a similar indecency ban for channels that cable companies must provide free to local governments and community groups. The court also ruled 6 to 3 that Congress cannot require cable companies to scramble signals of channels that air sexually explicit programs for everyone except subscribers who request access in writing.

Prosecution bias. In a case involving cocaine prosecutions, the court on May 13 ruled that statistics were insufficient proof that the federal government was deliberately threatening African American defendants with harsher sentences than white defendants. The justices voted 8 to 1 that a federal trial judge wrongly threw out cases against five men charged with distributing crack cocaine. The judge had dismissed the cases when prosecutors refused to explain why crack-cocaine defendants were far more often African American, while powdered-cocaine defendants tended to be white.

Under federal law, prison sentences are longer for offenses involving crack cocaine, which is more often associated with violent crime. The justices said African American defendants who claim they are being singled out based on their race must show that large numbers of white crack-cocaine defendants who could be charged in federal court are being prosecuted in state courts, where they get more lenient treatment.

Criminal law. On June 13, 1996, the justices upheld the federal prison sentences of two former police officers in the 1991 beating of Los Angeles motorist Rodney King. Voting 9 to 0 on key parts of the decision, the justices said the 30-month sentences given to former officers Stacey C. Koon and Laurence M. Powell were valid even though they were lower than the 70 to 87 months required by the federal sentencing guidelines. In 1993, Koon and Powell were convicted of violating King's civil rights.

Civil forfeiture. In two cases involving drug-related crimes, the court on June 24 upheld the federal government's power to seize defendants' property as well as to impose penalties, such as prison sentences. The justices ruled that seizures known as civil forfeitures do not violate the Fifth Amendment protection against being punished twice for a single crime. They voted 9 to 0 to uphold the government's seizure of hundreds of thousands of dollars in cash from two men convicted of running a major drug ring in California. In the case of a Michigan man whose residence was seized before he was convicted of growing and processing marijuana, the justices voted 8 to 1 to uphold the seizure.

☐ Linda P. Campbell and Geoffrey A. Campbell

See also **Civil rights; Courts.** In *World Book,* see **Supreme Court of the United States.**

Sweden

Sweden underwent a generational change of leadership in 1996 as Goran Persson, the 47-year-old, former finance minister, succeeded the retiring 61-year-old Ingvar Carlsson as prime minister on March 21. The changeover followed a December 1995 decision by the ruling Social Democratic Party to designate Persson as the successor to Carlsson, who had led the party since the assassination of former Prime Minister Olof Palme in 1986.

Economy. On taking office, Persson promised to maintain tight budget policies in order to slash the government's huge deficit while cutting the country's 8 percent unemployment rate in half by the year 2000. His task was complicated by an economic slowdown, however. The European Union (EU) predicted the economy would grow by just 1.2 percent in 1996, compared with 3.0 percent in 1995.

Persson's successor as finance minister, Erik Asbrink, introduced a fresh package of spending cuts and tax increases in April 1996 to reduce the deficit by $1.2 billion over two years. The measures were designed to enable Sweden to eliminate the deficit by 1998. In June 1996, the government proposed measures to reduce unemployment, including an expansion of adult and higher education and tax incentives for small businesses.

European Union issues. The new government adopted an ambiguous stance toward EU plans for monetary union. Persson claimed that the deficit re-

ductions would qualify Sweden for participation in the EU single currency, scheduled to begin in 1999, but he declined to commit the government to participate or to fix the value of the crown to other EU currencies, as Finland did. His caution reflected public skepticism toward deeper Swedish involvement in EU policies as well as fear of repeating past mistakes. Sweden briefly fixed the crown's value in the early 1990's but abandoned the policy in the face of massive currency speculation in 1992. The government also indicated a softening of Swedish neutrality by joining with Finland to propose that EU members work together in international peacekeeping.

Palme killing. The investigation into the 1986 assassination of former Prime Minister Olof Palme was suddenly revived in September, following claims of a South African connection. Eugene De Kock, the head of an apartheid-era police hit squad, alleged in a Pretoria court that a former South African spy, Craig Williamson, had been involved in the killing. Palme had been an outspoken critic of apartheid, and Swedish police had heard previous claims of a possible South African motive but failed to uncover any evidence. Palme was shot in downtown Stockholm while walking home with his wife from a movie theater. The failure to find the killer had been a source of national frustration.   ☐ Tom Buerkle

See also **Europe** (Facts in brief table). In *World Book,* see **Europe; European Union; Sweden.**

Swimming

Swimming. The United States Swimming Team dominated their events at the 1996 Summer Olympics in Atlanta, due in part to the poor performance of China's women swimmers. Chinese women won 12 of 16 titles in the 1994 world championships, raising charges that they used illegal steroids. But they won just one gold medal in Atlanta, probably the result of extensive drug testing.

Olympic Games. After a poorer-than-expected showing in the Olympic trials, held March 6-12 in Indianapolis, American swimmers believed they would win only 21 medals at the 1996 Olympics, of which only 4 would be gold medals. Instead, the U.S. swimming team won 26 medals in Atlanta, far more than its nearest rivals: Australia (12), Germany (12), Russia (8), Hungary (6), and China (6). U.S. swimmers won 13 gold medals (7 by women and 6 by men).

Twenty-three-year-old Amy Van Dyken of Englewood, Colorado, won four gold medals, the most by an American female swimmer in one Olympics. Tom Dolan, a 20-year-old University of Michigan senior from Arlington, Virginia, won gold in the men's 400-meter individual medley.

Aleksandr Popov of Russia narrowly defeated Gary Hall, Jr., of Tucson, Arizona, in the men's 50-meter and 100-meter freestyles, but Hall outswam Popov in two relay races. Each finished with two gold and two silver medals. Others who won two individual gold medals were Denis Pankratov of Russia (men's 100-meter and 200-meter butterfly), Danyon Loader of New Zealand (men's 200-meter and 400-meter freestyle), and Penny Heyns of South Africa (women's 100-meter and 200-meter breast-stroke). Hungary's Krisztina Egerszegi won the women's 200-meter backstroke for the third consecutive Olympics.

In the final meet of a career that produced three gold medals in 1988 and one in 1992, 24-year-old Janet Evans of Los Angeles won no medals. She barely missed qualifying for the women's 400-meter freestyle final and placed 6th in the 800-meter final.

An unexpected star was 26-year-old Michelle Smith of Ireland, who won gold medals in the women's 400-meter freestyle (4:07.25), 200-meter individual medley (2:13.93), and 400-meter individual medley (4:39.18) and bronze in the 200-meter butterfly. Although Smith passed many drug tests, rivals speculated that her sudden improvement was due to her use of banned, performance-enhancing drugs.

World records. Four of the year's five world records were set at the Olympics—by Pankratov in the men's 100-meter butterfly, Fred deBurghgraeve of Belgium in the men's 100-meter breast stroke (preliminaries), a U.S. team anchored by Hall in the men's 400-meter medley relay, and Heyns in the women's 100-meter breast-stroke (preliminaries).

□ Frank Litsky

See also **Olympic Games: The 1996 Olympics.** In *World Book*, see **Swimming.**

Switzerland experienced its sixth straight year of economic stagnation in 1996, unleashing an unprecedented wave of corporate restructuring. Economic output was expected to grow by only 0.5 percent as a strong Swiss franc depressed exports.

On March 7, Swiss drug companies Ciba-Geigy AG and Sandoz AG announced plans to merge. The new company, Novartis AG—the world's second-largest drug maker with sales of $30 billion—planned to slash 13,000 jobs, 10 percent of its work force. The news shocked employees in Basel, home to both companies, which stood to suffer many of the cuts.

In April, Credit Suisse, the nation's second-largest bank, proposed a merger with Union Bank of Switzerland (UBS), the country's largest. Although UBS rejected the bid, competitive pressures forced major shakeups in the industry. Credit Suisse announced plans to cut 5,000 jobs; UBS, 800 jobs; and Swiss Bank Corp., the third-largest bank, 1,700 jobs.

In September, the government agreed to waive banking secrecy laws and appoint a panel to determine whether Swiss banks still hold gold stolen by Nazi Germany from occupied nations and Holocaust victims. Paul Volcker, former chairman of the U.S. Federal Reserve System, began a search for the funds of Holocaust victims after a May agreement between Swiss banks and Jewish groups. □ Tom Buerkle

See also **Europe** (Facts in brief table). In *World Book*, see **Switzerland.**

Syria. The May election of Israeli Prime Minister Benjamin Netanyahu, who rejected the previous Israeli government's formula of exchanging land for peace, stalled the Syrian-Israeli peace negotiations during 1996. In June, Netanyahu called Syria a terrorist state. He proposed that Israel would withdraw troops from southern Lebanon if Syria, which controls Lebanon, disarmed militant Hezbollah (Party of God) guerrillas there. Syrian President Hafiz al-Asad openly rejected the proposal on August 7. Syria had hoped for the return of the Golan Heights, which Israel captured from Syria during the Six-Day War in 1967.

A 1996 United States State Department report listed Syria among countries that supported terrorism. The U.S. accused Syria of harboring the militant Kurdistan Workers Party (PKK) and radical parties opposed to the Arab-Israeli peace process.

Numerous explosions in major Syrian cities during May and June shook the regime. Syria blamed Turkey for the violence. It arrested 600 people, mostly ethnic Turks, and deployed military units to its border with Turkey. Relations between the neighbors were already strained by disputes over water rights to the Euphrates River, by a 1996 agreement between the Turkish and Israeli militaries, and by previous Syrian claims to a Turkish province.

□ Christine Helms

See also **Middle East** (Fact in brief table). In *World Book*, see **Syria.**

Taiwan held the first direct, democratic election for a national leader in Chinese history on March 23, 1996, when Li Teng-hui garnered 54 percent of the vote to win the presidency. His main opponent, Peng Ming-min of the Democratic Progressive Party (DPP), won only 21 percent of the vote. Li, the head of the Kuomintang (KMT) party, had been elected president previously by an indirect procedure in 1990.

Independence from China was a key issue in the election. In 1949, Communists drove Chiang Kai-shek's KMT government from mainland China to the nearby island of Taiwan. Since then, officials of both Taiwan and mainland China claimed to represent all of China. But in recent years, a movement led by the DPP argued for declaring Taiwan a separate and independent nation, a position that angered China, which claims Taiwan. During the 1996 campaign, China tried to intimidate Taiwan voters by conducting military exercises in the waters separating the two regions. Observers thought voters avoided Peng for fear that his election would provoke China into attempting to crush the Taiwanese independence movement. After his loss, Peng resigned the DPP leadership and was succeeded by Hsu Hsin-liang. The party moderated its independence stand in order to broaden its appeal to voters.

In his inaugural speech on May 20, Li stated that China should face the fact that the Taiwanese do not want to live under Communist rule. Li offered

Supporters gather in March in Taipei, Taiwan, below portraits of President Lee Teng-hui (left) and Vice President Lien Chan (right), candidates for Taiwan's first direct election.

to make a "journey of peace" to Beijing, China's capital, to meet the president and Communist Party leader, Jiang Zemin. China spurned this offer.

Seeking recognition. Only 30 countries had established diplomatic relations with Taiwan by 1996. Thus, throughout 1996, Taiwan worked to obtain official recognition from nations that already had diplomatic ties with mainland China. Senior Taiwanese officials visited Ukraine on August 19 and Indonesia on September 4. Taiwan and China competed for recognition from some small, impoverished African countries by giving them economic aid and advice.

The economy was expected to grow 5.8 percent in 1996. Forecasts were higher before election-based tensions with China discouraged trade and investment, but business recovered by summer. Although trade between Taiwan and China was officially banned, it was conducted via other nations. Taiwan proposed ways to trade more directly, and on August 20, China published regulations that opened some ports to direct shipping from Taiwan.

Typhoon tragedy. The worst typhoon in 30 years hit Taiwan on July 31, killing 44. The storm flooded large areas. ☐ Henry S. Bradsher

See also **Asia** (Facts in brief). In *World Book,* see Taiwan.

Tajikistan. See Asia.
Tanzania. See Africa.

Taxation. Tax cuts became a key issue in the 1996 United States presidential campaign. Although partisan differences blocked approval of major tax cuts, President Bill Clinton and the Republican-led U.S. Congress agreed on several tax measures to benefit small business, self-employed people, and parents of adopted children.

The candidates' plans. Former Senator Robert Dole, the Republican candidate for president, proposed a 15-percent income tax cut as the centerpiece of his economic program. Dole also backed a 50-percent reduction in taxes on profits from the sale of stock or other assets and repeal of a 1993 increase in taxes on social security benefits for higher-income retirees. His plan included a $500 tax credit for parents for each child under the age of 18.

Clinton criticized Dole's proposal as a "risky $550-billion scheme" that would explode the budget deficit and raise interest rates. The president's plan included an annual $500-per-child tax credit and a single $1,500 tax credit to offset the first two years of college tuition or a $10,000 tax deduction to offset four years of college tuition costs.

Tax measures passed. Several tax measures were approved by the Republican-controlled Congress and the Democratic president in 1996. As part of a bill raising the federal minimum wage, tax write-offs for investment in business equipment were raised from $17,500 a year to $25,000. Smaller firms were autho-

rized to start simplified pension plans requiring employers to contribute if workers set aside up to $6,000 a year tax-free savings. A single $5,000 tax credit was provided for parents adopting a child.

Health insurance-related reductions. Clinton on August 21 signed a health insurance reform bill that contained several new tax breaks. It raised the tax deduction for insurance costs for the self-employed from 30 percent to 80 percent and authorized a four-year test of 750,000 tax-free medical savings accounts for workers in smaller firms, uninsured people, and the self-employed.

Failed measures. Republicans in Congress tried, but failed, to repeal a 4.3 cent-a-gallon increase in gasoline taxes approved as part of Clinton's 1993 economic package. The House of Representatives voted for a temporary repeal, but the bill died when the Senate failed to act on it. A proposed constitutional amendment to require a two-thirds majority vote to enact legislation to increase federal taxes failed in the House.

The Clintons' taxes. Meanwhile, President Clinton and his wife, Hillary, paid $75,437 in federal income taxes on earnings of $316,074 in 1995. The Clintons also paid $3,400 in back taxes and interest to correct mistakes in estimating taxes owed on their Whitewater real estate investment in the 1980's.
☐ William J. Eaton

In *World Book,* see Taxation.

Telecommunications. AT&T Corp., the long distance telephone giant, shocked the corporate world on Jan. 2, 1996, by announcing the elimination of 40,000 jobs, the largest single job cut ever in the telephone industry. AT&T later said that only 18,000 employees would actually be laid off.

Telecommunications Act. While 1996 began on a grim note for the telecommunications world, the mood quickly improved after the United States Congress made a number of major revisions to laws governing the industry. On February 1, Congress approved a massive revision of the nation's 62-year-old Communications Act. The revised law deregulated large segments of the telecommunications industry, clearing the way for telephone and cable operators to enter each other's businesses; it also removed many restrictions on the ownership of broadcast properties. When President Bill Clinton signed the measure into law on February 8, a multibillion-dollar flurry of corporate mergers and acquisitions was ignited. Four of the nation's "Baby Bells" were among the biggest deal-makers.

On February 27, US West of Englewood, Colorado, purchased Continental Cablevision of Boston for $10.8 billion; Pacific Telesis of San Francisco and SBC Communications of San Antonio merged on April 1, in a deal worth $16.7 billion; and Bell Atlantic of Atlanta and Nynex of New York City merged in a $22.7 billion deal on April 22.

Telecommunications

Radio and television. Radio led the deregulatory revolution. The new law removed company ownership limits, leaving in place only restrictions within individual radio markets. On March 4, Infinity Broadcasting Corporation of New York City, the nation's largest owner of radio stations, bought 12 stations in 5 U.S. markets for $410 million. The biggest radio deal of the year, however, was announced on June 20, when Pittsburgh-based Westinghouse Electric Corporation acquired Infinity for $4.9 billion. The deal joined the two largest radio networks, creating a goliath of 83 radio outlets.

The ownership of TV stations had also been restricted under the 1934 Communications Act. Under the new law, owners could possess as many stations as they wished, as long as their stations did not reach more than 35 percent of the population. On June 5, Barry Diller, the former head of Paramount Pictures, won Federal Communications Commission (FCC) approval of his purchase of 12 television stations. The stations were to be the core of a new television network Diller planned to form.

New channels. Ted Turner, chairman of Atlanta-based Turner Broadcasting System (TBS) and founder of the Cable News Network (CNN), announced in February the launch of a new cable sports channel that would combine elements of CNN and *Sports Illustrated,* the weekly sports magazine. The channel, which debuted in December, was part of a collaborative effort between Turner and media giant Time Warner Inc. The two companies completed a $7.5 billion merger in October.

In July, General Electric Company's NBC television network and computer software giant Microsoft Corporation launched MSNBC, a 24-hour news and information cable channel. MSNBC also established a Worldwide Web site, offering additional news and information and enabling viewers to interact with the cable channel.

FCC presses for education. Although the U.S. Congress largely deregulated the broadcasting industry, government influence did not end entirely. On August 8, the Federal Communications Commission (FCC) unanimously resolved to require television stations to air three hours of children's educational programming weekly beginning in fall 1997.

Policing the Internet. On June 12, a U.S. District Court in Philadelphia blocked a federal government attempt to regulate information distributed on the Internet, the global computer network. The court declared key parts of the Communications Decency Act, which became law in February, unconstitutional. The act had made it a crime to distribute "indecent or patently offensive material" online. Congress passed the law partly to protect children from sexually-explicit articles, photographs, and other material on the Internet. □ Tim Jones

See also **Internet.** In *World Book,* see **Telecommunications.**

Television. The Telecommunications Reform Bill, the most sweeping legislation affecting the United States telecommunication industry in 62 years, was signed into law on Feb. 8, 1996, by President Bill Clinton. The law lifted controls on cable television rates, eased restrictions on mergers between media companies, and opened competition among cable television companies. The law also required manufacturers to equip most new televisions by 1998 with a *V-chip,* an electronic device that can block violent, sexually explicit, or other programming parents consider unsuitable.

The V-chip figured into a June 1996 ruling by the U.S. Supreme Court that lifted some programming restrictions on cable channels. The court declared unconstitutional parts of the 1992 Helms Amendment to the Cable Television Consumer Protection and Competition Act, which required cable operators to scramble sexually explicit programming on commercially leased channels unless viewers specifically requested access. V-chip technology made such a law unnecessary, the justices decided.

Ratings system. In an effort to help adults monitor the TV-viewing habits of children, President Clinton, an advocate of the V-chip, met with TV executives in February to discuss a TV ratings system similar to the ratings used for motion pictures. The executives agreed to implement such a system in 1997. On Dec. 19, 1996, industry leaders announced a system with six categories, including two for programs specifically for children. The four major broadcast networks—ABC, CBS, NBC, and Fox—said that they would begin using the new system on Jan. 1, 1997.

Mega-merger. On Sept. 12, 1996, the Federal Trade Commission (FTC) officially approved the Time Warner Inc. purchase of the Turner Broadcasting System (TBS), which owned several cable networks, including TNT and the Cable News Network (CNN). Time Warner was the world's largest communications company and the nation's second largest cable operator. As part of the $7.5-billion deal—one of the largest media buy-outs in history—the FTC demanded that the Time Warner cable system carry a second 24-hour news channel to compete with CNN.

The choice of that all-news channel in New York City, however, triggered a major political and legal fight. Time Warner chose to carry the all-news MSNBC, a Microsoft Corporation and National Broadcasting Corporation (NBC) joint venture that debuted in July in 22 million households nationwide. Shut out was the Fox News Channel, which was launched on October 8 by the Fox Broadcasting Company. Fox found allies in New York officials, including the governor, a U.S. senator, and the mayor of New York City, who threatened to give Fox one of the city's public-access channels. When Time Warner sued the city, the city filed a countersuit.

Cable gains, networks losses. In 1996, cable TV continued to flex its muscles. National cable companies collected $2.1 billion in advertising revenues during the first six months, up 25.7 percent over the same period in 1995. Cable channels also made their biggest viewer gains ever in the 1995-1996 season, capturing 30 percent of the prime-time audience, up from 25 percent the previous year. Viewers, however, paid for the privilege. After the passage of the telecommunications act, cable operators raised prices: up 13 percent by Tele-Communications Inc., the largest U.S. cable company; and up 10 percent by Time Warner.

In contrast to cable's success, the four major broadcast networks—the American Broadcasting System (ABC), CBS Inc., NBC, and Fox—lost prime-time audience, which fell from 65 percent of viewers during the 1994-1995 season to a record low of 61 percent in 1995-1996. NBC was the most successful of the broadcast networks, running five out of the six highest-rated shows for most of the 1995-1996 season, including "E.R.," "Seinfeld" and "Friends."

"N.Y.P.D. Blue," a gritty police drama, continued to rank among the most popular network series in 1996 and receive critical acclaim.

Television

NBC was the only broadcast network to increase viewership. Its ratings were also boosted by the 1996 Olympic Games in Atlanta, Georgia, which began July 19. Despite complaints about delayed coverage and soap-operalike commentary, NBC's coverage of the games attracted 22 percent of the prime-time audience, compared to a 17.5 percent share for the 1992 Olympics in Barcelona, Spain.

New programs. Several new shows of the 1995-1996 season were based on hit films: "Dangerous Minds" (ABC), about a teacher in an inner-city school; "Clueless" (ABC), loosely based on the Jane Austen classic *Emma*; and "The Big Easy" (USA Network), about cops in New Orleans, Louisiana. Dramas about the paranormal abounded, led by Fox's highly successful "The X-Files." Other supernatural contenders included "Early Edition" (CBS), about a man who receives his newspaper a day before it is published; "Millennium" (Fox), about a telepathic sleuth; "Dark Skies" (NBC), about aliens responsible for political assassinations; and "The Pretender" (NBC), about a genius hunted by government agents. Hitting a lighter note was "Third Rock from the Sun," a *sitcom* (situation comedy) about an alien family sent to study earthlings. A midseason replacement in January 1996, it became a regular part of NBC's fall line-up.

Old faces and new. Several veteran sitcom stars returned to TV after a few years' absence. Michael J. Fox of the long-running "Family Ties" starred in ABC's "Spin City," about the travails of a deputy mayor in New York City. Bill Cosby was back in "Cosby," reunited with his TV wife, Phylicia Rashad, on CBS. Rhea Perlman, the salty waitress of "Cheers," returned as a widow attending college on CBS's "Pearl." She co-starred with British actor Malcolm McDowell.

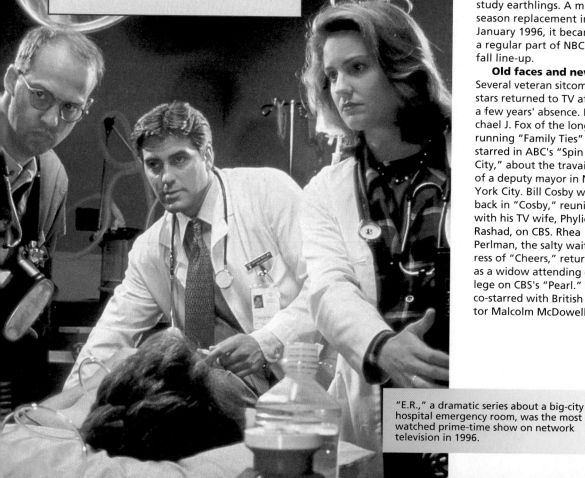

"E.R.," a dramatic series about a big-city hospital emergency room, was the most watched prime-time show on network television in 1996.

McDowell was one of several motion-picture actors trying out the small screen. Former teen star Molly Ringwald was one of three working-class girls in "Townies" on ABC. Actress Brooke Shields had the title role in "Suddenly Susan" (NBC), playing a magazine writer. Comedienne Lily Tomlin joined the long-running CBS hit "Murphy Brown," playing Murphy's (Candace Bergen's) new boss.

Network expansions. In September 1996, USA, prime time's most popular cable channel, added four new series to its mix of syndicated reruns and made-for-TV movies. Its first original series, "Silk Stalkings," had been a cult favorite for five years. In April, Nickelodeon launched a 24-hour version of Nick at Nite—Nick at Nite's TV Land. Nickelodeon's characteristic campy, vintage programming extended even to the commercials, which were recycled from television's distant and not-so-distant past.

The United Paramount Network (UPN), which debuted in January 1995, added a third night of programming and introduced six new series aimed chiefly at black viewers. One of the shows "Moesha," starring pop singer Brandy, quickly became a hit. Time Warner's WB network added a third night of programming and five new series, most of which featured predominately black casts.

Specials. There were historical themes to several notable miniseries. *Andersonville,* broadcast in March on TNT, depicted conditions at the infamous Civil War Confederate prison camp. Feature filmmaker John Frankenheimer directed the $18-million production. Ken Burns, director of popular miniseries on the Civil War and baseball, returned to television as producer of *The West,* broadcast in September on the Public Broadcasting System (PBS). The eight-part series featured Burns's characteristic vintage photographs and period music. Interspersing historians' analysis with the reading of historical letters, the series depicted the settling of the American frontier in the 1800's and early 1900's. PBS also aired *Genesis: A Living Conversation,* a 10-part series that began in October. Each episode examined a story from the Bible's Old Testament.

Departures. In January 1996, Phil Donahue, pioneer of audience participation talk shows, announced his retirement, after 29 years in broadcasting. His show, which had lost favor with audiences interested in more sensational fare, had been dropped by stations in such major outlets as New York City, San Francisco, and Los Angeles. In April, CBS canceled "Murder, She Wrote," starring Angela Lansbury as a mystery writer and sleuth, after a 12-year run. In July, former NBC news anchor John Chancellor, a 41-year veteran of television news, died of stomach cancer at age 68.   □ Troy Segal

See also **Supreme Court of the United States; Telecommunications.** In *World Book,* see **Cable; Television.**

Tennessee. See State government.

Tennis. Germany's Steffi Graf and America's Pete Sampras remained the world's leading tennis players in 1996. The 27-year-old Graf dominated women's tennis, winning three of the year's four grand-slam tournaments. Sampras, 24 years old, won one grand slam—the United States Open—for men.

Women. Graf missed the first grand-slam tournament, the Australian Open in Melbourne, following foot surgery. In the final round of that tournament, on January 27, Monica Seles of the United States defeated Anke Huber of Germany, 6-4, 6-1. It was the fourth Australian Open title in six years for the 22-year-old Seles, who missed the 1994 and 1995 tournaments after being stabbed by an assailant during a tournament in April 1993 in Hamburg, Germany. Seles was sidelined for 15 weeks with an injured left shoulder sustained at the Australian Open.

Although Graf was often distracted and in tears because her father was being tried in Germany on tax charges, she returned to the game following surgery, and her tennis was near impeccable. In grand-slam tournaments, she successively won the French Open (for the fifth time), Wimbledon (for the seventh time), and the United States Open (for the fifth time). She also won her fifth Lipton title and her ninth German Open.

Graf defeated Arantxa Sanchez Vicario of Spain in two grand-slam finals—by 6-3, 6-7, 10-8 at the French Open June 8 in Paris and by 6-3, 7-5 at Wimbledon July 6 in England. In the U.S. Open on September 8 in New York, Graf defeated Seles, 7-5, 6-4.

Fifteen-year-old Martina Hinges, a Swiss born in what was then Czechoslovakia, emerged as a future star in 1996. Hinges reached the final of the Italian Open, the semifinals of the United States Open, and the quarterfinals of the Australian Open, and she won the Wimbledon doubles title with Helena Sukova of the Czech Republic.

Men. The year began and ended with Pete Sampras ranked first by the computer, but Thomas Muster of Austria and Andre Agassi of the United States were ranked first at various times in between during the year. Muster's success came almost exclusively on clay courts, and Sampras, Agassi, and other professional players decried a system that allowed a specialist to be ranked first in the world.

Sampras was shaken by the illness of his coach, Tim Gullikson, who died in May of brain cancer at age 44. Several times during matches, Sampras broke down on the court in tears. His tennis was sometimes erratic, and he was eliminated in the semifinals of the French Open, the quarterfinals of Wimbledon, and the third round of the Australian Open.

Boris Becker of Germany, who last won a grand-slam title in 1991, won the Australian Open, defeating Michael Chang of the United States, 6-2, 6-4, 6-2, in the final. Sixth-seeded Yevgeny Kafelnikov of Russia beat Michael Stich of Germany, 7-6, 7-5, 7-6, in the French Open final. Unseeded Richard Krajicek of the Netherlands defeated unseeded MaliVai Washington of the United States, 6-3, 6-4, 6-3, in the Wimbledon final.

Before the U.S. Open began, players were in an uproar because the men's draw had been made before the seedings were announced, and the seedings did not follow the rankings. Foreign players said this allowed tournament officials to rig the draw to favor Americans. While tournament officials stood by the seedings, they redid the draw.

Sampras had a scare in the quarterfinals when he fought off a match point in a fifth-set tie-breaker against Alex Corretja of Spain in a match that lasted 4 hours and 9 minutes. In the final, Sampras beat Chang, 6-1, 6-4, 7-6, for his fourth U.S. Open title. It was Sampras's eighth grand-slam title, more than any other active player.

Team. The United States began its Davis Cup quest when Chang and Todd Martin led a 4-1 victory over Mexico. But because such stars as Sampras, Agassi, and Chang decided to skip the Davis Cup to prepare for the Olympics, Martin and Washington played singles, and the Americans lost, 3-2. In the final, November 29 to December 1, in Malmo, Sweden, France defeated Sweden. In the Fed Cup final for women, September 28 and 29, in Atlantic City, New Jersey, Seles and Lindsay Davenport led the United States to a 5-0 sweep of Spain.　□ Frank Litsky

In *World Book,* see **Tennis.**

Terrorism. On April 3, 1996, Theodore J. Kaczynski, the alleged Unabomber, was arrested at his remote cabin near Lincoln, Montana. The Unabomber's 17-year bombing campaign killed 3 people and injured 23 others. During 1996, charges were filed against Kaczynski for 7 of the 17 bombings or bomb threats.

In January, David Kazcynski, the suspect's brother, had provided the U.S. Federal Bureau of Investigation (FBI) with the lead. David Kazcynski had suspected his brother when he found old letters from his brother that were similar in tone and content to the Unabomber's 35,000-word antitechnology manifesto, published by *The Washington Post* in 1995.

Oklahoma City bombing trials. In February 1996, federal judge Richard P. Matsch agreed to move the trials of Timothy McVeigh and Terry Nichols, suspects in the 1995 bombing of the Oklahoma City federal building, to Denver, Colorado. The bombing on June 19, 1995, killed 168 people. The defense attorneys had argued that prejudice in Oklahoma against the defendants would not allow the two men to receive a fair trial. In October 1996, Matsch also agreed to try the two men separately.

Militia movements. In 1996, several people belonging to citizen militias were arrested or convicted for plotting violence against the U.S. government. On April 26, in Crawford County, Georgia, Bureau of Alcohol, Tobacco, and Firearms agents arrested two members of the Militia-at-Large for the Republic of Georgia for allegedly conspiring to build pipe bombs to use in a war against the federal government. On June 27, a federal grand jury in Phoenix, Arizona, indicted 12 members of the Viper Militia for plotting to bomb the local offices of the FBI, the Internal Revenue Service, Immigration and Naturalization Services, and other federal agencies. In Bellingham, Washington, on July 30, the FBI arrested eight members of a militia for conspiring to make and possess explosives, allegedly to arm themselves against the government. In West Virginia on October 11, FBI agents arrested seven members of the West Virginia Mountaineer Militia for allegedly plotting attacks on local federal buildings, including the FBI's fingerprint center in Clarksburg, West Virginia. On November 6, a federal grand jury in Macon, Georgia, convicted three members of the so-called 112th Georgia Militia of conspiracy for stockpiling explosives to use against the U.S. government.

International terrorism conferences. In February and March, four bombings by Hamas (Islamic Resistance Movement), which uses violence to pursue its goals of replacing Israel with an Islamic Palestinian state, claimed the lives of 61 people and injured hundreds of others in Israel. The bombings were a retaliation for the January 1996 assassination of bomb maker Yahya Ayyash.

In response to the threat of terrorism to the Israeli-Palestinian peace negotiations, Egypt and the United States sponsored a one-day antiterrorism summit in Sharm ash Shaykh, Egypt. Although the pledges of national leaders were mostly symbolic, the event was notable for bringing together leaders from 27 countries, including Israel and 14 Arab nations.

In Paris in June and July, leaders from the Group of Seven nations—France, Germany, Italy, Japan, Russia, the United Kingdom, and the United States—agreed to pursue measures to combat terrorism: monitoring the use of the Internet (the worldwide computer network) by terrorists; improving extradition procedures; developing standards for tracing sources of explosives; and restricting the production, sale, and export of firearms and explosives.

U.S. antiterrorism law. In response to increased terrorism at home and abroad, President Bill Clinton signed into law in April legislation that allocated $1 billion over a four-year period for law enforcement programs fighting terrorism. The law also made it easier to deport suspected terrorists; required the use of *taggants* (detection agents) in explosives, making them easier to trace; and barred alleged terrorist groups from raising money in the United States.　□ Richard E. Rubenstein

See also **Armed forces; Colombia; Egypt; India; Israel; Mexico; Middle East; Northern Ireland; Pakistan; Peru; Saudi Arabia; Turkey; United Kingdom.** In *World Book,* see **Terrorism.**

Texas. See **Houston; State government.**

Israeli soldiers and police, outside a Tel Aviv shopping mall, investigate the site of a March 4 suicide bombing, which killed 14 people and injured 130.

During the March funeral of Sangwal Mahidol, traditionally dressed soldiers escort the remains of the mother of two Thai kings past the Grand Palace in Bangkok.

Thailand held elections on Nov. 17, 1996, for the lower house of the National Assembly. The New Aspiration Party, 1 of 13 political parties in the race, won the election by two seats. Chavalit Yong-chaiyudh, head of the New Aspiration Party, formed a six-party coalition that held 221 of the 393 seats in the Assembly. Chavalit was then appointed the new prime minister by King Bhumibol Adulyadej.

Surprise election. On September 28, then Prime Minister Banharn Silapa-archa dissolved the National Assembly and called for November elections in a move that surprised and angered some of his coalition partners. A week earlier, he agreed to resign after the House defeated a motion of no-confidence against his scandal-plagued government. The legislators had expected to form a new ruling coalition without holding elections.

Controversial government. Banharn's Chart Thai party had come to power by winning the most seats, 92 out of 391, in 1995 elections. Almost all of his support came from rural areas, where patronage was strong and vote-buying was reportedly rampant. Banharn pieced together a coalition despite charges of election irregularities. A hostile press in the capital, Bangkok, accused his Cabinet of incompetence and corruption, and two senior Chart Thai members were denied Cabinet posts because the United States accused them of drug trafficking.

In May 1996, Banharn defeated a no-confidence motion that focused on charges that a deputy miniter had used illegally obtained land to get bank loans. During the summer, two parties quit the coation. One party bolted after the justice minister claimed that $90 million in bribes had been paid to the government in return for three bank licenses.

Chavalit then forced Banharn's resignation because he wanted to be prime minister, a post he hasought since 1990, when he retired as commander the Thai army. Chavalit stated that elections could give him a mandate as prime minister, though he was strongly supported by the military and reminded many civilian observers of old-style politics in Thailand. Since the 1930's, Thai armed forces had rpeatedly seized and lost power and interfered with civilian regimes.

The economy was expected to grow about 8 percent in 1996, the lowest rate since 1986. Much Thailand's economic expansion had been based on low-wage labor, but in 1996, labor costs were risinwhich benefited such low-wage competitors as China and Indonesia at Thailand's expense.

King Bhumibol Adulyadej celebrated his 50th anniversary on the throne on June 9, 1996. The 68-year-old king, the world's longest-reigning living monarch, was long beloved in Thailand as a nationsymbol of unity.   □ Henry S. Bradsh

See also **Asia** (Facts in brief table). In *World Boo* see **Thailand**.

Theater. In 1996, a mini-renaissance of musicals and a tempest of controversy about the 50th annual Antoinette Perry (Tony) Awards made for more interest, activity, and headlines than the American theater industry had seen in years. The musical seemed in big trouble in prior seasons. Not one home-grown musical of note premiered on or off Broadway in 1995, but just a year later, the playing field seemed transformed.

The new wave of musicals began in January 1996, when Jonathan Larson's *Rent,* a rock opera updating the story of Giacomo Puccini's *La Bohème* to present-day New York City, opened off-Broadway at the New York Theatre Workshop. A story of young love and early death in the age of AIDS, *Rent* was a sure-fire tear-jerker even before the ironic twist of fate surrounding the show. The 35-year-old playwright died of an *aortic aneurysm* (ruptured blood vessel) the night before the show's first performance. His death denied the musical theater one of its more promising young talents. Critics welcomed *Rent* as the landmark musical of the decade, in the same league as *Hair* and *A Chorus Line.* After a sellout run downtown, *Rent* headed to Broadway, earning the 1996 Pulitzer Prize for drama and turning its cast of talented young unknowns into stars.

The year's other major new musical, *Bring in 'Da Noise, Bring in 'Da Funk,* also started out downtown, at the Joseph Papp Public Theater. Part dance concert, part historical overview, part rap gig, *Bring in 'Da Noise* told the story of African Americans through a raw, up-to-the-minute style of tap dance, which its young company called *hittin'. Bring in 'Da Noise* played to rave reviews and sellout audiences downtown and also was transferred to Broadway, making a star of its 22-year-old lead performer and choreographer, Savion Glover, whom many critics have called the world's best tap dancer.

Tony Awards hype. In May, *Rent* and *Bring in 'Da Noise,* as expected, collected Tony Award nominations for best musical, but the other two nominees in that category, *Swingin' on a Star* and *Chronicle of a Death Foretold,* came as major surprises. Both were little-known and long-closed productions that had originated in nonprofit theaters. The nominations had been expected to go to two lavish Broadway-born spectacles, *Victor/Victoria* and *Big.*

Victor/Victoria's star, Julie Andrews, resentful that no one else from her hit musical had been nominated for a Tony, turned down her best-actress nomination in a dramatic post-performance speech that made national headlines. But Andrews may have had the last laugh. Despite its Tony boycott, *Victor/Victoria* did record-breaking business at the box office in the weeks following the Tonys, proving that star power, not awards, was still the strongest audience draw on Broadway.

Further Tony Awards controversy ensued when producer David Merrick sought a court injunction to stop voting in the best score of a musical category. Merrick argued that it was unfair of the nominating committee to consider only 4 of the 16 songs from his production of Rodgers and Hammerstein's *State Fair,* which appeared as a motion picture in 1945 and 1962. Merrick lost his case, but the off-stage drama made for one of the most dramatic Tony Awards in years.

Off-Broadway shows. Although the Broadway news drew attention—and audiences—away from off-Broadway shows, there were some highlights in the city's smaller theaters. In February, a hothouse flower of a musical called *Floyd Collins* opened at Playwrights Horizons. Composer and lyricist Adam Guettal and director Tina Landau turned the true story of a 1920's Kentuckian, who was trapped in a cave and died, into a meditation on our country's fascination with tragedy and a tribute to the power of imagination. Composer Polly Pen's musical adaptation of a 1920's silent film about a Moscow housing shortage, *Bed & Sofa,* also received excellent reviews at the Vineyard Theatre.

The American premiere of British playwright Caryl Churchill's drama about a collision between contemporary Britain and the spirit world, *The Skriker,* had a well-received run at the Joseph Papp Public Theater. Signature Theater devoted its 1995–1996 season to the work of African American playwright Adrienne Kennedy, who won the 1964 Obie award for playwriting, an award for off-Broadway theater

---

Tony Awards winners in 1996

Best Play, *Master Class,* Terrence McNally.
Best Musical, *Rent.*
Best Play Revival, *A Delicate Balance.*
Best Musical Revival, *The King and I.*
Leading Actor in a Play, George Grizzard,
  A Delicate Balance.
Leading Actress in a Play, Zoe Caldwell, *Master Class.*
Leading Actor in a Musical, Nathan Lane,
  A Funny Thing Happened on the Way to the Forum.
Leading Actress in a Musical, Donna Murphy,
  The King and I.
Featured Actor in a Play, Ruben Santiago-Hudson,
  Seven Guitars.
Featured Actress in a Play, Audra McDonald,
  Master Class.
Featured Actor in a Musical, Wilson Jermaine Heredia,
  Rent.
Featured Actress in a Musical, Ann Duquesnay,
  Bring in 'Da Noise, Bring in 'Da Funk.
Direction of a Play, Gerald Gutierrez,
  A Delicate Balance.
Direction of a Musical, George C. Wolfe,
  Bring in 'Da Noise, Bring in 'Da Funk.
Book of a Musical, Jonathan Larson, *Rent.*
Original Musical Score, Jonathan Larson, *Rent.*
Scenic Design, Brian Thomson, *The King and I.*
Costume Design, Roger Kirk, *The King and I.*
Lighting Design, Jules Fisher and Peggy Eisenhauer,
  Bring in 'Da Noise, Bring in 'Da Funk.
Choreography, Savion Glover, *Bring in 'Da Noise,
  Bring in 'Da Funk.*
Regional Theater, Alley Theater, Houston, Texas.

Theater

sponsored by New York City's *Village Voice*. Although the belated Broadway premiere of Sam Shepard's 1978 Pulitzer Prize-winning *Buried Child* had a disappointing run in 1996, Signature devoted its 1996–1997 season to a retrospective of Shepard's work.

A presidential election year brought a run of political plays on and off Broadway in the fall: Lincoln Center produced Christopher Durang's *Sex and Longing,* starring Sigourney Weaver, at Broadway's Cort Theater; Douglas McGrath's one-man show *Political Animal* came to the off-Broadway Westside Theater; and Theresa Rebeck's *View of the Dome* played at the New York Theatre Workshop.

New York's international festivals. The summer of 1996 saw the successful launch of the Lincoln Center Festival, New York's first major summer international multiarts festival. Its well-received theater offerings included the complete plays of Samuel Beckett, produced by the Gate Theatre of Dublin, and the long-awaited American premiere of the British experimental ensemble Theatre de Complicitie with *The Three Lives of Lucie Cabrol.*

The Brooklyn Academy of Music's 1996 Next Wave Festival, which ran from September through December, featured *Chimere,* a production by the Zingaro Equestrian and Musical Theatre, a French company featuring 26 horses, 22 performers, and 10 musicians; *The Beatification of Area Boy* by Nobel Prize-winning Nigerian playwright Wole Soyinka;

and French Canadian director Robert Lepage's *The Seven Streams of the River Ota,* an eight-hour epic about Hiroshima as seen through the eyes of a photographer who survived the atomic blast.

Regional Theater. Perhaps the most talked-about regional production of the year was a musical version of *Faust,* the legendary character who made a pact with the devil. With music by pop composer Randy Newman, *Faust* enjoyed a sellout run at Chicago's Goodman Theatre in the fall of 1996.

British playwright Patrick Marber's *Dealer's Choice,* a play about a compulsive gambler, was another regional hit. After its American premiere at the Olympic Arts Festival in Atlanta, Georgia, it played at New Haven, Connecticut's Long Wharf Theatre in late 1996 and seemed destined for a Broadway run.

Shakespeare revisited. In August in Great Britain, William Shakespeare's *The Two Gentlemen of Verona* inaugurated London's new Globe Theatre, a replica of the playhouse that was destroyed in 1644. The round, three-story, open-air theater brought the original Globe back to life—complete with a thatched roof and the *bear pit* in the center for standing audience members. Although the actors had to compete with the noise of airplanes overhead and motor boats on the River Thames, the performances of *The Two Gentlemen* restored the lively interaction between audience members and performers that was a part of the theater experience in the 1600's.

Theater goers fill the new Globe Theatre in London after it opened in August. The new Globe is a replica of the Shakespearian theater destroyed in 1644.

Death of a legend. If Jonathan Larson's death was the galvanizing event of the early theatrical year, the death of legendary producer Bernard Jacobs on August 27 at the age of 80 was the signpost event of late 1996. Jacobs, along with Gerald Schoenfeld, ran the Shubert Organization, the oldest and most powerful producing organization in the country. For 24 years, Jacobs and Schoenfeld were responsible for much of what opened on Broadway, including shows such as *Cats* and *A Chorus Line*.

Racial tension in theater. In June at the annual Theatre Communications Group (TCG) conference for nonprofit theaters, African American playwright August Wilson gave an unexpected jolt with his controversial keynote address. Wilson decried inequalities in funding for minority theaters and the inability of critics to analyze the work of playwrights whose works address the themes of a minority culture. Wilson's most controversial remarks centered on *color-blind* casting (casting actors in roles regardless of race), which he compared to having slaves "summoned to the plantation house to entertain the slave owner." Wilson's words were a harsh reminder of the unresolved racial tensions that plague American culture, but many at the conference remained confident that theater could air those conflicts and provide a resolution. ☐ Karen Fricker

In *World Book,* see **Shakespeare; Theater.**

Togo. See Africa.

Toronto experienced a transitional year in 1996. Ontario's largest city showed signs of pulling out of the economic recession that hit Canada in the early 1990's. But the unemployment rate in Metropolitan Toronto—Toronto proper and the four cities and one borough that surround it—stubbornly hovered between 9 and 10 percent throughout the year. In addition, Metro Toronto struggled with the impact of an austerity program imposed by a Progressive Conservative provincial government that had pledged to reduce the deficit and cut taxes. The budget-cutting triggered a five-week strike and one of the largest demonstrations in Toronto's history.

The good news. Several basic economic indicators showed improvement in 1996. In September, the number of people in Metro Toronto receiving welfare fell below 100,000 for the first time since 1991, though tighter eligibility rules accounted for part of the drop. Housing starts in Metro Toronto and surrounding communities rose from 15,200 in 1995 to 22,800 in 1996. Sales of automobiles, refrigerators, and other durable goods rose by 15 percent in the same period. Office vacancy rates, 25 percent in 1992, fell to 18.6 percent in 1996.

Budget backlash. A plan by the government of Ontario's Premier Mike Harris to lay off more than 10,000 civil servants triggered a strike that began on February. At least 50,000 members of the Ontario Public Service Employees' Union (OPSEU), most of them based in the Toronto area, stayed off the job until late March. Despite the strike, essential services were maintained. Although the OPSEU won some concessions on job security and on benefits for discharged workers, the government announced on April 11 that it would proceed with the layoffs, which represented 13 percent of public employees.

The Harris government's deficit-fighting austerity program, which included a 20-percent reduction in provincial grants to municipalities and a 21.6-percent reduction in payments to welfare recipients, gave some relief to taxpayers in 1996. The program, which was included in the budget approved by the government in May, gave a 7 percent reduction in provincial income taxes. The budget also cut funds for Metro Toronto's public transportation system, hospitals, schools, and libraries.

In late October, tens of thousands of people converged on downtown Toronto for union-led demonstrations against the budget cuts. On October 25, protesters shut down Toronto's public transportation system. Picket lines at 300 other sites delayed or halted the delivery of other government services. On October 26, at least 75,000 people joined in a 3-mile (5-kilometer) march—one of the largest in Toronto's history—from downtown Toronto to the provincial legislature in Queen's Park. Despite the demonstrations, Harris refused to alter his austerity program and said he would seek additional budget cuts in 1997.

Subway developments. On Sept. 29, 1996, the Metropolitan Council, which provides most of Metro Toronto's transit services, voted to complete the 3.7-mile (5.3-kilometer) Sheppard Avenue subway. The Sheppard line was the only survivor among four rapid transit lines proposed in 1990. On August. 15, the council, concerned that the Harris government might cut funds for public transportation, had voted to build the line's tunnels but not to fund tracks, stations, or trains. The provincial government agreed to pay $511 million (Canadian dollars) of the $875-million project. Metro Toronto would pay for the rest.

Regional reorganization. On January 16, a task force charged by the provincial government with proposing a new system of government for the Greater Toronto Area (GTA) recommended replacing the GTA's regional governments with one ruling body called the Greater Toronto Council. The GTA currently encompassed five regional governments as well as the governments of 30 cities and towns. The task force offered 51 recommendations for reorganizing the GTA.

Al Leach, Ontario's minister of municipal affairs, passed the report to several committees composed of private citizens and elected officials. The committees were charged with restructuring the GTA by 1997 as well as making recommendations for reorganizing municipal governments throughout Ontario.

☐ David Lewis

In *World Book,* see **Toronto.**

Toys and games. Retail toy sales in the United States in 1996 rose nearly 5 percent over 1995 sales, making it one of the best sales years since the beginning of the decade. Some industry watchers speculated that the presidential election fueled sales, since election years are usually good ones for retailers. Others theorized that consumers' increasing demand for competitive pricing sent more and more shoppers to discount stores for all their holiday buying needs. Apparently, toy shoppers were often able to find what they needed, or wanted, at the discounts: Approximately 42 percent of all toy purchases were made at the large, mass merchandising discount chains.

Going for the gold. Several toy manufacturers joined the winning team with toys inspired by the 1996 Summer Olympic Games held in Atlanta, Georgia. The Hasbro Toy Group of Pawtucket, Rhode Island, introduced Olympic greats Nadia Comaneci, Bruce Jenner, and Florence Griffith-Joyner into their Starting Lineup brand of sports action figures. Another set of Starting Lineup action figures depicted the members of the United States Olympic basketball team—the "Dream Team."

Olympic Gymnast Barbie from Mattel Incorporated of El Segundo, California, wore a red, white, and blue leotard bearing an official 1996 torch logo and sported a gold medal. The jointed doll could perform flips, cartwheels, and somersaults using a special tumbling-belt accessory.

Beanie Babies, the latest incarnation of the homely bean-bag, were among the most popular toys of 1996.

The official team mascots for Atlanta's Olympic Games were the Cabbage Patch Kids OlympiKids, available in two styles: one from Mattel Incorporated; and a handmade OlympiKid from Original Appalachian Artworks Incorporated of Cleveland, Georgia. Part of the purchase price of the dolls went to the support of the U.S. Olympic Team.

Out of this world. Again in 1996, outer space was a big theme in movies and TV, and the toy industry followed suit. Kids scooped up toys inspired by *Independence Day,* the summer movie thriller. Trendmasters Incorporated of St. Louis, Missouri, produced the *Independence Day* toys.

September 1996 was the 30th anniversary of the original "Star Trek" television show. To the delight of doll collectors everywhere, Mattel Incorporated rolled out a special Barbie & Ken Star Trek Gift Set. Packaged together, the dolls were authentically dressed as crew members of the *U.S.S. Enterprise,* for the space ship featured in the science-fiction series.

Chicago Bulls basketball player Michael Jordan brought his star power to a blockbuster motion picture, *Space Jam,* which combined a live-action Jordan with animated Looney Tunes characters. Toys based

on the movie, including a talking Michael Jordan doll from Playmates Toys, Incorporated, of La Mirada, California, were big hits.

Thrills and designer fashions. Video games continued to score a hit. Nintendo of America of Redmond, Washington, premiered the long-awaited Nintendo Ultra 64 in late September. The "next generation" of video-game hardware, Nintendo Ultra 64 featured a power-packed 64-bit microprocessor capable of producing dazzling visual effects, such as sophisticated 3D imaging. It was a hot holiday favorite with older children and teens.

Goosebumps, a series of adventure books published by Scholastic Incorporated of New York, sent shivers and tingles up the spines of young readers. Videocassette versions proved popular, as did Goosebumps games, manufactured by Milton Bradley Company of East Longmeadow, Massachusetts. Many children chose Melanie's Main Mall, manufac-

Among games, one of the most popular items in 1996 was Nintendo Ultra 64—the "next generation" of video-game hardware, capable of 3D imaging.

tured by Cap Toys Inc. of Bedford Heights, Ohio, as a 1996 favorite. The play-set included a working escalator, fountain, and revolving door. Mattel's Barbie Fashion Designer enabled creative, technically minded children to design fashions for Barbie on their computers.

From simple to sophisticated. Beanie Babies—stuffed toys that don't talk, walk, sing, or appear in a major motion picture—were among the most popular toys of 1996. These simple, floppy, bead-filled critters produced by Ty Inc. of Oak Brook, Illinois, appealed especially to young children, and their extremely modest price appealed to adults. Pinchers the Lobster, Twigs the Giraffe, and Lucky the Ladybug joined nearly 80 others in the line, spreading "Beaniemania" across the country. For children who wished to videotape their Beanie Babies collection for posterity, Tyco Toys, Inc. of Mt. Laurel, New Jersey, introduced the Video-Cam. Weighing under one pound and offering one-button operation, the VideoCam enabled children, ages 6 to 12, to record black-and white video images for playback.

Surf's up. Traveling on the information super-highway, surfing the net, and playing a favorite video game all became easier with the 1996 introduction of the Sega Saturn Net Link, by Sega of America, Inc. of Redwood City, California. A modem and custom-designed Internet browser, this Internet peripheral plugged into the Sega Saturn, the company's 32-bit microprocessor video-game hardware system. Net Link enhanced the video-game system for networked gaming, electronic mail, on-line chats, World Wide Web connections, and other services. Trivia buffs could now square off against counterparts from around the globe, playing Trivial Pursuit Interactive. Hasbro Interactive Worldwide, premiered this new live, multiplayer version of the popular board game in 1996 through an exclusive arrangement with America Online, one of the leading companies that provided access to the Internet global computer network. □ Diane P. Cardinale

In *World Book,* see **Doll; Game; Toy.**

Track and field. Michael Johnson, a 28-year-old American, had been a world-class sprinter since 1989. Svetlana Masterkova, a 28-year-old Russian, had been a world-class middle-distance runner before she took a two-year maternity leave in 1994. In 1996, both won two Olympic gold medals and were among track and field's outstanding athletes.

Johnson. In 1996, Johnson became the first man to win gold medals in both the 200-meter and 400-meter sprints at one Olympics. (At the 1984 Olympics, Valerie Brisco-Hooks became the first person to win both events.) Johnson had won both events at the U.S. championships in 1995, and, in 1996, he won every 400-meter final he raced, stretching his streak to 57 since 1989. He lost only two 200-meter finals in 1996, both to Namibia's Frank Fredericks. At Johnson's urging, the International Amateur Athletic Federation (IAAF), track and field's world governing body, adjusted the Olympic 200-meter and 400-meter time schedules to different days, to make his quest for a double victory more feasible.

At the U.S. Olympic trials, held June 14 through 23 in Atlanta, Georgia, Johnson won the 400 meters in 43.44 seconds, the third-fastest time ever. Then he won the 200 in world-record time—19.66 seconds.

At the Olympics, Johnson won the 400 in 43.49 seconds. In the 200 final, he defeated Fredericks by 4 meters in 19.32 seconds, setting his second world record in five weeks. That final was Johnson's eighth race in seven days. He passed up an almost sure gold medal in the 4x400-meter relay because of a strained right thigh, but the United States won without him.

Masterkova. On August 14 in Zurich, Switzerland, Masterkova set a world record in her first mile of 4 minutes 12.56 seconds. Nine days later in Brussels, Belgium, she set a world record of 2:28.98 for 1,000 meters. She also ran the year's fastest times for 800 meters (1:56.04) and 1,500 meters (3:56.77). In the Olympics, she beat the favorites—Maria Mutola of Mozambique in the 800 meters and Hassiba Boulmerka of Algeria and Sonia O'Sullivan of Ireland in the 1,500 meters—to win both gold medals.

Olympics. The United States won 23 medals in track and field, followed by Russia with 10, and Kenya with 8. The United States won 13 gold medals to 3 each for Russia, Germany, and France. Masterkova was not the only women's double winner. France's Marie-José Perec won the women's 200 meters in 22.12 seconds and the 400 in 48.25 seconds.

American Gail Devers became the second woman to win the 100 meters in successive Olympics (Wyomia Tyus did so in 1964 and 1968). In a thrilling, three-way photo finish, Devers and Merlene Ottey of Jamaica both finished in 10.94 seconds. Ottey's head crossed the finish line first, but Devers's torso was first to the tape, and so Devers won the gold. Gwen Torrence of the United States finished third at 10.96 seconds. Canada's Donovan Bailey won the men's 100 meters in world-record 9.84 seconds. In

Track and field

that event, Linford Christie of Great Britain was disqualified after making two false starts.

Jackie Joyner-Kersee, the 34-year-old American seeking her third consecutive gold medal in the women's heptathlon, withdrew after one event because of an old hamstring injury, but she returned in the women's long jump and won a bronze medal. Sergei Bubka, the 32-year-old Ukrainian who has broken the world pole vault record 35 times outdoors and indoors, withdrew during qualifying rounds because of a damaged Achilles tendon.

Grand Prix. Daniel Komen, a men's 5,000-meter runner from Kenya, and Russian-born hurdler Ludmila Enquist of Sweden won the $200,000 overall prizes in the Grand Prix series. Komen, age 20 years, also set a world record of 7:20.67 for 3,000 meters.

Four of those Grand Prix meets—in Oslo, Norway; Zurich, Switzerland; Brussels, Belgium; and Berlin, Germany—were known as the *Golden Four*. Any athletes who swept an event in the four meets would share 20 one-kilogram (2.2-pound) gold bars. Five athletes did—Fredericks in the men's 200 meters, Wilson Kipketer of Denmark in the men's 800 meters, Jonathan Edwards of Great Britain in the men's triple jump, Lars Riedel of Germany in the men's discus throw, and Stefka Kostadinova of Bulgaria in the women's high jump.   □ Frank Litsky

See also **Olympic Games** special report: **The 1996 Olympics.** In *World Book,* see **Track and field.**

Transportation. The first private trains to operate in the United Kingdom in almost 50 years began running on Feb. 4, 1996, as part of the government's plan to privatize the nation's rail system. The plan, detailed in the Railways Act of 1993, separated the operation of trains from ownership of track and signaling systems. Private companies bid for franchises to operate trains over the network for periods of from 7 to 15 years. Railtrack, the company formed to operate the track, was privatized in May 1996 with the sale of more than $2.6 billion in shares.

European railroads. Elsewhere in Europe, government-owned railroads were also opened up to competition and an influx of private capital. Italy, Austria, Germany, and the Netherlands all took steps toward separating railroad operations from ownership of track and signaling. Germany, which had planned to privatize Deutsche Bahn, its state-owned railroad, by 1999, invested about $10 billion in the system in 1996 to speed up the privatization process.

Canadian railroads. On July 1, 1996, the Canada Transportation Act went into effect, reducing regulatory oversight of the railroads. The act allowed railroads to withdraw unprofitable services and sell off abandoned lines without the approval of the Canadian Transportation Agency. The purpose of the act was to encourage the formation of private, short-line railways to provide shippers more competitive service. After the act went into effect,

World outdoor track and field records established in 1996

Men

Event	Holder	Country	Where set	Date	Record
50-km walk	Thierry Toutain	France	Hencourt, France	September 29	3:40:57.9
100 meters	Donovan Bailey	Canada	Atlanta, Georgia	July 27	9.84
200 meters	Michael Johnson	U.S.A.	Atlanta, Georgia	August 1	19.32
3,000 meters	Daniel Komen	Kenya	Rieti, Italy	September 1	7:20.67
2 miles	Daniel Komen	Kenya	Lappeenranta, Finland	July 14	8:03.54
10,000 meters	Salah Hissou	Morocco	Brussels, Belgium	August 23	26:38.08
Javelin throw	Jan Zelezny	Czech Republic	Jena, Germany	May 25	323 ft. 1 in. (98.48 m)

Women

Event	Holder	Country	Where set	Date	Record
1,000 meters	Svetlana Masterkova	Russia	Brussels, Belgium	August 23	2:28.98
1 mile	Svetlana Masterkova	Russia	Zurich, Switzerland	August 14	4:12.56
Pole vault	Emma George	Australia	Sapporo, Japan	July 14	14 ft. 7¼ in. (4.45 m)
Hammer throw	Mihaela Melinte	Romania	Cluj, Romania	May 12	227 ft. 9 in. (69.42 m)

m = meters

Source: USA Track and Field

All 1,700 residents of Weyauwega, Wisconsin, are fored to evacuate the town after a freight train carrying 1 million pounds (452,000 kilograms) of propane derailed on March 4.

Calgary-based Canadian Pacific Limited's CP Rail System announced that it would withdraw service from about 25 percent of its network, primarily in eastern Canada and in the midwestern and northeastern United States. Similarly, Montreal-based Canadian National Railways, which was privatized in 1995, announced that it planned to cut 25 percent of its service by 1999.

Magnetic levitation train. In April and May 1996, the German government approved the construction of the world's first magnetic levitation train. The train, to be completed in 2005, was designed to travel from Hamburg to Berlin in less than an hour. Conventional trains in the mid-1990's completed the same distance in three hours. A magnetic levitation train has no motor on board. Electromagnets in the track react with magnets on the train to move the train forward. The interaction of the magnets also levitates the train above the track.

Railroad consolidation. On July 3, the Surface Transportation Board, a successor agency to the Interstate Commerce Commission, approved the acquisition of Southern Pacific Rail Corp. of San Francisco by Union Pacific Corp. of Bethlehem, Pennsylvania. The $5.4 billion purchase made the Union Pacific the nation's largest railroad and decreased the number of major railroad companies west of the Mississippi River from five to two. In the eastern United States, a bidding war broke out in October for Philadelphia-based Conrail, Inc. A bid of $8.4 billion by CSX Transportation Corp. of Jacksonville, Florida, was countered with a $9.15 billion bid by Norfolk Southern Corp. of Norfolk, Virginia.

Ocean shipping. On Sept. 24, 1996, the U.S. Senate passed the Maritime Security Act, authorizing $1 billion in funding for the U.S. private merchant marine fleet over the next 10 years. The House of Representatives had passed the bill in 1995. The act,

which replaced a program that provided $200 million in annual funding to ocean-shipping lines, also eliminated trade-route and service restrictions. Proponents of the act hoped that it would help ensure the future of the U.S. merchant marine, which had dwindled from more than 2,000 active vessels in the 1940's to only 300 by 1996.

Freighter accident. A freighter owned by a Hong Kong shipping company but registered in Liberia crashed into a pier in the Riverwalk shopping district of New Orleans, Louisiana, on Dec. 14, 1996. More than 100 people were injured and damage to a multi-story shopping mall, hotel, and other businesses was estimated at $250 million. ☐ Ian Savage

See also **Automobile, Aviation.** In *World Book,* see **Bus; Electric railroad; Subway; Transportation.**

Trinidad and Tobago. See **West Indies.**

Tunisia. See **Middle East.**

Turkey. The chain of *secular* (not associated with a religion) governments that had ruled Turkey since the founding of the modern state in 1923 was broken on June 28, 1996, when Necmettin Erbakan, leader of a Muslim group called the Welfare Party (Refah), formed a coalition government and became prime minister. His coalition partner was former Prime Minister Tansu Ciller, who was made deputy prime minister and foreign minister. The coalition narrowly won approval by 278 votes in the 550-seat parliament on July 8.

Turkey had been politically unstable since 1995, partly due to rivalry between Islamists with popular support, on the one hand, and pro-Western, secular politicians and the military, on the other. Erbakan's party won the largest percentage of the vote—21.8 percent—in parliamentary elections in December 1995 but failed to win a ruling majority. Divisions among secularists and charges of political corruption added to the instability. Ciller formed a coalition government in March 1996 with Mesut Yilmaz, leader of the center-right Motherland Party, which fell apart in June due to internal bickering. Ciller herself refused in 1996 to account for $6.5 million that disappeared before the government led by her fell in September 1995.

Economy. Turkey's political problems fueled economic instability in 1996. Erbakan's announcement in July that 7 million government employees and pensioners would receive a 50-percent pay raise was expected to worsen inflation, already running at more than 85 percent. Foreign debt rose to at least $73 billion in early 1996, up nearly $8 billion from the previous year. Turkey's 1996 trade deficit was expected to exceed $20 billion.

Kurds. Abdullah Ocalan, head of the militant Kurdish Workers Party (PKK), warned on March 21 that he would renew a campaign of urban violence in Turkey. Between July and October 29, female suicide bombers killed 20 people in separate attacks in the towns of Tunceli, Adana, and Sivas.

Some 20,000 people have died since the PKK began a campaign in 1984 to establish an independent Kurdish state in Turkey. The conflict reportedly has drained Turkey of an estimated $8 billion annually since 1984.

U.S. relations. Erbakan initially sought to calm the concerns of the United States about his government. He persuaded parliament in late July 1996 to approve a five-month renewal of Operation Provide Comfort, a U.S.-led military alliance set up at the end of the 1991 Persian Gulf War to protect Iraqi Kurds from Iraq. Turkey hoped to win U.S. support for its request to buy Iraqi oil if Iraq received permission from the United Nations to sell oil for humanitarian goods.

The United States, however, was highly critical of Erbakan's efforts to improve Turkey's relations with states accused of terrorism and human rights violations. In August 1996, Erbakan signed a $20 billion gas deal with Iran. He traveled to Libya and Nigeria in early October in an effort to improve economic ties. Erbakan's trip to Libya, where Libyan leader Muammar Muhammad al-Qadhafi condemned Turkey's treatment of Kurds, angered many Turks. Erbakan survived a parliamentary vote of confidence in mid-October, however.

Israel. Arab countries and Iran condemned Turkey for signing a military agreement with Israel, which became public in April when Israeli F-16 fighter aircraft began a joint training exercise in Turkey. The agreement, which Turkey had signed in February, also allowed naval visits, shared intelligence, and joint training at military academies. In August, the two countries signed a defense industry cooperation accord.

Aegean Sea. A crisis was narrowly averted in late January when the United States convinced Turkey and Greece to withdraw warships from around a rocky island in the Aegean Sea that was claimed by both. Tension between the two countries increased in recent years due to rival claims to islands in the Aegean Sea and to Turkey's charge that Greece had aided the PKK. □ Christine Helms

See also **Erbakan, Necmettin; Greece; Iraq; Libya; Middle East** (Facts in brief table). In *World Book,* see **Kurds; Turkey.**

Turkmenistan. See Asia.

Uganda. See Africa.

Ukraine in 1996 experienced political and economic turmoil surrounding the adoption of a new constitution and a new currency. The year ended with a controversial agreement with neighboring Russia to resolve a long-standing dispute over the former Soviet Black Sea naval fleet.

On May 27, President Leonid Kuchma dismissed Prime Minister Yevhen Marchuk, citing Marchuk's weak support for economic reform. In his place, Kuchma named a political ally, Pavlo Lazarenko. The former deputy prime minister pledged to give renewed attention to Ukraine's pressing economic challenges, including payment of back wages and attracting greater foreign investment.

Political and constitutional crises. In early 1996, Ukraine was the only former Soviet republic that had failed to adopt a new, post-Soviet constitution. Ukrainian leaders had agreed in June 1995 to a "constitutional agreement" dividing political power between the president and the *Rada* (parliament) until a new constitution could be ratified. In March 1996, a constitutional committee submitted a draft constitution to the Rada. Liberals complained that the draft concentrated too much power in the presidency, while nationalists complained that it offered autonomy to the province of Crimea, which is largely populated with ethnic Russians.

In June 1996, the speaker of the Rada, Oleksander Moroz, triggered a crisis when he claimed that the June 1995 constitutional agreement had expired. Fearing a prolonged political battle, Kuchma called for a national referendum to ratify the constitution. Kuchma's proposal energized the Rada, which feared that a public referendum would render its input irrelevant. On June 28, 1996, the Rada, after a 23-hour session, adopted the new constitution.

In the wake of his victory, Kuchma renominated Lazarenko as prime minister. Lazarenko repeated his earlier promises to address economic reforms and stressed the need to fight corruption in the government and economy. On July 16, Lazarenko survived an assassination attempt when a bomb exploded near his car. Officials blamed the attack on Lazarenko's anticorruption pledge.

New currency and economic reforms. On September 2, Ukraine introduced a new unit of currency—the *hryvna*. Ukrainian leaders hoped that by replacing the *karbovanet*—a temporary currency used since 1992—the country would gain new monetary stability that would, in turn, encourage greater foreign investment. To ensure time for the hryvna to gain acceptance and to combat illegal currency speculation, the government announced a price freeze for the month of September 1996. The introduction of the currency, however, went so smoothly that the karbovanet was phased out ahead of schedule and the price freeze was lifted on September 16.

Lazarenko announced his government's three-year economic program on October 15. The plan showed signs of political compromise, perhaps to ensure its passage by the liberal-dominated Rada. The program retreated from earlier promises to the International Monetary Fund (IMF) to close dozens of unprofitable coal mines and to end state protection of selected industrial and agricultural sectors. However, IMF and World Bank support remained essential for Ukraine's economic growth.

Relations with Russia. In October, President Kuchma and Russian Prime Minister Viktor Chernomyrdin announced an agreement to end the long-simmering dispute over the division of the former Soviet Black Sea naval fleet. The fleet was based at the Crimean port city of Sevastopol, and both Russia and Ukraine had claimed control of both the naval base and the fleet. Tensions rose in September and October, as prominent Russian leaders reasserted Russia's claims to Sevastopol. In response, Ukrainian politicians appeared to harden their opposition to any form of compromise. Strong objections to any agreement were voiced in both countries, and by the end of 1996, no agreement on the fate of the port or the former Soviet fleet in the Black Sea was reached. The Black Sea fleet dispute remained the final obstacle to the signing of a friendship treaty between Russia and Ukraine. □ Steven L. Solnick

See also **Europe** (Facts in brief table). In *World Book*, see **Ukraine**.

Unemployment. See Economics; Labor.

United Kingdom. In 1996, John Major survived as prime minister of Great Britain with the backing of only a small majority in the House of Commons. With the Conservatives far behind the Labour Party in the polls, Major delayed the general election until the last possible moment—May 1997.

Government scandals. On Feb. 23, 1996, Peter Thurnham became the third Conservative Member of Parliament (MP) in four months to quit the party, cutting the government's majority margin to two. Thurnham criticized the government's handling of a report it had commissioned from Senior Judge Sir Richard Scott on the sale of weapons to Iraq in the 1980's. At that time, the government had banned the sale of arms to both Iran and Iraq, which were at war. Scott concluded that the government had secretly allowed some sales of British weapons to Iraq. His report accused William Waldegrave, then a foreign office minister, of repeatedly misleading the House of Commons. On Feb. 26, 1996, the Commons voted to accept the government's report.

Rod Richards, a junior Welsh-office minister, was forced to resign on June 2 after it was found that he was having an affair. Richards, a married man with three children, was the 16th insider or parliamentary aide forced to resign over private or business behavior since Major became prime minister in 1990.

On Oct. 16, 1996, the House of Commons approved an investigation into allegations that former minister William Hamilton had accepted money from Mohammed al-Fayed, owner of Harrods, the fashionable London department store, in return for furthering al-Fayed's interests in the House of Commons. The role of the paymaster general, David Willetts, in the affair was also to be investigated.

Conservative Party issues. On April 10, the Conservatives lost a parliamentary by-election in south Staffordshire, in central England, normally a party stronghold. A 22 percent swing gave the seat to Labour and cut the government's majority to one. In local elections on May 2, the Conservatives lost 578 council seats, half of their preelection total.

The European Union (EU), an organization of 15 Western European states that promotes internal economic and political cooperation, continued to create bitter divisions within the Conservative Party. MP's who opposed closer integration with the EU pressured Major to campaign during the next general election on a pledge that the United Kingdom (U.K.) would not join the European Monetary and Economic Union (EMU), a 1992 pact establishing a common currency and central bank among EU members scheduled to begin in 1999. But Major insisted that the government would only make up its mind when the precise terms of EMU were known.

A new political party was launched by billionaire Sir James Goldsmith in March 1996. The Referendum Party had one aim—to hold a *referendum* (a bill submitted to the direct vote of the people) on the U.K.'s membership in the EU. Conservatives feared that the new party could make the difference between the Conservatives winning or losing the next election.

Beef crisis. Relations with the European Union plummeted when the British government revealed that people who ate beef from cattle with the neurological disease bovine spongiform encephalopathy (BSE) may risk developing Creutzfeldt-Jakob disease (CJD), a fatal, degenerative disease of the human brain. In the March 20 announcement, Health Secretary Steven Dorrell stated that a new strain of the disorder had been found in the U.K. in 10 people under the age of 42 and that it may be linked to the consumption of infected beef. The cattle were believed to have contracted BSE after being fed the remains of sheep infected with scrapie, a condition similar to BSE. As panic spread, beef consumption plummeted, and foreign governments banned British beef.

At an EU meeting on April 3, the U.K. agreed to a large-scale slaughter of cattle. In return, the EU promised to cover 70 percent of the cost of compensating farmers for the loss of their livestock. The EU, however, rejected a demand by the U.K. to lift the ban on British beef exports. On May 21, Major retaliated by using the U.K. veto to block EU decisions on a variety of matters. In a compromise reached on June 20, EU leaders agreed to lift the export ban in stages if Britain adopted new safety measures, including the slaughter of up to 4 million animals believed to be at risk of the disease. Britain did not present plans for a slaughter until December, however, and there was little sign of a lifting of the ban at year-end.

Economy. The government hoped that improvements in the economy would create good will in voters. Consumers spent more, unemployment fell, interest rates were at a 30-year low, and housing values rose in 1996. Manufacturing gained strength, and inflation was unusually low by historical standards. Responsibility for translating the economic recovery into Conservative votes rested with Chancellor of the Exchequer (treasury head) Kenneth Clarke. Clarke had cut interest rates four times since December 1995, to less than 5.8 percent, giving millions of homeowners the cheapest home loans in a generation. But the last cut in June 1996 incurred the wrath of the Bank of England, which feared that inflationary pressures might begin to build.

Opposition difficulties. The Labour Party, far ahead in the polls after abandoning many of its left-wing policies, had its own difficulties. On Jan. 8, 1996, an industrial tribunal declared unlawful Labour's policy of choosing parliamentary candidates in some constituencies from women-only lists. The party had introduced the policy to boost the number of women MP's. But a tribunal in Leeds declared that this discriminated against men, and the party was forced to abandon the policy.

Dunblane massacre. On March 13, a gunman killed 16 children and a teacher at Dunblane, Scotland, in the U.K.'s worst mass murder of modern times. Thomas Hamilton, a local man, opened fire on a class of 5- and 6-year-olds in the gymnasium of the elementary school. He injured 12 other children and 2 teachers before killing himself. Hamilton had previously complained of a public conspiracy to bar him from organizing youth activities.

On August 13, six Conservative MP's on the 11-member House of Commons home affairs committee outvoted Labour members and rejected a total ban on handguns. They said that the problems posed by the 200,000 legally held handguns in the U.K. were far outweighed by those caused by the much greater numbers of unlicensed guns. Hamilton, however, had been armed with four legally held guns. Opinion polls showed almost three-quarters of all Britons were in favor of a ban. The government later did ban all handguns larger than .22 caliber and the keeping of weapons at home.

Unlawful sentencing of children. On May 2, the High Court ruled that Home Secretary Michael Howard had acted unlawfully in raising the minimum sentences that two 10-year-old child murderers would have to serve. The boys were sentenced to indefinite detention for battering 2-year-old James Bulger to death in February 1993. The trial judge had recommended a minimum sentence of eight

Debris from a June 16 bomb blast lies scattered in the central shopping district of Manchester, England. The bomb, believed to have been planted by the IRA, injured more than 200 people.

years. Under English law, the final decision rested with the home secretary, and Howard increased the sentence to 15 years. Lawyers for the boys argued successfully that Howard had wrongly treated them as adults. Howard said that he would appeal.

New divorce law. The Family Law Bill, designed to stem the rising tide of marriage breakups in England and Wales, was passed by parliament on June 17, 1996. The law, the most fundamental divorce reform in 30 years, ended "quickie" divorces and introduced "no fault" divorces, in which neither party is assigned blame, after an 18-month waiting period to allow for "reflection and consideration."

Royal divorces. On April 17, the judgement of divorce for Queen Elizabeth's second son, Prince Andrew, and his wife Sarah was given after a hearing in a London courtroom. It automatically became absolute six weeks later. The couple had been separated since 1992.

On July 12, 1996, the divorce of Prince Charles, eldest son of Queen Elizabeth II, and Princess Diana was announced after more than three years of separation. The divorce became final on August 28. Diana relinquished any claim to becoming queen. She was to continue to be known as Diana, Princess of Wales, as long as she did not remarry. But she lost the title "Her Royal Highness," and so would no longer be an official part of the royal family, despite being the mother of a possible future king.

Opinion polls showed that the number of people who believed that the U.K. would be worse off without a royal family dropped from 77 percent in 1984, the year of Charles and Diana's wedding, to 34 percent in the mid-1990's. In an effort to restore public confidence, a so-called "way ahead" committee, headed by the queen and her husband, Prince Philip, their children, and senior palace officials, met to consider a number of reforms. These included ending the monarch's status as head of the Church of England and allowing the monarch to marry a Roman Catholic.

Royal apology. Queen Elizabeth and Prince Philip visited Poland and the Czech Republic in late March. In Prague, the queen formally apologized for the U.K.'s role in the 1938 appeasement of Nazi Germany that led to the end of democracy in what was then Czechoslovakia.

Stone of Scone. John Major unexpectedly announced in July that the historic Stone of Scone was to be returned to Scotland. Edward I had seized the stone, an ancient symbol of the Scottish monarchy, and had it placed under a throne in Westminster Abbey in London in 1296. The stone was returned to Edinburgh in November.   ☐ Ian Mather

See also **Europe** (Facts in brief table); **Farm and farming** Special Report: **Mad Cow Disease; United Kingdom** Special Report: **Will the British Monarchy Survive?** In *World Book,* see **United Kingdom.**

Royal scandals, on levels unprecedented in modern times, have brought into question the future role of the once mighty British monarchy.

Will the
BRITISH MONARCHY
Survive?

By Robert Huston

As the year 2000 approaches, Europe's royal houses—in Belgium, Denmark, Liechtenstein, Luxembourg, Monaco, the Netherlands, Norway, Spain, Sweden, and the United Kingdom—have found themselves in a varied state of readiness for the next millennium. Paradoxically, one of the longest established *dynasties* (line of kings or queens—the United Kingdom's House of Windsor—is under the greatest pressure for reform.

For Queen Elizabeth II, whose reign began in 1952, the view from Buckingham Palace may be grander than from any other European palace—but it is grimmer. Elizabeth described 1992 as her *annus horribilis* (year of horrors) after the separation of her two eldest sons, Prince Charles and Prince Andrew, from their respective wives, the former Lady Diana Spencer and Sarah Ferguson. The year 1996, however, may

have been worse for the Queen.

On August 28, 1996, at the High Court in London, one of the most highly publicized divorces of the century was made final with the stamping of a *decree absolute* (final divorce document), ending the 15-year marriage of Charles and Diana, the Prince and Princess of Wales. The decree would appear to have concluded one of the saddest chapters in the history of the royal family of the United Kingdom (UK). It would not, however, end speculation about the future of the monarchy in the UK.

Unlike other monarchies in Europe, the House of Windsor was asked to justify its very existence. During the 1990's, the public became increasingly disillusioned with a family that was once revered. Three of the queen's four children failed in marriage: Charles, Andrew (who also divorced in 1996), and Princess Anne (who was divorced from Mark Phillips in 1992). Once admired as a model family, the Windsors seemed to slip in stature as well as popularity. The British monarchy, at one time the most secure in Europe, appeared to stagger under the accumulated weight of years of scandal and rumor.

In one of her many ceremonial roles, Queen Elizabeth II, *left,* presides over the opening of Britain's parliament. Troubles in her royal family, such as the strained relations that eventually led to the divorce of her son and heir to the throne Prince Charles from Princess Diana, caused speculation about whether the monarchy could—or should—survive in the modern world.

The royal family exposed

A major factor in the public's disillusionment was undoubtedly the divorce of the Prince and Princess of Wales, and the way in which the events leading to their final break took place. Conducted with much bitterness and often blatant manipulation of the media by both parties, the marriage breakdown was made worse by persistent reports—and Charles's own eventual admission—of his long-time relationship with a married woman, Camilla Parker Bowles. The prince's admission of the affair cost him public respect and affection.

Prince Charles, unlike his sister, Princess Anne, failed to end his marriage with dignity or detachment from the glare of adverse publicity. Considered to be a thoughtful and caring—if distant—man, Charles still suffered much criticism in the years before the divorce. After the couple's separation, church leaders and prominent commentators openly debated the correctness of having a divorced king as the official head of the Church of England, the established religion of the United Kingdom. A king, who had remarried, would hardly be better, as far as the general public was concerned. Polls conducted in 1996 by mass-

Realm of the British Monarchy

The British monarch remains the head of state of the United Kingdom and 15 other countries, including Canada, Australia, and New Zealand.

market newspapers in the UK indicated that the divorced heir to the throne marrying a divorcée (Camilla Parker Bowles also divorced her husband) was *not* a prospect that most British citizens were prepared to accept. In one poll, 43 percent of the national population and 62 percent of regular Church of England members stated that a remarried heir to the throne should not become monarch. In fact, the British public showed a growing, general disenchantment with Prince Charles as the future king. Many felt that he should remove himself from the line of succession so that, on the death of his mother, the crown would pass to his eldest son, Prince William.

At the same time, the Princess of Wales—once the object of almost unqualified public adoration—attracted her own negative publicity. Diana is a self-confessed victim of *bulimia,* an eating disorder charact-terized by eating binges followed by self-induced vomiting or purging with laxatives. She was regarded by many as either unable or unwilling to adjust to the routine of the royal family, and she used the television to announce extramarital indiscretions. Her behavior—with that of the Duchess of York, Diana's former sister-in-law—was relentlessly report-ed in the media. Mass coverage, which once glamorized the young roy-als, turned on them, exposing their indiscretions.

The shattering of an image

Before the difficulties of the 1990's, the last major crisis the Windsors faced was the abdication of Edward VIII. In 1936, Edward shocked the world by giving up the throne for Wallis Simpson, a twice-divorced American woman whom he wanted to marry. After a national radio broadcast to announce his abdication, Edward left the country and married Mrs. Simpson in 1937. Edward and Wallis were given the titles of Duke and Duchess of Windsor, and they lived in exile in Europe. George VI, father of Queen Elizabeth II, ascended to the throne.

George VI and his consort Queen Elizabeth, now the Queen Mother,

The author

Robert Huston is a free-lance writer, who has written extensively about the British royal family.

did much to repair the damaged prestige of the monarchy after the abdication of Edward VIII. During World War II (1939-1945), King George and Queen Elizabeth made a positive contribution to the UK's war effort. They and their daughters, Princess Elizabeth and Princess Margaret, remained in London through the worst of the *blitz* (the German bombing of London from September 1940 to May 1941). They made patriotic broadcasts to the nation, and they visited bomb sites, military installations, and factories. Princess Elizabeth, the present queen, became a driver for army personnel. The royal family emerged from the war with its reputation greatly enhanced. When Queen Elizabeth II was crowned in 1953, public reverence was so high that nobody dreamed of criticizing the monarch. Even the media exercised strict self-censorship.

Loss of the Empire

The monarchy's unassailable post-war position was, however, under threat because the society, both at home and abroad, over which the monarch reigned was undergoing huge and rapid change. From the end of the 1950's, the remnants of the British Empire, one of the greatest in world history, began to disappear, and the monarchy's world status weakened as a result. Many British colonies in Africa and the Caribbean became independent nations. Although some former colonies, such as Canada, Australia, and New Zealand, retained the queen as head of state (represented by a governor general), most former colonies became fully independent republics. By 1996, only 14 UK dependencies remained, and one of these, Hong Kong, was due to revert to Chinese rule in 1997. Of the 53 independent countries remaining within the Commonwealth of Nations, 21 were monarchies, but only 16 retained the queen as head of state. (The Commonwealth of Nations is a group of countries and their dependencies that were formerly under British rule and that are now independent but joined economically to the United Kingdom.)

The position of the monarchy, with the major exception of Australia, has been in question far less in the Commonwealth countries than at home. Ironically, this may partly have been the result of the royal family's own efforts to build a more popular base of support at home—and in so doing, inadvertently undermining their own elevated status. By the late 1960's, a new breed of palace public relations officers were attempting to make the monarchy more accessible—in effect, to sell royalty to the public. In 1969, the British Broadcasting Corporation (BBC) was allowed to make "Royal Family," a television film that went "behind the scenes" to show the queen and her family at work and play. When the film showed members of the royal family as ordinary, the nation's view of them began to change radically.

The historian Ben Pimlott, whose biography *The Queen* appeared in 1996, asked: "Once the royal family got into the business of revealing secrets, could it pick and choose? In later years, many looked back and said the film started the rot." The more the media were told about the private life of royalty, the more they wanted to know.

The monarchy through time

Turmoil involving a British monarch or members of his or her family is not a new phenomenon.

HENRY VIII

Henry VIII had six wives, but fathered only three legitimate children and only one male heir. He married his first wife, Catherine of Aragon, his older brother's widow, in 1509. By 1525, she was 40 years old and had only one surviving child, Mary. Henry wanted a male heir. He eventually petitioned the pope to annul the marriage on the grounds that it was not lawful to wed one's brother's widow. When Pope Clement VII refused, Henry broke England's ties with the Roman Catholic Church and in 1533 established the Church of England in its stead with himself as head.

In 1533, Henry married Anne Boleyn, who gave birth to another heir, Elizabeth. Henry, however, wanted a son. Anne Boleyn was beheaded in 1536 on charges of adultery and incest. Henry's next wife, Jane Seymour, died shortly after giving birth to the long-awaited male heir, Edward. Henry's fourth marriage, to Anne of Cleves, was quietly annulled. Catherine Howard, his fifth wife, was beheaded on grounds of adultery. Henry remained married to Catherine Parr, the sixth wife, until his death in 1547.

All three of Henry's children ruled England: Edward VI who died in 1553 at age 16; Mary I, dubbed "Bloody Mary" for her violent persecution of Protestants; and Elizabeth I, whose long and successful reign (1558–1603) is called the Elizabethan Age.

Charles I, crowned in 1625, believed in the *divine right of kings,* the notion that a monarch's right to rule is granted directly by God. The belief, not shared by most of Charles's subjects, triggered conflict with Parliament, the king's only source of funds. The clash eventually escalated into civil war between subjects loyal to Charles and those who sided with the Puritan-dominated Parliament, led by Oliver Cromwell. When the Puritans decisively defeated the loyalist forces, Charles I was tried for treason, found guilty, and on Jan. 30, 1649, beheaded. The monarchy was abolished, and Great Britain remained a republic until 1660, when Parliament invited the former king's son, Charles II, to take the throne.

CHARLES I

The queen's riches

From the 1970's onward, the queen's wealth became the subject of increased interest to the public and hence the media. During the 1960's, the British economy boomed, and the queen's personal fortune multiplied as a result. Her status as one of the richest persons on earth was enhanced by the fact that she paid no taxes. Yet the queen and members of her family—as far removed as cousins—continued to receive annual payments from the public purse under a system called the Civil List.

In fact, the queen's sizable private fortune dated back to the reign of Queen Victoria (1819-1901), who with her husband, Prince Albert, invested their money wisely. Much of the money that Victoria and Albert invested, however, had come from the public purse through the Civil List. The tax-free status of the monarch was an even more recent feature of royal wealth, having been established for George VI in 1937. A monarch with enormous private wealth was not a centuries-old tra-

GEORGE IV

In 1785, at the age of 23, the Prince of Wales (later George IV) secretly married a Roman Catholic woman. The marriage was later invalidated because members of the royal family under age 25 needed the king's permission to marry. In 1795, the prince's father, George III, offered to cover the prince's debts if the prince agreed to marry a German cousin, Caroline of Brunswick-Lüneburg. However, neither the prince nor his bride could abide being in each other's presence, and they lived apart as much as possible. Both were also careless about keeping their marriage vows. When George ascended to the throne in 1820, Caroline arrived from Italy to claim her rights as queen consort. A bill was introduced before the House of Lords to deprive her of her title and dissolve the marriage on the grounds of adultery, but it was withdrawn due to popular regard for Caroline. In 1821, she tried to attend George's coronation ceremony, but she was refused entry. The conflict was resolved when Caroline died the following month.

When Edward VIII became king in 1936, he had already fallen in love with Wallis Simpson. Mrs. Simpson was an American, a divorcée, and married to a man whom she planned to divorce to marry the king. To make matters worse, the Church of England, of which Edward was the head, did not officially recognize divorce, and so Mrs. Simpson, in the eyes of the church, was still married to her first husband. With the church, the prime minister, the leaders and people of the dominions, and the king's own family all opposed to his marriage to Mrs. Simpson, Edward, on Dec. 11, 1936, *abdicated* (formally renounced) the throne. In a radio broadcast, he explained, "I have found it impossible to carry on the heavy burden of responsibility and to discharge the duties of king as I would wish to do without the help and support of the woman I love." He then left for France, where he and Mrs. Simpson married and lived in exile for much of the rest of their lives. After Edward's death in 1972, historians with access to the papers of the king's ministers and contemporaries concluded that the abdication was not entirely voluntary. The king's careless disregard for state confidentiality and his attitude toward totalitarian regimes appear to have placed him on a collision course with his own government and its prime minister, Stanley Baldwin.

EDWARD VIII

dition, as so many had believed, but a relatively recent phenomenon. In 1969, when the queen made an official request for an increase in the Civil List, her position as a multimillionaire was already widely known. Republican Labor politician William Hamilton called the queen's request for a "raise" the "most insensitive and brazen pay claim in the last 200 years."

The queen's status as a nontaxpayer was a highly contentious issue until 1992, when Buckingham Palace finally took action by announcing that the queen would begin paying taxes in 1993. Other gestures were made. Queen Elizabeth occasionally traveled in an ordinary railway carriage instead of the royal train, and she gave up sole use of the royal yacht, *Britannia*. The much criticized Civil List was cut back, so that fewer extended family members of the royal family received money from the public purse. However, many British citizens continued to believe that the monarchy had not adjusted to modern demands quickly enough.

Europe's wiser royals

Much criticism of the British royals focused on comparisons with the other European monarchs, who steered their way into the 1990's without high-profile scandal. The monarchies in continental Europe showed a wiser way, critics claimed, and they did so by evolving rules of survival in the age of democracy and mass media.

The first of these rules—one that the British royal family did adhere to—is to keep out of politics. In the UK, the three "dignified functions" of the monarch as identified by the Victorian political writer Walter Bagehot have remained stable for more than a century: the right to be consulted, the right to encourage, and the right to warn. Constitutional experts, however, maintained that the monarch's power was wider than the "dignified functions."

On the European continent, where shifting coalitions across several political parties have long been common, a monarch may exercise greater influence on government than the constitution implies, simply by being above the changeable, day-to-day world of politics. In Spain, King Juan Carlos led his country firmly into democracy after decades of dictatorship. After succeeding to the restored throne in 1975, Juan Carlos used his official powers to build a parliamentary democracy—stripping himself of his own constitutional power in the process. In 1981, the king's cool conduct in the face of an attempted military *coup d'état* (takeover) confirmed his democratic credentials. Since his accession to the throne, he has used his powers when situations required it. Otherwise, he remained removed from contemporary politics.

A second rule of successful monarchies is to maintain family discipline. In the Netherlands, Queen Beatrix, often called "the general manager of the kingdom," exerted influence through regular family meetings. Her son, Crown Prince Willem-Alexander—known to the Dutch press as the Prince of Fun—apparently caused concern within the Dutch palace. However, there have also been claims that Beatrix rules with a will of iron, and there has been little evidence that her son is a threat to the reputation or stability of the Dutch royal house.

The third rule of modern successful monarchies is to maintain a lifestyle that is appropriate, but relatively modest. While European royals other than the Windsors were also counted among Europe's richest people, they for the most part avoided extravagant lifestyles. Conspicuous consumption, especially at taxpayer's expense, was shunned. Most contemporary European monarchs live and work in publicly owned palaces, and only the monarch and his or her heir are maintained by public taxes. Other family members were expected to support themselves. Europe's monarchs learned that while they must live in a style that distinguishes, they must not live so lavishly as to attract adverse criticism.

In the UK, the queen and her family became aware of public resentment about the costs of maintaining the monarchy. In 1994, Prince Charles claimed in a newspaper interview that some European royalty were, in fact, "grander, more pompous, more hard to approach" than the British royal family. However, in 1996, the Dutch royal family, the most expensive of the monarchies on the European continent, cost the state an estimated $57 million in 1996. The British royal family cost the UK an estimated $155 million in 1996.

The final rule of a modern monarch is to show a closeness to the people, yet maintain a dignified distance. Of Spain's Juan Carlos, a Spanish commentator declared: "A king has to be distant, yet close. He has to be modern and traditional at the same time. He has to be informal, but not middle class." Royal watchers have suggested that Prince Charles might follow the example of his cousin Juan Carlos.

The future

Republicanism—the belief in the principles of a republic, without a monarch—has not been a policy of any of the major political parties in the UK. However, Republicanism was a issue in other Commonwealth countries. Of those countries that expressed allegiance to Queen Elizabeth, Canada and Australia were the largest and most important. While Canada traditionally has been firmly loyal to the crown, the separatist movement in Quebec placed Canada's future and its relationship with the crown in question. In Australia, the Labor government, led during the early 1990's by Prime Minister Paul Keating, favored breaking ties with the British monarchy. Keating promised a referendum on the subject by 2001. But Labor lost the general election of March 1996, and a Liberal government under John Howard, a monarchist, took power. Plans to sever ties with the British monarch were shelved. Yet republican feelings remained strong in Australia, particularly among the young.

Within the UK, the pressure on the royal family to reform itself remained high. In August 1996, the press revealed the existence of a so-called "think tank" made up of the queen, her husband Prince Philip, Prince Charles, and senior household members. Its task was to consider changes necessary to prepare the monarchy for the next millennium. Among the matters reportedly under discussion were the possible repeal of a 300-year-old law that forbids the monarch to marry a Roman Catholic, the rights of female family members in the line of succession, and the monarch's relationship with the Church of England.

Regardless of the more impassioned extremes of public opinion, most experts agreed that Queen Elizabeth II will reign until she dies. Abdication, often advocated by sections of the press, has never been on her agenda. The ghosts of Edward's 1936 abdication have long haunted a family desperate to maintain, rather than jeopardize, its fragile stability. Whether Charles will reign as Charles III when the time comes remains to be seen. The heir to the throne faced an uphill struggle to rebuild and restore his reputation. To recover with dignity will be a difficult—but essential—requirement, both for Charles and the institution of monarchy. ■ ■ ■

Prince Charles appears before the cameras, *below,* with his eldest son William, the next in the line of succession after Charles.

United Nations. The world's seven richest industrialized countries—the so-called "Group of 7" (G-7)—demanded reform of the United Nations (UN) at their annual summit meeting June 27-29, 1996, in Lyon, France. The communiqué from the United States, Japan, Germany, France, Italy, Great Britain, and Canada called for refocusing the UN's priorities in the areas of poverty, employment, housing, education, health, advancement of women, protection of children, and humanitarian aid. It stressed the need to reduce the number of high-ranking positions in the UN and to appoint a single undersecretary of development to cut duplication of efforts.

Following the G-7 communiqué, the UN undersecretary in charge of administration and management, Joseph E. Connor, said that about 1,000 posts had already been cut to reduce the number of professionals working at secretariats in New York, Vienna, and Geneva to 9,000. Connor also noted that the UN budget of $2.6 billion for 1995 and 1996 had already been reduced by $250 million to hold the budget at *zero nominal growth* (no increase or negligible increase). The organization faced severe financial problems in 1996, forcing Connor to borrow money to pay for daily activities in the secretariats. As of October, more than 130 of the 185 UN members still owed nearly $2.5 billion, with the United States as the largest debtor, owing $1.5 billion in past and current payments.

Secretary-General. Another problem that beset the organization was the deterioration of the relationship between UN Secretary-General Boutros Boutros-Ghali and the Clinton Administration. On June 20, State Department spokesman Nicholas Burns announced that the United States would veto the reelection of Boutros-Ghali, whose tenure ended on December 31, for a second five-year term. Burns charged that Boutros-Ghali had not instituted sufficient reforms to reinvigorate the organization. On November 19, the United States cast its veto in the first vote held by the UN Security Council while the other 14 members voted in favor of Boutros-Ghali's reelection. Despite the veto, African countries supported the Egyptian diplomat until December 2, when Paul Biya, chairman of the Organization of African Unity, advised them to nominate other candidates. On December 13, the Council chose Kofi Annan of Ghana as the next secretary-general.

General Assembly. The 185 countries of the Assembly began the 51st annual session on September 18 under a new president, Ambassador Razali Ismail of Malaysia. More than 150 presidents, prime ministers, foreign ministers, and heads of delegations addressed the body on more than 160 issues.

Many of the country representatives present at the Assembly demanded the enlargement of the UN Security Council so that it would better reflect the importance of developing countries and new economic powers. The Security Council consists of 15 member countries, 5 of which—the United States, Russia, France, Great Britain, and China—are permanent members, and 10 of which serve two-year terms. The proposed changes would increase the number of permanent members to include such countries as Japan and Germany and allow more countries to serve as nonpermanent members.

Security Council for 1997. On October 21, the General Assembly elected Japan, Costa Rica, Kenya, Sweden, and Portugal to serve two-year terms in the Security Council beginning Jan. 1, 1997. Those countries replaced Indonesia, Honduras, Botswana, Germany, and Italy, which ended their terms on Dec. 31, 1996. In addition to the 5 permanent members and the 5 newly elected nonpermanent members, the 15-nation Security Council also consisted of Egypt, Guinea-Bissau, South Korea, Poland, and Chile, countries whose nonpermanent terms were set to end on Dec. 31, 1997.

Nuclear explosion ban. On Sept. 10, 1996, the General Assembly voted 158 to 3 to adopt the Comprehensive Test Ban Treaty (CTBT), an agreement that requires signatories to ban all nuclear explosions. A partial nuclear test ban treaty had been signed by the United States, the former Soviet Union, the United Kingdom, and other countries in 1963, banning nuclear explosions everywhere except underground. On Sept. 24, 1996, President Bill Clinton, representing the United States, was the first to sign the treaty. He was followed by the foreign ministers of Russia, France, Great Britain, and China. By November, more than 120 countries had signed the CTBT, and the parliament of Fiji had ratified it, being the first country to do so. The treaty was to go into effect when the legislatures of 44 countries—those capable of making nuclear weapons—had ratified it.

Iraq. On May 20, Iraq signed an agreement with the UN to carry out UN Resolution 986, popularly known as the oil-for-food deal. Under the resolution, Iraq was to be allowed to sell a limited quantity of oil worth $2 billion over a 6-month period. All the revenues were to be deposited in a UN escrow account in Paris. The UN was to monitor revenues, assuring that 50 percent was used to purchase food and medicine for needy Iraqis; 30 percent to compensate victims of the 1991 Gulf War, which was triggered by the Iraqi invasion of Kuwait; 15 percent to help the Kurds in northern Iraq; and 5 percent to cover costs of UN operations in Iraq.

Resolution 986 was intended to alleviate the suffering of ordinary Iraqis, which Iraq had claimed was caused by the economic sanctions imposed on the country after its troops invaded Kuwait. Under the terms of the agreement, UN experts were to be deployed in Iraq to monitor the oil exports and ensure that the government equitably distribute the humanitarian supplies to the Iraqi civilians rather than appropriating them for its own use. On Sept. 1, 1996, Boutros-Ghali suspended the deployment of the inspectors after Iraqi troops launched a military campaign against the northern city of Irbil, held by the pro-Iranian Kurdish group Patriotic Union of Kurdistan. On September 3 and 4, the U.S. Air Force and Navy fired 44 cruise missiles against Iraq's military installations in southern Iraq in retaliation for the Irbil attack. Iraq finally accepted UN conditions in the oil-for-food deal on November 25, and the agreement went into effect on December 10.

Former Yugoslav republics. Throughout 1996, the UN assumed a different role in the former Yugoslav republics than it had in the previous four years, during which its forces were engaged in the futile task of separating warring factions in Bosnia-Herzegovina and other former Yugoslav republics. In 1996, the UN was in charge of the civilian and police program of the peace agreement of December 1995, which ended the war. About 60,000 international troops under North American Treaty Organization command were responsible for the military program.

On Sept. 4, 1996, local ethnic Serb, Croat, and Muslim communities in Bosnia-Herzegovina elected a collective three-member presidency to govern a republic still divided along ethnic lines and suffering from the destruction of war. On September 29, the Organization of Security and Cooperation in Europe certified elections that it helped organize, though it acknowledged that the elections were neither free nor democratic. The Security Council on October 1 lifted economic sanctions against Serbia and Montenegro, the remaining republics of Yugoslavia. The sanctions had been imposed in 1992 to protest Serb support of the ethnic war in Bosnia-Herzegovina.

The UN International Criminal Tribunal for the Former Yugoslavia continued to gather evidence of war crimes committed by the warring factions in Bosnia-Herzegovina. In July 1996, the tribunal, for the second time, indicted Bosnian Serb leader Radovan Karadžić and his military commander, General Ratko Mladić, of genocide and crimes against humanity. The tribunal indicted and issued international arrest warrants for more than 70 Serbs, Croats, and Muslims and on November 29 sentenced a Croat to 10 years in prison for his participation in the Bosnian Serb Army massacre of more than 1,200 unarmed Muslims at Srebrenica in Bosnia-Herzegovina, in 1995. It was the first war-crime prosecution since the trials in Nuremburg, Germany, and Tokyo following World War II (1939-1945).

Habitat II. The UN organized an international conference in Istanbul, Turkey, from June 3 to 14, 1996, to focus attention on the housing crisis affecting at least 500 million urban dwellers worldwide. Representatives of more than 150 nations participated in the International Conference on Human Settlements, or Habitat II, the first such conference since the 1976 Vancouver meeting. The conference set broad guidelines for governments to improve living conditions and water and sanitation services and to reduce poverty and environmental hazards.

Human development. On July 17, 1996, the UN Development Program published a report decrying the widening gap between rich and poor in many countries around the world. The report noted that people in 89 countries were economically worse off in 1996 than they had been 10 years ago. The report also listed 174 countries that had done the most to improve human development, particularly in terms of education and living conditions. Canada was at the top of the list, followed by the United States, Japan, the Netherlands, and Norway.

Child abuse. The Swedish government, together with the UN Children's Fund (UNICEF), held a five-day World Congress Against Commercial Exploitation of Children in Stockholm in August. The conference urged governments to end the practice in their countries of using children in the sex industry and of commercially exploiting children in general. According to UNICEF sources, more than 1 million children were forced into prostitution around the world each year. They were either sold for sexual purposes or used in child pornography. As of November 1996, the Convention on the Rights of the Child, which gives children the right to protect themselves against all forms of sexual exploitation, had been ratified by 187 countries.　　　　□ J. Tuyet Nguyen

In *World Book,* see **United Nations.**

United States, Government of the. The longest United States government shut-down in history ended on Jan. 6, 1996, when Democratic President Bill Clinton signed a stopgap spending bill to halt a 21-day stand-off with the Republican-controlled Congress. The shut-down had begun Dec. 16, 1995, when a previous stopgap spending bill had expired and Clinton and Republican leaders failed to agree on a budget. The January 1996 spending bill allowed 280,000 furloughed federal workers to return to their jobs and assured back pay to 480,000 others who worked without pay to provide essential government services during the confrontation.

The day after the furloughed workers returned to their jobs, a winter storm dubbed the "Blizzard of '96" dumped 17 inches (43 centimeters) of snow on Washington, D.C., closing down federal offices for three more days.

A spirit of compromise eventually developed between Republican leaders in Congress and the Clinton Administration, producing agreement on hard-fought budget issues and other legislation, including new laws dealing with welfare, immigration, terrorism, telecommunications, farm policy, health care, the minimum wage, and the safety of drinking water. While President Clinton accepted larger spending cuts than he preferred, Republicans moderated their views on a number of social issues.

Investigations of alleged misdeeds in the Administration were conducted in 1996 by the U.S. Justice Department and congressional subcommittees. Records relating to First Lady Hillary Rodham Clinton's legal work in the mid-1980's, missing for two years, were unexpectedly found in the White House family quarters in January 1996. Hillary Clinton testified before a federal grand jury later that month, the first time the wife of a president had done so. The grand jury sought to determine whether she had acted improperly by representing Madison Guaranty Savings & Loan when she and her husband were partners with the owners of the Whitewater Development Corp., an Arkansas real estate project. Senate Republican investigators also charged that Mrs. Clinton had played a role in the questionable firing of seven employees of the White House travel office in 1993.

In April 1996, President Clinton testified on videotape for the defense in the trial of James McDougal and Susan McDougal, former owners of Madison Guaranty Savings & Loan and the Clintons' partners in the Whitewater venture. The McDougals were convicted of fraud and conspiracy, crimes unrelated to the Whitewater investment.

White House aides also admitted that they obtained more than 600 Federal Bureau of Investigation (FBI) files, including sensitive records on prominent Republi-

cans. White House officials said the files were acquired as the result of a bureaucratic mistake, but Republican critics remained skeptical.

Unabomber suspect arrested. One of the most intensive manhunts in the history of the Federal Bureau of Investigation (FBI) ended on April 3 with the arrest of Theodore J. Kaczynski, the suspected "Unabomber." Evidence connected this elusive terrorist to 16 bombings that killed 3 people and wounded 23 others between 1978 and 1995. Kaczynski, 53, a former mathematics professor, was arrested at his remote Montana cabin after his brother, David, provided the tip that linked him to the crimes. On June 18, Kaczynski was charged with 10 felonies, including 2 counts of murder, in connection with the bombings. He pleaded not guilty. On June 28, he was charged with three more bombings.

Other terrorism developments. In January, a federal judge sentenced 10 militant Muslims following their 1995 convictions for plotting to bomb the United Nations (UN) headquarters and other landmarks in New York and to kill political leaders. Egyptian cleric Sheik Omar Abdel Rahman, accused of leading the terrorist group, and El Sayyid Nosair were sentenced to life in prison with no possibility of parole. Eight others were sentenced to prison terms ranging from 25 to 57 years.

A federal jury in New York on September 5 convicted Ramzi Ahmed Yousef and two other Muslim

Gloria Ward (second from right) with her children, leaves the Freemen compound in Montana on June 6, a week before the rest of the antigovernment group surrender to the FBI.

men of conspiring to bomb 12 U.S. airliners flying Pacific Ocean routes to protest American support of Israel.

A federal judge ruled in February that the trials of Timothy McVeigh and Terry Nichols—charged with planting a bomb in April 1995 that destroyed a federal building in Oklahoma City, killing 168 people—would be held in Denver on the grounds that an impartial jury could not be found in Oklahoma City.

In July 1996, federal agents filed conspiracy charges against all 12 members of an Arizona group known as the Viper Militia. A six-month undercover investigation had revealed that the group had planned to blow up several federal, state, and local government buildings.

In Montana, 16 members of an antigovernment group called the Freemen surrendered to the FBI on June 13, ended an 81-day standoff. Most group members faced charges for allegedly passing phony money orders and checks, and allegedly threatening federal judges with violence.

Several plane crashes prompted government action in 1996. On July 17, Trans World Airlines (TWA) flight 800 exploded and crashed into the Atlantic Ocean not long after take-off from Kennedy International Airport in New York City. All 230 people aboard were killed. Although by year's end the National Transportation Safety Board (NTSB) had not determined the cause of the crash, early suspicions that the explosion was the work of terrorists could not be ruled out. As a result, in September, President Clinton proposed that aviation security measures be tightened at U.S. airports. The proposal included increasing the federal role in airport security, implementing new screening methods to detect suspicious passengers, and installing 54 high-tech bomb detection systems at airports throughout the country.

On May 11, a ValuJet airliner crashed in the Florida Everglades, killing 110 people. An investigation found that a fire started by oxygen containers in a cargo bay caused the crash. In June, the Federal Aviation Administration (FAA) grounded ValuJet because of "serious deficiencies" in its maintenance operations. The carrier resumed operations in September with Department of Transportation approval.

In March, the U.S. Treasury introduces a new $100 bill, the first new design of U.S. paper currency in 68 years.

Foreign relations. In its annual report on human rights, released in March, the State Department criticized China for "widespread and well-documented" abuses, including the use of torture, the large number of crimes eligible for the death penalty, intolerance of political dissent, and a family planning policy prohibiting couples from having more than one child.

In February, Cuban air force fighters shot down two unarmed, Miami-based private planes over international waters. Four members of a Cuban American group opposing President Fidel Castro of Cuba were killed. In response to the downing, President Clinton imposed stronger sanctions against Cuba, suspending all charter flights between the United States and Cuba, and limiting travel of Cuban diplomats.

The incident also persuaded Clinton to sign a controversial bill that would allow U.S. citizens to sue foreign companies that have acquired or sold American-owned property later seized after the 1959 Cuban revolution. The law angered U.S. allies in Europe, Canada, and Mexico, which protested that the United States was interfering in legal business operations.

Attempting to counter Iraq's military action in a Kurdish-controlled region in northern Iraq, the United States on Sept. 3 and 4, 1996, staged two missile attacks on military sites in southern Iraq. B-52 aircraft and two warships fired a total of 44 missiles.

Responding to increased criticism of U.S. troops

deployed on the island of Okinawa, the United States agreed on April 15 to return part or all of 11 U.S. military bases to Japan within seven years.

In January, Attorney General Janet Reno and the commissioner of the Immigration and Naturalization Service (INS), Doris M. Meissner, announced that the United States would step up its efforts to prevent illegal immigration across the border between the United States and Mexico. Three hundred additional Border Patrol agents were assigned to California and Arizona, along with 350 military and law-enforcement personnel.

The United States on July 11 revoked the visa of Colombian President Ernesto Samper Pizano on grounds that he financed his 1994 election campaign with $6 million in contributions from a drug cartel centered in the city of Cali, Colombia. The United States had not denied entry to a democratically elected foreign leader since it barred Austrian President Kurt Waldheim in 1987 because of evidence that he persecuted Jews while serving in the German army during World War II (1939–1945).

Louis Farrakhan, leader of the Nation of Islam, a religious organization sometimes called the Black Muslims, drew the attention of the U.S. government for a tour he made in January and February of Libya, Iraq, Iran, Nigeria, and other countries shunned by Washington for terrorist associations or human rights abuses. During the trip, Farrakhan reportedly held discussions with Libyan leader Muammar Mohammad al-Qadhafi regarding plans to work together on political lobbying efforts in the United States. The Justice Department responded by alerting Farrakhan that participating in such lobbying efforts would require him to register as a foreign agent. Farrakhan also accepted a $250,000 award from a Libyan organization and reported that Qadhafi had pledged $1 billion in aid for his organization. On August 28, the U.S. Treasury Department ruled that Farrakhan would not be permitted to accept these funds.

Trade deficit grows. The Department of Commerce reported in February that the U.S. trade deficit for 1995 increased to $111.04 billion, 4.5 percent over the 1994 figure. It was the largest annual trade deficit since 1988. In a related development, a threatened trade war was averted in June 1996, when the United States and China agreed on ways to curb illegal copying of American musical recordings, videos, and other copyrighted materials.

Measures against tobacco use. The government took action in 1996 against the marketing and sale of tobacco products to young people. President Clinton on August 23 approved regulations issued by the Food and Drug Administration (FDA) to classify nicotine as an addictive drug. New regulations put strict limits on cigarette advertising and required people under the age of 27 to produce photo identification when buying cigarettes over the counter.

Federal spending
United States budget for fiscal 1996*

	Billions of dollars
National defense	265.4
International affairs	13.7
General science, space, technology	17.9
Energy	2.9
Natural resources and environment	22.8
Agriculture	9.0
Commerce and housing credit	– 10.5
Transportation	38.6
Community and regional development	11.4
Education, training, employment, and social services	50.8
Health	118.9
Social security	349.7
Medicare	174.2
Income security	225.3
Veterans' benefits and services	37.0
Administration of justice	17.6
General government	12.0
Interest	241.1
Undistributed offsetting receipts	– 37.6
Total budget outlays	**1,560.2**

*Oct. 1, 1995, to Sept. 30, 1996.
Source: U.S. Department of the Treasury.

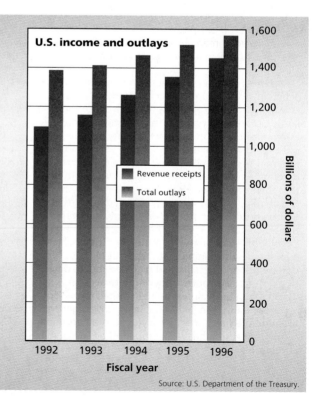

U.S. income and outlays

Revenue receipts
Total outlays

Billions of dollars

Fiscal year

Source: U.S. Department of the Treasury.

Selected agencies and bureaus of the U.S. government*

Executive Office of the President
President, Bill Clinton
Vice President, Albert Gore, Jr.
White House Chief of Staff, Leon E. Panetta†
Presidential Press Secretary, Michael McCurry
Assistant to the President for Domestic Policy, Carol H. Rasco
Assistant to the President for National Security Affairs, W. Anthony Lake
Assistant to the President for Science and Technology, John H. Gibbons
Council of Economic Advisers—Joseph E. Stiglitz, Chairman
Office of Management and Budget—Franklin D. Raines, Director
Office of National Drug Control Policy—Barry R. McCaffrey, Director
U.S. Trade Representative, Charlene Barshefsky (acting)

Department of Agriculture
Secretary of Agriculture, Daniel R. Glickman

Department of Commerce
Secretary of Commerce, Mickey Kantor†
Bureau of Economic Analysis—J. Steven Landefeld, Director
Bureau of the Census—Martha F. Riche, Director

Department of Defense
Secretary of Defense, William J. Perry†
Secretary of the Air Force, Sheila E. Widnall
Secretary of the Army, Togo D. West, Jr.
Secretary of the Navy, John H. Dalton
Joint Chiefs of Staff—
General John Shalikashvili, Chairman
General Ronald R. Fogleman, Chief of Staff, Air Force
General Dennis J. Reimer, Chief of Staff, Army
Admiral Jay L. Johnson, Chief of Naval Operations
General Charles C. Krulak, Commandant, Marine Corps

Department of Education
Secretary of Education, Richard W. Riley

Department of Energy
Secretary of Energy, Hazel R. O'Leary†

Department of Health and Human Services
Secretary of Health and Human Services, Donna E. Shalala
Public Health Service—Philip R. Lee, Assistant Secretary
Centers for Disease Control and Prevention—David Satcher, Director
Food and Drug Administration—David A. Kessler, Commissioner
National Institutes of Health—Harold Varmus, Director
Surgeon General of the United States, Audrey F. Manley

Department of Housing and Urban Development
Secretary of Housing and Urban Development, Henry G. Cisneros†

Department of the Interior
Secretary of the Interior, Bruce Babbitt

Department of Justice
Attorney General, Janet Reno
Bureau of Prisons—Kathleen M. Hawk, Director
Drug Enforcement Administration—Thomas A. Constantine, Administrator
Federal Bureau of Investigation—Louis J. Freeh, Director
Immigration and Naturalization Service—Doris M. Meissner, Commissioner
Solicitor General, Walter E. Dellinger (acting)

Department of Labor
Secretary of Labor, Robert B. Reich†

Department of State
Secretary of State, Warren Christopher†
U.S. Ambassador to the United Nations, Madeleine K. Albright

Department of Transportation
Secretary of Transportation, Federico F. Peña†
Federal Aviation Administration—David R. Hinson, Administrator
U.S. Coast Guard—Admiral Robert E. Kramek, Commandant

*As of Dec. 31, 1996.
†Has announced resignation.

Department of the Treasury
Secretary of the Treasury, Robert E. Rubin
Internal Revenue Service—Margaret Milner Richardson, Commissioner
Treasurer of the United States, Mary Ellen Withrow
U.S. Secret Service—Eljay B. Bowron, Director
Office of Thrift Supervision—vacant

Department of Veterans Affairs
Secretary of Veterans Affairs, Jesse Brown

Supreme Court of the United States
Chief Justice of the United States, William H. Rehnquist
Associate Justices—

John Paul Stevens	David H. Souter
Sandra Day O'Connor	Clarence Thomas
Antonin Scalia	Ruth Bader Ginsburg
Anthony M. Kennedy	Stephen G. Breyer

Congressional officials
President of the Senate pro tempore, Strom Thurmond
Senate Majority Leader, Trent Lott
Senate Minority Leader, Thomas A. Daschle
Speaker of the House, Newt Gingrich
House Majority Leader, Dick Armey
House Minority Leader, Richard A. Gephardt
Congressional Budget Office—June E. O'Neill, Director
General Accounting Office—Charles A. Bowsher, Comptroller General of the United States
Library of Congress—James H. Billington, Librarian of Congress

Independent agencies
Central Intelligence Agency—John M. Deutch, Director†
Commission on Civil Rights—Mary Frances Berry, Chairperson
Commission of Fine Arts—J. Carter Brown, Chairman
Consumer Product Safety Commission—Ann Winkelman Brown, Chairman
Corporation for National Service—Harris Wofford, Chief Executive Officer
Environmental Protection Agency—Carol M. Browner, Administrator
Equal Employment Opportunity Commission—Gilbert F. Casellas, Chairman
Federal Communications Commission—Reed E. Hundt, Chairman
Federal Deposit Insurance Corporation—Ricki Helfer, Chairman
Federal Election Commission—Lee Ann Elliott, Chairman
Federal Emergency Management Agency—James Lee Witt, Director
Federal Reserve System Board of Governors—Alan Greenspan, Chairman
Federal Trade Commission—Robert Pitofsky, Chairman
General Services Administration—David J. Barram, Administrator (acting)
International Development Cooperation Agency—J. Brian Atwood, Director (acting)
National Aeronautics and Space Administration—Daniel S. Goldin, Administrator
National Endowment for the Arts—Jane Alexander, Chairman
National Endowment for the Humanities—Sheldon Hackney, Chairman
National Labor Relations Board—William B. Gould IV, Chairman
National Railroad Passenger Corporation (Amtrak)—Thomas M. Downs, Chairman
National Science Foundation—Neal F. Lane, Director
National Transportation Safety Board—James E. Hall, Chairman
Nuclear Regulatory Commission—Shirley A. Jackson, Chairman
Peace Corps—Mark D. Gearan, Director
Securities and Exchange Commission—Arthur Levitt, Jr., Chairman
Selective Service System—Gil Coronado, Director
Small Business Administration—Phillip Lader, Administrator
Smithsonian Institution—I. Michael Heyman, Secretary
Social Security Administration—Shirley S. Chater, Commissioner
U.S. Arms Control and Disarmament Agency—John D. Holum, Director
U.S. Information Agency—Joseph D. Duffey, Director
U.S. Postal Service—Marvin T. Runyon, Postmaster General

Resignations and appointments. In January, President Clinton nominated Army General Barry R. McCaffrey to replace Lee P. Brown as the new director of the Office of National Drug Control Policy.

Jeffrey K. Harris, director of the National Reconnaissance Office (NRO), the agency that builds spy satellites, and his deputy, Jimmie D. Hill, were asked to resign in February amid reports of financial mismanagement. Auditors found $2 billion in unspent government funds in a secret, NRO account.

In February, President Bill Clinton appointed Alan Greenspan, chairman of the Federal Reserve Board, to a third four-year term. Clinton named Alice Rivlin, the director of the Office of Management and Budget, to be vice chairman of the Federal Reserve and Laurence H. Meyer, an economic consultant, to another board vacancy. Clinton selected Franklin D. Raines to replace Alice Rivlin as director of the Office of Management and Budget.

On June 5, President Clinton nominated Admiral Jay L. Johnson as chief of naval operations. Johnson replaced Admiral Jeremy M. (Mike) Boorda, who took his own life on May 16.   □ William J. Eaton

See also **Aviation; Clinton, Bill; Congress of the United States; Farm and farming; Iraq; Terrorism; Welfare.** In *World Book,* see **United States, Government of the.**

Uruguay. See **Latin America.**

Utah. See **State government.**

Uzbekistan. Western investment flowed into Uzbekistan in 1996, as the government continued an economic reform program begun in 1994. Increased activity by Western firms brought Uzbekistan new respect on the world stage. Despite lingering concerns over Uzbekistan's human rights record, President Islam Karimov met with United States President Bill Clinton in Washington in June 1996. In August, Karimov announced his intention to protect human rights and permit opposition parties to operate.

Much foreign investment in Uzbekistan in 1996 came in the form of joint ventures with Uzbek firms. European, Japanese, and Korean companies were particularly active, and American companies were considering more than $1 billion in investments in Uzbekistan's oil and gas sector.

Karimov also attempted to define new national myths and ideologies to replace the Communist symbols used when Uzbekistan was part of the Soviet Union. He declared 1996 the "year of Tamerlane (Timur the Lame)," recalling the legendary ruler of a powerful empire of the late 1300's and ealry 1400's that included modern Uzbekistan. The government also attempted to reinforce Uzbekistan's orientation toward the Turkish world by creating an Islamic broadcasting channel to emphasize Uzbekistan's religious and cultural heritage.   □ Steven L. Solnick

In *World Book,* see **Uzbekistan.**

Vanuatu. See **Pacific Islands.**

Venezuela. In 1996, the Venezuelan government introduced measures to encourage investment in the country's flagging economy. In January, the oil industry, which was nationalized in 1976, granted contracts to 13 foreign companies for the development of crude oil fields.

On April 15, 1996, President Rafael Caldera Rodríguez announced a new free-market strategy that lifted controls of foreign exchange and interest rates. The program raised the sales tax from 12.5 to 16.5 percent and the price of gasoline by 470 percent.

A 20-percent surge in oil prices between July and October brought Venezuela an extra $2.5 billion in revenue. With an unexpected 4.6-percent budget surplus, the government did not need to draw upon all of a $1.4-billion credit announced on July 12 by the International Monetary Fund, an agency of the United Nations.

Former President Carlos Andrés Pérez, who was impeached in 1993, was sentenced in May 1996 for misusing $17 million during his second term in office, which began in 1989. Having served most of the sentence while awaiting a verdict, Pérez was released in September 1996.   □ Nathan A. Haverstock

See also **Latin America** (Facts in brief table). In *World Book,* see **Venezuela.**

Vermont. See **State government.**

Vice President of the United States. See **Gore, Albert, Jr.**

Vietnam. Rather than risk factional fighting by selecting younger officials, the ruling Communist Party decided in 1996 to retain its aging leadership. More than 1,100 delegates to the eighth party congress held in June in Hanoi, the national capital, decided that power would be turned over to a younger generation only gradually.

Same trio of power. The congress reelected General Secretary Do Muoi, age 79; President Le Duc Anh, age 75; and Prime Minister Vo Van Kiet, age 73. The trio represented a geographical balance between north and south Vietnam and an ideological balance between conservatives, who feared losing party control, and reformers, who advocated a more capitalistic economy for the nation. Officials suggested that instead of serving out their five-year terms, the three would prepare others to eventually take over. However, on November 16, President Anh was incapacitated by a stroke and hospitalized.

The congress restricted the political process by creating a five-member standing committee within the party politburo that was to make daily decisions. In addition to the three top leaders, the committee included Le Kha Phieu, head of the army's political department, and Nguyen Tan Dung, deputy minister of the interior, who supervised police and intelligence work. The new 18-member politburo, which was enlarged by 2 members, had 6 military and security officials and a woman member for the first time.

Crackdown. Worried about what it called "cultural pollution" from abroad, the government tried to ban certain music and other types of popular culture from the West. The government prohibited the use of non-Vietnamese words in signs. But the atheistic Communist leadership also removed many obstacles to private religious worship in a country with many Buddhists, Confucians, and Roman Catholics.

Foreign investment was sought to provide jobs as staffs were cut by the army, civil service, and state-owned industries, all large employers in a Communist system. Taiwan, Japan, Hong Kong, Singapore, and other countries had invested about $20 billion in Vietnam since the late 1980's. But the population grew 2 percent annually, and many peasants were leaving overcrowded farms to seek work in urban areas, adding pressure for more investment and jobs. Rigid rules, corruption, and inadequate infrastructure discouraged many foreign investors, however. Businessmen surveyed by a consultant firm in Hong Kong said Vietnam was one of the most difficult places in Asia for doing business.

Economic growth, which had averaged 8.5 percent since 1993, slowed in 1996. Inflation rose sharply late in the year. □ Henry S. Bradsher

See also **Asia** (Facts in brief table). In ***World Book,*** see **Vietnam.**

Virginia. See State government.
Vital statistics. See Census; Population.

Washington, D.C. An audit of the 1995 fiscal
year, presented to the U.S. Congress on Feb. 2, 1996, revealed that Washington's fiscal crisis had worsened. While the city government reduced deficit spending from $335.4 million in 1994 to $54.5 million in 1995, the deficit was still $378.5 million. In 1995, this financial crisis had led Congress to appoint a financial control board to oversee the city. The city's continuing financial problems in 1996 raised doubts about whether home-rule government could survive.

Neglected services. Washington residents, already plagued by potholes and inadequate services, faced reports in January that police were holding bake sales to raise money for office supplies. In the winter and spring, federal government shutdowns, which blocked the distribution of federal appropriations to the city, crippled services further. Andrew Brimmer, chairman of the financial control board, testified before Congress in March, "No one should underestimate our financial plight."

The city was unprepared for the January 7 blizzard that dumped more than 17 inches (43 centimeters) of snow. Many streets remained unplowed a week after the storm. The city four years before had owned more than 100 plows and contracted for the use of an additional 240. In January 1996, the city had 50 plows available. With the entire yearly snow removal budget of $2.1 million used within days, the city ground to a halt until warm weather melted the snow.

The AIDS Memorial Quilt, representing more than 37,000 victims of the disease, is displayed on the National Mall in Washington, D.C., in October 1996.

Washington

In July, residents learned that city water had failed federal safety standards at least four times in the previous 12 months. After years of neglect, the city's water pipes and reservoirs needed $200 million to $400 million in repairs. In response to the crisis, large amounts of chlorine were dumped into the water.

Recommended solutions. Various groups offered solutions to the problems facing Washington's city government, but no changes were made. Local officials, including Mayor Marion S. Barry, Jr., favored statehood, which was opposed by Congress. Republicans in the U.S. House of Representatives recommended returning the city to congressional control. The Committee for the Capital City, a citizens' group, promoted plans to have the city, with the exception of the federal capital area, join the state of Maryland. Eleanor Holmes Norton, the city's nonvoting member of Congress, proposed a bill giving residents of Washington a flat federal income tax, designed to lure new residents and businesses to the city and thus reverse the declining tax base.

Vermeer exhibit. Despite Washington's long list of troubles, a number of notable cultural events took place in 1996. From Nov. 12, 1995, to Feb. 11, 1996, the National Gallery of Art hosted the largest modern exhibition of Jan Vermeer, a Dutch artist who lived in the 1600's. Washington was the only American city to host the event, which drew international audiences and attention. Large crowds lined up each morning around the West Wing of the National Gallery for coveted tickets.

Cultural birthdays. In September, the John F. Kennedy Center for the Performing Arts celebrated its 25th anniversary. The Kennedy Center houses the National Symphony and the Washington Opera, as well as showcasing drama and dance. Wolf Trap Farm Park, the official summer home of the National Symphony, also celebrated its 25th anniversary in 1996. Located in Vienna, Virginia, a few miles outside of Washington, Wolf Trap is the only national park devoted to the performing arts.

In August, the Smithsonian Institution celebrated its 150th anniversary. To mark the event, the Smithsonian sent an exhibit of more than 300 of its most famous objects—from Dorothy's ruby slippers from *The Wizard of Oz* to Thomas Edison's light bulb and George Washington's sword—on a 12-city tour of the country.

In May, the Smithsonian Institution also approved the architectural plans for its newest museum, the National Museum of the American Indian. The building, which is scheduled to open in 2002, has been designated to fill the last open space available as a construction site on the National Mall.

☐ Robert Messenger

See also **Art; City.** In *World Book,* see **Washington, D.C.**

Washington (state of). See **State government.**

Water. The drought that began over the western Great Plains of the United States in the autumn of 1995 persisted throughout most of the region into the summer of 1996. From western Nebraska south to northern Mexico, the drought—the worst since the 1930's—was disastrous for agriculture. In Oklahoma, many farmers plowed under their wheat.

The drought was also a disaster for cattle ranchers. In Texas, which has the largest cattle industry of any state, at least 40 percent of all pasture was too dry for grazing. The federal government declared 130 counties disaster areas, enabling ranchers to apply for emergency federal funds to buy cattle feed.

Farmers who grew irrigated crops, such as cotton, increased the pumping of ground water. The practice led to a drop in water levels in the Ogallala Aquifer, a massive layer of fine sediments holding water in the southern region of the Great Plains.

Finally, in mid-August, Hurricane Dolly swept up from the Gulf of Mexico, bringing rain to the region. The rain, however, came too late to save the wheat crop. Many ranchers had also sold off their cattle because they could not afford to continue to buy feed.

San Diego taps a new source. In July 1996, San Diego announced that it had forged a draft agreement to acquire water from the Imperial Irrigation District, which supplies water to the farmers of Imperial Valley 120 miles (190 kilometers) east of San Diego. How the water would be transferred, including the possibility of constructing new aqueducts, had yet to be determined. The San Diego Water Authority, which serves more than 2.6 million people, hoped to annually buy 400,000 acre-feet of water for the next 50 to 100 years. An acre-foot is approximately 326,000 gallons (1.2 million liters), about the amount of water a family of four would use in a year.

San Diego had depended on Los Angeles for up to 90 percent of its water since the 1940's, when it joined the Metropolitan Water District of Los Angeles. Los Angeles gets water via an aqueduct from the Sacramento Valley, 685 miles (1,102 kilometers) to the north. Since the late 1980's, Los Angeles had passed various water conservation measures. All of southern California faced future water shortages, according to 1996 announcements by state officials.

Drinking water see-saw. On July 2, 1996, officials in Washington, D.C., announced that for the fourth time in a year tests showed that city water supplies contained bacteria levels that violated federal standards. The next day, the officials recommended that elderly people and others with weakened immune systems boil their drinking water. On July 4, city health officials called off the drinking water alert, announcing that new tests showed the water had been safe all along. But in July, testing again disclosed the presence of bacteria, and extra chlorine was added to kill any organisms. ☐ Iris Priestaf

See also **Farm and farming; Weather.** In *World Book,* see **Water.**

Weather. Extremes—heavy snow and rain, record cold, and drought—characterized weather in the United States during the winter of 1996. Particularly hard hit were the Pacific Northwest and the Northeast, where excessive precipitation caused significant property damage and loss of life. Dry conditions in the South and Southwest resulted in extensive damage by wildfires.

Blizzards on East Coast. The season began with the blizzard of January 6 to 9. Millions of people in the urban corridor from Washington, D.C., to Boston, as well as in the Middle Atlantic States, were affected by the storm. The region was paralyzed with up to 35 inches (89 centimeters) of snow. Air traffic was halted at all major hubs, and city snow crews in both Philadelphia and Washington ran out of spaces to dump the snow removed from streets. Especially hard hit was southeastern Pennsylvania, where wind-blown snow drifts towered over 10 feet- (3 meters-) high. At least 150 deaths were attributed to the blizzard. Less than a week later, another storm brought heavy snow to parts of the Northeast. This additional snowfall set a monthly record at Harrisburg, Pennsylvania, where snow depths measured 39 inches (99 centimeters).

New snowfall records were set in many cities, including Boston, with 108 inches (274 centimeters); New York City, with 76 inches (193 centimeters); Washington's Dulles Airport, with 62 inches (157 centimeters); and Marquette, Michigan, with 226 inches (574 centimeters).

Flooding in Northeast. In late January, serious flooding occurred in the Northeast, when heavy rain fell onto a deep snow pack. Moist winds brought warm air that melted several feet of snow in less than 24 hours. The rapid discharge of meltwater combined with several inches of rain brought many major rivers and tributaries to flood stage. Significant flooding occurred in the Delaware, Susquehanna, upper Ohio, Potomac, and James river basins. River crests as high as 20 feet (6 meters) above flood stage forced more than 200,000 people from their homes. At least 42 deaths were attributed to the flooding, which caused more than $1 billion in damages.

Flooding in Northwest. The flooding that occurred in the Pacific Northwest in early February rivaled the devastation of the Northeast flood. An active storm track brought large amounts of rain to the region between the 5th and 9th, with rainfall of 12 to 20 inches (30 to 50 centimeters) common along windward mountain slopes in the Cascades. In addition, the unseasonably warm air that accompanied the rain caused rapid snowmelt, with Mt. Hood in Oregon, losing 58 inches (147 centimeters) of snow during 4 days. Flooding was considered to be the most severe since 1964, with the Columbia and Willamette rivers cresting between 7 and 18 feet (2 and 5 meters) above flood stage. The Northwestern states of Washington, Oregon, Montana, and Idaho were all declared federal disaster areas, and total damage estimates climbed above $600 million.

Bitter cold in February. A bitterly cold air mass poured over the northern Plains and upper Middle West in early February. At least 320 daily record lows were set during the Arctic outbreak, with record lows for the month set in four states. In Tower, Minnesota, the temperature dropped to -60 °F (-51 °C) on February 2; in Elkader, Iowa, the temperature dropped to -47 °F (-44 °C) on the 3rd; in Elizabeth, Illinois, the temperature fell to -35 °F (-37 °C) on the 3rd; and in Graeme, Rhode Island, the temperature fell to -25 °F (-32 °C) on the 5th.

Drought. The persistently dry weather that began in the autumn of 1995 reached a climax in late February 1996 across Texas and the southern Plains, when a bout of hot, breezy weather sparked wildfires, charring nearly 300 square miles (77,700 hectares) of forest and rangeland. Throughout the entire Southern and Southwestern United States, unseasonably warm and dry weather continued into spring, causing wildfires that charred more than 1 million acres (405,000 hectares).

Spring tornadoes in the east-central United States caused several deaths and considerable property damage, particularly in northwestern Arkansas and east-central Illinois. More than 110 tornadoes touched down between April 18 and 21.

Summer. Lightning from dry thunderstorms combined with heat and long-term dryness fueled wildfires across the West in June. By the end of the month, wildfires had consumed more than 2 million acres (809,000 hectares) of forests across six states. Meanwhile, slow-moving thunderstorms produced localized flash flooding from the western Great Lakes to the Middle Atlantic States.

Periods of torrential rain affected parts of Virginia, Maryland, and Pennsylvania, causing short-lived but severe floods that washed out numerous bridges, forced road closures, and inundated many houses. Meanwhile, Tropical Storm Arthur, the first of the Atlantic hurricane season, dropped up to 5 inches (13 centimeters) of rain on the South Carolina coast, but caused little damage.

Cool and wet conditions continued to cover many areas east of the Rockies during July. In eastern Quebec, Canada, torrential rains led to flash flooding along the Saguenay River July 19-22. More than 12,000 people were evacuated from their houses and 10 died in the disaster.

In the United States, heavy rains in the Northeast resulted in the second wettest June-July period in 102 years of record keeping. Some of the rain fell as Hurricane Bertha moved up the Eastern Seaboard. Bertha raked across the northeastern Antilles in the West Indies on July 8. Several days later, the remnants of the storm dropped 5 to 8 inches (13 to 20 centimeters) of rain from South Carolina to Maine.

On July 12, Bertha, a rare July hurricane, lashes a pier at Garden City, South Carolina. One of the first of more than a dozen Atlantic tropical storms and hurricanes in 1996, Bertha produced winds clocked at 115 miles (185 kilometers) per hour.

Weather 1996

From January's record-breaking snowfalls on the East Coast to the driest winter and spring on record in the panhandles of Texas and Oklahoma, 1996 was a year of extremes.

Volunteers deliver water to residents near Edgewood, Texas, an area hard hit by drought in 1996. In the first six months of the year, Southwestern and Great Plains states suffered the driest winter and spring since 1895, when the keeping of weather records was begun.

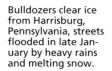

Bulldozers clear ice from Harrisburg, Pennsylvania, streets flooded in late January by heavy rains and melting snow.

Significant Weather Events of 1996

- **January 6-9.** A blizzard dumps 2 to 4 feet (61 to 122 cm) of snow over 12 mid-Atlantic and New England states, paralyzing much of the East Coast.

- **January 18-21.** Heavy rains and melting snow in the Northeast unleash floods that force tens of thousands from their homes.

- **February 2.** Arctic air blasts the northern plains, sending temperatures as low as -60 °F (-51 °C).

- **February 9.** Heavy rains and melting snow in the Northwest trigger record floods in Washington, Oregon, Idaho, and Montana.

- **April 14 & 21.** A tornado tears across three north-central Arkansas counties, leaving 7 dead. A week later, 4 more die when tornadoes rip through western Arkansas.

- **July 19-22.** Torrential rains in eastern Quebec lead to severe flooding along the Saguenay River, killing 10 people and causing $436 million in damage.

- **September 5.** Hurricane Fran slams 115-mile- (185-km-) per-hour winds into Cape Fear, North Carolina. Blowing in a northwesterly direction, the storm cuts a destructive swath as far inland as Harpers Ferry, West Virginia.

- **November 9-14.** A late autumn storm dumps 50 inches (127 centimeters) of snow on Shaker Heights, a suburb of Cleveland, Ohio.

Sunbathers in Marquette, Michigan, gather ice from Lake Superior in late May. A long, cool spring kept water temperature in the Great Lakes unusually low well into summer.

Clusters of slow-moving thunderstorms dropped exceptionally heavy rain in mid-July from the Missouri River valley to Illinois and Indiana. In a 24-hour period on July 17 and 18, nearly 17 inches (43 centimeters) of rain fell in Aurora, Illinois, establishing new state record. The same storm intensified into an unusually strong low pressure system that produced wind gusts to 154 miles (248 kilometers) per hour atop Mount Washington in New Hampshire. This was the strongest gust ever recorded in summer on New England's tallest mountain.

In contrast, exceptional heat and dry weather persisted through July and into autumn over most Western states. By the end of October, wildfires had consumed 6 million acres (2.4 million hectares) nationwide, the largest area in one year since 1952.

Although August 1996 was not as wet as the early summer in the Middle Atlantic States, the relatively cool, wet season kept temperatures below 90 °F (32 °C) more often than normal. For the first time in more than 100 years, temperatures in New York City's Central Park did not reach 90 °F in June or July.

Autumn. On September 5, Hurricane Fran became the third tropical cyclone of the season to land along the southern coast of North Carolina. Wind gusts of 115 miles (185 kilometers) per hour were recorded near the coast. The remnants of Fran moved into the central Appalachians, where severe flooding resulted from torrential rain. The Potomac and Shenandoah rivers crested 2 to 21 feet (1 to 6 meters) above flood stage, forcing evacuations in adjacent sections of Maryland, Virginia, West Virginia, and Washington, D.C.

A *northeaster* (a storm with effects similar to a hurricane, but with less concentrated winds) swept along the Northeast Coast of the United States on October 18 to 21. As many as 18 inches (46 centimeters) of rain fell on some communities from eastern Pennsylvania to northern New England. Records were set at Boston and Portland, Maine, for greatest 24-hour rainfall.

In early November, heavy snow buried parts of northeastern Ohio and western Pennsylvania. Chardon, Ohio, east of Cleveland, received 69 inches (175 centimeters) of snow between the 9th and 14th. The weight of the snow brought down power lines, disrupting electricity for thousands of residents.

In mid-November, a powerful storm brought rain, snow, and mud slides to parts of the Pacific Northwest. The area was hit again in the last week of December by two major storms, which dropped 2 feet (61 centimeters) of snow on western Washington. By December 31, rain and melting snow caused mud slides and floods in Washington and Oregon. Eleven people died in the storms and property damage exceeded $125 million.   □ Fred Gadomski and Todd Miner

See also **Disasters.** In *World Book,* see **Weather.**

Weightlifting. See Sports.

Welfare. President Bill Clinton signed legislation on Aug. 22, 1996, that radically revised the United States welfare system, abolishing the main federal welfare program, known as Aid to Families with Dependent Children (AFDC). AFDC, in effect since 1935, guaranteed federal cash assistance to poor families with children. Clinton, who had vetoed two earlier versions of the reform legislation, claimed that the new law carried out his 1992 campaign pledge to "end welfare as we know it."

Reduced federal role. The new law gave lump-sum payments to the 50 states to design and carry out their own programs for the poor. The law required states to cut off benefits for most families after five years on the welfare rolls and to reduce benefits to poor families if the head of the household failed to get a job within two years. The law also eliminated most federal benefits for legal immigrants and cut $24 billion from the federal food stamp program over six years.

The changes in the welfare system were expected to reduce federal spending on welfare by $55 billion over the next six years. At the signing ceremony, Clinton said that the bill was a way "to make welfare what it was meant to be: a second chance, not a way of life." The president promised, however, to seek changes in some provisions, particularly the elimination of benefits to legal immigrants who were not U.S. citizens and the cuts in the food stamp program.

Impact on states. The new law made the states responsible for developing their own systems for assisting poor families and contained relatively few federal mandates. States that failed to place welfare recipients in jobs would be penalized with smaller federal payments. Each state was required to spend on antipoverty programs at least 75 percent of what it spent on such programs in 1994. Bonus payments would be provided to states that reduced the number of children born to unwed mothers. But benefits would be cut by 25 percent for women who failed to identify the fathers of their children.

Criticism. Opponents charged that the law would plunge at least 1 million more children into poverty. Democratic Senator Daniel Patrick Moynihan of New York said that there was no evidence that such an overhaul would succeed and that it would put children at risk. Clinton sought to avert some of these concerns by demanding, and winning, a battle with Congress to continue Medicaid, the government health-care program for the poor, and to spend $14 billion for child care to make it easier for poor parents to work.

Other critics pointed out that reducing the federal role in caring for the poor could mean higher payments by states and cities to alleviate poverty. Many doubted that jobs could be found for all former welfare recipients.   □ William J. Eaton

In *World Book,* see **Welfare.**

West Indies. In July 1996, in Bridgetown, Barbados, leaders of the 14 member nations of the Caribbean Community (CARICOM) agreed to further integrate their economies. The leaders elected to adopt more economically sound methods for running their countries' respective airline industries, make social security benefits transferable among the 14 countries, and create a $50-million Caribbean investment fund to promote private investment in the region.

Following their meeting, CARICOM leaders sought unsuccessfully to persuade the United States to grant their region the same free-trade status held by Mexico and Canada, U.S. partners in the North American Free Trade Agreement. CARICOM leaders claimed that a partnership was necessary to offset a nearly 90 percent drop in U.S. economic assistance to member nations since 1986.

Dominican elections. On Aug. 16, 1996, Leonel Fernández Reyna, 42, of the Dominican Liberation Party, began a four-year term as president of the Dominican Republic. Fernández pledged to root out government corruption remaining from Joaquín Balaguer Ricardo's 7-term, 30-year presidency.

Fernández, who attended elementary and high school in New York City, had returned in 1971 to the Dominican Republic, where he earned a law degree and worked as a journalist and professor. During his campaign, which saw unprecedented activism among New York City's immigrant Dominican population, Fernández pledged to work for closer ties with the United States. While he contrasted his youth and vigor with the 89-year-old outgoing President Balaguer, Fernández's slim victory in the June 30, 1996, runoff election was dependent on Balaguer's endorsement.

St. Lucia. In April, Vaughn Lewis, 55, of the ruling United Workers' Party, became St. Lucia's new prime minister. Lewis, the former director-general of the Organization of Eastern Caribbean States, was selected by his predecessor, John Compton, who was awarded the honorary, noncabinet post of senior minister.

St. Kitts and Nevis. In May, the U.S. Justice Department charged four citizens of the two-island nation, Saint Christopher (commonly called St. Kitts) and Nevis, with conspiracy to smuggle cocaine into the United States. The four men were allegedly linked to a drug operation, which included two sons of former Deputy Prime Minister Sidney Morris, and to the 1994 murder of another of Morris's sons and a companion.

In July 1996, Vance Amory, the premier of Nevis—hoping to achieve "respect for the little guy"—introduced legislation in Nevis's National Assembly calling for independence from St. Kitts. If the legislation were to be passed by the assembly, two-thirds of Nevis's registered voters would need to approve a referendum for the island to secede.   □ Nathan A. Haverstock

See also **Latin America** (Facts in brief table).

West Virginia. See State government.

Wisconsin. See State government.

Wyoming. See State government.

Yugoslavia. Although officially a federal republic, Yugoslavia in 1996 continued to be dominated politically by Serbia. The former Yugoslavia, which comprised six republics, broke apart in 1991. The two remaining republics—Serbia and Montenegro—formed a new Yugoslavia in 1992, but by 1996 most countries still had not recognized this federation. Yugoslavia had a president and a prime minister, but Slobodan Milošević, the president of Serbia, held the most political power.

On June 26, facing the threat of reimposed United Nations (UN) sanctions against Yugoslavia, Milošević and other Yugoslav leaders issued an ultimatum demanding the resignation of Bosnian Serb leader Radovan Karadzić, who officially stepped down in July. But Milošević continued to resist international pressure to secure the arrest of Karadzić and his military commander, General Ratko Mladić. Both were under a UN indictment for war crimes.

Milošević was reelected president of the Socialist Party of Serbia on March 2, with 1,795 out of 1,799 party delegates voting for him. Milošević's government continued to hinder opposition parties, which never the less gained increasing support.

A September poll showed that the opposition had the support of 28.5 percent of the Serbian public, compared with 24.2 percent for the Socialists. But the Socialists retained their parliamentary majority after the November elections, ensuring that Milošević would remain as president of Serbia.

Huge antigovernment demonstrations took place daily in Belgrade, the capital, in November and December. Opposition leaders accused the Socialists of election fraud. In November local elections, opposition parties won majorities in several local districts. However, the regime canceled the election results in most of the districts that it had lost. In late December, after several weeks of ignoring the protests, Milošević arranged a counter-demonstration by his supporters, who were bused in from other parts of Serbia. Violence erupted, and opposition leaders accused Milošević of causing the clash as an excuse to bring in the police to crush the protests.

Yugoslavia established diplomatic relations with Macedonia in April and with Croatia in September. On October 3, Yugoslavia and Bosnia-Herzegovina also agreed to establish diplomatic relations. The UN Security Council formally ended sanctions against Yugoslavia October 1, but it did not reverse Yugoslavia's suspension from the General Assembly.

Serbia's inflation rate reached 120 percent in 1995 and 1996, and unemployment stood at 50 percent. The end of UN sanctions did not ease economic burdens, and many workers received no wages for long periods of time.   □ Sharon L. Wolchik

See also **Bosnia-Herzegovina; Croatia; Europe** (Facts in brief table); **United Nations.** In *World Book*, see **Yugoslavia.**

Yukon Territory. See Canadian Territories.

Zaire. Zaire's political situation deteriorated dramatically in 1996. In November, hundreds of thousands of refugees abandoned camps in Zaire and started for home amidst the chaos of war. Most of the refugees were of the Hutu ethnic group and had left Rwanda in 1994 after the Tutsi, another ethnic group, defeated the Hutu in a civil war that included the mass murder of Tutsi at the hands of Hutu.

Politics. While President Mobutu Sese Seko held onto power in 1996, his extended absences in Europe for medical treatment raised speculation about his health and about a possible successor. Mobutu's prime minister, Kengo wa Dondo, impressed the international community as an able leader, especially in bringing inflation under control. However, the impasse between Mobutu and Etienne Tshisekedi, the main leader of the opposition, continued in spite of attempts made in 1996 to resolve differences.

Slide into chaos. Zaire's affairs in 1996 were largely dominated by the refugees, over 1 million Rwandans and many thousands of Burundians, who refused to leave the camps along Zaire's eastern border. In August, Zaire and Rwanda agreed to cooperate in *repatriating*, or sending home, refugees. But an orderly repatriation became impossible when sporadic fighting broke out in September.

The Tutsi, a minority in Zaire, fought militias made up of Hutu refugees, aided by Zaire government troops. Zaire rebel militias, opposed to the Mobutu regime, fought Zaire army regulars. The army also engaged the army of Rwanda.

In late October and early November, as the Zairian and Rwandan armies lobbed artillery fire across the border, the international community considered possible interventions. The United States proposed a peacekeeping force under the auspices of the United Nations (UN). While this proposal found little support among Western powers, the UN, in early November, did send a special envoy to the region.

The exodus. In mid-November, the situation changed dramatically when Hutu militias attacked refugee camps near Goma, routing the government army and shutting down the camps. After more than two years, the embattled refugees in eastern Zaire began to move. Hundreds of thousands poured across the border into Rwanda. So massive was the exodus that its progress could be tracked by satellite. Canada proposed air-dropping food to starving refugees still in Zaire. Meanwhile, the situation in eastern Zaire remained extremely unstable. Observers feared the rapid collapse of the Zairian army could lead to the downfall of Mobutu or even the breakup of Zaire. □ Mark DeLancey

See also **Africa** (Facts in brief table); **Rwanda.** In *World Book*, see **Zaire.**

Zambia. See **Africa.**

Zimbabwe. See **Africa.**

Zoology. See **Biology.**

Zoos and aquariums across the United States welcomed the public to a large number of new, naturalistic exhibits in 1996. Aquatic animals and Asian wildlife provided dominant themes.

Baywatch. California's Monterey Bay Aquarium opened "Outer Bay" in March. At the three-story centerpiece gallery, visitors observed approximately 50 marine species through the world's largest single-pane window—an acrylic panel 15 feet (4.6 meters) tall and 54 feet (16.5 meters) wide. The 1-million-gallon (3.8 million-liter) tank housed blue and soupfin sharks, green sea turtles, and giant ocean sunfish, which can grow to 10 feet (3 meters) in length and weigh more than 3,000 pounds (1,360 kilograms). The tank also housed California barracudas, pelagic stingrays with wingspans of 3 feet (9 meters), and fast-swimming open-ocean fishes.

Chicago swamps. Brookfield Zoo in suburban Chicago opened "The Swamp: Wonders of Our Wetlands" in March. Visitors entered a Southern cypress "swamp" at sunrise. Mist rose from the water as animals gave voice to the morning. Green and little blue herons, white ibis, and snowy egrets stalked shallow waters. A winding boardwalk through towering, mossy cypress trees offered views of wood storks with 5-foot (1.5-meter) wingspreads, anhingas (or snakebirds) clinging to logs as they dried their wings, a colony of big brown bats roosting in a tree, and American alligators cruising the water.

Kentucky's Asian islands. In July, the Louisville Zoo in Kentucky began transporting visitors to Asian jungle habitats with the opening of "Islands." Inside facsimiles of Indonesian ceremonial huts, glass walls opened on the exhibit's cornerstone—three separate habitats found along a tropical forest stream. The forest replicas harbored orangutans, Malayan tapirs, a Sumatran tiger, siamang gibbons, and wild pigs called babirusas. "Islands" was the world's first zoo exhibit that allowed the animals to move through controlled passageways from one habitat to another, enabling them to encounter a variety of settings and foods, much as they would in the wild.

Monkeyshines. The Denver Zoo in July opened "Primate Panorama." A forested trail wound past the island home of rare lemurs from Madagascar and the West African habitat of a troop of mandrills. Another area afforded "moonlit" views of nocturnal species, such as slender lorises from India. Other displays showcased Southeast Asian primates, such as white-handed gibbons, and a variety of African monkeys. Sumatran orangutans climbed through the branches of a large, tree-filled area representing an Indonesian rain forest. The largest area, a forest home for gorillas, included a replica of a central West African village with a *shamba* (farm) and its vegetable garden, providing natural forage for the gorillas and realistically illustrating human encroachment on the wild. □ Eugene J. Walter, Jr.

In *World Book*, see **Zoo.**

1996

Dictionary Supplement

A list of new words added to the 1997 edition of *The World Book Dictionary* because they have been used enough to become a permanent part of our ever-changing language.

definition

spell | ing

word

wèrd), *n.*, *v.* –*n.*
 und or a group of
s that has meaning
an independent
speech; vocable:
ak words when
. A free form which
phrase is a word.
, then, is a free
form which does not
consist entirely of . . .
lesser free forms; in
brief, a word is a
minimum free form
(Leonard Bloomfield).

dictionary

dic|tion|ar|y (dik´shə ner´ē), *n.*, *pl.* –ar|ies.
1. a book that explains the words of a language,
or some special kind of words. It is usually arranged
alphabetically. One can use a dictionary to find out
the meaning, pronunciation, or spelling of a word.

1. a way of pronouncing:
pro|nun|ci|a|tion
a foreign pronunciation.

sup|ple|ment
(sup´lə mənt), *n.* 1. Something added to complete a thing,
or to make it larger or better.

A a

all-wheel-drive (ôl´whēl´drīv), *n.* a four-wheel drive transmission in a motor vehicle: [*Audi's*] *Quattro all-wheel-drive vehicle has been a champion in competitive endurance car racing since its introduction* (Vanity Fair).

alternative weapon, a weapon designed to control or disable without killing: *Attorney General Reno . . . became enthusiastic about alternative weapons after she was forced to take some of the blame for the Branch Davidian nightmare* (Spy Magazine).

an|nus hor|ri|bilis or **An|nus Hor|ri-bilis** (an´əs hô rē´bə lis), *pl.* **an|ni hor|ri|bile** or **An|ni Hor|ri|bile** (an´ī hô rē´bə lē), *Latin.* a horrible year; a year of disasters: *Leading national figures have been asking serious questions about an annus horribilis that had seen Germany dragged into an economic crisis* (Manchester Guardian Weekly).

B b

bench|mark (bench´märk´), *v.t.* to compare with others in order to establish a relative standard, as of performance: *In preparing for the marketing transition . . . they benchmarked a variety of other companies* (Investor's Business Daily).

big tent, **1** accommodating differing opinions within an organization: *The pro-choice faction had been led to believe . . . that the party would lean at least a little toward the "big tent" concept* [*of*] *its late chairman, Lee Atwater* (Time). **2** tolerance of differing opinions: *Nobody ever . . . asks him* [*House speaker Gingrich*] *on the record if these characters and these ideas are really part of the 'big tent' that is said to enclose Republicanism* (Christopher Hitchens).

Bork or **bork** (bôrk), *v.t.* to campaign vigorously against a public figure by attacking the person's beliefs and actions. [< Robert H. Bork, born 1927]

bot|tom|feed|er (bot´əm fē´dər), *n.* **1** a person who lives at the lowest level of society; poor and insignificant person: *Odets had been one of life's bottomfeeders, living off dimes and dreams as an actor with the Group Theatre* (New Yorker). **2** a person whose actions are disreputable: *Pickers have traditionally been the bottomfeeders of the antiques world, "taking things from people, like you were out hunting deer"* (International Herald Tribune).

brows|er (brou´zər), *n.* **1** a person or animal that browses. **2** computer software that allows the user to skim information lists before selecting an option: *Your provider may offer "browsers," more sophisticated services to help you weed through information and get to specific topics* (Business Mexico).

BSE, bovine spongiform encephalopathy.

C c

cli|ent-serv|er (klī´ənt sér´vər), *adj.,* or **cli|ent server**, of or relating to a computer network linking many personal computers to one master computer that provides backup support: *All these companies sell to the "client-server market," . . . computer systems that split up work between a network of desktop computers and "host" machines that manage the network* (Wall Street Journal).

clock speed, the number of cycles per second at which a computer's hardware operates, usually expressed in megahertz: *"Clock speed" refers to how many times the innards of the microprocessor tick each second* (Personal Computing).

colo|nia, *n.* (kə lō´nē ə), *n.* a Hispanic-American community of poor residents, lacking the services and regulation of local government, especially along the border of the United States and Mexico: *In the colonias near El Paso, for example, an estimated 30,000 people have no safe drinking water, and 53,000 lack sewers* (World Book Year Book).

complexity, *n.* Mathematics, Physics. **1** the level of random disorder out of which a relatively stable condition will evolve in a series of events: *Complexity . . . holds that even the wildest disorder may eventually cohere into a pattern—as when the teeming molecules of the young earth united in the arrangement that became life* (Time). **2** the study of complex systems: *One of complexity's main buzz words is "self-organization"* (Time).

D d

de|at|trib|ute (dē´ə trib´yüt), *v.t., v.i.,* **-ut|ed, -ut|ing.** to consider a person as no longer the creator of a particular artistic work: *The Met's curators take the view that the urge to deattribute has got out of hand* (New York Times).

document, *n.* information stored as a unit on a computer: *"Our view is that a document is anything that contains information that you need to access"* (Financial Times).

—*adj.* of or relating to information stored in a computer: *MBE centers . . . offer a wide variety of clerical services—including packaging, document translation . . .* (Business Mexico).

E e

e|co-dump|ing (ē´kō dum´ping, ek´ō-), *n.* the practice of reducing manufacturing cost of a product by neglecting or ignoring environmental regulations: *One issue that is bound to come up in discussions of trade and the environment is "eco-dumping"* (Business Mexico).

electronic town hall, a public meeting in which groups in different localities are able to interact by means of a communications system: *Speaking at an electronic town hall in Charlotte, North Carolina, last week, Clinton blamed the volatile financial markets* (Time).

extreme fighting, a contest of bare-knuckle fighting with few or no rules: *New York City would see its first extreme fighting tournament, . . . in which two men pummel each other until one is knocked unconscious or beaten into submission* (New York Times).

F f

fifteen, *n., adj.* **fifteen minutes (of fame)**, a brief period of celebrity: *The pathetic film extra Kato Kaelin won and lost his fifteen minutes; parlaying a slight acquaintance with the superstar defendant into . . . the grand sum of $50,000 for spilling the beans* (London Review of Books).

flame, *v.t. Slang.* to scorn, insult, or dispute with angrily on a computer network: *Don't flame people for bad grammar or spelling errors* (Time).

flat-screen (flat´skrēn´), *adj.* = flat-panel: *Flat-screen televisions have been the stuff of science fiction since the early 1950s* (Wall Street Journal).

G g

gated community, a housing development to which public access is restricted, usually by means of a private security force: *Residential-improvement districts clearly stem from an exclusionary impulse . . . It's a move toward L.A.-style 'gated communities'* (New York Magazine).

H h

home page, a display of information found at a particular site on a computer network: *Emery Web site gets a home page, an introductory screen with graphics and text resembling a page from a slick magazine* (New York Times).

Human Genome Project, a plan to identify all human genes and to show where each gene is located on a specific chromosome: *Today we are . . . embarrassed by the crudity of the genetic arguments that link genes to IQ and IQ to race or class . . . but the erroneous claims made for the Human Genome Project . . . do not allay such politically malignant attitudes* (Gabriel Dover).

I i

identity politics, political actions or principles based on ethnic or racial identity, or other special interest: *Identity politics . . . leads a group to envision itself as necessarily alienated from American culture at large, and . . . victimized by the ideas . . . it opposes* (Robert S. Boynton).

-intensive, *combining form.* requiring the use of large amounts of ____, as in *labor-intensive, capital-intensive, advertising-intensive,* or *data-intensive.*

J j

jungle music, fast-paced percussive dance music produced on synthesizers that create distorted effects and irregular rhythms: *Jungle music has multiple roots . . . elements of hip-hop, techno and reggae fused to create a distinctively British sound* (New York Times).

L l

liberal nationalism, nationalism that avoids encouraging ethnic or religious chauvinism: *In the campaign he* [*Mr. Parizeau*] *and Lucien Bouchard, . . . had painstakingly cast the movement in the image of liberal nationalism. "Ours is not an ethnic nationalism . . . the 'nation québécoise' is constituted by the people as a whole"* (Andrew Sark).

line dance, a country dance in which dancers face each other arranged in two lines and perform repetitive steps: *Learn some of the most popular traditional line dances . . . as seen on the country channel TNN* (Brewster Adult Education).

418

M m

ma|fi|ya or **maf|yi|a** (mä′fē yä, mäf′ yē ə), *n.* organized crime in Russia: *It is now conventional wisdom that mafiya extortion and official corruption of every sort are inflicting much damage on the Russian economy* (London Review of Books). [Russian, from English *Mafia*]

meg|a|church (meg′ə chėrch′), *n.* an extremely large group of persons with the same religious beliefs, usually expressing a fundamentalist philosophy: *Some of the largest megachurches are writing their own music, publishing their own religious education books and holding training conferences* (New York Times).

N n

net asset value, the value of a closed-end fund's securities after expenses are deducted: *A closed-end fund's shares are fixed in number and have two prices: The one at which they trade on the market and their net asset value* (New York Daily News).

nonconventional weapon, any nuclear, chemical, or biological weapon: *This new terrorism poses unprecedented dangers, especially because of Iran's drive to develop nonconventional weapons* (New York Times).

nonlethal weapon, any weapon designed primarily to disable rather than to kill: *There's a wide variety of these new nonlethal weapons . . . crowd-control 900, pinpointed laser beams . . . and tightly targeted microwaves* (Spy Magazine).

O o

orbital debris, any thing lost in space that orbits the earth, including equipment or parts, as of a spacecraft, artificial satellite, etc.; space junk: *Johnson, a leading authority on orbital debris, has found no confirmed case of injury or significant property damage from space junk* (USA Today).

P p

path dependence, the theory that one particular choice will determine a series of results: *A hypothesis called "path dependence" . . . suggests that, in choosing standards and technologies, our market-based economy frequently locks us into bad solutions* (Investor's Business Daily).

peer-to-peer (pir′tü pir′, -tə-), *n., adj.*
—*n.* a computer network having direct communication between users without a central server: *With peer-to-peer . . . each PC . . . acts as both a client and a server* (Financial Times).
—*adj.* of or having to do with a computer network that uses direct communication: *Intel is working on developing . . . technology that moves away from the client/server architecture and uses advanced peer-to-peer architecture* (Tom Foremski).

pre|ex|ist|ing or **pre-ex|ist|ing condition** (prē′ig zis′ting), any disease or

medical problem a person develops prior to seeking coverage of health insurance: *Many Americans may also wonder whatever happened to . . . the rules intended to keep insurance companies from denying coverage on grounds like "preexisting conditions"* (New York Times).

purine nucleoside phosphorylase, an enzyme that keeps T cells functioning by cleansing them of contaminants: *Purine nucleoside phosphorylase . . . cleans up metabolic debris that would otherwise build up inside the T cells and shut them down* (Jane E. Brody).

Q q

quad-scan (kwod′skan), *adj.* able to scan a CD-ROM four times faster than an audio compact disc is scanned: *The CD-ROM player is a quad-scan model and can quickly be swapped with the included floppy disk drive* (Stephen Manes).

quad-speed (kwod′spēd), *adj.* spinning a CD-ROM at four times the speed of an audio compact disc; quadruple-speed: *Better CD-ROM drives are now what's called quad-speed* (Personal Computing).

quantum interference or **quantum interference excitation**, a technique to control the excitation of molecules by the use of two interfering laser beams, which are passed through hydrogen gas in order to adjust the wavelength of each laser: *The mechanism that allows the physicists to control the reaction precisely is called quantum interference—the mutual interference of two laser beams as they excite hydrogen iodide molecules to break up in two different ways* (Malcolm W. Browne).

R r

race card racial prejudice, especially when used as part of a plan or strategy: *Simpson's lawyers have been playing the vaunted race card looking for that one juror who could hang his hat on a cockeyed conspiracy theory* (Richard Cohen).

reality check, a proof or test of the truth of a belief or opinion by comparison with known fact: *Bayles heaps scorn on those artists who disagree with her, calling them . . . in need of a reality check* (Atlantic).

Ro|din|i|a (rō din′ē ə), *n.* a hypothetical supercontinent that existed in the late Pre-Cambrian period. The supercontinents of Laurasia (North America, Europe, and Asia) and Gondwanaland (South America, Africa, India, Australia, and Antarctica) were formed from it. *The chief evidence . . . consists of the presence on all modern continents of sections of an ancient mountain range . . . that apparently spanned Rodinia* (World Book Year Book). [< Russian *rod* (it) to beget (as the source of, or begetting of, all later land masses) + *-inia,* as in *Sardinia*]

S s

server, *n.* a central computer that stores and sends information to, or provides backup support for, workstations on a network: *The traditional mainframe . . . has found a new role as a corporate information warehouse or large-scale enterprise network server* (Financial Times).

site, *n.* a location for particular information on a computer network: *Programmers are designing specialized software that allows parents to select what sites on computer networks their children can visit* (Steve Lohr).

soft money 1 campaign funds given indirectly to a candidate for federal office through a political party: *Critics of the current fund-raising system say soft money has become a convenient way of circumventing the limits on contributions to a candidate* (New York Times). **2** any funds used as a means of indirect support: *All Baylor scientists . . . must raise part or all of their salaries and fringe benefits through grants . . . most or all researchers are on this "soft money"* (Washington Post).

surf, *v.i.* to look at a series of things in quick succession, especially on a computer or television screen: *Many online users are happy to surf through these services, checking out specs in Road & Track or downloading photos* (Time). —*v.t.* to look at in quick succession, especially on a computer or television screen: *to surf the Internet.*

T t

toggle, *n., v.* to select or operate (something) by switching: *Toggle either switch up for a higher gear or down for a lower gear* (New York Post). —*v.i.* **1** to select by switching: *Toggle via menu commands between voice and data instantly* (Global Computer Supplies). **2** *Figurative.* to switch or shift: *The Citadel men's approach to women seems to toggle between extremes of gentility and fury.* (New Yorker).

U u

ultimate fighting, = extreme fighting: *The competition, called extreme or ultimate fighting, pits two bare-knuckled fighters who punch, kick and brawl their way toward an often bloody denouement* (Dan Barry).

W w

walk-by shooting, an act or instance of shooting a person while walking past: *. . . describing a successful walk-by shooting. "I hop a fence and I'm gone"* (New York Times).

win-win (win′win′), *adj.* **1** of benefit to all parties involved: *Mr. Perlmutter says it is a classic win-win situation. "I can take on more complex cases . . . And [the firm] . . . gets access to my clients* (New York Times). **2** without negative consequences; beneficial: *Jeanne Nathan . . . described the rumored AT&T-Sony deal as "win-win for the city of New York" because the AT&T jobs would remain while Sony would be making a high-profile commitment to New York* (New York News Day).

X x

xen|o|trans|plan|ta|tion (zen′ō trans′-plan tā′shən, -plän-), *n.* an act or instance of transplanting an animal organ or tissue into a human being: *The unusual operation may foreshadow the return of permanent animal-to-human transplants, a procedure called xenotransplantation* (Science News).

Pronunciation Key: hat, āge, cãre, fär; let, ēqual, tėrm; it, īce; hot, ōpen, ôrder; oil, out; cup, pu̇t, rüle; child; long; thin; ᴛнen; zh, measure; ə represents **a** in about, **e** in taken, **i** in pencil, **o** in lemon, **u** in circus.

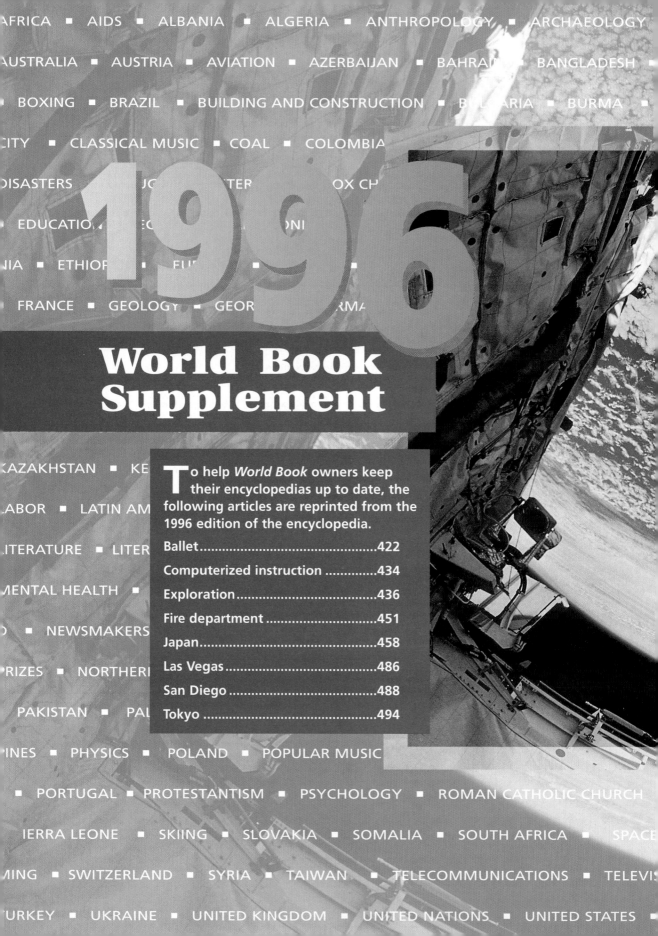

AFRICA ▪ AIDS ▪ ALBANIA ▪ ALGERIA ▪ ANTHROPOLOGY ▪ ARCHAEOLOGY

AUSTRALIA ▪ AUSTRIA ▪ AVIATION ▪ AZERBAIJAN ▪ BAHRAIN ▪ BANGLADESH ▪

▪ BOXING ▪ BRAZIL ▪ BUILDING AND CONSTRUCTION ▪ BULGARIA ▪ BURMA ▪

CITY ▪ CLASSICAL MUSIC ▪ COAL ▪ COLOMBIA

DISASTERS ▪ UC TER OX CH

▪ EDUCATIO EC NI

IA ▪ ETHIOP FU ▪

▪ FRANCE ▪ GEOLOGY ▪ GEOR RMA

World Book Supplement

To help *World Book* owners keep their encyclopedias up to date, the following articles are reprinted from the 1996 edition of the encyclopedia.

KAZAKHSTAN ▪ KE

LABOR ▪ LATIN AM

LITERATURE ▪ LITER

MENTAL HEALTH ▪

▪ NEWSMAKERS

PRIZES ▪ NORTHERN

PAKISTAN ▪ PAL

INES ▪ PHYSICS ▪ POLAND ▪ POPULAR MUSIC

▪ PORTUGAL ▪ PROTESTANTISM ▪ PSYCHOLOGY ▪ ROMAN CATHOLIC CHURCH

IERRA LEONE ▪ SKIING ▪ SLOVAKIA ▪ SOMALIA ▪ SOUTH AFRICA ▪ SPACE

MING ▪ SWITZERLAND ▪ SYRIA ▪ TAIWAN ▪ TELECOMMUNICATIONS ▪ TELEVIS

TURKEY ▪ UKRAINE ▪ UNITED KINGDOM ▪ UNITED NATIONS ▪ UNITED STATES

A classical ballet combines graceful, skilled dancers with beautiful music and elaborate scenery. *The Sleeping Beauty, above,* ranks among the most popular works in ballet. This production features dancers from the United Kingdom's Royal Ballet, one of the world's best-known companies.

Ballet

Ballet is a form of theatrical dance that uses formal, set movements and poses characterized by elegance and grace. Ballet dancers usually hold their bodies straight and lifted up. Ballet technique is based on positions in which the dancer's legs rotate outward from the hip joint and the feet turn outward. This rotation is called *turnout.*

An individual work or performance is called a ballet if it features ballet dancing. A ballet may tell a story, express a mood, illustrate the music that accompanies it, or simply portray movement. A ballet may consist of a full-length story, or it can be made up of short works, often in different styles. Ballets are sometimes included in other theatrical works, such as musical comedies and operas. *Choreographers* (creators of dances) arrange the steps and movements that form the complete work.

Ballet is a living art that can vary from performance to performance. Different dancers bring different qualities to their roles. The production will be affected by the harmony among performers, especially between the principal male dancer and the *ballerina* (leading female dancer). Throughout ballet history, some remarkable partnerships have developed, such as the one that began in the 1960's between Russian-born dancer Rudolf Nureyev and English ballerina Dame Margot Fonteyn. These pairings emerge when the partners show a particular understanding of each other, look good together physically, and perform in a complementary way.

Although dancing is the most important feature of a ballet, the presentation usually includes music, scenery, and costumes. Many ballets are collaborations among choreographers, set and costume designers, and composers. Ballets are performed by groups called *companies* or *troupes.* The *artistic director* of the company selects the *repertory* (ballets to be performed). The artistic director may also be the troupe's choreographer.

Ballet dancers perform many movements that are difficult for the body. However, when these movements are well executed, they look easy. Ballet dancers have always been known for their ability to control their bodies. Skilled dancers can perform complex turns, make magnificent leaps, and maintain control whether moving slowly or with great speed. Some dancers are also known for their dramatic and expressive skills or for their sensitivity to the phrasing of the music.

Ballet has become increasingly athletic over time, requiring greater flexibility and strength. Male dancers were once known primarily for their leaps, turns, and skills at partnering ballerinas. Now men have gained recognition for flexibility, high leg kicks, and other feats rarely attempted by earlier dancers. Female dancers were once known largely for dancing *on point* (on their toes) with the support of special shoes. Now female dancers also perform strong, complex leaps.

Training for ballet

The ideal ballet dancer has a well-proportioned body, with long legs and a slender torso. A dancer needs flexi-

Terms used in ballet

WORLD BOOK illustrations by Linda Worrall, Bernard Thornton Artists

Adagio, *uh DAH joh* or *uh DAH zhee oh,* is a series of slow, sustained movements in a ballet lesson to develop balance, line, and grace. It is also a slow dance in which the female partner performs difficult feats of balancing.

Allegro, *uh LAY groh* or *uh LEHG roh,* is a series of quick, lively movements.

Arabesque, *AR uh BEHSK,* is a pose in which one leg is raised and extended with a straight knee either in front of or behind the dancer, with the arms held in any of various positions.

Attitude is a pose in which one leg is raised and bent either behind or in front of the dancer with the knee higher than the foot.

Ballerina is a leading female dancer.

Barre, *bahr,* is a round wooden or metal rod that may be attached to a studio wall, or freestanding and portable. Dancers use the barre for support during ballet exercises.

Center work is the series of exercises performed in the second half of a class, without the support of a barre.

Choreography, *KAWR ee AHG ruh fee,* is the arranged movements that make up a ballet. The creator of the movements is a *choreographer.*

Corps de ballet, *KAWR duh ba LAY,* is the group of dancers who perform as an ensemble.

Danseur, *dahn SUR,* is a male dancer.

Divertissement, *dee vehr tees MAHN,* is a series of dances designed to show technical skill. It is inserted into many story ballets, but it is not necessarily related to the plot.

Entrechat, *ahn truh SHAH,* is a jump in which the dancer rapidly crosses the legs in front of and behind each other a number of times.

Jeté, *zheh TAY,* is a jump from one foot to the other with an outward kick of the leg. A *grand jeté* is a large forward leap, passing from one foot to the other.

Pas de deux, *PAH duh DU,* is a dance for two people, usually a man and a woman.

Pirouette, *PIHR u EHT,* is a full turn completed on one foot.

Plié, *plee AY,* is a bend of the knees. It is one of the most basic exercises in a ballet class.

Point work is dancing on the tips of the toes with the support of special ballet shoes.

Port de bras, *pawr duh BRAH,* is the technique of moving the arms. It is also the name of the exercise through which this technique is developed or displayed.

Relevé, *ruh luh VAY,* is raising the body by lifting the heels.

Révérence, *ray vay RAHNS,* is a bow or series of bows at the end of a class.

Rond de jambe, *rawn duh ZHAHNB,* is a ballet exercise in which one leg makes a circling motion on the floor or in the air.

Tendu, *tahn DOO,* is a ballet exercise in which the foot is "stretched" away from the body but still touches the floor.

Turnout is the basic position of the legs and feet in ballet. The legs are completely turned outward, with the feet forming a straight line with the heels together.

Tutu is a ballerina's skirt. It is made of layers of net fabric.

Arabesque

Attitude

Grand jeté

Pirouette   Plié

Martha Swope

Partnering brings together a principal male dancer and a ballerina. The partners frequently display their skills in a specially choreographed duet within a ballet called a *pas de deux, above.*

bility, strength, discipline, and control. The dancer also must have a good sense of rhythm and musical phrasing plus dramatic expressiveness. However, many ballet dancers do not start with ideal bodies. They work hard for years to achieve the physical qualities needed for ballet.

Ballet requires years of training that should begin when the dancer is a child, usually about 8 years old. Dancers continue to take classes throughout their careers to maintain their skills.

The ballet teacher. In choosing a teacher, the student or parent should carefully consider the instructor's background and experience. Teachers without the proper qualifications can cause the student harm, and even physical injury. Poor teaching will delay a dancer's progress, forcing him or her to unlearn the incorrect lessons before mastering proper technique. Many teachers are active or retired performers. However, good teachers need not have been ballet dancers themselves.

Some ballet companies operate their own schools, training students for eventual membership in the company. They usually admit children as students after auditions. Other companies hold classes open to the public.

The ballet studio. A ballet class typically takes place in a special studio designed for ballet dancers. The best studios have a flexible wooden floor, which is less jarring to a dancer's body than a concrete surface. The studio should provide unobstructed spaces, plentiful mirrors, and wooden or metal rods called *barres* that are attached to a wall. A barre can also be free-standing or portable. Dancers use the barre for support.

A ballet class usually lasts about 90 minutes. Ideally, a class will have live music to accompany the dancers during their exercises. Often, recorded music is used.

The class normally begins with exercises at the barre. Time spent on the barre varies, depending on the goals of the class. Sometimes barre work occupies most of the class time. It may also serve merely as a quick warm-up. The work at the barre is the most basic part of a dancer's training, and it is a daily routine for professional dancers.

The first exercise will usually include *pliés* (knee bends) at various depths and in various positions. Other exercises include *tendus*, in which the leg is extended and the foot is stretched to a point position while in contact with the floor, and *relevés*, in which the dancer raises the feet from a flat to a point or half-point position.

WORLD BOOK photo by Molly Winkelman

A ballet studio is equipped with metal or wooden rods called *barres* that are attached to a wall. Dancers use a barre for support while they practice. A studio also includes mirrors and a flexible wooden floor. The studio should provide enough space to allow the dancers to work without interfering with each other.

Dancers also practice traditional arm movements known as *ports de bras,* either separately or combined with other exercises. The exercises are designed to warm up the muscles, loosen the joints, build strength, and increase the dancer's coordination. The activities will increase in complexity and range as students advance in their knowledge and ability.

The second part of the class is devoted to *center work,* which takes place in the center of the studio, without the support of the barre. Dancers first perform slow combinations to test their balance and to build strength. These combinations include exercises in shifting from one foot to the other, changing the direction of the body in space, and moving the arms through *ports de bras.* Center work may include an *adagio,* a long slow combination that frequently involves large slow movements of one leg while balancing on the other. The dancers may also practice ballet turns. Center exercises usually build in speed and end with *allegro* work, which consists of fast and lively jump combinations.

Near the end of the class, dancers move across the floor and practice steps, turns, and jumps. A class traditionally concludes with dancers returning to the center of the floor. They perform a brief bow or series of bows called *révérence* to thank their teacher and the accompanist for the class.

In addition to basic ballet classes, advanced dancers may also attend special classes in such skills as partnering techniques and point work. They may also study other styles of dance and movement, such as folk dancing and pantomime.

Point work. Traditionally, point work has been reserved for female dancers. Some male dancers study it, though performing opportunities are limited to a few character or comic roles or to troupes in which men perform female roles.

A student usually needs at least three years of study to gain sufficient strength for point work. The dancer should be old enough to ensure that the feet have developed sufficiently. Point work is danced with special shoes that provide foot support, but the technique still requires knowledge, skill, and strength. Beginning students usually start with simple exercises that are part of regular classroom routine. They wear point shoes for only part of the class. As they advance, students attend classes devoted entirely to point work.

A dancer's life

A ballet career can offer enormous satisfaction, but it is also strenuous and difficult. Job opportunities for ballet dancers are limited and salaries are low, except for a few superstars. Performing careers tend to be short, and dancers are always vulnerable to injury. Although some performers dance for many years, ballet is basically for young adults.

After the first years of training, students preparing for a professional career may take three to six ballet classes a week. Professional dancers try to attend at least one class a day. It can be difficult to combine ballet training with regular school. Many young dancers interested in a professional career choose to skip or postpone college. They believe the college years from the late teens to the early 20's are too valuable in the short career of a dancer to devote the time to anything but ballet.

Design of a ballerina's shoe

A ballerina's point shoe is handmade from leather or canvas and covered with satin. The shoe is fastened onto the foot with ankle ribbons. Additional support comes from a reinforced inner sole. The hard toe is a layer of fabric mixed with special glue.

WORLD BOOK illustrations by Barbara Cousins

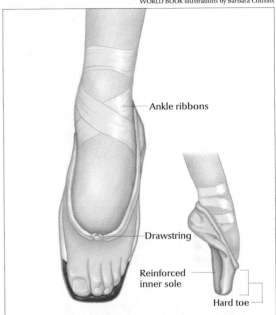

Ankle ribbons

Drawstring

Reinforced inner sole

Hard toe

WORLD BOOK photo by Molly Winkelman

Center work usually follows warm-ups at the barre in a ballet class. The dancing takes place in the center of the studio. Small groups of dancers practice jumps, turns, and other exercises.

The five ballet positions

Every ballet movement and pose begins with the feet in one of five positions. The legs and feet should be turned out from the hip in each position to permit greater freedom of movement. The toes should be flat on the floor. When the heels are flat on the floor, the body weight should be balanced equally on both legs. There are also five positions of the arms. The proper arm position should produce a clear line that runs from the shoulder to the fingertips. The pictures on this page illustrate the most common combinations of feet and arm positions. Beginning ballet students should memorize the five positions of the feet and arms. They cannot begin training without this knowledge.

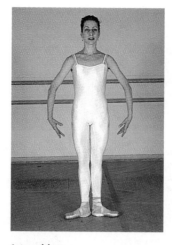

1st position

2nd position

3rd position

4th position

5th position

WORLD BOOK photos by Molly Winkelman

After dancers retire, some become teachers or rehearsal directors who help stage ballets. Others may become dance administrators, designers, historians, physical therapists, photographers, or critics. Some become *notaters*—that is, people who preserve ballets by writing down the patterns and steps through a system of graphic symbols.

Kinds of ballet

The most familiar type of ballet is the full-length story ballet. Many of the great story ballets originated in the 1800's. One example is *Coppélia* (1870), choreographed by Arthur Saint-Léon to music by Léo Delibes, both of France. Another is *The Nutcracker* (1892), choreographed by Lev Ivanov to music by Peter Ilich Tchaikovsky, both of Russia. These ballets have *librettos* (stories) that were created specially for the work. Many ballets use existing stories. For example, fairy tales are the basis for *The Sleeping Beauty* (1890) by Marius Petipa, a French-born

choreographer who worked in Russia, and *Cinderella*, in versions by several choreographers. *Daphnis and Chloë* (1912) by the Russian-born choreographer Michel Fokine is adapted from an ancient Greek story.

Story ballets typically have two or more acts separated by intermissions. They usually feature elaborate sets and costumes and often include pantomime as well as different types of dancing. Sometimes all the dancing relates to the story. In some ballets, a *divertissement* may be injected. A divertissement is a dance segment intended to display a dancer's technical skill. Many story ballets are love stories. Most such ballets feature dramatic solos and romantic *pas de deux* (duets) by the principal dancers, who play the lovers.

A ballet program may consist of several shorter works, which may vary greatly in style and scope. Some shorter ballets describe a brief incident rather than tell a complete story. Some poetic ballets evoke moods and meanings without telling a story. A ballet may be in

© Jack Vartoogian

The choreographer, *center,* creates a ballet by arranging the steps and other movements that form the complete work. A choreographer also teaches the movements to the dancers. Some ballet companies employ a resident choreographer who is responsible for creating new ballets for the troupe's repertoire.

spired by images or events from daily life or from art and music. Ballets may focus purely upon movement. They may explore the shapes, forms, and energies that belong uniquely to ballet, or they may utilize other dance styles. A ballet may set out purely to entertain, or it may try to deal with serious social issues.

Choreography

Choreographers vary in how they create a ballet. Some create material on their own. Others come to rehearsal with only a general idea of what they want, and they then work with the dancers to develop the ballet. Choreographers must consider the scenery, costumes, and music and how these elements will fit the dancing.

Often a company's repertory will consist of works by different choreographers. Some troupes employ a resident choreographer who is responsible for creating new ballets. The most successful works often come from choreographers who work with a group of dancers over time. Frequently a dancer will be a source of inspiration for a choreographer.

Sets and costumes

A ballet's sets and costumes are often designed by the same person. Some famous artists have designed ballets, including the Spanish-born painters Pablo Picasso and Salvador Dali. Painted backdrops and side panels have traditionally been the setting for ballets. Many modern designs have employed simple structures or scenic effects created with lighting alone. Occasionally, a designer uses film or video projections. The most successful designs create mood without obstructing the stage space the dancers require.

Costumes have changed during the history of ballet, and the changes have affected how the dancers move. In the early days of ballet, female dancers wore heavy skirts

This Labanotation records the first measure of the "Sugar Plum Fairy" variation from the ballet *The Nutcracker* (1892), choreographed by Marius Petipa of France. The photographs show the dancer's chief movements to this music.

Starting position

Labanotation courtesy Dance Notation Bureau, Inc; WORLD BOOK photos

Labanotation is a system of recording all the movements in a ballet. The center vertical line in the diagram above represents the center of a dancer's body. The symbols to the left of the line stand for movements of the left side of the body, and the symbols to the right stand for those of the right side. The distance from the center line indicates the part of the body to be moved, and the shape of each symbol indicates the direction of movement. The symbol's length specifies the speed of movement.

that reached the floor. During the 1800's, ballerinas began to wear skirts called *tutus,* made of lightweight net. Those tutus that extended below the knee were known as *romantic tutus. Classical tutus* were much shorter, often reaching no lower than the top of the thighs. Since the early 1900's, shorter and lighter costumes have allowed dancers more freedom to carry out complex movements. Today, dancers sometimes perform in close-fitting leotards and tights that show the entire body. Costumes today may range from informal rehearsal outfits to elaborate constructions.

Music

Music and dance are usually considered inseparable, though ballets have been performed to experimental sounds and even to silence. The greatest choreographers have been sensitive to music, and many had musical training. They create steps and movements that work in partnership with the music. The creation of a ballet score almost always involves discussion and collaboration between the composer and the choreographer.

During the early history of ballet, music composition went hand in hand with dance composition. But as ballets become independent theatrical forms, music was reduced in importance. Serious composers did not often write dance music. In the late 1800's, the Russian composer Tchaikovsky wrote several beautiful ballet scores that restored the reputation of music composed specifically for ballet. In the 1900's, Igor Stravinsky, another Russian-born composer, continued this tradition by writing 15 ballet scores that greatly influenced the art form.

Many ballets are set to music already composed for concert rather than theatrical performance. The music may provide the inspiration for the ballet. All types of music can be used, including classical, rock, and jazz.

Preserving a ballet

A ballet does not have a firm text, as does a book or the written score of a musical composition. Choreographers often do not document their works. As a result, a ballet's choreography can easily be lost. Even if a choreographer makes no changes in a work, the steps and style may become altered as new dancers learn and perform them. Dancers may change the choreography intentionally or unintentionally. They may forget movements and lose details of the work. Sometimes choreographers change a ballet to keep it fresh. A choreographer may want to try a different approach or make adjustments to accommodate a dancer's strengths and weaknesses.

Throughout ballet history, there have been efforts to develop systems of notation that would preserve the steps and patterns of a dance. Choreographers often develop personal systems of keeping notes. Although much of what we know about earlier dances comes from such systems and notes, they all were incomplete.

In the 1920's, a Hungarian choreographer and teacher named Rudolf von Laban developed a system called *Labanotation* to analyze and record dance movement in great detail. However, Labanotation is complex and requires a specially trained notater, an expense many choreographers cannot afford.

Film, videotape, and television broadcasts have helped preserve ballets, but they are only partly successful. They cannot provide the detail and thoroughness a dancer requires to learn a work. Computer graphics can be a tool for dance analysis and are even being used to create choreography. Other resources that can help preserve ballets include verbal descriptions by choreographers, performers, spectators, and critics; photographs; and musical scores.

History

The birth of ballet. Ballet originated in Italy in the 1400's and 1500's, during a cultural movement called the Renaissance. At that time, Florence and other powerful Italian cities made up nearly independent units called *city-states.* The wealthy families who ruled the city-states did much to promote the arts. The ruling families com-

Modern sets and costumes are often simpler than those used in the elaborate productions of classical ballets. The dancers shown at the left wear informal black costumes. They are performing on an empty stage with lighting replacing sets to create a mood.

peted with one another in giving costly, fancy entertainments that included dance performances. The dancers were not professional. They were nobles of the court who danced to please their ruler.

Catherine de Médicis, a member of the ruling family of Florence, became queen of France in 1547. She introduced into the French court the same kind of entertainment she had known in Italy. The dances were staged by Balthasar de Beaujoyeulx, who moved from Italy in 1555 and became Catherine's servant and dancing master.

Many historians consider the first ballet to be Beaujoyeulx's *Ballet Comique de la Reine,* performed in Paris in 1581 in honor of a royal wedding. It was a magnificent spectacle that lasted more than five hours. The ballet included specially composed music, singing, and spoken verse as well as dancing. Because dance technique was limited, Beaujoyeulx relied on lavish costumes and scenery to impress the audience. The ballet was a great success and was widely imitated in other European courts.

Italian dancing masters taught European courtiers how to dance, and they wrote manuals that preserved many steps for modern historians. Choreography was based on the social dances of the 1500's, such as the fast-paced *courante,* the lively *galliard,* and the stately *pavan.*

Because dancing was an activity of the royal court, it emphasized refinement, elegance, and grace. Women wore such long, heavy dresses that their movements were difficult to see. Men's clothes gave them more freedom for fancy footwork and jumps. Performers often wore masks. Many ballets dealt with love and tales from Greek and Roman mythology. In England, court spectacle took the form of *masques.* This entertainment, which reached its peak in the early 1600's, often included music and dancing as well as dialogue by leading writers.

The rise of professional ballet. As ballet developed, it required greater skill. As a result, professional dancers began to replace courtiers, who became the audience rather than the performers.

The *Ballet Comique de la Reine* helped make Paris a center of the ballet world. King Louis XIV, who ruled France from the mid-1600's to his death in 1715, promoted ballet further during his reign. Louis enjoyed dancing both as a spectator and as a participant. In 1661, he founded the Royal Academy of Dancing, and in 1669, the Royal Academy of Music. The music academy, soon known as the Paris Opéra, established a dancing school in 1672. Ballet as a profession can be dated from this period. Through serious training, professional dancers developed skills that had been impossible for amateurs, and dancing became more athletic and lively.

Louis's dancing master was Pierre Beauchamps (or Beauchamp). Beauchamps is credited with defining and naming many of the ballet steps used today, including the five positions of the feet. Most ballet steps have French names because of France's central role in developing the art form.

In the early 1700's, two famous ballerinas in Paris came to represent the two main styles in ballet. Marie Sallé gained fame for her dramatic expressiveness. Her rival, Marie Camargo, was known for her technical brilliance. Camargo shortened her skirts to make her steps more visible.

Professional dancers gradually moved from royal courts to performing for the general public in theaters. Dancers, teachers, and choreographers traveled from country to country. One of the greatest companies formed during this period was the Russian Imperial Ballet of St. Petersburg, now widely known as the Kirov Ballet. Its ballet school was founded in 1738.

Ballet d'action. By the mid-1700's, a number of dance masters had developed the *ballet d'action,* a French phrase meaning *ballet with a story.* This form told a story through dance and pantomime without the aid of spoken words as in earlier ballets.

Jean Georges Noverre was the most famous promoter of ballet d'action. In an influential book called *Letters on Dancing and Ballet* (1760), Noverre wrote that technical skill should not be emphasized for its own sake. Noverre insisted that ballets should combine plot, music, and dancing in a unified whole. He urged ballet dancers to stop using masks, wigs, and bulky costumes to help explain plot and character. Noverre claimed that skillful dancers could express these story elements using only their bodies and faces.

The subject matter of story ballet began to change from its previous emphasis on mythology. Noverre still created ballets based on Greek myths and drama, but other choreographers started to explore different themes. Jean Dauberval, a Noverre pupil, dealt with ordinary people in his comic ballet about young lovers, *La Fille mal gardée (The Ill-Guarded Girl).* It was first produced in 1789 and is one of the oldest ballets still performed today. In Italy, Salvatore Viganò drew on historical characters, such as Joan of Arc and Richard the Lion-Hearted, for some of his works.

Romantic ballet. In the early 1800's, the romantic period developed in ballet. The stories in romantic ballet emphasized escape from the real world into distant lands or into a dreamlike world of the supernatural. During this period, ballet technique expanded, especially for women, who began to dance on their toes. The development of point dancing during the romantic period was a direct result of the increased fascination with dreams and enchantment. Elevation on the toes suggested a lifting away from an earthly state into a supernatural world. Carlo Blasis of Italy became perhaps the most important ballet teacher of the 1800's. His writings further defined and expanded ballet techniques, influencing later generations of dancers.

In Paris, the Italian choreographer Filippo Taglioni created the first romantic ballet, *La Sylphide* (1832), for his daughter, Marie. She danced the role of the *sylphide,* a fairylike being, in a costume that set a new fashion for ballerinas. It included a light, white skirt that ended halfway between the knee and ankle. Her arms, neck, and shoulders were bare. Marie Taglioni, with her dreamlike style, became the greatest star of Paris ballet. Her chief rival was the Austrian ballerina Fanny Elssler, who also danced in Paris. Elssler's style expressed strong human feelings. She became famous for her lively character dances, particularly the *cachucha,* a Spanish dance performed with castanets. Elssler's *cachucha* caused a sensation when she first danced it in 1836.

The outstanding ballet of the romantic period was *Giselle* (1841), choreographed by Jean Coralli and Jules Perrot. The ballet tells the story of a peasant girl who falls in love with a nobleman in disguise. She goes in

Engraving (1582) by an unknown artist; Bibliothèque Nationale, Paris

Ballet Comique de la Reine, an influential early ballet, was performed in Paris in 1581. King Henry III of France and his court watched the spectacle in a decorated palace hall, *above.*

sane and dies after discovering that he is already engaged and has betrayed her. The part of Giselle requires both expressive and technical skill and remains one of the most challenging roles in a ballerina's repertory.

Paris was the capital of the ballet world throughout the romantic period, which lasted through the mid-1800's. However, many dancers and choreographers who trained and worked in Paris took their techniques to cities outside France. For example, August Bournonville, a Danish dancer and choreographer, worked in Paris before taking over the Royal Danish Ballet in 1830. He developed a light, open, buoyant style that remains popular in Denmark today.

Ballet in Russia. During the 1800's, a number of choreographers and dancers settled in Russia. Perhaps the most important was the French choreographer Marius Petipa. He moved to Russia in 1847 and served as the ballet master for the Russian Imperial Ballet of St. Petersburg from 1870 to 1903. Petipa helped make St. Petersburg the world center of ballet by the late 1800's. He specialized in creating spectacular choreography for women, notably the leading role in *The Sleeping Beauty* (1890) and the first and third acts of *Swan Lake* (1895).

The St. Petersburg company produced some of the greatest dancers in ballet history. The best known include Anna Pavlova and Vaslav Nijinsky. Pavlova became famous for the graceful, poetic, spiritual quality of her dancing. Nijinsky elevated the status of male dancers and thrilled audiences with his spectacular leaps.

Both Pavlova and Nijinsky later danced with a famous Russian touring company, Sergei Diaghilev's Ballets Russes. Diaghilev, one of the world's greatest producers of ballets, established the company in Russia in 1909. Diaghilev was interested in new developments in ballet and attracted some of the most important modern artists and composers of his time to collaborate on ballets. His choreographers included George Balanchine, Michel Fokine, Léonide Massine, Nijinsky, and Nijinsky's sister Bronislava Nijinska.

With Diaghilev's company, Fokine had the opportunity to carry out his ideas. In many ballets of the time, story-telling scenes alternated with pantomime and displays of technical dancing. Fokine wanted all the elements in a ballet to contribute to the story. He urged that all the arts in ballet be blended into a harmonious whole.

For the Ballets Russes, Fokine created such brilliant works as *Scheherazade* (1910), *The Firebird* (1910), and *Petrouchka* (1911). He also created one of the first one-act ballets without a story, *Chopiniana* (1907), renamed *Les Sylphides* (1909), to music by Polish composer Frédéric Chopin. Nijinsky also choreographed major experimental works for the Ballets Russes, especially *Afternoon of a Faun* (1912) and *The Rite of Spring* (1913). Both works caused a sensation at their premieres in Paris.

The Ballets Russes never actually performed in Russia. However, the company brought a Russian spirit and artistry to dance that thrilled audiences throughout the world. In Europe, its huge popularity revitalized ballet. The company also kindled enthusiasm about ballet in areas that had no strong tradition of ballet, such as South America. The Ballets Russes broke up after Diaghilev's death in 1929. His dancers and choreographers joined companies in many parts of the world, and they influenced ballet wherever they went.

Engraving (1781) by John Boydell; Courtesy of the Dance Collection, New York Public Library at Lincoln Center, Astor, Lenox and Tilden Foundations

The ballet d'action developed in the mid-1700's. These ballets told stories through dance and pantomime, omitting the spoken words of earlier ballets. Jean Georges Noverre became the leader of the form with such works as *Jason and Medea* (1763).

Russia became part of the Soviet Union in 1922, and the Soviet Union maintained a strong reputation for training dancers for much of the 1900's. From the late 1940's to the early 1990's, the Soviet Union and its Communist allies competed with the non-Communist nations of the West for power and international influence. During this period of rivalry, known as the *Cold War,* the two leading Soviet ballet companies, the Kirov and the Bolshoi, had some of the world's most technically accomplished dancers. They occasionally toured outside the Soviet Union, dazzling Western audiences with their skill. The leading Soviet dancers included Rudolf Nureyev, Maya Plisetskaya, and Galina Ulanova.

In 1961, Nureyev defected to the West while the Kirov was performing in Paris. Ballerina Natalia Makarova defected from the Kirov in 1970, and Mikhail Baryshnikov in 1974. All three refugees became important forces in Western ballet, dancing as guest artists and staging works from the Russian repertory. Nureyev and Baryshnikov eventually became artistic directors of major companies—Nureyev with the Paris Opéra Ballet and Baryshnikov with the American Ballet Theatre.

The Soviet Union broke apart in 1991, and economic difficulties undermined the health of ballet in Russia. These difficult conditions led many performers to leave their country and pursue careers in the West.

Ballet in England. Two major ballet companies were founded in England in the early 1900's. One was the Ballet Rambert, now called the Rambert Dance Company, originated by the Polish teacher Marie Rambert. The other was the Vic-Wells Ballet, directed by Dame Ninette de Valois. The company later became the Sadler's Wells Ballet and is now called the Royal Ballet. Sir Frederick Ashton, who worked with this company, became England's leading choreographer. He created ballets with no story (*Symphonic Variations,* 1946), dramatic works (*A Month in the Country,* 1976), and playful ballets (*Tales of Beatrix Potter,* 1971). Ashton choreographed many ballets for the great English ballerina Dame Margot Fonteyn. Together they created a British ballet style known for its dignity and sensitivity to musical phrasing. Other leading dancers who worked under Ashton included Antoinette Sibley and Anthony Dowell, who formed a famous partnership. Dowell became director of the Royal Ballet in 1984. The Birmingham Royal Ballet, descended from the Royal Ballet's touring company, became a major company in its own right.

Ballet in the United States. After Diaghilev's death, George Balanchine worked briefly in Europe and then settled in the United States in 1933. There, he helped found the School of American Ballet and a troupe that became the New York City Ballet. Balanchine was one of the most important choreographers of the 1900's, creating a wide variety of traditional and experimental works. He became famous for ballets that centered on movement for movement's sake. He created ballets that were physical representations of the music and ballets that evoked a mood without trying to tell a story.

Balanchine was an important teacher, and he expanded the ballet vocabulary and point technique. Many of the finest ballerinas of the 1900's danced in his company, including Melissa Hayden, Maria Tallchief, Violette Verdy, and Suzanne Farrell. Notable male dancers under Balanchine included Jacques d'Amboise, Arthur Mitch-

Detail of a lithograph (about 1831) of Marie Taglioni in *Flore et Zéphire* after a painting by Chalon and R. J. Lane; New York Public Library at Lincoln Center

Marie Taglioni was one of the the most influential dancers of the romantic movement. She introduced a costume that included a light, white skirt that ended between the knee and ankle.

Courtesy of the Dance Collection, New York Public Library at Lincoln Center, Astor, Lenox and Tilden Foundations

Vaslav Nijinsky and Anna Pavlova were famous stars of Russian ballet during the early 1900's. He played a slave and she played the heroine, Armide, in *Le Pavillon d'Armide* (1907).

ell, Edward Villella, and Peter Martins. Most of his leading dancers became choreographers, teachers, and company directors throughout the world.

In 1940, a troupe that became the American Ballet Theatre (ABT) gave its first performance. The ABT joined the New York City Ballet as one of America's two major ballet companies. The ABT developed a repertory that included works by choreographers Agnes de Mille, Jerome Robbins, and Antony Tudor. The three explored various types of dramatic expression. De Mille's *Rodeo* (1942) is set in the Western United States and includes cowboy characters. Robbins's *Fancy Free* (1944) is a lighthearted work that follows three sailors on leave as they look for fun in New York City. Tudor's *Pillar of Fire* (1942) explores the psychological conflicts of a shy woman who fears that she will never marry.

In the mid-1900's, several ballet companies were established in New York City. The Joffrey Ballet (now the Joffrey Ballet of Chicago) was founded by choreographer Robert Joffrey in 1956. It was the first American troupe to invite a new generation of experimental choreographers to compose dances. Among the most notable were Laura Dean and Twyla Tharp. The Joffrey also encouraged important revivals and was among the first to perform ballets choreographed to rock music, such as Gerald Arpino's *Trinity* (1970).

In 1968, the African American dancer Arthur Mitchell established a dance school in the Harlem district of New York City. The school led to the founding of the Dance Theatre of Harlem. Mitchell dedicated his company to challenging the prejudice that black dancers were not suited to ballet. The Dance Theatre of Harlem presented a varied repertory, including works by black choreographers. The efforts of Mitchell and others encouraged many ballet troupes to become multiracial.

Ballet in Canada. Canada, like the United States, benefited from the arrival of European dancers, teachers, and choreographers during the mid-1900's. The National Ballet of Canada, founded in 1951, was first directed by the British dancer Celia Franca. The company gained even greater recognition under the directorship of the Danish dancer Erik Bruhn during the 1980's. The Latvian-born dancer Ludmilla Chiriaeff founded Les Grands Ballets Canadiens in 1958. Among its leading choreographers was Brian Macdonald. He also worked for the Royal Winnipeg Ballet, Canada's oldest major ballet company, founded in 1939.

Ballet in Europe. European ballet companies fared better financially than many North American companies in the late 1900's. Many benefited from government assistance. European dance groups welcomed talent from other countries. John Cranko, a South African who worked in England, and John Neumeier of the United States served as resident choreographers with German companies, beginning in the 1960's. Cranko raised the Stuttgart Ballet to world importance, and Neumeier brought international recognition to the Hamburg Ballet. Both created works with a strong literary and dramatic base. The French-born choreographer Maurice Béjart developed an athletic style for his troupe, Ballet of the 20th Century, based in Belgium and Switzerland. Jiří Kylían of the Czech Republic created a broad range of works as director of the Netherlands Dance Theatre.

The American Glen Tetley brought his modern style to companies in the Netherlands and Germany. Another American, Mark Morris, worked for several years in Belgium as resident choreographer of the Théâtre Royal de la Monnaie in Brussels. In France, the Paris Opéra Ballet was the focus of international attention in the 1980's, when Rudolf Nureyev became ballet director. Ballet in Denmark showed stability and artistic consistency throughout most of the 1900's. The Royal Danish Ballet, based in Copenhagen, preserved historical tradition with its dedication to the Bournonville style.

Ballet in musical comedies has been popular since the early 1900's. A number of leading ballet choreographers have created dances for Broadway musicals. In 1943, Agnes de Mille choreographed the dances for the famous musical *Oklahoma!*, including the extended dream ballet shown at the left.

Mikhail Baryshnikov, *center,* ranks among the world's leading ballet dancers. He helped found the White Oak Dance Project, a touring company, and became its featured performer. The company presents many dances by the American choreographer Mark Morris, including *Motorcade, left.*

© Tom Brazil

Recent developments. During the late 1900's, many ballet companies were founded throughout the world. In the United States, important companies established in Houston, Miami, and other cities joined older companies, such as the San Francisco Ballet, in raising the level of dancing throughout the country. After returning to the United States from Belgium, Mark Morris became choreographer for the White Oak Dance Project, a touring company he helped found with Mikhail Baryshnikov in 1990. Such companies provided more opportunities for dancers and choreographers and helped educate audiences. However, in spite of growing interest in ballet, U.S. companies struggled to survive in difficult economic times. They faced limited funding from local and federal government sources and from private support.

Critically reviewed by Katy Matheson

Related articles in *World Book* include:

Biographies

Ailey, Alvin	Markova, Dame Alicia
Ashton, Sir Frederick	Martins, Peter
Balanchine, George	Massine, Léonide
Baryshnikov, Mikhail	Mitchell, Arthur
Bruhn, Erik	Nijinsky, Vaslav
D'Amboise, Jacques	Nureyev, Rudolf
De Mille, Agnes	Pavlova, Anna
De Valois, Dame Ninette	Petipa, Marius
Diaghilev, Sergei	Petit, Roland
Dolin, Sir Anton	Robbins, Jerome
Fokine, Michel	Stravinsky, Igor
Fonteyn, Dame Margot	Taglioni, Marie
Hayden, Melissa	Tallchief, Maria
Joffrey, Robert	Taylor, Paul
Kaye, Nora	Tharp, Twyla
Kirstein, Lincoln	Villella, Edward Joseph

Other related articles

Art and the arts (picture: Mixed arts)	Manitoba (picture: Dancers of the Royal Winnipeg ballet)
Bolshoi Ballet	Russia (picture: Russian ballet troupes)
Dancing	
Degas, Edgar (picture)	

For a video on basic ballet movements, see the **Ballet** article in *The World Book Multimedia Encyclopedia* (CD-ROM).

Outline

Questions

When does a dancer perform a *révérence?*
What was the significance of the *Ballet Comique de la Reine?*
What is the purpose of the *barre?*
How did Jean Georges Noverre influence ballet?
What is *Labanotation?*
What African American dancer founded the Dance Theatre of Harlem?
What is the responsibility of the choreographer?
Who composed the first romantic ballet?
What is a *divertissement?* A *pas de deux?*
Who was Sir Frederick Ashton?

Additional resources

Level I
Bussell, Darcey, and Linton, Patricia. *The Young Dancer.* Dorling Kindersley, 1994.
Dufort, Antony. *Ballet Steps.* 2nd ed. Clarkson Potter, 1990.
McCaughrean, Geraldine. *The Random House Book of Stories from the Ballet.* Random Hse., 1995.
Medova, Marie-Laure. *Ballet for Beginners.* Sterling Pub., 1995.
Spatt, Leslie E. *Behind the Scenes at the Ballet: Rehearsing and Performing the Sleeping Beauty.* Viking, 1995.

Level II
Anderson, Jack. *Ballet & Modern Dance: A Concise History.* 2nd ed. Princeton Bk. Co., 1992.
Bremser, Martha, and Nicholas, Larraine, eds. *International Dictionary of Ballet.* 2 vols. St. James Pr., 1993.
Clarke, Mary, and Crisp, Clement. *Ballet: An Illustrated History.* Hamish Hamilton, 1992.
Kerner, Mary. *Barefoot to Balanchine: How to Watch Dance.* Anchor Bks., 1990.
Lawson, Joan. *Beginning Ballet.* 1977. Reprint. Routledge, 1994.

Computerized instruction is the use of a computer system to provide or supplement a learner's education. The student sits at a computer terminal. The computer screen displays lessons, questions, or other information, often with accompanying pictures or sound. The learner reacts by typing responses on the computer's keyboard or by moving a handheld control device called a *mouse.*

Computerized instruction has several advantages. It is *interactive*—that is, the student's responses determine what happens next. The computer responds to the learner immediately, acknowledging correct answers and giving additional explanation if needed. When a teacher instructs an entire class, the information may be too hard or too easy for some students. With computerized instruction, each student works at his or her own pace and level of ability. Teachers who use computers to provide some instruction may have more time to give extra attention to students who need it. Computerized instruction can even provide teachers with detailed information about each student's progress.

Computerized instruction can help students at all levels, from preschoolers through adult learners. Businesses, government, and the armed forces include computerized instruction in their training programs. People also use computers at home to acquire new skills. For example, there are computer programs to help bridge and chess players improve their play. This article chiefly discusses computerized instruction in schools.

How computerized instruction works

To use a computer for instruction—or for any other purpose—a user needs *hardware* and *software.* The physical equipment that makes up a computer system is called hardware. Computer software, also called a *program,* tells the hardware what to do and how to do it. Many instructional programs are recorded on a type of disc called a CD-ROM (*C*ompact *D*isc *R*ead-*O*nly *M*emory), which can store large amounts of data. Multimedia programs combine text, images, animation, and sound. Multimedia CD-ROM's are a popular learning tool. Common features enable users to click the mouse on a word to see a definition or hear a pronunciation or view a related illustration or video clip.

Approaches to computerized instruction differ in the amount of instruction provided by the computer. In some cases, a teacher provides most of the instruction and asks students to operate a program to supplement the lesson. For example, a history teacher might ask students to use a program to learn about political campaigns before a class presentation on elections. In other cases, the computer provides most of the instruction. Schoolchildren can operate this type of program independently without a teacher. For example, students in remote or isolated communities can take advantage of such a program when a teacher is not available.

Types of programs

Educational programs are divided into groups according to the teaching methods they use. Different types of programs include *drill-and-practice programs, tutorials, instructional games, simulations,* and *resource programs.* Some of the programs combine teaching methods.

Drill-and-practice programs imitate flashcards. Students often use drill-and-practice programs to master material learned from a teacher or another source. Examples of drill-and-practice programs include multiplication drills and vocabulary practice programs.

Tutorials give a learner a small amount of information and then ask a question about the material. If the student answers correctly, the program presents new material and questions. If the student gives a wrong answer, the program explains the error. Students can use tutorials in all subject areas.

Instructional games enable students to win a computer game by using information that they have learned. Many instructional games use printed materials to supply the content that players must learn to win. Students often play instructional computer games in social studies classes. In one popular series of games, students look up answers to geography or history questions to chase a criminal around the world or through time.

Simulations are computer models of realistic situations. Students make choices and watch how their choices affect outcomes. In one popular simulation, players design their own cities. Students decide how to provide public services, such as transportation and utilities. They determine how to use land and how much tax to charge residents. These decisions affect factors that influence the desirability of the city, including the cost of houses, the crime rate, and the amount of pollution.

Software companies often design simulations for mathematics, science, and social studies classes. Some schools have replaced science laboratories with simulations that enable students to perform experiments. For example, a biology class might learn anatomy from a simulated dissection of a frog instead of cutting up a real dead animal.

Resource programs give a learner access to *databases* (collections of useful information). Resource programs are a powerful tool for doing research. People can *search* (extract information from) databases in ways that meet their individual needs. For example, users can specify a subject or an author's name. One example of a resource program is an encyclopedia on CD-ROM, such as *The World Book Multimedia Encyclopedia.*

Databases may be *local* or *remote.* Local databases are available only to one computer or to a *local area network* of computers that are connected to one another and share software. Remote databases, also known as *on-line databases* or *on-line resources,* are stored on a computer at a different location. Computer operators gain access to remote databases using a device called a *modem,* which enables computers to communicate over telephone lines. After users search on-line databases, they often electronically copy information, or *download* it, to their own computer to examine later.

One of the most powerful and popular on-line resources is the Internet. The internet is a vast computer network over which governments, universities, businesses, and individuals exchange information. Although the Internet contains a wealth of data, images, and sounds, finding specific information can be difficult. Because no overall authority checks the accuracy of information, users must evaluate Internet sources carefully.

IBM Corporation

Computers in the classroom provide a powerful learning tool. Educational software extends the ways in which students can investigate many subjects. Computers also enable students to work at their own pace and to explore areas of individual interest.

Development of computerized instruction

Computerized instruction is based on a method of teaching called *programmed instruction.* Programmed instruction presents a sequence of material in small units that gradually increase in difficulty. Before computers were used for instruction, most programmed learning consisted of paper-and-pencil workbooks or tutorials. Students responded to questions and then were directed to different places in the tutorial, based on their answers. They had to learn the material in one unit before they could go on to the next. Many students found tutorials awkward to use.

Early teaching machines. During the 1920's, researchers developed *teaching machines* that could deliver programmed instruction. The first teaching machine was a mechanical testing device that asked multiple-choice questions, one at a time. The machine did not present a new question until the student pressed the correct lever.

By the early 1960's, teaching machines became more complex. They presented information on a small screen and used sound or light to indicate a correct response.

One of the first widespread uses of computerized instruction was PLATO (*P*rogrammed *L*ogic for *A*utomatic *T*eaching *O*perations), a project developed by the University of Illinois. PLATO was the first system that combined graphics with a touch-sensitive screen. By the early 1970's, many students were using PLATO instructional materials on large computers called *mainframes.*

The personal computer. Technological advances helped to produce smaller, faster, less expensive computers. By the late 1970's, electronics companies introduced *personal computers.* Unlike mainframes, personal computers were inexpensive enough for many individuals, families, and schools to purchase them. More students had access to computers, and they welcomed the novelty of computerized instruction. But most of the programs available at this time were poorly designed. Many were drill-and-practice programs that

required lots of memorization and used the computer screen as if it were a piece of electronic paper.

In the 1980's, new computer technology helped to revolutionize software. Computer manufacturers developed faster computers with more memory and improved color screens. Computer programmers added more colors, attractive graphics, and lively animation. CD-ROM drives made it possible for programs to easily provide audio and video information. By the late 1980's, a technology called *graphical user interface* made most instructional programs easier to use. This technology enables users to give the computer instructions by selecting a picture called an *icon* rather than by typing commands.

Trends in computerized instruction. The importance of computers continues to increase in schools and throughout society. Computerized instruction can help students learn and also help them acquire computer literacy. Many experts feel that skill and confidence in using computers are some of the most essential lessons that education can provide. Because these skills are so important, equal access to computers has become a topic of public debate. Experts feel that society must find ways to make computers and other expensive technologies available to schools of all income levels.

The technology of computerized instruction continues to advance. Software engineers are working with *artificial intelligence* to design programs that—like good teachers—ask interesting questions and respond to creative answers. Artificial intelligence enables a computer to process information in a manner similar to the way a person thinks.

As computerized instruction becomes more widespread in schools, many educators expect the role of a teacher to change. In a classroom where computers are used extensively, the teacher may no longer be the main source of information. Instead, the teacher may act as a facilitator, helping students locate, interpret, and share information.   Ward Mitchell Cates

See also **Audio-visual materials** (Computers).

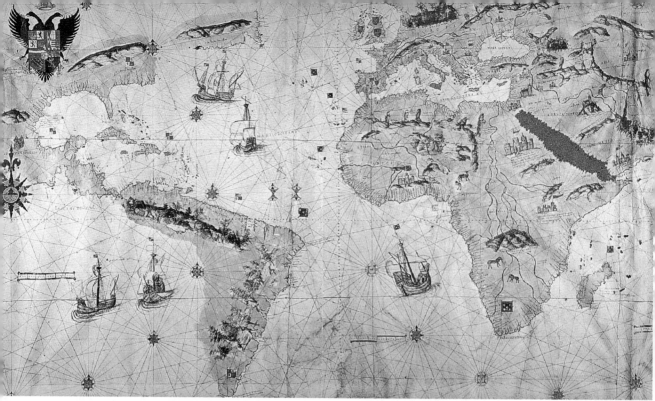

Granger Collection

Exploration has greatly increased knowledge of the world through the centuries. The map above provides a record of the world as Europeans knew it in the 1500's. The photograph below shows how part of the world actually looks from space.

Exploration

NASA

Exploration is one of the oldest and most widespread of human activities. People in all times and places have engaged in some form of exploration. Even children explore their immediate surroundings.

However, the people we usually think of as explorers are those individuals who traveled over long distances and to unfamiliar areas for certain purposes. For example, some explorers have sought to learn more about an unknown part of the world or have traveled for adventure. Others have hoped to gain fame or wealth for themselves or to expand their country's trade or territory. Still others have set out on expeditions to faraway lands for religious reasons.

In many cases, as explorers came upon places that were new to them, they encountered people who had been living in these areas for centuries. When Europeans began arriving in the Americas in the late 1400's, for example, they found the continents to be inhabited by the people who are now commonly called American Indians. Sometimes, the inhabitants helped explorers by acting as interpreters and providing information about geography and sources of food and water. More frequently, explorers tried to conquer or colonize newly found lands. In many cases, fighting broke out between the new arrivals and the local peoples.

Helen Delpar, the contributor of this article, is Professor of History at the University of Alabama and the editor of The Discoverers: An Encyclopedia of Explorers and Exploration.

People have engaged in exploration since prehistoric times. Prehistoric human beings crossed vast areas of land and water and eventually populated all the continents except Antarctica. Later navigators started out from the islands of Southeast Asia and settled Hawaii, New Zealand, and other Pacific Islands.

In ancient and medieval times, people from Europe, the Middle East, and Asia ranged far beyond their homelands to chart many areas new to them. Even so, as late as 1450, large parts of the world remained isolated from one another. Starting about that time, Europeans became the most active explorers in the world. They eventually explored the Americas, Siberia, the Pacific Islands, Australia, Africa, the Arctic, and Antarctica. By the early 1900's, most parts of the world had been explored and mapped. At that time, explorers turned their attention to two new frontiers—the ocean depths and space.

The first explorers

Most scholars believe that the earliest human beings originated in southern and eastern Africa. These early people and their nearest descendants are often considered the first explorers. They traveled far from their original homelands, settled Africa, and spread across Asia and Europe as well.

During the last ice age, from about 100,000 to 11,500 years ago, sea levels were lower than they are today, and several areas now separated by water were joined together. For example, what are now New Guinea and

Australia formed a single continent. As early as 50,000 years ago, the first seafaring explorers sailed from Southeast Asia to colonize these lands. Somewhat later, people from northeast Asia entered what is now Alaska. They traveled across a land bridge that connected North America and Asia where a waterway called the Bering Strait separates the two continents today. Scholars disagree on when human beings first crossed into the Americas and where they settled. However, by 10,000 years ago, people could be found in nearly all parts of North and South America.

At least 3,000 years ago, people from the islands of Southeast Asia set out on the first of many voyages on the Pacific Ocean. These seafarers sailed over long stretches of water in double canoes without the help of sophisticated navigational instruments. But they did have knowledge of the stars for navigation. They eventually settled Fiji, Hawaii, New Zealand, Samoa, Tahiti, Tonga, and other Pacific Islands. A few scholars believe that these early sailors discovered new islands by accident. But many others think that the early Pacific seafarers planned their voyages of exploration and colonization.

Ancient exploration

Ancient people living in the Middle East and along the shores of the Mediterranean Sea explored parts of Europe, Africa, and Asia. In the late 1400's B.C., Queen Hatshepsut (pronounced *hat SHEHP soot)* of Egypt sent an expedition by way of the Red Sea to a place called the

Ancient and medieval exploration

The map at the right shows how much of the world's lands (yellow) and seas (blue) were known to Europeans by the A.D. 1300's. The enlargement below shows the routes of some ancient and medieval expeditions, beginning with the Egyptian exploration of the 1400's B.C.—one of the first ever recorded.

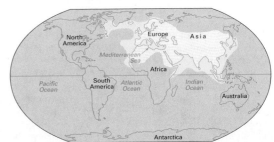

—·— Egyptians 1400's B.C.

- - - - Phoenicians 1100's B.C.

——— Carthaginians 400's B.C.

- - - - Alexander the Great 334-323 B.C.

—·— Pytheas 300's B.C.

——— Zhang Qian 128-126 B.C.

—·—·— Vikings 800's - 1000's

- - - - Marco Polo 1271-74

——— Ibn Batuta 1330-32, 1352-53

—··— Zheng He 1431-33

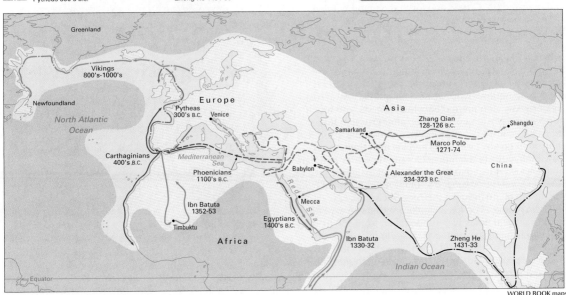

WORLD BOOK maps

Land of Punt. The exact location of Punt is not known. It may have been in southwest Arabia or the Somali coast of Africa.

The Phoenicians, whose main cities were on the coasts of what are now Israel, Lebanon, and Syria, sailed far into the Mediterranean Sea to conduct trade and establish colonies. About 500 B.C., the Carthaginian statesman and navigator Hanno set out with 60 vessels on an expedition that took him down the west coast of Africa, perhaps as far as what is now Sierra Leone or the Gulf of Guinea.

Granger Collection

Alexander the Great of Macedonia expanded ancient Greek knowledge of the world.

The Greeks expanded geographical knowledge by founding colonies, especially in Asia Minor, Italy, and southern France, and along the coast of the Black Sea. The Greeks were also the first people to write about past exploration and to describe the world as it was known to them. Herodotus *(hih RAHD uh tuhs)*, the great Greek historian of the 400's B.C., included much geographical information in his account of the war between the Persians and the Greeks.

One of the most important Greek explorers was Pytheas *(PIHTH ee uhs)*. During the 300's B.C., he sailed up the coasts of Spain and France and around the British Isles. He then probably entered the North Sea. Pytheas mentioned a land called Thule *(THOO lee)*, which was probably Norway. For many years, people in the Mediterranean region considered Thule to be the farthest inhabited part of the world to the northwest.

Also in the 300's B.C., Alexander the Great launched a military campaign that greatly expanded the world known to the Greeks. Alexander was the son of King Philip II of Macedonia, a country north of Greece. Philip had defeated the Greeks and formed a union between Greece and Macedonia. After Alexander succeeded his father, he set out to expand Macedonian and Greek power.

In 334 B.C., at the age of 22, Alexander led his army into what is now Turkey. Soon after, he won a victory over the Persian army. The young king then marched south to conquer Egypt. Next, he fought his way across western Asia, conquering Babylonia, Persia, and much of present-day Afghanistan. Soon after crossing the Indus River in what is now Pakistan, Alexander's soldiers refused to go any farther. He and his men then sailed down the Indus to the Indian Ocean. Alexander and part of the army returned to the Middle East by land. But Nearchus *(nee AHR kuhs)*, one of his officers, sailed from the mouth of the Indus to the Persian Gulf.

The Chinese. The most significant Chinese expeditions in ancient times were undertaken from 138 to 109 B.C. by Zhang Qian (pronounced *jahng chee ehn*, and also spelled Chang Ch'ien). Zhang traveled in the service of the Emperor Wudi (Wu-ti), who wished to develop diplomatic relations with people in western Asia. Zhang traveled as far as the river valley of the Amu Darya. This river flows into the Aral Sea in what is now Uzbekistan. Although Zhang's missions were not a diplomatic success, his reports expanded Chinese ideas of the world. They also laid the foundation for later trade between China and the Roman Empire, especially in silk.

The Romans. The Roman Empire reached its greatest extent about A.D. 100, when it stretched from Britain through much of Europe and the Middle East, and across Egypt and the rest of northern Africa. The Romans did not engage in much exploration. Through trade, however, they acquired information about some areas beyond their empire, such as the east coast of Africa and the Indian Ocean. Much of what was known about the world in ancient times was preserved in the writings of Ptolemy *(TAHL uh mee)*, a geographer and astronomer who lived in Egypt during the 100's.

Medieval exploration

After the collapse of the western Roman Empire in the late 400's, Europe was divided into small kingdoms and other states. For about the next 600 to 800 years, most Europeans had neither the means nor the desire to engage in exploration. During this same period, Muslims— that is, followers of the religion of Islam—established a huge empire that eventually extended throughout the Middle East and across northern Africa. Many Muslims became expert navigators. Muslim merchant ships with *lateen* (triangular) sails ranged throughout the Indian Ocean, going as far as East Africa and Southeast Asia.

By about the 1200's, the Chinese and Europeans had a renewed interest in exploration. By that time, explorers could find their direction more easily because of the development of the magnetic compass. Some scholars believe that the Chinese were the first to use the compass for navigation about 1100 and that it was quickly adopted by Muslims and northern Europeans. Others believe that Muslims and northern Europeans independently developed the use of the compass for ship navigation.

Granger Collection

A medieval Muslim map of the world shows Arab lands at the top. This map accompanied *The Book of Roger,* a geographical treatise completed by the Muslim explorer al-Idrisi in 1154.

Viking exploration. The most important European explorers from the fall of the Roman Empire to about the 1000's were the Vikings, who originally came from Scandinavia. About 800, they settled the Shetlands, the Faroes, and other islands in the North Atlantic Ocean. About 860, a storm drove a Viking ship to a large island that was later named Iceland. The Norse began to settle Iceland about 870, and it became the base for later voyages.

About 900, Gunnbjorn Ulfsson, a Viking leader, sighted Greenland. About 982, Eric the Red began exploring the coast of this huge island. Eric and other Vikings later established colonies there.

About 986, another Viking leader, Bjarni Herjolfsson *(BYAHR nee hehr YOHLF suhn)*, was driven off course while sailing from Iceland to Greenland. Herjolfsson sighted a coastline to the west—probably North America—but he did not land there. Instead, he went on to Greenland. About 1000, Leif Ericson, son of Eric the Red, led an exploring party to the land Herjolfsson had sighted. He set up a base at a place he called Vinland. No one knows exactly where Vinland was, but most experts believe that it lay in what is now the Canadian province of Newfoundland. Vikings made several other voyages to Vinland and established a colony there. But conflicts with the local peoples and other problems led the Vikings to abandon the colony about 1014.

Muslim exploration. Muslims studied the writings of ancient authorities and produced outstanding geographies and maps. During the 1100's, for example, al-Idrisi *(uhl ih DREE see)* traveled widely throughout the Middle East. After moving to the court of King Roger II of Sicily, al-Idrisi prepared an important geographical treatise, often called *The Book of Roger*. Completed in 1154, it surveyed all the countries of the world known to Europeans and Muslims of that time.

The most celebrated Muslim explorer was Ibn Batuta *(IHB uhn ba TOO tah)*, who was born in Morocco. From 1325 to 1354, he traveled as far as India and China. He also visited the Mali Empire in western Africa south of the Sahara. His account of his travels is often called *Rihla (Journey)*.

Chinese exploration. During the Middle Ages, Chinese explorers made long journeys throughout Asia and the Middle East. Until about the 1200's, most of these travels were religious *pilgrimages* (journeys to sacred places). The Buddhist monk Xuanzang (pronounced *shyoo an zahng*, and often spelled Hsuan-tsang), for example, set out in 629 for India, the birthplace of Buddhism. There, he visited many Buddhist holy places over a 16-year period and gathered much information about the history and geography of the region.

The largest Chinese expeditions took place during the early 1400's. From 1405 to 1433, Zheng He (pronounced *juhng huh*, and also spelled Cheng Ho) commanded seven expeditions involving dozens of ships. He sailed from the waters of the East China Sea to the Indian Ocean and to the East African coast. As a result of these voyages, China expanded diplomatic and commercial relations with more than 30 countries.

European exploration. During the mid-1200's, Europeans came into more direct contact with central and eastern Asia than ever before. At that time, most of Asia was ruled by the Mongols, a nomadic people who

Granger Collection

The astrolabe was one of the most important navigational instruments on voyages of discovery. The astrolabe, along with the quadrant, enabled sailors to determine latitude more accurately.

were superior fighters. European leaders hoped to convert the Mongols to Christianity and persuade them to become allies against Muslim rulers in the Middle East and northern Africa. In the 1240's and 1250's, several Franciscan friars, including John of Plano Carpini and William of Rubruck, visited the camp of the *khan* (Mongol leader) at Karakorum in what is now Mongolia. The friars failed to convert the khan to Christianity, but they brought back much information about eastern Asia.

The most famous European traveler in Asia in the 1200's was Marco Polo, a native of Venice. In 1271, when Marco was 17, he accompanied his father, Nicolò, and his uncle Maffeo to China. Nicolò and Maffeo Polo were merchants. They had visited China in the 1260's and had been well received by Kublai Khan, the Mongol emperor of China. During Marco's visit, he made such a favorable impression on Kublai Khan that the Mongol ruler sent him on official missions throughout the kingdom. After returning to Venice in 1295, Marco was taken prisoner during a conflict between Venice and Genoa. While in captivity, he dictated an account of his travels. This widely read book, called *Description of the World*, was the first to provide Europeans with detailed and accurate information about China's impressive civilization.

The great age of European exploration

By the 1400's, many Europeans wanted to buy products that came from Asia—jewels, silk, and such spices as cinnamon, pepper, and cloves, which were used to season and preserve food. As the Mongol Empire had begun to break down into smaller states during the 1300's, overland trade between Asia and Europe became increasingly disrupted and expensive.

By the mid-1400's, Turkish Muslims controlled much of the main overland route between Europe and Asia, but overland trade was still uncertain. Muslims also controlled the sea trade routes from Asia to the Middle East. In the Mediterranean, the Italian city of Venice held a monopoly on trade in spices and eastern luxury goods between the Muslim ports and the rest of Europe. As a result, other Europeans became eager to bypass the old overland and Mediterranean sea routes and find a direct ocean route to the *Indies,* as Europeans then called the eastern part of Asia. Europeans also hoped to make converts to Christianity and thereby strike a blow against the Muslims.

Portugal and Spain took the lead in launching voyages to discover a direct ocean route to the Indies. By 1500, ship designers in these countries had made long voyages possible by designing a new kind of ship, known as the *caravel.* The caravel combined square sails with the triangular lateen sails used by Muslims. Exploration by sea was also aided by the use of the *astrolabe* and the *quadrant,* instruments that enabled sailors to determine latitude more accurately. The expeditions of Portugal and Spain opened a great period of exploration and led to the colonization of America by Europeans.

Reaching the tip of Africa. During the early 1400's, Portuguese explorers concentrated their attention on the west coast of Africa. Prince Henry, a son of King John I of Portugal, became known as Henry the Navigator. He never went on a voyage of exploration himself, but he encouraged and sponsored many explorations. Henry wanted to increase Portugal's trade along the African coast and find the source of the gold that African Muslim traders had been carrying north from central Africa for centuries. He also hoped to find a legendary Christian kingdom that was supposed to exist somewhere in Africa.

Trip after trip, Henry's crews sailed farther and farther south along the African coast. By the time Henry died in 1460, the coast had been traced as far south as present-day Sierra Leone. During these voyages, the Portuguese collected gold dust and African captives who were sold into slavery. After 1500, when the settlement of the Americas created a demand for slaves, other Europeans began to sail to the west African coast to take part in the slave trade.

During the late 1400's, the Portuguese became increasingly hopeful of reaching the southern end of Africa. They believed that such a discovery would reveal a way of sailing to India.

In 1487, the Portuguese explorer Bartolomeu Dias (*BAHR tul uh MEH oo DEE uhs)* set out to find a route around Africa. As he sailed along the continent's southwestern coast, a violent storm blew his ships south of the tip of the continent. Dias then turned east and sailed into the Indian Ocean in early 1488 without sighting the tip of Africa. After turning north again, Dias reached the east coast of Africa, but his crew then forced him to return to Portugal. On the return voyage, he saw a point of

The great age of European exploration — European knowledge of the world greatly expanded during the 1400's and 1500's, as shown by the yellow and blue areas on this map. European explorers of the time sailed around Africa to Asia and began to map the Americas.

WORLD BOOK map

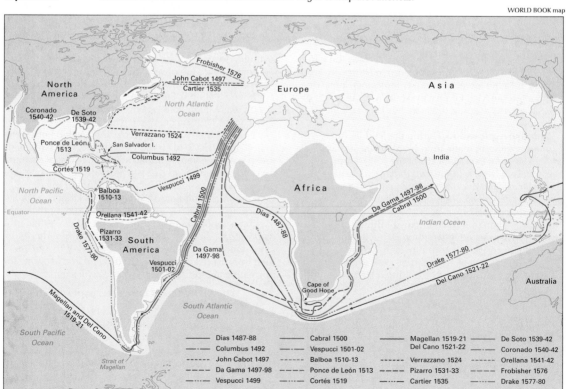

land jutting out from the continent's southern tip. The Portuguese named it the Cape of Good Hope because its discovery indicated hope that a sea route to India had been found.

Columbus reaches America. While the Portuguese were searching for an eastward sea route to Asia, Christopher Columbus, a sea captain from Genoa, looked to the west. Columbus developed a plan to reach Asia by sailing across the Atlantic Ocean. He was convinced that his plan would work. However, he underestimated the distance between western Europe and Japan—and he did not know that a large land mass lay in the way.

Columbus tried without success to persuade the Portuguese to give him command of a westward expedition. In 1485, he went to Spain. He eventually persuaded Queen Isabella to support his plan. He was given three small vessels: the *Niña,* the *Pinta,* and the *Santa María.* He assembled a crew of about 90 men and boys for the voyage.

Columbus left Palos, Spain, on Aug. 3, 1492. After a stop at the Canary Islands, off the west coast of Africa, the expedition headed westward across the Atlantic. The crew sailed for more than a month without seeing land. Finally, on October 12, an island was sighted.

Columbus landed on the island, which is one of the Bahamas. He also visited two other islands—Cuba and Hispaniola (now shared by Haiti and the Dominican Republic). Columbus believed that he had reached the Indies, and so he called the people he met Indians. He started his return trip to Spain in January 1493 and reached Palos in March.

The voyage around Africa. News of Columbus's discoveries caused much excitement in Spain. But the Portuguese did not believe that Columbus had reached the Indies because he had not brought back spices or other known Asian products. They remained convinced that the best route to Asia would be found by sailing around Africa.

In 1497, King Manuel I of Portugal chose the Portuguese navigator Vasco da Gama *(VAHS koh duh GAM uh)* to sail all the way to Asia. On July 8, da Gama set out from Lisbon, Portugal, with four ships and a crew of about 170. Instead of sailing close to the west African coast, he swung out into the Atlantic to find the most favorable winds. He rounded the Cape of Good Hope on November 22 and then sailed into the Indian Ocean. At Malindi, in present-day Kenya, he found an experienced Arab pilot, Ahmad Ibn Majid *(AHM ahd IHB uhn MAH jihd),* who agreed to show the way to India.

The Portuguese reached Calicut on the southwest coast of India on May 20, 1498. Calicut's Hindu ruler was not interested in the goods da Gama brought to trade. The Muslim merchants there were not happy to see da Gama, whom they considered a possible business rival. But the explorer obtained some gems and spices, including pepper and cinnamon, to take back to Portugal to prove he had reached Asia. Da Gama made a second voyage to Calicut in 1502. He arrived with a fleet of 20 ships, bombarded the town, and established Portuguese rule there.

Exploring the New World. Columbus made three more voyages across the Atlantic from 1493 to 1504. He explored what are now Jamaica, Puerto Rico, and

Granger Collection

The caravel was used by Spanish and Portuguese sailors for ocean exploration and trade during the 1500's and 1600's. Caravels combined square sails with triangular *lateen* sails.

Trinidad, and the coasts of Venezuela and Central America. Columbus always believed that he had been in or near Asia, but it gradually became clear that he had come upon lands previously unknown to Europeans.

In 1497, John Cabot, an Italian navigator, became the first European to visit the northeast coast of North America since the Vikings. Sailing in the service of King Henry VII of England, Cabot landed on the east coast of Canada or on the coast of Maine. Cabot's voyage helped lay the foundation of English claims to North America.

Other explorers began to visit South America. In 1500, two explorers independently reached the area where the Portuguese colony of Brazil would later be established. They were Vicente Yáñez Pinzón *(bee THEHN teh YAH nyehth peen THAHN),* a Spaniard who had commanded the *Niña* on Columbus's first voyage; and Pedro Álvares Cabral *(PAY throo AHL vuh reesh kuh BRAHL),* a Portuguese captain on his way to India. Pinzón also explored the mouth of what would later be called the Amazon River.

Amerigo Vespucci *(uh MEHR uh goh veh SPOO chee),* a merchant and navigator born in Italy, made two voyages along the eastern coast of South America from 1499 to 1502. He was the first person to refer to the lands he had visited as a "New World." In 1507, a German geographer placed a Latin version of Vespucci's first name—that is, *America*—on a map of the newly found southern continent. This name was later applied to North America as well.

In 1513, the Spanish explorer Vasco Núñez de Balboa *(VAHS koh NOO nyayth day bal BOH uh)* led an expedition across what is now Panama from its Atlantic coast to its Pacific coast. He became the first European to see the eastern shore of the Pacific Ocean. His finding helped prove that the New World was indeed a huge land mass lying between Europe and Asia.

Magellan's globe-circling expedition. In 1517, Ferdinand Magellan *(muh JEHL uhn),* a Portuguese navigator, asked King Charles I of Spain to sponsor a voyage to Asia by way of South America. King Charles agreed because the Portuguese controlled the route around Africa. If Magellan was successful, Spain would have its own route to Asia. At the time, Magellan did not know how large South America is.

Magellan sailed from Spain on Sept. 20, 1519. He had five ships and a crew of about 240. After reaching the northeast coast of Brazil, he sailed southward until he arrived at what is now Puerto San Julián, Argentina. He spent several months there and farther south at what is now Puerto Santa Cruz, Argentina, during the Southern Hemisphere's winter.

Magellan set sail from Puerto Santa Cruz on Oct. 18, 1520. Three days later, the ships entered a passage now known as the Strait of Magellan at the southern tip of South America. On November 28, three of the five ships sailed out of the strait into the Pacific Ocean. One of the other two ships had been wrecked in a storm, and one had turned back to Spain.

In the Pacific, the explorers sailed for more than three months without sighting any land except two uninhabited islands. Food ran out, and the sailors ate oxhides and rats to stay alive. In March 1521, Magellan reached what is now Guam, where he was able to gather supplies. He then sailed to the present-day Philippine Islands. There, he became involved in a conflict among the islanders. Magellan was killed in a battle on April 27, 1521.

After Magellan's death, the expedition abandoned one of the ships. The other two sailed to the Spice Islands (now part of Indonesia). One of these ships, the *Victoria,* then sailed west under the command of Magellan's lieutenant, Juan Sebastián del Cano *(hwahn seh BAS tee AHN dehl KAHN oh).* The ship crossed the Indian Ocean and sailed around the Cape of Good Hope. Badly damaged and with only 18 Europeans and 3 or 4 Indonesians aboard, the *Victoria* reached Spain on Sept. 6, 1522, having completed the first trip around the world.

Spain's conquests in the New World. During the early 1500's, Spanish explorers pushed across most of Central and South America. They unintentionally brought with them smallpox and other diseases that were unknown in the Americas. As a result, thousands of Native Americans, who had no resistance to these diseases, sickened and died from them. The Spanish explorers established colonies in the new lands. Royal officials, Roman Catholic priests, and settlers arrived soon after the explorers. The Indians typically were forced to work for the Spaniards. The Spaniards also brought sugar cane, wheat, and other new plants to the Americas, as well as horses, cattle, sheep, and other domestic animals. The Spaniards took back to Europe many plants that were unknown there, such as corn and potatoes.

One of the most important Spanish expeditions in the New World was commanded by Hernando Cortés *(kawr TEHZ),* who left Cuba in 1519 with more than 600 men. He sailed to what is now the Mexican state of Yucatán, which was a center of Maya civilization. Cortés moved along the coast of Mexico and then inland to Tenochtit-

From the *Codex Duran* (1520); The National Library, Madrid (Granger Collection)

Spanish soldiers attacked Aztec Indians in 1520, *above.* The Spaniards and Indians fought many bloody battles as the Spaniards pushed across Central and South America in the 1500's.

lan (now Mexico City), the capital of the Aztec empire. Along the way, he met an Indian woman named Malinche, who the Spaniards called Doña Marina. Malinche, who knew both the Maya and the Aztec languages, served as an interpreter for Cortés.

By 1521, Cortés had subdued the Aztec and taken permanent control of their empire. Mexico then became a base for Spanish exploration of Central America and what is now the southern United States.

Several Spanish expeditions also explored and conquered much of South America. From 1527 to 1529, Sebastian Cabot, a son of John Cabot, explored one of the continent's great water systems by sailing up the Rio de la Plata and the Paraná and Paraguay rivers in present-day Argentina and Paraguay. Cabot was looking for a "white king" whose realm was supposed to be rich in silver. Other explorers searched for a fabulous golden kingdom in South America, especially in what are now Colombia and Venezuela. This kingdom was usually called *El Dorado,* which means "the gilded one."

In 1532 and 1533, the Spanish explorer Francisco Pizarro *(frahn SIHS koh pih ZAHR oh)* conquered the Inca Indians. From their home in what is now Peru, the Inca ruled an empire that included parts of what are now Colombia, Ecuador, Bolivia, Chile, and Argentina. From 1535 to 1537, Diego de Almagro *(DYAY goh deh ahl MAHG roh),* a member of Pizarro's party, explored parts of what are now Bolivia and Argentina and crossed the Andes Mountains into Chile. In 1541 and 1542, Francisco de Orellana *(frahn SIHS koh deh oh ray YAH nah),* another veteran of Pizarro's expedition, sailed from the Andes Mountains down the mighty Amazon River to its mouth on the Atlantic Ocean in Brazil.

During the 1500's, Spaniards explored much territory that became part of the United States. In 1513, Juan Ponce de León *(hwahn PAWN say day lay AWN)* sailed from Puerto Rico and landed on the east coast of Florida. He then sailed around the southern tip of Florida and into the Gulf of Mexico. He next explored the southwest coast of Florida before returning to Puerto Rico.

In 1539, an expedition of more than 600 people led by Hernando de Soto *(dih SOH toh)* sailed from Cuba to the west coast of Florida. In search of gold, this expedition traveled through what is now the southern United States, including Georgia, Alabama, Mississippi, and Arkansas. The explorers found no gold, but they became the first Europeans to reach the Mississippi River. After de Soto died of fever in 1542, the survivors of the expedition sailed down the river and eventually reached Mexico by way of the Gulf of Mexico.

In 1540, Francisco Vásquez de Coronado set out from Campostela near the west coast of Mexico on an expedition to find the legendary Seven Cities of Cibola. These supposedly rich and flourishing cities were thought to lie north of Mexico City. Coronado traveled through what are now Arizona, New Mexico, Texas, Oklahoma, and Kansas. He found no important cities, but his expedition and that of de Soto gave Europeans a good idea of the width of North America.

The search for a northern passage. During the 1500's, the known sea routes to Asia were long, and they were controlled by Spain and Portugal. As a result, Europeans from other nations tried to find alternate—and shorter—routes. Some explorers looked for a Northwest Passage—that is, a strait or other body of water that would allow ships to sail through North America to reach Asia. Others looked for a Northeast Passage north of Europe. However, none of the explorers of the time found a Northwest or Northeast Passage, and the search continued for centuries.

In 1524, King Francis I of France sent Giovanni da Verrazzano *(joh VAHN ee dah vehr uh ZAH noh),* an Italian navigator, to North America to find a passage to Asia. Verrazzano explored the east coast from about Cape Fear in present-day North Carolina to Newfoundland. But he did not find a passage.

Jacques Cartier *(zhahk kahr TYAY),* a French explorer, also failed to find a passage during two voyages he made from 1534 to 1536. However, he became the first Euro-pean to see the St. Lawrence River in what is now Canada and helped establish French claims to this region.

Several English explorers also looked unsuccessfully for a Northwest Passage in North America. From 1576 to 1578, Martin Frobisher made three voyages and reached what is now Frobisher Bay in northeastern Canada. In 1585, John Davis, another English navigator, discovered and explored what are now Davis Strait between Green-land and Canada and Cumberland Sound in northeastern Canada.

English merchants sent three expeditions in search of a Northeast Passage from 1553 to 1580. However, these expeditions got only as far as the Kara Sea north of Russia before they turned back. Willem Barents *(WIHL uhm BAR uhnts),* a Dutch navigator, looked for the Northeast Passage during the 1590's. He sailed farther north than any other European had in a recorded voyage and explored what is now Spitsbergen and other islands in the Arctic Ocean.

Linking the globe

By 1600, the Spanish had explored, and established colonies in, Central and South America and parts of North America. Spain tried to claim all of North America, but the French and English set up their own colonies and explored much of the continent themselves. Meanwhile, Russians were moving east to explore what are now Siberia and Alaska. During the 1700's and 1800's, European explorers gradually filled in the outlines of the areas that were still unknown to them. They mapped the Pacific Ocean, worked their way through the interiors of Australia and Africa, and reached the Arctic and Antarctic regions. Finally, in the 1900's, they raced to reach the North and South poles.

The French and English in North America. During the 1600's, the French and English began to found colonies in what are now Canada and the United States. The French and English, like the Spanish before them, unknowingly introduced smallpox and other new diseases into the areas they controlled. As before, many Indians died from these diseases. The French and English also traded with the Indians for the skins of beaver and other animals. Traders learned much about the land from the Indians, who often acted as interpreters and guides.

Samuel de Champlain *(sham PLAYN),* a French explorer and geographer, charted the Atlantic coast from Cape Breton Island in Canada to Martha's Vineyard in what is now Massachusetts. In 1608, he founded the city of Quebec as a fur-trading post. Over the next eight years,

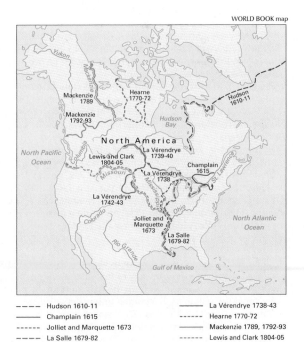

WORLD BOOK map

----- Hudson 1610-11	——— La Vérendrye 1738-43
——— Champlain 1615	------ Hearne 1770-72
------ Jolliet and Marquette 1673	——— Mackenzie 1789, 1792-93
---- La Salle 1679-82	------ Lewis and Clark 1804-05

The exploration of North America by Europeans in the 1600's and 1700's revealed the continent's shape and much of the interior. American explorers pushed westward in the early 1800's.

he traveled extensively and learned about the rivers and lakes of the region. In 1609, Champlain became the first European to reach the lake in present-day New York, Vermont, and Quebec that now bears his name.

The French also explored the great river known as the Mississippi. In 1673, Louis Jolliet *(Iwee JOH lee eht)*, a fur trader, and Jacques Marquette *(zhahk mahr KEHT)*, a Roman Catholic priest, reached the river near what is now Prairie du Chien, Wisconsin. They paddled canoes southward to the place where the Mississippi meets the Arkansas River. In 1682, René-Robert Cavelier, Sieur de La Salle *(luh SAL)*, led an expedition that sailed down the Illinois River. He began at a point near present-day Peoria, Illinois, and then traveled down the Mississippi to its mouth at the Gulf of Mexico. He claimed the entire region drained by the Mississippi for France and named it Louisiana in honor of King Louis XIV.

The first permanent English settlement in North America was founded at Jamestown, Virginia, in 1607. By the end of 1670, English settlements had been established in 12 of what were to become the 13 original colonies. The first permanent settlement in the 13th, Georgia, was founded in 1733.

England also claimed much of what is now eastern Canada. This claim was based in part on a voyage of the English navigator Henry Hudson, who was looking for a Northwest Passage. In 1610, Hudson sailed through a strait in northeastern Canada into a large body of water he thought was the Pacific Ocean. It was really a huge bay now known as Hudson Bay.

Crossing North America. During the 1700's, French and British explorers blazed new trails westward across the northern parts of North America. They also discovered the northern limits of the continent.

In 1738 and 1739, the French-Canadian fur trader Pierre Gaultier de Varennes, Sieur de La Vérendrye, *(lah vay RAHN dree)*, and his sons explored what are now Manitoba and North Dakota. In 1742 and 1743, two of the sons, Louis-Joseph and François, traveled as far as present-day Montana and Wyoming.

From 1770 to 1772, the British explorer Samuel Hearne explored the land between what are now Churchill, Manitoba, and the Coppermine River in the present-day Northwest Territories. The Coppermine flows into the Arctic Ocean.

Alexander Mackenzie, an agent of a fur-trading company called the North West Company, made further explorations of northern North America. In 1789, he traveled north from the western tip of Lake Athabasca in present-day Alberta to the mouth of the river now named after him. In 1792 and 1793, he made a famous journey from Lake Athabasca across the Rocky Mountains to the Pacific Ocean.

Two U.S. Army officers, Meriwether Lewis and William Clark, began an important expedition to the Pacific Northwest in 1804. In May of that year, they set out from St. Louis and traveled up the Missouri River. They spent the winter with Mandan Indians near what is now Bismarck, North Dakota. There, they met Sacagawea *(sah KAH guh WEE uh)*, a Shoshone woman who agreed to be their interpreter. The following spring, the expedition continued up the Missouri and crossed the Rockies. Once past the mountains, the explorers pushed to the Columbia River. They followed the river to the Pacific Ocean, reaching it in November 1805. Lewis and Clark returned to St. Louis in 1806. They brought back with them valuable information about the land, plant and animal life, and peoples they encountered on their journey.

The Russians in Siberia. The exploration of what is now called Siberia—the vast region in northern Asia between the Ural Mountains and the Pacific Ocean—began in 1581. That year, Yermak Timofeyevich *(yur MAHK ty-ihm uh FYAY uh vyich)*, a Russian military leader, conquered the ruler of a territory called Sibir just east of the Ural Mountains. The name *Siberia* was then applied to the entire region.

During the early 1600's, Russians moved eastward across Siberia. They came upon Lake Baikal in 1643. By 1650, Russians had reached the Sea of Okhotsk in the northern Pacific and had rounded the Chukchi Peninsula in northeastern Asia. In the late 1690's, a Russian soldier named Vladimir V. Atlasov *(AT luh sawf)* conquered the peoples of the Kamchatka Peninsula on the Pacific coast of what is now eastern Russia.

In 1728, Vitus Bering *(VEE tus BAIR ihng)*, a Danish seaman in the service of Russia, led an expedition that sailed from Kamchatka north through the strait now named after him. But he did not see North America because of dense fog. In 1741, Bering headed a larger expedition. He and his chief lieutenant, Aleksei I. Chirikov *(CHIHR yuh kuhf)*, sailed on different ships. Both men saw the coast of Alaska. Bering also sighted what is now Mount St. Elias and landed briefly on Kayak Island. As a result of Bering's voyages, Russia claimed Alaska. In 1784, the Russians established the first European colony there, on Kodiak Island.

Exploring the Pacific. Several Spanish and English navigators had explored the Pacific after Magellan's voyage, but this vast ocean was still largely unknown to Europeans in 1600. In the 1600's and 1700's, Dutch, English, and French navigators sailed throughout the Pacific. They discovered many islands. European voyagers also hoped to find the mysterious *Terra Australis Incognita* (Unknown Southern Continent). The Europeans of the time believed this legendary large and fertile continent lay in the South Pacific as a counterweight to the northern continents of Europe and Asia.

After 1750, two developments made long Pacific voyages safer than they had been. First, sailors realized that lemons and other fresh fruits and vegetables would prevent *scurvy*. This disease, which is caused by a lack of vitamin C, had been responsible for many illnesses and deaths on earlier voyages. Captains now tried to have supplies of these foods on hand for their crews. Second, in the late 1700's, navigators began to use the *chronometer*, a device that enabled them to determine longitude more accurately. As a result, it was possible for them to pinpoint their position at sea and to establish the exact location of newly found islands.

In the early 1600's, the Dutch gained control of what is now Indonesia. This area became the starting point for Dutch voyages of exploration in the Pacific. From 1606 to 1636, Willem Jansz *(WIHL uhm YAHNS)* and other Dutch navigators reached the coast of Australia, but they did not establish colonies there. In 1642 and 1643, the Dutch navigator Abel Janszoon Tasman *(AH buhl YAHN sohn TAZ muhn)* reached the island now called Tasmania, which is named after him, and sighted New Zealand. In 1644, he made a voyage during which he explored Australia's northern and western coasts.

During the second half of the 1700's, the French and the British were the most active in exploring the Pacific. In 1766, Louis-Antoine de Bougainville *(lwee ahn TWAHN duh boo gahn VEEL)* began what would be the first French voyage around the world. In January 1768, Bougainville entered the Pacific by way of the Strait of Magellan. In April, he reached the island of Tahiti, which had been visited the year before by Samuel Wallis, a British explorer. Bougainville's later account of the island's people and climate made Tahiti seem like an earthly paradise to many Europeans.

Bougainville was the first European to see several islands in the Pacific, including the island in the Solomon group now named after him. In addition, among Bougainville's crew was probably the first woman to sail around the world. This young Frenchwoman, named Jeanne Baret *(zhahn bah RAY),* sailed with Bougainville disguised as a male servant to one of the scientists on the expedition. Her true identity was not revealed until after the expedition had reached Tahiti.

The greatest explorer of the Pacific was James Cook, a British naval officer who made three long voyages from 1768 to 1779. These voyages provided much scientific information about the waters and islands of the Pacific and contributed to European colonization of Australia and other territories. Cook's first voyage was mainly a scientific expedition, but Cook also had orders from the British Navy to try to find the Unknown Southern Continent. He did not find it, but he did explore New Zealand and the eastern coast of Australia.

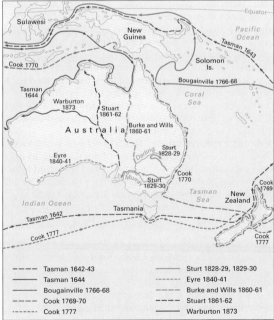

Tasman 1642-43
Tasman 1644
Bougainville 1766-68
Cook 1769-70
Cook 1777
Sturt 1828-29, 1829-30
Eyre 1840-41
Burke and Wills 1860-61
Stuart 1861-62
Warburton 1873

WORLD BOOK map

The European exploration of Australia began with sea voyages that reached the area during the 1600's and 1700's. Explorers crossed the interior of the continent in the 1800's.

Cook was instructed to look for the Unknown Southern Continent during his second voyage as well. In 1773 and 1774, he crossed the Antarctic Circle and went farther south than any other explorer up to that time. But he could not find an Unknown Southern Continent. During his third voyage, Cook set out to look for an outlet of the Northwest Passage in the northern Pacific. In 1778, he sailed north through the Bering Strait until ice blocked his way. He found no outlet. The following year, Cook was killed in a dispute with the local peoples on the island of Hawaii.

Exploring Australia's interior. The exploration of Australia began soon after the British established a colony for convicts near what is now Sydney in 1788. The British often fought with the original inhabitants of Australia, who are known as Aborigines. In addition, thousands of Aborigines died from diseases unknowingly introduced by the Europeans. However, some Aborigines acted as guides and pointed out sources of food and water to explorers.

At first, exploration was centered on the areas around Sydney. In January 1829, an expedition led by Charles Sturt, a British Army officer, reached the Darling River. In 1829 and 1830, Sturt led a second expedition during which he sailed down the Murrumbidgee and Murray rivers to the sea near present-day Adelaide.

Exploration of the interior of Australia was difficult and dangerous because much of the region is desert. The British explorer Edward John Eyre (pronounced *air)* became the first European to make a major overland journey from east to west. His expedition in 1840 and 1841 closely followed the southern coast of Australia. The first European party to cross Australia from south to north was led by Robert O'Hara Burke, an Irish-born explorer; and William John Wills, a British-born explorer. Burke and Wills left Melbourne in 1860 and reached the Gulf of Carpentaria in 1861. On their return trip, they starved to death. Meanwhile, John McDouall Stuart, a Scottish-born explorer, was also trying to cross Australia. Stuart made several unsuccessful attempts before making a round trip between the southern and northern coasts in 1861 and 1862.

The exploration of Africa. By the late 1700's, Europeans were familiar with the coasts of Africa, but the interior of the continent remained a mystery to them. Penetration of the interior was difficult because of the harsh terrain in many places and the presence of deadly diseases, such as malaria and dysentery. Despite these obstacles, Europeans explored most of Africa south of the Sahara during the late 1700's and the 1800's. During the late 1800's, exploration was combined with conquest, and Europeans became the rulers of most of the African continent.

During the late 1700's and early 1800's, European explorers tried to solve a mystery that had puzzled geographers for centuries. Ancient writers had mentioned an important African river called the Niger. But they had not known where the river began, in what direction it flowed, and where it ended. In 1796, Mungo Park, a Scottish explorer, reached the Niger near Ségou, in what is now Mali. He determined that it flows from west to east. In 1830, Richard Lemon Lander, a British explorer, sailed down the Niger to its mouth in the Gulf of Guinea. During the 1820's, Alexander Gordon Laing, a Scottish

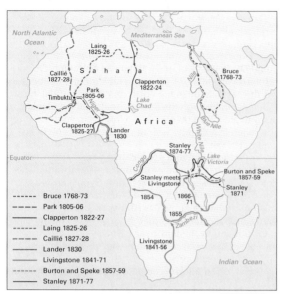

WORLD BOOK map

Exploring the interior of Africa. During the 1700's and 1800's, European expeditions explored the regions of the great rivers of Africa—the Congo, Niger, Nile, and Zambezi. Explorers also crisscrossed the western and southern parts of the continent.

Granger Collection

"Dr. Livingstone, I presume?" With those words, reporter Henry Morton Stanley, *left*, greeted explorer David Livingstone, *right*, at their famous meeting in 1871. Stanley went to Africa to find Livingstone, who had not been heard from for several years.

explorer, and René Caillié *(ruh NAY cah YAY)*, a Frenchman, separately visited the city of Timbuktu, near the Niger in Mali.

By the late 1700's, Europeans were familiar with the lower Nile, which is formed by the meeting of the Blue Nile and the White Nile at what is now Khartoum, in Sudan. But the source of the river was a mystery. In 1770, James Bruce, a Scottish explorer, reached the source of the Blue Nile in the mountains of Ethiopia.

In 1857, the British explorers Richard Francis Burton and John Hanning Speke began to search for the source of the White Nile. In 1858, they reached Lake Tanganyika, which is bordered by what are now Burundi and Tanzania in the east and Zaire and Zambia in the west. Arabs in the region told Burton and Speke about another large lake nearby. Speke went alone to look at the lake and became convinced that it was the source of the Nile. He named it Lake Victoria in honor of Queen Victoria of Britain. This lake, known as Victoria Nyanza in Africa, lies partly in what are now Kenya, Tanzania, and Uganda.

Speke returned to Lake Victoria in 1862 and identified the source of the Nile as a large waterfall at the lake's northern end. This waterfall is now submerged by the Owen Falls Dam. Burton and others believed that Speke was wrong, but later explorers proved him right.

During the early 1860's, a British explorer named Samuel White Baker explored many rivers of eastern Africa with his companion, Florence, who later became his wife. In 1864, they became the first Europeans to reach what are now called Lake Albert (Albert Nyanza) and Murchison Falls.

The most famous European explorer in Africa was David Livingstone *(LIHV ihng stuhn)*, a Scottish missionary. From 1854 to 1856, he became the first European to cross Africa. He followed the Zambezi River during part

of his journey from what is now Angola to Mozambique. In 1855, he became the first European to see the Victoria Falls on the Zambezi River. In 1859, during a later expedition in southeast Africa, he reached Lake Nyasa, also known as Lake Malawi. From 1866 until his death in 1873, Livingstone explored the lakes and rivers of central Africa.

In 1869, Henry Morton Stanley, a reporter, received an assignment from the publisher of the *New York Herald* to go to Africa to find Livingstone. Livingstone had not been heard from in several years. The story of how Stanley found Livingstone near Lake Tanganyika in 1871 captured the imagination of people around the world (see **Stanley and Livingstone**). Stanley became an important explorer himself. From 1874 to 1877, he crossed central Africa from east to west and explored the Congo River. His explorations during the 1880's helped answer questions about the Congo and Nile rivers.

Arctic exploration. By 1800, a great deal was known about the Arctic regions because of the discoveries of early explorers. However, no one had as yet found either the Northwest Passage or the Northeast Passage. During the 1800's, European explorers accomplished both of these goals. Attention then turned to reaching the North Pole.

The severe cold and ice of the Arctic made exploration there extremely dangerous. Ships could get trapped in ice or destroyed by it. Food was scarce, and starvation was a real danger if explorers used up their supplies.

In the early 1800's, the British Navy began to send expeditions to try to find a Northwest Passage in Arctic waters north of Canada. In 1819, William Edward Parry, a British naval officer, found an entrance to the Northwest Passage in the Canadian Arctic. He sailed through Lancaster Sound as far west as Melville Island.

In 1845, Sir John Franklin left England with two ships and 128 men to continue the search for the passage. By 1848, nothing had been heard from Franklin and his men. The British then began sending ships to look for them, but the remains of the expedition were not found until 1859. Franklin and his crew had died after their ships became jammed in the ice. From 1850 to 1854, Robert McClure, an officer in command of one of the search ships, traveled from the Bering Strait to the Atlantic Ocean. He claimed that he had found the Northwest Passage. But he had sailed on several ships and had gone part of the way on heavy sleds. As a result, it was not clear whether a single ship could make its way through the passage. This feat was accomplished from 1903 to 1906 when Roald Amundsen *(ROH ahl AH muhn suhn)*, a Norwegian explorer, sailed from the Atlantic Ocean to the Bering Strait.

Meanwhile, Nils Adolf Erik Nordenskjöld *(nihls AH dawlf AY rihk NOOR duhn SHOOLD)*, a Swedish explorer, completed the Northeast Passage from Europe to Asia. In July 1878, he sailed east from Tromsø, Norway, and reached the Pacific Ocean a year later.

During the late 1800's, many explorers tried to reach the North Pole. At first, many people believed that there was open water in the Arctic Ocean and that the North Pole might be reached by ship. It soon became clear, however, that the Arctic Ocean has a permanent cover of ice. As a result, explorers would have to cross the ice by sled to reach the pole.

From 1898 to 1905, Robert E. Peary, an American explorer, led two expeditions to try to reach the North Pole. He began his third expedition in 1908 and headed north to the pole from Ellesmere Island in the Canadian Arctic in early 1909. Peary is usually credited with reaching the North Pole on April 6, 1909, accompanied by his chief assistant, Matthew A. Henson, and four Inuit. Upon returning to the United States, Peary learned that another American explorer, Frederick A. Cook, claimed that he had reached the pole a year before Peary, on April 21, 1908. Most experts decided that Peary's story was more believable than Cook's, but the dispute has never been definitely settled.

The invention of the airplane and other technological advances in the 1900's brought new methods of polar exploration. In 1926, Richard E. Byrd, an American naval officer, and Floyd Bennett, an American pilot, claimed they flew from Svalbard to the North Pole and back in a three-engine airplane, though some scholars today dispute that claim. Also in 1926, a team of explorers flew from Svalbard to Alaska by way of the North Pole in an airship called the *Norge.* The explorers included Umberto Nobile *(um BER taw NOH bee lay)*, an Italian Air Force officer, who piloted the craft; Lincoln Ellsworth, an American civil engineer; and Roald Amundsen, who had earlier sailed through the North-west Passage. In 1958, the U.S. nuclear-powered submarine *Nautilus* passed underneath Arctic ice to the position of the North Pole.

The exploration of Antarctica. By the early 1800's, Antarctica remained the only continent still unknown to the world. But this uninhabited frigid continent was difficult to reach and explore because it is surrounded by stormy, ice-filled waters and is covered by a thick layer of ice.

Nobody knows who first saw the Antarctic continent.

But many historians divide the credit among three individuals known to have sighted Antarctica on separate voyages in 1820. These three are Edward Bransfield, a British naval officer; Nathaniel Brown Palmer, an American sea captain; and Fabian von Bellingshausen, of the Russian Imperial Navy.

Several countries sent expeditions to Antarctica to carry on scientific research. In 1840, an American naval officer named Charles Wilkes led an expedition that charted part of the coast of the continent. From 1839 to 1843, James Clark Ross, a British naval officer, commanded an expedition that sailed into what is now called the Ross Sea. Ross discovered the volcanoes Mount Erebus and Mount Terror, which he named after his ships, *Erebus* and *Terror.* He continued southward until his progress was blocked by a massive barrier of ice now known as the Ross Ice Shelf.

During the late 1890's and early 1900's, Belgium, Britain, Germany, and Sweden sent scientific expeditions to explore the continent. Robert Falcon Scott, a British naval officer, led an expedition from 1901 to 1904 that discovered what is now called Edward VII Peninsula. Scott's expedition used sleds pulled by dogs to travel deep into the interior of the continent.

In 1911, two groups of explorers raced across Antarctica to reach the South Pole. One group was led by Amundsen and the other by Scott. Amundsen reached the pole on Dec. 14, 1911, about five weeks before Scott. Scott and the four other members of his group who reached the pole died on the return trip.

During the 1920's, aircraft began to be used to explore Antarctica. George Hubert Wilkins, an Australian explorer, made the first Antarctic airplane flight in 1928. The same year, Byrd went to Antarctica with three airplanes and built a base on the Ross Ice Shelf called Little America. He used the planes to carry on long-range exploration. On Nov. 28 and 29, 1929, he led the first flight over the South Pole. Bernt

Brown Brothers

Roald Amundsen of Norway led the first group of explorers to reach the South Pole. They arrived there on Dec. 14, 1911.

Balchen, a Norwegian American pilot, flew the plane over the pole.

During the 1950's, many nations built bases on Antarctica from which to conduct scientific research. In 1957 and 1958, an expedition led by Vivian Fuchs *(fyooks)*, a British geologist, accomplished the first overland crossing of Antarctica. The members of the expedition used snow tractors and dog teams to make the crossing. Their journey covered 2,158 miles (3,473 kilometers) and took 99 days.

In 1989 and 1990, Will Steger of the United States led a team of explorers from six nations across Antarctica. The

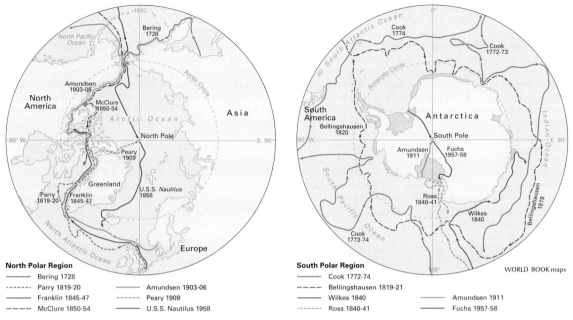

North Polar Region

—— Bering 1728			
------ Parry 1819-20		—— Amundsen 1903-06	
—— Franklin 1845-47		----- Peary 1909	
– – – McClure 1850-54		—— U.S.S. Nautilus 1958	

South Polar Region

WORLD BOOK maps

—— Cook 1772-74			
– – – Bellingshausen 1819-21			
—— Wilkes 1840		—— Amundsen 1911	
------ Ross 1840-41		—— Fuchs 1957-58	

Exploration of the frigid polar regions began during the 1700's. However, explorers did not reach the North Pole until 1908 or 1909 and did not arrive at the South Pole until 1911.

expedition, which traveled by dog sled and ski, was the first to cross the continent without motorized vehicles.

The new frontiers

Throughout history, the unknown has attracted explorers to the earth's farthest and most isolated places. Today, this same urge continues to draw men and women toward the newest frontiers of exploration: the ocean depths and outer space.

Deep-sea exploration. Early explorers and geographers were curious about the seas and the life forms that lived in them. They often took *soundings* (measurements) of the depth of the oceans. They also tried to determine deep-sea temperatures and used dredges to bring marine life to the surface.

The first expedition devoted entirely to the study of the sea was organized in 1872 by Britain's Royal Navy and the Royal Society of London, a British scientific association. A naval vessel called the *Challenger* was specially equipped for the expedition and placed under the command of Captain George S. Nares. Charles Wyville Thomson, a Scottish naturalist, was put in charge of the civilian scientists. The *Challenger* spent more than three years at sea and traveled nearly 70,000 miles (113,000 kilometers). The expedition made hundreds of soundings, gathered much information about the ocean floor, and discovered many marine organisms.

In the early 1900's, the development of *echo sounders* made it easier to determine the depth of the ocean. These devices were based on the principle that sound waves travel through water at a known rate. Echo sounders enabled navigators to make continuous measurements while a ship was moving and gave a much clearer picture of the ocean floor.

In the mid-1900's, explorers and scientists began to get firsthand views of the underwater world. In 1943,

Jacques-Yves Cousteau *(zhahk eev koo STOH)*, a French naval officer, and Émile Gagnan *(ay MEEL GAHN yahn)*, a French engineer, invented the *aqualung*. This device allowed divers to breathe air from canisters on their backs and to move freely underwater.

In the late 1900's, divers penetrated deep into the ocean with the help of improved suits and breathing apparatus. In 1979, for example, Sylvia A. Earle, an American marine biologist, made a record-breaking dive by descending 1,250 feet (381 meters) to the ocean floor off Hawaii. She wore a kind of diving suit called a *Jim-suit.*

Deep-sea explorers in the 1900's also used piloted submersibles to study the oceans. In 1934, William Beebe *(BEE bee)*, an American naturalist, and Otis Barton, an American engineer, descended 3,028 feet (923 meters) into waters off Bermuda in a vehicle called a *bathysphere.*

The Swiss physicist Auguste Piccard *(oh GOOST pee KAHR)* made a major contribution to ocean exploration during the 1940's. He invented a diving vehicle known as a *bathyscaph,* which could descend farther than any craft of its day. In 1960, Piccard's son Jacques and Donald Walsh of the U.S. Navy used a bathyscaph to dive into the Mariana

© Seth Resnick

Sylvia A. Earle of the United States made a record-breaking ocean dive near Hawaii in 1979.

Trench, a valley in the Pacific Ocean floor that is the lowest known place in the world. They reached the bottom at a point 35,800 feet (10,911 meters) beneath the surface of the water.

By the late 1900's, marine geologist Robert D. Ballard and other scientists had developed new types of exploring equipment, including remotely operated diving vessels and robots, to study the sea. In the late 1970's, Ballard and a team of explorers discovered strange worms and other life forms living near hot water vents on the Pacific Ocean floor. In 1985, Ballard and French oceanographer Jean-Louis Michel led a team of French and American explorers who found the wreckage of the *Titanic,* which had sunk in the North Atlantic in 1912.

For more information on deep-sea exploration, see **Ocean** (Exploring the ocean).

Space exploration. The rockets first used for space exploration were developed for warfare during World War II (1939-1945). For example, Germany developed a rocket-powered missile called the V-2. Some of these missiles were captured by the United States and used to launch exploratory instruments after the war.

After World War II ended, the United States and the Soviet Union engaged in an intense rivalry known as the Cold War. The two nations built increasingly powerful rocket-powered missiles, including ones that could fly across continents.

The space age began on Oct. 4, 1957. That day, the Soviet Union launched Sputnik 1, the first artificial satellite, into orbit around the earth. On Jan. 31, 1958, the United States sent up its first space satellite, Explorer 1.

Most space exploration has been conducted by mechanical and electronic robots. Starting in the late 1950's, spacecraft carrying no crew have been sent to the moon and various planets to gather information that cannot be obtained in any other way. In 1977, the United States launched Voyager 1 and Voyager 2, two identical spacecraft with powerful telescopic cameras. From 1979 to 1981, both craft flew near Jupiter and Saturn. Voyager 2 flew past Uranus in 1986 and Neptune in 1989. Both spacecraft sent back data and photographs that greatly enriched scientists' knowledge of these planets. The United States launched the Hubble Space Telescope in 1990. This orbiting telescope provides sharper pictures of heavenly bodies than other telescopes do.

The first person to travel in space was Yuri Gagarin, a Soviet Air Force officer. On April 12, 1961, he circled the earth one time in a spacecraft called Vostok I. On Feb. 20, 1962, John H. Glenn, Jr., a U.S. Marine test pilot, became the first American to orbit the earth. His Friendship 7 spacecraft circled the planet three times. During the rest of the 1960's, the United States conducted a series of programs directed toward landing astronauts on the moon. On July 20, 1969, U.S. astronauts Neil A. Armstrong and Edwin E. Aldrin, Jr., became the first people to set foot on the moon. During the next three years, 10 other U.S. astronauts landed on the moon.

In 1981, the United States launched its first *space shuttle,* a vehicle that takes off like a rocket and lands like an airplane. The world's first permanent space station, the Soviet Union's Mir, went into orbit in 1986. At first, the United States planned to launch its own space station. But after the breakup of the Soviet Union and the end of the Cold War in 1991, the United States decided to com-

Jeff Hester and Paul Scowen (Arizona State University/NASA)

Images from the Hubble Space Telescope show stars forming from clouds of gas. The orbiting Hubble, launched in 1990, aids in the exploration of one of the final frontiers—space.

bine its space station program with Russia's. In 1996, for example, Shannon Lucid, an American astronaut and biochemist, was launched into space on a space shuttle and spent more than six months on Mir.

The United States, Russia, and other countries plan to assemble an international space station by 2002. It is supposed to house six crew members and contain seven science laboratories. This program promises exciting opportunities for further discovery. It also makes clear that the future of exploration, like space itself, has no known limits.   Helen Delpar

Related articles. For biographies of space explorers, see the *Related articles* listed in the **Astronaut** article. See also:

American explorers

Andrews, Roy Chapman	Gray, Robert
Bartlett, Robert Abram	Henson, Matthew Alexander
Beebe, William	Lewis, Meriwether
Bennett, Floyd	Long, Stephen Harriman
Bonneville, Benjamin de	MacMillan, Donald Baxter
Bridger, Jim	Muir, John
Byrd, Richard Evelyn	Palmer, Nathaniel Brown
Clark, William	Peary, Robert Edwin
Colter, John	Pike, Zebulon Montgomery
Cook, Frederick Albert	Roosevelt, Theodore, Jr.
Eielson, Carl Ben	Smith, Jedediah Strong
Ellsworth, Lincoln	Stephens, John Lloyd
Fairchild, David Grandison	Wilkes, Charles
Frémont, John Charles	

Canadian explorers

Bernier, Joseph Elzéar	McKay, Alexander
Fraser, Simon	Thompson, David
Mackenzie, Sir Alexander	

English explorers

Baffin, William
Baker, Sir Samuel White
Burton, Sir Richard Francis
Cook, James
Dampier, William
Davis, John
Drake, Sir Francis
Franklin, Sir John
Frobisher, Sir Martin
Fuchs, Sir Vivian Ernest
Gilbert, Sir Humphrey
Gosnold, Bartholomew

Hearne, Samuel
Henday, Anthony
Hudson, Henry
Kingsley, Mary Henrietta
Parry, Sir William Edward
Puget, Peter
Raleigh, Sir Walter
Ross, Sir James Clark
Scott, Robert Falcon
Vancouver, George
Wallace, Alfred Russel

French explorers

Bienville, Sieur de
Brulé, Étienne
Cartier, Jacques
Champlain, Samuel de
Cousteau, Jacques-Yves
Groselliers, Sieur des
Iberville, Sieur d'
Jolliet, Louis
La Salle, Sieur de

La Vérendrye, Sieur de
Le Sueur, Pierre-Charles
Marquette, Jacques
Monts, Sieur de
Nicolet, Jean
Radisson, Pierre Esprit
Roberval, Sieur de
Tonty, Henri de

Italian explorers

Cabot
Columbus, Christopher
Kino, Eusebio Francisco

Polo, Marco
Verrazzano, Giovanni da
Vespucci, Amerigo

Norwegian explorers

Amundsen, Roald
Eric the Red

Ericson, Leif
Nansen, Fridtjof

Portuguese explorers

Cabral, Pedro Álvares
Da Gama, Vasco
Dias, Bartolomeu

Henry the Navigator
Magellan, Ferdinand
Queirós, Pedro Fernandes de

Spanish explorers

Ayllón, Lucas Vásquez de
Balboa, Vasco Núñez de
Cabeza de Vaca, Álvar Núñez
Cabrillo, Juan Rodríguez
Coronado, Francisco
  Vásquez de
Cortés, Hernando
De Soto, Hernando

Jiménez de Quesada, Gonzalo
Menéndez de Avilés, Pedro
Narváez, Pánfilo de
Oñate, Juan de
Orellana, Francisco de
Pizarro, Francisco
Ponce de León, Juan

Other explorers

Alexander the Great
Barents, Willem
Bering, Vitus
Emin Pasha
Estevanico
Hennepin, Louis
Hillary, Sir Edmund Percival
Ibn Batuta
McClure, Sir Robert John
  Le Mesurier

Nordenskjöld, Nils Adolf
  Erik
Park, Mungo
Piccard
Pytheas
Shackleton, Sir Ernest Henry
Stanley and Livingstone
Tasman, Abel Janszoon
Wilkins, Sir Hubert

Other related articles

Africa (History)
Antarctica (Exploration)
Arctic (Exploration)
Astronaut
Australia (History)
Balloon (History)
Caravel
Cibola, Seven Cities of
Colonialism
El Dorado

Fur trade
Geography
Latin America (History)
Lewis and Clark expedition
Map (History)
Northwest Passage
Ocean (Exploring the ocean)
Ptolemy
Ship (History)
Space exploration

Trade route
Vikings

Vinland

Outline

I. The first explorers
II. Ancient exploration
  A. The Phoenicians
  B. The Greeks
  C. The Chinese
  D. The Romans
III. Medieval exploration
  A. Viking exploration
  B. Muslim exploration
  C. Chinese exploration
  D. European exploration
IV. The great age of European exploration
  A. Reaching the tip of Africa
  B. Columbus reaches America
  C. The voyage around Africa
  D. Exploring the New World
  E. Magellan's globe-circling expedition
  F. Spain's conquests in the New World
  G. The search for a northern passage
V. Linking the globe
  A. The French and English in North America
  B. Crossing North America
  C. The Russians in Siberia
  D. Exploring the Pacific
  E. Exploring Australia's interior
  F. The exploration of Africa
  G. Arctic exploration
  H. The exploration of Antarctica
VI. The new frontiers
  A. Deep-sea exploration
  B. Space exploration

Questions

Why did Europeans become eager to find a direct sea route to Asia during the 1400's?

What technological developments made long voyages possible by 1500?

Who was the most celebrated Muslim explorer? Where did he travel?

What are some of the effects the arrival of Europeans had on American Indians and Australian Aborigines?

Who was probably the first woman to sail around the world?

What obstacles made exploration of the interior of Africa difficult?

Who were the leaders of the first European party to cross Australia from south to north?

What are echo sounders? How did they help deep-sea exploration?

Who was the first European to see the eastern shore of the Pacific Ocean?

How did the Cold War affect the coming of the space age?

Reading and Study Guide

See *Exploration* in the Research Guide/Index, Volume 22, for a *Reading and Study Guide.*

Additional resources

Level I

Matthews, Rupert. *Explorer.* Knopf, 1991. Discusses exploration from ancient to modern times.

Saari, Peggy, and Baker, Daniel B., eds. *Explorers and Discoverers: From Alexander the Great to Sally Ride.* 4 vols. Gale Research, 1995.

Starkey, Dinah. *Scholastic Atlas of Exploration.* Scholastic, 1994.

Stefoff, Rebecca. *Accidental Explorers: Surprises and Side Trips in the History of Discovery.* Oxford, 1993.

World Explorers. 32 vols. Chelsea Hse., 1990-1994. Each volume covers one explorer or group of explorers.

World's Great Explorers. 20 vols. Childrens Pr., 1990-1992. Most volumes cover one specific explorer.

Level II

Baker, Daniel B., ed. *Explorers and Discoverers of the World.* Gale Research, 1993.

Bohlander, Richard E., ed. *World Explorers and Discoverers.* Macmillan, 1992.

Austin Fire Department

Fighting fires is one of the most important tasks of a fire department. Many firefighters and a variety of equipment are needed to put out a large building fire, such as the one shown above.

Fire department

Fire department is one of the most important organizations in a community. Fire departments battle fires that break out in homes, factories, office buildings, stores, and other places. Firefighters risk their lives to save people and protect property from fires.

The men and women who work for fire departments also help people who are involved in many kinds of emergencies besides fires. For example, firefighters rescue people who may be trapped in cars or trains after an accident. They aid victims of such disasters as tornadoes, floods, hurricanes, and earthquakes.

Fire departments work to prevent fires by enforcing fire safety laws. They also teach people about possible fire dangers in their homes and places of work. Every year, fires kill thousands of people, injure thousands more, and destroy billions of dollars worth of property. To reduce the damage caused by fires, local fire departments need the support of the people in the community.

Until the 1800's, fires often destroyed whole settlements. When a fire broke out, all the people in the community rushed to the scene. They formed a row from a source of water to the fire and passed buckets of water from one person to another to put the fire out. As cities and towns grew larger, volunteer and paid fire depart-

Robin Paulsgrove, the contributor of this article, is Fire Chief for the city of Austin, Texas.

ments were organized. Today, fire departments in most industrialized nations have well-trained men and women and a variety of modern firefighting equipment.

The work of a fire department

Firefighting. The two basic firefighting units in most fire departments are engine companies and ladder companies. Engine companies operate trucks called *engines,* which carry a pump and hoses for spraying water on a fire. Ladder companies use *ladder trucks,* which carry ladders of various lengths. Ladder trucks also have a hydraulically extendable ladder or elevating platform to rescue people through windows or to spray water from a raised position. Both kinds of trucks also have other rescue equipment and firefighting tools. At a fire, engine and ladder companies work together under the direction of an officer of the fire department.

After an alarm is received, the engine and ladder companies hurry to the fire. They often arrive within a few minutes after receiving the alarm. The officer in command quickly sizes up the situation and directs the firefighters into action. Their first and most important task is to rescue people who may be trapped in the building.

The members of the ladder company search for anyone who may be trapped. In some buildings, they use ladders to rescue people through windows. However, the ladders on most trucks extend up to only about eight stories. Firefighters use stairs or elevators to get to people trapped on floors above the reach of the ladders.

Meanwhile, members of the engine company connect a hose from their pump to a nearby fire hydrant. They then stretch hose lines from the pump to the building on fire. Their first concern is to keep the flames from spreading. The firefighters direct water on the fire until it is out. They also spray water on any nearby buildings that are in danger of catching fire. Ladder company members ventilate the building to let out the smoke, heat, and gases that build up during a fire. They open or break windows and sometimes cut holes in the roof or walls. If the building were not ventilated, the heat and the pressure of the gases could cause an explosion.

The ladder company also tries to save any furniture or other property not damaged by the fire. The members spread canvas or plastic covers over such property to prevent water damage. This process is called *salvage.* Finally, in a process called *overhaul,* the ladder company searches the building for hidden sparks that might cause another blaze.

After the fire is out, the firefighters try to find out exactly where and how the fire started. The officer in charge makes out a report that gives all the important facts about the fire. The report includes information on injuries, the cause of the fire, and the estimated cost of repairing the damage.

Emergency rescue operations. Large fire departments have rescue companies to handle nonfire emergencies. For example, rescue workers may be called to free people trapped under the wreckage of a fallen building or in a car after an accident. Rescue workers sometimes have to break through walls or cut through metal doors to reach an injured person. Many large fire departments have specialized teams to rescue people who are stranded underwater or in swift-flowing water, or on cliffs and in other high places.

Rescue companies may also go to major fires. At a building fire, for example, the rescue workers help the ladder company get people out of the building. They give first aid to people overcome by smoke or suffering from burns.

Emergency medical operations. Many fire departments provide medical care in nonfire emergencies before the patient is taken to the hospital. These departments make up an important part of their community's Emergency Medical Services (EMS) system. In the United States, EMS systems are set up in accordance with federal and state guidelines to provide quick prehospital care to victims of injury or sudden illness. Medical emergencies other than fires account for most alarm responses in a majority of the fire departments that belong to an EMS system.

Some fire departments provide only a basic, "first response" service. A private company or another emergency department then provides more advanced treatment and transports the patient to the hospital. Other fire departments have *paramedic units,* whose members receive training for many kinds of medical emergencies. Paramedic units operate ambulances and use communication equipment to stay in touch with a nearby hospital. Under the direction of a physician, they may use advanced medical equipment and administer drugs. They may also transport the patient to the hospital.

Arson investigations are conducted by local fire departments in most cases. Arson is the crime of purposely setting fire to a building or other property. Fire departments gather evidence in cases where arson is suspected. The evidence may then be used in court.

Fire prevention and fire safety. To help prevent fires and reduce fire losses, local fire departments inspect public buildings. They also teach people about fire safety. Many fire departments have a separate division that handles fire prevention and fire safety programs.

Public building inspections. Most cities have a fire safety code that applies to such buildings as theaters, department stores, schools, and hospitals. These codes specify that the buildings should not be made of materials that burn easily. The codes also require portable fire extinguishers, a certain number of exits, and other fire safety features in public buildings.

Many fire safety codes require large buildings to have built-in *sprinkler systems* and special water lines to which fire hoses can be attached. A sprinkler system consists of a network of pipes that is installed throughout a building. The pipes carry water to nozzles in the ceiling. The heat from a fire causes the nozzles directly above the fire to open and spray water. The sprinklers put out or control most fires before the fire department arrives. Many fire safety codes also require high-rise

Austin Fire Department

A firefighter ventilates a burning building by breaking windows in the structure. Ventilation may be necessary to release a build-up of smoke and gases that could cause an explosion.

Austin Fire Department

Fire department paramedics treat people needing emergency medical care and may rush them to a hospital. The paramedics operate ambulances that carry medical equipment and drugs.

structures to have fire alarm systems.

Fire department officials inspect public buildings to enforce the local code. The officials check the operating condition of the fire protection systems. They note the number and location of exits and fire extinguishers. The inspection also covers housekeeping practices and many other matters that affect fire safety. Fire department inspectors may also review plans for a new building to make sure it meets the safety code.

Public education programs. Many fire departments work with other local agencies to teach people how to prevent fires and what to do during a fire. In some communities, fire department officials serve as instructors or advisers in fire safety courses in schools. For example, they may use a portable model of a house to show students how to safely leave a burning building.

The National Fire Protection Association has developed many educational materials, including a *Learn Not to Burn* course of study for schools. The association is a private, nonprofit organization based in Boston that develops fire safety standards and publishes fire prevention materials for the United States and Canada. A similar group called the Fire Prevention Canada Association, based in Ottawa, also provides fire prevention and training programs.

Most of the deaths caused by fires occur in private homes. Many home fires are caused by leaving the kitchen when food is cooking, disposing of cigarettes improperly, misusing portable heating equipment, and placing flammable or combustible items too close to heat sources. To make your home safer, check the heating and air-conditioning systems and the cooking equipment. Look for unsafe practices, such as overloading electric outlets or running electric cords under a rug.

It is important to know what to do if a fire breaks out. To leave the home safely and quickly in case of fire, families are advised to make escape plans and to practice fire drills. For other instructions, see the table *What to do in case of fire* in this article.

Fire departments advise people to install smoke detectors in their homes. Smoke detectors are devices that sound an alarm if a small amount of smoke enters their sensors. Smoke detectors are attached to the ceiling or wall in several areas of the home. Fire protection experts recommend at least one detector for each floor of a residence. Most home fires that result in deaths occur at night when the family is asleep. Smoke detectors will awaken the family before the flames and the smoke build up to the point where escape is impossible.

Fire departments also recommend that people have portable fire extinguishers in their homes. A person must be sure, however, to call the fire department before trying to extinguish a fire. It is also important to use the right kind of extinguisher for the type of fire involved. For example, a water extinguisher cannot put out a grease fire. Such a fire can be fought with a special extinguisher. For more information on the kinds of fires and extinguishers, see the article **Fire extinguisher.**

Fire department equipment

The most important equipment of a fire department includes (1) communication systems, (2) fire trucks, and (3) special fire vehicles. In addition, the firefighters themselves require special protective clothing.

What to do in case of fire

1. **Leave the building immediately.** Children should not attempt to fight fires. Adults may use a fire extinguisher on a small fire if it seems safe to do so.
2. **Never open a door that feels hot.** Before opening any door, touch it briefly with the back of your hand. If the door feels hot, the fire on the other side may be blazing fiercely. You could be killed by the heat and smoke if you opened the door. Try another escape route or wait for help.
3. **Crawl on the floor when going through a smoky area.** Smoke and heated gases tend to rise, and so they will be thinnest near the floor.
4. **Do not run if your clothes catch fire.** Running fans and spreads flames. Roll on the floor to smother the flames.
5. **Do not return to the building.** After you have escaped, call the fire department. If people are trapped inside, wait for the fire department to rescue them.

Communication systems are necessary to alert fire departments to the outbreak of a fire. Most fire alarms are telephoned to the fire department. Many communities have introduced 9-1-1 as the telephone number to call in emergencies. This number can be dialed from almost any telephone and from most pay phones without a coin.

Most other alarms are sent from automatic signaling devices, which are installed in many public buildings. These devices include smoke and heat detectors that are wired to send an alarm automatically to an alarm monitoring center. A sprinkler system can also be wired to alert the fire department automatically.

Alarm headquarters in a small fire department may consist of one switchboard operator. Most large fire departments have a computerized system of receiving alarms, notifying fire stations, and transmitting data to computer terminals in fire trucks. Each fire truck has a two-way radio for communication with the *dispatcher* (official who sends the truck out) and the fire department officer in charge at the emergency scene.

Fire trucks. Many fire departments have several different types of fire trucks. The main types are (1) engines,

Howard M. Paul, Emergency Stock

A fire department dispatcher at a 9-1-1 center receives alarms reporting the outbreak of a fire. The dispatcher alerts the appropriate fire station, which sends firefighters to the scene.

(2) ladder trucks, and (3) rescue trucks.

Engines have a large pump that takes water from a fire hydrant or other source. The pump boosts the pressure of the water and forces it through hoses.

Engines carry several sizes of hoses and nozzles. Many also have a small-diameter hose called a *booster line,* which is wound on a reel. The booster line is used chiefly to put out small outdoor fires. Engines used for fighting grass or brush fires carry a tank of water and such tools as shovels and rakes.

Ladder trucks. There are two kinds of ladder trucks—*aerial ladder trucks* and *elevating platform trucks.* An aerial ladder truck has a metal extension ladder mounted on a turntable. The ladder can be raised as high as 100 feet (30 meters), or about eight stories. An elevating-platform truck has a cagelike platform that can hold several people. The platform is attached to a lifting device that is mounted on a turntable. The lifting device consists of either a hinged *boom* (long metal arm) or an extendable boom made of several sections that fit inside each other.

The boom on the largest trucks can extend 150 feet (46 meters). A built-in hose runs the length of the boom and is used to direct water on a fire. In most cases, a pump in a nearby engine generates the pressure needed to spray the water. However, ladder trucks called *quints* have their own pumps.

Ladder trucks are equipped with portable ladders of various types and sizes. They also carry *forcible entry tools,* which firefighters use to gain entry into a building and to ventilate it to let out smoke. Common forcible entry tools include axes, power saws, and sledge hammers.

Rescue trucks are enclosed vehicles equipped with many of the same kinds of forcible entry tools that ladder trucks carry. But rescue trucks also carry additional equipment for unusual rescues. They have such tools as oxyacetylene torches, for cutting through metal, and hydraulic jacks, for lifting heavy objects.

Rescue trucks may also carry other hydraulic tools. With a *hydraulic rescue tool,* commonly known by the trade name Jaws of Life, firefighters can apply a large

Three kinds of fire trucks The illustrations below show a rescue truck, an engine, and an aerial ladder truck. Rescue trucks carry tools for unusual rescues. The other two kinds of trucks are used to spray water on a fire. An aerial ladder truck can also be used to rescue people through the windows of a burning building.

WORLD BOOK illustrations by Greg Maxson, Precision Graphics

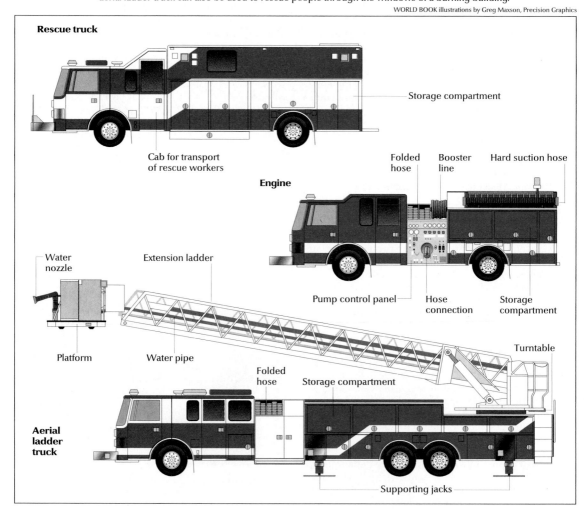

Rescue truck

Storage compartment

Cab for transport of rescue workers

Engine

Folded hose

Booster line

Hard suction hose

Pump control panel

Hose connection

Storage compartment

Water nozzle

Extension ladder

Platform

Water pipe

Folded hose

Storage compartment

Turntable

Aerial ladder truck

Supporting jacks

A firefighter's clothing

Firefighters wear special clothing to protect themselves from fire and other hazards. The clothing includes such garments as fire-resistant pants and coat, heavy leather gloves, and a helmet. An air supply may be carried in a tank strapped to the back.

Austin Fire Department

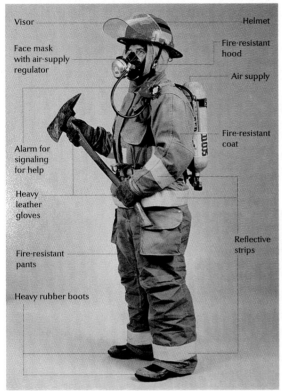

- Visor
- Helmet
- Face mask with air-supply regulator
- Fire-resistant hood
- Air supply
- Fire-resistant coat
- Alarm for signaling for help
- Heavy leather gloves
- Reflective strips
- Fire-resistant pants
- Heavy rubber boots

Some equipment carried on fire trucks

Fire trucks carry a variety of *forcible entry tools,* such as axes, sledge hammers, and crowbars, which are used to gain entry into a building or room. Other equipment on fire trucks includes ropes, bolt cutters, smoke ejectors, and hydraulic rescue tools.

WORLD BOOK illustrations by Yoshi Miyake

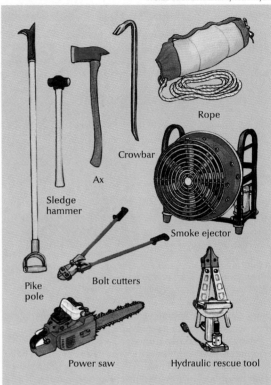

- Rope
- Crowbar
- Ax
- Sledge hammer
- Smoke ejector
- Pike pole
- Bolt cutters
- Power saw
- Hydraulic rescue tool

amount of pressure to two objects to squeeze them together or pry them apart. The tool is often used to free people trapped in automobiles and other vehicles after an accident. Rescue trucks also carry small hand tools, such as crowbars and saws, and ropes and harnesses for rescuing people from water or high places. In addition, they carry medical supplies and equipment.

Special fire vehicles include *airport crash trucks* and *hazardous materials trucks.* Airport crash trucks are engines that spray foam or dry chemicals on burning aircraft. Water is ineffective against many aircraft fires, such as those that involve jet fuel, gasoline, or certain metals.

Hazardous-materials units carry tools to stop gas leaks, and supplies to absorb or clean up spills of dangerous liquids or solids. These trucks also have equipment to prevent the spread of liquid spills that can contaminate the environment. Hazardous materials include pesticides, fertilizers, and other chemicals as well as gasoline, natural gas, and other fuels. Many hazardous-materials emergencies involve truck or train wrecks in which a dangerous substance is accidentally spilled.

Protective clothing. Firefighters require special clothing for protection against flames, falling objects, and other hazards. They wear coats and pants made of fire-resistant material. Other clothing includes special boots, gloves, and helmets. Firefighters also use a

breathing apparatus to avoid inhaling smoke and toxic gases. The apparatus consists of a face piece connected to a small air tank strapped on the firefighter's back.

On rare occasions, firefighters must walk through flames. For instance, they may do so when rescuing passengers from a burning airplane. In such situations, they wear *heat-reflective suits.* These suits are fire resistant and coated with aluminum or another metal to reflect heat. Hazardous-materials trucks may carry *fully encapsulating suits* to protect firefighters from dangerous chemicals. These one-piece suits cover everything the firefighters wear, including their footwear and breathing apparatus.

Kinds of fire departments

Thousands of volunteer and paid fire departments protect communities throughout much of the world. Most of these departments are volunteer organizations. Special-purpose departments are maintained by certain government agencies and some private industries.

Volunteer departments provide protection mainly in small towns and rural communities. They are staffed by men and women who serve part time. Some departments have a few paid firefighters but rely chiefly on volunteers. When a fire breaks out, the volunteers leave their jobs or homes and rush to the fire station. In some

Howard M. Paul, Emergency Stock

A fully encapsulating suit provides special protection for firefighters who deal with hazardous chemicals. The one-piece suit covers everything the firefighter wears, including an air tank.

departments, the volunteers receive a small sum for their work, but in others they receive no pay.

Many volunteer departments have only enough equipment and volunteers for routine fires. Others have excellent equipment. In case of a major fire, departments from neighboring communities help one another. Most volunteer departments are headed by a fire chief, who is either appointed by the mayor or elected by members of the department.

Paid departments serve chiefly in larger cities. Some are organized on a county, district, or regional level. All are staffed by full-time firefighters.

Paid fire departments in large cities have many firefighting companies, which operate from neighborhood fire stations. Each company is commanded by a captain or a lieutenant. Several companies make up a *battalion* or a *district*. Battalions may be further grouped into *divisions*. Large departments also have separate staffs that work in such areas as fire prevention, training, communications, and arson investigations. A fire chief, who is appointed by the mayor or some other city official, directs the entire fire department.

Special-purpose departments. The governments of many countries maintain fire departments at military bases and other large federal installations. Many governments also maintain firefighting units to watch for and deal with forest fires. Some industrial plants, such as those that manufacture fuels or explosives, organize their own fire departments. In addition, all major airports have a fire department to fight aircraft fires.

History

One of the first firefighting organizations was established in ancient Rome. Augustus, who became emperor in 27 B.C., formed a group called the *vigiles*. The vigiles patrolled the streets to watch for fires. They also served as the police force in Rome.

Scholars know little else about the development of firefighting organizations in Europe until after the Great Fire of London in 1666. This fire destroyed much of the city and left thousands of people homeless. Before the fire, London had no organized fire protection system. After the fire, insurance companies in the city formed private fire brigades to protect their clients' property. Insurance company brigades would fight fires only at buildings the company insured. These buildings were identified by a badge or sign.

Fire protection in North America developed in a tradition of communities helping themselves. Citizens organized volunteer fire companies, even in the largest cities. To put out a fire, the members formed lines called *bucket brigades* to pass buckets of water from nearby wells. Another row of volunteers passed back the empty buckets.

Peter Stuyvesant, the governor of New Netherland, a Dutch colony in the area of present-day New York, made one of the first efforts to establish a fire prevention system. In 1648, he appointed four fire wardens to inspect homes and check chimneys for fire hazards. In 1658, Stuyvesant began one of the first community alarm systems. He appointed men to patrol the streets at night and watch for fires. The men were called the *rattle watch* because they shook wooden rattles to alert the people whenever a fire was discovered.

In 1679, Boston established the first paid fire department in the American Colonies. The first fire safety regulations in Canada were adopted in 1734 in Montreal and Quebec, which were then ruled by France. In 1736, Benjamin Franklin founded the American Colonies' first volunteer fire department in Philadelphia. In 1763, Montreal established the first such organization in Canada, called the Fire Club.

In the mid-1700's, fire companies in North America acquired their first practical fire pumps, which were made in Europe. Firefighters had to fill the pumps with pails of water and operate and haul them by hand. However, the pumps enabled crews to fight a fire by shooting a steady stream of water from a safe distance.

By the early 1800's, most U.S. and Canadian cities and towns had volunteer fire companies. The companies required large numbers of volunteers to haul the hand pumps and hose carts to fires. In many cities, prominent citizens belonged to the volunteer companies, which became powerful social and political organizations.

In the mid-1800's, steam-powered pumping engines pulled by horses began to replace hand pumps. The steam pumpers required fewer people to operate them. As a result, many larger cities could switch from volunteer to paid fire departments. From 1910 to 1930, gasoline-powered vehicles replaced horse-drawn fire engines. Since then, many improvements have been made in the equipment and methods used in firefighting.

Recent developments. In the 1970's, fire departments began to put greater emphasis on preventing fires and educating the public about fire safety. In 1974, the United States government established the National Fire Prevention and Control Administration in the Department of Commerce. The agency became the

Steam pumpers pulled by horses were used by fire departments from the mid-1800's to the early 1900's. At the time, they were a major improvement over the hand pumps formerly used.

United States Fire Administration (USFA) in 1978 and was transferred to the independent Federal Emergency Management Agency. The USFA works to improve fire prevention and education, firefighting technology, and firefighter health and safety. It also operates the National Fire Academy in Emmitsburg, Maryland. The academy administers training programs for firefighters and others who work in the field of fire prevention and control. Another government agency, the Consumer Product Safety Commission, develops fire safety information for consumers.

During the 1980's and 1990's, fire departments became more involved in providing emergency medical care, highway accident rescue, hazardous materials handling, and other emergency services. The change of focus coincided with a reduction in the number and size of fires. This reduction resulted from improved public education and better fire safety codes.

Careers

The requirements for becoming a paid firefighter vary from one fire department to another. In general, an applicant must be at least 18 years old and in excellent physical condition. The applicant must also pass a written test.

After being accepted by a fire department, a probationary firefighter takes a training program that may last up to six months. The program covers such subjects as fire behavior, firefighting strategy, forcible-entry rescue techniques, and emergency medical skills. The entire probationary period usually lasts one year. After this period, a firefighter may receive more advanced training in such areas as rescue work and fire prevention.

Many fire departments provide continuing education programs for firefighters. In addition, many community colleges offer courses in subjects related to fire protec-

tion. Fire department managers often have bachelor's and advanced degrees in such fields as management and public administration.   Robin Paulsgrove

Related articles in *World Book* include:

Arson	Fire extinguisher	Paramedic
Emergency Medical Services	Fire prevention	Safety
	Fireproofing	Smoke detector
Fire	Forestry (Fire)	Thermography
Fire drill		

Outline

I. The work of a fire department
  A. Firefighting
  B. Emergency rescue operations
  C. Emergency medical operations
  D. Arson investigations
  E. Fire prevention and fire safety
II. Fire department equipment
  A. Communication systems
  B. Fire trucks
  C. Protective clothing
III. Kinds of fire departments
  A. Volunteer departments
  B. Paid departments
  C. Special-purpose departments
IV. History
V. Careers

Questions

What rules should a person follow in case of fire?
What service does the United States Fire Administration provide?
How did the early American colonists fight fires?
What is the purpose of a hydraulic rescue tool, commonly known by the trade name Jaws of Life?
What duties does an engine company perform at a building fire? A ladder company?
Why do fire departments inspect buildings?
What are paramedic units?
How do sprinkler systems work?
Why must firefighters ventilate a burning building?

Tony Stone Images

Japan is rich in both advanced technology and natural beauty. Japan's *shinkansen,* also called the "bullet train," speeds to its destination through fertile fields, *above.* Lovely Mount Fuji, a volcanic peak considered sacred by many Japanese people, seems to float in the background.

Japan

Japan is an island country in the North Pacific Ocean. It lies off the east coast of mainland Asia across from Russia, Korea, and China. Four large islands and thousands of smaller ones make up Japan. The four major islands—Hokkaido, Honshu, Kyushu, and Shikoku—form a curve that extends for about 1,200 miles (1,900 kilometers). About 126 million people are crowded on these islands, making Japan one of the most densely populated countries in the world.

The Japanese call their country *Nippon* or *Nihon,* which means *source of the sun.* The name *Japan* may have come from *Zipangu,* the Italian name given to the country by Marco Polo, a Venetian traveler of the late 1200's. Polo had heard of the Japanese islands while traveling through China.

Mountains and hills cover most of Japan, making it a country of great beauty. But the mountains and hills take up so much area that the great majority of the people live on a small portion of the land—narrow plains along the coasts. These coastal plains have much of Japan's best farmland and most of the country's major cities. Most of the people live in urban areas. Japan's big cities are busy, modern centers of culture, commerce, and industry. Tokyo is the capital and largest city.

Gary D. Allinson, the contributor of this article, is Professor of Modern Japanese History at the University of Virginia and the author of Japanese Urbanism *and* Japan's Postwar History.

Japan is one of the world's economic giants. Its total economic output is exceeded only by that of the United States. The Japanese manufacture a wide variety of products, including automobiles, computers, steel, television sets, textiles, and tires. The country's factories have some of the most advanced equipment in the world. Japan has become a major economic power even though it has few natural resources. Japan imports many of the raw materials needed for industry and exports finished manufactured goods.

Life in Japan reflects the culture of both the East and the West. For example, the favorite sporting events in the country are baseball games and exhibitions of *sumo,* an ancient Japanese style of wrestling. Although most Japanese wear Western-style clothing, many women dress in the traditional *kimono* for festivals and other special occasions. The Japanese *no* and *kabuki* dramas, both hundreds of years old, remain popular. But the Japanese people also flock to see motion pictures and rock music groups. Many Japanese artworks combine traditional and Western styles and themes.

Early Japan was greatly influenced by the neighboring Chinese civilization. From the late 400's to the early 800's, the Japanese borrowed heavily from Chinese art, government, language, religion, and technology. During the mid-1500's, the first Europeans arrived in Japan. Trade began with several European countries, and Christian missionaries from Europe converted some Japanese. During the early 1600's, however, the rulers of Japan decided to cut the country's ties with the rest of the world. They wanted to keep Japan free from outside influences.

Japan's isolation lasted until 1853, when Commodore

Paul Chesley, Tony Stone Images

A Tokyo railway station, the busy Shinjuku station, *above,* is crowded with commuters. It handles millions of riders a day.

Gavin Hellier, Tony Stone Images

A farm in central Hokkaido grows rice. Farmland is limited in Japan because mountains and hills cover most of the country.

Matthew C. Perry of the United States sailed his warships into Tokyo Bay. As a result of Perry's show of force, Japan agreed in 1854 to open two ports to U.S. trade.

During the 1870's, the Japanese government began a major drive to modernize the country. New ideas and manufacturing methods were imported from Western countries. By the early 1900's, Japan had become an industrial and military power.

During the 1930's, Japan's military leaders gained control of the government. They set Japan on a program of conquest. On Dec. 7, 1941, Japan attacked United States military bases at Pearl Harbor in Hawaii, bringing the United States into World War II. The Japanese won many early victories, but then the tide turned in favor of the United States and the other Allied nations. In August 1945, U.S. planes dropped the first atomic bombs used in warfare on the Japanese cities of Hiroshima and Nagasaki. On Sept. 2, 1945, Japan officially surrendered, and World War II ended.

World War II left Japan completely defeated. Many Japanese cities lay in ruins, industries were shattered, and Allied forces occupied the country. But the Japanese people worked hard to overcome the effects of the war. By the 1970's, Japan had become a great industrial nation. The success of the Japanese economy attracted attention throughout the world. Today, few nations enjoy a standard of living as high as Japan's.

Government

Japan is a constitutional monarchy with a parliamentary government. The Constitution, which took effect in 1947, guarantees many rights to the people, including freedom of religion, speech, and the press. It awards the vote to all men and women age 20 and older. The Constitution establishes three branches of government—the executive, the legislative, and the judicial.

National government. Japan's emperor is considered a symbol of the nation. The emperor performs some ceremonial duties specified in the Constitution, but he does not possess any real power to govern. The emperor inherits his throne.

The Diet is the national legislature, the highest lawmaking body of Japan. The Diet consists of two houses, the House of Representatives and the House of Councillors. The representatives have slightly more power under the Constitution than the councillors do.

The House of Representatives has 500 members who are elected to serve terms of up to four years. Three hundred representatives are elected directly from 300 electoral districts. The other 200 are chosen under a system called *proportional representation,* which gives a political party a share of seats in the Diet according to its share of the total votes cast.

The House of Councillors has 252 members. They are chosen in two ways—100 from the nation as a whole and 152 from small districts. Councillors serve six-year terms.

The prime minister is the head of the executive branch of the government. The prime minister leads the government and represents Japan abroad. Members of the Diet elect the prime minister, who must be a civilian and an elected member of the Diet. The prime minister selects members of the Cabinet to help govern the country. At least half the Cabinet ministers must be members of the Diet.

Japan in brief

General information

Capital: Tokyo.
Official language: Japanese.
Official name: *Nippon* or *Nihon* (Source of the Sun).
National anthem: "Kimigayo" ("The Reign of Our Emperor").
Largest cities: (1990 census)

Tokyo (8,163,573)	Sapporo (1,671,742)
Yokohama (3,220,331)	Kobe (1,477,410)
Osaka (2,623,801)	Kyoto (1,461,103)
Nagoya (2,154,793)	

Japan's flag, adopted in 1854, is a red sun on a white background. The Japanese call the country *Nippon* or *Nihon,* meaning *source of the sun.*

The imperial mon (badge) consists of a chrysanthemum with 16 petals. This symbol of the imperial family dates back hundreds of years.

Land and climate

Land: Japan lies in the North Pacific Ocean off the east coast of mainland Asia. It lies across from Russia, Korea, and China. Japan has four main islands—Hokkaido, Honshu, Kyushu, and Shikoku—and thousands of smaller ones. Mountains and hills cover most of the country. Narrow plains lie along the coasts. Most of the Japanese people live on the coastal plains.

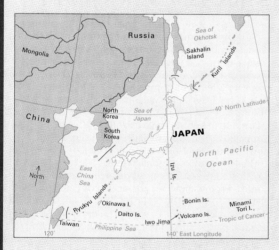

Area: 145,870 sq. mi. (377,801 km²). The four main islands—Hokkaido, Honshu, Kyushu, Shikoku—stretch about 1,200 mi. (1,900 km) from northeast to southwest. *Coastline*—5,857 mi. (9,426 km).
Elevation: *Highest*—Mount Fuji, 12,388 ft. (3,776 m) above sea level. *Lowest*—sea level.
Climate: Central and southern Japan have hot summers, mild winters, and moderate precipitation in all seasons. Daytime high temperatures average about 86 °F (30 °C) in the hottest month, August, and about 46 °F (8 °C) in January, the coldest month. Hokkaido, northern Honshu, and high mountain areas are much colder than the rest of the country in winter and cooler in summer.

Government

Form of government: Parliamentary democracy with ceremonial emperor.
Ceremonial head of state: Emperor.
Head of government: Prime minister.
Legislature: Diet of two houses: 500-member House of Representatives and 252-member House of Councillors.
Executive: Prime minister (chosen by Diet), assisted by Cabinet (chosen by prime minister).
Political subdivisions: 47 prefectures.

People

Population: *Estimated 1996 population*—126,320,000. *1990 census*—123,611,167. *Estimated 2001 population*—128,412,000.
Population density: 866 persons per sq. mi. (334 per km²).
Distribution: 78 percent urban, 22 percent rural.
Major ethnic/national groups: Almost entirely Japanese. Small minority of Koreans and some Chinese.
Major religions: Shinto, the native religion of Japan, and Buddhism. Not many Japanese strictly practice either religion, but almost everyone engages in some practices or rituals based on these two religious traditions. Small percentage of population is Christian.

Population trend

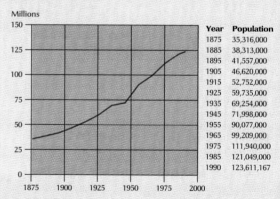

Year	Population
1875	35,316,000
1885	38,313,000
1895	41,557,000
1905	46,620,000
1915	52,752,000
1925	59,735,000
1935	69,254,000
1945	71,998,000
1955	90,077,000
1965	99,209,000
1975	111,940,000
1985	121,049,000
1990	123,611,167

Economy

Chief products: *Agriculture*—cabbage, Chinese cabbage, hogs, mandarin oranges, milk, potatoes, poultry and eggs, rice, strawberries, tea, white radishes. *Fishing*—clams, eels, mackerel, oysters, pollock, salmon, sardines, scallops, squid, tuna. *Manufacturing*—automobiles, cement, chemicals, computers, iron and steel, optical equipment, paper and newsprint, processed foods, television sets, textiles, tires, watches. *Mining*—coal.
Money: *Basic unit*—yen. For the price of the yen in U.S. dollars, see **Money** (table: Exchange rates). See also **Yen.**
Foreign trade: *Major exported goods*—chemicals, electronic equipment, iron and steel, motor vehicles, office machinery, scientific and optical equipment. *Major imported goods*—chemicals, electrical equipment, fish and shellfish, machinery, metal ores, petroleum. *Main trading partners*—China, Germany, South Korea, Taiwan, United States.

Local government. The nation is divided into 47 political units called *prefectures*. The residents of each prefecture elect a governor and representatives to a prefectural legislative assembly. The residents of each city, town, and village also elect a mayor and a local council.

Politics. Japan has several political parties. The Liberal Democratic Party is the largest. Other important political parties include the New Frontier Party, the New Harbinger Party, and the Social Democratic Party of Japan.

Courts. The Supreme Court is the nation's highest court. It consists of 1 chief justice and 14 associate justices. The Cabinet names, and the emperor appoints, the chief justice. The Cabinet appoints the associate justices. Every 10 years, the people have an opportunity to remove a justice from the court by voting in a referendum.

The Supreme Court oversees the training of Japan's judges and attorneys. It also administers the national system of courts. The court system includes 8 regional high courts; 50 district courts; many summary courts, which handle minor offenses and small claims without the formal procedures of other courts; and numerous family courts, which handle domestic cases.

Armed forces. The Constitution prohibits Japan from maintaining military forces to wage war. But Japan does have a Self-Defense Agency created to preserve Japan's peace, independence, and national security. A civilian member of the Cabinet heads the agency. The agency oversees an army, a navy, and an air force consisting of about 240,000 members. All service is voluntary.

People

Japan is one of the world's most populous nations. About 90 percent of the people live on the coastal plains, which make up only about 20 percent of Japan's territory. These plains ranks among the most thickly populated places in the world. Millions of people crowd the big cities along the coasts, including Tokyo, Japan's capital and largest city. The Tokyo metropolitan region, which includes the cities of Yokohama and Kawasaki, is the most populous urban area in the world.

Ancestry. The Japanese are descended from peoples who migrated to the islands from other parts of Asia. Many of these peoples came in waves from the northeastern part of the Asian mainland, passing through the Korean Peninsula. Some ancestors of the Japanese may have come from islands south of Japan.

Historians do not know for certain when people first arrived in Japan. But by about 10,000 B.C., the Japanese islands were inhabited by people who hunted, fished, and gathered fruits and plants for food. This early culture is known as the *Jomon,* which means *cord-marked,* because the people made pottery that was covered with the impressions of ropes or cords.

About 300 B.C., a new, settled agricultural society began to replace the Jomon. This culture is called the *Yayoi,* after the section of modern Tokyo where remains of the culture were found. The Yayoi people grew rice in irrigated fields and established villages. They cast bronze into bells, mirrors, and weapons. The Japanese people of today are probably descended from the Yayoi. In fact, scholars believe that by A.D. 100 the people living throughout the islands closely resembled the present-day Japanese in language and appearance.

Chinese, Koreans, and a group of people called the *Ainu* (pronounced *EYE noo*) make up the largest minority groups in Japan. The country has about 70,000 Chinese,

Dave Bartruff

The Ainu may have been Japan's original inhabitants. Most of them now live on Hokkaido, the country's northernmost island.

Mike Yamashita

An Osaka street scene reflects the common ancestry of most Japanese. Many ancestors of the Japanese came from the Asian mainland. Others may have come from islands south of Japan. The nation has a few small minority groups, such as the Ainu.

Japan map index

Prefectures

Aichi ....6,690,603 .H 6
Akita ....1,227,478 .D 7
Aomori ......1,482,873 .D 8
Chiba ....5,555,429 .H 7
Ehime ....1,515,025 .I 3
Fukui ....823,585 .G 6
Fukuoka ......4,811,050 .I 2
Fukushima ...1,546,295 .F 8
Gifu ....2,066,529 .G 5
Gunma ....1,966,265 .G 6
Hiroshima ...2,849,847 .H 3
Hokkaido .....5,643,647 .B 8
Hyogo ....5,405,040 .H 4
Ibaraki ......2,845,382 .G 7
Ishikawa .....1,164,628 .G 5
Iwate ....1,416,928 .E 8
Kagawa ....1,023,412 .H 4
Kagoshima ...1,797,824 .J 2
Kanagawa ....7,980,391 .H 7
Kochi ....865,034 .I 4
Kumamoto ...1,840,326 .I 2
Kyoto ....2,602,460 .H 5
Mie ....1,792,514 .H 5
Miyagi ....2,248,558 .E 8
Miyazaki .....1,168,907 .I 2
Nagano ....2,156,627 .G 6
Nagasaki .....1,562,959 .I 1
Nara ....1,375,481 .H 5
Niigata ......2,474,583 .F 6
Oita ....1,236,942 .I 3
Okayama ......1,925,877 .H 4
Okinawa‡ 1,222,398
Osaka ....8,734,516 .H 5
Saga ....877,851 .I 2
Saitama ......6,405,319 .G 7
Shiga ....1,222,411 .H 5
Shimane ......781,021 .H 3
Shizuoka .....3,670,840 .G 7
Tochigi ......1,935,168 .H 6
Tokushima ....831,598 .I 4
Tokyo ....11,855,563 .H 7
Tottori ......615,722 .G 4
Toyama ....1,120,161 .G 6
Wakayama .....1,074,325 .I 5
Yamagata .....1,258,390 .E 7
Yamaguchi ....1,572,616 .H 2
Yamanashi ....852,966 .G 6

Cities and towns

Abashiri ......44,285 .B 9
Abiko* ....120,628 .G 7
Ageo* ....194,947 .G 7
Aizuwaka-
  matsu ....119,080 .F 7
Akashi* ....270,722 .H 4
Akishima* .....105,372 .G 7
Akita ....302,362 .D 7
Ako ....52,349 .H 4
Amagasaki .....498,999 .H 5
Anan ....60,752 .I 4
Anjo ....142,251 .H 5
Aomori ....287,808 .D 7
Asahigawa .....359,071 .B 8
Asaka* ....103,617 .G 7
Ashikaga ......167,686 .G 7
Ashiya* ....87,127 .H 4
Atsugi* ....197,283 .G 7
Beppu ....130,334 .I 2
Chiba ....829,455 .G 7
Chigasaki* ....201,675 .G 7
Chofu* ....197,677 .G 7
Choshi ....87,884 .G 8
Daito* ....126,460 .H 5
Ebetsu ....90,328 .B 8
Ebina* ....155,822 .G 7
Fuchu* ....209,396 .G 7
Fuji ....222,490 .H 6
Fujieda* ......119,815 .H 6
Fujimi* ....85,698 .G 7
Fujinomiya* ...117,092 .H 6
Fujisawa ......350,330 .H 7
Fukaya* ....89,123 .G 7
Fukui ....252,743 .G 5
Fukushima .....277,528 .F 7
Fukuyama ......365,612 .H 4
Funabashi .....533,270 .G 7
Gamagori* .....85,580 .H 6
Gifu ....410,324 .G 5
Ginowan* 69,206
Habikino* .....115,049 .H 5
Hachinohe .....241,057 .D 8
Hachioji* .....466,347 .G 7
Hadano* ....155,620 .G 7
Hagi ....52,741 .H 2
Hakodate ......307,249 .C 7
Hamada ....51,070 .H 3
Hamamatsu .....534,620 .H 6
Hanamaki ......69,885 .E 8
Handa* ....92,883 .H 6
Higashi-
  kurume* .....113,818 .G 7
Higashi-
  murayama* ...134,002 .G 7
Higashiosaka ..518,319 .H 5
Hikone ....94,205 .H 5
Himeji ....454,360 .H 4
Hino* ....165,928 .G 7
Hirakata* .....390,788 .H 5
Hiratsuka .....245,950 .H 7

Hirosaki ......174,704 .D 7
Hiroshima .....1,085,705 .H 3
Hitachi ....202,141 .G 7
Hofu ....117,634 .H 3
Hoya* ....91,563 .G 7
Ibaraki ....254,078 .H 5
Ichihara ......257,716 .G 7
Ichikawa* .....436,596 .G 7
Ichinomiya ....262,434 .H 5
Iida* ....92,402 .G 6
Iizuka ....81,868 .I 2
Ikeda* ....104,218 .H 5
Imabari ....123,114 .H 3
Inazawa* ......94,480 .H 5
Iruma* ....137,585 .G 7
Isahaya ....88,374 .I 2
Ise ....104,164 .H 5
Isesaki* ......115,938 .G 6
Ishinomaki ....121,976 .E 8
Itami* ....186,134 .H 4
Ito ....70,195 .H 7
Iwaki ....355,812 .F 8
Iwakuni ....109,530 .H 3
Iwamizawa* ....81,665 .B 8
Iwatsuki* .....106,462 .G 7
Izumi ....146,127 .E 7
Izumi* ....137,633 .H 5
Izumisano* ....91,563 .H 5
Izumo ....80,748 .H 3
Joetsu ....130,116 .F 6
Kadoma* ....142,297 .H 5
Kagoshima .....536,752 .J 2
Kakamiga-
  hara* ....129,680 .G 5
Kakogawa* .....239,803 .H 4
Kamagaya* .....85,705 .G 7
Kamaishi ......60,005 .E 8
Kamakura* .....174,307 .G 7
Kanazawa ......442,868 .G 5
Kariya* ....120,126 .H 6
Kashihara* ....115,550 .H 5
Kashiwa* ......305,058 .G 7
Kashiwazaki ...86,020 .F 6
Kasugai ....266,599 .H 5
Kasukabe* .....188,823 .G 7
Katsuta* ......109,825 .G 7
Kawachina-
  gano* ....180,767 .H 5
Kawagoe ....304,854 .G 7
Kawaguchi* ....438,680 .G 7
Kawanishi* ....141,253 .H 4
Kawasaki ......1,173,603 .G 7
Kimitsu* ......84,311 .G 7
Kiryu ....126,446 .G 7
Kisarazu* .....123,433 .G 7
Kishiwada .....188,563 .H 5
Kitakyushu ....1,026,455 .H 2
Kitami ....107,247 .B 9
Kobe ....1,477,410 .H 4
Kochi ....317,069 .I 4
Kodaira* ......164,013 .G 7
Kofu ....200,626 .G 6
Koganei* ......105,899 .G 7
Kokubunji* ....100,982 .G 7
Komaki* ....124,441 .H 5
Komatsu ....106,075 .G 5
Konan* ....92,048 .H 5
Koriyama ......314,642 .F 7
Koshigaya* ....285,259 .G 7
Kumagaya ......152,124 .G 7
Kumamoto ......579,306 .I 2
Kurashiki .....414,693 .H 4
Kurayoshi .....52,349 .H 4
Kure ....216,723 .H 3
Kuroiso ....49,742 .F 7
Kurume ....228,347 .I 2
Kusatsu* ......87,543 .H 5
Kushiro ....205,639 .B 9
Kuwana* ....94,730 .H 5
Kyoto ....1,461,103 .H 5
Machida* ......349,050 .G 7
Maebashi ......286,261 .G 6
Maizuru ....98,779 .H 5
Marugame ......74,273 .H 4
Masuda ....54,050 .H 3
Matsubara* ....135,919 .H 5
Matsudo* ......456,210 .G 7
Matsue ....142,956 .G 3
Matsumoto .....200,715 .G 6
Matsuyama .....443,322 .I 3
Matsuzaka .....118,725 .H 5
Mihara ....85,975 .H 3
Minoo* ....122,120 .H 5
Misato* ....128,376 .G 7
Mishima* ......105,418 .H 6
Mitaka* ....165,564 .G 7
Mito ....234,968 .G 7
Miyako ....61,013 .E 8
Miyakonojo ....130,153 .J 2
Miyazaki ......287,352 .J 2
Moriguchi* ....157,372 .H 5
Morioka ....235,434 .E 7
Muroran ....117,855 .C 7
Musashino* ....139,077 .G 7
Nagano ....347,026 .G 6
Nagaoka ....185,938 .F 6
Nagare-
  yama* ....140,059 .G 7
Nagasaki ......444,599 .I 1
Nagoya ....2,154,793 .H 5
Naha‡ 304,836
Nara ....349,349 .H 5
Narishino* ....151,471 .G 7
Nemuro ....40,675 .B 10

Neyagawa* .....256,524 .H 5
Niigata ....486,097 .F 6
Niihama ....129,149 .I 4
Niiza* ....138,919 .G 7
Nishinomiya* ..426,909 .H 4
Nishio* ....91,930 .H 6
Nobeoka ....130,624 .I 2
Noda* ....114,475 .G 7
Noshiro ....59,167 .D 7
Numazu ....211,732 .H 7
Obihiro ....167,384 .B 9
Odawara ....193,417 .H 7
Ogaki ....148,281 .H 5
Oita ....408,501 .I 3
Okaya ....61,750 .G 6
Okayama ....593,730 .H 4
Okazaki ....306,822 .H 6
Okinawa‡ 105,845
Ome* ....125,960 .G 7
Omiya ....403,776 .G 7
Omuta ....150,453 .I 2
Onomichi ......100,642 .H 3
Osaka ....2,623,801 .H 5
Ota* ....139,801 .G 6
Otaru ....163,211 .B 8
Otsu ....260,018 .H 5
Oyama ....142,262 .G 7
Saga ....169,963 .I 2
Sagamihara* ...531,542 .G 7
Saiki ....54,709 .I 3
Sakado* ....87,586 .G 7
Sakai ....807,765 .H 5
Sakata ....100,811 .E 7
Sakura* ....144,688 .G 7
Sanjo ....86,325 .F 7
Sano ....80,753 .H 7
Sapporo ....1,671,742 .B 8
Sasebo ....244,677 .I 2
Sayama* ....157,309 .G 7
Sendai ....918,398 .F 7
Seto ....126,340 .H 6
Settsu* ....86,332 .H 5
Shibata ....77,219 .F 7
Shimizu ....241,523 .H 6
Shimonoseki ...262,635 .H 2
Shiogama ......61,825 .F 8
Shizuoka ......472,196 .H 6
Soka* ....206,132 .G 7
Suita ....345,206 .H 5
Suzuka ....174,105 .H 5
Tachikawa* ....152,824 .G 7
Tajimi* ....84,829 .G 5
Takamatsu .....329,684 .H 4
Takaoka ....175,466 .G 5
Takarazuka* ...201,862 .H 4
Takasago* .....91,434 .H 4
Takasaki ......236,461 .G 7
Takatsuki .....359,867 .H 5
Takefu ....69,148 .G 5
Takikawa ......52,005 .B 8
Tama* ....144,489 .G 7
Tanabe ....70,827 .I 5
Tanashi* ......71,333 .G 7
Tatebayashi* ..75,141 .G 7
Tateyama ......56,035 .H 7
Tochigi* ......86,289 .G 7
Toda* ....76,960 .G 7
Tokai* ....95,278 .H 6
Tokorozawa* ...303,040 .G 7
Tokushima .....263,356 .H 4
Tokuyama ......110,900 .H 3
Tokyo ....8,163,573 .H 7
              †11,927,457 .G 7
Tomakomai .....160,118 .B 8
Tondabaya-
  shi* ....110,447 .H 5
Tottori ....142,467 .G 4
Toyama ....321,254 .G 6
Toyohashi .....337,982 .H 6
Toyokawa* .....111,730 .H 6
Toyonaka* .....409,837 .H 5
Toyota* ....332,336 .H 6
Tsu ....157,177 .H 5
Tsuchiura* ....127,471 .G 7
Tsukuba ....22,860 .G 7
Tsuruga ....65,670 .G 5
Tsuruoka ......143,396 .E 7
Tsuyama ....86,835 .H 4
Ube ....175,053 .H 2
Ueda ....119,435 .G 6
Uji ....177,010 .H 5
Urasoe‡ 81,612
Urawa ....418,271 .G 7
Urayasu* ......115,675 .G 7
Usa ....52,216 .I 2
Utsunomiya ....426,795 .G 7
Wakayama ......396,553 .H 5
Wakkanai ......51,854 .A 8
Yachiyo* ......148,615 .G 7
Yaizu* ....112,186 .H 6
Yamagata ......249,487 .F 7
Yamaguchi .....129,461 .H 2
Yamato* ....194,866 .G 7
Yamatokori-
  yama* ....89,624 .H 5
Yao* ....277,568 .H 5
Yatsushiro ....108,135 .I 2
Yokkaichi .....274,180 .H 5
Yokohama ......3,220,331 .G 7
Yokosuka ......433,358 .H 7
Yonago ....131,435 .G 4
Yonezawa ......93,725 .F 7
Yono* ....71,598 .G 7
Zama* ....112,102 .G 7

*Does not appear on map; key shows general location.
†Population of metropolitan area, including suburbs.
‡Does not appear on map; on Okinawa.
Sources: 1990 census for prefectures and cities with populations over 100,000; 1985 census for other places.

Japan political map

Legend:
- National park (N.P.)
- International boundary
- Prefecture boundary
- Expressway
- Road
- Express railroad
- Other railroad
- ⊛ National capital
- ★ Prefectural capital
- • Other city or town

WORLD BOOK map

Map labels: Jixi · Lake Khanka · 45° · Suifenhe · Ussuriysk · CHINA · Artem · Vladivostok · Nakhodka · Najin · 130° · NORTH KOREA · Kimchaek · 40° North Latitude · Hamhung · Wonsan · Chunchon · Kangnung · SOUTH KOREA · Wonju · Ullung I. · Chongju · Taejon · Andong · Kimchon · Pohang · Oki Islands · Taegu · Dozen Is. · Chinju · Ulsan · Matsue · Izumo · Masan · Pusan · Shimane · Western Channel · Korea Strait · Eastern Channel · Hamada · Miyoshi · Tsushima · Iki · Masuda · Hiroshima · Onomichi · Yamaguchi · Hagi · Kure · Iwakuni · Inland · Kitakyushu · Shimonoseki · Hofu · Ube · Tokuyama · TOKAIDO · Imabari · Fukuoka · Yukuhashi · Suo Sea · Iyo Sea · Matsuyama · Karatsu · Iizuka · Nakatsu · Ehime · Hirado I. · Imari · Saga · Hita · Beppu · Usa · Yawatahama · ASHIZURI-UWAKAI N.P. · Sasebo · Oita · Uwajima · Goto Islands · Nagasaki · Omuta · ASO N.P. · Saiki · Nakamura · SAIKAI N.P. · Kumamoto · UNZEN-AMAKUSA N.P. · Yatsushiro · Nobeoka · Amakusa Sea · Hitoyoshi · Miyazaki · Amakusa Is. · Minamata · Kyushu · Koshiki Islands · Sendai · Kagoshima · Miyakonojo · Kushima · East China Sea · KIRISHIMA-YAKU N.P. · Makurazaki · Kanoya · Shibushi Bay · Kagoshima Bay · 130°

Okinawa Prefecture lies south of the main islands.

Scale: 0 — 100 — 200 (miles); 0 — 100 — 200 — 300 — 400 (kilometers)

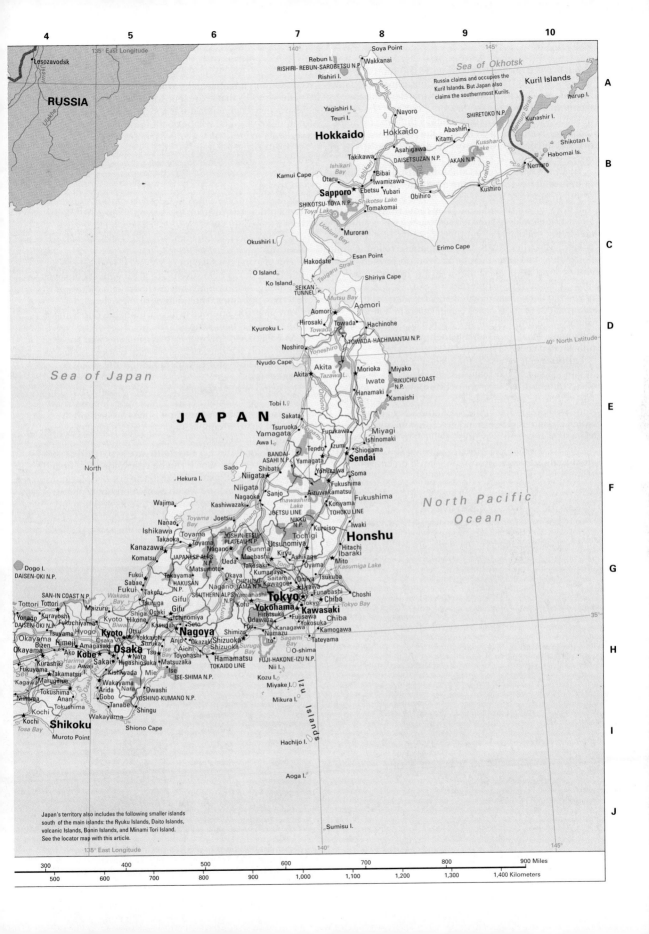

4   **5**   **6**   **7**   **8**   **9**   **10**

135° East Longitude   140°   145°

RUSSIA

Lesozavodsk

Ulakhe

Sea of Okhotsk

Rebun I.
Soya Point
Wakkanai
RISHIRI - REBUN - SAROBETSU N.P.
Rishiri I.

Russia claims and occupies the
Kuril Islands. But Japan also
claims the southernmost Kurils.

Kuril Islands

Iturup I.

Yagishiri I.
Teuri I.
Nayoro
SHIRETOKO N.P.
Kunashir I.

Hokkaido   Hokkaido
Takikawa
Asahigawa
Abashiri
Kitami
Shikotan I.
DAISETSUZAN N.P.
Kamui Cape
Ishikari Bay
Otaru
Bibai
Iwamizawa
AKAN N.P.
Kussharo Lake
Habomai Is.
Nemuro

Sapporo
Ebetsu
Yubari
Obihiro
Kushiro
SHIKOTSU-TOYA N.P.
Shikotsu Lake
Tomakomai
Toya Lake
Uchiura Bay
Muroran

Okushiri I.
Erimo Cape

Hakodate
Esan Point
O Island
Ko Island
Taugaru Strait
Shiriya Cape
SEIKAN TUNNEL
Mutsu Bay

Aomori
Aomori
Hirosaki
Towada
Hachinohe
Kyuroku I.
Towada
TOWADA-HACHIMANTAI N.P.
40° North Latitude

Noshiro
Yoneshiro
Nyudo Cape
Miyako
Akita
Akita
Morioka
Tazawa L.
Iwate
RIKUCHU COAST N.P.

Sea of Japan
Hanamaki
Kamaishi

Tobi I.
Sakata
Omono

J A P A N
Tsuruoka
Furukawa
Miyagi
Yamagata
Izumi
Ishinomaki
Awa I.
Tendo
Shiogama
BANDAI-ASAHI N.P.
Yamagata
Sendai
Sado
Shibata
Yonezawa
Soma
Niigata
Aizuwakamatsu
Hekura I.
Niigata
Sanjo
North Pacific
Nagaoka
Inawashiro Lake
Fukushima
Wajima
Kashiwazaki
JOETSU LINE
Fukushima
Ocean
Nanao
Joetsu
NIKKO N.P.
Koriyama
Toyama Bay
TOHOKU LINE
Ishikawa
Toyama
JOSHIN-ETSU PLATEAU N.P.
Kuroiso
Iwaki
Takaoka
Nagano
Utsunomiya
Honshu
Kanazawa
JAPANESE ALPS N.P.
Ueda
Tochigi
Hitachi
Komatsu
Matsumoto
Maebashi
Gunma
Kiryu
Ibaraki
Fukui
CHICHIBU N.P.
Takasaki
Ashikaga
Mito
Sabae
HAKUSAN N.P.
Okaya
Saitama
Oyama
Kasumiga Lake
Fukui
Takefu
Nagano
YAMA N.P.
Kumagaya
Tsukuba
Dogo I.
Tsuruga
SOUTHERN ALPS
Kawagoe
DAISEN-OKI N.P.
Wakasa Bay
Shiga
N.P.
Yamanashi
Omiya
Funabashi
Gifu
Urawa
Choshi
Maizuru
Biwa
Ogaki
Kofu
Tokyo
Tottori
SAN-IN COAST N.P.
Hikone
Yokohama
Kawasaki
Chiba
Tottori
Kurayoshi
Kyoto
Otsu
Ichinomiya
Hiratsuka
Fujisawa
Tokyo Bay
Yonago
Fukuchiyama
Seto
Fuji
Yokosuka
35°
DAISEN-OKI N.P.
Tsuyama
Kyoto
Kasugai
Nagoya
Odawara
Kanagawa
Kamogawa
Okayama
Hyogo
Yokkaichi
Shimizu
Ito
Bizen
Suzuka
Anjo
Shizuoka
Sagami Bay
Tateyama
Osaka
Okayama
Ako
Itami
Okazaki
Shizuoka
O-shima
Himeji
Kobe
Nara
Aichi
Toyohashi
Kurashiki
Amagasaki
Mie
Hamamatsu
Matsuzaka
Kozu I.
Fukuyama
Sakai
Higashiosaka
TOKAIDO LINE
Kagawa
Awaji
Kishiwada
Mie
Ise
FUJI-HAKONE-IZU N.P.
Niijima
Takamatsu
Harima Sea
ISE-SHIMA N.P.
Miyake I.
Niihama
Wakayama
Nara
Owashi
Tokushima
Arida
Gobo
YOSHINO-KUMANO N.P.
Mikura I.
Anan
Gobo
Kochi
Tokushima
Tanabe
Kochi
Wakayama
Shingu
Tosa Bay
Shikoku
Shiono Cape
Muroto Point

Izu Islands

Hachijo I.

Aoga I.

Japan's territory also includes the following smaller islands
south of the main islands: the Ryukyu Islands, Daito Islands,
volcanic Islands, Bonin Islands, and Minami Tori Island.
See the locator map with this article.

Sumisu I.

135° East Longitude   140°   145°

300   400   500   600   700   800   900 Miles
500   600   700   800   900   1,000   1,100   1,200   1,300   1,400 Kilometers

North

about 675,000 Koreans, and about 15,000 Ainu. Most of the Ainu live on Hokkaido, the northernmost of Japan's main islands. Many Ainu have intermarried with the Japanese and adopted the Japanese culture. The rest of the Ainu are ethnically and culturally different from the Japanese. Some scholars believe the Ainu were Japan's original inhabitants, who were pushed northward by the ancestors of the present-day Japanese people.

Japan's minority groups suffer from prejudice. But the people who have suffered the most injustices are a group of Japanese known as the *burakumin*. The burakumin number about 3 million. They came from *buraku* (villages) traditionally associated with such tasks as the execution of criminals, the slaughter of cattle, and the tanning of leather. According to Japanese religious traditions, these tasks and the people who performed them were considered unclean. As a result, the burakumin—though not ethnically different from other Japanese—have long been discriminated against. Many of the burakumin live in segregated urban slums or special villages. The burakumin have started an active social movement to achieve fair treatment, but they have had only limited success so far.

Language. Japanese is the official language of Japan. Spoken Japanese has many local dialects. These local dialects differ greatly in pronunciation. However, the Tokyo dialect is the standard form of spoken Japanese. Almost all the people understand the Tokyo dialect, which is used in schools and on radio and television. Many Japanese can also speak English to some extent. A number of Japanese words, such as *aisu kuriimu* (ice cream) and *guruupu* (group), are based on English.

Where the people of Japan live

Most of Japan's people live near the coasts. The Pacific coast from Tokyo to Kobe is the most densely populated area. The mountainous interiors of the islands are thinly settled.

WORLD BOOK map

Persons per sq. mi.	Persons per km²
More than 1,000	More than 386
400 to 1,000	154 to 386
100 to 400	39 to 154
Less than 100	Less than 39

Sapporo

Tokyo
Kyoto Yokohama Kawasaki
Nagoya
Hiroshima Kobe Osaka
Kitakyushu
Fukuoka

Written Japanese is considered one of the most difficult writing systems in the world. It uses Japanese phonetic symbols that represent sounds as well as Chinese characters. Each character is a symbol that stands for a complete word or syllable. Schools in Japan also teach students to write the Japanese language with the letters of the Roman alphabet.

Way of life

City life. About three-fourths of the Japanese people live in urban areas. Most of the urban population is concentrated in three major metropolitan areas: (1) the Tokyo metropolitan region, which also includes the cities of Kawasaki and Yokohama; (2) Osaka; and (3) Nagoya.

The prosperity of Japanese society is visible in these cities. The downtown streets are filled with expensive, late-model automobiles and are lined with glittering high-rise buildings. The buildings house expensive apartments, prosperous firms, fashionable department stores, and elegant shops.

Most Japanese people who live in cities and suburbs enjoy a high standard of living. Many work in banks, hotels, offices, and stores. Others hold professional or government jobs.

Housing in metropolitan areas includes modern high-rise apartments and traditional Japanese houses. The houses are small because land prices are extremely high. Tokyo, for example, has some of the most expensive land in the world.

In traditional homes, the rooms are separated by sliding paper screens, which can be rearranged as needed. Straw mats called *tatami* cover the floors. People sit on cushions and sleep on a type of padded quilt called a *futon*. Today, many Japanese apartments and houses have one or more rooms fitted with carpets instead of tatami and containing Western-style chairs and tables.

Dave Bartruff

Apartment buildings in Osaka provide homes for many of the city's residents. Most Japanese people live in urban areas, and Japan's largest cities are among the most crowded in the world.

Japan's big cities, like those in many other countries, face such problems as overcrowding and air and water pollution. However, crime and poverty are not as common in Japan as they are in most Western nations.

Rural life. Only about one-fourth of the Japanese people live in rural areas. Farm families make up most of the rural population. In rural areas along the coasts, some Japanese make their living by fishing and harvesting edible seaweed.

Most families in rural areas live in traditional Japanese-style wooden houses like those in the cities. Housing is cheaper in the countryside than in cities, but it is still expensive by international standards.

Japan's rural areas face an uncertain future. Only about 15 percent of farm households live on their farming incomes alone. By taking second and third jobs, farmworkers maintain an average household income slightly higher than that of urban workers. But rural populations have declined as the children of farmers leave to work in Japan's cities.

Clothing. Some well-to-do Japanese buy designer-made garments, but the majority of the people purchase more moderately priced clothing. The styles they buy are similar to those worn in the United States and Western Europe.

For business and professional men, typical workday wear consists of a dark suit, white shirt, conservative tie, black shoes, and a dark woolen overcoat for winter. Younger men sometimes wear patterned sport coats and colorful ties. When not at work, Japanese men typically wear slacks and a casual shirt or sweater.

Most working women wear a skirt, blouse, and jacket to the office. Most women who do not work outside the home dress in moderately priced dresses or blouses with skirts or slacks when at home or in their own neighborhood. While in a major city shopping area or business district, many of these women wear expensive imported dresses or skirts, blouses, and jackets. For accessories, they wear fine jewelry and silk scarves.

On special occasions, such as weddings, funerals, or New Year's celebrations, Japanese women may dress in the traditional long garment called a *kimono*. A kimono is tied around the waist with a sash called an *obi* and worn with sandals known as *zori*.

Most Japanese children wear uniforms to school. The uniforms often consist of a black or navy jacket worn with matching shorts, skirt, or slacks. On weekends, Japanese children dress in the latest casual styles from Europe and the United States or in T-shirts printed with Japanese cartoon characters.

Food and drink. Many Japanese families eat at restaurants on weeknights and weekends as well as on special occasions. Favorite dining spots include Japan's new casual family restaurants. Roads and superhighways are lined with such American establishments as Denny's and McDonald's and similar Japanese-owned chains called Skylark and Lotteria.

When dining at home, most older people eat traditional Japanese foods. They drink tea and eat rice at almost every meal. They supplement the rice with fish, *tofu* (soybean curd cake), pickled vegetables, soups made with *miso* (soybean paste), and on occasion, eggs or meat.

Younger people eat fewer of the traditional foods. Like their elders, they eat fish, but they also like to eat beef, chicken, and pork. They eat more fruit, including imported kiwi and grapefruit as well as the apples, oranges, pears, and strawberries grown in Japan. They also consume larger amounts of eggs, cheese, and milk than their parents. Instead of rice, many prefer bread, doughnuts, and toast. In fact, by 1990, total rice consumption in Japan had dropped to about half its level in 1960.

Overall, younger people now take in significantly more protein and fat then their grandparents did. The

John Launois, Black Star

A traditional Japanese house blends with the natural beauty surrounding it. Many such houses in Japan feature lovely gardens, graceful tile roofs, and sliding paper screens between rooms.

Paul Chesley, Tony Stone Images

Paul Chesley, Tony Stone Images

Japanese meals reflect the culture of both the East and the West. Many people enjoy dining at home in traditional Japanese style, *above,* and many enjoy eating out. Casual family restaurants are favorite dining places, and fast-food establishments, *left,* are also popular throughout Japan.

nutritional change has helped make the members of the younger generation an average of 3 to 4 inches (8 to 10 centimeters) taller than their grandparents.

Recreation. Japanese people are energetic sports enthusiasts. Schools encourage children to enjoy sports, and adults spend large sums on athletic equipment and membership fees. Baseball, bowling, golf, gymnastics, and tennis attract large numbers of participants, and many Japanese are good swimmers and runners. Another popular sport is *kendo,* a Japanese form of fencing in which bamboo or wooden sticks are used for swords. Many Japanese also practice *aikido, judo,* and *karate,* traditional martial arts that involve fighting without weapons. Spectator events, such as baseball, horse racing, soccer, and the Japanese form of wrestling called *sumo,* are also popular.

Hobbies are another important leisure time activity for Japanese men and women. Popular hobbies include performing the tea-serving ceremony, chanting medieval ballads, or *ikebana* (flower arranging). Many Japanese study with masters of these arts to improve their skills.

Travel is a favorite leisure pursuit. Every year, millions of Japanese visit foreign countries. Within Japan, popular travel destinations include temples or shrines, hot springs, and famous historical sites.

Other leisure pursuits common in Japan include watching television, playing video games, and listening to recorded music. The Japanese also like to read books and magazines. Many workers read during the hours spent commuting by train between homes in the suburbs and jobs in the city.

Men in Japan often spend their free time after work socializing in small groups. They stop off at little shops, restaurants, and bars to have a snack together and a drink of *sake* (Japanese-style rice wine) or beer.

The Japanese celebrate many festivals during the year. One of the most popular celebrations in Japan is the New Year's Festival, which begins on January 1 and ends on January 3. During the festival, the Japanese dress up, visit their friends and relatives, enjoy feasts, and exchange gifts.

Religion. Many Japanese people say they are not devout worshipers and do not have strong religious beliefs. However, nearly everyone in Japanese society engages in some religious practices or rituals. Those practices are based on the two major religious traditions in Japan, Shinto and Buddhism.

Shinto means *the way of the gods.* It is the native religion of Japan and dates from prehistoric times. Shintoists worship many gods, called *kami,* that are found in mountains, rivers, rocks, trees, and other parts of nature. Shinto also involves ancestor worship.

In 1868, the Japanese government established an official religion called State Shinto. State Shinto stressed patriotism and the worship of the emperor as a divine being. The government abolished State Shinto after World War II, and the emperor declared he was not divine.

Today, fewer than 3 percent of Japanese practice strict traditional Shinto. But almost all Japanese perform some Shinto rituals. Many people visit Shinto shrines to make offerings of fruit, rice, prayers, and other gifts to the gods. In return, they may ask the gods for favors, such as the safe birth of a child, success on examinations, or good health. Japanese people typically invite Shinto priests to preside at weddings and to offer blessings for the New Year or for the construction of new buildings.

Buddhism came to Japan from India via China in the 500's. Buddhism has a more elaborate set of beliefs than Shinto, and it offers a more complicated view of humanity, the gods, and life and death. Generally, Buddhists believe that a person can obtain perfect peace and happiness by leading a life of virtue and wisdom. Buddhism stresses the unimportance of worldly things. Many Japanese turn to Buddhist priests to preside at funerals and other occasions when they commemorate the dead.

A variety of religious groups called New Religions developed in Japan during the 1800's and 1900's. Many of these religions combine elements of Buddhism, Shinto, and in some cases, Christianity. In addition, a small percentage of the Japanese population is Christian.

Gender roles. Japanese society imposes strong expectations on women and men. The society expects women to marry in their mid-20's, become mothers soon afterward, and stay at home to attend to the needs of their husband and children. Women often have a dominant role in raising children and handling the family finances. Men are expected to support their fami-

lies as sole breadwinners. To make this possible, Japanese employers provide male workers with family allowances.

Most Japanese men accept this idea of their place in society, and many women do, too. But in practice, the majority of Japanese women do hold jobs at one time or another. Most women work before they marry, and many of them return to the labor force after their children are in school or grown. In addition, some Japanese women work while their children are young.

Altogether, about 50 percent of all Japanese women over age 15 are in the labor force at any one time. But because of the society's expectations about gender roles, female employees earn lower incomes and receive fewer benefits than male employees do, and have almost no job security.

The traditional ideas about gender roles have begun to change in Japan, most quickly among younger women. Many women in their early 20's are reluctant to give up their jobs and income. As a sign of that change, an increasing number of Japanese women are postponing marriage until they are in their late 20's or early 30's.

A driving range with three levels enables large crowds of Japanese golfers to practice their swing. Golf is a popular sport in Japan, and the country has many golf courses.

Sumo wrestlers parade around the ring before an exhibition of this Japanese style of wrestling. Sumo tournaments attract large, enthusiastic crowds. Many matches are televised.

Shinto and Buddhism are the two major religious traditions in Japan. The procession shown on the left above is part of a Shinto festival. Many Japanese Buddhists visit the *Daibutsu* (Great Buddha), a huge bronze statue of Buddhism's founder in Kamakura, *above right*.

Education. Japanese society places an extremely high value on educational achievement, particularly for males. The Japanese measure educational achievement chiefly by the reputation of the university a student attends. The student's grades or field of study are less important as signs of success. Under most circumstances, any student who graduates from a top-ranked university has a big advantage over other college graduates in seeking employment. Families work hard to get their children into a good university, starting when the youngsters are in junior high school.

After six years at an elementary school, almost all Japanese children continue for another three years at a junior high school. Education at public schools is free during these nine years for children 6 to 14 years of age.

Japanese elementary and junior high school students study such subjects as art, homemaking, the Japanese language, mathematics, moral education, music, physical education, science, and social studies. In addition, many junior high school students study English or another foreign language. Students spend much time learning to read and write Japanese because the language is quite difficult. The country has an exceptionally high literacy rate, however. Almost all adults can read and write.

Public school students attend classes Monday through Friday and half a day on Saturday, except for two weeks each month when they have Saturdays off. The Japanese school year runs from April through March of the next year. Vacation is from late July through August.

During the last two years of junior high school, many students focus on attaining admission to a high school with a good record of getting its graduates into top universities. Many of the most successful high schools are expensive private institutions that require incoming stu-

dents to pass a difficult entrance examination. To prepare for the test, many eighth- and ninth-grade students spend several hours each day after school taking exam-preparation classes at private academies called *juku*.

Students attend senior high school for three years. Classes include many of the same subjects studied in junior high school, along with courses to prepare students for college or train them for jobs. While in high school, a student may continue to study at a juku as preparation for the entrance exam to a university.

Students work on a lesson with their teacher, *above*. Education is valued highly in Japan. Even before entering high school, students begin to focus on getting into a well-regarded university.

Japan has more than 500 universities and about 600 technical and junior colleges. The most admired institutions are the oldest national universities, the University of Tokyo and the University of Kyoto. Two private universities, Keio University and Waseda University in Tokyo, are also highly regarded.

After students are admitted to one of these four universities, they tend to pay more attention to extracurricular activities than to their classwork. Simply being at a top university will ensure job interviews at the country's best firms.

Because Japanese society does not expect a woman to be the family's main wage earner, the educational experience for girls is more limited. About half of the women who get college educations attend technical or junior colleges rather than universities. In contrast, nearly all men who get a college degree attend universities. At the graduate level, male students outnumber females 2 to 1.

Japanese students consistently score well on international tests of science and mathematics skills. But many Japanese are concerned about the disadvantages of their educational system. Parents feel that it places too much emphasis on memorization and taking exams. Most would prefer to have their children educated in a more creative environment that requires less time in classrooms. Many Japanese politicians and business people agree that their educational system has flaws.

The arts

For hundreds of years, Chinese arts had a great influence on Japanese arts. A Western influence began about 1870. However, there has always been a distinctive Japanese quality about the country's art.

Music. Most forms of Japanese music feature one instrument or voice or a group of instruments that follow the same melodic line instead of blending in harmony. Japanese instruments include the lutelike *biwa*; the zitherlike *koto*; and the three-stringed banjolike *samisen*, or *shamisen*. Traditional music also features drums, flutes, and gongs. Performances of traditional music draw large crowds in Japan. Most types of Western music are also popular. Many Japanese cities have their own professional symphony orchestras that specialize in Western music.

Theater. The oldest form of traditional Japanese drama is the *no* play, which developed during the 1300's. *No* plays are serious treatments of history and legend. Masked actors perform the story with carefully controlled gestures and movements. A chorus chants most of the important lines in the play.

Two other forms of traditional Japanese drama—*bunraku* (puppet theater) and the *kabuki* play—developed during the late 1600's. In puppet theater, a narrator recites the story, which is acted out by large, lifelike puppets. The puppet handlers work silently on the stage in view of the audience. *Kabuki* plays are melodramatic representations of historical or domestic events. *Kabuki* features colorful costumes and makeup, spectacular scenery, and a lively and exaggerated acting style.

The traditional types of theater remain popular in Japan. But the people also enjoy new dramas by Japanese playwrights, as well as Western plays.

Literature. Japan has a rich literary heritage. Much of the country's literature deals with the fleeting quality of human life and the never-ending flow of time. Murasaki Shikibu, a lady-in-waiting to the empress, wrote *The Tale of Genji* during the early 1000's. This long novel is generally considered the greatest work of Japanese fiction and possibly the world's first novel.

Sculpture. Some of the earliest Japanese sculptures were *haniwa*, small clay figures made from the A.D. 200's to 500's. Haniwa were placed in the burial mounds of important Japanese people. The figures represented animals, servants, warriors, weapons, and objects of everyday use.

Japanese sculptors created some of their finest works for Buddhist temples. The sculptors worked chiefly with wood, but they also used clay and bronze. The most famous bronze statue in Japan, the Great Buddha at Kamakura, was cast during the 1200's.

Paolo Koch, Photo Researchers

Kabuki, a traditional form of Japanese drama, features chanting, music, colorful costumes and makeup, and a lively and exaggerated acting style. Kabuki plays are melodramatic portrayals of historical or domestic events. The Japanese developed kabuki theater during the 1600's.

Wood-block print by an unknown Japanese artist (1800's); Art Resource

Landscape prints, such as the wood-block print above, flourished in Japan in the 1800's. Printmaking is still popular in Japan.

Painting. Early Japanese painting dealt with Buddhist subjects, using compositions and techniques from China. From the late 1100's to the early 1300's, many Japanese artists painted long picture scrolls. These scrolls realistically portrayed historical tales, legends, and other stories in a series of pictures. Ink painting flourished in Japan from the early 1300's to the mid-1500's. Many of these paintings featured black brush-strokes on a white background.

During the mid-1500's and early 1600's, a decorative style of painting developed in Japan. Artists used bright colors and elaborate designs and added gold leaf to their paintings. From the 1600's to the late 1800's, artists created colorful wood-block prints. Printmaking is still popular in Japan.

Architecture. Many architectural monuments in Japan are Buddhist temples. These temples have large tile roofs with extending edges that curve gracefully upward. Traditional Shinto shrines are wooden frame structures noted for their graceful lines and sense of proportion. The simple style of Shinto architecture has influenced the design of many modern buildings in Japan. Japanese architecture emphasizes harmony between buildings and the natural beauty around them. Landscape gardening is a highly developed art in Japan.

Other arts. Japan ranks among the world's leading producers of motion pictures. Many Japanese films have earned international praise. The Japanese have long been famous for their ceramics, ivory carving, lacquerware, and silk weaving and embroidery. Other traditional arts include flower arranging, *cloisonné* (a type of decorative enameling), and *origami* (the art of folding paper into decorative objects).

Robert Glaze, Artstreet

The National Stadium of Tokyo shows the influence of traditional Japanese architecture in the gracefully curving lines of the structure's roof. The stadium, designed by the Japanese architect Kenzo Tange, was constructed in 1964 for the Summer Olympic Games held in Tokyo that year.

Paul D. Thrash

Mount Fuji, framed by cherry blossoms, symbolizes the great natural beauty of Japan. Fuji is Japan's highest and most famous peak, and many Japanese people climb it each year. Fuji is part of a chain of volcanoes on the island of Honshu, the largest of Japan's four main islands.

The land

Japan is a land of great natural beauty. Mountains and hills cover about 70 percent of the country. In fact, the Japanese islands consist of the rugged upper part of a great mountain range that rises from the floor of the North Pacific Ocean. Jagged peaks, rocky gorges, and thundering mountain waterfalls provide some of the country's most spectacular scenery. Thick forests thrive on the mountainsides, adding to the scenic beauty of the Japanese islands.

Japan lies on an extremely unstable part of the earth's crust. As a result, the land is constantly shifting. This shifting causes two of Japan's most striking natural features—earthquakes and volcanoes. The Japanese islands have about 1,500 earthquakes a year. Most of them are minor tremors that cause little damage, but severe earthquakes occur every few years. Undersea quakes sometimes cause huge, destructive waves, called *tsunami*, along Japan's Pacific coast. The Japanese islands have more than 150 major volcanoes. Over 60 of these volcanoes are active.

Numerous short, swift rivers cross Japan's rugged surface. Most of the rivers are too shallow and steep to be navigated. But their waters are used to irrigate farmland, and their rapids and falls supply power for hydroelectric plants. Many lakes nestle among the Japanese mountains. Some lie in the craters of extinct volcanoes. A large number of hot springs gush from the ground throughout the country.

The Japanese islands have a total land area of about 145,834 square miles (377,708 square kilometers). The four main islands, in order of size, are Honshu, Hokkaido, Kyushu, and Shikoku. Thousands of smaller islands and islets lie near these major islands. Japan's territory also includes the Ryukyu and Bonin island chains. The Pacific Ocean lies to the east and south of Japan. The Sea of Japan washes the country's west coast. Japan's four chief islands have 4,628 miles (7,448 kilometers) of coastline.

Honshu, Japan's largest island, has an area of 87,805 square miles (227,414 square kilometers). About 80 percent of the Japanese people live on Honshu.

Three mountain ranges run parallel through northern Honshu. Most of the people in this area live in small mountain valleys. Agriculture is the chief occupation. East of the ranges, along the Pacific, lies the Sendai Plain. West of the mountains, the Echigo Plain extends to the Sea of Japan.

The towering peaks of the Japanese Alps, the country's highest mountains, rise in central Honshu. Southeast of these mountains lies a chain of volcanoes. Japan's tallest and most famous peak, Mount Fuji, or Fujiyama, is one of these volcanoes. Mount Fuji, which is inactive, rises 12,388 feet (3,776 meters) above sea level. The Kanto Plain, the country's largest lowland, spreads

Hokkaido extends the farthest north of any of Japan's main islands. It is mostly covered with forested mountains and hills. Hokkaido's chief agricultural region, dotted with small rural communities like the one at the left, lies in the southwestern part of the island.

Mike Yamashita

east from the Japanese Alps to the Pacific. This lowland is an important center of agriculture and industry. Tokyo sprawls over the southern part of the Kanto Plain. Two other major agricultural and industrial lowlands—the Nobi Plain and Osaka Plain—lie south and west of the Kanto region.

Most of southwestern Honshu consists of rugged, mountainous land. Farming and fishing villages and some industrial cities lie on small lowlands scattered throughout this region.

Hokkaido, the northernmost of Japan's four major islands, covers 30,144 square miles (78,073 square kilometers). It is the country's second largest island but has only about 5 percent of Japan's total population. Much of the island consists of forested mountains and hills. A hilly, curved peninsula extends from southwestern Hokkaido. Northeast of this peninsula is the Ishikari Plain, Hokkaido's largest lowland and chief agricultural region. Smaller plains border the island's east coast. The economy of Hokkaido depends mainly on dairy farming, fishing, and forestry. The island is also a popular recreational area. Long winters and heavy snowfall make Hokkaido ideal for winter sports.

Kyushu, the southernmost of the main islands, occupies 14,114 square miles (36,554 square kilometers). After Honshu, Kyushu is Japan's most heavily populated island, with about 11 percent of the population. A chain of steep-walled, heavily forested mountains runs down the center of the island. Northwestern Kyushu consists of rolling hills and wide plains. Many cities are found in this heavily industrialized area. Kyushu's largest plain and chief farming district is located along the west coast.

The northeastern and southern sections of Kyushu have many volcanoes, high lava plateaus, and large deposits of volcanic ash. In both regions, only small patches

Burt Glinn, Magnum

Kyushu is the southernmost of Japan's main islands. Rugged terrain covers much of the island. Farmers grow some crops on level strips of land cut out from the sides of lava plateaus.

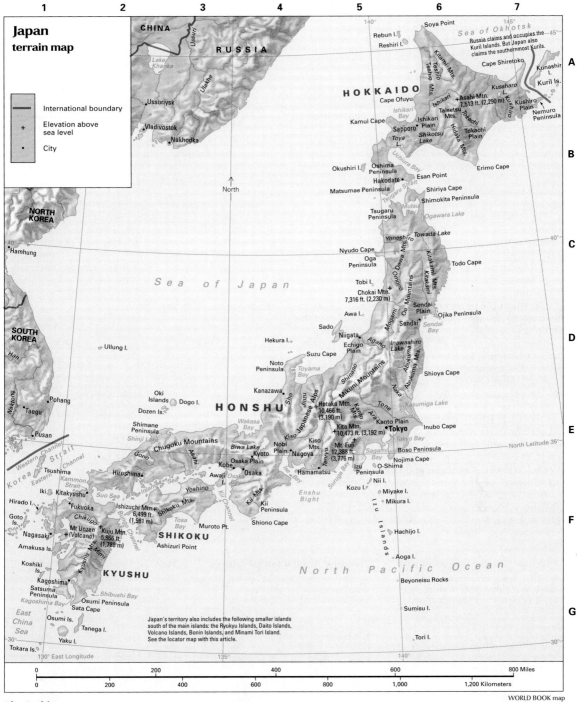

Japan
terrain map

WORLD BOOK map

Physical features

Abukuma Mountains ....D 6	Honshu (island) ....E 4
Agano River ....D 5	Inawashiro Lake ....D 5
Amakusa Islands ....F 1	Inland Sea ....F 2
Asahi Mountain ....A 6	Ise Bay ....E 4
Awaji Island ....F 3	Ishikari Plain ....B 6
Biwa Lake ....E 4	Izu Islands ....F 5
Boso Peninsula ....E 5	Izu Peninsula ....F 5
Bungo Channel ....F 2	Japanese Alps ....E 4
Chugoku Mountains .....E 3	Kagoshima Bay ....G 1
Echigo Plain ....D 5	Kammon Strait ....F 1
Enshu Bight ....F 4	Kanto Mountains ....E 5
Erimo Cape ....B 6	Kanto Plain ....E 5
Esan Point ....B 6	Kasumiga Lake ....E 6
Goto Islands ....F 1	Kii Channel ....F 3
Hidaka Mountains ......B 6	Kii Mountains ....F 4
Hokkaido (island) .....A 6	Kii Peninsula ....F 4

Kitakami Mountains ....C 6	Osaka Plain ....E 4
Kitami Mountains ......A 6	O-shima (island) ......E 5
Korea Strait ....E 1	Oshima Peninsula ......B 5
Kushiro Plain ....A 7	Osumi Islands ....G 1
Kyushu (island) ....G 1	Osumi Peninsula ....G 2
Kyushu Mountains ......G 1	Ou Mountains ....D 6
Mikuni Mountains ......D 5	Sado (island) ....D 5
Mount Fuji ....E 5	Sagami Bay ....E 5
Mutsu Bay ....C 6	Satsuma Peninsula .....G 1
Nemuro Peninsula ......B 7	Sea of Japan ....C 3
Nobi Plain ....E 4	Sendai Bay ....D 6
Noto Peninsula ....D 4	Sendai Plain ....D 6
Oga Peninsula ....C 5	Shikoku (island) ......F 3
Ojika Peninsula ....D 6	Shikoku Mountains .....F 3
Oki Islands ....E 3	Shimane Peninsula .....E 2
Okushiri Island ....B 5	Shimokita Peninsula ...C 6

Shiono Cape ....F 4
Soya Point ....A 6
Suo Sea ....F 2
Suruga Bay ....E 5
Tanega Island ....G 1
Teshio Mountains ......A 6
Tokachi Plain ....B 6
Tokyo Bay ....E 5
Tone River ....E 5
Toyama Bay ....D 5
Tsugaru Peninsula .....C 5
Tsugaru Strait ....B 5
Tsushima (islands) ....E 1
Uchiura Bay ....B 5
Wakasa aBay ....E 4
Yaku Island ....G 1

of land along the coasts and inland can be farmed. Farmers grow some crops on level strips of land cut out from the steep sides of the lava plateaus.

Shikoku, the smallest of the main Japanese islands, covers 7,049 square miles (18,256 square kilometers). About 3 percent of the Japanese people live on the island. Shikoku has no large lowlands. Mountains cross the island from east to west. Most of the people live in northern Shikoku, where the land slopes downward to the Inland Sea. Hundreds of hilly, wooded islands dot this beautiful body of water. Farmers grow rice and a variety of fruits on the fertile land along the Inland Sea. Copper mining is also important in this area. A narrow plain borders Shikoku's south coast. There, farmers grow rice and many kinds of vegetables.

The Ryukyu and Bonin islands belonged to Japan until after World War II, when the United States took control of them. The United States returned the northern Ryukyus to Japan in 1953 and the Bonins in 1968. In 1972, it returned the rest of the Ryukyu Islands, including Okinawa, the largest and most important island of the group.

More than 100 islands make up the Ryukyus. They extend from Kyushu to Taiwan and have about 1¼ million people. The Ryukyu Islands consist of the peaks of a submerged mountain range. Some of the islands have active volcanoes. The Bonins lie about 600 miles (970 kilometers) southeast of Japan and consist of 97 volcanic islands. About 1,900 people live on the islands.

Climate

Climates in Japan vary dramatically from island to island. Honshu generally has warm, humid summers. Winters are mild in the south and cold and snowy in the north. Honshu has balmy, sunny autumns and springs. Hokkaido has cool summers and cold winters. Kyushu and Shikoku have long, hot summers and mild winters.

Two Pacific Ocean currents—the Kuroshio and the Oyashio—influence Japan's climate. The warm, dark-blue Kuroshio flows northward along the south coast and along the east coast as far north as Tokyo. The Kuroshio has a warming effect on the climate of these regions. The cold Oyashio flows southward along the east coasts of Hokkaido and northern Honshu, cooling these areas.

Seasonal winds called *monsoons* also affect Japan's climate. In winter, monsoons from the northwest bring cold air to northern Japan. These winds, which gather moisture as they cross the Sea of Japan, deposit heavy snows on the country's northwest coast. During the summer, monsoons blow from the southeast, carrying warm, moist air from the Pacific Ocean. Summer monsoons cause hot, humid weather in the central and southern parts of Japan.

Rain is abundant throughout most of Japan. All areas of the country—except eastern Hokkaido—receive at least 40 inches (100 centimeters) of rain yearly. Japan has two major rainy seasons—from mid-June to early July and in September and October. Several typhoons strike the country each year, chiefly in late summer and early

Average monthly weather

	Tokyo						Sapporo				
	Temperatures				Days of rain or snow		Temperatures				Days of rain or snow
	F°		C°				F°		C°		
	High	Low	High	Low			High	Low	High	Low	
Jan.	46	30	8	-1	8	Jan.	28	12	-2	-11	26
Feb.	48	30	9	-1	8	Feb.	30	12	-1	-11	23
Mar.	54	36	12	2	13	Mar.	36	19	2	-7	23
Apr.	63	46	17	8	14	Apr.	52	32	11	0	13
May	70	54	21	12	14	May	61	41	16	5	14
June	75	63	24	17	16	June	68	50	20	10	13
July	82	70	28	21	14	July	75	59	24	15	13
Aug.	86	72	30	22	13	Aug.	79	61	26	16	13
Sept.	79	66	26	19	17	Sept.	72	52	22	11	17
Oct.	68	54	20	12	14	Oct.	61	39	16	4	17
Nov.	61	43	16	6	10	Nov.	46	28	8	-2	19
Dec.	52	34	11	1	7	Dec.	34	18	1	-8	25

Average January temperatures

In winter, winds from the mainland of Asia bring cold weather to northern Japan. Winters are mild in the south.

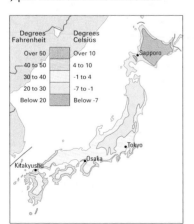

Degrees Fahrenheit	Degrees Celsius
Over 50	Over 10
40 to 50	4 to 10
30 to 40	-1 to 4
20 to 30	-7 to -1
Below 20	Below -7

Average August temperatures

In summer, most of Japan has hot, humid weather. Ocean currents flowing near the islands bring warm, moist air.

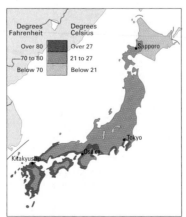

Degrees Fahrenheit	Degrees Celsius
Over 80	Over 27
70 to 80	21 to 27
Below 70	Below 21

Average yearly precipitation

Japan has abundant rainfall. Winds called *monsoons* bring rain in summer. In winter, snow falls over much of Japan.

WORLD BOOK maps

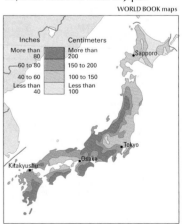

Inches	Centimeters
More than 80	More than 200
60 to 80	150 to 200
40 to 60	100 to 150
Less than 40	Less than 100

fall. The heavy rains and violent winds of these storms often do great damage to houses and crops.

Economy

Japan is one of the most economically powerful nations in the world. The size of its economy ranks second only to that of the United States in terms of its *gross domestic product* (GDP). The GDP is the total value of all goods and services produced within a country yearly. Japan is also a major participant in the international economy. It is one of the world's leading countries in the value of its exports and imports. On average, Japanx.ese families enjoy one of the highest income levels in the world, and their assets and savings are among the world's largest.

Key elements in Japan's economic success are manufacturing and trade. The country has few natural resources, so it must buy such necessities as aluminum, coal, lead, and petroleum. To pay for those imports, the government has adopted a strategy of exporting manufactured goods of high value.

Manufacturing. Japan's manufactured products range from tiny computer components to giant ocean-going ships. The most important manufactured products are cars and trucks, electronic products, and communications and data processing equipment. Other products include cement, ceramics, clothing, fabricated metal products, food products, plastics, textiles, steel, tires, and watches and other precision instruments.

Japan's manufacturing *sector* (portion of the economy) plays a major role in the Japanese economy. Manufacturing industries have consistently employed about 25 percent of the Japanese labor force and generated about 30 percent of the country's gross domestic product.

An especially important part of Japan's manufacturing sector is known as the *large-firm sector.* It includes such well-known companies as NEC Corporation, Nissan Motor Company, Sony Corporation, Toshiba Corporation, and Toyota Motor Corporation. Most of the large manufacturing firms assemble parts and components into a finished product such as a car, computer, or television set. The large firms then sell the product at a significantly higher price than the cost of the components.

Another part of the manufacturing sector consists of tens of thousands of small factories. Most of these companies make the parts or components that large firms assemble into finished products.

A core group of Japanese managers and skilled workers in the large-firm sector have secure jobs, earn high wages, and enjoy generous benefits. But some workers in the large-firm sector and many in the small factories have less job security, lower wages, and fewer benefits.

Manufacturing in Japan is concentrated in five main regions. For the location of each region and a listing of its main products, see the map titled *Economy of Japan* in this section of the article.

Construction. The construction sector consists of several giant national firms, hundreds of medium-sized regional firms, and thousands of small local firms. The sector employs about 10 percent of Japan's labor force and generates about 9 percent of the GDP.

The industry grew dramatically after World War II, when construction firms were needed to rebuild Japan's

Japan's gross domestic product

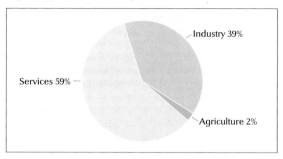

Japan's gross domestic product (GDP) was $3,670,000,000,000 in 1992. The GDP is the total value of goods and services produced within a country in a year. *Services* include community, social, and personal services; finance, insurance, and real estate; government; transportation and communication; wholesale and retail trade; and utilities. *Industry* includes construction and manufacturing. *Agriculture* includes agriculture, forestry, and fishing.

Production and workers by economic activities

Economic activities	Percent of GDP produced	Employed workers	
		Number of persons	Percent of total
Manufacturing	30	15,690,000	24
Community, social, & personal services	18	15,110,000	23
Finance, insurance, & real estate	15	2,620,000	4
Wholesale & retail trade	14	14,360,000	22
Construction	9	6,190,000	10
Transportation & communication	6	3,850,000	6
Government	3	2,040,000	3
Utilities	3	330,000	1
Agriculture, forestry, & fishing	2	4,110,000	6
Mining	*	60,000	*
Total	100	64,360,000	100

*Less than one-half of 1 percent.
Figures are for 1992.
Source: Japan Center for Economic Research.

ruined cities and demolished factories. Later, the nation's growing economy brought a constant demand for new shops, offices, factories, roads, harbors, airports, houses, apartments, and condominiums. In the 1990's, most of the largest firms began to expand internationally. Today, Japanese construction firms build such large projects as hotels and office buildings throughout the world. They handle many projects in other parts of Asia, the United Kingdom, and the United States.

Mining. Japan has a wide variety of minerals, but supplies of most are too small to satisfy the nation's needs. The chief mining products are coal, copper, lead, limestone, manganese, silver, tin, and zinc.

Agriculture. Throughout much of Japan's history, agriculture was the mainstay of the Japanese economy. As late as 1950, the agricultural sector employed 45 percent of the labor force. But as Japan's industries grew, the economic importance of agriculture declined. By the end of the 1900's, farmworkers made up less than 6 percent of the labor force, and they produced less than 2 percent of the GDP.

Because Japan is mountainous, only about 15 percent of the land can be cultivated. To make their farmland as productive as possible, Japanese farmers use irrigation, improved seed varieties, fertilizers, and modern machinery. Farmers grow some crops on *terraced fields*—that is, on level strips of land cut out of hillsides.

Japan's farmers are able to produce almost all the eggs, potatoes, rice, and fresh vegetables eaten in Japan. They also produce 50 to 80 percent of the dairy products, fruit, and meat. However, they raise only a tiny share of the animal feed, beans, and wheat that Japan needs. The nation must import the agricultural products that its farmers cannot supply.

For decades, government policies have kept crop prices high, especially for rice. Those policies help ensure that Japan has an adequate supply of food, and they protect rural communities from the sudden loss of income. But most Japanese consumers want to reduce the government subsidies so that food becomes less expensive. Other nations want Japan to stop protecting its agricultural sector, so that foreigners can sell rice and other farm products to the Japanese.

Fishing industry. Japan is one of the most important fishing nations in the world. Japanese fishing crews catch large amounts of bonito, carp, eel, mackerel, pollock, sardines, trout, and tuna. Other products of Japan's fishing industry include crabs and other shellfish and squid. Workers also harvest oysters and edible seaweed from "farms" in coastal waters.

The fishing industry began to decline in the 1950's. Pollution and international restrictions on ocean catches have reduced the quantity and value of the Japanese catch. Today, few young people enter the industry.

Service industries. Taken altogether, service industries generate almost 60 percent of Japan's GDP and employ more than 60 percent of the labor force. Japan's leading service industries include community, social, and personal services; finance, insurance, and real estate; and wholesale and retail trade. Other service industries that contribute to Japan's economy are government, utilities, and transportation and communication.

Many of the workers in the service industries are highly educated and well-paid. They hold such positions as bankers, financial analysts, civil servants, engineers, teachers, accountants, doctors, and lawyers. Most of these workers are men, and they—as well as managers in the manufacturing industry—are known as *sarariman* (salarymen). In general, salarymen receive generous incomes and benefits, and they enjoy good job security until they retire in their late 50's or early 60's.

However, a number of other workers in the service industries earn lower salaries and have fewer benefits and little job security. They work in such businesses as department stores, movie theaters, restaurants, and the small retail establishments often called "Mom-and-Pop shops." Such shops sell food, clothing, household necessities, and a variety of other goods. The little shops are far more numerous in Japan than in the United States or Western Europe. But they are disappearing as giant discount stores force them out of business.

Energy sources. Japan requires large amounts of energy to power its factories, households, offices, and motor vehicles. But the nation must import most of the fuel required to produce that energy. Japan has virtually no

natural supplies of petroleum. Hokkaido and Kyushu contain fairly large deposits of coal, but its quality is poor, and the deposits are difficult to mine.

Nevertheless, Japan ranks among the world's leading consumers of electric power. Power plants that burn coal, natural gas, or petroleum produce about 65 percent of Japan's electric power. Nuclear power plants supply about 25 percent of the country's electric power, and hydroelectric plants about 10 percent.

Japan had hoped to build many more nuclear power plants to decrease its reliance on imported fuels. However, a 1995 accident at an experimental nuclear reactor raised questions about the future of the expansion program.

International trade. In many ways, the driving force of Japan's economy is international trade. By trading with other nations, Japan obtains the raw materials it does not have and finds buyers for the expensive, high-quality manufactured goods its workers produce.

Japan's largest single import is crude oil. Other major imports include chemicals, fish and shellfish, and metal ores. Japan buys many of its imports from Asian nations with small populations and few consumers. Some of

Orion Press

Thousands of Japanese cars on a huge wharf near Nagoya await shipment to other countries. Automobiles are among Japan's most important manufactured products.

Japan's trading partners are relatively poor. As a consequence, Japan is seldom able to sell to its trade partners enough manufactured goods to maintain an equal balance of imports and exports.

To find buyers for Japan's expensive products, the nation looks to wealthy countries in North America and Western Europe. Since the end of World War II, the United States has bought the largest share of Japan's exports. In the 1950's, the United States purchased inexpensive Japanese textile products. Later, it began to buy more costly goods, such as automobiles and communications and computer equipment.

The United States sells Japan many American goods in return, including expensive items, such as computers and medicines. However, Japanese trade barriers place restrictions on many imports. By the 1980's, the United States was buying far more from Japan that it was selling to it. The inequality led to a large trade imbalance between the two nations. In the early 1990's, a similar imbalance arose between Japan and the nations of North and East Asia and Western Europe.

Japan's trade surpluses enabled it to accumulate huge reserves of foreign currency, in an amount that was second only to the foreign reserves of the United States. Japan used some of its reserves to invest in factories, banks, businesses, and real estate in the United States and many other countries.

Just as Japan was reaping these successes, Canada, the United States, and Western Europe were suffering economic slowdowns. People in other nations began to envy and resent Japan for its trade surpluses, large reserves of foreign currencies, and heavy investment in other countries. Under pressure, Japan began to lift some of its trade barriers.

Transportation. Japan has a modern transportation system, including airports, highways, railroads, and coastal shipping. All the major cities have extensive local transit networks that include buses, trains, and subways.

An eight-company business unit known as Japan Railways Group operates about 75 percent of Japanese railroads. Trains traveling between Honshu and Hokkaido go through an undersea tunnel called the Seikan Tunnel. At 33.5 miles (53.9 kilometers) long, it is the world's longest transportation tunnel.

Japan's commercial fleet is one of the world's largest. Japan's chief ports are Chiba, Kobe, Nagoya, and Yoko-

Economy of Japan

Manufacturing is the single most important economic activity in Japan. This map shows the nation's five major industrial regions and lists the chief products of each region. Japan's croplands, forest lands, mineral deposits, and fishing products are also indicated on the map.

Fishing is an important industry in Japan. Fish are a chief source of protein in the Japanese diet. The dockworkers at left are handling a huge tuna catch.

hama. Hundreds of smaller ports and harbors enable coastal shippers to serve every major city in Japan.

Japan has many airports. Tokyo International, also called Haneda, is Japan's busiest airport. It and the Osaka airport rank among the world's busiest. Much of the foreign air traffic to and from Tokyo arrives at New Tokyo International Airport, also called Narita Airport. Kansai International Airport, which was built on an artificial island in Osaka Bay, opened in 1994.

Communication. Japan has thriving publishing and broadcasting industries. The nation has more than 100 daily newspapers. Each year, Japanese publishers produce tens of thousands of new books and periodicals, including popular comic books, called *manga*, for both adults and children. Virtually every Japanese household has at least one color television set and one or more radios.

The Japanese government operates the postal system. The country's telegraph and telephone systems are privately owned.

History

Early days. People have lived on the islands of Japan for more than 30,000 years. The earliest inhabitants lived by hunting and gathering food and made tools out of stone. Historians refer to the period of Japanese history between about 10,000 and about 300 B.C. as the Jomon era. During this time, people lived in small villages of about 50 people. To obtain food, they hunted for deer and boar, fished, and gathered nuts and berries. The main artifacts these people left behind were pots with markings made by cords or ropes. *Jomon* means *cord-marked.*

Near the end of the Jomon era, people in Japan learned new ideas and new technologies from contact with Korea and China. The Japanese learned how to grow rice in irrigated fields, and they began to settle in communities near the rice paddies. They also learned how to make tools and weapons out of bronze and iron.

Rice fields cover many hillsides in rural Japan. Farmland is limited because so much of the country is mountainous. But farmers grow most of the rice eaten in Japan.

This period is called the Yayoi era (about 300 B.C. to about A.D. 300).

By the end of the Yayoi era, different groups of extended families began to struggle for power in the Yamato Plain. The plain lies southeast of modern Kyoto. When the leaders of these groups died, their relatives buried them in large tombs called *kofun* that were often shaped like keyholes. The period of Japanese history from about 300 to 710 is often known as the Kofun era. It is also sometimes called the Yamato period. The tombs were surrounded with small clay sculptures called *haniwa*. Many haniwa are figurines of warriors or sculptures of bows and arrows, a sign that warfare had become an important part of Japanese society.

Chinese influence. In the 600's and 700's, one of the extended family groups began to dominate the others, and it declared itself Japan's imperial household. By tradition, the imperial family has no family name. The head of the imperial house, whose given name was Kotoku, became emperor in 645.

The next year, the imperial family began a program called the Taika Reform. The program involved constructing capital cities and organizing Japanese society following the example of China. The imperial family created a central government and official bureaus and adopted a system of land management similar to China's. Under this system, most people worked as farmers on land the government owned. In return, the farmers paid taxes to the government and provided labor, including service in the government's small armies.

To justify its claim to authority, the imperial family relied not on China but on ancient Japanese beliefs. Japanese histories written in the 700's maintain that the family had descended from the gods who created the Japanese islands in Japanese mythology. The family's presumed descent was through Amaterasu, the Japanese sun goddess.

Heian era. In 794, the imperial household moved to a new capital city called Heian-kyo, located at the site of today's Kyoto. During the next 400 years, Heian-kyo was the center of Japan's government and nobility.

During the Heian era, a male in the imperial household ruled as emperor. The male heads of noble families assisted the emperor by administering the government, collecting tax revenues, maintaining small armies, and judging legal disputes. These officials earned generous incomes and lived in large mansions in the capital city.

The ruling nobles used their leisure time primarily to observe nature and write poetry. Female members of the nobility, who were barred from holding office, had the most time for these pursuits. Women produced the era's most famous writings, including *The Tale of Genji*.

During the Heian era, the leading noble families undermined the power of the emperor and his government. One such family was the Fujiwara, who gained power by intermarrying with the imperial family.

Creation of private estates. As the central government's power declined during the Heian era, a new type of institution emerged—the *shoen* (private estate). Private estates were plots of land whose owners were free from government interference and taxation. The government began to establish these estates in the 700's to provide Buddhist temples and Shinto shrines with income to fund their religious activities. Gradually, the religious institutions became major landholders.

During the 700's, the government also began to allow tax exemptions to those who developed new lands for growing rice. The aristocratic families and religious institutions that had enough wealth to develop new lands acquired large holdings. Later, the Fujiwara and other high-ranking families in Heian-kyo used their influence to obtain ownership of other public lands. In the late 1000's, even retired emperors began taking land. By the 1200's, about half of the rice-growing land in Japan had been converted into private estates.

As the influence of the private estate owners increased, the power of the central government declined. With less public land, the government had less tax revenue to support its activities. The government and the aristocrats in Heian-kyo had to rely on bands of professional soldiers called *samurai* to protect the land and keep order in the countryside.

Important dates in Japan

c. 300 B.C.-c.A.D. 300 During the Yayoi era, new ideas and new technologies from China and Korea began to be used.

645 One family declared itself Japan's imperial family. Its head, Kotoku, became emperor.

646 The Taika Reform began. It set up a central government controlled by the emperor.

794 Heian-kyo (now Kyoto) became the capital.

1192 Minamoto Yoritomo became the first shogun. He established a military government headquartered in Kamakura.

1500's Japan endured a long period of wars among regional lords.

1603 The Tokugawa family began its more than 250-year rule.

1630's Japan closed itself off from the outside world.

1853 Commodore Matthew C. Perry of the United States arrived with a small fleet. This visit and a second one in 1854 led to the opening of Japanese ports to international trade.

1867 Revolutionaries overthrew the shogun and restored power to the emperor.

1868 On January 3, the emperor officially announced the return of imperial rule. The Meiji period began. Tokyo became the capital, and Japan began working to develop modern industries and to strengthen its military.

1895 Japan took control of Taiwan from China and began to build an empire.

1923 An earthquake struck the Tokyo-Yokohama area. The earthquake and the fires and *tsunami* (huge, destructive sea wave) that followed caused about 143,000 deaths and destroyed large areas of the two cities.

1931 Japan seized the Chinese province of Manchuria.

1937 Japan began a war with China. The fighting became part of World War II.

1941 Japan attacked U.S. bases at Pearl Harbor in Hawaii.

1945 The United States dropped atomic bombs on Hiroshima and Nagasaki. Japan surrendered to the Allies, and the Allied occupation of Japan began. It lasted until 1952.

1947 Japan's democratic Constitution went into effect.

1980's-1990's Opposition to Japan's international trade policies became strong in the United States, Canada, and some other countries.

1990's Japan's vigorous economy suffered a recession.

1993 The Liberal Democratic Party, which had ruled Japan since the party was founded in 1955, lost its majority in parliament for the first time. Japan began a period of political instability and frequent changes of government.

Rise of the shogun. By the 1100's, two large military clans—the Taira and the Minamoto—had armies of samurai under their command. Both clans were descendants of the noble families at court. In the late 1100's, the Taira and Minamoto clashed in a series of battles for power. The Minamoto finally emerged victorious in the 1180's.

The Minamoto established a new military government headquartered in Kamakura, a town in eastern Japan far from Heian-kyo. In 1192, the head of this military government, Yoritomo, was given the title of *shogun*, a special, high-ranking military post granted by the emperor. His military government became known as a *shogunate*.

Although Yoritomo was the emperor's special commander, he established his own separate bases of power. He assumed control of the administration of justice. He began to place nobles who had sworn loyalty to him on private estates and appointed others to oversee the remaining public lands. In this way, the shogun began to influence both areas of power in Japan—the imperial government and the private estates.

By the early 1200's, Japan's political situation had become highly unstable. The imperial government's influence was limited and declining. Private estate owners were struggling to retain control over their lands as the shogun's ambitious supporters expanded their influence.

The next 200 years brought waves of conflict and change. First, the Minamoto family lost its influence to members of the Hojo family, who ruled as agents in the name of the Minamoto shoguns. Then the military government in Kamakura fell to the superior force of another clan, the Ashikaga. The Ashikaga established a new military government in Kyoto in the 1330's. Gradually, the clan lost control of the nobles under its command. By the 1460's, Japan had no effective central political authority.

Warring states period. In the century after the 1460's, Japan was an armed camp. Peasants in the countryside were forced to take up swords to protect their communities. Temples with large landholdings trained their own armies of warrior-monks to protect their assets. Some estate owners gathered private armies of samurai to guard their lands. Samurai without masters roamed the country offering to fight for pay.

The most powerful samurai became regional lords called *daimyo*. They exercised control over many armed warriors and governed large areas of farmland. They fought each other for military supremacy during the 1500's, as Japan sank into a long period of civil war.

In 1549, Saint Francis Xavier, a missionary from Portugal, arrived in Japan and introduced a new element into this unstable scene. Xavier and a few other priests had come to convert the Japanese populace to Christian beliefs. The missionaries also intended to help Portuguese traders sell European luxury goods and up-to-date weapons to the Japanese.

The priests had little success in converting the Japanese to Christianity. But the traders found eager customers among the daimyo in southern Japan. The guns they sold were an explosive addition to the civil wars.

One regional lord who made much use of the weapons was Oda Nobunaga. Oda was a ruthless warrior

Detail of *The Burning of the Sanjo Palace* (late 1200's), an ink painting with colors on paper by an unknown Japanese artist; Museum of Fine Arts, Boston, Fenollosa-Weld Collection

Rival families fought for control of the Japanese government during the 1100's. Two large military clans—the Taira and the Minamoto—met in battle in 1160, *above*. The Taira won and ruled Japan until the Minamoto defeated them in 1185. The Minamoto established a military government. In 1192, the emperor gave the title *shogun* (great general) to the clan leader, Minamoto Yoritomo.

with a keen desire for power. In the 1560's, he gathered a large coalition of forces under his command and led them to Kyoto. He brought order to the capital district. He was beginning to impose control on other areas of Japan when he was killed in 1582.

Oda's successor, Toyotomi Hideyoshi, took up the task of uniting the nation. Toyotomi carried out several reforms with far-reaching effects. He disarmed the peasantry. He brought many of the unruly samurai under his control. And he surveyed most of the usable farmland in the country. Toyotomi tried to extend his power to Korea in the 1590's. Twice he tried to conquer Korea, but both times he failed.

Tokugawa period. Toyotomi was succeeded by a noble named Tokugawa Ieyasu, who had also served Oda Nobunaga. In 1603, the emperor gave Tokugawa Ieyasu the title of shogun. For the next 265 years, leaders of the Tokugawa house governed Japan as shogun.

The Tokugawa shogun presided over a delicately balanced system of authority. The shogun directly controlled about 25 percent of the farmland in the country. He also licensed foreign trade, operated gold mines, and ruled the major cities, including Kyoto, Osaka, and the shogun's capital—Edo, which is now Tokyo.

The Tokugawa shogun had to share authority with the daimyo, who controlled the remaining 75 percent of Japan's farmland. The number of daimyo during the Tokugawa period averaged about 270. Each of these daimyo governed his own *han* (domain). In each han, the daimyo, not the shogun, issued laws and collected taxes. During the Tokugawa era, Japan thus had only a partially centralized government.

By the early 1600's, Japan was also home to five groups of foreigners: the Portuguese, Spanish, English, Dutch, and Chinese. Their presence disturbed the shogun, in part because the Tokugawa did not support Christianity, the religion of most of the outsiders. In addition, the shogun wanted to control Japan's international trade to prevent any daimyo from gaining too much wealth and power through trade with the outsiders.

For these reasons, the Tokugawa had most foreigners expelled from Japan during the 1630's under orders known as *seclusion edicts.* Only a few Dutch and Chinese traders were allowed to remain in Japan to conduct their business. But they could live only in the distant city of Nagasaki. That town served as Japan's sole window on the European world until the mid-1800's.

Japan had now put an end to centuries of internal wars and had closed itself off from the rest of the world. During this period of peace and isolation, the nation began to pursue its own course of development.

At this time, Japan laid the foundation for its future economic growth. People in all walks of life developed a strong work ethic and devotion to their craft and duty. Hard-working farmers in the countryside and merchants in the cities saved money and learned to invest it wisely. Trading firms in the large cities developed skills in finance, organization, and personnel management.

Entertainment and the arts also flourished, particularly in Edo. In the 1700's, Edo became one of the world's largest cities. It developed thriving industries to entertain the many samurai and merchants living there. Entertainers perfected the form of stage drama called *kabuki* and the puppet theater called *bunraku.* The entertain-

Detail of *The Opening of Japan* (mid-1920's?), a water color by Ogata Gassan; Kurihama Administration Center (International Society for Educational Information, Tokyo, from the Consulate General of Japan, Chicago)

An American mission led by Commodore Matthew C. Perry arrived in Japan in 1853. The United States government sent Perry to open diplomatic and trade relations with the Japanese. Japan had been closed off from the rest of the world since the 1600's. In 1858, partly as a result of Perry's efforts, Japan signed trade treaties with the United States and other Western countries.

ment districts, called *ukiyo* (the floating world), became the subjects of a new Japanese art style named *ukiyo-e*. The colorful wood-block prints depicted the men and women of the entertainment districts.

But the Tokugawa era was also a time of critical difficulties. The military government grew dull and strict. It discouraged individual freedoms and slowed commercial development. Government financial problems led to cuts in the income of samurai. Their declining incomes added to the samurai's growing dissatisfaction with Japan's rigid social structure, which prevented them from rising to better stations in life. Finally, poor harvests and harsh lords drove many peasants to join together in protest.

Renewed relations with the West. In 1853, renewed contact with the West led directly to sweeping changes. That year, a small fleet of American naval vessels sailed into the bay south of Edo. The fleet's commander, Matthew C. Perry, asked Japan to open its ports to international trade.

The shogun rebuffed Perry, but Perry returned in 1854. After many discussions, Japan allowed the United States to station a negotiator, Townsend Harris, in the small port of Shimoda, far from Edo. In 1858, Harris succeeded in his negotiations on behalf of the United States, and Japan signed a treaty of commerce. The treaty permitted trade between the two countries, called for opening five Japanese ports to international commerce, and gave the United States the right of *extraterritoriality*. This right enabled American citizens to be governed only by U.S. laws while they were on Japanese soil.

Many Japanese disapproved of the treaty and similar agreements signed later. To them, the treaties were unequal, because Japan had granted extraterritoriality and other privileges that were not given to the Japanese in turn. The treaties enraged many samurai, who attacked and killed some foreign officials. The samurai also plotted to overthrow the shogunate.

Meiji period. In 1867, a small group of samurai and aristocrats overthrew the shogunate and restored the emperor to his previous position at the head of the government. The revolutionaries disapproved of the trade treaties and wanted to increase Japan's security and well-being in what they considered a dangerous and competitive world. They acted without support of the Japanese people.

On Jan. 3, 1868, the emperor officially announced the return of imperial rule. The emperor, a teen-ager named Mutsuhito, adopted *Meiji,* meaning *enlightened rule,* as the name for the era of his reign. He reigned from 1868 to 1912, a span of time known as the *Meiji period.* The revolution that placed him in power is known as the *Meiji restoration.*

In practice, however, the leaders of the revolution and their successors ruled the country, not the emperor. The leaders adopted the slogan "Enriching the Nation and Strengthening the Military" as their guiding policy. By enriching Japan, the new leaders believed they would enable the nation to compete with the Western powers.

To compete in the late 1800's meant building modern industries. And so Japan embarked on an ambitious program of economic development. The nation invested

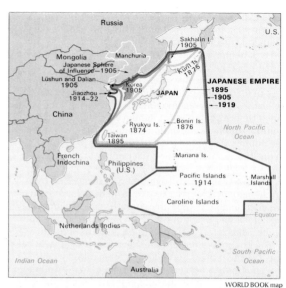

WORLD BOOK map

Japan expanded its territory in the late 1800's and early 1900's as a result of three wars: the first Chinese-Japanese war (1894-1895), the Russo-Japanese War (1904-1905), and World War I (1914-1918). By 1919, Japan was a world power.

in coal mines, textile mills, shipyards, cement factories, and many other modern enterprises.

Few of these ventures were successful, however. In the 1880's, the government began selling its industries to private companies. Some of these companies, such as the Mitsui and Sumitomo groups, were old merchant houses that had been in business since the 1600's. Others, such as the Mitsubishi group, sprang up after the Meiji restoration. From the 1880's to the 1940's, these business enterprises grew large and rich. These conglomerates became known as *zaibatsu.*

Most zaibatsu were owned and operated by a single family or a family group. They created many related ventures, especially in banking, insurance, international trade, manufacturing, and real estate. The zaibatsu cooperated with the government to promote its aim of enriching the nation. But they remained private enterprises that enriched themselves at the same time.

The second strategy of the Meiji leadership was to strengthen Japan's military. Former samurai took charge of a modern military recruited from the sons of farmers. With the advice of European military experts, the government built naval shipyards and assembled military arsenals. Within 20 years after the Meiji restoration, Japan had developed the best military force in East Asia.

From 1868 to 1889, government leaders also experimented with different methods of organizing the nation's political institutions. In 1889, they produced Japan's first Constitution. This document made the emperor the head of the government and established a cabinet of ministers and a legislature with two houses. The Constitution spelled out the rights and duties of the citizens, and it created a system of courts.

Under this Constitution, the powers of the Japanese people were extremely limited. The leaders of the restoration and their appointees continued to hold real power. These men now served in official roles as prime ministers and Cabinet members.

Another aim of the new government was to reorganize society. The nation removed the restrictions that had prevented people from pursuing any occupation they desired. New laws made the family the basic unit of society and males the heads of households. Some of these laws limited women's rights more drastically than they had been during the Tokugawa era of the 1600's to mid-1800's.

Finally, the government established an ambitious system of public education. By the early 1900's, Japan offered free elementary education to most young people. More advanced, specialized schooling was available to students who had the money and talent to proceed further. This school system made it possible for many people to improve their status in society. It greatly assisted Japan's economic development. The schools also cultivated in students a strong sense of national pride and superiority.

Imperialism. In due course, the Meiji government's emphasis on military might and the educational system's emphasis on Japanese superiority led to war. In 1895, Japan began to build an empire like those of Britain and other European powers. Three Asian regions were the initial targets of Japanese expansion: Taiwan, Korea, and Manchuria.

After defeating China in a short war, Japan assumed control over Taiwan in 1895. The Japanese then exploited Taiwan as an agricultural colony producing rice and sugar.

Korea fell under Japanese control in 1910, following a bitterly fought war between Japan and Russia in 1905. Japan exploited Korea for its rice and its potential to develop industries. Remembering stories of Toyotomi's invasions in the 1590's, Koreans fiercely resented

Japan's colonization. The Japanese treated them badly in return.

The Russo-Japanese War also gave Japan a small foothold in Manchuria. There, Japan's army of occupation gradually expanded its control.

World War I began in 1914. Japan, as an ally of Britain, at once declared war on Germany. The war gave Japan an opportunity to enlarge its empire slightly. More important, the war gave Japan an economic advantage in India and the rest of Asia. As Western nations became preoccupied with the war in Europe, they stopped their investment and trade in the East. Japanese exporters and manufacturers took that opportunity to move into Indian and other Asian markets. The zaibatsu expanded, and Japan's economy boomed.

Rise of militarism. The 1920's were a time of great difficulties for Japan. After the war, Western nations reestablished trade with India and the rest of Asia, and the Japanese economy suffered. In 1923, a terrible earthquake struck the Tokyo-Yokohama area and led to the deaths of about 143,000 people. A worldwide depression during the late 1920's further hurt the Japanese economy.

About this time, China began to strengthen its administration in Manchuria. Japan feared it might lose the rights it gained in the Russo-Japanese War.

Japan's prime minister and other government leaders could not deal with the problems troubling Japan. Officers in the Japanese army decided to take matters into their own hands. In 1931, the Japanese occupation force took control of Manchuria. At home, nationalist groups began to threaten members of the government who opposed the army. On May 15, 1932, nationalists assassinated Prime Minister Tsuyoshi Inukai.

By 1936, Japan's military leaders were in firm control of the government. As Japanese armies marched across China and into Southeast Asia, the United States grew

AP/Wide World

Emperor Hirohito, *on the white horse,* reviewed Japanese troops in 1938. Japan's military had become increasingly powerful during the 1930's. By 1936, military leaders held firm control of Japan's government.

increasingly concerned. Meanwhile, Japan moved toward closer relations with Nazi Germany and Fascist Italy by signing anti-Communist pacts with the two nations.

World War II began in Europe in September 1939. In September 1940, Japanese troops occupied the northern part of French Indochina. When they moved into the southern part of Indochina the next year, the United States cut off its exports to Japan.

In the fall of 1941, General Hideki Tojo became prime minister of Japan. Japan's military leaders began preparing to wage war against the United States.

Japanese bombers attacked the U.S. military bases at Pearl Harbor in Hawaii on Dec. 7, 1941. They also bombed U.S. bases on Guam and Wake Island and in the Philippines. The bombing brought the United States into war against Japan and Japan's European allies, Germany and Italy.

Japan quickly won dramatic victories in Southeast Asia and in the South Pacific. By 1942, the Japanese empire spanned much of the area from the eastern edge of India through Indonesia, and from the Aleutian Islands near Alaska to the Solomon Islands in the South Pacific Ocean.

The Japanese fleet suffered its first major setback in May 1942, when the United States fought the Battle of the Coral Sea to a draw. The U.S. victory in the Battle of Midway the following month helped turn the tide in favor of the United States. As Japanese defeats increased, political discontent in Japan grew. On July 18, 1944, Prime Minister Tojo's Cabinet fell.

Early in 1945, the battle for the Japanese homeland began. American bombers hit industrial targets, and warships pounded Japanese coastal cities. American submarines cut off the shipping of vital supplies to Japan. On August 6, the United States dropped the first atomic bomb ever used in warfare on the city of Hiroshima. Two days later, the Soviet Union declared war on Japan and invaded Manchuria and Korea. The next day, U.S. fliers dropped a second and larger atomic bomb on Nagasaki.

Japan agreed to surrender on August 14. The next day, Emperor Hirohito announced to the Japanese people that Japan had agreed to end the war. On Sept. 2, 1945, Japanese officials officially surrendered aboard the battleship U.S.S. *Missouri* in Tokyo Bay.

Japan lost all its territory on the mainland of Asia. It also lost all the islands it had governed in the Pacific. The nation kept only its four main islands and the small islands nearby. In the 1950's, 1960's, and 1970's the United States returned to Japan the Bonin Islands, Iwo Jima, and the Ryukyu Islands. Russia still occupies the Kuril Islands.

Allied military occupation. Japan's defeat brought foreign occupiers to its shores for the first time in its long history. Under the direction of U.S. General Douglas MacArthur, the occupation force carried out a sweeping set of reforms inspired by American ideals. The Japanese government served only to carry out MacArthur's orders.

Under the occupation, more than 5 million Japanese troops were disarmed. The Allies tried 25 Japanese leaders for war crimes. Seven of the leaders, including former Prime Minister Tojo, were executed. The rest were sent to prison.

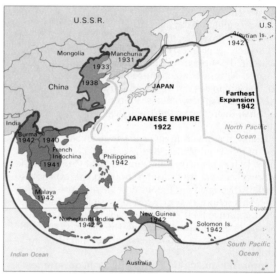

WORLD BOOK map

The Japanese empire in 1942 reached its greatest extent. In 1931, Japan conquered Manchuria and then advanced into other parts of China and Southeast Asia. The map above shows the stages of Japanese expansion from 1931 to 1942.

The Allied occupation force began reforms in 1946, when MacArthur and his advisers drew up a new Japanese Constitution. Under this document, the emperor lost all real power and became merely a symbol of the state. The two-part legislature became Japan's supreme lawmaking body. A civilian prime minister, chosen by majority vote in the legislature, became head of the government. The rights of the people increased dramatically compared with those granted by the Meiji Constitution.

The American occupiers also began economic and social reforms. They redistributed farmland, legalized labor unions, and encouraged new laws giving women and children greater rights. The Americans also reorganized Japan's educational system to make it more democratic.

In 1951, Japan signed a peace treaty with 48 nations that went into effect on Aug. 28, 1952. The Allied occupation officially ended on that day.

Postwar boom. The Japanese economy suffered greatly from World War II. Allied bombing destroyed many of the nation's factories and nearly leveled most large cities. Many Japanese were forced out of work. Much of the population lived in dire conditions in small rural villages, and they depended on friends and neighbors to survive.

Japan was almost closed off from the outside world because many of its trading ships had been destroyed. The value of its currency, the *yen,* dropped so low that Japan could not afford to purchase many foreign goods.

Recovering from these losses took about a decade of effort. The United States provided financial assistance, but the Japanese national government played the central role in promoting reconstruction.

After the war, the government began to guide and direct the nation's industries. The government formed the Ministry of International Trade and Industry to identify the industries in Japan that needed to be developed. Then the Ministry of Finance directed investment funds toward these enterprises. The Japanese tradition of working hard, saving money, and investing wisely helped the nation become economically stable. By the mid-1950's, the output of most Japanese industries matched their prewar levels.

From 1955 to 1993, a single conservative party called the Liberal Democratic Party (LDP) dominated national politics. The LDP consistently won the most seats in the Diet as well as in the prefectural and local assemblies. The party strongly advocated Japan's economic growth, and it put into effect many successful policies.

Many social changes occurred during the postwar years. Fewer and fewer people stayed in rural areas to earn a living by farming. Instead, they moved to cities and became workers in manufacturing or service industries. Families saw their incomes doubling and tripling within a generation.

Cooperation and harmony continued to be prized ideals in Japan. But the pressures to conform to society's expectations were less apparent in large cities than in the small villages. Young people felt freer to be individuals than their parents and grandparents had.

Even the imperial family took part in some changes. In 1959, Crown Prince Akihito broke tradition by marrying a commoner, Michiko Shoda, the daughter of a wealthy industrialist. In 1971, Emperor Hirohito and Empress Nagako visited Western Europe. It was the first time a reigning emperor had ever left Japan.

Political changes. Emperor Hirohito died in 1989, and his son, Akihito, began to reign. It soon began to appear that Akihito's era would be a time of unsettling political and economic change.

Troubles for Japan's long-term ruling political party, the LDP, began in the 1980's. A number of leading government figures were accused of raising campaign funds illegally. Some were tried and convicted of corruption. Voters began to turn against the LDP. In mid-1993, the party lost its majority in the Diet.

For nearly 10 months, a coalition of seven other parties governed Japan. The coalition passed important laws reforming the election system, but its members could not overcome their differences on other issues.

The LDP returned to power in mid-1994, ruling in alliance with the Social Democratic Party of Japan and the New Harbinger Party. In late 1994, most of the opponents of the governing coalition formed the New Frontier Party. By the mid-1990's, Japan's political parties had gathered into two large factions, one composed of the LDP and its allies, the other a coalition of opposition parties. Conflicts among and within the parties continued, however. Japanese party politics were expected to remain unstable for some time.

Economic troubles also arose in the late 1980's, as Japanese manufacturers began finding it difficult to sell their products abroad. Japan's strong currency, high real estate values, and high labor costs all made Japanese goods expensive to overseas customers. Japanese manufacturers also had to compete with low-cost businesses from newly developing nations.

At the same time, the Japanese banking system began to suffer because the banks had made many loans during the late 1980's that failed as real estate prices dropped in the 1990's. The result of Japan's problems in trade and finance was a recession, a period when the economy virtually stopped growing. In the 1990's, Japan's unemployment rate rose, average household incomes nearly stopped growing, and consumer spending declined.

Other wealthy nations, including the United Kingdom and Germany, also suffered economic problems in the 1990's. Therefore, Japan's relative economic position in the world did not change dramatically. But economic anxiety spread throughout Japan as businesses and workers tried to maintain their competitive edge.

Gary D. Allinson

Related articles in *World Book* include:

Biographies

Akihito	Minamoto Yoritomo
Hideyoshi	Mutsuhito
Hirohito	Tojo, Hideki
Jimmu Tenno	Yamamoto, Isoroku
Kurosawa, Akira	Yukawa, Hideki
Miki, Takeo	

Cities

Hiroshima	Osaka
Kobe	Sapporo
Kyoto	Tokyo
Nagasaki	Yokohama
Nagoya	

History

Boxer Rebellion	Perry, Matthew Calbraith
China (History)	Russo-Japanese War
Chinese-Japanese wars	Samurai
Colombo Plan	Shogun
Gentlemen's agreement	Taira
Kamakura period	World War I (Fighting else
Kamikaze	where)
MacArthur, Douglas	World War II
Manchuria	Yamato period
Mikado	

Arts and recreation

Architecture (Japanese architecture; picture)	Japanese print
Dancing (Oriental dancing; picture)	Judo
	Kite
Doll (Doll festivals and customs; picture)	Lacquerware
	Martial arts (Japanese martial arts)
Drama (Japan; picture)	Music (Asian music)
Flower (Flower arranging; pictures)	Origami
	Painting (Japanese painting; pictures)
Furniture (Japan)	
Japanese literature	Sculpture (Japan; picture)

Other related articles

Ainu	Kuroshio
Asia (Way of life in East Asia)	Labor movement (Labor around the world)
Bamboo	
Bonin Islands	Library (Australia and the Far East)
Buddhism	
Chrysanthemum	Mount Fuji
Clothing (pictures)	National park (Japan)
Flag (picture: Historical flags of the world)	Navy (World War II)
	Nisei
Food (picture)	Okinawa
Hara-kiri	Ryukyu Islands
Japan, Sea of	Shinto
Japanese language	Space exploration (Japan)
Jinrikisha	Toyota Motor Corporation
Kuril Islands	

Las Vegas is the largest city in Nevada and one of the most popular tourist destinations in the United States. It is famous for its hotels, gambling casinos, and 24-hour entertainment. The city attracts about 30 million visitors a year. Las Vegas lies in a valley in southern Nevada.

The city is the county seat of Clark County. It is the center of the fastest growing metropolitan area in the United States. Many people move to the Las Vegas area every month. Large areas of vacant desert in the valley are developed each year.

Las Vegas was founded as a water stop for steam locomotives on the route of what is now the Union Pacific Railroad. The site consisted of grassland fed by springs, and the name of the city comes from two Spanish words meaning *the meadows.*

The city. The bright lights of two Las Vegas streets are world famous. Fremont Street, in downtown Las Vegas, is the major casino-hotel district within the city limits. The Las Vegas Strip, a portion of Las Vegas Boulevard just outside the city limits, is famous for its large resort hotels and casinos.

Las Vegas is home to many of the largest and most elaborate hotels in the world. The MGM Grand Hotel/Casino, with over 5,000 guest rooms, is the world's largest hotel. Dozens of pirates and other actors stage outdoor battles every evening in front of Treasure Island hotel and casino. Ancient Egypt comes to life at the Luxor, a pyramid-shaped hotel complete with a replica of the tomb of the famous King Tutankhamen.

The Las Vegas metropolitan area includes Clark and Nye counties in Nevada, and Mohave County in Arizona. About half of the urban area popularly referred to as Las Vegas is outside the city limits. Other large cities in Clark County include Henderson, North Las Vegas, and Boulder City. Popular attractions near the city include Hoover Dam, one of the largest dams in the world; and Lake Mead, one of the world's largest artificially created lakes and the main source of water for the metropolitan area. Engineers formed Lake Mead by building Hoover Dam across a canyon of the Colorado River.

People

Ethnic groups. About 75 percent of the city's residents are white, and about 9 percent are black. People of Hispanic descent—who may be white, black, or of mixed ancestry—make up about 11 percent of the city's population and are the largest minority group in metropolitan Las Vegas. The approximately 5 percent remaining consist of people of American Indian, Asian, or other ancestry.

Education. The Clark County School District operates about 185 public elementary and secondary schools. The area also has about 50 church-supported and other private schools.

The University of Nevada, Las Vegas, is the city's best-known institution of higher education. Other schools of higher learning include the Community College of Southern Nevada, with campuses in Las Vegas, North Las Vegas, and Henderson.

Cultural life

The arts. The Nevada Dance Company and the Nevada Opera perform at the University of Nevada, Las Vegas. The university also hosts an annual series of concerts by visiting orchestras. Hotels offer big-name entertainment and elaborate production shows.

Museums and libraries. The Clark County Heritage Museum in nearby Henderson features exhibits on southern Nevada's history, including an unrestored ghost town and an outdoor railroad. Interactive displays at the Lied Discovery Children's Museum provide fun facts about the sciences, arts, and humanities. The Nevada State Museum and Historical Society includes exhibits on the natural history and art of southern Nevada. Displays at the Liberace Museum include many of the famous pianist's showy costumes, rare pianos, and antique cars.

The Las Vegas-Clark County Library District operates many branch libraries throughout the metropolitan area. The University of Nevada, Las Vegas, also has a library.

Recreation. Metropolitan Las Vegas has numerous parks and golf courses. It is one of the few metropolitan areas selected to host two major Professional Golfers' Association of America (PGA) events each year, the Las Vegas Invitational and the Las Vegas Senior Classic. The National Finals Rodeo is held in Las Vegas every December. The city also hosts numerous world championship boxing matches and professional bowling tournaments.

Economy

Industry. Las Vegas depends heavily on tourism and convention business. The tourist industry ranks as the city's largest employer and generates more revenue than any other industry. The Las Vegas Convention Center is the largest single-level convention facility in the United States. More than $2\frac{1}{2}$ million people attend conventions in Las Vegas every year.

The U.S. government is also a major employer in the area. The Nevada Test Site, a nuclear weapons testing facility operated by the U.S. Department of Energy, is north of Las Vegas. Also north of the city is the Nellis Air Force Base, home of a precision flying group called the Thunderbirds, and the Nellis Air Force Range.

Transportation and communication. Las Vegas's McCarran International Airport is the largest airport in Nevada. The city is also served by the Union Pacific Railroad and many trucking lines. Las Vegas has two daily newspapers, the *Las Vegas Review-Journal* and the *Las Vegas Sun.* About 10 regular television stations, 1 cable television system, and over 30 radio stations serve the city.

Facts in brief

Population: *City*—258,295 (1990 census). *Metropolitan area*—852,737 (1990 census).
Area: *City*—85 sq. mi. (220 km²). *Metropolitan area*—39,370 sq. mi. (101,969 km²).
Climate: *Average temperature*—January, 45 °F (7 °C), July, 90 °F (32 °C). *Average annual precipitation* (rainfall, melted snow, and other forms of moisture)—4 in. (10 cm). For the monthly weather in Las Vegas, see **Nevada** (Climate).
Government: Council-manager. *Terms*—Four years for the mayor and the four council members. City manager is appointed by the council and the mayor.
Founded: 1905. Incorporated as a city in 1911.

The Las Vegas Strip is best known for its large, luxurious hotels and nonstop entertainment. These attractions have made the city one of the leading tourist destinations in the United States. Las Vegas is Nevada's largest city.

Las Vegas News Bureau

Government

Las Vegas has a council-manager form of government. The voters elect a mayor and four council members to four-year terms. The mayor and council appoint a city manager to carry out their policies and administer the day-to-day operations of the city. The city's chief sources of revenue include sales taxes, property taxes, and taxes on gambling.

Clark County is governed by seven commissioners who are elected to four-year terms. The commissioners select a county manager to administer county government.

History

Early days. Paiute Indians lived in what is now the Las Vegas area at the time white people arrived. The first non-Indians to settle in the area were missionaries sent by Mormon leader Brigham Young in 1855. The Mormons created a settlement and tried to convert the Paiutes to their religious beliefs. The Mormons abandoned the area in 1858.

Las Vegas was founded in 1905 when a railroad company auctioned off land there. In 1910, the town had a population of about 1,000. It received a city charter in 1911.

Rapid growth. Two developments in 1931 set the stage for rapid growth in Las Vegas. That year, the state legalized casino gambling. Also in 1931, construction began on Hoover Dam, which would supply water and electric power for much of the Pacific Southwest. The dam was dedicated in 1935.

Las Vegas's population had passed 8,400 by 1940. Nellis Air Force Base began as a gunnery school in 1941, during World War II. Las Vegas's first big gambling casino opened in 1946. By 1950, the city's population had almost tripled, reaching nearly 25,000. To attract patrons to the casinos, Las Vegas hotels offered lavish entertainment. Many of the shows featured famous singers, comedians, or other performers, as well as chorus lines of beautiful women in elaborate costumes. By the mid-1950's, gambling and entertainment had made Las Vegas one of the leading tourist attractions in the United States.

By 1960, the city reached a population of about 64,000. The population nearly doubled over the next 10 years as the casino industry continued to prosper. The city's growth prompted the development of the Southern Nevada Water Project (now the Robert B. Griffith Water Project) from 1967 to 1983 to pump more water from Lake Mead.

Recent developments. Las Vegas's population reached almost 260,000 by the 1990 census and continued to climb after the census. Many of the problems facing Las Vegas's city government are a result of the rapid population growth. The desert city has a high rate of water usage per person. The metropolitan area's share of water from the Colorado River and Lake Mead is not sufficient for continued growth. The county and city governments helped form the Southern Nevada Water Authority, which is working to develop water conservation programs and find new sources of water.

The Las Vegas area's population growth has led to crowded classrooms. In response, the Clark County School District has placed some schools on double sessions or year-round schedules. The population growth also has increased traffic congestion, air pollution, and crime.

Until the late-1900's, gambling was illegal in most parts of the United States outside Nevada. But many state governments then began legalizing some forms of gambling to raise revenues for their operations. In response to the new competition, Las Vegas gaming companies began building larger, themed hotels to attract more visitors.   Charles Zobell

Downtown San Diego lies on San Diego Bay, one of the world's finest natural harbors. The city is a popular tourist destination, as well as an important hub of operations of the United States Navy.

San Diego

San Diego, California, is the sixth largest city in the United States and an important base of operations for the U.S. Navy. The city lies in the southwestern corner of the country and is bordered by the Pacific Ocean on the west and by Mexico on the south.

San Diego has experienced dramatic growth since the mid-1900's. In 1940, it ranked 43rd in population among U.S. cities. But by 1990, it had jumped to 6th. Among the cities in California and on the Pacific Coast, only Los Angeles is larger.

San Diego has one of the finest natural deepwater harbors in the world. The harbor, which is on San Diego Bay, serves oceangoing ships and United States Navy vessels. The city is a major tourist center. The San Diego Zoo and Sea World each attract millions of visitors every year. San Diego has a thriving arts community, with numerous museums and theaters.

The city is sometimes called *The Birthplace of California.* It was founded in 1769, when Spanish soldiers built California's first *presidio* (military fort) on the site. The Spaniards chose the location because of the fine harbor. That same year, a Franciscan priest, Junípero Serra, established California's first mission within the presidio.

The city

Layout of San Diego. San Diego covers 324 square miles (839 square kilometers). It is the seat of San Diego County. The city's southern boundary forms part of the border between the United States and Mexico. Los Angeles lies about 125 miles (200 kilometers) to the north.

Downtown San Diego extends inland from San Diego Bay to Balboa Park—the site of the famed San Diego Zoo. The Community Concourse, a modern civic center, lies in the heart of the busy downtown area. It includes the City Administration Building as well as the Civic Theatre, the city's largest theater. The San Diego Convention Center has a nautical design in keeping with its location on the harbor's edge. Horton Plaza, named for downtown developer Alonzo E. Horton, is a multilevel shopping and dining complex. The 16-block Gaslamp Quarter, also downtown, has been restored to its appearance during the late 1800's.

San Diego's original downtown was established a few miles northwest of the present downtown. This area is known as Old Town. A number of historic buildings that made up the original downtown have been restored or reconstructed. They surround a plaza at Mason Street and San Diego Avenue. Just northeast of Old Town is Presidio Park, the site of the original presidio.

Point Loma, a peninsula that forms part of the entrance to San Diego Bay, is a popular tourist destination. It includes the Old Point Loma Lighthouse and the Cabrillo National Monument. First lit in 1855, Old Point Loma is one of the oldest lighthouses on the Pacific Coast. It honors Juan Rodríguez Cabrillo, a Portuguese explorer who sailed into San Diego Bay in 1542.

The geography of the San Diego area includes numerous canyons and mesas. Some neighborhoods were built in the canyons, and others overlook them. In some areas, canyons separate neighborhoods.

Many of San Diego's most fashionable neighborhoods and resort areas overlook the Pacific Ocean. Such areas within the city include La Jolla (pronounced *luh HOY uh*), Mission Beach, and Pacific Beach.

San Diego's mild, sunny climate helps make the city a popular vacation spot. Temperatures average 69 °F (21 °C) in summer and 56 °F (13 °C) in winter. Precipitation totals only about 10 inches (25 centimeters) yearly.

The metropolitan area of San Diego extends over the entire county. It covers 4,205 square miles (10,891 square kilometers) and includes 17 incorporated cities and towns besides San Diego. One of the best-known suburbs is the resort town of Coronado, on a peninsula in San Diego Bay. The San Diego-Coronado Bay Bridge, which is about 2¼ miles (3.5 kilometers) long, connects Coronado to downtown San Diego. Other suburban San Diego communities include Carlsbad, Chula Vista, Del Mar, El Cajon, Escondido, Imperial Beach, La Mesa, National City, Oceanside, Santee, and Vista.

San Diego's suburbs also offer numerous points of in-terest. Perhaps the most famous is San Diego Wild Animal Park, a wildlife preserve in Escondido. Also in Escondido, San Pasqual Battlefield State Historic Park commemorates the 1846 Battle of San Pasqual. This was the most significant battle fought in California during the Mexican-American War. Visitors to Chula Vista can tour the Chula Vista Nature Center, one of the few remaining salt marsh habitats on the Pacific Coast. The marsh is regularly flooded by seawater at high tide. A famous site in Oceanside is Mission San Luis Rey de Francia. Established in 1798, it was once the largest and most prosperous of the California missions.

People

Ethnic groups. San Diego has wide cultural diversity. About 20 percent of the city's residents were born out-

City of San Diego

San Diego is a naval and aerospace center. The map at the right shows major landmarks in and around the city. The map below shows the Pacific coast from Los Angeles to Mexico.

━━━	City boundary
── ──	County boundary
─ ── ─	International boundary
═══	Expressway
────	Road or street
────	Railroad
✈	Airport
▪	Point of interest
▨	Park
▨	Military area

San Diego and Los Angeles area

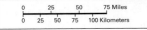

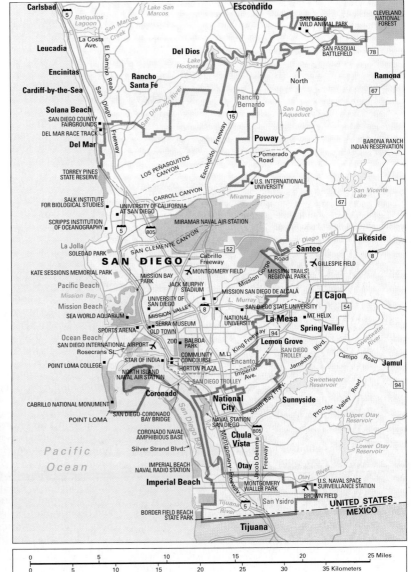

Facts in brief

Population: *City*—1,110,549. *Metropolitan area*—2,498,016.
Area: *City*—324 sq. mi. (839 km²), including 15 sq. mi. (40 km²) of inland water. *Metropolitan area*—4,205 sq. mi. (10,891 km²).
Climate: *Average temperature*—January, 56 °F (13 °C); July, 69 °F (21 °C). *Average annual precipitation* (rainfall, melted snow, and other forms of moisture)—10 in. (25 cm).
Government: Council-manager. *Terms*—4 years for the mayor and 8 other council members; manager appointed.
Founded: 1769. Incorporated as a city in 1850.

Largest communities in the San Diego area

Name	Population	Name	Population
San Diego	1,110,549	San Diego	
Chula Vista	135,163	Country Estates†	77,000
Oceanside	128,398	Vista	71,872
Escondido	108,635	Carlsbad	63,126
El Cajon	88,693	Encinitas	55,386

†Unincorporated. Source: U.S. Bureau of the Census.

Symbols of San Diego. The flag includes the city seal and the date 1542, when the explorer Juan Rodríguez Cabrillo sailed into San Diego Bay. The bell tower on the middle of the seal, *right,* symbolizes the influence of missionaries on the city's early development.

side the United States, and 30 percent speak a language other than English at home. Non-Hispanic whites make up about 60 percent of the city's population. Hispanics, who may be white, black, or of mixed ancestry, make up about 20 percent. The majority of Hispanics in San Diego are of Mexican heritage. African Americans account for about 10 percent. Together, Asians and Pacific Islanders also make up about 10 percent of the population. San Diego County includes 18 American Indian reservations, representing several Indian nations. Some American Indians reside in the city.

Housing. Housing costs in San Diego rank among the highest in the United States. The region's dwellings include elegant Craftsman-style houses built in the 1920's and 1930's. These houses feature intricately carved cabinets and woodwork. Some older neighborhoods have many ornate, Victorian-style homes. After World War II ended in 1945, a housing boom introduced numerous, more affordable two- and three-bedroom bungalows. Spanish influences, such as *stucco* (rough plaster) walls and red tile roofs, appear on both older and newer houses.

San Diego has several military facilities. The thousands of military personnel stationed there contribute to a shortage of good low-cost housing. The city also faces

the problem of providing shelter for its large group of homeless people.

Education. The city of San Diego operates about 155 public schools that serve about 130,000 students. The rest of San Diego County has about 430 public schools with approximately 380,000 students. Many church-supported and other private schools also operate in the county.

San Diego has a number of colleges and universities. The University of California at San Diego, in La Jolla, is part of the University of California system. The city's famous Scripps Institution of Oceanography is part of the university. San Diego State University is part of the California State University system. Other colleges and universities in the area include the University of San Diego, National University, Point Loma Nazarene College, and United States International University.

Social problems. Like many large cities, San Diego faces the problems of poverty and homelessness. Numerous public and private organizations work to provide shelter and social services. San Diego County maintains two schools for homeless children. Both of the schools are downtown, where the homeless population is largest.

The city's location close to the Mexican border creates both benefits and problems for the city. Mexican residents and tourists who cross the border from Mexico into San Diego County frequently shop in the San Diego area, spending more than $2.5 billion a year. However, some Mexicans come to the United States to work without immigration papers that they need to hold jobs legally. Operation Gatekeeper, a United States Border Patrol program, was introduced in 1994 to make illegal entry into the United States more difficult. The program calls for more patrols, improved fences, and other measures to guard the border against illegal immigration.

Cultural life

The arts. The Civic Theatre downtown is the home of the San Diego Opera. Major theater performances in San Diego are staged at the La Jolla Playhouse and the Old Globe Theatre in Balboa Park. Both theaters have sent successful plays to Broadway. The Old Globe, part of the Simon Edison Center for the Performing Arts, produces plays by the great English dramatist William Shakespeare each summer.

Suburban performing arts centers include the Poway Center for the Performing Arts in Poway and the California Center for the Arts in Escondido. Both are in northern San Diego County.

Museums and libraries. San Diego has a wide variety of interesting museums, many in Balboa Park. Among the museums in the park are the San Diego Museum of Art, which features paintings by European masters; and the Timken Museum of Art, which owns a valuable collection of Russian religious art. Also in the park, the Museum of Photographic Arts houses contemporary and historic photo exhibits. The Centro Cultural de la Raza features Mexican, Mexican American, and American Indian visual and performing arts; and the Reuben H. Fleet Space Theater and Science Center offers science exhibits, a planetarium, and a large-format motion-picture theater. Both are in Balboa Park as well.

WORLD BOOK photo by David R. Frazier

Balboa Park includes a wide variety of interesting museums, scenic gardens, and the famous San Diego Zoo. Several buildings in the park, including the Botanical Building, *left,* were constructed to house the Panama-California Exposition, an international fair. San Diego hosted the exposition in 1915 and 1916.

Along the wharf, the Maritime Museum features the *Star of India,* an iron sailing ship built in the 1860's. In Presidio Park, the Junípero Serra Museum has exhibits on early San Diego history. The Museum of Contemporary Art in La Jolla displays modern painting, sculpture, and photography. A branch of the museum is in downtown San Diego. Also in La Jolla, the Stephen Birch Aquarium-Museum displays marine life from around the world in more than 30 aquariums.

The San Diego public library system consists of the Central Library downtown and branches throughout the city. The San Diego County library system allows suburban libraries throughout the county to share books and other materials with one another.

Recreation. San Diego's mild climate allows residents to enjoy an outdoor lifestyle all year long. San Diego County has 70 miles (112 kilometers) of ocean beaches. The city of San Diego has about 175 parks. Mission Bay Park, one of the largest parks, covers more than 4,600 acres (1,850 hectares). It includes an aquatic park with areas for fishing, swimming, and boating. The park is also home to Sea World, a 150-acre (60-hectare) marine park featuring dolphins, sharks, penguins, and killer whales. The restored Giant Dipper roller coaster is in nearby Belmont Park. It was built in 1925.

The famous San Diego Zoo is in Balboa Park. It is known for its work in preserving endangered species of animals. It houses about 4,000 animals of about 900 species in a 100-acre (40-hectare) garden of tropical plants and flowers. The zoo also operates the popular San Diego Wild Animal Park in Escondido, which features a guided 5-mile (8-kilometer) monorail "safari."

The San Diego Padres of the National League play baseball at Jack Murphy Stadium. The National Football League's San Diego Chargers also play there.

The Mexican city of Tijuana lies about 15 miles (25 kilometers) south of downtown San Diego. It is a favorite destination of visitors to the area. Tijuana's attractions include gift shops, restaurants, nightclubs, bullfights, and horse races.

The Palomar Observatory, which houses the huge Hale Telescope, has a visitor's gallery and offers guided tours. The observatory stands on Palomar Mountain, about 45 miles (70 kilometers) northeast of downtown San Diego. Also northeast lies the Anza-Borrego Desert State Park, which has hiking and driving trails through 600,000 acres (240,000 hectares) of California desert. A spectacular array of wildflowers bloom there in March and April.

WORLD BOOK photo by David R. Frazier

San Diego Zoo is one of the city's most popular attractions. Windows at the zoo's modern hippopotamus display, *above,* enable visitors to view the animals below the surface of the water.

Economy

Manufacturing ranks as the San Diego area's largest industry in terms of revenue. However, the industry employs only about 10 percent of the county's workers. The area's major manufacturers build ships and make medical instruments and electronic and oceanographic equipment.

The armed forces and other government agencies make up San Diego's second largest industry. About one-fifth of San Diego residents are employed by the government. Many residents work at the huge San Diego Naval Base.

Tourism is San Diego's third largest revenue-producing industry. San Diego attracts millions of visitors a year. Spending by visitors contributes heavily to the economy. Tourism generates many jobs related to dining, lodging, shopping, and recreation.

Several major health and medical research firms are based in the San Diego area. The area ranks among the largest centers for biotechnology in the United States. About 100 companies in this field apply technology to solve problems in biology and medicine. More than 55,000 small businesses operate in the metropolitan area, most employing fewer than 100 people.

San Diego County ranks among the top 25 counties in the United States in the market value of its agricultural production. It is one of the world's leading avocado growing areas.

Transportation and communication. Major airlines operate out of San Diego International Airport. Passenger railroads and several steamship lines serve the city as well. San Diego Transit buses serve the city. The San Diego Trolley system carries about 15 million passengers a year between southern and eastern parts of the county and downtown San Diego.

San Diego has one daily newspaper, the *San Diego Union-Tribune*. About 40 radio stations, 7 regular television stations, and several cable TV systems serve the metropolitan area. The *San Diego Daily Transcript* publishes news of interest to the local business community.

Government

San Diego has a council-manager form of government. Voters elect a mayor and eight other City Council members to four-year terms. The council appoints a city manager, who serves as administrative head of the government. Property and sales taxes are the chief source of San Diego's income.

San Diego County is governed by a five-member Board of Supervisors. Board members are elected to four-year terms. The Board of Supervisors appoints a

WORLD BOOK photo by David R. Frazier

San Diego Bay plays an important role in the regional economy of San Diego. The bay serves U.S. Navy ships, ocean liners, and fishing and sightseeing boats, as well as recreational vessels. The huge San Diego Naval Base employs thousands of area residents.

chief administrative officer to handle the day-to-day affairs of government.

History

Early years. Indians lived in what is now the San Diego area long before Europeans arrived. The Spaniards called the Indians the Diegueño. Juan Rodríguez Cabrillo was probably the first European to enter the region. Cabrillo, a Portuguese explorer in the service of Spain, sailed into what is now San Diego Bay in 1542. An expedition led by the Spanish explorer Sebastián Vizcaíno reached the area on Nov. 10, 1602. Vizcaíno's flagship was called the *San Diego* (Spanish for Saint Didacus). On November 12, the feast day of San Diego de Alcalá, a Spanish saint, priests with the expedition said Mass. The bay was named San Diego, probably to honor the flagship and the feast day.

No white settlers came into the area until 1769. That year, Spanish soldiers from Mexico constructed a presidio on a hill near San Diego Bay. Junípero Serra, a Franciscan priest, established California's first mission within the presidio that same year. The mission, the presidio, and—later—the city were also given the name San Diego. Mission San Diego de Alcalá was the first of 21 missions established in California. Junípero Serra established eight more missions in California before his death in 1784.

In 1774, the mission was rebuilt about 5 miles (8 kilometers) up the valley, closer to an Indian village. The new location also had a better water supply for crops. During the early 1800's, colonists began settling at the bottom of the hill on which the presidio stood. This is the area now known as Old Town.

The trading of cattle hides became an important activity in the area during the early 1800's. San Diego's port helped make the settlement a center of the Pacific Coast hide trade. Located close to a migration route for gray whales, the port also was a base for whaling ships from the 1850's to the 1870's.

San Diego was organized as a town in 1834. It adopted a city charter in 1850, the same year that California became a state. By 1860, San Diego had a population of 731. A businessman named Alonzo E. Horton purchased land along eastern San Diego Bay in 1867. He laid out an area called New Town, which soon became the new center of the town.

Growth. The California Southern Railroad provided the first rail link to San Diego from the eastern United States in 1885. Its arrival created a land boom. Business expanded rapidly. By 1887, the city's population had jumped to about 40,000. But the boom ended suddenly, and by 1890 the population of San Diego had fallen to about 16,000.

During the early 1900's, a growing demand for tuna led to the establishment of large fish canneries in San Diego. Several companies built their canneries there because of the city's port facilities and location close to tuna-fishing waters.

In 1915 and 1916, San Diego hosted the Panama-California Exposition, an international fair. The event brought worldwide attention to the city and made Balboa Park a popular tourist attraction.

Military center. San Diego's rapid development as a major naval center occurred largely because of World War I (1914-1918). The San Diego Naval Base and North Island Naval Air Station both opened in 1917, the year the United States entered the war. By 1920, 75,000 people lived in the city. San Diego became the headquarters of the 11th Naval District in 1922.

Consolidated Aircraft Corporation (now called General Dynamics), a major aircraft and defense manufacturer, moved to San Diego in 1935. Other contractors and related companies soon followed. By 1940, San Diego's population had passed 200,000.

In the 1940's, the armed forces and defense contractors became the dominant forces in San Diego's economy. After the United States entered World War II in 1941, San Diego's airplane plants attracted thousands of workers from throughout the country. The armed services also built new military facilities in the city. Thousands of people received military training in San Diego before serving overseas. Many of these people returned to live in the San Diego area after the war ended in 1945. They enjoyed the area's mild climate and numerous outdoor recreation opportunities. By 1950, the population of San Diego had risen to more than 330,000.

Economic changes brought more diversity to San Diego's economy in the second half of the 1900's. Competition from Japanese and South American tuna canneries and a decline in the aircraft industry hurt the city's economic base in the 1950's. But gains in missile production and shipbuilding helped make up the loss.

Large-scale unemployment followed a further decline in the aircraft and spacecraft manufacturing industry in the early 1960's. Civic leaders established programs to broaden San Diego's economic base. Development of several new industrial parks for factories and warehouses helped attract many new industries. In the 1970's, San Diego grew as a center of health science and medical research activities.

The decline of Cold War tensions in the late 1980's and an economic recession in the early 1990's led to a further decline in the role of defense in San Diego's economy. In 1994, the Martin Marietta Corporation, a major defense contractor, left San Diego, eliminating many jobs. That same year, General Dynamics Corporation, the region's largest civilian employer, announced plans to close its San Diego-based Convair division. Cuts in the federal defense budget resulted in a decision to close the San Diego Naval Training Center by the end of the 1990's. However, the emergence of new high-technology companies in San Diego helped reduce the economic impact.

Other recent developments. San Diego completed several major development projects in the 1980's and 1990's, including Horton Plaza and the San Diego Convention Center. The city also experienced another dramatic increase in population during this period. By 1990, the city's population had climbed to about 1,100,000, and the metropolitan area had about $2\frac{1}{2}$ million people.

Karen Lin Clark

Related articles in *World Book* include:

California (pictures)
Hispanic Americans (picture)
Palomar Observatory
San Diego Marine Corps
  Recruit Depot
San Diego Naval Base

Scripps Institution of
  Oceanography
Serra, Junípero
Tijuana
Zoo (picture)

Tokyo at night glows with light. The city is Japan's capital and one of the largest and most crowded cities in the world. The busy Ginza district, *above,* in central Tokyo, has many restaurants and shops.

Tokyo

Tokyo is the capital of Japan and one of the largest cities in the world. It is part of a huge urban area that also includes the port city of Yokohama and the manufacturing cities of Chiba and Kawasaki. This area, known as the Tokyo metropolitan region, is the largest urban center in the world. It has an estimated population of more than 28 million people.

Tokyo itself is one of the busiest and most crowded cities in the world. It is the home of the Japanese emperor and the headquarters of the national government. It is Japan's center of business, culture, and education. Its many banks, commercial establishments, and industries help make Japan one of the richest nations in the world.

Tokyo has tall buildings, freeways jammed with traffic, and more neon signs than probably any other city in the world. The people of this Asian city listen to American jazz and rock music, and they eat at restaurants that offer everything from hamburgers to the finest European dishes. Many residents go to baseball games and watch movies and television shows from Western countries.

Gary D. Allinson, the contributor of this article, is Professor of Modern Japanese History at the University of Virginia and the author of Japanese Urbanism *and* Suburban Tokyo.

In spite of such outside influences, however, Japanese tradition remains strong in Tokyo. Large numbers of Tokyo's people take part in dances and parades during the city's many traditional festivals, some of which have been held for hundreds of years. They go to city parks to enjoy the beauty of the cherry trees and lotus blossoms. They visit historic shrines and temples and attend traditional plays and wrestling matches.

Tokyo traces its beginning to 1457, when a powerful warrior built a castle there. It became the Japanese capital in 1868. Tokyo was almost destroyed twice—by a terrible earthquake in 1923 and by air raids in the 1940's during World War II. But the city began growing rapidly after the war.

Facts in brief

Population: *City, or ward area*—8,163,573. *Tokyo Metropolitan Prefecture*—11,927,457. *Tokyo metropolitan region*—28,447,000.
Area: *City, or ward area*—223 sq. mi. (578 km²); *Tokyo Metropolitan Prefecture*—832 sq. mi. (2,156 km²); *Tokyo metropolitan region*—1,089 sq. mi. (2,820 km²).
Altitude: 80 ft. (24 m) above sea level.
Climate: *Average temperature*—January, 39 °F (4 °C); July, 76 °F (24 °C). *Average annual precipitation* (rainfall, melted snow, and other forms of moisture)—58 in. (147 cm).
Government: *Chief executive*—governor (4-year term). *Legislature*—127-member assembly (4-year terms).
Founded: 1457.

About one-fourth of the people of Japan live in the Tokyo area. Tokyo itself has become extremely crowded, and its housing costs are among the highest in the world. It also faces such problems as pollution and some of the world's heaviest traffic.

The city

Tokyo lies on the southeastern coast of Honshu, Japan's largest island. The city stands in the southern part of a sprawling lowland called the Kanto Plain, a rich agricultural and industrial area. Mount Fuji, Japan's highest and most famous peak, lies about 60 miles (97 kilometers) to the southwest. On clear days, people in Tokyo have a spectacular view of the beautiful mountain, which seems to "float" on the horizon.

The city, or ward area. The city of Tokyo is divided into 23 units called *wards*, and it is often called the *ward area*. It is bordered by the Edo River on the northeast, by an inlet of the Pacific called Tokyo Bay on the east, and by the Tama River on the south. The Sumida River flows into Tokyo Bay in the eastern part of the city.

The Imperial Palace, where the Japanese emperor lives, stands near the center of the city. The town that became Tokyo grew up in this area.

East from the palace to Tokyo Bay, the land is low and flat. Many of Tokyo's chief business, commercial, and industrial districts are in this area. The Marunouchi district, an area of tall office buildings southeast of the palace, is Tokyo's business and financial center.

Part of eastern Tokyo is jammed with office buildings and apartment buildings made of concrete and steel. The oldest and poorest residential sections of Tokyo are also located in the eastern part of the city.

Much of far eastern Tokyo is filled-in land on what

had been part of Tokyo Bay. Some of this land lies below sea level. The low-lying areas are always in danger of floods, especially during heavy rains. Dikes have been built along the waterfront and the riverbanks. But the filled-in land sinks lower every year, mainly because of the removal of large amounts of ground water for industrial use. The dikes sink along with the land, making flood control difficult.

West of the Imperial Palace, the land becomes hilly. The chief residential sections of the city are in the west. The residences include large apartment buildings like those in Western cities and simple one- or two-story wooden buildings, the traditional Japanese houses. Many of the wooden houses are small and plain by Western standards. In some sections, rich families and poor families live in the same neighborhood, and their houses are plain and look much alike. But the western part of the city also has luxurious residential sections where the wealthy live.

Tokyo, unlike most other Japanese cities, no longer has large numbers of buildings in the ancient Japanese style that is most familiar to Westerners. This style features low, graceful lines and roofs turned up at the edges. Most of the remaining buildings in this style are religious shrines or temples.

The Tokyo Metropolitan Prefecture is one of 47 prefectures in Japan. Prefectures are the country's main units of regional government. The Tokyo prefecture is called *Tokyo-to* in Japanese. Most prefectures are called *ken*. Tokyo is called a *to* in order to indicate its special status as the nation's capital.

The Tokyo Metropolitan Prefecture is made up of four areas: (1) the city, or ward area, (2) about 25 suburban cities west of the ward area, (3) several towns in a

Tokyo area

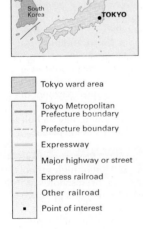

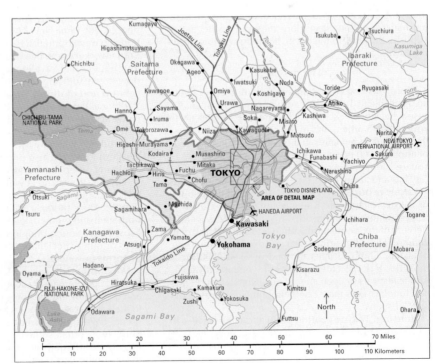

- Tokyo ward area
- Tokyo Metropolitan Prefecture boundary
- Prefecture boundary
- Expressway
- Major highway or street
- Express railroad
- Other railroad
- Point of interest

WORLD BOOK map

A Tokyo family relaxes at home in the evening, *left.* The father and son play a Japanese version of chess, called *shogi.* The food, the furnishings of the home, and the family's clothing reflect a combination of Asian and Western influences that is typical of life in Tokyo.

Paul Chesley, Tony Stone Images

mountainous area on the far western edge of the prefecture, and (4) the Izu Islands and the Bonin Islands, two small island groups in the Pacific Ocean, south of the prefecture. Nearly all of the prefecture's residents live in the ward area or the suburban cities.

The Tokyo metropolitan region is the world's largest urban center. It consists of most of the Tokyo Metropolitan Prefecture and parts of three neighboring prefectures—Kanagawa, Chiba, and Saitama. Kanagawa, to the south, includes the port city of Yokohama and the manufacturing city of Kawasaki. Chiba, on the east, has many large manufacturing cities and residential suburbs. Saitama, to the north, has many rapidly growing towns.

The people

More jobs and educational and cultural opportunities are available in Tokyo than anywhere else in Japan. As a result, the city constantly attracts people—especially the young—from other parts of the country. Tokyo is one of the most crowded cities in the world. It has an average of about 37,000 people per square mile (14,000 per square kilometer)—nearly twice as many as New York City has and about three times as many as Bombay has.

Ethnic groups and religion. Almost all the people of Tokyo are Japanese. Koreans and Chinese are the largest minority groups, but they make up less than 1 percent of the population. Shinto and Buddhism are the chief religions throughout Japan. Tokyo has hundreds of historic Shinto shrines and Buddhist temples. But most residents visit these places of worship only for public festivals or such special occasions as weddings and funerals. Less than 2 percent of the city's residents are Christians.

Housing. Tokyo's soaring population has created a strong demand for housing. In the past, most Tokyo residents lived in small, one- or two-story wooden houses, each with its own yard or garden. As the population

grew, many apartment buildings were constructed in the city in an attempt to provide housing for all the people. Even so, a housing shortage continued. The limited amount of housing and land in the city center drove up rents and land prices. Many people—even if they could find housing—could not afford to pay for it. As a result, Tokyo's outlying areas have experienced a building boom since the 1960's.

The Tokyo prefecture has begun financing the construction of low-rent housing projects. One such project, called Tama New Town, houses about 200,000 people. But Tama New Town, like many other Tokyo housing developments, is far from the downtown area. Some workers who live in outlying areas spend up to four hours a day traveling to and from their jobs in downtown Tokyo.

Food and clothing. Many Tokyo residents enjoy traditional Japanese foods. Popular Japanese dishes include *sukiyaki* (beef cooked with vegetables), *tempura* (fish and vegetables fried in batter), and *sushi* (vinegar-flavored rice with raw fish or vegetables). Chinese and Western foods are also popular in Tokyo, and the city has many American fast-food restaurants.

On the streets and at work, most of the people wear Western-style clothing. Some older women still wear a *kimono.* The kimono, a traditional Japanese garment of both men and women, is a long robe tied with a sash. Most Tokyo young people wear a kimono only on holidays or other special occasions. Most students wear uniforms to school.

Education. The Tokyo Metropolitan Prefecture has about 1,500 elementary schools, 900 junior high schools, and 500 senior high schools. Most of these schools are in the ward area and the suburbs. Some parts of Tokyo do not have enough schools for the rapidly growing population. But in some old sections of the city center that are now largely occupied by businesses, many of the schoolhouses stand nearly empty.

The prefecture has about 120 four-year colleges and universities and 80 junior colleges. More than a third of Japan's college students attend these institutions.

Social problems, such as poverty and crime, exist in Tokyo. But they are not as severe as they are in many other large cities. Because of Tokyo's strong economy, most people can find jobs. In addition, the local and national governments provide aid for people who cannot support themselves. Tokyo's crime rate is much lower than the crime rate in most other large cities. Also, because Tokyo has no large minority groups, the city has few major problems stemming from racial or other social differences.

Demonstrations are often held in Tokyo to protest such matters as political, educational, and environmental policies. They have sometimes resulted in violence.

Cultural life and recreation

Few cities in the world can match Tokyo as an international center of culture and entertainment. Tokyo's cultural institutions and favorite leisure-time activities reflect the culture of both the East and the West.

The arts. Many of Japan's finest artists and craftworkers live and work in Tokyo. Some still use the styles and methods of their ancestors to create beautiful paintings

on paper or silk and colorful wood-block prints. But many Tokyo artists create paintings and sculptures using Western styles and methods.

Tokyo is the center of Japanese drama, music, and other performing arts. Two traditional types of Japanese drama, *no* and *kabuki,* rank as favorite forms of entertainment in Tokyo. For descriptions of these colorful plays, see **Drama** (Japan).

Several professional symphony orchestras that specialize in Western music perform in Tokyo. Other Tokyo musical groups present concerts of traditional music, featuring such Japanese instruments as the three-stringed *samisen,* or *shamisen,* and a kind of harp called a *koto.*

Japan's motion-picture industry is also centered in Tokyo. Japanese movies have been praised by audiences throughout the world.

Museums and libraries. Some of Japan's finest museums and libraries are in Tokyo. The Tokyo National Museum, the largest museum in Japan, has a valuable collection of Asian art. The National Museum of Modern Art specializes in works by modern Japanese artists. The National Museum of Western Art houses a large collection of works by Western artists. The National Science Museum focuses on scientific discoveries.

Central Tokyo

The map at the right shows the central part of Tokyo and its major landmarks. The Imperial Palace stands near the center of the city in beautiful parklike grounds. Ueno Park, which lies northeast of the palace, is one of the city's most popular parks. It includes a zoo and several museums and art galleries.

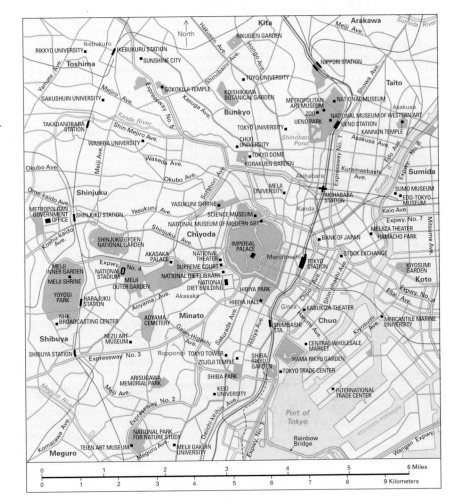

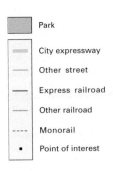

- Park
- City expressway
- Other street
- Express railroad
- Other railroad
- Monorail
- Point of interest

Superstock

An actor in a *no* play performs a story with gestures and movements. The no play is a traditional form of Japanese drama. Tokyo is Japan's center of drama, music, and other performing arts.

Tokyo's public library system includes a central library and two branches. The National Diet Library ranks as the country's largest library. The library's first responsibility is to provide research and reference assistance to Japan's *Diet* (parliament). It also serves many other needs, including those of scholars.

Recreation. Exhibitions of *judo* and *sumo,* which are Japanese forms of wrestling, rank as favorite sporting events. Western sports, including baseball, bowling, golf, ice skating, soccer, tennis, and track and field, are also popular. Baseball is the most popular sport in Tokyo. Home games of the Yomiuri Giants professional baseball team and many other sports events are held in the 50,000-seat Tokyo Dome. Tokyo's largest stadium, the National Stadium, is the site of many important track and field events. It seats about 72,000 spectators.

Tokyo also has many amusement parks and nightclubs. *Karaoke* bars, where the guests themselves sing on stage to recorded music, are popular.

Visitor's guide

Large numbers of tourists visit Tokyo the year around. In early April, the city's famous cherry trees are in bloom. Autumn in Tokyo usually brings pleasantly mild weather. The city's many festivals are other tourist attractions. These include the exciting parade of Tokyo's firefighters on January 6 and the lively Sanja Festival in the Asakusa district in mid-May.

Tourists can choose from many fine hotels and restaurants in Tokyo. Many of the hotels are built and furnished in Western style. Others are Japanese-style hotels called *ryokan.* They have such traditional features as sliding paper-paneled doors called *shoji,* mats called *tatami* that cover the floors, and heavy quilts called *futon* that serve as beds. Tokyo has thousands of restaurants. Many of these restaurants specialize in Japanese or other Asian dishes, and many others serve Western foods.

This section of the article describes a few of the interesting places to visit in Tokyo. See other sections of the article for discussions of additional places of interest.

The Imperial Palace is the home of Japan's emperor. It stands near the center of the city and consists of several low buildings and beautiful parklike grounds. Stone walls and a series of wide moats separate it from the rest of the city. The palace is open to the public only two days of the year—January 2 and the emperor's birthday. Thousands of Japanese come to pay their respects to the emperor on these two days.

Government buildings. The National Diet Building, a concrete and granite structure with a tall central tower, stands southwest of the Imperial Palace. It is the meeting place of Japan's parliament. The Tokyo Metropolitan Government Office stands in the western part of the city, in an area called the Shinjuku district. This striking concrete building, designed by Japanese architect Kenzo Tange, has twin 48-story towers. It houses the offices of the governor of the Tokyo prefecture and various government agencies. An observation deck at the top is open to visitors. The Shinjuku district has many skyscrapers, including hotels, department stores, and office buildings.

Tokyo Tower, a 1,092-foot (333-meter) steel tower that ranks as the city's tallest structure, stands south of the Imperial Palace. The Tokyo Tower houses radio and television broadcasting studios and has two observation platforms.

Parks and gardens attract many visitors. Ueno Park, northeast of the palace, is one of the city's most popular parks. Its spring displays of cherry blossoms and summer displays of lotus blossoms are outstanding. The park includes Tokyo's largest concert hall, several museums and art galleries, a zoo, a temple and shrine built during the 1600's, and tombs of Japanese rulers.

Several Japanese-style gardens in Tokyo are open to the public. Korakuen Garden and Rikugien Garden—both north of the palace—are two of the oldest and most famous gardens. Many people visit Tokyo's gardens to admire their beautifully landscaped grounds and relax at their teahouses.

Shrines and temples attract millions of worshipers and tourists yearly. The shrines are Shinto places of worship, and the temples are Buddhist.

Meiji Shrine, in a wooded parkland near the Shinjuku district, is one of the best-known shrines in Japan. Many Japanese visit it on New Year's Day, one of the few times when most Japanese women wear traditional dress in public. The Yasukuni Shrine stands northwest of the palace. It is dedicated to Japan's war dead and draws huge crowds of worshipers for special festivals in April and October.

Tokyo also has a number of famous Buddhist temples, including the historic Kannon Temple in the Asakusa district at the northeastern outskirts of the city. The temple traces its origins to the 600's, though the present buildings were constructed in the 1950's. Colorful souvenir

Baseball is the most popular sport in Tokyo and a favorite pastime throughout Japan. Tokyo's professional baseball team, the Yomiuri Giants, plays home games at the Tokyo Dome. At left, the Giants, in white uniforms, face the Yokohama Whales.

Dave Bartruff

shops line the approach to the temple. During the Sanja Festival, held in the temple area in mid-May, people parade in traditional Japanese costumes.

Other places of interest. Several well-known districts are near the Imperial Palace. The Ginza district, southeast of the palace, ranks as one of Tokyo's liveliest and most colorful districts. It is famous for its stores and nightclubs. The Kanda district, northeast of the palace, is known for its many bookstores. The Akihabara district, north of Kanda, features hundreds of shops that sell electronics products. The Asakusa district, site of the Kannon Temple, is north of Akihabara. Asakusa is one of Tokyo's oldest entertainment sections. It includes amusement parks, theaters, and restaurants.

The Tokyo Central Wholesale Market, also known as Tsukiji Market, is east of the Ginza. This lively place is the largest fish market in Asia.

A theme park called Tokyo Disneyland, in the Chiba Prefecture, is a top tourist attraction. The park was built on filled-in land in Tokyo Bay.

Economy

Tokyo is one of the world's most important centers of economic activity. It has long been a center of Japanese manufacturing. Since the 1970's, however, such service industries as finance, trade, and communication have become even more important. Many of Japan's business corporations, including the giant automakers Nissan Motor Company and Honda Motor Company, have their headquarters in Tokyo.

Manufacturing. The manufacture of electronics equipment is one of Tokyo's leading industries. Some of the world's largest electronics firms, including Hitachi Limited and the Toshiba, Sony, and NEC corporations,

have their headquarters in Tokyo. These huge companies and many small ones in the city make cassette recorders, compact disc players, computers, fax machines, radios, television sets, video recorders, and other electronics products. Many of these products are exported.

Publishing and printing is also a leading industry in Tokyo. Most of Japan's publishing companies have their headquarters in the city. Much of the material published in Tokyo is also printed there.

Other important products made in Tokyo include chemicals, food, furniture, and paper. Several Tokyo companies rank among the 25 largest manufacturing firms in the world.

Yokohama and Kawasaki also have many manufacturing plants. Products made in the metropolitan region include automobiles, chemicals, iron and steel, machinery, metal products, petroleum products, and ships.

Finance. Tokyo is one of the world's major financial centers. The Tokyo Stock Exchange ranks among the largest stock exchanges in the world. Businesses and industries throughout Japan depend on Tokyo banks for loans. The Bank of Japan, the nation's central bank, has its headquarters in Tokyo. Controlled by the national government, the Bank of Japan regulates the nation's entire banking system. Tokyo also has many commercial banks. The largest commercial banks have branches or offices in many Japanese and foreign cities. Tokyo is also the nation's center for such consumer services as financial planning and credit management.

Trade. Thousands of companies in Tokyo deal in international trade. These firms handle almost half of Japan's export business and more than half of the nation's import business. The 40-story Tokyo Trade Center displays various types of Japanese goods for international buyers.

The Tokyo Stock Exchange is one of the largest stock exchanges in the world. The exchange and Tokyo's many banks help make the city a center of world finance.

Guy Marche, FPG

The Tokyo International Trade Center sponsors displays of international goods that attract millions of visitors from all over the world each year.

Because Tokyo has a relatively shallow harbor, most large ships that enter Tokyo Bay dock at Yokohama. The Port of Yokohama ranks as Japan's largest port. Railroads, trucks, and barges carry large quantities of freight between the two cities. Chiba and Kawasaki also have port facilities.

Transportation. Motorists in Tokyo drive many more automobiles than the freeways and streets can handle effectively, and severe traffic jams occur frequently. The prefecture government is trying to provide more public transportation as a substitute for automobile travel. The Tokyo Bay Bridge and Tunnel is being built to help relieve traffic congestion.

Tokyo's public transportation system includes railroad, subway, and bus lines. An extensive network of rail lines crisscrosses the Tokyo metropolitan region. High-speed electric trains link Tokyo with Osaka and other cities. These trains, called *shinkansen* or "bullet trains," carry passengers at speeds of up to 130 miles (209 kilometers) per hour.

Tokyo's commuter trains rank among the fastest and most efficient in the world. Nearly 10 million passengers cram aboard them each day. During rush hours, employees called *oshiya* (pushers) work at the main train stations. Their job involves shoving passengers into crowded trains to make more room (see **City** [picture: Travel in cities]). The Shinjuku commuter station ranks as one of the busiest railway stations in the world. It handles millions of riders a day.

Tokyo has two major airports. Tokyo International Airport, also called Haneda Airport, lies in the far south-

ern part of the city. It handles mainly domestic traffic. A *monorail* (single-rail train) operates between central Tokyo and Tokyo International Airport. Most international flights use the New Tokyo International Airport, also called Narita Airport. It is in Narita, about 40 miles (64 kilometers) east of central Tokyo.

Communication. Tokyo's many television and radio stations make the city a broadcasting center. Japanese programs as well as American and European programs with Japanese sound tracks appear on TV. Tokyo's newspaper companies publish more than 25 daily papers.

Government

The governor is the chief official of the Tokyo Metropolitan Prefecture. The people elect the governor to a four-year term. The chief lawmaking body is the Metropolitan Assembly. It has 127 members, whom the voters elect to four-year terms. Each ward, suburb, and other community in the prefecture has at least one representative in the Assembly. The prefecture government also includes a board of education, police and fire departments, and many other agencies.

The wards, suburbs, towns, and villages of the Tokyo Metropolitan Prefecture all have some form of local government. Each elects a council and a mayor or other administrators. However, the prefecture government limits the powers of these local officials. It makes *ordinances* (rules) for all the communities in the prefecture. It also provides police protection and certain other public services for the entire area. But it provides some services, including fire protection and sanitation facilities, for the ward area only.

Local governments must provide services that are not supplied by the prefecture government. They may collect some tax money for these projects, and they receive additional funds from the prefecture and national governments.

History

Early development. The earliest settlement in the Tokyo area for which there is any evidence dates from A.D. 737. Archaeologists uncovered the remains of a Buddhist temple and monastery that had been built there at that time. However, Tokyo marks 1457 as its beginning. In that year, a warrior named Ota Dokan built a castle there. The area had military importance because it overlooked both Tokyo Bay and the Kanto Plain. Dokan worked in the service of a powerful warrior family, one of several who ruled parts of Japan. He built his castle where the Imperial Palace now stands. A town named Edo (now called Tokyo) grew up around the castle.

The development that made the town Japan's chief city began in 1590. In that year, a warrior named Tokugawa Ieyasu made Edo his headquarters. In 1603, Ieyasu became *shogun* (military ruler) of Japan. Edo became the nation's political center. But Kyoto, a city southwest of Edo and the home of the emperor, remained the official capital. By the early 1800's, Edo had grown into a city of over a million people. Ieyasu and his descendants ruled as shogun in Edo until 1867.

Western influence. Beginning in the early 1600's, Japan closed itself off from normal contact with the rest of the world. This policy was known as the *sakoku* (closed country) rule. The government allowed ships from Holland and from China to trade in Japan, but only occasionally and only at the port of Nagasaki. It prohibited Japanese people from traveling to other countries.

In 1853, United States naval officer Commodore Matthew C. Perry arrived at Tokyo Bay on a mission for the U.S. government. His goal was to open diplomatic and trade relations with Japan. Perry sailed into Tokyo Bay with four warships and began talks with Japanese rulers. He returned with more warships the next year and signed a treaty of friendship with the rulers. Partly as a result of Perry's efforts, Japan signed trade treaties with the United States and other Western countries in 1858. The treaties marked the start of modern Western influence in Japan.

Emperor Mutsuhito—who took the title *Meiji,* meaning *enlightened rule*—did much to further Westernization. He took control of Japan from the shogun in 1867. He transferred the capital from Kyoto to Edo in 1868 and moved into the Edo castle. Edo was renamed *Tokyo,* which means *eastern capital.* After 1868, Japan—especially Tokyo—rapidly adopted Western styles and inventions. By the late 1800's, Tokyo began to look like a Western city.

Earthquake and reconstruction. On Sept. 1, 1923, a violent earthquake shook the Tokyo area. Buildings collapsed and fires broke out throughout Tokyo. About 120,000 residents of the city died in the disaster, and most of central Tokyo was destroyed. The city was rebuilt during the next 20 years.

At the time of the earthquake, Tokyo consisted of 15 wards in the vicinity of the Imperial Palace. After the disaster, areas outside the 15 wards began to develop. In 1932, the city took over many of the areas and made them wards, establishing the present city limits.

World War II brought destruction to Tokyo again. American bombers first attacked the city in April 1942. The heaviest raids occurred from March to August of 1945, when Japan announced its intention to surrender. The bombs destroyed about one-third of Tokyo. Hundreds of thousands of people were killed or listed as missing. Thousands fled the city. Tokyo's population dropped from about 7,350,000 in 1940 to about 3,500,000 in 1945. In 1943, Tokyo and communities west of it formed the Tokyo Metropolitan Prefecture.

Rebuilding the city. The people of Tokyo began to rebuild their city after the war, but without much planning. Buildings went up wherever there was room. Tokyo's economy began booming a few years after the war. Population growth accompanied economic growth, and the population of the city nearly tripled between 1945 and 1960. In 1964, Tokyo was host to the Summer Olympic Games. In preparation for the games, the city started a construction program that included new freeways and hotels, and the monorail.

Tokyo's rapid growth made it one of the world's largest cities and gave it a strong economy. But the growth, along with a lack of planning, helped cause such problems as housing shortages, pollution, and traffic jams.

In 1966, the prefecture government started a series of plans to help solve Tokyo's problems. The plans set goals

Wood-block print (1856); Victoria and Albert Museum, London (Art Resource)

Moonlit Street Scene in Edo is one of many prints of the city created in the 1800's by Japanese artist Hiroshige. Edo was renamed Tokyo in 1868, when it became Japan's capital.

The Imperial Palace is the home of the Japanese emperor. It stands in a beautiful park-like setting near the center of Tokyo. Stone walls and moats separate the palace grounds from the rest of the city. The settlement that became Tokyo was established in this area.

Mike Yamashita

for improving public housing, purifying the polluted air and river water, reducing street noise and traffic jams, and increasing sanitation facilities. Parts of the Tokyo prefecture were set aside for public housing and other community projects. To ease overcrowding, the government has encouraged the development of new suburban towns. A number of such towns are growing rapidly. For example, Tsukuba, which lies about 30 miles (50 kilometers) northwest of Tokyo, was completed in 1979 as a center for scientific research and teaching. The city now has about 50 research institutes and two universities dedicated to technological studies.

Recent developments. By the 1990's, Tokyo's air was significantly cleaner. The city had also reduced water pollution by building better sewage and waste-disposal plants. Overcrowding and soaring land prices remained serious problems, however. In the early 1990's, both the national and prefecture governments began drafting new land and tax laws in an attempt to make housing more affordable. Because the city's overcrowding had become so severe, some Japanese leaders began to study the possibility of moving the national government out of Tokyo.

In 1995, the Tokyo Metropolitan Prefecture began construction of a huge development on reclaimed land along Tokyo Bay. When completed, the project will include office buildings, cultural facilities, and an international convention center. Gary D. Allinson

Related articles in *World Book* include:

Architecture (picture: The Tokyo Cathedral)
Asia (picture: Two Asian street scenes)
Bonin Islands
Japan (with pictures)
Shogun
World War II (The tide turns; Closing in on Japan)
Yokohama

Outline

I. **The city**
   A. The city, or ward area
   B. The Tokyo Metropolitan Prefecture
   C. The Tokyo metropolitan region
II. **The people**
   A. Ethnic groups and religion
   B. Housing
   C. Food and clothing
   D. Education
   E. Social problems
III. **Cultural life and recreation**
   A. The arts
   B. Museums and libraries
   C. Recreation
IV. **Visitor's guide**
V. **Economy**
   A. Manufacturing
   B. Finance
   C. Trade
   D. Transportation
   E. Communication
VI. **Government**

Index

How to use the index

This index covers the contents of the 1995, 1996, and 1997 editions of *The World Book Year Book*.

Each index entry gives the edition year and the page number or numbers—for example, **Avalanche, Colorado, 97:** 234-235. This means that information on this topic may be found on pages 234 through 235 of the 1997 *Year Book.*

The "see" and "see also" cross references—for example, the two at the end of the **Aviation** heading—refer the reader to other entries in the index.

When there are many references to a topic, they are grouped alphabetically by clue words under the main topic. For example, the clue words under **Aviation disasters** group the references to that topic under numerous subtopics.

The indication (il.) means that the reference on this page is to an illustration only, as in the **Baader, Andreas** picture on page 433 of the 1996 edition.

When a topic such as **BAHRAIN** appears in all capital letters, this means that there is a *Year Book* Update article entitled Bahrain in at least one of the three volumes covered by this index. References to the topic in other articles may also appear after the topic name.

When only the first letter of a topic, such as *Bakke* **case** is capitalized, this means that there is no article entitled *Bakke* case but that information on this topic may be found in the edition and on the pages listed.

An index entry followed by *WBE* refers to a new or revised *World Book Encyclopedia* article in the supplement section, as in **BALLET:** *WBE,* **97:** 422. This means that a *World Book Encyclopedia* article on the Ballet begins on page 422 of the 1997 *Year Book.*

Index

A

Index

Index

Index

Index

Index

514

Index

Index

518

Index

520

Index

Acknowledgments

The publishers acknowledge the following sources for illustrations. Credits read from top to bottom, left to right, on their respective pages. An asterisk (*) denotes illustrations and photographs that are the exclusive property of *The Year Book*. All maps, charts, and diagrams were prepared by *The Year Book* staff unless otherwise noted.

6 © Philippe Renault, Gamma/Liaison; AP/Wide World
7 NASA
8 AP/Wide World; AP/Wide World; © Tim Graham, Sygma
9-10 AP/Wide World
12 © Allan Tannenbaum, Sygma
14 © Mathieu Polak, Sygma
16 © Tim Graham, Sygma
19 © Derek Pruitt, Gamma/Liaison
20 © *Miami Herald* from Gamma/Liaison
22 Reuters/Archive Photos
24 © J.O. Atlanta from Gamma/Liaison
26 © L. Stone, Sygma
27 Steve Liss © *Time* Magazine
28 NASA
30 AP/Wide World
32 © Gifford, Gamma/Liaison
35 © Cynthia Johnson, Gamma/Liaison
36-39 Reuters/Archive Photos
44 © Scott Daniel Peterson, Gamma/Liaison
49 AP/Wide World; © Eric Miller, Impact Visuals
50 © Mark Peters, Sipa Press
52 © Henry Hurtak, Sygma; Reuters/Archive Photos
56-57 Agence France-Presse
59 AP/Wide World
61 Anne Glenn, University of Cincinnati
63 AP/Wide World
66 *Girl with the Pearl Earring* (1660-1665) oil on canvas by Jan Vermeer; Mauritshuis, The Hague, Netherlands (SCALA/Art Resource)
69 AP/Wide World
73 NASA
74 AP/Wide World
78 General Motors Corporation; Jaguar Motor Company
79 Chrysler Corporation; Toyota Motor Corporation; Ford Motor Company
81 Airbus Industries of North America
86-89 AP/Wide World
91 W. Jack Jones, Ph.D.
93 Reuters/Archive Photos
97 David Portnoy, NYT Pictures
99-100 Reuters/Archive Photos
103 M. Slaughter, *The Toronto Star*
104 Reuters/Archive Photos
111 Chris Swartz; Peter Sibbald
114-119 AP/Wide World
122 UPI/Corbis-Bettmann
125 Corbis-Bettmann
126 © Greg Girard, Contact Press Images; © Dilip Mehta, Contact Press Images
127 © Dilip Mehta, Contact Press Images
129 © Greg Girard, Contact Press Images; Xinhua News Agency from Sygma
130 Corbis-Bettmann
136 Reuters/Archive Photos
138-140 AP/Wide World
142 AP/Wide World; University of Pennsylvania Archives
144 Smithsonian Institution; UPI Corbis-Bettmann; University of Pennsylvania's School of Engineering and Applied Science; Stuart Wilson, University of Pennsylvania
146 Corbis-Bettmann; Bureau of the Census
149 Stephen Crowley, NYT Pictures
152 Architect of the Capitol
155-157 AP/Wide World
159 © Zoran Milich, Gamma/Liaison
162 Nan Melville, NYT Pictures
164 UPI/Corbis-Bettmann; Corbis-Bettmann; UPI/Corbis-Bettmann
165 Springer/Corbis-Bettmann; Archive Photos; Steve Van Warner; UPI/Corbis-Bettmann
166 AP/Wide World; AP/Wide World; Corbis-Bettmann; AP/Wide World
167 UPI/Corbis-Bettmann; Archive Photos
168 AP/Wide World
169 © George Rose Gamma/Liaison
170 Archive Photos
171 MGM from Archive Photos
173 AP/Wide World
174 © Steve Liss, Gamma/Liaison
177-188 AP/Wide World
190 AP/Wide World; © Jim Bourg, Gamma/Liaison; © Rick Friedman, Black Star
192 AP/Wide World; © Gifford, Gamma/Liaison; AP/Wide World
194 Reuters/Archive Photos
198 WORLD BOOK photo
201 AP/Wide World
202 Reuters/Archive Photos
208 Jim Wilson, NYT Pictures
210 © Paul Ashton, SouthWest News Service from Sygma
212 CLV/Eurelios/SPL from Photo Researchers; Linda Detwiler, USDA; Richard T. Johnson
214 © Marc Clertot, Gamma/Liaison
215 © Jacob Sutton, Gamma/Liaison
216 © Murdo MacLeod
219 © William Stevens, Gamma/Liaison; Marshall Field & Co. (Jeff Guerrant*); © Olympia, Gamma/Liaison
222-230 AP/Wide World
234 © Al Bello, Allsport
236 AP/Wide World
238 © Todd Warhsaw, Allsport
243-253 AP/Wide World
256 © Jeff McNally, Tribune Media Services
259 AP/Wide World
263-265 Reuters/Archive Photos
268 Illustration by Peggy Rathmann. Reprinted by permission of G.P. Putnam's Sons from *Officer Buckle and Gloria*, ©1995 by Peggy Rathmann
269 Reprinted by permission of the American Library Association
272 Steve Goldstein, NYT Pictures
278-281 AP/Wide World
285 20th Century Fox From Shooting Star
288-90 AP/Wide World
292 Monica Almeda, NYT Pictures
293 Reuters/Archive Photos
294 © Robert Allison, Contact Press Images
299 Lamont-Doherty Earth Observatory
300 © David Madison, Duomo
303 © Mike Powell, Allsport
306 © Rick Rickman, Duomo
307 © Al Bello, Allsport
309 © Rick Rickman, Duomo
310 © Chris Cole, Duomo
314-318 AP/Wide World
323 © Philippe Renault, Gamma/Liaison
324 Metronome Collection from Archive Photos
325 UPI/Corbis-Bettmann
332-334 AP/Wide World
335 Reuters/Archive Photos
338 AP/Wide World
340 © Andy Hernandez, Gamma/Liaison
343 © Daniel Sheehan, Black Star; © Alexandra Avakian, Contact Press Images; © Lise Sarfati, Contact Press Images
345 © Bill Swersey, Gamma/Liaison; AFP/Corbis-Bettmann
346 AFP/Corbis-Bettmann
348 © Bill Swersey, Gamma/Liaison
349 © Steven Levy, Contact Press Images
355 Agence France-Presse
357 AP/Wide World
360 NASA
362 AP/Wide World
369 © Manoosher, Sygma
371-374 AP/Wide World
377 ABC from Shooting Star
378 NBC from Shooting Star
381-382 AP/Wide World
354 Richard Kalina
386 © Ty Inc.; Nintendo of America
389-392 AP/Wide World
394 © Tim Graham, Sygma; © Sygma
398 *Portrait of Henry VIII* (1532) oil on canvas by Hans Holbein the Younger (Corbis-Bettmann); *Portrait of Charles I Hunting* (about 1635) oil on canvas by Sir Anthony Van Dyek; The Louvre, Paris (SCALA/Art Resource)
399 *Portrait of George IV* (1819) by Sir Thomas Lawrence; Vatican Museums (Corbis-Bettmann); UPI/Corbis-Bettmann)
401 © Tim Graham, Sygma
404 AP/Wide World
405 U.S. Treasury Department
409-413 AP/Wide World
420 NASA

A Preview of 1997

January

S	M	T	W	TH	F	S
			1	2	3	4
5	6	7	8	9	10	11
12	13	14	15	16	17	18
19	20	21	22	23	24	25
26	27	28	29	30	31	

1 New Year's Day.

1-2 **Major college football bowl games** played by top teams.

6 **Epiphany** celebrated by many Christians to commemorate the visit of the Magi.

85th anniversary of admission of New Mexico as the 47th state of the Union.

7 **Christmas** observed as national holiday in Russia.

10 **Ramadan,** a Muslim holiday that consists of a month of fasting, begins.

19 **190th anniversary of birth of Robert E. Lee** celebrated as a legal holiday in most Southern States.

20 **Martin Luther King, Jr., Day.**

23 **260th anniversary of birth of John Hancock,** first signer of the Declaration of Independence.

Tu B'Shvat, a Jewish arbor day, celebrated by Jews throughout the world by donating funds to plant trees in Israel.

26 **Super Bowl XXXI** played in New Orleans.

160th anniversary of admission of Michigan as the 26th state of the Union.

February

S	M	T	W	TH	F	S
						1
2	3	4	5	6	7	8
9	10	11	12	13	14	15
16	17	18	19	20	21	22
23	24	25	26	27	28	

1 **African American History Month,** or Black History Month, begins.

2 **Ground-Hog Day** celebrated. According to legend, if a ground hog emerges and sees its shadow, six weeks of winter weather will follow.

Boy Scouts of America Anniversary Week begins.

7 **The Chinese Year of the Ox** begins, marking lunar year 4695 of the Chinese calendar.

9 **Shrovetide** begins, a time of confession and festivity before Lent.

11 **150th anniversary of birth of Thomas A. Edison.**

12 **Ash Wednesday** celebrated by many Christians to mark beginning of Lent.

Abraham Lincoln's Birthday.

14 **Valentine's Day.**

17 **Presidents' Day** celebrated, to honor George Washington, Abraham Lincoln, and other U.S. presidents.

22 **265th anniversary of birth of George Washington.**

24 **415th anniversary of adoption of the Gregorian Calendar** by most Roman-Catholic nations of Europe.

March

S	M	T	W	TH	F	S
						1
2	3	4	5	6	7	8
9	10	11	12	13	14	15
16	17	18	19	20	21	22
23	24	25	26	27	28	29
30	31					

1 **National Women's History Month** begins, to celebrate the achievements of women.

2 **Save Your Vision Week** begins, to promote awareness of the importance of eye health.

3 **150th anniversary of birth of inventor Alexander Graham Bell.**

7 **World Day of Prayer.**

8 **Total solar eclipse** visible in East Asia, Arctic regions, Alaska, and western Canada.

10 **Girl Scout Week** begins.

Commonwealth Day observed in Canada.

13 **Deaf History Month** begins, to celebrate the achievements of deaf Americans.

16 **170th anniversary of founding of first African American newspaper** in the United States.

Camp Fire Boys and Girls Week begins.

17 **St. Patrick's Day.**

20 **Spring** begins with the vernal equinox at 8:55 a.m. (E.S.T.).

23 **Palm Sunday** celebrated by many Christians to mark triumphal entry of Jesus into Jerusalem, when palm branches were strewn before Him.

28 **Good Friday** celebrated by many Christians, to mark the crucifixion of Christ.

30 **Easter** celebrated by many Christians, to mark the resurrection of Christ.

April

S	M	T	W	TH	F	S
		1	2	3	4	5
6	7	8	9	10	11	12
13	14	15	16	17	18	19
20	21	22	23	24	25	26
27	28	29	30			

1 **April Fools' Day.**

Alcohol Awareness Month begins, to raise awareness of underage drinking.

6 **Daylight-saving time** begins at 2:00 a.m. in most areas of the United States.

7 50th anniversary of death of **Henry Ford.**

13 **National Library Week** begins.

15 85th anniversary of sinking of the *Titanic.*

16 130th anniversary of birth of aviator **Wilbur Wright.**

21 **Passover,** or Pesah, begins, to celebrate the deliverance of the ancient Israelites out of Egypt.

22 **Professional Secretaries Day.**

25 **Arbor Day** celebrated in the United States.

27 **Easter** observed by Eastern-Orthodox Christians.

175th anniversary of birth of **Ulysses S. Grant,** Civil War general and U.S. president.

28 **Workers Memorial Day** celebrated in the United States in memory of workers injured or killed on the job.

National Day of Mourning celebrated in Canada in memory of workers killed or injured on the job.

30 185th anniversary of admission of **Louisiana** as the 18th state of the Union.

May

S	M	T	W	TH	F	S
				1	2	3
4	5	6	7	8	9	10
11	12	13	14	15	16	17
18	19	20	21	22	23	24
25	26	27	28	29	30	31

1 **May Day.**

Law Day celebrated in the United States.

Mental Health Month begins, to heighten public awareness of mental health.

3 **Kentucky Derby** is run.

4 **Be Kind to Animals Week** begins.

5 **Cinco de Mayo** celebrated, to commemorate a battle in which Mexican forces in 1862 defeated invading French troops.

6 **National Nurses' Week** begins.

National Teacher Day.

8 **World Red Cross Day.**

11 **Mother's Day.**

14 390th anniversary of founding of **Jamestown, Virginia,** the first permanent English settlement in North America.

17 **Armed Forces Day.**

18 **Pentecost** observed by many Christians.

19 **Victoria Day** observed in Canada.

21 70th anniversary of **Charles Lindbergh's solo flight** across Atlantic Ocean.

22 **Immigrant's Day** celebrated in Canada, to recognize contributions of immigrants.

25 **Trinity Sunday** celebrated by many Christians to commemorate the Holy Trinity.

26 **Memorial Day** celebrated in the United States.

29 80th anniversary of birth of **John F. Kennedy.**

June

S	M	T	W	TH	F	S
1	2	3	4	5	6	7
8	9	10	11	12	13	14
15	16	17	18	19	20	21
22	23	24	25	26	27	28
29	30					

1 **Hurricane season** begins in the Atlantic Ocean, the Caribbean Sea, and the Gulf of Mexico.

National Safe Boating Week begins.

5 **United Nations World Environment Day.**

8 **Children's Sunday** observed by many Christian congregations.

130th anniversary of birth of architect **Frank Lloyd Wright.**

9 **National Little League Baseball Week** begins.

11 **Shavuot, Jewish Pentecost,** celebrated.

13 Only Friday the 13th of 1997.

14 **Flag Day** celebrated in the United States, to commemorate the 1777 adoption of the Stars and Stripes.

15 **Father's Day.**

21 **Summer** begins in Northern Hemisphere with the summer solstice at 4:20 a.m. (E.S.T.).

22 **Deaf-Blindness Awareness Week** begins, to celebrate anniversary of Helen Keller's birth.

24 **Saint John the Baptist Day** celebrated by many Christians.

July

S	M	T	W	TH	F	S
		1	2	3	4	5
6	7	8	9	10	11	12
13	14	15	16	17	18	19
20	21	22	23	24	25	26
27	28	29	30	31		

1 **Canada Day** celebrated, to commemorate confederation of Upper and Lower Canada with certain Maritime provinces to form the Dominion of Canada in 1867.

3 **60th anniversary of disappearance of Amelia Earhart** over the Pacific Ocean during her around-the-world flight.

4 **Independence Day** celebrated in the United States.

5 **Independence Day** celebrated in Venezuela.

10 **Independence Day** celebrated in the Bahamas.

11 **United Nations' World Population Day** celebrated, to focus attention on issues involving population growth.

230th anniversary of birth of John Quincy Adams, 6th U.S. president.

13 **Festival of Lanterns** begins in Japan, with religious rites in memory of the dead.

14 **Bastille Day** celebrated in France.

20 **Space Week** begins, to commemorate the U.S. landing on the moon on July 20, 1969.

Independence Day in Colombia.

26 **150th anniversary of independence of Liberia.**

28 **Independence Day** celebrated in Peru.

August

S	M	T	W	TH	F	S
					1	2
3	4	5	6	7	8	9
10	11	12	13	14	15	16
17	18	19	20	21	22	23
24	25	26	27	28	29	30
31						

3 **505th anniversary of the beginning of Columbus' first voyage**.

4 **Coast Guard Day** observed, to celebrate founding of the U.S. Coast Guard in 1790.

Canadian Civic Holiday observed in Alberta, British Columbia, Manitoba, New Brunswick, Ontario, Saskatchewan, and the Northwest Territories.

6 **Summer** is half over.

9 **All-American Soap Box Derby** run in Akron, Ohio.

Intertribal Indian Ceremonial, a major festival, begins in Gallup, New Mexico, and continues through August 17.

United Nations World Indigenous People Day.

10 **Independence Day** celebrated in Ecuador.

13 **575th anniversary of birth of William Caxton**, the man who produced the first book printed in English.

15 **50th anniversary of independence of India.**

18 **Little League World Series** for 11- and 12-year-olds begins in Williamsport, Pennsylvania.

National Aviation Week begins.

19 **National Aviation Day** celebrated, to commemorate the Wright brothers' contributions to aviation.

26 **Women's Equality Day** celebrated, to commemorate 19th Amendment to the U.S. Constitution, granting women the right to vote.

September

S	M	T	W	TH	F	S
	1	2	3	4	5	6
7	8	9	10	11	12	13
14	15	16	17	18	19	20
21	22	23	24	25	26	27
28	29	30				

1 **Labor Day** celebrated in the United States and Canada.

Childhood Cancer Month begins, to focus public support on efforts to find cures for childhood cancers.

Partial solar eclipse visible from Indian Ocean and in Australia and New Zealand.

7 **175th anniversary of Brazilian Independence** from Portugal.

15 **National Hispanic Heritage Month** begins.

Independence Day celebrated in Costa Rica, El Salvador, Guatemala, Honduras, Mexico, and Nicaragua.

16 **Total lunar eclipse** visible in many areas of the world.

18 **Independence Day** celebrated in Chile.

20 **Banned Books Week** begins, to emphasize freedom of the press.

Religious Freedom Week begins.

22 **Autumn** begins with the autumnal equinox at 7:56 p.m. (E.S.T.).

25 **100th anniversary of birth of William Faulkner,** renowned American writer.

October

S	M	T	W	TH	F	S
			1	2	3	4
5	6	7	8	9	10	11
12	13	14	15	16	17	18
19	20	21	22	23	24	25
26	27	28	29	30	31	

1 **Rosh Ha-Shanah** begins, to celebrate the Jewish New Year, 5758.

National Crime Prevention Month begins.

5 **National Newspaper Week** begins.

Fire Prevention Week begins.

8 **National Children's Day.**

9 **Leif Ericson Day.**

10 **Yom Kippur,** the Jewish Day of Atonement, begins at sundown.

11 **General Pulaski Memorial Day** celebrated, to recognize role of Polish cavalry officer Casimir Pulaski in the American Revolution.

12 **Partial solar eclipse** visible in Europe, Iceland, North Africa, and parts of northeast Canada.

13 **Columbus Day** celebrated in the United States.

Thanksgiving observed in Canada.

15 **Sukkot,** Jewish Feast of Tabernacles, begins.

18 **130th anniversary of transfer of Alaska** from Russia to the United States.

Sweetest Day.

24 **United Nations' Day.**

26 **Daylight-saving time** ends and standard time resumes at 2:00 a.m.

31 **Halloween.**

National UNICEF Day observed, to raise awareness of the lives of children in the developing world.

November

S	M	T	W	TH	F	S
						1
2	3	4	5	6	7	8
9	10	11	12	13	14	15
16	17	18	19	20	21	22
23	24	25	26	27	28	29
30						

1 **All Saints' Day.**

National Alzheimer's Disease Month begins.

National Diabetes Month begins.

National Epilepsy Awareness Month begins.

2 **New York City Marathon** is run.

All Souls' Day.

3 **Independence Day** observed in Panama.

4 **Election day** in the United States.

5 **Guy Fawkes Day** celebrated in England to commemorate the foiling of a plot in 1605 to blow up the Houses of Parliament.

9 **Remembrance Day** celebrated in the United Kingdom.

125th anniversary of great Boston fire.

11 **Veterans Day** celebrated in the United States.

Remembrance Day celebrated in Canada.

16 **American Education Week** begins, to call attention to the importance of public education in the United States.

National Geography Awareness Week begins.

90th anniversary of admission of Oklahoma as 46th state of the Union.

20 **Great American Smokeout** celebrated, to urge smokers to stop smoking for at least one day.

21 **National Adoption Week** begins.

27 **Thanksgiving** celebrated in the United States.

30 **Advent** begins for many Christians.

December

S	M	T	W	TH	F	S
	1	2	3	4	5	6
7	8	9	10	11	12	13
14	15	16	17	18	19	20
21	22	23	24	25	26	27
28	29	30	31			

1 **United Nations' World AIDS Day celebrated,** to focus attention on prevention and control of AIDS.

5 **215th anniversary of birth of Martin Van Buren,** eighth U.S. president.

6 **St. Nicholas Day** celebrated in Europe with gift giving.

Independence Day celebrated in Finland.

7 **Pearl Harbor Day** celebrated, to commemorate the 1941 bombing of the U.S. fleet in Hawaii by the Japanese.

10 **Human Rights Day.**

180th anniversary of admission of Mississippi as 20th state of the Union.

21 **Winter** begins in the Northern Hemisphere with the winter solstice at 3:07 p.m. (E.S.T.).

24 **Hanukkah,** the eight-day Jewish Feast of Lights, begins.

25 **Christmas** observed by many Christians.

355th anniversary of birth of Sir Isaac Newton, English scientist who formulated the theory of gravity.

26 **Kwanzaa,** an African American family observance based on African harvest festivals, begins and continues through Jan. 1, 1998.

Boxing Day observed in Great Britain and Canada.

31 **New Year's Eve.**